T0205279

Communications in Computer and Information Science 1463

More information about this series at http://www.springer.com/series/7899

Krystian Wojtkiewicz · Jan Treur ·
Elias Pimenidis · Marcin Maleszka (Eds.)

Advances in Computational Collective Intelligence

13th International Conference, ICCCI 2021
Kallithea, Rhodes, Greece, September 29 – October 1, 2021
Proceedings

Editors
Krystian Wojtkiewicz
Wrocław University of Science and Technology
Wrocław, Poland

Jan Treur
VU Amsterdam
Amsterdam, The Netherlands

Elias Pimenidis
University of the West of England
Bristol, UK

Marcin Maleszka
Wrocław University of Science and Technology
Wrocław, Poland

ISSN 1865-0929 ISSN 1865-0937 (electronic)
Communications in Computer and Information Science
ISBN 978-3-030-88112-2 ISBN 978-3-030-88113-9 (eBook)
https://doi.org/10.1007/978-3-030-88113-9

This Springer imprint is published by the registered company Springer Nature Switzerland AG
The registered company address is: Gewerbestrasse 11, 6330 Cham, Switzerland

Preface

This volume contains the proceedings of the 13th International Conference on Computational Collective Intelligence (ICCCI 2021), held in Rhodes, Greece, during September 29 – October 1, 2021. Due to the COVID-19 pandemic the conference was organized in a hybrid mode which allowed for both on-site and online paper presentations. The conference was hosted by the Democritus University of Thrace, Greece, and jointly organized by Wrocław University of Science and Technology, Poland, in cooperation with the IEEE SMC Technical Committee on Computational Collective Intelligence, the European Research Center for Information Systems (ERCIS), the University of Piraeus, Greece, and the International University-VNU-HCM, Vietnam.

Following the successes of the first ICCCI (2009) in Wrocław, Poland, the second ICCCI (2010) in Kaohsiung, Taiwan, the Third ICCCI (2011) in Gdynia, Poland, the 4th ICCCI (2012) in Ho Chi Minh City, Vietnam, the 5th ICCCI (2013) in Craiova, Romania, the 6th ICCCI (2014) in Seoul, South Korea, the 7th ICCCI (2015) in Madrid, Spain, the 8th ICCCI (2016) in Halkidiki, Greece, the 9th ICCCI (2017) in Nicosia, Cyprus, the 10th ICCCI (2018) in Bristol, UK, the 11th ICCCI (2019) in Hendaye, France, and the 12th ICCCI (2020) in Da Nang, Vietnam, this conference continued to provide an internationally respected forum for scientific research in the computer-based methods of collective intelligence and their applications.

Computational collective intelligence (CCI) is most often understood as a subfield of artificial intelligence (AI) dealing with soft computing methods that facilitate group decisions or processing knowledge among autonomous units acting in distributed environments. Methodological, theoretical, and practical aspects of CCI are considered as the form of intelligence that emerges from the collaboration and competition of many individuals (artificial and/or natural). The application of multiple computational intelligence technologies such as fuzzy systems, evolutionary computation, neural systems, consensus theory, etc., can support human and other collective intelligence, and create new forms of CCI in natural and/or artificial systems. Three subfields of the application of computational intelligence technologies to support various forms of collective intelligence are of special interest but are not exclusive: the Semantic Web (as an advanced tool for increasing collective intelligence), social network analysis (as the field targeted at the emergence of new forms of CCI), and multi-agent systems (as a computational and modeling paradigm especially tailored to capture the nature of CCI emergence in populations of autonomous individuals).

The ICCCI 2021 conference featured a number of keynote talks and oral presentations, closely aligned to the theme of the conference. The conference attracted a substantial number of researchers and practitioners from all over the world, who submitted their papers for the main track and nine special sessions.

The main track, covering the methodology and applications of CCI, included knowledge engineering and Semantic Web, social networks and recommender systems, collective decision-making, data mining and machine learning, computer vision techniques, and natural language processing, as well as the Internet of Things: technologies and applications. The special sessions, covering some specific topics of particular interest, included cooperative strategies for decision making and optimization, IoT and computational technologies for collective intelligence, smart industry and management systems, machine learning in real-world data, knowledge-intensive smart services and their applications, swarms of UAVs, low resource languages processing, computational collective intelligence and natural language processing, and computational intelligence for multimedia understanding.

We received over 230 papers submitted by authors coming from 45 countries around the world. Each paper was reviewed by at least three members of the international Program Committee (PC) of either the main track or one of the special sessions. Finally, we selected 60 best papers for oral presentation and publication in one volume of the Lecture Notes in Artificial Intelligence series and 58 papers for oral presentation and publication in one volume of the Communications in Computer and Information Science series.

We would like to express our thanks to the keynote speakers: Plamen Angelov from Lancaster University, UK, Yannis Manolopoulos from the Open University of Cyprus, Cyprus, Daniele Nardi from Sapienza Università di Roma, Italy, and Andrzej Skowron from the Systems Research Institute of Polish Academy of Sciences, Poland, for their world-class plenary speeches.

Many people contributed toward the success of the conference. First, we would like to recognize the work of the PC co-chairs and special sessions organizers for taking good care of the organization of the reviewing process, an essential stage in ensuring the high quality of the accepted papers. The workshop and special session chairs deserve a special mention for the evaluation of the proposals and the organization and coordination of the nine special sessions. In addition, we would like to thank the PC members, of the main track and of the special sessions, for performing their reviewing work with diligence. We thank the Local Organizing Committee chairs, publicity chair, Web chair, and technical support chair for their fantastic work before and during the conference. Finally, we cordially thank all the authors, presenters, and delegates for their valuable contribution to this successful event. The conference would not have been possible without their support.

Our special thanks are also due to Springer for publishing the proceedings and to all the other sponsors for their kind support.

It is our pleasure to announce that the ICCCI conference series continues to have a close cooperation with the Springer journal Transactions on Computational Collective Intelligence, and the IEEE SMC Technical Committee on Transactions on Computational Collective Intelligence.

Finally, we hope that ICCCI 2021 contributed significantly to the academic excellence of the field and will lead to the even greater success of ICCCI events in the future.

September 2021

Krystian Wojtkiewicz
Jan Treur
Elias Pimenidis
Marcin Maleszka

Organization

Organizing Committee

Honorary Chairs

Arkadiusz Wójs	Wrocław University of Science and Technology, Poland
Fotios Maris	Democritus University of Thrace, Greece

General Chairs

Ngoc Thanh Nguyen	Wrocław University of Science and Technology, Poland
Lazaros Iliadis	Democritus University of Thrace, Greece

Program Chairs

Costin Bădică	University of Craiova, Romania
Ilias Maglogiannis	University of Piraeus, Greece
Gottfried Vossen	University of Münster, Germany

Steering Committee

Ngoc Thanh Nguyen	Wrocław University of Science and Technology, Poland
Shyi-Ming Chen	National Taiwan University of Science and Technology, Taiwan
Dosam Hwang	Yeungnam University, South Korea
Lakhmi C. Jain	University of South Australia, Australia
Piotr Jędrzejowicz	Gdynia Maritime University, Poland
Geun-Sik Jo	Inha University, South Korea
Janusz Kacprzyk	Polish Academy of Sciences, Poland
Ryszard Kowalczyk	Swinburne University of Technology, Australia
Toyoaki Nishida	Kyoto University, Japan
Manuel Núñez	Universidad Complutense de Madrid, Spain
Klaus Solberg Söilen	Halmstad University, Sweden
Khoa Tien Tran	International University-VNUHCM, Vietnam

Special Session Chairs

Bogdan Trawiński — Wrocław University of Science and Technology, Poland
Elias Pimenidis — University of the West of England, UK

Doctoral Track Chairs

Marek Krótkiewicz — Wrocław University of Science and Technology, Poland
Christos Makris — University of Patras, Greece

Organizing Chairs

Antonis Papaleonidas — Democritus University of Thrace, Greece
Krystian Wojtkiewicz — Wrocław University of Science and Technology, Poland
Adrianna Kozierkiewicz — Wrocław University of Science and Technology, Poland

Publicity Chairs

Antonios Papaleonidas — Democritus University of Thrace, Greece
Marcin Maleszka — Wrocław University of Science and Technology, Poland

Webmaster

Marek Kopel — Wrocław University of Science and Technology, Poland

Local Organizing Committee

Anastasios-Panagiotis Psathas — Democritus University of Thrace, Greece
Dimitris Boudas — Democritus University of Thrace, Greece
Vasilis Kokkinos — Democritus University of Thrace, Greece
Marcin Jodłowiec — Wrocław University of Science and Technology, Poland
Rafał Palak — Wrocław University of Science and Technology, Poland
Marcin Pietranik — Wrocław University of Science and Technology, Poland

Keynote Speakers

Plamen Angelov	Lancaster University, UK
Yannis Manolopoulos	Open University of Cyprus, Cyprus
Daniele Nardi	Sapienza Università di Roma, Italy
Andrzej Skowron	Systems Research Institute, Polish Academy of Sciences, Poland

Special Session Organizers

CCINLP 2021: Special Session on Computational Collective Intelligence and Natural Language Processing

Ismaïl Biskri	University of Québec à Trois-Rivières, Canada
Nadia Ghazzali	University of Québec à Trois-Rivières, Canada

CSDMO 2021: Special Session on Cooperative Strategies for Decision Making and Optimization

Piotr Jędrzejowicz	Gdynia Maritime University, Poland
Dariusz Barbucha	Gdynia Maritime University, Poland
Ireneusz Czarnowski	Gdynia Maritime University, Poland

IOTCTCI 2021: Special Session on Internet of Things and Computational Technologies for Collective Intelligence

Octavian Postolache	Instituto de Telecomunicações, ISCTE-IUL, Portugal
Madina Mansurova	Al-Farabi Kazakh National University, Kazakhstan

IWCIM 2021: International Workshop on Computational Intelligence for Multimedia Understanding

Davide Moroni	National Research Council of Italy (CNR), Italy
Maria Trocan	Institut Supérieur d'Électronique de Paris, France
Behçet Uğur Töreyin	Istanbul Technical University, Turkey

KISSTA 2021: Special Session on Knowledge-Intensive Smart Services and Their Applications

Thang Le Dinh	University of Québec à Trois-Rivières, Canada
Thanh Thoa Pham Thi	Technological University Dublin, Ireland
Nguyen Cuong Pham	University of Science, Ho Chi Minh City, Vietnam

LRLP 2021: Special Session on Low Resource Languages Processing

Ualsher Tukeyev	Al-Farabi Kazakh National University, Kazakhstan
Madina Mansurova	Al-Farabi Kazakh National University, Kazakhstan

MLRWD 2021: Special Session on Machine Learning in Real-World Data

Jan Kozak	University of Economics in Katowice, Poland
Krzysztof Kania	University of Economics in Katowice, Poland
Przemysław Juszczuk	University of Economics in Katowice, Poland
Barbara Probierz	University of Economics in Katowice, Poland

SIMS 2021: Special Session on Smart Industry and Management Systems

Marcin Fojcik	Western Norway University of Applied Sciences, Norway
Adam Ziębiński	Silesian University of Technology, Poland
Rafał Cupek	Silesian University of Technology, Poland
Dariusz Mrozek	Silesian University of Technology, Poland
Marcin Hernes	Wrocław University of Economics and Business, Poland

SUAV 2021: Special Session on Swarms of UAVs

Frédéric V. G. Guinand	Normandy University – UNIHAVRE, France
François Guérin	Normandy University – UNIHAVRE, France
Grégoire Danoy	University of Luxembourg, Luxembourg
Serge Chaumette	University of Bordeaux, France

Senior Program Committee

Plamen Angelov	Lancaster University, UK
Costin Bădică	University of Craiova, Romania
Nick Bassiliades	Aristotle University of Thessaloniki, Greece
Mária Bieliková	Slovak University of Technology in Bratislava, Slovakia
Abdelhamid Bouchachia	Bournemouth University, UK
David Camacho	Universidad Autonoma de Madrid, Spain
Richard Chbeir	University of Pau and Pays de l'Adour, France
Shyi-Ming Chen	National Taiwan University of Science and Technology, Taiwan
Paul Davidsson	Malmo University, Sweden
Mohamed Gaber	Birmingham City University, UK

Program Committee

Muhammad Abulaish	South Asian University, India
Sharat Akhoury	University of Cape Town, South Africa
Ana Almeida	GECAD-ISEP-IPP, Portugal
Bashar Al-Shboul	University of Jordan, Jordan
Adel Alti	University of Setif, Algeria
Taha Arbaoui	University of Technology of Troyes, France
Thierry Badard	Laval University, Canada
Amelia Bădică	University of Craiova, Romania
Hassan Badir	Ecole Nationale des Sciences Appliquees de Tanger, Morocco
Dariusz Barbucha	Gdynia Maritime University, Poland
Paulo Batista	Universidade de Evora, Portugal
Khalid Benali	University of Lorraine, France
Leon Bobrowski	Białystok University of Technology, Poland
Peter Brida	University of Zilina, Slovakia
Ivana Bridova	University of Zilina, Slovakia
Krisztian Buza	Budapest University of Technology and Economics, Hungary
Aleksander Byrski	AGH University of Science and Technology, Poland
Frantisek Capkovic	Institute of Informatics, Slovak Academy of Sciences, Slovakia
Kennedy Chengeta	University of KwaZulu Natal, South Africa
Raja Chiky	Institut Supérieur d'Electronique de Paris, France
Amine Chohra	Paris-East Créteil University, France
Kazimierz Choroś	Wrocław University of Science and Technology, Poland
Mihaela Colhon	University of Craiova, Romania
Jose Alfredo Ferreira Costa	Universidade Federal do Rio Grande do Norte, Brazil
Rafał Cupek	Silesian University of Technology, Poland
Ireneusz Czarnowski	Gdynia Maritime University, Poland
Camelia Delcea	Bucharest University of Economic Studies, Romania
Tien V. Do	Budapest University of Technology and Economics, Hungary
Rim Faiz	University of Carthage, Tunisia
Marcin Fojcik	Western Norway University of Applied Sciences, Norway
Anna Formica	IASI-CNR, Italy
Faiez Gargouri	University of Sfax, Tunisia

Mauro Gaspari	University of Bologna, Italy
K. M. George	Oklahoma State University, USA
Janusz Getta	University of Wollongong, Australia
Daniela Gifu	University "Alexandru loan Cuza" of Iasi, Romania
Antonio Gonzalez-Pardo	Universidad Autonoma de Madrid, Spain
Foteini Grivokostopoulou	University of Patras, Greece
Kenji Hatano	Doshisha University, Japan
Marcin Hernes	Wrocław University of Economics, Poland
Huu Hanh Hoang	Hue University, Vietnam
Frédéric Hubert	Laval University, Canada
Maciej Huk	Wrocław University of Science and Technology, Poland
Agnieszka Indyka-Piasecka	Wrocław University of Science and Technology, Poland
Joanna Jędrzejowicz	University of Gdańsk, Poland
Gordan Jezic	University of Zagreb, Croatia
Przemysław Juszczuk	University of Economics in Katowice, Poland
Petros Kefalas	University of Sheffield, Greece
Rafał Kern	Wrocław University of Science and Technology, Poland
Zaheer Khan	University of the West of England, UK
Marek Kisiel-Dorohinicki	AGH University of Science and Technology, Poland
Attila Kiss	Eotvos Lorand University, Hungary
Marek Kopel	Wrocław University of Science and Technology, Poland
Leszek Kotulski	AGH University of Science and Technology, Poland
Ivan Koychev	University of Sofia "St. Kliment Ohridski", Bulgaria
Jan Kozak	University of Economics in Katowice, Poland
Adrianna Kozierkiewicz	Wrocław University of Science and Technology, Poland
Dalia Kriksciuniene	Vilnius University, Lithuania
Dariusz Król	Wrocław University of Science and Technology, Poland
Marek Krótkiewicz	Wrocław University of Science and Technology, Poland
Jan Kubicek	VSB-Technical University of Ostrava, Czech Republic
Elżbieta Kukla	Wrocław University of Science and Technology, Poland

Julita Kulbacka	Wrocław Medical University, Poland
Marek Kulbacki	Polish-Japanese Academy of Information Technology, Poland
Kazuhiro Kuwabara	Ritsumeikan University, Japan
Halina Kwaśnicka	Wrocław University of Science and Technology, Poland
Philippe Lemoisson	French Agricultural Research Centre for International Development (CIRAD), France
Florin Leon	"Gheorghe Asachi" Technical University of Iasi, Romania
Mikołaj Leszczuk	AGH University of Science and Technology, Poland
Doina Logofatu	Frankfurt University of Applied Sciences, Germany
Juraj Machaj	University of Zilina, Slovakia
Bernadetta Maleszka	Wrocław University of Science and Technology, Poland
Marcin Maleszka	Wrocław University of Science and Technology, Poland
Urszula Markowska-Kaczmar	Wrocław University of Science and Technology, Poland
Adam Meissner	Poznań University of Technology, Poland
Héctor Menéndez	University College London, UK
Mercedes Merayo	Universidad Complutense de Madrid, Spain
Jacek Mercik	WSB University in Wrocław, Poland
Radosław Michalski	Wrocław University of Science and Technology, Poland
Peter Mikulecky	University of Hradec Králové, Czech Republic
Miroslava Mikusova	University of Zilina, Slovakia
Javier Montero	Universidad Complutense de Madrid, Spain
Dariusz Mrozek	Silesian University of Technology, Poland
Manuel Munier	University of Pau and Pays de l'Adour, France
Laurent Nana	University of Brest, France
Anand Nayyar	Duy Tan University, Vietnam
Filippo Neri	University of Napoli Federico II, Italy
Linh Anh Nguyen	University of Warsaw, Poland
Loan T. T. Nguyen	International University-VNUHCM, Vietnam
Sinh Van Nguyen	International University-VNUHCM, Vietnam
Thi Thanh Sang Nguyen	International University-VNUHCM, Vietnam
Adam Niewiadomski	Łódź University of Technology, Poland
Adel Noureddine	University of Pau and Pays de l'Adour, France
Agnieszka Nowak-Brzezińska	University of Silesia, Poland
Alberto Núñez	Universidad Complutense de Madrid, Spain

Olgierd Unold	Wrocław University of Science and Technology, Poland
Thi Luu Phuong Vo	International University-VNUHCM, Vietnam
Roger M. Whitaker	Cardiff University, UK
Izabela Wierzbowska	Gdynia Maritime University, Poland
Adam Wojciechowski	Łódź University of Technology, Poland
Krystian Wojtkiewicz	Wrocław University of Science and Technology, Poland
Drago Zagar	University of Osijek, Croatia
Danuta Zakrzewska	Łódź University of Technology, Poland
Constantin-Bala Zamfirescu	"Lucian Blaga" University of Sibiu, Romania
Katerina Zdravkova	University St Cyril and Methodius, Macedonia
Aleksander Zgrzywa	Wrocław University of Science and Technology, Poland
Haoxi Zhang	Chengdu University of Information Technology, China
Jianlei Zhang	Nankai University, China
Adam Ziębiński	Silesian University of Technology, Poland

Special Session Program Committees

CCINLP 2021: Special Session on Computational Collective Intelligence and Natural Language Processing

Ismaïl Biskri	Université du Québec à Trois-Rivières, Canada
Mounir Zrigui	Université de Monastir, Tunisia
Anca Pascu	Université de Bretagne Occidentale, France
Éric Poirier	Université du Québec à Trois-Rivières, Canada
Fatiha Sadat	Université du Québec à Montréal, Canada
Adel Jebali	Concordia University, Canada
Eva Hajiova	Charles University in Prague, Czech Republic
Khaled Shaalan	British University, Dubai, United Arab Emirates
Vladislav Kubon	Charles University in Prague, Czech Republic
Louis Rompré	Cascades, Canada
Rim Faiz	IHEC Carthage, Tunisia
Thang Le Dinh	Université du Québec à Trois-Rivières, Canada
Usef Faghihi	Université du Québec à Trois-Rivières, Canada
Amel Zouaq	Polytechnique Montréal, Canada

CSDMO 2021: Special Session on Cooperative Strategies for Decision Making and Optimization

Dariusz Barbucha	Gdynia Maritime University, Poland
Amine Chohra	Paris-East Créteil University, France

Ireneusz Czarnowski	Gdynia Maritime University, Poland
Joanna Jędrzejowicz	Gdansk University, Poland
Piotr Jędrzejowicz	Gdynia Maritime University, Poland
Edyta Kucharska	AGH University of Science and Technology, Poland
Antonio D. Masegosa	University of Deusto, Spain
Jacek Mercik	WSB University in Wrocław, Poland
Javier Montero	Complutense University of Madrid, Spain
Ewa Ratajczak-Ropel	Gdynia Maritime University, Poland
Iza Wierzbowska	Gdynia Maritime University, Poland
Mahdi Zargayouna	IFSTTAR, France

IOTCTCI 2021: Special Session on Internet of Things and Computational Technologies for Collective Intelligence

Octavian Postolache	Instituto de Telecomunicações, ISCTE-IUL, Portugal
Vítor Viegas	Portuguese Naval Academy, Portugal
Wolfram Hardt	Chemnitz University of Technology, Germany
Uyanga Sambuu	National University of Mongolia, Mongolia
Yadmaa Narantsetseg	Mongolian University of Science and Technology, Mongolia
Madina Mansurova	Al-Farabi Kazakh National University, Kazakhstan
Olga Dolinina	Yuri Gagarin State Technical University of Saratov, Russia
Vadim Zhmud	Novosibirsk State Technical University, Russia
Nadezhda Kunicina	Riga Technical University, Latvia
Jelena Caiko	Riga Technical University, Latvia
Mikhail Grif	Novosibirsk State Technical University, Russia
Baurzhan Belgibayev	Al-Farabi Kazakh National University, Kazakhstan
Sholpan Jomartova	Al-Farabi Kazakh National University, Kazakhstan
Assel Akzhalova	Kazakh-British Technical University, Kazakhstan
Aliya Nugumanova	S. Amanzholov East Kazakhstan State University, Kazakhstan

IWCIM 2021: International Workshop on Computational Intelligence for Multimedia Understanding

Enis Cetin	University of Illinois at Chicago, USA
Michal Haindl	Institute of Information Theory and Automation of the CAS, Czech Republic

Andras L. Majdik	MTA SZTAKI - Institute for Computer Science and Control, Hungarian Academy of Sciences, Hungary
Cristina Ribeiro	University of Porto, Porto, Portugal
Emanuele Salerno	National Research Council of Italy (CNR), Italy
Ales Prochazka	University of Chemistry and Technology, Czech Republic
Anna Tonazzini	National Research Council of Italy (CNR), Italy
Gabriele Pieri	National Research Council of Italy (CNR), Italy
Gerasimos Potamianos	University of Thessaly, Greece
Gorkem Saygili	Tilburg University, The Netherlands
Josiane Zerubia	Inria, France
Maria Antonietta Pascali	National Research Council of Italy (CNR), Italy
Marie-Colette van Lieshout	CWI Amsterdam, Netherlands
Marco Reggiannini	National Research Council of Italy (CNR), Italy
Nahum Kiryati	Tel Aviv University, Israel
Rozenn Dahyot	Trinity College Dublin, Ireland
Sara Colantonio	National Research Council of Italy (CNR), Italy
Massimo Martinelli	National Research Council of Italy (CNR), Italy
Shohreh Ahvar	Institut Supérieur d'Électronique de Paris, France
Tamás Szirányi	MTA SZTAKI - Institute for Computer Science and Control, Hungarian Academy of Sciences, Hungary

KISSTA 2021: Special Session on Knowledge-Intensive Smart Services and Their Applications

William Menvielle	Université du Québec à Trois-Rivières, Canada
Manh Chien Vu	Université du Québec à Trois-Rivières, Canada
Diarmuid O'Donoghue	Maynooth University, Ireland
Markus Helfert	Maynooth University, Ireland
Nhien-An Le-Khac	University College Dublin, Ireland
Joseph Timoney	Maynooth University, Ireland
Thuong Cang Phan	University of Cantho, Vietnam
Thanh Lam Hoang	IBM research, Dublin, Ireland
Thi My Hang Vu	University of Science, Ho Chi Minh City, Vietnam
Nam Le Nguyen Hoai	University of Science, Ho Chi Minh City, Vietnam
Nizar Bouguila	Concordia University, Canada
Jolita Ralyté	University of Geneva, Switzerland
Trung Bui	Adobe Research, USA
Elaine Mosconi	Université de Sherbrooke, Canada
Abdelaziz Khadraoui	University of Geneva, Switzerland

LRLP 2021: Special Session on Low Resource Languages Processing

Miguel A. Alonso	Universidade da Coruna, Spain
Pablo Gamallo	University of Santiago de Compostela, Spain
Nella Israilova	Kyrgyz State Technical University, Kyrgyzstan
Marek Kubis	Adam Mickiewicz University, Poland
Belinda Maia	University of Porto, Portugal
Madina Mansurova	Al-Farabi Kazakh National University, Kazakhstan
Gayrat Matlatipov	Urgench State University, Uzbekistan
Marek Miłosz	Lublin University of Technology, Poland
Diana Rakhimova	Al-Farabi Kazakh National University, Kazakhstan
Altynbek Sharipbay	L. N. Gumilyov Eurasian National University, Kazakhstan
Ualsher Tukeyev	Al-Farabi Kazakh National University, Kazakhstan

MLRWD 2021: Special Session on Machine Learning in Real-World Data

Rafał Skinderowicz	University of Silesia, Poland
Grzegorz Dziczkowski	University of Economics in Katowice, Poland
Marcin Grzegorzek	University of Lübeck, Germany
Ignacy Kaliszewski	Systems Research Institute, Polish Academy of Sciences, Poland
Krzysztof Kania	University of Economics in Katowice, Poland
Jan Kozak	University of Economics in Katowice, Poland
Przemysław Juszczuk	University of Economics in Katowice, Poland
Janusz Miroforidis	Systems Research Institute, Polish Academy of Sciences, Poland
Agnieszka Nowak-Brzezińska	University of Silesia, Poland
Dmitry Podkopaev	Systems Research Institute, Polish Academy of Sciences, Poland
Tomasz Jach	University of Economics in Katowice, Poland
Tomasz Staś	University of Economics in Katowice, Poland
Magdalena Tkacz	University of Silesia, Poland
Barbara Probierz	University of Economics in Katowice, Poland
Wojciech Wieczorek	University of Bielsko-Biała, Poland

SIMS 2021: Special Session on Smart Industry and Management Systems

Adam Ziębiński	Silesian University of Technology, Poland
Anne-Lena Kampen	Western Norway University of Applied Sciences, Norway

Artur Rot	Wrocław University of Economics and Business, Poland
Bogdan Franczyk	University of Leipzig, Germany
Damian Grzechca	Silesian University of Technology, Poland
Dariusz Frejlichowski	West Pomeranian University of Technology, Poland
Dariusz Mrozek	Silesian University of Technology, Poland
Helena Dudycz	Wrocław University of Economics and Business, Poland
Jarosław Wątróbski	University of Szczecin, Poland
Jerry Chun-Wei Lin	Western Norway University of Applied Sciences, Norway
Knut Øvsthus	Western Norway University of Applied Sciences, Norway
Marcin Fojcik	Western Norway University of Applied Sciences, Norway
Marcin Hernes	Wrocław University of Economics and Business, Poland
Mieczysław Owoc	Wrocław University of Economics and Business, Poland
Mykola Dyvak	Ternopil National Economic University, Ukraine
Paweł Weichbroth	Gdansk University of Technology, Poland
Piotr Gaj	Silesian University of Technology, Poland
Rafał Cupek	Silesian University of Technology, Poland
Krzysztof Hauke	Wrocław University of Economics and Business, Poland
Łukasz Łysik	Wrocław University of Economics and Business, Poland
Piotr Tutak	Wrocław University of Economics and Business, Poland
Maciej Huk	Wrocław University of Science and Technology, Poland
Piotr Biernacki	Silesian University of Technology, Poland
Ewa Walaszczyk	Wrocław University of Economics and Business, Poland
Krzysztof Lutosławski	Wrocław University of Economics and Business, Poland
Krzysztof Tokarz	Silesian University of Technology, Poland

SUAV 2021: Special Session on Swarms of UAVs

Pierre Avanzini	Squadrone System, France
Pascal Bouvry	University of Luxembourg, Luxembourg
Serge Chaumette	University of Bordeaux, France

Grégoire Danoy	University of Luxembourg, Luxembourg
Simon G. Fabri	University of Malta, Malta
Isabelle Fantoni	CNRS, Nantes, France
Paola Flocchini	University of Ottawa, Canada
Antonio Franchi	University of Twente, The Netherlands
François Guérin	Normandy University, France
Frédéric V. G. Guinand	Normandy University, France
Chouaib El Houssein Harik	NIBIO, Norway
Samira Hayat	University of Klagenfurt, Austria
Sanaz Mostaghim	Otto-von-Guericke University, Germany
Giuseppe Prencipe	University of Pisa, Italy

Contents

Social Networks and Recommender Systems

Collective Decision-Making

Computer Vision Techniques

Cybersecurity Intelligent Methods

Data Mining and Machine Learning

Machine Learning in Real-World Data

Internet of Things and Computational Technologies for Collective Intelligence

Smart Industry and Management Systems

Social Networks and Recommender Systems

Identifying Key Actors in Organizational Social Network Based on E-Mail Communication

Dariusz Barbucha(✉) and Paweł Szyman

Department of Information Systems, Gdynia Maritime University, Morska 83, 81-225 Gdynia, Poland
d.barbucha@umg.edu.pl, p.szyman@wznj.umg.edu.pl

Abstract. Nowadays a lot of diverse systems in many different fields can be described as complex network and they are the focus of interest in many disciplines such as politics, marketing, social systems. Using different network analysis tools may provide many interesting observations about the structure of the network, dynamics of the network over the time and the role of selected nodes in the network. The paper focuses on organizational social network based on email communication between employees within the organization. Such network has a form of a network including a set of vertices, referring to persons employed in this organization, and a set of edges, defining information flow between these persons using an email communication channel. The main contribution of the paper is to discover main properties of the email-based social network of public organization located in Poland and to identify key actors in it using social network analysis tools. An important part of the analysis is also a comparison of the obtained results with real structure of the organization. The experiment confirmed that analysis of email traffic within an organization may derive information that can be usable for organizational management purposes.

Keywords: Organization · Information management · Email communication · Centrality · Social network analysis

1 Introduction

Last years one can observe a growing interest of researchers in social network analysis (SNA) of organizational structures, where actors (people or units of the organization) are represented in the form of nodes in the network, and relationships or information flow between these actors are represented in the form of edges between nodes in the network. It is assumed that actors are linked to each other by social ties, and these relations are the core of the organizational network approach. Thanks to the SNA, it is possible for example to detect emerging communities or describe and visualize structural bottlenecks, critical connections, irregular communication patterns, and isolated actors. SNA is often seen as a

K. Wojtkiewicz et al. (Eds.): ICCCI 2021, CCIS 1463, pp. 3–14, 2021.
https://doi.org/10.1007/978-3-030-88113-9_1

potential tool for detection of distinct groups or subgroups inside hierarchies in the organization and to determine the positions and the roles of selected persons in a given organization [3].

A representative form of an organizational social network can be a network based on different digital forms of communication within an organization. In case of email communication, a number of individuals can be linked according to their interaction in terms of messages sent and received, while a number of interactions, their frequency, and the time differences may reveal information about the strength of bilateral relationships [4]. Growing interest observed in social networks based on digital forms of communication within the organization in the past decade [3,5,9,12] stems from the fact that emails represent a major source of electronic communication in the organization. It is expected that analysis of such organizational social network may bring a lot of interesting observations related to selected aspects of organization and its activity.

This paper focuses on the organizational social network of one of the public organizations located in Poland. It has been constructed by extracting the anonymized data referring to email communication between persons employed in this organization. The main contribution of the paper is to discover main properties of the network and to identify actors playing key roles in it, using SNA tools. An important part of the analysis is also a comparison of the obtained results with real structure of the organization.

The rest of paper is organized as follows. Section 2 focuses on the problem of identification of key actors in a social network using different centrality measures. Section 3 refers to a group of organizational social networks inferred from email communications. It presents main components of these networks and refers to tasks analyzed and solved by different researchers and business practitioners. Section 4 presents assumptions, goal and details of experiment which has been carried out to analyze a social network extracted from email communication in public organization in Poland and identifying a set of actors playing key role in it. Finally, Sect. 5 concludes the paper, provides analysis of the results of the experiment and presents directions for future work.

2 Identifying Key Actors in a Social Network

2.1 Key Actors

Using SNA tools and discovering the role of selected nodes in the social network allows us to identify the individuals that act as key actors, players or influencers [7,13,14]. The natural way of identifying key players in a social network seems to be using measures which focuses on identifying "central" nodes in such networks. Some of them used in the analysis presented in the paper have been briefly described below.

2.2 Centrality Measures in a Social Network

Centrality can be seen as a one of fundamental concepts in network analysis and it has a long history in social network analysis. It refers to such attributes of nodes or group of nodes in a network as power, importance or influence. Although there exists a lot of measures and classifications of centrality approaches, one of the most important is classifications provided by Freeman [6]. He defined three centrality measures referring to [2]:

1. The number of edges that are directly incident upon that node (being central means being active within the network, that is, maintaining many ties) - *degree centrality.*
2. The length of (usually shortest) paths that have that node as one of their end nodes (being central means being efficient or independent of go-betweens by having short distances to other vertices in the network) - *closeness centrality.*
3. The proportion of (usually shortest) paths that have that node as one of their inner nodes (being central means being an important go-between, that is, being part of many paths between other vertices in the network) - *betweenness centrality.*

Let we assume that a social network be denoted by $G = (V, E)$, where V represents a set of nodes (also called vertices or actors in terms of social network nomenclature), and E - set of edges (also called ties) between nodes. Let n and m are the number of vertices and edges for G, respectively. Moreover, let A be an adjacency matrix of G, where each element $a_{ij} \in A$ is equal to 1 if $(i, j) \in E$ (i and j are neighbors), otherwise it is equal to 0.

Degree Centrality. As defined by Freeman [6], *degree centrality* can be measured as the number of edges incident upon a given node. In graph theory, it directly refers to the degree of the node $i \in V$. Degree centrality can be computed as the marginals of the adjacency matrix A as stated in Eq. (1).

$$DC(i) = \sum_{j \in V \setminus \{i\}} a_{ij} \tag{1}$$

Degree centrality reflects a popularity or an importance of the node in the network. The nodes with more direct connections to others, compared to those with fewer, hold a more prominent place in the network. On the other hand, the nodes with high degree centrality are highly exposed to flowing information or spreading disease in networks. Besides the simplicity and usefulness of degree centrality measure, its fundamental limitation is its local view of the network topology.

Closeness Centrality. Other view on importance of the node in the social network is presented by *closeness centrality* measure. Instead of focusing on the number of direct connections a particular node to others, it emphasizes its indirect connections to other nodes using the idea of shortest paths between two nodes. If one can reach the most other nodes (persons) in the network via shortest paths, one can conclude that the node is better connected, in terms of closeness centrality, that another node which has to traverse longer paths to reach the same other nodes (persons).

Freeman [6] argued that the power of a node (person) in a social network in terms of closeness centrality is inversely proportional to the sum of its distances to all the other persons in that social network. So, denoting d_{ij} as a distance from i to j $(i, j \in V)$, the closeness centrality of a node $i \in V$ is computed as stated in Eq. (2).

$$CC(i) = \frac{1}{\sum_{j \in V \setminus \{i\}} d_{ij}} \tag{2}$$

Betweenness Centrality. Opposite to degree centrality, which refers to a number of direct connections to other nodes, or closeness centrality, which refers to ability to reach a lot of other nodes by traversing relatively small distances, the *betweenness centrality* measure assumes that the importance of the node stems from the fact of being "in-between" the indirect communications of other nodes in graph. It refers to the number of walks that any actor needs a given actor to reach any other actor. Nodes that stand in these brokerage place in the network, occupy an important position, in term of this measure.

Following Freeman [6], the betweenness centrality version of power and importance of a node is assumed to be proportional to the fraction of shortest paths between all possible pairs of nodes that are passing through that node. Assuming that $g_{jk(i)}$ denotes the number of shortest paths from node j to k which are passing through node i and g_{jk} denotes the total number of shortest paths from node j to k, the betweenness centrality of a node $i \in V$ is defined as in Eq. (3).

$$BC(i) = \sum_{j=1 (j \neq i)}^{n} \sum_{k=1 (k \neq i)}^{j-1} \frac{g_{jk}(i)}{g_{jk}} \tag{3}$$

As it was stated, this measure represents the brokerage power of a person in a social network. It can be also a good indicator of the expected amount of communication load a node which has to handle. One can say that a person with high betweenness centrality has higher control over the information flowing across the network.

Other Centrality Measures. Among other popular centrality measures used to analyze social and complex networks one can list for example: *eigenvector centrality*, *PageRank centrality* and *Katz centrality*. They can be seen as generalizations or special cases of any of the three abovementioned fundamental measures.

3 Organizational Social Networks Based on Email Communication

As it was mentioned, an organizational social network may have different forms depending on a source and a form of information used to its construction. One of the most representative one is a social network based on different digital forms of business communication within an organization, especially using electronic mail channel. In such network, a number of employees (represented by nodes in a network) can be linked (represented by edges in a network) according to their interaction in terms of messages sent and received. Moreover, the number of interactions and their frequency may reveal information about the strength of bilateral relationships (represented for example as a weight on an the edge) [4].

Social networks inferred from email communications may be used to examine how organizational entities interact with each other, characterizing the many informal connections that link different roles together. Leading roles within organizations are often more linked to the number of relationships an individual within a network is at the center of than their actual job description [3].

Studies using email have become popular in social network analysis in the past decade, and much work has been done on this subject ranging from organizational design to operational efficiency and change management. Among them, one can point the work of Creamer at al. [5], Biswas and Biswas [1], and Nawaz et al. [12]. They aimed at extracting social hierarchies from electronic communication data [5], focused on ego-centric community estimation, to detect reachability and isolability in the actors within networks [1], and studied the problem of grouping of individuals with similar neighborhood and communication behavior using email metadata, such as number of sent and received emails, subject length, text, email and attachment sizes, and the date and time [12]. Email-organizational social network analysis has been also provided by Gloor et al. [8], where they measured team creativity and collaborative innovation through longitudinal social signals, using electronic records of interpersonal interactions like emails, Kolli and Narayanaswamy [10], where email communication network for crisis detection in a large organization was analyzed, and Merten and Gloor [11] who aimed at recognizing a possible sources of stress caused by email.

This paper contributes to analysis of organizational social network based on email communication by focusing on identifying key actors in such network.

4 Study on Organizational Social Network Based on Email Communication in Public Organization

The aim of the study was to examine the organizational social network based on email communication in one of the public organization located in Poland in terms of discovering the role of selected nodes in the network and to determine which of them plays a key role in the network. The results obtained during the experiment have been compared with an organizational structure of investigated organization respecting the roles playing by employees identified by the nodes in the network.

The organization studied in this section is a middle-sized public organization located in Poland. It has five departments additionally divided into 4–6 smaller units each with hierarchical structure.

The studied social network was generated using anonymized email traffic data obtained from server logs of the organization. The data were collected from January to June 2020 (6 months). Anonymized data about all incoming and outgoing email of the organization included: the (anonymized) sender, the (anonymized) receiver, and the timestamp of the message dispatch. In order to transfer the set of email messages into a network, each (anonymized) email address has been assigned to a single node. An undirected edge between nodes i and j has been established if an actor represented by node i sent (or received) at least one message to (from) an actor represented by node j ($i, j \in V$).

For the purpose of study, it has been decided to observe in details a single unit of the organization, where 91 persons have been employed and represented in the network. The number of messages sent and received within the selected unit was equal to 10 364, whereas the number of messages sent and received within the whole organization in the observed period was equal to 251 129 (see Table 1).

Table 1. Main characteristics of the data referring to email communication between employees within the organization

Category	January - June 2020
Number of messages sent and received within the whole organization	251 129
Number of messages sent and received within the selected organizational unit	10 364

For the purpose of the experiment, the *R* tool with the *iGraph* package was used [15]. Whereas *R* is a general purpose language used for statistical calculations and visualization of research results, *iGraph* provides a set of data types and appropriate social network property analysis functions. To identify persons who plays key role in the network it has been decided to use three function referring to centrality measures: `degree(graph)`, `closeness(graph)`, and `betweenness(graph)`.

Using *R* to analyze the social network requires preparation of relevant input data in CSV format. The data have been saved as an edge list, which is one of the more common ways to represent a chart. During the analysis after the data were loaded, it was necessary to convert them into a data frame (`graph.data.frame()`), from which the loaded communication network can be mapped in the form of a graph. The next step was to use the previously selected centrality measures and apply them by launching appropriate functions in *R*.

Table 2 presents selected detailed results limited to 20 (out of 91) the most important vertices identified by three functions with highest values calculated by each function. Moreover, visualization of organizational social networks based on email communication with using degree, closeness, and betweenness centrality measures are presented in Fig. 1, Fig. 2 and Fig. 3, respectively. Let us remind that numbers presented in columns denoted by vertex are labels that hide the email addresses.

Table 2. Results of computational experiment referring to email communication between employees within the organization regarding centrality

Betweenness		Degree		Closeness	
Vertex	Measure value	Vertex	Measure value	Vertex	Measure value
1	401.7364	**1**	35	**1**	0.00641
28	178.3609	**40**	31	28	0.00610
81	150.2756	**28**	28	67	0.00595
40	143.8153	82	25	**33**	0.00578
45	130.3590	19	24	**45**	0.00578
4	124.8592	8	23	36	0.00578
33	122.6270	**27**	23	68	0.00578
27	114.1669	**72**	23	44	0.00575
73	110.2344	2	22	**27**	0.00572
72	107.0353	7	22	**4**	0.00572
67	106,4562	**33**	22	57	0,00568
79	98,2287	69	22	**40**	0,00565
82	95,0158	5	21	**72**	0,00565
21	92,8466	21	20	41	0,00562
22	88,1084	**45**	20	52	0,00562
59	87,4566	**4**	19	59	0,00559
8	83,1771	6	19	81	0,00552
68	75,1055	18	19	34	0,00552
88	73,9119	22	19	65	0,00552
44	70,5588	41	19	79	0,00549

When analyzing the results obtained for the whole network (91 vertices) and presented in the Table 2 and Fig. 1, Fig. 2 and Fig. 3, one can conclude that every person arising in the network has at least one connection with some other person (it means that at least one email was sent or received by her/him). In fact, the number of contacts ranges from 8 to 35. Of course, this fact is evidenced by the degree centrality. The second measure (closeness) for individual vertices shows that the email network studied here is dense and strongly connected. The values observed for all vertices in the network are very similar and range from 0.00446 to 0.00641. The last measure (betweenness) allows us to distinguish persons with high influence on the distribution of information within the network. In the case of our network, a significant differences between vertex have been observed. The highest value of betweenness is equal to 401,7364 the lowest - 0,33101.

Deeper analysis of the results presented in the Table 2 provided additional interesting observation. First observation is that in most cases, three different measures give different rankings of nodes. Although it may be not surprising taking into account specific features of these measures, two nodes (1 and 28 -

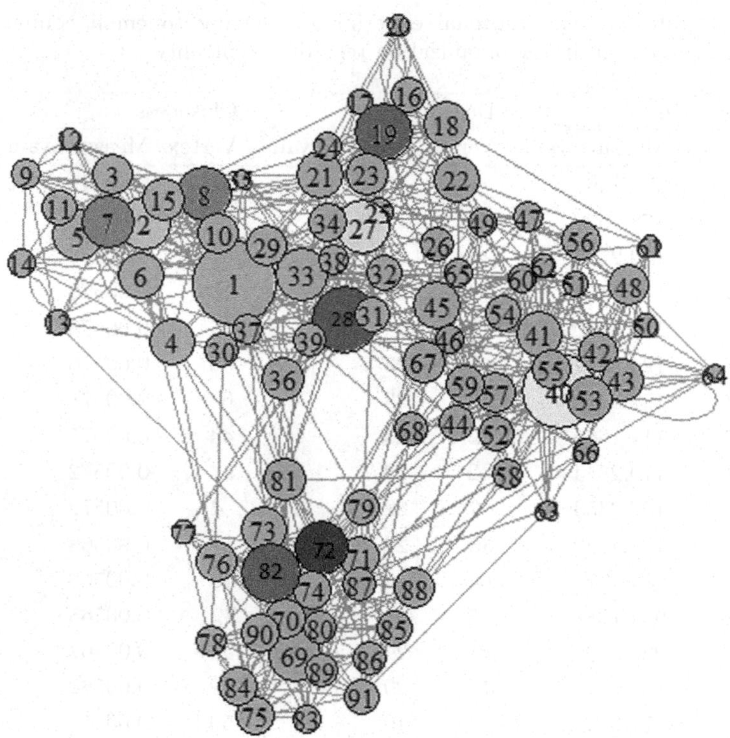

Fig. 1. Visualization of the organizational social network based on email communication using degree centrality - experiment results

written in bold font in the Table 2) have a prominent position in all rankings. It means that these persons may be responsible for distributing information among employees or occupying an important position in the organization. Focusing our observation on vertex 1 one can conclude that it has the highest number of connections with other people in the network. Additionally, this vertex is characterized by definitely the highest intermediation, which may indicate that it is a key person in the network. She/he can be treated as a bridge in communication with other people in the network. If we compare the values of betweenness of the first node - 1 (401 736) with the value of the second node - 28 (178 360) in the ranking, significant difference can be observed. As a consequence, removing the key vertex 1 could significantly affect the flow of information in the organization.

The next observation from the obtained results is that only three vertex (1, 28, 27) can be found in the group of the top 10 nodes of all rankings, and additional five (4, 33, 40, 45, 72) - when we consider top 20 nodes of all rankings. It may suggest, that persons represented by these vertices may also occupy an important position in the organization.

Because of the fact that the above three measures refer to centrality but focuses on a little different aspects of it, it has been also decided to carried out

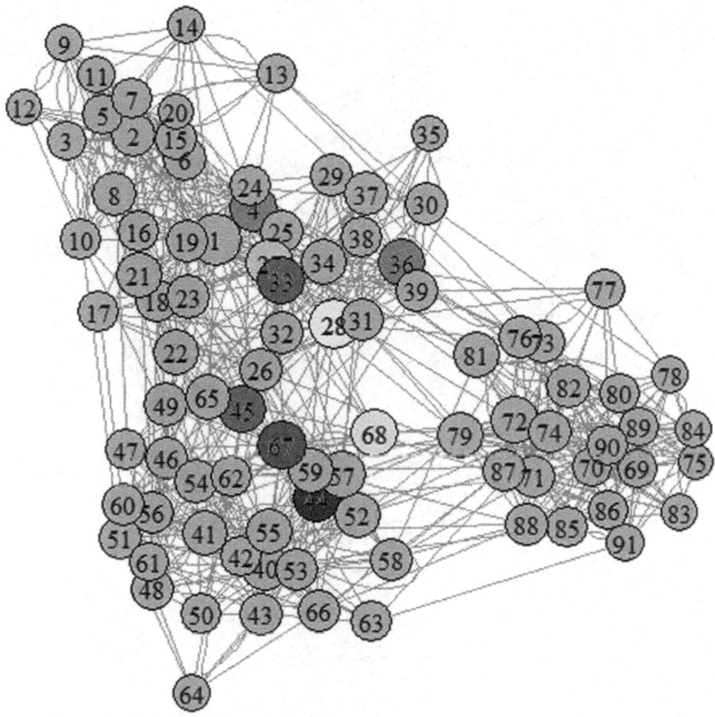

Fig. 2. Visualization of the organizational social network based on email communication using closeness centrality - experiment results

an experiment where the correlation between results obtained by using these measures has been observed. The results of the calculation are presented in Table 3. Analysis of these results allows us to conclude that all three measures are highly correlated. The values of correlation coefficients between all measures range from 0.80 to 0.85.

Table 3. Results of computational experiment referring to email communication within the organization - correlation between centrality measures used

	`degree()`	`closeness()`	`betweenness()`
`degree()`	1.00	0.81	0.85
`closeness()`	0.81	1.00	0.80
`betweenness()`	0.85	0.80	1.00

Having in mind the above results, it has been decided to analyze them from the organization perspective and taking into account the roles played by persons represented by the abovementioned vertices in our organizational social network.

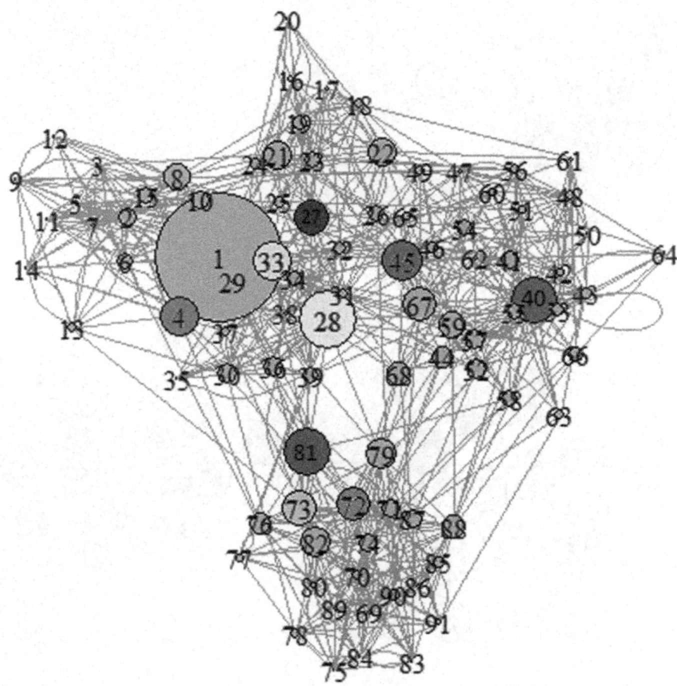

Fig. 3. Visualization of the organizational social network based on email communication using betweenness centrality - experiment results

In most cases, the analysis confirmed the importance of them, especially person denoted by node 1 is a secretary in one of the biggest and important organizational unit and 28 is a vice-chair of one of the departments of the organization. The rest of the mentioned vertices refer to management staff of the whole organization (vertex 4), management staff of the unit (vertices: 40, 72), or secretary in one of the units (vertices: 27, 45).

The results presented here demonstrates that information derived from analysis of email traffic within an organization can be usable for organizational management purposes.

5 Conclusions

Different communication channels between employees in the organization can be used as a data source to distinguish the network of relationships. The paper focuses on identifying key actors in social network based on email communication in public organization. The study uses the main centrality measures: degree, betweenness, and closeness. By analyzing and interpreting the indicated measures in the social network, it has been shown that they can play an important role in identification of people who play an important role and have a significant impact on the functioning of the organization. What important, such information can be usable for organizational management purposes.

Future work will aim at identifying key players in the organizational network based on emails exchanged by employees within the longer period (whole year), additionally divided into smaller periods (months) and using different measures of centrality. It will allow us to check how the vertex centrality measures and the structure of the organization changed over time. The second aspect is that the dataset we used covers internal email traffic limited to the organization. Of course, it is suitable only for the analysis of the internal patterns of email communication within an organization. An interesting extension of the research would be similar analysis referring also to external email communication, which would probably provide more valuable observations from a business perspective.

References

1. Biswas, A., Biswas, B.: Investigating community structure in perspective of ego network. Expert Syst. Appl. **42**, 6913–34 (2015)
2. Borgatti, S.P., Everett, M.G.: A graph-theoretic perspective on centrality. Soc. Netw. **28**(4), 466–84 (2006)
3. Christidis, P., Gomez-Losada, A.: Email based institutional network analysis: applications and risks. Soc. Sci. **8**, 306 (2019)
4. Christidis, P.: Intensity of bilateral contacts in social network analysis. Information **11**, 189 (2020)
5. Creamer, G., Rowe, R., Hershkop, S., Stolfo, S.J.: Segmentation and automated social hierarchy detection through email network analysis. In: Zhang, H., et al. (eds.) SNAKDD/WebKDD -2007. LNCS (LNAI), vol. 5439, pp. 40–58. Springer, Heidelberg (2009). https://doi.org/10.1007/978-3-642-00528-2_3
6. Freeman, L.C.: Centrality in social networks conceptual clarification. Soc. Netw. **1**(3), 215–39 (1979)
7. de la Fuente, D., Vega-Rodriguez, M.A., Perez, C.J.: Identifying key players in large social networks by using a multi-objective artificial bee colony optimization approach. Appl. Soft Comput. **77**, 176–187 (2019)
8. Gloor, P.A., Almozlino, A., Inbar, O., Lo, W., Provost, S.: Measuring team creativity through longitudinal social signals. arXiv:1407.0440 (2014)
9. Gloor, P.A., Fronzetti Colladon, A.: Measuring organizational consciousness through e-Mail based social network analysis. In: 5th International Conference on Collaborative Innovation Networks COINs15, Tokyo, Japan, 12–14 March (2015). http://www.ickn.org/documents/COINs15_organizationalConsciousness_final.pdf
10. Kolli, N., Narayanaswamy, B.: Analysis of e-mail communication using a social network framework for crisis detection in an organization. Procedia Soc. Behav. Sci. **100**, 57–67 (2013)
11. Merten, F., Gloor, P.: Too much e-mail decreases job satisfaction. Procedia Soc. Behav. Sci. **2**, 6457–65 (2010)
12. Nawaz, W., Khan, K.U., Lee, Y.K.: A multi-user perspective for personalized email communities. Expert Syst. Appl. **54**, 265–83 (2016)
13. Zhao, K., Yen, J., Greer, G., Qiu, B., Mitra, P., Portier, K.: Finding influential users of online health communities: a new metric based on sentiment influence. J. Amer. Med. Inform. Assoc. **21**(e2), e212–e218 (2014)

14. Zhu, Z.: Discovering the influential users oriented to viral marketing based on online social networks. Physica A **392**(16), 3459–3469 (2013)
15. https://cran.r-project.org/web/packages/igraph/igraph.pdf,16.04.2021

Social Recommendation for Social Networks Using Deep Learning Approach: A Systematic Review

Muhammad Alrashidi[1], Ali Selamat[1,2,3,4](✉), Roliana Ibrahim[1], and Ondrej Krejcar[4]

[1] School of Computing, Faculty of Engineering, Universiti Teknologi Malaysia (UTM), 81310 Skudai, Malaysia
aselamat@utm.my

[2] Media and Games Center of Excellence (MagicX), Universiti Teknologi Malaysia (UTM), Jalan Sultan Yahya Petra, 54100 Kuala Lumpur, Malaysia

[3] Malaysia Japan International Institute of Technology (MJIIT), Universiti Teknologi Malaysia Kuala Lumpur, Jalan Sultan Yahya Petra, 54100 Kuala Lumpur, Malaysia

[4] Faculty of Informatics and Management, Center for Basic and Applied Research, University of Hradec Kralove, Rokitanskeho 62, 500 03 Hradec Kralove, Czech Republic

Abstract. The increasing popularity of social networks indicates that the vast amounts of data contained within them could be useful in various implementations, including recommendation systems. Interests and research publications on deep learning-based recommendation systems have largely increased. This study aimed to identify, summarize, and assess studies related to the application of deep learning-based recommendation systems on social media platforms to provide a systematic review of recent studies and provide a way for further research to improve the development of deep learning-based recommendation systems in social environments. A total of 32 papers were selected from previous studies in five of the major digital libraries, including Springer, IEEE, ScienceDirect, ACM, Scopus, and Web of Science, published between 2016 and 2020. Results revealed that even though RS has received high coverage in recent years, several obstacles and opportunities will shape the future of RS for researchers. In addition, social recommendation systems achieving high accuracy can be built by using a combination of techniques that incorporate a range of features in SRS. Therefore, the adoption of deep learning techniques in developing social recommendation systems is undiscovered.

Keywords: Machine learning · Deep learning · Recommendation · Social media

1 Introduction

When a wide range of choices are open, making a decision is difficult. With information overload on the internet, particularly on social media platforms, finding accurate and appropriate data has become extremely difficult. As a result, users prefer decision-making assistance that is automatically easy and personalized. A recommender system,

K. Wojtkiewicz et al. (Eds.): ICCCI 2021, CCIS 1463, pp. 15–29, 2021.
https://doi.org/10.1007/978-3-030-88113-9_2

also known as a recommendation engine or portal, is a type of knowledge filtration process that aims to determine a user's "rating" or "preference" for an object [1]. The word "item" is used to describe what the framework suggests to consumers. A recommendation system focuses primarily on a certain category of item, and its architecture, graphical user interface, and key recommendation methodology are all tailored to offer useful and meaningful tips for that item. Social media has become very important for news, marketing, and advertising. Therefore, the huge amount of data generated from social media is valuable. Approximately 35% of purchases on Amazon and 75% of movies watched on Netflix are generated by recommendation systems [2]. Despite the potential value of recommendation systems, many studies suggest some future challenges in this field, such as using a combination of techniques to develop a hybrid model for social recommendation as a future work [3].

Deep learning (DL) is a subdivision of artificial intelligence that has progressed rapidly in recent years. It contains several kinds of processing layers, where each layer is utilized for the extraction of more complex features and fed to the next layer as input. DL models work the same way as the human brain learns and processes information [4]. The training process of DL models is classified into supervised and unsupervised learning. Deep neural networks, convolutional neural networks, deep autoencoders, restricted Boltzmann machines, and recurrent neural networks are some of the prominent DL models currently utilized for social media recommendation systems. Recently, interests and research publications on DL recommender systems have remarkably increased. Numerous studies have been conducted to review DL-based recommendation systems [5–7]. Although the previous studies provide a great summarization and analysis of the highest-quality academic papers based on DL-based recommendation systems, no study has investigated the various features of social networks essential in the generation of successful recommendations. As a result, a thorough study and examination of state-of-the-art related publications concentrating on social recommendation systems using DL are greatly needed to help appreciate the fundamental benefits and challenges of these approaches in helping researchers seek to develop a recommendation system for social media.

Hence, this paper aimed to identify, summarize, and assess current research works related to social recommendation systems using DL algorithms. The established research gaps and potential research directions are the expected outcomes.

The following are the study's major contributions, as determined by data collection and synthesis from 32 reviewed papers:

- The potential research gaps for social recommendation systems are identified using DL algorithms.
- Several social application domains, datasets, and evaluation metrics used in various social recommendations are presented.

2 Review Methodology

2.1 Research Questions

As previously mentioned, various studies have been conducted to review DL-based recommendation systems. However, the number of reviewed papers in implementing

DL for social recommendation is very limited. This study aims to identify, summarize, and assess studies related to the application of DL-based recommendation systems on social media. Therefore, a systematic literature review (SLR) was conducted following the [8] guideline.

The following research questions are restricted to DL in social recommendation because the responses to these questions would allow us to perform primary studies and build a new framework for some of the open problems found in this study.

- **RQ1**: Which DL techniques have been implemented on social RSs in previous studies?
- **RQ2**: Which social network datasets have been included in the study?
- **RQ3**: What application domains have been used in previous studies?
- **RQ4**: What are the metrics used for evaluating the performance of social RSs?

2.2 Search Procedure

An automatic search of the major digital libraries, including Springer, IEEE, ScienceDirect, ACM, Scopus, and Web of Science, was carried out to collect the appropriate publications for this study. Due to their popularity and being a rich source of research papers, these libraries were selected. This SLR searched for articles published between 2016 and 2020. Various combinations of keywords were used to refine the scope of the search. The following question was eventually determined:

"("recommendation system" OR "recommender system" OR "recommendation" OR "recommender") AND ("machine learning" OR "DL" OR "deep") AND ("social")"

2.3 Paper Selection

Study Scrutiny. Many papers were collected from electronic sources to obtain a thorough overview of this area. After each paper's abstract and methodology pages were read, the results of the search were filtered according to the selection criteria. Papers written in the English language only and papers that could answer at least one research question were included. In addition, papers published from 2016 to 2020 only and publications from conferences and journals only were included in this study. Figure 1 shows the paper selection process using PRISMA guidelines [9]. The selection of papers was based on six international journals and four research questions. The selection process comprised four stages: identification, screening, eligibility, and inclusion. The first stage was based on the automatic search and resulted in 590 papers. After screening, which was based on duplication and inaccessibility removal, 75 papers remained. A total of 32 papers were retrieved after passing all four stages, as shown in Fig. 1.

Quality Assessment. The papers selected were then scored according to the method of quality assessment defined by [10]. The quality of a paper was assessed by a list of questions adopted by [11]. The search was further refined by rating each criterion as: 2 (completely), 1 (partly), or 0 (none). Each study obtained a total score calculated for each criterion. Only those studies that had a score ≥ 9 were selected. The final subset of papers, including 32 papers, was identified. The researcher read these papers carefully, and the research questions were answered.

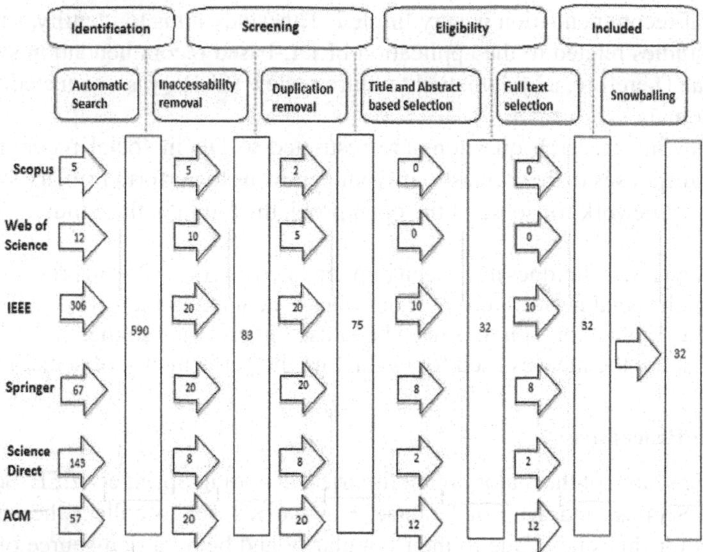

Fig. 1. Paper selection process

2.4 Threats to Validity

The rigorous assessment of an SLR's validity is one of the frameworks for ensuring the degree of empirical value of its results [12]. This SLR was supported by considering the four common forms of TTVs, namely, constructing validity, internal validity, external validity, and conclusion validity, as proposed by [12]. The first step was constructing validity by paper scrutiny and quality assessment. The research questions and inclusion and exclusion criteria were clearly identified. In internal validity, an unbiased paper collection process was ensured by using a manual and automatic search technique to find papers that were exhaustively relevant to the topics of interest. External validity was reduced in the third phase by looking for papers written between 2016 and January 2020 to generalize the study's results. Finally, conclusion validity was controlled using the procedures and techniques used in this research in accordance with the authors' guidelines [9, 10].

2.5 Data Extraction and Data Synthesis

In this study, various parameters were considered for the selection of relevant research papers to be included. For performing the research papers' complete study, various aspects and attributes of these studies were divided into columns, which were collated together to form a spreadsheet. Such information clusters included author names and year of publication, title of the paper, application domain, social network dataset, DL model, RS technique, and metrics used. The final subset of papers, including 32 papers, was identified, as shown in Table 1. The researcher read these papers carefully, and the research questions were answered.

Table 1. Selected studies of social RS using deep leaning.

References	Authors and year of publication	Application domains	Social network dataset	Deep learning model	Additional RS technique	Metric used
[13]	Wan (2020)	Social recommendation	Epinions, Flixter	Deep Learning	Matrix Factorization	Root Mean Squared Error (RMSE), F1 score, Coverage (COV)
[14]	Tahmasebi et al. (2020)	Movie	Twitter	Autoencoder	Collaborative filtering and content-based filtering	Mean Absolute Error (MAE), and RMSE
[15]	Pan et al. (2020)	Learning social Representations	Epinions and Ciao datasets	Autoencoder	Collaborative filtering	MAE and RMSE
[16]	Gao et al. (2020)	Microblogs and social network	Sina Weibo and Twitter	DNN	Collaborative filtering	Precision and Recall
[17]	Pramanik (2020)	Venue recommender	Meetup and Yelp	DeepCoNN	Collaborative Topic Regression based Ranking (CTR) Matrix Factorization-Based Ranking (MFR)	Recall and Mean Inverse Rank (MIR)
[18]	Zhang (2019)	Social images	NUS-WIDE object + Flickr	CNN	Tag Tree	Precision and Recall
[19]	C C, N. and Mohan (2019)	Semantic social Information	Github	Autoencoder	Collaborative Filtering	MAE and RMSE
[20]	Lei (2019)	Attention-aware recommendation	Yahoo Movies, Amazon Video Games and Amazon Movies and TV	Deep Learning	Collaborative Filtering	Mean Average Precision (MAP), Recall@N
[21]	Zhang (2019)	Movie recommendation	MovieLens	Bayesian Network	Matrix Factorization, Collaborative Filtering	RMSE, Precision@10

(*continued*)

Table 1. (*continued*)

References	Authors and year of publication	Application domains	Social network dataset	Deep learning model	Additional RS technique	Metric used
[22]	Shamsoddin (2019)	Product prediction	Amazon	Deep Learning	Collaborative Filtering	MAE, RMSE, Positive Predictive Rate (PPV), Recall, Accuracy (ACC) and Mathew's Correlation Coefficient (MCC)
[23]	Garg (2019)	Session-based recommendation	Yoochoos, Diginetica, RetailRocket	Deep Learning	Neighborhood-Based Methods	MRR@K (Mean Reciprocal Rank) and Recall@K,
[24]	Chen (2019)	Context-ware recommendation	MovieLens, Last.fm	Deep Learning	Collaborative Filtering	F1-score
[25]	Lemei (2019)	Personalized news recommendation	Adressa, Last.fm and Weibo-Net-Tweet	Deep Neural Network	User Interest Modelling	MRR@K, Recall@K, Precision@K, F1 score
[26]	Song (2019)	Social recommendation	Douban, Delicious, Yelp	Deep Learning	Matrix Factorization	Recall@K and Normalized Discounted Cumulative Gain (NDCG)
[27]	Wu ((2019)	Recurrent recommender Systems	Netflix and MovieLens	Deep Learning	Collaborative Filtering	RMSE, MAE
[28]	Qu (2018)	Friend recommendation	Sina Weibo	DNN		RMSE
[29]	Lu (2018)	Reviews	Yelp, Amazon	Deep Learning	Matrix Factorization	MSE
[30]	Malte (2018)	Session-based recommendation	E-commerce Datasets, Media Datasets	Deep Learning	Matrix Factorization	Hit rate, MRR, Catalog COV, and Average Popularity (POP)

(*continued*)

Table 1. *(continued)*

References	Authors and year of publication	Application domains	Social network dataset	Deep learning model	Additional RS technique	Metric used
[31]	Neamanee (2018)	Time-aware	MovieLens	Deep Learning		MAE, COV
[32]	Niu (2018)	Image recommendation	Flickr YFCC100M	Deep Learning	Matrix Factorization	Precision@K, Recall@K
[33]	Liang (2018)	Implicit feedback	MovieLens-20M, Netflix-price, Million Song	Deep Neural Network	Collaborative Filtering	Recall@K, NDCG@K
[34]	Wei (2017)	Movie	Netflix	Autoencoder	Collaborative Filtering	RMSE
[35]	Deng (2017)	Trust-aware recommendation	Epinions and Flixster	Autoencoder	Matrix Factorization	RMSE
[36]	Dang and Ignat (2017)	User trust relations	Epinions and Ciao	DNN		MAE and RMSE
[37]	Ngu yen (2017)	Tag recommendation	NUS-WIDE and Flickr-PTR	Deep Neural Network	Content-Base	F1@K, AUC
[38]	Zheng (2017)	Reviews recommendation	Yelp, Beer, Amazon	Deep Learning	Collaborative Filtering	MSE
[39]	Wang (2017)	Article recommendation	Own dataset Created	Deep Learning	Content-Base	AUC, Precision, Recall, F1 Score
[40]	Cao (2017)	Top-n recommendation	MovieLens, Netflix and Yelp	Deep Learning	Collaborative Filtering	Accuracy, Precision, Recall
[41]	Hidasi (2016)	Session-based recommendations	VIDXL, CLASS	Deep Learning	Matrix Factorization	Recall@K, MRR@K
[42]	Tan (2016)	Quote recommendation	Quote dataset	Deep Learning	Content-Base	MRR, Recall@K, NDCG@K
[43]	Lee (2016)	Quote Recommendation	real twitter dialogue	Deep Neural Network	Content-Base	MRR, Recall@K, NDCG@K, Hit@K
[44]	Zhou (2016)	Profile recommendation	ILSVRC-2012	Deep Learning	Content-Base	Distance

3 Results and Discussion

In this section, the findings are presented in this process to answer research questions based on data collected from selected studies. This section comprises four main subsections. The first subsection describes the various techniques of DL that were used in social RSs. The second subsection lists various datasets, and the third section discusses the domain of DL techniques used in recommendation systems. The last subsection details the various evaluation metrics utilized to assess the DL-based RS's accuracy (ACC).

Moreover, the keywords used in the articles were examined and displayed in Fig. 2. VOSviewer software was used to extract the relation between the co-occurrence of keywords that related to the research topic.

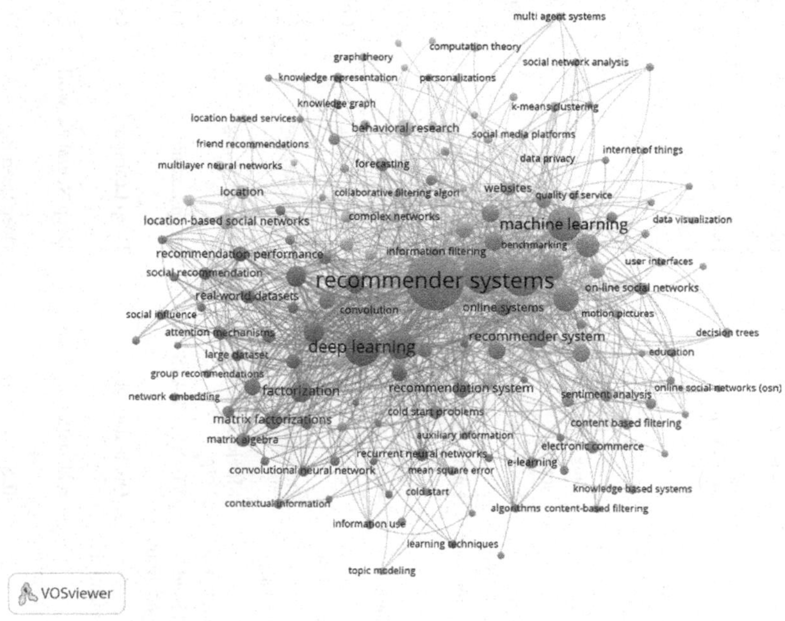

Fig. 2. Frequency of keywords in the publications

3.1 Social RSs using Deep Learning

RQ1: Which DL techniques have been implemented on social RSs in previous studies?

This subsection identifies the result of RQ1, which helps to classify the studies that were based on the DL social recommendation system that were part of this review. Figure 3 illustrates the distribution of journal articles by publication year from 2016 to 2020. The number of studies using DL techniques for recommendation systems was identified through a graph for this SLR. Different studies have used different DL techniques for recommendation systems. For example, Wan et al. [13] used two DMF techniques to extract the features from the ranking of user objects, namely, (i) linear DMF and (ii) non-linear DMF, to improve the loading ACC; furthermore, Deep-Marginalized Denoising Autoencoder was used to approximate the user factor matrix factorized from the user-item ranking matrix by extracting the latent representation in the secret layer from the trust relationship matrix. Another study [20] proposed a MARS by using convolutional neural networks. A study [22] introduced SN-CFM based on DL for the prediction of high customer recommendation on the similarity of the customers and the goods in the neighborhood. A researcher [26] introduced a session-based recommendation system by using different DL techniques: RNN, KNN, and Neural Attentive Recommendation Machine. A study [33] defined a variant autoencoder by using a deep latent Gaussian model. Another study [23] presented the recommendation for Sequence and Time Aware using session-based k-nearest-neighbors. However, although RS has received high coverage in recent years, several obstacles and opportunities will remain to shape the future of RS for researchers. The adoption of DL techniques in developing social recommendation systems has not been fairly investigated.

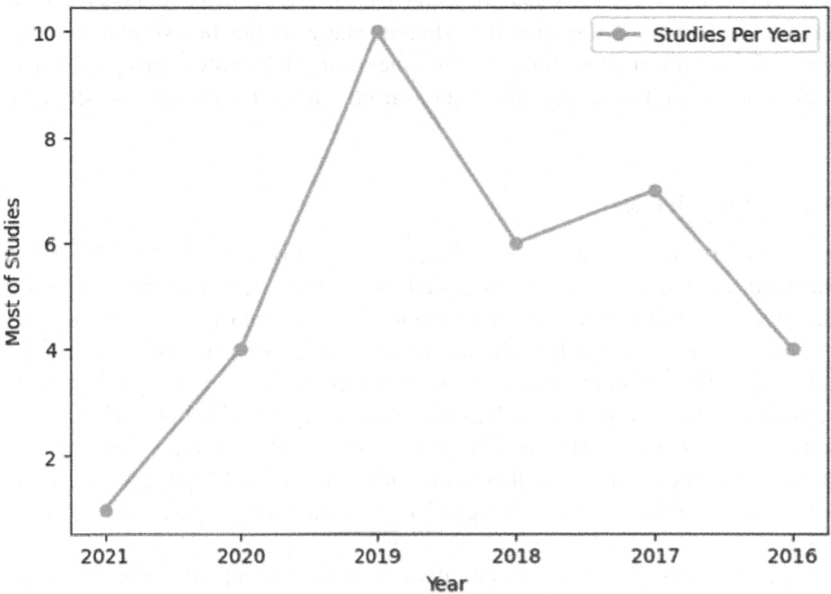

Fig. 3. Distribution of studies per year

3.2 Social Networks Dataset

RQ2: Which social network dataset have been included in the study?

The 38 datasets are mentioned in Table 1. We list the domain for each and the studies that used it. At least one dataset was used in each of the studies found. An analysis can use more than one dataset in some cases. Table 1 shows that the Movie Lens [24, 27, 28, 31, 33] and Yelp [17, 26, 29, 38, 40] datasets proved, based on the chosen papers, to be the most widely used datasets, although Epinions [13, 15, 35, 36], Twitter [14, 16, 25, 43], and Amazon [20, 22, 29, 38] were also classified as the most popularly used datasets. Furthermore, the table shows that several separate publicly available databases were used for the DL-based RS assessment. Finally, the majority of the studies relied on publicly accessible databases for their study. In conclusion, most of the studies used socially available datasets in their research, whereas most of the researchers also focused on creating or extracting their own dataset.

3.3 Application Domains

RQ3: What are the application domains used in the previous studies?

Various studies have introduced differing domains for the recommendation system. As shown in Table 1, many application domains presented from 2016 to 2020 are listed with the dataset. In recent times, recommendation systems have been applied to many domains, which is gaining more interest day by day. Session-based [23, 25, 26, 30, 41], attention-aware [20], trust-aware [35, 36], context-aware [24], friendship aware [28], and time-aware [23, 31] recommendations have been used. Various studies used various datasets for the corresponding domain, whereas many studies had similar datasets and domains but used different techniques. In conclusion, this shows strong evidence that the field is active and attracting the attention of a growing number of scholars and practitioners.

3.4 Evaluation Metrics

RQ4: What are the metrics used for evaluating the performance of social RSs?

The main objectives of any recommendation system are efficiency and excellent performance. A variety of metrics have been developed and used in various ways to measure the efficiency of the RS. Numerous parameters are used for the evaluation of DL techniques, as listed in this analysis and presented in this section. The distribution of the examined studies in terms of prediction metrics is presented in Fig. 4. Figure 4 shows the metrics used between 2016 and 2020, which indicates that the number of studies used a number of metrices, where recall was the most used metric. Figure 4 is based on 17 metric parameters, which were used to evaluate classification, rating prediction, ranking, and other recommendations.

Classification metrics, which essentially determine the degree of correct classification of objects, depending on the user's interest, are another type of metric used to test the precision of the RS. The magnitude of the error in the users' ranking forecast is normally ignored in these metrics. Recall, precision, F1 measure, and ACC are some of the most widely used measurement criteria in this case. The percentage of the user's favorite objects that are available is clearly depicted by recall. In general, the ACC represents the user's favorite objects. The F1 measurement is a compromise between recall and precision. ACC is a simple calculation that compares the true positive and negative rates.

Rating prediction metrics: The key goal of rating prediction parameters is to determine how well the RS will predict how users will rate products. However, by comparing various algorithms using ranking predictive metrics, one can determine which has the lowest number of errors. These measurement metrics determine the recommendation's correctness in terms of error. MSE, RMSE, and MAE are the three evaluation parameters we observed in this SLR. The discrepancy between the expected and actual ratings was computed using these metrics. As a result, lower metrics values indicate increased performance.

Ranking metrics: The ACC metric is the ranking metric that tests how well RS does when recommending the lists of objects that are ordered by users when the order of the items on the list is important. The rating parameters for the RS evaluations used in the review papers are as follows. NDCGs show that the items having more ranking are completely satisfied than poorly rated items. The Hit ratio is a metric that determines when a customer goal preference appears in the high-ranked list of recommendations. Mean reciprocal ranks evaluate the place of ratings of customers' desired choices in the RS. Finally, mean average precision takes into account the precisions of the first K-recommended graded products.

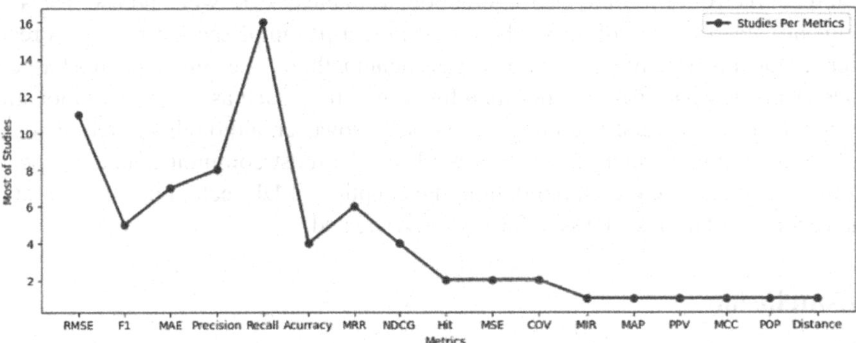

Fig. 4. Distribution of studies per metric

4 Recommendations and Future Research Directions

The primary target of any RS that is designed to take into account many user experiences is user satisfaction. Although RS has received high coverage in recent years, some obstacles and opportunities will shape the future of RS for researchers. In addition, social recommendation systems achieving high ACC can be built by using a combination of techniques that incorporate a range of features in SRS. The challenge of advancement in science and technology faced by RS is observed in this SLR in various forms, including user profile drift, item demand drift, change in quality management system and fames, revolution in material precepts of objects, energetic attention within the communal, seasonality, unstable user–object favoritism, vagaries in measurement tools, permanent and temporary churning, and high volatility. State-of-the-art historical models in RS have not been sufficiently versatile to address all dynamism problems encountered in the field of RS. A solution that is sufficiently versatile to satisfy equally lengthy and short-term consumer likings is ideal. Most RS temporal models can only predict consumer behavior for potential suggestions based on their preferences at a certain time period. Few studies overlook the importance of previous experiences, and in most situations, may also have an effect when making recommendations. Methods for detecting shift points must be considered, in which observed modifications can only be evaluated using those techniques and carrying out the required procedures.

Here is a requirement to understand the point identification methods that observed modifications that can simply be evaluated by using certain methods and conducting a detailed test. Thereafter, the requisite act can be occupied and also updating or discarding the model when the modification is definite. Another open problem in modeling the idea that drifts in RS is that concept drifts often arise in various ways and at several times, necessitating different ways to deal with them. As a result, a detailed investigation of DL techniques' full abilities to develop current RS models is required as a possible research path. Another thing to note is the assessment technique used to measure the success of RS programs, given that nearly all the experiments analyzed were assessed using offline methods. In addition, if offline evaluation is thought to be less expensive and has no bias in reaction from dynamic user interaction, as in the case of web and user trials, the findings are always contradictory when used in real-life implementations. As a result, further research is urgently needed on assessment methods to evaluate results based on various evaluation parameters other than fine estimation, such as real-time, innovation, coverage, luck, and diversity, among others [45]. However, although a range of studies on DL-based recommendation systems work on the most common domains, such as e-commerce and movie recommendation, the adoption of DL techniques in developing social recommendation systems is fairly uninvestigated.

5 Conclusion

In this review, an SLR was conducted to review and analyze recent studies on social recommendation systems using DL algorithms. A search of the major digital libraries, including Springer, IEEE, ScienceDirect, ACM, Scopus, and Web of Science, was carried out to collect the appropriate publications for this study. The main results of the review discovered. Current approaches of recommendation systems based on DL techniques in studies published between 2016 and 2020 were reviewed and examined. This SLR aimed to provide and assist academics and researchers in relevant fields to gain a comprehensive understanding of recommendation systems based on DL. This SLR examined some of the most urgent open issues and some potential possible extensions. In recent decades, both DL and recommender mechanisms have become hot research topics. Every year, a significant number of new strategies and models emerge. We hope that this survey will provide readers with a thorough understanding of the main facets of this area and an explanation of the most significant developments and shed light on future research.

Acknowledgements. This work was supported/funded by the Ministry of Higher Education under the Fundamental Research Grant Scheme (FRGS/1/2018/ICT04/UTM/01/1). The authors sincerely thank Universiti Teknologi Malaysia under Research University Grant Vot-20H04 and Malaysia Research University Network Vot 4L876, for the completion of the research. The work is also partially supported by the SPEV project (ID: 2102–2021), Faculty of Informatics and Management, University of Hradec Kralove. We are also grateful for the support of Ph.D. students

Michal Dobrovolny and Sebastien Mambou in consultations regarding application aspects from Hradec Kralove University, Czech Republic.

References

1. Ricci, F., Rokach, L., Shapira, B.: Recommender Systems Handbook (2011)
2. McKinsey & Company: How Retailers can keep up with Consumers, https://www.mckinsey.com/industries/retail/our-insights/how-retailers-can-keep-up-with-consumers
3. Shokeen, J., Rana, C.: A study on features of social recommender systems. Artif. Intell. Rev. **53**(2), 965–988 (2019). https://doi.org/10.1007/s10462-019-09684-w
4. Shokeen, J., Rana, C.: Social recommender systems: techniques, domains, metrics, datasets and future scope. J. Intell Inf. Syst. **54**(3), 633–667 (2019). https://doi.org/10.1007/s10844-019-00578-5
5. Da'u, A., Salim, N.: Recommendation system based on deep learning methods: a systematic review and new directions. Artif. Intell. Rev. **53**, 2709–2748 (2020). https://doi.org/10.1007/s10462-019-09744-1
6. Batmaz, Z., Yurekli, A., Bilge, A., Kaleli, C.: A review on deep learning for recommender systems: challenges and remedies. Artif. Intell. Rev. **52**(1), 1–37 (2018). https://doi.org/10.1007/s10462-018-9654-y
7. Zhang, S., Yao, L., Sun, A., Tay, Y.: Deep learning based recommender system: a survey and new perspectives. ACM Comput. Surv. **52**, 1–35 (2019). https://doi.org/10.1145/3285029
8. Kitchenham, B., Pearl Brereton, O., Budgen, D., Turner, M., Bailey, J., Linkman, S.: Systematic literature reviews in software engineering – a systematic literature review. Inf. Softw. Technol. **51**, 7–15 (2009). https://doi.org/10.1016/j.infsof.2008.09.009
9. Moher, D., Liberati, A., Tetzlaff, J., Altman, D.G.: Preferred reporting items for systematic reviews and meta-analyses: the PRISMA statement. PLoS Med. **6**, e1000097 (2009). https://doi.org/10.1371/journal.pmed.1000097
10. Review, A.S.: Applied sciences recommender system based on temporal models, pp. 1–27 (2020)
11. Del Carpio, A.F., Angarita, L.B.: Trends in software engineering processes using deep learning: a systematic literature review. In: 2020 46th Euromicro Conference on Software Engineering and Advanced Applications (SEAA), pp. 445–454. IEEE (2020)
12. Zhou, X., Jin, Y., Zhang, H., Li, S., Huang, X.: A map of threats to validity of systematic literature reviews in software engineering. In: 2016 23rd Asia-Pacific Software Engineering Conference (APSEC), pp. 153–160. IEEE (2016)
13. Wan, L., Xia, F., Kong, X., Hsu, C.-H., Huang, R., Ma, J.: Deep matrix factorization for trust-aware recommendation in social networks. IEEE Trans. Netw. Sci. Eng. **8**, 511–528 (2021). https://doi.org/10.1109/TNSE.2020.3044035
14. Tahmasebi, H., Ravanmehr, R., Mohamadrezaei, R.: Social movie recommender system based on deep autoencoder network using Twitter data. Neural Comput. Appl. **33**(5), 1607–1623 (2020). https://doi.org/10.1007/s00521-020-05085-1
15. Pan, Y., He, F., Yu, H.: Learning social representations with deep autoencoder for recommender system. World Wide Web **23**(4), 2259–2279 (2020). https://doi.org/10.1007/s11280-020-00793-z
16. Gao, J., Zhang, C., Xu, Y., Luo, M., Niu, Z.: Hybrid microblog recommendation with heterogeneous features using deep neural network. Expert Syst. Appl. **167**, 114191 (2021). https://doi.org/10.1016/j.eswa.2020.114191

17. Pramanik, S., Haldar, R., Kumar, A., Pathak, S., Mitra, B.: Deep learning driven venue recommender for event-based social networks. IEEE Trans. Knowl. Data Eng. **32**, 2129–2143 (2020). https://doi.org/10.1109/TKDE.2019.2915523
18. Zhang, J., Yang, Y., Zhuo, L., Tian, Q., Liang, X.: Personalized recommendation of social images by constructing a user interest tree with deep features and tag trees. IEEE Trans. Multimed. **21**, 2762–2775 (2019). https://doi.org/10.1109/TMM.2019.2912124
19. Nisha, C.C., Mohan, A.: A social recommender system using deep architecture and network embedding. Appl. Intell. **49**(5), 1937–1953 (2019). https://doi.org/10.1007/s10489-018-1359-z
20. Zheng, L., et al.: MARS: memory attention-aware recommender system. In: 2019 IEEE International Conference on Data Science and Advanced Analytics (DSAA), pp. 11–20. IEEE (2019)
21. Zhang, R., Mao, Y.: Movie recommendation via markovian factorization of matrix processes. IEEE Access. **7**, 13189–13199 (2019). https://doi.org/10.1109/ACCESS.2019.2892289
22. Shamshoddin, S., Khader, J., Gani, S.: Predicting consumer preferences in electronic market based on IoT and Social Networks using deep learning based collaborative filtering techniques. Electron. Commer. Res. **20**(2), 241–258 (2019). https://doi.org/10.1007/s10660-019-09377-0
23. Garg, D., Gupta, P., Malhotra, P., Vig, L., Shroff, G.: Sequence and time aware neighborhood for session-based recommendations. In: Proceedings of the 42nd International ACM SIGIR Conference on Research and Development in Information Retrieval, pp. 1069–1072. ACM, New York (2019)
24. Chen, H., Li, J.: Adversarial tensor factorization for context-aware recommendation. In: Proceedings of the 13th ACM Conference on Recommender Systems, pp. 363–367. ACM, New York (2019)
25. Zhang, L., Liu, P., Gulla, J.A.: Dynamic attention-integrated neural network for session-based news recommendation. Mach. Learn. **108**(10), 1851–1875 (2019). https://doi.org/10.1007/s10994-018-05777-9
26. Song, W., Xiao, Z., Wang, Y., Charlin, L., Zhang, M., Tang, J.: Session-based social recommendation via dynamic graph attention networks. In: Proceedings of the Twelfth ACM International Conference on Web Search and Data Mining, pp. 555–563. ACM, New York (2019)
27. Wu, X., Shi, B., Dong, Y., Huang, C., Chawla, N. V.: Neural tensor factorization for temporal interaction learning. In: Proceedings of the Twelfth ACM International Conference on Web Search and Data Mining, pp. 537–545. ACM, New York (2019)
28. Qu, Z., Li, B., Wang, X., Yin, S., Zheng, S.: An efficient recommendation framework on social media platforms based on deep learning. In: 2018 IEEE International Conference on Big Data and Smart Computing (BigComp), pp. 599–602. IEEE (2018)
29. Lu, Y., Dong, R., Smyth, B.: Coevolutionary recommendation model. In: Proceedings of the 2018 World Wide Web Conference on World Wide Web - WWW 2018, pp. 773–782. ACM Press, New York (2018)
30. Ludewig, M., Jannach, D.: Evaluation of session-based recommendation algorithms. User Model. User-Adap. Inter. **28**(4–5), 331–390 (2018). https://doi.org/10.1007/s11257-018-9209-6
31. Neammanee, T., Maneeroj, S.: Time-aware recommendation based on user preference driven. In: 2018 IEEE 42nd Annual Computer Software and Applications Conference (COMPSAC), pp. 26–31. IEEE (2018)
32. Niu, W., Caverlee, J., Lu, H.: Neural personalized ranking for image recommendation. In: Proceedings of the Eleventh ACM International Conference on Web Search and Data Mining, pp. 423–431. ACM, New York (2018)

33. Liang, D., Krishnan, R.G., Hoffman, M.D., Jebara, T.: Variational autoencoders for collaborative filtering. In: Proceedings of the 2018 World Wide Web Conference on World Wide Web - WWW 2018, pp. 689–698. ACM Press, New York (2018)
34. Wei, J., He, J., Chen, K., Zhou, Y., Tang, Z.: Collaborative filtering and deep learning based recommendation system for cold start items. Expert Syst. Appl. **69**, 29–39 (2017). https://doi.org/10.1016/j.eswa.2016.09.040
35. Deng, S., Huang, L., Xu, G., Wu, X., Wu, Z.: On Deep learning for trust-aware recommendations in social networks. IEEE Trans. Neural Netw. Learn. Syst. **28**, 1164–1177 (2017). https://doi.org/10.1109/TNNLS.2016.2514368
36. Dang, Q.-V., Ignat, C.-L.: dTrust: a simple deep learning approach for social recommendation. In: 2017 IEEE 3rd International Conference on Collaboration and Internet Computing (CIC), pp. 209–218. IEEE (2017)
37. Nguyen, H.T.H., Wistuba, M., Grabocka, J., Drumond, L.R., Schmidt-Thieme, L.: Personalized deep learning for tag recommendation. In: Kim, J., Shim, K., Cao, L., Lee, J.-G., Lin, X., Moon, Y.-S. (eds.) PAKDD 2017. LNCS (LNAI), vol. 10234, pp. 186–197. Springer, Cham (2017). https://doi.org/10.1007/978-3-319-57454-7_15
38. Zheng, L., Noroozi, V., Yu, P.S.: Joint deep modeling of users and items using reviews for recommendation. In: Proceedings of the Tenth ACM International Conference on Web Search and Data Mining, pp. 425–434. ACM, New York (2017)
39. Wang, X., et al.: Dynamic attention deep model for article recommendation by learning human editors' demonstration. In: Proceedings of the 23rd ACM SIGKDD International Conference on Knowledge Discovery and Data Mining, pp. 2051–2059. ACM, New York (2017)
40. Cao, S., Yang, N., Liu, Z.: Online news recommender based on stacked auto-encoder. In: 2017 IEEE/ACIS 16th International Conference on Computer and Information Science (ICIS), pp. 721–726. IEEE (2017)
41. Hidasi, B., Quadrana, M., Karatzoglou, A., Tikk, D.: Parallel recurrent neural network architectures for feature-rich session-based recommendations. In: Proceedings of the 10th ACM Conference on Recommender Systems, pp. 241–248. ACM, New York (2016)
42. Tan, J., Wan, X., Xiao, J.: A neural network approach to quote recommendation in writings. In: Proceedings of the 25th ACM International on Conference on Information and Knowledge Management, pp. 65–74. ACM, New York (2016)
43. Lee, H., Ahn, Y., Lee, H., Ha, S., Lee, S.: Quote recommendation in dialogue using deep neural network. In: Proceedings of the 39th International ACM SIGIR conference on Research and Development in Information Retrieval, pp. 957–960. ACM, New York (2016)
44. Zhou, J., Albatal, R., Gurrin, C.: Applying visual user interest profiles for recommendation and personalisation. In: Tian, Q., Sebe, N., Qi, G.-J., Huet, B., Hong, R., Liu, X. (eds.) MMM 2016. LNCS, vol. 9517, pp. 361–366. Springer, Cham (2016). https://doi.org/10.1007/978-3-319-27674-8_34
45. Aggarwal, C.C.: An introduction to recommender systems. In: Recommender Systems, pp. 1–28. Springer, Cham (2016). https://doi.org/10.1007/978-3-319-29659-3_1

Session Based Recommendations Using Char-Level Recurrent Neural Networks

Michal Dobrovolny[1], Jaroslav Langer[1], Ali Selamat[1,2,3], and Ondrej Krejcar[1(✉)]

[1] Faculty of Informatics and Management, Center for Basic and Applied Research, University of Hradec Kralove, Hradec Kralove, Czech Republic
{michal.dobrovolny,jaroslav.langer,ondrej.krejcar}@uhk.cz

[2] Malaysia Japan International Institute of Technology (MJIIT), Universiti Teknologi Malaysia Kuala Lumpur, Jalan Sultan Yahya Petra, 54100 Kuala Lumpur, Malaysia
aselamat@utm.my

[3] School of Computing, Faculty of Engineering, Universiti Teknologi Malaysia (UTM), 81310 Skudai, Malaysia

Abstract. The use of long short-term memory (LSTM) for session-based recommendations is described in this research. This study uses char-level LSTM as a real-time recommendation service to test and offer the optimal solution. Our strategy can be used to any situation. Two LSTM layers and a thick layer make up our model. To evaluate the prediction results, we use the mean of squared errors. We also put our recall and precision metrics prediction to the test. The best-performing network had roughly 2000 classes and was a trainer for the last year of likes on an image-based social platform. On twenty objects, our best model had a recall value of 0.182 and a precision value of 0.061.

Keywords: Neural networks · Session-based filtering · Deep learning · Recommender systems · Long short-term memory · Collaborative filtering

1 Introduction

Consumers are now exposed to a wide range of products thanks to recommendation systems in many current applications. Typically, such systems present the customer with a list of suggested things or estimate how much each item might cost. These technologies assist users in identifying appropriate items and making selections from the collection's desired items. [6]

Forecasting is one of the most important tasks that people are attempting to complete. It is difficult to predict a long-term or mid-term bid. The methods are evolving at a breakneck pace. We strive to analyze the patterns of repetition and forecast the next cycle using a modern power system. Algorithms of Neural network (NN) can search and represent both structured and not structured data – for instance, natural language processing, time series or image data [1,14]. In

K. Wojtkiewicz et al. (Eds.): ICCCI 2021, CCIS 1463, pp. 30–41, 2021.
https://doi.org/10.1007/978-3-030-88113-9_3

image data processing can be found examples about fixing an image [19,21], compression [16], super-resolution [3,11], image classification [2,13], forecasting [5] session based recommendations [4]. Many tournaments include NN algorithms as the first place finisher. Image and time series processing is a well-developed field. Picture interpretation, image damage repair, image style, and fake image generation are only a few examples. Researchers experiment with a variety of models to enhance them.

In this paper, we aimed to see if the long short-term memory (LSTM) is capable of automating and providing real-time recommendations for content. We created a deep learning algorithm to generate user content and tested it in terms of precision and recall on collaborative filtering.

It is organized as follows: Content recommendation is covered in Sect. 2. The text "evaluation metrics" can be found in Sect. 3. We outline the approach we are using to employ LSTM for session-based recommendations as well as our dataset in Sect. 4. Results are discussed in the Sect. 5. In the last section of the paper, we summarize our findings and make some concluding remarks about our future work plans.

2 Methods of Content Recommendation

Collaborative filtering is a technology that is built at the core of many modern recommendation engines, including those from Amazon, Netflix, and Spotify. It identifies and matches people based on their needs for knowledge and tastes. By participating in collaborative filtering, users who utilize the system may share their assessments and views of each item they consume with other system users, helping them make better decisions about which items to select. The collaboration filtering framework offers useful personalized recommendations in return for new products.

There are several methods, some of which are more advanced than others. Autoencoders, Boltzmann machines, and multi-layer perceptrons are commonly used for a recommendation.

2.1 Autoencoders

Autoencoder is a type of neural network that can be used to learn a compressed representation of raw data.

An autoencoder is built from an encoder and a decoder sub-model. When sending, the encoder compresses the information, and when receiving, the decoder attempts to recreate the information that was sent. The model is saved and the decoder is thrown away after training [8,12,17].

Overall, autoencoders are made up of three parts: In an encoder, there is an input layer and a hidden layer; the bottleneck is the data reservoir, and in a decoder, there is a learned or compressed representation of the information. – the part that starts from hidden layer and ends with output layer [8,12], as shown on following figure.

We can take an unlabeled dataset and frame it as a supervised learning problem tasked with outputting $(\widehat{x})$, a reconstruction of the original input x. This network can be trained by minimizing the reconstruction error, $(x, \widehat{x})$, which measures the differences between our original input and the consequent reconstruction.

There are several main use cases for auto-encoders such as: Data compression, Denoising data, Classification and Collaborative Filtering (Recommendation) [8,12].

In this paper, author will focus on the last one-use case - Collaborative Filtering. There are many autoencoders model implementations.

Some of them will be described and explained.

AutoRec. The AutoRec algorithm allows users to be placed directly into low-dimensional space, and instead of having to explicitly embed users/items into the low-dimensional space, it utilizes the interaction matrix as the input, which is then reprocessed to provide the output.

AutoRec is different from a conventional auto-encoder. Instead of learning the hidden representatives, AutoRec focuses on learning or re-construction of the output layer. It uses an interaction matrix partially observed as the input to recreate the completed evaluation matrix. Meanwhile, missing entries from the information are re-constructed for recommendation in the output layer. [15]

DeepRec. Autoencoders DeepRec extends the AutoRec idea. A deep self-encoder consists of two deep-belief network symmetrical, which typically have four or five shallow net encoding layers and a second set of four or five layers, which comprise the half decoding.

The layers are Restricted Boltzmann Machine (RBM), the building blocks of deep-belief networks.

A deep-belief network can be defined as a stack of restricted Boltzmann machines, in which each RBM layer communicates with both the previous and subsequent layers. The nodes of any single layer don't communicate with each other laterally [10].

Collaborative Denoising Autoencoders is represented as a one-hidden-layer neural network. Collaborative Denoising Autoencoder (CDAE) consists of 3 layers, including the input layer, the hidden layer and the output layer as is shown on next figure.

CDAE extends idea of classic Denoising Autoencoders where key difference a latent vector for the user. In the input layer, there are in total $I + 1$ nodes, where each of the first I nodes corresponds to an item, and the last node is a user specific node (the red node in the figure), which means the node and its associated weights are unique for each user $u \in U$ in the data [20].

Variational Autoencoders. Is the autoencoder's special application. A probabilist way to describe an observation in latent space is provided by Variational Autoencoder (VAE). The encoder is designed to describe the probability distribution for each latent attributes, not to build an encoder that produces one value to describe each latent state attribute.

The encoder model in VAE generates parameters describing a distribution for each dimension of latent space rather than directly output values for latent state as in a standard autoencoder. The decoder model then creates a latent vector from these defined distributions and then develops an original input reconstruction.

3 Evaluation of Recommendation Systems

We decided to measure different metrics as evaluation measurements. The The Mean absolute error (MAE) and Mean squared error (MSE) are calculated, which are also calculated during training on the set. We have also decided to measure and recall methods for decision support.

3.1 Mean Absolute Error

The average difference between the recommender's predicted value and the user's actual value is mean absolute error. First, we calculate the error by removing for each user the forecast values and actual ratings and then take the mean of all errors to calculate MAE.

MAE shows how far from the current score the predicted score is. We do not want to cancel the negative sign, as its name suggests. Since we do not want positive or negative values, we just want to know the difference between true and forecast values.

Zero MAE means that between predicted and actual ratings no difference is found, and that the model is accurately predictable. The less the MAE, the better. In our case, MAE is 1.5, which is near zero and indicates that our model accurately predicts film ratings for any given user.

3.2 Mean Squared Error

MSE is MAE similar and the only difference is that we square the negative sign instead of taking the absolute error.

MAE helps to reduce the results so that there will be a major difference even in a small change. This also suggests that the recommendation system has been good if MSE is near zero, as otherwise it won't have such a small MSE.

3.3 Precision

The number of items selected which are relevant is precision. If our recommender system chooses three items, two of which will be relevant, then 66% precision. As shown in the Fig. 1 .

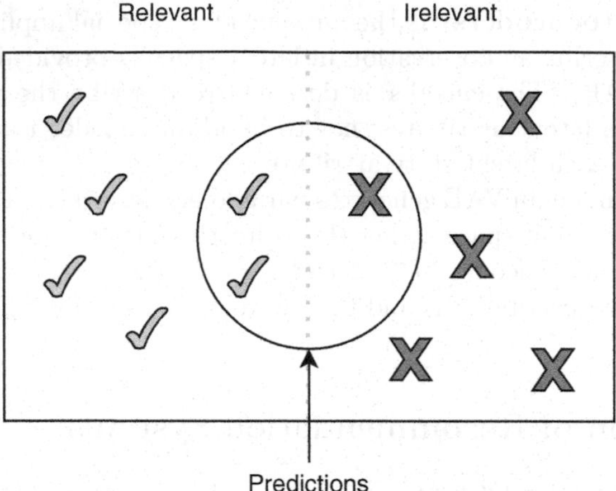

Fig. 1. Precision is the number of space items that have been correctly selected. The relevant items are on the left and irrelevant on the right. On the right.

Precision involves finding the best items for the user, if more useful items are available than you would like [6].

$$precision = \frac{|\{retrieved\ ids\} \cap \{relevant\ ids\}|}{|\{retrieved\ ids\}|} \tag{1}$$

3.4 Recall

The reminder is the number of selected items. If six items are included in the recommendation, from which two relevant items are selected, then a reminder is 33 percent. As can be seen in the Fig. 1. The recall is about not missing useful items [6].

$$recall = \frac{|\{relevant\ ids\} \cap \{retrieved\ ids\}|}{|\{relevant\ ids\}|} \tag{2}$$

4 Using the LSTM as a Recommender System

We've got a text, for example,'I love college, university life.' Divide the two sentences with",“ separate them in two words and separate them in space. Two sequences with lengths of three are produced as follows. “I love the university is life,” LSTM results will be like. From the grammar perspective, the result is stupid and pure. The logic remains here, however.

4.1 Recurrent Neural Networks

Every second, humans do not start to think. We understand that we build on previous knowledge by doing anything. We don't throw all away and begin to think from scratch. We understand each word in other words during the reading.

There is no memory in traditional neural networks. Just imagine, for example, that the network is trying to solve a classification problem. Classify all frames of a film, to be correct. All points must be described on the timeline. In the context of a film, it is impossible to understand if the network has no information concerning previous events in the film.

RNN is an architecture for the network that addresses this problem. A loop for the network to persist in information is included in the RNN. A loop can be used to pass information from step to step [9].

This loop reduces the understanding of a recurrent neural network. We can imagine recurring networks as multiple copies of the same network for a better experience. From the previous network every new one has been created. Take it as a loop.

4.2 Long Short-Term Memory

LSTM is intended to prevent the problem of long-term dependence. For long periods, they retain information. All RNNs have a type of loop-like repeating module, as we described in the last part. Like a repeater module, LSTM also has a loop. Figure 2 shows the architecture of the LSTM cell.

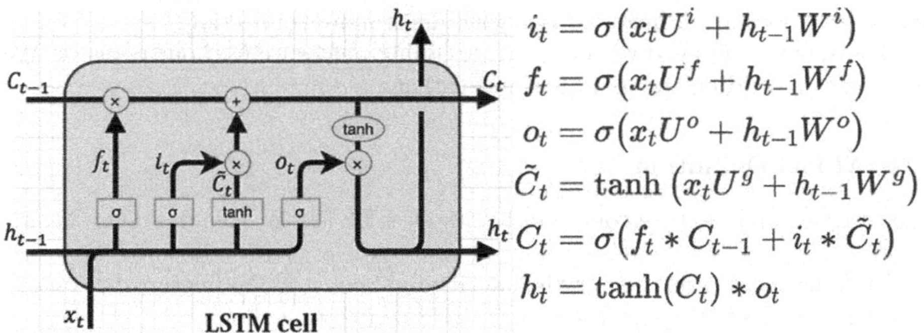

Fig. 2. An illustration of LSTM cell with memory pipe [18]

Cline is the critical component of an LSTM cell. C is a pipeline for memory. LSTM may add or delete gate-regulated memory information. Gates x and + are a way to optionally consider information. A real number between zero and one is output in the σ layer. The effect of information is this value. Null is without impact, and one is very important.

4.3 Data Preparation

The LSTM is the ideal time series as described. The trick is therefore to transform our information into a series of steps.

For example, we need to transform the pictures in sequence from a list when we have a list of images the user wants. If we have three users we can look at a user's likes on an image as a phrase of IDs. For a certain period, each of them has a history of love. What's the next one, we want to predict? [4]

Let's make a shopping list text story. The clients buy milk, bread, cheese, eggs. They are also available.

Regarding our previous work in article Session based recommendations using Recurrent neural networks - Long short-term memory [4], we continued and changed from word-level LSTM to char-level LSTM. This change allows us to use a much bigger dataset with a higher number of ids. We are using a dataset of 4325 stories from the social platform.

4.4 Dataset Transformations

To over-perform, our previous performance described in article [4]. We decided to normalise our inputs to the same length words. To achieve this we count the full length of unique words and then we create new ids with closes numbers. For instance, if we have in our input about 2000 of words, we will create new ids in the range 1000 – 10000. This allows us to control the length of words.

The pseudo ids must be sorted. We have sorted it alphabetically so that the number of connections to learn is reduced. We don't think that sorting is necessary if we have a huge dataset with much more connection.

The input is changed with one-hot encoding before we feed our network. We don't use embedding the main reason for that.

4.5 Model Definition

Our starting architecture contains the stateless LSTM layer and a dense layer.

LSTM long short-term memory is described in Sect. 4.2. We finetuned networks with three or four layers as the result Table 1 of testing shows.

Dense Layer. The dense layer is defined by the size of the number of classes. Dense layer purpose is to predict which class is the next one to recommend.

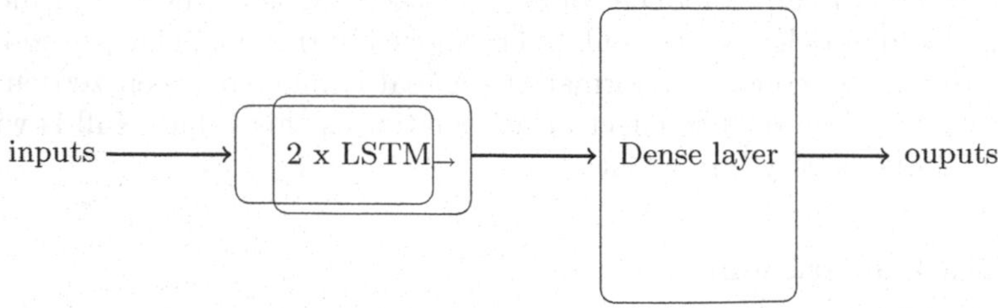

Fig. 3. Our model architecture contains two LSTM layers and dense layer.

For the hyperparameter finetuning described in Table 1 we used the optimisation framework Optuna. We run ten trials to find the best architecture. In Table 1 are described the results in numbers. The best performing one we selected for future testing was bold line with dropout rate 0.2, three layers and 1024 cells. The best performing trial is marked by bold text.

Table 1. Results of hyperparametric optimization.

Dropout	Layers	Hiddens	Embeding	Loss	Acurracy	Time	Epochs
0.5	4	768	–	1.13	67	9 h 20 m	–
0.5	4	512	–	0.94	71	7 h 14 m	–
0.5	3	512	–	0.99	71	5 h 40 m	240
0.5	3	768	–	0.93	77	10 h 35 m	210
0.5	3	1024	–	–	–	Unfinished	Unfinished
0.2	4	768	–	1.06	69	7 h 2 m	200
0.2	3	768	–	0.72	78	5 h	200
0.2	4	512	–	0.84	78	8 h	221
0.2	3	512	–	0.92	76	5 h 50 m	200
0.2	3	**1024**	–	**0.68**	**78**	8 h 10 m	251
0.2	3	768	256	0.69	75	6 h 31 m	221

5 Results and Discussions

As described below, our experiment is applicable to any dataset. Our results are outlined in this section.

5.1 Experiment

The first step is a dataset creation. Any positive user feedback can be used to form our data set. They liked it in our case. For example, purchasing products could be an alternative. We group this list of products by user as a list of identifiers sorted alphabetically. We use new generated pseudo ids to sort the dataset alphabetically. These ids are produced while the data set described in Sect. 4.4 is pre-possessed.

In accordance with the procedure described in Sect. 4.3, we will transform this dataset. Let us therefore quantify the classes. This number shows the size of neurons that are input and output.

We define our model from the number of characters obtained. That is, 12 characters are numbered. The input and output neurons of our model will be 12. Two LSTM layers are to be hidden.

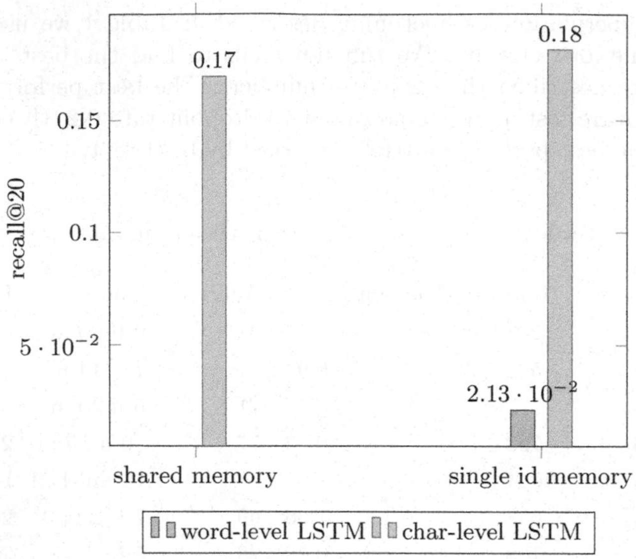

Fig. 4. Compared recall@20 values for word and char level LSTM.

We will then conduct supervised training that teaches our network connections. We tested two different ways of predicting the next item during the evaluation. Our test shows that the user initializes the single memory more effectively. In Algorithm 1 below the algorithm described this single memory initialization.

Algorithm 1: Memory initialisation per id

Result: list of predicted ids
initialisation of LSTM memory;
while *count of predicted ids* ¡ *limit* **do**
  make prediction;
  add prediction to ids;
end

We tested the initialization of the memory by id as a reverse method. The results are 7 % worse in this method. The Algorithm 2 describes this method.

Algorithm 2: Memory initialisation per id

Result: list of predicted ids
while *count of predicted ids* ¡ *limit* **do**
  initialisation of LSTM memory;
  make prediction;
  add prediction to ids;
end

5.2 Recall and Precision Results

Table 2 shows result of our model. We evaluated on our dataset with metrics as precision described in Sect. 3.3 and recall described in Sect. 3.4.

Table 2. Word LSTM, char level LSTM in two prediction modes compared on our dataset.

Method	Memory initialisation	Recall@20	prec@20
Word LSTM	Single memory initialization	0.0213	0.0052
Char-level LSTM	Memory initialised every id	0.170	0.056
Char level LSTM	**Single memory initialization per user**	0.182	0.061

Generally LSTM, RNN and NN are very demanding in terms of performance. Two cards with a total of 7 934 CUDA cores are available on our computer. This card is one of the best-performing NVIDIA card games. We decided to use NVIDIA cards only due to the framework support. One of our 1080TI cards is a graphics clock rate of 11 176 MB and a clock rate of 1607 MHz. Another is a 2080TI with a graphics memory of 11019 MB and a max clock rate of 1545. The processor used is i7-8700 with a clock of 3.20 GHz.

We used Python in version 3.8.2 as a programming language. The web-based Jupyter Notebook was our programming environment in Python. Our key framework is PyTorch. We used PyTorch Lightning for quick prototyping. PyTorch Lightning is a high quality frame on top of PyTorch with higher abstraction. We used the framework Optuna for the finishing of our model.

6 Conclusions and Future Work

Collaborative filtering is a key area and has a large number of possible architectures in machine learning. They are all highly advanced. They all have certain advantages and disadvantages. A solution to remove certain disadvantages can be used with LSTM.

In recommendation systems, LSTM models could be used. They also have their limitations, however – for example, data ordering.

With regard to our preparation of data, we made a text trick for a phrase list. We have also created a pseudo ID to maintain similar word lengths.

We must have sufficient data or more important connections between classes for predictions done on LSTM network. It will fail by overfitting or getting a week model if we have a small data set.

When we train our model on previously marked correct user data, we get that model to make real-time forecasts.

Future work will focus on a comparable dataset experiment. For example the film [7]. For example. We want to compare our model with other models like autoencoders or Boltzmann machines on this dataset.

Acknowledgment. The work and the contribution were supported by the SPEV project "Smart Solutions in Ubiquitous Computing Environments", University of Hradec Kralove, Faculty of Informatics and Management, Czech Republic.

References

1. Abdel-Nasser, M., Mahmoud, K.: Accurate photovoltaic power forecasting models using deep LSTM-RNN. Neural Comput. Appl. **31**(7), 2727–2740 (2017). https://doi.org/10.1007/s00521-017-3225-z
2. Ciresan, D., Meier, U., Schmidhuber, J.: Multi-column deep neural networks for image classification. In: 2012 IEEE Conference on Computer Vision and Pattern Recognition (CVPR), pp. 3642–3649. IEEE, New York (2012). wOS:000309166203102
3. Dobrovolny, M., Mls, K., Krejcar, O., Mambou, S., Selamat, A.: Medical image data upscaling with generative adversarial networks. In: Rojas, I., Valenzuela, O., Rojas, F., Herrera, L.J., Ortuño, F. (eds.) IWBBIO 2020. LNCS, vol. 12108, pp. 739–749. Springer, Cham (2020). https://doi.org/10.1007/978-3-030-45385-5_66
4. Dobrovolny, M., Selamat, A., Krejcar, O.: Session based recommendations using recurrent neural networks - long short-term memory. In: Nguyen, N.T., Chittayasothorn, S., Niyato, D., Trawiński, B. (eds.) ACIIDS 2021. LNCS (LNAI), vol. 12672, pp. 53–65. Springer, Cham (2021). https://doi.org/10.1007/978-3-030-73280-6_5
5. Dobrovolny, M., Soukal, I., Lim, K.C., Selamat, A., Krejcar, O.: Forecasting of FOREX price trend using recurrent neural network - long short-term memory, pp. 95–103 April 2020. 10.36689/uhk/hed/2020-01-011, http://hdl.handle.net/20.500.12603/212
6. Gunawardana, A., Shani, G.: Evaluating recommender systems. In: Ricci, F., Rokach, L., Shapira, B. (eds.) Recommender Systems Handbook, pp. 265–308. Springer, Boston (2015). https://doi.org/10.1007/978-1-4899-7637-6_8
7. Harper, F.M., Konstan, J.A.: The movielens datasets: history and context. ACM Trans. Interact. Intell. Syst. **5**(4), 1–19 (2016). https://doi.org/10.1145/2827872
8. Hinton, G.E., Salakhutdinov, R.R.: Reducing the dimensionality of data with neural networks. Science **313**(5786), 504–507 (2006). https://doi.org/10.1126/science.1127647, wOS:000239308600057
9. Hochreiter, S., Schmidhuber, J.: Long short-term memory. Neural Comput. **9**(8), 1735–1780 (1997). https://doi.org/10.1162/neco.1997.9.8.1735
10. Kuchaiev, O., Ginsburg, B.: Training deep autoencoders for collaborative filtering. arXiv:1708.01715 (2017)
11. Ledig, C., et al.: Photo-realistic single image super-resolution using a generative adversarial network. In: 30th IEEE Conference on Computer Vision and Pattern Recognition (CVPR 2017), pp. 105–114. IEEE, New York (2017). wOS:000418371400012
12. Liu, W., Wang, Z., Liu, X., Zeng, N., Liu, Y., Alsaadi, F.E.: A survey of deep neural network architectures and their applications. Neurocomputing **234**, 11–26 (2017). https://doi.org/10.1016/j.neucom.2016.12.038, wOS:000395221800002
13. Mambou, S., Krejcar, O., Selamat, A., Dobrovolny, M., Maresova, P., Kuca, K.: Novel thermal image classification based on techniques derived from mathematical morphology: case of breast cancer. In: Rojas, I., Valenzuela, O., Rojas, F., Herrera, L.J., Ortuño, F. (eds.) IWBBIO 2020. LNCS, vol. 12108, pp. 683–694. Springer, Cham (2020). https://doi.org/10.1007/978-3-030-45385-5_61

14. Pena-Barragan, J.M., Ngugi, M.K., Plant, R.E., Six, J.: Object-based crop identification using multiple vegetation indices, textural features and crop phenology. Remote Sens. Envir. **115**(6), 1301–1316 (2011). https://doi.org/10.1016/j.rse.2011.01.009
15. Sedhain, S., Menon, A.K., Sanner, S., Xie, L.: AutoRec: autoencoders meet collaborative filtering. In: Proceedings of the 24th International Conference on World Wide Web, WWW 2015 Companion, pp. 111–112. Association for Computing Machinery, Florence, May 2015. https://doi.org/10.1145/2740908.2742726
16. Sun, Y., Chen, J., Liu, Q., Liu, G.: Learning image compressed sensing with subpixel convolutional generative adversarial network. Pattern Recogn. **98**, 107051 (2020). https://doi.org/10.1016/j.patcog.2019.107051, http://www.sciencedirect.com/science/article/pii/S003132031930353X
17. Vaiyapuri, T., Binbusayyis, A.: Application of deep autoencoder as an one-class classifier for unsupervised network intrusion detection: a comparative evaluation. PeerJ Comput. Sci. **6**, e327 (2020). https://doi.org/10.7717/peerj-cs.327 wOS:000599181100001
18. Varsamopoulos, S., Bertels, K., Almudever, C.G.: Designing neural network based decoders for surface codes, p. 13 (2018)
19. Wolterink, J.M., Leiner, T., Viergever, M.A., Isgum, I.: Generative adversarial networks for noise reduction in low-dose CT. IEEE Trans. Med. Imaging **36**(12), 2536–2545 (2017). https://doi.org/10.1109/TMI.2017.2708987, wOS:000417913600013
20. Wu, Y., DuBois, C., Zheng, A.X., Ester, M.: Collaborative denoising auto-encoders for top-n recommender systems. In: Proceedings of the Ninth ACM International Conference on Web Search and Data Mining WSDM 2016, pp. 153–162. Association for Computing Machinery, San Francisco, California February 2016. https://doi.org/10.1145/2835776.2835837
21. Yang, Q., et al.: Low-dose CT image denoising using a generative adversarial network with wasserstein distance and perceptual loss. IEEE Trans. Med. Imaging **37**(6), 1348–1357 (2018). https://doi.org/10.1109/TMI.2018.2827462, wOS:000434302700006

Collective Decision-Making

Hybridization of Metaheuristic and Population-Based Algorithms with Neural Network Learning for Function Approximation

Zhen-Yao Chen(✉)

Department of Business Administration, Hungkuo Delin University of Technology, No. 1, Ln 380, Qingyun Road, New Taipei City 23654, Taiwan
keyzyc@gmail.com

Abstract. This paper attempts to improve the learning representation of radial basis function neural network (RBFNN) through metaheuristic algorithm (MHA) and evolutionary algorithm (EA). Next, the ant colony optimization (ACO)-based and genetic algorithm (GA)-based approaches are employed to train RBFNN. The proposed hybridization of ACO-based and GA-based approaches (HAG) algorithm incorporates the complementarity of exploration and exploitation abilities to reach resolution optimization. The property of population diversity has higher chance to search the global optimal instead of being restricted to local optimal extremely in two benchmark problems. The experimental results have shown that ACO-based and GA-based approaches can be integrated intelligently and develop into a hybrid algorithm which aims for receiving the best precise learning expression among relevant algorithms in this paper. Additionally, method assessment results for two benchmark continuous test function experiments and show that the proposed HAG algorithm outperforms relevant algorithms in term of preciseness for learning of function approximation.

Keywords: Hybrid algorithm · Radial basis function neural network · Artificial colony optimization · Genetic algorithm · Function approximation

1 Introduction

The typical optimization approaches such as linear and nonlinear programming [29], which are based on optimization formulation, would not be the best option for the intelligent forecasting models due to their nature of inherent limitations and complexity of obtained objective function [38]. Studies have also shown that the metaheuristic (MH) algorithms (MHAs), which primarily include evolutionary and swarm intelligence (SI) based algorithms, have been applied to search the feasible solutions for these complicated predictive models in the past two decades [38].

Further, researchers have devoted to improving the precision of models through modifying and developing them with new approaches [3]. One possible approach to improve precision is to integrate the model with robust optimization MHAs such as genetic programming (GP), genetic algorithm (GA), and ant colony optimization (ACO)

K. Wojtkiewicz et al. (Eds.): ICCCI 2021, CCIS 1463, pp. 45–56, 2021.
https://doi.org/10.1007/978-3-030-88113-9_4

to minimize deviation and increase the accuracy of the model [27, 34]. However, evolutionary algorithms (EAs) mimetic the evolutionary procedure in nature where the global area optimal are obtained through generating new offspring that inherit the properties from the parents' population. The set of candidate solution is improved gradually until satisfying the termination criteria. As such, throughout generation, the probability of achieving advanced results near the global area optimal will raise, however obtaining approximation of the global optima with high preciseness is not guaranteed [32].

On the other hand, the common mechanism of artificial neural networks (ANNs) is built based on the behavior within the neurons of human brains. This biological behavior was first modeled in several mathematical equations by McCulloch & Pitts [26] in 1943. Their paper has become an innovative work and it opens a new era of computational intelligence [2]. Moreover, the radial basis function (RBF) neural network (RBFNN) was proposed by Duda & Hart [9] in 1973. It exists a number of dominances over other types of NNs: excellent approximation capabilities, easier network constitutions and algorithms with faster learning capability [28]. Further, Zhang & Liao [39] in 2014 examined the prediction performance of RBFNN and hybrid fuzzy clustering (HFC) algorithm. The HFC algorithm has shown better performance over the former [39]. In addition, the representation of RBFNN depends upon the relevant parameters of nonlinear kernel functions for RBFNN. At the meantime, not many efforts have been made to hybrid several MH and population-based algorithms with trained RBFNN where exists gaps to improve in term of the fitting preciseness for function approximation. Accordingly, this study intends to propose a HAG algorithm for training RBFNN and make adequate performance verification and comparison. The proposed HAG algorithm incorporates the local and global area search abilities for problem resolution. Next, the HAG algorithm utilizes two benchmark continuous test functions, which are usually adopted in the literature to be the contrast of algorithm expression in the experiment.

The remainder of this study is organized as follows. Section 2 presents the literature review related to this paper, while the proposed HAG algorithm is introduced and illustrated in Sect. 3. Sections 4 discussed the experimental and assessment results. The study ends by the concluding remarks in Sect. 5.

2 Literature Review

A number of soft computing (SC) techniques normally named as MHAs have been emerged as the outputs for this research field that considered to imitate the biological processes, the group behavior of agents and survival of the fittest and so on, for the optimization problems [14]. Further, swarm-based algorithms exist the features of information sharing among multiple individuals, capability of being collaboration, self-organized, and learning during generations to fulfill efficient seeking procedures [37]. This section presents general background associated to this study, including MH and population-based algorithms for RBFNN learning.

MHAs are inspired from nature and ACO is one of the instances, have been well applied to numerous different optimization problems [10]. In Savsani et al. [31] in 2014, ACO algorithm developed by Dorigo [8] in 1996 was utilized on the simulation of collaboration mechanism of real-world ant colonies. Ants have the inclination to seek the shortest route between their nest and sources of food. Consider an optimization problem as a multi-layer topology. In which, the count of nodes within specific layer is equivalent to the count of detachment values corresponding to the design variables and the count of layers is equivalent to the number of design variables. Next, ACO has fascinated much concentration in the domains of discrete problems due to its population-based search ability as well as robustness and simplicity. ACO uses heuristic technique to generate a well initial solution and decides an appropriate search tendency according to the experience. While it is deserving to note that this strategy often brings a well solution for ACO, it leads to ACO trapped in local optimal as trade-off [19].

EAs imitate rules in natural evolution operators. GA is inspired through Darwinian evolutionary principle, which is the most broadly used EA [11]. One of beforehand works to imitate the appearance to seek the global area extreme values of an optimization task was done in 1975 by Holland [15] in 1992 when he introduced his GA, which simulates the evolutionary theory proposed through Darwin [12]. Next, GA is a random search approach through the Darwinian evolutionary principle, adopting procedures such as natural selection, reproduction, mutation and crossover. Early, an initial stochastic population was established, after that several solutions are sorted through their objective function and then, the first probability of them are transmitted to the next generation. Later, any two solution sets are chosen adopting the Roulette wheel (RW) selection and are merged to establish new offsprings. The procedure employed in establishing the new population is the mutation step. Lastly, objective value estimation of the new population should be fulfilled [30]. Further, gene choice permits us to comprehend the situations of a cell influenced through an illness. Especially, gene choice is a principle through selecting the most dominant genes that can valid forecast the class to which a cell specimen belongs to [30].

The ACO is a probabilistic approach to solve computational tasks. It provides the optimal solution by the paths of graph although it perhaps be fall into a local area optimal solution and is different from a global area optimal one [21]. On the other hand, Holland (1975) developed the GA, which is a population-based and stochastic-based optimization approach. The model was built based on nature-inspired evolutionary procedures such as natural selection, inherit, crossover and mutation [1]. Next, a hybrid algorithm of GA and ACO (i.e., GA-ACO algorithm) was proposed by Luan et al. [25] in 2019 and was adopted to resolve the linear programming model for supplier extract task. The GA-ACO algorithm applies the superiorities of GA with high initial accelerate convergence and the advantages of ACO with valid and parallelism feedback. As for the GA-ACO algorithm, the solutions generated through GA will be utilized to determine the initial produced pheromones for ACO [25].

3 Methodology

RBFNN is normally premeditated as a three-layered construction composed by input, hidden, and output layers [36], in which the RBF interpolation is formulated as [17]:

$$u(x) = \sum_{i=1}^{N} w_i \xi_i(\|x - x_i\|_2), \tag{1}$$

where w_i are the weights value, ξ_i is the RBF, and $\|x - x_i\|_2$ denotes the Euclidean distance between the new point x and a sample point x_i. The RBFs ξ_i, used in this work is the Gaussian basis function:

$$\xi(r) = e^{-(\varepsilon r)^2}, \tag{2}$$

where r is the Euclidean distance between a vector of RBFNN input layer and a center of RBFNN hidden layer, and ε is the width factor determining the size of the RBF [36].

Further, as one class of topical kernel function (KF), the parameter ε of RBF resolves the width of the KF. Merely the selected point in sight of the trial point may influence on the yield of the function. In other words, RBF function has partial features and capability on interpolation [35]. Thus, the nonlinear function of the RBFNN hidden layer adopted is the Gaussian basis function shown in Eq. (2). Additionally, a typical hidden node in a RBFNN is characterized through its center, which is a vector where its number of dimensions is the number of inputs to the node. Then, the framework for the proposed HAG algorithm is illustrated in Fig. 1.

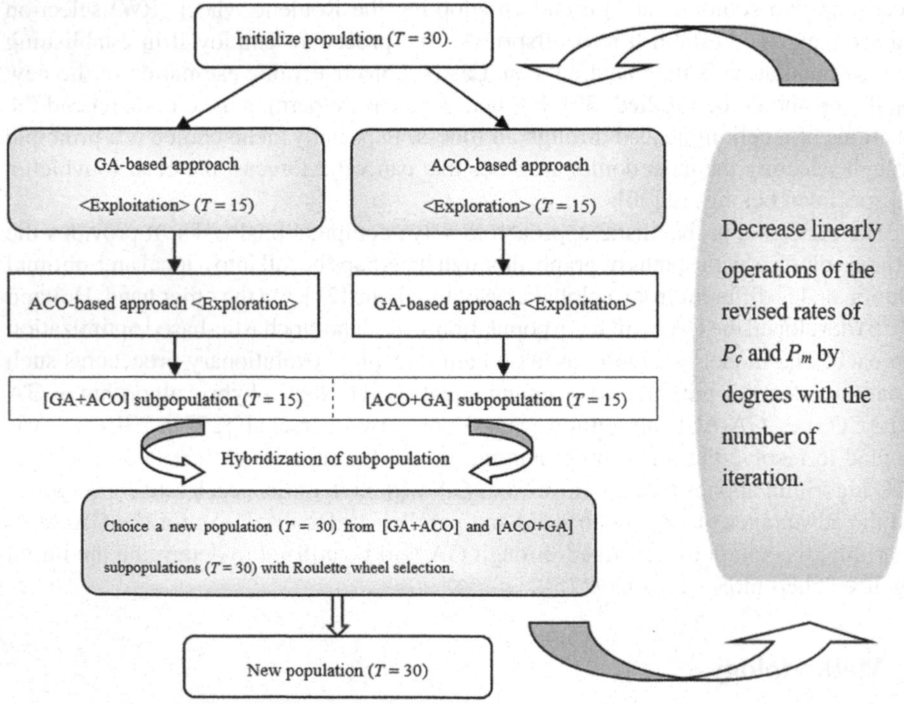

Fig. 1. The framework for the proposed HAG algorithm

3.1 The Detailed Description of the Proposed HAG Algorithm

This paper focused on training and tuning the corresponding parameters for RBFNN. The best solution of parameter values set can be received and adopted in the proposed HAG algorithm with the RBFNN to solve the problem for function approximation. The purpose is to receive the maximum of a fitness function regarding the parameters of the RBFNN (i.e., the hidden node center, width, and weight between the hidden and output layers). The inverse of mean absolute error (MAE) (i.e., MAE^{-1}) is adopted as fitness function. The fitness values for the HAG algorithm in the experiment are calculated by maximizing the MAE^{-1} defined as Eq. (3):

$$Fitness = MAE^{-1} = N \cdot \left(\sum_{i=1}^{N} |y_i - \hat{y}_i| \right)^{-1}, \tag{3}$$

where y_i is the actual output; $\hat{y}_i$ is the predicted output of the learned RBFNN for the ith testing pattern; N is the number of the testing set. Therefore, RBFNN can be trained to approximate two benchmark functions to a higher degree of precision. Next, the progress procedures for the HAG algorithm was then executed and summarized as follows.

(1) **Initialization:** The initialization corresponding to nature random selection assures the diversity among units (i.e., ants in ACO-based approach; chromosomes in GA-based approach) and benefits the evolutionary procedure hereafter. An initial population with a number of units is produced and the initializing procedures are as follows.

   (a) Each unit in the initial population is the set of positions for neuron (i.e., $c^t_{i,j}$) and width (i.e., d^t_i) on RBFNN, defined in a matrix form. The results are adopted as the number of neurons in RBFNN.
   (b) The weights w_i are obtained by resolving the linear relationship [17]: where $\mathrm{A} = A_{ij} = \xi_i(\|x - x_i\|_2)$ and $u = u(x_i)$ are the investigated function values at the specimen points. The chosen RBFs will generate a positive-definite matrix $\Re$, thus assuring a sole solution to Eq. (4) [17].
   (c) The fitness value of unit matrix in population is calculated through Eq. (3) (i.e., MAE^{-1}).

(2) **ACO-based approach** [8, 31]:
   Let the ant nest include K ants. In the origination of the optimization procedure, all paths are initialized with an equivalent quantity of pheromone. In each generation, ants begin at the nest node, traverse across the varying layers from the first to the last layer, and finish at the target node [31]. Through following Eq. (5), each ant may determine only one node in every layer [8].

In which, P^k_{ij} indicates the probability of selecting j as the next intent aim for ant k located at node i, τ_{ij} is the pheromone trial and α is the pheromone sensitiveness.

In case the route is finish, the ant precipitates some pheromone on the route based on the locally trial updating rule given through Eq. (6):

$$Aw = u \tag{4}$$

$$P_{ij}^{k} = \begin{cases} \dfrac{\tau_{ij}^{\alpha}}{\sum \tau_{ij}^{\alpha}} \text{ if } j \in K_i^k \\ 0 \text{ if } j \notin K_i^k \end{cases} \tag{5}$$

$$\tau_{ij} = \tau_{ij} + \Delta\tau^{k}, \tag{6}$$

where $\Delta\tau^k$ is the pheromone accumulation via kth ant on the route it has transited.

When all the ants fulfill their routes, the pheromones on the global area best route are revised utilizing the globally trial updating rule given through Eq. (7):

$$\tau_{ij} = (1-\rho)\tau_{ij} + \sum_{k=1}^{K} \Delta\tau_{ij}^{k}, \tag{7}$$

where ρ is the pheromone attenuating (exhalation) rate, $\Delta\tau_{ij}^k$ is the pheromone precipitated via the best ant k on the route ij estimated as $Q \cdot (fitness^k)^{-1}$, and Q is a constant [8]. Furthermore, for the population in ACO-based approach, the ant concludes better solution by referencing itself and other ants, determines the proceeding direction and therefore is able to explore in a global search space.

(3) **Duplication:** The population promoted via the learning of ACO-based approach [8, 20] is replicated and is named as ACO population.
(4) **GA-based approach:** The approach of GA evolution that includes crossover and mutation operators in the population of ACO-based approach learning is called [GA+ACO] subpopulation. The operators used in GA-based approach are as follows.

    (a) Further, each row of the chosen paired C_t will execute crossover operator with P_c.
    (b) Through the mutation operator, the values are substituted via randomly chosen values from the range of the search domain in each dimension, which keeps the diversity and produces new solutions.

(5) **Reproduction:** The [ACO+GA] and [GA+ACO] subpopulations are hybridization after the refined evolution. Units with same quantity from the initial population are randomly chosen via the proportional RW selection [13] for the evolution hereafter. Thus, by applying ACO-based and GA-based approaches to conduct exploration and exploitation in the solving space respectively, it is expected to obtain the optimal solution with their best complementary properties.

Additionally, owing to the feature of local search with GA-based approach, whether what the fitness values of the units in population are, them entirely have the chances to make progress with some genetic operators and enter into the next iteration of population to perform. GA-based approach then is able to exploit the potential solution.

(6) **Termination:** The HAG algorithm will not stop returning to step (2) unless a specific number of iterations has been reached.

In summary, executing an evolution program via the ACO-based approach would receive a promoted progress population, which is better than the initial population. Moreover, the advantage of the feature of global search in ACO-based approach allows wider exploration on dimension domain among different experiments and the solving space is able to be expanded. On the other hand, as the HAG algorithm progresses, the members of the population evolve gradually. In this way, the HAG algorithm accords the essence of GA-based approach, assures the genetic diversity in the refinement of future evolution, and makes progresses to obtain a new promoted population. Besides, through the GA-based approach within the HAG algorithm to calculate the fitness values of unit parameters solution in the population, the better solutions will be received gradually. Accordingly, the solution space in population could be improved progressively and converge regarding to the global optimal solution.

4 Experimental Results

This section focused on training and tuning the corresponding parameters in RBFNN for function approximation problem. The objective is to receive the maximum of a fitness function concerning the parameters of the RBFNN. The intention is then to solve the suitable values of the parameters from the setting domain in the experiment. The proposed HAG algorithm will gradually be able to train and thus receive a set of solutions for parameter values.

4.1 Benchmark Problems Experiment

Continuous test function induces excellent approximation to recompense RBFNN for the outcome of nonlinear mapping relation. This paper applies two continuous test functions that are usually used in the literature to be the comparative benchmark of estimated algorithms. As such, the experiment contains the following two benchmark problems, including Rosenbrock and Griewank [4] continuous test functions are listed in Table 1.

Table 1. Two benchmark continuous test functions [4] adopted in this experiment

Benchmark continuous test function	Equation	Initial range
Rosenbrock	$f(x) = \sum_{i=1}^{D-1} \left[100(x_{i+1} - x_i^2)^2 + (x_i - 1)^2\right]$	[−30, 30]
Griewank	$f(x) = \sum_{i=1}^{n} \frac{x_i^2}{4000} - \prod cos\left(\frac{x_i}{\sqrt{i}}\right) + 1$	[−100, 100]

4.2 Parameter Setup

In the proposed HAG algorithm, four parameters (i.e., pheromone trail, pheromone decay rate, crossover probability, and mutation probability), which have major impact on calculation results are analyzed. Besides, this paper also referred to the related literature for the range of the parameters' value setting. Next, the setup of the parameters for HAG algorithm is tuned by referring to the Taguchi experimental design [33] with analysis mode substitute for using trial and error procedure [38]. After, the maximum number of iterations is set at 1,000 to set as termination condition in the experiment. Finally, the appraisal of the parameters setting for the proposed HAG algorithm was conducted with the content listed in Table 2.

Table 2. Parameter setup for the proposed HAG algorithm

Parameter	Description	Value
E	The maximum number of iterations	1000
g_t	The number of the RBFNN hidden node centers	[1, 50]
d_i^t	The width of RBFNN hidden layer	[1000, 40000]
δ	The learning rate of the RBFNN	0.3
T	Population size	30
K	The number of ant	100
τ	The pheromone trail	0.5
α	The pheromone sensitiveness	0.8
ρ	The pheromone attenuating rate	0.3
Q	A constant	0.65
P_c	Crossover probability	[0.4, 0.5]
P_m	Mutation probability	[0.01, 0.05]

4.3 Performance Assessment and Comparison

The learning of all algorithms on several solutions of parameter values set (i.e., hidden node center, width, and weight) for RBFNN that are generated by the population during the operation of the progress procedure in the experiment are discussed in this section. Consequently, 1000 randomly generated data sets are divided into three parts to train RBFNN which are training set (65%), testing set (25%), and validation set (10%) [24] respectively, and in which we can assess the learning status and tune the parameters' setting. Next, this study uses these algorithms to resolve the best solution of parameter values set for RBFNN, and it randomly generates unrepeatable 65% training set from 1000 generated data and input the set to RBFNN for training. With the same approach, it randomly generates unrepeatable 25% testing set to inspect unit parameters' solution in population and further calculates the fitness value. RBFNN has adopted 90% dataset in learning stage at this point. After 1000 iterations in the evolution process, the best solution of parameter values set for RBFNN are received. Finally, it randomly generates unrepeatable validation set (10% dataset) to certify how the unit parameters solution approximates the two benchmark problems and record the RMSE values to justify the learning status of RBFNN. Once the data refining steps presented above have completed, all algorithms are ready to execute. The learning and validation stages mentioned above were carried out 50 times before the average RMSE (i.e., RMSE_{avg}) values were calculated. The values of the RMSE_{avg} and standard deviation (SD) for all algorithms calculated from the experiment are listed in Table 3.

Table 3. Result comparison among relevant algorithms adopted in this experiment

Benchmark problem Competitive algorithm	Rosenbrock		Griewank	
	Training set	Validation set	Training set	Validation set
RBFNN [5]	12046.37 ± 1361.53	12971.61 ± 2624.59	27.87 ± 2.79	28.21 ± 3.82
GA-based [15]	1672.38 ± 378.17	2592.16 ± 253.21	19.59 ± 16.47	54.27 ± 17.38
ACO-based [8]	1235.05 ± 147.61	1986.38 ± 362.53	7.34 ± 13.27	51.16 ± 10.37
GA-ACO [25]	914.52 ± 21.18	627.72 ± 29.02	6.38 ± 3.27	15.06 ± 4.15
HAG	**707.36 ± 13.28**	**590.02 ± 23.59**	**5.47 ± 2.83**	**13.51 ± 2.65**

In Table 3, the results demonstrate that HAG algorithm obtains the smallest values with stable expression during the entire training process of the experiment. Thus, RBFNN is able to receive the single parameters' solution from the evolution learning process in population, which has realized the situation with optimal function approximation. When the training of RBFNN by the HAG algorithm is accomplished, the unit with the best solution of parameter values set in learning stage is the RBFNN setting in certain. Additionally, the HAG algorithm shows robust learning within two benchmark problems and shows remarkable approximation results.

5 Conclusions

This paper proposed the HAG algorithm through incorporating ACO-based and GA-based approaches, which offers the settings of RBFNN parameters. The experimental results shown that ACO and GA algorithms can be integrated intelligently and develop into a hybrid algorithm which is designed for receiving the best precise learning expression among all algorithms in this study. Additionally, method assessment results for two benchmark continuous test function experiments and show that the proposed HAG algorithm outperformed other algorithms in preciseness of function approximation.

References

1. Al-Obaidi, M.A., Li, J.P., Kara-Zaïtri, C., Mujtaba, I.M.: Optimisation of reverse osmosis based wastewater treatment system for the removal of chlorophenol using genetic algorithms. Chem. Eng. J. **316**, 91–100 (2017)
2. Al-Roomi, A.R., El-Hawary, M.E.: Universal functions originator. Appl. Soft Comput. **94**, 106417–106448 (2020)
3. Ansari, M., Othman, F., El-Shafie, A.: Optimized fuzzy inference system to enhance prediction accuracy for influent characteristics of a sewage treatment plant. Sci. Total Environ. **722**, 137878–137890 (2020)
4. Bilal, M.P., Zaheer, H., Garcia-Hernandez, L., Abraham, A.: Differential evolution: a review of more than two decades of research. Eng. Appl. Artif. Intell. **90**, 103479–1034502 (2020)
5. Chen, S., Cowan, C.F.N., Grant, P.M.: Orthogonal least squares learning algorithm for radial basis function networks. IEEE Trans. Neural Netw. **2**(2), 302–309 (1991)
6. Chen, S., Wu, Y., Luk, B.L.: Combined genetic algorithm optimization and regularized orthogonal least squares learning for radial basis function networks. IEEE Trans. Neural Netw. **10**(5), 1239–1243 (1999)
7. Denker, J.S.: Neural network models of learning and adaptation. Physica D. **22**, 216–232 (1986)
8. Dorigo, M., Maniezzo, V., Colorni, A.: Ant system: optimization by a colony of cooperating agents. IEEE Trans. Syst. Man Cybern. Part B (Cybern.) **26**(1), 29–41 (1996). https://doi.org/10.1109/3477.484436
9. Duda, R.O., Hart, P.E.: Pattern Classification and Scene Analysis. John Wiley and Sons, New York (1973)
10. Dzalbs, I., Kalganova, T.: Accelerating supply chains with Ant Colony Optimization across a range of hardware solutions. Comput. Ind. Eng. **147**, 106610–106623 (2020)
11. Faramarzi, A., Heidarinejad, M., Stephens, B., Mirjalili, S.: Equilibrium optimizer: a novel optimization algorithm. Knowl. Based Syst. **191**, 105190–105210 (2020)
12. Ghafil, H.N., Jarmai, K.: Dynamic differential annealed optimization: new metaheuristic optimization algorithm for engineering applications. Appl. Soft Comput. **93**, 106392–106410 (2020)
13. Goldberg, D.E.: Genetic Algorithms in Search Optimization and Machine Learning. Addison-Wesley, Boston (1989)
14. Hamzaday, A., Baykasoglu, A., Akpinar, S.: Solving combinatorial optimization problems with single seekers society algorithm. Knowl. Based Syst. **201–202**, 106036–106065 (2020)
15. Holland, J.H.: Adaptation in Natural and Artificial Systems: An Introductory Analysis with Applications to Biology, Control, and Artificial Intelligence. MIT Press, Cambridge (1992)

16. Islam, J., Vasant, P.M., Negash, B.M., Laruccia, M.B., Myint, M., Watada, J.: A holistic review on artificial intelligence techniques for well placement optimization problem. Adv. Eng. Softw. **141**, 102767–102786 (2020)
17. Jakobsson, S., Andersson, B., Edelvik, F.: Rational radial basis function interpolation with applications to antenna design. J. Comput. Appl. Math. **233**(4), 889–904 (2009)
18. Jugulum, R., Taguchi, S., et al.: Computer-Based Robust Engineering: Essentials for DFSS. ASQ Quality Press, Milwaukee (2004)
19. Kefayat, M., Ara, A.I., Niaki, S.A.N.: A hybrid of ant colony optimization and artificial bee colony algorithm for probabilistic optimal placement and sizing of distributed energy resources. Energ. Convers. Manage. **92**, 149–161 (2015)
20. Kozak, J., Boryczka, U.: Multiple boosting in the Ant colony decision forest meta-classifier. Knowl. Based Syst. **75**, 141–151 (2015)
21. Lin, Y.K., Yeh, C.T., Huang, P.S.: A hybrid ant-tabu algorithm for solving a multistate flow network reliability maximization problem. Appl. Soft Comput. **13**, 3529–3543 (2013)
22. Lin, C.F., Wu, C.C., Yang, P.H., Kuo, T.Y.: Application of Taguchi method in lightemitting diode backlight design for wide color gamut displays. J. Disp. Technol. **5**(8), 323–330 (2009)
23. Liu, B., Aliakbarian, H., Ma, Z., Vandenbosch, G.A.E., Gielen, G., Excell, P.: An efficient method for antenna design optimization based on evolutionary computation and machine learning techniques. IEEE Trans. Antennas Propag. **62**(1), 7–18 (2014)
24. Looney, C.G.: Advances in feedforward neural networks: demystifying knowledge acquiring black boxes. IEEE Trans. Knowl. Data Eng. **8**(2), 211–226 (1996)
25. Luan, J., Yao, Z., Zhao, F., Song, X.: A novel method to solve supplier selection problem: hybrid algorithm of genetic algorithm and ant colony optimization. Math. Comput. Simul. **156**, 294–309 (2019)
26. McCulloch, W.S., Pitts, W.: A logical calculus of the ideas immanent in nervous activity. Bull. Math. Biophys. **5**(4), 115–133 (1943)
27. Naghibi, S.A., Ahmadi, K., Daneshi, A.: Application of support vector machine, random forest, and genetic algorithm optimized random forest models in groundwater potential mapping. Water Resour. Manage. **31**(9), 2761–2775 (2017)
28. Qasem, S.N., Shamsuddin, S.M., Zain, A.M.: Multi-objective hybrid evolutionary algorithms for radial basis function neural network design. Knowl. Based Syst. **27**, 475–497 (2012)
29. Rao, R.V., Rai, D.P., Balic, J.: A multi-objective algorithm for optimization of modern machining processes. Eng. Appl. Artif. Intell. **61**, 103–125 (2017)
30. Salehpoor, I.B., Molla-Alizadeh-Zavardehi, S.: A constrained portfolio selection model at considering risk-adjusted measure by using hybrid meta-heuristic algorithms. Appl. Soft Comput. **75**, 233–253 (2019)
31. Savsani, P., Jhala, R.L., Savsani, V.: Effect of hybridizing biogeography-based optimization (BBO) technique with artificial immune algorithm (AIA) and Ant colony optimization (ACO). Appl. Soft Comput. **21**, 542–553 (2014)
32. Sulaiman, M.H., Mustaffa, Z., Saari, M.M., Daniyal, H.: Barnacles mating optimizer: a new bio-inspired algorithm for solving engineering optimization problems. Eng. Appl. Artif. Intell. **87**, 103330–103342 (2020)
33. Taguchi, G., Chowdhury, S., Wu, Y.: Taguchi's Quality Engineering Handbook. Wiley, Hoboken (2005)
34. Tayfur, G.: Modern optimization methods in water resources planning, engineering and management. Water Resour. Manage. **31**(10), 3205–3233 (2017)
35. Tian, Z.: Short-term wind speed prediction based on LMD and improved FA optimized combined kernel function LSSVM. Eng. Appl. Artif. Intell. **91**, 103573–103596 (2020)
36. Urquhart, M., Ljungskog, E., Sebben, S.: Surrogate-based optimisation using adaptively scaled radial basis functions. Appl. Soft Comput. **88**, 106050–106066 (2020)

37. Yang, Z., Li, K., Guo, Y., Ma, H., Zheng, M.: Compact real-valued teaching-learning based optimization with the applications to neural network training. Knowl. Based Syst. **159**, 51–62 (2018)
38. Yin, X., Niu, Z., He, Z., Li, Z.S., Lee, D.: An integrated computational intelligence technique based operating parameters optimization scheme for quality improvement oriented process-manufacturing system. Comput. Ind. Eng. **140**, 106284–106298 (2020)
39. Zhang, F., Liao, Z.: Gold price forecasting based on RBF neural network and hybrid fuzzy clustering algorithm. In: Jiuping, X., Fry, J.A., Lev, B., Hajiyev, A. (eds.) Proceedings of the Seventh International Conference on Management Science and Engineering Management, pp. 73–84. Springer, Heidelberg (2014). https://doi.org/10.1007/978-3-642-40078-0_6

Valentino Braitenberg's Table: Downhill Innovation of Vehicles via Darwinian Evolution

Sahand Shaghaghi(✉), Owais Hamid, and Chrystopher L. Nehaniv

Systems Design Engineering, University of Waterloo, Waterloo, Canada
{s2shagha,omabdulh,cnehaniv}@uwaterloo.ca

Abstract. Evolution has been a topic of interest that has been explored extensively throughout recent history. Ever since the proposal of the evolutionary theory by Darwin, there have been attempts made to validate, extend, explore and exploit the different aspects of this theory. This study sets forth methods to explore elements of what has been proposed by Darwinian evolution using Braitenberg vehicles, simple machines with sensory-motor couplings in an environmental context. In this study, a simulation environment is set up based upon the descriptions of neurophysiologist Valentino Braitenberg. This simulation environment is then utilized to carry out the thought experiments envisioned by Braitenberg for the simplest nontrivial kinds of vehicles. The methodology and results for the carried out experiments are detailed in this paper. Apart from an understanding of whether the environmental setup affects evolution, specifically the number of light sources (stimuli) and location of these light sources, the experiments show an interesting trend regarding dynamic equilibrium of the evolutionary process, the ramifications of which might not have been understood well enough previously. It is concluded that ecological setup, as well as the initial genetic makeup of the vehicles, play a crucial role in the evolution of vehicles in scenarios laid out in this study. Further, the placement of stimuli (location of lights) and the number of the stimuli have a visible effect on the survivability of vehicle types (species).

Keywords: Braitenberg vehicles · Multi-agent robotics · Evolutionary robotics

1 Introduction

This paper explores the topic of evolution as laid out by the neuroscientist and biological cyberneticist Valentino Braitenberg. In his book *Vehicles: Experiments in Synthetic Psychology* [2], Braitenberg sets forth methods for experimentation

This work was supported by University of Waterloo's Social and Intelligent Robotics Research Lab (SIRRL).

K. Wojtkiewicz et al. (Eds.): ICCCI 2021, CCIS 1463, pp. 57–72, 2021.
https://doi.org/10.1007/978-3-030-88113-9_5

with concepts relating to the evolutionary process through experiment number 6 "Selection, the Impersonal Engineering", a thought experiment instantiating Darwinian evolution. Here a population of vehicles, each with various coupled sensory-motor connections determining its behaviour, may roam and interact with other vehicles and stimuli on a large table, while those that fall off its edge are replaced by variants of those surviving on the table. While the evolutionary scenario of Braitenberg's table is widely known, to our knowledge, our study here represents the first faithful experimental implementation of his scenario to directly and empirically study the implications of this classic thought experiment.

For this exploration, a simulation environment utilized by [16] is further improved upon. The main aim is to produce a faithful realization of what has been discussed by Braitenberg in the simplest non-trivial case where vehicles each have two frontal sensors and two rear motors, coupled with either ipsilateral or contralateral wiring, either positive or negative transduction of sensory stimulation to motor activation, by a monotonic transfer function.

2 Overview

The Darwin-Wallace theory of evolution is a ground-breaking development that made waves through the scholarly community at the time of its publication and onwards. Among those taking inspiration from Darwin's theory of evolution is Valentino Braitenberg in order to understand the mechanisms of intelligent behaviour and *"let the problem of the mind dissolve in your mind"*. In his experiment 6, Braitenberg [2] sets forth a methodology for the exploration of the evolutionary processes through simple controllable steps. This experiment builds on the previous thought experiments and previous vehicles described in this book, whose behaviour observers might describe as "Love", "Fear", "Aggression", or "Exploration". The positive (respectively, negative) and ipsilateral (respectively, contralateral) sensory-motor couplings in these vehicles give rise to stimulus-seeking or stimulus-avoiding behaviours of different vehicles (e.g. positive or negative phototaxis, with acceleration or deceleration in the vehicles, which to the observers could suggest different classes of affect and behaviour).

Here the bi-wheel platforms designed through the previous experiments in this book are set up for an evolutionary process. Various vehicles of relatively similar physical characteristics but different sensor types, connections and connection constants are set up for a Darwinian evolutionary scenario. The world set forth here is one with physical limits (referred to in the book as 'cliffs') of which the vehicles could fall off ('splash'). The vehicles which avoid the edge and do not splash are prime candidates for the next iteration of the evolutionary process (selection with inheritable variation). Characteristics that have contributed to survival are thus used impersonally to 'design' the next vehicle iterations by blindly copying a survivor on the table. This process is then repeated in an ongoing manner, which leads to an evolution of sorts. Braitenberg mentions that these next vehicle iterations may not be precisely the same due to the builders' limited capabilities and sloppiness. As such, mutations and hybrids would be a possibility. The plan as laid out by Braitenberg is used as a framework for our experimental setup.

2.1 Darwinian Evolution

Prior to Darwin, the consensus regarding the interconnected nature of living beings was the presence of divine intervention. Through his theory of evolution by natural selection, Darwin was able to change the public perception in this regard. In 1859, Darwin released the first edition of *On the Origins of the Species* [4] through which he popularized the idea of descent with modification. In such a context, desired traits are carried on through evolution, and undesirable traits are not carried forward.

Part of Darwin's genius was his ability to distinguish the main building components of evolution. This includes the "process of slow, gradual transformation of species" [9] understood by Darwin. What truly distinguishes Darwin's explanation of evolution from the previous theories is his causal explanation of the processes involved [14]. This goes against what was proposed prior to him by the likes of Jean-Baptiste Lamarck (1873) who proposed evolution by requiring a complexifying force (driving living beings up "a ladder of progress") and a separate adaptive force (based on use-and-disuse, and inheritance of acquired traits). Darwin's theory's simplicity is what makes it unique, and this simplified theoretic approach is what is also pursued in this study. These causal factors of Darwinian evolution comprise the basic ingredients of the experiments laid out in this study. Darwin and the people following in his footsteps have emphasized the connection between life and evolutionary adaptation [1]. Evolutionary biologist Maynard Smith [11] characterizes as "alive" individuals in evolving populations, i.e., with multiplication (reproduction), heredity and variation under the action of natural selection. These characteristics are exactly what has been explored in Braitenberg's Experiment 6, with the caveat that reproduction has been simplified to making a "rough copy" of a surviving individual. The other aspect of evolution which has been emphasized in this experiment is the environment in which the population lives. The importance of the varying environment in conjunction with natural selection has been emphasized by Cairns-Smith [3] in the sense that evolution is closely related to the medium it is taking place at. Braitenberg, citing the difficulty of trying to determine the mechanism responsible for any observed behaviour, characterized this use of evolution as "*downhill innovation*" in contrast to "*uphill analysis*": "*It is much more difficult to start from the outside and try to guess internal structure just from the observation of behaviour..., analysis is more difficult than invention.*" [2, p. 20].

2.2 Braitenberg Vehicles

In the series of simulations laid out in this paper, bi-wheeled dual-sensor Braitenberg vehicles are utilized, including archetypal vehicles Braitenberg described that observers tend to attribute affect and behaviour showing "Fear", "Aggression", "Love", and "Exploration" to. All of these vehicles have two sensors and two motors. In these vehicles, each sensor connects to one of the motors. This connection is either to the same side wheel's motor (ipsilateral) or the opposite side wheel's motor (contralateral). These vehicles' behaviour could give the impression of high-level emotions using low-level connections and sensorimotor transfer functions. For example, the vehicle bearing the affect of "Fear" utilizes sensor connections to motors on the same side. Both sensors have positive connections to the motors meaning that as the sensors get closer to the excitement source, the motors will spin faster. This would then lead to the motor closer to the excitement source spinning faster than the other motor and hence the vehicle moving away from the source of the excitement.

An exciting aspect of "Vehicles" that makes it unique is its exploration of evolutionary robotics. Braitenberg emphasizes the need to create an environment in which his proposed vehicles can operate and either succeed or splash. These successes or failures then would be used for the creation of the next iteration of vehicles. As such, every iteration would be more capable of facing life-threatening environmental cues. Again, this is closely modelled after observations of the evolutionary process in natural organisms.

Ever since Braitenberg in the 1980s, efforts have been made to merge evolution and Braitenberg type vehicles, e.g. Salomon [13] used evolutionary strategies to evolve controllers and receptive fields for physical Khepera robots, and Pichler [12] has explored affect and emotions as the dictating factors in the evolving ecological and morphological diversity in evolutionary robotics. Complementary to such studies, our work represents the first attempt at faithful implementation of Braitenberg's original thought experiment.

3 Research Questions

What has been explored in this study is the question of how the environment would affect the evolution, specifically positioning of the stimuli sources in the environment and environment size. Since this is an initial exploratory study, no hypothesis has been established or tested. However, several questions are investigated:

1. Is the evolutionary process contingent upon the spatial location of the sources of stimuli?
2. Is the evolutionary process contingent upon the number of stimuli sources?
3. Is the evolutionary process contingent upon the size of the table (environment)?

3.1 Vehicle Assignments

Ten vehicles are initialized, possessing different characteristics (genetic makeup). These characteristics include left and right wheel rotational speed constants and

Table 1. Initializations of the ten vehicles used in these experiments. The first four vehicles are the archetypes introduced by Braitenberg. The remaining six vehicles are not specific archetypes and variants of the four mentioned archetypes. Right and Left Wheel values are base rotational speed constants for each wheel. Right and Left Sensor values indicate constant multipliers for each sensor activation added to the connected wheel. Connection type indicates whether the sensor connections to motors are either ipsilateral or contralateral. Note that these transfer functions are all monotonic ("the more sensor activation, the more velocity", or "the more, the less") and linear.

Colour	Vehicle name	Right wheel	Left wheel	Right sensor	Left Sensor	Connection Type	Connection Value	Observer-attributed affect/behavior
Red	II.cntr.pos.R	1	1	1	1	contra	pos	Aggression
Blue	II.ipsi.neg.Bl	5	5	−0.4	−0.4	ipsi	neg	Love
Green	II.ipsi.neg.G	1	1	3	3	ipsi	pos	Fear
White	II.cntr.neg.W	4	4	−0.2	−0.2	contra	neg	Exploration
Pink	II.cntr.neg.P	3	3	−0.4	−0.4	contra	neg	-
Yellow	II.cntr.mix.Y	3	3	−0.9	0.9	contra	mix	-
Cyan	II.cntr.pos.C	1	2	1	3	contra	pos	-
Magenta	II.cntr.pos.M	1	4	2	2	contra	pos	-
Aquamarine	II.cntr.pos.A	1.2	1	0.5	0.5	contra	pos	-
Brown	II.cntr.pos.Br	2	2	0.2	0.2	contra	pos	-

left and right sensor multiplier constants (Table 1). The first four vehicles are archetypal vehicles introduced by Braitenberg, but the remainder of the ten vehicles are variants of the four mentioned archetypes. Each vehicle is assigned a unique colour and name (Table 1). The II.ipsi.neg.G vehicle's behaviour suggests the observer-attributed affect of "Fear". This vehicle is repelled by light. This could be seen in sensor connections and values. The presence of a light source alters II.ipsi.neg.G vehicle's travel trajectory by steering it off the light source. The II.cntr.pos.R vehicle is attracted towards light sources and would aggressively approach the light source with increasing velocity and acceleration. The II.ipsi.neg.Bl vehicle's behaviour suggests the observer-attributed affect of "Love". A II.ipsi.neg.Bl vehicle is attracted to light and would stop in the vicinity of a light source in light source adoration. The II.cntr.neg.W vehicle's behaviour suggests the observer-attributed affect of "Exploration". This vehicle type is also repelled by light sources. Here in the light source's presence, the vehicle would turn around and travel in the opposite direction of light presence. As stated, the rest of the vehicles are variants of the four initial archetypes. II.cntr.neg.P is a variation of II.cntr.neg.W. II.cntr.mix.Y is not a variation of any of the above. It tends to rotate around itself, as would become apparent in the upcoming experiments. II.cntr.pos.R, II.cntr.pos.M, II.cntr.pos.A and II.cntr.pos.Br are all variations of the II.cntr.pos.R vehicle even though with differences in sensor multiplier values and wheel constant values.

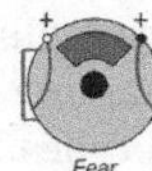

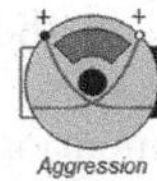

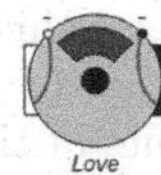

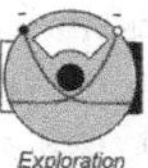

Fig. 1. Wiring connection schemata of Braitenberg vehicles of type II (bi-wheeled with two frontal sensors [16]) whose behaviour towards the stimulus suggests "Love" (II-ipsilateral-negative), "Fear" (II-ipsilateral-positive), "Aggression" (II-contralateral-positive), and "Exploration" (II-contralateral-negative).

4 Simulation Environment Implementation

It was decided to use a simulation environment vs physical implementation due to test repeatability advantages, leading to better chances of progress in experimentation with the simulation environment. The source code [16] is written in the JavaScript programming language and is executable as an HTML page (http://www.harmendeweerd.nl/braitenberg-vehicles/). This code is designed to simulate experiments 2 and 3 of *Vehicles*. As such, alterations to the code were needed to achieve the desired evolutionary processes prescribed by Braitenberg.

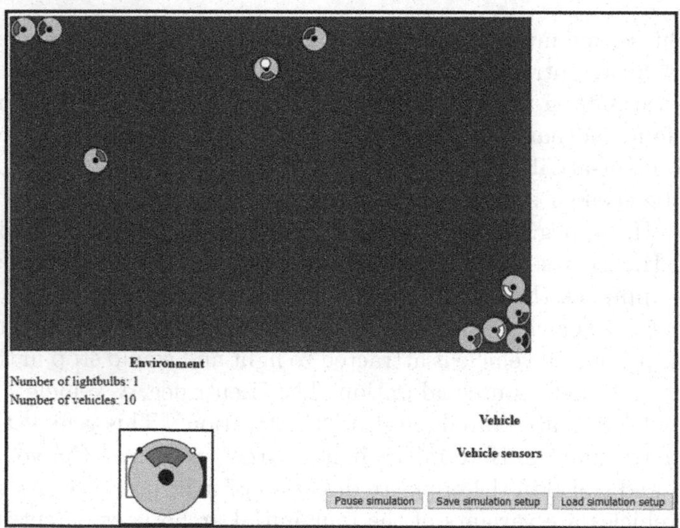

Fig. 2. Altered GUI before the edge fall module was implemented. Here, the ten initialized vehicles reach the edges of the table but don't splash.

The environment (tabletop) is surrounded by edges since evolution needs the turn-over of generations whereby space is created for new variants of surviving individuals when another individual perishes ('splash', when it falls off the table). There are no obstacles other than other vehicles present in the environment. Vehicles are composed of two wheels and two sensors sensitive to light stimuli.

A sensor could either be connected to the right wheel or the left wheel [[16], Fig. 1]. The source code is set up such that when a vehicle reaches the edge of the canvas (tabletop), it will not be able to go beyond this edge (Fig. 2). For this study, this attribute of the source code needed to be altered so when a vehicle reaches the edge, it can splash and be replaced with a new mutated variant of a surviving vehicle (https://github.com/patrickshas/Braitenberg_Exper). The newly implemented code then at random selects a vehicle other than the current vehicle to create a new mutant vehicle. As a vehicle splashes, it is instantaneously replaced with a vehicle having the characteristics of one of the remaining vehicles on the table, with variations. The new vehicles have the same make-up as the originating vehicle except for their sensor multiplier constant values (sensors attracted to light). A random multiplication factor is used for the generation of the new senor multiplier constant values. Here, this multiplication factor is a random number between 0.9 and 1.1. In this sense, the experiments proposed here investigate single characteristic (gene) evolutionary processes relating to the light attraction. Vehicle size also had to be experimented with to mitigate unnecessary vehicle pile-ups, which could hinder the experiments. Here the goal was not to entirely eliminate pile-ups but to set a balance.

5 Method

5.1 Evaluation Method

Throughout the simulation scenario iterations, it is crucial to monitor what is taking place in the simulation environment to determine the characteristics of the evolutionary process. Here, both qualitative and quantitative analysis were utilized. In the first sub-study, each setup's evolutionary process was monitored for observation of emergent patterns such as the dominant species and the vehicle movement types during and after the culmination of the evolutionary process, using video logging. In a second sub-study quantitative analysis was conducted in order to monitor and analyze the evolutionary process.

5.2 Variability

Here, the source of genetic variation acts on the value of the sensor connection weights. These are varied by a multiplier using a random coefficient in the vehicle mutation function in the methodology. This random coefficient is the instigator for the creation of "rough copies" or variants of surviving vehicles. For the present experiment's purposes, this random coefficient is a randomly selected float value between 0.9 and 1.1. As such, both sensor constant multiplier values of the surviving vehicle selected for replacing a dead vehicle are multiplied by the random coefficient in the process of creating a rough copy. A more narrowly set coefficient value (e.g. 0.99 to 1.01) would lead to a smaller deviation from the original multiplier values, and a higher coefficient value would lead to a higher deviation from the original multiplier values. Sources of environmental variability include table size, distribution of light sources, and the interactions with other members of the changing population.

Vehicle mutation in the methodology cumulatively instigates the generation of new vehicles that are different from the parent vehicle from which it originated due to the above-mentioned random coefficient not being 1. This then leads to the generation of variability in the evolutionary process. The generation of variation is crucial for evolvability. A slow variation generation process over numerous evolution steps could somewhat resemble what is proposed through Darwinian evolution. On the other hand, sensorimotor connectivity and other values are inherited without change in the current set-up, so that there is a ongoing selection among the the ten vehicle types (or species) of Table 1. An independent variable manipulated in this work is *environmental configuration* (number and locations of light sources).

5.3 Dependent Variables

A log of dependent variables is recorded for each evolutionary run at the time of each splash using the Node.js API and includes each vehicle's living time and the vehicle's type. Type is an index between 1 and 10 which refers to connectivity type the vehicle has descended from.

5.4 Procedures and Measures

This study is composed of two sub-studies comprised of qualitative and quantitative experiments:

Qualitative Experiments. Here, predefined scenarios entailing a specific table size and light locations are utilized. Each scenario is run ten times (ten trials). These scenarios were video logged and manually observed to determine emergent patterns.

These scenarios (conditions) are:

1. No light sources.
2. One light source, with the light source placed in the four corners of the table.
3. Two light sources, with the formation of the light sources varied.
4. Three light sources, with the formation of the light sources varied.
5. Four light sources, located in four corners with the distance from the edges varied. Here, the size of the tabletop is also experimented with.

For each condition, the lights are placed in different formation and spatial location in relation to the table, so the effects of these formations could be observed. In the case of two and tree lights, formation was varied by choosing different combination of table corners and placing of the lights. In the case if four lights, distance was varied by moving of the lights, placed in the four corner areas of the table, closer and farther from the corner edges in the different conditions. The video recordings for this sub-study are available at: https://www.mediafire.com/folder/5rqeljddjic32/Br_06.

Quantitative Experiments. A second set of experiments using predefined scenarios similar to the previous sub-study entailing specific number of lights and light locations were conducted while logging the previously mentioned data into a database:

Generational Species Types Data Analysis. Additional infrastructure was put in place to record desired data into a NoSQL database. This includes a Node.js server, an API and a NoSQL database. The data recorded is the number of existing vehicles of each type at the beginning of each evolutionary splash iteration for each given scenario run. This data is transmitted to a database as JSON objects which is then used for plotting and analysis (Fig. 3).

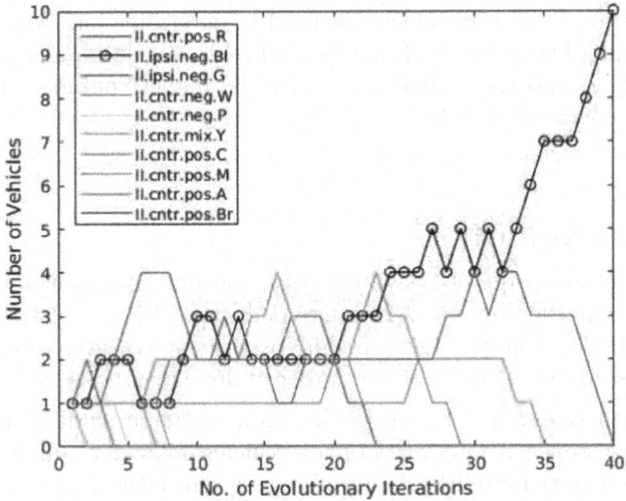

Fig. 3. Evolutionary trends for a sample run with one light located at the lower right area of the table. Here, II.ipsi.neg.Bl achieves evolutionary dominance at the 40th iteration.

Similar scenarios (conditions) to the qualitative study are utilized here: one light, two light, etc. which emphasize the placing of stimuli sources in different locations in the environment. For our experiments, we perform 30 runs for each condition, and the data coming from one vehicle type is aggregated (the mean is calculated) over the 30 runs. If the runs are not of the same length, padding is performed with the last value padding the rest of the column. (Fig. 4, upper-left) shows how the average remaining values of each vehicle type play out over up to 30 evolutionary iterations (splash-replacements).

Further, we look at which vehicle types (species) survive until the end across the 30 runs. This information is graphed in (Fig. 4, middle-left) which shows that vehicle II.ipsi.neg.Bl, for instance, has survived in approximately 55% of all runs, the most of all types. Finally, (Fig. 4, lower-left) plots the distribution of vehicle types survived at the end of each of the 30 runs. For instance, three vehicle types survived at the end of each run approximately 20% of the 30 runs.

For a few of these conditions, we conducted both 30 and then 60 run experiments to ensure that in both instances the results are the same (i.e., the system has converged to an equilibrium dynamic). Since the system dynamics in our experiments are probabilistic and not deterministic, it was vital to ensure that a dynamic equilibrium has been reached at the end of each run. To this end 60 runs of the same condition was compared against a 30 runs of said condition to see if there is any noticeable difference between the two in terms of results. Each run lasted 10 min. This time frame was chosen after the 30 run quantitative study, and is well beyond the time during which significant evolutionary change would take place.

Dominant vehicle types were determined as follows: For each condition, the vehicle counts after the last splash are used to determine the dominant vehicle type in each run. The number of members of each vehicle type is then sorted in descending order, and the vehicle type with the highest number of members is chosen as the dominant vehicle.[1]

6 Results

6.1 Quantitative Study

In order to conduct a quantitative analysis, specific visualizations of the data gathered through the Node.js API was conducted (Fig. 4). All the generated plots are available at https://github.com/patrickshas/Braitenberg_Exper/wiki. Through the study of these plots a number of observations were made:

1. In almost all cases, the vehicles come to a dynamic equilibrium within 30 evolutionary steps with majority of the vehicles no longer falling off the table. This was not anticipated by Braitenberg. In effect the dynamic equilibrium means that evolution comes to a halt. For example, in the case of the condition presented in (Fig. 4, left column) only a few of the runs fully converge to a dominant vehicle type. Majority of the runs come to a dynamic equilibrium on average (mean) at $\mu = 4451$ simulator clock cycles ("loops") with standard deviation (SD) of 2523 loops. A 10 min run is comprised of 12,000 loops.
2. Evolutionary dominance of vehicle types in different conditions is highly dependent on the the number and location of the light sources placed on the tabletop.
3. There are vehicle types (species) which perform well in many of the scenarios.
4. The edge conditions (locating of light sources closer to the table edge) cause the biggest variation in species dominance.

Overall, the quantitative results point towards contingency of the evolutionary process on location and number of the lights with certain vehicle types tending to persist to dynamic equilibrium in many scenarios (e.g. II.cntr.neg.P).

[1] If this type is not unique, dominance could be shared between two or more types. However in our experiments, no case of equal numbers of members for first and second place vehicle types are found.

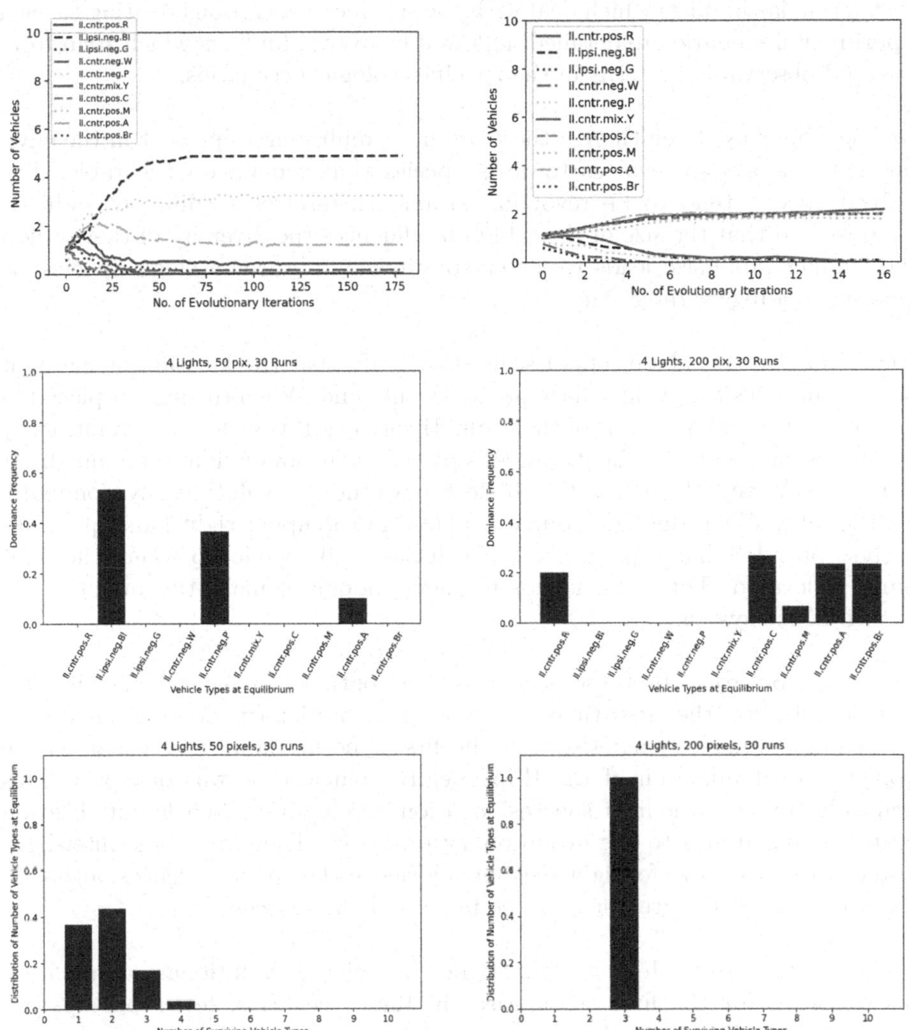

Fig. 4. Illustrative results from the quantitative sub-study for two ecological scenarios involving 4 lights placed 50 (left column) vs. 200 (right column) pixels from each corner of the table, respectively; where vehicles radius = 5 pixels. Upper row: time course of average vehicle numbers for each vehicle type, per condition; due to dynamic equilibria not all runs have the same number of evolutionary iterations, as such, separate runs' results are padded for processing. Middle row: Dominant vehicle types present at the last iteration of the evolutionary process. Vertical axis indicates the fraction of runs and horizontal axis indicate the dominant species type. Lower row: Fraction of runs a set number of vehicle species is present at the end of each evolutionary process.

6.2 Qualitative Study: Granular Findings

First, granular findings which deal with the specific observations relating to each experimental scenario are detailed, followed by overall findings which stem from repeated observable patterns in the specific ecological scenarios.

No Light Sources. Even though there are no stimuli sources present in the environment, the system evolves towards species that remain on the table. The evolved species tend to be revolving around themselves in different radii. It was observed that the size of the tabletop influences the diversity of the species. The smaller table size leads to faster convergence towards a single species, as opposed to a bigger table size.

One Light Source. These sets of scenarios clarify that the location of the light source influences the evolutionary process's outcome. When the light is placed in the lower left hand quadrant of the table, II.cntr.neg.P vehicle type evolutionary dominates, and when the light source is placed in the lower right hand quadrant II.cntr.pos.A, and II.cntr.pos.C vehicle types tend to evolutionarily dominate. Additionally, When the light source is placed in the upper right hand quadrant or the upper left hand quadrant, the vehicles tend to pile up where the light source is located. This behaviour is frequent enough to make this an emergent pattern of the system.

Two Light Sources. In these scenarios, we continue to see vehicle pile-ups. Additionally, for the first time, there is an evolutionary domination of the II.cntr.neg.P vehicle type. Also, For the first time in one of the scenarios, the evolutionary domination of the II.ipsi.neg.Bl vehicle type was observed. This then indicates that the light sources' location in relation to vehicle initialization locations contributes to the evolutionary processes. There are some inter-light source travel instances for light seeking vehicles in the above scenarios, although not often, due to the greater distance between light sources.

Three Light Sources. Here, the II.cntr.pos.R vehicles' evolutionary domination was observed for the first time. Also, in these scenarios, fewer pile-ups are observed. This is mainly due to the availability of more light sources in the environment.

Four Light Sources. As the number of light sources is increased, it is observed that there are fewer pile-ups and that the variety in species is still protected. In these sets of scenarios higher amount of inter-light travel is observed. In one of the scenarios, the II.cntr.neg.P vehicle is observed to succeed evolutionarily. In another scenarios, the evolutionary succession of II.cntr.mix.Y vehicle is seen. Here, an emergent pattern is observed. II.cntr.mix.Y is momentarily dominant just to be replaced with another vehicle type. In a final scenario, as the lights are moved closer to the edge, and the experiment arena size is reduced, species' behaviour becomes more homogeneous.

Overall Findings. The experimental sequence was initiated using no stimuli sources (no lights) and then moving to a higher number of stimuli sources consecutively. With the addition of stimuli sources, the placing of the stimuli sources in the environment and the table's size were experimented with.

1. The outcome of the evolutionary experiments is closely related to environmental settings. The vehicle types' succession and domination are different depending on the number of the lights, location of the lights, distance of the lights from the edge and size of the arena.
2. The outcome of the evolutionary experiments is also closely related to the Vehicles' genetic makeup.
   - Species not inherently attracted to the light never persist in the course of evolution, where a source of stimuli (light source) present. These species tend to go extinct in the first few evolutionary iterations.
   - Some species attracted to the light are present more frequently in most scenarios (e.g. II.cntr.pos.C).
3. Larger tabletop sizes and greater light source numbers help with the maintenance of diversity.
4. Smaller arena size and lights closer to the edge lead to faster convergence towards a dominant vehicle type. Here drift convergence [10] and Darwinian evolution work in tandem. Since the population is limited (ten vehicles) and comparatively small, there is an element of limited evolvability at play. Forcing environmental conditions towards edge cases then facilitates the manifestation of both drift convergence and Darwinian evolution in full force. It should also be noted that when moving away from edge cases, there tends to be an emergence of evolutionary instances without convergence. Many such examples occur with two or more different species persisting together through an evolutionary run in dynamic equilibrium behaviour.

Addtional emergent patterns were observed as well:

1. In scenarios with bigger table surface size, sometimes a specific vehicle type evolves/dominates for a certain time before dying down and being replaced by another vehicle type.
2. An emergent behaviour of the system is vehicles getting stuck in clusters (pile-up) at or near a light source (resembling a local maxima). The vehicles stuck in these pile-ups are then guaranteed to persist and, if not displaced, to persist in the course of evolution. Other types of observed dynamic equilibria included vehicles rotating around themselves, and periodic travel between lights.

7 Critical Analysis

As seen in the experimental results, the prescribed process by Braitenberg leads to a form of the evolutionary process that is influenced by Darwinian evolution and drift convergence. A critical notion that needs to be addressed in this context is drift convergence [10] since the population in present experiments is finite and small. It is fair to say that drift convergence plays an essential role in the evolution of dominant species in our scenarios. However, drift convergence is not the only force at play. Darwinian evolutionary processes prescribed by Braitenberg work in conjunction with ecological dynamics whereby evolutionary change comes to a halt when vehicles maintain a dynamic equilibrium with none falling off the table. This can prevent convergence to a single species type. This interplay among equilibrium dynamics, Darwininian evolution and drift convergence yields different outcomes in different trial runs of the same scenario while also exhibiting persistent patterns of domination of specific species in those scenarios.

This study in part explores the driving force responsible for the evolutionary process in Braitenberg's table scenarios. The vehicles are evolved based on the characteristic which makes them viable for survival. Bad (maladaptive) features resulting from inheritable information ('genes') in the environmental context lead to splashes, and good (well-adapted) features lead to staying on the table. These features are then regenerated and reinforced in the new vehicles through the replacement of the splashed vehicles. Random variation facilitates the evolution and tuning of the specific good traits (inheritable genes) beyond what the initial gene assignment affords the species. This random coefficient factor generation facilitates the generation of variability in the system. It should be noted that the creation of "rough copies" is just one approach towards achieving variability and evolvability. This "rough copies" creation methodology has been offered by Braitenberg since it instantiates what is described by Darwin in his evolutionary theory. It is also in line with Braitenberg's "Law of uphill analysis and downhill invention" approach [2] toward understanding possible mechanisms underlying an observed animal's or system's behaviour: Invention, the mimicking and simulation using simple behavioural control systems through iterative design and/or evolution, can lead to better insight into understand those systems than external analysis.

An occurrence that Braitenberg did not anticipate in his writings is the occurrence of dynamic equilibrium, a constant case in our experiments. In the case of dynamic equilibrium, the system's evolutionary process comes to a relevantly quick stop without evolutionary convergence to a single type which would otherwise eventually occur through drift convergence.

One of the issues associated with the experimental setup proposed here is the loss of diversity while achieving convergence. This is mainly due to the small population size and repeated sampling of this limited population. This is in line with the variations selection process originally discussed by Darwin and Wallace [5], and more recently [7]. Additionally, it is not always granted that the evolved members of a breed ("species") would be similar to the original ones. In the evolutionary design explored in this study, the evolution towards a dominant species is probabilistic in nature. The evolution towards a specific dominant species is not always guaranteed. The exact same setup could lead to the evolutionary domination of two completely different species. What these species have in common with each other is their evolved genetic makeup which affords them the ability to stay on top of the table (survive) given the environmental constraints.

In this study, concepts of affordance [6] and Umwelt [15] also come into play. The Umwelt of vehicles in the designed system is the tabletop and stimuli sources (lights) together with the vehicle's sensorimotor embodiment. The experience of staying on top of the table relates to the affordances that the environment can afford the set of the initial vehicle types. Mainly this affordance could be interpreted as falling vs not falling, and as such, the species as a whole evolves not to fall off the tabletop since the traits in the non-falling species are reinforced. When another affordance presents itself, that affordance gets a chance to be present in the evolutionary process. This secondary affordance in our case is either light 'adoration' (the case with the II.ipsi.neg.Bl vehicle) or light following (the case with the II.cntr.pos.R, II.cntr.pos.C, and II.cntr.pos.A vehicles). The evolutionary traits relevant to these affordances evolve side by side with the non-splash desire affordance. Different environmental (Umwelt) setups dictate which affordances take prevalence.

8 Conclusion and Future Work

We have conducted Darwinian evolution on Braitenberg's table using the simplest non-trivial kind of bi-wheeled vehicles with two frontal sensors (with both sensors responding to the same sort of stimuli). Even in such setting, we see a diversity of resulting evolved populations of vehicles and classes of behaviours depending on the environmental conditions (distribution of light sources), that allow either for convergence to a dominant type, or continued balance with the coexistence of more than one "species" (vehicles sharing a sensory-motor configuration topology). Following Braitenberg's thought experiments further, it would next be natural to implement and examine scenarios that:

1. Investigate more sensor pair types present in same bi-wheeled vehicles (Vehicle 3c [2, p. 12]), allowing sensitivity to different classes and modalities of stimuli, such as moisture, chemical gradients, different frequencies of electromagnetic radiation (see "Values" [2, p. 14]).
2. Allow non-monotonic connections in the transfer functions (Vehicle 4a [2, p. 15]), for more complex behavioural reactions. These additional dimensions for evolution can be expected to increase the evolvability of the Braitenberg's table scenario.
3. Incorporate mechanisms to continue the evolutionary process beyond dynamic equilibrium, e.g. periodic environmental perturbations that guarantee continued turn-over of generations of vehicles.
4. Extend the traits under evolutionary variation to include connection topology and other parameters, and allow for hybridization between surviving vehicle types.

In conclusion, the experiment conducted here could serve as the basis for broader studies that could investigate the evolutionary characteristics of these fast-evolving species. To achieve this task, there is a need for more rigorous experimentation and analysis of the logged data to determine and validate emergent patterns of behaviour and the underlying vehicle architectures achieving them in a particular environmental setting.

References

1. Bedau, M.A.: The nature of life. In: Boden, M. (ed.) The Philosophy of Artificial Life, pp. 332–357. Oxford University Press (1996)
2. Braitenberg, V.: Vehicles: Experiments in Synthetic Psychology. MIT Press, Cambridge (1986)
3. Cairns-Smith, A.G.: Seven Clues to the Origin of Life: A Scientific Detective Story. Cambridge University Press, Cambridge (1990)
4. Darwin, C.: On the Origin of Species by Means of Natural Selection, or Preservation of Favoured Races in the Struggle for Life. John Murray, London (1859). https://search.library.wisc.edu/catalog/9934839413602122
5. Darwin, C., Wallace, A.: On the tendency of species to form varieties; and on the perpetuation of varieties and species by natural means of selection. J. Proc. Linn. Soc. London, Zool. **3**(9), 45–62 (1858)
6. Gibson, J.J.: The theory of affordances. In: The Ecological Approach to Visual Perception, vol. 8, pp. 127–137, Lawrence Erlbaum Associates, Hillsdale (1979)
7. Gildenhuys, P.: Natural selection. In: Zalta, E.N. (ed.) The Stanford Encyclopedia of Philosophy, Winter edn. (2019)
8. de Lamarck, J.B.D.M.: Philosophie Zoologique, vol. 1, publ: F. Savy (1873)
9. Lennox, J.: Darwinism. In: Zalta, E.N. (ed.) The Stanford Encyclopedia of Philosophy, Metaphysics Research Lab, Stanford University, Fall edn. (2019)
10. Maynard Smith, J.: Evolutionary Genetics. Oxford University Press, Oxford (1989)
11. Maynard Smith, J.: The Theory of Evolution. Cambridge Univ, Press (1993)
12. Pichler, P.P.: Natural Selection, Adaptive Evolution and Diversity in Computational Ecosystems. Ph.D. thesis, Adaptive Systems Research Group, University of Hertfordshire (2009)
13. Salomon, R.: Scaling behavior of the evolution strategy when evolving neuronal control architectures for autonomous agents. In: Angeline, P.J., Reynolds, R.G., McDonnell, J.R., Eberhart, R. (eds.) EP 1997. LNCS, vol. 1213, pp. 47–57. Springer, Heidelberg (1997). https://doi.org/10.1007/BFb0014800
14. Sloan, P.: Darwin: From origin of species to descent of man. In: Zalta, E.N. (ed.) The Stanford Encyclopedia of Philosophy, Metaphysics Research Lab, Stanford University, Summer edn. (2019)
15. von Uexküll, J.: Streifzüge durch die Umwelten von Tieren und Menschen. Verlag von J. Springer, Berlin (1934)
16. de Weered, H.: Braitenberg vehicles. http://www.harmendeweerd.nl/braitenberg-vehicles/ (2016). Accessed 14 Mar 2021

Testing for Data Quality Assessment: A Case Study from the Industry 4.0 Perspective

Dariusz Król[1(✉)] and Tomasz Czarnecki[2]

[1] Department of Applied Informatics, Wroclaw University of Science and Technology, Wroclaw, Poland
dariusz.krol@pwr.edu.pl

[2] Faculty of Computer Science and Management, Wroclaw University of Science and Technology, Wroclaw, Poland

Abstract. Driven by the significant improvement of technologies and applications into smart manufacturing, this paper describes a way of analyzing and evaluating the quality of real-world industrial data. More precisely, it focuses on developing a method for determining the quality of production data and performing analysis of quality in terms of KPIs, such as OEE index and its sub-indicators, i.e. availability, quality rate and efficiency. The main purpose of the work is to propose a method that allows determine the quality of the data used to calculate production efficiency scores. In addition to the requirements imposed upon properly selected measures, we discuss possibilities of verifying the validity and reliability of these sub-indicators in relation to major production losses. The method for data quality assessment, developed in terms of the provided real data gathered from the factory shop-floor monitoring and management systems, was tested for its correctness. Our research has shown that an analysis of the quality of production data can reveal strengths and weaknesses in the production process. Finally, based on our single-unit intrinsic case study results, we discuss results learned on data quality assessment from an industry perspective and provide recommendations in this area.

Keywords: Big data · Data quality · Key performance indicators · Knowledge engineering · Smart manufacturing · Quality management

1 Introduction

During the long history, the world has witnessed several industrial revolutions over the years and the fourth revolution is currently underway. New smart production lines and ICT technologies have radically changed working conditions and business expectations in the era of Industry 4.0. With the increasing amount of industrial data available nowadays, it has become critical to benefit from them and maximize the efficiency of production.

Along with the automation of industry through integration of service-oriented architecture, AI, proactive maintenance systems, here comes production data

K. Wojtkiewicz et al. (Eds.): ICCCI 2021, CCIS 1463, pp. 73–85, 2021.
https://doi.org/10.1007/978-3-030-88113-9_6

that allows manufacturers to calculate and analyze several key performance indicators (KPIs). At first glance, it may seem that the production indicators are relatively simply interpretable, and therefore readable and understandable. The performance index, however, typically consists of many components. This, in turn, may distort the final interpretation. To have a clear and transparent conclusion, every single component should be analyzed. One of the factors deteriorating the final score of the indicator may generate problems, obstacles that occur during production process. The more complex the index is, the more in-depth analysis is required - from the general to the detailed level.

A central tenet of this work reflected our paramount intention for linking research more directly to practice. We are currently dealing with the fourth industrial revolution often referred to in short as Industry 4.0 or I4.0. It is recognizable by the use of ICT technologies for fostering industry-science cooperation. It brings digitalization that allows us to connect production, its processes and enable their interaction in real time. Devices can communicate with each other and transfer the information about themselves. New level of interaction and production automation is possible by technologies such as IoT, cloud/edge computing or big data analytics. Networking of various devices and systems leads to intelligent factories in which the production could be almost autonomous. The current industrial sector has many tremendous applications such as predictive maintenance, improved coordination and optimization of production processes, better decision making in real time. Factories that implement I4.0 solutions can thus reduce production costs, easily and quickly identify various anomalies in their production processes, as well as make faster business decisions.

Because data are so pervasive and play a critical role in omnifarious applications, to date, a myriad of studies have examined data quality [2,4,5,7]. Poor quality of data applied in any domain can lead to decisions being made more on subjective judgments, rather than data-driven objective conclusions. From the Industry 4.0 perspective, maintaining the intrinsic quality of manufacturing data is often recognized as crucial to effective asset management, and still it is seen as challenging and problematic [1,11,12]. The last advances have lead to the development and use of numerous smart techniques for data quality assessment. For instance, we can examine the quality of data based on correlations with indicators and its components [8].

As you can see from the above examples, the most essential component in achieving more effective management is producing better quality data. Therefore, the main contribution of this paper is to identify the quality of industrial data and to analyze the possibility of obtaining better quality of the data. We focus on developing a method that allows to determine the quality of the data used to calculate production efficiency indicators. By data quality assurance we mean the whole of planned and systematic procedures that take place before, during, and after data collection, to guarantee the quality of data-driven decisions that will drive the business forward. Our main result is to prove that improving the quality of data may have an impact on improving the production indicators. To perform our evaluation, we used a real large-scale dataset. To be useful, manufacturing data must be of good quality. Some aspects of this approach evolved from previously published research [6,8].

This paper presents a systematic methodology demonstrated in a case study. A detailed examination on a specific case is a useful process, but like everything else it has strengths and weaknesses. We decided to apply a single-unit intrinsic case study [6]. There are a number of advantages in using it. First, research on single case can help identify variables and hypotheses that have been left out of existing theories and may also uncover different errors that may exist in other cases. Particularly, it may help to explain the complexities of the factory shop-floor situations which may not be captured through theoretical and experimental research. Second, we can use causal mechanisms to give both quantitative and qualitative analyses of the data for better explanations of real cases. But on the other hand, case studies may come under strong criticism. For example, not to be rigorous, use a small number of subjects, depends on a single case and show an inability to generalize the overall results. Despite these, we considered to offer a study using 'how', 'what' and 'why' questions. This in turn can help replicate the findings from our case to another, similar to that used by researchers on multiple simulations and experiments. Several studies have attempted to look at data quality using a real-world case study [9], however they did not report such practical approach strict related to the overall equipment effectiveness (OEE) performance [10].

The remainder of this paper is structured around the following main questions: *How to develop a method of improving production efficiency scores by increasing the quality of industrial data? What are the potential consequences of data quality loss (gain) events? Why does the improvement of the quality of some data improve significantly the OEE value?*

2 Quality of Industrial Data: Unit of Analysis

The OEE-based score is the one of the most desirable index for manufacturers to improve their productive effectiveness. The formula is calculated by multiplying three sub-indexes: availability efficiency (A), performance efficiency (E) and product quality efficiency (QR) and is generally represented by a percentage.

In order to calculate the OEE index [3], the following components are required:

$$A = \frac{APT}{PBT}, \; E = \frac{PRI * PQ}{APT}, \; QR = \frac{PQ - RQ}{PQ} \tag{1}$$

where

- A denotes the ratio of the time planned for a specific task/order/activity to the time which was actually spent on that task,
- APT stands for actual production time based on a machine's work time events,
- PBT stands for planned busy time based on a machine's work time events,
- E denotes the ratio of available time to actual work time,

- PRI stands for planned run time based on products' completion events,
- PQ stands for produced quantity based on products' completion events,
- QR denotes the ratio of produced good products to all produced products,
- RQ stands for rejected quantity based on products' completion events.

None of the above indexes does not reach a value greater than 1, however, it can happen as a result of false PRI estimation. Then the performance index is limited to 1. The OEE index is a product of three indexes:

$$OEE = A * E * QR = \frac{PRI * (PQ - RQ)}{PBT} \tag{2}$$

The calculation of the OEE index consists mainly of information on the production time and the quantity of manufactured products. This information is usually delivered directly from the shop floor sensors, or Enterprise Resources Planning (ERP) systems, where the transactions with the produced quantities are logged in either manually or automatically in permanent storage. Additional information, such as PRI, is declared by the manufacturer in relation to, for instance, the machine's work calendar, its planned busy time. It is similar with the PBT measure, which is estimated for a given work order or operation that is performed on the machine and determines the production time of a unit of a given product.

At first glance calculating the OEE index looks quite simple and transparent but in fact, it is not. The OEE value does not always indicate a reliable result and there might be some issues with calculating it. For instance, it could be lack of sufficient data, which leads to calculating OEE on the basis of not all sub-indicators or even distortions in data that certainly require a deeper analysis. We could not rely only on the final result of OEE, therefore there was a need to examine the quality of the OEE itself and all its sub-components. Data quality analysis in the context of industrial data will help to identify the anomalies and therefore calculate the proper OEE value. Another element in assessing the effectiveness of an enterprise is the identification of problems that occur in individual production places. Also it should be noted that these problems are not related to the quality of industrial data provided. We assume that the quality of the data is sufficient for the reliability of the components of the OEE index. Based on the knowledge of the OEE sub-indexes (A, E, Q), it may happen that at first place, there are some problems related to the availability of the machine due to frequent failures, and at second place - problems with low efficiency of the workers due to insufficient experience, while at the third position - problems with the quality of manufactured goods.

Table 1 gives a summary of major production losses, factors that adversely affect the efficiency of the production process. This list completed with impacts and practical remarks may be helpful in undertaking remedial actions by the manufacturer. Taking proper action may by facilitated based on the approach to

Table 1. Loss characteristics, impacts, and management practices.

Loss category	Impact on the OEE index	Event	Remark
Equipment failure	Availability efficiency (A)	– Tool failure – Hardware failure – Unplanned maintenance	Identification of the boundary between failure and micro-downtime, idling and minor stoppage is still challenging
Setup and adjustment	Availability efficiency (A)	– Configuration and setup time – Material shortage – Absence of the operator – Startup time – Other corrections	These losses may be reduced by scheduling software, that can manage configuration and setup time
Idling and minor stoppage	Performance efficiency (E)	– Locked product flow – Locked material flow – Jam – Sensor lock – Locking of supplies – Cleaning, inspection and lubrication	Usually, it includes breakups, repairs and maintenance to five minutes that do not require any operation involvement
Reduced speed	Performance efficiency (E)	– Rough work – Work below maximum efficiency – Work below nominal efficiency – Equipment spent – Operator inefficiency	The maximum speed may stop the process
Defects in process	Product quality efficiency (QR)	– Defective product – Damage caused during processing – Incorrect configuration	Defects may occur during the startup or other early production phase. It can be caused due to incorrect configuration or incorrect startup time
Reduced yield	Product quality efficiency (QR)	– Defective parts – Damage caused during processing – Incorrect installation	Reduced yield accounts for the defective parts rejected during warm-up, startup or other early production

enterprise management which is known as TQM [1]. One of TQM tools, called Ishikawa diagram, which is the corresponding cause and effect graph, is showed in Fig. 1. It shows the potential causes of OEE losses: (A) breakdowns, set ups and adjustments, small stops, startups rejects, (E) reduced speeds, (QR) production rejects, i.e. scraps and reworks. This is a graphical analysis of the impact of the factors having negative effect on the overall efficiency index listed in Table 1.

In terms of data quality, problems can arise in several places. Information on the quantities produced may be reported with a delay, which significantly affects the result of the quality ratio component Q. In the case of the efficiency factor E, there may be errors in the estimation of the PRI value, which in some cases exceeds the permissible upper value of the sub-indicator. This may

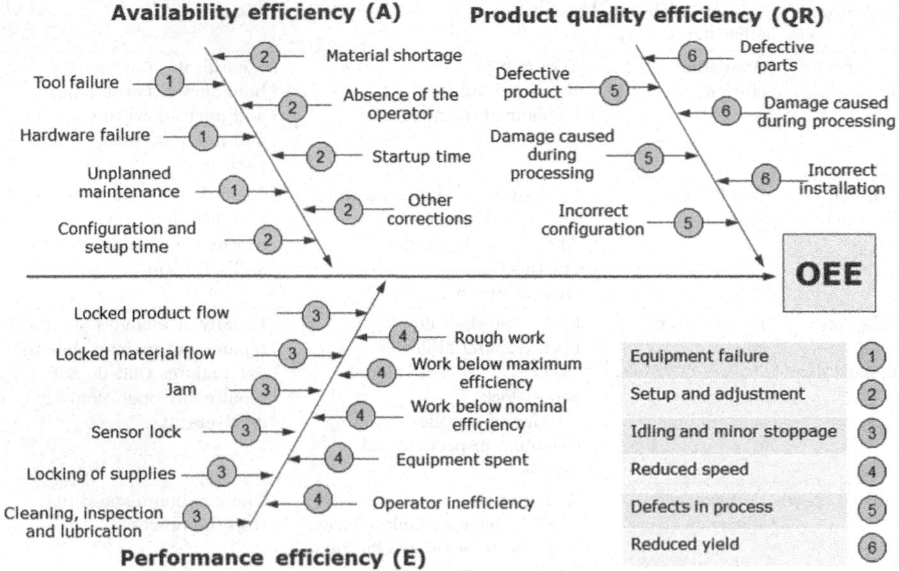

Fig. 1. Ishikawa diagram of OEE with A, E and QR branches.

also be influenced by incorrect, incomplete, late reported information on the quantities produced, for example, if this information is not being submitted from the machine but depends on the human factor. Regarding the availability factor A, problems can arise in the event of a machine busy time misplanning or a disturbance on the machine's signal collection process, which, in turn, leads to erroneous estimates of the actual machine APT.

3 The Conundrum of the Results

This section reviews the performed data quality validation experiments. It consists of calculating KPIs and analyzing their quality. In the experimental part, the shop floor real data were used, which come from a factory that produces wire, staples and nails. In this section, step by step process of extracting, transforming and calculating data is explained.

The general outline of the experiment includes: (1) analysis of the data obtained from the sensors and maintenance systems, (2) database structure absorption and data integration, (3) verification and selection of data from 20 production units, (4) calculation of OEE values, (5) developing a method to test data quality, (6) measuring data quality, (7) analysis of output data and verification of the correctness of the developed method.

The production data contained in the database which was created for the experiments comes from two separate systems. In the context of calculating the indicators that make up OEE, data about the produced quantities and the work signals are extremely important. Below is a graph showing the number of the work signals related to the machines and another graph showing the number of produced quantities. In both cases, data for the full time period between January 2019 and July 2020, are presented.

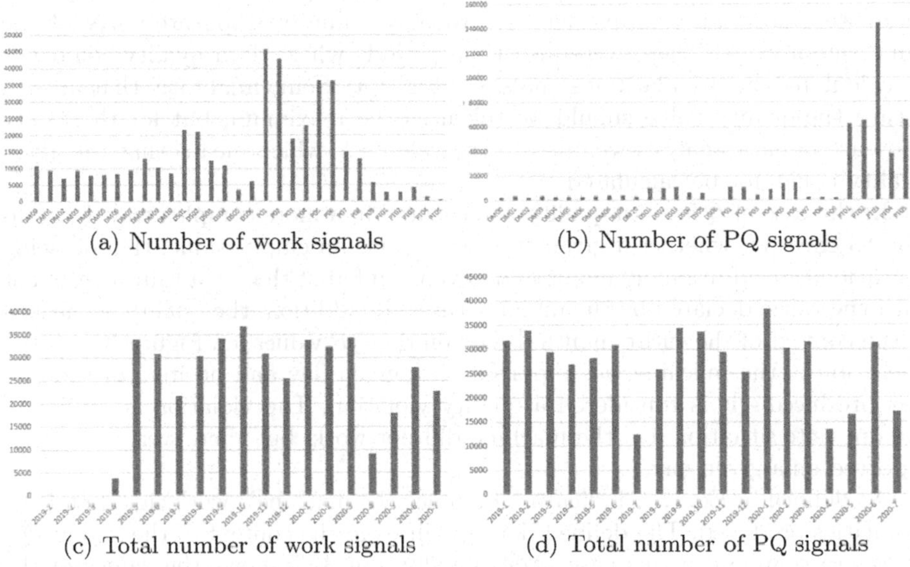

(a) Number of work signals

(b) Number of PQ signals

(c) Total number of work signals

(d) Total number of PQ signals

Fig. 2. Uncertainty in signals distributed to machines: (a-b) tracked to different machines, (c-d) tracked to all machines over several months.

The clustered column charts presented in Fig. 2(a) and 2(b) depict an interesting relationship for conveyor belt machines (PT01–PT04). For the full period, these machines from this group had the fewest occurrences of work signals and the most recorded events related to the number of quantities produced. In turn, as shown in Fig. 2(c) there were actually no work signal events during the first three months of 2019 for any of the machines. The slight presence of events in January 2019 (6 total number of work signals), no events in the next two months and the growing number of events since April indicate a potential problem in data delivery. The probable reason for the lack of data is a failure of one of the subsystems supplying data from machines to the manufacturing execution systems (MES) database. The factory did not have any production downtime, which is confirmed by another chart on the quantities produced by month presented in Fig. 2(d). According to the quantities produced, which originates from the ERP system, the production line was working all the time. The failure related to the signals supplied to the MES system was fixed in April 2019. Based on these sparse findings, it can be assumed that the data between May 2019 and July 2020 is suitable for further analysis. Therefore, in this time period, it will be possible to calculate OEE index,

In the case of data quality for the A area, the situation can be interpreted as zero-one. For days for which the machine signal quality could be computed, there were no quality drops due to erroneous value or duplicate entry of the same signal value. There were also time periods where data quality could not be calculated due to a lack of signals, see Fig. 2(a). Some might say that in such a case the quality value should be taken as the maximum, but for the safety and ease of data analysis we operate the value -1, which means that the given quality could not be calculated.

In the case of QR, data quality is measured in a more complex way. In addition to checking whether a given transaction has an empty value, the following conditions are additionally monitored: a value different than 0, a value consistent with the range declared by the manufacturer. In addition, the quality is checked in the context of the entire month, based on the QR values, cf. Figure 2(c). If the operation of the machine was reported on a given day and no item of product was produced - it is considered a quality violation. The violation is similar in the opposite situation, i.e. the machine did not work, but there were quantities reported on a given day.

As defined in Eq. 1, E indicator combines the machine's work signal and the quantities produced. The defined data qualities in the context of the A and QR areas are common in this case. Additionally, Fig. 3(e) shows the values of the index exceeding the maximum of 1. This is related to the situation when the machine had a very low value of the actual working time and a large number of reported quantities produced. The value of the planned time of producing a item unit also affects the result, because it can be incorrectly estimated, which leads to overestimated results. Moreover, the value of the efficiency index cannot be calculated in the case when the actual machine working time on a given day is 0.

4 Discussion

The following section considers findings from our case study. These findings are discussed in the context of (4.1) validity and reliability, and (4.2) better industrial quality characteristics.

4.1 Validity and Reliability

In every scientific study, questions are raised about whether the study is valid and reliable. We applied construct validity, external validity and reliability mechanisms in this study. In general, validity refers to whether there is substantial evidence that the theoretical paradigm correctly corresponds to observation: (a) having the correct measurement (construct validity), (b) identifying the study context for which the results can be generalized (external validity). On the other hand, reliability focuses on whether the process of the study is consistent and can be replicated with the same results. In our case, construct validity is included since this study gathers data from multiple sources (the factory shop-floor monitoring and management systems) whereas external validity is accomplished by the fact that we use of theory presented in the ISO 22400 standard and based on the literature review. To ensure the reliability of data (1) we use the Internet of Things technology and provide real-time information about equipment status, (2) we transfer data from shop floor level into public cloud computing repository (Microsoft Azure). We believe that investigating more industrial data can improve production efficiency score.

4.2 Industrial Quality Characteristics

This section addresses the question of how data quality can be improved. Usually, it depends on the environment, data and the purpose for which they are collected. First, when we combine data from different sources that are not unequivocally consistent with each other, it should be checked whether the data sets can be correctly associated with each other.

The actual good and scrap quantities data from the ERP system contain information about the machine code/name. However, in the case of data collected in the MES system, we have potential machine codes in various production tables, which caused the problem of their unambiguous connection to ERP data. Only an additional analysis of the data completeness concerning machine names, signals and the number of entries (events) allowed to determine which of the duplicates is the correct one. But in order to avoid potential quality problems, to ensure unambiguous connections between data from different systems, we have added information about the machine's work center.

Another very important issue related to the produced quantities is the correct estimation of the *PRI* value, cf. Sect. 2. During the calculations of the production efficiency index, it was noticed that the upper limit of the index value was exceeded repeatedly. Therefore, we come to another aspect of the data anomaly, which may indicate that the machine was not working at all or very briefly, but it produced a large number of items. This may happen for a variety of reasons, one of them relating to the hardware. It may be a failure of the system transmitting information (e.g. data bus, machine controller) about the machine's work to the MES system. The data on machine signals should be updated after the failure has been repaired. The second aspect of this situation is a human factor, because the data on the quantities are reported manually. This information may be entered with a delay or inaccuracy. The best solution would be that the quantities should also be derived from machine signals, because only then the data would be maintained on a regular basis.

After analyzing the results of the experiments statistically and qualitatively, we identified the following steps to increase the efficiency sub-indicators:

- Availability efficiency (A) - for days with no machine's work signal reported, the last value from the previous day was repeated in a given day.
- Product quality efficiency (QR) – reported quantities that exceeded the maximum value of the desired value range have been reduced.
- Performance efficiency (E) - the PRI value was limited and re-estimated so that the final value of the efficiency index did not exceed the maximum value.

Table 2. Correlations between *speed* and OEE for conveyor belt machines.

Production unit	Signal	Margin	Inertia	Correlation power
PT01	PT01_Speed	1	2	0.36
PT02	PT02_Speed	1	2	−0.76
PT03	PT03_Speed	1	3	−0.17
PT04	PT04_Speed	1	3	−0.43

By using the Production Unit Performance Management Tool (PUPMT), we are able to name the input signals that affect the OEE indicator to complete the characteristics of data [8]. As the result, Table 2 presents a list of 4 settings of the best correlations between input signal *speed* and the OEE value for conveyor belt machines (PT01–PT04). The coincidence of changes of *speed* is related to the inertia, which determines the time shift between the input-output observations and the margin of inertia defining the period in which the given change affects the selected production unit. The last column lists the actual strength of the correlation, where we use the Pearson correlation to compute the power. In our case, only PT01, PT02, and PT04 units and their *speed* values should be checked for any anomalies. From this, it emerged that no significant anomalies were reported for the specified study period.

After that, the OEE index and all sub-indexes were recalculated. All results of the tests of PT01 unit, before (baseline) and after (growth) improvement for April 2020 are plotted in Fig. 3. Only for testing purposes, the growth of total quality is set to the maximum.

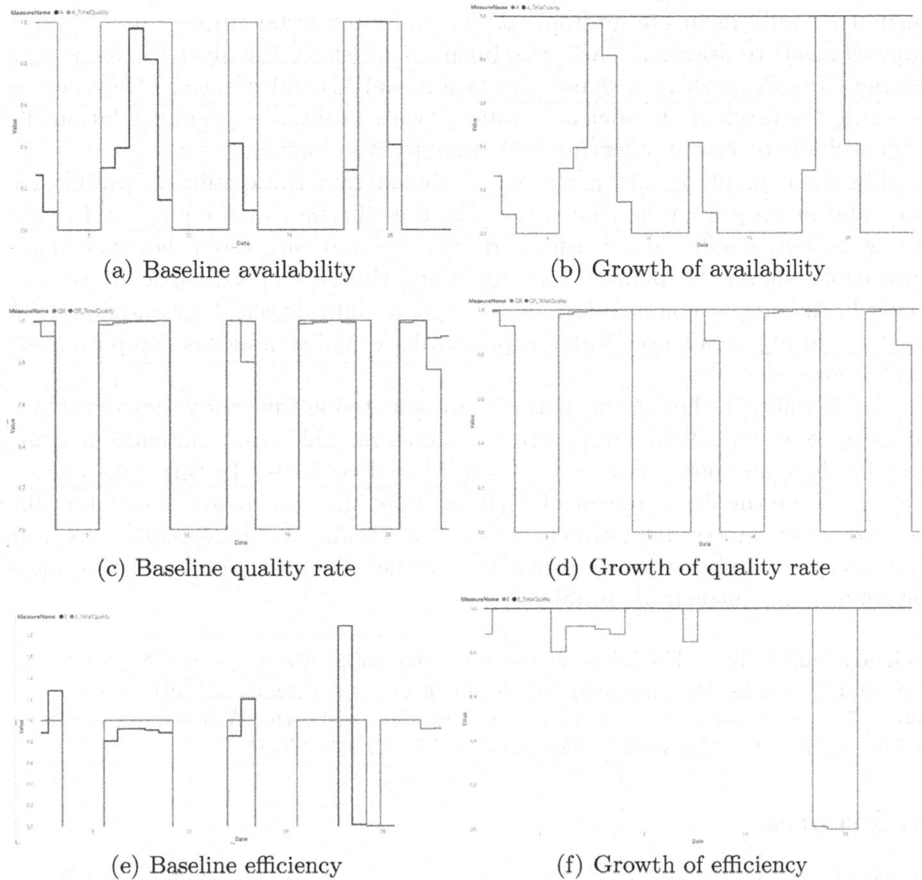

(a) Baseline availability (b) Growth of availability

(c) Baseline quality rate (d) Growth of quality rate

(e) Baseline efficiency (f) Growth of efficiency

Fig. 3. Sub-indexes: availability (A), quality rate (QR), efficiency (E) before (left) and after (right) improvement.

5 Concluding Remarks

In this paper, the main concern is single-unit intrinsic case study on data quality. We investigated the different aspects of data quality that have an impact on the efficiency of production.

The method for the improvement OEE scores was demonstrated and validated using a case study focusing on a real-world examination scenario. The findings and observations compiled during the study highlighted several important points. Firstly, while analytics of standard models deliver quit limited operational insights, detailed testing of KPIs can facilitate the process of identifying correlations. From our case study, it appears that in the case of automatic data collection from a shop floor, the losses are mostly systematic, but the real causes are not easily come-at-able. Secondly, given the better I4.0 technology which translates into better analyzes, there is a significant need to adopt new standards that fully facilitate interoperability and integration through data quality improvements to draw more accurate business decisions. Finally, permanent data testing through boosting a signal correlation analysis and selecting of key factors affecting the production efficiency could provide profitable recommendations by the emphasis placed on affecting real-time decision-making.

The focal point of this study was to investigate the quality of production data and develop a method for improving the efficiency of the process. In view of the current results, some tests and strategies are suggested, however, some limitations should be pointed out, including the lack of a holistic framework towards the deep recommendations to support data-driven decision-making. A very promising area to overcome common data quality issues is computational intelligence.

Furthermore, although the methods investigated in this study were developed and applied to industrial data, these techniques may also show potential in other specific domains, not necessarily closely related to KPIs. Testing data quality may influence the development of early warning and control systems, inter alia, to analyze telemetry data, which are used in making swift decisions. We hope that the presented case study provides some new insights and some more ideas for solving this intractable problem.

Acknowledgments. The initial research for this paper was supported in part by the National Centre for Research and Development under contract no. POIR 01.01.01-00-0687/17-00. The preparation of this paper was funded by the Wrocław University of Science and Technology under block grant no. 8211104160/K45.

References

1. Ahuja I.: Total productive maintenance. In: Ben-Daya, M., Duffuaa, S., Raouf, A., Knezevic, J., Ait-Kadi, D. (eds) Handbook of Maintenance Management and Engineering. Springer, London (2009) . https://doi.org/10.1007/978-1-84882-472-0_17
2. Cai, L., Zhu, Y.: The challenges of data quality and data quality assessment in the big data era. Data Sci. J. **14**, 1–10 (2015)
3. Chung, Y., Krishnan, S., Kraska, T.: A data quality metric (DQM): how to estimate the number of undetected errors in data sets. In: Proceedings of the VLDB Endowment, pp. 1094–1105 (2017)
4. Cichy, C., Rass, S.: An overview of data quality frameworks. IEEE Access **7**, 24634–24648 (2019)
5. Corrales, D.C., Corrales, J.C., Ledezma, A.: How to address the data quality issues in regression models: a guided process for data cleaning. Symmetry **10**(4), 99 (2018)
6. Crowe, S., Cresswell, K., Robertson, A., et al.: The case study approach. BMC Med. Res. Methodol. **11**(100), 1–9 (2011)
7. Das, S., Saha, B.: Data quality mining using genetic algorithm. Int. J. Comput. Sci. Secur. IJCSS **3**(2), 105–112 (2009)
8. Król, D., Skowroński, J., Zareba, M., Bartecki, K.: Development of a decision support tool for intelligent manufacturing using classification and correlation analysis. In: 2019 IEEE International Conference on Systems, Man and Cybernetics (SMC), pp. 88–94 (2019)

9. Marta-Pedroso, C., Freitas, H., Domingos, T.: Testing for the survey mode effect on contingent valuation data quality: a case study of web based versus in-person interviews. Ecol. Econ. **62**(3), 388–398 (2007)
10. O'Donovan, P., Bruton, K., O'Sullivan, D.T.: Case study: the implementation of a data-driven industrial analytics methodology and platform for smart manufacturing. Int. J. Prognostics Health Manage. **7**, 1–22 (2016)
11. Simard, V., Rönnqvist, M., Lebel, L., Lehoux, N.: A general framework for data uncertainty and quality classification. IFAC PapersOnLine **52**(13), 277–282 (2019)
12. Viswanadham, N., Narahari, Y.: Performance Modeling of Automated Manufacturing Systems. Prentice-Hall Inc, Upper Saddle River (1992)

Hybrid Biogeography-Based Optimization Algorithm for Job Shop Scheduling Problem with Time Lags and Single Transport Robot

Madiha Harrabi[1](✉), Olfa Belkahla Driss[2], and Khaled Ghedira[3]

[1] LARIA Laboratory, Ecole Nationale des Sciences de l'Informatique, Université de la Manouba, Manouba, Tunisia

[2] LARIA Laboratory, Ecole Supérieure de Commerce de Tunis, Université de la Manouba, Manouba, Tunisia
olfa.belkahla@isg.rnu.tn

[3] ESPRIT School of Engineering Tunis, Ariana, Tunisia
khaled.ghedira@isg.rnu.tn

Abstract. We are interesting for the Job shop Scheduling Problem with Time Lags and Single Transport Robot (JSPTL-STR). This problem is a new extension of the Job shop Scheduling Problem, in which, we take into account two additional constraints; the minimum and maximum time lags constraints between finish and start time of two operations and transportation time constraints of different operations between different machines using a single robot. After the completion of an operation on a machine, it needs to be transported using transport robot to the next machine taking some time. The objective is to determine a feasible schedule of machine operations and transport operations with minimal makespan (Completion time of the last operation executed). This problem belongs to a category of problems known as NP-hard problem. Biogeography-Based Optimization (BBO) algorithm is an evolutionary algorithm inspired by the migration of species between habitats. It has successfully solved optimization problems in many different domains and has demonstrated excellent performance. To assess the performance of the proposed algorithm, a series of experiments on new proposed benchmark instances for JSPTL-STR are performed.

Keywords: Optimization · Scheduling · Job shop · Time lags

1 Introduction

The scheduling problem is one of the most encountered problems in the management of production system. It occurs in all the economic domains, from computer engineering to manufacturing techniques. The Job Shop Problem with Time Lags and Single Transport Robot (JSPTL-STR) is a special case of the classical Job shop problem, it arises in many real-life scheduling applications

K. Wojtkiewicz et al. (Eds.): ICCCI 2021, CCIS 1463, pp. 86–98, 2021.
https://doi.org/10.1007/978-3-030-88113-9_7

such as steel industry, chemical reactions, hoist-scheduling problems, perishable product production and in biotechnology and chemistry.

JSPTL-STR as a new sub-problem in a Job shop environment where additional minimum and maximum Time Lags constraints between operations are considered and jobs have to be transported between machines by a single transport robot. The addition of time lag constraints between operations and transportation time of operations between machines makes difficult even the usually simple task of finding a feasible schedule. This problem belongs to NP-hard combinatorial optimization problems that need "strong" resolution method. The Biogeography Based Optimization algorithm was successfully used for solving many scheduling problems in the literature. We propose a Hybrid Biogeography-Based Optimization algorithm (HBBO) for solving the JSPTL-STR problem with makespan minimization. In the proposed HBBO, the effective greedy constructive heuristic is adapted to generate the initial population of habitat. Moreover, a local search metaheuristic is investigated in the mutation step in order to ameliorate the solution quality and enhance the diversity of the population. To assess the performance of HBBO, a series of experiments on well-known benchmark instances for job shop scheduling problem with time lag constraints are performed. The reminder of the paper is organized as follows. Section 2 presents the related works, in Sect. 3, we present the problem formulation. In Sect. 4, the disjunctive graph model is given. In Sect. 5, we give the basic concepts of BBO algorithm. In Sect. 6, we present the adaptation of HBBO algorithm for our problem. Section 7 analyzes the performance results of HBBO when applied to solve instances of benchmark problems. At last, we come to our conclusion and some possible future directions.

2 Related Works

We study the Job shop Scheduling Problem with Time Lags and Single Transport Robot which is a new extension of Job shop Scheduling problem and consists of two sub-problems; the Job shop Scheduling Problem with Time Lags and the Job shop Scheduling Problem with Single Transport Robot. Time lag means the waiting-time constraints between two consecutive operations in the same job or between two operations of different jobs. Two kinds of time lag constraints can be used in several fields of industrial applications of Job shop, either minimum or maximum time lags. Minimum time lag constraints can be corresponded to overlap time, storage time, transit time, communication time between processes of a computer system, etc. Maximum time lags can be used to demand the waiting time between operations must not be overly long to avoid deterioration of products. Minimum and maximum time lag constraints arise in many real-life scheduling applications such as: steel industry, chemical reactions, hoist-scheduling problems, perishable product production and biotechnology and chemistry problems.

Different methods were proposed for solving the Job shop Scheduling Problem with Time Lags in the literature. Caumond et al. [4–6] and [7] introduced different metaheuristics such as tabu search algorithm, genetic algorithm and memetic algorithm. Deppner [9] proposed some heuristics for solving the Job shop problem with additional time lags constraints. Karoui et al. [21] investigated a Climbing

Discrepancy Search method. Artigues et al. [2] proposed a job insertion heuristic and generalized resource constraint propagation mechanisms. González et al. [10] proposed a scatter search procedure combining the path relinking and the tabu search metaheuristic. Harrabi et al. [12–17] and [18] proposed a variety of metaheuristics, hybrid approaches, and distributed models using multi-agent system. Lacomme et al. [23] and [24] proposed some dedicated constraint propagation and greedy randomized priority rules. Different methods were proposed for solving the Job shop Scheduling Problem with Single Transport Robot. Hurink and Knust [19] and [20] proposed a tabu search metaheuristic. Lacomme et al. [22] proposed a branch and bound procedure combined with a discrete events simulation model. Caumond et al. [8] proposed a mixed integer linear program and a heuristic branch and bound approach. Afsar et al. [1] proposed a disjunctive graph modeling and a Greedy Randomized Adaptive Search Procedure with an Evolutionary Local Search procedure (GRASP × ELSE) for solving the Job shop problem with time lags and transportation constraints and they considered the waiting time between operations as the transportation time of operations.

In this paper, we propose the first resolution of the Job shop Scheduling Problem with Time Lags and Single Transport Robot using the Hybrid Biogeography-Based Optimization algorithm combined with greedy heuristic in the initialisation step and local search procedure in the mutation step.

3 Problem Formulation

The formulation of Job shop Scheduling problem with Time Lags and Single Transport Robot is an extension of the Lacomme's formulation [23] extended by adding the transportation time constraints. The JSPTL-STR involves a set of jobs that should be processed on a set of machines. Each job i consists of a sequence of operations; (i, j) denotes the jth operation of job i. Every operation must be assigned to a unique machine without interruption. For some pairs of operations (i, j) and (i', j') there are minimum and maximum time lag constraints respectively denoted by $TL^{min}_{(i,j),(i',j')}$ and $TL^{max}_{(i,j),(i',j')}$ restricting the distance between the end of (i, j) and the start of (i', j') to the interval $[TL^{min}_{(i,j),(i',j')}, TL^{max}_{(i,j),(i',j')}]$. Additionally, each job J_i (J_1, ... , J_n) is composed of n_{i-1} transport operations $\{T_{i,1}, T_{i,2}, \ldots, T_{i,n_{i-1}}\}$ to be made by a robot R from one machine to another. They occur if a job changes from one machine to another, i.e. if job J_j is processed on machine M_k and afterwards on machine M_l, a transportation time T_{jkl} arises. We assume that all transportations have to be done by a single transport robot R which can handle at most one job at a time.

Solving the JSPTL-STR consists in sequencing all operations on the machines, such that the following constraints are satisfied:

(i) Precedence constraints for operations of the same job;
(ii) Minimum and Maximum Time Lag constraints;
(iii) Each machine processes at most one operation at a time;
(iv) The robot can transport at most one operation at a time;

The objective is to find a schedule that minimizes the makespan which is the total completion time C_{max} = Max C_i where C_i is the finish time of job i.

4 Disjunctive Graph Model

The disjunctive graph model for the classical Job shop problem developed by Roy and Sussmann [28] was extended to the Job shop Scheduling Problem with Single Transport Robot by Hurink and knust [20] which incorporate the scheduling of the robot into the model. We extend this representation by adding arcs for time lags between operation into the model.

In the disjunctive graph, each operation is modeled by a node and an arc from operation (i, j) to operation (i', j') represents the minimum distance between the start time of these two operations. It corresponds to the binary constraint: $t_{i'j'} - t_{ij} \geq l_{(ij),(i'j')}$ where $l_{(ij),(i'j')}$ is the length of the arc. Maximum time lag from an operation (i, j) to an operation (i', j') is represented by an arc with negative length which corresponds to the duration of (i, j) plus the maximum time lag value. Minimum time lag constraints are modeled by extra arc from operation (i, j) to operation (i', j') and it is weighted with the processing time of (i, j) plus the minimum time lag value. When no time lags are specified (for example, between one operation and the dummy operation of the graph), it is possible to assume, without loss of generality, to have null minimum time lags and infinite maximum time lags. Additionally, transport operations are introduced for all needed transports as additional vertices in the disjunctive graph and requiring that these operations have to be processed by the robot. Furthermore, the empty moving times are modeled as sequence-dependent setup times. The disjunctive graph G = (V, C ∪ D_M ∪ D_R) consists of a set of vertices V containing all operations (machine operations and transport operations) and two dummy nodes 0 and *, a set of conjunctions C representing the job orders, disjunctions for the machines (D_M) and the robot (D_R). For each job J_j (j = 1, ..., n) we introduce n_j −1 so-called transport operations t_{ij} (i = $1, \ldots, n_{j-1}$) with precedences $O_{ij} \rightarrow T_{ij} \rightarrow O_{i+1,j}$. The processing time of T_{ij} is equal to the transportation time of job J_j from machine μ_{ij} to $\mu_{i+1,j}$, i.e. p(T_{ij}) = T_{jkl}, when $\mu_{ij} = M_k$, $\mu_{i+1,j} = M_l$.

Example. We consider an instance of Job shop Scheduling Problem with Time Lags and Single Transport Robot given in Table 1 with 3 jobs and 3 machines. So we have 9 "ordinary" operations and 6 "transport" operations. Transportation times of robot between each pairs of machines is 5.

The minimum and maximum time lags between operations of different jobs are:

$$TL^{min}_{(O11),(O13)} = 36 \qquad TL^{max}_{(O11),(O13)} = 95$$

$$TL^{min}_{(O11),(O22)} = 15 \qquad TL^{max}_{(O11),(O22)} = 50$$

$$TL^{min}_{(O21),(O31)} = 13 \qquad TL^{max}_{(O21),(O31)} = 35$$

The corresponding disjunctive graph is given in Fig. 1.

Table 1. Example of instance Job shop J

	Operation 1	Operation 2	Operation 3
job1	M1, 10	M2, 35	M3, 25
job2	M1, 15	M3, 16	M2, 12
job3	M3, 11	M1, 12	M2, 21

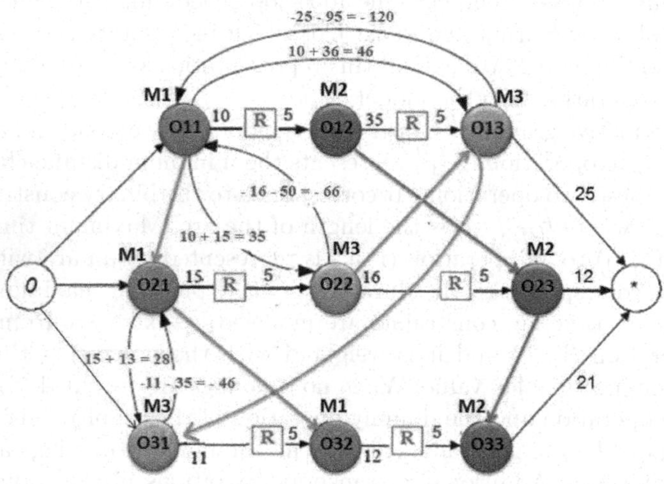

Fig. 1. Disjunctive graph model

5 Biogeography-Based Optimization

BBO algorithm, proposed in 2008 by Simon [29], is inspired by the mathematics of biogeography and mainly the work from MacArthur and Wilson [26]. Later, a large amount of theoretical, methodological, and practical studies on BBO have come into being. The two main concepts of BBO are Habitat Suitability Index (HSI) and Suitability Index Variables (SIVs). Features that correlate with HSI include rainfall, diversity of topographic features, land area, and temperature. Moreover, SIVs are considered as the independent variables of the habitat. The two main operators of BBO are migration and mutation. Migration operator, including immigration and emigration, bridges the communication of habitats in an ecosystem. Deciding whether or not a habitat performs emigration or immigration is up to its HSI. Mutation operator is used to enhance the diversity of the population, which helps to decrease the chances of getting trapped in local optima.

BBO algorithm was successfully used for solving many scheduling problems. Rabiee et al. [27] developed a modified BBO algorithm for hybrid flow shop scheduling problem. Habib et al. [11] introduced a new BBO algorithm for solving the flexible Job shop scheduling problem. Wang et al. [30] proposed a hybrid BBO algorithm for Job shop scheduling problem. Yang [31] investigated a modified

BBO algorithm with machine-based shifting decoding strategy for solving the flexible Job shop scheduling problem. Lin et al. [25] introduced a hybrid discrete BBO algorithm for flow shop scheduling problem.

In this work, we use an Hybrid BBO algorithm for the Job shop Scheduling Problem with Time Lags and Single Transport Robot with makespan minimization.

6 Hybrid BBO Algorithm for JSTL-STR Problem

6.1 Representing Habitat

The Job shop Scheduling Problem with Time Lags and Single Transport Robot is composed of two types of operations: the machine operations and the transport operations, that's why the representation is encoded in two vectors: firstly, a vector V1 contains the machine operations sequence with length L1 equal to the total number of machine operations and where each index represents the selected operation to be processed on machine indicated at position p. Secondly, a vector V2 contains the machine operations and transport operations sequence with length L2 equal to the total number of machine operations and transport operations and where each index represents the selected machine operation or transport operation indicated at position p. See Fig. 2.

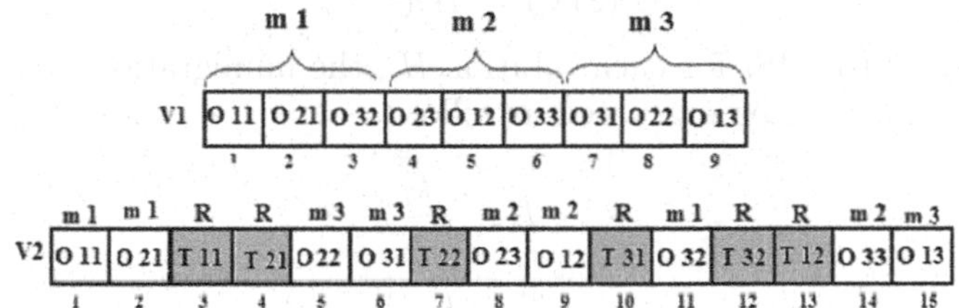

Fig. 2. Habitat representation

6.2 Initialisation of Population

The BBO algorithm starts with population habitats. According to the chosen parameter Population Size (PS), an initial population containing PS individuals is generated using the greedy algorithm [32] in order to get out of a local optimum and provide a good exploration of the search space. This heuristic is one of the popular methods to solve hard optimization problems. It is easy to be implemented and expanded and it produces solutions with good quality.

6.3 Selection Strategies

This step is one of the distinctive steps of BBO with other algorithms, which is executed through two different strategies, one for migration and one for mutation. To explain the selection strategies for migration, we should firstly define the immigration rate λ_i and the emigration rate μ_j. During the migration process, we face two types of selection. Firstly, we should determine whether a special habitat H_i should be immigrated or not. To do so, a simple comparison of λ_i with a random number is done. Secondly, we should select habitat H_i for emigrating to H_j. During the mutation process, a habitat H_i selected to be mutated according to a simple comparison of the mutation probability with a random number.

6.4 Migration Operator

Migration is a probabilistic operator that is used for modifying each solution H_i by sharing features among different solutions. The idea of a migration operator is based on the migration in biogeography which shows the movement of species among different habitats. Solution H_i is selected as immigrating habitat with respect to its immigration rate λ_i, and solution H_j is selected as emigrating habitat with respect to its emigration rate μ_j. It means that a solution is selected for immigrating or emigrating depends on its immigration rate λ_i, or emigration rate μ_j; the migration process can be shown as:

$$H_i(\mathrm{SIV}) \leftarrow H_j(\mathrm{SIV})$$

After calculating the HSI for each solution H_i, the immigration rate λ_i and the emigration rate μ_j can be evaluated as follows:

$$\lambda_i = I(1 - \frac{k_i}{n}) \tag{1}$$

$$\mu_j = E(\frac{k_i}{n}) \tag{2}$$

In (1) and (2), k_i represents the rank of the ith habitat after sorting all habitats according to their HSIs. It is clear that since more HSI represents a better solution, more k_i represents the better solution. Therefore, the 1st solution is the worst and the nth solution is the best. I is the maximum immigration rate and E the maximum emigration rate which are both usually set to 1, n is the number of habitats in the population. The two rates, λ_i and μ_j are the functions of fitness or HSI of the solution. Since, according to the biogeography, the SIVs of a high-HSI solution tend to emigrate to low-HSI solutions, a high-HSI solution has a relatively high μ_j and low λ_i, while in a poor solution, a relatively low μ_j and a high λ_i are expected. Figure 3 illustrates an example of migration operator of BBO for the Job shop Scheduling Problem with Time Lags and Single Transport Robot.

As mentioned earlier, the SIVs from a good habitat tend to migrate into a poor habitat. This migration operator is performed probabilistically based

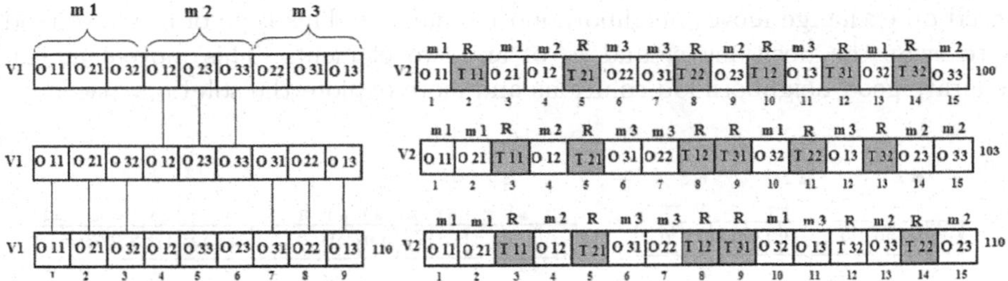

Fig. 3. Migration operator of BBO algorithm

on immigration and emigration rates. In this example, we will explain how the migration is implemented in our BBO algorithm. Consider dealing with an instance of Job shop Scheduling Problem with Time Lags and Single Transport Robot presented in Table 1. Suppose, based on immigration and emigration rates, that an immigrating habitat $H_i = (O_{11}, O_{21}, O_{32}, O_{12}, O_{23}, O_{33}, O_{22}, O_{31}, O_{13})$ and an emigrating habitat $H_e = (O_{11}, O_{21}, O_{32}, O_{12}, O_{33}, O_{23}, O_{31}, O_{22}, O_{13})$. The migration process is: $H_e(\text{SIV}) \leftarrow H_i(\text{SIV})$

SIVs of H_i will be randomly selected and replace randomly selected SIVs of H_e. Assuming SIVs of H_i (O_{12}, O_{23}, O_{33}) are selected to replace SIVs of H_e (O_{12}, O_{33}, O_{23}). Therefore, the migration process consists in:

(1) SIVs of machine 2 H_i (O_{12}, O_{23}, O_{33}) migrate into H_e to replace SIVs of H_e (O_{12}, O_{33}, O_{23}).
(2) SIVs of H_i (O_{12}, O_{23}, O_{33}) replace SIVs of H_e (O_{12}, O_{33}, O_{23}).
(3) SIVs (O_{11}, O_{21}, O_{32}) of machine 1 and SIVs (O_{31}, O_{22}, O_{13}) of machine 3 from H_e remain at original places.
(4) Therefore, the new habitat, $H_n = (O_{11}, O_{21}, O_{32}\ O_{12}, O_{23}, O_{33}, O_{31}, O_{22}, O_{13})$ is produced.

6.5 Mutation Operator

Mutation is a probabilistic operator that randomly modifies a solution's SIV based on its priory probability of existence. Mutation is used to enhance the diversity of the population, which helps to decrease the chances of getting trapped in local optima. Solutions with very high HSI and very low HSI are both equally improbable, while medium HSI solutions are relatively probable to mutate. Namely, a randomly generated SIV replaces a selected SIV in the solution H_m according to a mutation probability. Note that an elitism approach is employed to save the features of the habitat that has the best solution in BBO process. The habitat with the best solution has a mutation rate of 0.

In this step of the algorithm, we choose to use the local search procedure based on exchange moves neighborhood mechanism. This step starts using the solution result of migration step as the initial solution then, applying the neighborhood structure to generate a modified solution. Figure 4 illustrates an example of mutation operator of BBO. We propose to use a local search procedure based on exchange moves neighborhood mechanism. This type of neighborhood is to swap the positions p_i and p_j of any two elements. This movement can generate good neighborhood solutions and more explore the solution space.

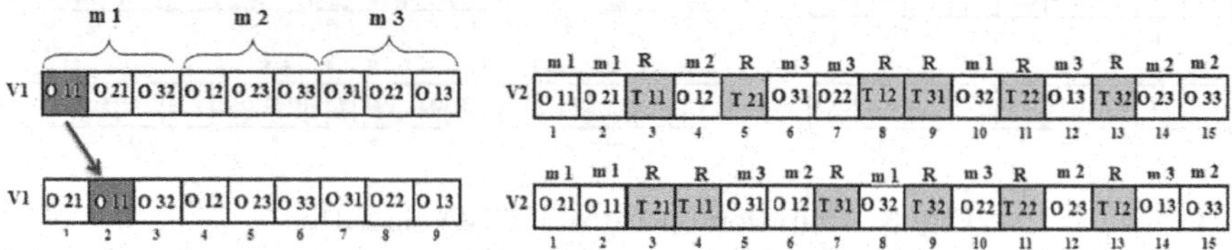

Fig. 4. Mutation Operator of BBO

As mentioned earlier, the local search mutation mechanism is performed by replacing a selected SIV of a habitat with other generated SIV. In our example the mutation process consists in:

(1) SIV O_{11} is chosen to mutate.
(2) Assume that the new SIV which is randomly generated is O_{21}. SIV O_{11} is replaced with O_{21}.
(3) SIV O_{21} takes the place of O_{11}.
(4) The resulting mutated habitat is produced.

7 Experimental Results

We study for the first time the Job shop Scheduling problem with Time Lags and Single Transport Robot and we propose a new data set of benchmarks. The studied problem is composed of two sub-problems; the Job shop Scheduling Problem with Time Lags constraints and the Job shop Scheduling Problem with Single Transport Robot. For this reason, the new benchmark data set is based on benchmark from the literature of these two sub-problems. In fact, we combine benchmark data set of Carlier [3] for Job shop Scheduling Problem with Generic Time Lags and data set of Hurink and Knust [20] for Job shop Scheduling Problem with Single Transport Robot. For instances of Carlier, we add the full and empty moving transportation time of single robot between machines from Hurink and Knust data set [20]. In Table 2, we give results of Hybrid Biogeography-Based Optimization algorithm used for solving Carlier's instances of Job shop Scheduling Problem with Time Lags and Single transport Robot. We give for each instances the name, size, results of CPLEX linear programming model, results of classic Biogeography-Based Optimization algorithm and results of Hybrid Biogeography-Based Optimization.

Each instance is executed 20 times then, we return the average. The experimental parameters used are:

- Number of iterations: 200
- Population size: 75
- Immigration rate: 0.7
- Emigration rate: 0.3
- Mutation rate: 0.5

Table 2. Makespan results for Carlier instances

Instances	Size	CPLEX	BBO	HBBO
car6-D5-d1	8 × 6	9551	10886	10629
car6-D5-t1	8 × 6	9573	10861	10653
car6-D5-t2	8 × 6	9689	10914	10648
car6-T1-d1	8 × 6	9664	10921	10684
car6-T1-t1	8 × 6	9550	10944	10870
car6-T1-t2	8 × 6	9712	10873	10672
car6-T5-d1	8 × 6	9596	10852	10623
car6-T5-t1	8 × 6	9587	10981	10668
car7-D5-d1	7 × 7	8964	11065	10814
car7-D5-t1	7 × 7	8982	10974	10892
car7-D5-t2	7 × 7	8965	10982	10904
car7-T1-d1	7 × 7	8943	11027	10987
car7-T1-t1	7 × 7	9054	11083	10946
car7-T1-t2	7 × 7	8972	10985	10932
car7-T5-d1	7 × 7	8995	10961	10917
car7-T5-t1	7 × 7	9027	10976	10951
car8-D5-d1	8 × 8	11427	12584	12326
car8-D5-t1	8 × 8	11490	12646	12406
car8-D5-t2	8 × 8	11429	12681	12574
car8-T1-d1	8 × 8	11545	12643	12360
car8-T1-t1	8 × 8	11596	12517	12433
car8-T1-t2	8 × 8	11613	12627	12569
car8-T5-d1	8 × 8	11564	12536	12428
car8-T5-t1	8 × 8	11572	12587	12406

Analysis of Results

In order to prove the efficiency of the proposed Hybrid Biogeography-Based Optimization, it was evaluated by using 24 instances of problem generated from Carlier [3] benchmark instances for Job shop Scheduling Problem with Generic Time

Lags combined with Hurink and Knust [20] benchmark for Job shop Scheduling Problem with Single Transport Robot. These problem instances are commonly utilized for benchmarking the Job shop Scheduling Problem with Time Lags and Single Transport Robot with the objective of minimizing makespan.

Results show that the Hybrid Biogeography-Based Optimization gives solutions near of the optimal solutions founded using CPLEX for most of the instances. Moreover, it's clear that the Hybrid BBO was improved using greedy heuristic and local search algorithm and was able to enhance the BBO results for all tested instances of the problem.

8 Conclusion

During the last decades, different new types of algorithms have been developed for solving optimization problems. Biogeography-Based Optimization is a new simulated bio-inspired intelligent algorithm which has some features that are unique to other biology-based optimization methods. We propose an Hybrid Biogeography-Based Optimization algorithm combined with greedy heuristic and local search procedure for solving the Job shop Scheduling Problem with Time Lags and Single Transport Robot, which is an NP-hard problem and the obtaining of a feasible solution is a difficult problem. According to an analysis and comparisons of the test results of HBBO through different instances of Job shop Scheduling Problem with Time Lags and Single Transport Robot, this algorithm can better solve most of instances. Due to good results of the proposed HBBO algorithm, it can be used to solve other extensions of our problem. We can develop the hybridization of BBO with other algorithms such as ACO, PSO or GA in order to solve the same problem.

References

1. Afsar, H.M., Lacomme, P., Ren,L., Prodhon, C., Vigo, D.: Resolution of a job-shop problem with transportation constraints: a master/slave approach. In: IFAC Conference on Manufacturing Modelling, Management and Control (2016)
2. Artigues, C., Huguet, M., Lopez, P.: Generalized disjunctive constraint propagation for solving the job shop problem with time lags. Eng. Appl. Artif. Intell. **24**, 220–231 (2011)
3. Carlier, J.: Ordonnancements a contraintes disjunctives. RAIRO Recherche operationelle/Operations Research **12**, 333–351 (1978)
4. Caumond, A., Lacomme, P., Tchernev, N.: Proposition d'un algorithme génétique pour le job-shop avec time-lags. ROADEF **5**, 183–200 (2005)
5. Caumond, A., Gourgand, M., Lacomme, P., Tchernev, N.: Métaheuristiques pour le pro-blème de job shop avec time lags: Jm—li, s j(i)—Cmax. In: 5ème conférence Francophone de Modélisation et SIMulation (MOSIM'04). Modélisation et simulation pour l'analyse et l'optimisation des systèmes industriels et logistiques, Nantes, France, pp. 939–946 (2004)

6. Caumond, A., Lacomme, P., Tchernev, N.: Feasible schedule generation with extension of the Giffler and Thompson's heuristic for the job shop problem with time lags. In: International conference of Industrial Engineering and Systems Management, pp. 489–499 (2005)
7. Caumond, A., Lacomme, P., Tchernev, N.: A memetic algorithm for the job-shop with time-lags. Comput. Oper. Res. **35**, 2331–2356 (2008)
8. Caumond, A., Lacomme, P., Moukrim, A., Tchernev, N.: An MILP for scheduling problems in an FMS with one vehicle. Eur. J. Oper. Res. **199**(3), 706–722 (2009)
9. Deppner, F.: Ordonnancement d'atelier avec contraintes temporelles entre opérations. Ph.D. thesis, Institut National Polytechnique de Lorraine (2004)
10. González, M.A., Oddi, A., Rasconi, R., Varela, R.: Scatter search with path relinking for the job shop with time lags and set up times. Comput. Oper. Res. **60**, 37–54 (2015)
11. Rahmati, S.H.A., Zandieh, M.: A new biogeography-based optimization (BBO) algorithm for the flexible job shop scheduling problem. Int. J. Adv. Manufact. Technol. **58**, 1115–1129 (2012). https://doi.org/10.1007/s00170-011-3437-9
12. Harrabi, M., Olfa, B.D.: MATS–JSTL: a multi-agent model based on Tabu search for job shop problem with time lags. In: Núñez, M., Nguyen, N.T., Camacho, D., Trawiński, B. (eds.) ICCCI 2015. LNCS (LNAI), vol. 9329, pp. 39–46. Springer, Cham (2015). https://doi.org/10.1007/978-3-319-24069-5_4
13. Harrabi, M., Belkahla Driss, O., Ghedira, K.: Competitive agents implementing parallel Tabu searches for job shop scheduling problem with time lags. In: IASTED International conference on Modelling, Identification and Control, 848–052 MIC (2017)
14. Harrabi, M., Belkahla Driss, O., Ghedira, K.: Combining genetic algorithm and Tabu search for job shop scheduling problem with time lags. In: IEEE International Conference on Engineering, MIS (2017)
15. Harrabi, M., Belkahla Driss, O., Ghedira, K.: A multi-agent model based on hybrid genetic algorithm for job shop scheduling problem with generic time lags. In: ACS/IEEE International Conference on Computer Systems and Applications, AICCSA (2017)
16. Harrabi, M., Driss, O.B., Ghedira, K.: A greedy biogeography-based optimization algorithm for job shop scheduling problem with time lags. In: Graña, M., et al. (eds.) SOCO'18-CISIS'18-ICEUTE'18 2018. AISC, vol. 771, pp. 489–499. Springer, Cham (2019). https://doi.org/10.1007/978-3-319-94120-2_47
17. Harrabi, M., Belkahla Driss, O., Ghedira, K.: A modified biogeography-based optimization algorithm with improved mutation operator for job shop scheduling problem with time lags. Logic J. IGPL, jzaa037 (2020). https://doi.org/10.1093/jigpal/jzaa037
18. Harrabi, M., Belkahla Driss, O., Ghedira, K.: A hybrid biogeography-based optimization for job shop scheduling problem with generic time lags. J. Sched. (2021, in press). https://doi.org/10.1007/s10951-021-00683-w
19. Hurink, J., Knust, S.: A Tabu search algorithm for scheduling a single robot in a job-shop environment. Discrete Appl. Math. **119**(12), 181203 (2002)
20. Hurink, J., Knust, S.: Tabu search algorithms for job-shop problems with a single transport robot. Eur. J. Oper. Res. **162**(1), 99111 (2005)
21. Karoui, W., Huguet, M.-J., Lopez, P., Haouari, M.: Méthode de recherche à divergence limitée pour les problèmes d'ordonnancement avec contraintes de délais. In: ENIM IFAC Conférence Internationale de Modélisation et Simulation (2010)

22. Lacomme, P., Moukrim, A., Tchernev, N.: Simultaneous job input sequencing and vehicle dispatching in a single-vehicle automated guided vehicle system: a heuristic branch-and-bound approach coupled with a discrete events simulation model. Int. J. Prod. Res. **43**(9), 1911–1942 (2005)
23. Lacomme, P., Huguet, M.J., Tchernev, N.: Dedicated constraint propagation for Job-Shop problem with generic time-lags. In: 16th IEEE Conference on Emerging Technologies and Factory Automation, Toulouse, France (2011). IEEE catalog number: CFP11ETF-USB
24. Lacomme, P., Tchernev, N.: Job-shop with generic time lags: a heuristic based approach. In: 9th International Conference of Modeling, Optimization and Simulation - MOSIM (2012)
25. Lin, J.: A hybrid discrete biogeography-based optimization for the permutation flow shop scheduling problem. Int. J. Prod. Res. **54**(16), 1–10 (2016)
26. MacArthur, R., Wilson, E.: The Theory of Biogeography. Princeton University Press, Princeton (1967)
27. Rabiee, M., Jolai, F., Asefi, H., Fattahi, P.: A biogeography-based optimization algorithm for a realistic no-wait hybrid flow shop with unrelated parallel machines to minimize mean tardiness. Int. J. Comput. Integr. Manufact. **29**, 1007–1024 (2016)
28. Roy, B., Sussmann, B.: Les problèmes d'ordonnancement avec contraintes disjonctives. Technical report, SEMA (1964)
29. Simon, D.: Biogeography-based optimization. IEEE Trans. Evol. Comput. **12**, 702–713 (2008)
30. Wang, X., Duan, H.: A hybrid biogeography-based optimization algorithm for job shop scheduling problem. Comput. Ind. Eng. **73**, 96–114 (2014)
31. Yang, Y.: A modified biogeography-based optimization for the flexible job shop scheduling problem. Math. Prob. Eng. **2015**, 1–10 (2015)
32. Helman, P.: A theory of greedy structures based on K-ary dominance relations. Technical Report CS89-11, University of New Mexico, Department of Computer Science (1989)

Computer Vision Techniques

Deep Component Based Age Invariant Face Recognition in an Unconstrained Environment

Amad Asif, Muhammad Atif Tahir(✉), and Mohsin Ali(✉)

FAST School of Computing, National University of Computer and Emerging Sciences, Karachi Campus, Islamabad, Pakistan
{k173064,atif.tahir,mohsin.ali}@nu.edu.pk

Abstract. Age Invariant face recognition is one of the challenging problems in pattern recognition. Most existing face recognition algorithms perform well under controlled conditions where the data set is collected with careful cooperation with the individuals. However, in most real-world applications, the user usually has little or no control over environmental conditions. This paper proposes efficient deep component-based age-invariant face recognition algorithm in an unconstrained environment. The algorithm detects face from an image, align the face and extract the facial components (eye, mouth and nose). Each facial component is then trained using deep neural network. Thus, deep features are extracted from each component. Support vector machine is then used in classification stage. Experiments are conducted on two challenging benchmarks: AgeDb30 and Pins-Face. Results have shown significant improvement when compared with the state of the art baseline approach.

Keywords: Age invariant face recognition · CNN · SVM · RestNet-50

1 Introduction

The objective of an automatic face recognition system is to categorize the individuals using the full face present. Various factors such as face pose, illumination and ageing [5,18] effect the overall performance of the face recognition system. Use of Component-Based Face Recognition (CBFR) [9] techniques can significantly help overcome some of these challenges. Component-based face recognition focuses on certain sub facial regions such as nose, eyes, mouth or ears [1]. Component-based face recognition's basic idea is to compensate for the changes that occur due to the change in pose and age by preserving the individual facial component's shape and size. Change in illumination that alters the facial features only affects parts of the face [20], therefore component-based face recognition helps to maintain and even improve the overall accuracy. Face components such as nose, eyes, ears and lips are usually unaffected by age, makeup, pose, expression and facial hair [3,10,14]. This

K. Wojtkiewicz et al. (Eds.): ICCCI 2021, CCIS 1463, pp. 101–113, 2021.
https://doi.org/10.1007/978-3-030-88113-9_8

is part of the reason why classifiers designed to recognise specific components of the face perform better than classifiers designed to recognise the full face [1]. There are several challenges to face recognition which include illumination, pose, expression, ageing as well as low resolution images. A variation in illumination has a prominent effect on the appearance of the facial features. The facial features change drastically under different lighting conditions and the performance declines for unfamiliar lighting conditions. Facial recognition systems are highly sensitive to change in facial pose, a change in pose affects the features that are extracted from the detected face and the overall accuracy of the model. Facial expressions are generated as a result of the contract and expansion of facial muscles. This deforms the pivotal features of the face such as nose, eyes, lips and skin texture. As the individual ages, the facial features and textures change drastically over time and the features computed for the training model may no longer be similar to existing features.

In this paper, we propose a method for age-invariant face recognition using Component-based Convolution Neural Network (CNN) [2]. Deep features are extracted using Deep Neural Network from each component. Features from each component are combined and Support Vector Machine is then used during classification. We focus on three important components of the face, the eyes pair, nose and the lips, that individuals are considered to form an association and recognition. Experiments are conducted on two challenging benchmarks: AgeDb30 (mainly age invariant face recognition dataset) and Pins-Face (Uncontrolled environment data set). Results have indicated significant increase in performance when compared with baseline approach.

This paper is organized as follows. Section 2 reviews the existing approaches followed by proposed methodology in Sect. 3. Experiments and results are presented in Sect. 4. Section 5 concludes the paper.

2 Literature Review

In this section, we will review some state of the art papers in Face recognition based on deep learning. Convolution Neural Networks (CNN) is the most common type of deep learning architecture currently being used in Face Recognition. The facial features obtained are robust to intra-class variations such as facial expressions, pose, age and illuminating changes. One drawback of using this technique is that a huge volume of data is needed for training, which may not always be available. Fortunately, there are several publicly available data sets [7,19] for training and validation purposes. There are several approaches to solving the face recognition problem with deep learning, one approach assumes it as a problem of classification, and here each individual represents a separate class in the classification problem. After completing the training phase, the classification layer is discarded and using the features obtained from the previous layer identify if the individual is part of the training set or unknown identity. The CNN model can be fine-tuned using a loss function [22].

Zhou et al. studied the effect the number of training images per class has on the accuracy of the model; the best accuracy was obtained when adding 10,000 images per class. Another approach to face recognition is by using different components of the face for recognition purpose [21]. The authors in proposed an approach of using each component of the face in association with transfer learning and showed that the information obtained from full-face classification can be transferred to the classification of different facial components. For association and recognition, three important facial components the ears, eyes and nose are used. Even though each component and the face belong to a separate domain, common knowledge is shared between them and that in turn is used to transfer the information obtained from one part to another [4].

The authors of VarGNet proposed a novel network design mechanism for efficient embedded computing. Their design proposes to fix the number of channels in a group convolution, instead of the existing practice of fixing the total group numbers. It is a lightweight network that is friendly to the embedded hardware. The input to the network is the entire face components, cropped and aligned. This is a generic network that is also used in object classification [11].

Authors presented a system ArcFace that uses a deep convolution network to create a mapping of the facial image after normalising the pose into feature vector embedding. These embedding are such that the same person features have a small distance while images of two different individuals have a significant distance between them. The novel supervisor signal,(ArcFace) that is additive angular margin, that understands a better interpretation geometrically than the existing supervision signals. Due to these features obtained through arc face are significantly more discriminating [8].

In Hassan et al., invariant feature extraction method for Component-based Facial Recognition is proposed. The model consists of two steps: pre-processing and feature extraction. Pre-processing stage consists of detecting facial landmarks and aligning the facial components around the extracted landmarks, then cropping these facial components. Features are extracted using HOG and LBP.

3 Proposed Methodology

In this section, we will discuss our proposed method. The proposed algorithm is inspired with HOG-LBP component based architecture recently proposed by [8]. Our main novelty is the investigation of RestNet-50 based features instead of HOG-LBP based features. We will first briefly explain architecture proposed in followed by the proposed methodology.

3.1 HOG-LBP Based Feature Extraction

Figure 1 shows the traditional component based face recognition model. Individual components of the face are extracted using facial landmark points. The Local Binary Pattern (LBP) and the Histogram of Gradient (HOG) features are extracted from the each of the segmented facial components, this step is followed by random subspace principal component analysis and cosine distance.

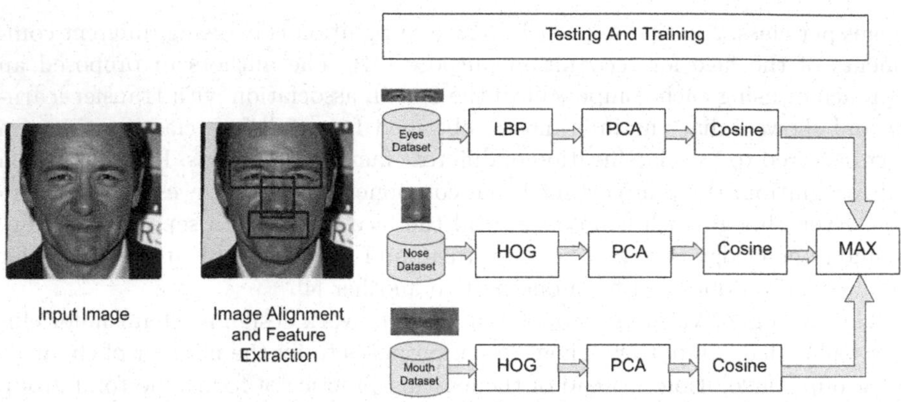

Fig. 1. Model for traditional component based face recognition

Facial alignment is one of the pre-processing steps implemented that uses the inclination angle of the face. This method consists of two main stages, first involves applying pre-processing on the image and then extract features from these images. The input size of each image is 250 × 250 resolution, The first step of pre-processing is to detect the 66 facial landmarks, thus accurately extract the individual components of the face. Clockwise and anticlockwise rotations are applied to accurately align the face before segmenting out specific components of the face.

The next step is matching the facial components where we use cosine distance for Principal Component Analysis features that are trained on two dissimilar separated descriptors. [6] proposed method of extracting the features of each component individually and then combine those, however authors rely on voting each descriptor features per component as a result of pre-experiments. This incurs lower complexity in terms of processing time and also results in overall increase in performance. The HOG and LBP features are extracted for each component of face and we utilize a path of 8 × 8 without overlapping. The features extracted using the histogram of gradients and local binary patterns are then concatenated together and forming two individual feature vectors for each component of the face. The dimension of features extracted from LBP are four times the length of features extracted from HOG; therefore, for every four LBP neighboring feature, the mean value is used to sample a point.

For component matching, one image is taking for each pair and compare it with the 40 impostor images (here each image of individual is 1 year older than the testing image). If between the genuine pairs the cosine distance is less than all of the 40 measures the output decision is set to one, otherwise the decision is set to 0.

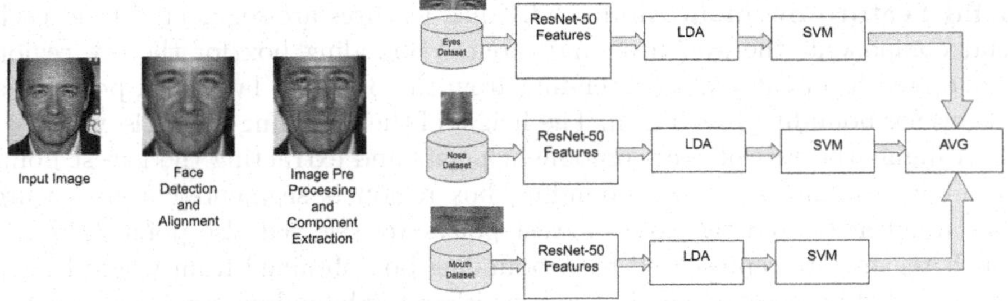

Fig. 2. Framework for component based face recognition

3.2 Proposed Deep Component Based Age-Invariant Face Recognition Using ResNet-50

The block diagram for the proposed framework for component based face recognition under transfer learning for age invariant face registration is shown in Fig. 2. Once the face detector segments out the face from the facial image in the wild, segmented images can have different sizes. We first resize the original image to 255 × 255× 3 and then feed this image to the convolution neural network to extract the features. The extracted features from the neural network are fed to the combined Fisher's Linear Discriminant Analysis and regularization block for dimensional reduction and diminish probability distribution between the multiple classes. For the classification of extracted features, Support Vector Machines (SVM) classifier is used during classification stage [5]. Different components of the proposed architecture are explained below.

Landmark Extraction. The input size of each image is 250 × 250 resolution, The first step of pre-processing is to detect the 66 facial landmarks, the two outer landmarks of eye components are used to align the face horizontally with the appropriate angle of rotation. This allows us to accurately extract the individual components of the face.

Face Alignment. Face recognition under a variation of poses refers to recognizing face images of different poses. Face recognition systems have historically struggled with accurately recognising and matching faces under different poses of the same individual. Proposed method using the features of the face to detect the eyes regions, instead however for horizontal alignment of face, the detected landmark points of left and right outer corners of the 2 eyes are used. Clockwise and anticlockwise rotations are applied if the facial image is not horizontally aligned, the rotation is based on the angle calculated. Once the inclination angle of an image is correctly calculated then image alignment takes place [16].

Facial Feature Segmentation. Individual features are segmented from each facial component, the eye, nose and mouth. Bounding box for the eye region is extracted from the region extending from the 37 to 43 landmark point as a rectangular bounding box region. The height of the bounding region is extracted by arranging the pair of eyes component points and extracting the lowest point and highest point. The nose bounding box region is segmented from feature point number 29, and the nose's lowest points are selected also point 32 to 36. Mouth regions are represented by a bounding box obtained from where length is represented by points 49 and 55 and width of the bounding box is represented by the highest and lowest points of the mouth.

Histogram Equalisation. In image processing histogram equalisation is one of the most common technique for image pre-processing [17]. The idea here is to obtain an enhanced image by stretching and redistributing the original histograms making use of the entire range of discrete levels of the image. Histogram equalization is the most frequently used histogram normalization technique where we change the histogram image to a histogram that is constant for all bright values. Histogram equalisation cannot however improve all the parts of the face especially if the illuminations on the face are irregularly spawned. This can cause some details on individual's face to over brighten. Histogram equalisation is applied selectively on images where quality of image can be improved by use of histogram equalisation.

ResNet-50. We use ResNet-50 [12] for extracting features from images. ResNets, belong to deep neural network family having the same structure but with different depths. Using the residual unit the resnet avoids degradation as network's depth increases. It is a well known architecture to extract deep features from images. The structure of residual learning unit in ResNet is a feed forward network which is capable of adding new inputs in the network and thus generating new outputs through a shortcut connection. The main advantage of ResNet is it produces better results with higher accuracy with out increasing complexity. Figure 3 shows the basic architecture of ResNet-50.

We have made use of transfer learning via feature extraction, when performing feature extraction, we treat the pre-trained network as an arbitrary feature extractor, allowing the input image to propagate forward, stopping at pre-specified layer, and taking the outputs of that layer as our features.

CNN Based Face Component Feature Extraction. In deep learning the Convolution Neural Networks (CNN) belong to a class of networks most often applied to visual image analysis. The neural network's feed forward phase serves to visualize data in the image working in the same way as the human visual cortex. Convolution Neural Networks are categorized as semi-supervised to unsupervised technique for feature extraction. The features extracted are without any prior information about the input. The main composition of CNN is an

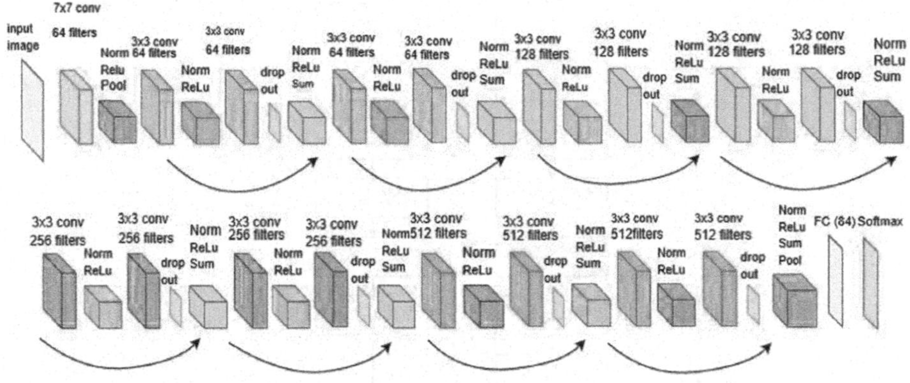

Fig. 3. Residual Net architecture

input layer, a number of convolution layers, a pooling layer and finally the fully connected layer.

Transfer learning allows us to utilize an existing pre-trained classifier as a starting point for a new classification. We will make use of transfer learning via feature extraction. When performing feature extraction, we treat the pre-trained network as an arbitrary feature extractor. We first fine tune the network's weights by training it on MS-Celeb-1M [7] data set, allowing more specific facial features to be extracted. The input image is then allowed to propagate forward, stopping at pre specified layer, and taking the outputs of that layer as our features. We remove the soft max layer from the network and utilize the activation at this layer. Using ResNet, our output layer has a volume size of $7 \times 7 \times 2048$. Treating the output as a feature vector, we simply flatten it into a list of $7 \times 7 \times 2048 = 100{,}352$ dimensional vector. The output features from CNN are highly discriminating but also very high dimensional, meaning training classifier directly on features will be very expensive in computation and memory. Fisher's Linear Discriminant Analysis (FLDA) allows to obtain dimension reduction at the same time conserving the maximum inter class discriminating information. At this time the CNN has extracted features for us and they have been dimensional reduced, CNN's are non-linear models capable of learning non-linear features that are already robust and discriminate, but also very large and high dimensional. We, therefore, need a fast model that can be trained on top of the features, linear models tend to be very fast to train. We use the SVM classifier that works well with unstructured data and is less prone to over fitting.

4 Experiments and Results

Our algorithm is compared with the state of the art Component based HOG-LBP feature extraction technique [8]. Experiments are conducted on individual components of the face as well as when all components of the face are combined.

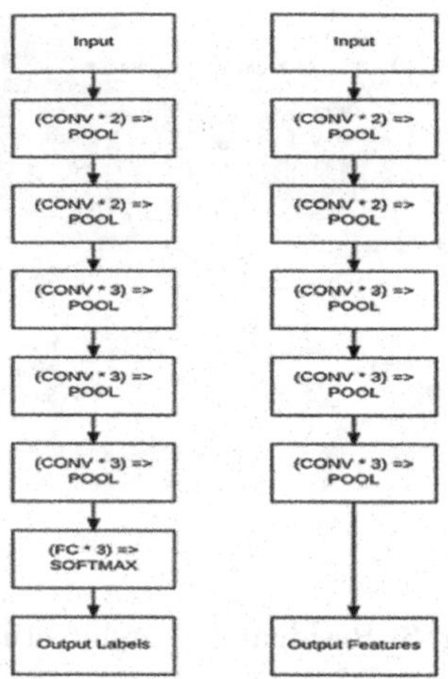

Fig. 4. Using convolution neural network as a classifier vs feature extractor

4.1 Evaluation Criteria

In order to access the performance of the algorithm and the various experiments that are performed the evaluation metric used is the accuracy. Accuracy is a good evaluation metric when the importance of each class is equally important and we want to focus on the true positives and true negatives.

4.2 Datasets

Experiments are conducted on the following data sets.

AgeDb-30 Data Set. For the experiment of component-based age invariant face recognition the AgeDB-30 [13] data set is used. All the images in the data set are collected from images in the wild over the internet. The data set contains a total of 16,488 images of 568 individuals with noise-free labels of identity and age, accurate to a year. At the time of the paper to the best of the author's knowledge, there does not exist a publicly available data set that has individually segmented out facial components the eyes, nose, mouth and half faces [(right, left) half and (left, right)diagonal]. Therefore each of these individual data sets is prepared using images from the AgeDb-30 data set using a set of tools and scripts. From this, a subset of 3 data sets (eyes, nose and mouth) were prepared. For experiments, the first n age groups are used in training while the individual's oldest $(t - n)$ images are used for testing. Here t represents the total number of images for one class.

Pins Face Data Set. The data set contains images that have been accumulated from Pinterest and faces cropped. The data set consists of images of 105

celebrities and there are a total of 17534 images. The images are taken in an unconstrained environment where the individual has no control over the parameters such as pose, lighting, illumination, angle, occlusion and background. From the full face data set the individual data sets are prepared to segment out specific components of the face nose, eye and mouth using a set of tools and scripts. These factors make the data set the perfect candidate for validating the performance of the algorithm in an unconstrained environment. The data set also contains images of individuals with a range of age spectrum, the images are not accurately labelled with age so this data set will not be used for age invariant validation of the method. The training and testing images are randomly sampled for each class. To avoid bias in the data set each experiment is repeated 5 times where data set for training and testing are randomly generated each time for experiments. The results reported in the next section are the average of results obtained from the 5 experiments.

4.3 Experiments on Individual Components of the Face

Table 1. Recognition comparison between baseline and proposed method on PinsFace dataset. Here, 90% data points are used for training while 10% used for testing.

Face components	Proposed method (%)	Baseline method (%)
Eyes	92.60	75.36
Nose	85.60	69.16
Mouth	92.90	74.13
Eyes + Nose + Mouth	94.90	78.76

PinsFace Dataset. Eyes are regarded as essential part of face recognition, humans are able to often identify an individual with high confidence simply by looking at the eyes. This data set however contains several individuals with spectacles or sun glasses on. Spectacles distort the eye side of the face and the spectacles frame also obscures part of the eyes. Sun glasses on the other hand completely obscures the eyes making it nearly impossible to recognise the individual using the eyes. Images such as these were excluded from the experiments. Makeup around the eyes and eyebrows especially for the female subjects also deform the features around the eyes making the task more challenging, such images are not excluded from the experiments. The lips and the region around them is an essential region when it comes to identifying the individual. Images in this data set do pose a challenge to recognition where the lips region is covered with heavy makeup. The makeup alters the structure and texture of the region and provides a challenge as features learned in training phase can be different to the testing set with a different makeup applied. Experiments showed that the mouth component indeed plays in important role in face recognition, the highest of 92.9% accuracy is obtained any there is a very gradual decrease in accuracy as the number of images used for recognition decreases. Nose present another important component of the face. While the nose itself is not as discriminating as the eye and mouth component it's importance should still not be undermined. Nose component acts as the center of face and features are evenly spread around this component. The nose features unlike the eyes and mouth components do not carry the most robust features of the face and are affected with significant change in pose, especially with tilt greater than 15° in left or right direction.

Table 2. Recognition comparison between baseline and proposed method on AgeDb-30 dataset. Here, 90% data points are used for training while 10% used for testing.

Face components	Proposed method accuracy (%)	Baseline method accuracy (%)
Eyes	91.60	71.36
Nose	85.10	64.36
Mouth	91.10	72.36
Eyes + Nose + Mouth	93.70	74.86

AgeDb-30 Dataset. The eye component of the face is regarded as a passive component, meaning it is not one that degrades significantly as the human ages. Eyes also capture the emotional expressions and non verbal signs. Radji et al., in their experiments showed that eyebrows combined with the eyes serve as an important for recognition and the absence of eyebrows from the image can significantly deteriorate the performance of the system [16]. Features extracted using deep learning technique are more robust to changes in lighting compared to features extracted using HOG and LBP. Nose is another important component for face recognition, nose acts as the center of information where information is balanced in all directions. Paul et al. showed that mouth is another passive identifier of the face that is not greatly degraded with ageing and captures the emotion on the face [15].

4.4 Experiments on Full Face

Experiments are conducted by combining features extracted from all three components of the face, the eye, nose and mouth. **PinsFace dataset** Results indicate that the highest classification accuracy is achieved when features extracted from all three components of the face are combined before classifying the individuals using SVM classifier. The data set contained a number of individuals with eyes occluded by glasses or features around the eye masked by makeup around the eyes. By combining the features of the three components together we were able to obtain a greater recognition accuracy when compared to individual components. When combining multiple facial components we were able to obtain maximum of 94.9%. Table 1 summarises results for recognition rates between the baseline and the proposed method for individual components of the face as well as the combined components of the face. Figure 5 shows the effect of varying the training size. Here, fraction of dataset used for training and testing was varied from 90% training to 50% of data set used for training. Results of experiments are summarised in 5.

There is slight decrease in performance when the number of training points are reduced to 50% of the whole data. **AgeDb-30 dataset** Experiments for full face recognition were repeated on the AgeDb-30 dataset. When all components of the face were combined the maximum accuracy of 93.7%. Experiments were also conducted to study the effect of size of dataset used for training and results are shown in Fig. 6.

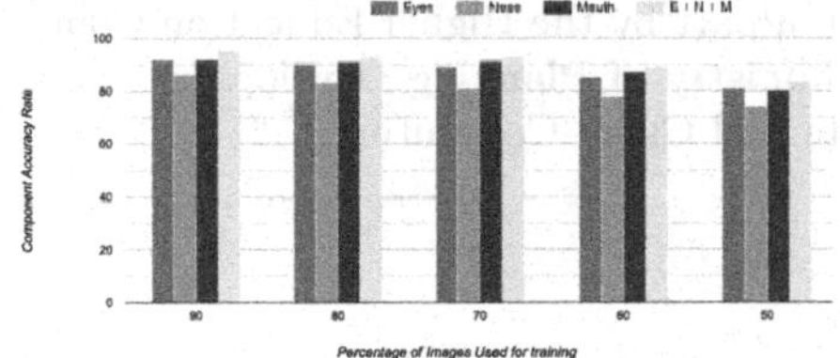

Fig. 5. Effect of holdout approach using ResNet-50 on Pins Data Set

Fig. 6. Using ResNet-50 on AgeDb-30 Data Set

Table 3. Results summary table for PinsDb data set.

Face component	Total images	Total individuals	True prediction	False prediction	Accuracy (%)
Eye component	16972	105	15716	1256	92.6
Nose component	17320	105	14879	2503	85.6
Mouth component	17382	105	16090	1140	92.9
Eyes + Nose + Mouth	17410	105	16524	886	94.9

Table 4. Results summary table for AgeDb-30 data set.

Face component	Total images	Total individuals	True prediction	False prediction	Accuracy (%)
Eye component	16393	588	15016	1377	91.6
Nose component	16420	588	13973	2447	85.1
Mouth component	16390	588	14931	1459	91.1
Eyes + Nose + Mouth	16432	588	15396	1036	93.7

5 Conclusion

In this paper, we proposed a method of deep component based face recognition. ResNet-50 is employed to extract the discriminating features of the faces and the support vector machine classifier (SVM) is used to classify the extracted features. After tuning the model, we performed experiments on AgeDB and Pins Face data sets. We found that the proposed method performs well when singular components of the face are used to recognise the face and the highest accuracy is achieved when all components of the face are combined. Experiments were also conducted to study the effect of varying the number of images used for training. We concluded that features extracted using deep learning techniques are more discriminating and superior to features extracted using classical machine learning techniques.

Acknowledgment. This work was supported in part by the Higher Education Commission (HEC) Pakistan, and in part by the Ministry of Planning Development and Reforms under the National Center in Big Data and Cloud Computing.

References

1. Al-Ghamdi, B.A.S.: Recognition of human face by face recognition system using 3D. J. Inf. Commun. Technol. (JICT) **4**(2), 8 (2010)
2. Albawi, S., Mohammed, T.A., Al-Zawi, S.: Understanding of a convolutional neural network. In: 2017 International Conference on Engineering and Technology (ICET), pp. 1–6. IEEE (2017)
3. Choraś, M.: The lip as a biometric. Pattern Anal. Appl. **13**(1), 105–112 (2010). https://doi.org/10.1007/s10044-008-0144-8
4. Deng, J., Guo, J., Xue, N., Zafeiriou, S.: ArcFace: additive angular margin loss for deep face recognition. In: Proceedings of the IEEE/CVF Conference on Computer Vision and Pattern Recognition, pp. 4690–4699 (2019)
5. Du, S., Ward, R.K.: Adaptive region-based image enhancement method for robust face recognition under variable illumination conditions. IEEE Trans. Circ. Syst. Video Technol. **20**(9), 1165–1175 (2010)
6. Gold, J.M., et al.: The perception of a familiar face is no more than the sum of its parts. Psychon. Bull. Rev. **21**(6), 1465–1472 (2014). https://doi.org/10.3758/s13423-014-0632-3
7. Guo, Y., Zhang, L., Hu, Y., He, X., Gao, J.: MS-Celeb-1M: a dataset and benchmark for large-scale face recognition. In: Leibe, B., Matas, J., Sebe, N., Welling, M. (eds.) ECCV 2016. LNCS, vol. 9907, pp. 87–102. Springer, Cham (2016). https://doi.org/10.1007/978-3-319-46487-9_6
8. Hassan, A., Viriri, S.: Invariant feature extraction for component-based facial recognition. Int. J. Adv. Comput. Sci. Appl. (2020)
9. Heisele, B., Ho, P., Poggio, T.: Face recognition with support vector machines: global versus component-based approach. In: Proceedings Eighth IEEE International Conference on Computer Vision, ICCV 2001, vol. 2, pp. 688–694. IEEE (2001)
10. Heisele, B., Koshizen, T.: Components for face recognition. In: Sixth IEEE International Conference on Automatic Face and Gesture Recognition, 2004. Proceedings, pp. 153–158. IEEE (2004)

11. Kute, R.S., Vyas, V., Anuse, A.: Component-based face recognition under transfer learning for forensic applications. Inf. Sci. **476**, 176–191 (2019)
12. Mo, N., Yan, L., Zhu, R., Xie, H.: Class-specific anchor based and context-guided multi-class object detection in high resolution remote sensing imagery with a convolutional neural network. Remote Sens. **11**(3), 272 (2019)
13. Moschoglou, S., Papaioannou, A., Sagonas, C., Deng, J., Kotsia, I., Zafeiriou, S.: AgeDB: the first manually collected, in-the-wild age database. In: Proceedings of the IEEE Conference on Computer Vision and Pattern Recognition Workshops, pp. 51–59 (2017)
14. Nixon, M.S., Bouchrika, I., Arbab-Zavar, B., Carter, J.N.: On use of biometrics in forensics: gait and ear. In: 2010 18th European Signal Processing Conference, pp. 1655–1659. IEEE (2010)
15. Paul, S.K., Uddin, M.S., Bouakaz, S.: Face recognition using eyes, nostrils and mouth features. In: 16th International Conference on Computer and Information Technology, pp. 117–120. IEEE (2014)
16. Radji, N., Cherifi, D., Azrar, A.: Importance of eyes and eyebrows for face recognition system. In: 2015 3rd International Conference on Control, Engineering & Information Technology (CEIT), pp. 1–6. IEEE (2015)
17. Raj, S., Kumar, S., Raj, S.: An improved histogram equalization technique for image contrast enhancement, January 2015. ResearchGate
18. Sellahewa, H., Jassim, S.: Face recognition in the presence of expression and/or illumination variation. In: Fourth IEEE Workshop on Automatic Identification Advanced Technologies (AutoID 2005), pp. 144–148. IEEE (2005)
19. Sun, Y., Wang, X., Tang, X.: Deep learning face representation from predicting 10,000 classes. In: Proceedings of the IEEE Conference on Computer Vision and Pattern Recognition, pp. 1891–1898 (2014)
20. Wang, Y.Q.: An analysis of the viola-jones face detection algorithm. Image Process. On Line **4**, 128–148 (2014)
21. Zhang, Q., et al.: VarGNet: variable group convolutional neural network for efficient embedded computing. arXiv preprint arXiv:1907.05653 (2019)
22. Zhou, E., Cao, Z., Yin, Q.: Naive-deep face recognition: touching the limit of LFW benchmark or not? arXiv preprint arXiv:1501.04690 (2015)

Hybrid Vision Transformer for Domain Adaptable Person Re-identification

Muhammad Danish Waseem(✉), Muhammad Atif Tahir(✉), and Muhammad Nouman Durrani(✉)

National University of Computers and Emerging Sciences, Karachi, Pakistan
{k190887,atif.tahir,muhammad.nouman}@nu.edu.pk
http://nu.edu.pk/

Abstract. Person re-identification refers to finding person images taken from different cameras at different times. Supervised re-id methods rely on labeled dataset, which is usually not available in real word situations. Therefore, a procedure must be devised to adapt unseen domains in an unsupervised manner. In this work we have proposed a domain adaptation methodology by using hybrid Vision Transformers and incorporating Cluster loss along with the widely used Triplet loss. Our proposed methodology has shown to improve results of exiting unsupervised domain adaptation methods for person re-id.

Keywords: Person re-identification · Domain adaptation · Vision transformer

1 Introduction

Person re-identification (re-id) is the task of finding the same person in the images taken from different cameras or images taken from the same camera at different times. It has significant usage in video surveillance applications. Person re-id is a difficult task due to the varying poses and lightning conditions, low resolution of images taken from CCTV cameras, changing background, and occlusion. Hence, it is required to learn a robust representation of a person body.

Supervised Deep Learning methods [1] along with Attention mechanism [2] have shown to produce good results on re-id datasets. But supervised methods does not perform well in real world scenarios. This is due to the reason, that supervised methods rely on large labeled datasets, but in an open world situation, such large number of labels are not available. To increase the performance of a supervised model in an unseen domain, it should be able to adapt to the new domains without having large number of labels, with the help of an unsupervised domain adaptation method.

For computer vision tasks, Convolutional Neural Networks (CNNs) are a defacto standard. CNNs are able to learn strong representations from images, where initial layers learn low level features such as edges and deeper layers learn higher level feature such as persons clothing textures. But CNNs does not provide a

K. Wojtkiewicz et al. (Eds.): ICCCI 2021, CCIS 1463, pp. 114–122, 2021.
https://doi.org/10.1007/978-3-030-88113-9_9

mechanism to learn long range dependencies of pixels, as they use a small kernel window, which moves around the image one step at a time. Attention Mechanism was introduced for Natural Language processing (NLP) tasks, which provided a way to learn long range dependencies among words in a long text. Attention mechanisms were then adopted to be used along with CNNs [2] to learn local or global attention weights, which tells how much each pixel should attend to other pixel of the image. CNNs along with Attention mechanism have produced superior results in supervised person re-identification, but they are not explored widely in unsupervised person re-id. This has motivated us to explore Attention mechanism for unsupervised domain adaptation for person re-id.

Recently, Vision Transformers [3] which use attention schemes, have demonstrated results comparable to CNN architecture results on Imagenet, which is a benchmark dataset for image classification task. Vision Transformer uses the Transformer model [4], originally proposed for the NLP tasks, with minimal changes, and used it for the image classification task. CNNs have been benefited by a decade long research and they perform well on images because they have prior image related inductive biases such as translational equivariance. On the other hand, recently proposed Vision Transformers does not have such prior inductive biases, therefore, they require a huge amount of data to generalize well.

In this work we have used Vision Transformer encoder along with CNN to reduce the need for large amount of data. The training is divided in two phases. In the first phase we performed supervised pre-training of the hybrid Vision Transformer encoder on a source dataset. In the second phase, we used unsupervised domain adaptation approach [5] and trained our model on the target dataset for several iterations. In each iteration, the embedding for global (full body) and local (upper and lower body) were extracted from the Vision Transformer encoder. These embedding are then assigned pseudo-labels using DBSCAN [6] clustering. This generates a new dataset with cluster IDs as the person IDs. This dataset is then used to train the encoder again by incorporating Triplet loss [7] and Cluster loss [8]. Using Vision Transformer generated features resulted increase in mean average precision (mAP) and cumulative matching characteristics (CMC) scores. Lastly, we used K-reciprocal re-ranking [9] to further improve mAP and CMC scores.

This work is organized as follows. Section 2 reviews state of the art papers followed by proposed methodology in Sect. 3. Experiments and results are conducted in Sect. 4. Section 5 concludes this paper.

2 Related Work

Robust feature representation learning is important for person re-id. Person re-id works can be categorized into global and local features representation learning. Global features are extracted from the full image of a person. [10] is a widely adapted work, which pose re-id task as a multi class classification problem, where each person ID represents a class. Images generated through GANs are also used to improve representation learning. [11] proposed to train jointly the generative module along with the re-id discriminative module. Local representation learning is performed by splitting the person images horizontally or by body part based splitting. Part-based Convolutional Baseline (PCB) [12] learns one classifier for each horizontal split of the image. [5] combined both global and local feature for more robust representation learning.

Attention mechanisms are studied extensively for person re-identification [1]. Attention is used to provide mechanism to the model to focus more on the foreground. Pixel level attention was used in [13] to learn robust feature representation from misaligned images. [14] used Attention for suppressing the background by using mask guided attention.

Several methods [1] has been proposed for unsupervised domain adaptation (UDA) for person re-id. Usually for UDA, first the model is trained on a source dataset in a supervised manner. Latter, the model is trained on a target dataset without the labels. Self-Similarity-Grouping (SSG) [5] is a simple yet effective approach for UDA. SSG divided the person image horizontally into two parts. One global and two local embedding were then extracted from the CNN based encoder. These embedding were separately clustered and assigned a cluster id. Triplet loss was used to train the model with the generated pseudo labels.

Vision Transformer (ViT) [3] is a new class of architectures for computer vision. ViT divides the input image into small patches of equal size. These patches are then flattened and assigned a positional embedding, which are then passed to the transformer layers, where attention weights are calculated. A Transformer consists of several attention blocks along with batch norm layers and skip connections.

Person re-id share several aspects with face recognition task, therefore many face recognition techniques are also applied in person re-id. Triplet loss, proposed by FaceNet [7] is widely used in person re-id task. Triplet loss minimizes the distance between an anchor image and a positive image, and maximizes the distance between anchor and a negative sample.

3 Methodology

Our methodology consists of two phases. In first phase, we trained our model on source dataset and in the second phase we fine tune the model on target dataset. Figure 1 show the unsupervised domain adaptation approach using hybrid Vision Transformer.

3.1 Supervised Pre-training

We used Market1501 [15] as the source dataset. We used pre-trained Resnet50 [16] model, which was trained on [17], as the backbone for generating the patch embeddings. During all the iterations in all phases, all the layers of Resnet backbone were kept frozen. If we open layers of Resnet encoder, the model will become very deep and we do not have sufficient data to train such deep network, and the model will have the tendency to over-fit quickly. Our experiments showed

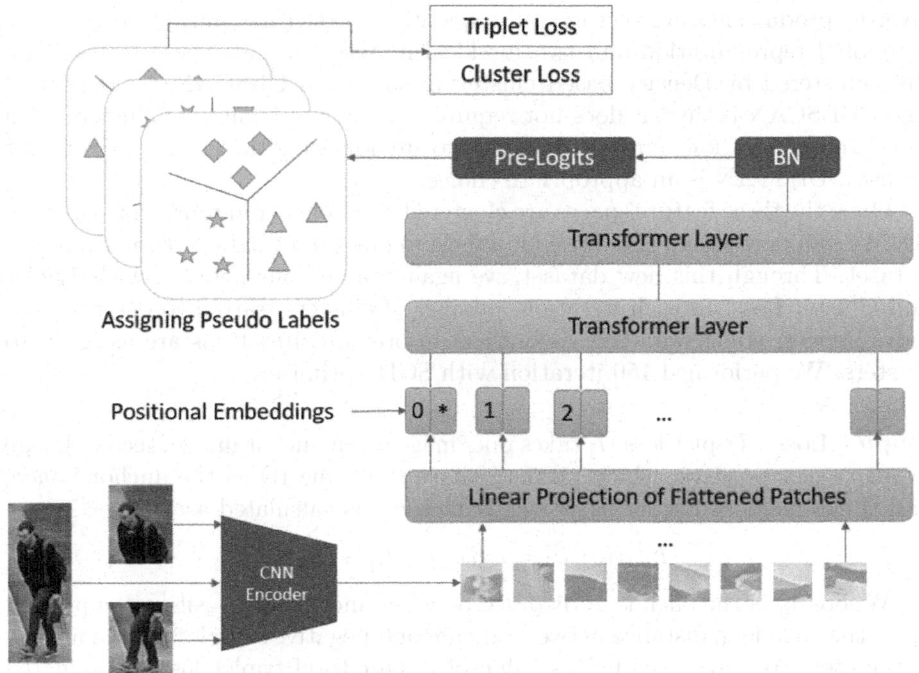

Fig. 1. Input image is divided into two parts. Full image and image parts are given to a CNN encoder to generate patch embeddings, which are then passed to ViT along with positional embeddings. Features generated by the final layers are clustered. Three clusters are formed by global, upper part, and lower part embeddings. Triplet loss and Cluster Loss is used to train the model on generated cluster ids.

that using a pre-trained backbone to generate patch embeddings produce better results than using the raw patches. We trained Hybrid ViT on Market1501 with Cross Entropy loss and Triplet loss for 70 epochs. We used Adam optimizer [18] and kept batch size of 32.

3.2 Unsupervised Adaptation

We used the domain adaptation approach proposed in [5]. We split images in two parts i.e. upper body and lower body for getting local features, and used full image to attain global feature representation. These three images were input to resnet50 to produce 16 by 16 patch embeddings. Patch embeddings are than flattened and concatenated with positional embeddings. Positional embeddings help transformer layers to know where a patch lies in relation to the other patches. Vision Transformer has 8 attention blocks. Before passing input to each attention block, layer normalization is done and all blocks are connected with a skip connection from the previous block. Finally, the output of the last attention block is passed to the batch normalization layer, whose output is passed to the linear layer to produce feature vectors. Subsequently, we get three output vectors, one for global representation and two for local representations. These features are then clustered by Density based clustering algorithm DBSCAN [6]. Benefit of using DBSCAN is that, it does not require to know the number of clusters. And since we do not know number of ids, as we are not using the labels of the target dataset, DBSCAN is an appropriate choice.

Once the three feature spaces are clustered, each cluster id represents a person ID. We can now assign these pseudo labels to our target dataset to make a new dataset. Through this new dataset, we again trained our network with Triplet and Cluster Loss. In each iteration, number of clusters started to decrease and more images, which were left as outliers in previous iterations are assigned to clusters. We performed 150 iteration with SGD optimizer.

Triplet Loss. Triplet loss [7] takes one image as an anchor image, second image as an anchor positive, which means it have the same ID as the anchor image, and third image as anchor negative. Triplet loss is calculated as:

$$L_{tri}(i, j, k) = max(\rho + d_{ij} - d_{ik}, 0) \tag{1}$$

Where $\mathrm{d_{ij}}$ is the euclidean distance between anchor and positive sample and $\mathrm{d_{ik}}$ is the euclidean distance between anchor and negative sample. ρ is the margin parameter. We have used 0.5 as value of ρ. Our total triplet loss is calculated by summing the triplet loss of global and local embeddings. Training with easy triplets can hurt the discriminative ability of the model. To alleviate this issue, we used hard batch triplet loss in which a sample in a batch with maximum distance to the anchor is selected as the negative sample.

Cluster Loss. We have used Cluster loss which was proposed in [8] to increase inter-cluster distances and decrease the intra-cluster distances. Cluster loss is calculated as:

$$Lb_c = \sum_{i}^{P} max((d_i^{intra} - d_i^{inter} + \alpha), 0) \tag{2}$$

Where $\mathrm{d^{intra}}$ is the distance between f(x) to the mean of the cluster. f(x) is the feature which is farthest to the cluster mean. And $\mathrm{d^{inter}}$ is calculated by taking the distance of a cluster mean with another cluster mean which is nearest to that cluster.

The total Loss is the aggregation of Triplet and Cluster loss.

3.3 Re-ranking

During the testing phase, list of images are retrieved from the gallery of images, given a query image. Re-ranking can be used to further improve the retrieval results. We have used K-reciprocal re-ranking [9] approach. Given a query image and a retrieved list of nearest neighbours, two images are k-reciprocal when both are ranked top k in the respective retrieved lists when each image is used as a query itself. Therefore it is an indication that both images are a true match.

4 Experiment Results

4.1 Datasets

We used Market1501 [15] as our source dataset and DukeMTMC-reid [19] as target dataset. Table 1 show details of these datasets.

Table 1. Datasets used in our experiments.

Dataset	Year	No. of IDs	No. of Images	No. of Cameras
Market1501	2015	1,501	32,668	6
DukeMTMC-reid	2017	1,404	36,411	8

4.2 Evaluation Metrics

Cumulative Matching Characteristics (CMC) and Mean Average Precision (mAP) are two widely used evaluation metrics in person re-identification works. CMC measures the probability that the retrieved images are in top-k matched results. CMC is accurate when there is only one match in the gallery for each query. In person re-id datasets, several images taken from different cameras for each id are available in the gallery set. mAP is useful when there are more than one match for a query in the gallery set. It evaluates the average retrieval performance of a model. We have used mAP and rank-1 CMC scores to compare our results.

4.3 Compared Methods

We have compared the results of Vision transformer with Resnet [16] and EfficientNet [20] after training on the source dataset and directly testing on the target dataset without training on the target dataset to measure the generalization ability of these models. We also compared our pre-adaptation results with SNR [21] which is mainly a domain generalization technique for object and person re-identification. After adaptation on the target dataset, we compared our results with SSG [5] which is a domain adaptation approach for person re-identification. SSG used Resnet50 as the encoder and used Triplet loss for training.

4.4 Results and Discussion

For computer vision related tasks convolutional neural networks are considered to be most effective and used widely across the domain. Our experiments show that Vision Transformers also perform well on image data and can even outperform CNN based networks in some cases. When tested on target dataset after being trained on a source dataset, ViT resulted in 8.9% increase in mAP and

10% increase in Rank-1 CMC score, compared to Resnet50. This shows that ViT has a good generalization ability. This generalization ability of ViT also helped in producing higher scores after the adaptation phase.

We also compared our results with SNR [21]. SNR first remove the style from images by normalizing them. This style removal also removes some discriminative information from the images. SNR restitute this information back to the network so that the model can have a good generalization ability along with the discriminative ability. Hybrid ViT (Resnet + ViT) performed better than SNR out of the box.

Through our experiments we observed that, if we use a model pre-trained on Imagenet to directly adapt on person re-id dataset, it does not perform well. By training on a source re-id dataset prior to the adaptation, model learns features related to a person dataset and hence perform much better in the adaptation phase.

Table 2. Result on market1501 as source dataset and Dukemtmc-reid as target dataset.

Method	mAP - R1 Before adaptation	mAP - R1 After adaptation
Resnet50 [16]	17.6–34.9	–
EfficientNet-B5 [20]	22.9–44.0	–
ViT [3]	26.5–45.0	–
SNR [21]	33.6–55.1	–
SSG [5]	16.1–30.5	53.4–73.0
Proposed work	**35.2–55.8**	**68.3–81.4**
Proposed work (after re-ranking)	–	**71.8–84.0**

Table 2 shows comparison of CNN architectures and Vision transformer (ViT) when tested on the target dataset before adaptation. Clearly ViT performs better than convolutional based models and shown to have better generalization ability. Our methodology uses the domain adaptation approach of SSG [5] and by using Vision Transformers along with Cluster loss we have acquired significant improvement in our results.

5 Conclusion

We have demonstrated the use of Vision Transformer in unsupervised domain adaptation for person re-identification. We have incorporated Cluster loss which effectively helped in decreasing intra-cluster and increasing inter-cluster distances. Using CNN backbone for generating patch embeddings for Vision Transformer is also a useful approach for reducing the need for huge dataset, as the original ViT was trained with 300 Million images and than fine tuned on

Imagenet. Vision Transformers are a new class of architecture and have shown promising performance. Future research will increase their efficiency and usage in other areas of computer vision as well.

References

1. Zheng, L., Yang, Y., Hauptmann, A.G.: Person re-identification: past, present and future (2016)
2. Yang, F., Yan, K., Lu, S., Jia, H., Xie, X., Gao, W.: Attention driven person re-identification. Pattern Recogn. **86**, 143–155 (2019)
3. Dosovitskiy, A., et al.: An image is worth 16 × 16 words: transformers for image recognition at scale (2020)
4. Vaswani, A., et al.: Attention is all you need (2017)
5. Fu, Y., Wei, Y., Wang, G., Zhou, Y., Shi, H., Huang, T.S.: Self-similarity grouping: a simple unsupervised cross domain adaptation approach for person re-identification. Presented at the proceedings of the IEEE/CVF international conference on computer vision (2019)
6. Kriegel, H., Kröger, P., Sander, J., Zimek, A.: Density-based clustering. Wiley Interdiscip. Rev. Data Min. Knowl. Discov. **1**, 231–240 (2011)
7. Schroff, F., Kalenichenko, D., Philbin, J.: FaceNet: a unified embedding for face recognition and clustering. Presented at the proceedings of the IEEE conference on computer vision and pattern recognition (2015)
8. Alex, D., Sami, Z., Banerjee, S., Panda, S.: Cluster loss for person re-identification. Presented at the proceedings of the 11th Indian conference on computer vision, graphics and image processing (2018)
9. Zhong, Z., Zheng, L., Cao, D., Li, S.: Re-ranking person re-identification with k-reciprocal encoding. Presented at the proceedings of the IEEE conference on computer vision and pattern recognition (2017)
10. Zheng, L., Zhang, H., Sun, S., Chandraker, M., Yang, Y., Tian, Q.: Person re-identification in the wild. Presented at the proceedings of the IEEE conference on computer vision and pattern recognition (2017)
11. Zheng, Z., Yang, X., Yu, Z., Zheng, L., Yang, Y., Kautz, J.: Joint discriminative and generative learning for person re-identification. Presented at the proceedings of the IEEE/CVF conference on computer vision and pattern recognition (2019)
12. Sun, Y., Zheng, L., Yang, Y., Tian, Q., Wang, S.: Beyond part models: person retrieval with refined part pooling (and a strong convolutional baseline). Presented at the proceedings of the European conference on computer vision (ECCV) (2018)
13. Li, W., Zhu, X., Gong, S.: Harmonious attention network for person re-identification. Presented at the proceedings of the IEEE conference on computer vision and pattern recognition (2018)
14. Song, C., Huang, Y., Ouyang, W., Wang, L.: Mask-guided contrastive attention model for person re-identification. Presented at the proceedings of the IEEE conference on computer vision and pattern recognition (2018)
15. Zheng, L., Shen, L., Tian, L., Wang, S., Wang, J., Tian, Q.: Scalable person re-identification: a benchmark. Presented at the proceedings of the IEEE international conference on computer vision (2015)
16. He, K., Zhang, X., Ren, S., Sun, J.: Deep residual learning for image recognition. Presented at the proceedings of the IEEE conference on computer vision and pattern recognition (2016)

17. Deng, J., Dong, W., Socher, R., Li, L.-J., Li, K., Fei-Fei, L.: ImageNet: a large-scale hierarchical image database. Presented at the 2009 IEEE conference on computer vision and pattern recognition (2009)
18. Kingma, D.P., Ba, J.: Adam: a method for stochastic optimization (2014)
19. Ristani, E., Solera, F., Zou, R., Cucchiara, R., Tomasi, C.: Performance measures and a data set for multi-target, multi-camera tracking. Presented at the European conference on computer vision (2016)
20. Tan, M., Le, Q.: EfficientNet: rethinking model scaling for convolutional neural networks. Presented at the International Conference on Machine Learning (2019)
21. Jin, X., Lan, C., Zeng, W., Chen, Z., Zhang, L.: Style normalization and restitution for generalizable person re-identification. Presented at the proceedings of the IEEE/CVF conference on computer vision and pattern recognition (2020)

Recognition of Changes in the Psychoemotional State of a Person by the Video Image of the Pupils

Marina Boronenko, Oksana Isaeva(✉), Yuri Boronenko, Vladimir Zelensky, and Pavel Gulyaev

Yugra State University, 16 Chekhov Street, 628012 Khanty-Mansiysk, Russia
{w_selenski,P_Gulyaev}@ugrasu.ru

Abstract. We are looking for a relationship between electrodermal activity and the amplitude of fluctuations in the size of the pupils, depending on the magnitude of the stress (stress state) experienced. Studies have been carried out on the psychophysiological reactions of a person (emotions) arising in response to external stress factors (stimuli). For this, a device was used to register changes in pupil size and galvanic skin response. It turned out that the change in the values of galvanic skin response and pupil size correlates ($p = 0.9$) in the presence of emotions (all other things being equal). The result of measuring galvanic skin reaction (GSR) shows that the level of attention during the test to some stimuli was higher than to others. This means that the first stimuli may be more significant for the subject than the second. The results obtained make it possible to link the galvanic skin response and the pupil response in response to the stimulus material. Our research also shows that the pupil diameter signal has a good discriminating ability to detect changes in the psychological state of a person. The results can be useful for the development of Computer Vision and Artificial Intelligence.

Keywords: Pupillogram · Galvanic skin reaction · Computer vision

1 Introduction

In the modern world, technologies and methods are being actively developed to improve the interaction between man and technology. In our research, we strive to create methods and algorithms that will allow artificial intelligence to assess the psycho-emotional state of a person, to predict his behavior. Computational collective intelligence can be considered as a means of optimizing artificial intelligence. One area of application of collective intelligence is data mining. Before analyzing the information, you first need to get it. One of the most popular methods for obtaining data is obtaining various information from images. Therefore, psychological and behavioral analysis using video files is gaining popularity. In the future, we plan to create an intelligent security system based on the results of an automated analysis of the sequence of pupil images received from video cameras.

K. Wojtkiewicz et al. (Eds.): ICCCI 2021, CCIS 1463, pp. 123–133, 2021.
https://doi.org/10.1007/978-3-030-88113-9_10

2 Related Work

2.1 Behavior Recognition

Y. Matsumoto, T. Ogasawara and A. Zelinsky [1] describe a behavior recognition system based on real-time stereophonic face tracking and gaze detection to simultaneously measure head position and gaze direction. A key aspect of the system is the use of real-time stereo vision along with a simple algorithm that is suitable for real-time processing. The authors were able to significantly simplify the algorithm for fitting a 3D model to obtain a full 3D head pose compared to conventional systems that use a monocular camera.

Batchuluun G. et al. [2] propose a method of behavior recognition based on a fuzzy system that combines prediction and recognition of behavior. For daytime and nighttime behavioral recognition, a dual visible light camera system (far infrared light) is used to capture 12 datasets, including 11 different types of human behavior in various surveillance environments. Experimental results, together with collected datasets and an open database, have shown that the proposed method provides a higher accuracy of behavior recognition compared to traditional methods.

Gunes H., Piccardi M. [3] present an approach to automatic visual recognition of expressive facial and upper body gestures from video sequences suitable for use in a vision-based affective multimodal structure. Face and body movements are recorded simultaneously by two separate cameras. For each video sequence, separate expressive frames from both the face and the body are manually selected for analysis and recognition of emotions. First, individual classifiers are trained individually. Second, we integrate information about facial expressions and emotional body gestures at the performance level and at the decision-making level. In the experiments carried out, the classification of emotions using two modalities achieved a higher recognition accuracy than the classification using only the individual modality of the face or body.

T. Baltrusaitis, A. Zadeh, YC Lim and L. Morency [4] present OpenFace 2.0, a tool for computer vision and machine learning researchers, as well as for the emotional computing community and people interested in creating interactive applications based on behavior analysis. persons. OpenFace 2.0 is an extension of the OpenFace toolbox that can more accurately determine face landmarks, assess head posture, recognize facial action units, and assess gaze. The computer vision algorithms that make up the core of OpenFace 2.0 demonstrate state-of-the-art performance in all of the above tasks. In addition, the tool is capable of working in real time and can be operated from a simple webcam without special equipment.

E. Laksana, T. Baltrušaitis, L. Morency and J. P. Pestian [5] investigate non-verbal facial behavior to distinguish between control patients, mentally ill and suicidal patients. For this task, the authors used a balanced corpus containing interviews of men and women with and without suicidal ideation and/or mental disorders from 3 different hospitals. In their experiments, the authors studied smiling, frowning, raising eyebrows, and head movements. They investigated both the origin of such behavior and how it was carried out. It was found that descriptors of facial behavior, such as the percentage of smiles associated with contraction of the orbicular muscles of the eyes (Duchenne smile), had statistically significant differences between the suicidal and non-suicidal groups. Experiments have also shown that the stage of the interview in which these facial features appear affects their ability to discriminate.

In the above-described works, the behavior of the person is used to predict human behavior. However, when analyzing the behavior of a person, there may be problems with the interpretation of the results obtained. Since a person can easily reproduce the "necessary" expression on his face, that is, hide true feelings and emotions. And a person is not able to control the change in the size of the pupils. This is the advantage of our method of recognizing changes in the psychoemotional state of a person from the video image of the pupils.

2.2 Emotion/stress Assessment Methods

As you know, people have a different character, temperament, upbringing, culture. Emotional expression differs significantly even in the same situation. Therefore, to justify the opposite conclusion that the pattern of facial movements is an expression of a particular emotional state, four criteria must be met: reliability, specificity, generalizability and reliability [6].

Methods for assessing emotions based on changes caused by the autonomic nervous system (ANS) are more objective. These methods include measurements of galvanic skin response (GSR) [7]. However, the main disadvantage of this method is that it is a contact method.

Pedrotti M. et al. [8] propose a method based on wavelet transform and neural networks to establish a connection between pupil behavior and psychological stress (accuracy 79.2%). The proposed method was tested by recording pupil diameter and electrodermal activity during simulated driving. Self-report indicators were also collected. Significant correlations were found between stress and dynamics of pupil size. At the same time, the electrodermal activity did not change accordingly. At the same time, it is also known about the generality of the mechanisms of mental regulation of human activity and functional states. This is expressed in a single time scale of the course of regulation processes at different levels.

Based on the above, we can conclude that there is a dependence of the size of the pupil on the emotional state of a person. GSR is one of the most accurate ways to measure emotional state. Thus, for the transition from the contact method to the non-contact method, it is necessary to prove the relationship between GSR and the pupillary response. Our purpose: to test the presence of a correlation between the emotional state measured by GSR and the pupillary response.

3 Experimental Method and Technique

3.1 Experimental Setup

The rejection of the null hypothesis in favor of the observations made indicates that we observe the manifestation of emotions with a certain degree of probability. Even under laboratory conditions, the human brain can be affected by factors other than the stimulus material.

During the experiment, changes in pupil size and galvanic skin response (GSR) were recorded (Fig. 1). Components of the installation: a video camera that records changes in the size of the pupil; a video camera that records changes in the values of the GSR parameters; hardware and software complex "Activation-6". Video cameras ZWO ASI 120MC-S with the following technical characteristics (Table 1).

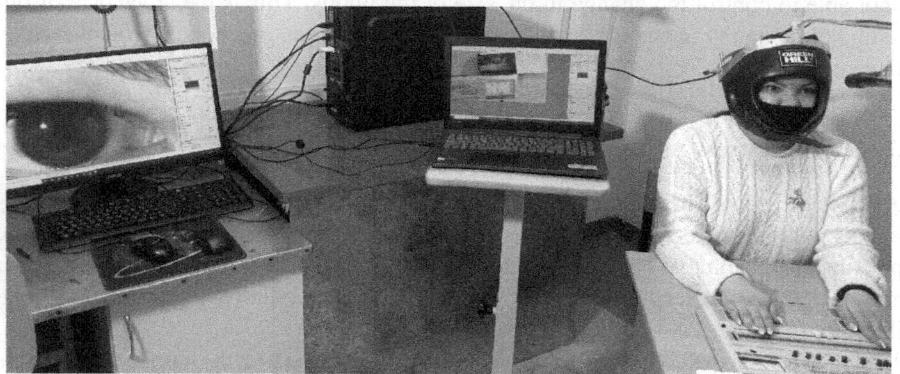

Fig. 1. Experimental setup for recording changes in pupil size and galvanic skin response.

Table 1. Technical characteristics of the ZWO ASI 120MC-S video camera.

Parameter	Value	Supported resolution
Chromaticity	RGB	Binning 1 × 1: 1280 × 960 - 60FPS 1280 × 720 - 98FPS 1280 × 600 - 116FPS 1280 × 400 - 168FPS 960 × 960 - 74FPS 1024 × 768 - 90FPS 1024 × 400 - 160FPS 800 × 800 - 85FPS 800 × 640 - 106FPS 800 × 480 - 141FPS 640 × 480 - 133FPS 512 × 440 - 145FPS 512 × 400 - 158FPS 480 × 320 - 196FPS 320 × 240 - 254FPS Binning 2 × 2: 640 × 480 - 45FPS
The matrix	ARO130CS	
Matrix size	4.8 × 3.6 mm	
Megapixels	1,2	
Resolution	1280 × 960	
Pixel size	3.75 μm	
Readout noise	4.0 e	
Maximum pixel efficiency	13,000 e	
Quantum efficiency	75%	
ADC bit width	12 bits	
Maximum shooting speed	240 fps	
Holding time	0.064–2000 s	

The experiment involved student volunteers (19–23 years old), a total of 52 people (boys - 29, girls - 23). All had normal vision, or corrected with glasses or lenses. When analyzing video files containing a pupillary reaction, cases of strange behavior of the pupils were revealed. This data was discarded and was not taken into account. A total of 5 series of experiments were carried out. In each series, the participants and their number did not change. Illumination during the measurements did not change. Pupillary reaction was recorded by a video camera, which has a rigid coordinate connection with the head. At the same time, diagnostics of the psychoemotional state was carried out using the device "Activatiometer-6", which registers the galvanic skin response (GSR). A feature of the device is its ability to take into account the contribution of activation of each hemisphere to the general psychoemotional state. The readings of the device were also recorded on a video camera. To link the GSR response to the stimulus material, a mirror was placed in the viewing area of the video camera. The mirror reflected the monitor on which the test objects were demonstrated. The stimulus to which the pupillary reaction occurred was determined by the reflection of the monitor on the surface of the eye.

Stimulus material (test objects) was demonstrated on the slides of the presentation. Calibration is needed to distinguish an emotional response from a non-emotional response. For such calibration, plain slides were used as stimulus material, which in the overwhelming majority of cases did not evoke emotion.

3.2 Analysis of Video Files

The preparation of images, processing and contouring of the pupils were carried out using the FiJi program (ImageJ). In order to highlight the pupil in the resulting video files, you first need to carry out high-quality contouring. When processing images "manually", the analysis procedure takes a rather long period of time. But the open-source program FiJi (ImageJ) allows you to write macros, which greatly speeds up the work. A portion of the pupil contouring algorithm is presented below.

```
//run("Brightness/Contrast...");
run("Apply LUT", "stack");
run("Colour Deconvolution", "vectors=H&E");
run("Mean", "block_radius_x=10 block_radius_y=10 stack");
run("Apply LUT", "stack");
run("Remove Outliers...", "radius=30 threshold=0 which=Dark stack");
```

The processing algorithm will vary depending on the color of the iris of the eyes, illumination. The evolution of the image is shown in Fig. 2.

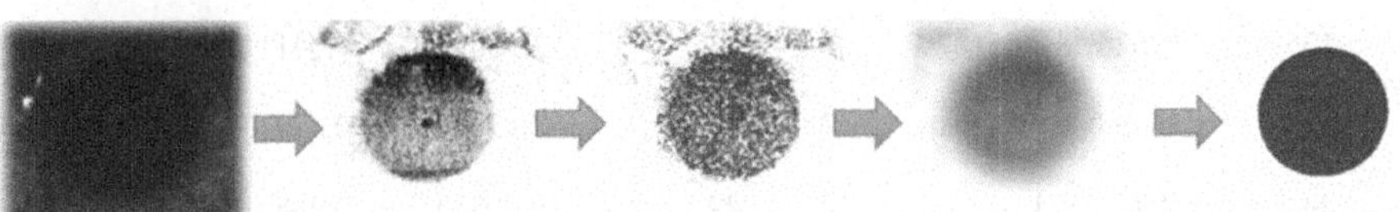

Fig. 2. Contouring algorithm for brown eyes with clearly defined pupil contour. (Color figure online)

Preliminary improvement of the video file quality allows to increase the signal-to-noise ratio (signal – to retina, noise – to pupil) by an order of magnitude. The results were visualized using the Origin2021 software.

4 Experiment Results

Calibration allows not only to establish the correct spatial scale, but also to interpret the results. For calibration, monophonic slides were used, to which an emotional response was not expected. Therefore, the stressful state caused by stimuli should be absent. Therefore, GSR and pupillograms should not contain areas caused by emotional outburst (tension). However, in some cases, deviations of the reaction from normal were observed. Subsequently, it turned out that the subjects were distracted by their thoughts. Also, to compare the reactions, an audio message was made to five subjects while viewing the calibration slides (which was individually selected and targeted). In response to the message, the subject gave an answer. According to the standard method [9], the control of GSR made it possible to reveal a lie. Comparative analysis of pupillary reaction and GSR allows you to check the correctness of the decoding technique. Thus, three types of reactions were observed: absence of emotions (calibration state), accidental distraction to one's thoughts, reaction to a sound message.

Testing the null hypothesis that the pupillary response in cases with and without a sound message was the same, was carried out for each subject separately (example in Table 2). Alternative Hypothesis: The samples come from different populations. At the

Table 2. Post-hoc analysis.

	Dunn's Test				Wilcoxon-Nemenyi-McDonald-Thompson Test			
	Sum Rank Diff	Z	Prob	Sig	Sum Rank Diff	Z	Prob	Sig
DH DI	−263	5.44851	5.07934E-7	1	−263	7.70536	0	1
DH DJ	−152	3.14895	0.01639	0	−152	4.45329	0.01425	0
DH DK	−67	1.38802	1	0	−67	1.96296	0.63936	0
DH DL	−128	2.65175	0.08008	0	−128	3.75014	0.06185	0
DI DJ	111	2.29956	0.21473	0	111	3.25207	0.1465	0
DI DK	196	4.06049	4.89705E-4	1	196	5.7424	2.70068E-4	1
DI DL	135	2.79676	0.05162	0	135	3.95522	0.04111	0
DJ DK	85	1.76093	0.78251	0	85	2.49032	0.39913	0
DJ DL	24	0.4972	1	0	24	0.70315	0.98821	0
DK DL	−61	1.26372	1	0	−61	1.78717	0.71481	0

0.01 level, the populations are significantly different. The rejection of the null hypothesis in favor of the observations made indicates that we observe the manifestation of emotions with a certain degree of probability. Even under laboratory conditions, the human brain can be affected by factors other than the stimulus material.

When decoding GSR, it can be seen that the response on the curve has several peaks A, B (Fig. 3). This reaction can occur if, in the process of comprehending information (or simply contemplating an empty slide), memories arose that became a stimulus that caused unplanned emotional stress. The usual reaction begins in 1,2–2 s, memories can be somewhat delayed in time.

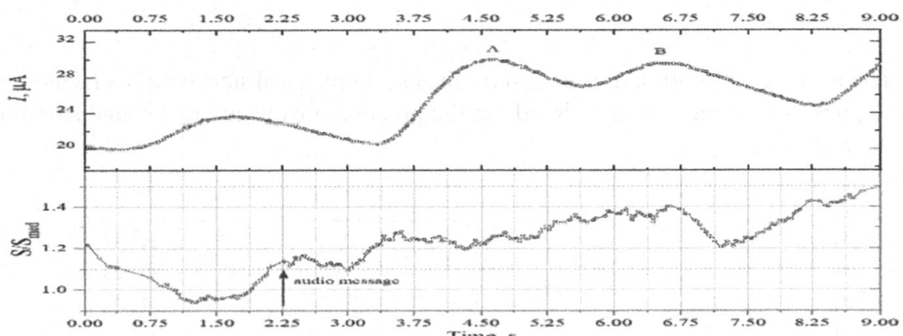

Fig. 3. Pupillogram, GSR, obtained when the subject's attention is switched from the calibration slide to sound information.

As is known [10], the priority function that triggers a change in the mental state is attention. It is this function that has a stable connection with the functioning of the autonomic nervous system of the body. Its activity can be monitored for individual "external" indicators using the GSR. It is also known that a violation of the synchronicity of the pupillary reaction and GSR can occur either when RA GSR reflect not the processes of regulation of functional states, but the processes of homeostasis of the physiological systems of the body, or with artifact saccades. Because on the graphs the synchronicity is observed, then it can be concluded that the registered reaction is due to a change in the psychophysical state.

We are looking for a relationship between electrodermal activity and the amplitude of fluctuations in the size of the pupils, depending on the magnitude of the stress (stress state) experienced. The strength of stress depends on the significance of the stimulus. We believe that the impact of a one-color slide is equivalent to no impact (unless, of course, there is no emotional hypersensitivity to color). To take into account the possible distraction of the subjects on their thoughts, measurements of the effect of monochromatic slides were carried out 5 times. Descriptive statistics of one of the participants for whom the audio message was made (Table 3).

Table 3. Descriptive statistics.

	N total	Mean	Standard deviation	Sum	Minimum	Median	Maximum
Normalized2	628	1.00019	0.06634	628.11773	0.78595	1.00174	1.16664
Normalized4	565	0.99396	0.11799	561.58982	0.69706	1.0034	1.20996
Normalized6	622	1.00548	0.05756	625.40565	0.89761	1	1.14638
Normalized8	532	1.0057	0.043	535.03439	0.90926	1	1.1342
Normalized10	466	1.01248	0.07136	471.81468	0.86311	1.00313	1.16289

The results of the correlation analysis of the psychophysical state (stress) and the size of the pupils of the participants directly in the process of exposure to a sound stimulus are shown in Fig. 4:

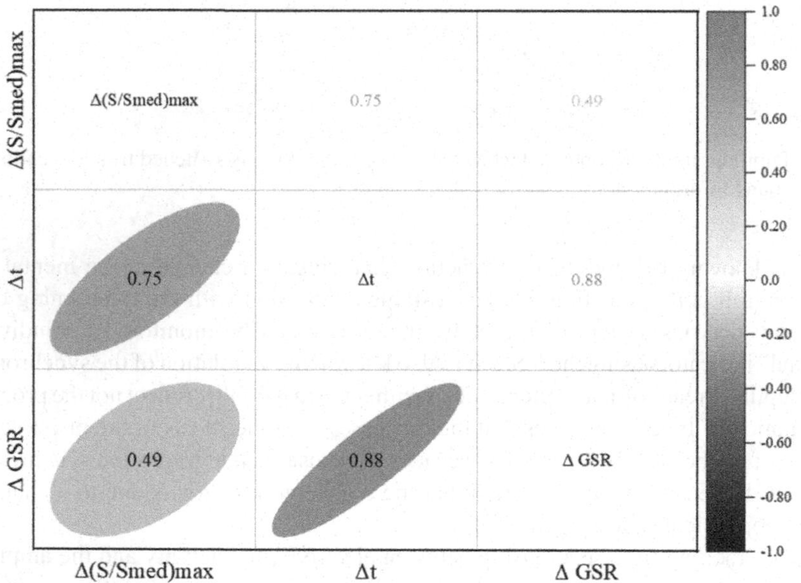

Fig. 4. Spearman's correlation.

Correlation is significant at the 0.05 level. Thus, there is a significant correlation between the duration of pupil dilation and galvanic skin response (0.88). The results obtained make it possible to link the galvanic skin response and the response of the pupils in response to the stimulus material.

When compared with the results of participants who were not exposed to a significant stimulus, the correlation was significantly reduced (Table 4).

Table 4. r-Spearman. Rank correlations (pairwise deletion) alternative hypothesis H1: $r \neq 0$.

VAR vs. VAR	N	Rho	t	p-value
Δ(S/Smed)max vs.| Δt	28	−0.2262	−1.1839	0.2472
Δ(S/Smed)max vs. |Δ GSR	29	−0.1636	−0.8617	0.3965
Δt vs.| Δ GSR	28	−0.0474	−0.2422	0.8105

A similar reaction manifested itself precisely when the stimulus material was not emotionally colored. Thus, if there is no emotional reaction, then GSR does not correlate with changes in pupil size.

5 Discussion

In the context of the spreading coronavirus infection, remote sensing technologies are becoming more and more relevant in the world. For remote diagnostics of a person's psychoemotional state, specialized expensive equipment is needed, which not all people can afford. The proposed method makes it possible to remotely control changes in the size of the pupils and assess the psychoemotional state of a person remotely without specialized equipment. This article describes the results of attaching a video camera to a helmet on the head. Earlier, we showed the possibility of not fixing the video camera [11], but here we use a standard method to simplify the data processing procedure.

It was shown in [11] that the use of a video camera without infrared illumination in the absence of head fixation leads to distortion of the track. Therefore, it needs to be corrected. To do this, you need to make a transition from a coordinate system associated with a fixed head to a coordinate system associated with a moving center of the pupil. In this case, the stimulus material was demonstrated from a laptop screen located at a distance of no more than 1 m. At such a distance, the brightness of the displayed images is important, because affects the size of the pupils. To eliminate this effect, it is necessary to convert the image materials used as a stimulus into equal brightness (brightness fluctuations were no more than 0.7%). The results of testing the hypothesis about the identity of the results obtained by fixed and free video cameras showed that At the 0.01 level, the populations are not significantly different. Currently, the resolution of video cameras in gadgets is becoming more and more. Therefore, in the future, the application of the proposed method is quite realistic.

The results give hope that the size of the pupil can serve as a pattern for remote diagnostics of the psychophysical state of a person. In video surveillance systems, it is possible to obtain a set of data on pupil reactions, synchronized with the Eye tracker [12] with reference to test objects. This will make it possible to conduct a comprehensive analysis of the mental state of a person, to identify a depressive state and to detect people showing emotions that are characteristic of law and order violators. This will come in handy in modern security systems, where biometric personal identification is increasingly used. Also, the video images of the pupil can be used for the fatigue and stress recognition system of the driver. This will avoid accidents caused by inattention, drowsiness or poor health of the driver [13].

6 Main Results and Conclusions

The research of psychophysiological reactions of a person (emotions) under the influence of external stress factors (stimuli) has been carried out. The response (psychophysical reaction) to the stimulus was measured by GSR and pupillometry. A search for a correlation between the emotional state, measured by GSR and pupillary response, has been carried out. Installed:

- Galvanic skin response and long-term increase in pupil size correlate ($p = 0.9$), subject to the presence of emotion, and all other things being equal. The level of attention during the test to some stimuli was higher than to others, which, in turn, indicates that they are more significant for the subject than the second. An oral questioning confirms the hypothesis. To more significant stimuli, the emotional response measured by the size of the pupils and GSR are in good agreement.
- When interpreting the results, it is necessary to take into account that even in laboratory conditions, in addition to the planned stress factor (stimulus material), a random factor can influence. The random factor can be due to an unplanned coincidence of circumstances, the subject's train of thought, his physical condition, etc.

The results can be useful for the development of Computer Vision and Artificial Intelligence.

Acknowledgment. The study was carried out with the financial support of the Russian Foundation for Basic Research in the framework of the research project 18-47-860018 p_a.

References

1. Matsumoto, Y., Ogasawara, T., Zelinsky, A.: Behavior recognition based on head pose and gaze direction measurement. In: Conference: Intelligent Robots and Systems (IROS 2000), Takamatsu, Japan, vol. 3, pp. 2127–2132 (2000). https://doi.org/10.1109/IROS.2000.895285.
2. Batchuluun, G., et al.: Fuzzy system based human behavior recognition by combining behavior prediction and recognition. Expert Syst. Appl. **81**, 108–133 (2017). https://doi.org/10.1016/j.eswa.2017.03.052
3. Gunes, H., Piccardi, M.: Bi-modal emotion recognition from expressive face and body gestures. J. Netw. Comput. Appl. **30**(4), 1334–1345 (2007). https://doi.org/10.1016/j.jnca.2006.09.007
4. Baltrusaitis, T., Zadeh, A., Lim, Y.C., Morency, L.: OpenFace 2.0: facial behavior analysis toolkit. In: 13th IEEE International Conference on Automatic Face & Gesture Recognition, Xi'an, China, pp. 59–66. IEEE (2018). https://doi.org/10.1109/FG.2018.00019
5. Laksana, E., Baltrušaitis, T., Morency, L., Pestian, J.P.: Investigating facial behavior indicators of suicidal ideation. In: 12th IEEE International Conference on Automatic Face & Gesture Recognition, Washington, DC, USA, pp. 770–777. IEEE (2017). https://doi.org/10.1109/FG.2017.96
6. Melnikova, O.T., Khoroshilov, D.A.: Modern criterion systems for the validity of qualitative research in psychology. Natl. Psychol. J. **2**(14), 36–48 (2014). https://doi.org/10.11621/npj.2014.0205

7. Montagu, J.D., Coles, E.M.: Mechanism and measurement of the galvanic skin response. Psychol. Bull. **65**(5), 261–279 (1966). https://doi.org/10.1037/h0023204
8. Pedrotti, M., et al.: Automatic stress classification with pupil diameter analysis. Int. J. Hum. Comput. Interact. **30**(3), 220–236 (2014). https://doi.org/10.1080/10447318.2013.848320
9. Tsagarelli Yu, A.: Systemic Diagnostics of a Person and the Development of Mental Functions. Knowledge, Kazan (2009)
10. Kostin, A.N., Golikov, Y.Y.: Conceptual foundations of the joint analysis of EOG and GSR for the study of mental regulation of activity and functional states. In: Experimental Psychology in Russia: Traditions and Perspectives, pp. 515–519 (2010)
11. Boronenko M.P., Isaeva O.L., Zelensky V.I..: Method for increasing the accuracy of tracking the center of attention of the gaze. In: 2021 International Symposium on Electrical, Electronics and Information Engineering (ISEEIE 2021), Seoul, Republic of Korea, New York, NY, USA, p. 6. ACM (2021). https://doi.org/10.1145/3459104.3459172
12. IMOTIONS Homepage. https://imotions.com/blog/capturing-life-as-it-happens-an-online-field-study-in-politics/. Accessed 26 June 2021
13. Sautin M.G., Gamayunov P.P.: Driver fatigue recognition system. In: Actual Issues of the Organization of Road Transport and Traffic Safety: A Collection of Materials of the International Scientific and Practical Conference, vol.355, pp.147–151 (2018)

Morphological Analysis of Histopathological Images Using Deep Learning

Artur Zawisza, Martin Tabakov(✉), Konrad Karanowski, and Krzysztof Galus

Faculty of Computer Science and Management, Department of Computational Intelligence, Wroclaw University of Science and Technology, Wroclaw, Poland

{artur.zawisza,martin.tabakow}@pwr.edu.pl, {254533, 253060}@student.pwr.edu.pl

Abstract. In this study, we introduce a morphological analysis of segmented tumour cells from histopathology images concerning the recognition of cell overlapping. The main research problem considered is to distinguish how many cells are located in a structure, which is composed of overlapping cells. In our experiments, we used convolutional neural network models to provide recognition of the number of cells. For the medical data used: Ki-67 histopathology images, we achieved a high f1-score result. Therefore, our research proves the assumption to use convolutional neural networks for morphological analysis of segmented objects derived from medical images.

Keywords: Convolutional neural networks · Digital histopathology · Morphological analysis · Morphological image processing · Medical images · Histopathology images

1 Introduction

Cancer is a major healthcare problem worldwide, with a growing rate every year. We can distinguish breast cancer as the most frequent cancer among the women population [22]. In breast cancer screening and grading procedures, the Ki-67 biomarker is an important factor for the immunohistochemical assessment of the cancer proliferation rate [17]. A very common problem in digital histopathology, considering the Ki-67 index evaluation, is to recognize the type of the considered tumour cells and the accurate number of cells used for Ki-67 index calculation. Recently, deep learning techniques mostly based on convolutional neural networks (CNN), were applied successfully in order to provide Ki-67 index evaluation. Gamma mixture model with expectation-maximization applied in deep learning process was proposed in [20], model called PathoNet for Ki-67 immunostained cell detection and classification was proposed in [16], MobileUnet model used for segmentation of Ki-67 images was introduced in [12] or other dedicated convolutional neural networks models [24, 27]. Nevertheless, the success of any CNN model is determined of the correctly prepared training sets.

K. Wojtkiewicz et al. (Eds.): ICCCI 2021, CCIS 1463, pp. 134–145, 2021.
https://doi.org/10.1007/978-3-030-88113-9_11

In our research, we focus on the very specific problem of cell overlapping in histopathology images. The procedure of histology slide preparation cannot avoid the overlap of tissue cells, which after image acquisition with a digital microscope are shown as large irregular structures. The most common such structures are random combinations of two or three overlapping cells. If a considered cell recognition problem is sensitive to the accurate number of cells, it becomes a considerable problem. An image segmentation algorithm can rarely separate accurately all segmented histology structures into cells. Of course, separation of segmented objects is a well-known problem in image analysis, which is the step of morphological image processing after segmentation and the pre-processing of the recognition process [5]. Morphological image processing is widely used in medical image analysis as segmentation post-processing [14]. The problem of separation of segmented cells or other structures is handled as well [4, 13]. Nevertheless, the application of CNN models for this particular problem seems to be a new approach. Therefore, our goal is to apply known CNN models for the classification of overlapped cancer cells considering the number of cells in the segmented structures.

The rest of the paper is organized as follows: in Sect. 2, the data used and the CNN models applied are explained, in Sect. 3 the research experiment is presented, in Sect. 4 we show the achieved results, and finally, Sects. 6 and 5 draw discussion and conclusions.

2 Materials and Methods

2.1 Materials

We used the SHIDC-BC-Ki-67 histopathology image dataset introduced in [16]. The dataset consists of 2357 histopathology images, labelled by expert pathologists. It contains microscopic tru-cut biopsy images of malignant breast tumours of the invasive ductal carcinoma type. Below in Fig. 1, we show some example of the dataset considered.

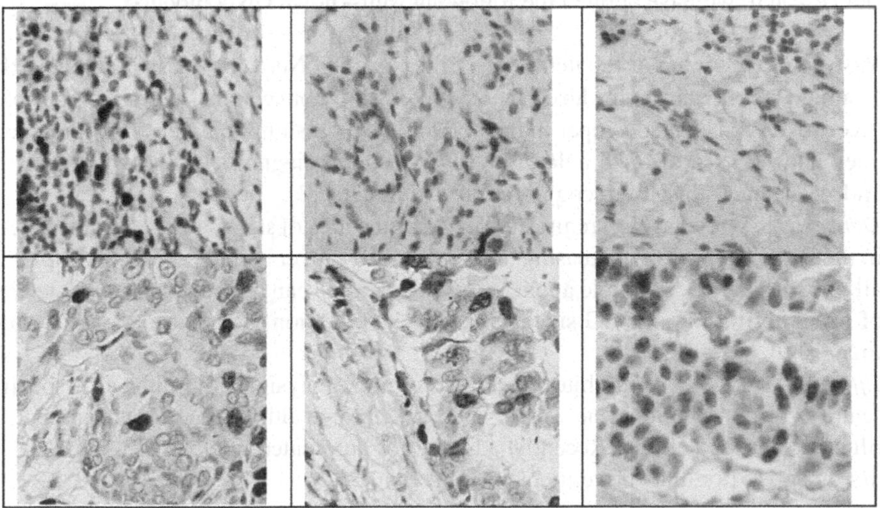

Fig. 1. Example images from the SHIDC-BC-Ki-67 dataset.

As we can see, the problem of overlapping cells is present in almost every image. By cell overlapping, we mean the connection of significant parts of the surface area of the cells. It can become a significant recognition problem if we need the accurate count of cells in the diagnostic process. The calculation of the Ki-67 proliferation index is a perfect example of such a problem. Below in Fig. 2, we show some overlapping cells, which should be taken into consideration in order to calculate the accurate Ki-67 index value.

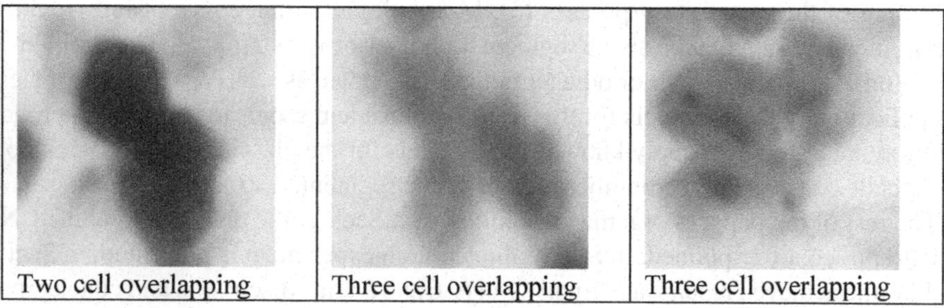

Fig. 2. Cell overlapping.

Considering the above problem, our research goal was to verify whether CNN models are capable of a classification of a given image, into classes of one, two or three cells in the cell overlap scenario.

2.2 Methods

In our research, we have applied the following well-known CNN models:

- *ResNet-18* [7] – One of the iterations of the Residual Network (ResNet) model. The assumed architecture introduced the so-called skip connections that pass input of a layer to a layer located deeper in the network. This assumption allows building very deep networks. In medical field, used for ultrasound diagnosis of thyroid disease [6] and Alzheimer's disease recognition in MRI images [3],
- *DenseNet* [8] – DenseNet architecture expands the idea of skip connections introduced in the ResNet model by increasing their number so a layer is connected to the inputs of all previous layers. Example applications in medicine can be found as well: detection of atrial fibrillation in ECG signals [18] or classification of osteosarcoma histology images [9],
- *EfficientNet* [26] – An architecture based on the analysis of the impact of specific features of convolutional networks, such as depth, width or resolution (number of filters), on its scalability. Recently, adopted for automated, image-based COVID-19 diagnosis [15] or diabetic retinopathy detection [2],

- *GoogLeNet* [25] – Introduced by Google and winner of ImageNet2014 competition. It has been used successfully in medical image classification [11] and artefact removal for sparse-viewed Computed Tomography (CT) [28],
- *MobileNetV2* [19] – A network dedicated for limited resources applications e.g. mobile devices. Reduces costs by usage of so called depthwise separable convolutions that have similar performance of regular convolutional layers with reduced number of parameters. In medical field, applications can be found in cervical precancerous lesions [1] and histopathological biopsy image [10] classification,
- *VGG-11* [23] – A version of a model which took the 2nd place in the ImageNet2014 competition. Reduced size of the kernels allows to increase the network's depth. Used as a part of CT image denoising system [29] and automatic instrument segmentation in robot-assisted surgery [21].

For accurate training, any deep model needs a large training dataset. The acquisition of large amounts of data is a major problem in medical applications. Training of such neural network models from scratch requires tens of thousands of samples as a bare minimum, which rarely is provided by physicians.

The above problem is addressed by two major techniques: data augmentation and transfer learning.

Data augmentation refers to the process of generation of new data samples by disturbing samples taken from the original dataset. In case of images these perturbations are created by e.g. small, random rotations of the images; addition of Gaussian noise, etc.

Transfer learning is an approach that utilizes networks that have been already trained. It is based on an assumption that knowledge gathered by a network in one problem can be utilized in some other, similar problem. The process can be divided into a few steps:

1. A trained deep model is modified by removing some of its output layers,
2. New, randomly initialized layers are added in their place,
3. The network is being trained using the target dataset with its layers from the original model being unaffected by the process,
4. After some learning, the whole network is trained using the target dataset.

The layers saved in step number one have the role of *feature extractors* (pre-processors) of the new dataset. The goal of the third step is to train newly added layers with respect to the target dataset and finally, the fourth step, called *fine-tuning*, allows corresponding adjustment of the image filters applied in the input layers (the convolutional layers).

The above procedure, among other techniques, approximates the procedure of accurate training of deep models without the need of large datasets.

In our research, we applied data augmentation assuming the following image transformations: rotations by $\pm 5°$ and horizontal flipping. Additionally, Gaussian noise was added and transfer learning was applied as well. The output layer of each deep model considered was replaced and next, fine-tuning was applied. Further details of the research experiments are given in the section below.

3 Experiments

For the purpose of our experiments, we have prepared a dataset consisting of three types of cells, single-separated cells, double-two overlapping cells and triple-three overlapping cells. We have created our training and test datasets manually using labelled histopathology dataset introduced in [16]. The number of training and test data are shown in Table 1.

Table 1. Training and test data for each class

Types of cells	Training data	Test data
Single (image resolution: 100 × 100 pixels)	776	28
Double (image resolution: 120 × 120 pixels)	118	20
Triple (image resolution: 160 × 160 pixels)	76	24

Below, in Fig. 3 we show some sample images of the types of cells considered.

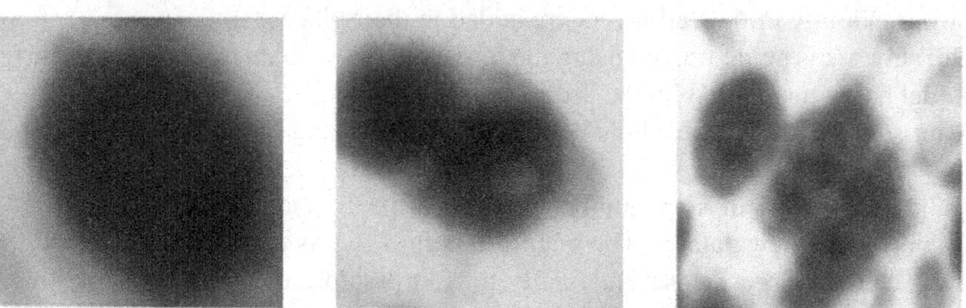

Fig. 3. Types of cells for classification: single, double and triple respectively.

The training procedure of the deep models considered involved k-folded cross validation (with $k = 5$) for each epoch and incorporated early stopping to prevent overfitting. Cross-entropy was selected as a loss function for the optimization process. The optimization was done with Adam optimizer. The training process, visualizing corresponding epochs with respect to achieved average values of loss, accuracy and f-score for each model are shown in Fig. 4 (a)–(f). The experiments were conducted with the parameters shown in Table 2.

Table 2. Parameter values of the models applied.

Batch size	4 images
Optimizer	Adam: $\beta_1 = 0.9$; $\beta_2 = 0.999$
Learning rate:	0.00001
Maximal number of iterations:	15
Early stopping wait time [#iterations]	7

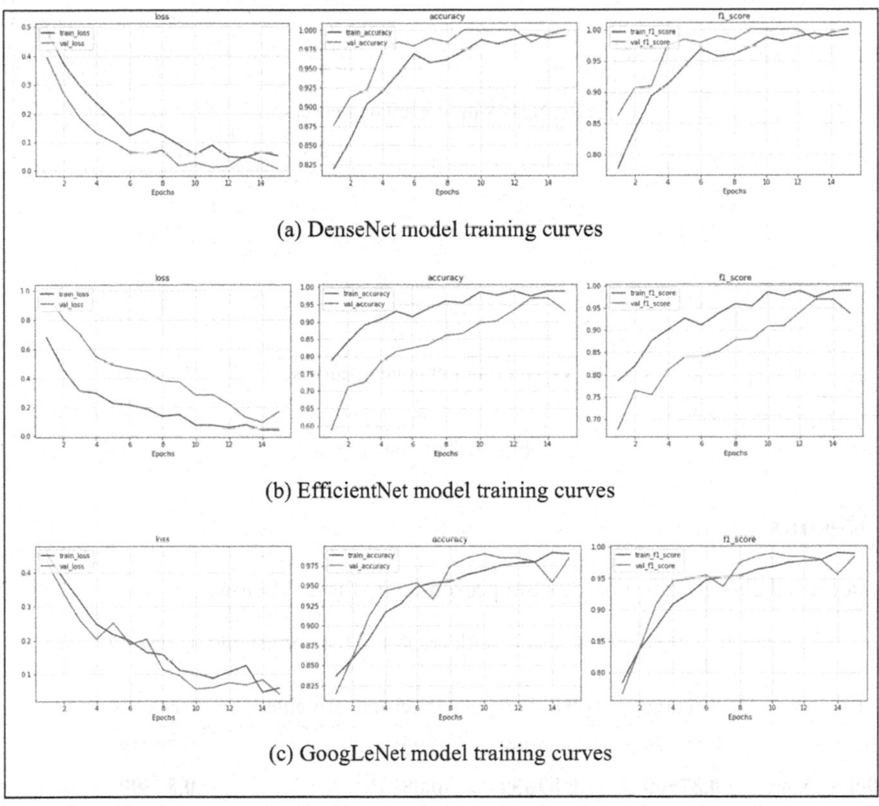

(a) DenseNet model training curves

(b) EfficientNet model training curves

(c) GoogLeNet model training curves

Fig. 4. (a)–(f). Training curves for each deep model considered.

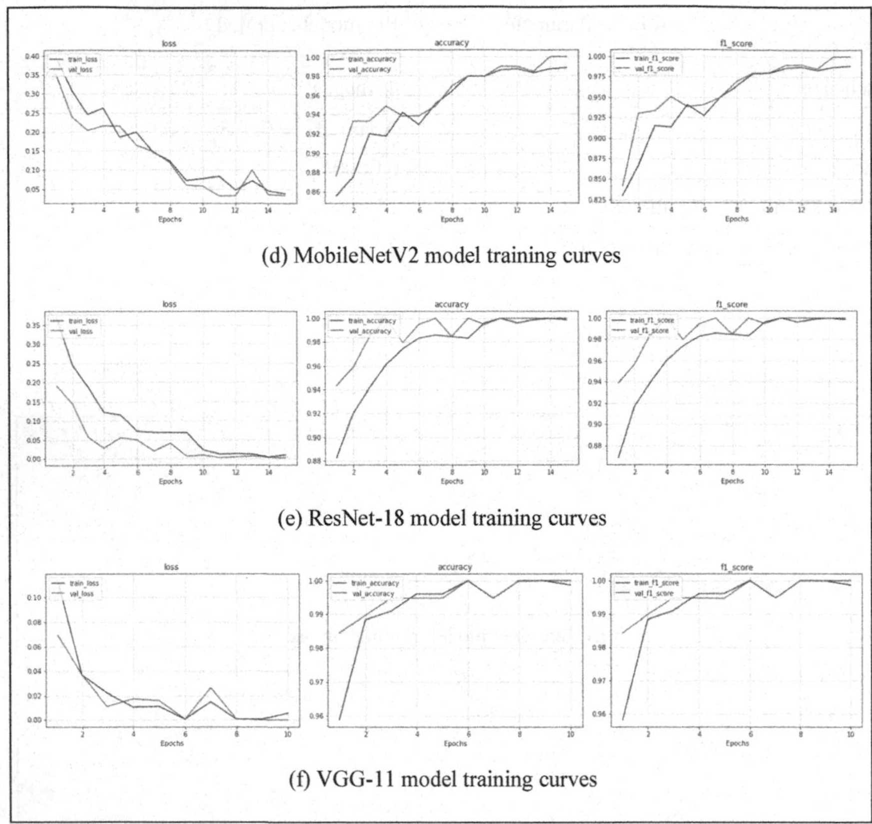

(d) MobileNetV2 model training curves

(e) ResNet-18 model training curves

(f) VGG-11 model training curves

Fig. 4. continued

4 Results

The achieved classification results are presented in Table 3 below.

Table 3. Classification results with respect to the corresponding test sets

Model	Accuracy	F1-score	Precision (weighted)	Recall (weighted)
DenseNet	0.77778	0.77968	0.80193	0.77778
EfficientNet	**0.87500**	**0.87639**	**0.88131**	**0.87500**
GoogLeNet	0.76389	0.76650	0.78938	0.76389
MobileNetV2	0.77778	0.78131	0.79060	0.77778
ResNet18	0.81944	0.81334	0.82747	0.81944
VGG11	0.81944	0.81503	0.83188	0.81944

We achieved best results for the EfficientNet model. Additionally, in Fig. 5 (a) – (f) we show some examples of correctly and incorrectly classification predictions for the deep models considered.

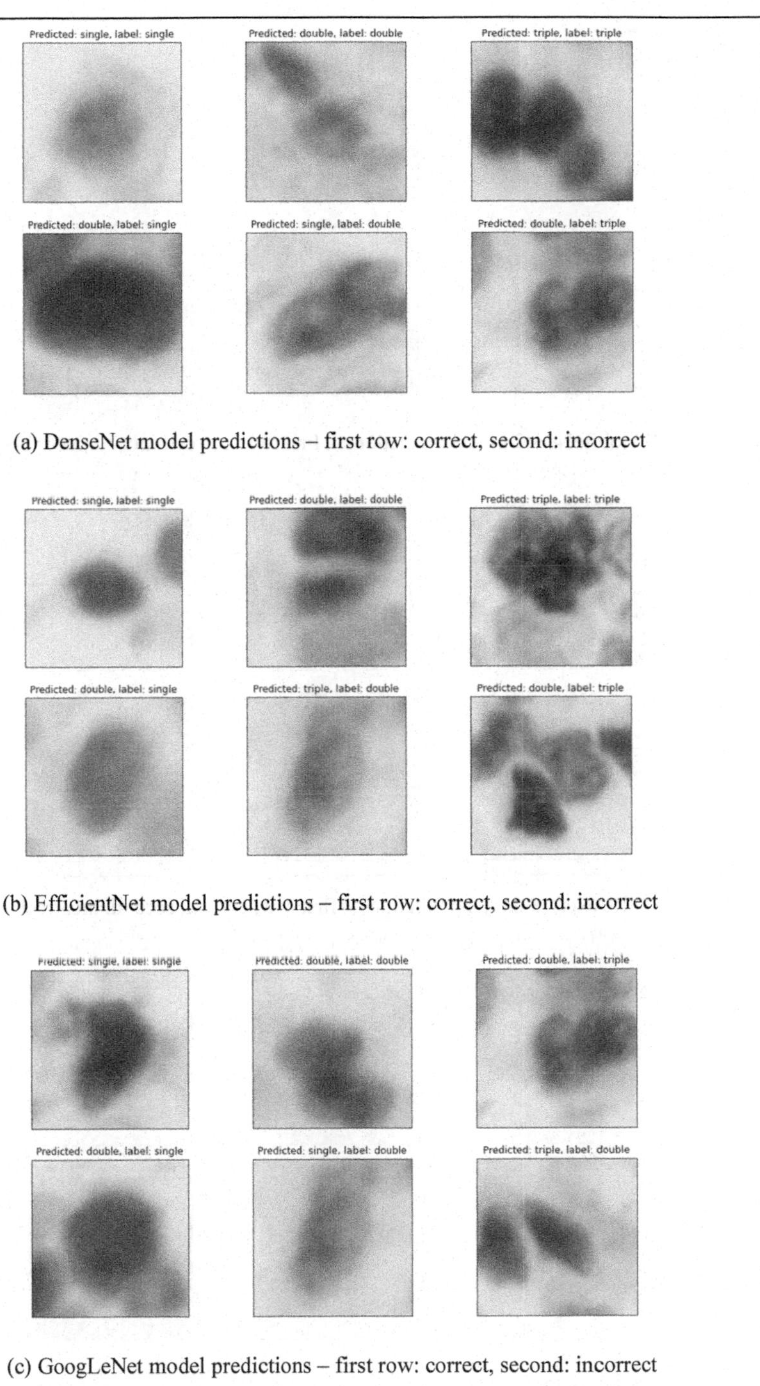

(a) DenseNet model predictions – first row: correct, second: incorrect

(b) EfficientNet model predictions – first row: correct, second: incorrect

(c) GoogLeNet model predictions – first row: correct, second: incorrect

Fig. 5. (a) – (f) Prediction examples

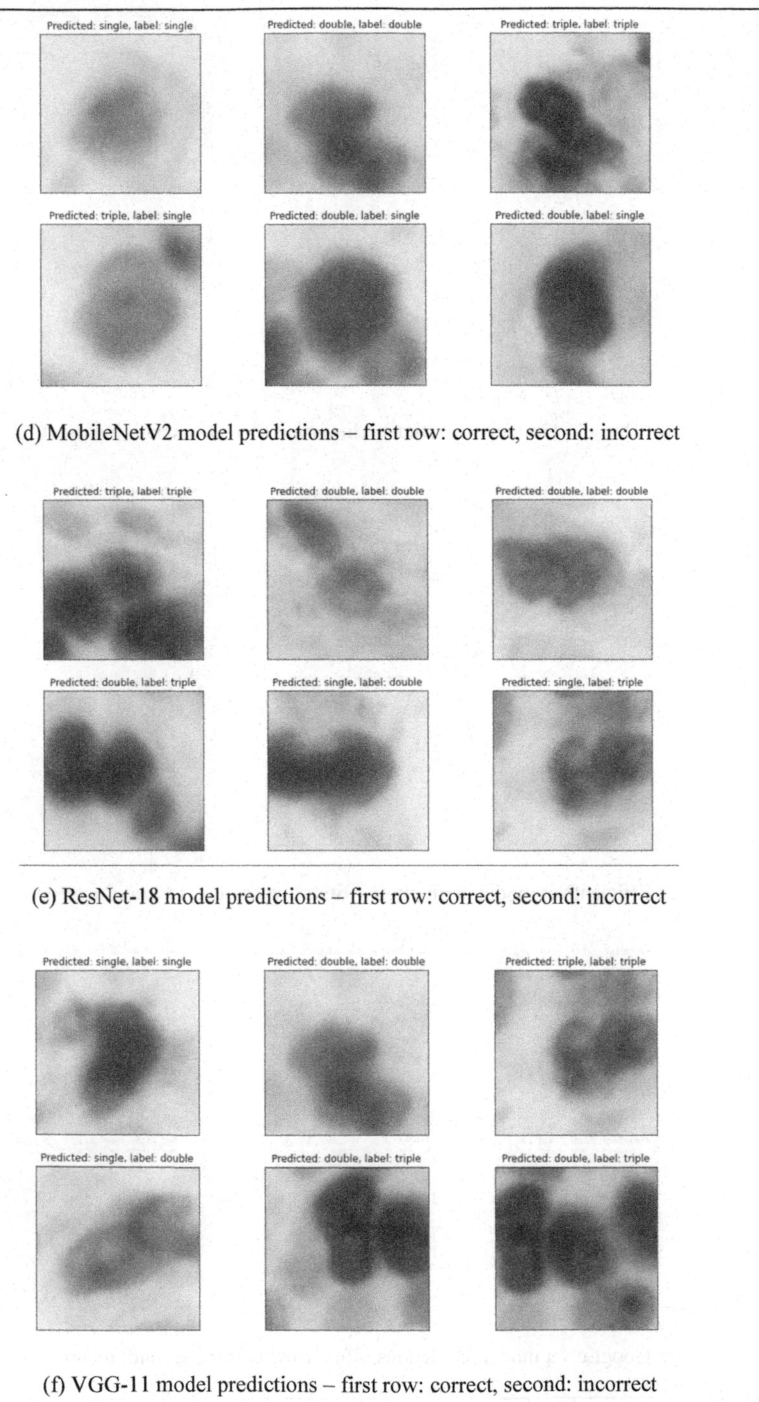

(d) MobileNetV2 model predictions – first row: correct, second: incorrect

(e) ResNet-18 model predictions – first row: correct, second: incorrect

(f) VGG-11 model predictions – first row: correct, second: incorrect

Fig. 5. continued

5 Discussion

Authors believe this research support the claim that deep learning models can be used with a success for morphological image processing of medical images. We achieved promising results, despite the relatively small number of data used in our experiments.

The strongest evidence lies within mislabeled test samples as presented in Fig. 6. This result shows that model learnt 'the idea of a cell' even if the dataset label was misleading. The model was able to correctly recognize the number of the cells in the sample. The incorrect label was probably a result of a semi-automatic data preparation which incorrectly cropped the original image.

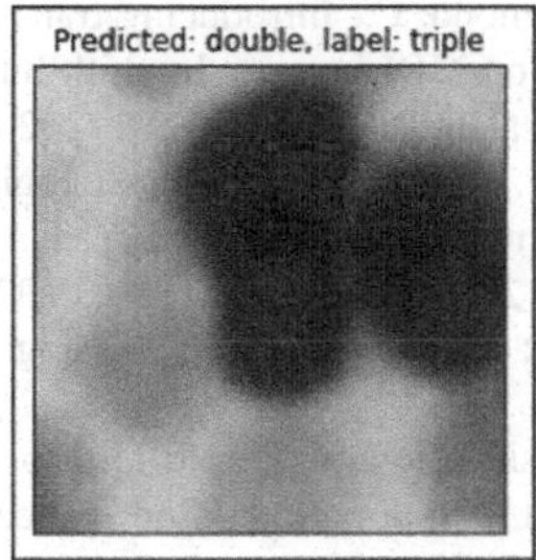

Fig. 6. A correct prediction against a mislabeled image as seen in Fig. 5 (f).

Our target was the specific problem of cell counting in histopathology structures with cell overlapping. In further research, we aim to improve our data sets both: in terms of histopathology data, but also in terms of data augmentation procedures. Additionally, we intend to improve the transfer learning applied by initial learning on histopathology data. Because of the lack of easily accessible data, for the purpose of this research, we applied initial learning on well-known image data sets, but not related to the research topic. Nevertheless, we still achieved good classification results. We believe that this paper gives new possibilities in the field of morphological image processing as the applied segmentation algorithms in medical image analysis do not have to be perfectly accurate. The recognition of cells in cell overlapping structures can be done within post-processing, by applying corresponding CNN models.

6 Conclusions

In this research, we applied successfully well-known CNN models in morphological image processing. We have achieved the best result with the EfficientNet model. Our research assumption and the achieved results prove the possibility to introduce new CNN applications in medical image analysis. As further work, we intend to evolve the morphological image processing proposed in terms of the data augmentation and the transfer learning process.

Acknowledgement. This work was supported by the statutory funds of the Department of Computational Intelligence, Faculty of Computer Science and Management, Wroclaw University of Science and Technology.

References

1. Buiu, C., Dănăilă, V.-R., Răduţă, C.N.: MobileNetV2 ensemble for cervical precancerous lesions classification. Processes **8**(5), 595 (2020)
2. Chetoui, M., Akhloufi, A.M.: Explainable diabetic retinopathy using EfficientNET. In: 42nd Annual International Conference of the IEEE Engineering in Medicine & Biology Society (EMBC). IEEE (2020)
3. Ebrahimi, A., Suhuai, L., Raymond, C.: Introducing transfer leaming to 3D ResNet-18 for Alzheimer's disease detection on MRI Images. In: 35th International Conference on Image and Vision Computing New Zealand (IVCNZ). IEEE (2020)
4. Fouad, S., Landini, G., Randell, D., Galton, A.: Morphological separation of clustered nuclei in histological images. In: Campilho, A., Karray, F. (eds.) ICIAR 2016. LNCS, vol. 9730, pp. 599–607. Springer, Cham (2016). https://doi.org/10.1007/978-3-319-41501-7_67
5. Gonzalez, R.C., Woods, R.E.: Digital Image Processing. 4th Edn. MedData Interactive, Pearson (2018)
6. Guo, M., Yongzhao, D.: Classification of thyroid ultrasound standard plane images using ResNet-18 networks. In: IEEE 13th International Conference on Anti-counterfeiting, Security, and Identification (ASID). IEEE (2019)
7. He, K., Zhang, X., Ren, S., Sun, J.: Identity mappings in deep residual networks. In: Leibe, B., Matas, J., Sebe, N., Welling, M. (eds.) ECCV 2016. LNCS, vol. 9908, pp. 630–645. Springer, Cham (2016). https://doi.org/10.1007/978-3-319-46493-0_38
8. Huang, G., Liu, Z., Van Der Maaten, L., Weinberger, K.Q.: Densely connected convolutional networks. In: IEEE Conference on Computer Vision and Pattern Recognition (CVPR), pp. 2261–2269 (2017)
9. Huang, Z., Zhu, X., Ding, M., Zhang, X.: Medical image classification using a light-weighted hybrid neural network based on PCANet and DenseNet. IEEE Access **8**, 24697–24712 (2020)
10. Kassani, S.H., Kassani, P.H., Wesolowski, M.J., Schneider, K.A., Deters, R.: Classification of histopathological biopsy images using ensemble of deep learning networks. arXiv preprint arXiv:1909.11870 (2019)
11. Kumar, A., Kim, J., Lyndon, D., Fulham, M., Feng, D.: An ensemble of fine-tuned convolutional neural networks for medical image classification. IEEE J. Biomed. Health Inform. **21**(1), 31–40 (2016)
12. Lakshmi, S., Vijayasenan, D., Sumam, D.S., Sreeram, S., Suresh, P.K.: An integrated deep learning approach towards automatic evaluation of Ki-67 labeling index. In: Proceedings of the TENCON, IEEE Region 10 Conference (TENCON), Kochi, India, 17–20 October, pp. 2310–2314 (2019)
13. Lim, K.-T., Park, S.-H., Kim, J., Seonwoo, H., Choung, P.-H., Chung, J.H.: Cell image processing method for automatic cell pattern recognition and morphological analysis of mesenchymal stem cells-an algorithm for cell classification and adaptive brightness correction. J. Biosyst. Eng. **38**, 55–63 (2013)
14. Lotufo, R.A., Rittner, L., Audigier, R., Machado, R.C., Saúde, A.V.: In: Deserno, T. (eds.) Biomedical Image Processing. Biological and Medical Physics, Biomedical Engineering. Springer, Heidelberg (2010). https://doi.org/10.1007/978-3-642-15816-2
15. Marques, G., Deevyankar, A., de la Torre Díez, I.: Automated medical diagnosis of COVID-19 through EfficientNet convolutional neural network. Appl. Soft Comput. **96**, 106691 (2020)

16. Negahbani, F., Sabzi, R., Pakniyat Jahromi, B., et al.: PathoNet introduced as a deep neural network backend for evaluation of Ki-67 and tumor-infiltrating lymphocytes in breast cancer. Sci. Rep. **11**, 8489 (2021)
17. Ragab, H.M., Samy, N., Afify, M., Maksoud, Nl. Abd El., Shaaban, H.A.M.: Assessment of Ki-67 as a potential biomarker in patients with breast cancer. J. Genet. Eng. Biotechnol. **16**, 479–484 (2018)
18. Rubin, J., Parvaneh, S., Rahman, A., Conroy, B., Babaeizadeh, S.: Densely connected convolutional networks for detection of atrial fibrillation from short single-lead ECG recordings. J Electrocardiol. **51**(6S), S18–S21 (2018)
19. Sandler, M., Howard, A., Zhu, M., Zhmoginov, A., Chen, L.-Ch.: MobileNetV2: inverted residuals and linear bottlenecks. In: Proceedings of the IEEE Conference on Computer Vision and Pattern Recognition (CVPR), pp. 4510–4520 (2018)
20. Saha, M., Chakraborty, C., Arun, I., et al.: An advanced deep learning approach for Ki-67 stained hotspot detection and proliferation rate scoring for prognostic evaluation of breast cancer. Sci. Rep. **7**, 3213 (2017)
21. Shvets, A., Rakhlin, A., Kalinin, A.A., Iglovikov, V.: Automatic instrument segmentation in robot-assisted surgery using deep learning. In: 17th IEEE International Conference on Machine Learning and Applications (ICMLA). IEEE (2018)
22. Siegel, R.L., Miller, K.D., Fuchs, H.E., Jemal, A.: Cancer statistics, 2021. CA Cancer J. Clin. **71**, 7–33 (2021)
23. Simonyan, K., Zisserman A.: Very deep convolutional networks for large-scale image recognition. In: 3rd International Conference on Learning Representations (ICLR) (2015)
24. Swiderska-Chadaj, Z., Gallego, J., Gonzalez-Lopez, L., Bueno, G.: Detection of Ki67 hotspots of invasive breast cancer based on convolutional neural networks applied to mutual information of H&E and Ki67 whole slide images. Appl. Sci. **10**, 7761 (2020)
25. Szegedy, C., Liu, W., Jia, Y., et al.: Going deeper with convolutions. In: Proceedings of the IEEE Conference on Computer Vision and Pattern Recognition (2015)
26. Tan, M., Quoc, L.: Efficientnet: Rethinking model scaling for convolutional neural networks. In: International Conference on Machine Learning. PMLR (2019)
27. Valkonen, M., Isola, J., Ylinen, O., Muhonen, V., Saxlin, A., Tolonen, T., Nykter, M., Ruusuvuori, P.: Cytokeratin-supervised deep learning for automatic recognition of epithelial cells in breast cancers stained for ER, PR, and Ki-67. IEEE Trans. Med. Imaging. **39**(2), 534–542 (2020)
28. Xie, S., Zheng, X., Chen, Y., et al.: Artifact removal using improved GoogLeNet for sparse-view CT reconstruction. Sci Rep. **8**(1), 6700 (2018)
29. Yang, Q., Yan, P., Kalra, M.K., Wang, G.: CT image denoising with perceptive deep neural networks. ArXiv170207019 Cs [Internet] (2017)

Developing a Three Dimensional Registration Method for Optical Coherence Tomography Data

Bansari Vadgama(✉), Doina Logofatu(✉), and Peter Thoma(✉)

Frankfurt University of Applied Sciences, 60318 Frankfurt am Main, Germany
{logofatu,peter.thoma}@fb2.fra-uas.de

Abstract. This work proposes a registration method for stitching different overlapping Optical Coherence Tomography (OCT) data. The algorithm is based on the basic procedure of image registration where key points and descriptors are located, feature matching is established and transformed using a homographic transformation to obtain the resultant registered images. Image similarity techniques such as mean square error, structural similarity index, and peak signal to noise ratio are the three basic approaches that are used for the analysis of these registered OCT images from the OCT datasets. An algorithm for locating the differences in the registered images against reference and target images is also demonstrated. Similarity measures and image differentiation approach provide a general analysis regarding the appropriateness of the image registration algorithm. The same methods are also used for the analysis of the optical coherence tomography volume scans. The analysis on the similarity of the images also shows that images with the highest similarities have the highest possibilities to be close to each other and can be further used for the registration. The analysis comprises the comparison of two optical coherence tomographic volumes.

Keywords: Image registration · Image similarity · Image differentiation · Optical coherence tomography

1 Introduction

In the biological system, Optical Coherence Tomography, widely known as OCT, has been introduced to have noninvasive cross-sectional imaging [2]. OCT is also known as high resolution optical imaging technique [1,3]. Tomographic techniques are meant for providing image slices of a three-dimensional object [4]. OCT has a wide range of applications in the medical field, but OCT has promising results in ophthalmology. OCT is considered a gold standard in diagnosing retinal diseases in ophthalmology [5].

Image registration can be defined as an approach for overlapping two or more images of the same scene taken at different times from different viewpoints by the

Frankfurt University of Applied Sciences.

K. Wojtkiewicz et al. (Eds.): ICCCI 2021, CCIS 1463, pp. 146–158, 2021.
https://doi.org/10.1007/978-3-030-88113-9_12

same or different sensors [5]. Overall, image registration can be divided into four parts: feature detection, feature matching, transform model estimation, and image resampling and transformation [5]. Image registration has a wide field of applications such as in remote sensing, image registration is necessary in multispectral classification, and environmental monitoring, change detection[5]. In the biomedical field, image registration is applied with imaging techniques such as Computed Tomography (CT), OCT, and Nuclear Magnetic Resonance [5].

Organoids are a 3D structure that is a collection of tissues derived from human stem cells [6]. Organoids can be classified as stem cells that are cultured in a 3D space in the presence of appropriate exogenic factors. These resultant structures, widely known as organoids, imitate the architecture of a particular organ in vitro [7]. OCT has been used in the research and analysis of organoids. In a 3D structure, tracking of the exposure-response in mammary epithelial organoids is implemented using OCT [8]. OCT imaging technology is adapted for analyzing the internal structures of human placenta-derived trophoblast organoids [9].

The research work and implementation are based on developing a three-dimensional (3D) registration technique for stitching two volumes of optical coherence tomography (OCT) data. A registration method has been proposed, which can expand the maximum volume that can be visualized. With OCT, it is possible to analyze a 3D structure, which can be further processed in the form of 2D sectional images. A possible field of application for the 3D registration of OCT data is the visualization of large 3D cell cultures. However, due to data availability issues, testing, analysis, and implementation have been performed on the OCT data of microlens and scotch tape data instead of the organoid. One of the main concerns here is identifying a higher similarity score or lower dissimilarity score to find images adjacent to each other for image registration. The implementation scope focuses on various issues related to the 3D registration technique, image comparison, identifying similarities and dissimilarities area between OCT images, analyzing these images, and finding similarity and dissimilarity measure w.r.t. various statistical techniques such as Mean Square Error (MSE), Structural Similarity Index (SSIM), and Peak Signal to Noise Ratio (PSNR). One approach is a direct one which is the image registration methodology, and the other one is an indirect approach where images with the highest similarity results can be used for the registration methodology. The discussed methods are also helpful in figuring out if images from the two different data sets have many similarities based on the OCT scans taken at different angles. An algorithm for locating the differences amongst the images also aids the performance of image similarity, which is also demonstrated as a part of the analysis.

2 Related Work

There exists much research and methodologies for 2D image registration. On the other hand, research in the direction of 2D-3D image registration is still growing. Other than OCT, image registration has been also implemented on imaging techniques such as X-Ray, MRI, Ultrasound, and CT [11,12]. An automated 3D registration approach for OCT was proposed by Yu Gan, Wang Yao, Kristin M. Myers, and Christine P. Hendon [9]. They proposed an image registration method for multiple overlapped OCT data into a single volume [9]. A nonrigid hierarchical approach for 3D medical image registration has also been proposed by Sunyeong Kim and Yu-Wing Tai [10]. Approaches such as distance coefficient mutual information (DCMI) and distance weighted mutual information (DWMI) have also been used for 2D/3D image registration [11].

Hybrid elastic registration algorithms are also used to register 3D gel electrophoresis images with the help of both, landmark, as well as intensity-based information [13]. Nonrigid registration methods are also presented for the registration of OCT images [14]. Artificial Intelligence (AI) and Machine Learning (ML) techniques have also been used for image registration. Quicksilver is a fast deformable image registration approach that is developed using a deep encoder-decoder network and this network acts as a predictive model [15]. An image registration algorithm consisting of a convolutional neural network (CNN) has also been proposed for the registration of retinal OCT images [16]. Srikar Appalaraju and Vineet Chaoji proposed an approach called SimNet which is based on a deep Siamese network and curriculum learning for figuring out the image similarities [17]. Deep learning techniques are also proposed which detect similarity metrics from the datasets of the images [18]. Unsupervised adversarial similarity networks have also been proposed for image registration and similarity detection [19]. Image differentiation method based on deep neural networks with unsupervised feature learning has also been proposed [20]. The amalgamation of various ML algorithms can also be used for detecting the changes in the images [21].

The image registration algorithm that has been proposed in this paper, includes feature detection, feature matching, transform model estimation, and the last one, image resampling and transformation. Feature detection has been done with the help of Oriented FAST and Rotated BRIEF (ORB). Feature matching has been established here with the help of brute force matcher and hamming distance measurement. The homographic transformation has been achieved here with the help of the RANSAC algorithm.

3 Experiment

3.1 Image Slicing

In the first step, images are sliced. In this module, 2D images are generated by slicing 3D OCT data along the X, Y, and Z-axis. These resultant sliced images along the X, Y, and Z-axis are later used for image registration, locating image differences, and finding image similarities. It forms the basis for experimental results. Microlens dataset consists of a total of 926 images with 128 slices across the X-axis, 670 slices across the Y-axis, and again 128 slices across Z-axis. The Scotch tape dataset consists of 3,388 images, with 1,694 images for the top view and 1,694 images for the bottom view. The top view and bottom view of OCT volumes are sliced across X, Y, and Z-axis. The top view and bottom view contain 512 slices across X-axis, 670 slices across Y-axis, and 512 slices across Z-axis.

3.2 Image Registration

In the second step, image registration is implemented. This algorithm aims to stitch multiple OCT images, however, two at a time, and produce a resultant registered image out of the two given images (Fig. 1).

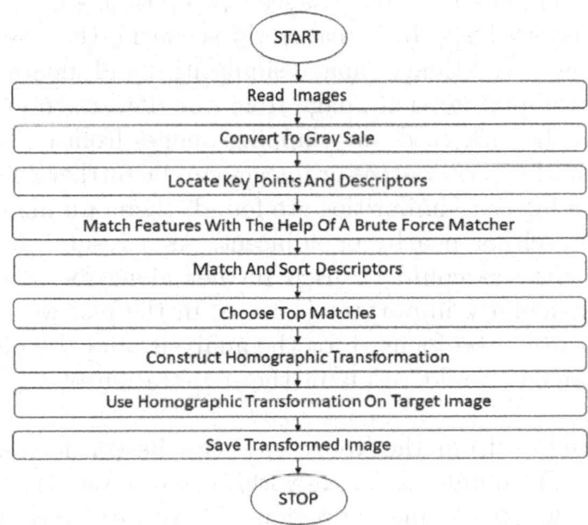

Fig. 1. Flowchart for the image registration algorithm

Initially, reference and targeted images are read and converted to grayscale. In the next step, key points and descriptors are located. Now, feature matching is established between the descriptors of the images with the help of brute force matching and sorted based on the hamming distance measurement. From these matches, the topmost 90% matches are selected by eliminating the noisy matches. At last, a homographic transformation is made on the targeted image by creating a homographic matrix with the help of the chosen matches.

3.3 Image Differentiation

It is not easy to differentiate OCT images since many times it does not have easily identifiable changes. As a result, the image differentiation algorithm is used for identifying the changes in the registered, base, and target images. Initially, a given set of images are imported and converted to grayscale. In the next step, the threshold for image differences is accomplished, and contours are found to acquire the difference of the images.

3.4 Image Similarity

The concept of image similarity is used to aid the results of image registration. In this module, image similarity is measured in terms of MSE, SSIM, and PSNR. In general, the algorithm takes a couple of images from a given set and checks the similarity score for MSE, SSIM, and PSNR. The usefulness of this concept is further explained below.

- The image similarity approach analyzes the results of image registration and verifies if the results are satisfactory.
- Image registration aims to stitch images. Two datasets of OCT volumes are necessary for the analysis. In a real-world scenario, the two datasets could have overlapping areas. Hence, image similarities and identicalness could be figured out by comparing each image from one dataset to every image from another dataset. In such cases, overlapping images from both datasets could be figured out, and adjacent areas or images can be further analyzed. Hence, if images with the highest similarities are found, there are higher chances that those images are either nearby or adjacent. As a result, these images with the highest similarities could be used further along for image registration. This case is particularly important because, in the real world, only slices of the OCT scans would be focused for the analysis, and the highest similarity results of the images could result in the registration of adjacent images or nearby images.
- The same procedure from the above case can be considered with different regions of the OCT volume. In a real-world scenario, the datasets may consist of volumetric images from different regions. There are chances that the volume could vary with perspective to angles, rotation, noise, unordered, and many other factors. Therefore, to ease the analysis process here, different sections of the images have been taken, and the same scenario from the above case has been applied.
- An amalgamation of approaches can also be done. For instance, image differentiation can be located based on image similarity, and similar volume regions can be identified.
- OCT scans showing higher similarities could be used further for testing other innovative image registration approaches.

4 Experimental Analysis

4.1 Image Registration

For microlens dataset, image registration is performed on first 21 images which are the OCT slices taken over Y-axis. Registered image is the resultant registered image of any two consecutive images from the dataset of 21 images. The resultant registered images are analyzed with the help of MSE, SSIM, and PSNR.

Graphs for the analysis of MSE, SSIM, and PSNR are given in Figs. 2, 3, and 4. Four image comparisons have significant lowest values for MSE; these values are

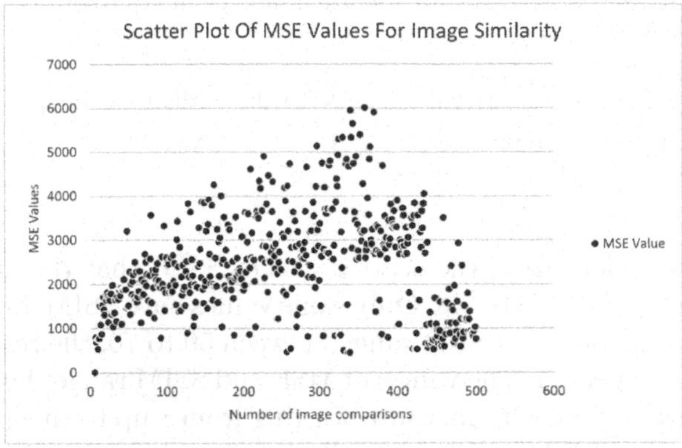

Fig. 2. Scatter plot of MSE values distribution for image comparisons of microlens OCT image registration

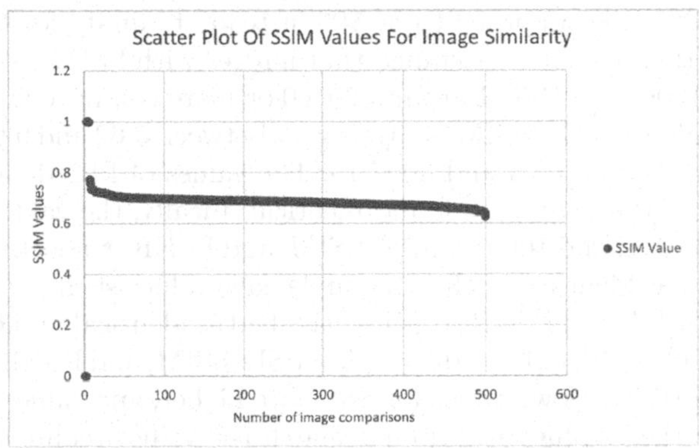

Fig. 3. Scatter plot of SSIM values distribution for image comparisons of microlens OCT image registration

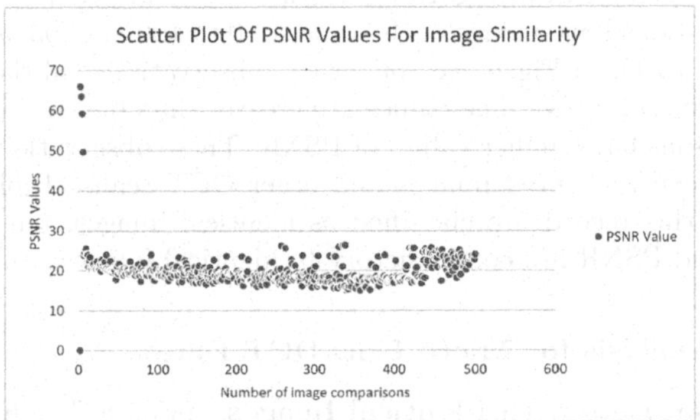

Fig. 4. Scatter plot of PSNR values distribution for image comparisons of microlens OCT image registration

Table 1. Similarity Score Analysis for identical images in microlens dataset indicating a FP

MSE value	SSIM value	PSNR value	Identical images
0.3	0.99	58.13	Yes

less than 3. It is evident from the scatter plot of SSIM that the majority of the SSIM values are between 0.6 to 0.8. Only some values have SSIM around 0.9. Only four values in the graphs for PSNR range between 50 to 70, the rest of the values are not as high as expected. The values of MSE and SSIM ranges between 0 and 1. For MSE, the lowest similarity measure starting from 1 up to the highest similarity measure of 0. For SSIM, the lowest similarity measure starting from 0 up to the highest similarity measure 1. The values of PSNR ranges from 0 to 100. For PSNR, the lowest similarity measure starting from 0 up to the highest similarity measure of infinity. However, for simpler understanding and analysis, the highest similarity measure of PSNR is supposed to be 100 instead of infinity for the analysis in the implementation. It can be assumed that images with SSIM greater than 0.6, MSE less than 1000, and PSNR around 50–60 or more can have greater similarities. Here, the values for the SSIM analysis vary between 0.62 and 0.99. The values for MSE ranges between 0.04 and 6007.10. The values of PSNR ranges between 56.86 and 15.11. Two images are found identical. Ideally, the values for identical images should be 0, 1, and 100 for MSE, SSIM, and PSNR, respectively. However, images identified as identical in the first tuple have values such as 0.08, 0.99, and 63.48 for MSE, SSIM, and PSNR. Images classified as identical in the second tuple also have values like 0.23, 0.99, and 59.24 for MSE, SSIM, and PSNR, respectively. Here values for MSE are low, values for SSIM are higher, and values for PSNR are also higher, but these values still do not match the values required for the ideal identicalness. In a realistic scenario, there are very rare chances of images being identical. Therefore, it can be classified as a false positive(FP) (Table 1).

Graphs in Figs. 5, 6, and 7 illustrate the scatter plot of the distribution of values for image comparisons regarding MSE, SSIM, and PSNR, respectively. In Fig. 5, 6 observations have values in the range of 0 to 100, and 93 observations lie between 100 and 200. In Fig. 6, except for two observations, all the comparisons have higher values of SSIM. The values are greater than 0.8. In Fig. 7, only four image comparisons have higher values of PSNR. These observations show higher similarity between registered images and other OCT scans. Table 2 displays a FP. Images in this record are classified as identical images, but the values of MSE, SSIM, and PSNR are contradictory to identical images.

4.2 Image Analysis for Micro Lens OCT Data

Analysis of Datasets with Identical Images. Two OCT volumes are compared in this analysis. The first dataset consists of 20 images, and the second dataset also consists of 20 images. Both the datasets have ten common OCT scans. Common OCT images are identified with 0, 1, and 100 values for MSE,

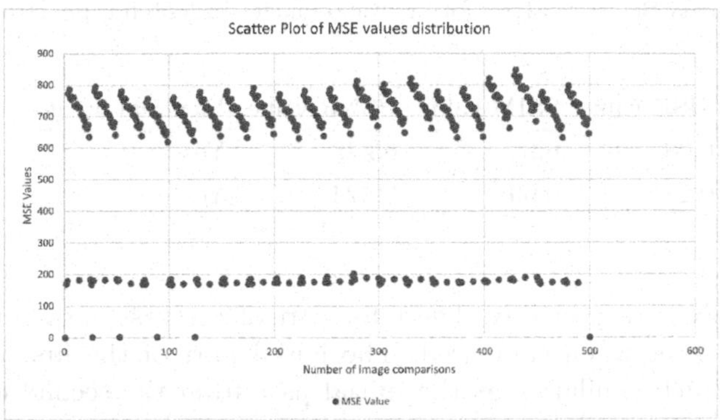

Fig. 5. Scatter plot of MSE values distribution for image comparisons of scotch tape OCT image registration

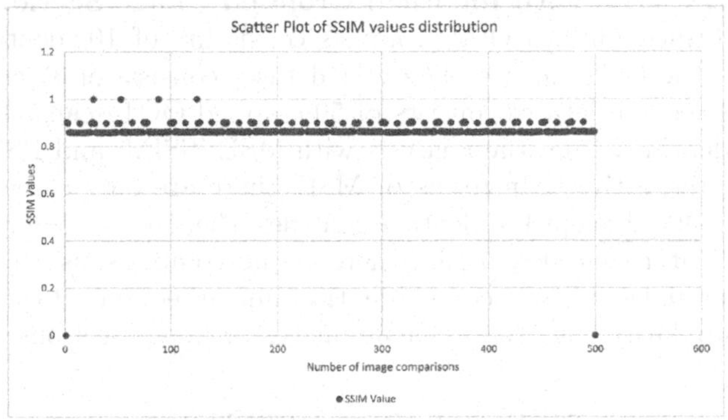

Fig. 6. Scatter plot of SSIM values distribution for image comparisons of scotch tape OCT image registration

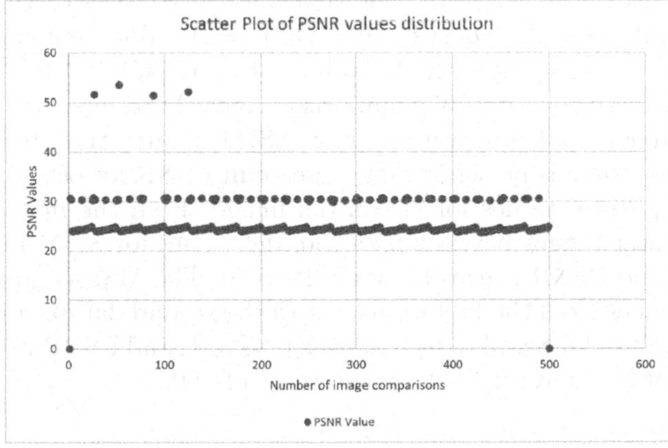

Fig. 7. Scatter plot of PSNR values distribution for image comparisons of scotch tape OCT image registration

Table 2. Similarity Score Analysis for identical images in scotch tape dataset indicating a FP

MSE value	SSIM value	PSNR value	Identical images
0.08	0.99	63.48	Yes
0.23	0.99	59.24	Yes

SSIM, and PSNR, respectively. The later part of the first dataset is similar to the second dataset when compared. The initial part of the first dataset does not show as much similarity as the initial part from the second dataset. The common set of images also shows more similarity with images in proximity than the distant images.

Analysis of Datasets with Identical Cropped Image Sections. Analysis has been performed on two OCT volumes consisting of 10 identical cropped sections out of the OCT images. The first dataset consists of 35 cropped OCT scans, and the second dataset consists of 50 cropped OCT scans. The identical matches are identified from the analysis with MSE, SSIM, and PSNR equal to 0, 1, and 100, respectively. In terms of MSE, there are only three comparison scores less than 300. Except for identical matches, there are no comparisons with SSIM scores greater than 0.8. Again, there are no comparisons except identical matches having higher PSNR scores. Identical image sections of the images also show a little similarity with their nearby images or image sections.

4.3 Image Analysis for Scotch Tape OCT Data

Analysis of Datasets with Identical Images. Analysis has been done on two OCT volumes sharing some identical scans. There is a total of 10 identical OCT images common in both datasets. The first dataset consists of 20 OCT scans, and the second dataset also consists of 20 OCT scans. Ten identical sections are identified from the analysis with the values of 0, 1, and 100 for MSE, SSIM, and PSNR, respectively. Total 37 comparisons have MSE less than 300. Except for two comparisons, all observations have SSIM greater than 0.8. Except for identical images, there is no significant increase in PSNR for other observations. The MSE comparison values for the initial images from the first dataset with the second dataset ranges between 600–700, the values for SSIM range between 0.85 and 0.86, and PSNR ranges between 24 to 30. The MSE comparison values for the later images from the first dataset with the second dataset range between 200–700. The values for SSIM range between 0.85 to 1, and PSNR ranges between 24 to 28 with only one record having the value of 100.

Analysis of Datasets with Identical Cropped Image Sections. Two OCT volumes having identical cropped sections from OCT images are used for the analysis. There are ten identical image sections common in both datasets. The first dataset consists of 50 cropped OCT sections, and the second dataset consists of 60 cropped OCT sections. The analytical results for identical image comparisons are 0, 1, and 100 for MSE, SSIM, and PSNR. Many values have lower similarity scores for MSE, but only identical sections have the lowest similarity scores. All other comparisons have similarity scores greater than 300. Except for identical sections, there are no other comparisons having SSIM values greater than 0.8. Also, no image comparisons have a higher similarity score for PSNR except identical sections.

5 Experimental Summary

This section gives a detailed summary involving the entire experiment. Initially, the 3D OCT data is sliced in the X, Y, and Z-axis. The resultant axial images form the sample datasets for the algorithms. An algorithm is implemented which registers OCT images. This algorithm is used to register the scans taken out of the 3D OCT volume. The image registration algorithm has been implemented on 3D OCT datasets of microlens and scotch tape. The algorithm works successfully on both datasets. The resultant registered images are analyzed and compared against the OCT images used for the registration. These analytical reports show many similarities in MSE and SSIM, but PSNR does not show any significant results for the comparisons. Many image comparisons with MSE values are less than 300 and SSIM greater than 0.8, indicating the highest similarities in the registered and other OCT images in both the datasets. On the other hand, some FP are classified as identical images for registered and other OCT images. However, these records should be considered as comparisons with the highest similarities but not identical images due to their contradicting values of MSE and SSIM instead of 0 and 1, respectively. Hence, the analysis concludes that the image registration algorithm is employed correctly.

Further analysis has also been done on the 3D OCT volume of the microlens and scotch tape dataset. The analysis is classified into two types of image comparisons for both the datasets: analysis of datasets with common images and analysis of datasets with common cropped image sections. Identical images and cropped image sections are identified with the values 0,1, and 100 for MSE, SSIM, and PSNR, respectively.

- Datasets with identical OCT volume: Here, identical OCT volumes from both datasets are recognized. The identical images, which are common in both the datasets, showed a maximum number of similarities in MSE and SSIM with the images in their proximity. The proportion of similarities decreases as the proximity increases.
- Datasets with identical cropped OCT image sections: Here, identical OCT volumes from both datasets are recognized. The cropped image sections do not show many similarities with other sections overall. Higher similarities are observed but individually in terms of MSE or SSIM, not together. Image comparisons showing the highest similarities in terms of MSE and SSIM are rarely observed.

The analysis shows that the lowest similarities are primarily observed in the image comparisons. However, the highest similarities are observed when MSE is less than 300, SSIM is greater than 0.85, and PSNR should be as high as possible, especially with current algorithms; it should be at least higher than 90. Observations with image similarity scores are found and can be classified as examples of images or image sections with higher similarity. It can also be concluded from the analysis that images that are in proximity of each other or consecutive images show a higher number of similarity scores in terms of MSE and SSIM compared to distant images.

In a real scenario, when the images are compared, similarity scores can assist greatly in deciding whether images are nearby. Cropped image sections represent any arbitrary section from the image. There is a high probability that OCT datasets will have images that are not aligned, tilted, with some degrees of rotation, and much more in a realistic situation. As a result, cropped image sections are used as a reference for testing the algorithm on the sample datasets. This similarity analysis can be used with the whole images or image sections for checking the nearness of the images or their sections. The highest similarity results obtained after analyzing the similarity scores of the image comparisons can be used further for registering the images with the proposed algorithm. The results can also be used as sample images in the development of any other image registration approaches. Additionally, the similarity measures are also helpful for analyzing and verifying the registered images. In this case, similarity scores help figure out how much similarity exists between the reference, target, and registered images. Also, image differentiation algorithms are very much beneficial, especially in this scenario. It aids the resultant analysis of differentiating the specific area of the images altered in the registered images. As a result, similarity scores and altered regions can both be identified with the help of the prevailing methods. The analysis also states that similarity measures such as MSE and SSIM yield relevant results. However, the PSNR approach failed to provide the desired results.

6 Conclusion and Future Work

The proposed registration algorithm works successfully for registering images. An algorithm is a step-by-step approach by slicing the 3D OCT data and registering the slices to get the resultant registered images. Furthermore, similarity approaches are used for analyzing the result of the registration. MSE, SSIM, and PSNR are the three concepts used in calculating image similarities. However, MSE and SSIM have proven to yield significant results compared to PSNR. Images tend to have a higher number of similarities where MSE is less than 300 and SSIM is greater than 0.85. Additionally, similarity approaches are also used on the raw datasets to find the OCT volume having the highest similarity. The resultant images can be further used for registration in the proposed algorithm or sample datasets in other innovative registration methods. The proposed image registration approach can also be further developed to aggregate more datasets.

Deep Learning can also be used to develop methods for the aggregation of larger datasets and image registration. Further development can be established using machine learning approaches such as deep neural networks and other algorithms in image similarity detection, image registration, and identifying image differences for 3D OCT data.

References

1. Podoleanu, A.G.: Optical coherence tomography. Br. J. Radiol. **78**(935), 976–988 (2005). PMID: 16249597
2. Huang, D., et al.: Optical coherence tomography. Science **254**(5035), 1178–1181 (1991)
3. Podoleanu, A.G.: Optical coherence tomography. J. Microsc. **247**(3), 209–219 (2012)
4. Fercher, A.F., Drexler, W., Hitzenberger, C.K., Lasser, T.: Optical coherence tomography-principles and applications. Rep. Prog. Phys. **66**(2), 239 (2003)
5. Zitová, B., Flusser, J.: Image registration methods: a survey. Image Vis. Comput. **21**(11), 977–1000 (2003)
6. Browne, A.W., et al.: Structural and functional characterization of human stem-cell-derived retinal organoids by live imaging. Invest. Ophthalmol. Vis. Sci. **58**, 3311–3318 (2017)
7. Sun, Y., Ding, Q.: Genome engineering of stem cell organoids for disease modeling. Protein Cell **8**(5), 315–327 (2017). https://doi.org/10.1007/s13238-016-0368-0
8. Yang, L., Yu, X., Fuller, A.M., Troester, M.A., Oldenburg, A.L.: Characterizing optical coherence tomography speckle fluctuation spectra of mammary organoids during suppression of intracellular motility. Quant. Imaging Med. Surg. **10**(1), 76 (2020)
9. Gan, Y., Yao, W., Myers, K.M., Hendon, C.P.: An automated 3D registration method for optical coherence tomography volumes. In: 2014 36th Annual International Conference of the IEEE Engineering in Medicine and Biology Society, pp. 3873–3876 (2014)
10. Kim, S., Tai, Y.: Hierarchical nonrigid model for 3D medical image registration. In: 2014 IEEE International Conference on Image Processing (ICIP), pp. 3562–3566 (2014)
11. Wang, L., Gao, X., Zhang, R., Xia, W.: A comparison of two novel similarity measures based on mutual information in 2D/3D image registration. In: 2013 IEEE International Conference on Medical Imaging Physics and Engineering, pp. 215–218. IEEE (2013)
12. Huang, X., et al.: Dynamic 2D ultrasound and 3D CT image registration of the beating heart. IEEE Trans. Med. Imaging **28**(8), 1179–1189 (2009)
13. Worz, S., Winz, M.-L., Rohr, K.: Geometric alignment of 2D gel electrophoresis images using physics-based elastic registration. In: 2008 5th IEEE International Symposium on Biomedical Imaging: From Nano to Macro, pp. 1135–1138. IEEE (2008)
14. Lee, S., Lebed, E., Sarunic, M.V., Beg, M.F.: Exact surface registration of retinal surfaces from 3-D optical coherence tomography images. IEEE Trans. Biomed. Eng. **62**(2), 609–617 (2015)
15. Yang, X., Kwitt, R., Styner, M., Niethammer, M.: Quicksilver: fast predictive image registration-a deep learning approach. NeuroImage **158**, 378–396 (2017)

16. Arikan, M., Sadeghipour, A., Gerendas, B., Told, R., Schmidt-Erfurt, U.: Deep learning based multi-modal registration for retinal imaging. In: Suzuki, K., et al. (eds.) ML-CDS/IMIMIC -2019. LNCS, vol. 11797, pp. 75–82. Springer, Cham (2019). https://doi.org/10.1007/978-3-030-33850-3_9
17. Appalaraju, S., Chaoji, V.: Image similarity using deep CNN and curriculum learning (2017)
18. Wang, J., et al.: Learning fine-grained image similarity with deep ranking. In: Proceedings of the IEEE Conference on Computer Vision and Pattern Recognition, pp. 1386–1393 (2014)
19. Fan, J., Cao, X., Xue, Z., Yap, P.-T., Shen, D.: Adversarial similarity network for evaluating image alignment in deep learning based registration. In: Frangi, A.F., Schnabel, J.A., Davatzikos, C., Alberola-López, C., Fichtinger, G. (eds.) MICCAI 2018. LNCS, vol. 11070, pp. 739–746. Springer, Cham (2018). https://doi.org/10.1007/978-3-030-00928-1_83
20. Zhao, J., Gong, M., Liu, J., Jiao, L.: Deep learning to classify difference image for image change detection. In: 2014 International Joint Conference on Neural Networks (IJCNN), pp. 411–417. IEEE (2014)
21. Chan, J.C.-W., Chan, K.-P., Yeh, A.G.-O.: Detecting the nature of change in an urban environment: a comparison of machine learning algorithms. Photogram. Eng. Remote Sens. **67**(2), 213–226 (2001)

Which Gameplay Aspects Impact the Immersion in Virtual Reality Games?

Marek Kopel(✉) and Marta Rutkowska

Faculty of Computer Science and Management, Wroclaw University of Science and Technology, wybrzeze Wyspiańskiego 27, 50-370 Wroclaw, Poland
marek.kopel@pwr.edu.pl

Abstract. In this paper a comparison of two implementations of the same game is presented: a VR (virtual reality) version and a traditional one, meaning with no VR hardware used. The implementations' design - made specially for this research - is the result of the analysis of many state-of-the VR games. The comparison's goal is to find the aspects of gameplay that impact user immersion in a video game. Each extracted aspect is covered by a question in a post experiment questionnaire and discussed before final conclusions are drawn.

Keywords: Virtual reality · Non-VR · Traditional · Video game · Immersion

1 Introduction

Over the last decade the latest wave of VR hardware from HTC, Valve and Oculus, but also by Microsoft (Windows Mixed Reality) and Sony (Playstation VR) has been changing the video game industry in a more and more extensive way. Since last year, its popularity has additionally increased due to COVID 19 restrictions. Nevertheless, there are still many challenges to overcome before an HMD (Head-Mounted Display) becomes a default hardware for a regular player. Today VR games offer some killer gameplay mechanics that cannot be replicated in any traditional (non-VR) environment and seem to be designed specially for VR, e.g. slicing with a sword or shooting a longbow. But the non-VR gameplay has many more mechanics that are still a challenge to implement in VR without breaking the immersion. Even with something as crucial as navigation without causing a VR sickness [8] or preventing users from "walking through walls" [4]. In this research we try to look at gameplay mechanics that work best in VR or non-VR environments and find the factors that are responsible for breaking the immersion when the mechanics is ported to the other platform.

2 Related Works

For a long time now immersion has been considered as important as interactivity in VR systems [6]. In [1] authors do a VR literature review and distinguish 3 types

K. Wojtkiewicz et al. (Eds.): ICCCI 2021, CCIS 1463, pp. 159–171, 2021.
https://doi.org/10.1007/978-3-030-88113-9_13

of system: non-immersive, immersive (using HMD) and semi-immersive (using stereo image monitors). One of the objectives in [2] is to determine conceptual rationale (purpose) for immersive VR implementations. The findings contained: the purpose of skill training, the optimization of interactivity between users and objects, highlighting of objects in both the virtual or real world but also the purposes of engagement, safety, convenience, team building, and suggestion. Authors also claim the immersion to be one of three features for full VR experience. The other two are interaction and imagination. In [5] authors indicate that player's frustration encompass both positive and negative aspects and the positive frustration is desirable for developers due to it improving the immersion and motivation in games and comes from players learning through frustration.

2.1 Gameplay Aspects that Impact Immersion and VR Sickness

Literature analysis allowed to extract essential aspect of video games that may impact immersion. All those aspect drove the design and implementations of games used in this research. Moreover, those aspect highlight the most important differences between immersion in traditional platform and VR. Those aspect are: difficulty of the game, sensations regarding movement activities, sensations regarding interaction activities, intuitive game controls, feeling of freedom in the game world, physical involvement, physical discomfort, intuitive user interface, sounds, graphics effects, emotional experiences, technical problems. All of those are covered by post-experiment questionnaire in Subsect. 3.4. This kind of tools for VR research is widely used [7].

The research objective is to investigate weather an implementation of a video game in VR allows for a stronger sense of immersion for the player and what gameplay aspects (factors) work along or against that including causing the VR sickness.

3 The Experiment

Since the research subject is to compare immersion in a traditional video game and its implementation in VR, a special experimental environment - in the form of a game - has been designed and implemented. This experimental environment was developed for VR and non-VR platform, after analysis of state-of-the-art VR games (i.e. Half-Life: Alyx, Beat Saber, Lone Echo) and VR adaptations of non-VR games (i.e. SuperHot, HellBlade, Skyrim VR, Fallout 4 VR). Determining the level of immersion is based on the user's assessment of his experiences, emotions, commitment, sense of realism, as well as impressions from individual elements of the game. On this basis, conclusions are drawn regarding the differences in the sense of immersion between the VR and non-VR implementations of the same game.

The most important feature of the designed experimental environment is that it should be designed for two platforms: a VR platform and a traditional desktop computer platform. The experimental environment in the form of a game should have the same functionalities, but appropriately adapted to a given platform. These functionalities should be selected to adequately address the differences between VR and non-VR games. Then it is possible to demonstrate the most significant differences in the experiences and sense of immersion of the examined person. An important aspect in the vision of the designed experimental environment is also ensuring the possibility of collecting appropriate data on the feelings of the examined person. This can be achieved by preparing questionnaires that should appear at appropriate moments in the game. These questionnaires contain questions that are be strictly related to the subject of research.

3.1 The Environment Implementation - a VR and a Non-VR Game

In order to implement the experimental environment Unity Engine in version 2019.4 was used. The programming language used was C# version 7.3. All 3D models as well as textures, graphic effects and 2D graphics have been prepared independently. The sounds used in the game are royalty free. The libraries used for the graphics purposes were ProBuilder and UModeller. Thanks to them, it was possible to prepare the research environment from the graphic side.

Appropriate libraries and tools were also used. The most important library from the perspective of the implementation of the experimental environment was the Unity XR library [3]. This library allows programming games using Unity Engine for VR platforms. Thanks to the XR library, it is possible to connect a VR headset to the game, as well as to operate the goggles and controllers.

Fig. 1. Screenshots of the two corresponding experiment environment implementations: non-VR (left) and VR (right) showing interacting with objects. In non-VR the player is informed in the right lower part of the UI that he is crouching. White circle in the middle of the screen indicates the interaction cursor. In VR the cube is grabbed with a virtual hand.

The objective of the experiment game is to move from the starting point to the finish point without being spotted by opponents (cameras) positioned in the play area. To facilitate the transition from point A to point B, the player can use appropriate objects that can temporarily reduce the alertness of the cameras. To avoid being spotted by an enemy, player can use multiple game mechanics. The first one is hiding behind objects. This mechanic allows the player to avoid being seen by a camera. For example, if the player is hidden behind an object in the game that would obscure him from the camera's point of view, he would not be detected by the camera.

Another game mechanic that allows the player to avoid being seen by cameras is to place objects in the camera's view field, for example by throwing them. Screenshots of interaction with cubes in VR and non-VR implementations are shown in Fig. 1. The camera, during detecting a suspicious object, will stop there for a certain time to detect it. During this time, the player can try to sneak past the camera. After the set time to recognize the object, the camera continues scanning the area, ignoring the previously placed object, because having recognized it, it remembers it and is no longer sensitive to it (Fig. 2).

Fig. 2. Screenshot comparison of shooting a projectile with smoke into the camera's view field on non-VR (left) and VR (right) platform. In non-VR the gun is attached to the camera (is always visible in the same way), so aiming (with a white dot in the middle) means moving the camera. In VR version the gun (being held in right hand) is independent of the camera and aiming is done by moving the gun itself (without the need of moving player's head, i.e. moving the camera.

On of the aspects which is taken under the consideration during the experiment is user interface and its intuitiveness. To interact with the user interface on the traditional platform player is using the mouse movement and left-clicks on the interface elements. To enter text on the screen (for example, in the case of entering the participant's ID), the player has to use the keyboard. Interaction with the interface in the main menu is presented in Fig. 3.

User interface in VR uses a laser pointer leading from the controller to the front. To interact with the objects on the interface, laser pointer was used with the help of a trigger button. In order to enter text on the screen (for example, in the case of entering the ID of the participant), the player has to use a virtual keyboard, implemented especially for this purpose.

The user interface for the questionnaires was implemented in accordance with the designed interface prototype for the experimental environment. There were a maximum of three questions on one page of the questionnaire. The implementation of the questionnaire in non-VR platform has been presented in Fig. 4.

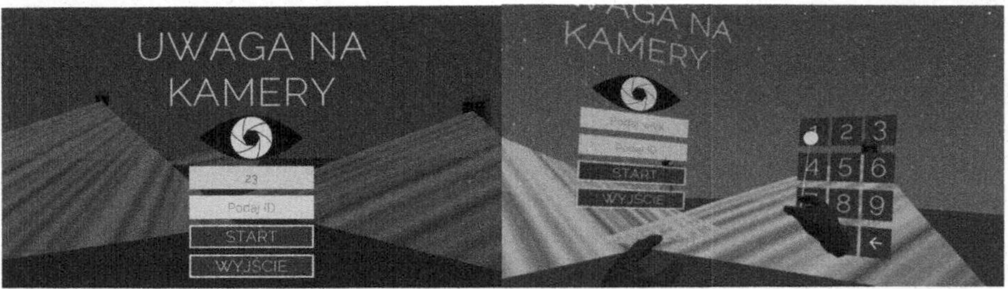

Fig. 3. Comparison of user interface in non-VR (left) and VR (right) implementation. In non-VR the user can input his age using physical keyboard. In VR the user cannot see any real world objects, so there is a virtual keyboard he can use to input data.

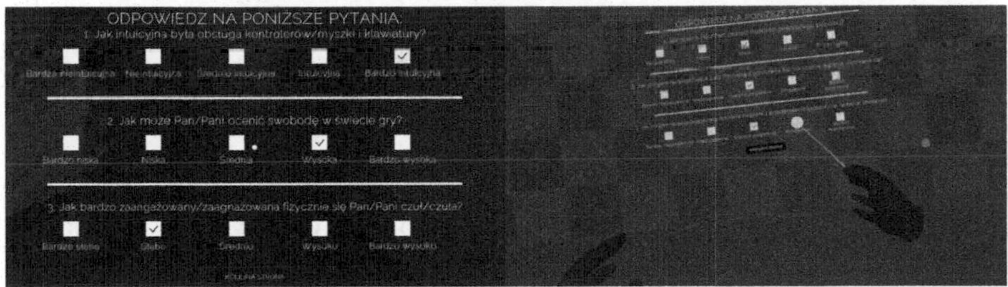

Fig. 4. User interface of the post experiment questionnaire in the non-VR platform. In non-VR the questionnaire works like a traditional desktop form. In VR the questionnaire checkboxes are placed on a virtual wall and user can check the boxes with a virtual beam.

3.2 Experiment Procedure

As part of the research, two empirical research methods were used: questionnaires and observation of the respondents. In the prepared research environment questions were displayed in the form of questionnaires, to which the respondent had to answer.

The second method was observation of the research participants during the experiment. All significant observations from the perspective of the conducted research were noted. These comments were mainly related to behavior, reactions, problems encountered, verbal comments, motor skills etc.

3.3 Research Group

The research was conducted on 26 people. Each of them operated in the research environment on two platforms: VR and traditional one. Thirteen people started the experiment on the traditional platform, and the remaining thirteen started with VR (starting the research by all people from the same platform could have an impact on the results for the other platform).

The profile of the examined person was the same. The examined person had previous experiences with VR and is familiar with playing video games. Participant also uses new technologies on a daily basis, such as a computer or smartphone. Most of the respondents were 20–30 years old, with high physical fitness. None of the respondents had contraindications in the form of serious diseases (e.g. epilepsy) or body injuries.

In the study for the traditional platform, equipment in the form of a desktop computer was used. All participants used the same equipment in the form of a monitor, mouse, keyboard and headphones. In the study for the VR platform, the Oculus Quest 2 VR headset was used with its controllers. The cable-less experience and the high-enough resolution are the main factors for the choice. Moreover the hardware aspects are outside of this research scope.

3.4 The Questionnaire

The questionnaire appearing in the research environment was used to collect data on the feelings of the participant during the game. This survey and the questions contained therein were built on the basis of a literature analysis and an analysis of existing video games made in VR and non-VR versions. The questions were divided into two groups: questions about the subject of research, which is immersion, and questions about the participant profile, for example about his experience with VR games. The questionnaire consisted of 15 questions. The questions asked in the research environment were the same in the non-VR and VR versions. They are listed below:

1. How do you evaluate the difficulty of the level you have overcome?
2. How enjoyable and engaging were the sensations of moving, turning, crouching, hiding?
3. How enjoyable and engaging was the experience with the objects? (lifting, throwing, shooting)?
4. How intuitive was the use of the controllers (in case of virtual reality)/mouse and keyboard (in case of traditional platform)?
5. How can you evaluate the freedom in the game world?
6. How much did you feel physically involved?
7. Was there any physical discomfort during the game (like nausea, headaches, eye strain)?
8. How intuitive and pleasant was the use of the user interface?
9. How realistic were the sounds in the game?
10. How pleasant were the graphics effects and models in the game?
11. How high were your emotional experiences (like adrenaline, satisfaction)?
12. How many technical problems were encountered?
13. How experienced are you with virtual reality games?
14. How experienced are you with video games in general?

The answers to those questions were from range 1 to 5, and were customized depending on the question. For example, answers to the question "How do you evaluate the difficulty of the level you have overcome?" the answer range from 1 to 5 is interpreted as from "very easy" to "very difficult".

4 Results

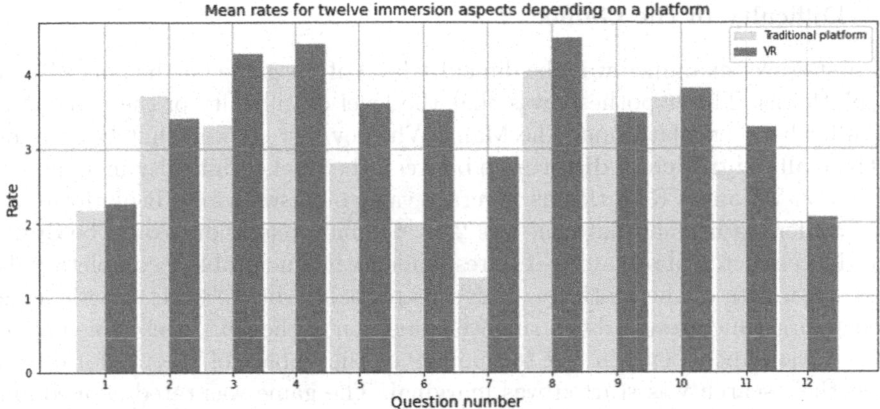

Fig. 5. Average rating of the aspects impacting immersion in non-VR (orange) and VR (red) environments. All answer's are ranging from 1 to 5. For the legend of horizontal axis please refer to the questions in Sect. 3.4. (Color figure online)

The collected data consisted of answers given by 26 people on each of the two platforms, which made up 52 records in the table. One person was not able to finish the experiment due to VR motion sickness. This person was also taken into the consideration. Each participant had previous experiences with virtual reality and is medium to highly advanced in playing video games (covered by question 14). The data analysis was performed from three perspectives: a comprehensive comparison of the results for two platforms, a comparison of the results for two platforms in terms of the advancement of the test person with VR technology and from the perspective of comparing the results for two platforms depending on whether the test person started the study from the non-VR or the VR platform. Average experiment session length per one participant was 25 min. Each participant played once on the VR platform and once on the traditional platform. The break between playing on another platform was approximately 1 min.

In the case of advancement of the subject with VR technologies, it was assumed that the person considered highly experienced with VR, when asked "How experienced are you with VR games?", answered "high" or "very high". People who answered "not at all", "little" or "average" were considered as not advanced with VR technology. The distribution of these people was as follows. There was 8 participants advanced in the VR technology and 18 not advanced.

Because the data (even divided into sets related to a specific question) did not come from a normal distribution, the non-parametric Mann-Whitney test was used to analyze the collected data. The data was processed and analyzed using the Python programming language, using pandas, numpy, statistics, and matplotlib libraries. The results of twelve examined aspects of immersion were presented in Fig. 5.

4.1 Difficulty of the Game

The first aspect examined was the difficulty level of the game for the non-VR and VR platforms. The hypothesis was that the level of difficulty of the game does not differ between platforms. The Mann-Whitney test showed that there is **no statistically significant difference** between the level of difficulty in gameplay on the non-VR and VR platforms. Average value of answers for VR platform was 2.27 and for traditional platform was 2.18. Similar conclusions could be drawn from the conducted observation. The respondents had no problem completing the game, regardless of the platform. This was probably due to their experience in video games, which resulted in a smooth transition to the next levels. The impact of the advancement level in VR technology or the impact of the platform from which the research was started was marginal. The game was rated as medium-easy. It can therefore be concluded that the player did not experience frustration with the level of difficulty that would affect the sense of immersion. VR games are usually considered more difficult but the research conducted does not confirm this. It can therefore be concluded that in terms of the level of difficulty, the **level of immersion between the platforms was similar**.

4.2 Sensations Regarding Movement Activities

Another aspect examined, was the sensations of moving, turning, crouching and hiding from opponents. The statistical test showed that there are significant differences in sensations related to motor activities between VR and non-VR platforms. The one-sided test showed that the experiences were found to be **more enjoyable on the non-VR platform**. Average value of answers for VR platform was 3.4 and for traditional platform was 3.71. From the observation of the respondents in the context of their mobility, it was shown that people who play the game on the VR platform often had problems with maintaining stable staying position. They also indicated nausea and balance problems. This is a frequently reported problem with VR. One of the respondents was unable to complete the VR study due to malaise related to physical activities. People advanced in using VR did not report this problem verbally as often as people inexperienced in this technology. To sum up, the assessment of feelings related to motor activities showed significant dependencies in terms of the tested immersion. The sensations related to movement were indicated as more pleasant on the non-VR platform, and this was mainly due to the motion sickness in VR. Additionally, an important observation is the relationship between the assessment of sensations related to motor activities and the advancement of the participant with VR. People who use VR more often found movement in VR more enjoyable. Getting used to the VR results in player feeling smaller effect of motion sickness, which unfortunately happens very often to people who use VR rarely.

The presented results translate into a conclusion about the **bad influence of "motion sickness", resulting from movement in VR, on immersion**.

4.3 Sensations Regarding Interaction Activities

The next examined aspect concerned the interaction experience in the game, such as picking up objects, rotating, holding, throwing, stacking them, and also firing smoke projectiles. At the beginning, the results of the game were compared for the traditional platform and the VR platform for all respondents. Conducting a statistical test showed that there are significant differences in the feelings associated with the interactions. The one-sided test showed that interactions were found to be **more enjoyable on the VR platform**. Average value of answers for VR platform was 4.27 and for traditional platform was 3.31. In the case of comparing the experiences of interacting with objects, for people advanced with VR technology, no significant differences were found for the VR platform. However, non-advanced people indicated interactions with objects as more enjoyable in the non-VR game than in VR. In addition, people highly familiar with VR technology indicated more strongly that interactions with objects in VR were more pleasant than on a traditional platform, compared to unfamiliar people. Nevertheless, both groups clearly rated the experiences of interacting with objects better for the VR platform than for the desktop platform. From the analyzed data related to the assessment of experiences from interaction with objects, it can be concluded that this aspect differed significantly between the two platforms. The respondents indicated the VR platform as providing a more pleasant, better experience related to interactions with objects, which **is a very important aspect of video games immersion**.

4.4 Intuitive Game Controls

The low intuitiveness of the controls is mentioned as a considerable problem in VR games, reducing the feeling of immersion due to frustration. The conducted research showed that the intuitiveness of using the controllers (in the case of VR) or the mouse and keyboard (in the case of the non-VR platform) was at a very high level - the respondents found it intuitive towards a very intuitive one. Moreover, the statistical test showed significant differences between the intuitive operation of the controllers or the mouse and keyboard for the two platforms. The respondents indicated **the VR platform as more intuitive to control**. Average value of answers for VR platform was 4.4 and for traditional platform was 4.12. Interestingly, people not advanced in VR technology statistically rated the intuitiveness of using the mouse and keyboard better on the non-VR platform compared to VR. Veterans of VR games had the opposite impressions. For them, it was the handling of controllers in VR that seemed more intuitive. In summary, the controls on VR were considered more intuitive, which definitely **translates into a greater sense of immersion on the VR platform**. This observation may be due to the similarity of VR controllers to the hand. The grip button used to grasp objects really resembles that of clenching hand on an object, and the trigger button is a perfect representation of the trigger in a gun. The controls with the mouse and keyboard do not resemble actual gestures, but are widely popularized in video games. For those reasons, high intuitiveness is not surprising.

4.5 Feeling of Freedom in Game World

Conducting statistical tests on data regarding the freedom of the respondents in the game world showed that the **VR platform is characterized by a clearly higher sense of freedom**. Average value of answers for VR platform was 3.6 and for traditional platform was 2.81. With assessment of higher freedom in the VR game world, it can be concluded that the **sense of immersion for this aspect is also higher for VR**. VR allows for more free manipulation of objects and exploration of the game world. In the case of a desktop computer, the player feels limited by the space in which he is (sitting on a chair, looking at the monitor). In the case of HMD and controllers, the boundaries of the game world are much wider.

4.6 Physical Involvement

Physical involvement is a factor that distinguishes the researched platforms. When playing a game adapted to VR, the player usually takes a standing position, has to reach for objects, throw them, bend down and perform other physical activities. Games on non-VR platform do not require high physical involvement. The player is usually sitting, and his movement is reduced to moving the mouse and pressing the keyboard keys. Physical involvement allows player to reflect activities that are performed in the real world, requiring some movement. On the other hand, high physical involvement can have the effect of distracting the player. In the case of the conducted research, it was shown that physical involvement **differed statistically between the two platforms, indicating that it was higher on VR**. However, the physical involvement in VR was found to be moderate, which may mean that it was not intense enough to distract or frustrate the player. Average value of answers for VR platform was 3.52 and for traditional platform was 2.0. People advanced in VR games felt more physically involved playing VR than non-advanced people. On the other hand, they also felt physically involved in performing activities on the traditional platform than non-advanced people. However, both groups indicated that physical involvement was significantly higher in VR. Summarizing the conducted analysis in the context of physical involvement, it can be concluded that higher physical involvement, but of moderate intensity, observed for the VR platform, has a **positive effect on the perceived immersion, as it simulates activities performed in the real world**.

4.7 Physical Discomfort

One of the most important aspects of the study was physical discomfort. This factor, as shown by the analysis, has a negative impact on the perceived immersion.

The analysis of the collected data showed that there are statistically significant differences in the perceived physical discomfort between the two tested platforms. The one-sided test found that **physical discomfort, such as nausea, headache and eye strain, is higher in VR**. In the case of the non-VR platform, the physical discomfort was assessed as very low (of average 1.27), while for the other platform, it was assessed as average (of average 2.88). The high rate of malaise in people tested while **playing VR translates into a reduction in their sense of immersion**. Physical discomfort distracts the subject and reminds the subject of the real world, which is undesirable when the goal is to achieve a high level of immersion.

4.8 Intuitive User Interface

One of the factors indicated as a factor influencing the sense of immersion is the intuitive use of the user interface. Non intuitive UI frustrates players. The analysis of the collected data showed that there are significant differences between the intuitive operation of the user interface between the examined platforms. One-sided analysis showed that the **respondents indicated the interface in VR was more intuitive**. This is a surprising result because the implementation of the user interface on the non-VR platform was a standard implementation. However, this result is good for both platforms and ranks between "intuitive" and "very intuitive". Average value of answers for VR platform was 4.48 and for traditional platform was 4.04. In conclusion, the use of the user interface has been found to be more intuitive for VR. Both platforms, however, showed a high level of intuitiveness, which **did not have a negative impact on the obtained immersion**.

4.9 Sounds

The sounds in the game are one of the most important factors influencing the perceived immersion. Realistic sounds are those that are spacious and well suited to the environment. However, the obtained **results did not show any significant differences** between the realism of sounds on non-VR and VR platforms. For both platforms, the sounds were considered medium realistic to realistic. This may be due to the not very advanced range of sounds used in the experimental environment and the focus of the subjects on other aspects of the game. Average value of answers for VR platform was 3.48 and for traditional platform was 3.46. Despite the lack of significant differences, it can be concluded that the sounds in the game on both platforms **did not have an adverse effect on the perceived immersion**. The important conclusion, however, is that the sounds in the game should be fine-tuned. After all, the sense of hearing is very important in the context of the perceived immersion and should be properly stimulated.

4.10 Graphics Effects

Graphic effects are another aspect of video games that has a significant impact on the level of immersion. The analysis of game reviews showed that **the poorer quality of graphics effects experienced on VR is a factor that has a very negative impact on immersion** compared to the same game on the traditional platform. However, the conducted research **did not show a significant difference** between the perception of graphic effects in the game. The result was on a similar level for both platforms. As in the case of sounds in the game, the lack of significant differences confirms the similarity between the perceived level of immersion, resulting from the experience related to the graphics in the game on both platforms. Average value of answers for VR platform was 3.8 and for traditional platform was 3.69.

4.11 Emotional Experiences

Emotional experiences were indicated at the level of analysis as a significant aspect influencing immersion. Data analysis showed that there are statistically significant differences between the level of experienced emotions. **The VR platform was indicated by the respondents as a platform that provides higher emotional experiences**. Average value of answers for VR platform was 3.28 and for traditional platform was 2.69. During the observations, it was noted that the subjects shouted various phrases during the VR experiment, indicating their fear or feeling of adrenaline. In addition, several people mentioned during the VR test that they are afraid of the height at which they are located. Such behavior did not take place during the traditional platform walk-through and proves higher intensity of emotions in contact with VR. Since the respondents clearly indicated that emotional experiences are higher during the game in VR, it translates into the level of immersion, where **the high intensity of emotions positively influences the perceived immersion**.

4.12 Technical Problems

In the case of technical problems, the analysis showed that they are **a big problem in the case of perceived immersion**. Errors in the game remind players of dealing with the artificial world created by the computer. They are a frequent cause of the loss of the realism of the presented world (which translates directly into the perceived immersion) and should be avoided. Statistical analysis showed that there were **no significant differences** between the indicated number of technical problems by the respondents. It can also be seen that the result was close to the answer "few errors". Average value of answers for VR platform was 2.08 and for traditional platform was 1.88.

5 Conclusions

Summarizing the conducted survey and observation, conclusions can be drawn on the comparison of immersion in a non-VR and VR game respectively. The implemented research environment (a VR and a traditional 3D games created from scratch for the research) gave the possibility to obtain all the necessary data, and the observation additionally strengthened the conclusions drawn. Based on the collected data, it was possible to obtain answers about the differences in the level of immersion for both platforms. The conducted research also helped to identify the factors that have the greatest impact on the immersion experienced by people participating in the experiment. In seven out of twelve aspects, VR has shown an advantage in perceived immersion. In two of the twelve, the traditional platform has shown higher sense of immersion. In three aspects, it was not possible to decide which platform performed better in the study. Considering the importance of these aspects as equal, it can be calculated that: 58% of the aspects indicate the VR platform as more immersive; 17% of the aspects indicate the non-VR platform as more immersive; for 25% of the aspects it cannot be stated which platforms is more immersive. It is also worth noting that people who are highly familiar with VR technology express a stronger tendency to feel a high level of immersion than people unfamiliar with VR. People who are advanced in using VR can cope with physical discomfort better. To sum up, it can be concluded that VR allows players to obtain a higher level of immersion compared to non-VR video games.

References

1. Cipresso, P., et al.: The past, present, and future of virtual and augmented reality research. Frontiers Psychol. **9**, 2086 (2018)
2. Concannon, B.J., e al.: Head-mounted display virtual reality in post-secondary education and skill training. Frontiers Educ. **4**, 80 (2019)
3. Fleck, P., Schmalstieg, D., Arth, C.: Creating IoT-ready XR-WebApps with Unity3D. In: The 25th International Conference on 3D Web Technology, pp. 1–7 (2020)
4. Kopel, M., Stanasiuk, B.: How to handle head collisions in VR. In: Fujita, H., Fournier-Viger, P., Ali, M., Sasaki, J. (eds.) IEA/AIE 2020. LNCS (LNAI), vol. 12144, pp. 626–637. Springer, Cham (2020). https://doi.org/10.1007/978-3-030-55789-8_54
5. Nylund, A., Landfors, O.: Frustration and its effect on immersion in games (2015)
6. Ryan, M.L.: Immersion vs. interactivity: virtual reality and literary theory. SubStance **28**(2), 110–137 (1999)
7. Schwind, V., et al.: Using presence questionnaires in virtual reality. In: Proceedings of the 2019 CHI conference on human factors in computing systems, pp. 1–12 (2019)
8. Ziegler, P., et al.: Simulator sick but still immersed. In: 2018 IEEE Conference on VR and 3D UI, pp. 743–744. IEEE (2018)

4. [illegible]
5. [illegible] virtual reality [illegible]
6. [illegible]

Innovations in Intelligent Systems

Is Wikipedia Easy to Understand?: A Study Beyond Conventional Readability Metrics

Simran Setia(✉), S. R. S. Iyengar, Amit Arjun Verma, and Neeru Dubey

Indian Institute of Technology, Ropar, India
{2017csz0001,sudarshan,2016csz0003,neerudubey}@iitrpr.ac.in

Abstract. Wikipedia has emerged to be one of the most prominent sources of information available on the Internet today. It provides a collaborative platform for editors to edit and share their information, making Wikipedia a valuable source of information. The Wikipedia articles have been duly studied from an editor's point of view. But, the analysis of Wikipedia from the reader's perspective is yet to be studied. Since Wikipedia serves as an encyclopedia of information for its users, its role as an information securing tool must be examined. The readability of a written text plays a major role in imparting the intended comprehension to its readers. Readability is the ease with which a reader can understand the underlying piece of text. In this paper, we study the readability of various Wikipedia articles. Apart from judging the readability of Wikipedia articles against standard readability metrics, we introduce some new parameters related specifically to the comprehension of the text present in Wikipedia articles. These new parameters, combined with standard readability metrics, help classify the Wikipedia articles into comprehensible and non-comprehensible classes through the SVM classification technique.

Keywords: Readability · Wikipedia articles · Knowledge gaps · Comprehension · Crowdsourced

1 Introduction

Wikipedia is undoubtedly a vast source of information. At present, Wikipedia houses 6 million articles in 293 languages[1]. Since Wikipedia is one of the biggest producers of information, it serves as a source of information for readers around the world. As of February 2, 2020, the aggregate page views are around 5 billion for all Wikipedia articles[2]. The number of page views suggests the huge crowd of readers that Wikipedia experiences. One of the studies states that the majority of the crowd is involved in reading the information present on Wikipedia [31]. As an instance, the *Coronavirus* outbreak generated many page views for the

[1] https://en.wikipedia.org/wiki/Wikipedia:Statistics.
[2] https://tools.wmflabs.org/siteviews.

K. Wojtkiewicz et al. (Eds.): ICCCI 2021, CCIS 1463, pp. 175–187, 2021.
https://doi.org/10.1007/978-3-030-88113-9_14

concerned Wikipedia page[3]. On the contrary, the Wikipedia article on Coronavirus witnessed only 196 editors. The difference in the number of producers (editors) and consumers (readers) establishes the need to analyze Wikipedia from a reader's perspective. The first and foremost parameter to engage readers on a text document is its readability. Readability is the ease of understanding a piece of text. Higher readability of a piece of text can increase the probability of conveying the correct information to readers with minimum reading effort. The commonly used readability metrics like the Flesch-Kincaid readability test, Coleman Liau index, and Automated readability index help to quantify the readability of the text [19]. They output the US grade level, i.e., the number of education years required to understand a piece of text. As per the scores obtained from the aforementioned readability metrics, there are significant concerns about the readability of Wikipedia articles [18]. But, it should be noted that these readability metrics take into account the surface level parameters like the average number of syllables, average number of words, and average number of sentences to calculate the readability score [29]. These readability metrics are based on the assumption that shorter words and sentences are easy to read and comprehend [19]. However, the aforementioned surface level parameters do not capture the subjective parameters related to the comprehension of the text, such as the completeness of information and writing style of the article. Hence, in this study, we introduce some subjective parameters that affect the comprehension of the text present in Wikipedia articles. Some of the past studies consider some subjective measures like the popularity of the words present in the underlying text. For Example, the probability distribution of each word present in the text is calculated across topics like history, science, entertainment, and across genres like travel documents, government documents, and technical documents. These probability distributions calculated across different topics and genres capture the popularity of the words present in the text, which is directly related to the readability of the text [11]. In this paper, we discuss some subjective parameters related to the completeness and writing style of the underlying information, which apprehends the comprehension of the text present in the Wikipedia articles. These parameters are calculated using renowned NLP techniques like topic modeling through LDA, text segmentation.

2 Related Work

2.1 Importance of Reading Wikipedia

Several research studies have been conducted on Wikipedia ranging from studying the collaboration dynamics to the quality of Wikipedia articles [23,26]. However, only 20% of the research studies focus on Wikipedia's readers [22]. As stated earlier, readers form a major chunk of Wikipedia users. Prior studies also state that reading is an indicator of the quality of Wikipedia articles [6]. Also, the readers are no more considered as free riders [24]. Reading is termed as legitimate

[3] https://tools.wmflabs.org/topviews.

peripheral participation because some readers gravitate towards more prominent roles like the editor of the Wikipedia articles [2]. Hence, it is essential to study the readability of Wikipedia articles to impart a better reading experience to most Wikipedia users.

2.2 Limitations of Standard Readability Metrics

Readability metrics are devised to measure the difficulty encountered while reading the article. The current readability metrics are based on surface-level parameters that do not capture the underlying text's degree of comprehension. Many objections have been raised against the existing readability formulas. In [8], the authors object that reading difficulty is related to the background of the reader as well as the inherent difficulty of the subject matter. The authors also state that if we try to modify the text to achieve a specific readability level, it does more harm than good to the text in terms of comprehensibility. It has been found that the text documents written by a conscientious writer are more readable than the ones written by someone trying to make a text fit a readability level defined by the formula.

2.3 New Readability Metrics

Many researchers have come up with new readability metrics that take into account many subjective parameters apart from surface-level parameters. In [29], the authors claim that the readability metrics should be sensitive to the text content and surface-level parameters. The content information is captured through the unigram language model. In addition to this, the authors design a statistical model in which the model parameters are learnt from the text corpora itself. The text corpora include K-8 science documents. As an instance, the metrics like sentence length is found to be more useful than word length for such corpora. A new readability metric is designed specifically for k-8 science web documents based on the unigram language model and sentence length statistical model. In [12], authors take natural language parameters like syntactic features, features based on language models, and lexical features to learn the readability level of a text document. This new readability model is found to predict the readability level of the underlying document accurately. Similarly, it has also been argued that the readability of documents should also take into account the intended audience. For example, financial documents are bound to have complex words which can be easily understood by investors and financial analysts. In [17], the authors design a new readability metric for financial documents. One of the other studies focuses on designing a new metric to quantify the difficulty level of online health information documents [16]. Also, in [34], the authors focus on the readability of technical documents. The new readability metric for technical documents is related to the document's scope and the cohesion of the concepts present. The scope of the document deals with coverage of domain-specific terms in the document, and cohesion deals with the relatedness of the concepts present in the document. In addition to this, authors have also measured the readability of other types of documents like graphic documents like graphs and maps, entry documents like forms [20]. Similarly, we introduce some new comprehension pointers which affect the comprehension of text present in Wikipedia articles.

3 Data Set

The Wikipedia quality assessment scheme categorizes the Wikipedia articles based on various quality measures like language quality, the layout of the article[4]. The different categories identified are Featured Articles (FAs), Good Articles (GAs), A articles, B articles, C articles, Start Articles, and Stub Articles in decreasing order of their quality. We select 1000 random FAs, GAs, B articles, C articles, Start articles, and Stub articles as a part of the data set. The A category articles are very few, and hence, 1000 random articles from the rest of the categories except category A articles are chosen. This amounts to 6000 Wikipedia articles in total as a part of the data set.

4 Comprehension Pointers

There are many cognitive theories explaining the process of text comprehension by readers. The theories describe that the knowledge present in the text must be coherent with the background knowledge of the reader [9,13,14,21,32]. If these two knowledge sources are not coherent, then the text comprehension is unsuccessful. Hence, the information present must resonate with the background knowledge of the reader. It should be noted that a platform like Wikipedia encounters readers with varied educational backgrounds. To execute successful text comprehension on Wikipedia, we must not assume any background knowledge from the reader. The information present in the Wikipedia articles should be self-sufficient in knowledge. If a text conveys all the information assuming no background knowledge from the reader, the readers can easily comprehend information present in the text. In order to quantify the entirety of the information given, it is essential to do some quality checks on the content of the text apart from calculating the surface level metrics. There are often missing pieces of information in the text, which hinder the comprehension of the underlying text. We refer to these missing pieces of information as knowledge gaps. For example, while explaining the area and perimeter of a circle, the concept of radius must be explained to the reader. The concept of radius, if missing in the text, is termed as a knowledge gap. These knowledge gaps are important to identify for successful text comprehension on a platform like Wikipedia. We define the knowledge gap parameter to quantify the knowledge gaps in a Wikipedia article.

---

[4] https://en.wikipedia.org/wiki/Wikipedia:Content_assessment.

- Knowledge Gaps Parameter: Knowledge gaps are identified with an assumption of no prerequisite knowledge expected from the reader. In order to quantify the knowledge gaps, the given Wikipedia article is divided into segments using the semantic word embedding [1,28]. Text segmentation is used to split the text in wiki articles into contiguous coherent sections called segments of the text. Once the segments are obtained, LDA (Latent Dirichlet Allocation) is applied to each of the segments, which are used to figure out the topic of the corresponding text [4]. For a piece of text, LDA outputs a set of keywords along with their probability distribution. This set of keywords, along with probability distribution, is a *topic* inferred through LDA. Hellinger distance is then applied to calculate the semantic distance between the probability distributions of subsequent segments. Hellinger distance is the probabilistic analog of Euclidean distance and is used to calculate the similarity between the probability distributions [3]. The lesser the Hellinger distance, the more similar the probability distributions are. If the Hellinger distance between any two subsequent segments is more than 0.5, then there is a knowledge gap between the two segments. The threshold of 0.5 has been defined empirically. The knowledge gap parameter is the ratio of the number of knowledge gaps to the total number of segments in the Wikipedia article. The Start and Stub articles are deficient in information, and thus, many of them have very few number of segments (in the range of 2–3). Hence, Start and Stub articles must score high on the knowledge gap parameter. Since the total number of segments weighs down the knowledge gap parameter, it very well captures the deficiency of information in such articles. According to the results obtained, the featured articles experience the least knowledge gap parameter followed by Good Articles (as depicted in Fig. 1). The reason for such a behavior is that Featured articles are self-sufficient in knowledge, leaving little scope for knowledge gaps to be present in the concerned articles.

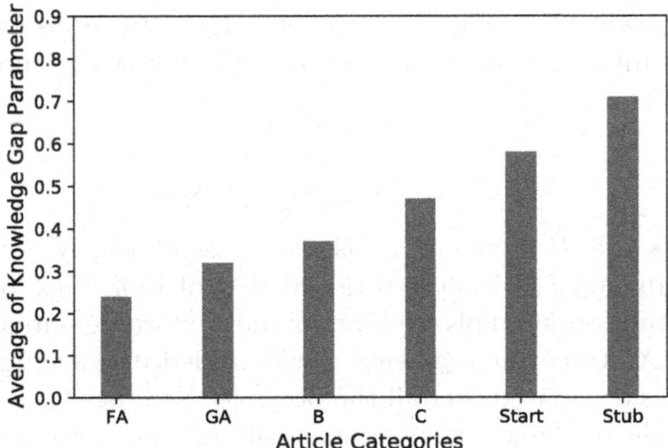

Fig. 1. The above figure represents the average knowledge gap parameter for 5 different category articles in Wikipedia.

- Crowdsourced Parameters: Wikipedia articles are the product of several edits done by a bunch of editors. As mentioned in the past literature, an author's writing style influences the comprehension of the underlying text [25]. In case of collaboratively written articles, the comprehension of the underlying text is dependent on the writing style of all the participating authors. Hence, in contrast to conventional documents written by a single author, the comprehension pointers in Wikipedia articles must consider their crowdsourced nature. We define two parameters to capture the crowdsourced nature of the Wikipedia articles, named, Stylistic Coefficient and Edit Coefficient.
  - Stylistic Coefficient: Every author has his unique writing style [7]. This leads to many stylistic inconsistencies in a collaboratively authored article [10]. As per the past literature, stylistic inconsistencies affect the comprehension of the text present in the article [25]. This is because the stylistic differences are best identified using the frequency of content features like parts-of-speech (POS) tags, function words, and punctuation symbols [10]. The text documents with a higher frequency of POS tags, function words, and punctuation symbols tend to contain more information, which leads to poor comprehension of the underlying text by the reader [11]. The stylistic coefficient is captured by the frequency of POS tags, function words, and punctuation symbols. A higher stylistic coefficient indicates poor comprehension of the underlying text.

    The POS tags are used to tag the words present in the sentence [27]. The tag specifies whether the specific word is a noun, adjective, verb, and so on. Function words are used to classify the words as determiners, conjunctions, prepositions, pronouns, auxiliary verbs, and question words [5]. Also, we consider 29 punctuation symbols including !, $,.,;, and so on. To quantify the stylistic differences in the text, we first divide the Wikipedia article into segments around the stylistic differences. The stylistic change is identified using the change in frequency of POS tags, function words, and punctuation symbols in the text. The segmentation is carried out using a greedy algorithm. The greedy algorithm is used to divide the given text into segments by maximizing the following score function:

$$s^0 = S_0$$

$$s^{t+1} = min_{(i \in [1,N])} f(S_t \cap S_i)$$

    where s^i is the ith segment, S_i is the ith sentence, N is the total number of segments, $f(X)$ is the total number of POS tags, function words, and punctuation symbols present in the text represented by the set of sentences X. Once the segments are identified, the average frequency of POS tags is calculated over all the possible POS tags for a particular segment. Similarly, the average frequency of function words and punctuation symbols are calculated for a particular segment. The average frequency of POS tags for an article is calculated by taking the average frequency of POS tags over all the segments. The average frequency of function words and punctuation symbols for an article are calculated in a similar fashion. We then calculate the average of the POS tags, function words, and punctuation symbols for each of the article categories. As per the results obtained, the highest average for the aforementioned parameters is observed in B and C articles (as depicted in Fig. 2). The Featured Articles (FAs) and Stub articles have a relatively lower average for all the parameters. The Good Articles (GAs) have a higher average than FAs. The Start articles have a higher average than Stub articles. Hence, there is a higher frequency of the POS tags, function words, and punctuation symbols for B and C articles. In other words, B and C articles experience a high stylistic coefficient. As stated above, a higher frequency of POS tags, function words, and punctuation symbols indicate much more information is conveyed in the text, which leads to poor comprehension. The probable reason is relatively lower number of segments present in B and C articles as compared to FAs and GAs. We found that the total number of POS tags, function words, and punctuation symbols are more or less the same in FAs, GAS, B articles, and C articles. However, the information present in FAs, GAs is written in a more elaborative manner, which leads to more number of segments and a lower stylistic coefficient. The Stub articles have limited content, which leads to low frequency of POS tags, function words, and punctuation symbols.

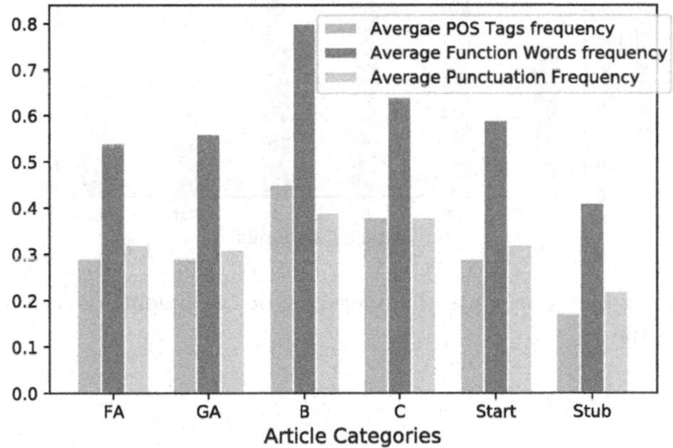

Fig. 2. The above figure represents the average frequency of all POS tags, function words and punctuation symbols over all segments for 5 different category articles in Wikipedia

- Edit Coefficient: The Edit coefficient of Wikipedia articles measures the degree of editing performed on the current text present in the article. It is calculated as the ratio of the number of text bytes to the number of edits of a Wikipedia article. More text bytes per edit suggests that the underlying text has not been subjected to an adequate amount of editing. The information present in a Wikipedia article may be enough. But if it is not subjected to rigorous editing, then there is a higher probability of errors in the article. The errors can be inaccurate information or grammatical errors that affect the comprehension of articles. The edit coefficient is coined by keeping in mind Linus's law [15]. Linus's law states that "Given enough eyeballs, all bugs are shallow". Hence, the articles should have a low edit coefficient in order to achieve the desired comprehension. The B and C articles have a higher edit coefficient as compared to other category articles (as depicted in Fig. 3). FAs are self-sufficient in terms of information and, thus, have more content as compare to other category articles. FAs have more text bytes and more number of edits as compared to other categories. On the contrary, Start and Stub article have a lesser number of text bytes and a lesser number of edits as compared to other categories. For GA, B, and C articles, the number of text bytes is relatively more than Start and Stub articles, but the number of edits is lesser than FAs. Such behavior in B and C articles leads to a higher edit coefficient.

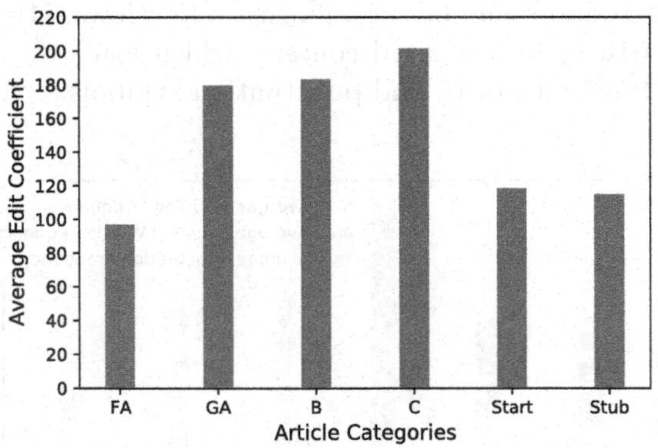

Fig. 3. The above figure represents the average edit coefficient for 5 different category articles in Wikipedia.

5 Impact of Comprehension Pointers

To quantify the effect of each of the above-mentioned comprehension pointers on the readability of Wikipedia articles, we apply the SVM classification with comprehension pointers as the features. The classification process is used to classify Wikipedia articles into comprehensible and non-comprehensible articles. SVM is used instead of other classification models like Random Forest, Naive Bayes because the accuracy of the SVM classifier obtained is more than other classifiers.

In order to define the gold standard for comprehensible articles in Wikipedia, we use the data set curated by Singer et al. [30]. In this particular data set, 30,000 responses are collected from the readers of various Wikipedia articles. For every response, the following information is collected from the readers:

- Motivation for reading the Wikipedia article: intrinsic learning/bored/ random/work/school/current event/media/other
- Information need: overview/fact/in-depth
- Prior knowledge regarding the Wikipedia article: Familiar/Unfamiliar

For comprehensible articles, we consider those articles if the particular reader is unfamiliar with the underlying topic of Wikipedia article, information need is in-depth, and the motivation is school-related work. This is because, as stated earlier, we do not assume any knowledge possessed by the reader while defining the knowledge gap parameter. Also, in-depth information need and school-related work as the motivation behind reading the article correlate with long-sessions spent while reading the Wikipedia articles [30]. As per the past studies, long reading time correlates with good comprehension scores for a particular age-group [33]. Thus, we consider those articles as the comprehensible ones that school students read with no prior information and an in-depth need for information. We collect a data set of 1000 such articles. The data set of non-comprehensible articles comprises of 166 FAs, 166 GAs, 166 B articles, 166 C articles, 166 Start articles, and 166 Stub articles. Such distribution of different category articles is selected to construct a balanced data set of articles belonging to comprehensible and non-comprehensible categories. We apply linear SVM classification model with Knowledge Gap Parameter, Average POS tags frequency, Average function words frequency, Average punctuation symbols frequency, and Edit coefficient as the features and obtain linearly separable decision boundary (as depicted in Fig. 4). The testing training ratio for the SVM classifier is 0.33. According to the results obtained, we obtain an accuracy of 79%. The classification report is depicted in Table 1. The relative importance of each of the features is depicted in Table 2. As evident from the table, the most important feature is the knowledge gap parameter, followed by the stylometric coefficient. The parameters related to the stylometric coefficient hold more or less the same importance. Also, the least important feature is the edit coefficient. Hence, we can conclude that it is very important to have a low knowledge gap parameter to achieve the desired degree of comprehension of a Wikipedia article.

Table 1. Classification evaluation report

Classes	Precision	Recall	F1-score	Support
0	0.89	0.70	0.78	349
1	0.73	0.91	0.81	315

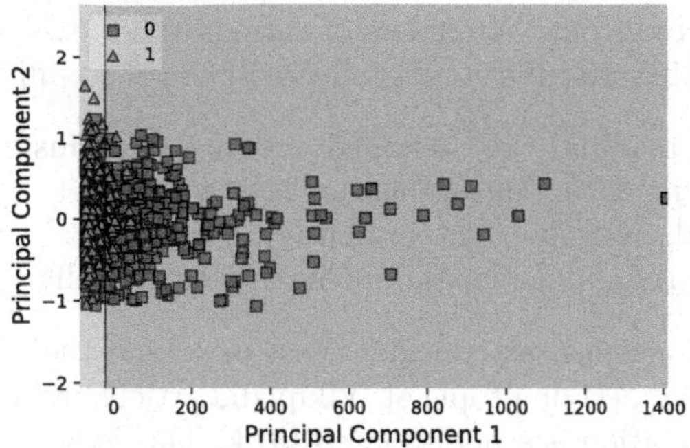

Fig. 4. The above figure represents the decision boundary calculated for the classification of Wikipedia articles into comprehensible and non-comprehensible classes. Here, Class 1 represents the comprehensible class, and Class 0 represents the non-comprehensible class. Since the SVM linear classification model is based on 5 features, it is not possible to visualize the classification on a 2D space. So, we apply PCA to reduce the features to a 2D space. A linear separable boundary between Class 0 and Class 1 instances suggests the aptness of the linear SVM model.

Table 2. Linear SVM coefficients observed for various features.

Features	Linear SVM coefficients
Edit coefficient	−0.033
Average POS tags frequency	0.38
Average function words frequency	0.41
Average punctuation symbol frequency	0.45
Knowledge gap parameter	1.96

6 Discussion

The importance of readers in the Wikipedia environment is well understood. They form the majority of Wikipedia users. They are not only consumers of information, but some also contribute towards the editing of Wikipedia articles [2]. The most important feature of a Wikipedia article that a reader desires is the good readability of the concerned article. The readability of the article is related to the comprehension of the text present in the article. According to the previous studies, Wikipedia articles score low on readability. To tackle the readability issues, Wikipedia has come up with new projects like Simple Wikipedia, which focuses on the development of Wikipedia articles that are easy to understand. However, the articles on Simple Wikipedia are not as exhaustive in information as their corresponding articles on Wikipedia[5]. The previous studies also judge the readability of the Wikipedia articles based on conventional readability methods like Flesch-Kincaid, Coleman Liau, and ARI. These conventional readability

[5] https://simple.wikipedia.org/wiki/Main_Page.

methods are based on surface-level parameters like the number of words, number of sentences. An article's readability must take into account the comprehension of text perceived by the reader of the article. As pointed by past theories, comprehension of the underlying text is judged with the help of subjective parameters like knowledge gaps [9,13,14,21,32]. The knowledge gap parameter captures the missing pieces of information, which hinders the text comprehension by a reader. In addition to this, the crowdsourced nature of Wikipedia articles must be considered while quantifying the comprehension of the underlying article. The stylistic coefficient and edit coefficient capture the crowdsourced nature of Wikipedia articles. As per the results obtained, different category articles show different behavior on evaluation based on the comprehension pointers. Further, to quantify the relative effect of the comprehension pointers on Wikipedia articles, we apply a linear SVM classification model with comprehension pointers as the features and output as the comprehensible or non-comprehensible class of each of the Wikipedia articles. The coefficients figured out through SVM classification suggest the knowledge gap parameter as the most important comprehension pointer for Wikipedia articles. The knowledge gaps, when eclipsed in a Wikipedia article, enhances its comprehensibility and hence, readability. Also, the stylistic coefficient is the second most important comprehension pointer required to enhance readability. The least important feature, i.e., Edit Coefficient, suggests that a low number of text bytes per edit does not necessarily lead to a good degree of comprehension of Wikipedia articles. Hence, we can conclude that conventional readability parameters should not solely judge the readability of Wikipedia articles. The readability of Wikipedia articles should instead be a product of comprehension pointers like the knowledge gap parameter, stylistic coefficient, edit coefficient, and many more.

7 Limitations

As discussed above, the knowledge gap parameter is an important parameter that should be considered to enhance the comprehension of Wikipedia articles. It should be noted the Wikipedia articles consist of hyperlinks to other Wikipedia pages called wiki links. If there exists a knowledge gap between two segments of an article, the knowledge gap could be eclipsed by the article pointed by the wiki link. However, we do not consider the wiki links to calculate the knowledge gap parameter. Hence, it represents a limitation of our work.

8 Conclusion and Future Work

The fact that longer sentences are difficult to comprehend forms the underlying principle of judging the readability of Wikipedia articles in past studies. But, it should be noted that the knowledge gaps present in an article are another notable obstacle towards the comprehension of the text present in the article. The low value of the knowledge gap parameter in FAs is evident from the exhaustive knowledge present in the articles. On the contrary, the rest of the article categories in Wikipedia show poor performance in terms of the knowledge gap parameter. Since FAs form a small population of Wikipedia articles, there are significant concerns about the readability of Wikipedia. Hence, the removal of knowledge gaps can serve as a remedy for the better comprehension of Wikipedia articles. As a part of future work, we plan to devise ways for predicting the knowledge gaps present in Wikipedia articles by considering the wiki links.

References

1. Alemi, A.A., Ginsparg, P.: Text segmentation based on semantic word embeddings. arXiv preprint arXiv:1503.05543 (2015)
2. Antin, J., Cheshire, C.: Readers are not free-riders: reading as a form of participation on Wikipedia. In: Proceedings of the 2010 ACM Conference on Computer Supported Cooperative Work, pp. 127–130 (2010)
3. Beran, R., et al.: Minimum Hellinger distance estimates for parametric models. Ann. Stat. **5**(3), 445–463 (1977)
4. Blei, D.M., Ng, A.Y., Jordan, M.I.: Latent Dirichlet allocation. J. Mach. Learn. Res. **3**, 993–1022 (2003)
5. Brill, E.: Transformation-based error-driven learning and natural language processing: a case study in part-of-speech tagging. Comput. Linguist. **21**(4), 543–565 (1995)
6. Bryant, S.L., Forte, A., Bruckman, A.: Becoming Wikipedian: transformation of participation in a collaborative online encyclopedia. In: Proceedings of the 2005 international ACM SIGGROUP Conference on Supporting Group Work, pp. 1–10 (2005)
7. Yang, C.C., et al. (eds.): PAISI 2007. LNCS, vol. 4430. Springer, Heidelberg (2007). https://doi.org/10.1007/978-3-540-71549-8
8. Davison, A., Kantor, R.N.: On the failure of readability formulas to define readable texts: a case study from adaptations. Read. Res. Q., 187–209 (1982)
9. Gernsbacher, M.A.: Language Comprehension as Structure Building. Psychology Press (2013)
10. Graham, N., Hirst, G., Marthi, B.: Segmenting documents by stylistic character. Nat. Lang. Eng. **11**(4), 397–416 (2005)
11. Jatowt, A., Tanaka, K.: Is Wikipedia too difficult? Comparative analysis of readability of Wikipedia, simple Wikipedia and Britannica. In: Proceedings of the 21st ACM International Conference on Information and Knowledge Management, pp. 2607–2610 (2012)
12. Kate, R.J., et al.: Learning to predict readability using diverse linguistic features. In: Proceedings of the 23rd International Conference on Computational Linguistics, pp. 546–554. Association for Computational Linguistics (2010)
13. Kendeou, P.: A general inference skill. In: Inferences During Reading, pp. 160–181 (2015)
14. Kintsch, W.: The role of knowledge in discourse comprehension: a construction-integration model. Psychol. Rev. **95**(2), 163 (1988)
15. Leicht, N.: Given enough eyeballs, all bugs are shallow-a literature review for the use of crowdsourcing in software testing. In: Proceedings of the 51st Hawaii International Conference on System Sciences (2018)
16. Leroy, G., Helmreich, S., Cowie, J.R., Miller, T., Zheng, W.: Evaluating online health information: beyond readability formulas. In: AMIA Annual Symposium Proceedings, vol. 2008, p. 394. American Medical Informatics Association (2008)

17. Loughran, T., McDonald, B.: Measuring readability in financial disclosures. J. Financ. **69**(4), 1643–1671 (2014)
18. Lucassen, T., Dijkstra, R., Schraagen, J.M.: Readability of Wikipedia. First Monday (2012)
19. McCallum, D.R., Peterson, J.L.: Computer-based readability indexes. In: Proceedings of the ACM 1982 Conference, pp. 44–48 (1982)
20. Mosenthal, P.B., Kirsch, I.S.: A new measure for assessing document complexity: The PMOSE/IKIRSCH document readability formula. J. Adolesc. Adult Literacy **41**(8), 638–657 (1998)
21. Myers, J.L., O'Brien, E.J.: Accessing the discourse representation during reading. Discourse Process. **26**(2–3), 131–157 (1998)
22. Okoli, C., Mehdi, M., Mesgari, M., Nielsen, F.Å., Lanamäki, A.: The people's encyclopedia under the gaze of the sages: a systematic review of scholarly research on Wikipedia. Available at SSRN 2021326 (2012)
23. Piscopo, A., Simperl, E.: What we talk about when we talk about Wikidata quality: a literature survey. In: Proceedings of the 15th International Symposium on Open Collaboration, pp. 1–11 (2019)
24. Preece, J., Nonnecke, B., Andrews, D.: The top five reasons for lurking: improving community experiences for everyone. Comput. Hum. Behav. **20**(2), 201–223 (2004)
25. Rexha, A., Kröll, M., Ziak, H., Kern, R.: Authorship identification of documents with high content similarity. Scientometrics **115**(1), 223–237 (2018). https://doi.org/10.1007/s11192-018-2661-6
26. Rezgui, A., Crowston, K.: Stigmergic coordination in Wikipedia. In: Proceedings of the 14th International Symposium on Open Collaboration, pp. 1–12 (2018)
27. Schmid, H.: TreeTagger-a language independent part-of-speech tagger (1994). http://www.ims.uni-stuttgart.de/projekte/corplex/TreeTagger/
28. Setia, S., Iyengar, S., Verma, A.A.: QWiki: need for QnA & Wiki to Co-exist. In: Proceedings of the 16th International Symposium on Open Collaboration, pp. 1–12 (2020)
29. Si, L., Callan, J.: A statistical model for scientific readability. In: Proceedings of the Tenth International Conference on Information and Knowledge Management, pp. 574–576 (2001)
30. Singer, P., et al.: Why we read Wikipedia. In: Proceedings of the 26th International Conference on World Wide Web, pp. 1591–1600 (2017)
31. Swartz, A.: Who writes Wikipedia. Raw Thought **4** (2006)
32. Tzeng, Y., Van Den Broek, P., Kendeou, P., Lee, C.: The computational implementation of the landscape model: modeling inferential processes and memory representations of text comprehension. Behav. Res. Methods **37**(2), 277–286 (2005)
33. Wallot, S., O'Brien, B.A., Haussmann, A., Kloos, H., Lyby, M.S.: The role of reading time complexity and reading speed in text comprehension. J. Exp. Psychol. Learn. Mem. Cogn. **40**(6), 1745 (2014)
34. Yan, X., Song, D., Li, X.: Concept-based document readability in domain specific information retrieval. In: Proceedings of the 15th ACM International Conference on Information and Knowledge Management, pp. 540–549 (2006)

Compatibility Checking of Business Rules Expressed in Natural Language Against Domain Specification

Bogumila Hnatkowska(✉)

Wroclaw University of Science and Technology, Wyb. Wyspiańskiego 27, 50-370 Wrocław, Poland
Bogumila.Hnatkowska@pwr.edu.pl

Abstract. Business rules play an important role in software development. They are usually expressed in natural language, sometimes with the use of sentence templates such as RuleSpeak. The rules should be consistent with other artifacts representing the same domain, e.g. business glossary. Typically, business rules are written in a text editor. Such editors only offer basic support such as grammar spelling. They do not check compliance of business rules with a business glossary or more complex artifacts, e.g. domain diagrams. The goal of this paper is to propose a method of compatibility checking of business rules expressed in natural language with the domain specification. Checking is done at the syntax level. It is assumed that the domain is specified by a class diagram and a glossary. The compatibility checking is a heuristic method, the usefulness of which has been demonstrated by several experiments. At that point, the method application is limited to business rules relating to at most two classes and/or two attributes/roles.

Keywords: Business rules · Natural language · Compatibility · Domain · Class diagram · Glossary

1 Introduction

Business rules are an important part of business modeling. Together with the glossary and domain model, they form a set of useful artifacts with many potential applications, including software development.

A domain glossary is a list of terms with their informal definitions and aliases (synonymous names). A domain model is "a product of domain analysis that provides a representation of the requirements of the domain" [1]. It can show structure, functions, information flow, and more. In further, we limit our interest to the domain structure, which is usually represented graphically, in the form of a diagram. The diagram represents glossary entries, i.e. domain entities and relationships among them, including generalizations, compositions, aggregations, and associations. The diagram can take the form of an Entity Relationship Diagram (ERD), UML class diagram, or a concept diagram [2]. The following assumes that the domain is represented by a class diagram. This notation is commonly used for business/system structure representation.

K. Wojtkiewicz et al. (Eds.): ICCCI 2021, CCIS 1463, pp. 188–198, 2021.
https://doi.org/10.1007/978-3-030-88113-9_15

Business rules represent constraints on the way the domain behaves or is structured. As business rules are read by many different stakeholders (business experts, business analysts, developers, testers) they should be clearly expressed. Typically, they are expressed in natural language or controlled natural language, e.g. SBVR SE [3]. Natural language gives freedom to business rules writers, but this freedom can lead to a very complex structure, difficulty in reading, and business rules misinterpretation. Controlled languages can be processed by computers, but their use (due to their limited grammar) can be difficult and cumbersome. RuleSpeak® can be seen as a solution that gives you concise, understandable business rules without too many limitations. RuleSpeak® is a well-known and popular set of sentence templates, promoted by Business Rule Solution, LLC [4]. The templates are very simple. Each contains one modal verb that defines the nature of the business rule, e.g. … 'must' …, … 'must not' … 'if' … RuleSpeak® is not a controlled language unlike The RuleSpeak® Business Rule Notation defined in the annex H of the Semantics of Business Vocabulary and Business Rules ([5]). The guidelines explain how to use these templates effectively. They were an inspiration to the business rule patterns catalog [6].

Regardless of the notation used to express business rules, they must be consistent with other artifacts, especially the business glossary and domain specification (e.g. class diagram). According to the Business Rules Manifesto [7], rules must be defined based on facts (relations), and facts must be built based on terms (glossary entries).

The paper presents a method of checking the compatibility of business rules written in natural language with the domain specification. Natural language may follow RuleSpeak or SBVR SE guidelines, but the rules don't need to be fully consistent with them. The method is intended to work in the early stages of modeling. It should be light, effective (fast), and work with agile models. The method – at that moment – can check sentences referring to at most two entities/attributes. The consistency relates to the syntax, not the semantic level.

The paper is structured as follows. Section 2 presents the related works. Section 3 provides a motivating example. The method is presented in Sect. 4 and its verification in Sect. 5. The last Sect. 6 concludes the paper.

2 Related Works

There exist many tools to help you define business rules according to a specific controlled natural language (English). Examples include RuleCNL [8], SBVR Lab 2.0 [9], RuleXpress [10], or DSL based [11]. The expressiveness of the natural language is limited by the closed grammar the writer must use. The tools usually also support the definition of the business domain, i.e. domain terms and facts. Some allow for a graphical definition (UML-like notation). The tools offer many useful features such as syntax colors or code completion. But none of them can test business rules expressed in free, natural language.

According to the best author's knowledge, there are no tools that check the syntactic correctness of business rules written in free natural language with business vocabulary and a domain diagram. A similar problem was tackled in [12], where the authors tried to translate business rules written in free natural language to the SBVR SE formalism, assuming that the domain is described by a UML class diagram. The basic way to process natural sentences is similar to the method proposed in this paper (tokenization, tagging). The accuracy of the solution was not impressive (92% for simple rules and 90% for complex rules – with generalizations). It should be mentioned, however, that the issue under discussion was different. Another research from the same area is [13], in which the authors propose a method of translating natural language constraints to the OCL language, using SBVR SE as an intermediate representation. The results were even worse than previously mentioned (average precision equal to 87%).

3 Motivating Example

Suppose we have a domain specification defined as a class diagram – see Fig. 1 – and our glossary introduces the following aliases: customer – client, account – bank account.

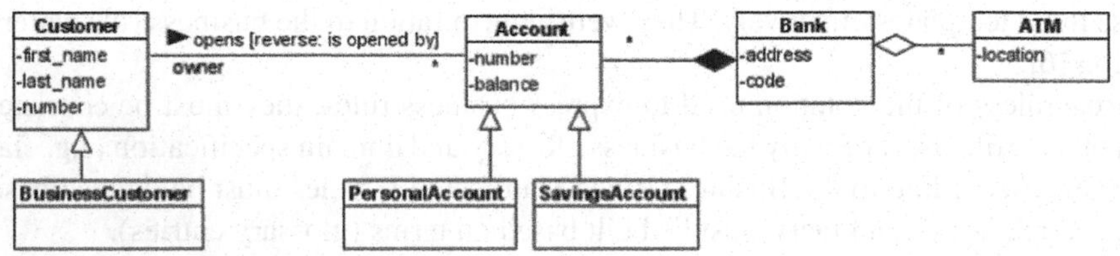

Fig. 1. Exemplary domain specification

We are interested in a method that would allow checking if business rules written in free natural language are consistent with the domain definition. Rules are assumed to be generally correct English sentences that can refer to the elements of the class diagram in various ways. The scope of checking is limited to terms, facts, and their relationships.

Below there is a list of business rule versions with the same semantics. All the rules are compatible with the class diagram from Fig. 1:

- Number of each customer must be unique
- Customers' numbers must be unique
- Each client's number is unique
- Number of clients should be unique
- Customers' numbers should be different
- It is necessary that the number of each customer is unique
- Number of each account owner must be unique

A navigation expression written in natural language can go through inherited dependencies, e.g.

- Each personal account must be opened by exactly one client.
- A bank should compose at least 2 savings accounts

Examples of incorrect business rules (not based on terms/facts from Fig. 1) are shown below. The underlined words indicate tokens not compatible with the class diagram.

- Each account should belong to at most 1 person
- Each ATM must be owned by one bank
- It is obligatory that an ATM has an address defined

4 Compatibility Checking Method

4.1 Class Diagram – Assumptions

A class diagram is a namespace for its content. This means that class names must be unique. Each class can have more than one alias defined, but aliases must also be unique.

A class name is assumed to be a singular noun expression, consisting of one or more words. In the case of compound name, e.g. Bank Account, the name can be written as: 'bank account', 'bank_account' (the texts can include any number of capital letters), or 'BankAccount' (capital letters allow recognition of word boundaries).

A class is a namespace for its features (attributes and navigable association roles). It is assumed that the features are represented by noun expressions written in the same way as the class name, however, the plural form is acceptable.

Only binary relationships are processed. A composition or aggregation cannot have a name in contrast to an association. The name of an association should be a verb expression written in the same way as the class name, e.g. 'opens', 'be opened', 'be_opened'. An association may have its reverse name defined, e.g. for the association between Customer and Account called 'opens', the reverse name can be 'is opened by'. All associations may have multiplicities and role names defined at their ends. Role names are noun expressions. The multiplicity is not being processed at that moment.

4.2 Business Rules – Assumptions

A business rule is a sentence written in English. The style may resemble RuleSpeak or SBVR SE (see Sect. 3 for examples).

To express the fact that one is navigating through aggregation or composition, special expressions should be used. For example: 'Account must be included in a bank', 'The bank contains zero or more accounts'. The list of possible expressions can be set by the user.

The business rule is assumed to be syntactically correct (or almost correct). At that moment, the business rule should be a simple sentence relating to at most two glossary terms (classes) and/or two features. An author of the business rule can navigate through at most one association.

4.3 Method

The proposed evaluation method works at the post-processing stage – it checks the compliance of a business rule with a domain specification after the rule has been written (not on the fly). It is a heuristic method that limits its interest to navigation perspective (syntax level). For example, for the rule "Customer's name is always unique", the method will check whether 'name' is a feature defined in the 'Customer' class and whether the 'Customer' class is present on the class diagram. The "heuristic" notion is used here in the context of decision-making problems. We have to decide if a business rule is consistent or not with a given class diagram. The "rule of thumb" heuristic strategy is effectively used here. It is an inference strategy relying on one piece of information, ignoring other available sources [15]. The findings do not always have to be correct.

The method goes through the activities presented on the activity diagram in Fig. 2. Their results will be explained with a small example.

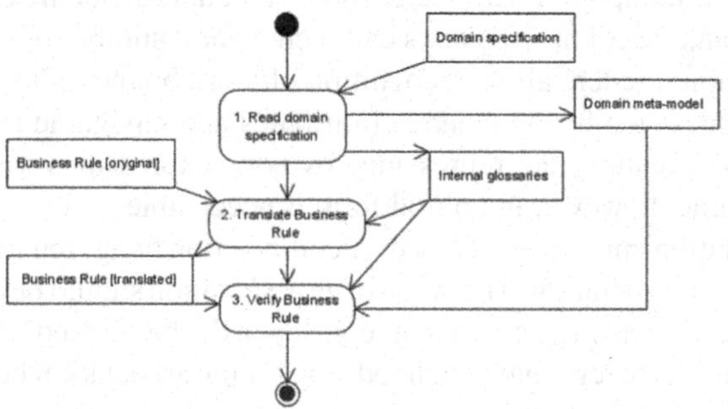

Fig. 2. Verification method – activity diagram

Suppose the business rule to be checked is "Customer's number is always unique" and we want to check its compliance with a part of the class diagram presented in Fig. 1 (the class diagram is limited to the *Customer* class only).

In the first step, the domain specification is read and kept in an internal meta-model. The structure of the meta-model is simple – see Fig. 3. Its instance (Fig. 4) will be used further to check the business rule compatibility with the class diagram.

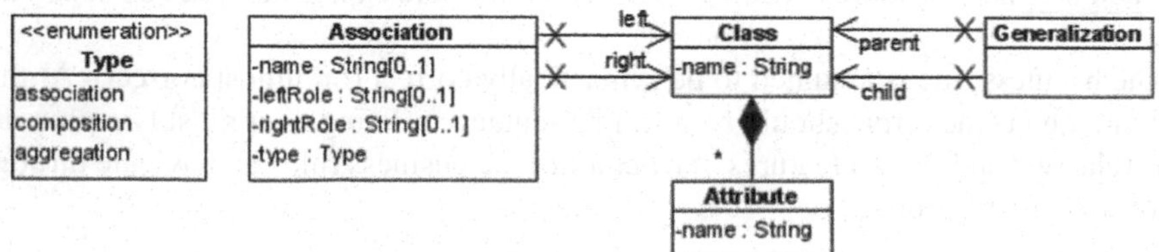

Fig. 3. Class diagram meta-model

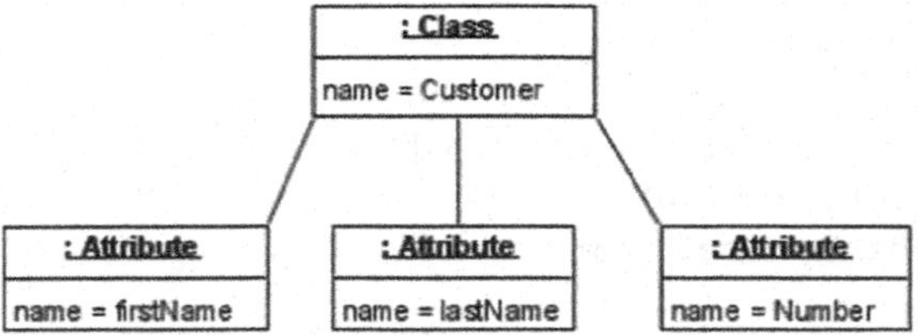

Fig. 4. Meta-model instance example

The domain specification is also translated into a set of glossaries – in this step, the following glossaries are created: *classes* (class names and their aliases, role names), *attributes* (name of attributes), *associations* (name of associations including their reverse versions with expressions to represent compositions and aggregations), and *total* (union of other glossaries). All complex names are stored as sequences of words, e.g. 'BankAccount' is stored as 'bank account', e.g. glossary = {classes: {customer}, attributes: {first name, last name, number}, associations: {include, contain, be included, be contained}, total: {customer, first name, last name, number, include, contain, be included, be contained}}.

The second activity removes meaningless elements (particles, modal verbs, punctuations, units) from the business rule in its original version and translates any remaining token to its basic form (lemma). This step is done with the help of an external tagger (spacy, model 'en_core_web_sm'), e.g. "Customer's name be unique".

The main processing takes place in the third activity, which is presented in the pseudocode (Listing 1). This activity verifies the conformance of the translated business rule with the meta-model instance. *FindMappings* is a recursive function that generates all sequences of possible matches of business rule tokens to the total glossary entries along with a list of categories they belong to (CL for a class, ATR for an attribute, ASS – for an association). This is a heuristic function that tries to find the most similar match. Note that one can get more than one match, especially when the business rule uses complex expressions. For example, when the dictionary contains the entries: 'bank' (CL), 'bank account' (CL), 'account' (CL), the expression 'Bank account' can be represented as a sequence of: 'bank' (CL) and 'account' (CL) entries or simply 'bank account' (CL) entry. The sequence may still contain tokens not presented in the glossary, e.g. 'Customer's name' is represented as a sequence of 'customer' (CL), 's' (no category), 'name' (ATR). One token can belong to many categories, e.g. 'name' can represent a class and an attribute. One additional category was defined (NOUN) to represent nouns outside the glossary.

```
Verify Business Rule
Requires:
      Business rule (BR) - list of tokens,
      Internal glossary (G),
      Meta-model instance (cdi)

begin
  mappings ← empty
  FindMappings(mappings, empty, BR, G, 0)
  is_satisfied ← false
  foreach mapping in mappings do
      categorized_mappings ← empty
      CategorizeMappings(categorized_mappings, empty, mapping, 0)
      foreach categorized_mapping in categorized_mappings do
            test ← VerifySentence(categorized_mapping, cdi)
            if test then
                  is_satisfied ← true
                  break
  return is_satisfied
end
```

Listing 1. Main phase of verification method

The *CategorizeMappings* function works similarly to *FindMappings.* Its purpose is to flatten the mapped tokens so they belong to only one category. Let assume that a mapping contains tokens: 'customer' (CL), 's' (no category), 'name' (ATR, CL). The *CategorizeMappings* function will produce all combinations of tokens (lists) with a category defined, i.e. ['customer' (CL), 'name' (ATR)], and ['customer' (CL), 'name' (CL)]. Each combination is checked by the *VerifySentence* function. If the function returns true, processing completes successfully. If the function fails for all token combinations, the compatibility check result is set to false.

The *VerifySentence* function does two things. First, it checks if the token combination is valid. A valid combination cannot contain a token from the NOUN category and must match one of the specified patterns. Below is a list of the considered patterns (ATR – attribute, ASS – association, CL – class) along with a validation rule the pattern enables:

- Pattern 1: ATR CL or CL ATR – *checkOneAttribute*
- Pattern 2: ATR CL ATR CL or CL ATR CL ATR or CL ATR ATR CL or ATR CL CL ATR – *checkTwoAttributes*
- Pattern 3: CL ASS CL – *checkAssociation*

The pattern search is defined by a state machine – see Fig. 5. "ST" label is used to represent the fact that there are no more tokens to be processed.

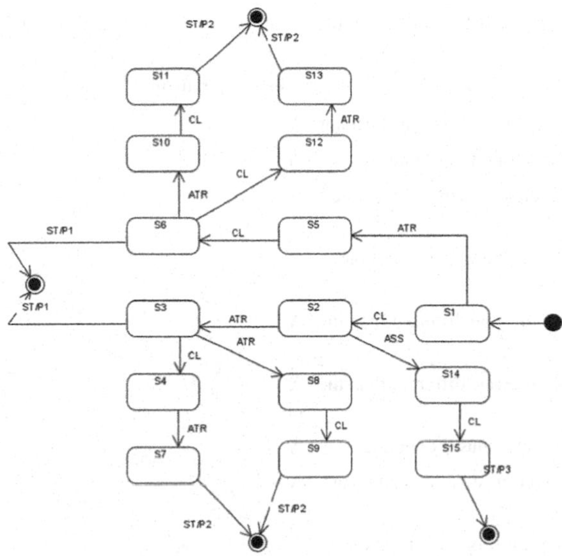

Fig. 5. Finding a pattern based on processing a combination of tokens

When a pattern is found, the *VerifySentence* function replaces synonyms of tokens with their basic form and runs the proper verification function. For example, *checkOneAttribute* takes a meta-model instance (*cdi*), attribute, and class as input, and returns true if the attribute, according to *cdi*, belongs to the class or one of its parents, false otherwise. The *checkTwoAttributes* function calls *checkOneAttribute* twice at each end and additionally checks whether there exists a binary relationship between classes on *cdi* (if the classes are different) or whether one class is represented by a role name at the end of association, starting at the second class. The *checkAssociation* function checks if an association with a given name links two classes or their parents; one of the classes can be represented by a role name.

5 Method Verification

The method has been implemented in Python according to its description given in Sect. 4.

The method has been verified by a set of business rules inspired by [14]. The set consists of 40 rules – 30 valid and 10 invalid. The list of exemplary rules (15 valid and 10 invalid) was given in Table 1. The domain specification is presented in Fig. 1. Additionally, the following synonyms for classes have been defined: customer – client.

The invalid rules are valid English sentences (with one exception, 'cutomer' except of 'customer'), but they are inconsistent with the class diagram given.

Table 1. Extract from the business rule set used for method verification

Id	Business rule	Class	Comment
1	Each bank must compose at least one account	V	
2	Client must open at most one account	V	
3	It is possible, that a buyer opens at most one account	V	
4	An account must be included in at most one bank	V	
5	Location of an Atm must be different than the address of a bank	V	
6	Location of an Atm must be different than the bank's address	V	
7	Each customer's number must be unique	V	
8	Each personal account must be opened by at most one client	V	
9	A business customer must open at least one personal account	V	
10	A buyer must open at most one account	V	
11	Personal account must be opened by one business customer	V	
12	A personal account must be opened by one business customer	V	
13	An atm must be aggregated in at most one bank	V	
14	A bank must accumulate at least one atm	V	
15	An account must be included in at most one bank	V	
16	Each person must open one bank account	I	Wrong class name
17	First name of customer must be different than customer family name	I	Wrong attribute name
18	Customer must open at most one customer account	I	Wrong class name
19	It is necessary that each account belongs to one client	I	Wrong association name
20	Cutomer must open at least one account	I	Wrong class name
21	Account must be given by exactly one owner	I	Wrong association name
22	It is necessary that each account is opened by exactly two guests	I	Wrong class/role name
23	Each bank's first name must be unique	I	Wrong attribute localization
24	Bank aggregates many parts	I	Wrong class name (parts outside the diagram)
25	Bank contains many ATM	I	Wrong dependency (verb)

The tool correctly classified all rules except one: "Cutomer must open at least one account". The tool is insensitive to minor syntax errors (cutomer instead of customer) what can be seen as an advantage. The performance is as follows (TP: 30, TN: 9, FP: 1, FN: 0, Accuracy = 98%, Precision = 97%).

The way of processing 2 examples (rule 23 and rule 25) is given below.

The translated 23th rule looks like this: bank 's first name be unique. The categorized list of tokens: {'pos': 0, 'value': 'bank', 'cat': < Category.CLL: 1 >}, {'pos': 2, 'value': 'first name', 'cat': < Category.ATT: 2 >}. This sequence matches the first pattern for which the *chekOneAttribute* function is enabled. It returns false because the *first name* attribute is not defined for the *Bank* class.

The translated 25th rule looks like: bank contains ATM. The categorized list of tokens: {'pos': 0, 'value': 'bank', 'cat': < Category.CLL: 1 >}, {'pos': 1, 'value': 'contain', 'cat': < Category.ASS: 1 >}, {'pos': 3, 'value': 'atm', 'cat': < Category.CLL: 1 >}. This sequence matches pattern 3, but the *checkAssociation* function returns false because there is no composition between Bank and ATM classes.

6 Summary

The paper deals with the problem of compatibility between a set of business rules written in free natural language with the business domain. It is assumed that the specification is given in the form of a class diagram extended by a glossary of class synonyms. The method is light and efficient, prepared to work with agile models (class diagrams contain only basic data). It does not require writing rules strictly according to a specific grammar which leaves much more freedom to specifiers. This is a heuristic method trying to find out if the business rule is built on facts and terms.

The method may have problems classifying correctly rules with many verbs, only one of which is correct. At that moment, invalid verb tokens (outside the domain) are skipped by the processing mechanism. Only the correct one is taken into consideration. Such a solution is sufficient for the considered cases – when the business rule is a singular sentence (one verb) referring to at most two classes/attributes.

The method performance is very good. The only false positive classification occurred for the sentence with a slight misspelling, which can be treated as a desired side effect.

In further, the method will be extended to handle complex sentences. The complex sentence, except for many verbs in different tenses, can contain possessive pronouns, e.g. his, its. The author also wants to include elements of verifying the semantics of sentences.

References

1. ISO/IEC/IEEE 24765: Systems and software engineering – Vocabulary
2. Hnatkowska, B., Walkowiak-Gall, A.: Towards Definition of a unified domain meta-model. In: Kosiuczenko, P., Zieliński, Z. (eds.) KKIO 2018. AISC, vol. 830, pp. 86–100. Springer, Cham (2019). https://doi.org/10.1007/978-3-319-99617-2_6
3. Hnatkowska, B., Hnatkowska, A.: Usability of the business rules specification languages. In: 2020 IEEE International Conference on Systems, Man, and Cybernetics (SMC), pp. 905–911 (2020)

4. RuleSpeak: Let the business people speak rules!. http://www.rulespeak.com/en/
5. OMG: Semantics of Business Vocabulary and Business Rules (SBVR), v1.4 Annex H - The RuleSpeak® Business Rule Notation (2016)
6. Hnatkowska, B., Rodríguez, J.M.Á.: Business rule patterns catalog for structural business rules. In: Software Engineering: Challenges and Solutions - Results of the XVIII KKIO 2016 Software Engineering Conference 2016 held at September 15–17 2016 in Wroclaw, Poland, pp. 3–16 (2016)
7. Business Rules Group: Business Rules Manifesto. https://www.brcommunity.com/brg/BRManifesto.pdf (2003)
8. Feuto Njonko, P.B., Cardey, S., Greenfield, P., El Abed, W.: RuleCNL: a controlled natural language for business rule specifications. In: Davis, B., Kaljurand, K., Kuhn, T. (eds.) CNL 2014. LNCS (LNAI), vol. 8625, pp. 66–77. Springer, Cham (2014). https://doi.org/10.1007/978-3-319-10223-8_7
9. SBVR Lab 2.0. http://www.sbvr.co/
10. RuleArts. RuleXpress. http://www.rulearts.com/rulexpress-solution/
11. Feuto, P.B., Cardey, S., Greenfield, P., Abed, W.E.: Domain specific language based on the SBVR standard for expressing business rules. In: 17th IEEE International Enterprise Distributed Object Computing Conference Workshops, pp. 31–38 (2013)
12. Bajwa, I.S., Lee, M., Bordbar, B.: SBVR business rules generation from natural language specification. In: AAAI Spring Symposium: AI for Business Agility (2011)
13. Bajwa, I.S., Lee, M., Bordbar, B.: Translating Natural Language Constraints to OCL. School of Computer Science, University of Birmingham, B15 2TT (2011)
14. Młynarczyk, K.: Badanie zgodności reguł biznesowych w języku naturalnym z diagramem domenowym (Compatibility checking of business rules in natural language with a domain diagram), Wroclaw University of Science and Technology, Master Thesis, not published (2020)
15. Del Camp, C., Pauser, S., Steiner, E., et al.: Decision making styles and the use of heuristics in decision making. J. Bus. Econ. **86**, 389–412 (2016)

Agent-Based Modeling and Simulation of Citizens Sheltering During a Tsunami: Application to Da Nang City in Vietnam

Nguyen-Tuan-Thanh Le[1(✉)], Phuong-Anh-Hung-Cuong Nguyen[2], and Chihab Hanachi[3]

[1] Thuyloi University, 175 Tay Son, Dong Da Dist, Hanoi, Vietnam
thanhlnt@tlu.edu.vn
[2] PVI, Hanoi, Vietnam
[3] IRIT Laboratory, University Toulouse 1 Capitole, 2 Rue du Doyen-Gabriel-Marty, Toulouse, France
Chihab.Hanachi@ut-capitole.fr

Abstract. Humans have witnessed several tsunamis throughout their history with tremendous human, environmental and material damage. Vietnam, because of its special geographic location in Southeast Asia, might be affected by tsunamis. Although the risk of tsunami in Vietnam is low, it does exist. Therefore, people must be well prepared if a tsunami strikes. Minimizing the damage caused by a tsunami, both for humans and infrastructure, is the most important duty of the authorities and the scientists. The objective of our research is to evaluate and measure the tsunami impacts on citizens and tourists according to their awareness of the situation and moving strategies towards shelters. We follow the agent-based modeling and simulation (ABMS) approach and illustrate it through a case study applied to Da Nang city, Vietnam, using the NetLogo platform and geo-spatial information.

Keywords: Tsunami evacuation · Agent-based modeling and simulation · Multi-agent systems

1 Introduction

During human history, we have recorded several tsunamis causing tremendous damage. In Japan, for example, the 2011 Tōhoku earthquake and tsunami, which occurred at 14:46 JST on 11 March, lasted only six minutes, but caused serious damage with 15,863 people killed, 5,901 people injured, 4,414 people missing and 114,591 destroyed houses [6].

Vietnam, with the particular geographic location in Southeast Asia and a long coastline along the whole country, might be affected by tsunamis, caused by earthquakes at the Manila Trench [19]. Historically, there are no reliable recorded documents about tsunamis occurring in Vietnam, according to [3]. However, from 2018, tsunami warning monitoring systems have been installed on the coasts of

K. Wojtkiewicz et al. (Eds.): ICCCI 2021, CCIS 1463, pp. 199–211, 2021.
https://doi.org/10.1007/978-3-030-88113-9_16

Quang Nam and Da Nang provinces. The risk of tsunamis in Vietnam is low, but exists, and therefore the government and people must be well prepared if a tsunami occurs [2].

Minimizing the damage caused by tsunamis, both for humans and infrastructure, is the most important duty of the authorities and the scientists. Raising public awareness about tsunamis and educating people to evacuation strategies to protect themselves, will help to reduce the impact of a tsunami. Therefore, evacuation drills are necessary to experiment with different evacuation strategies in order to find out the best one. However, such drills require mobilizing a lot of people and huge resources. Instead, we can use a computer-based evacuation model for educational purposes [18].

The agent-based modeling and simulation (ABMS) approach has been applied by researchers for decades to model and simulate tsunami evacuation [9,10,14,15]. However, their models often focused on few aspects of tsunami evacuation, e.g., the dynamics of pedestrians or/and vehicles. As a consequence, they did not provide complete insight into the matter, e.g., the dynamics of a tsunami, dynamics of other stakeholders (e.g. rescuers) and different moving strategies as our work does.

In addition, real drills, with the participation of local authorities and others stakeholders (e.g., the navy, marine police, fire police, border protecting forces, etc.), including disaster mitigation, search and rescue tasks, as the one that took place in Da Nang city in 2011 [22], mostly aim to focus on the coordination of the functional agencies. In our work, we focus on citizens and tourists moving strategies, that are, in our opinion, the main objects of evacuation task during a tsunami.

In this paper, we model, simulate and analyze the sheltering of people (citizens and tourists, pedestrians or with a vehicle) to face a tsunami located in Da Nang city. We follow the agent-based modeling and simulation (ABMS) approach, using the NetLogo platform. **The contributions** of our work are twofold:

1. A model representing the several concepts involved in the simulation and their links. It also includes the behavior of citizens and tourists (possibly inside cars) with different levels of awareness on the area in which they evolve;
2. A simulation framework on top of which several runs have been conducted to compare different moving strategies of these agents in a geo-spatial setting.

Our model also takes into account the behavior of functional agencies (e.g., rescuers and their awareness of the shelter location) and the tsunami dynamics based on its velocity, height, and number of segments.

The remainder of this paper is organized as follows. We first present the background on ABMS in Sect. 2. The state of the art, about computer-based support for crisis management and notably for tsunami evacuation assistance, is discussed in Sect. 3. Our ABMS model for tsunami evacuation and the corresponding simulation results are described in Sect. 4. Finally, a discussion about our work and a conclusion, including future work, are provided.

2 Background on Agent-Based Modeling and Simulation

It is not always possible or may be very difficult to define theoretical laws (e.g., mathematical equations) for understanding and analyzing complex phenomena due to their numerous components and the non-linearity of their interactions. Agent-based Modeling and Simulation (ABMS for short) is recognized as an alternative and bottom-up approach to study complex systems (e.g., tsunamis, floods, transportation, epidemiology, etc.). Indeed, it proposes to abstract a system as a collection of autonomous entities, called *agents* [10,16], able to interact to reproduce collectively the behavior of a complex system. Moreover, agents may have very simple behavior (reactive agent, e.g., ants) or exhibit cognitive and goal-oriented behavior (e.g., bidder) with high-level interactions (e.g., contract net protocol). Also new organizations or phenomena can emerge from these interactions [10]. For example, while each citizen, taken individually, follows a set of simple movement rules, a panic or a self-organization phenomena can emerge from the collective interactions of the citizens.

ABMS has three main interesting features supporting crisis and disaster management at the different steps of a crisis life-cycle management (mitigation, preparedness, response and recovery) [7]:

1. It first makes the reproduction of past situations possible to understand and explain better what has occurred.
2. It can also help to explore what-if scenarios by playing on values of several parameters such as actors' behavior, their mental states and interactions, the environment context and its dynamic,... In this case, it can help to anticipate issues or emergent phenomena such as panics, or discover the benefits of mutual aid between citizens or self-organization advantages.
3. Finally, ABMS provides means to explore different strategies regarding alternative emergency plans or communication policies.

In addition, if coupled with geographic information system, ABMS makes the visualization of these phenomena possible and can be of great use to stakeholders for deciding collectively and in real time (response phase) action plans to be taken, defining policies or adapting strategies. Once a plan is decided, ABMS can help to calibrate it, allocate the necessary resources and analyze potential vulnerabilities and risks linked to this plan.

Finally, the ABMS approach offers different points of view on crisis or disaster phenomena, such as:

1. Macro view underlying global interesting situations, collective emergent behavior or organizations, key performance indicators,...
2. Micro view zooming on a specific agent behavior or a given geographic location,...
3. A topic-oriented view focusing on risks, damages, environment or specific tasks, such as evacuation, sheltering, feeding, search or rescue.

From an implementation point of view, several ABMS platforms are available on top of which one can build his own model. Among the most well-known platforms, are NetLogo [20], GAMA [15], AnyLogic for general purposes, or for specific purposes, SUMO (urban mobility), MATSim (transport simulation), etc. The complete classification of ABMS platforms based on the computational strength and model development efforts is presented in [1].

3 State of the Art

Software tools are widely adopted by crisis management stakeholders to improve their cooperation, support their decisions, understand disaster situations better, anticipate risks and adapt their crisis resolution plans.

Several generic software platforms have been developed to help and support cooperation during one or several steps of the crisis life-cycle. [7] provides a review of several cooperative platforms (WORKPAD, SoKNOS, INDIGO or USHAHIDI, HAC-ER,...) and in particular explains how they help to coordinate stakeholders and/or ease cooperation with volunteers and citizens.

Regarding simulation, Agent-Based Modeling and Simulation (ABMS) is one of the main approaches which led to the development of several simulators. These simulators have been most of the time developed on top of Netlogo or GAMA platforms. Such simulators, devoted to a specific phenomenon (tsunami, earthquake, flooding, or bushfires,...), model a precise environment and more or less complex and heterogeneous human behaviors (reactive to cognitive, basic interactions to high levels protocols).

In [11], the authors provide an interesting state of the art of such ABMS approaches and explain the interest of BDI (Believe-Desire-Intention) agent architecture to support complex decisions integrating emotions.

More recently, Geographic Information Systems (GIS) have been coupled with ABMS systems in order to add a spatio-temporal dimension to simulations, see [4] for a review. This is the approach followed in our paper. This coupling lets the users have a more realistic view of the environment structure (roads, rivers, seas, buildings,...) and its evolution, but also of the agents' movements inside the environment. Moreover, emerging phenomena, such as traffic congestion, floods, crowd movements or panic, may be more easily visible by the users of a simulator.

Regarding tsunami modeling, as discussed in [10], three approaches have been explored: geographic information systems, system dynamics and discrete element methods. However, these approaches encountered difficulties in providing complete insight about the tsunami evacuation problem, as demonstrated in [10]. ABMS has proved to be more relevant, notably for modeling and simulating evacuation [12]. [14,15] used a hybrid modeling approach to develop an agent-based model of pedestrian evacuation in Nha Trang city, Vietnam. Their model improved speed and realism in pedestrian dynamics and collision avoidance behaviors by combining micro and macro modeling. However, their work did not take into account the dynamics of vehicles and other stakeholders (e.g., rescuers). LE et al. [8] combined genetic algorithms and linear programming in an ABMS setting in order to optimize the sign placement for tsunami evacuation, while in our work we focus on the influence of awareness of citizens and tourists on the efficiency of their evacuation towards shelters. Several other works [9,10,13,17] developed an agent-based model for tsunami evacuation that takes into account tsunami flooding and interactions between vehicles and pedestrians. However, their work left out the dynamics of other stakeholders (e.g., rescuers).

In conclusion, our work develops a holistic agent-based model, including geospatial information, for tsunami evacuation. We consider several aspects: the dynamics of tsunamis, the tourists, citizens and vehicles movement strategies and also rescuers strategies. In addition, tourists and rescuers have variable degrees of awareness of the situation which allows to study the impact of awareness on evacuation efficiency.

4 Modeling and Simulating Tsunami Evacuation in Da Nang City

4.1 Hypothetical Situation

Our research is based on the real rehearsal that took place in Son Tra district, Da Nang city, in 2011, with the participation of 6,600 people [22]. The hypothetical situation was: "There is a 8.8 magnitude earthquake off the East Sea, from Luzon Island of the Philippines, which causes a tsunami with waves up to 6 meters high along the coast of Da Nang city. As soon as they receive alert of an impending tsunami, evacuees (i.e., residents and tourists) will try to move quickly to the shelters arranged inland."

The main purpose of our research is to find out the best evacuation strategy to minimize the number of casualties, by maximizing the number of people evacuated into shelters.

NetLogo [20], one of the most popular multi-agent platforms, is used to model and simulate tsunami evacuation. It is a useful platform to develop rapidly efficient prototypes.

4.2 Conceptual Representation of the Agents and the Environment

In our model, we consider 15 concepts involved in the tsunami evacuation, represented as classes in the UML diagram of Fig. 1, including: **Tsunami**, **Segment**, **Area**, **Shelter**, **Road**, **Building**, **Agent**, **AdultLocal** (or AdultCitizen), **AdultTourist**, **Child**, **Rescuer**, **Vehicle**, **Car**, **Motorbike** and **Boat**.

The study *Area* consists of *Shelters*, *Roads* and *Buildings*. The *Tsunami* is composed of several *Segments* which might have different velocities, heights and depths. The *Agent* class is extended by the *AdultLocal*, *AdultTourist*, *Child*, *Rescuer* and *Vehicle* classes. We consider three types of vehicles: *Car*, *Motorbike* and *Boat*.

4.3 Concept Implementation

The study *area*, corresponding to the spatial components, is represented by a 360 × 360 squares, corresponding to 129600 patches. The agents can move on

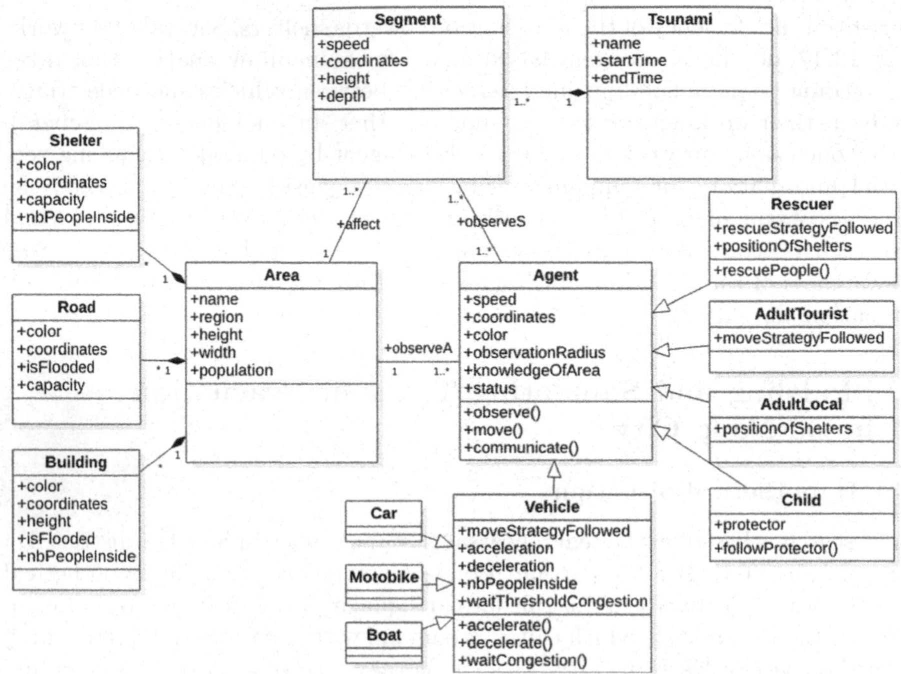

Fig. 1. The UML conceptual representation of our tsunami evacuation model.

patches. Each patch, in the study area, may be in one of the three following states: 1) *flooded*, i.e., if it is inside a segment of tsunami; 2) *safe in shelter*, i.e., if it is in a shelter; and 3) *safe and out of shelters*, i.e., if it is out of shelters and not flooded.

A *shelter*, placed inland and normally at high positions, such as mountains, is represented by a small green square. Each shelter has a limited capacity, meaning that if the current number of people in a given shelter exceeds its capacity, the other people cannot go inside this shelter and must move and find another one. In our model, we define the shelters coordinates and capacity in a csv file.

A *building* in its life-cycle belongs to one of two states: 1) *destroyed*, meaning that it is inside a segment of tsunami; and 2) *safe*, meaning that it is outside the tsunami.

The *roads* are highlighted by white patches. The coordinates of roads and buildings are taken from a shapefile of Da Nang city, extracted from OpenStreetMap.

The *tsunami* is presented by vertical blue patches. It moves inland from the East Vietnam Sea, i.e. from the right of screen, and consists of some segments. Each tsunami segment has four attributes: 1) *speed*; 2) *coordinates*; 3) *height*; and 4) *depth*. The velocity v of a segment depends on its depth, as defined by $v = \sqrt{gd}$ where g is the acceleration of gravity and d is the depth. When a segment approaches the coast, its speed will decrease gradually. The segment will stop when its speed reaches 0. The greater the speed when approaching the coast, the more inland the segment will go. To implement the dynamics of the tsunami, we have reused and improved a public code, available at [21].

Our evacuation model consists of *agents*, which have one of three states in their life-cycle: 1) *dead*, i.e. within the tsunami; 2) *safe*, i.e. evacuated to a shelter; and 3) *in-danger*, i.e. moving to a shelter. In addition, each agent has attributes, such as *speed*, *knowledge of area* (awareness), *observation radius* that is useful to find the way to a shelter. The actual speed of each agent is generated randomly on the basis of *human average speed* parameter using a Gaussian distribution. The initial position of the agents is also generated randomly.

The *adult locals* (adult citizens), extended from Agent class, have full knowledge of the study area. They know the position of shelters, so they can quickly move to a shelter using the shortest path.

Contrary to adult locals, *adult tourists* have partial knowledge of the study area. Therefore, they have to use an efficient moving strategy that helps to increase their survivability. In our model, we implemented three moving strategies for adult tourists: 1) *wandering*, i.e., the tourists move randomly, i.e. they choose next patch randomly; 2) *following rescuers/locals*, i.e., if the tourists see a rescuer or a local, they will follow this rescuer/local; and 3) *following crowd*, i.e., if the tourists see a moving crowd, they will follow this crowd.

A *child*, extended from Agent class, must be protected by his parents. He/she always follows his/her parents during the evacuation.

The *vehicles*, extended from Agent class, have *acceleration* and *deceleration* attributes that help to increase or decrease their speed by given values, depending on the current situation on the road. Although the most popular vehicle in Vietnam is the motorbike, in our model, we only consider the cars that have different behaviors. If a car has to stop for a long time, because of a congestion, the people inside this car could go outside and move to a shelter by foot. As tourists, the cars follow a moving strategy that helps go to a shelter quickly and efficiently. In our model, we implemented three strategies for cars: 1) *always go ahead*, i.e., they follow the chosen route and if there is a congestion, they will stand in place and wait until the congestion is over; 2) *change direction when congestion*, i.e., they will find another route if there is a congestion; and 3) *go out when congestion*, i.e., if there is a congestion, people will get out of their cars and evacuate on foot.

The *rescuers*, i.e., military or police, have the duty to take people to safe places. In addition to their knowledge of the area, inherited from Agent class, they feature a specific attribute, called *positionOfShelters*, that make them aware of the shelters positions. In order to rescue as many people as possible, they have to follow an efficient strategy. In our model, for simplicity reasons, their strategy for finding people is a random moving. Once the rescuers have found people, they move to the shelters following the shortest path.

We do not implement the *Motorbike*, *Boat* and *Child* class in our current version.

4.4 Model Interface

The interface of our model is composed of three components: 1) *View component*; 2) *Input component*; and 3) *Output component.*

The View component is illustrated in Fig. 2. It presents the study area (with roads, buildings, shelters), the agents dynamics and the tsunami dynamics.

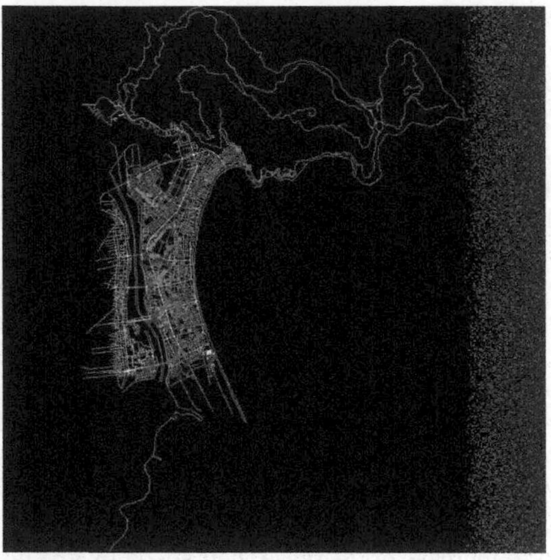

Fig. 2. The View component of our model, in which white curves represent roads, the blue region on the right represents tsunami and the colorful circles represent agents. (Color figure online)

The Input component is shown in Fig. 3. It allows the user to calibrate global parameters for the agents (e.g., quantity, average speed, moving strategy), as well as parameters for the tsunami (e.g., average speed, number of segments). The *tsunami_approach_time* parameter corresponds to the moment when a tsunami approaches the study area. In fact, at the beginning of a run, when people receive a tsunami alert, they start to evacuate.

The Output component consists of several *monitors* and *plots* to present real-time statistics about agents (adult locals, adult tourists, cars, rescuers states), buildings, and tsunami dynamics during the simulation.

4.5 Comparing Tourists Moving Strategies

Our holistic model can be used to discover several aspects of tsunami evacuation. Among them, finding the good moving strategy for agents to reduce the damage caused by tsunami, is an important task.

In our model, we implement three moving strategies for tourists and three moving strategies for cars. In the scope of this paper, we will compare the evacuation strategies of tourists who are the most vulnerable agents when a tsunami

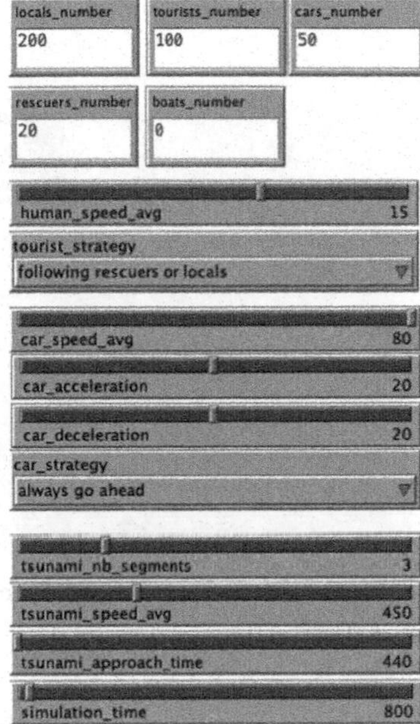

Fig. 3. The Input component of our model to set up the values of the parameters

occurs. We performed ten simulations for each tourist strategy. The other global parameters are the same, but the actual speed of each agent and tsunami segment are generated randomly, following a Gaussian distribution. Indeed, in this current version, we do not use the depth information to calculate the speed of tsunami segments. Also, as soon as a tsunami segment reaches the coast, we decrease its speed randomly. In addition, the initial positions of the agents are chosen randomly.

Figure 4 shows the comparison of simulation results (i.e., number of dead, evacuated and in-danger tourists), when we try different moving strategies for 100 adult tourists. In comparison to other strategies, we can see that the *following rescuers/locals* strategy features significant improvements in the number of evacuated tourists, and it reduces also the number of dead tourists.

Additionally, in general, the result of *following crowd* strategy is better than the *wandering* strategy. However, in some runs, when tourists employ the *following crowd* strategy, most of them die. It makes sense because sometimes the crowd acts just like a "blind" agent.

4.6 Influence of Awareness on Tsunami Impact

Figure 5 shows the comparison of the percentages of casualties while Fig. 6 shows the percentages of evacuated locals and tourists during an arbitrary run. While the locals are aware of the positions of the shelters, the tourists are not. We use the *following rescuers/locals* strategy for the tourists. They have to find first

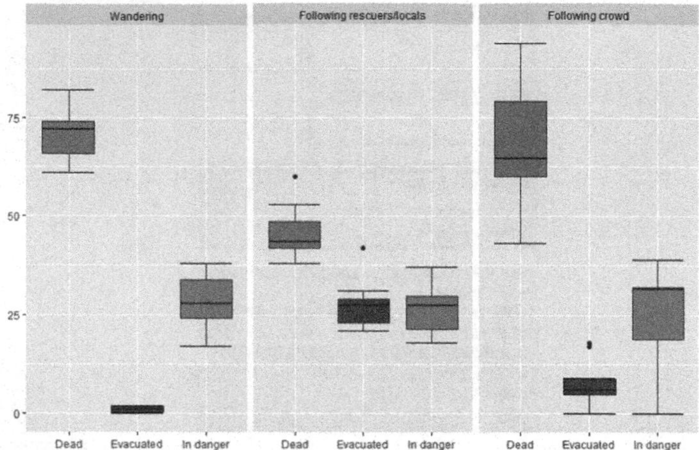

Fig. 4. Comparison of three tourists moving strategies according to the number of dead, evacuated and in-danger people

a rescuer or a local before following him/her. This explains why tourists have a higher percentage of casualties (Fig. 5) and a less percentage of saved lives (Fig. 6).

These simulations clearly show the advantages of the awareness factor since the tsunami has less impact on locals (who are aware of the shelters positions) than on tourists, even if these ones follow rescuers or locals.

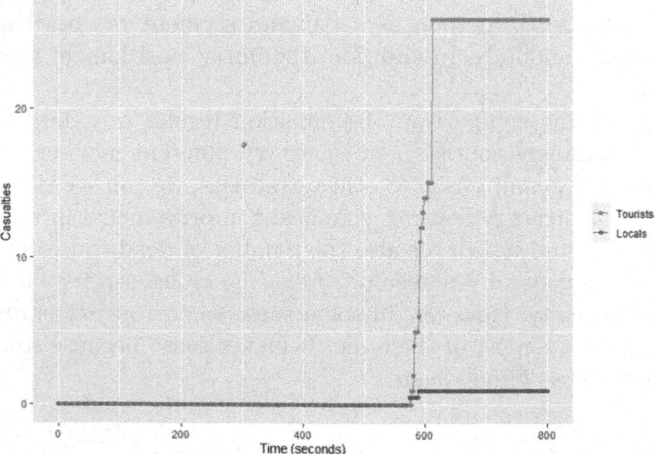

Fig. 5. The real-time percentage of casualties of locals and tourists during an arbitrary run.

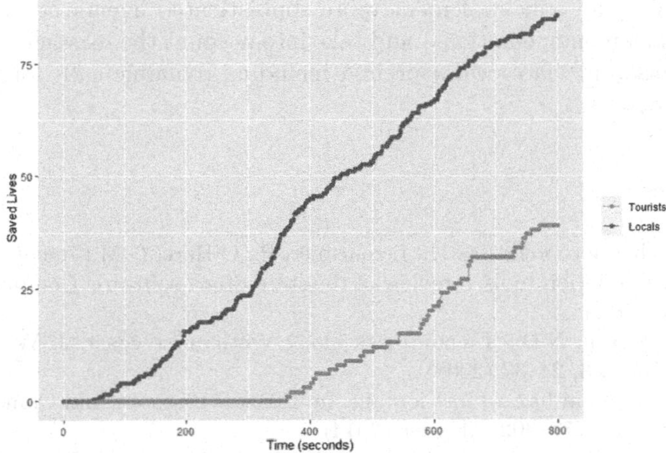

Fig. 6. The real-time percentage of evacuated locals and tourists during an arbitrary run.

5 Discussion and Conclusion

In this paper, we have presented a tsunami evacuation model, developed on top of an agent-based modeling and simulation paradigm, for Da Nang city, Vietnam.

The simulator described constitutes a proof-of-concept and allows interesting conclusions. The number of casualties are affected by several factors, such as the speed of the tsunami and agents, the initial position of agents, the radius of observation, public awareness about shelters and tsunami, etc. However, following the right moving strategy and raising awareness are the key factors that can help tourists to survive.

On the basis of the simulation results, we recommend that the tourists do not follow a crowd when a tsunami occurs. Instead, they should follow locals or rescuers. If tourists are informed about the shelters positions before the tsunami occurs, it will probably increase their chances of survival.

Our holistic model is useful for authorities to obtain the complete insight of tsunamis evacuation problems by experimenting scenarios through simulations, for example. It could help them to make adequate decisions (e.g., about communication policy towards citizens and tourists, adapting shelters positions). Moreover, we believe that our approach can be easily reused for other types of disasters and other areas.

In future work, we will improve the accuracy of our simulation results by increasing the number of runs and agents. Indeed, due to the constraints of computation time, we only considered 10 runs for each strategy in this work. However, we believe that the above results do reflect the effectiveness of each strategy accurately but do not underline potential phenomena such as panics, people cooperation and self-organization.

Additionally, we will implement more sophisticated agents behaviors (e.g., psychological elements, emotions) and take into account the messages exchanged between agents and via crowd-sourcing, including dynamic calls for volunteers to help the citizens.

References

1. Abar, S., Theodoropoulos, G.K., Lemarinier, P., O'Hare, G.M.: Agent based modelling and simulation tools: a review of the state-of-art software. Comput. Sci. Rev. **24**, 13–33 (2017)
2. Ca, V.T., Xuyen, N.D.: Tsunami risk along Vietnamese coast. J. Water Resour. Environ. Eng. **23**, 24–33 (2008)
3. Ca, V.T.: Tsunami hazard in Vietnam. In: Coastal Disasters and Climate Change in Vietnam, pp. 277–302. Elsevier (2014)
4. Crooks, A.T., Heppenstall, A., Malleson, N.: Agent-based Modelling. In: Huang, B. (ed.) Comprehensive Geographic Information Systems, vol. 1, pp. 218–243. Elsevier, Oxford (2018)
5. Ferber, J., Gutknecht, O., Michel, F.: From agents to organizations: an organizational view of multi-agent systems. In: Giorgini, P., Müller, J.P., Odell, J. (eds.) AOSE 2003. LNCS, vol. 2935, pp. 214–230. Springer, Heidelberg (2004). https://doi.org/10.1007/978-3-540-24620-6_15
6. Koketsu, K., et al.: A unified source model for the 2011 Tohoku earthquake. Earth Planet. Sci. Lett. **310**(3–4), 480–487 (2011)
7. Le, N.T.T.: Coordination models for crisis resolution: discovery, analysis and assessment. Doctoral dissertation, Université Toulouse 3 Paul Sabatier (2016)
8. Le, V.M., Chevaleyre, Y., Zucker, J.D., Vinh, H.T.: Speeding up the evaluation of casualties in multi-agent simulations with Linear Programming application to optimization of sign placement for tsunami evacuation. In: The 2013 RIVF International Conference on Computing & Communication Technologies-Research, Innovation, and Vision for Future, pp. 215–220. IEEE (2013)
9. Mas, E., Suppasri, A., Imamura, F., Koshimura, S.: Agent-based simulation of the 2011 great east japan earthquake/tsunami evacuation: an integrated model of tsunami inundation and evacuation. J. Nat. Disaster Sci. **34**(1), 41–57 (2012)
10. Mas, E., Koshimura, S., Imamura, F., Suppasri, A., Muhari, A., Adriano, B.: Recent advances in agent-based tsunami evacuation simulations: case studies in Indonesia, Thailand, Japan and Peru. Pure Appl. Geophys. **172**(12), 3409–3424 (2015)
11. Mancheva, L., Adam, C., Dugdale, J.: Multi-agent geospatial simulation of human interactions and behaviour in bushfires. In: International Conference on Information Systems for Crisis Response and Management (2019)
12. Munadi, K., Nurdin, Y., Dirhamsyah, M., Muchalil, S.: Multiagent based tsunami evacuation simulation: a conceptual model. In: The Proceedings of 2nd Annual International Conference Syiah University 2012 & 8th IMT Uninet Biosciences Conference, pp. 254–259 (2012)
13. Mostafizi, A., Wang, H., Cox, D., Dong, S.: An agent-based vertical evacuation model for a near-field tsunami: choice behavior, logical shelter locations, and life safety. Int. J. Disaster Risk Reduct. **34**, 467–479 (2019)

14. Anh, N.T.N., Daniel, Z.J., Du, N.H., Drogoul, A., An, V.D.: A hybrid macro-micro pedestrians evacuation model to speed up simulation in road networks. In: Dechesne, F., Hattori, H., ter Mors, A., Such, J.M., Weyns, D., Dignum, F. (eds.) AAMAS 2011. LNCS (LNAI), vol. 7068, pp. 371–383. Springer, Heidelberg (2012). https://doi.org/10.1007/978-3-642-27216-5_28
15. Nguyen, T.N.A., Zucker, J.D., Nguyen, M.H., Drogoul, A., Nguyen, H.P.: Simulation of emergency evacuation of pedestrians along the road networks in Nhatrang city. In: IEEE RIVF International Conference on Computing & Communication Technologies, Research, Innovation, and Vision for the Future, pp. 1–6 (2012)
16. Russell, S., Norvig, P.: A Modern Approach. Artificial Intelligence, pp. 25–27. Prentice Hall (1995)
17. Wang, H., Mostafizi, A., Cramer, L.A., Cox, D., Park, H.: An agent-based model of a multimodal near-field tsunami evacuation: decision-making and life safety. Transp. Res. Part C: Emerging Technol. **64**, 86–100 (2016)
18. Wafda, F., Saputra, R.W., Nurdin, Y., Munadi, K.: Agent-based tsunami evacuation simulation for disaster education. In: International Conference on ICT for Smart Society, pp. 1–4 (2013)
19. Thao, N.D., Takagi, H., Esteban, M. (eds.): Coastal Disasters and Climate Change in Vietnam: Engineering and Planning Perspectives. Elsevier, Amsterdam (2014)
20. Wilensky, U., Rand, W.: An Introduction to Agent-Based Modeling - Modeling Natural, Social, and Engineered Complex Systems with NetLogo. The MIT Press, Cambridge (2015)
21. Rizqiya, P.: Tsunami evacuation model (2013). https://modelingcommons.org/browse/one_model/3477#model_tabs_browse_procedures. Accessed 30 June 2021
22. ThanhNien News: Vietnam holds first-ever tsunami drill (2011). https://thanhniennews.com/society/vietnam-holds-firstever-tsunami-drill-10052.html. Accessed 30 June 2021

Effect of Dialogue Structure and Memory on Language Emergence in a Multi-task Game

Kasun Vithanage[1,2](✉), Rukshan Wijesinghe[1], Alex Xavier[1], Dumindu Tissera[1], Sanath Jayasena[1], and Subha Fernando[2]

[1] CODEGEN QBITS Lab, University of Moratuwa, Moratuwa, Sri Lanka
sanath@cse.mrt.ac.lk

[2] Department of Computational Mathematics, University of Moratuwa, Moratuwa, Sri Lanka
subhaf@uom.lk

Abstract. In language emergence, neural agents engage in finite-length conversations using a finite set of symbols to reach a given goal. In such systems, two key factors can determine the dialogue structure; the size of the symbol set and the conversation length. During training, agents invent and assign meanings to the symbols without any external supervision. Existing studies do not investigate how these models behave when they train under multiple tasks requiring different levels of coordination and information exchange. Moreover, only a handful of work discusses the relationship between the dialogue structure and the performance. In this paper, we formulate a game environment where neural agents simultaneously learn on heterogeneous tasks. Using our setup, we investigate how the dialogue structure and the agent's capability of processing memory affect the agent performance across multiple tasks. We observed that memory capacity non-linearly affects the task performances, where the nature of the task influences this non-linearity. In contrast, the performance gain obtained by varying the dialogue structure is mostly task-independent. We further observed that agents prefer smaller symbol sets with longer conversation lengths than the converse.

1 Introduction

Humans use language to create practical effects in the environment and in the mindset of coordinating parties [1]. It raises the utilitarian definition of language understanding and emphasizes language as a tool for accomplishing tasks. Frequently, language emergence setups consist of discretely connected neural networks, known as agents in this context [5,14,15]. These agents act like players in a signaling game and cooperate to achieve certain non-linguistic tasks. In doing so, they emerge native communication methods that are required to accomplish the given tasks. By allowing neural agents to develop their own communications [6,16], such setups direct supervised language learning towards unsupervised language emergence.

Supported by CODEGEN QBITS Lab.

K. Wojtkiewicz et al. (Eds.): ICCCI 2021, CCIS 1463, pp. 212–224, 2021.
https://doi.org/10.1007/978-3-030-88113-9_17

Partial observability of inputs is a crucial characteristic of these games. At least, some of the agents cannot observe the total amount of necessary information to achieve the task. Agents must engage in finite-length conversations by sampling from a finite-sized symbol set to get the required information. Initially, symbols do not mean anything to the agents. They should come to a mutual agreement regarding what is meant by a symbol. Hence, during the training, agents must formulate and assign meanings to the symbols by themselves. Our emergent language is not a natural language or a formal language in the ordinary sense, but a token-based communication that frequently appears in language emergence literature [8,14–16].

Studies in task-based language emergence have progressed through two distinct paths [5]. One of those paths studies emergent communications as a means of supporting better coordination among multi-agent systems [16,19]. The other path mainly investigates the dynamics of language emergence [4,5], which is also the main focus of this research.

Traditional setups investigate scenarios where agents train to attain a single task or multiple tasks in isolation. However, this paper introduces a novel game that facilitates agents in simultaneously learning multiple structurally different tasks. It is similar to how humans use natural language. Instead of focusing on a unique task, humans use language to accomplish goals requiring various levels of coordination. We follow a naturally favorable game structure by simulating a turn-taking dialogue between two participants, where agents can interchange between speaker and listener roles. Our intention is not to argue that multi-task settings improve or hinder language emergence but to investigate how memory capacity and dialogue structure affect the agent behavior in such a multi-task setting.

Our setup contains three tasks that are based on the same input and output domains. Nonetheless, the requirements of information exchange and inter-agent coordination for *correctly* solving them is different from each other. Hence, in this sense, we denote our environment as a multi-task environment for convenience. Our tasks take the form of a question-answering game. Agent receives a question and an image as local inputs, where the question is the same for both the agents. After understanding the question and observing the image, they start to communicate using a finite set of symbols. In the end, each of them provides their answers to the given question. Our observations show that agents respond to different questions (tasks) uniquely, depending on the memory capacity.

The dialogue structure of this game is determined by the size of the symbol set and the conversation length. If agents have large symbol sets, they can possibly connect compositional concepts with single symbols. For example, the words *green* and *square* are atomic concepts, where *green square* is compositional. When agents have surplus symbols, they can assign single symbols to composite concepts like *green square*, in addition to the atomic concepts. An increase in conversation length provides agents more time to coordinate with each other. Thus, understanding the behavior of the agents under these two parameters is of crucial importance. Previous studies have shown that increasing both of these values gives higher performance [3]. However, we observe that, under normal training settings, agents prefer longer dialogue lengths and smaller vocabularies than the converse.

2 Related Work

Several interesting pieces of research have already been conducted to investigate the dynamics of language emergence [5,15]. But unlike [5,15], we do not use a referential game setup. In referential games, agents could develop lexicons denoting low-level properties of the images like pixel intensity [2]. Thus higher performance may not indicate good communication or protocols. Our game follows the paradigm of classification games [13], which ensures that symbols are associated with sufficiently rich meanings to predict the final labels.

Previous studies have explored the dynamics of emergent languages using different blends of matrices and parameters. For example, determining the relationship between the compositionality and the generalization [3], the relationship between bandwidth, capacity, and compositionality [7,17], mutual entropy minimization pressure [13], anti-efficient encoding [4], representations developed by the agents during emergent language development [2], the effect of message length, conversation length, and the information-theoretic content [5]. In this paper, we use a different blend, focusing on investigating the effect of the memory capacity and the dialogue structure across multiple heterogeneous tasks requiring different levels of coordination. We elaborate on the emerging effects in terms of the performance and the nature of the evolved protocols.

Several studies discuss the effect of symbol set size and conversation length. According to them, increasing both the conversation length and the symbol set size is more effective [8,12]. Instead of solely investigating these parameters in isolation, we also analyze their combined effect on heterogeneous tasks. Moreover, we elaborate on how agents prefer certain combinations of symbol set sizes and conversation lengths over others. Previous works that investigate factors like capacity, bandwidth, and memory, employ tasks that require uni-directional communication [3,7,17]. In our setups, we make some of the tasks require bi-directional communication essentially for correctly achieve them. Our agents are symmetric in their structure and can interchange between speaker and listener roles.

3 Model

CLEVR Dataset. We use CLEVR [11] dataset in our experiments. CLEVR images are highly compositional, where each image is a combination of multiple objects, and each object is again a combination of a set of core attributes. Objects are 3–D geometrical shapes, and characterized by physical attributes such as *color*, *size*, *shape*, and *material*. In a given image, 5–10 objects can be present at once.

3.1 Overview

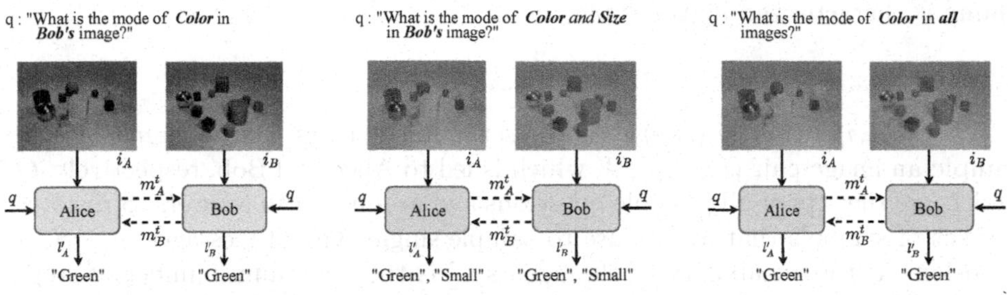

Fig. 1. Category Q1. (Color figure online)

Fig. 2. Category Q2. (Color figure online)

Fig. 3. Category Q3. (Color figure online)

Questions. Our game contains two agent players whom we denote as *Alice* and *Bob*. Each player receives a CLEVR image and a question q. The question requires agents to find out the mode value of a given attribute. Questions have the following structure: "What is the mode of *attribute(s)* in *reference agent(s)* image(s)?". For an example refer Fig. 1, "What is the mode of *color* in *Bob's* image?" is the question. The answer to this question is "Green" because most of the objects in Bob's image are green in color. If all values for the given attribute have the same frequency, all respective values are indicated in the answer instead of omitted. Although the questions are interpreted using words, what agents receive is a binary vector that contains the attribute(s) and reference agent(s).

Game Play. After receiving inputs, agents start to communicate bidirectionally with each other. They carry out three actions during the communication phase, 1) listen to the incoming message from its peer, 2) transmit a message to its peer, 3) produce a memory update. This process regarding message generation, receiving, and transmission is further explained in Sect. 3.3. Each message consists of a single symbol sampled from a finite set of symbols. Dialogue can continue up to a predefined number of steps. No prior meaning is assigned to any of the symbols. Hence, during the training, agents have to formulate and assign meanings to the symbols. At the end of the dialogue, both agents should provide the answer to the given question. (see Fig. 1, 2, and 3 for a high level overview of the game).

Question Categories. We model the game as a cooperative game. Based on the parameters *attribute(s)* and *reference agent(s)*, tasks can belong to 3 categories. If the question contains a single attribute and one reference agent, it belongs to the category $Q1$ (see Fig. 1). Questions that contain two attributes and one reference agent belong to the category $Q2$ (see Fig. 2). The category $Q3$ (see Fig. 3) contains questions with a single attribute and both the agents as references. In $Q2$, the mode of two attributes is found independently from each other.

3.2 Game Framework

Game is characterized by the tuple,

$$G = \langle I, Q, S, T, L, L' \rangle \tag{1}$$

$I = \{(i_A, i_B)_1, \ldots, (i_A, i_B)_N\}$ is the set of image pairs. During gameplay, we sample an image pair $(i_a, i_B) \in I$, which is fed to Alice and Bob, respectively. Q and L are the sets of all possible questions and ground truth answers. S denotes the set of symbols that agents use to sample single symbol messages $m \in S$. S functions as the vocabulary of the agents. T is the maximum number of steps permitted within a dialogue. L' is the set of predicted answers for the question set Q.

Set R contains all the possible variations of reference(s) that a question can contain;

$$R = R_1 \cup R_2 \tag{2}$$

$$R_1 = \{Alice, Bob\} \tag{3}$$

$$R_2 = \{x : x \subseteq R_1 and \mid x \mid= 2\} \tag{4}$$

Similarly, the set P contains all variations of the attribute(s).

$$P = P_1 \cup P_2 \tag{5}$$

$$P_1 = \{Color, Size, Shape, Material\}; \tag{6}$$

$$P_2 = \{x : x \subset P_1 and \mid x \mid= 2\} \tag{7}$$

The set Q is defined as the union of the 3 Cartesian products that represent individual question categories, where each question $q \in Q$ is an ordered pair (p, r) such that $p \in P$ and $r \in R$. A question is sampled from one of the three categories and given to both the agents during the gameplay.

$$Q_1 = P_1 \times R_1 \tag{8}$$

$$Q_2 = P_2 \times R_1 \tag{9}$$

$$Q_3 = P_1 \times R_2 \tag{10}$$

$$Q = Q_1 \cup Q_2 \cup Q_3 \tag{11}$$

Each symbol in S is represented as a one-hot encoded vector of size k.

$$S = \left\{ x : x \in \{0,1\}^k, \sum_{i=1}^{k} x_i = 1 \right\} \tag{12}$$

We define D, which denotes the set of all possible dialogues that can occur between two agents, where each dialogue is defined as an ordered T-tuple. The cardinality of D is controlled by the size of the symbol set $\mid S \mid= k$ and the maximum number of steps per dialogue T, where $\mid D \mid=\mid S \mid^{2T}= k^{2T}$.

$$D = \Big\{((m_A^0, m_B^0), \ldots, (m_A^t, m_B^t), \ldots, (m_A^{T-1}, m_B^{T-1})) : m_A^t, m_B^t \in S, \\ t \in [0, \ldots, T-1]\Big\} \quad (13)$$

The ground-truth set L consists of c dimensional vectors and the map between I, Q, is given as,

$$L : I \times Q \rightarrow \{0,1\}^c \quad (14)$$

We parameterize *Alice* and *Bob* as neural networks with parameters θ_A and θ_B. Agents are symmetric in design but do not share their parameters. Our agents take images, question, hidden state $h \in H$ from the previous time step, and an incoming message as inputs. Agents produce two outputs during the message passing.

First, they output a message sampled from the symbol set, and secondly, they produce a hidden state vector that carries information to the next step of the game. Each agent predicts an answer $l' \in L'$ for the given question at the end of the dialogue.

$$\theta : I \times Q \times H \times S \times \mathbb{1}[t = T] \rightarrow H \times S \times L' \quad (15)$$

3.3 Agent Architecture

We developed identical neural agents with feed-forward neural networks and long short-term memory (LSTM) [9]. Within each agent, there are two LSTM cells stacked together and two feed-forward neural networks functioning as decoders for the hidden state of the last LSTM cell. Gameplay during step $t < T$ for any of the two agents is as follows: First, the given question q, image i, and the incoming message m_{in}^{t-1} is concatenated to form a single input I_{input}.

$$I_{input} = \text{concatenate}\left[q, i, m_{in}^{t-1}\right] \quad (16)$$

The concatenated input is then fed into the stacked LSTM cells.

$$h_1^t, c_1^t = \text{LSTM}\left(h_1^{t-1}, c_1^{t-1}, I_{input}\right) \quad (17)$$

$$h_2^t, c_2^t = \text{LSTM}\left(h_2^{t-1}, c_2^{t-1}, h_1^t\right) \quad (18)$$

A decoder network D_S observes h_2^t and outputs a set of logits $p_m^t = D_S\left(h_2^t\right)$, which is used to sample a single symbol from the set S, creating the output message m_{out}^t. The sampled single symbol message is then transmitted to the other agent as a one-hot encoded vector. At the end of the dialogue $t = T$, the hidden state h_2^T is fed in to $D_{L'}$, which produce a set of logits $p_{l'}^T = D_{L'}\left(h_2^T\right)$ predicting the answer $l' \in L'$. We calculate the loss by comparing the ground-truth answer $l \in L$ and the predicted answer l' to backpropagate [18] through the agents.

Each value in the answer vector $l' \in L'$ is treated as the probability indicating a positive response for a particular value of an attribute. Since each CLEVR scene contains 8 *colors*, 3 *shapes*, 2 *sizes*, and 2 *materials* as attribute values, we represent the output of the agents and the corresponding ground-truth $l \in L$ as vectors with 15 dimensions.

Gumbel-Softmax Approximation. Since discrete outputs are not differentiable, we use Gumbel-Softmax [10] approximation, which is a continuous relaxation of a discrete categorical distribution. Using logits p_m^t, we obtain the vector "y", where each element j of y is calculated according to the Eq. 19. During the forward pass, we obtain the argmax value of the vector to obtain the discrete message m_{out}^t which consists of a single symbol. The original continuous approximation y is used for the backpropagation. Gumbel noise $\epsilon = -\log(-\log(u))$ is added to the log value of the logits p_m^t, before applying the softmax operation and $u = U(0, 1)$ is sampled from the uniform distribution. $(p)_j^t$ represent the jth element of the p_m^t.

$$G(y)_j = \frac{\exp((\log(p)_j^t + \epsilon)/\tau)}{\sum_{i=0}^{k} \exp((\log(p)_i^t + \epsilon)/\tau)} \tag{19}$$

3.4 Coordination and Information Exchange

Kharitonov *et al.* [13] showed that due to the entropy minimization pressure, the emergent protocols tend to be as simple as the task they are developed for. Within a single episode, to succeed in category Q_2, agents have to exchange information about two attributes, wherein category Q_1, the task can be completed by referring to a single attribute. Thus, even if agents converge to the most straightforward possible protocols, two question categories require different amounts of information exchange.

Q_1 and Q_2 questions can be achieved by either uni-directional or bi-directional information exchange. If the question "What is the mode of *color* and *shape* in *Alice's* image?" is given, Alice can simply transmit the necessary information (mode value of color and shape) directly to Bob. In this case, feedback from Bob is not essential. However, this may not always be the case, and agents can choose between uni-directional and bi-directional communication at their sole discretion. Q_3 questions need to refer only to a single attribute, but the level of coordination is significantly higher than a Q_1 question. Q_3 questions essentially require bi-directional cooperation because questions are based on input scenes given to both the agents.

4 Experiments and Results

4.1 Overview

Instead of directly using pixel images, we used *scene graphs* provided with the CLEVR images. Scene graphs explicitly and symbolically represent the attributes of objects in a given CLEVR image [11]. Then, scene graphs were transformed into vectors before being fed into the model, preventing the model from focusing on processing pixels that do not correlate with the language emergence. Questions were represented as binary encoded vectors. The decoder networks D_S and $D_{L'}$ were two-layer feed-forward neural networks, where their first layers contained a node count equal to $2h_2$. The final layers of the two networks had a node count equal to the size k of the symbol set and 15, respectively.

We trained our agents on all tasks (Q_1, Q_2, Q_3) simultaneously. We first selected 4 different values for the cardinality of the dialogue set D. Then, different configurations for the symbol set size k and dialogue length T were arranged for each cardinality as in Table 1. Although they have different dialogue structures with varying k and T parameters, they represent the same cardinality k^{2T}. We selected 5 hidden state sizes $(128, 256, 512, 1024, 2048)$ for LSTM cells, per each configuration in Table 1, totalling 55 unique experiments.

Table 1. Dialogue structure.

Cardinality (k^{2T})	Configuration (k, T)
10^4	$(10, 2), (10^2, 1)$
10^8	$(10, 4), (10^2, 2), (10^4, 1)$
10^{12}	$(10, 6), (10^2, 3), (10^3, 2)$
10^{16}	$(10, 8), (10^2, 4), (10^4, 2)$

We trained a single model for 100 epochs, used the Adam optimizer with a learning rate of 1×10^{-5}, and applied a learning rate decay of 0.6 after 80 epochs. At each trial, performance was measured separately for each of the three categories. Our questions were based on 4 attributes (*color*, *shape*, *material*, and *size*) that constitutes objects within the CLEVR dataset. We used F1-score as an evaluation metric to evaluate the performance of agents. Moreover, we measured the average entropy of the distribution of symbols exchanged within a single dialogue in nats per round under each question category.

In a similar sense to [7,17], we do not provide a rigorous interpretation for the memory capacity of the agents. The efficiency of manipulating the memory is important as the size of the memory. Despite this, we use the hidden state size h of the LSTM cells in our results as an indication for the memory capacity of an agent for the sake of simplicity, assuming that LSTM cells with larger hidden state sizes are more effective than cells with smaller hidden state sizes.

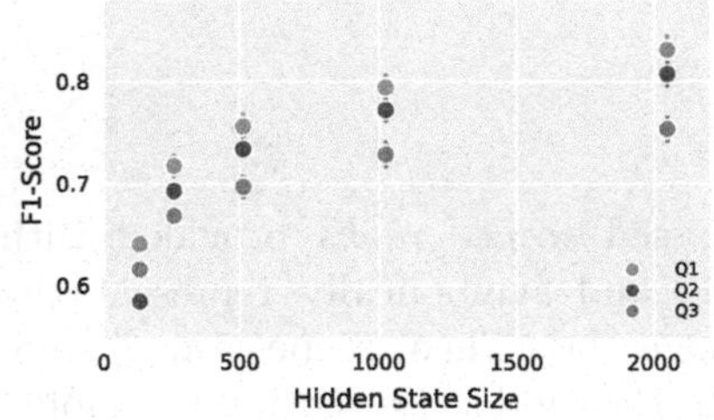

Fig. 4. F1-Score against hidden state size.

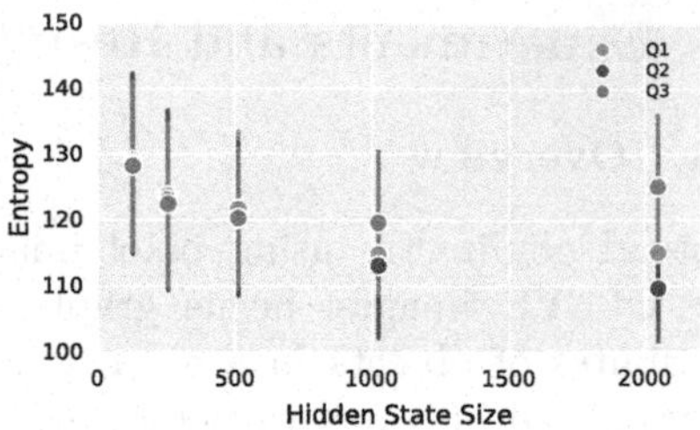

Fig. 5. Entropy against hidden state size

4.2 Effect of Memory

F1-Score. We averaged all trial runs for a particular hidden state size to investigate the effect of memory on the behavior of the agents (see Fig. 4). Error bars represent the standard error of the mean(SEM). In general, performance increases with the hidden state size across all three question groups, but the gain of the performance is not identical across the three categories, signifying that the effect of memory capacity on the performance is task-dependent. Q_1 and Q_2 shows a similar variation of F1-Score, where Q_3 behaves more differently.

Entropy. For the first three hidden state sizes (128, 256, 512), the entropy value for all three categories are nearly identical (see Fig. 5). As the memory capacity increase, entropy gets reduced under all three categories, from 128 to 1024. After that, entropy for Category 3 starts to increase, where entropies for other categories further decrease. Then at the hidden state size of 2048 entropy for Q_3 questions, get diverged significantly from the others. At this point, there is a considerable gap between all three entropy values. Counter-intuitively, we observe that entropy value for Q_1 is greater than that of Q_2, although Q_2 inquire about two attributes while Q_1 only concerned about a single attribute.

Behaviour of the Emergent Protocols. Given the behavior of the entropy and F-1 scores, we can expect that at lower memory capacities, agents use similar protocols for all three question types. Initially, agents may not have enough memory complexity to register separate protocols for the three tasks. Observations of the entropy suggest that the recurrent memory capacity of the agents enables the identification of differences between tasks.

The considerable entropy reduction at the initial stages (128, 256, 512) may be caused by protocols becoming more concise with the increasing complexity of the agents (F1-Score increases, while the entropy of the information exchanged reduces). Although agents could not establish well-specified protocols for individual question groups (thus displaying very similar entropy values), it is still possible to fine-tune the existing protocol to a certain extent by reducing noise and other unwanted transmissions. After the hidden size of 512, agents may be registering more specific protocols for Q_3. These protocols should be more concise. Nevertheless, they specifically address the high demand for coordination in Category Q_3 effectively. Hence, as the hidden state size increase, agents may begin to share more useful information, counteracting the entropy reduction caused by protocols becoming more concise, explaining the increase of entropy for Q_3 questions at larger ($h = 2048$) hidden state sizes.

4.3 Effect of the Dialogue Structure

Cardinality of the Dialogue Set. We averaged the F1-Scores across all the hidden state sizes for a given cardinality in the dialogue set D and plot the behavior in a semi-log scale (see Fig. 6). The error bars represent the standard error of the mean. A noticeable gain in the score can be observed across all question categories. Previous works [3,17] have shown that increasing the available space for dialogue usually makes a better performance. We further observed that our performance increases are parallel to each other. Moreover, the corresponding entropy values (see Fig. 7) are identical across all question types, where increased cardinality has not caused entropy values to be different from each other. This behavior shows that changing the size of the dialogue space affects performance in a task-independent way. However, this effect is somewhat counterintuitive because by looking at the types of tasks, one could expect that tasks requiring higher coordination like category Q_3 should get more advantage of the increased cardinality.

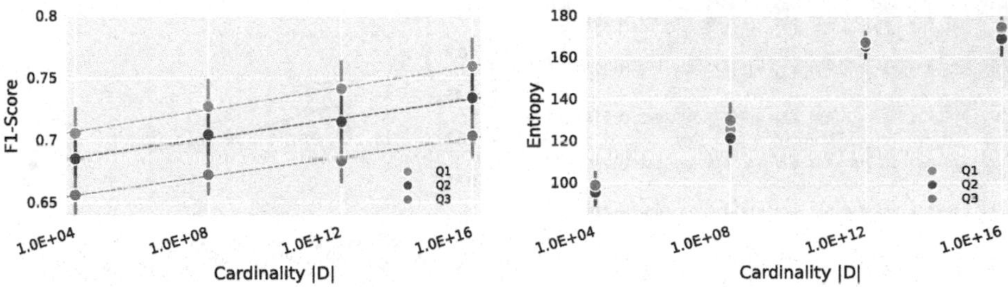

Fig. 6. F1-Score against cardinality $|D|$.

Fig. 7. Entropy against cardinality $|D|$.

Dialogue Configuration. If we consider combinations of dialogue length and symbol set size, agents generally perform better with longer dialogue lengths and smaller symbol set sizes than the converse (see Fig. 8). This effect is strong enough to counter the advantage offered by the increased agent memory capacity. For example, consider the agent performance in (10, 8) configuration with the hidden state size of 512; it comfortably surpasses all performance values indicated in bandwidth configuration (10000, 2) regardless of the agent capacity. The maximum F1-Score under configuration (10000, 2) is 0.76, which is achieved with a hidden state size of 2048. But with 512 hidden state units, agents could achieve a F1-score of 0.79 in configuration $(10, 8)$.

This behavior is seen among all task categories regardless of their complexity (see Fig. 8). Importantly, the extent of this effect is similar across all question types. We hypothesize that if we consider the two-agent system spanning over the entire dialogue length as a single neural network, the dialogue length is analog to the network depth. Hence, increasing dialogue length dramatically increases the performance. Besides, increasing the recurrent memory capacity permits agents to utilize the increased dialogue length more effectively. For example, the gain of F1-score for transitioning from $(100, 1)$ to $(10, 8)$, at a hidden state size of 128 is 10.17%. However, at a hidden state size of 2048, the gain of performance is 21.12%.

Extreme Dialogue Configurations. Then we investigated the impact of extreme dialogue configurations on the performance (see Table 2). The results show that it can still outperform most other combinations with much larger symbol sets even at these extremes. But it lags behind $(10, 8)$ combination and $(10, 6)$ combination on some occasions. We hypothesize the performance decrease is due to having a minimal symbol set (2 is the least possible meaningful size for the symbol set). Thus, the effect of symbol set size is not null, but after reaching a barely sufficient number of symbols (e.g., 10), it is certainly beneficial to have a longer dialogue length.

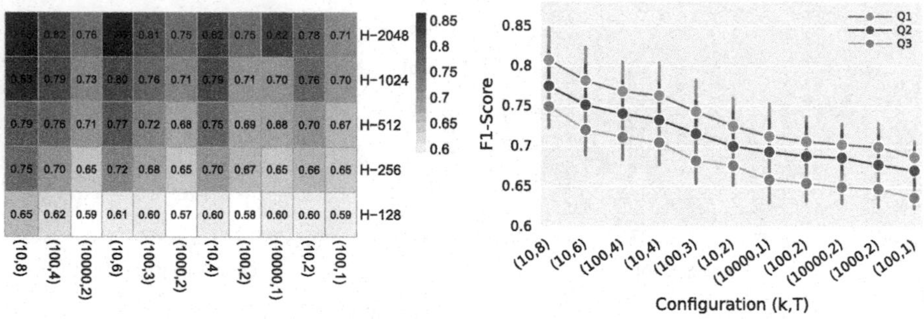

Fig. 8. Variation of agent performance with dialogue structure

5 Discussion

In this paper, we investigated how memory capacity and dialogue structure affect language emergence in a multi-task environment. In our environment, agents faced heterogeneous tasks that require different levels of information exchange and coordination. We trained our agents on three types of tasks simultaneously, where agents can communicate bi-directionally, making our setup more naturally

Table 2. Mean F1-Scores for extreme dialogue configurations. All values are shown with SEM.

Configuration	Cardinality	Q1	Q2	Q3
$(10, 8)$	1×10^{16}	$\mathbf{0.81 \pm 0.04}$	$\mathbf{0.78 \pm 0.04}$	$\mathbf{0.75 \pm 0.02}$
$(2, 33)$	$\mathbf{7.38 \times 10^{19}}$	0.79 ± 0.03	0.74 ± 0.04	0.73 ± 0.03
$(2, 27)$	1.8×10^{16}	0.78 ± 0.03	0.74 ± 0.03	0.73 ± 0.03
$(10, 6)$	1×10^{12}	$\mathbf{0.78 \pm 0.04}$	$\mathbf{0.75 \pm 0.05}$	$\mathbf{0.72 \pm 0.03}$
$(2, 20)$	$\mathbf{1.1 \times 10^{12}}$	0.77 ± 0.03	0.72 ± 0.04	0.71 ± 0.03

plausible. Using our setup, we have made novel insights into the dynamics of language emergence in previously unexplored aspects.

Through our experiments, we showed that memory capacity is affecting the system performance in a task-dependent manner. Memory capacity determined to what extend agents could establish specific and efficient protocols for individual tasks. Our findings showed that there is an entropy minimization pressure acting on the agent communication channel, which is affected by the nature of the task and the capacity of the agents. As capacity increased, protocols get much more precise and clean. Furthermore, we observed that when the agent complexity increases, they differentiated the tasks better and converged towards more specific but efficient methods of information exchange.

Then we observed that the size of the dialogue space is affecting the agents in a task-independent way. The performance of the system significantly depended on the configuration of the conversation structure. Under normal training settings, combinations of smaller symbol sets with a longer conversation length gave better results than the converse. Inspiring by this behavior, we propose to study the relationship between the dialogue length of a multi-agent game setup, analogous to the depth of a typical neural network. We hope that if such an analogy can be established, it would provide a better way of understanding the behavior of neural agents in a language emergence game in terms of the dialogue structure.

Acknowledgments. We thank Dr. Ranga Rodrigo and Dr. Jayathu Samarawickrama for arranging insightful discussions.

References

1. Austin, J.: How to Do Things with Words Harvard University Press. Cambridge, MA (1962)
2. Bouchacourt, D., Baroni, M.: How agents see things: on visual representations in an emergent language game. arXiv preprint arXiv:1808.10696 (2018)
3. Chaabouni, R., Kharitonov, E., Bouchacourt, D., Dupoux, E., Baroni, M.: Compositionality and generalization in emergent languages. arXiv preprint arXiv:2004.09124 (2020)

4. Chaabouni, R., Kharitonov, E., Dupoux, E., Baroni, M.: Anti-efficient encoding in emergent communication. arXiv preprint arXiv:1905.12561 (2019)
5. Evtimova, K., Drozdov, A., Kiela, D., Cho, K.: Emergent communication in a multi-modal, multi-step referential game. arXiv preprint arXiv:1705.10369 (2017)
6. Foerster, J.N., Assael, Y.M., de Freitas, N., Whiteson, S.: Learning to communicate to solve riddles with deep distributed recurrent q-networks. arXiv preprint arXiv:1602.02672 (2016)
7. Gupta, A., Resnick, C., Foerster, J., Dai, A., Cho, K.: Compositionality and capacity in emergent languages. In: Proceedings of the 5th Workshop on Representation Learning for NLP, pp. 34–38 (2020)
8. Havrylov, S., Titov, I.: Emergence of language with multi-agent games: learning to communicate with sequences of symbols. In: Advances in Neural Information Processing Systems, pp. 2149–2159 (2017)
9. Hochreiter, S., Schmidhuber, J.: Long short-term memory. Neural Comput. **9**(8), 1735–1780 (1997)
10. Jang, E., Gu, S., Poole, B.: Categorical reparameterization with Gumbel-Softmax. arXiv preprint arXiv:1611.01144 (2016)
11. Johnson, J., Hariharan, B., van der Maaten, L., Fei-Fei, L., Lawrence Zitnick, C., Girshick, R.: CLEVR: a diagnostic dataset for compositional language and elementary visual reasoning. In: Proceedings of the IEEE Conference on Computer Vision and Pattern Recognition, pp. 2901–2910 (2017)
12. Jorge, E., Kågebäck, M., Johansson, F.D., Gustavsson, E.: Learning to play guess who? And inventing a grounded language as a consequence. arXiv preprint arXiv:1611.03218 (2016)
13. Kharitonov, E., Chaabouni, R., Bouchacourt, D., Baroni, M.: Entropy minimization in emergent languages. In: International Conference on Machine Learning, pp. 5220–5230. PMLR (2020)
14. Lazaridou, A., Hermann, K.M., Tuyls, K., Clark, S.: Emergence of linguistic communication from referential games with symbolic and pixel input. arXiv preprint arXiv:1804.03984 (2018)
15. Lazaridou, A., Peysakhovich, A., Baroni, M.: Multi-agent cooperation and the emergence of (natural) language. arXiv preprint arXiv:1612.07182 (2016)
16. Mordatch, I., Abbeel, P.: Emergence of grounded compositional language in multi-agent populations. In: Thirty-Second AAAI Conference on Artificial Intelligence (2018)
17. Resnick, C., Gupta, A., Foerster, J., Dai, A.M., Cho, K.: Capacity, bandwidth, and compositionality in emergent language learning. arXiv preprint arXiv:1910.11424 (2019)
18. Rumelhart, D.E., Hinton, G.E., Williams, R.J.: Learning representations by back-propagating errors. Nature **323**(6088), 533 (1986)
19. Sukhbaatar, S., Fergus, R., et al.: Learning multiagent communication with back-propagation. In: Advances in Neural Information Processing Systems, pp. 2244–2252 (2016)

Towards Smart Customer Knowledge Management Systems

Thang Le Dinh[1(✉)] and Nguyen Anh Khoa Dam[1,2]

[1] Business School, Université du Québec a Trois-Rivières, Trois-Rivières, Québec, Canada
{Thang.Ledinh,Nguyen.Anh.Khoa.Dam}@uqtr.ca

[2] The University of Danang, University of Science and Technology, Da Nang, Vietnam

Abstract. Nowadays, customer focus is one of the most important challenges of enterprises in identifying customer needs and providing suitable products and services to customers. Customer focus gives prominence to knowledge about, for, and from customers. Customer knowledge management and transfer – at the right time, in the right place, and with the right quality – enable enterprises to survive in today's business environment. This paper presents the concept of smart customer knowledge management and proposes a conceptual framework for studying and designing smart customer knowledge management systems based on the design science method.

Keywords: Customer knowledge management · Context-ware · Customer intelligence · Knowledge management system

1 Introduction

Nowadays, customer focus is one of the most important challenges of enterprises in identifying customer needs and providing suitable products and services to customers. Customer knowledge, which is defined as the knowledge about customers, knowledge for customers, and knowledge from customers, becomes crucial in offering customized products and services to customers [1]. Customer knowledge management and transfer, which should be available at the right time, in the right place, and with the right quality, enable enterprises to survive in today's business environment and to enhance their growth and competitiveness [2].

Enterprises are overwhelmed to take advantage of customer knowledge for smart services [3, 4]. However, designing a smart service system as a customer knowledge management system is a perplexing task [5, 6]. The challenges arise from identifying relevant types of customer data, sources, customer knowledge, and applications [4, 7, 8]. In this paper, we present the concept of smart customer knowledge management and then propose a conceptual framework for studying and designing smart customer knowledge management systems (SCKMS) based on the design science method.

The rest of the paper is organized as follows. Section 2 presents smart customer knowledge management. Section 3 proposes a conceptual framework for designing smart customer knowledge management systems. Section 4 illustrates the proposed framework

K. Wojtkiewicz et al. (Eds.): ICCCI 2021, CCIS 1463, pp. 225–238, 2021.
https://doi.org/10.1007/978-3-030-88113-9_18

with the specific case of the SCKMS for a cultural organization. Section 5 provides some conclusions and future research work.

2 Smart Customer Knowledge Management Systems

This section discusses customer knowledge management systems and then presents the concept of smart customer knowledge management systems.

Customer Knowledge Management Systems. Customer knowledge management system (CKMS) is the integration of customer relationship management systems (CRM) and knowledge management systems (KMS) [4, 9]. In CKMS, KMS is applied to manage and transform customer data into customer knowledge, which is then applied to operations of CRM [10, 11]. The purpose of CKMS is to capture, share, and apply customer knowledge [12]. CKMS steps further with the integration of the diverse sources of massive data such as webs, social media, and the Internet of Things [8]. The revolution of massive data also witnesses the convergence of traditional CKMS technologies with real-time, open-source technologies and machine learning [4, 13].

Customer knowledge management systems emphasize the role of absorptive capability to capture, share, and apply customer knowledge. Absorptive capability is defined as the ability to acquire and learn from, about, and with customer knowledge and then apply it to the decision-making process. Due to absorptive capability, enterprises will be able to absorb customer knowledge, merging it with the organizational process and knowledge, and transform it into a firm's knowledge [12].

Smart Customer Knowledge Management Systems. This paper seeks to answer the following research question: *"How to design a smart customer knowledge management system?"*. To respond to this question, the paper begins with the principles of customer knowledge management systems and then continues with the overall architecture of smart customer knowledge management systems.

Knowledge management systems (KMS) are defined as a class of IT-based information systems applied to manage organizational knowledge to support and enhance the organizational processes of knowledge creation, storage/retrieval, transfer, and application [14]. In the context of customer knowledge management systems (CKMS), organizational knowledge can be *knowledge for customers, knowledge from customers,* and *knowledge to customers* [15].

Inside CKMS, knowledge is considered as objects, which can be stored and manipulated [14, 16]. Thus, the system supports the process of knowledge development in order to transfer data into information and information into knowledge [16]. Indeed, the CKMS provides links among knowledge objects to create the breadth and depth of knowledge development [14].

Outside CKMS, knowledge is also a condition of access to information [14]. Therefore, the role of CKMS is to provide effective search and retrieval mechanisms for locating relevant information. In this case, CKMS can be considered a service system [17] that provides services relative to knowledge, information, and data to different stakeholders of the value creation network [18].

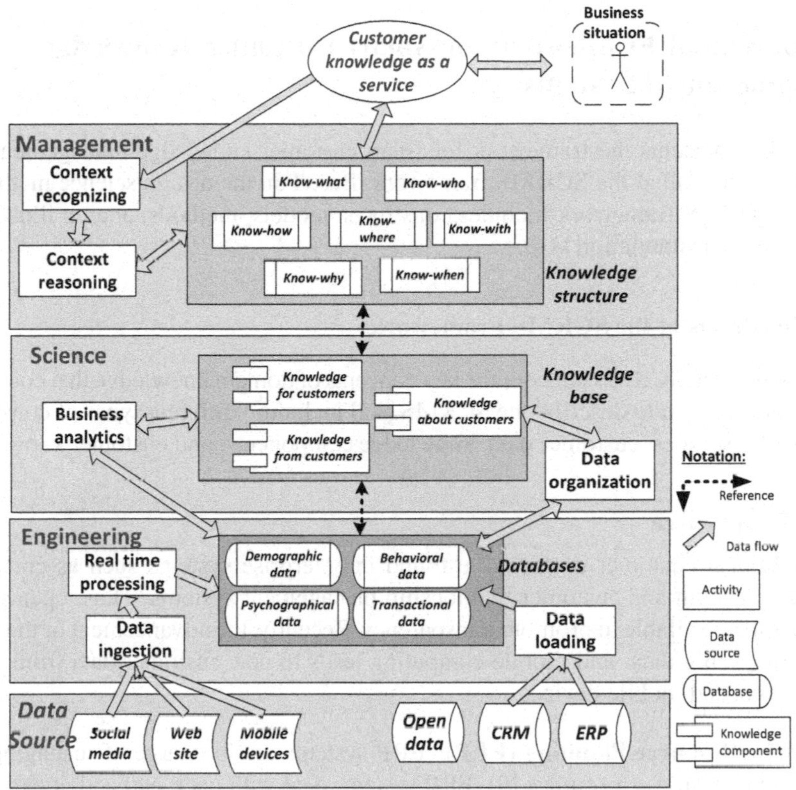

Fig. 1. Overall architecture of an SCKMS.

The purpose of this study is to propose an SCKMS that can provide smart services. In this paper, smart services are capable of actively adapting and responding based on the circumstance of interests [19, 20]. Moreover, the SCKMS becomes a smart service system, which is capable of learning, dynamic adaptation, and decision-making based upon data received, transmitted, and/or processed to improve its response to a future situation [21].

Figure 1 presents the overall architecture of a smart customer knowledge management system. To provide customer knowledge as a service, SCKMS includes the three levels of the service science perspective: Management, Science, and Engineering [17]. The *Engineering level* concerns the transformation of low-level data sources and unorganized data into purposed data. The *Science level* deals with the transformation of data into useful information by organizing information in the knowledge structure and creating new insights based on different techniques of business analytics. The *Management level* focuses on the transformation of information into actionable knowledge, which is represented by different knowledge components [16]. The following section presents more detail about the three levels of SCKMS.

3 Conceptual Framework for Smart Customer Knowledge Management Systems

This section presents the framework for smart customer knowledge management systems, hereafter called the SCKMS framework. Based on the design science methodology, the SCKMS framework includes constructs, models, methods, and an illustrative example as an instantiation [16].

3.1 Constructs of the SCKMS Framework

Constructs of the SCKMS concern the key concepts of domain knowledge that constitute a conceptualization to describe the SCKMS [42] including different types of constructs such as data sources, customer data, knowledge components, and customer knowledge.

3.1.1 Data Source

The traditional customer data can be found in enterprise systems such as enterprise resource planning and customer relationship management systems. Thus, open public data becomes available to promote transparency. Recently, the advancement of the Internet of things, big data, and mobile computing leads to new customer data from social media, Web, and mobile devices.

Enterprise Resource Planning (ERP). ERP systems are in charge of managing and streamlining business resources [9]. ERP systems deal with back-end activities related to finance, manufacture, logistics, and human resources [22]. To put it differently, *knowledge for customers* is applied to these back-end activities to offer optimal products and services for customers. ERP systems also generate a significant amount of knowledge about customers through the business process of using, organizing, and sharing customer knowledge [23].

Customer Relationship Management (CRM). CRM the foremost source of customer data, particularly transactional data [5, 24]. CRMs provide all types of transactional data, including calls to customer support lines [25]. Nowadays, CRM systems can be integrated with social media to adapt to the rise of massive data [4, 13]. Social CRMs connect social media with operations of traditional CRM such as sales, marketing, and service [11]. As such, social CRM systems are also able to track the number of likes, tweets, retweets, views [4, 24].

Open Public Data. In order to promote transparency, several governments have made public data available for reuse [26]. Open public data are not only considered as an economic asset, which contributes to new products and services. They are also seen as a key driver in the increase in citizen participation in political and social life [26].

Social Media. The era of massive data is characterized by social media in which customers create a significant amount of data on digital platforms [13]. Social media contribute customer data related to socio-demography and behaviors of users and followers for CKMS is a great data source for *knowledge from customers,* which reflects in the number of likes, shares, and comments as well as the number of impressions and reaches on social media [4, 24]. Nowadays, executives put trust in content and sentiment analysis in interpreting dialogues or content of users to understand their attitude and satisfaction towards products or brands [4, 11].

Web Sites. Websites provide clickstream data through customer interactions [25]. Google Analytics can provide interesting insights on customer knowledge. Nowadays, interviews and questions are also conducted on web-based platforms to collect knowledge about customers towards experiences with the products and services [4, 24].

Mobile Devices. Along with websites, mobile devices such as cellphones or smart devices can provide spatial data that identifies the geographical locations of users [11, 27]. Spatial data release *knowledge from* and *about customers* with information on time, location, and activities of customers. Based on spatial data, service providers can offer location-based services in a real-time manner [23, 25].

3.1.2 Customer Data

Customer data can be imported and processed from different data sources and stored as databases in SCKMS. The era of massive data has acknowledged a significant amount of data created through interactions between enterprises and customers on digital platforms [28]. From the perspective of customer focus, customer data can be categorized into demographic, behavioral, transactional, and psychographic data.

Demographic Data. Demographic data identify customer profiles and segmentation [29]. Customers can be divided into different segments based on criteria such as age, gender, profession, location, income, and marital status [29, 30]. Enterprises rely on CRM systems, social media, and open public data (such as U.S. Census Bureau) as primary sources for this type of data.

Behavioral Data. Behavioral data examine customer behaviors through their interactions with enterprises and products on websites, social media, and mobile devices [31, 32]. Typical examples of behavioral data are clickstream data, add-to-favorites, add-to-cart data [33, 34]. The proliferation of social media contributes a large amount of behavioral data through customers' likes, shares, and comments.

Transactional Data. Transactional data demystify customer purchases [35, 36]. Examples of transactional data would be purchased items, amount, frequency, payment methods [30, 34]. Transactional data come from diverse sources, including transaction records, sales reports, invoices, billing records, CRM systems [33, 37].

Psychographic Data. Psychographic data touch upon customer emotions, lifestyles, and preferences [36, 38]. Psychographic data are the integration of demographic, behavioral, and transactional data to uncover purchasing motivations and satisfaction [39]. Nowadays, data scientists apply text mining on social media to acquire psychographic data [13, 36].

3.1.3 Customer Knowledge

Customer data are organized to become useful information that is rich in relationship to represent customer knowledge. As mentioned above, customer knowledge can be classified into three types: knowledge about customers, knowledge for customers, and knowledge from customers [40].

Knowledge About Customers. Knowledge about customers is the understanding of customer behaviors and preferences [5, 24]. Knowledge about customers is derived from transactional data of customers (from ERP and CRM systems) such as purchasing activities [4, 13]. In other words, knowledge about customers involves customer satisfaction to gain insights on customer experience with products/services [12, 27]. Enterprises make use of knowledge about customers to learn about customer profiles by identifying similar patterns in transactional data [11, 41]. Then, knowledge about customers is applied to customer segmentation to define the most relevant customer segments due to knowledge on customer lifetime values [6, 7].

Knowledge for Customers. Knowledge for customers is developed by enterprises to satisfy the needs of customers [5, 12]. Knowledge for customers relates to knowledge on markets, products, or suppliers [13, 42]. Knowledge for customers aligns internal organizational information with external information; consequently, customers can position a product or a brand so that they understand the place of the product/brand in the market [15]. Enterprises rely on knowledge for customers to identify product benefits for customers [27]. From the marketing perspective, knowledge for customers is communicated to customers so that they can perceive values toward attributes and features of products/services [24].

Knowledge from Customers. Knowledge from customers is customers' knowledge on products, services, marketing, and supports of an enterprise and its competitors [5, 13]. Knowledge from customers is generated through customer interactions with enterprises [12]. Enterprises often neglect the role of customer co-creation in the innovation process even though this type of customer knowledge has significantly influence marketing results [7]. Interaction between customers and service providers creates a significant amount of knowledge for product development and service improvement. Knowledge from customers is believed to outperform knowledge about customers in capturing customer behaviors and preferences [25]. Organizational culture and incentives play an important role in stimulating knowledge from customers [6]. Since customers are considered as knowledge development partners [43], this type of knowledge aims at facilitating interaction between customers and the enterprise to develop new knowledge such as new product/service developments [15]. The era of big data emphasizes the role of customers in co-creating knowledge with service providers [24].

3.1.4 Knowledge Components

In order to facilitate the interpretation and to support business decisions, customer knowledge is linked and organized based on knowledge components to construct the knowledge structure [14]. The proposed knowledge components for SCKMS are know-what, know-how, know-who, know-why, know-with, know-when, and know-where [14, 16, 44]. Table 1 presents the knowledge components and their characteristics.

Table 1. Knowledge components in an SCKMS.

Knowledge component	Description	Focus	Related customer knowledge
Know-what	Declarative knowledge that describes knowledge artefacts, which are known and related to a phenomenon of interest	Products and services	Knowledge for customer
Know-how	Procedural knowledge that describes the understanding of the generative processes constituting phenomena	Business activities	Knowledge about customer
Know-who	Know-who refers to individuals, groups, or organizations that participate in the value creation network	Customer	Knowledge about customer
Know-why	Causal knowledge that describes the understanding of principles of the underlying phenomena	Business rules	Knowledge about customer

(*continued*)

Table 1. (*continued*)

Knowledge component	Description	Focus	Related customer knowledge
Know-with	Relational knowledge that describes the understanding of how products and services relate to other products and services	Business activities	Knowledge from customer
Know-when	Conditional knowledge that describes when a product or service may be purchased	Business activities	Knowledge from customer
Know-where	Situational knowledge that describes where a product or service may be purchased	Business activities	Knowledge from customer

3.2 Model of the SCKMS Framework

The model of the SCKMS framework aims at expressing the relationships between the constructs [45], which are represented based on the simplified UML notation [46].

As presented in Fig. 2, each class represents a construct. There are different types of relationships between classes such as specialization, dependency, composition, and reference. Four key constructs of this framework include Data source, Database, Knowledge base, and Knowledge components. Databases are created from different data sources; knowledge bases are organized from databases; and knowledge components are used to represent knowledge from knowledge bases. As one can observe in Fig. 2, there are different specializations of key constructs. Each construct can be referenced to constructs at higher and lower levels.

Furthermore, there are relations between constructs at the same level. For instance, a *know-how* is an activity performed on a set of *know-what* for a *know-who* at (time) a *know-when in (a location) know-where.* A *know-why* is a business rule that is defined on a set of *know-what* and a set of conditions on a *know-how.*

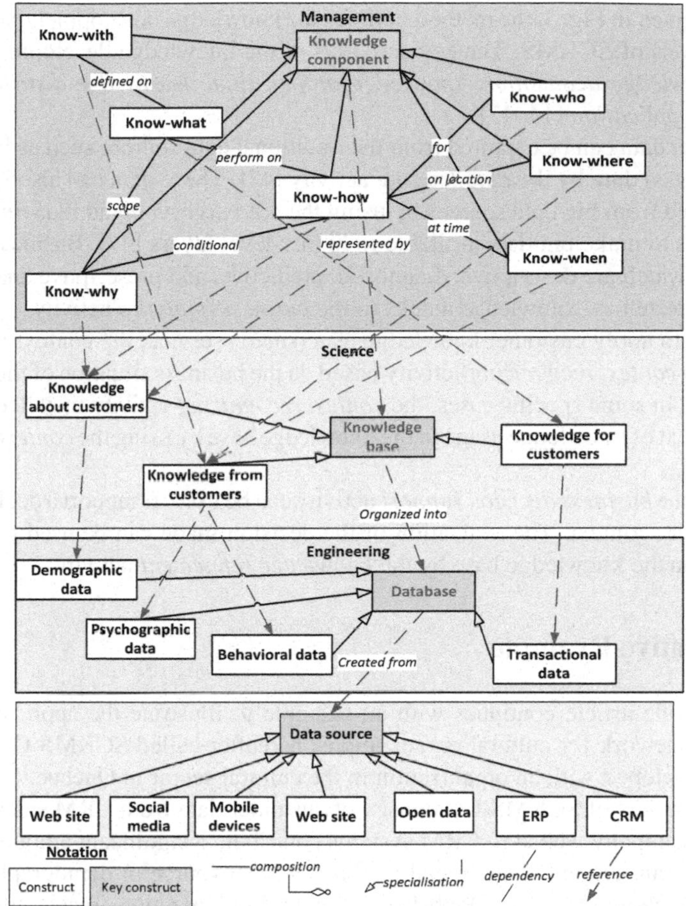

Fig. 2. Model of the SCKMS framework.

3.3 Method of the SCKMS Framework

The method covers a set of interrelated activities of the knowledge development process to develop constructs and establish relationships among constructs [45].

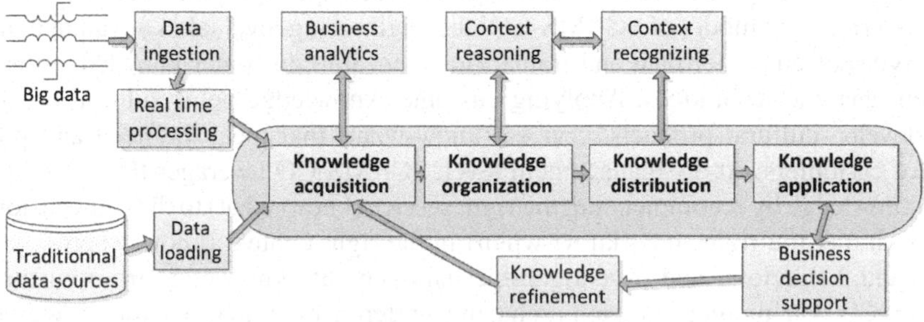

Fig. 3. Method of the SCKMS framework.

As presented in Fig. 3, the method outlines the knowledge development process over the three levels of SCKMS. The key activities of the knowledge development process include *knowledge acquisition*, *knowledge organization*, *knowledge distribution*, and *knowledge application* [14, 47].

Customer data can be captured from the traditional data sources such as ERP, CRM, and public open data by the *data loading* activity [47]. These data can also be captured and processed from big data sources by using the *data digestion* and *real-time processing* activities to make big data available to higher-level layers [47]. Business analytics techniques, which are descriptive, diagnostic, predictive, and prescriptive analytics, can be used to create new knowledge thanks to the *business analytics* activity.

In order to apply customer knowledge as a (smart) service, the context needs to be identified by *context recognizing* activity based on the business situation of the requested service [48]. In some specific cases, the *context recognizing* activity may determine the similar context of knowledge usage in the knowledge base by using the *context reasoning* activity [48].

Finally, the *business decision support* activity can be used to support a decision based on a particular context. The evaluation of the decision made can be used to refine the knowledge in the knowledge base by the *knowledge refinement* activity.

4 Illustrative Example

This part of the article continues with an example to illustrate the application of the SCKMS framework for cultural organizations, hereafter called SCKMS-CO, which is currently developed with an organization in the cultural sector in Québec, Canada.

The constructs of SCKMS-CO consist of customer data from CRM systems, social media, and company websites. CRM systems contribute a significant amount of demographic and transactional data. Social media is a great source of demographic, behavioral, and psychographic data. Websites of cultural organizations record transactional data along with behavioral data through user interactions. The most common data are transactional. In the cultural sector, demographic data comes from customer profiles. As the nature of the cultural sector depends on funding, cultural customers can be donors and other stakeholders. Many cultural organizations tend to use social media, particularly Facebook, Twitter, and Instagram to acquire demographic and behavioral data (the numbers of likes, shares, retweets, comments). Text mining through comments is still a challenging task for cultural organizations to acquire psychographic data.

Concerning the model of SCKMS-CO, the engineering level takes advantage of different types of customer data and transforms them into customer knowledge through different analytic techniques. Applying customer knowledge helps cultural organizations develop cultural products/services (know-what) that meet the need and preferences of customers. At the management level, SCKMS-CO leverages the value of customer knowledge by recommending the right service (know-what) to the right customers (know-who) at the right time (know-when) in the right context (know-where). On the other hand, behavioral and psychographic data generate knowledge from customers. SCKMS-CO can predict similar purchasing preferences among customer segments. Accordingly, business rules among similar products/services and customers (know-why) can be found. Based on the know-why component, SCKMS-CO can function as a recommender system that makes recommendations based on related cultural contents or users with similar preferences. Transactional data give prominence to knowledge for customers. Purchasing behaviors that reflect through customer transactions help cultural organizations determine products/services (know-what) that customers are interested in. At the science level, knowledge about customers, from customers, and for customers can facilitate business rules or business models that support the internal decision-making processes. In the current situation of the COVID-19 pandemic, cultural organizations in Québec, particularly ones in the performing arts domain, have shown a great interest in applying and visualizing customer knowledge towards digital dashboards for data-driven decisions.

In terms of the method of SCKMS-CO, customer data are acquired from different data sources. Through descriptive, diagnostic, predictive, prescriptive analytics, customer knowledge is acquired and organized by *context reasoning* activities. Descriptive analytics is relevant to explore historical data and transforms them into knowledge through different techniques such as business reporting, descriptive statistics, and visualization [29]. Diagnostic analytics explains why something happened. As the characteristics of predictive analytics are to forecast future possibilities, it would make customer knowledge more actionable [32]. On the other hand, prescriptive analytics proposes the most optimal solutions for specific practical scenarios through simulations and optimization [30]. Once customer data are converted into customer knowledge through analytics, it is visualized through digital dashboards or reports that can be accessed by employees and managers. Therefore, customer knowledge is distributed and applied to support the decision-making process across cultural organizations.

5 Conclusion

The great potential of customer knowledge as a smart service has stimulated the research motivation of the paper. This study aims at proposing a framework for smart customer knowledge management systems through the lens of design science, called the SCKMS framework. Through the paper, the authors have clarified the detailed artefacts relevant to the SCKMS framework, including constructs, model, method, and an example as an instantiation. The validation of the SCKMS has been conducted through an ongoing project with organizations in the cultural sector in Québec, Canada. According to our knowledge, this study is one of the first that addresses smart customer knowledge management as smart service systems.

In terms of research contributions, this study has leveraged the value of customer knowledge as a smart service corresponding to the circumstance of interests. Giving the matrix of customer knowledge applications, the SCKMS would assist enterprises to stay on track in developing and optimizing smart services. Furthermore, customer knowledge, including knowledge about customers, from customers, and for customers can stimulate customer insights such as business rules, models, or dashboards to support the decision-making process. From the perspective of customers, the SCKMS would facilitate the process of supporting customers to find the right products/services at the right time in the right context. To put it another way, the SCKMS supports customers to filter out misleading information and efficiently search for the right information.

For future work, a customer intelligence framework for customer journey management will be developed. This framework can be considered as a part of the SCKMS and will be experienced with a case study, whose objective is to map and optimize customer journeys for cultural organizations in Québec, Canada.

References

1. Sain, S., Wilde, S.: Customer Knowledge Management. Springer, Cham (2014). https://doi.org/10.1007/978-3-319-05059-1
2. Wilde, S.: Customer knowledge management. In: Improving Customer Relationship Through Knowledge Application. Springer Science & Business Media, Heidelberg (2011).https://doi.org/10.1007/978-3-642-16475-0
3. Khodakarami, F., Chan, Y.E.: Exploring the role of customer relationship management (CRM) systems in customer knowledge creation. Inf. Manage. **51**(1), 27–42 (2014)
4. Castagna, F., Centobelli, P., Cerchione, R., Esposito, E., Oropallo, E., Passaro, R.: Customer knowledge management in smes facing digital transformation. Sustainability **12**(9), 3899 (2020)
5. Zanjani, M.S., Rouzbehani, R., Dabbagh, H.: Proposing a conceptual model of customer knowledge management: a study of CKM tools in British dotcoms. Management **7**(8), 19 (2008)
6. Khosravi, A., Hussin, A.R.C.: Customer knowledge management antecedent factors: a systematic literature review. Knowl. Process. Manag. **25**(1), 12–30 (2018)
7. Fidel, P., Schlesinger, W., Cervera, A.: Collaborating to innovate: effects on customer knowledge management and performance. J. Bus. Res. **68**(7), 1426–1428 (2015)
8. Tseng, S.-M.: The effect of knowledge management capability and customer knowledge gaps on corporate performance. J. Enterp. Inf. Manage. **29**(1), 51–71 (2016)
9. Chan, J.O.: Big data customer knowledge management. Commun. IIMA **14**(3), 5 (2014)
10. Bueren, A., Schierholz, R., Kolbe, L.M., Brenner, W.: Improving performance of customer-processes with knowledge management. Bus. Proc. Manage. J. **11**(5), 573–588 (2005)
11. Taghizadeh, S.K., Rahman, S.A., Mosharref Hossain, M.: Knowledge from customer, for customer or about customer: which triggers innovation capability the most? J. Knowl. Manage. **22**(1), 162–182 (2018)
12. Taherparvar, N., Esmaeilpour, R., Dostar, M.: Customer knowledge management, innovation capability and business performance: a case study of the banking industry. J. Knowl. Manage. **18**(3), 591–610 (2014)
13. He, W., Zhang, W., Tian, X., Tao, R., Akula, V.: Identifying customer knowledge on social media through data analytics. J. Enterp. Inf. Manage. **32**(1), 152–169 (2019)
14. Alavi, M., Leidner, D.E.: Review: knowledge management and knowledge management systems: conceptual foundations and research issues. MIS Quart. **25**(1), 107 (2001)
15. Smith, H.A., McKeen, J.D.: Developments in practice XVIII-customer knowledge management: Adding value for our customers. Commun. Assoc. Inf. Syst. **16**(1), 36 (2005)
16. Le Dinh, T., Rickenberg, T.A., Fill, H.-G., Breitner, M.H.: Towards a knowledge-based framework for enterprise content management. In: 2014 47th Hawaii International Conference on System Sciences, pp. 3543–3552. IEEE (2014)
17. Le Dinh, T., Pham, T.T.T.: Information-driven framework for collaborative business service modelling. Int. J. Serv. Sci. Manag. Eng. Technol. **3**(1), 1–18 (2012)
18. Le Dinh, T., Leonard, M.: A conceptual framework for modelling service value creation networks. In: 2009 International Conference on Network-Based Information Systems, pp. 463–468. IEEE (2009)

19. Geum, Y., Jeon, H., Lee, H.: Developing new smart services using integrated morphological analysis: integration of the market-pull and technology-push approach. Serv. Bus. **10**(3), 531–555 (2015)
20. Le, D.T., Thi, T.T.P., Pham-Nguyen, C., Nam, L.N.H.: Towards a context-aware knowledge model for smart service systems. In: Nguyen, N.T., Hoang, B.H., Huynh, C.P., Hwang, D., Trawiński, B., Vossen, G. (eds.) ICCCI 2020. LNCS (LNAI), vol. 12496, pp. 767–778. Springer, Cham (2020). https://doi.org/10.1007/978-3-030-63007-2_60
21. Medina-Borja, A.: Editorial column—smart things as service providers: a call for convergence of disciplines to build a research agenda for the service systems of the future. In: INFORMS (2015)
22. Campbell, A.J.: Creating customer knowledge competence: managing customer relationship management programs strategically. Ind. Mark. Manage. **32**(5), 375–383 (2003)
23. Parry, G., Graves, A.: The importance of knowledge management for ERP systems. Int. J. Logistics Res. Appl. **11**(6), 427–441 (2008)
24. Del Vecchio, P., Secundo, G., Passiante, G.: Analyzing Big Data through the lens of customer knowledge management: Evidence from a set of regional tourism experiences. Kybernetes **47**(7), 1348–1362 (2018)
25. Garcia-Murillo, M., Annabi, H.: Customer knowledge management. J. Oper. Res. Soc. **53**(8), 875–884 (2002)
26. Hellberg, A.-S., Hedström, K.: The story of the sixth myth of open data and open government. Trans. Gov. People, Process Policy (2015)
27. Chen, Y.-H., Su, C.-T.: A Kano-CKM model for customer knowledge discovery. Total Qual. Manag. Bus. Excell. **17**(5), 589–608 (2006)
28. Ramaswamy, V., Ozcan, K.: Digitalized interactive platforms: turning goods and services into retail co-creation experiences. NIM Mark. Intell. Rev. **11**(1), 18–23 (2019)
29. France, S.L., Ghose, S.: Marketing analytics: methods, practice, implementation, and links to other fields. Expert Syst. Appl. **119**, 456–475 (2018). https://doi.org/10.1016/j.eswa.2018.11.002
30. Erevelles, S., Fukawa, N., Swayne, L.: Big Data consumer analytics and the transformation of marketing. J. Bus. Res. **69**(2), 897–904 (2016)
31. Rawson, A., Duncan, E., Jones, C.: The Truth about customer experience. Harvard Bus. Rev. (2013)
32. Dam, N.A.K., Le Dinh, T., Menvielle, W.: A service-based model for customer intelligence in the age of big data. In: AMCIS 2020 Proceedings, vol. 9 (2020)
33. Chen, H., Chiang, R.H.L., Storey, V.C.: Business intelligence and analytics: from Big Data to big impact. MIS Quart. **36**, 1165–1188 (2012)
34. Fan, S., Lau, R.Y.K., Zhao, J.L.: Demystifying Big Data analytics for business intelligence through the lens of marketing mix. Big Data Res. **2**(1), 28–32 (2015). https://doi.org/10.1016/j.bdr.2015.02.006
35. Anshari, M., Almunawar, M.N., Lim, S.A., Al-Mudimigh, A.: Customer relationship management and Big Data enabled: personalization & customization of services. Appl. Comput. Inf. **15**(3), 94–101 (2019)
36. Holmlund, M., Van Vaerenbergh, Y., Ciuchita, R., Ravald, A., Sarantopoulos, P., Ordenes, F.V., Zaki, M.: Customer experience management in the age of Big Data analytics: a strategic framework. J. Bus. Res. **116**, 356–365 (2020)
37. Sivarajah, U., Kamal, M.M., Irani, Z., Weerakkody, V.: Critical analysis of Big Data challenges and analytical methods. J. Bus. Res. **70**, 263–286 (2017). https://doi.org/10.1016/j.jbusres.2016.08.001
38. Lafrenière, D.: Digital transformation: start with the customer, not IT! Les Affaires (2020)
39. Hong, T., Kim, E.: Segmenting customers in online stores based on factors that affect the customer's intention to purchase. Expert Syst. Appl. **39**(2), 2127–2131 (2012)

40. Gibbert, M., Leibold, M., Probst, G.: Five styles of customer knowledge management, and how smart companies use them to create value. Eur. Manag. J. **20**(5), 459–469 (2002)
41. Shaw, M.J., Subramaniam, C., Tan, G.W., Welge, M.E.: Knowledge management and data mining for marketing. Decis. Support Syst. **31**(1), 127–137 (2001)
42. Gebert, H., Geib, M., Kolbe, L., Brenner, W.: Knowledge-enabled customer relationship management: integrating customer relationship management and knowledge management concepts. J. Knowl. Manag. (2003)
43. Dam, N.A.K., Le Dinh, T., Menvielle, W.: Customer co-creation through the lens of service-dominant logic: a literature review. In: AMCIS 2020 Proceedings, vol. 29 (2020)
44. Garud, R.: On the distinction between know-how, know-what, and know-why. Adv. Strateg. Manag. **14**, 81–102 (1997)
45. March, S.T., Smith, G.F.: Design and natural science research on information technology. Decis. Support Syst. **15**(4), 251–266 (1995)
46. Rumbaugh, J., Jacobson, I., Booch, G.: The unified modeling language. Ref. Manual (1999)
47. Le Dinh, T., Phan, T.-C., Bui, T.: Towards an architecture for big data-driven knowledge management systems. In: Twenty-second Americas Conference on Information Systems (2016)
48. Le Dinh, T., Dam, N.A.K.: Smart data as a service. In: Proceedings of the International Conference on Exploring Service Science (IESS) 2.1 (2021)

Cybersecurity Intelligent Methods

The Proposition of Balanced and Explainable Surrogate Method for Network Intrusion Detection in Streamed Real Difficult Data

Mateusz Szczepanski[1,2], Mikołaj Komisarek[1,2], Marek Pawlicki[1,2(✉)], Rafał Kozik[1,2], and Michał Choraś[1,2,3]

[1] ITTI Sp. z o.o., Poznan, Poland
[2] UTP University of Science and Technology, Bydgoszcz, Poland
marek.pawlicki@utp.edu.pl
[3] FernUniversitaet in Hagen, Hagen, Germany

Abstract. Handling the data imbalance problem is one of the crucial steps in a machine learning pipeline. The research community is well aware of the effects of data imbalance on machine learning algorithms. At the same time, there is a rising need for explainability of AI, especially in difficult, high-stake domains like network intrusion detection. In this paper, the effects of data balancing procedures on two explainability procedures implemented to explain a neural network used for network intrusion detection are evaluated. The discrepancies between the two methods are highlighted and important conclusions are drawn.

Keywords: Machine learning · Explainability · Data imbalance

1 Introduction, Context and Rationale

The number of technologies based on machine learning implementations is growing ever faster. By the same token, the amount of data in various real-life domains increases exponentially year after year. Data scientists are building increasingly complex models based on a multitude of features. All these factors contribute to the increasing complexity in translating the results brought by machine learning models. The explanation of prediction or classification results is sometimes hard even for experienced experts. In the domains where AI already exceeds human benchmarks, the capability to explain the model reasoning could provide valuable insights [8]. This is a significant challenge, as people who work in relevant industries utilising artificial intelligence techniques are not able to correctly identify the contributors to the decision process. In network intrusion detection systems (NIDS), the security operators fairly frequently only receive the list of nearly a hundred values with a label explaining that the AI component believes that this feature set suggests an attack. Along with data privacy [19] and AI fairness [8], explainability is one of the most pressing societal issues pertaining

K. Wojtkiewicz et al. (Eds.): ICCCI 2021, CCIS 1463, pp. 241–252, 2021.
https://doi.org/10.1007/978-3-030-88113-9_19

to artificial intelligence. This work is a joint effort between the H2020 SIMARGL and the H2020 SPARTA projects. One of the focuses of the SIMARGL project is on providing protection against cyberthreats with the use of ML techniques. Security operators using ML require a degree of explainability. Explainability, on the other hands, is one of the facets of AI handled by the SPARTA project.

There is a specific set of demands for an explainability system in NIDS and, generally, in the cybersecurity domain. Though a degree of transparency is needed, it should not be introduced at the cost of performance or the system's security. Therefore, an appropriate solution must be proposed. Because of their model-agnostic nature, combined with low-overhead and no impact on the model's performance, two surrogate-type local explanations: LIME [21] and Hybrid Oracle-Explainer [26] are explored and compared in the context of cybersecurity. Specifically, this paper aims to verify their stability and assess their usefulness as a method to explain NIDS classification. Furthermore, this work is the first of its kind to investigate the impact of various data balancing approaches, which are commonly used in real-life scenarios, on the explanations generated by surrogate type techniques.

The article is structured as follows: In the second section, a brief overview of the existing solutions in both data balancing and xAI is presented. Section three describes the used methodology along with the used dataset, the balancing methods and the characteristics of the neural network. Finally, section four presents the results and an evaluation of the impact of data balancing on the selected xAI methods. The paper ends with conclusions and future plans.

1.1 The Impact of Data Imbalance

The problem of imbalanced data is a well-established research problem in the machine learning community [12,13,20]. Nathalie Japkowicz and Shaju Stephen in their paper [11] list and answer three important questions. Firstly, how the imbalanced data factor influences the relationship between concept complexity, size of the training set and class imbalance level. The second point of article describes the basic resampling methods and evaluates how those affect the classifiers, comparing their effectiveness. Finally, Japkowicz and Stephen prove that the data imbalance problem occurs not only in decision trees but also in neural networks and Support Vector Machines.

The authors of [24] review the topics related to the problem of data imbalance. Additionally, the authors provide a breakdown of the different strategies for balancing a dataset. The first of these is the under-sampling technique, which aims to reduce the number of samples from the majority class to balance the data distribution. This strategy is explored in depth in [5,10] and [23].

The next evaluated approach is over-sampling, a strategy which inflates the number of minority class samples. One of the most proliferated methods of this class is SMOTE [7]. In this method, synthetic samples are introduced along the line segments joining the k minority class nearest neighbours. The SMOTE approach was used in a number of research works, including [9], where it is employed to solve the imbalance problem in smart home data. The authors conclude that the minority classes are better distinguished by ML algorithms after balancing with the SMOTE method. An array of data balancing methods has been identified in research. Some of those techniques are described in-depth in [5].

1.2 XAI

To better illustrate the subject of explainability and its use cases, the authors of [3] define and characterize this domain. Furthermore, they explain the most commonly used phrases and nomenclature concerning explainability, such as Understandability, Comprehensibility, Interpretability, Explainability, and Transparency. The authors also noted the gap between academia and the business sector in AI environments, so it is so important to continuously improve explainability and make it easier for the ordinary user to better and faster understand the prediction or classification results of an algorithm.

To help close the gap between the academia, the authors of [25] created an extensive reference point, which provides both a theoretical overview of the field of xAI and presents the practical ways by which explainability can be introduced into the project.

There are many available xAI techniques to select. Thus authors of [3] have proposed a comprehensive taxonomy for them. They start with a distinction between inherently transparent models and those that need to rely on external means to achieve some degree of transparency. To the first category belong linear models, decision trees, or expert-based systems, while the second creates a broad family of post-hoc explanations techniques. Post-hoc explanations, according to the definition, 'aim at communicating understandable information about how an already developed model produces its predictions for any given input [3].' Those are firstly divided between model agnostic and model-specific techniques.

Model-specific techniques are designed to work with the particular algorithm and sacrifice flexibility to allow for a higher level of fidelity. There are some methods designed for shallow models like support vector machines within this category, but the main focus is on deep learning. Model agnostic techniques, on the other hand, are not limited to one method or group. Therefore they offer great flexibility at the cost of fidelity. Those can be divided even further, but subcategories pivotal for this work are [3,25]:

1. **Explanation by simplification** - Denotes the methods where a new, simpler model is built. It resembles the original and keeps a similar performance score, but its complexity has been lowered. Those methods can also be called surrogate-type explanation techniques [6].
2. **Local explanations** - These techniques segment the solution space and provide explanations in simpler sub-spaces, usually in the neighbourhood of the model's predictions [15].
3. **Feature relevance explanations** - Those methods calculate relevance scores for the model's input variables to assess the importance of each feature for the prediction.

Since this paper is aimed at checking the effect of balancing on the techniques of explainability, referring to the paper [18] would provide a good example and suggestions for the methods. The authors work with data representing financial fraud. They use SMOTE and then explanatory methodologies such as LIME [22], SHAP [16] and LRP [14] The authors conclude that the data that has been balanced using the SMOTE technique maintains high accuracy without altering the feature correlation for the explanation process.

Just as in financial fraud, ML algorithms in NIDS are, by the nature of the domain, often trained with data balanced using the accepted balancing methods. Thus, if the ML models used in NIDS are to be augmented with explainability, the effect of data balancing procedures on xAI needs to be researched.

In the following work, two local surrogate type-explanations will be evaluated: **Local interpretable model-agnostic explanations (LIME)** and **Oracle Explainer**. The functioning of LIME is independent of the model. Therefore, it can be applied to any regression or classification model. In addition, it is a visualization technique that helps explain individual predictions. The approach of LIME is based on the principle that any complex model is linear at the local scale [21]. Another technique uses a comprehensible decision tree [6] to try to explain a highly accurate but opaque model. This approach was explored for NIDS in [26], and will be the base explainer of this work. The method will be referred to as **"Oracle Explainer"**

2 Methodology

2.1 Data

Four tests were conducted using samples from the recent Internet of Things (IoT) cybersecurity dataset [2]. It contains network traffic from IoT devices, having 20 scenarios with malware capture and three with benign traffic. All samples were obtained from real hardware in a controlled network environment. While the full dataset features 16 classes, for the purposes of this experiment only two were chosen. It was done to frame the experiment in the context of anomaly detection and be able to clearly compare and asses outputs of both explanation methods.

Any "-" values were turned to '0' and rows with NaN were deleted. The samples of Benign traffic were taken from concatenation of scenarios 1, 7, 8, 34, 35, 36, resulting in 469 395 data points, while the samples of C&C attack were taken from scenario 43 and count 3 490 data points. Also, one randomly selected sample from each category was cut to observe how behaviour of explanatory algorithms changes between tests.

After thorough feature selection from the original 21 features, the following 8 were used:

- **proto** - Communication protocol.
- **duration** - Duration of package transition.
- **orig_pkts** - Number of packets that the originator sent.
- **orig_ip_bytes** - Number of IP level bytes that the originator sent.

- **resp_pkts** - Number of packets that the responder sent.
- **resp_bytes** - The number of payload bytes the responder sent.
- **orig_bytes** - The number of payload bytes the originator sent.
- **resp_ip_bytes** - Number of IP level bytes that the responder sent.

2.2 Research Process

Research conducted in this work are based on 4 scenarios:

1. **Imbalanced** - data used to train the model is not balanced, making it the "Default" scenario,
2. **Undersampled** - data is undersampled using Random Subsampling,
3. **Oversampled** - data is oversampled using SMOTE [7],
4. **Over- and Undersampled** - data is first oversampled and then undersampled with SMOTEEN [4] from imblearn.

Each test followed an identical pipeline. First, samples were shuffled randomly to improve the quality of clusters used by the decision trees in the Oracle-Explainer. [26]. The feature columns, with exception of column "proto" which was one-hot encoded, were afterwards scaled using StandardScaler. Label columns on the other hand were encoded by LabelEncoder offered by [1]. Subsequently, the dataset was split into train and test set with the test size equal to 25% of all data points. Then, the in case of tests 2, 3 and 4, selected balancing algorithm was utilised. Just before training of the Artificial Neural Network (ANN), the clusters, centroids and decision trees necessary for the Oracle-Explainer were prepared. The details of this procedure are available in [26]. For this research, in all cases, the representativity parameter is set to 0.2, while the maximal depth of decision trees is limited to 3 levels.

It should also be noted that the version used here is modified with a mechanism ensuring the retrieved decision tree has more than just one class in it. Also, wherever possible, the random seed was set to 0 to ensure reproducibility.

The ANN used in the experiment had 2 dense layers with 64 and 32 neurons each. Both of them used ReLU as the activation function, while the output layer utilised Softmax. The Categorical cross-entropy loss function was used, while ADAM with the learning rate equal to 0.1 was the optimizer. Model performance in each test was measured, using the prepared test set.

Then, the general model performance was investigated to see how different balancing methods had affected its accuracy. Furthermore, the obtained model was used to generate predictions for two xAI test samples cut from the dataset beforehand, as mentioned earlier in this section. The samples were transformed with the same encoders and scalers as the rest of the dataset. Finally they were fed to the two selected explainability methods, LIME [21] and the Oracle-Explainer [26], to generate interpretations of model predictions.

Afterwards, the output of the LIME method for the two samples between trials is evaluated. This is to find out if, and to what degree, the importance of the features changes - according to LIME. The Oracle-Explainer generated explanations undergo a similar examination in the following subsection.

2.3 Technology

The tests were conducted using Python 3.7. The list of all important modules used for the research is presented in Table 1, with the exception of dtreeviz [17], which had to be manually altered.

Table 1. Important modules used in the project with versions

Module	Version
matplotlib	3.3.3
imbalanced-learn	0.7.0
mlxtend	0.18.0
tensorflow	2.4.0
scikit-learn	0.23.2
lime	0.2.0.1
dask[complete]	2021.1.0
pandas	1.2.0
numpy	1.19.5
graphiz	0.16

3 Results

The results obtained during tests are gathered, compared and summarised in this section.

3.1 Model Performance Comparison

In Table 2, all the results of the models for every experiment are combined. Though the model trained with the imbalanced dataset achieved the highest accuracy, in a situation with big discrepancies between amounts of samples this can be a very misleading metric. By looking at other metrics, it becomes clear that it practically classified all samples as benign. The accuracy metric was included in Table 2 for the sake of keeping the paper self-contained. The two xAI test samples were also classified as benign, which is only true for xAI test sample I. The other one should be classified as the C&C. High recall for the benign class combined with very low recall for the C&C class suggest that the classifier puts all the samples into the benign class. A decrease in precision for the benign class supports this assertion.

Balancing dataset through undersampling or oversampling helps tackle the very low recall, though at the price of accuracy and precision. The model trained on undersampled data recognises the attacks very well (100% recall), but also misclassifies the benign samples (7% precision). Since there are only 874 C&C samples in the test set, even a few mistreated benign samples lead to a considerable drop in precision.

The SMOTEEN procedure used in test case "over- and undersampled" has the lowest recall score of all the balancing methods. This, along with high execution time and significant drop in precision, made it the worst-performing balancing method in this experiment.

Finally, it should be noted that there was no case where both of the xAI test samples had been correctly classified.

Table 2. Model performance for differently balanced dataset

Dataset	Imbalanced	Undersampled	Oversampled	Over- and undersampled
Accuracy	99%	91%	91%	97%
Imbalance ratio train set	1:134	1:1	1:1	1:2
Imbalance ratio test set	1:134	1:134	1:134	1:134
Precision Benign	99%	100%	100%	100%
Precision C&C	100%	7%	7%	12%
Recall Benign	100%	91%	91%	97%
Recall C&C	1%	100%	100%	54%
Test sample I classification	Benign	C&C	C&C	Benign
Test sample II classification	Benign	C&C	Benign	Benign

3.2 LIME Explanations Comparison

Table 3 presents three most important features highlighted by LIME for both samples in each test scenario. "*Feature*" column shows the name of the chosen feature and whether or not it was bigger than some discovered threshold value, while "*Score*" presents its impact on final prediction. Positive value can be interpreted as an argument for the given prediction, while negative as an argument against it. Features are sorted by absolute value of their score.

The analysis of the table clearly shows that the importance of the features between tests changes. For example, in case of the imbalanced dataset, the most important sign that a class belongs to the benign traffic was duration lesser than −0.02, while for undersampled dataset it was resp_pkts lesser or equal to −0.05. The duration then had become the most significant for the oversampled dataset, to again fall behind in last test case.

A similar dynamic holds for the second test sample. Here also, depending on the balancing approach used, the importance of the features changes. For case with unbalanced dataset resp_ip_bytes bigger than −0.06 was the most significant feature, along with duration bigger than −0.02. But after undersampling dataset resp_ip_bytes lost to orig_bytes and duration even started to be treated as a negative indicator.

Table 3. LIME scores

Dataset	Importance	Sample			
		Benign		C&C	
		Feature	Score	Feature	Score
Imbalanced	1	duration ≤ −0.02	0.04	resp_ip_bytes > −0.06	0.05
	2	resp_bytes ≤ −0.10	0.02	duration > −0.02	0.04
	3	orig_pkts ≤ −0.11	0.10	orig_pkts ≤ −0.11	−0.03
Undersampled	1	orig_bytes ≤ −0.09	−0.33	orig_bytes ≤ −0.09	0.42
	2	resp_pkts ≤ −0.05	0.32	resp_ip_bytes > −0.06	0.30
	3	resp_ip_bytes ≤ −0.06	0.25	resp_pkts > −0.05	0.29
Oversampled	1	duration ≤ −0.02	0.60	resp_bytes ≤ −0.10	−0.48
	2	resp_bytes > −0.10	0.51	resp_ip_bytes > −0.06	0.48
	3	resp_ip_bytes ≤ −0.06	0.49	resp_pkts > −0.05	−0.36
Over- and Undersampled	1	resp_bytes ≤ −0.10	0.62	resp_bytes ≤ −0.10	−0.51
	2	duration ≤ −0.02	0.59	resp_ip_bytes > −0.06	0.48
	3	resp_ip_bytes ≤ −0.06	0.57	resp_pkts > −0.05	−0.26

3.3 Oracle-Explainer Explanations Comparison

Table 4 presents prediction paths obtained from Oracle-Explainer for the two test samples in each test scenario. It must be noted that the Oracle-Explainer finds the closest explanation to the label provided by the opaque model based on the feature vector and the label returned by the oracle. This is the reason why the same explanations are returned for samples assigned to the same category.

Table 4. Prediction paths of Oracle-Explainer

Sample	Imbalanced dataset	Undersampled dataset	Oversampled dataset	Over- and undersampled dataset
Benign	duration < 0.27 proto_tcp ≥ 0.50 duration < 0.18	orig_ip_bytes ≥ 0.02	orig_ip_bytes ≥ 0.15 resp_ip_bytes < 0.84	duration < 0.27 duration < 0.07
C&C	duration < 0.27 proto_tcp ≥ 0.50 duration < 0.18	orig_ip_bytes ≥ 0.02	orig_ip_bytes ≥ 0.15 resp_ip_bytes ≥ 0.84	duration < 0.27 duration < 0.07

For the Oracle-Explainer, a pattern similar to the one noticed with LIME reemerges, that is: depending on the samples distribution within the dataset, different explanations are generated. Or, in case of decision trees specifically, splits are made using distinct features and values, leading to creation of dissimilar prediction paths. The starkest evidence of this is in the comparison of a prediction path for the unbalanced dataset with the one made based on the undersampled data. The former utilises three distinct nodes, while the latter is based only on the feature orig_ip_bytes and whether or not its value is smaller than 0.02. This phenomenon only becomes clearer with further investigation of gathered results.

Interestingly enough, both LIME and the Oracle-Explainer often consider different features to explain the same sample in the same test case. Though it may be expected, since both algorithms work in distinct ways, it can easily confound a user or an analyst. How to explain model behaviour, when the explanations diverge? It is definitely something that demands further investigation and can have a profound impact on the surrogate type approaches and their practical usage.

3.4 Conclusion and Discussion

The objective of this research is to propose an explainable surrogate-type method that would work well in the context of NIDS and difficult data. For NIDS, used ML methods are often trained on data balanced with the evaluated balancing methods. Two xAI techniques were investigated and compared to see what kind of explanations they can generate for the same samples, based on data treated with various balancing methods. The evaluation assesses their usefulness in providing explanations of highly-accurate black box models to security operators and potentially discover weaknesses.

The results of the experiments indicate that, depending on the dataset balance in class distribution, the chosen surrogate type methods will procure different explanations. Furthermore, methods do tend to diverge when explaining the same sample in each test scenario. It is a potential problem that has to be tackled for real-life implementations.

Balancing approaches have the potential of creating new neighbourhoods for each sample, which is reflected in the results obtained by methods that rely on creating simpler, local models.

Divergence in explanations can be a direct consequence of the different nature of methods used. For example, LIME trains a linear model in the neighbourhood of explained sample to derive the impact of the attributes. On the other hand, Oracle-explainer, which is based on the comprehensible decision trees [6], generates decision trees on clusters made from the dataset and then presents the appropriate one based on the centroid closest to the sample. Since both methods use different approaches to the neighbourhood and explaining algorithm, their explanations can differ.

To conclude, surrogate type methods can effectively provide NIDS with some degree of explainability. Those are model agnostic, convenient approaches with small overhead that generate comprehensible explanations for the human operator. However, as the results of this work prove, it must be remembered that those methods only approximate complex model decisions and, in the end, show their 'point of view'. Furthermore, those methods for effective use should be used in groups, and best expanded with an interface to provide the user with one cohesive explanation.

4 Summary

This paper has investigated the use of local surrogate-type explanations and assessed their value for NIDS. It has, as the first of its kind, researched the impact of data balancing methods on their output. Furthermore, it has highlighted the problem of divergent explanations for these kind of methods in this setting.

Acknowledgments. This work is partially funded under the SPARTA project, which has received funding from the European Union's Horizon 2020 research and innovation programme under grant agreement No. 830892. This work is also partially funded under SIMARGL project, which has received funding from the European Union's Horizon 2020 research and innovation programme under grant agreement No. 833042.

References

1. Scikit-learn official website. https://scikit-learn.org/stable/. Accessed 21 Feb 2020
2. Parmisano, A., Sebastian Garcia, M.J.E.: A labeled dataset with malicious and benign IoT network traffic, 22 January 2020
3. Barredo Arrieta, A., et al.: Explainable artificial intelligence (XAI): concepts, taxonomies, opportunities and challenges toward responsible AI. Inf. Fusion **58**, 82–115 (2020) https://doi.org/10.1016/j.inffus.2019.12.012. http://www.sciencedirect.com/science/article/pii/S1566253519308103
4. Batista, G.E., Bazzan, A., Monard, M.C.: Balancing training data for automated annotation of keywords: a case study. In: WOB (2003)
5. Batista, G.E.A.P.A., Prati, R.C., Monard, M.C.: A study of the behavior of several methods for balancing machine learning training data. SIGKDD Explor. Newsl. **6**(1), 20–29 (2004). https://doi.org/10.1145/1007730.1007735
6. Blanco-Justicia, A., Domingo-Ferrer, J.: Machine learning explainability through comprehensible decision trees. In: Holzinger, A., Kieseberg, P., Tjoa, A.M., Weippl, E. (eds.) CD-MAKE 2019. LNCS, vol. 11713, pp. 15–26. Springer, Cham (2019). https://doi.org/10.1007/978-3-030-29726-8_2
7. Chawla, N.V., Bowyer, K.W., Hall, L.O., Kegelmeyer, W.P.: Smote: synthetic minority over-sampling technique. J. Artif. Int. Res. **16**(1), 321–357 (2002)
8. Choraś, M., Pawlicki, M., Puchalski, D., Kozik, R.: Machine learning – the results are not the only thing that matters! what about security, explainability and fairness? In: Krzhizhanovskaya, V.V., et al. (eds.) ICCS 2020. LNCS, vol. 12140, pp. 615–628. Springer, Cham (2020). https://doi.org/10.1007/978-3-030-50423-6_46
9. Hamad, R.A., Kimura, M., Lundström, J.: Efficacy of imbalanced data handling methods on deep learning for smart homes environments. SN Comput. Sci. **1**, 204 (2020)
10. Hirabayashi, A., Condat, L.: Torwards a general formulation for over-sampling and under-sampling. In: 2007 15th European Signal Processing Conference, pp. 1985–1989 (2007)
11. Japkowicz, N., Stephen, S.: The class imbalance problem: a systematic study. Intell. Data Anal. **6**(5), 429–449 (2002)

12. Kozik, R., Pawlicki, M., Choraś, M.: Cost-sensitive distributed machine learning for netflow-based botnet activity detection. Secur. Commun. Networks **2018**, 8753870:1–8753870:8 (2018). https://doi.org/10.1155/2018/8753870
13. Ksieniewicz, P., Woźniak, M.: Imbalanced data classification based on feature selection techniques. In: Yin, H., Camacho, D., Novais, P., Tallón-Ballesteros, A.J. (eds.) IDEAL 2018. LNCS, vol. 11315, pp. 296–303. Springer, Cham (2018). https://doi.org/10.1007/978-3-030-03496-2_33
14. Lapuschkin, S., Binder, A., Montavon, G., Klauschen, F., Müller, K.R., Samek, W.: On pixel-wise explanations for non-linear classifier decisions by layer-wise relevance propagation. PLoS ONE **10**, e0130140 (2015). https://doi.org/10.1371/journal.pone.0130140
15. Laugel, T., Renard, X., Lesot, M., Marsala, C., Detyniecki, M.: Defining locality for surrogates in post-hoc interpretablity. CoRR abs/1806.07498 (2018), http://arxiv.org/abs/1806.07498
16. Lundberg, S.M., Lee, S.I.: A unified approach to interpreting model predictions. In: Proceedings of the 31st International Conference on Neural Information Processing Systems. NIPS 2017, Red Hook, NY, USA, pp. 4768–4777. Curran Associates Inc. (2017)
17. Parr, T., Grover, P.: Explained.ai. https://explained.ai/decision-tree-viz/index.html. Accessed 21 Feb 2020
18. Patil, A., Framewala, A., Kazi, F.: Explainability of smote based oversampling for imbalanced dataset problems, pp. 41–45 (2020). https://doi.org/10.1109/ICICT50521.2020.00015
19. Pawlicka, A., Jaroszewska-Choras, D., Choraś, M., Pawlicki, M.: Guidelines for stego/malware detection tools: Achieving GDPR compliance. IEEE Technol. Soc. Mag. **39**(4), 60–70 (2020). https://doi.org/10.1109/MTS.2020.3031848
20. Pawlicki, M., Choraś, M., Kozik, R., Hołubowicz, W.: On the impact of network data balancing in cybersecurity applications. In: Krzhizhanovskaya, V.V., et al. (eds.) ICCS 2020. LNCS, vol. 12140, pp. 196–210. Springer, Cham (2020). https://doi.org/10.1007/978-3-030-50423-6_15
21. Ribeiro, M.T., Singh, S., Guestrin, C.: "why should I trust you?": explaining the predictions of any classifier. In: Proceedings of the 22nd ACM SIGKDD International Conference on Knowledge Discovery and Data Mining, San Francisco, CA, USA, 13–17 August 2016, pp. 1135–1144 (2016)
22. Ribeiro, M.T., Singh, S., Guestrin, C.: "why should i trust you?": explaining the predictions of any classifier. In: Proceedings of the 22nd ACM SIGKDD International Conference on Knowledge Discovery and Data Mining. KDD 2016, pp. 1135–1144, Association for Computing Machinery, New York (2016). https://doi.org/10.1145/2939672.2939778
23. Sokol, K., Flach, P.: Explainability fact sheets: a framework for systematic assessment of explainable approaches. In: Proceedings of the 2020 Conference on Fairness, Accountability, and Transparency, FAT* 2020, pp. 56–67. Association for Computing Machinery, New York (2020). https://doi.org/10.1145/3351095.3372870
24. Sui, H., Yang, B., Zhai, Y., Qu, W., Zhai, Y., An, B.: The problem of classification in imbalanced data sets in knowledge discovery. In: 2010 International Conference on Computer Application and System Modeling (ICCASM 2010), vol. 9, pp. V9–658-V9-661 (2010). https://doi.org/10.1109/ICCASM.2010.5622948

25. Szczepański, M., Choraś, M., Pawlicki, M., Pawlicka, A.: The methods and approaches of explainable artificial intelligence. In: Paszynski, M., Kranzlmüller, D., Krzhizhanovskaya, V.V., Dongarra, J.J., Sloot, P.M.A. (eds.) ICCS 2021. LNCS, vol. 12745, pp. 3–17. Springer, Cham (2021). https://doi.org/10.1007/978-3-030-77970-2_1
26. Szczepański, M., Choraś, M., Pawlicki, M., Kozik, R.: Achieving explainability of intrusion detection system by hybrid oracle-explainer approach. In: 2020 International Joint Conference on Neural Networks, IJCNN 2020, Glasgow, United Kingdom, 19–24 July 2020, pp. 1–8. IEEE (2020). https://doi.org/10.1109/IJCNN48605.2020.9207199

Behavioral Anomaly Model for Detecting Compromised Accounts on a Social Network

Antonin Fuchs[1(✉)] and Miroslava Mikusova[2]

[1] Department of Business Intelligence, Ringier Axel Springer SK, a.s., Bratislava, Slovakia
antonin.fuchs@ringieraxelspringer.sk

[2] Faculty of Operation and Economics of Transport and Communications, University of Zilina, Zilina, Slovakia
miroslava.mikusova@fpedas.uniza.sk

Abstract. The previous two decades have given birth to a new popular phenomenon - online social networking. Its range, diversity and constantly growing impact on our lives provides space for the creation of new and profitable, highly professionalized industry of cybercrime. It is based on phishing, social engineering, brute force password guessing or malware collecting passwords. The aim is to penetrate another's account and monetize it by blackmailing, searching for cryptocurrency wallets, obtaining passwords, influencing public opinion in favor of an idea, or at least sending spam. Today's hackers are well organized into massive, internally specialized criminal networks recruited from the best IT specialists, and as the latest results of the British investigative initiative Bellingcat show, they are also often the cornerstone of the ongoing hybrid war. On top of this, in February 2021, the "mother of all breaches" appeared on the darknet - the COMB database - consisting of 3.2 billion of unique pairs of emails and cleartext passwords. This is a clear and present danger for every user of any social network and their providers have to act immediately to protect accounts of their users. This paper describes how a social network operator with 250,000 daily active users deals with the problem of account compromise by deploying anomaly detection responsive to sudden changes in the behavior of a user trying to log in to the account.

Keywords: On-line social network · Login data · Anomaly model · Compromised acccount · Phishing

1 Introduction

Online social media and social platforms are the same as crowded places in the real world - squares, pubs, stadiums with many different people with different motives and different levels of vigilance. People use it to build or maintain social relations with those with similar interests [1] to share knowledge, opinions, and experiences; seek information and resources; and expand personal connections [2]. The most popular social media like Facebook, YouTube or WhatsApp already highly exceeded 2 billion active users each [3] and average spent time in last 8 years increased from 90 min to 145 min per day [4].

K. Wojtkiewicz et al. (Eds.): ICCCI 2021, CCIS 1463, pp. 253–265, 2021.
https://doi.org/10.1007/978-3-030-88113-9_20

The more time people spend in their online presence, the more valuable content they create, the more personal information they share with their trusted friends [5] the more they increase the overall value of their account not only for themselves but also for professional cybercriminal groups armed with password collecting malware.

The compromised account is not only very unpleasant for its owner due to the loss of privacy and personal information, but also causes significant economic damage to social network operators. A real account with history looks very trustworthy and is much more difficult to detect with automated systems, so it is more suitable for sending spam and phishing messages than new accounts registered for this purpose.

Penetration into old and forgotten accounts from long time ago, which were primarily used as an alternative mail for password recovery, often allows access to much more valuable, currently used accounts. Email account compromise (EAC) and Business Email Compromise (BEC) also opens the door to highly effective, social engineering based financial frauds when e.g. compromised account of boss orders someone to make a very high payment.

According to FBI Crime Report in the year 2020 they have received 19,369 official BEC/EAC complaints with adjusted loses over $1.8 billion [6]. The same report says that number of identity theft between 2019 and 2020 almost tripled from 16,053 to 43,330 and also phishing has doubled from 114,702 complaints to 241,342.

The situation with compromising user accounts is complicated by the fact that most of the users are indolent and lazy to create and remember strong passwords and they even re-use the same passwords between different services. Many obsolete or non-professional service providers do not follow basic rules of secure handling of user passwords and do not pay attention to regular updates of their systems to patch known exploits. The minimal rule that every service provider must follow is to never store user passwords as plaintext but at least to store only hashes of salted passwords and create them on individual bases – the same "word" for different user generates a different hash.

According to technological server Cybernews.com [7] on Tuesday, 2-nd February 2021, huge database named Compilation of Many Breaches shortly COMB (or sometimes PWCOMB2021) was leaked on a popular hacking forum. It contained billions of user credentials from past leaks from Netflix, LinkedIn, Exploit.in, Bitcoin and many other services. The leak was comparable to the Breach Compilation of 2017, in which 1.4 billion credentials were leaked but this updated version contained more than 3.2 billion unique pairs of cleartext emails and passwords.

The database included hundreds of thousands (more than 250,000 existing and probably at least the same amount of already deleted) accounts of users belonging to Ringier Axel Springer owned popular social network Pokec.sk. Only 2 days after the COMB appeared on darknet, about 1,600 Pokec accounts of users sharing the same credentials with untrustworthy services were compromised. The breach was made possible by nothing less than the collective human ignorance but the network provider was the one who had to mitigate the damages – to suspend the accounts, provide users with additional form of verification, inform authorities about the security incident and to take precautionary measures for the future.

The Business Intelligence Department (formerly Data Mining & Big Data) took on the task to analyze the breaches, learn from it and to propose measures to reduce human-caused security incidents in the future. We decided to continue on our previous theoretical work from 2016 [8] where we reviewed very inspiring different approaches in several areas such as detection of fake accounts [9, 10], detection of regular compromised accounts [11, 12], detection of high profile compromised accounts [13], phishing website detection [14].

The approach proposed by Egele et al. [11] detects sudden changes in user behavior based on computation of frequencies of various features extracted from Twitter messages and Facebook posts. This set of individual features is combined with identification of account groups which experience similar changes within a short period of time.

This approach inspired us to create algorithm calculating the level of usual or anomalous behavior by extracting key features during login process. Each login of a user creates a set of values, and that set is compared to previous sets of values for the user to detect the anomaly and calculate the anomaly score. If the anomaly score is higher than a given threshold, the login is considered to be suspicious and user is challenged to provide additional information which was shared only between user and provider. In this case it is the mobile number associated with the account.

Other systems may be further involved to evaluate the actual behavior of the entire population and to detect: currently malicious IP addresses or unusual, obsolete or incorrect UserAgents and take additional measures such as SMS with one-time access code sent to the associated mobile number. The detailed description of deployed algorithm for detection of the malicious IP addresses is not the main scope of this paper and will be described just very briefly.

The resulting proposal is a passive alternative to 2FA (two-factor authentication) in which the user does not care too much about security of his account but in the background the operator ensures safe usage and intervenes only if login is unusual.

2 The Social Network

2.1 History

In the Slovak Republic, the largest online community where people can meet others and chat with their friends is the online social network Pokec. About 5.46 million people live in the Slovak Republic [15] and the network is visited by more than 250,000 people per day, spending an average of 122 min on the network.

Pokec was founded in 1997 originally as a dating site. 2 years later a simple free e-mail service and chat was added and brand Pokec.sk (meaning Chat in colloquial Slovak) was established. This chat gained great popularity among Slovak scientists and university students, who at that time were the only ones with access to a very expensive Internet.

Due to the evolving infrastructure, the availability of computers, the growth of computer literacy and the fall in the price of the Internet, its penetration among the population kept increasing in following years. Global competition did not yet exist and three local players specializing in three different segments covered all the needs of the Slovak internet market – Zoznam.sk search in directory of webpages; SME.sk news; and Pokec.sk social networking.

Pokec continued to grow until 2009, when the first real global competitor – Facebook appeared in Slovakia. Despite the different focus – the chat represents an anonymous virtual adventure since the arrival of a strong competitor, the user base is gradually declining.

In 2010, Pokec – and the entire network of other subsequently developed successful services – became a subsidiary of the Swiss-German publishing houses Ringier AG and Axel Springer AG and as a part of the same international group started to closely cooperate with the sister Polish dating portal Sympatia.pl.

In 2014, Pokec won twice in a row the prestigious international award Superbrands [16] as the best perceived Slovak brand. At that time, it still had 700,000 daily users who wrote 10 million messages a day. As a really strong local player, Pokec soon became the target of individual local criminals and also huge international cyber-gangs.

In 2015, Ringier Axel Springer Slovakia s.r.o. transforms into a modern data-driven company and establishes the Data Mining & Big Data Department. The first task was to build a data infrastructure capable of processing at least 15,000 events per second. On the one hand, the department provides analyses for the strategic decision-making of the company and at the same time proposes various algorithms that e.g., increase the safety of users. The Department has broadened the focus, hired more employees and in 2021 was renamed to Business Intelligence Department.

The department also works closely with Slovak state institutions such as the Police or the National Security Agency of SR. By cooperating with an academic sphere on various big data and machine learning projects [17, 18], it also wants to contribute to the improvement of this industry.

2.2 Threats

Spam, phishing and financial frauds belong to the most common threats that the social network must face. In recent years, however, this network has also been discovered by organized gangs from abroad, which create thousands of new registrations per month.

"Nigerian scam" adapted for dating environment from IP addresses of Togo, Senegal, Benin and Nigeria with focus on abandoned women in their fifties. Charming US Army generals promise them a fairy-tale life for a "wedding certificate" after the already non-existent war in Lybia ends. "Russian Brides" using Russian or TOR IPs, on the other hand, focus on financially secure older men.

Especially from the Vietnamese IPs Pokec regularly faces very diverse and massive attacks. E.g. registering Pokec-email accounts for the purpose of registering new fake accounts on Facebook. Hijacking of Facebook accounts through old compromised Pokec accounts used as recovery emails on Facebook. And recently appearing attempts to infiltrate old Pokec accounts through malware-collected databases on third-party servers – so called COMB or "Compilation of Many Breaches" [7].

The use of the same passwords by our users on various insecure sites and a lax approach to security is the main source of Pokec's problems with compromising our accounts, and therefore we are testing different approaches to solve this problem.

2.3 Local Community

Pokec is mostly a local Slovak community with Czech and Hungarian minority. According to internal data audits, more than 95% of accesses are from Slovak IP addresses, 3% from Czech and 2% are IPs from all over the world.

Restrict to a language used by only 5 million people is a disadvantage in terms of machine learning, where there is a number of well-developed NLTK tools for English, but almost none for Slovak. On the other hand, for security reasons this is a huge advantage.

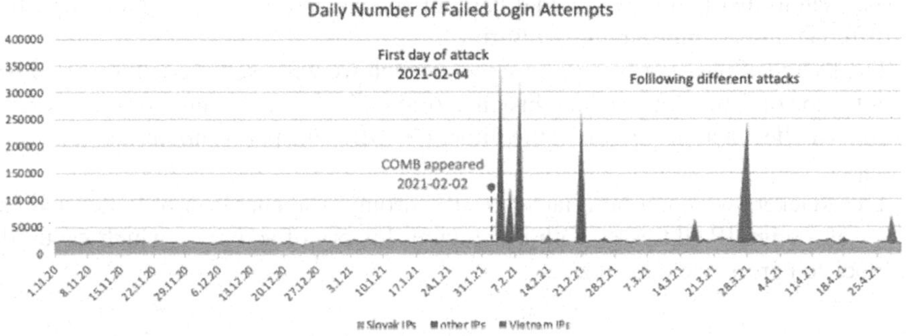

Fig. 1. Number of failed login attempts into existing accounts between November 2020 and May 2021 split into attempts from local and foreign IP addresses.

Figure 1 shows consistent and very predictable trend of natural amounts of typos while user submits his/her credentials resulting in login failure between November 2020 and beginning of February 2021. 250,000 daily active users usually generate about 20,000 login failures (and about 1 million successful logins).

The absolute majority of failed logins comes from Slovak IP addresses and only small portion from other countries where Pokec users live – Czech Republic, Austria, Germany, Hungary and UK. We used this to our advantage to analyze, detect and later label endangered and compromised accounts to evaluate the proposed algorithm.

2.4 The COMB Attacks

Within 48 h after the COMB appeared, number of unsuccessful logins has jumped from 20,000 to 350,000 attempts. More than 250,000 existing accounts were subject of one or more attempts to access it using formerly correct passwords collected from different sites.

The most of these accounts were very old - registered between 2008 and 2009. Lot of them were already abandoned but many are still in use. Among 350,000 attempts during the first day of attack only about 1,600 were successful. Fortunately, attackers just tried to unsuccessfully search the email content for strings related to bitcoin wallets and did not take over the compromised accounts for future harmful actions. This gave the operator sufficient time to take rescue measures.

In addition, there was probably at least twice or three times more attempts to log in to already deleted accounts, which are not captured in the Fig. 1. These numbers depict a huge range of malware-stolen data collected in COMB during last decade. We can say, that in our case attackers failed, but there are other services where this attack might be much more successful and destructive. Most of the COMB data was very outdated and worthless but COMB still provides a huge database of real passwords relevant to brute force dictionary attacks.

The attacks continued in the following weeks and our thorough retrospective analysis revealed important facts:

A) There were different attacking groups with a very clear "modus operandi" - which we used to distinguish individual parallel attacks and even to assign attacks from different days to the same group/script.
B) The source of passwords was the same – which we will use for upcoming real-time detection of future attacks like this one, to actualize table of dangerous IP addresses and to collect actual version of the future COMB. This part is not the subject of this paper.
C) The attackers were not familiar with such strong local character of Pokec and used set of foreign IP addresses with no previous history of activity – which we used to label compromised accounts.

3 The Anomaly Detection

3.1 Input Data Used for Model

The analysis of attacks with a special focus on the first day revealed that it was very easy to define which IP addresses are part of the attack. Attackers deployed more than 3,500 different IP addresses to confuse our systems but:

A) completely omitted Slovak, Czech, Hungarian and Austrian IPs; instead they used very exotic countries like Singapore, Bhutan, Indonesia etc.
B) none of used IP addresses had any previous history; no other logins before the first day of attack.
C) usual ratio is 50 successful logins to 1 failure; ratio of this set of IP was about 220 failures to 1 success.
D) All attempts had the same UserAgent. Unfortunately, in this case it was the most recent version of Chrome and the most common browser at the time.

Combination of these factors helped us to easily find all the deployed IP addresses, all accounts which were endangered or compromised and even to restore part of the COMB which concerns the Pokec users. As a byproduct of this analysis, we created a table with combination of iduser + hashes of all passwords that were checked by attackers. These users should not be allowed to change his/her password to fit this set of hashes in the future.

As the next step we have selected all 257,824 users successfully logged in during the first day of attack and populated a new auxiliary SQL table with all their logins during previous 90 days. The new Auxiliary Table of Logins (AToL) contains more than 110 million records of logins extracted from original eventUserLogin in the structure provided in Table 1.

Table 1. Structure of Auxiliary Table of Logins (AToL).

Column	Example	Description
date	2020-12-10 15:51:55	Human readable date-time
iduser	199177	Internal identifier of the user
user_logins	38	Current order of login
ip_country	SK	Country of IP extracted from IP
ip_country_ord	38	Order of this particular item
ip_country_dist	1	Number of distinct items until now
ip_net_name	GPRS-PAT-195091018	IP provider extracted from IP
ip_net_name_ord	6	Order of this particular item
ip_net_name_dist	4	Number of distinct items until now
ip	195.91.18.42	IP converted to string form from IP
ip_ord	6	Order of this particular item
ip_dist	4	Number of distinct items until now
ip_part_1_2	195.91	First 2 segments of the IP string
ip_part_1_2_ord	6	Order of this particular item
ip_part_1_2_dist	4	Number of distinct items until now
device	Sony XQ-AU52	Device name extracted from UserAgent
device_ord	37	Order of this particular item
device_dist	2	Number of distinct items until now
os_version	Android 10	Operating system + version extracted from UserAgent
os_version_ord	37	Order of this particular item
os_version_dist	2	Number of distinct items until now
browser	Pokec.sk	Browser extracted from UserAgent
browser_ord	37	Order of this particular item
browser_dist	2	Number of distinct items until now

In the above example this was the 38-th successful login of the user 199177. He has logged in from Slovakia and this country is the only one he logs from (number of distinct countries is 1) it also implies that this is his 38-th successful login from Slovakia. On the other hand, until now he used 4 different IP addresses and this particular login is his 6-th with current IP address.

Before we decided to consider this set of features, we had performed wide set of supplementary analysis. One focused on the usual variability of different features. The aim was to define small number of features which are very various in population but at the same time very consistent for an individual user. It was also very important to define the minimal number of logins sufficient to build the behavioral profile of each active user and the maximal number of last logins to consider. The more logins we remember the more demanding and costlier will be the final production. Last but not least we also had to follow the privacy and GDPR regulations of European Union and adjust the timeframe for deleting old data with it – another analysis of average number of successful logins during different periods of time was conducted.

Finally, we decided to work with the last 90 days and calculate the profile for users with no more than 50 most recent logins. We solved the problem with the minimal number of logins necessary to build the behavioral profile with SMS verification in the initial stages of building profile and adding this innovation to the original anomaly calculation [8].

The analysis of IP variability yielded interesting results and following example very clearly explains the way how we decided which features would be used in the anomaly checking algorithm. The average number of different IPs used by each user during 90 days is 7.52. This high number is often caused by telecom operators when balancing the load of mobile internet traffic by providing the least loaded IP from reserved range e.g. "85.237.234.123". The usage of this IP is not the choice of the user but the high variability of IP would uselessly increase the anomaly of IP feature of particular user. Variability of the first 3 segments of IP (e.g. "85.237.234") decreased to 4.69, of the first 2 segments (e.g. "85.237") was 2.57 and the average number of different first segments (e.g. "85") was only 2.45 per user.

Variability of the first segment of IP for user is small and provides very consistent profile of his usual behavior, but there is also a very high chance – 1:255 – that the attacker unintentionally uses the same segment and anomaly of this feature will not appear at all. In contrast, the variability of the first 2 segments only slightly increases from 2.45 to 2.57 per user but rapidly decreases the chance for attacker to use the IP with the same two segments. The statistical chance is 1:65,025 but in reality, in most cases the foreign attacker must share the same, usually a very small local internet provider, which is even more unlikely (Fig. 2).

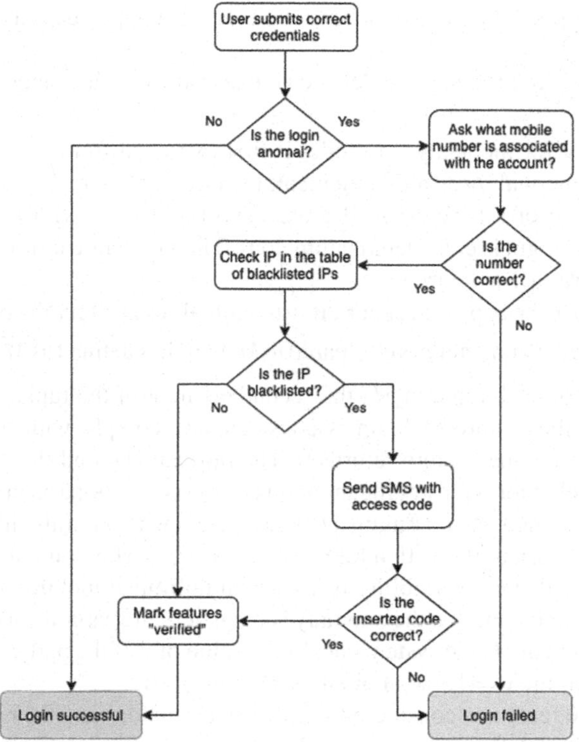

Fig. 2. Updated flow of the process of user login considering the anomaly detection and deploying additional proof of ownership – alternative to 2FA.

3.2 Training and Evaluation of the Models

Training: the input for the training were features extracted from logins and previously shown in the Table AToL. The finally considered 5 feature models could be grouped into Device related (device, os_version and browser) and Location related (country and ip_part_1_2).

Each feature model is represented as a set M. Each element of M is a tuple <*fv,c,v*>. *fv* is the value of a feature (e.g., "Sony XQ-AU52" for the device model, or "SK" for the country model). Parameter *c* stands for the number of logins in which the specific feature value *fv* was present and *v* is binary identification if the feature value has been verified by an additional user action.

In our case the user action means providing the correct mobile number when asked or to provide the correct access code sent to his mobile number if the user tried to log in using dangerous IP address.

Each model also stores the total N number of messages that were used for training.

Evaluating a New Login. When calculating the anomaly score for a new login, we want to evaluate whether this event violates the behavioral profile of a user for the given 5 models. In general, a login is considered more anomalous if the value for a particular feature did not appear at all in the stream of a user, or it appeared only a small number of times.

The anomaly score for each model is calculated in following steps:

1. The feature *fv* for the analyzed model is first extracted from the login event. If M contains a tuple with *fv* as a first element, then the tuple <*fv*,*c*,*v*> is extracted from M where value of v is set to 0. If there is no tuple in M with *fv* as a first value, this feature of login is considered anomalous. The procedure terminates here and an anomaly score of 1 is returned.
2. In the next step, the approach checks if *fv* is anomalous at all for the behavioral profile being analyzed. Parameter c is compared to M, which is defined as $\overline{M} = \sum_{i=1}^{\|M\|} c_i \big/ N$ where c_i is, for each tuple in $\overline{M}$, the second element of the tuple. If c is greater or equal to $\overline{M}$, the feature of login is considered to comply with the profile of the model and an anomaly score returns 0. The rationale behind this that user already proved this behavior with significant number of items. Comparison with the average probability also helps to distinguish between users with naturally high variability of features (e.g., variability of IP address of user often surfing on public wi-fis to save limited data and small variability of user with unlimited mobile internet and using the same IP) and to milden the anomaly score where the natural variability is higher.
3. If the c is less than $\overline{M}$, the system checks the value of v. If the particular feature value was validated; the $v = 1$; the anomaly score returns 0.
4. Otherwise the feature is considered somewhat anomalous and the relative frequency f of *fv* is calculated as $f = c_{fv} \big/ N$. The system returns an anomaly score of the feature model as $1 - f$.

To calculate the overall anomaly score, we simply added the partial anomalies together to evaluate the results and continued with different approaches to calculate it and used different weights to reach the best results. After comparing a few different approaches, we have found that the first and the simplest approach provided the best results which in combination with additional SMS verification are good enough to be ready for further real-time tests on the production data in beta testing environment.

3.3 Testing the Final Anomaly Score Thresholds

AToL provided a valuable resource for many different analyses, but the main question was how useful this approach could be to serve as the active security feature against the future COMB-like attacks.

A subset of all logins was selected from AToL table, for users who were previously labeled as the victims of the first COMB attack and had the history of at least 10 logins before the day of attack. We were unable to simulate the responses of users to SMS challenge in the first stages of behavioral profile building when the lack of historical data would result in high anomalies and SMS requests. Instead, we decided to focus on the more valuable – active victims with already existing behavioral profile of at least 10 logins in last 90 days.

The testing subset consisted of 43,799 successful login records of 1,003 active users (at least 10, but max 50 most recent records) with 1,447 labeled records of confirmed infiltration.

The goal was to find the threshold of overall anomaly score which ensures to detect almost all penetrations (~100% sensitivity) while only a least necessary amount of logins will trigger additional security actions (max. specificity).

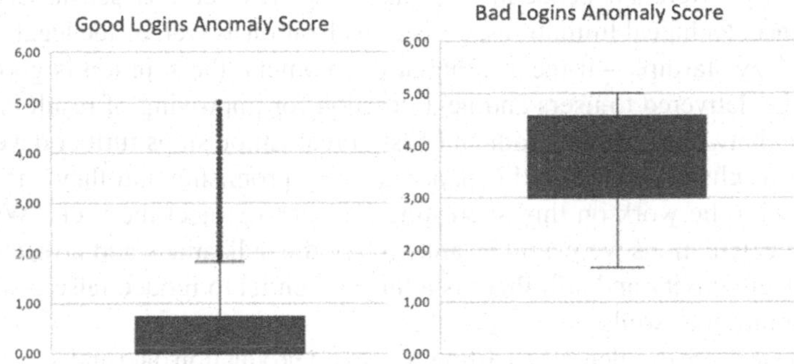

Fig. 3. Boxplot of anomaly score distribution for valid logins and penetrated logins.

The Fig. 3 shows that even the simple calculation of the anomaly score inspired by original work of Egele et al. and adopted to detect behavioral changes during the process of user login can very precisely distinguish between correct and penetrated logins.

Fig. 4. Ratio between sensitivity and specificity at the different thresholds of the final anomaly score

The final ratios of sensitivity and specificity in the Fig. 4 revealed that by the threshold with value 1.7 the proposed algorithm would stop 99.86% of COMB penetrations and only 9.04% of logins would trigger the additional security measures uselessly.

In absolute numbers the false positives represent 3,829 records, but only 637 of them are the first-in-row anomalies. This means that if the users were challenged to provide the correct mobile number the innovative element of "feature value verification" would be deployed and the subsequent 3,192 false positives would be considered as a correct login.

4 Conclusions

In this paper we have tested the core of innovative approach to prevent bulk penetrations to user accounts which combines profile of usual behavior of user with detection of sudden changes in it and as a result automatically triggers passive from of two-factor authentication.

The paper mediates the business approach of the real provider of social network which is slightly different to academic approach. The provider must sensitively consider user experience, technical limitations, costs of realization as well as the legal issues and acts as the "lazy startup" – it means, that at the moment, the solution is good enough and it must be delivered to users and next iteration for improving of result is prepared until the ratio between potential gain and cost of realization stops further development.

The first results presented in this paper are very promising and they encourage us to continue with the work on this interesting project to protect the users. With a very simple set of calculations we would be able to face the bulk attack and protect our users with 99,86% effectivity and still there is a huge potential to reduce false positives and cost of the solution as well.

The next steps are to calculate real-time scores on production data and to test different weights to decrease number of false positives while detecting maximum of penetrations. The big future challenge will be to prove good results of this algorithm also on domestic phishing activities which are much more inconspicuous and subtle because the attack is usually targeted very individually and conducted from IP addresses of local providers which decreases the level of presented anomaly score.

References

1. Obar, J.A., Wildman, S.: Social media definition and the governance challenge: an introduction to the special issue. Telecommun. Policy **39**(9), 745–750 (2015)
2. Xiao, C., Freeman, D. M., Hwa, T.: Detecting clusters of fake accounts in online social networks. In: ACM Workshop on Artificial Intelligence and Security, pp. 91–101 (2015)
3. Statista Portal. Most popular social networks worldwide as of January 2021, ranked by number of active users (2021). https://www.statista.com/statistics/272014/global-social-networks-ranked-by-number-of-users. Accessed 16 Feb 2021
4. Statista Portal. Daily time spent on social networking by internet users worldwide from 2012 to 2020. https://www.statista.com/statistics/433871/daily-social-media-usage-worldwide. Accessed 17 Jan 2021
5. Stringhini, G., Kruegel, C., Vigna, G.: Detecting spammers on social networks. In: Annual Computer Security Applications Conference, pp. 1–9. Association for Computing Machinery, Austin (2010)
6. Internet Crime Report 2020. https://www.ic3.gov/Media/PDF/AnnualReport/2020_IC3Report.pdf. Accessed 21 May 2021
7. Cybernews. https://cybernews.com/news/largest-compilation-of-emails-and-passwords-leaked-free. Accessed 12 Apr 2021
8. Bohacik, J., Fuchs, A., Benedikovic, M.: Detecting compromised accounts on the Pokec online social network. In: 2017 International Conference on Information and Digital Technologies (IDT), pp. 56–60. IEEE, Zilina (2017)

9. Cao, Q, Sirivianos, M., Yang, X., Pregueiro, T.: Aiding the detection of fake accounts in large scale social online services. In: Proceedings of the 9th USENIX Conference on Networked Systems Design and Implementation, pp. 1–14. USENIX Association, San Jose (2012)
10. Gao, H., Hu, J., Wilson, C., Li, Z., Chen, Y., Zhao, B.Y.: Detecting and characterizing social spam campaigns. In: ACM SIGCOMM Conference on Internet Measurement, pp. 35–47. Association for Computing Machinery, New York (2010)
11. Egele, M., Stringhini, G., Kruegel, C., Vigna, G.: COMPA: detecting compromised accounts on social networks. In: Network and Distributed System Security Symposium. The Internet Society, San Diego (2013)
12. Ruan, X., Wu, Z., Jajodia, Z.: Profiling online social behaviors for compromised account detection. IEEE Trans. Inf. Forensics Secur. **11**(1), 176–187 (2015)
13. Egele, M., Stringhini, G., Kruegel, C., Vigna, G.: Towards detecting compromised accounts on social networks. IEEE Trans. Dependable Secure Comput. **14**(4), 447–460 (2017)
14. Aburrous, M.R.M.:Design and Development of an Intelligent Association Classification Mining Fuzzy Based Scheme for Phishing Website Detection with an Emphasis on E-Banking. University of Bradford eThesis, UK (2010)
15. Statistical Office of the Slovak Republic, How Many of Us Are There, What Households We Form. Statistical Office of the Slovak Republic, Slovakia, 14p (2021)
16. Superbrands. https://www.brandsearch.superbrands.com/wp-admin/admin-ajax.php?juwpfisadmin=false&action=wpfd&task=file.download&wpfd_category_id=1096&wpfd_file_id=96011&token=5417907906f57d0d940b86d2f53c6da9&preview=1. Accessed 15 Mar 2021
17. Racko, J., Machaj, J., Brida, P.: Wi-fi fingerprint radio map creation by using interpolation. Procedia Eng. **192**, 753–758 (2017)
18. Stefanik, A., Grznar, P., Micieta, B.: Tools for continual process improvement - simulation and benchmarking. In: Proceedings of the 14th International Symposium of the Danube-Adria-Association-for-Automation-and-Manufacturing, pp. 443–444. Bosnia & Hercegovina, Sarajevo (2003)

Adversarial Attacks on Face Detection Algorithms Using Anti-facial Recognition T-Shirts

Ewa Lyko and Michal Kedziora(✉)

Faculty of Computer Science and Management, Wroclaw University of Science and Technology, Wroclaw, Poland
michal.kedziora@pwr.edu.pl

Abstract. Purpose of the paper was to analyze adversarial attacks on face detection algorithms with the use of anti-facial recognition T-shirts. In the research we also checked whether the methods used to attack detectors of objects are effective in attacking face detectors. Research has been proposed to verify the safety of computer vision algorithms on the example of face detection. An attempt was made to attack the object detector with 63 prepared examples. Each of the examples contained a specially generated adversarial pattern, which was then placed on the T-shirt in a digital version or in the form of a physically printed sheet applied to the T-shirt.

Keywords: Computer vision · Adversarial attack · Face detection

1 Introduction

Successfully carried out attacks in the field of object detection pose a potential threat to computer vision systems using adversarial pattern printed on T-shirt. The growing popularity of computer vision based systems is contributing to an increased interest in attacking and deceiving intelligent algorithms. Therefore, it should be considered whether there is a possibility of generalizing attacks on face detectors and thus a wider breach of the security of computer vision systems.

The work includes photos in which an attempt was made to deceive the detector of objects and not detect a person by using a adversarial pattern applied to a T-shirt or to a cardboard held at the height of the T-shirt. Then, the effectiveness of attacks was tested on the example of 3 face detectors: MS Azure, Face++ and DeepAI. Thus, an attempt was made to test whether the methods aimed at the object detector can be generalized in face detectors.

In the scientific literature, can be also found examples that compile the work of other researchers along with a description of the results of their attacks. This work goes one step further, because in addition to the literature review, research has been proposed to verify the safety of computer vision algorithms on the example of face detection.

K. Wojtkiewicz et al. (Eds.): ICCCI 2021, CCIS 1463, pp. 266–277, 2021.
https://doi.org/10.1007/978-3-030-88113-9_21

The remainder of this paper is structured as follows. In Sect. 2, theoretical foundations of the described research problem were discussed, i.e. algorithms used in the detection of objects and in face detection were presented. In the Sect. 3, scientific articles related to the topic discussed in this paper were indicated. Then, in Sect. 4, the methodology of the research was presented. The results of the research were collected and analyzed in Sect. 5. In the last section, i.e. 6, conclusions from the research were drawn and further directions of work development were indicated.

2 Object Detection and Face Detection

As part of the research carried out in this paper, examples of attacks targeting object detectors were considered. Then their effectiveness was tested on face detectors. Therefore, the algorithms used for both cases will be presented.

2.1 Object Detection Algorithms

Object detection is an important computer vision task that deals with detecting instances of visual objects of a certain class (such as humans, animals, or cars) in digital images. The objective of object detection is to develop computational models and techniques that provide one of the most basic pieces of information needed by computer vision applications: What objects are where? [13]. For the detection of objects are used, among others, algorithms such as:

- Region Based Convolutional Neural Network (R-CNN),
- Fast Region Based Convolutional Neural Network (Fast R-CNN),
- You Only Look Once (YOLO).

The first of the aforementioned algorithms, R-CNN, is discussed in the work [5]. This method works by selecting 2000 regions using selective search, and then operations are performed on individual regions. Each position is inserted into the convolutional neural network (CNN) and the result is a 4096-dimensional feature vector. The output CNN layer consists of extracted ceilings, which are then fed into the SVM to classify the presence of an object in a given region. Importantly, the algorithm also takes into account the shift values in order to increase the precision of detection within the region (it may happen that, for example, a half of a human face is in one area and the other half in another).

Another of the mentioned methods is Faster R-CNN, which is devoted to scientific works such as [10] and [11]. This algorithm improves on R-CNN by speeding up the uptime by not having to specify 2000 regions. An image is sent to CNN in order to generate a convolutional feature map (and not a region proposal as was the case in R-CNN). In Faster R-CNN, slow selective searches have been eliminated, and the region positions are known by the a separate network itself.

The last of the methods discussed is YOLO, that is You Only Look Once. The operation of the mentioned algorithm is described in the article [7]. Contrary to the previous two algorithms, the network does not look at the entire image, but only a part of it (those that contain the object with high probability) - a single neural convolutional network predicts frames limiting the object and the probabilities of individual classes for boxes.

2.2 Face Detection Algorithms

Face detection can be defined as follows: Given an arbitrary image, the goal of face detection is to determine whether or not there are any faces in the image and, if present, return the image location and extent of each face [1].

In the research paper [1], the following division of techniques used in face detection was proposed:

- Knowledge-based methods,
- Feature invariant approaches,
- Template matching methods,
- Appearance-based methods.

The first of the discussed methods are knowledge-based methods. These methods, based on rules, define people's knowledge of what a typical face is (rules usually define relationships between facial features). An example of such a rule is that the face in the photo includes a nose, a mouth and two eyes symmetrical to each other.

The second category of methods described are feature invariant approaches. The purpose of the described algorithm is to find such structural features that they remain even when the face conditions, position or point of view change. The features are then used to find the location of the face.

The third distinguished category are template matching methods. They work by computing the correlation between the input image and the stored standard face patterns that describe the entire face or individual facial features. They are calculated independently for the face contour, mount, eyes, and nose. The correlation value will determine whether or not a face is included in the input image.

The last group highlighted are appearance-based methods, which are mainly used to detect faces, based on learned models. Unlike the previous method (template matching), the models are taught on a set of training photos. Of course, they should be representative, i.e. include photos containing various variations in the appearance of the face. Discriminant functions and distribution models are used. The algorithms used in this category include Neural Networks, Support Vector Machines, Naive Bayes Classifier and Hidden Markov Model.

3 Related Works

The scientific literature in the field of generating contradictory examples is expanding every year. The attacks include, inter alia, object detectors, image classifiers, face detectors or face recognition algorithms. It has been scientifically proven that deep learning algorithms are vulnerable to adversarial attacks. In most of studies, researchers focus on attacks on static objects, by attaching adversarial patches to this objects. Usually these are, for example, stickers attached to the stop sign, pictures attached to cardboard or glass frames.

Article [2] shows that it is possible to attack the classifier via feeding adversarial photos obtained from a camera in mobile phone to an ImageNet Inception classifier [3]. In another work, scientists [8] have proven that a small change in input data can result in misclassification. In their work, they focused on proving that a slight alteration, more precisely applying black and white stickers to the stop sign, caused the object to be misclassified. Yet another example is the results of work [15] in which an effective attack on facial recognition was carried out by using glasses printed on the face. Another work describes generating universal adversarial patches, the addition of which will destroy the operation of state-of-the-art face detectors [19]. Researchers generated patches that can be applied to two different scenarios. The first is when the attacker wants to trigger a "false alarm" by generating a patch that will be recognized as a face and the real face will go unnoticed. The second scenario covers situations where the attacker aims to avoid any face detection.

An article that is closely related to the research conducted in this work is [12]. The method of attacking an object detector with the use of a specially generated pattern and placed on a cardboard was presented. The cardboard was usually held above the waist, on the background of a T-shirt or sweatshirt. According to the results presented by the researchers, it can be seen that this type of attack is effective. However, the scientific article [4] proved that the proposed solution is not always effective.

Paper [4] presents a different and innovative approach to the discussed topic. The authors of the work focused on a non-rigid object such as a T-shirt. Scientists have studied the effects of wearing an adversarial shirt on detectors of people recognition based on deep neural networks.

The human body, when walking, makes movements that cause certain deformations (wrinkles) to appear on the clothes we wear. Designing a adversarial T-shirt that accommodates such distortions is a challenge. Due to the fact that the adversarial T-shirt worn by a human is not a static object, it is necessary to model the deformation by Thin Plate Spline Mapping (TPS). TPS is a relatively effective tool with which it is possible to model coordinate transformations. The TPS interpolant $f(x, y)$ has form [18]:

$$f(x, y) = a_1 + a_x x + a_y y + \sum_{i=1}^{p} w_i U(\| (x_i, y_i) - (x, y) \|) \tag{1}$$

where $U(r) = r^2 log(r)$, (x_i, y_i) are locations in the plane (control points), with $i = 1, 2, ..., p$, a_1, a_x, a_y, w_i are the TPS parameters. Through a set of control points with given positions TPS learns a parametric deformation mapping from an original image x to a target image z.

The goal is to mis-detect by detectors, frames that are perturbed with the universal adversarial perturbation. Scientists in their work focused on designing such a adversarial T-shirt that allows for erroneous recognition by both a single detector and multiple detectors (using min-max optimization). In case of an ensemble attack there were used two different object detectors: YOLO-v2 and Faster R-CNN (simultaneously), both pretrained on COCO dataset.

Scientists launched the attack in the digital world and physical world. Both training data and test data were collected for the study. The dataset consisted of a total of 2003 video frames in 40 different recordings. The recordings were made in 4 different scenes: 3 indoor and 1 ourdoor. The video shows a person with a T-shirt printed with a checkerboard pattern (videos are 5 to 10 s long). From the training dataset the desired adversarial pattern is learnt. The tests were carried out using the adversarial T-shirt proposed by T. Goedeme, S. Thys and W. Van Rast in [12] (without TPS transformation) and adversarial T-shirt proposed by the researchers in the present article (with TPS transformation).

The attack was considered successful when 2 conditions were met. The first is that the person wearing the adversarial T-shirt has not been detected. The second one is that the person wearing the standard outfit has been correctly detected. As a result of the research in digital world, interesting results were obtained, because for both detectors YOLO-v2 and Faster R-CNN achieved high attack efficiency. When attacking a single detector, in the case of YOLO-v2, the percentage success of the attacks was 74% when using a adversarial T-shirt with TPS transformation and only 24% when using a adversarial T-shirt without TPS transformation. In case of Faster R-CNN, the percentage success of the attacks was 61% when using a adversarial T-shirt with TPS transformation and only 22% when using a adversarial T-shirt without TPS transformation. In the case of a ensemble attack, when the attack was aimed at Faster R-CNN, the effectiveness was achieved at 47%, and when the attack was YOLO-v2 at 53%.

Conducting research in the physical world first required the preparation of an appropriate T-shirt by printing a adversarial pattern on a white T-shirt. Patterns with and without TPS transformation were used again. In the case of these studies, they were performed taking into account 3 specific scenarios: indoor, outdoor and for the environment, which was not included in the training data. The best results were achieved for YOLO-v2 inside with adversarial T-shirt with TPS transformation - 64% attack efficiency. The individual results are summarized in the Table 1. Based on the results obtained, it should be noted that it is important to add the TPS transformation to the adversarial T-shirt.

Additionally, studies were carried out to check the effectiveness of attacks depending on the distance and angle of the camera. The high effectiveness of the attack was achieved up to about 4 m and an angle of 20°. Above 30°, there is a sharp drop due to the occlusion of the adversarial pattern. At a distance of about 5 m, there is a clear decrease in the effectiveness of attacks due to the fact that the camera cannot clearly see the pattern on the T-shirt.

Table 1. Attack success rate of adversarial T-shirts in physical world, source: [4]

Method	Model	Indoor	Outdoor	New scenes	Average
Adversarial without TPS	Fast R-CNN	15%	16%	12%	14%
Adversarial with TPS		50%	42%	48%	47%
Adversarial without TPS	YOLO-v2	19%	17%	17%	18%
Adversarial with TPS		64%	47%	59%	57%

In addition, the authors of the studies performed tests to check the effectiveness of the attack depending on the position of the person and the environment in which the person is located. In the case of the human position, the sitting, crouched and running position was checked with the camera pointing straight at the person at a distance of no more than 2 m. The best results were achieved for running in a standing position (attack effectiveness 63%), then for the crouching position (attack effectiveness 53%), and the worst and relatively low effectiveness for the sitting position (attack effectiveness 32%). In the case of tests taking into account the environment, 3 scenes were selected: a car park, a busy intersection with cars and pedestrians, and a room with many other elements. The best results were achieved for the room (attack effectiveness 73%), then for the car park (attack effectiveness 65%), and the worst results were achieved, but still relatively high for the intersection (attack effectiveness 54%).

In conclusion, it should be noted that a bit more than just a adversarial T-shirt is needed to paralyze a real-world people detector. Features such as low resolution, posture changes and occlusions are important. Nevertheless, the successes achieved by the adversarial T-shirt during the real-time attacks show new insights into designing practical adversarial human wearables in physical world.

4 Methedology

The aim of the research was to check whether the methods used to attack detectors of objects, which consist in not detecting a person, are effective in attacking face detectors.

Choosing the right research environment is not a trivial matter. Today, there are many different solutions available on the internet from different vendors. For example, some solutions offer better face detection performance with age attributes, while other solutions are better at determining facial emotions. Due to the nature of the research, the aspect of this comparison can be omitted as only face detection is important. The following detectors were used for further research: MS Azure Cognitive Service [16], Face++ [9] and DeepAI [6].

The first service used to conduct the research was MS Azure Cognitive Service, which offers AI algorithms that detect, recognize and analyze human faces in images. It is built on industry-leading Azure security. According to the product website, Microsoft invests more than $1 billion annually in cybersecurity research and solutions, and employs more than 3,500 security experts who are focused on data protection and privacy, making it a reliable and trustworthy solution. In addition, the services of this provider are used by companies such as Cloudinary, GrayMeta, Prism Skylabs or Uber.

The second solution used in the research was the service offered by Megvii known as Face++. Megvii is a Chinese technology company that specializes in the development of image recognition and deep learning software. An aspect that contributed to the choice of this solution was the fact that Megvii manages one of the world's largest research institutes specializing in computer vision. In addition, according to the information on the company's website, since 2017 Megvii has won a total of 40 world championships related to the field of science of artificial intelligence in various leading international competitions. Including a three-time title at the International Conference on Computer Vision's Common Objects in Context (COCO) Challenge.

The third solution used in the study was the Facial Recognition API provided by DeepAI. Unlike the previous two companies, DeepAI is a small enterprise with up to 10 employees and based in San Francisco, USA. DeepAI started its operations relatively recently, in 2017. According to information posted on LinkedIn, DeepAI's mission is to accelerate the transition of the world to artificial intelligence, including by accessing the latest results from the world of machine learning and artificial intelligence [14].

Group of examples selected for testing as part of the described work are T-shirts containing specially generated patterns aimed at preventing the object detection as a human being. Scientists from Northeastern University, MIT-IBM Watson AI Lab and the Massachusetts Institute of Technology have designed a pattern to trick a specific deep neural network [4]. Designing such a pattern is not easy, because the T-shirt is not a flat object, its shape adapts to the human body. Therefore, as part of the research, scientists recorded a person who was walking and wearing a T-shirt with a specially prepared checkerboard pattern. From the movement of each square, scientists were able to determine how the T-shirt wrinkles and moves with the human body. Information about this behavior was then incorporated into the design of adversarial examples (shown in the Fig. 1 a).

A year earlier, 3 scientists from Belgium published their research work on generating adversarial patterns in order to deceive the human detection system [12]. At the time of an attack, the intruders could pass unnoticed through the surveillance system, only thanks to the hand-held cardboard plate with a pattern pointing towards the cameras. The Fig. 1 b shows an exemplary photo taken during the research, indicating that the person dressed as normal was recognized as a person, while the person standing next to him, holding the previously described pattern, remained unnoticed by the object detection system.

In the context of research carried out as part of a work, the disadvantage of the discussed solution is that it assumes knowledge about the object detection algorithm (attacks are not directed to face detection). Nevertheless, due to the fact that this is a very interesting approach and it is worth checking the vulnerability of face detection algorithms to attacks using the proposed approach, 46 photos have been used for research, on which a person with a prepared T-shirt or pattern was presented.

The successes in fooling the object detector, which were described in the discussed articles [4] and [12], contributed to the increased interest in this topic. A manifestation of such interest is the appearance of T-shirts advertised as "Adversarial Anti-Facial Recognition Invisibility Camouflage" [17]. In the product description, can be found information that the T-shirt is to confuse the object detector. Therefore, the research used 17 photos from the online store where adversarial T-shirts can be bought (an example photo was presented in the Fig. 1 c).

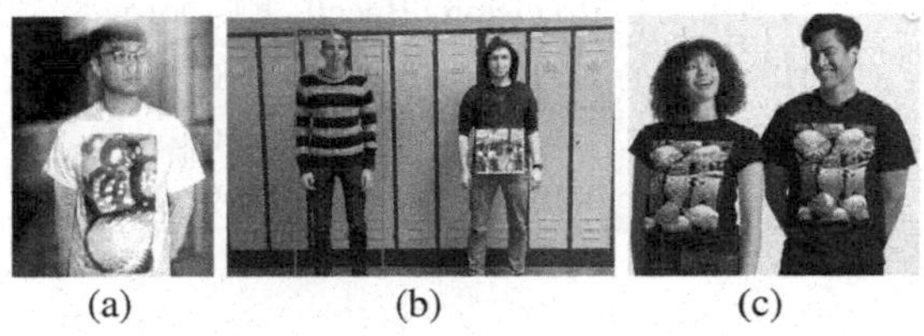

Fig. 1. (a) adversarial T-shirt, source: [4] (b) adversarial pattern during test, source: [12] (c) T-shirts from online store, source: [17]

5 Experiments

Carrying out research on the safety of face detectors using photos in which an attempt was made to attack the object detector began with the preparation of 63 examples. Each of the examples contained a specially generated adversarial pattern, which was then placed on the T-shirt in a digital version or in the form of a physically printed sheet applied to the T-shirt. All the patterns used came from the following articles: [4] - 7 different patches and [12] - 4 different patches (in total 46 images with 52 faces). In addition there are 17 examples of T-shirts from online store (in total 21 faces).

Detailed research results obtained for examples from scientific articles or using formulas contained in them are presented in Table 2. Examples of T-shirts from the online store are not included in these results. As can be seen very interesting results have been obtained. Both MS Azure and Face++ achieved full detection correctness, which means that the services detected the face in the place where it was actually located and there was no mistake during the detection related to the lack of detection of the face or its detection in the wrong place. Therefore, the precision and recall measure was 1.00 and thus the F1-score was 1.00. This shows that the security of these two detectors has not been compromised and thus the attacks proved to be ineffective.

The situation was slightly different for the DeepAI detector. Unlike the previous two detectors, the detector made a mistake in detecting a face where it was not, which caused the precision to drop to 0.98. As with the other detectors, no faces were missed during detection, which influenced the score of 1.00 for recall. Thus, the F1-score was 0.99. It is worth noting that this is still a very high detection result, which suggests that the detector's security has not been breached.

Table 2. Precision, recall and F1-score for images where the target of the attack was an object detector by services

Service	Object detector		
	Precision	Recall	F1-score
MS Azure	1.00	1.00	1.00
Face++	1.00	1.00	1.00
DeepAI	0.98	1.00	0.99

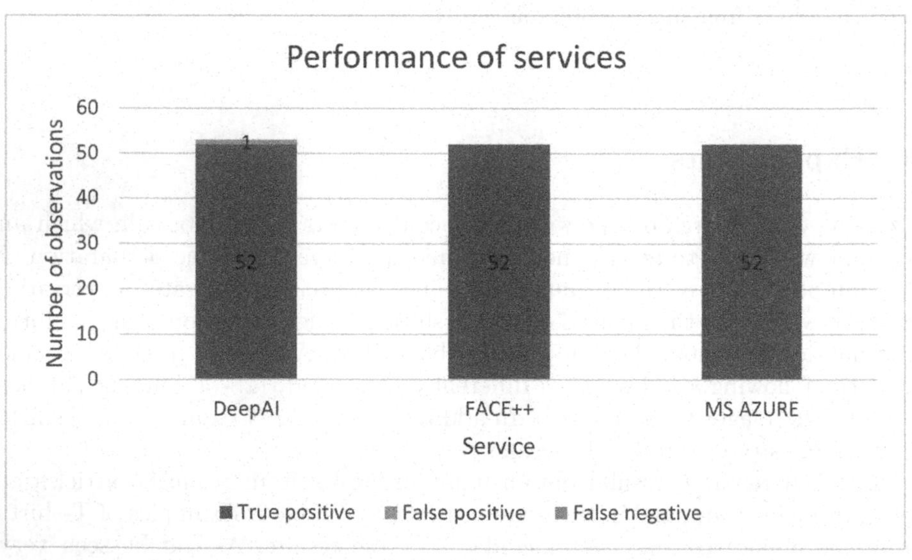

Fig. 2. Performance of detection by services, does not include examples of T-shirts from the online store

To see exactly how this translates into the number of observations, Fig. 2 presents a list of true positive, false positive, and false negative measures for each of the services on examples of photos from scientific articles (does not include examples of T-shirts from the online store). Thanks to this, it is possible to notice that the erroneous detection for DeepAI happened only once. After the processed photos have been checked in detail, the wrong example was presented in Fig. 3. As can be seen in the printed pattern, a face was detected in the upper right corner even though it was not there. The pattern for which the detection error was recorded was taken from a research paper [12].

Fig. 3. Photo with detected one face to much by DeepAI service during attack on face detector (blue frame - MS Azure, orange frame - Face++, yellow frame - DeepAI) (Color figure online)

A separate summary of the research was carried out for examples of T-shirts from online stores. Table 3 contains detailed detection results obtained by MS Azure, Face++ and DeepAI. As can be seen, each of the detectors showed the full correctness of the position. Each of the faces in the photo has been correctly located and none has been incorrectly detected or omitted. Therefore, the precision and recall measure was 1.00 and thus the F1-score was 1.00.

Table 3. Precision, recall and F1-score for t-shirts from online store where the target of the attack was an object detector by services

Service	Object detector (t-shirts from online store)		
	Precision	Recall	F1-score
MS Azure	1.00	1.00	1.00
Face++	1.00	1.00	1.00
DeepAI	1.00	1.00	1.00

6 Conclusion and Future Work

Based on the results obtained, it can be assumed that attacks of this type do not pose a threat to the face detector. The potential security breach occurred only once for one detector, DeepAI. It concerned face detection within a specially generated patch. The occurrence of such a situation once in 52 observations does not make it possible to unequivocally state that the error that occurred was caused by an successfully conducted attack by generating a pattern. As already discussed, despite the fact that the attacks were not directed at the face detector, it was decided to use examples in which an attempt was made to cheat the object detector. It was decided to choose this group of photos because they were attacks aimed at the detection of a person whose face is an essential part of body. In addition, it should be mentioned that the generated pattern was intended to not detect a human, and in the case of this face examination, not to detect a face elsewhere, as is the case, for example, in the article [19].

An interesting aspect of the research was checking the correctness of detection for T-shirts from an online store, in which they appeared as a result of publishing research results of scientific articles on generating adversarial patterns. Thus, for about $20, every person in the world can become the owner of such an item. Nevertheless, as this research has shown, the attacks performed are ineffective for face detection systems. Thus, it should be noted that T-shirts offered by many online stores do not pose a threat to face detection systems.

Nevertheless, the overall detection efficiency was very high, which suggests that the security of systems that use face detection using one of the detectors in question is not compromised in the event of such an attack. Additionally, since the selected detectors are developed by independent companies with different financial outlays, it can be assumed that the obtained safety results can be generalized for a larger number of detectors.

Due to the fact that as part of research, the effectiveness of face detection was tested for methods aimed at attacking object detectors and not detecting a human being, another idea for the development of works may be related to this area. An interesting issue and worth investigating is the repetition of the research carried out on contradictory T-shirts, not on face detectors, but on object detectors. Despite the fact that DeepAI did not provide such a service at the time of writing, Face++ and MS Azure offer this service. T-shirts are a very interesting aspect of the research due to their invisibility during an attack by people who are not immersed in the secrets of the method. The aforementioned imperceptibility is interesting because the attacks examined in this paper usually required so much interference in the face area, which may result in a lower chance of using such attacks in real scenarios.

References

1. Ahuja, N., Kriegman, D., Yang, M.: Detecting faces in images: a survey. IEEE Trans. Pattern Anal. Mach. Intell. **24**, 34–58 (2002). https://doi.org/10.1109/34.982883
2. Bengio, S., Goodfellow, I., Kurakin, A.: Adversarial examples in the physical world (2016)
3. Bernstein, M., et al.: ImageNet large scale visual recognition challenge. Int. J. Comput. Vis. **115**, 1–42 (2015)
4. Chen, H., et al.: Evading real-time person detectors by adversarial t-shirt (2019)

5. Darrell, T., Donahue, J., Girshick, R., Malik, J.: Rich feature hierarchies for accurate object detection and semantic segmentation (2014)
6. DeepAI: Facial Recognition API. https://deepai.org/machine-learning-model/facial-recognition. Accessed 02 Feb 2021
7. Divvala, S., Farhadi, A., Girshick, R., Redmon, J.: You only look once: unified, real-time object detection. In: Proceedings of the IEEE Conference on Computer Vision and Pattern Recognition, pp. 779–788 (2016)
8. Evtimov, I., et al.: Robust physical-world attacks on deep learning visual classification, pp. 1625–1634 (2018). https://doi.org/10.1109/CVPR.2018.00175
9. Face++: Facial recognition. https://www.faceplusplus.com. Accessed 02 Feb 2021
10. Girshick, R.: Fast R-CNN (2015)
11. Girshick, R., He, K., Ren, S., Sun, J.: Faster R-CNN: towards real-time object detection with region proposal networks (2016)
12. Goedeme, T., Thys, S., Rast, W.V.: Fooling automated surveillance cameras: adversarial patches to attack person detection, pp. 49–55 (2019). https://doi.org/10.1109/CVPRW.2019.00012
13. Guo, Y., Shi, Z., Ye, J., Zou, Z.: Object detection in 20 years: a survey (2019)
14. LinkedIn: Deepai. https://www.linkedin.com/company/deepai. Accessed 28 Mar 2021
15. Lujo, B., Mahmood, S., Reiter, M.K., Sruti, B.: Accessorize to a crime: real and stealthy attacks on state-of-the-art face recognition. In: Proceedings of the 2016 ACM SIGSAC Conference on Computer and Communications Security, pp. 1528–1540. CCS 2016. Association for Computing Machinery, New York (2016)
16. Microsoft: Azure Cognitive Services. https://azure.microsoft.com/en-us/services/cognitive-services. Accessed 02 Feb 2021
17. RedBubble: Adversarial Anti-Facial Recognition Invisibility Camouflage Classic T-Shirt. https://www.redbubble.com/i/t-shirt/Adversarial-Anti-Facial-Recognition-Invisibility-Camouflage-by-el-em-cee/48303486.IJ6L0.XYZ. Accessed 05 Apr 2021
18. Belongie, S., Donato, G.: Approximate thin plate spline mappings (2001). https://doi.org/10.1007/3-540-47977-5_2
19. Wei, F., Yang, X., Zhang, H., Zhu, J.: Design and interpretation of universal adversarial patches in face detection (2019)

Security and Scalability in Private Permissionless Blockchain: Problems and Solutions Leading to Creating Consent-as-a-Service (CaaS) Deployment

Hanna Grodzicka, Michal Kedziora(✉), and Lech Madeyski

Faculty of Computer Science and Management, Wroclaw University of Science and Technology, Wroclaw, Poland
michal.kedziora@pwr.edu.pl

Abstract. The purpose of this paper is to analyze the security and scalability problems occurring in private permissionless blockchain systems. The consent management system (CMS) based upon Hyperledger Fabric (HLF), was implemented in the selected blockchain-as-a-service (BaaS), and therefore led to consent-as-a-service (CaaS) deployment. The experiments results assessed to what level the network transaction throughput is affected by changing the world state size, which indicates scalability of chosen blockchain system implementation. Additional experiments with the IBM Blockchain Platform and the FastFabric framework (a HLF modification) were performed to prove the possibility to achieve transaction throughput comparable to the Ethereum blockchain network.

Keywords: Blockchain scalability · Permissionless blockchain · Blockchain security

1 Introduction

Utilising blockchain undergoes in several business areas. For example, in supply chain management (SCM) it enables to track product or service subsequent states in the business flow. Business partners can join the blockchain network to either read or write information to the ledger history. Blockchain properties (security, immutability) were found suitable for creating CMS [2,8,11,16,31,32]. However, the main and inherent limitation to the technology to overcome is scalability. A relatively new idea among cloud vendors is embracing blockchain to an offer. Such solutions are named Blockchain as a Service (BaaS). In this paper, BaaS term refers to every kind of service directly supported by the cloud services provider, including those available in their marketplace. BaaS is already used by well-known companies, mostly for the SCM purpose and seems to be applicable in a narrow target group for specifically defined requirements. However, there is a gap in research over BaaS since the idea of providing the blockchain network infrastructure, as well as the technology itself, is relatively new. None of them

K. Wojtkiewicz et al. (Eds.): ICCCI 2021, CCIS 1463, pp. 278–289, 2021.
https://doi.org/10.1007/978-3-030-88113-9_22

discussed related works considers the blockchain services in detail. The offers from network cloud providers tend to be treated collectively without testing solutions and without distinguishing their level of support.

Our paper addresses this gap by first surveying security and scalability problems occurring in private permissionless blockchain systems, as well as solutions to them, and then recreating a scalable blockchain system using several cloud environments. The emphasis is put on the blockchain systems hosted by cloud vendors in the form of BaaS. The currently available solutions offered by the most appreciated cloud providers are reviewed. The most promising services are tested for the real deployment of the CMS described by Agarwal et al. [2]. Implementing the CMS atop BaaS leads to CaaS. Through experiments, the proposed system's replication ability and its scalability are examined, along with assessing the feasibility of the CMS development in the provided cloud environment. An additional objective is to provide theoretical knowledge by introducing blockchain technology and performing a survey on its scalability, security and the emerging blockchain cloud services.

Paper structure is as follows. Blockchain technology is introduced in Sect. 1. Section 2 is a comprehensive survey which gathers information on various blockchain types, their favourable properties and main concerns. It shows and assesses the problems and solutions to scalability and security of blockchain systems and the current state of the distributed ledger technology (DLT) software. The possible and real-world blockchain use cases are analysed with paying particular attention to Consentio CMS whose originators are Agarwal et al. [2]. Section 3 presents results obtained by performing the scalability experiments on the CMS in the selected BaaS platform and its findings. The experience gained through testing various cloud services is summarised by estimating its costs, identifying the encountered problems and key differences. In Conclusions, the main assumptions of this research are pointed out and recapitulated, with identifying some future directions.

2 Related Work

With the growth of interest in blockchain technology from companies and institutions, the need for privacy and the ability to decide who can participate in a blockchain-based network arisen. Since Bitcoin and other cryptocurrencies used a completely public network, private and regulated solutions have been proposed. Hence the new terms introduced were permissioned as opposed to permissionless, as well as a private and public dichotomy. Not all of the research papers make a distinction between the four types of blockchain. Some, like [26,30], consider only private and public or permissioned and permissionless as two leading blockchain categories. Another prevalent approach is associating public blockchain with permissionless, and private with permissioned [17,20,21,24]. However, some recent publications [1,5,14] do distinguish those and acknowledge the existence of public permissioned and private permissionless blockchains as well, or just use a general *hybrid* term to categorise those recently emerging blockchains [21].

The Ethereum team (with "Vitalik" Buterin) introduced a *Scalability Trilemma* which states that an ideal blockchain system should have three characteristics: scalability, security and decentralisation. According to the trilemma, a blockchain system can have only two out of the three, e.g., improving scalability reduces a security level or the decentralised network on-chain [15]. There is a trade-off between getting a higher degree of one property and sacrificing the other ones. The concept has probably derived from the CAP theorem which applies to distributed systems, thus for blockchain as well. CAP stands for Consistency, Availability and Partition Tolerance. Any distributed system can have at most two of these aspects. It indicates that there cannot be a system that simultaneously: provides the same view of data to all the nodes, always responds to a user's request and works as expected despite the arbitrary physical network partitioning triggered by network failures.

Xie et al. [29] address the blockchain scalability issue to three fields: throughput, storage and networking. Throughput in the public blockchain is many times lower compared to the traditional payment methods. In 2013, Visa had the capability of handling more than 24000 transactions per second (TPS) [27]. Four years later it had the capacity of over 65000 TPS [28]. Meanwhile, Bitcoin can only process 3.3–7 [7] and Ethereum 7–15 transactions in the same amount of time [15]. It is worth noticing that the numbers are rather theoretical since they determine network capabilities – not the average TPS. As of December 15, 2019, Ethereum Blockchain Explorer shows an average of 7.2 TPS [12] and Ethereum's co-founder, Buterin, states that it will not scale to more than 15 TPS.

A limited throughput for Bitcoin is caused by its block size bound to 1 MB [4] and a long block interval time, i.e., time of confirming a transaction, including it in a block. An expected latency is 10 min [7] to create sufficient security. For comparison, another leading credit card company, Mastercard, claims to have the transaction processing speed below 500 ms [19]. Public permissionless blockchains like Bitcoin or Ethereum tend to use proof-of-work as a consensus mechanism. The resulting latency is the cost of propagating block over the decentralised network and utilising a relatively expensive consensus protocol, which is required to prevent Sybil attacks (e.g., 51% attack). An increasing block size seems to be an obvious solution to this problem. However, it results in a higher computing power requirement for confirming transactions, which leads to the risk of network centralisation by supercomputers.

Another point made by Xie et al. is storage scalability. A conventional blockchain system requires a node to store the complete transaction history. A current Bitcoin's blockchain size reaches 240 GB [6]. Therefore, a full node requires vast amounts of storage. The last scalability issue, related to networking, is the data transmission delay. In the Bitcoin model, each transaction broadcasts twice – first after creation (and moving to a transaction pool) and second after transmitting within a mined block.

Often omitted is the fact that the scalability issue should be addressed primarily to permissionless blockchains [29]. A transaction approval usually takes a few minutes. The problem is worse in public permissionless since every node is a validator. In public permissioned, as in any private blockchains, only selected nodes can validate. Permissioned blockchain systems can perform significantly better, sometimes even close to permissioned networks, such as Visa, Mastercard or PayPal, due to a low number of nodes and utilising different consensus algorithms. Latest Corda Enterprise release achieved 2580 TPS [22], while Hyperledger Fabric was once tested by IBM researchers to perform 3500 TPS [3,25] and others did manage to increase the throughput up to 20000 TPS [13] by proposing some architectural changes to the platform to reduce bottlenecks. The numbers are promising, but permissioned blockchain relies on having a trusted authority. Increasing both scalability and security violates decentralisation by allowing a middle-man, which seems to be just what Scalability Trilemma addresses. Permissioned blockchains are controversial because the original blockchain assumptions put an emphasis on the idea of having a purely distributed system, and their existence seems to be a step back to centralisation. Holochain, with its *agent-centric* approach, even claims not to be blockchain, but a decentralised technology (a P2P application framework) utilising hash chains [9]. Major scalability solutions try to improve research areas such as network efficiency, storage, data usage and a consensus algorithm [10].

Public blockchains suffer from many scalability issues, and the private ones tend to be centralised by an intermediary. Permissionless is not secure, since it allows nodes to be anonymous and permissioned may lead to centralisation as well. Another challenge in the blockchain system is security and data privacy. While decentralisation is a desirable feature, it leads to trouble in maintaining data integrity. Timeliness of transactions can affect both system's performance and security. One of the possible attacks is double-spending – a data integrity violation that may appear in purely distributed peer-to-peer (P2P) systems like blockchain. Malicious peers are a threat to the network, and even there are machine learning (ML) efforts made to detect them [23]. Allowing peers to verify new transactions is a way to prevent transferring ownership more than once. However, to verify transactions, their log has to be transparent. One of the most prominent blockchain technical limitations addressed by [10] Drescher is lack of privacy. The system has to reconcile two opposite concepts: transparency and privacy. Hence, it is not an appropriate solution to use cases that necessitate a high level of privacy. If a solution is needed for homogeneous environment where everyone trusts each other and has a full control over a flow of data, and the environment itself is not exposed to any external threats – blockchain is going to be a very slow and disturbing database. The technology becomes relevant if dealing with a lack of trust in the network. Then the responsibility is spread over many members, and each of them has a reason not to let the system break (either by an attack or by entering incorrect information). Moreover, even when discrediting some servers, there is always a dozen or more servers that allow regaining balance. However, convincing competitors to rely on technology and entrust an intellectual property to machines is challenging. That is why consortia are created. It is the authority and independence of the leaders that guarantee comfortable conditions for solving problems – regardless of market relations.

Drescher perceives the blockchain security model to be yet another limitation. Users identification, authentication and authorising their transactions require a pair of keys. A public key is an account number or, in terms of cryptocurrency, a wallet address. A private key is used to generate a unique digital signature to confirm *who* makes the transaction. Blockchain uses powerful cryptography methods. Its security model is not a problem itself. Unlike centralised applications in the P2P system, there are no security procedures to revoke access to the account when one looses their own private key. The situation is not rare. Most users store their private keys on the computer where it is prone to be stolen either by malware or hard disk failure [18]. Few ways to avoid losing the key is creating its backup or using offline storage. If the user fails to keep the key in a safe place, there is no way to reset it like most real-world systems allow to do with a password.

3 Experiments

Besides blockchain's widespread use in cryptocurrency, its attributes for private permissionless variation seem especially suitable for CMS. Agarwal et al. [2] presented in their article a CMS named *Consentio* implemented in Hyperledger Fabric. The need to track and manage consent to private data is considered in three areas: gathering electronic health records, smart infrastructure (smart cities) and within social media applications. The authors have emphasised creating a scalable system deploying blockchain back-end for CMS which was not within the scope of prior studies in this area. For this reason, it was decided to reproduce Consentio blockchain network and experiments. The proposed system is promising, because of:

- the ability to translate complex requirements of CMS to Fabric key-value world state;
- achieving high transaction throughput and making the system easy to scale for deployments (where an increasing number of individuals and resources defines scalability);
- ensuring low latency and therefore preventing double-spending by disallowing to have two or more transactions with the same key in the same block.

Despite the listed favourable properties, Agarwal et al. [2] made the article easy to reproduce thanks to precise descriptions and by providing the smart contract source code in their study. Transaction throughput was evaluated locally through micro-benchmarking on five servers connected by a switch. With all the details given, it should be possible to move the Consentio infrastructure involving a single endorser, orderer, peer, four clients and smart contracts for Individual-oriented World State (IWS) world state design into a cloud environment.

3.1 Testing Environment

Consentio comes along with sample implementation in Hyperledger Fabric. Agarwal et al. [2] has emphasised creating a scalable system deploying blockchain back-end for CMS, what was not a scope of prior studies in this area.

The aim is to implement CMS atop BaaS and therefore creating CaaS using Consentio chaincode. The main requirement for Consentio is Hyperledger Fabric framework, which narrows the selection of possible blockchain cloud services. Three cloud platforms that fulfilled the requirements will be compared: AKS (Azure), AMB (AWS) and IBM Blockchain Platform. With template solution from Microsoft Azure, the deployment failed at the beginning due to unknown error (no information was provided in the correlation ID). With Amazon's fully-managed service it was possible to build a simple network. However, in experiment planning, the new requirement for the system was discovered. One of the operations from Consentio chaincode needs a CouchDB backend database for a peer. As opposed to LevelDB that operates faster, this state database permits rich queries of data if the data has been modelled in a smart contract as JSON. AMB does not support CouchDB, even though HLF incorporates it. Ultimately, IBM Blockchain Platform could handle both deployment and experiments.

In Fig. 1 the results of continuous writing 100 transactions by four local users are shown. They can be regarded as a measure of infrastructure performance. Each transaction held just one key-value pair. The measured time is a period between the earliest and latest created transaction in a single block created. 20000 with one value per each key have been sent. The world state key space (a number of key-value pairs in the registry) reached size of 11280.

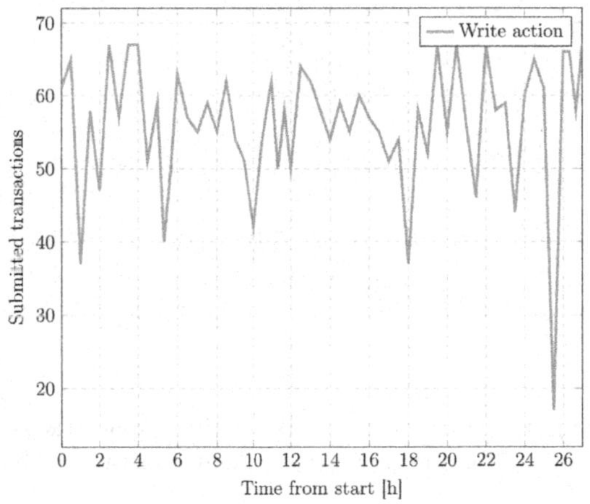

Fig. 1. Percent of submitted transactions in a single block (block size 100)

A single time measurement for TPS calculation was done differently, which considers time for creating a single block. It includes a range from creation of the first block to a last timestamp of submitted transaction. Figure 2 present accordingly read and write actions.

Table 1. Differences in volume between Consentio system and reproduction experiments

	Original	Reproduction
World state key space	20000	4000
Keys added in transaction	100	1
Value space per key	1; 100; 500; 1K; 5K; 10K	1; 2; 3; 4; 5; 6; 7; 8; 9; 10
Key space per transaction	100	10
Block size	100	20
Sent transactions	100000	4000

Red dashed line determines the average throughput which for *read* reached 1.02 and for *write* 1.55 TPS. With the statistical significance of 5%, margins of error equal:

- Read: 1.0244 ± 0.0297 TPS.
- Write: 1.5395 ± 0.1110 TPS.

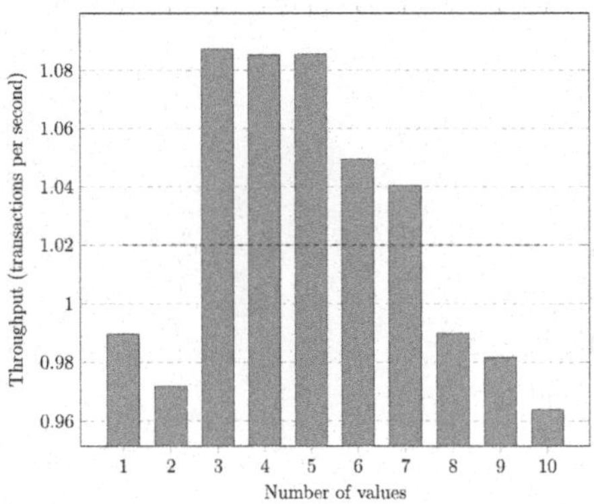

Fig. 2. Read throughput performance vs. size of value space (keys touched per transaction is kept constant at 100 and key space is kept constant at 4000)

3.2 Results

With proper setup to replicate a write throughput experiment, the testing script for submitting transactions using four users, each one having 25 threads (100 threads total), has been run. The IBM Blockchain Platform infrastructure could not handle such overload. Node.js Fabric SDK returned errors caused by the inability to contact the peer. Web UI available through the console was nearly unreachable at the time of sending transactions. Approximately 56% of written transactions were appended to each block, when others were lost due to insufficient resources. Ultimately, the world state key space reached a size of 11280 instead of 20000.

Some of Consentio experiments were repeated though (on the new channel, but for lower volumes, which are pointed out in Table 1). Among the three designs, the IWS world state was tested. Besides, the infrastructure still differs from the original one. Except for using IBM Kubernetes free cluster with 4 CPU and 2 GB of RAM to host the blockchain network, the four clients have been run on the MacBook Pro 2019 with Intel Core i5-8279U 2.4 GHz (4 cores) and 16 GB of RAM. The Internet connection used to communicate with the blockchain network was symmetrical with the download rate of 8.1 Mbps and 8.0 Mbps upload. The client application utilises Fabric SDK in Node.js to connect to HLF v1.4 blockchain network set up on IBM Blockchain Platform. Agarwal et al. [2] did not mention the client application SDK used for their experiments.

Considering experiments the replication and the first attempt of Consentio CMS reproduction for the same volume for which achieved transaction throughput was lower than in Bitcoin network (3.13 TPS) with 56.4% rate of successfully submitted transactions, insufficiencies in three areas have been examined compared to the Consentio network: physical resources, a blockchain framework and a network connection.

Table 2. Number of unsuccessful transactions during read or write to the world state containing a certain number of values per key

Values	1	2	3	4	5	6	7	8	9	10	Average
Read	1	5	0	0	1	0	1	3	0	0	1.10
Write	2	2	0	0	1	0	0	7	2	3	1.55

In the case of physical resources, the free tier offered by IBM cloud vendor could not handle the desired traffic. Another considerable difference gap concerns the difference in blockchain framework used – in the study it was plain HLF. In their experiments, Agarwal et al. [2] used FastFabric, which was mentioned earlier. Gorenflo et al. [13] introduced this HLF v1.2 modification in 2019. At the time, it enabled improving the transaction throughput from 3000 TPS (for baseline HLF v1.2) to 20000 TPS, which was shown through benchmarking. Assuming the improvement resulting from FastFabric to scale linearly, Consentio deployed in HLF would achieve 6–7 times fewer TPS – presumably around 900 TPS on average for both reading and writing. The gap between the original and reproduction experiments results is not significantly diminished when applying the same calculations for the obtained throughput. TPS of 7.7 for reading and 10.85 for writing are the highest values likely with FastFabric. The last limitation is network connection.

In Consentio experiments, 1 Gbit/s switch connected the servers. The isolated environment guaranteed comparatively a stable level of exchanged data.

In reproduction, the requests were sent through an Internet connection with approximately 125 times worse throughput. Also, every request was sent from Wroc?aw (Poland) to the cluster in the city of Dallas (United States). The connection type and the distance led to high latency. As claimed in the Consentio paper [2], the proposed CMS is replicable and indeed scalable. Physical testing infrastructure was almost adequately efficient to handle requests of the selected volumes. Minor reservations relate to occasional errors, which resulted in failing to add a transaction or in an inability to read the world state. *Lost* transactions for both read and write corresponding to the value iterations in Fig. 2 are presented in Table 2. Lost transactions account for roughly 0.03% of the total transactions made.

4 Discussion

Initially, for Consentio, all three experiments aimed to be repeated. In reproduction, key differences are physical infrastructure (that is much less technically advanced) and using plain HLF v1.4 instead of FastFabric [13] framework. Also, transaction times have been expected to increase because of the ongoing endorsement process. Despite the differences in physical infrastructure, the framework used, the presence of Endorser, these factors should not be meaningful in reproduction. Consentio experiments prove that the proposed system is scalable. With obviously decreased TPS values, the same measurements have been expected to show the linear trend.

Despite significant fluctuations of the obtained TPS values occurring in the results of actual reproduction, they do not seem to correlate to the increasing value space of the world state. However, TPS might have been affected by the network connection. The throughput reaches its overhead in the middle of Fig. 2. The number of values ranging from 3 to 7 gave results above the average in both cases. Measurements for the interval were done at night between 11 PM and 9 AM the following day. Reduced internet traffic at the time could have had an impact on them.

Regarding the cloud blockchain solutions, the definition of BaaS is yet vague. There are different levels and types of support for DLT. For instance, a blog post describing a simple blockchain network deployment (that might even come as a configured Docker container) using any web infrastructure needs to be distinguished from fully-managed blockchain services. These usually comprise extensive documentation, web UI, online video or interactive tutorials, and technical support.

When deciding on certain BaaS, one usually has to seek precise information about frameworks included. Like in the case of Amazon QLDB, their versions are rarely mentioned explicitly until creating a final configuration to deploy or paying attention to hyperlinks to framework's documentation in the deployment guide.

BaaS customers of the discussed platforms prefer to use permissioned blockchains for SCM. Due to blockchain's technology data-centric approach, it is especially convenient for multistakeholder governance.

The key results of this empirical study are:

- Recreating the Consentio blockchain network was fully possible with one of the tested BaaS platforms, the IBM Blockchain Platform.
- Using the cloud environment and a similar configuration to Consentio with four client users (one hundred threads total) continuously writing transactions to the blockchain, it took about 27 h to get a key space of 11280. During that process approximately only 56% of sent transactions were submitted due to insufficient resources.
- For overall lower volumes, the experiment for reading consent had average of 1.02 TPS and 1.55 TPS for writing. However, with FastFabric framework (a HLF variation), the highest values likely are estimated to be 6–7 higher, i.e. 7.7 TPS for reading and 10.85 TPS for writing.
- The results suggest that the network transaction throughput is not affected by changing the world state size, which proves the Consentio CMS to be a scalable system in this sense.

5 Conclusion and Future Work

Our paper aimed to fill the gap in the research over BaaS by making the following contributions. First by implementing a scalable blockchain system in a cloud environment. Second by surveying security and scalability problems occurring in private permissionless blockchain systems and solutions to them. The most promising services have been tested for the real deployment of the CMS, and led to creating CaaS. Through experiments, the proposed system's replication ability and its scalability have been examined, along with assessing the feasibility of the CMS development in the provided cloud environment. Considering the experiments replication, insufficiencies in three areas have been examined: physical resources, a blockchain framework and a network connection. All the factors combined led to high latency in transaction throughput for both reading and writing. Using the cloud environment and a similar configuration to Consentio with four client users (one hundred threads total) continuously writing transactions to the blockchain, it took about 27 h to get a key space of 11280 with approximately 44% of lost transactions due to limited resources. For overall lower volumes, the experiment for reading consent reached an average of 1.02 TPS and 1.55 TPS for writing. However, with FastFabric framework (a Hyperledger Fabric variation), the highest values likely are estimated to be 7.7 TPS for reading and 10.85 TPS for writing which is a similar throughput to Ethereum cryptocurrency. Nevertheless, the throughput results obtained are thousands of times lower, which indicates the insufficiency of the provided infrastructure. Future directions indicate that more advanced technical infrastructure for Consentio deployment would enable to reproduce all the experiments for the same volumes. In IBM Blockchain Platform, investing in a more powerful Kubernetes cluster should improve the throughput results. Independently, adding more peers to the blockchain network would increase the ability to endorse the transactions (assuming endorsement policy that does not require all peers).

References

1. Acharya, V., Yerrapati, A.E., Prakash, N.: Oracle Blockchain Quick Start Guide: A Practical Approach to Implementing Blockchain in Your Enterprise. Packt Publishing Ltd (2019)
2. Agarwal, R.R., Kumar, D., Golab, L., Keshav, S.: Consentio: managing consent to data access using permissioned blockchains. arXiv preprint arXiv:1910.07110 (2019)
3. Androulaki, E., et al.: Hyperledger fabric: a distributed operating system for permissioned blockchains. In: Proceedings of the Thirteenth EuroSys Conference, p. 30. ACM (2018)
4. Badr, B., Horrocks, R., Wu, X.B.: Blockchain By Example: A Developer's Guide to Creating Decentralized Applications using Bitcoin, Ethereum, and Hyperledger. Packt Publishing Ltd (2018)
5. Belotti, M., Božić, N., Pujolle, G., Secci, S.: A Vademecum on blockchain technologies: when, which, and how. IEEE Commun. Surv. Tutorials **21**(4), 3796–3838 (2019)
6. Blockchain Luxembourg: Blockchain Size (2017). https://www.blockchain.com/charts/blocks-size. Accessed 14 Sep 2019
7. Croman, K., et al.: On scaling decentralized blockchains. In: Clark, J., Meiklejohn, S., Ryan, P.Y.A., Wallach, D., Brenner, M., Rohloff, K. (eds.) FC 2016. LNCS, vol. 9604, pp. 106–125. Springer, Heidelberg (2016). https://doi.org/10.1007/978-3-662-53357-4_8
8. Dias, J.P., Sereno Ferreira, H., Martins, Â.: A blockchain-based scheme for access control in e-health scenarios. In: Madureira, A.M., Abraham, A., Gandhi, N., Silva, C., Antunes, M. (eds.) SoCPaR 2018. AISC, vol. 942, pp. 238–247. Springer, Cham (2020). https://doi.org/10.1007/978-3-030-17065-3_24
9. Donath, M.: Holochain Docs (2019). https://developer.holochain.org/docs/what-is-holochain/what-is-holochain. Accessed 06 Jan 2020
10. Drescher, D.: Blockchain Basics: A Non-Technical Introduction in 25 Steps. APRESS, New York (2017)
11. Ekblaw, A., Azaria, A., Halamka, J.D., Lippman, A.: A case study for blockchain in healthcare: "MedRec" prototype for electronic health records and medical research data. In: Proceedings of IEEE Open & Big Data Conference, vol. 13, p. 13 (2016)
12. Etherscan: Ethereum (ETH) Blockchain Explorer (2020). https://etherscan.io. Accessed 25 Apr 2020
13. Gorenflo, C., Lee, S., Golab, L., Keshav, S.: Fastfabric: scaling hyperledger fabric to 20,000 transactions per second. In: 2019 IEEE International Conference on Blockchain and Cryptocurrency (ICBC), pp. 455–463. IEEE (2019)
14. Huertas, J., Liu, H., Robinson, S.: Eximchain: supply chain finance solutions on a secured public, permissioned blockchain hybrid. Eximchain White Paper 13 (2018)
15. Hummer: Sharding FAQ (2017). https://github.com/ethereum/wiki/wiki/Sharding-FAQ. Accessed 12 Dec 2019
16. Jesus, V.: Towards an accountable web of personal information: the web-of-receipts. IEEE Access **8**, 25383–25394 (2020)
17. Lai, R., Chuen, D.L.K.: Blockchain-from public to private. In: Handbook of Blockchain, Digital Finance, and Inclusion, vol. 2, pp. 145–177. Elsevier (2018)
18. Malanov, A.: Problems and risks of cryptocurrencies (2017). https://www.kaspersky.com/blog/cryptocurrencies-intended-risks/20034/. Accessed 24 Feb 2020

19. Mastercard International Incorporated: Mastercard Transit Solutions Guide (2018). https://graphic.mastercard.com/acquirer-newsletter/issue12/pdf/14-f-mastercard-transit-solutions-guide.pdf. Accessed 14 Dec 2019
20. Novotny, P., et al.: Permissioned blockchain technologies for academic publishing. Inf. Serv. Use **38**(3), 159–171 (2018)
21. Onik, M.M.H., Miraz, M.H.: Performance analytical comparison of Blockchain-as-a-Service (BaaS) platforms. In: Miraz, M.H., Excell, P.S., Ware, A., Soomro, S., Ali, M. (eds.) iCETiC 2019. LNICSSITE, vol. 285, pp. 3–18. Springer, Cham (2019). https://doi.org/10.1007/978-3-030-23943-5_1
22. R3 Limited: Sizing and performance - Corda Enterprise 4.3 (2018). https://docs.corda.r3.com/sizing-and-performance.html. Accessed 22 Dec 2019
23. Rahouti, M., Xiong, K., Ghani, N.: Bitcoin concepts, threats, and machine-learning security solutions. IEEE Access **6**, 67189–67205 (2018)
24. Sánchez, D.C.: Raziel: private and verifiable smart contracts on blockchains. arXiv preprint arXiv:1807.09484 (2018)
25. Schatsky, D., Arora, A., Dongre, A.: Blockchain and the five vectors of progress. Deloitte Insights (2018)
26. Swanson, T.: Consensus-as-a-service: a brief report on the emergence of permissioned, distributed ledger systems. Report, available online (2015)
27. Visa Inc.: The technology behind Visa (2013). Accessed 14 Dec 2019
28. Visa Inc.: Visa Fact Sheet (2017). Accessed 14 Dec 2019
29. Xie, J., Yu, F.R., Huang, T., Xie, R., Liu, J., Liu, Y.: A survey on the scalability of blockchain systems. IEEE Netw. **33**(5), 166–173 (2019). https://doi.org/10.1109/MNET.001.1800290
30. Yaga, D., Mell, P., Roby, N., Scarfone, K.: Blockchain technology overview. arXiv preprint arXiv:1906.11078 (2019)
31. Zhang, Y., Kasahara, S., Shen, Y., Jiang, X., Wan, J.: Smart contract-based access control for the Internet of Things. IEEE Internet of Things J. **6**(2), 1594–1605 (2018)
32. Zyskind, G., Nathan, O., et al.: Decentralizing privacy: using blockchain to protect personal data. In: 2015 IEEE Security and Privacy Workshops, pp. 180–184. IEEE (2015)

Data Mining and Machine Learning

EMaxPPE: Epoch's Maximum Prediction Probability Ensemble Method for Deep Learning Classification Models

Javokhir Musaev[1(✉)], Ngoc Thanh Nguyen[2], and Dosam Hwang[1(✉)]

[1] Yeungnam University, Daegu, Republic of Korea
[2] Wroclaw University of Science and Technology, Wroclaw, Poland
Ngoc-Thanh.Nguyen@pwr.edu.pl

Abstract. As deep learning (DL) is evolving rapidly, implementing the knowledge of DL into various fields of human life and the effective usage of existing data insights are becoming crucial tasks for a majority of DL models. We are proposing to ensemble maximum prediction probabilities of different epochs and the epoch which achieved the highest accuracy for classification problems. Our suggestion contributes to the improvement of DL models using the pre-trained and skipped results from epochs. The maximum prediction probability ensemble of epochs increases the prediction space of the entire model if the intersection of prediction scope of any epoch is smaller than the one that has the biggest prediction scope. Using only the best epoch's prediction probabilities for classification cannot use the other epochs' knowledge. To avoid bias in this research, a simple CNN architecture with batch normalization and dropout was used as a base model. By ensembling only maximum prediction probabilities of different epochs, we managed to use 50% of the lost data insight from the epochs, thereby increasing the total accuracy by 4–5%.

Keywords: Prediction probabilities of epochs · Maximum prediction probability · Epoch ensemble · Deep learning ensemble

1 Introduction

Recently, ensemble learning has been primarily studied as a part of machine learning tools. Machine learning focuses on the automatization of tasks using minimal human knowledge. Instead of using existing algorithms, it was targeting to increase the role of creating new algorithms. Nevertheless, new algorithms to solve different problems are still an optimal solution if it can be developed. In a row of the field's growth's sources like creating new models, data preprocessing tools, increasing capability of dataflow, and new approaches to input data, ensemble techniques serve the same for improving the final training results as those we counted. According to [1], the amount of data that we have today has grown tremendously. Smartphones, social networks, and sensors are the source of generating data. Deep learning (DL) was started with the idea of developing new algorithms or models using data and the ground truth. The uniqueness of DL is

K. Wojtkiewicz et al. (Eds.): ICCCI 2021, CCIS 1463, pp. 293–303, 2021.
https://doi.org/10.1007/978-3-030-88113-9_23

that universal forms of solution or models were achieved after training using data and labels. After DL achieved serious results that could be applied to real life projects and gained popularity in different fields, large amounts of financial resources for research were directed to the development of DL. In our research, we study ensemble learning and try to contribute to the growth of DL. To address the limited computational resource issue, various methods were suggested in different fields, as discussed in [2]. Ensemble learning is beneficial for various branches of modern economy and human life. Starting from the financial sector to healthcare, the DL ensemble learning model was applied in many forms, e.g., a multistage neural network ensemble learning approach for banking, as discussed in [3], or prediction of oil price and others, as discussed in [4].

AMaxPPE represents ensemble of maximum prediction probabilities of different epochs into corresponding class of the model that achieved the highest accuracy. The reason to use other epochs' prediction probabilities was each epoch can obtain better results for different input data. Generalization of epochs true prediction scope for data can reach better accuracy than the best epochs accuracy. In our research we tried to solve generalization problem of DL for classification.

Our research consists of the following sections: related works in Sect. 2, research problem, proposed solution, experiment, and conclusion. In related works, we review the current research status in the world and the history of evaluation, i.e., possible applications of ensemble learning and future studies related to ensemble learning methods. Research problem includes highlighting existing problems that are partially solved or could not be solved by previous studies. In the next part, we propose a solution to the problem, i.e., implementation of maximum prediction probability application during the ensemble result of the safer DL model that can change the overall accuracy. The experiment section includes all our training results and evaluation metrics that we used to compare our proposed solution to the underlying problem.

2 Related Works

Numerous research were conducted on ensemble learning and applied to various fields. [5] and [1] applied ensemble learning to neuromuscular disorder prediction and data stream classification, [6] used it for hyperspectral imaging, and [7] studied DL ensemble for diabetic retinopathy. Multi-step forecasting for big data time series based on ensemble learning was studied in [8]. In [9], ensemble DL model for novel COVID-19 on computer tomography images was studied. In this study, approximately 15% of the noisy images were removed from the training set during preprocessing. The images were acquired from published journal datasets and Ningxia medical university hospital. In approximately 7500 images that were used, 2500 images were of COVID-19 patients, 2500 images were of normal lungs, and the remaining 2500 were computer tomography images of tumors. They suggested an ensemble of AlexNet, GoogleNet, and ResNet to classify the images. In their study, the authors used relative voting classification to diagnose the images. The relative voting system chooses images that are classified by a majority of models in an ensemble, or in our case, two models. If the majority part of the ensemble predicts the image as an infected image, then the model returns the same result. This shows how relative voting system works in an ensemble model. As pre-trained models of

AlexNet, GoogleNet, and ResNet were used, they compared the results of the ensembled model with each of the underlying models. As a result, 99.054% accuracy was achieved after training the ensembled model. From AlexNet, GoogleNet, and ResNet models, it improved to 0.89%, 0.80% and 0.49%, respectively. In [10], ensemble learning-based structural health monitoring by Mahalanobis distance metrics was suggested, where they classified ensemble learning into two classes. The first class is parallel ensemble learning, whereas the second class is sequential ensemble learning. Another approach to improve the accuracy of classification tasks was suggested in [11] using EL. Imbalanced classes in datasets play a significant role in the final results. A different number of classes in a dataset can lead the training model to be biased towards the classes with a significantly huge number of instances. The classic form of ensemble learning includes weighted average ensemble[1], where meta-learners and their appropriate weights identify the prediction probability of each class for the Cifar10 dataset. Using four different models and their weights, the average result increased to 1.323%. In individual models, they were 0.9269%, 0.9422%, 0.9090%, and 0.9135%. Ensemble learning was also applied in biomedicine [12]. Diseases like cancer still do not have a reliable treatment method. The only effective solution is early diagnosis of cancer using all resources. For this purpose, computer vision was used to classify informative gene data to detect cancer earlier. An ensemble of five different classification models [12] along with RNA-seq data sets of three different classes of cancers, i.e., lung adenocarcinoma, stomach adenocarcinoma, and breast invasive carcinoma, were used for this purpose.

The other works did not learn epochs prediction scope and its effect to final classification result. Our proposed method can use 50% of other epochs' prediction advantages. The importance of ensemble learning in various fields can be observed from the aforementioned studies. Different independent results and decentralized solutions for DL were proposed by ensemble learning because it can use the features learnt from different models, structures, training datasets, and combinations of models. Another advantage of ensemble learning is the unobstructed application of learned feature knowledge in any field, from self-driving to biomedicine, etc. Nevertheless, there are several studies that analyzed ensemble learning and its performance advantage over single DL models.

3 The Proposed Methodology

This section contains comprehensive information about EMaxPPE and the structure of EMaxPPE. Our proposed model has consist of following steps:

1. Preparing data
2. Training classification model for 5 epochs and save prediction probabilities of test set
3. Training classification model for 10 more epochs and save prediction probabilities of test set
4. Training classification model for 15 more epochs and save prediction probabilities of test set

[1] https://towardsdatascience.com/the-power-of-ensembles-in-deep-learning-a8900ff42be9.

5. Training classification model for 20 epochs and save prediction probabilities of test set
6. At the final step we take maximum of prediction probabilities from step 2, step 3 and step 4 and add them into the corresponding prediction class of step 5. This ensemble represents EMaxPPE. Then we can classify input image using EMaxPPE.

An overview of the proposed model is shown in Fig. 1. In the initial step, we set the batch size, input image size, number of classes, and number of epochs for the proposed model. Then, the data was loaded into the model after preprocessing and normalization.

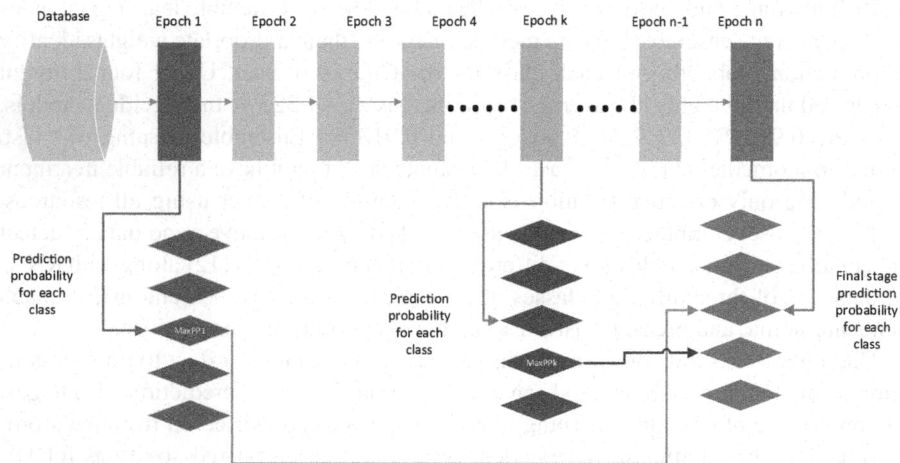

Fig. 1. Proposed method: EMaxPPE method

The next step includes a CNN model with batch normalization, max pooling, and a 3×3 filter size. The model for the proposed method includes a convolutional layer with 32 nodes, 3×3 filter, and ReLU activation function followed by batch normalization. Then, 2×2 max pooling was used and 2 consecutive convolutional layer blocks with batch normalization and max pooling were used. Before the final layer, 256 and 128 dense layers were used with ReLU function, and at the and 10 classification nodes with softmax activation functions were classified. Then, the architecture was trained 5, 10, 15, and 20 times.

We proposed an ensemble of different epoch prediction probabilities of the same model (model described in Fig. 1). This model calculates the intersection union of the true prediction space of the chosen epoch and considers the size ensemble model to return the result.

It is an ensemble of the best prediction accuracy of the epoch and maximum prediction probability of another epoch, which has a lower prediction probability. [9] can be considered as an encouraging source to develop a new ensemble learning method. The relative voting method suggested in [9] has many similarities to our method. However, instead of voting we are considering the highest prediction probability of a certain class and adding it to the corresponding class of the epoch that has highest accuracy.

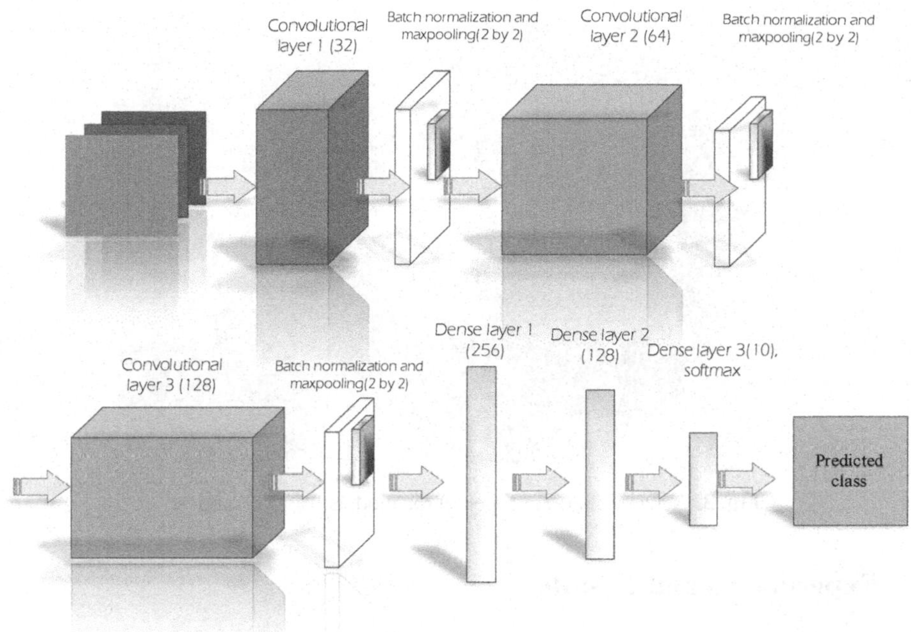

Fig. 2. Training model architecture

The impact of choosing the highest probability in the prediction of an epoch is presented in Fig. 2. Each space represents different true prediction space of an epoch. Space "a" represents the highest accuracy prediction scope of the epoch. Similarly, spaces "b" and "c" show the prediction space with lower accuracy and smaller scopes of two different epochs. If we analyze the intersection union, it is obvious that different epochs achieve better results using different data. For instance, intersection of scope "a" and scope "b" do not reach the full size of the smaller scope. This means that the smaller scope can provide a better prediction than the bigger scope on the data that is beyond the intersection in the smaller scope (Fig. 3).

Generally, all the achieved models after a few trainings provide good results only on certain part of the dataset. However, to acquire all the knowledge in a dataset, we need to gather different models that learn different parts of the dataset. Nevertheless, training different models is an expensive and time consuming process. Therefore, instead of training two or more models, we can use the existing knowledge that can increase the overall result of our model. Moreover, by understanding classification results, we can completely understand how maximum prediction probability works.

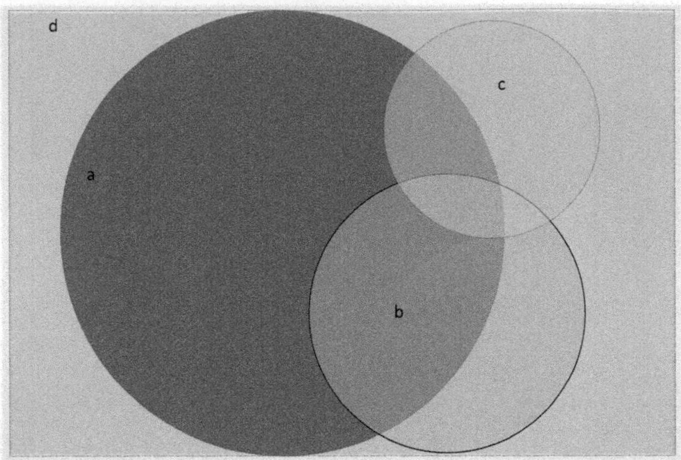

Fig. 3. True prediction scopes of the models: "a", "b" and "c"

4 Experiments and Results

In this section, we provide comprehensive information about the experiments and their results. This section also includes test results of the used model and dataset. Its comparison to our base model and the evaluation is the main part of this section.

4.1 Dataset

We used a popular dataset from the image classification field. A sufficient number of images and reliable labeled data make the Cifar10[2] dataset that was collected by Alex Krizhevsky, Vinod Nair, and Geoffrey Hinton popular in classification tasks. Additionally, the size of the dataset is advantageous for training. The detailed description of the classification can be seen in Table 1. We did not change the image size in the dataset. To avoid any bias from preprocessing, we used minimum preprocessing tools. The images were normalized by 255. Additionally, Cifar10 can help us test the potential results of the proposed method on light datasets. For a simple CNN and dense layer model, using this dataset is very convenient. The results obtained can be easily divided into different scopes and detailed evaluation results of the method can be selected.

Table 1. Cifar10[a] dataset description.

Dataset name	Cifar10
Total number of images	60000

(*continued*)

[2] https://www.cs.toronto.edu/~kriz/cifar.html.

Table 1. *(continued)*

Dataset name	Cifar10
Size of images	32 × 32 × 3
Train set	50000
Test set	10000
Size of dataset	163 mb (python version)
Class names	"airplane", "automobile", "bird", "cat", "deer", "dog", "frog", "horse", "ship", "truck"

[a]https://www.cs.toronto.edu/~kriz/cifar.html.

4.2 Baseline Model

In our study, we chose the first step or the best result of our own model as a baseline model. Using the same model architecture to evaluate the method is very reasonable. The proposed method can be compared with different ensemble methods or based on the best performance. We chose the best performance as the results of other related studies were approximately 1% better than their best performance. The aim of this research was to achieve more than 3% increase in the best performance. In this study, we chose different epochs as base models and the main one that achieves the best result without using EMaxPPE.

4.3 Training Setup

We formulated the model of the proposed method using Python 3.6.12 and Python 2.1.0 of the TensorFlow framework. The experiments were performed using a 12 GB NVidia Titan-XP GPU with CUDA 10.2 on a computer with an Intel core-i5 7th generation CPU and 32 GB of RAM. In our training, we initialized weights randomly, and then saved the model in each step and continued training for the next interval of epochs. Additionally, we used the Adam optimizer with a default learning rate of 0.001 and epsilon 1e − 07. We used sparse categorical loss function for our training and chose 5 epochs for the first step followed by an additional 10, 15, and 25 epochs. We trained the model in different intervals of epochs to achieve epochs that learn various parts of the dataset.

4.4 Evaluation Metrics

A majority of computer vision tasks include evaluation metrics like training loss, test loss, accuracy, IoU, etc. For our case, we used training validation loss, accuracy, and test accuracy. Finally, we calculated the unique true predictions for each model.

Accuracy is calculated as follows:

$$\text{Accuracy} = \frac{TP + TN}{TP + TN + FP + FN} \tag{1}$$

TP-true predicted positive results

TN-true predicted negative results
FP-false predicted positive results
FN-false predicted negative results

Unique true prediction for each model (UP) is calculated as follows:

$$UP_n = TP_n + TN_n - TP_m - TN_m \tag{2}$$

n-model index by epoch
m-model index by epoch

4.5 Experimental Results and Discussions

In our training, we included evaluation metrics, such as training validation losses, accuracies, and test accuracy. In the final step, we calculated the unique prediction scope of each model. Figure 4 presents the training and validation losses, which are the main tools to evaluate during the training process. Additionally, Fig. 4 presents the losses for each model or, as we structured, for each interval of epochs. As our model began to move from the early training steps, it began learning training data better. However, overfitting of training data can be observed from the second, third, and fourth interval or models that difference the losses of training and the validation set increases.

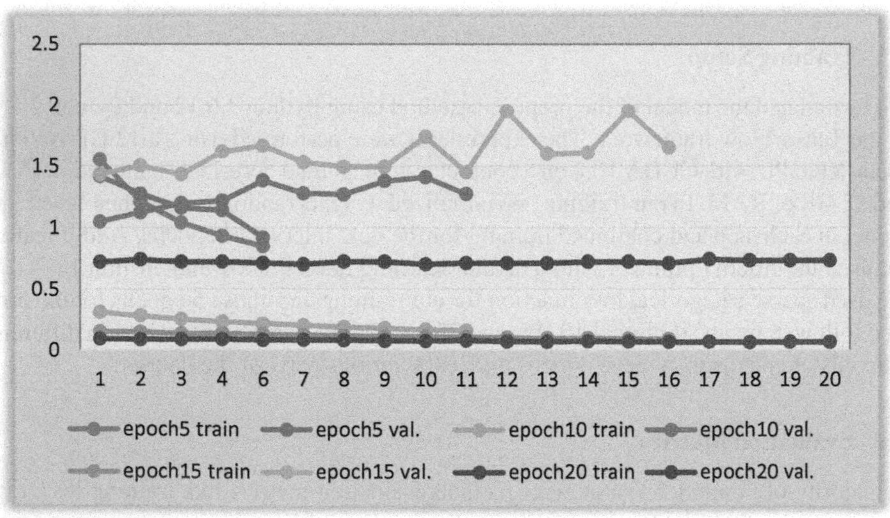

Fig. 4. Training and validation loss for different intervals of training

Figure 5 shows how the aforementioned overfitting problem reflects the accuracy. Accuracy of the training set can reach 99 percent in very short steps of training. However, the validation score decreases more than expected. For model 1, model 2, model 3, and model 4, our validation accuracies were 69%, 72%, 72%, and 73%, respectively. While the results for the validation set were very close, our prediction of the test set provided us much better results than the validation set. The reason to achieve better result was using prediction ability of other epochs for input image.

Table 2. Test accuracies for each epoch or model.

Model	Accuracy
Modell (epoch5)	68.2%
Model2 (epoch10)	71.8%
Model3 (epoch15)	72.85%
Model4 (epoch20)	71.6%
EMaxPPE model	75.61%

Table 2 shows the test accuracies of each model, where model 1 achieves 68.2% accuracy, whereas the other three models achieve 71.8%, 72.85%, and 71.6%, respectively. Model 1 has lower accuracy than model 5, but it can work better for 10.51% different images then model 5, according to Table 3. Model 2 has 9.59% different true predicted images than true predicted images by model 5, and this is the main reason for our method that returns better accuracy.

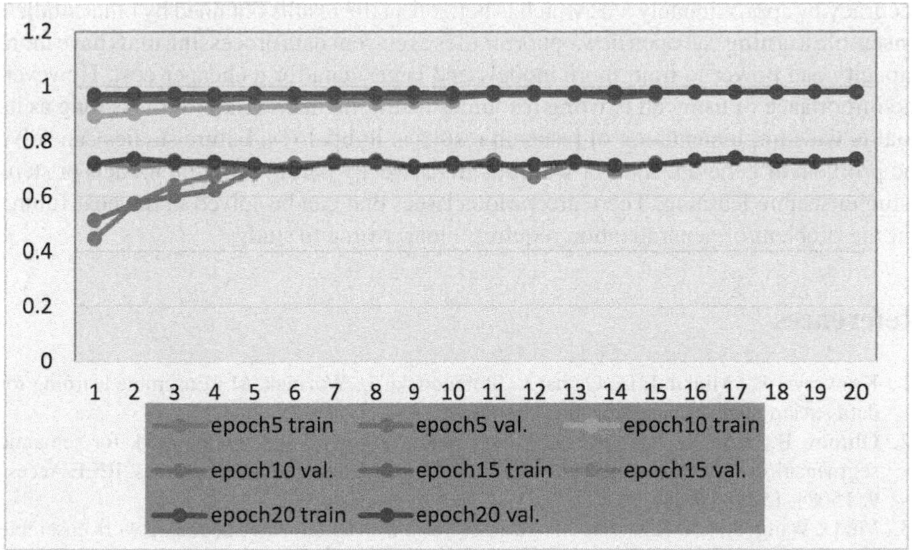

Fig. 5. Training validation accuracy for different intervals of training

Table 3 provides the scope of true predicted images of each model. Even with very close accuracies, each model learned approximately 10% different images from each other. Furthermore, the last column ensemble of maximum prediction probability of lower accuracy models and best models corresponding to class prediction probabilities returned approximately 3% better result. The reason to achieve a better result for our method is the differences of true predicted images between models.

Table 3. Test accuracies for each epoch or model.

	Model 1	Model 2	Model 3	Model 4
Model 1	0	0.1007	0.982	0.1051
Model 2	0.1341	0	0.0895	0.0959
Model 3	0.1324	0.0903	0	0.0839
Model 4	0.1341	0.0915	0.0787	0

5 Conclusion and Future Work

In conclusion, we can say that applying EMaxPPE can provide better results than an ensemble of two differently trained models. Additionally, using the existing knowledge can contribute more than what is expected from this model. In our method, we used maximum epoch prediction probabilities to achieve better results and we increased our accuracy by approximately 3%, which is better than the results obtained by other studies. Ensemble learning can open new opportunities as current data processing units have more capacity and power to train more models and larger data for a cheaper cost. However, the importance of using all existing resources is still the main task of DL. As long as its goal is wide implementation of research results in lights IoTs. Future studies can solve the problem of generalization or learning all dataset by part in different models or steps using ensemble learning. There are various issues that can be solved in the near future, but the problem of generalization requires a longer time to study.

References

1. Krawczyk, B., Minku, L.L., Gama, J., Stefanowski, J., Woźniak, M.: Ensemble learning for data stream analysis: a survey. Inf. Fusion **37**, 132–156 (2017)
2. Olimov, B., Kim, J., Paul, A.: REF-Net: robust, efficient, and fast network for semantic segmentation applications using devices with limited computational resources. IEEE Access **9**, 15084–15098 (2021)
3. Yu, L., Wang, S., Lai, K.K.: Credit risk assessment with a multistage neural network ensemble learning approach. Exp. Syst. Appl. **34**(2), 1434–1444 (2008)
4. Zhao, Y., Li, J., Yu, L.: A deep learning ensemble approach for crude oil price forecasting. Energy Econ. **66**, 9–16 (2017)
5. Khamparia, A., et al.: A novel deep learning-based multi-model ensemble method for the prediction of neuromuscular disorders. Neural Comput. Appl. **32**(15), 11083–11095 (2018)

6. Chen, Y., Wang, Y., Gu, Y., He, X., Ghamisi, P., Jia, X.: Deep learning ensemble for hyperspectral image classification. IEEE J. Select. Top. Appl. Earth Observ. Remote Sens. **12**(6), 1882–1897 (2019)
7. Qummar, S., et al.: A deep learning ensemble approach for diabetic retinopathy detection. IEEE Access **7**, 150530–150539 (2019)
8. Galicia, A., Talavera-Llames, R., Troncoso, A., Koprinska, I., Martínez-Álvarez, F.: Multistep forecasting for big data time series based on ensemble learning. Knowl. Based Syst. **163**, 830–841 (2019)
9. Zhou, T., Lu, H., Yang, Z., Qiu, S., Huo, B., Dong, Y.: The ensemble deep learning model for novel COVID-19 on CT images. Appl. Soft Comput. **98**, 106885 (2021)
10. Sarmadi, H., Entezami, A., Saeedi Razavi, B., Yuen, K.V.: Ensemble learning-based structural health monitoring by Mahalanobis distance metrics. Struct. Control Health Monitor. **28**(2) (2021)
11. Chen, Z., Duan, J., Kang, L., Qiu, G.: Class-imbalanced deep learning via a class-balanced ensemble. IEEE Trans. Neural Netw. Learn. Syst. 1–15 (2021)
12. Xiao, Y., Wu, J., Lin, Z., Zhao, X.: A deep learning-based multi-model ensemble method for cancer prediction. Comput. Methods Prog. Biomed. **153**, 1–9 (2018)
13. Sagi, O., Rokach, L.: Ensemble learning: a survey. WIREs Data Mining Knowl. Discov. **8**(4) (2018). https://doi.org/10.1002/widm.1249.

Convolutional Neural Networks with Dynamic Convolution for Time Series Classification

Krisztian Buza(✉) and Margit Antal

Department of Mathematics-Informatics, Sapientia Hungarian University of Transylvania, Targu Mures, Romania
buza@biointelligence.hu, manyi@ms.sapientia.ro

Abstract. Due to its prominent applications, time series classification is one of the most important fields of machine learning. Although there are various approaches for time series classification, dynamic time warping (DTW) is generally considered to be a well-suited distance measure for time series. Therefore, in the early 2000s, techniques based on DTW dominated this field. On the other hand, deep learning techniques, especially convolutional neural networks (CNN) were shown to be able to solve time series classification tasks accurately. Although CNNs are extraordinarily popular, the scalar product in convolution only allows for rigid pattern matching. In this paper, we aim at combining the advantages of DTW and CNN by proposing the *dynamic convolution* operation and *dynamic convolutional neural networks* (DCNNs). The main idea behind dynamic convolution is to replace the dot product in convolution by DTW. We perform experiments on 10 publicly available real-world time-series datasets and demonstrate that our proposal leads to statistically significant improvement in terms of classification accuracy in various applications. In order to promote the use of DCNN, we made our implementation publicly available at https://github.com/kr7/DCNN.

Keywords: Time series classification · Dynamic convolution · Convolutional neural networks · Dynamic time warping

1 Introduction

Time series classification is the common denominator of numerous recognition tasks in various domains ranging from biology, medicine and healthcare over astronomy and geology to industry and finance. Such tasks include signature verification, speech recognition, earthquake prediction or the diagnosis of heart diseases based on electrocardiograph signals. Due to the aforementioned applications, and many others, time series classification is one of the most prominent fields of machine learning.

In the last decades, various approaches have been introduced for time series classification, including methods based on neural networks, Bayesian networks, hidden Markov models, genetic algorithms, support vector machines, decision

K. Wojtkiewicz et al. (Eds.): ICCCI 2021, CCIS 1463, pp. 304–312, 2021.
https://doi.org/10.1007/978-3-030-88113-9_24

trees, frequent pattern mining and hubness-aware classifiers, see e.g. [4,6,7,11, 13,14,20] and [3,17] for introductory surveys. However, one of the most surprising results states that the simple k-nearest neighbor classifier using dynamic time warping (DTW) as distance measure is competitive (if not superior) to many other classifiers. In particular, Xi et al. compared various time series classifiers and concluded that 1-nearest neighbor with DTW "is an exceptionally competitive classifier" [19]. Although, this result dates back to 2006, the observation has been confirmed by many researchers who used DTW in their approach and achieved high accuracy, see e.g. [15,17] and the references therein. The primary reason why DTW is appropriate for time series classification is that DTW is an elastic distance measure in the sense that it allows for shifts and elongations while matching two time series.

Although DTW is a well-suited distance measure for time series classification, meanwhile state-of-the-art solutions are based on deep learning techniques, see e.g. [8,18,20,21]. Especially, recent convolutional neural networks (CNNs) perform well for time series classification tasks, in many cases they outperform the previous baseline of kNN-DTW, see [7] for a review on CNNs for time series classification. Convolution is intended to act as local pattern detector, however, convolution itself only allows for rigid pattern matching by design. Therefore, convolutional layers are usually followed by pooling layers in state-of-the-art CNNs. While these pooling layers may alleviate the aforementioned issue of rigidity in pattern matching to some extent, as we will explain in Sect. 3.1 in detail, this solution is inherently limited and the resulting operation is somewhat irregular in terms of its ability to account for translations of local patterns.

In this paper, we aim at exploiting the flexibility of DTW in convolutional neural networks. In particular, in order to allow for local shifts and elongations, we replace the dot product in the first convolutional layer by DTW and call the resulting operation *dynamic convolution*. We perform experiments on publicly available real-world time-series datasets and demonstrate that our proposal leads to statistically significant improvement in terms of classification accuracy in various applications.

The remainder of the paper is organized as follows. A short review of related work on time series classification with CNNs and the embedding of DTW into neural networks is given in Sect. 2. This is followed by the definition of dynamic convolution and its integration with CNNs in Sect. 3. In Sect. 4, we describe the datasets, experimental protocols, and compare the results obtained by CNNs using conventional and dynamic convolutional layers. The last section presents the conclusions.

2 Related Work

Works that are most closely related to ours fall into two categories: (i) methods based on convolutional neural networks for time series classification and (ii) approaches that integrate DTW with neural networks.

As for the former, we refer to the recent survey of Fawaz et al. [7] and we point out that our approach is orthogonal to convolutional network architectures as it can be used with any convolutional network by replacing the (first) convolutional layer by our dynamic convolution.

Regarding the approaches that integrate DTW with neural networks, we point out the works of Iwana et al. [10] and Cai et al. [5] who used DTW to construct features. In contrast, Afrasiabi et al. [1] used neural networks to extract features and used DTW to compare the resulting sequences. Shulman [16] proposed "an approach similar to DTW" to allow for flexible matching in case of the dot product. In our current work, we propose to use DTW instead of modifying the dot product.

Most closely related to our work is probably the DTW-NN approach, in case of which the authors considered neural networks and replaced "the standard inner product of a node with DTW as a kernel-like method" [9]. However, they only considered multilayer perceptrons (MLP). In contrast, we focus on convolutional networks.

3 Our Approach

In this section, we describe the proposed approach in detail. We begin this section by discussing the limitations of "usual" convolution and max pooling. This is followed by the definition of *dynamic convolution*. Subsequently, we will discuss how the "usual" convolution can be replaced by dynamic convolution and how the weights (parameters) of dynamic convolution can be learned.

3.1 Convolution and Max Pooling

In CNNs, convolutional layers act as local pattern detectors and they are often followed by max pooling layers. Max pooling layers allow for some flexibility in pattern matching by hiding the exact location of a pattern within the time series. In other words: even if the pattern is shifted by a few positions, depending on the window size used in the max pooling layer, the activation of the layer may remain unchanged. However, max pooling is only able to establish this robustness in pattern matching if the pattern is shifted within the max pooling window: if the pattern is located at the boundary of the max pooling window, even if it is shifted just by one position outside the max pooling window, the activation of the max pooling layer will change. This is illustrated in Fig. 1 where the same pattern has been shifted by one position to the left and right. In the former case, the activation of the max pooling layer remains unchanged, whereas in the later case, the activation of the max pooling layer changes to a non-negligible extent. We argue that this behavior is somewhat irregular as one would expect the same changes regardless whether the pattern is shifted to the left or to the right.

More importantly, while convolution with max pooling may account for minor translations (even if its behaviour is somewhat irregular), we point out that there may be other types of temporal distortions as well, such as elongations within local patterns, that can not be taken into account by the dot product in convolution.

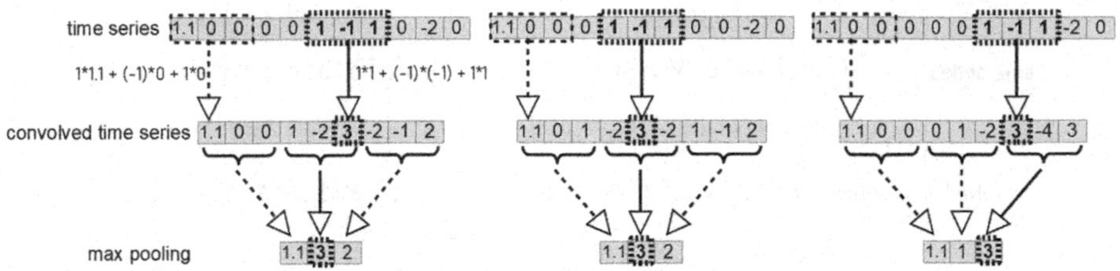

Fig. 1. Convolution with max pooling allows for a limited and, more importantly, irregular robustness against translations of local patterns. The convolutional kernel in the top is expected to detect 'V'-shaped local patterns. In the left, the pattern has been detected at one of the central positions in the time series which is reflected by the high activation of the max pooling layer at the second position (see the highlighted '3'). In the time series depicted in the center of the figure, the pattern has been translated by one position to the left. The activation of the max pooling layer remains unchanged indicating the robustness against small translations. On the other hand, in the time series in the right, the same pattern has been translated by one position to the right (compared to its original location in the time series in the left), and the activation of the max pooling layer changed.

3.2 Dynamic Convolution

The main idea behind dynamic convolution is to replace the calculation of dot products (or inner products) in convolution by the calculation of DTW distances between the kernel and time series segments. This is illustrated in Fig. 2. We omit the details of the calculation of DTW distances, as it has been described in various works, see e.g. [3] or [17].

Regarding dynamic convolution in neural networks, we propose to use dynamic convolution in the first hidden layer (i.e., directly after the input layer). We call the resulting model *dynamic convolutional neural network* or *DCNN* for short.

In order to determine the parameters of the dynamic convolutional layer, we propose to train an analogous neural network with "usual" convolution in the first hidden layer and use its learned kernel as kernel of the dynamic convolution. With *pre-training phase of DCNN*, we refer to the aforementioned process of training the analogous neural network with "usual" convolution in its first hidden layer. Once the pre-training is completed, the weights (parameters) of dynamic convolution are frozen (i.e., they do not change anymore), and other layers of DCNN can be trained by various optimization algorithms, such as stochastic gradient descent or Adam [12]. In order to implement training efficiently, the activation of the dynamic convolutional layer may be pre-computed (as the weights of dynamic convolution do not change after pre-training).

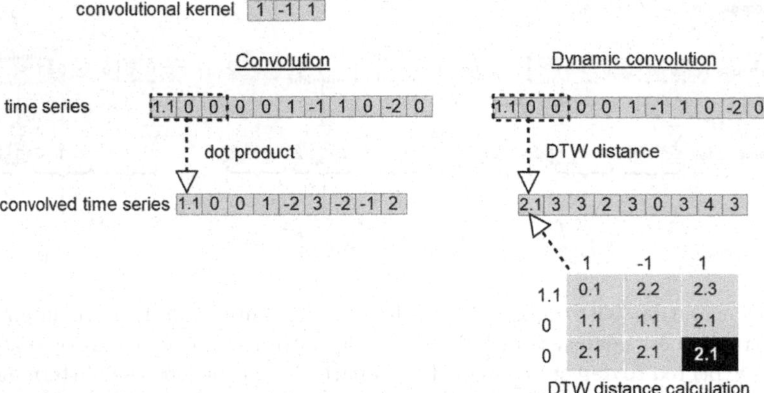

Fig. 2. Convolution (left) vs. dynamic convolution (right). In case of dynamic convolution, instead of the dot product (or inner product), DTW distances between the kernel and time series segments are calculated.

4 Experimental Evaluation

The goal of our experiments is to examine whether the proposed dynamic convolution improves the accuracy of neural networks in the context of time series classification.

Data: We performed experiments on real-world time series datasets that are publicly available in "The UEA & UCR Time Series Classification Repository" [2]. The datasets used in our experiments are listed in the first column on Table 1.

Experimental Settings: In order to assess the contribution of dynamic convolution, we trained two versions of the same networks: *with* and *without* dynamic convolution, and compared the results. In the former case, the first hidden layer was a dynamic convolutional layer (with DTW calculations), whereas in the later case, we used the "usual" convolution (with dot product).

To account for the fact that dynamic convolution may be used in various neural networks, we assessed the contribution of dynamic convolution in case of two different neural networks:

- *Net1* is a simple convolutional network, containing a single convolutional layer with 10 filters, followed by a max pooling layer with window size of 2, and a fully connected layer with 100 units.
- *Net2* contains a convolutional layer with 25 filters, followed by a max pooling layer with window size of 2, a second convolutional layer with 10 filters, a second max pooling layer with window size of 2 and a fully connected layer with 100 units.

Table 1. Average accuracy ± its standard deviation (calculated over 10 folds) for the neural networks with "usual" convolution (denoted as CNN) and dynamic convolution (denoted as DCNN). The best out of the both networks is denoted by bold font. In each case we also provide a symbol •/∘ denoting if the observed difference is statistically significant (•) or not (∘) according to paired t-test at significance level (p-value) of 0.05.

Dataset	Net1		Net2	
	CNN	DCNN	CNN	DCNN
Adiac	0.506 ± 0.061	**0.575 ± 0.046** •	0.558 ± 0.052	**0.640 ± 0.055** •
ArrowHead	0.886 ± 0.064	**0.896 ± 0.083** ∘	**0.900 ± 0.062**	0.887 ± 0.082 ∘
Beef	0.733 ± 0.170	**0.800 ± 0.163** •	0.700 ± 0.180	**0.783 ± 0.130** •
EarthQuakes	0.725 ± 0.042	**0.733 ± 0.069** ∘	0.699 ± 0.072	**0.731 ± 0.063** ∘
ECG200	0.870 ± 0.050	**0.890 ± 0.044** ∘	0.865 ± 0.084	**0.870 ± 0.064** ∘
FiftyWords	0.702 ± 0.033	**0.714 ± 0.045** ∘	0.686 ± 0.034	**0.715 ± 0.027** •
Plane	0.981 ± 0.032	**0.990 ± 0.029** ∘	0.976 ± 0.032	**0.995 ± 0.014** •
SwedishLeaf	0.864 ± 0.041	**0.883 ± 0.027** •	0.862 ± 0.036	**0.881 ± 0.033** ∘
WordSynonyms	0.682 ± 0.031	**0.714 ± 0.050** •	0.681 ± 0.049	**0.727 ± 0.047** •
Yoga	0.951 ± 0.013	**0.960 ± 0.012** •	0.945 ± 0.022	**0.959 ± 0.008** ∘

In both cases, the output layer contains as many units as the number of classes in the dataset. Both in case of Net1 and Net2, we experimented with the aforementioned two versions, i.e., with and without dynamic convolution in the first hidden layer. Although, there may be other neural networks that are better suited for a particular time series classification task, we observed that both Net1 and Net2 lead to accurate models in the examined tasks and we point out that the primary goal of our experiments was to assess the contribution of dynamic convolution. We implemented both Net1 and Net2 in pytorch. In order to calculate DTW distances quickly, we used a function that was implemented in Cython. We executed the experiments in Google Colab.[1]

We performed experiments according to the 10-fold cross-validation protocol and report average classification accuracy together with its standard deviation for both versions of Net1 and Net2 in Table 1. Additionally, we used paired t-test at significance level (p-value) of 0.05 in order to assess whether the observed differences are statistically significant (denoted by •) or not (denoted by ∘).

Codes: In order to assist reproduction of the results, we published our code in our GitHub repository

https://github.com/kr7/DCNN

in form of IPython notebooks that can be directly executed in Google Colab.

[1] https://colab.research.google.com.

Results: As one can see in Table 1, in half of the examined cases, DCNN significantly outperforms CNN. In the remaining cases, where the difference is statistically insignificant, DCNN still usually performs better than CNN, the only exception is the experiment with Net2 on the ArrowHead dataset. These results indicate that the proposed dynamic convolution may indeed improve the accuracy of convolutional neural networks.

Discussion: We point out that both Net1 and Net2 contain max pooling layers. Therefore, our results also demonstrate that "usual" convolution with max pooling was not able to account for all the temporal distortions that are present in the data. This is inline with our expectations based on our analysis in Sect. 3.1 where we discussed the rigidity of the dot product and pointed out that max pooling only has a limited ability to account for translations, however, it can not take elongations into account.

Training Time and Complexity: The method to train DCNN consists of two phases: in the first (pretrain) phase, a CNN is trained; whereas in the second phase, the weights of DCNN (except for the weights of the dynamic convolutional layer) are learned. Therefore, the overall training time is roughly twice of the training time of a single CNN. However, as pointed out in Sect. 3.2, the activation of the dynamic convolutional layer may be precomputed, i.e., it needs to be computed only once, even if the network is trained for many epochs in the second phase. Therefore, the second phase of training may actually be slightly faster than the training of an analogous CNN.

In the sense of complexity theory, under the assumptions that the number of convolutional filters in the dynamic convolutional layer is a constant, the sizes of each of them is a (small) constant and the length of time series is constant as well, the time required for computation of the activation of the dynamic convolutional layer is constant which does not change the complexity of training in the sense of algorithm theory. Also training two networks instead of one, is just a multiplication by a constant factor of 2 which again does not change the complexity in the sense of algorithm theory. Therefore, the theoretical complexity of training DCNN is the same as training a "usual" CNN.

5 Conclusions and Outlook

In this paper we introduced dynamic convolution as an alternative to the "usual" convolution operation. Dynamic convolutional layers can be used within various neural networks. We performed experiments in context of time series classification on publicly available real-world datasets. The results are very promising: they show that dynamic convolution is indeed competitive with "usual" convolution, moreover, the neural networks using dynamic convolutional layers systematically, often statistically significantly, outperform analogous neural networks with "usual" convolutional layers. In principle, the proposed neural networks with dynamic convolution may be used for any time series classification tasks, such as handwriting recognition, signature verification, ECG-based diagnosis of various heart diseases, etc. In order to assist reproduction of our work and to promote using dynamic convolutional layers in various applications, we published our codes.

As future work, we plan to perform experiments with additional neural network architectures, such as deeper neural network, or networks with residual connections. Moreover, in order to examine the generality of our results, we plan to experiment with further datasets as well.

References

1. Afrasiabi, M., Mansoorizadeh, M., et al.: DTW-CNN: time series-based human interaction prediction in videos using CNN-extracted features. Visual Comput. **36**(6), 1127–1139 (2020)
2. Bagnall, A., Lines, J., Vickers, W., Keogh, E.: The UEA & UCR time series classification repository. www.timeseriesclassification.com
3. Buza, K.: Time series classification and its applications. In: Proceedings of the 8th International Conference on Web Intelligence, Mining and Semantics, pp. 1–4 (2018)
4. Buza, K.: Asterics: projection-based classification of EEG with asymmetric loss linear regression and genetic algorithm. In: 2020 IEEE 14th International Symposium on Applied Computational Intelligence and Informatics (SACI), pp. 35–40. IEEE (2020)
5. Cai, X., Xu, T., Yi, J., Huang, J., Rajasekaran, S.: DTWNet: a dynamic time warping network. In: Advances in Neural Information Processing Systems, vol. 32 (2019)
6. Esmael, B., Arnaout, A., Fruhwirth, R.K., Thonhauser, G.: Improving time series classification using hidden Markov models. In: 2012 12th International Conference on Hybrid Intelligent Systems (HIS), pp. 502–507. IEEE (2012)
7. Ismail Fawaz, H., Forestier, G., Weber, J., Idoumghar, L., Muller, P.-A.: Deep learning for time series classification: a review. Data Min. Knowl. Disc. **33**(4), 917–963 (2019). https://doi.org/10.1007/s10618-019-00619-1
8. Guzy, F., Woźniak, M.: Employing dropout regularization to classify recurring drifted data streams. In: 2020 International Joint Conference on Neural Networks (IJCNN), pp. 1–7. IEEE (2020)
9. Iwana, B.K., Frinken, V., Uchida, S.: DTW-NN: a novel neural network for time series recognition using dynamic alignment between inputs and weights. Knowl. Based Syst. **188**, 104971 (2020)
10. Iwana, B.K., Uchida, S.: Time series classification using local distance-based features in multi-modal fusion networks. Pattern Recogn. **97**, 107024 (2020)
11. Jankowski, D., Jackowski, K., Cyganek, B.: Learning decision trees from data streams with concept drift. Procedia Comput. Sci. **80**, 1682–1691 (2016)
12. Kingma, D.P., Ba, J.: Adam: a method for stochastic optimization. arXiv preprint arXiv:1412.6980 (2014)
13. Lines, J., Davis, L.M., Hills, J., Bagnall, A.: A shapelet transform for time series classification. In: Proceedings of the 18th ACM SIGKDD International Conference on Knowledge Discovery and Data Mining, pp. 289–297 (2012)

14. Pavlovic, V., Frey, B.J., Huang, T.S.: Time-series classification using mixed-state dynamic bayesian networks. In: Proceedings. 1999 IEEE Computer Society Conference on Computer Vision and Pattern Recognition (Cat. No PR00149), vol. 2, pp. 609–615. IEEE (1999)
15. Radovanović, M., Nanopoulos, A., Ivanović, M.: Time-series classification in many intrinsic dimensions. In: Proceedings of the 2010 SIAM International Conference on Data Mining, pp. 677–688. SIAM (2010)
16. Shulman, Y.: Dynamic time warp convolutional networks. arXiv preprint arXiv:1911.01944 (2019)
17. Tomašev, N., Buza, K., Marussy, K., Kis, P.B.: Hubness-aware classification, instance selection and feature construction: survey and extensions to time-series. In: Stańczyk, U., Jain, L.C. (eds.) Feature Selection for Data and Pattern Recognition. SCI, vol. 584, pp. 231–262. Springer, Heidelberg (2015). https://doi.org/10.1007/978-3-662-45620-0_11
18. Wang, Z., Yan, W., Oates, T.: Time series classification from scratch with deep neural networks: a strong baseline. In: 2017 International Joint Conference on Neural Networks (IJCNN), pp. 1578–1585. IEEE (2017)
19. Xi, X., Keogh, E., Shelton, C., Wei, L., Ratanamahatana, C.A.: Fast time series classification using numerosity reduction. In: Proceedings of the 23rd International Conference on Machine Learning, pp. 1033–1040 (2006)
20. Zhao, B., Lu, H., Chen, S., Liu, J., Wu, D.: Convolutional neural networks for time series classification. J. Syst. Eng. Electron. **28**(1), 162–169 (2017)
21. Zheng, Y., Liu, Q., Chen, E., Ge, Y., Zhao, J.L.: Time series classification using multi-channels deep convolutional neural networks. In: Li, F., Li, G., Hwang, S., Yao, B., Zhang, Z. (eds.) WAIM 2014. LNCS, vol. 8485, pp. 298–310. Springer, Cham (2014). https://doi.org/10.1007/978-3-319-08010-9_33

Enhancing Speech Signal Features with Linear Envelope Subtraction

Hao D. Do[1,2,3](✉), Duc T. Chau[1,2], Dung D. Nguyen[2,3], and Son T. Tran[1,2]

[1] University of Science, Ho Chi Minh City, Vietnam
[2] Vietnam National University, Ho Chi Minh City, Vietnam
[3] OLLI Technology JSC, Ho Chi Minh City, Vietnam
hao@olli-ai.com

Abstract. The common integral transforms present the speech signal to another space with a set of orthogonal basis vectors. The speech, in terms of nature, is a periodic signal so the basis vectors are periodic too, particularly the sinusoidal wave. In reality, after impacted by many outside agents, the speech signal is not always periodic. This leads to the fact that the traditional transforms such as Fourier or Wavelet transforms do not always perform well. In this research, we propose a new method in which the speech signal is processed to be periodic before transformed into the frequency domain. We first use linear regression to identify the linear envelope of the speech signal in the time domain, then subtract the signal with the identified linear function to horizontalize the speech signal. The feature vector we propose includes two parameters from the linear envelope and the standard feature vectors in the frequency domain. Experimental results show that our new method works well in many cases. It demonstrates the significant impact of the linear envelope and its improvement on the performances of the recognizers.

Keywords: Speech features · Linear envelope · Envelope subtraction

1 Introduction

The rightness of feature vector impacts directly the final performance of recognition models. If the feature vector presents the main and the most important information of data, the models can process the data so well. On the other hand, losing information or errors in the feature vector can cause failures in both learning and inferring steps of the models. In this research, we present a new approach to transform the speech data before extracting features to improve the quality of the feature vector.

In this research, we first show the negative impact of the non-periodic signal to Fourier transform and then suggest a new approach to periodicalize the speech signal before applying the integral transform to extract the feature vector. Practically, to identify the signal envelope, we apply a linear regression algorithm.

Supported by OLLI Technology JSC.

K. Wojtkiewicz et al. (Eds.): ICCCI 2021, CCIS 1463, pp. 313–323, 2021.
https://doi.org/10.1007/978-3-030-88113-9_25

After that, the signal will subtract with the envelope to form the detail signal. In the next step, the signal is shifted to form a zero-mean signal by subtracting with its expected value. Finally, it is transformed to the frequency domain via Fourier transform. The extracted feature vector includes three elements: the parameters of the linear envelope, expectation value, and all coefficients in the frequency domain.

Experimental results demonstrate an important discovery. The signal, after removing its linear envelope, becomes more informative with the speech-related recognizing model. The evidence is the decreasing error rates and the stability of the proposed method in many cases.

The main distributions of this research are at two aspects:

- Quantifying the impact of the linear envelope on the quality of extracted speech-related features.
- Proposing an effective approach for speech signal feature extraction.

The remaining of this work is organized as follows. Many related works of research will be listed in Sect. 2. Then Sect. 3 will present some analysis about the signal linear envelope and its negative impact on the signal feature. After that, Sect. 4 will present our approach to establishing a new framework for speech feature extraction. Finally, experimental results are described in Sect. 5. We will present some discussion in this section too.

2 Related Works

2.1 Integral Transforms

In many problems, especially the problems related to the speech signal, it is so difficult and complicated to reach a good solution with the original form of data. The process of transforming data from its first form to another form, which is better, more informative, more visible, is needed. The destination form, which is called the feature representation or many other names, should exploit some meaningful aspects of the data including properties, qualities, behaviors. In the original form, these aspects are hidden, so the transforming, which visualizes them to improve the input quality, plays a significant role in the success of a solution.

Integral transform [1,2] is a group of mathematical methods proposed to convert the data from its original form to another form, or data space to feature space, which is more informative for a particular purpose or application. The name for this group is integral transform because these methods are mainly designed and implemented via an integral operator. In general, the standard forward form for these transform is presented in the Eq. 1.

$$Tf(u) = \int_{t_1}^{t_2} f(t)K(t,u)dt \tag{1}$$

In another view, integral transform provides a new viewpoint to the data with more information, especially the hidden information. In Eq. 1, $f(t)$ is the data original form presented as a function with time-variable t. The hidden information is presented by $Tf(u)$ with u as the variable in the new space. In reality, both $f(t)$ and $Tf(u)$ can be the functions with one variable or multi variables. Function $K(t,u)$ is called the kernel or basic of the transform [3] [4]. This is the most important aspect of a transformation because it provides most of the information to describe the feature space and the way to transform. $K(t,u)$ is usually a class of orthogonal functions, which is aimed to build a feature space with orthogonal basic to maximum the meaning of its dimensions. Each value u is corresponding with one dimension in the feature space, thus, the dimension of the feature space is equal with the number of variable u joining the transform $Tf(u)$.

In mathematical essence, integral transform presents a data point of $f(t)$ into another space with the basic defined by kernel $K(t,u)$. The computation process is done with the integral transform. Because these two spaces, the original space, and the feature space, together with present one data point at the different spaces. So there is a mutuality between these two coordinates, and hence, the information and the meanings.

With Riemann-Lebesgue lemma [5,6], it is the truth that the main information of data is well preserved via an integral transform, or this transform is a lossless transform. This provides solid evidence for the existence of an inverse transform, which transforms the data from the feature space to the original space. There is no general form for the inverse transforms although all of them depend on the forward transform. In reality, most of the inverse transform is based on the inverse kernel $K^{-1}(t,u)$, or inverse basic of the forward transform as in Eq. 2.

$$f(t) = \int_{u_1}^{u_2} Tf(u)K^{-1}(t,u)du \tag{2}$$

The common transforms such as Fourier [7,8], Mellin [9–11], or Laplace, all have a long history. Their inverse forms are so similar to their forward forms. Moreover, these forms mostly depend on the logarithm function with nature base e. Via Euler equality, the relation of e^t and sine-shape functions are established, so this provides a foundation to exploit the hidden information of periodic time series data such as speech signal using integral transform.

Table 1. Some common integral transforms and their inverse forms

Transform	K	t_1	t_2	$^{-1}$	u_1	u_2
Fourier	$\frac{e^{-iut}}{\sqrt{2\pi}}$	$-\infty$	∞	$\frac{e^{iut}}{\sqrt{2\pi}}$	$-\infty$	∞
Mellin	t^{u-1}	0	∞	$\frac{t^{-u}}{2\pi i}$	$c-i\infty$	$c+i\infty$
Laplace	e^{-ut}	0	∞	$\frac{e^{ut}}{2\pi i}$	$c-i\infty$	$c+i\infty$

Table 1 lists some common integral transform with their forms and ranges of transform. The inverse kernel K^{-1} is mutual with the forward kernel K since their products are constants. On the other hand, all the kernel is based on exponential function with base e. This is an essential trick to speed up the computation process, especially with the process with many integral and derivation operators.

2.2 Our Motivation: The Lack of Considering the Appropriate of Integral Transform and Its Derivation to Signal Analysis

Excepting the vector from a deep neural network, most of the speech features [12–16] are established as follows:

- Applying an integral transform to transform the speech signal into another space
- Designing some extended operators to process data in the transformed space:
  - Mel scale
  - Filter bank
  - Statistics

It can be observed that the feature extracting process always begins with an integral transform. This means that the suitability of the integral transform to the speech signal defaults as right. The problem is whether or not the integral transform should be applied to the signal without any involvements. An integral transform is a traditional tool in mathematics with hundreds of years of history, so it is hard to modify or extend this side. On the other hand, due to the popularity of human speech, the variety of speech signals is big too. There can be a significant ratio of human speech distorted. These data cannot be transformed directly via some traditional transforms. The data should be pre-processed or pre-transformed before passed into the transform process. In this paper, we would like to propose a new paradigm for extracting speech features to make sure that the suitability of integral transform to speech signal is increased after the data is passed by our processor.

3 Impacts of Non-periodic Property to Signal Presentation in the Frequency Domain

3.1 Human Speech and Its Presentation in the Frequency Domain

Created by the vibration of the vocal tracts, human speech is usually presented as a sine-shape signal. Since most speech signal property depends on its main harmonies, the speech waveform is converted into the frequency domain via integral transforms such as Fourier transform, Wavelet transform, Cosine transform, etc. These transforms, in terms of nature, separate the speech signal into many sinusoidal elements, and then use their coefficients to form the representative vector. This means that each vector dimension presents one harmony in the speech, and the value in that dimension is corresponding with the coefficient of the harmony, or the amplitude of the sinusoidal wave.

Mathematically, the integral transform converts the signal into the frequency domain. In this space, let the basis vectors are the sinusoidal function, so each element in the frequency representation vector is corresponding with:

$$F(\omega_k) = \int_{-\infty}^{\infty} f(t)e^{-i\omega_k t}dt \tag{3}$$

If k is an integer arranged in $[0, n-1]$, the representation vector is a $n-dim$ point in the frequency space with $n - dim$. Each dimension presents one harmony, so the vector can present mostly fully the behavior of the speech signal with the n coefficients. The higher frequency ω_k is, the higher the speech tone is. It can be said that the frequency vector presents both the intensity and pitch of human speech.

Most of the important properties of human speech are presented clearly in the frequency domain, but this representation is not a uniform distribution. There are two aspects of the frequency domain that motivated the invention of some modern features such as Mel-cepstral or MFCC. The first is that the difference of harmonies in low frequency is much clearer than in high frequency. For an instance, the human can realize the difference of harmonies 700 Hz and 1000 Hz, but it is so difficult to distinguish the harmonies 10700 Hz and 11000 Hz. The perception of the human ear with speech frequency is not linear. To shrink the frequency distribution into linear form, the Mel scale is proposed. Mel is a tool to scale the spectral into a new form that is easier to analyze and recognize. Secondly, because only the low frequencies can be distinguished easily, they can be analyzed as a set of independent features. With the higher frequency, they should be clustered into groups to form one dimension in the feature space. This trick means that a filter bank with the wideband of each filter proportional to its central passband should be used. In the feature vector, the low index elements are corresponding with the low-frequency harmonies and the narrow passband. This distribution is similar to the nature of human speech.

3.2 Frequency of Non-periodic Signal and the Dependency of the Linear Envelope to the Signal Length

The Linear Envelope (LE) of a signal or a segment is the main trend in its range and is usually presented by a regression line. To compute this line, we use linear regression algorithm. Assuming:

$$a * x + b = LinearRegression(f(t)) \tag{4}$$

then a is the slope of LE for signal $f(t)$ while b presents the bias value. It can be said that (a, b) is the representation for LE of a signal.

LE of a signal mainly depends on its length, if the length is too short, the linear envelope is meaningful, even with a high threshold θ. On the other hand, when the length is large enough, the signal tends to distribute in the horizontal direction. Generally, an unnormal envelope only plays a key role with an average length and a large enough θ.

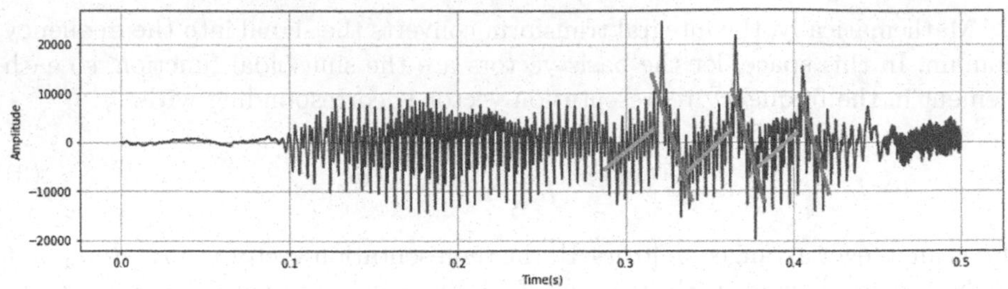

Fig. 1. A waveform with many linear envelope

Particularly, Fig. 1 presents an audio waveform with many linear envelopes. There are three envelopes with positive slopes (green lines) and three envelopes with negative slopes (red lines). The signal linear envelope is hard to exist in a long signal because if the signal is long enough, it tends to horizontal, and the slope is none. On the other hand, it usually distributes suddenly in a short signal segment. That motivates to define a new concept to describe the internal stability for a speech signal as follows:

Definition 1. *Linear Envelope Rate (LER) of a signal with a threshold θ is the ratio between the number of frames with slope higher than θ and the total frames in the signal:*

$$LER(signal, \theta) = \frac{\#frame, slope(LE(frame)) > \theta}{\#frame} \tag{5}$$

LER with a threshold θ of a signal present the ratio a the frames with high slope for their LE during the whole signal. Of course, this values can be vary for both the different speech data and the value for θ. With a θ too big, the LER values are mainly equal zero because most of the signal frames are horizontal. On the other hand, if we choose a near zero value for θ, the LER are too high and a lot of frames get a meaningful LE, and then the differences between each frames are not clear. So, to get a optimal choice for LE, θ should be assigned with a reasonable value.

Figure 2 presents the distribution of LER for the signal in TIMIT dataset [17] with the threshold $\theta = 0.001$. In our experiment, 0.001 is the best choice for θ because it balance the LER of different signals in the dataset. As can be observed in the figure, with the length over 50 ms, the LER values are too low. This means that with a long signal, the main trend is horizontal. With the very short frame, the LER is no meaningful even the ratio is high. With the range from 10 ms to 25 ms, the LER is high enough. This is a common length for speech frames in many systems such as speech recognition, speaker identification. It can be said that the phenomenon of LE, especially with a high LER, is meaningful and it is necessary to exploit to extract speech features more effectively.

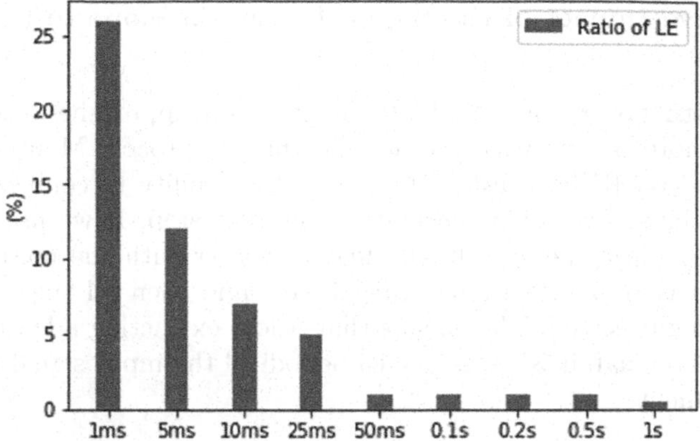

Fig. 2. Ratio of frames with Linear Envelope (LE) in TIMIT dataset

3.3 Impacted Range by Linear Envelope in the Frequency Domain to Speech Representation

Back to the simple beginning example, let us consider the impact of a linear function to a particular harmony. It is needed to compute the dot product of the signal $f(x) = sin(3x) + x$ with a sine-shape function $sin(nx)$. Let $ax + b$ and $sin(nx)$ represent the linear envelope for the signal and the harmony. Although the linear envelope of $f(x) = sin(3x) + x$ is $f_2(x) = x$, we use the form $ax + b$ for more general. The dot product for these two functions is computed by:

$$\langle ax + b, sin(nx) \rangle = \int_0^{2\pi} (ax + b) sin(nx) dx \tag{6}$$

$$\langle ax + b, sin(nx) \rangle = \frac{-2\pi a}{n} \tag{7}$$

The above result implies that the impact of the linear envelope is proportional with the slope of the LE and unproportional with the frequency. The spectral range can be impacted depends on the value of the slope and the minimum value that a computer can process. For example, if the minimum value that a computer can process is $2^{-32} \approx 0.25 \cdot 10^{-9}$, the threshold for the linear envelope is assumed as $\theta = 10^{-5}$, the maximum frequency that can be noise is:

$$n_{max} = \frac{2\pi 10^{-5}}{0.25 \cdot 10^{-9}} = \approx 25 \cdot 10^4 = 250.000\,\text{Hz} \tag{8}$$

Another example, if an application that needs to use the feature with the error under 10^-8, the frequency, which is impacted, is up to:

$$n_{max} = \frac{2\pi\theta}{10^{-8}} \approx 6.300\,\text{Hz} \tag{9}$$

From these examples, it can be seen that a wide range of signal spectrum can be changed under the negative impact of the linear envelope. It is needed to develop an effective processing method to avoid this effect.

3.4 Negative Impact of the Signal Linear Envelope to the Whole System

Although existing everywhere and affecting to many approaches, the problem of LE is much more serious with the deep learning approach. Many deep models mainly depend on RNN to take advantage of its ability to connect the results at many previous steps to process at the current step. If we use RNN or its variants to recognize the speech, the feature vector with the noises caused by the linear function cannot be recognized well, and then all the segment after cannot be recognized too. This means that before extracting a feature vector or transforming a signal, it is necessary to periodical the input signal by removing the linear element.

4 Periodicalizing Speech Signal with Envelope Subtraction

To exploit the role of the linear envelope, we design a new paradigm to extract the speech feature in the Algorithm 1.

Algorithm 1. Framework for speech feature extraction

```
1: procedure FEATURE EXTRACTION(f(x))
2:     nframe ← f(x)
3:     Feature ← {}
4:     for frame in nframe do
5:         frame ← frame * Windowfunction
6:         (a, b) ← LinearRegression(frame)
7:         frame ← frame − (ax + b)
8:         c ← Mean(frame)
9:         frame ← frame − Mean(frame)
10:        d ← GetFeature(frame)
11:        Feature ← Feature + (a, b, c, d)
12:    return Feature
```

In the algorithm, a, b are the coefficients for LE of a signal frame, c is the mean value in a frame, and d is popular feature for signal such as spectrum or MFCC. So, each frame is represented by three information including: main trend or LE, mean, and a normal feature vector.

The most improvement in this framework is step 7. This is the process of subtracting the linear envelope or a horizontalizing or periodicalizing step. Our interference removes the negative impacts of the linear envelope on the frequency coefficients. On the other hand, at step 10, there are many features that we can apply including spectrum, cepstrum, MFCC, etc. Not only the noises can be reduced, but the main frequency elements or speech formants are also enhanced.

5 Experimental Results

In this experiment, we aim to compare the accuracy of the recognition model when applying many features. We apply our proposed method, envelope subtraction (ES) with three well-known features including spectrum, cepstrum, and MFCC. Particularly, this experiment clarifies the impact of the linear envelope on the quality of the feature. We compare three groups of features:

- Original features, including spectrum, cepstrum, and MFCC
- ES Group: features processed with envelope subtraction, including ES Spectrum, ES Cepstrum, ES MFCC. In these features, we firstly identify the linear envelope by the linear regression model, and then we subtract the envelope to gain the processed signal. Finally, we extract in the remaining signal the features vector such as spectrum, cepstrum, and MFCC.
- LE Group: features inhanced with LE, including LE Spectrum, LE Cepstrum, LE MFCC. The method to extract these features is presented in Algorithm 1. The difference between this group with the second group above is the addition of linear regression coefficients of the linear envelope to the final feature vector.

In this experiment, we aim to specify the impact of the linear envelope on the quality of the extracted features. All these features are used in the speaker dialect recognition task for English with the TIMIT dataset. We mainly use DeepSpeech2 [18] as the recognition model. The result in detail is presented in the Table 2.

Table 2. Impact of linear envelope to speaker dialect recognition

Feature	Feature size	Error rate (%)
Original Spectrum	128	4.1
Original Cepstrum	128	3.3
Original MFCC	39	3.2
ES Spectrum	128	3.1
ES Cepstrum	128	2.9
ES MFCC	39	2.7
LE Spectrum	131	2.9
LE Cepstrum	131	2.8
LE MFCC	42	2.6

In Table 2, the results reflect clearly the positive impact of our proposed method in terms of error rate. The results in group two (ES features) are better than the original features in group 1. This implies that the signal, after subtracting with the linear envelope, presents more useful information for the machine learning model.

Moreover, the error rates in the final group (LE features) are the lowest. This means that the parameters in the linear envelope are meaningful and can be used for the recognizer. On the other hand, the difference between the second and the first group is significant, while the last two groups are too similar. We can infer that in our proposed method, the phase of subtracting the linear envelope plays a more important role than the LE coefficients because it impacts more to the final result. Although the information on the linear envelope is good, it only contributes a little bit of improvement overall.

6 Conclusion

In many cases, when the signal distributes in a clear trend in the time domain, we can exploit this envelope to strengthen the extracted features. In this research, we have proposed a new paradigm to extract a more meaningful feature for speech signals. The feature vector extracted by our approach contains three factors: signal linear envelope, expectation values, and a standard feature vector after subtracting the signal envelope. This combination provides the learning model more information for the recognizing tasks.

Experimental results show that the phase of subtracting the signal envelope contributes most to the improvements of the suggestion. On the other hand, although the parameters of the envelope have no significant impact, they hold a little meaningful information and provide more information for the recognizing model. In comparison with other standard methods, the proposed approach gain more positive results.

Acknowledgments. This research is funded by OLLI Technology JSC, Ho Chi Minh City, Vietnam.

References

1. Davies, B.: Integral Transforms and Their Applications. Springer, New York. https://doi.org/10.1007/978-1-4684-9283-5 (2002). ISBN 978-1-441-92950-1
2. Debnath, L., Bhatta, D.: Integral Transforms and Their Applications. Chapman and Hall/CRC (2016). ISBN 978-1-584-88575-7
3. Scholkopf, B., Smola, A.J., Bach, F.: Learning with Kernels Support Vector Machines, Regularization, Optimization, and Beyond. MIT Press. ISBN 978-0-262-53657-8 (2018)
4. Sergios, T.: Pattern Recognition. Elsevier (2008). ISBN 978-0-080-94912-3
5. Bochner, S., Chandrasekharan, K.: Fourier Transforms. Princeton University Press (1949)
6. Serov, V.: The Riemann–Lebesgue lemma. In: Fourier Series, Fourier Transform and Their Applications to Mathematical Physics. AMS, vol. 197, pp. 33–35. Springer, Cham (2017). https://doi.org/10.1007/978-3-319-65262-7_6
7. Pei, S.-C., Yeh, M.-H., Luo, T.-L.: Fractional fourier series expansion for finite signals and dual extension to discrete-time fractional Fourier transform. IEEE Trans. Signal Process. **47**(10), 2883–2888 (1999). https://doi.org/10.1109/78.790671

8. Snopek, K.M.: Relationship between the Cayley-Dickson fourier transform and the Hartley transform of multidimensional real signals. In: 40th International Conference on Telecommunications and Signal Processing (TSP), Barcelona, pp. 497–501 (2017). https://doi.org/10.1109/TSP.2017.8076036
9. Yang, J., Lu, Z., Tang, Y.Y., Yuan, Z., Chen, Y.: Quasi Fourier-Mellin transform for affine invariant features. IEEE Trans. Image Process. **29**, 4114–4129 (2020). https://doi.org/10.1109/TIP.2020.2967578
10. Zuo, X., Zhou, N.: Spectrum analysis on Mellin Transform and fractional Mellin transform. In 4th International Congress on Image and Signal Processing, Shanghai, China, pp. 2218–2222 (2011) https://doi.org/10.1109/CISP.2011.6100534
11. Cakir, S., Cetin, A.E.: Mel and Mellin-cepstral feature extraction algorithms for face recognition. Comput. J. **54**(9), 1526–1534 (2011). https://doi.org/10.1093/comjnl/bxq100
12. Do, H.D., Tran, S.T., Chau, D.T.: Speech source separation using variational autoencoder and bandpass filter. IEEE Access **8**, 156219–156231 (2020). https://doi.org/10.1109/ACCESS.2020.3019495
13. Do, H.D., Tran, S.T., Chau, D.T.: A variational autoencoder approach for speech signal separation. In: Nguyen, N.T., Hoang, B.H., Huynh, C.P., Hwang, D., Trawiński, B., Vossen, G. (eds.) ICCCI 2020. LNCS (LNAI), vol. 12496, pp. 558–567. Springer, Cham (2020). https://doi.org/10.1007/978-3-030-63007-2_43
14. Widyowaty, D.S., Sunyoto, A.: Accent recognition by native language using mel-frequency cepstral coefficient and K-nearest neighbor. In: 3rd International Conference on Information and Communications Technology (ICOIACT), Yogyakarta, Indonesia, pp. 314–318 (2020). https://doi.org/10.1109/ICOIACT50329.2020.9332026
15. Huang, Z., Epps, J., Joachim, D., Sethu, V.: Natural language processing methods for acoustic and landmark event-based features in speech-based depression detection. IEEE J. Sel. Top. Signal Process. **14**(2), 435–448 (2020). https://doi.org/10.1109/JSTSP.2019.2949419
16. Bhattacharjee, M., Prasanna, S.R.M., Guha, P.: Speech/music classification using features from spectral peaks. IEEE/ACM Trans. Audio Speech Lang. Process. **28**, 1549–1559 (2020). https://doi.org/10.1109/TASLP.2020.2993152
17. Nicolas, M., Javier, T., Javier, G., Jose, C., Doroteo, T.: STC-TIMIT generation of a single-channel telephone corpus. In: Proceedings of the Sixth International Language Resources and Evaluation, pp. 391–395 (2008)
18. Amodei, D., et al.: Deep speech 2: end-to-end speech recognition in English and Mandarin. In: Proceedings of the 33rd International Conference on International Conference on Machine Learning, vol. 48, pp. 173–182 (2016)

Entropy Role on Patch-Based Binary Classification for Skin Melanoma

Guillaume Lachaud(✉), Patricia Conde-Cespedes(✉), and Maria Trocan(✉)

ISEP - Institut Supérieur d'Électronique de Paris, 10 rue de Vanves, Issy les Moulineaux 92130, France
{glachaud,pconde,maria.trocan}@isep.fr

Abstract. In this paper, we split the region of interest of dermoscopic images of skin lesions in patches of different size and we analyze the impact of the entropy of the patches on patch-based binary classification using a convolutional neural network (CNN). Specifically, we analyze the distribution of entropy amongst the patches and we compare the training time of a classifier on subsets of the data with varying entropy. We find that the classifier converges faster on patches with higher entropy. Our entropy-based analysis is performed on skin lesion images from the ISIC archive.

Keywords: Entropy · Skin melanoma · Patch-based classification · Resnet

1 Introduction

Convolutional Neural Networks (CNNs) have become one of the most effective machine learning solutions for computer vision problems such as classification, object detection, face recognition, etc. More specifically, CNNs are extensively used for medical image processing tasks and their use in medical research care. The main goal of this field is to extract relevant clinical information or knowledge from medical images. One can mention, for instance, computer-aided diagnosis of cancer using classification methods [1]. Cancer is one of the leading causes of deaths worldwide [14]. However, if the cancer is diagnosed early, when the cancer has not spread, chances of survival are far greater than for later stages [19]. For this reason, there has been a lot of research focused on leveraging deep learning to improve cancer diagnosis and prognosis, especially in breast cancer [22], skin cancer [2], and lung cancer [11].

Typically, image classification tasks take as input the entire image. However, in some situations training an image patch, that is, a subset of the entire image, might be preferable. Not only is this less time consuming, but it can also improve the classifier performance in some particular situations. For instance,

K. Wojtkiewicz et al. (Eds.): ICCCI 2021, CCIS 1463, pp. 324–333, 2021.
https://doi.org/10.1007/978-3-030-88113-9_26

in [9], the authors claimed that in cancer subtypes classification, the decision is mostly based on cellular-level visual features observed on image patch scale. Another example where patch based classification was preferred over pixel based classification is presented in [17] where this approach was used for classification of breast histology. One can find other applications of patch-based classification in [16] and [24].

In information theory, entropy is a measure used to quantify the level of information contained in an object. The higher the entropy, the higher the information content of the image is. For example, an image of random noise will have a higher entropy that a unicolor image. Entropy is indicative of the minimum amount of storage that is required to preserve the full information of an object, which makes this measure particularly useful in data compression to estimate whether the compression algorithm is close to the best possible results [18].

Entropy has been successfully applied to a wide variety of tasks, including image reconstruction where we choose the image with the highest entropy out of all the possible images [20]. Furthermore, applications of maximum entropy are not restricted to images but also extends to other types of data such as text data, in which entropy is used to produce the most uniform probability distribution given the training data [12]. Additionally, entropy has been effectively studied for image texture analysis [25], which can also be used for texture synthesis.

In this paper, we study the role of entropy on the training time of a neural network. We use the region of interest of the image to maximize the relevance of the patches for the classification task. The use of patches instead of the whole image allows us to study the influence of entropy at different scales. To the best of our knowledge, we are the first to analyse the role of entropy on patch-based binary classification. However, it is relevant to mention that in [13], the authors have already focused on entropy for brain tumor patch based classification. Indeed, the authors resized MRI (Magnetic Resonance Imaging) images, split them in patches, and used the entropy of each patch as a feature for the image as well as the image moments.

The dataset we used in this study comes from the ISIC [1] archive (International Skin Imaging Collaboration). Because of the lethality of melanoma cancer, the ISIC project was created to help improve skin cancer diagnosis via imaging data. They started an annual challenge in 2016 [7], and from 2019 onwards, the challenges have focused on dermoscopic image classification, with multiple diagnostic categories [15]. The researchers who had the best results on the 2019 ISIC challenge [4] studied patch-based classification on the HAM10000 dataset [21] in [5]. They took multiple patches from each image and used an attention-based approach to combine the information from the patches and classify the image.

The paper is organized as follows: in Sect. 2 we describe the datasets and data pre-processing, analyze their entropy and we introduce the network architecture we used. Next, Sect. 3 shows the experimental results. Finally, Sect. 4 presents the conclusion and perspectives of this work.

[1] The data is publicly available at https://www.isic-archive.com.

2 Proposed Method

2.1 Dataset Description and Pre-processing

The ISIC archive database (see [15]) contains images of skin lesions which can be benign or malignant; other images can also have an unknown status. The image resolution varies across the datasets. The archive also has an API [2] which can be used to get information about images or to retrieve lesion masks created by expert users. Our goal is to perform binary classification using patches of images. Our target variable has two labels[3] indicating whether the lesion is *benign* or *malignant*.

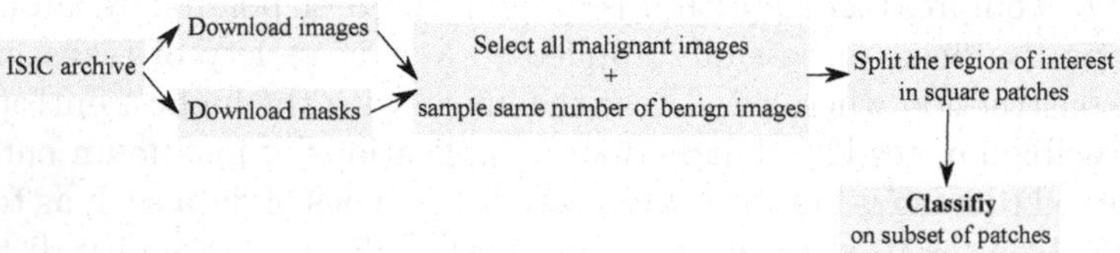

Fig. 1. Data pre-processing workflow

All the data pre-processing steps are described in Fig. 1:

1. First, using the API from the ISIC archive, we download all the images which have a mask.
2. Second, we take all the malignant images and we sample the same quantity of benign images from all the benign images with a mask.
3. Next, for each image, we take the region of interest, that is, the part where the lesion is, which is obtained from the mask, and we split this region in square patches of size 32×32, 64×64, 128×128 and 256×256. Figure 2 shows an example of an image and its mask, with patches of different size taken from the same image in Fig. 3. Table 1 indicates the total number of patches for each patch size. Since we took the same number of malignant and benign images, we have an imbalanced dataset with more malignant patches than benign ones. This is due to the fact that malignant lesions are often captured in higher resolution, because it is more important to get the best image quality when analyzing cancerous lesions than it is for benign ones.
4. Finally, we perform binary classification on patches.

---

[2] https://isic-archive.com/api/v1.

[3] Originally, the ISIC challenge had more refined categories. In this paper we use only 2.

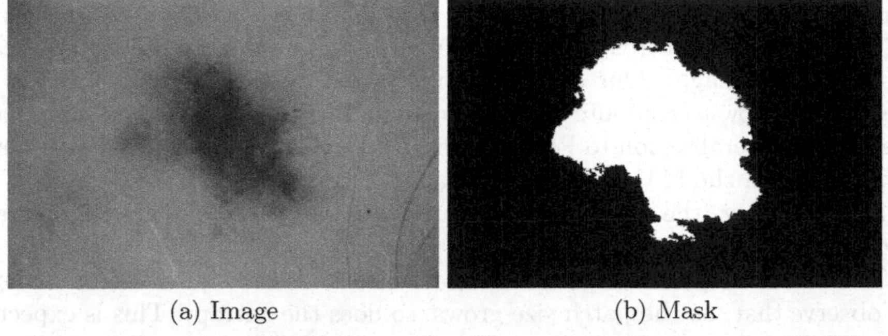

(a) Image (b) Mask

Fig. 2. Example of a malignant skin lesion

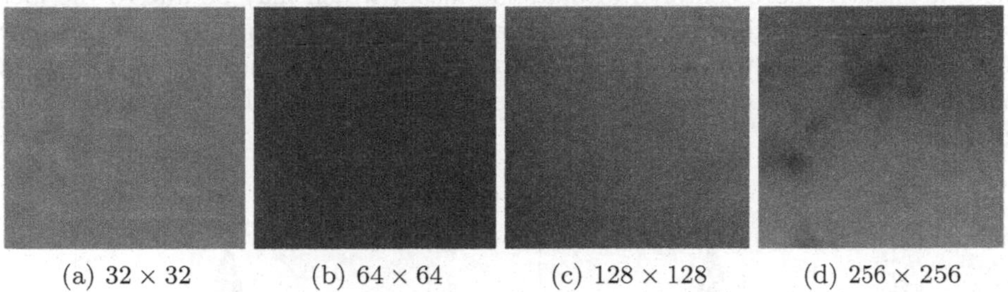

(a) 32 × 32 (b) 64 × 64 (c) 128 × 128 (d) 256 × 256

Fig. 3. Example of patches of size (a) 32 × 32, (b) 64 × 64, (c) 128 × 128, (d) 256 × 256, from Fig. 2

Table 1. Number of patches for different patch sizes

Patch size	Number of patches
32 × 32	4,886,969
64 × 64	1,173,052
128 × 128	270,821
256 × 256	58,253

2.2 Entropy

We are interested in the study of the behavior of the Shannon entropy [18] of the images. The formula used for the calculation of entropy is the following:

$$H = -\sum_{k=0}^{M} p_k \log_2(p_k) \tag{1}$$

where M is the highest intensity of a pixel (in our case, 255), and p_k is the probability associated with the pixel intensity k in the grayscale image. In practice, the entropy is computed using histograms to estimate the probabilities. The entropy can take values between 0 and $\log_2(255) \approx 8$. Although the images in the dataset are in the RGB format, the entropy is computed on the grayscale version of the images. Our choice was motivated by the fact that there is no consensus on how to compute the entropy of an RGB image: Eq. 1 does not have a canonical generalization to RGB images, while RGB conversion to grayscale is standardized in the ITU-R Recommendation BT.601-2.

Figure 4 shows the distribution of entropy amongst the patches for different patch sizes.

Table 2 shows the mean, standard deviation and some quantiles of entropy. We observe that, as the patch size grows, so does the entropy. This is expected because the more pixels we have, the more likely they are to have different intensities, which lead to a higher entropy. Also, the entropy for bigger patch sizes is slightly more centered around the mean, which may be due to the fact that bigger patch sizes will average some of the more extreme patches of smaller size. For example, instead of having multiple small patches of low and high entropy, a bigger patch containing all the small patches will have a more average entropy.

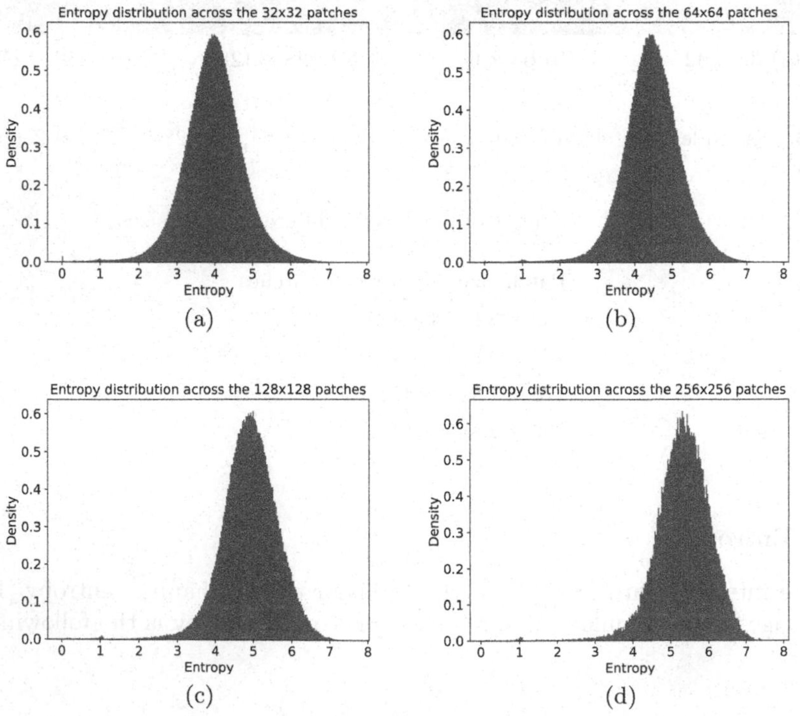

Fig. 4. Distribution of patch entropy. (a)–(d) are taken for square patches of size 32, 64, 128 and 256 pixels.

Table 2. Entropy statistics

Patch size	Mean	Standard deviation	Quantile			
			15	42.5	57.5	85
32	3.974	0.779	3.247	3.85	4.104	4.71
64	4.456	0.765	3.75	4.335	4.588	5.191
128	4.903	0.747	4.223	4.795	5.047	5.633
256	5.319	0.735	4.66	5.229	5.475	6.029

We are interested in the impact of the entropy behaviour on the training of a classifier: whether it is faster to train on a dataset with low entropy than with a dataset with standard entropy; and whether a dataset with higher entropy is harder to train on. We split the created patches in three groups for the four groups of patches:

- one containing the patches with entropy below the 15-th quantile, referred to as *low*.
- one with the patches entropy above the 85-th quantile, referred to as *high* and
- the last one with patches having entropy between the 42.5-th and 57.5-th quantiles, referred to as *intermediate*. Our choice for the quantile values is motivated by having the entropy be equally distant from the other groups, and keeping the same number of samples to make time comparisons meaningful.

We do this for each patch size, e.g. 32×32, 64×64, 128×128, 256×256.

2.3 Network Architecture and Tuning Parameters

Following [23] and [3] who compared classifiers for the same task and dataset, we use a ResNet50 for the classification. ResNet50 [8], is a 50-layer convolutional neural network, which contains *residual units* between convolutional blocks (stacks of convolutional layers) with identity mappings interspersed, to help propagate the gradient and mitigate the problem of vanishing and exploding gradients [6].

Though ResNets can be arbitrary deep, provided we have the computing resources to train the model, e.g. using 101 or 152 layers, we followed [23] and used the 50-layer version. Since we are interested in binary classification, e.g. whether the lesion is benign or malignant, we remove the last layer of the network, designed for multiclass classification, and replace it with a max pooling layer followed by a Dense layer with a *sigmoid* activation.

The optimizer used for the model is the Adam optimizer [10] with a learning rate of 0.001. We use a *binary cross-entropy loss* for the training.

The model is trained for 10 epochs, with early stopping if the validation loss stops decreasing after 3 consecutive epochs.

Each dataset is split in the following way for training: 90% for training, of which 20% goes to validation, and 10% for testing.

3 Results

All the experiments were performed on a device with a 3.60 GhZ Intel CPU, 32 Gb of RAM and an NVidia Titan XP, running on Ubuntu. The code was written in Python and Tensorflow. The computation of the entropy was done using Pillow.

To account for the fact that a neural network may take more time to converge based on the random initialization of the parameters, we train 10 instances of a ResNet50 on each dataset. We display the 30-th quantile, the median and the 70-th quantile of the training time of the instances in Table 3.

Table 3. Quantiles for the training time on datasets with varying entropy

Patch size	Entropy	Quantile of training time (in seconds)		
		30	50 (median)	70
32	High	1350.7	2013.2	2781.4
32	Intermediate	2000.4	2854.0	2855.3
32	Low	1534.9	2906.7	3078.5
64	High	291.0	382.9	441.9
64	Intermediate	331.0	402.3	498.8
64	Low	290.6	338.3	414.2
128	High	155.0	204.6	220.0
128	Intermediate	174.6	235.2	281.3
128	Low	204.8	255.0	255.4
256	High	142.4	152.2	189.7
256	Intermediate	171.3	171.8	204.8
256	Low	189.6	226.4	226.5

We see that the dataset with the highest entropy tends to be the fastest to converge. Since a higher entropy usually indicates that more information is present in the patch, we could expect the neural network to take longer to train. Conversely, a dataset with lower entropy would train faster because the patches would have less discriminating features, and the network would quickly classify them.

A possible explanation for this discrepancy is that patches with higher entropy might share a similar structure or have patterns not present for other patches, and thus are more recognizable by the network, while patches with lower entropy might have less salient features, which makes it harder for the classifier to classify them.

Concerning the training for the dataset with intermediate entropy, it seems to take longer to converge for smaller patch sizes compared to training on datasets with more extreme entropy, but reaches similar speeds in comparison with the other datasets when we increase the patch size. A reason for this could be that, for lower patch sizes, patches with average entropy might be more diverse than patches with lower or higher entropy, and the network will require more time to analyze the patterns. When the patches are bigger, a patch can be composed of smaller zones which vary greatly in entropy, but have an average entropy when we look at the entirety of the patch. Therefore, these patches would be easier to classify, which would lead to a faster training time.

4 Conclusion and Future Works

We studied the influence of entropy on the training time of a convolutional neural network applied to patch-based classification. We found that the CNN converges faster when using datasets with higher entropy, which might be due to the presence of patterns on these patches the network can detect. We also observe that performance of datasets with average entropy tend to improve, in comparison with the other datasets, when the patch size increases.

Some perspectives to this work can be to explore the use of segmentation to obtain the regions of interest, increasing the number of images we can work with, and see if the results are comparable. Another possibility can be to analyze the effects of resizing images on their entropy to quantify the loss of information, and the impact it can have on classification using resized images.

References

1. Anwar, S.M., Majid, M., Qayyum, A., Awais, M., Alnowami, M., Khan, M.K.: Medical image analysis using convolutional neural networks: a review. J. Med. Syst. **42**(11), 1–13 (2018). https://doi.org/10.1007/s10916-018-1088-1
2. Esteva, A., Kuprel, B., Novoa, R.A., Ko, J., Swetter, S.M., Blau, H.M., Thrun, S.: Dermatologist-level classification of skin cancer with deep neural networks. Nature **542**(7639), 115–118 (2017). https://doi.org/10.1038/nature21056
3. Favole, F., Trocan, M., Yilmaz, E.: Melanoma detection using deep learning. In: Nguyen, N.T., Hoang, B.H., Huynh, C.P., Hwang, D., Trawiński, B., Vossen, G. (eds.) ICCCI 2020. LNCS (LNAI), vol. 12496, pp. 816–824. Springer, Cham (2020). https://doi.org/10.1007/978-3-030-63007-2_64
4. Gessert, N., Nielsen, M., Shaikh, M., Werner, R., Schlaefer, A.: Skin lesion classification using ensembles of multi-resolution EfficientNets with meta data. MethodsX **7**, 100864 (2020). https://doi.org/10.1016/j.mex.2020.100864
5. Gessert, N., et al.: Skin lesion classification using CNNs with patch-based attention and diagnosis-guided loss weighting. IEEE Trans. Biomed. Eng. **67**(2), 495–503 (2020). https://doi.org/10.1109/TBME.2019.2915839
6. Glorot, X., Bengio, Y.: Understanding the difficulty of training deep feedforward neural networks. In: Teh, Y.W., Titterington, D.M. (eds.) Proceedings of the Thirteenth International Conference on Artificial Intelligence and Statistics, AISTATS 2010, Chia Laguna Resort, Sardinia, Italy, 13–15May 2010. JMLR Proceedings, vol. 9, pp. 249–256. JMLR.org (2010)

7. Gutman, D., et al.: Skin Lesion Analysis toward Melanoma Detection: A Challenge at the International Symposium on Biomedical Imaging (ISBI) 2016, hosted by the International Skin Imaging Collaboration (ISIC). arXiv:1605.01397 [cs] (May 2016)
8. He, K., Zhang, X., Ren, S., Sun, J.: Deep Residual Learning for Image Recognition. In: 2016 IEEE Conference on Computer Vision and Pattern Recognition (CVPR), Las Vegas, NV, USA, pp. 770–778. IEEE (2016). https://doi.org/10.1109/CVPR.2016.90
9. Hou, L., Samaras, D., Kurc, T.M., Gao, Y., Davis, J.E., Saltz, J.H.: Patch-based convolutional neural network for whole slide tissue image classification. In: 2016 IEEE Conference on Computer Vision and Pattern Recognition (CVPR), pp. 2424–2433 (2016). https://doi.org/10.1109/CVPR.2016.266
10. Kingma, D.P., Ba, J.: Adam: a method for stochastic optimization. CoRR abs/1412.6980 (2015)
11. Marentakis, P., et al.: Lung cancer histology classification from CT images based on radiomics and deep learning models. Med. Biol. Eng. Comput. **59**(1), 215–226 (2021). https://doi.org/10.1007/s11517-020-02302-w
12. Nigam, K., Lafferty, J., McCallum, A.: Using maximum entropy for text classification. In: IJCAI-99 Workshop on Machine Learning for Information Filtering, Stockholom, Sweden, vol. 1, pp. 61–67 (1999)
13. Ouchtati, S., Chergui, A., Mavromatis, S., Aissa, B., Rafik, D., Sequeira, J.: Novel method for brain tumor classification based on use of image entropy and seven hu's invariant moments. Traitement du Signal **36**(6), 483–491 (2019). https://doi.org/10.18280/ts.360602
14. Ritchie, H., Roser, M.: Causes of death. In: Our World in Data (2018)
15. Rotemberg, V., et al.: A patient-centric dataset of images and metadata for identifying melanomas using clinical context. Sci. Data **8**(1), 34 (2021). https://doi.org/10.1038/s41597-021-00815-z
16. Rousseau, F., Habas, P.A., Studholme, C.: A supervised patch-based approach for human brain labeling. IEEE Trans. Med. Imaging **30**(10), 1852–1862 (2011). https://doi.org/10.1109/TMI.2011.2156806
17. Roy, K., Banik, D., Bhattacharjee, D., Nasipuri, M.: Patch-based system for classification of Breast Histology images using deep learning. Comput. Med. Imaging Graph. **71**, 90–103 (2019). https://doi.org/10.1016/j.compmedimag.2018.11.003
18. Shannon, C.E.: A mathematical theory of communication. Bell Syst. Tech. J. **27**(3), 379–423 (1948). https://doi.org/10.1002/j.1538-7305.1948.tb01338.x
19. Siegel, R.L., Miller, K.D., Fuchs, H.E., Jemal, A.: Cancer statistics. CA Cancer J. Clin. **71**(1), 7–33 (2021). https://doi.org/10.3322/caac.21654
20. Skilling, J., Bryan, R.: Maximum entropy image reconstruction-general algorithm. Mon. Not. R. Astron. Soc. **211**, 111 (1984)
21. Tschandl, P., Rosendahl, C., Kittler, H.: The HAM10000 dataset, a large collection of multi-source dermatoscopic images of common pigmented skin lesions. Sci. Data **5**(1), 180161 (2018). https://doi.org/10.1038/sdata.2018.161
22. Yala, A., Lehman, C., Schuster, T., Portnoi, T., Barzilay, R.: A deep learning mammography-based model for improved breast cancer risk prediction. Radiology **292**(1), 60–66 (2019). https://doi.org/10.1148/radiol.2019182716
23. Yilmaz, E., Trocan, M.: Benign and malignant skin lesion classification comparison for three deep-learning architectures. In: Nguyen, N.T., Jearanaitanakij, K., Selamat, A., Trawiński, B., Chittayasothorn, S. (eds.) ACIIDS 2020. LNCS (LNAI), vol. 12033, pp. 514–524. Springer, Cham (2020). https://doi.org/10.1007/978-3-030-41964-6_44

24. Zhang, F., et al.: Lung nodule classification with multilevel patch-based context analysis. IEEE Trans. Biomed. Eng. **61**(4), 1155–1166 (2014). https://doi.org/10.1109/TBME.2013.2295593
25. Zhu, S.C., Wu, Y.N., Mumford, D.: Minimax entropy principle and its application to texture modeling. Neural Comput. **9**(8), 1627–1660 (1997). https://doi.org/10.1162/neco.1997.9.8.1627

Reinforcement Learning for Optimizing Wi-Fi Access Channel Selection

Hung Nguyen[1], Duc Long Pham[2], Mau Hien Doan[2], Thi Thanh Sang Nguyen[1](✉), Duc Anh Vu Dinh[1], and Adrianna Kozierkiewicz[3]

[1] School of Computer Science and Engineering, International University, VNU-HCMC, Vietnam National University, Ho Chi Minh City, Viet Nam
ITITIU15045@student.hcmiu.edu.vn, {nttsang,ddavu}@hcmiu.edu.vn

[2] Center for Information Services, International University, VNU-HCMC, Vietnam National University, Ho Chi Minh City, Viet Nam
{pdlong,dmhien}@hcmiu.edu.vn

[3] Faculty of Computer Science and Management, Wroclaw University of Science and Technology, Wroclaw, Poland
adrianna.kozierkiewicz@pwr.edu.pl

Abstract. Wi-Fi's success is largely a testament to its cost-effectiveness, convenience, and ease of integration with other networks. Wi-Fi allows a suddenly increased number of users to access network services within their networking environment from any convenient location. However, wireless networks have a frequent issue of losing packets caused by poor Wi-Fi signal, network interference, and long-distance connection. This study primarily analyses the mentioned Wi-Fi issues and demonstrates the solution to maintain a reliable network connection within an area including multiple access points and devices by using Reinforcement Learning (RL). The RL algorithm is developed to recommend appropriate channels for the access points in a wireless network environment. The case study of Wi-Fi access data at a university is examined to evaluate the proposed method. Experimental results have shown that the RL-based Wi-Fi access channel selection can achieve higher performance than manual channel selection.

Keywords: Wi-Fi access control · Wi-Fi channel selection · Reinforcement learning

1 Introduction

1.1 Background

The fast improvement of advanced technologies is transforming the way the world functions. Information technology offers humans the ability not only to interact with each other but also with computers. Researchers have now found a way to enable the computer to learn and function in a manner that humans often do. Even though the discovery did not go smoothly in the beginning, more and more researchers later showed the promise of the artificial intelligence of the computer, promising to change the way conventional

K. Wojtkiewicz et al. (Eds.): ICCCI 2021, CCIS 1463, pp. 334–347, 2021.
https://doi.org/10.1007/978-3-030-88113-9_27

systems used to work. The use of machine learning is one of the most significant contributions of the fourth industrial revolution. Machine learning is a field of study that gives computers the ability to learn without being explicitly programmed [1]. Machine intelligence depends on how large the quantities of training data are. The more available data that can be obtained regularly, the more precise the machine learning will be.

Standards-based wireless networks are a significant research subject in industries and universities. Huge amounts of work on multi-channel and routing protocols that concurrently use the various channels available in IEEE 802.11 have been done to improve the network bandwidth. During the implementation of multi-channel protocols, a few authors realized that Adjacent Channel Interference (ACI) between partially overlapping channels causes severe problems when used with 802.11 [2]. ACI occurs on an adjacent or partially overlapping channel when signals are sent. The channel bleeds over on an overlapping channel, which creates interference and noise. Particularly in a high-density zone, ACI negatively affects wireless networks, and this is the case of Frequency Interference (FI). To prevent FI, Reinforcement Learning (RL) can be used to decide which channels need to be assigned to the adjacent access points. Its applications could be applied to problems in the real world and recognize research ready for practical exploitation.

1.2 Problem Statement

As great as Wi-Fi is, it has major drawbacks because of how they operate. Since all wireless signals and networks use radio frequency transmissions, they are suffered from all of the same problems that plague other types of radio technology: interference from other radio wave transmitting devices, weaker signals caused by inappropriate installation of access points, channel overlap/cross-channel among neighbor APs and environmental noise as affected by radio signal devices. Weak Wi-Fi signal also results in data loss, leading to a slower than normal connection and decreased communication efficiency be-tween wireless LAN and local and remote devices.

For many organizations, an unreliable wireless connection is extremely frustrating. Using reinforcement learning, suitable channels can be allocated to access points (AP) to prevent channel interference so that users do not have to worry about slow connectivity to the internet.

2 Related Work

2.1 Wi-Fi

Over the last few years, Wi-Fi or Wireless Fidelity has expanded rapidly to become the most significant wireless network standard. As it functions in unlicensed frequency bands, anyone can build a wireless network and cover a wide area with high-speed wireless connectivity to a LAN and the Internet [3]. Wi-Fi uses various networking elements of the IEEE 802.11 protocol and is intended to communicate with Ethernet. It has different variants defined by numerous IEEE 802.11 standards, with radio frequency bands, maximum ranges, and achieved speeds being determined by various radio technologies.

Radio waves are used by Wi-Fi-enabled devices to transmit data to wireless AP, and the AP completes the connection to other LAN, WAN, or Internet devices.

The 2.4 GHz and 5 GHz frequency bands are utilized for Wi-Fi technology. Wi-Fi frequency bands are radio wave frequency ranges that are used to relay data in the wireless spectrum. The higher the frequency is, and the shorter the range of signals is. Therefore, the 2.4 GHz band is used when searching for more Wi-Fi coverage, and the 5 GHz band is used when looking for higher speeds. Smaller bands known as Wi-Fi channels are within these Wi-Fi frequency bands, and wireless networks use them to transmit and receive data. A certain number of Wi-Fi channels are available for the AP to choose, depending on which frequency band the AP uses. For example, 11 Wi-Fi channels are in the 2.4 GHz frequency band, and 25 Wi-Fi channels are in the 5 GHz frequency band.

By default, each Wi-Fi channel is assigned a 20 MHz portion, divided by 5 MHz in the frequency band in which they are located, and may also be grouped to form broader portions. The Wi-Fi channel width determines how much data can pass through and at what speed wider channels allow more data transmitted at higher speeds. Broader Wi-Fi channel widths (40 MHz and 80 MHz) are better used in the 5 GHz frequency band because there are more Wi-Fi channels and fewer overlapping channels (25 non-overlapping channels out of 45 channels). Therefore, the 5 GHz band is considered for being less crowded and can accommodate wide Wi-Fi channel widths which are 20 MHz, 40 MHz, and 80 MHz. However, in the 2.4 GHz frequency band, it is typically advised to use the channel width of 20 MHz since the 2.4 GHz band only is 100 MHz wide. And 11 channels with 20 MHz width will reduce channel overlap and signal noise.

One of the key causes of network interference is overlapping Wi-Fi channels, or adjacent-channels, which results in more unsatisfactory wireless performance. To eliminate the 2.4 GHz band adjacent-channel interference, only channels 1, 6 and 11 are utilized. They have enough space between their channel centers and do not overlap because they are far enough from each other (Fig. 1).

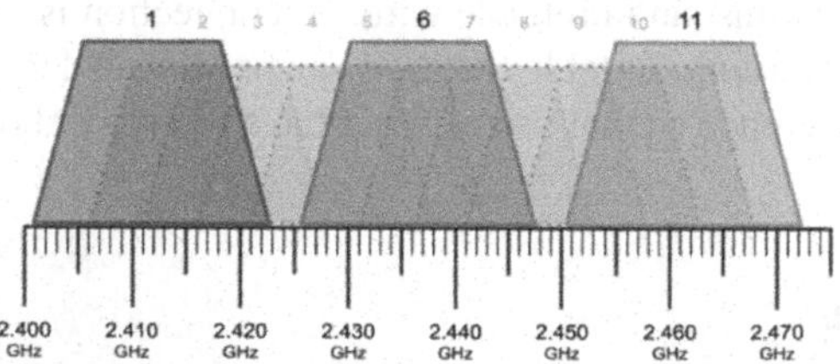

Fig. 1. Overlapping and non-overlapping channels on 2.4 GHz frequency band (Metageek) [4]

In the 5 GHz band, with the Wi-Fi channel width of 20 MHz, channels partially do not overlap, and there are 24 non-overlapping channels to work with, which is much easier to set up and choose a Wi-Fi channel for wireless access point or router.

2.2 Wireless Local Area Networks

Wireless LANs are clusters of wireless networking nodes capable of radio communications within a small geographic area, such as a campus or a university. WLANs are usually implemented as extensions to existing wired local area networks to enhance user mobility [5].

In a limited area, WLAN utilizes wireless communication to connect multiple devices to form a controlled LAN. WLAN provides links for connected devices to access the Internet using orthogonal frequency-division multiplexing technology. This allows users to move around and stay connected to the Internet network within the area.

Two types of equipment are composed of a WLAN: an AP and a station. A station is a personal computer or handheld device with a wireless Network Interface Controller (NIC) that connects to APs. To create links to WLAN, NICs use radio signals. The AP serves as a connector between wired and wireless networks. AP operates as a base station in the WLAN, connecting several stations to the wired network.

WLAN can be established with multiple APs if the range is not enough to cover a desirable area. Wireless stations cannot maintain connection when they are too far away from a Wi-Fi network. By using multiple access points and configuring them to use the same Service Set Identifier, they will all act as one extensive network, and clients will automatically switch between APs when needed while still sustaining connection to that WLAN [6].

2.3 Reinforcement Learning

Definition

Reinforcement Learning (RL) is a Machine Learning area that focuses on how the software agent shall take actions or make moves in an environment to enhance some prioritized rewards. RL algorithms research the behavior of agents and study to refine that behavior in such an environment. The learning process evolves with trial and error different from supervised learning. It is important to tell an agent what the right action is for any position it encounters [7]. Therefore, Reinforcement Learning has been used to address a dynamic multichannel access problem and achieved near-optimal performance in switching channels [8].

Markov Decision Process

Markov Decision Process (MDP) is a perceptive and basic methodology for decision-theoretical planning (DTP) and other learning difficulties in stochastic domains. An environment is modeled in MDP as a set of actions and states could be executed to regulate the system's state. The goal is to manage the system to ensure that some performance criterion is maximized. MDP provides a method to formulate sequential decision-making. This formulation is one of the fundamental issues that are solved in RL. The components of an MDP include Environment, Agent, States, Actions, and Rewards.

In an MDP, a decision-maker is called an agent. This agent is put in an environment and interacts with itself. Over time, the agent's interactions happen sequentially. The agent will be able to get a bit depiction of the state of the environment at each phase of the time, and given this depiction, that agent takes an action. The environment would then be moved to some next state and, as a consequence of the agent's previous action, that agent is granted a reward.

The course of choosing an action from a state-provided to the agent, moving to the next state, and earning a reward occurs consecutively repeatedly, which produces a path that illustrates the series of actions, rewards, and states. This is the task of the agent in the process to maximize the sum of rewards. Rewards are earned by taking actions in provided environment states. It implies that not just the instant reward, but also the accumulated rewards will obtain gradually, and the agent must maximize them.

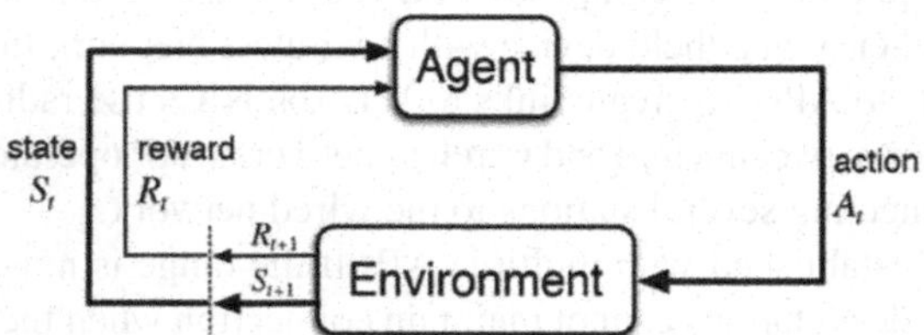

Fig. 2. Markov decision process illustration diagram (Source: Sutton and Barto)

As depicted in Fig. 2, there are a set of states $\boldsymbol{S}$, a set of actions $\boldsymbol{A}$ and a set of rewards $\boldsymbol{R}$ within an MDP. The agent observes the state of the environment $S_t \in \boldsymbol{S}$ at each time phase $t = 0, 1, 2, 3\ldots$ Based on the state S_t, the agent selects an action $A_t \in \boldsymbol{A}$. This gives us the state-action pair (S_t, A_t). In the next phase $t + 1$, the environment is changed to a next state $\boldsymbol{S_t} + 1 \in \boldsymbol{S}$. At this moment, the agent earns a reward $R_t + 1 \in \boldsymbol{R}$ for the action A_t the agent take from state S_t.

It is possible to consider this course of earning a reward as a function f. This function at each time t maps a state-action pair to a reward value: $f(S_t, A_t) = R_t + 1$. The orbit reflecting the concurrent course of picking action from a provided state, moving to the next state, then obtaining a reward is possibly illustrated as $S_0, A_0, R_1, S_1, A_1, R_2, S_2, A_2, R_3\ldots$

3 Methodology

3.1 Framework

The study proposes a framework implementing RL in order to optimize Wi-Fi access channel selection in a real-world Wi-Fi network. It includes three key components: pre-processing data, training, and testing, as shown in Fig. 3. The next section will describe the details of the components.

3.2 Pre-processing

Pre-processing Data

In this pre-processing unit, the raw datasets which are in CSV format are loaded into our implemented system. There are two types of input data: AP and Client data. The AP data is used to find the access point channels (2.4 GHz and 5 GHz channels) (Table 1); the Client data is used to determine the access point signal strength at each time stamp (Table 2).

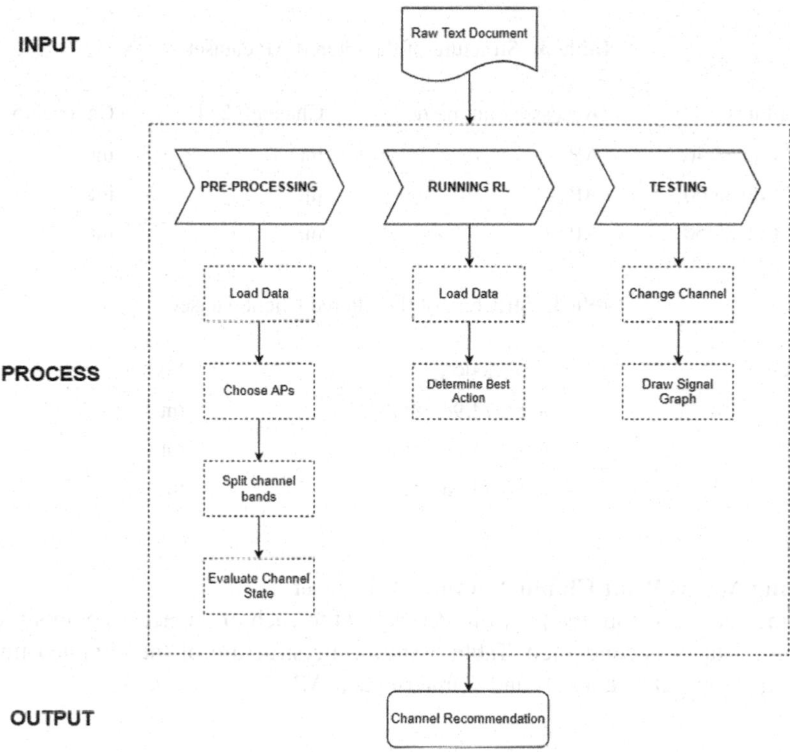

Fig. 3. Overview implementation of reinforcement learning

Table 1. Structure of the extracted access point dataset

MAC_address	Access_point_name	IP	Channel_2_4	Channel_5	Download_bytes	Upload_bytes
string	string	string	int	int	int	int

Choosing APs

A group of highly correlated access points is selected to change their channels. Due

Table 2. Structure of the extracted client dataset

Name	IP	Band	Bitrate_rx	Bitrate_tx	Last_name	Last_node	Signal	Traffic_down	Traffic_up
string	string	string	int	int	String	int	string	int	int

to using a MAC address, it is convenient to pick a group of access points on the same WLAN. For example, when a MAC address starts with ac:86:74, the following APs in the AP data and the Client data can be found, as shown in Tables 3 and 4.

Table 3. Structure of the filtered AP dataset

MAC_address	Access_point_name	Channel_2_4	Channel_5
ac:86:74:9e:58:40	AP_1	int	int
ac:86:74:d0:4a:60	AP_2	int	int
ac:86:74:0a:85:60	AP_3	int	int

Table 4. Structure of the filtered Client dataset

Last_name	Last_node	Signal
AP_1	ac:86:74:9e:58:40	int
AP_2	ac:86:74:d0:4a:60	int
AP_3	ac:86:74:0a:85:60	int

Assigning Access Point Channel to the AP Dataset

Assigning channels from the previous AP dataset to each of the access points found in the Client dataset is conducted. Table 5 shows the structure of the obtained final AP dataset, including the channels and signal of each AP.

Table 5. Structure of the final AP dataset

AP_name	AP_mac_address	Signal	Channel
AP_1	ac:86:74:9e:58:40	int	int
AP_2	ac:86:74:d0:4a:60	int	int
AP_3	ac:86:74:0a:85:60	int	int

Evaluating Access Point Channel States

The final step of pre-processing data is to evaluate access point channel states. The dataset of access point channel states needs to be converted into binaries. Every channel has two probable states which are good (1) or bad (0). At each time slot, we have multiple users select one channel to send a packet. Because of the limitations of collecting real datasets, this study evaluates the Wi-Fi channels only using the AP and client datasets, that is, basing on Wi-Fi signal strength receiving from clients. If a channel has a signal greater than or equal to -70 dBm, then it is in the good state; otherwise, that channel has a signal less than -70 dBm, then it is in the bad state.

3.3 Running Reinforcement Learning Algorithm

TensorFlow is used to run the RL algorithm. To begin the training, the first step is to create an initial state by choosing a random start state. The algorithm generates an initial state by randomly selecting M actions (a) (corresponding to the number of channels), observing the state of those actions (o), then appending those actions and observations to the initial state so in the format: $s = (a_{t-1}, o_{t-1} \ldots a_{t-M}, o_{t-M})$.

In the first episode, the algorithm uses the initial state as the input state to select the best action either by exploration or exploitation:

- By choosing the action based on exploration, the algorithm randomly selects an action in M actions ranging from 0 to $M - 1$.
- By choosing the action based on exploitation, the algorithm uses the input state to calculate Q-Values in the hidden layers and chooses the action with the optimal Q-Value $\max_{\pi} q_{\pi}(s, a)$ under policy π.

The algorithm then monitors the state of those chosen actions, calculates the reward r, generates the new state based on those actions, observations, input state and adds them to the replay memory for future use. The next input state will receive the value of that new state. The process repeats from $t = 0$ until done.

From the second episode onwards, the algorithm will use the state saved in the replay memory to calculate the actions, observations, rewards in the next state.

Next, the neural network weight θ is updated to decrease the network loss to minimize the error of the neural network. In training neural networks, it is unable to pass the entire dataset into the neural network at once since backpropagation requires the computation of many gradients and it can be computationally heavy. Therefore, it is necessary to divide the dataset into several batches. Calculation of the network loss by using a mini-batch of 32 samples is aimlessly selected from the replay memory.

The loss function is computed as follows: $Loss = (r + \gamma \max_{a'} Q(s', a') - Q(s, a))^2$, where, ($s'$, a') is the next state and action of (s, a), and γ is the discount factor which controls the contribution of rewards further in the future.

- The target Q-Value: The algorithm utilizes the new state in the replay memory to calculate the target Q-Values using the equation $q^*(s, a) = \mathrm{E}\,[R_{t+1} + \gamma \max_{a'} q^*(s', a')]$.
- The predicted Q-Value: The algorithm takes a random batch of samples in the replay memory. This batch is then inputted into the policy network. The policy network takes the current state and action from each data sample and predicts the Q-Value for that particular action.

The network then updates its weights by conducting the stochastic gradient descent to minimize the loss using the Adam algorithm [9] with the learning rate of 0.01 to optimize the model. Figure 4 depicts the Deep Q-Network flowchart. After a number of episodes, the best action will be determined from the replay memory. The best action is the best channel to be assigned to the interfered access point.

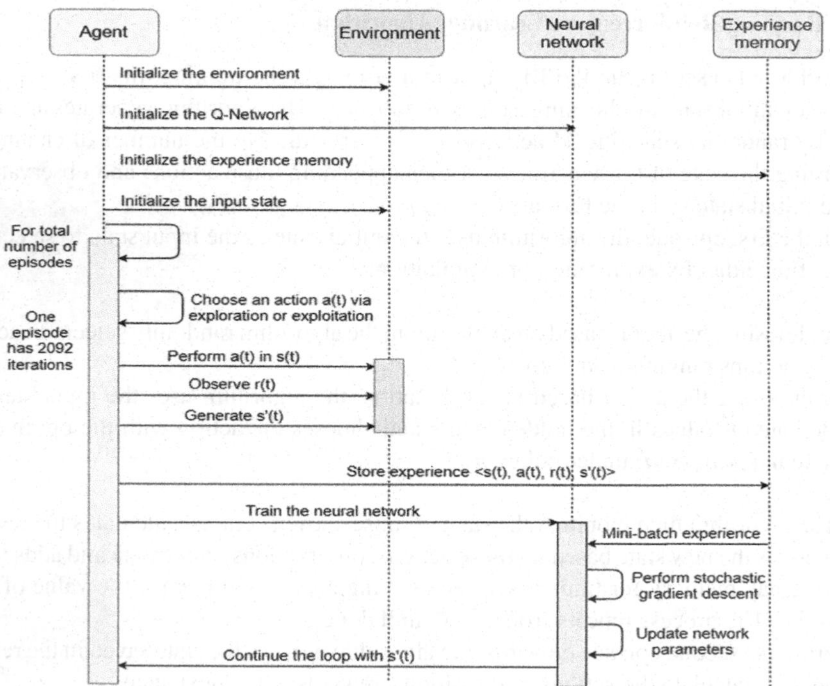

Fig. 4. Deep Q-network flowchart

4 Experiments and Results

4.1 Experiments

The AP datasets and client datasets are extracted from the Wi-Fi Controller of the International University, VNU-HCMC. They are described as below.

- The AP dataset: contains the access point's name, MAC address, channel, etc. (Fig. 5). This dataset consists of 15 records. It is noted that Channel_2_4 refers to 2.4 GHz channels, and Channel_5 refers to 5 GHz channels.
- The Client dataset: contains the connected AP name, AP MAC address, connection signal, etc. (Fig. 6). This dataset consists of 8943 records.

1	Access_Point_ID	MAC_Address	Access_Point_Name	Channel_2_4	Channel_5	Role	Firmware_Version	Mesh_Version
2	1438177	ac:86:74:e0:64:c0	IU'-OFFICE'-TV_2_Giua	1	157	gateway	6.4.15	batman'-adv
3	1437326	ac:86:74:9e:58:40	IU'-HCM'-A1_309_Unimart	1	149	gateway	6.4.15	batman'-adv
4	1436830	ac:86:74:d0:4a:60	IU'-HCM'-A1.308	6	44	gateway	6.4.15	batman'-adv
5	1446070	ac:86:74:0a:ee:10	IU'-HCM'-A1.306	5	48	gateway	6.4.15	batman'-adv
6	1447735	ac:86:74:e0:81:a0	IU'-HCM'-A2_407_Phai	11	153	gateway	6.4.15	batman'-adv
7	1445902	ac:86:74:d0:86:e0	IU'-HCM'-A2.307_Trai	11	149	gateway	6.4.15	batman'-adv

Fig. 5. Partial access point dataset

1	name	ip	last_name	last_node	signal
2	Les'-MBP'-3	10.239.28.240	IU'-HCM'-TV1'-Phai	ac:86:74:e0:80:e0	{"antenna1":0,"antenna2":0,"antenna3":0,"antenna4":0,"average":'-63}
3	iPad'-cua'-Thu	10.239.1.247	IU'-STUDY'-TV1_Ngoai	ac:86:74:0a:82:80	{"antenna1":'-89,"antenna2":'-89,"antenna3":0,"antenna4":0,"average":'-86}
4	LEs'-Air'-2	10.239.17.76	IU'-STUDY'-TV1_Ngoai	ac:86:74:0a:82:80	{"antenna1":'-90,"antenna2":'-90,"antenna3":0,"antenna4":0,"average":'-87}
5	DESKTOP'-IJSUL29	10.239.10.75	IU'-HCM'-TV1'-Trai	ac:86:74:e0:65:80	{"antenna1":0,"antenna2":0,"antenna3":0,"antenna4":0,"average":'-57}
6	LAPTOP'-5SPP06C1	10.239.1.122	IU'-HCM'-A1.306	ac:86:74:0a:ee:10	{"antenna1":'-63,"antenna2":'-68,"antenna3":0,"antenna4":0,"average":'-62}
7	LAPTOP'-H3BPCPO7	10.239.23.147	IU'-HCM'-A2.307_Trai	ac:86:74:d0:86:e0	{"antenna1":0,"antenna2":0,"antenna3":0,"antenna4":0,"average":'-54}

Fig. 6. Partial client dataset

Selecting APs

There are many WLANs in the International University, each WLAN has its Wi-Fi coverage extended by multiple access points. When deploying multiple APs on the same network, there is a chance that the neighboring access points may use overlap-ping channels which can cause channel interference.

Our objective is to find access points that are closed to each other, observe the performance of their channels and then change the channel of the access point that is interfered with or has a weak signal. For example, we can find the following four APs in the AP dataset. The APs are placed in four rooms as shown in Fig. 7.

The AP in room A1.306 is in Channel 5 and it interferes with the AP in room A1.308 which is in Channel 6. Therefore, we have to change the channel of the access point in A1.306. The channel interference occurs only in the 2.4 GHz band, while the 5 GHz band does not have channel interference.

1	MAC_Address	Access_Point_Name	Channel_2_4	Channel_5
2	ac:86:74:9e:58:40	IU'-HCM'-A1_309_Unimart	1	149
3	ac:86:74:d0:4a:60	IU'-HCM'-A1.308	6	44
4	ac:86:74:0a:85:60	IU'-HCM'-A1'-312'-NEW	11	36
5	ac:86:74:0a:ee:10	IU'-HCM'-A1.306	5	48

Access points Area Visualization

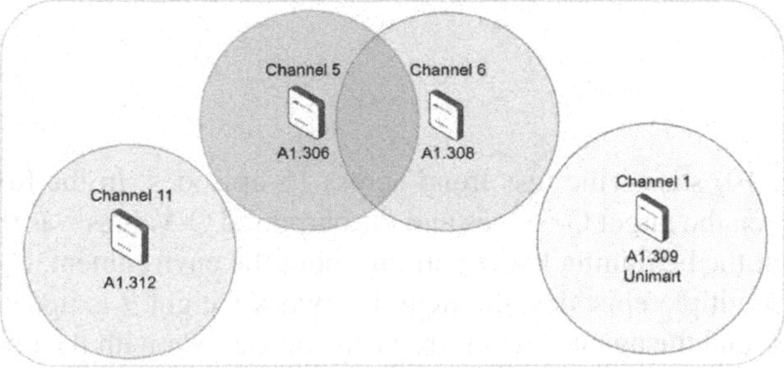

Fig. 7. Selecting APs from the AP dataset

Since the AP dataset is lacking signal information, we can find the signal information of APs from the Client dataset. A 2.4 GHz Client dataset is generated as Fig. 8, containing 8436 records (each room has 2106 records) with the signals of APs.

1	ap_name	ap_mac_address	last_seen	signal
2	IU'-HCM'-A1'-312'-NEW	ac:86:74:0a:85:60	2020-11-30 T 01:26	-87
3	IU'-HCM'-A1_309_Unimart	ac:86:74:9e:58:40	2020-11-30 T 01:30	-76
4	IU'-HCM'-A1.308	ac:86:74:d0:4a:60	2020-11-30 T 01:36	-74
5	IU'-HCM'-A1'-312'-NEW	ac:86:74:0a:85:60	2020-11-30 T 01:40	-85
6	IU'-HCM'-A1'-312'-NEW	ac:86:74:0a:85:60	2020-11-30 T 01:45	-76
7	IU'-HCM'-A1.306	ac:86:74:0a:ee:10	2020-11-30 T 02:05	-78
8	IU'-HCM'-A1'-312'-NEW	ac:86:74:0a:85:60	2020-11-30 T 02:10	-77
9	IU'-HCM'-A1_309_Unimart	ac:86:74:9e:58:40	2020-11-30 T 02:10	-71
10	IU'-HCM'-A1_309_Unimart	ac:86:74:9e:58:40	2020-11-30 T 02:10	-88
11	IU'-HCM'-A1_309_Unimart	ac:86:74:9e:58:40	2020-11-30 T 02:15	-73
12	IU'-HCM'-A1'-312'-NEW	ac:86:74:0a:85:60	2020-11-30 T 02:15	-83

Fig. 8. Selecting APs from the client dataset

Assigning Access Point Channels to the Filtered AP Dataset

Assigning channel index from the filtered AP dataset to each of the access points found in the filtered Client dataset (the channel index represents the real channel of an AP), is implemented as Fig. 9.

1	ap_mac_address	ap_name	channel_2_4	channel_5	channel_index
2	ac:86:74:9e:58:40	IU'-HCM'-A1_309_Unimart	1	149	0
3	ac:86:74:d0:4a:60	IU'-HCM'-A1.308	6	44	1
4	ac:86:74:0a:85:60	IU'-HCM'-A1'-312'-NEW	11	36	2
5	ac:86:74:0a:ee:10	IU'-HCM'-A1.306	5	48	3

Fig. 9. The signal and channel of APs in 2.4 GHz frequency band

Evaluating Access Point Channel States and Running RL Algorithm

Regarding to the proposed framework, the channel states are evaluated to be assigned good or bad values. After that, the RL algorithm is performed. The procedure takes over 720 iterations to complete 1 episode. After 15 episodes, the best action or channel is found from the replay memory. The following shows some experimental results.

4.2 Results

Average Loss

The graph (Fig. 10) shows the loss trend across 15 episodes. In the first episode, the difference between the target Q-Values and the outputted Q-Values was the most drastic since the agent at the beginning knew nothing about the environment. Over time, when the agent plays multiple episodes, the neural network weight θ is updated to decrease the network loss, and the agent can determine the best action with the optimal Q-Value. After 15 episodes, it can determine the best action from the replay memory to find the best channel. Given the used datasets, the best channel is Channel 11. Since Channel

11 is far enough from Channel 6 which is assigned to the neighboring access point in A1.308, they have sufficient space between their channel centers and do not overlap. Therefore, it ought to change the 2.4 GHz channel of the access point in A1.306 from Channel 5 to Channel 11.

Changing the access point in room A1.306 from Channel 5 to Channel 11 would make the Wi-Fi signal performance improved as shown as Fig. 11.

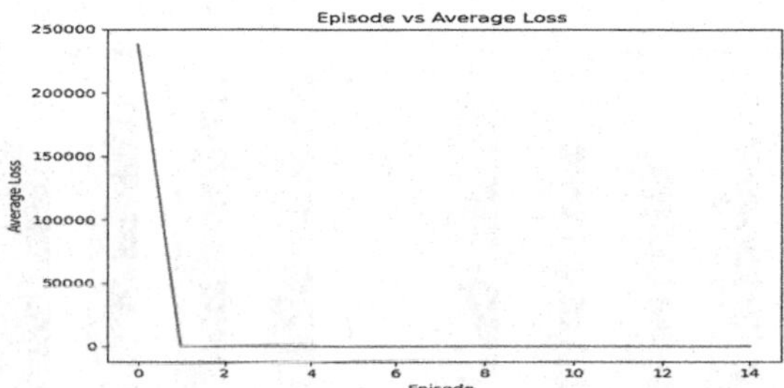

Fig. 10. Episode vs Average loss

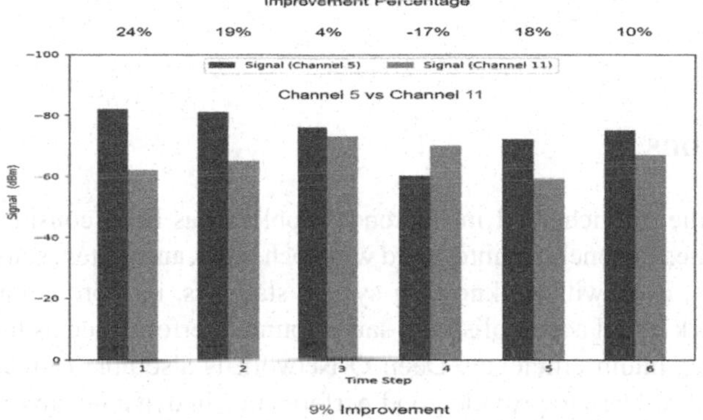

Fig. 11. Bar chart of signal quality of AP in A1.306

Before changing channels, the signal quality of the access point in A1.306 sometimes excessed the usable threshold due to the adjacent channel congestion. As the access point in A1.306 tried to talk to its clients, its transmissions became garbled because of the transmissions of the access point in A1.308. Signal above −70 dBm often results in unreliable packet delivery and poor connectivity. There is a 9% improvement in signal quality after changing from Channel 5 to Channel 11, the signal is regularly stable at around −60 to −70 dBm and can provide very reliable and timely delivery of data packets.

In addition, this study compares the performance of Wi-Fi signals when changing channels by human evaluation (Channel 5 to 1) and changing channels based on the proposed method (Channel 5 to 11). A human can change the channel of AP in A1.306 from 5 to 1, because Channel 1 is far from Channel 5, as Fig. 8, this may avoid signal overlap. However, the performance after changing the access point in A1.306 from Channel 5 to Channel 11 is 5% better than from Channel 5 to 1, as Fig. 12. This has shown that the proposed RL-based method would support choosing better channels for APs automatically over time.

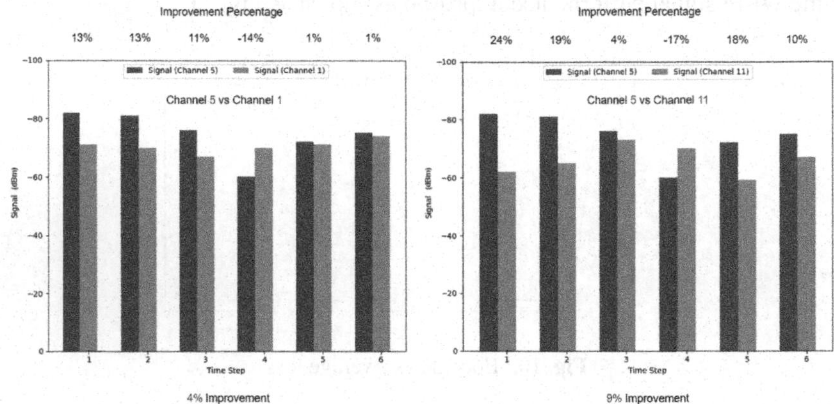

Fig. 12. Comparison the signal performance of Channel 1, 5 and 11 assigned to AP in A1.306

5 Conclusions

In this paper, the multichannel interference problem has been considered in a more realistic case when channels are interfered with each other, and system stats are uncertain. Via simulations, even without knowing system statistics, in more complicated cases, Deep Q-Network could accomplish the same optimal performance as humans and can achieve near-maximum efficiency. Deep Q-Network is also able to recognize system adjustments and re-learn to provide good performance in dynamic environments.

This proposed RL-based framework allows users to input the dataset of APs and Clients, the best channels will be then recommended for access points to achieve an optimal signal quality. In order to achieve better performance, a broad input dataset is required. And the use of RL for channel recommendation can bring many advantages for network administration.

Acknowledgements. This research is funded by International University, VNU-HCM under grant number T2020-02-IT.

References

1. Al Musawi, A.: Introduction to Machine Learning [Internet] (2018). https://www.researchgate.net/publication/323108787_Introduction_to_Machine_Learning
2. Zubow, A., Sombrutzki, R.: Adjacent Channel Interference in IEEE 802.11n. IEEE (2012)

3. Al-Alawi, A.I.: WiFi technology: future market challenges and opportunities. J. Comput. Sci. **2**(1), 13–18 (2006)
4. Why Channels 1, 6, and 11? | MetaGeek [Internet]. https://www.metageek.com/training/resources/why-channels-1-6-11.html. Accessed 10 Mar 2021
5. Dahiya, M.: Evolution of wireless LAN in wireless networks. Int. J. Comput. Sci. Eng. **9**, 109–113 (2017)
6. Tetz, E.: Wireless Network Routing with Multiple Access Points (APs) - Dummies [Internet]. https://www.dummies.com/programming/networking/cisco/wireless-network-routing-with-multiple-access-points-aps/. Accessed 10 Mar 2021
7. Hammoudeh, A.: A Concise Introduction to Reinforcement Learning (2018)
8. Wang, S., et al.: Deep reinforcement learning for dynamic multichannel access in wireless networks. IEEE Trans. Cognit. Commun. Netw. **4**(2), 257–265 (2018)
9. Kingma, D.P., Ba, J.: Adam: a method for stochastic optimization (2014). https://arxiv.org/abs/1412.6980

Emotiv Insight with Convolutional Neural Network: Visual Attention Test Classification

Chean Khim Toa[1](✉), Kok Swee Sim[1], and Shing Chiang Tan[2]

[1] Faculty of Engineering and Technology, Multimedia University, 75450 Melaka, Malaysia
[2] Faculty of Information Science and Technology, Multimedia University, 75450 Melaka, Malaysia

Abstract. The purpose of this paper is to use the low-cost EEG device to collect brain signal and use the neural network algorithm to classify the attention level based on the recorded EEG data as input. Fifteen volunteers participated in the experiment. The Emotiv Insight headset was used to record the brain signal during participants performing the Visual Attention Colour Pattern Recognition (VACPR) test. The test was divided into 2 tasks namely task A for stimulating the participant to be attentive and task B for stimulating the participant to be inattention. Later, the recorded raw EEG signal passed through a Notch filter and Independent Component Analysis (ICA) to filter out the noise. After that, Power Spectral Density (PSD) was used to calculate the power value of pre-processed EEG signal to verify whether the recorded EEG signal is consistent with the mental state stimulated during task A and task B before performing classification. Since EEG signals exhibit significantly complex behaviour with dynamic and non-linear characteristics, Convolutional Neural Network (CNN) shows great promise in helping to classify EEG signal due to its capacity to learn good feature representation from the signals. An accuracy of 76% was achieved, indicating the feasibility of using Emotiv Insight with CNN for attention level classification.

Keywords: Convolution neural network · Electroencephalogram · Emotiv insight · Visual attention colour pattern recognition (VACPR) test

1 Introduction

Visual attention is an important set of cognitive operations, which can filter out irrelevant information and select relevant information. In the learning process, whether a person being attentive or inattentive throughout instruction usually affect their learning efficacy [1]. Attentive behaviour can allow a person to stay on the task and acquired relevant information, while inattentive behaviour can cause a person to be unable to focus on the task. Inattentive occur due to external factors such as emotional stress and distraction. In academics, the teacher usually observes student's expressions during learning to determine their mental state. However, it is a burden for a novice teacher to teach and monitor all the student expressions at the same time. To effectively determine a person's mental state during the learning process, the use of EEG has become quite popular among the researchers. Tóth et al. [2] using the BrainAmp DC 64-channel EEG system to record

K. Wojtkiewicz et al. (Eds.): ICCCI 2021, CCIS 1463, pp. 348–357, 2021.
https://doi.org/10.1007/978-3-030-88113-9_28

the brain activity and study focusing attention and divided attention of the speech stream and the processing of speech under different time-scale and depth. Shestyuk et al. [3] used 32 active electrodes biopotential system and Biosemi ActiveTqwo DC-coupled amplifier to record the EEG signal of an individual. The signals were analysed using the power spectrum of the frequency bands to predict the population success rate of various TV shows and determine the cognitive processes (attention, memory, and motivation) that help with audio engagement with television shows. Aliakbaryhosseinabadi et al. [4] using 18 active electrode g.GAMMAcap system and g.USB amplifier to record the signals and find the time-frequency features to identify the user's attention variation during the motor task execution. Although the use of research-grade EEG systems with many channels can obtain more features from the recorded brain signal, the device is expensive and the set-up is quite tedious, less versatility outside the laboratory environment, and uncomfortable to wear by the user. Recently, there has been a use of consumer-grade EEG device for analysis of the mental state of a person. Tan [5] using the one channel NeuroSky Mindset to record the brain signal and detect the mental state during the word trials. Van Hal et al. [6] using the one channel NeuroSky Mindset to record the signal and then filtered it into alpha and beta frequency bands to detect the onset of sleep.

In this study, we use the Emotiv Insight to record the EEG signals during the participant performing the Visual Attention Colour Pattern Recognition (VACPR) test. Emotiv Insight is a device designed for daily usage with an advanced electrode that uses 5 channels to record the brain signal [7]. The recorded raw EEG signal was then passed through pre-processing such as Notch filter and Independent Component Analysis (ICA) to filter out artifact noise. Next, the Power Spectral Density (PSD) was used to calculate the power value of the pre-processed signal to verify whether the signal is consistent with the mental state stimulated during the VACPR test [8]. After that, a Convolution Neural Network (CNN) was used to perform the classification on the signals. CNN is a deep learning algorithm that takes input signals, learns the features through the convolutional layer, and performs the classification of attention level in a fully neural layer [9]. The aim of this paper is divided into two parts. First is to verify whether the collected EEG signal using Emotiv Insight is consistent with the mental state stimulated during the VACPR test (task A and task B). Second is to determine whether the accuracy of the EEG classification on the tasks is higher than the chance (50% for binomial problem) [10].

Section 2 of this paper describes the material and methods used for performing the experiment, collecting the brain signals, and analysing the signals. Section 3 shows the result obtained from the experiment and its discussion. Section 4 is a conclusion that highlights the finding in this research work.

2 Materials and Methods

2.1 Participants

The experiment was conducted on fifteen participants (10 males and 5 females; age from 21 to 26). All participants voluntarily participated in the experiment and they are all healthy. A consent form was given to them before participating in the experiment.

They were told that if they begin to feel unwell, they could stop the experiment. The experiment was performed for 4 weeks; in which they participated 1 day per week.

2.2 Consumer-Grade Electroencephalogram Device

The electroencephalogram device that used in this research is the Emotiv Insight headset shown in Fig. 1(a), which is a low-cost consumer-grade device designed to record daily brain activity. It consists of 5 channel electrodes with a 128 Hz sampling frequency. To determine the quality of EEG signals is under good condition, Emotiv Xavier Control Panel software was used as shown in Fig. 1(b). The software was used to check if the electrodes have properly touched the scalp of the head, as follows:

(a) Black colour indicates no signal received. The electrode may not yet touch the scalp.
(b) Red colour indicates bad signal quality. The electrode needs to adjust properly
(c) Orange colour indicates poor signal quality. The electrode needs to adjust properly
(d) Green colour indicates good quality. The electrode seems to be placed properly.

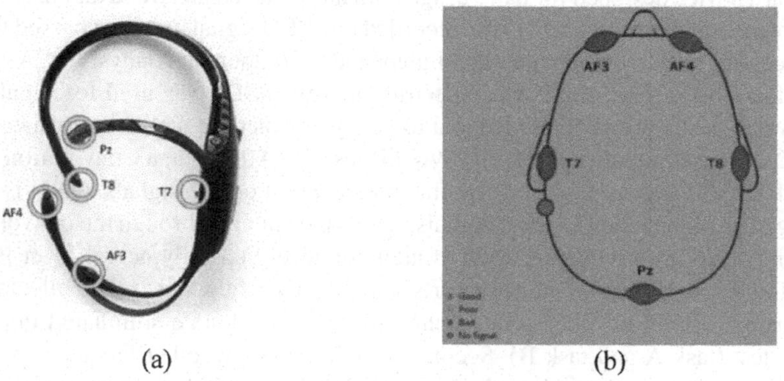

Fig. 1. (a) Emotiv Insight device and (b) EEG channel position

Emotiv Insight is using a polymer-based semi-dry electrode, which is comfortable and easier to wear by the participant. The set-up time is only 2 min. Besides, the device works wirelessly, which means that you can easily connect to the computer or smartphone to record the EEG signals. Table 1 shows the parameters of the headset.

Table 1. Parameters of Emotiv Insight

Parameter	Value
EEG channels	AF3, AF4, T7, T8, Pz
EEG references	CMS/DRL references on the left mastoid process
Sensor material:	Hydrophilic semi-dry polymer
Wireless	Bluetooth Low Energy
Sampling rate	128 Samples per second per channel
Resolution	14 Bits with 1 LSB = 0.51 μV
Frequency response	0.5–43 Hz, digital notch filters at 50 Hz and 60 Hz

2.3 Experimental Design

In this research, the visual attention colour pattern recognition (VACPR) test was designed and used as shown in Fig. 2. VACPR test is a type of perceptual test that requires visual attention to scan the environment and search for the targeted object. The design and concept of VACPR test are refer from PsyToolkit, a website that running cognitive-psychological experiments that maintained by a physiologist [11]. The use of the VACPR test can stimulate participants to be attentive or inattentive in a relatively short time. This can be done by dividing the test into 2 tasks (task A and task B).

For task A shown in Fig. 2(a), the purpose is to stimulate participants to be attentive. Participants were initially prompt for the targeted stimulus (TS) with random colour (red or blue) and pattern (vertical and horizontal) in each trial. Later, the participant needs to search for TS in the stimulus display (SD) filled with non-targets. The colour of all non-targeted stimulus is the same as the targeted stimulus, but with a different pattern. A similar concept also applies to task B shown in Fig. 2(b). The purpose of task B is to stimulate participants to be inattentive by including distractors and inducing emotional stress. Participants were initially prompt for the TS with random colour and pattern in each trial. After that, a distractor (same colour with different pattern, different colour with the same pattern, and different colour with different pattern) appeared in SD and the participant needs to find targeted stimulus among distractors. Figure 2(c) shows the stimulus sequence for task A and task B, in which duration of 500 ms will be given to the TS and the SD for each trial.

To collect the EEG signal when the participant performing the VACPR test, an experiment protocol was constructed as shown in Fig. 3. The duration of the experiment is about 180 s. Before the experiment, the participant was informed about the nature of the experiment. Then, the participant was given an instruction sheet that explains the experiment process. Later, the participant entered a closed room with a chair , table,

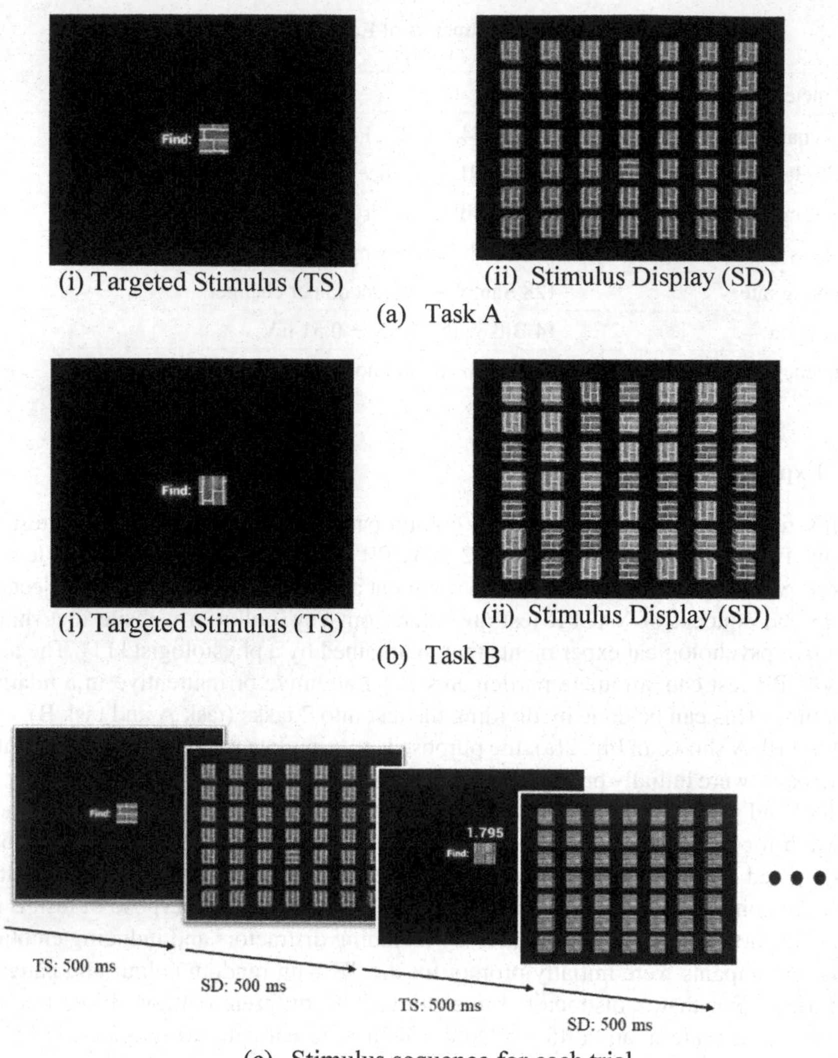

(i) Targeted Stimulus (TS) (ii) Stimulus Display (SD)

(a) Task A

(i) Targeted Stimulus (TS) (ii) Stimulus Display (SD)

(b) Task B

(c) Stimulus sequence for each trial

Fig. 2. Stimulus presented on each trial in the Visual Attention Colour Pattern Recognition (VACPR) test

computer, and EEG device prepared in advance. First, the participant wears the Emotiv Insight and rest for 30 s before starting to record. After that, the participant begins recording 60-s of task A. After finishing the first task, the participant was allowed to rest for 30 s. Afterward, the participant begins recording 60-s of task B. All recorded raw EEG data during the test was saved in the computer for further analysis.

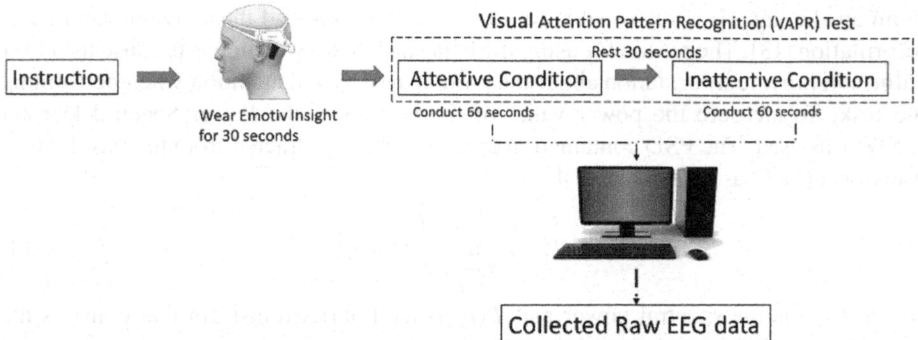

Fig. 3. Experiment protocol

2.4 EEG Signal Pre-processing

Since the raw EEG signal contains unwanted noise such as eye blinking, muscle movement, and line noise, there is a need to perform the pre-processing on the signals [12]. Figure 4 shows the pre-processing technique used in this research.

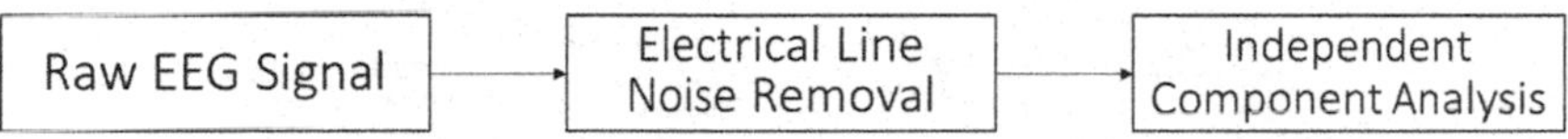

Fig. 4. Block diagram of EEG signal Pre-processing Technique

To remove the electrical line noise from the raw EEG signal, a digital notch filter is implemented. This filter filtering out the noise found at 50 Hz and 60 Hz.

$$G(x) = \frac{1 - 2\cos(50)x^{-1} + x^{-2}}{1 - 2r\cos(50)x^{-1} + r^2x^{-2}} \tag{1}$$

where x is the z-transform of raw EEG signal. Next, to eliminate the eye blinking and muscle movement, an Independent Component Analysis (ICA) is employed. The use of ICA is to separate mixture signals into their respective sources, thus can easily identify the noise in the signal. Equations 2 and 3 show the formulation of ICA.

$$S = Vx \tag{2}$$

$$V = \begin{bmatrix} \cos Ø & \sin Ø \\ -\sin Ø & \cos Ø \end{bmatrix} y^{-1} \begin{bmatrix} \cos\theta & \sin\theta \\ -\sin\theta & \cos\theta \end{bmatrix} \tag{3}$$

where S is the independent component, V is the matrix of independent component value, and x is the EEG input signal.

2.5 EEG Power Spectral Density

In this study, out of 5 frequency bands (delta, theta, alpha, beta, and gamma), only beta (13–30 Hz) are interested. Beta wave is a high frequency that is commonly observed in an awake state. It is responsible for conscious thinking and the active processing of information [13]. The reason for using the beta band in this research is because its power value can provide information about the participants' visual attention when performing the task. To measure the power value of the beta band, the Power Spectral Density (PSD) was used. The PSD contained in the beta band is extracted from the Fast Fourier transform (FFT) as shown in Eq. 4

$$P(f) = \lim_{N \to \infty} \frac{1}{N} |T(f)|^2 \tag{4}$$

where $P(f)$ is the spectral power and $T(f)$ is the Fourier transform that converts the signal from a time domain to a frequency domain.

2.6 Convolution Neural Network

In this research, the deep learning algorithm used is a Convolutional Neural Network (CNN) shown in Fig. 5, which uses pre-processed EEG signal as the input, learns important features from various aspects of the image, and distinguishes them from each other in the neural network [14].

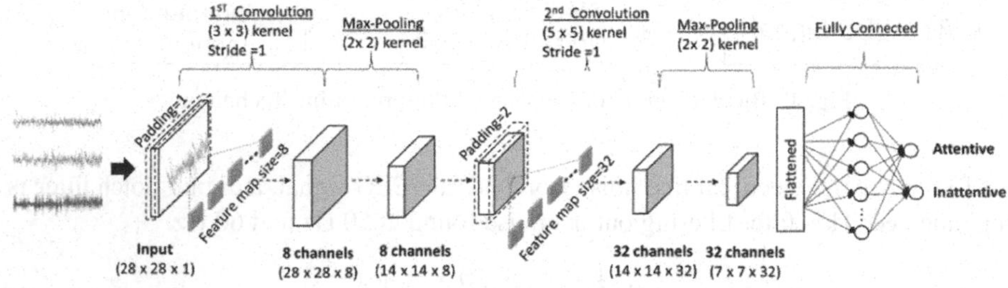

Fig. 5. The architecture of CNN

From the architecture, the EEG signal is initially converted into a 2-dimensional grayscale image and used as the input of CNN. Since the EEG signal exhibit significantly complex behaviour with dynamic and non-linear characteristics, 2 blocks of convolutional layer and pooling layer are used. In the convolutional layer, the image will go through convolution operation and using the kernel to extract the feature maps. Low-level features will be extracted by the first convolutional layer, but as layers are added, the architecture will slowly learn and extracted the high-level features. Besides, rectified linear unit (ReLu) is also used in the convolutional layer as an activation function that helps to speed up the training. For the pooling layer, it is used to reduce the size of the features. The purpose is to decrease the computational power required to process the data and obtain the significant features among the feature maps. Next, all the extracted features will be flattening and go through a fully connected layer to classify the learned feature into 2 classes which are attentive and inattentive. Furthermore, hyperparameter tuning has been done for CNN. First is the learning rate where the value is set to 1×10^{-4} to adjust the weight in network. Second is the epochs where the value is set to 20 to achieve a small gap between test error and training error. Third, the batch size is set to a value of 10. Fourth, a dropout is used to avoid the overfitting to the data in network.

3 Result and Discussion

3.1 Power Spectral Density in Beta Band

To verify that whether it is sufficient to use Emotiv Insight to record brain activities when participant performing the Visual Attention Color Pattern Recognition (VACPR) test, the Power Spectral Density (PSD) values of the low beta band and the high beta band for frontal and parietal channels (AF3, AF4, and Pz) are averaged and compared, as shown in Fig. 6. According to the study [15], a low beta band (12–20 Hz) is associate with focus and concentration, while a high beta band (20–30 Hz) is associate with significant stress and distraction.

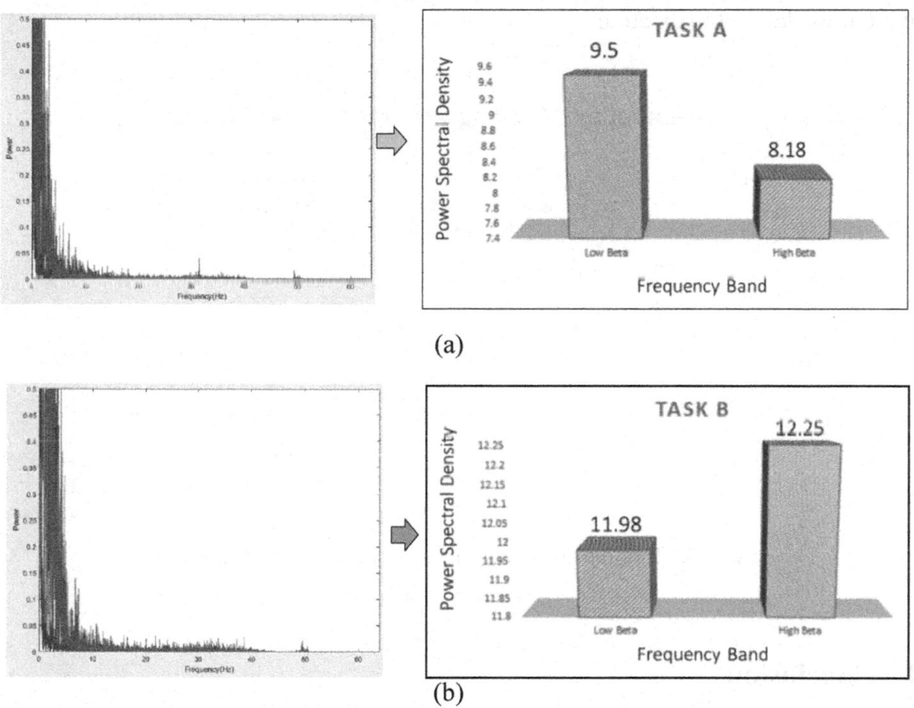

Fig. 6. Power spectral density in low and high beta bands

Figure 6 shows the PSD value obtained in 2 different tasks. Task A stimulates the participant to be attentive, while task B stimulates the participant to be inattentive. Based on Fig. 6(a), we can see that when the participant performing task A, the PSD value of the low beta band is greater than the PSD value of the high beta band, indicating that the collected EEG signal shows the participant is focusing on the task. As for Fig. 6(b), when the participant performing task B, the PSD value of the high beta band is greater than the PSD value of the low beta band, indicating that the collected EEG signal shows the participant is distracted and might emotionally stress. From the result, we can verify that the collected EEG signal using Emotiv Insight is satisfied the collectability requirement as the PSD value of the collected EEG signal is consistent with the mental state stimulated during task A and task B.

3.2 Accuracy Using Convolutional Neural Network (CNN) Classifier

After verifying that the use of Emotiv Insight in the VACPR test can provide significant information about the participant brain activity, the next step is to determine how accurate the classification of collected EEG signals in the VACPR test using the Convolutional Neural Network (CNN). Figure 7 shows the progress of training and testing accuracy.

Based on the graph, we can see that the EEG classification of VACPR tasks (task A and task B) can reach 76% accuracy, which is much better than chance (50% for binomial problem). This indicates that Emotiv Insight with CNN can provide good performance in attention level classification.

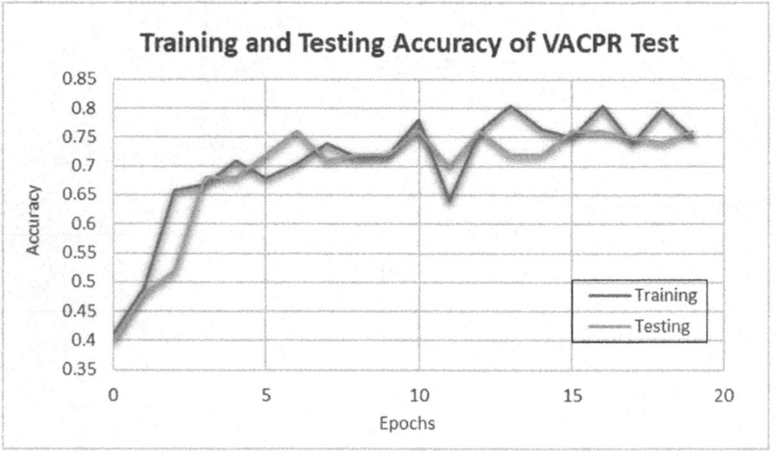

Fig. 7. Training and testing accuracy curve over 20 epochs

4 Conclusion

This research has presented some findings that involve the use of Emotiv Insight to capture the brain activity of participants and the use of Convolutional Neural Network (CNN) to classify attention level based on the collected EEG data. The Power Spectral Density (PSD) result shows that Emotiv Insight is reliably in capturing brain activity since the PSD value of the collected EEG signal is consistent with the mental state stimulated during task A and task B. For the EEG classification of 2 tasks, accuracy up to 76% was achieved which is higher than chance. Therefore, it is feasible to use Emotiv Insight with CNN for attention level classification.

References

1. Das, M., Bennett, D.M., Dutton, G.N.: Visual attention as an important visual function: an outline of manifestations, diagnosis and management of impaired visual attention. Br. J. Ophthalmol. **91**(11), 1556–1560 (2007). https://doi.org/10.1136/bjo.2006.104844
2. Tóth, B., et al.: Attention and speech-processing related functional brain networks activated in a multi-speaker environment. PLOS ONE **14**(2), e0212754 (2019)
3. Shestyuk, A.Y., Kasinathan, K., Karapoondinott, V., Knight, R.T., Gurumoorthy, R.: Individual EEG measures of attention, memory, and motivation predict population level TV viewership and Twitter engagement. PLoS ONE **14**(3), 1–27 (2019). https://doi.org/10.1371/journal.pone.0214507
4. Aliakbaryhosseinabadi, S., Kamavuako, E.N., Jiang, N., Farina, D., Mrachacz-Kersting, N.: Classification of EEG signals to identify variations in attention during motor task execution. J. Neurosci. Methods **284**, 27–34 (2017). https://doi.org/10.1016/j.jneumeth.2017.04.008
5. Tan, B.H.: Using a Low-cost EEG Sensor to Detect Mental States (2012)
6. Van Hal, B., Rhodes, S., Dunne, B., Bossemeyer, R.: Low-cost EEG-based sleep detection. In: 2014 36th Annual International Conference of the IEEE Engineering in Medicine and Biology Society (EMBC), 2014, pp. 4571–4574 (2014). https://doi.org/10.1109/EMBC.2014.6944641
7. Zabcikova, M.: Visual and auditory stimuli response, measured by Emotiv Insight headset. MATEC Web Conf. **292**, 01024 (2019). https://doi.org/10.1051/matecconf/201929201024
8. KumarAhirwal, M., londhe, D.N.: Power spectrum analysis of EEG signals for estimating visual attention. Int. J. Comput. Appl. **42**(15), 34–40 (2012). https://doi.org/10.5120/5769-7993
9. Jebelli, H., Khalili, M.M., Lee, S.: Mobile EEG-based workers' stress recognition by applying deep neural network. In: Mutis, I., Hartmann, T. (eds.) Advances in Informatics and Computing in Civil and Construction Engineering, pp. 173–180. Springer, Cham (2019). https://doi.org/10.1007/978-3-030-00220-6_21
10. Borst, J., Schneider, D., Walsh, M., Anderson, J.: Stages of processing in associative recognition: evidence from behavior, EEG, and classification. J. Cogn. Neurosci. **25**(12), 2151–2166 (2013). https://doi.org/10.1162/jocn_a_00457
11. Stoet, G.: PsyToolkit: a software package for programming psychological experiments using Linux. Behav. Res. Methods **42**(4), 1096–1104 (2010). https://doi.org/10.3758/BRM.42.4.1096
12. Lim, Z.Y., Sim, K.S., Tan, S.C.: An evaluation of left and right brain dominance using electroencephalogram signal. Eng. Lett. **28**(4), 1358–1367 (2020)
13. Gola, M., Magnuski, M., Szumska, I., Wróbel, A.: EEG beta band activity is related to attention and attentional deficits in the visual performance of elderly subjects. Int. J. Psychophysiol. **89**(3), 334–341 (2013). https://doi.org/10.1016/j.ijpsycho.2013.05.007
14. Toa, C.K., Sim, K.S., Tan, S.C.: Electroencephalogram-based attention level classification using convolution attention memory neural network. IEEE Access **9**, 58870–58881 (2021). https://doi.org/10.1109/ACCESS.2021.3072731
15. Abhang, P.A., Gawali, B.W., Mehrotra, S.C.: Chapter 3: Technical aspects of brain rhythms and speech parameters. In: Abhang, P.A., Gawali, B.W., Mehrotra, S.C. (eds.). Introduction to EEG- and Speech-Based Emotion Recognition, pp. 51–79. Academic Press, New York (2016)

Machine Learning in Real-World Data

Machine Learning in the Context of COVID-19 Pandemic Data Analysis

Anita Hrabia, Jan Kozak(✉), and Przemysław Juszczuk

Department of Machine Learning, University of Economics in Katowice, 1 Maja, 40-287, Katowice, Poland
{anita.hrabia,jan.kozak,przemyslaw.juszczuk}@ue.katowice.pl

Abstract. Recently a subject of COVID-19 pandemic-related predictions and models emerged as one of the crucial problems related to medicine and computer science. Acquired data carries the features of complex, difficult to analyze data. Moreover, often exponential growth of infected leads to the rapid growth of available data. Thus any approach related to cleaning and preprocessing data, as well as algorithm capable to deal with the prediction problem are crucial. It is especially important due to two main reasons: first of all, results acquired during the analysis and prediction could be used to contain the pandemic; moreover, such unprocessed, difficult data could be very important for different machine learning methods as a source of real-world, still-changing data. It should be clearly stated, that impact of the external factors, like capabilities of dealing with a pandemic, different country-dependent actions, and different virus mutations is an enormous challenge related to the data prediction.

In this article, we introduce an overview of different methods and approaches used in the context of the COVID-19 pandemic. Additionally, we estimate the quality of pandemic prediction on the basis of the polynomial regression. We investigate four different versions (dependent on the size of the train set) as well as test results on four different cases (situation in three different countries as well as the situation around the world).

Keywords: SARS-CoV-2 · COVID-19 · Polynomial regression · Machine learning for COVID-19

1 Introduction

Since detecting the first cases of COVID-19 in December 2019, people wouldn't expect, that during the four next months, the situation will change from difficult, to a global pandemic, which will paralyze the economy of most countries around the world for the next months. After over a year since the World Health Organization announced a global pandemic, people still struggle with the difficult situation, the virus takes thousands of lives every day and there is no global solution for this situation. Scientists from many different fields and disciplines try to overcome difficulties and deliver as much useful information as possible.

K. Wojtkiewicz et al. (Eds.): ICCCI 2021, CCIS 1463, pp. 361–374, 2021.
https://doi.org/10.1007/978-3-030-88113-9_29

Since the number of COVID-19 cases still rises, thus more and more solutions, which could improve the research over this new disease are proposed. Considering the fact, that machine learning gives opportunities related to prediction, classification, or analysis of large datasets, it is possible, that applying these methods becomes one of the concepts supporting the fight with pandemic [8,14]. In this article, we present a general review of the most popular solutions and methods available on this subject.

Taking into account a very dynamic course of the pandemic of SARS-CoV-2, we also investigate the concept, potentially capable to deal with such volatile data. Such a solution based on the regression will be presented in the experimental section of this article.

Previous research pointed out, that artificial intelligence and machine learning can derive a significant improvement in healthcare [2]. Thus it can be assumed, that in the case of COVID-19 it is reasonable to use machine learning methods as well. Of course, it is a concept among many different complex systems and methods allowing to derive support in the process of making decisions [15].

As it was mentioned before, we struggle with the pandemic situation for over a year, thus numerous approaches related to the use of machine learning are present in the widely discussed fight with the SARS-CoV-2 virus. These works include both review articles, interdiscyplinary works, as well as fully functional models [3,9,17,18]. We can also find different works related to the possible impact of artificial intelligence on vaccine production [7,13].

The goal of this article is the general review of articles based on the machine learning methods used in the problem of SARS-CoV-2 virus pandemic prediction. Next, we propose a solution based on the polynomial regression and we experimentally verify the results depending on the size of the learning and test sets. We rather focus on investigating the relatively simple approach rather than building the complex models. This seems to be especially crucial due to the fact, that in such a dynamic environment, the process of deriving approximate results seems to be far more important, than exact, time-consuming calculations.

The article is organized as follows: In the next section, we present the literature review of COVID-19 prediction work. The third section is focused on polynomial Regressions. The fourth section includes the numerical experiments of the generated results. The last sections include a short summary and details of future research.

2 Review of Works Related with the COVID-19 Pandemic Prediction

At present one of the newest and the most interesting subjects related with the real-world data is the COVID-19 disease caused by a SARS-CoV-2 virus. Mainly it is due to fact, that a newly discovered disease spread so quickly and have a relatively high death rate. Thus among researchers an intensive work towards deriving pandemic-related solutions allowing to better predict potential pandemic situation in future is very desirable.

2.1 Predicting the Growth and Trends for COVID-19 Pandemic

In the work [19] authors focused on using the machine learning along with the cloud computing to implement solutions related with tracking the possible actions focused on preventing pandemic spread. In the research, an improved mathematical model to analyze and prognose the potential pandemic rise was implemented. The model was based on the machine learning and used to predict potential COVID-19 thread in countries along the world. Authors shown, that using the iterative weighting for fitting Generalized Inverse Weibull distribution [4] a improved prediction can be achieved. In the article, an initial set of tools and possible research directions was proposed.

Among the crucial solutions proposed by authors was introducing the "social distancing". Authors suggested, that since there is no easily accessible vaccine, there is a need to introduce a solid mathematical background, which could be used to track the pandemic spread. Such action could be further used in the online dynamic environment capable to support decisions. A prediction model implemented with the use of the FofBus framework was used as well. This solution was used to present the detailed prognosis of COVID-19 patients, as well as the estimated number of cases along with the cured for the nearest future. Moreover, this approach was used to estimate the potential date for the pandemic end.

Authors focused on the data available on Our World in Data [10]. These data can be considered as the online data, due to daily updates taken from the World Health Organization. Machine learning models were used to potentilly increase the quality of prediction of new cases, however authors suggested, that the environment based on the cloud computing can be adapted to include large amount of data. Data could include detailed informaton as infomation from government hospitls, private health centers, which could potentialy sent the information from patients with positive COVID-19 result, population density, average age of patient, potential health amenities and other important pandemic-related information.

FInally, the extensions of the solution including mathematical modelling, machine learning and the cloud computing can help with active prediction of COVID-19 pandemic expansion. Moreover, a case study based on the virus spread across countries around world was presented. Using the proposed Weibull modell based on the iterative weighting, it was shown, that model is capable to perform statistically bether prognoses than basic Gauss model (since the second approach presented over-optimistic scenario).

2.2 Data Analysis Directed Towards Virus Detection

In the article [12] a different aspects related to COVID-19 were presented. Among the crucial element the visualisation of infection spread as well as the potential use of data analysis can be found. Authors expected, that these concepts could play an important role in examining COVID-19 features and possibly lead to bring closer the vaccine invention.

Authors in this paper performed the data analysis on the basis of well-known Johns Hopkins University. It is worth mentioning, that site with data includes not only the COVID cases, but also information about the incidence rate, case-fatality ratio, or testing rate (selected regions). In the mentioned article authors focused on comparision of the pandemic with other, recently observed epidemics – EBOLA, SRS, H1N1 and MERS available at Kaggle repository. It was shown, that in comparison to EBOLA, SARS and MERS number of people affected by deasase, the possible number of infections is higher. It the time of the publication, the H1N1 disease was still affecting the larger number of people than COVID, however this no longer true in 2021, where overall number of infections excedeed over 130 millions. In both: H1N1 as well as COVID-19 a such high number is cases is related with relatively low mortality for both diseases.

In article authors analyzed different machine learning algorithms used to automatic disease diagnostic. The classification methods were used to set the positive/negative decision class for patients. Considered methods were XGBoost, multilayer perceptrons (MLP), k-nearest neighbors (KNN), linear regression (LR) and decision trees (DT).

Ecentually, the possible use od the data analysis was presented. Among the crucial information one can find details about the possible infection zones with relatively higher number of infected patients. Additionally, a concept of system capable to observe the symptoms in case of people suspected towards COVID-19 and automatically predict the potential disease was proposed.

2.3 Real-Time Prediction and Risk Estimation for COVID-19 New Cases

A main goal of the work [1] was the generation of short-term (in real time) future prediction of future COVID-19 cases for multiple countries along with the risk estimation for selected contries with the highest number of cases. The presented idea assumed finding different, important demographic features of countries connected with some disease symptoms. To resolve the first issue, a hybrid approach based on the self-regresive, integrated model of moving average and prediction model based on Wavlet, which can generate short-term predeicions of confirmed cases. Authors assumed, that predictions of future increase of cases in different countries would be crucial to effectively distribute resources available in the healthcare. Moreover, it would be a potentially good early warning system. In the second problem, the optimal regression tree algorithm was used, to find the basic casual variables, which will significantly affect the fatality ratio in different countries. The initial prediction assumed the risk estimation for 50 countries.

In the article a classical and modern prediction methods were analyzed. The proposed research assumed the use of the hybrid models to generate short-term predictions for different countries. In the classical prediction of time series, the Autoregressive integrated moving average (ARIMA) model is used mainly to predict the linear time series. However, in the newest literature, the model based on the wavelet forecasting presented very good performance in the non-stationary modelling of time series. In such case, authors assumed, that combination of both models could improve the modelling of such complex autocorrelation structures in the COVID-19 datasets. Moreover, the standard deviation and variance of error could be minimized.

Due to fast-changing data acquired from pandemic situations, an estimated fatality ratio for 50 countries were calculated. This was done from the start of the pandemic to 4 April 2020. Conducted analysis was focused to deriving the set of possible variables, which could be crucial casual variables to estimating the COVID-19 risk for the most affected by pandemic countries. To estimate the risk a regression tree (RT) was used. The proposed method included the mechanism to feature selection, was easy ti interpret and assured the good visualisation. Acquired results were consistent with the claim, that overall number of cases as well as the age distribution has significantly affect the case fatality ratio.

2.4 Spatial Analysis in the Context of COVID-19 Pandemic

Authors [11] focused on the analysis of the numerical data for virus as well as the spatial information. To perform the analysis, self-organizing maps (SOM) were used. This method is in general extension of the classical unsupervised neural networks. The idea was to use the neural networks to classify the 199 countries as well as the 32 Mexico states to estimate, if there is dependency between the region and the number of cases.

Additionally, besides the use of SOM to visualize the groups based on the similarity, two popular diseases: diabetes and high blood presure were taken into account to estimate the quality of clasification derived by the self-organizing maps.

Analysis of the spatial evolution of pandemic around the world was presented. In general, the countries with similar COVID-19 cases were grouped in clusters.

2.5 Screening Tests and COVID-19 Prediction

In work [21] authors suggested, that an effective screening tests towards SARS-CoV-2 could lead to fast and effective diagnosis and can visibly decrease the burden of the healthcare system. A few different prediction models used to estimate the risk of infection were derived. Such models could potentially assist the medical personel around the world to select difficult cases – this is crucial due to overall healthcare resource limitations. Model presented by authors predicts the positive test result (for popular RT-PCR test) on the basis of 8 questions related to sex, age, potential contact with the infected, as well as the presence of first symptoms. Model was used in the Izreal in first moths of pandemic.

A different prediciton models connecting different features related to estimating the infection risk were discussed. This is due to fact, that for the most cases, the hospital personel is often forced to select patients, which could be admitted to hospital. These models used the concepts like computer tomography, clinical symptoms, laboratory tests and integration of above concepts. It was pointed out, that majority of previous models was based on the hospitalized patients, which affected the relatively low efficiency of models adapted towards screening tests.

2.6 Hybrid Machine Learning and Metaheuristics in the Prediction of COVID-19 Cases

A main goal of the article [20] was the future improvement of algorithms based on the hybrids of machine learning methods and nature-inspired algorithms. Authors note, that due to COVID-19 almost all countries were forced to introduce measures and regulations to prevent the virus spreading.

Authors proposed the prediction model representing the hybrid approach based on the machine learning, adaptive reasoning neuro-fuzzy system and metaheuristic based on the beetle antennae search. Authors noted, that extended search approach presented by the last algorithm can be used to estimate the parameters of adaptive system and overall improvement of the prediction model.

Improved algorithm was tested and verified on the basis of wide set of data. It was shown, that the proposed method outperforms original implementation. Further, proposed method was compared with other existing approaches, which were tested on the same data. Results of simulations and analysis shown, that the proposed method outperforms other complex approaches and can be usefull tool in the prediction of time series.

2.7 Early Risk Prediction for Patients on the Basis of Hospital Data

Authors in work [5] noticed, that despite the fact, that the epodemiological as well as clinical COVID-19 features were described relatively well, we still lack of information about the risk factors related with mild to severe organism response for COVID-19.

In this research authors analyzed 879 patients with positive SARS-CoV-2 result hospitalized in NHS Trust (London, England) in the period from 1 January to 26 May 2020. The vast majority of cases have place in March and April. Authors separated anonimized demographic data, physiological clinic variables as well as the laboratory results taken from the Electronic medical documentation (EMD). A multivariate logistic regression, Random forest and gradient boosted decision trees were used. To evaluate the early risk estimation, authors used the data acquired from the initial patient examination at hospital. A three clinical points were examined: admitting the patient at intensive care, invasive treatment, mechanical ventilation, and mortality at the hospital. Eventually such research lead to extract the crucial clinical features used to predict the future patient's condition.

Authors concluded, that among the COVID-19 patients, the machine learning could help in the early identification of patients with relatively bad prognossis with the use of the EMD and information colleced during the first patient visit at hospital. Additionaly, it was pointed out, that age of patient and oxygenation are the main indicators of poor prognosis.

3 Polynomial Regression

Regression can be found among the most popular machine learning models. Regression is used to predict the decision attribute presented as the real number. This is done on the basis of remaining attributes. In the case of classification, the value from finite (mostly small) set including decision attribute values is selected. Similarities between regressin and classification cover aspects such as: building the model, testing and predicion of unknown values on the basis of model built in step 1. Additionaly, to build a model, data is divided into testing and training set.

Among the differences between classificaion and regression it is worth mentioning, that in the case of regression, the value of the decision attribute is continuous, which for obvious reasons leads to difficulties in estimating the exact values of decision attribute in testing set. Moreover, in the case of regression, a prediction of value is made on the basis of calculating the new decision attribute value for a new case (in the classification a decision attribute value is set on the basis of assigning value from the available set of values.

Polynomial regression [16] is a specific form of linear regression. It allows to detect the non-linear dependencies between the output and input data. According to Eq. (1):

$$y = b_0 + b_1x + b_2x^2 + b_3x^3 + \cdots + b_nx^n + E \tag{1}$$

where y is the polynomial function, which will be used to prediction, x is the input variable, $b_0, b_1 \cdots b_n$ are regression coefficients (which we are looking for), n is the number of features, while E is the free element.

Polynomial regression is a form of regression, where a polynomial of n-th degree is used to find the correlation allowing for prediction. Predicion of values is made on the basis of weighted sum of features for the input data, which are raised to proper power as well as the free element.

In opposite to the classical linear regression, the polynomial regression can fit model to non-linear characteristic of the value distribution in given time. It allows to generate much more precise prediction related with the COVID-19. It is especially important due to fact, that prognozed COVID-19 aspects like number of cases or fatality ratio are not (and for sure won't be in future) linear. Models presented in the further part of this article analyzed by authors will be based on the third degree polynomial.

4 Experiments

Goal of this article was the review of works related with the COVID-19 cases prediction. However, in the experimental section we focus on the evaluating quality of prediction based on the polynomial regression. Additionally, we invesigated, what is the impact of the traind set on the quality of prediction.

4.1 Data Set

In the experiments we used real-world data including the number of confirmed cases for the COVID-19 [6]. In the first phase of experiments we selected data for 179 days starting from 1st September 2020. This date was used due to large number of new cases in successive months, and obviously shows great complexity and eventually difficulties with prediction.

For experiments we selected four datasets – it is related with different characteristics of data: China (country, where first cases were confirmed). Italy (country, in which the exponential growth of new cases was observed in the first pandemic wave), Poland (country, with relatively small number of cases in the first wave, however with massive growth of new cases in the second wave) and world.

Length of prediction will be equal to 26 days and these are validation data not taken into account during the process of generating the model. Remaining 153 days were used to learn the model – learning and testing. Experiments were conducted for four different cases: 50% train; 85% train, 99% train, and 99.5% train. It reflects a few cases related with the pandemic growth as well as a time, which is included in the analysis. The lesser the train data affects the shorten time for model train and vice versa. In the last case 152 days were used to train and test, and 26 days was used to predict data on the basis of derived model.

Polynomial regression was chosen for the experiments as the most common approach in the literature used for this type of time series plotting. Other machine learning algorithms are described in Sect. refsec:rev, but polynomial regression is analysed in detail. Unlike linear regression, polynomial regression can fit a model to the curvilinear characteristics of the distribution of instrument values over a given time period. This will make it possible to generate much more accurate predictions of the number of incidences of Covid-19. The assumptions of applicability are the same as in multiple regression, so, for example, the degree of the polynomial must be much lower than the number of observations. The models that will be presented in this paper are those containing degree 3 polynomial regression.

4.2 Results of Experiments

On Fig. 1 we can see the confirmed cases of COVID-19 in China, as well as the results for four prediction models based on the polynomial regression. Despite the differences between the actual and predicted cases (due to pandemic stage), the most relevant results were achieved in the case of model, for which data

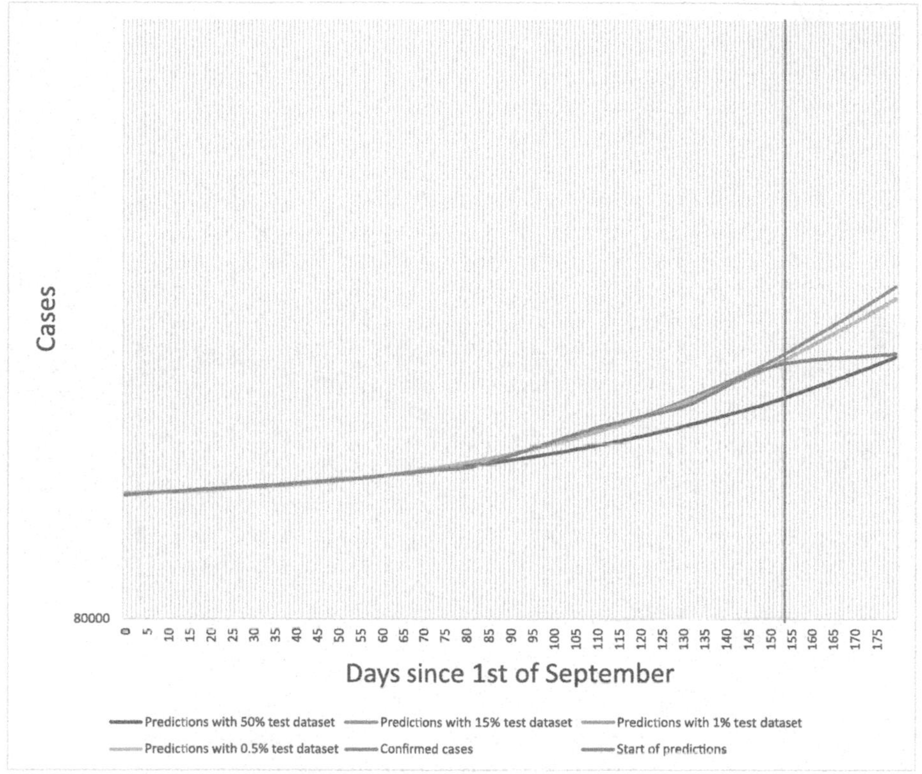

Fig. 1. Comparison of prediction of COVID-19 cases for China

were divided for 50% learn and 50% test data. Remaining models (in opposite to confirmed cases) indicated the visible rise of the number of COVID-19 cases. The highest differences was observed in the case of model including 85% of train data.

Figure 2 presents confirmed cases of COVID-19 in Italy, as well as the predictions made by different polynomial regression models. Despite the decreasing tendency, predictions closest to the actually observed number of cases was achieved by the model, in which train data was set to 99.5%. The only model, for which the predictions were similar to the actual reported cases (the rising tendency of confirmed cases) was achieved by the model including 50% of train data. Unfortunately, test data as well as the predictions differ a lot from the actual reported number of COVID-19 cases.

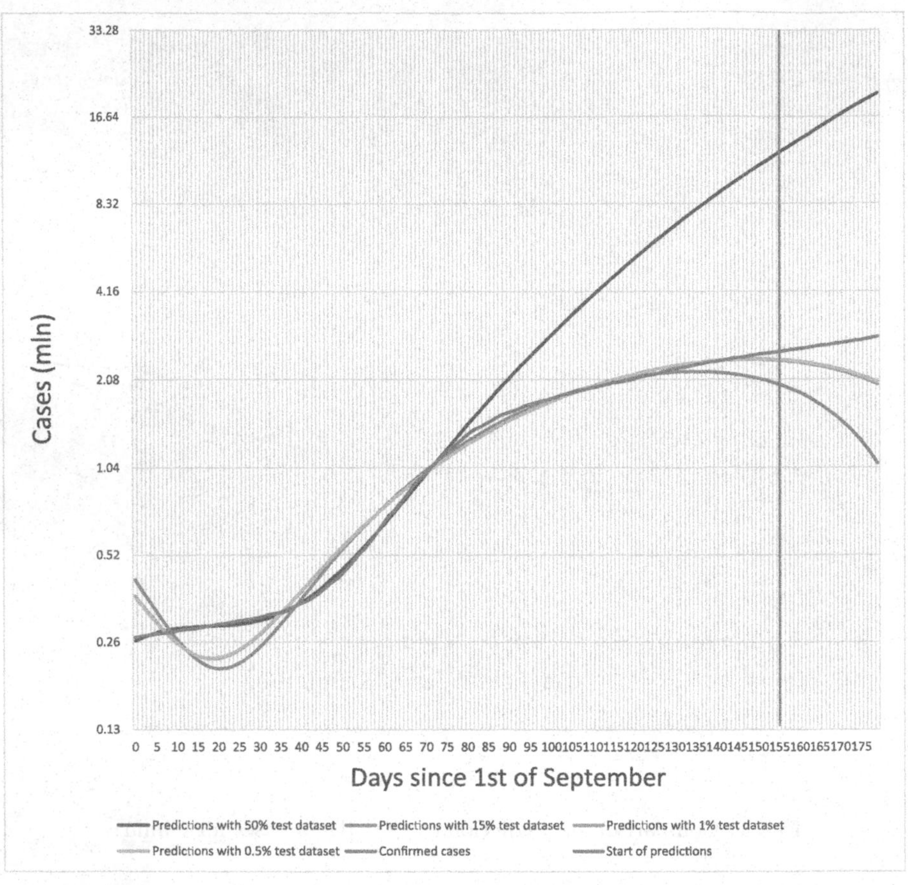

Fig. 2. Comparison of prediction of COVID-19 cases for Italy

Figure 3 presents the confirmed cases for COVID-19 in Poland as well as the results for four models. In this case, the best results were achieved for the model, where train data was equal to 99.5%, while slightly worse results were achieved for model with 99% (which was equal to 1 day shorter set). The worst data were obtained for the model with 50% of data in train set, however, it was the only model, for which the rising tendency (the same, as the actual trend) was observed.

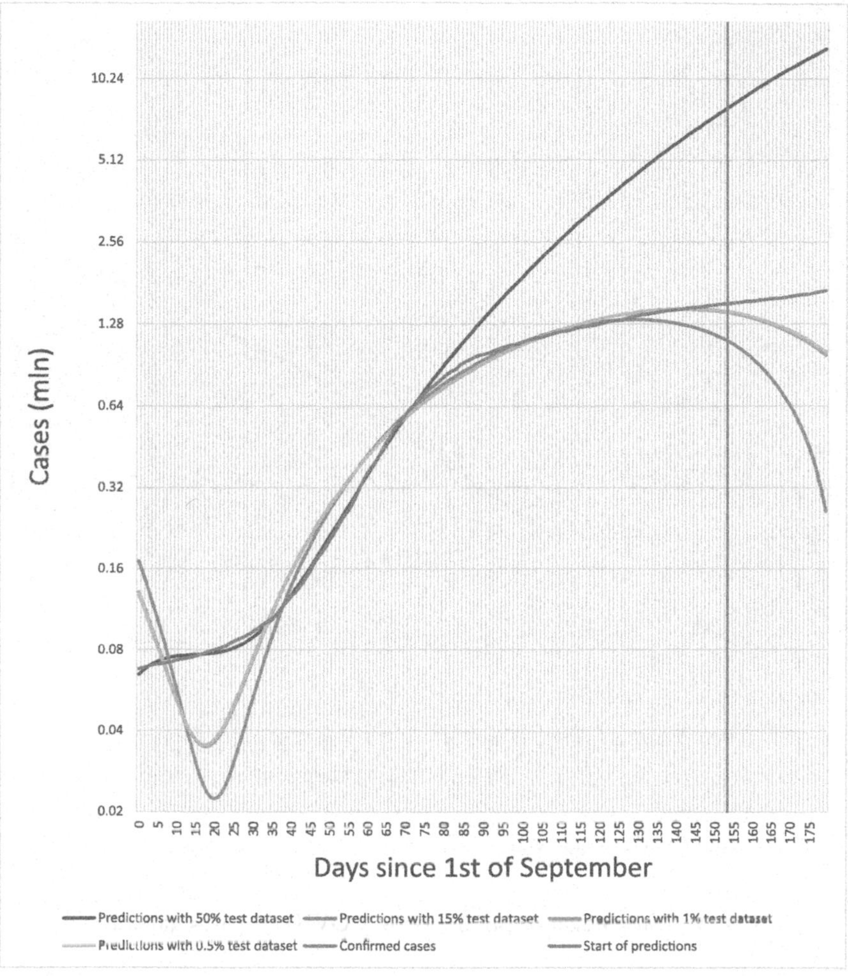

Fig. 3. Comparison of prediction of COVID-19 cases for Poland

At Fig. 4 the confirmed COVID-19 cases around the world were presented. The most similar results (to the actually observed number of cases) were achieved for the model, for which the train data was equal to 99%, however only slightly worse results were observed for the model with 99.5% data. Results in the case, where data was equal to 50% included the largest error (in comparison to actual number of confirmed cases).

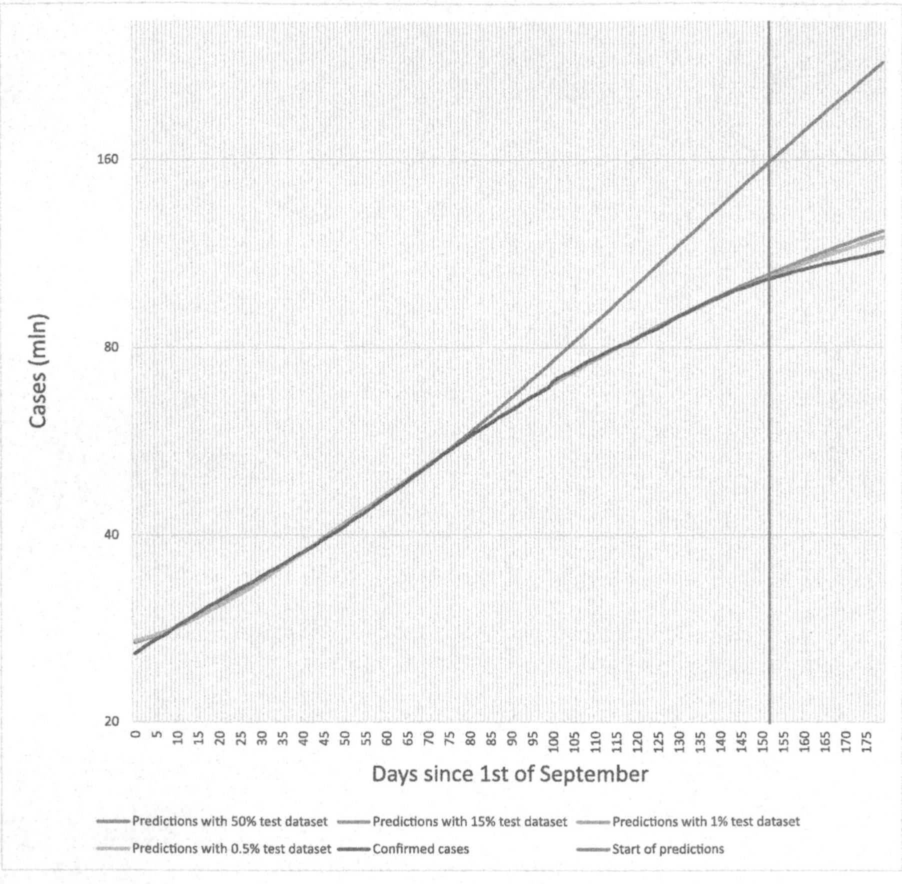

Fig. 4. Comparison of prediction of COVID-19 cases globally

5 Conclusions

The impact of the artificial intelligence, and even more, the machine learning methods on the making the pandemic-related decisions is undeniable. It should be pointed out, that at the beginning of the COVID-19 pandemic, acquired data and use of the different methods (both classical, as well as hybrid) had a visible impact on different fields of science related with the situation.

According to one of the goals of the article, a detailed review of selected pandemic-related articles was made. An experimental approach based on the polynomial regression was proposed as well.

It was experimentally verified, that in the case of polynomial regression, use of the large train test allows to better fit the unusual characteristic of positive COVID-19 cases. However, it was very difficult to detect the sudden rise of the cases at the second wave of the pandemic, and additional external actions (possibly related with need of more domain knowledge) could be needed. In the future additional methods, for example combined with classical linear regression, should be examined as well. Moreover, including the concepts based on the collective intelligence and other approximate methods could lead to a better fit the predictions. This seems to be extremely important due to fact, that a shape of function responsible for predicting future number of cases even in the moment, where several different vaccines are available, is still very difficult, and most of the classical methods fail to achieve sufficient results.

References

1. Chakraborty, T., Ghosh, I.: Real-time forecasts and risk assessment of novel coronavirus (covid-19) cases: a data-driven analysis. Chaos, Solitons Fractals **135**, 109850 (2020)
2. Davenport, T., Kalakota, R.: The potential for artificial intelligence in healthcare. Future Healthcare J. **6**(2), 94 (2019)
3. De Felice, F., Polimeni, A.: Coronavirus disease (covid-19): a machine learning bibliometric analysis. Vivo **34**(3 suppl), 1613–1617 (2020)
4. Hanook, S., Shahbaz, M.Q., Mohsin, M., Golam Kibria, B.: A note on beta inverse-weibull distribution. Commun. Stat. Theor. Methods **42**(2), 320–335 (2013)
5. Heldt, F.S., et al.: Early risk assessment for covid-19 patients from emergency department data using machine learning. Sci. Rep. **11**(1), 1–13 (2021)
6. Kaggle: Novel corona virus 2019 dataset (2020), data retrieved from. https://www.kaggle.com/sudalairajkumar/novel-corona-virus-2019-dataset
7. Kannan, S., Subbaram, K., Ali, S., Kannan, H.: The role of artificial intelligence and machine learning techniques: race for covid-19 vaccine. Archives of Clinical Infectious Diseases, vol. 15, no. 2 (2020)
8. Kushwaha, S., et al.: Significant applications of machine learning for covid-19 pandemic. Journal of Industrial Integration and Management, vol. 5, no. 4 (2020)
9. Lalmuanawma, S., Hussain, J., Chhakchhuak, L.: Applications of machine learning and artificial intelligence for covid-19 (sars-cov-2) pandemic: a review. Chaos, Solitons Fractals **139**, 110059 (2020)
10. Roser, M., Ritchie, H., Ortiz-Ospina, E., Hasell, J.: Coronavirus pandemic (covid-19). Our World in Data (2020). https://ourworldindata.org/coronavirus
11. Melin, P., Monica, J.C., Sanchez, D., Castillo, O.: Analysis of spatial spread relationships of coronavirus (covid-19) pandemic in the world using self organizing maps. Chaos, Solitons Fractals **138**, 109917 (2020)
12. Mondal, M.R.H., Bharati, S., Podder, P., Podder, P.: Data analytics for novel coronavirus disease. Inform. Med. Unlocked **20**, 100374 (2020)
13. Ong, E., Wong, M.U., Huffman, A., He, Y.: Covid-19 coronavirus vaccine design using reverse vaccinology and machine learning. Front. Immunol. **11**, 1581 (2020)
14. Pham, Q., Nguyen, D.C., Huynh-The, T., Hwang, W., Pathirana, P.N.: Artificial intelligence (ai) and big data for coronavirus (covid-19) pandemic: a survey on the state-of-the-arts. IEEE Access **8**, 130820–130839 (2020)
15. Phillips-Wren, G., Ichalkaranje, N.: Intelligent decision making: An AI-based approach, vol. 97. Springer Science & Business Media (2008). https://doi.org/10.1007/978-3-540-76829-6
16. Stigler, S.M.: Gergonne's 1815 paper on the design and analysis of polynomial regression experiments. Historia Math. **1**(4), 431–439 (1974) https://doi.org/10.1016/0315-0860(74)90033-0, https://www.sciencedirect.com/science/article/pii/0315086074900330

17. Sujath, R., Chatterjee, J.M., Hassanien, A.E.: A machine learning forecasting model for covid-19 pandemic in india. Stochast. Environ. Res. Risk Assess. **34**, 959–972 (2020)
18. Tárnok, A.: Machine learning, covid-19 (2019-ncov), and multi-omics. Cytometry **97**(3), 215 (2020)
19. Tuli, S., Tuli, S., Tuli, R., Gill, S.S.: Predicting the growth and trend of covid-19 pandemic using machine learning and cloud computing. Internet Things **11**, 100222 (2020)
20. Zivkovic, M., et al.: Covid-19 cases prediction by using hybrid machine learning and beetle antennae search approach. Sustain. Cities Soc. **66**, 102669 (2021)
21. Zoabi, Y., Deri-Rozov, S., Shomron, N.: Machine learning-based prediction of covid-19 diagnosis based on symptoms. NPJ Digit. Med. **4**(1), 1–5 (2021)

Web Scraping Methods Used in Predicting Real Estate Prices

Tomasz Jach[1,2(✉)]

[1] Department of Machine Learning, University of Economics in Katowice, 1 Maja 50, 40-287 Katowice, Poland
tomasz.jach@ue.katowice.pl
[2] HomeTime.ai, Katowice, Poland
http://www.hometime.ai

Abstract. Currently, a significant increase is observed in offers number related to, among others, with the real estate market. More and more clients are looking for real estate on dedicated portals. However, too much data and the number of websites related to the real estate market and the dependence of this market on many factors make it very difficult for the end user to have data presented in a single place. Therefore, a good solution is to prepare a tool that serves as an initial expert system helping to make the decision. In this paper we are using different web scraping methods to obtain data from the real estate market. For the Polish market, the data is either not free of charge or scattered around multiple different sources. The end goal is to make predictions about price; therefore, quality of data acquisition is crucial. The solution is to combine different methods of web scraping and crawling into a complete solution presented here as an actual use case study with guidelines and good practices. The presented systems is successfully running and being a data source for real estate market predictions.

Keywords: Web scraping · Real estate price evaluation · Case study · Data quality

1 Introduction

The real estate market is an enormous and intimidating place to be. It does not matter whether one wants to buy or sell a property; there is always the matter of uncertainty if the price is right. And simultaneously there are a lot of factors, most of them are changing in time, which have to be taken into account to make a proper decision. To some extent, most of the decision were made during a visit in a given property with emotions playing the major role. Before visiting a property, one has to go through a lot of offers scattered on different websites and other medias.

That's where the web scraping and crawling techniques might help. Crawling is a process of finding links on a given page pointing to specific resources of interest, while scraping is considered the download end extraction phase when

K. Wojtkiewicz et al. (Eds.): ICCCI 2021, CCIS 1463, pp. 375–387, 2021.
https://doi.org/10.1007/978-3-030-88113-9_30

an address is given. Constructing an efficient service which combines these two modules with a proper quality is a challenge. Despite having relatively many methods of doing that, the process of choosing the right one is daunting and often involves tailoring different methods and combining them into one.

For instance, the authors of [20] present the survey of different scrapping techniques. They do not apply them to a single use case, but rather point out the advantages and drawbacks of each one. They also scrap whole websites and do not extract individual information for a site. This is done in a second study ([11] where the example is far more comprehensive. Other researchers in [2] go one step further and use cloud-based computing in scraping big data. The problem of fast data acquisition and clean-up is also considered on a legal basis in [14]; the authors of [8] even consider bypassing both legal and programmatic restrictions to access data on Twitter.

Scrapping is done with multiple types of data: weather in South Sumatra [16], travel and hospitality research [6], companies and entrepreneurs [12] and of course finance [15]. This all leads to a conclusion, that data is often spread across multiple web pages and needs to be combined to become a proper data set: big enough and with sufficient quality.

In terms of web scraping methods, as it is going to be shown in the following sections, multiple methods exists today. The authors of [22] present the way of scrapping web-pages not involving the costly process of creating the DOM tree. This provided a performance boots, however for the cost of accuracy and loosing an information about the context of a search. The hospitality research article's [6] authors provide a skeleton Python code of web-scraping, which is unfortunately just a guideline and not a complete system. Apart from that, their solution is susceptible to small changes in DOM happening very often in real life applications. According to [19], web scrapping was understood as a simple process (called "pattern mining") of extracting headers and identifying them using HTML tags. This is also an ideal situation very seldom happening on real-life pages contain real estate adverts.

The following chapters are going to provide both the details, along with good practices during the evaluation and scrapping of a material used as a basis of a machine learning approach of finding the most accurate price for a real-estate (in contrast to prices shown in the adverts). The novelty of this paper includes the comprehensive and holistic approach to obtaining data from live web-pages which are subject to constant change of the underlying source and DOM structure.

Having the data set, there are numerous examples of successfully applying machine learning methods to different use cases, like involving trading [10]. This paper presents a solution developed by a growing startup, HomeTime.AI. We wanted to fill the niche and provide an accurate and easy to use prediction of a real estate price based on multiple factors, including the location, similarity between other properties and other non-trivial features.

After the initial design period, we wanted to validate our approach and test using real data. As the transnational prices in Poland are not easily accessible (one has to have a real state license), we have decided to validate the solutions using advertised prices presented in public and free-to-access web pages. The whole project is currently ongoing and in a state of real-time validation. During the last couple of months, we have already established some guidelines and good practices for this kind of task, which are shared in this paper.

The remainder of this paper is organized as follows. Section 2 explains the details of different web scraping methods. Multiple approaches are discussed with comments about real-life applications, pitfalls and obstacles to avoid. The following section explains the details and benefits from using machine-to-machine data exchange formats. Section 4 is a comprehensive case study of a working system using presented findings and approaches. The overall effectiveness metrics are shown and discussed here. Th paper is wrapped with conclusions containing future work propositions and a reference section.

2 Web-Scraping Methods

To transfer data from a web page to another destination, one has first to scrap this information. The term comes from reading, parsing and process the information found on a particular webpage. This process is usually fully automatic, as it takes a lot of time.

The web page extraction process can be divided into three main phases [4]. The first one, called crawling, is the phase in which the hyperlinks are identified and parsed. Not every link on a web page is worth following. For example, all the links which point to resources (images, cascade style sheets, JavaScript resources, etc.) are not worth downloading if one is interested in text extraction. The crawling process identifies the next links, which should be then followed to obtain more pages with meaningful content. This database of links is then used in the second phase - downloading.

Fetching the webpage requires either downloading the whole website using *cURL* or *wget* scripts or simulating a web browser and users' interactions. Frequently, a web pages design involves generated content that is only accessible after some user interaction, e.g. clicking a "Read more" link or starting the JavaScript snippet to load more content dynamically. That's why simulating the web browser with an artificial user is the closest to real browsing. However, this process is significantly slower than the separate download of the whole static page.

Once the fetch part is complete, the final task - extraction - may commence. This is the most challenging and crucial process, as the typical webpage can spawn multiple layers of embedment inside the Document Object Model [23]. Modern web pages are built to be easily readable by humans, but this comes with the drawback of being hard to process automatically. One man's drawback is another one's advantage, though - usually, the data presented on a web page is valuable, and most companies do not want to share it with others without a fee.

The extraction can be done in multiple ways [21]. Manual copy-paste, which uses a human reader which collects the necessary information by hand and moves it to a destination. This method, however very accurate, is not widely commonly used, as the resources needed are huge and usually do not justify the use of manual labour. However, if one must build a small database of information found on a web page that is particularly difficult to scrap automatically, this method might provide good results. Being present is often not enough - users ten to submit information in vastly different formats, which have to be taken into account. For instance, the area can be given in metrical (from a standard m^2, a to ha) and imperial units (which also vary). Even though, we are analysing the Polish market, the prices are often set in different European currencies.

In the early days of *HomeTime.AI*, we used this method to find out which information is present in most adverts. This way, we were able to identify the possible features of a machine learning model which had the least missing data. Despite this method being cumbersome and boring, it can provide multiple insights into the underlying data set when done by a trained specialist.

Text extraction using regular expressions is the first and least sophisticated method of automatic extraction. To perform it, one has to develop a series of regular expressions [9] which match and extract the desired data. This method is quite effective when the number of extracted information is relatively small, and the features have a predictable format.

For example, we use this method to extract information about the address of a property. The problem with this approach is that the addresses can be written using a different order of elements. One of insights after first data analysis was that in Poland people are less willing to provide real estate address in advertise. The typical address consists of a street, building number, zip code and a city. To find a proper one, we try to extract each of this information individually and identify the address part as the cluster on a webpage with the most number of hits for individual parts of an address. To find a street name, we use some common prefixes denoting a street (like *ul.*, *al.*, *pl.*). The zip code is the easiest one, as it is standardised across the whole country.

HTML parsing uses extra information provided by the HTML tags. The newest standard provides a special kind of semantic tags specially designed to make the webpage more readable by automatic scrapers[1]. In a real life application, these are often used when present. However, many web pages failed to accommodate this approach, as it is a fairly new standard.

Document Object Model (DOM) parsing is a method that we commonly used. The DOM is a hierarchical structure of a web page that can be thought of as a web page map. Each element is placed inside this tree-like structure and thus - can be easily found using tree traversing algorithms. Usually, one uses the xPath address to identify the single element unequivocally. This method, as shown in the [5] can be both highly effective and fast.

Being the go-to web scraping method, it is also the most blocked by websites. As the DOM traversing is done in a fully deterministic matter, web- sites often incorporate artificial empty HTML elements, such as `<div></div>` or `<span></span>` tags to change the xPath of a given element. This is benign

[1] See: https://www.w3schools.com/tags/tag_address.asp.

for the end-user using a web browser but provides a significant obstacle for an automatic crawler.

The real-life scenario of using xPath is to get a part of a web page that other methods then analyse. From our observations, most of the interesting parts of a webpage have a short path. This is true because the web pages are designed to keep users' limited focus on elements that are present vertically higher on o webpage (and thus - being earlier in DOM). Furthermore, this method can read the dynamically generated and content and - to some extent - simulate user's behaviour on a page.

Vertical aggregation platforms are specialised platforms that gather data from specific types of web pages that share a similar design. Usually, such platforms are crafted and tailored software that can scale to hundreds of thousands of scraps per second to extract information from a group of pages before any changes in page structure prohibits them from working correctly.

This approach is actively blocked by most of the sites with lots of valuable data by automatic methods which try to classify the traffic into two categories: human and bot traffic. The details of how to do it correctly and how bots pretend to be human are beyond the scope of this paper but can be found in [7,13,18].

The computer vision approach uses the premise that everything worth scraping is visible to the human eye. This family of methods does not rely on a page source, nor it does rely on the structure. Most of the time, a page is treated as an image that needs to be processed by Optical Character Recognition (OCR) software. This makes all the security measures discussed before obsolete and not applicable.

However tempting, these methods rely completely on the quality of OCR software. The quality of the input image is superb, but the semantics of a webpage has to be discovered - either by manually giving the positioning of the interesting parts of a page or by semantics discoveries (often also the regexp method).

All of the above methods use information that was not designed to be read automatically. Apart from some semantic HTML tags, each method tries to add context or find the meaning of a found text. On the other hand, modern web pages are usually separated into the back-end part (which is serving the information) and the front end (displaying it). The efficient way to exchange data between them uses machine-to-machine data formats, such as JSON or XML.

3 Machine-to-Machine Data Formats

When it comes to exchanging the data between two machine consumers, one must choose the proper format of messages. The first and most important factor is if the format of the messages should be read-only directly by machine interfaces or (for example, for debugging purposes) the format has to be understandable for humans. The machine-only formats are mostly serialised binary messages that need to be deserialised to be human-readable. Two of the most common ones include Avro and Google Protocol Buffers. Both of them are self-validated methods of messages serialisation and deserialisation with a great deal of performance [17]; however, they are not directly readable by humans.

JSON and XML are the two most popular data exchange formats which a person can directly view without deserialisation. XML documents contain tagged data. That is, every piece of information has to be labelled, creating a tree-like structure. In XML, tags define the structure and meaning of data: they tell what specific data is. By describing the structure and meaning of data, one can reuse that data in different ways. In other words, one can use a system to generate data and tag it with XML tags and then process that data on any other system, regardless of hardware platform or operating system. Portability is one of the reasons why XML has become one of the most popular data exchange technologies [3]. In some cases, XML becomes a standard domain language, as it happened with the real estate market in Australia[2].

Each information is labelled correctly and easy to understand by a human. Another observation shows that the amount of extra information (like closing and opening of tags) is significant and can influence the speed of processing this kind of messages. This addition does not occur when using the binary formats discussed above.

JSON (JavaScript Object Notation) is an open format for saving data structures. JSON consists of attribute-value pairs and array data types. Its notation is similar to JavaScript objects. The two primary parts that make up JSON are keys and values. Together they make a pair. A key is always a string enclosed in quotation marks, while a value can be a string, number, Boolean expression, array, or an object. Its advantages are popularity, simplicity of operation, the brevity of the syntax. It was created in 2001 [1].

4 Case Study: Adverts of Polish Real-Estate Market

In December 2020, a group of developers gathered around applying machine learning methods to predict the prices on a real estate market. They wanted to develop a universal solution, which will work on any property market - both for buying and selling and renting. In order to build an efficient model, real data had to be acquired. Unfortunately, the real transactional data for the Polish market is out of scope for a non-professional person who does not hold the real-estate market license. The process of obtaining it is long and involves multiple exams to be passed. The other option is to fill in the prices requests for each government agencies spread across the country. Every application filled in is an extra cost, both in time invested in preparing it and quite high fees for considering the application.

That is why the idea of gathering the offer prices emerged. To do that in an efficient and fast way, we had to develop a custom made set of crawlers and parsers to look for prices over the internet. The crawlers, however crucial, are

[2] https://help.realestate.com.au/hc/en-us/articles/115004127963-REAXML-Documentation.

out of the scope of this paper. It is enough to say that they identify the actual adverts on a page and are able to follow the links to obtain web addresses of properties with more than 99,9% effectiveness measured as the ratio between actual adverts overall identified links.

4.1 Manual Rewrite of Adverts

The first approach involved manual extraction of information found on multiple real-estate portals. This was a lengthy but needed process. We found out that all of the adverts fall into two categories during that period: filled in by professionals and by individuals. The first group of adverts is usually very well written. Most of the information is given directly, all the special fields (such as extra features of property) are also filled in. The professionals often use automatic programs to add many offers at once, which are very similar to each other. All the technical and numerical fields were submitted most of the time.

On the other hand, the property description was full of buzzwords and other attractive content, which surprisingly did not tell much about the property (or the neighbourhood). During that time, the specialised software for cleaning up the description was developed. This application took the description and extracted interesting keywords, providing the condensed and machine-readable form of an advert. We chose the JSON format to store the information due to its brevity and being readable by humans and machine interfaces. Apart from taking the keywords, the prototype of an advert scored was proposed. This score took the description of an advert and, by using the semantic analysis, was computing the "fairness factor" understood as the amount of real information inside an advert without the buzzwords.

The second group of adverts were the ones filled indirectly by the individual owners. Here, the opposite case was often observed: the description was full of concrete information, while the numeric and categorical values were often omitted.

It was quickly clear that most of the adverts on web pages are partially structured. Consider the fragments of advert pages shown on Fig. 1. All of the analysed portals have a part reassembling a table in which the summary of numerical and categorical values is shown.

4.2 Automatic Scraping of Adverts

After the first initial phase of manually scraping the adverts, we decided to write a set of scrapers for different sources of adverts. We used a hybrid approach combining multiple scraping methods described earlier.

After the first initial phase of manually scraping the adverts, we decided to write a set of scrapers for different sources of adverts. We used a hybrid approach combining multiple scraping methods described earlier. Initially, we have prepared the xPath internal database of web pages fragments with specific information, which was validated using hundreds of adverts. Our internal quality measure was set to 80% of hits using a particular record. In other words, an xPath

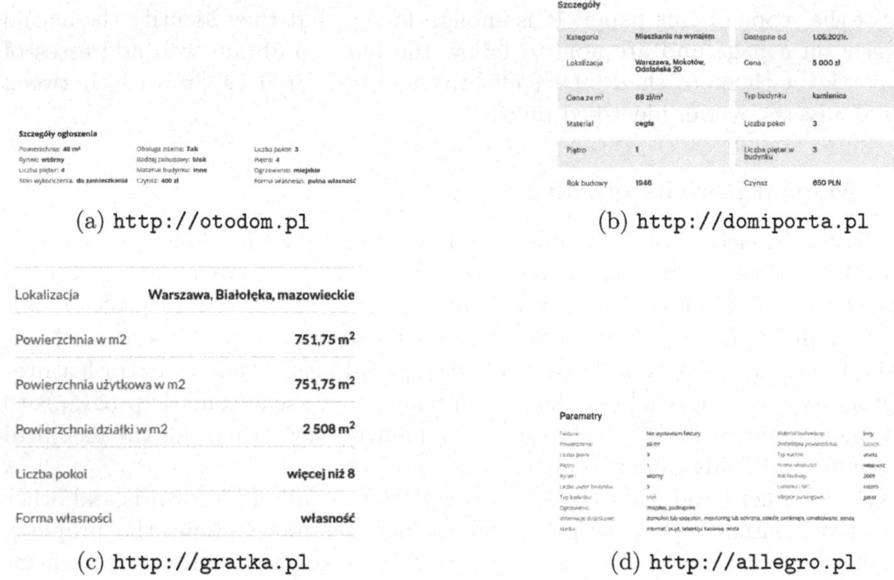

(a) `http://otodom.pl` (b) `http://domiporta.pl`

(c) `http://gratka.pl` (d) `http://allegro.pl`

Fig. 1. Fragments of adverts on different portals.

was considered valid when it allowed reading more than 80% of pages belonging to a single advert provider. This database should be dynamically validated, and when the quality measures are degraded, the manual input is required to find out the reason for failures. As mentioned before, the fragments chosen by this approach are broad, so small changes inside the DOM are not affecting the whole process.

The example of this database in JSON format is shown in Fig. 2:

This database is constantly updated and growing over time. In the future, the automatic way of finding the proper records will be proposed. The *baseUrl* points to a specific website which is redacted due to company secret policies.

Having the fragment of a web page with information about what to look at on that part, the actual extraction occurs. We use a combination of regular expressions, DOM traversing and repair mechanisms to find the proper values. For instance, although the number usually gives the floor number in a house of flats, a few advert providers are not validating the input of this field when a user is submitting an ad. This leads to the values of this field being inputted as text (e.g. "basement", "higher than 10 floors", "cellar", "garret"). This made the regexp approach wholly unusable, and we had to revert to fixing the exact xPath location of this field value. Apart from that, the machine learning model requires the numerical input here, so there's a repair function that takes the known phrases and changes them to a number.

It was crucial here that on every unsuccessful reading of a field, the parse should log the exact value and information about the advert, date, and metadata to fix it during the next run. This is an entirely automatic process followed by

```
{"service_1": {
    "baseUrl": "<redacted>",
    "xPaths": [
        {
        "section": "title",
        "xPath": "/html/body/div[3]/div[2]/div/div/div/div[3]/h1",
        "validFrom": "2020-12-01T00:00:00",
        "validTo": "2021-03-14T13:21:10",
        }
    ]
    }
}
```

Fig. 2. xPath database record example

manually adding the repair mappings, which boosted the overall accuracy of scraping significantly. From our experience, using the automatic repairs here (like the Levenstein distance to fix the typos or more sophisticated text mining) did not give better results and was vastly more difficult to design and develop.

Some of the elements on a webpage were already prepared for automatic reading. For instance, a few of the fields were given as valid JSON values but were hidden inside the comments in the HTML source. Identifying them was also a manual process but turned out to be a great success.

4.3 The Results and Metrics Used

In the real estate market, time is crucial. The second most valuable factor is accurate information. To have them both, we have developed our complete solution which starts with finding and scraping information from public sources, correcting it, enriching additional features and serving it to the end customer. Because of the nature of this process, the constant monitoring of different pieces is vital. One of the most important metrics is the scrap delay. When an advert goes online, it should be added to our internal database as soon as possible. On the other hand, however, the crawlers and scrapers have to respect the fairness and politeness thresholds that reassemble normal traffic on a given website. It is no use to scrap and crawl web pages with a full speed of a cloud provider just to be blocked immediately or cause problems in the source websites. Figure 3 shows the delay between the time of the advert showing up on the internet and it being scraped to our database. The time-series axis is set to present roughly an hour of traffic. It is clear that one of the services (shown with a yellow line) has far better delay times, usually measured in seconds. It is being scraped with a higher speed than the second one because of the far simpler webpage design. The size of a page is smaller by orders of magnitude (kilobytes vs megabytes), so is the DOM structure. This makes scraping and analysing information far more efficient, so we can scrap in a much shorter interval without impacting the

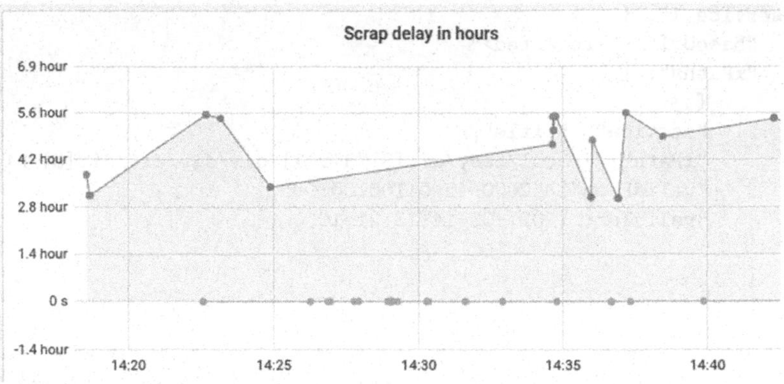

Fig. 3. Delay between advert showing up on the internet and it being scraped by our software. The two colors represent two different services. (Color figure online)

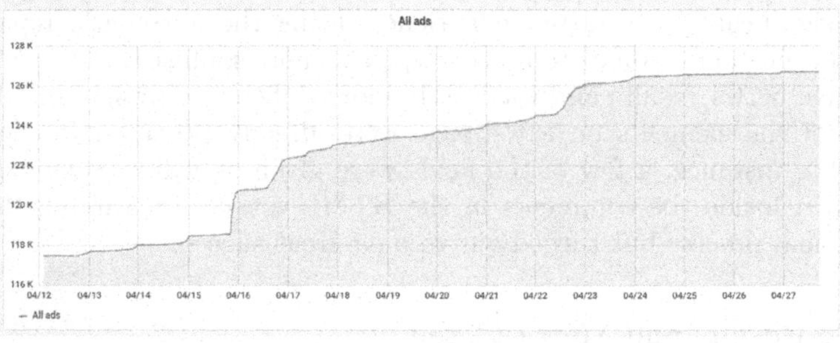

Fig. 4. The total number of adverts processed

normal service operation. The other service is scraped with a delay of a couple of hours. For the real opportunities in the real estate market, this time is currently subject to improvement.

Another interesting metric is the overall number of current adverts (Fig. 4) This measurement tells what is the size of the database used for our predictions and machine learning training. It is also the number of adverts which is currently active and ready to be bought. Both the total number matters, but also the slope of the curve. For instance, our software is capable of processing the bursts of adverts (see the point for April 15 around 20:00), usually added to the source services by agencies and professionals. This ads are reasonably similar to each other (most of the time, they are flats inside a single building), but usually, there are one or two offers which stand out and are more attractive than the others.

4.4 The Summary of the Proposed Machine Learning Model

The results of this paper are used to design and implement a machine learning algorithm which will estimate the "true" or "real" price of a real estate based on other properties ("features") which are similar in some way. Because of the limitation of using just the advertised prices as an input for training, this is still an estimation. Despite this fact, this approach is valid regardless of the prices used to estimate whether someone over- or under-priced in the advert. Using the transactional prices will be much more beneficial, however for Polish market it is a challenge to obtain these.

After much research and development, we established some minimal and necessary features which are essential to a low-error output of a machine learning model. This include: the exact location of a property, the usable area of the flat and the building type. Without this three features, the prediction error is far more greater, while the other factors such as heating type, date of construction or windows type are useful, but not crucial. Overall, we include this information as an input for the price estimation algorithm:

- Date of adding the advert
- The area of a property
- Construction date
- The number of rooms and total number of floors in a building
- A floor which the property is located at
- Condition of a property
- Ownership and building type (e.g. tenement house or a co-op apartment)
- Heating type, type of installed windows
- Exact address

There are other extra features used in HomeTime.AI solution, which further enhance the prediction, however the details exceed the scope of this paper. The exact address feature is also quite hard to obtain, as most of the adverts provide just a vague description with not enough accuracy, but we have found a few ways to increase the quality of this feature, mainly by combining multiple data source. The details of this approach will be presented in another paper.

The Table 1 present the percentage of missing values of a baseline solution (that is automatic scrapping with no improvements such as using context information, regexp extraction, DOM parsing, etc.) to the one currently used in HomeTime.AI.

Table 1. Percentage of missing values between different approaches

Type of a feature	Baseline solution	Improved solution
Area of property	3.68%	0.63%
Construction date	45.48%	32.66%
Number of rooms	24.89%	3.52%
Building type	40.48%	0.00%

5 Conclusions

Our proposed *HomeTime.AI* approach consisting of scrapers, crawlers and machine learning modules is now being in the validation phase. The current rapid growth of the company brings a lot of new ideas for the future. We want to speed up the crawling and scraping process for one of the underlying source services and use more sophisticated methods of semantic discovery of property description. Research and methods presented here were the foundations of a machine learning methods to predict the price. Because of the improvement in quality of data, this second step was possible. In the future we can find additional information in user-submitted texts and rely less on numerical data.

Also, the pictures inside the ads are interested in terms of extracting meaningful information using multi-label classification methods and multi-object detection. One can also extrapolate the real state of property not by taking it from the description (most of the people exaggerate with this value) but from the pictures themselves.

The ultimate goal of a system is to provide a user-friendly portal for the customers to ease a process of buying a property. This will be achieved by presenting them with an estimated price based on similar adverts and taking into account the current market status (thus, the date of adding an advert is crucial). Apart from that, the system will be able to merge duplicate adverts into a single one, regardless of the underlying data source. The solution is scalable in multiple ways: we are able to quickly add more data sources, such as additional advert sites or to quickly adapt the solution to a market in another country (some works have already been done and preliminary results show the same level of validity on one of the another European markets). Lastly, the scrappers and crawlers technologies combined with our experiences, allow to completely change the market to another good such as collectibles, single malt whisky or any other publicly tradable product.

References

1. Bray, T.: The JavaScript Object Notation (JSON) Data Interchange Format. RFC 8259, December 2017. https://doi.org/10.17487/RFC8259, https://rfc-editor.org/rfc/rfc8259.txt
2. Chaulagain, R.S., Pandey, S., Basnet, S.R., Shakya, S.: Cloud based web scraping for big data applications. In: 2017 IEEE International Conference on Smart Cloud (SmartCloud), pp. 138–143. IEEE (2017)
3. Chituc, C.M.: Xml interoperability standards for seamless communication: an analysis of industry-neutral and domain-specific initiatives. Comput. Ind. **92**, 118–136 (2017)
4. Glez-Peña, D., Lourenço, A., López-Fernández, H., Reboiro-Jato, M., Fdez-Riverola, F.: Web scraping technologies in an API world. Briefings Bioinform. **15**(5), 788–797 (2013). https://doi.org/10.1093/bib/bbt026
5. Gottlob, G., Koch, C., Pichler, R.: Efficient algorithms for processing xpath queries. ACM Trans. Database Syst. (TODS) **30**(2), 444–491 (2005)

6. Han, S., Anderson, C.K.: Web scraping for hospitality research: overview, opportunities, and implications. Cornell Hospitality Q. **62**(1), 89–104 (2021)
7. Haque, A., Singh, S.: Anti-scraping application development. In: 2015 International Conference on Advances in Computing, Communications and Informatics (ICACCI), pp. 869–874. IEEE (2015)
8. Hernandez-Suarez, A., Sanchez-Perez, G., Toscano-Medina, K., Martinez-Hernandez, V., Sanchez, V., Perez-Meana, H.: A web scraping methodology for bypassing twitter api restrictions. arXiv preprint arXiv:1803.09875 (2018)
9. Hosoya, H., Vouillon, J., Pierce, B.C.: Regular expression types for xml. ACM SIGPLAN Notices **35**(9), 11–22 (2000)
10. Juszczuk, P., Kozak, J., Kania, K.: Using similarity measures in prediction of changes in financial market stream data-experimental approach. Data Knowl. Eng. **125**, 101782 (2020). https://doi.org/10.1016/j.datak.2019.101782, https://www.sciencedirect.com/science/article/pii/S0169023X18306451
11. Karthikeyan, T., Sekaran, K., Ranjith, D., Balajee, J., et al.: Personalized content extraction and text classification using effective web scraping techniques. Int. J. Web Portals (IJWP) **11**(2), 41–52 (2019)
12. Kinne, J., Axenbeck, J.: Web mining of firm websites: a framework for web scraping and a pilot study for germany. ZEW-Centre for European Economic Research Discussion Paper, no. 18–033 (2018)
13. Krijnen, D., Bot, R., Lampropoulos, G.: Automated web scraping apis (2014). http://mediatechnology.leiden.edu/images/uploads/docs/wt2014_web_scraping.pdf. Accessed 25 Apr 2018
14. Krotov, V., Silva, L.: Legality and ethics of web scraping (2018)
15. Krotov, V., Tennyson, M.: Research note: scraping financial data from the web using the r language. J. Emerg. Technol. Account. **15**(1), 169–181 (2018)
16. Kunang, Y.N., Purnamasari, S.D., et al.: Web scraping techniques to collect weather data in south sumatera. In: 2018 International Conference on Electrical Engineering and Computer Science (ICECOS), pp. 385–390. IEEE (2018)
17. Maeda, K.: Performance evaluation of object serialization libraries in xml, json and binary formats. In: 2012 Second International Conference on Digital Information and Communication Technology and it's Applications (DICTAP), pp. 177–182. IEEE (2012)
18. Rovetta, S., Suchacka, G., Masulli, F.: Bot recognition in a web store: an approach based on unsupervised learning. J. Netw. Comput. Appl. **157**, 102577 (2020)
19. Salem, H., Mazzara, M.: Pattern matching-based scraping of news websites. In: Journal of Physics: Conference Series, vol. 1694, p. 012011. IOP Publishing (2020)
20. Saurkar, A.V., Pathare, K.G., Gode, S.A.: An overview on web scraping techniques and tools. Int. J. Future Revolution Comput. Sci. Commun. Eng. **4**(4), 363–367 (2018)
21. Sirisuriya, D.S., et al.: A comparative study on web scraping (2015)
22. Uzun, E.: A novel web scraping approach using the additional information obtained from web pages. IEEE Access **8**, 61726–61740 (2020). https://doi.org/10.1109/ACCESS.2020.2984503
23. Wood, L., et al.: Document object model (dom) level 1 specification. W3C Recommendation, vol. 1 (1998)

Combining Feature Extraction Methods and Principal Component Analysis for Recognition of Vietnamese Off-Line Handwritten Uppercase Accented Characters

Ha Hoang Quoc Thi[1] and Mau Hien Doan[2(✉)]

[1] Department of Mathematics, Teacher College, Can Tho University, Can Tho, Viet Nam
hhqthi@ctu.edu.vn

[2] Center for Information Services, International University, Vietnam National University (VNU-HCM), Ho Chi Minh City, Viet Nam
dmhien@hcmiu.edu.vn

Abstract. This paper proposes a blended model that is suitable for recognizing off-line handwritten accented characters in general and Vietnamese characters in particular. The recognition model linearly combines four extracting methods in the feature extraction period, including Zones density, Projection histogram, Contour profiles, and Haar wavelets. The set of features obtained will be applied with Principal Component Analysis (PCA) to retain useful features, reducing the recognition time. Additionally, a Support Vector Machine (SVM) is also utilised for training and recognition. The proposed model is tested on the dataset of 21174 samples with 99 Vietnamese off-line handwritten accented characters.

Keywords: Handwritten recognition · PCA · SVM

1 Introduction

In recent years, the strong development of artificial intelligence, specifically in the fields of machine learning and computer vision, helps people free up labor and automatic work. Complex handwritten character recognition is also accomplished through machine learning and computer vision, which helps to build recognition applications, converts from difficult to readable characters, allows storage and searches easily through digitization. Recognizing off-line handwritten characters is used for digitalizing characters and for many applications such as reading postal addresses, the automatic processing of forms, checks, and faxes [7]. Many researchers' big challenge is to build an appropriate system with a high accuracy rate in the shortest time [6]. Especially, recognizing Vietnamese characters is more difficult because of the following two reasons. First, Table 1 shows that the Vietnamese special characters accompanied with the five accents (acute,

K. Wojtkiewicz et al. (Eds.): ICCCI 2021, CCIS 1463, pp. 388–398, 2021.
https://doi.org/10.1007/978-3-030-88113-9_31

grave, hook, tilde, dot-below ("/", "\", "?", "~", "."), 99 characters including 10 numeric characters, and the 89 other characters as the combination of 29 Latin characters) are more complicated than other languages [8]. Second, the characteristics of handwritten characters cause difficulties in recognizing the positions of the accents. With the same letter, different people with different physical characteristics will write differently. It depends on writers' ages and their psychology as well. With the desire to find out and build an appropriate recognizing system for off-line Vietnamese characters, a new system known as the combination of the four feature extractions is proposed in the feature extraction step. They are Zones density, Projection histogram, Contour profiles, Haar Wavelet. Principal Component Analysis (PCA) is also used to retain the number of good features; in other words, PCA is applied to reduce recognizing time. In contrast, in training and recognizing characters, the Support Vector Machine (SMV) is used for classification. This paper has four sections: Sect. 1 is the introduction; Sect. 2 is the Recognition model of Vietnamese off-line handwritten accented characters; Sect. 3 Experiments - describes the experimental process; Sect. 4 Results and discussion, and the last section reports the conclusion of the current study.

Table 1. Ninety-nine Vietnamese characters

Type	Numbers	Letter
Numeric	10	0, 1, 2, 3, 4, 5, 6, 7, 8, 9
Vowel non-accented	12	A, Ă, Â, E, Ê, O, Ô, Ơ, U, Ư, I, Y
Consonant	17	B, C, D, Đ, G, H, K, L, M, N, P, Q, R, S, T, V, X
Vowel accented	60	Á, À, Ả, Ã, Ạ, Ắ, Ằ, Ẳ, Ẵ, Ặ, Ấ, Ầ, Ẩ, Ẫ, Ậ, É, È, Ẻ, Ẽ, Ẹ, Ế, Ề, Ể, Ễ, Ệ, Í, Ì, Ỉ, Ĩ, Ị, Ó, Ò, Ỏ, Õ, Ọ, Ố, Ồ, Ổ, Ỗ, Ộ, Ớ, Ờ, Ở, Ỡ, Ợ, Ú, Ù, Ủ, Ũ, Ụ, Ứ, Ừ, Ử, Ữ, Ự, Ý, Ỳ, Ỷ, Ỹ, Ỵ

2 The Recognition Model of Vietnamese Handwritten Accented Characters

Like many other recognizing systems, the current study's proposed system is conducted by three steps, as shown in Fig. 1.

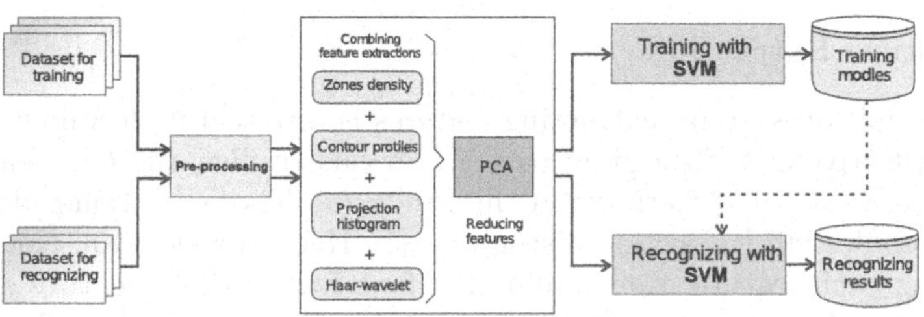

Fig. 1. The recognition model of Vietnamese off-line handwritten accented characters.

- Step 1: Creating a dataset for the recognition system, including collecting data and pre-processing data.
- Step 2: Extracting features in each sample to gain a set of values.
- Step 3: Using SVM to classify samples.

2.1 Dataset

That is a set of images with 22647 isolated samples of Vietnamese handwritten uppercase accented, in which 2160 samples are numeric characters, and the other 19487 samples are uppercase accented ones. Those samples are collected from 28 people; each person writes 99 characters, and each letter is written eight times on the face of an electronic board named DLA - 401. However, in the original dataset, some bad samples are eliminated because the writers write wrongly or erase or rewrite them in the same position. Therefore, the dataset remains the final number of 21174 samples. Those samples are binary with the black background and the white characters. They are distributed to 99 folders with the correspondent names of the characters.

Figure 2 illustrates some samples in the dataset with a height of 62 pixels and different widths. These samples must be standardized in the standard size of 64 × 64 pixels for feature extractions zones density, contour profiles, and projection histogram before being extracted features. Especially with the Haar Wavelet feature, samples have to be standardized in size of 32 × 32 pixels. The reason for this difference is when the size of samples is at 64 × 64 pixels for Haar Wavelet, the number of the obtained features are 64 × 64 = 4096, and it can cause negative effects on the execution time of the system.

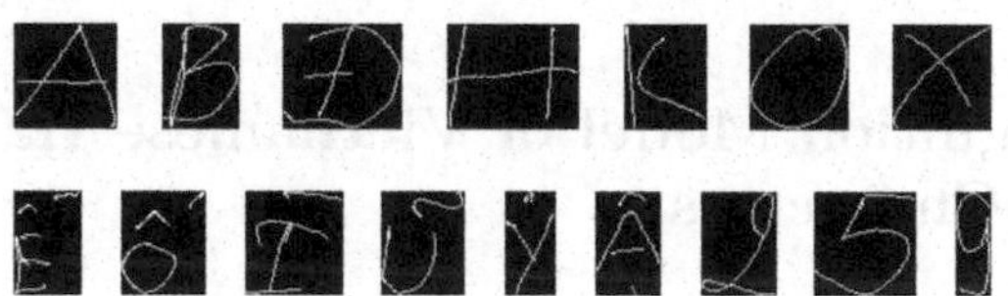

Fig. 2. Some samples in the dataset.

2.2 Feature Extraction

In the recognition system, extracting features is essential in deciding the whole system's effectiveness. According to the previous studies, the four features are appreciated as suitable methods in this study [6]. Those are Zones density [9], Contour profiles [4], Projection histograms [5], Haar Wavelet [10]. Not stopping at applying each feature, we combine the four features (the feature extracting combination). The feature combination is basically conducted as the following process. Firstly, each sample is applied four kinds of extraction method to get four sets of value. Secondly, the four sets of value are linearly combined to become a unique dataset. Those values are stored as vectors, which are called feature vectors.

In Zones density extraction, Fig. 3 shown that each sample 64 × 64 pixels is divided into $n \times m$ regions (n: the number of rows and m: the number of columns). Each region is a feature, and its value is the sum of white pixels. Therefore, each sample in $n \times m$ will give $n \times m$ features. In the current study, each sample is divided into $8 \times 8 = 64$ regions, equivalent to a set of 64 features. Besides, based on the way Vietnamese is written, most of them are done from left to right and from top to bottom. Hence, the feature values are arranged in the same order.

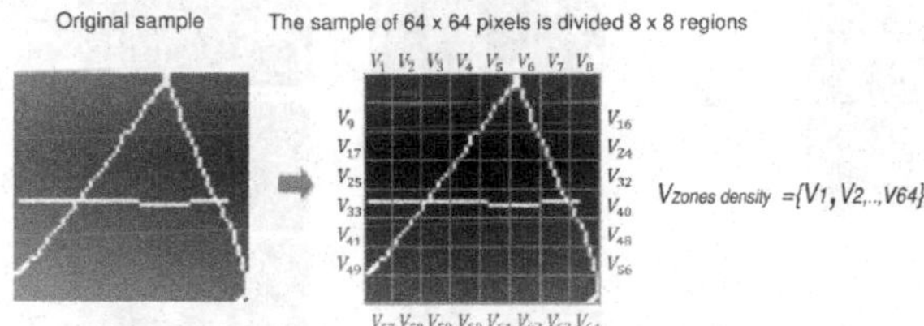

Fig. 3. The Zones density feature.

Each sample is scanned in Contour profiles extraction according to 4 directions: left, right, top and bottom. After scanning, in each direction, we get a set of continuous values. Each value is the distance - the number of black pixels - from the edge of the image to the first white pixel in that direction. The value's order is counted from left to right for the two directions, top and bottom. Therefore, a sample of 64 × 64 pixels will give 64 features on the left +64 features on the right +64 features on the top and 64 features on the bottom. There are 256 feature values, which is illustrated in Fig. 4.

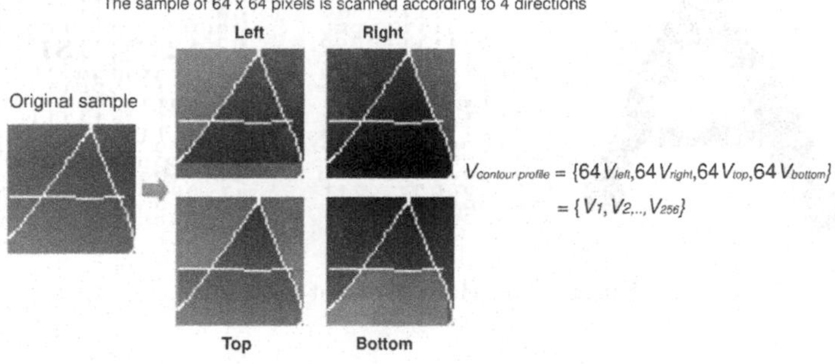

Fig. 4. The Contour profiles feature.

In Projection histogram extraction, white pixels in each sample will be projected on the four axes: horizontal, vertical and two diagonals. In each axis, we gain a set of values, in which each value is the number of white pixels projected on the axis. As a result, Fig. 5 shows that with 64×64 pixels, we get 382 features (64 horizontal features, 64 vertical features and $(64 + 64 - 1) \times 2$ diagonal features).

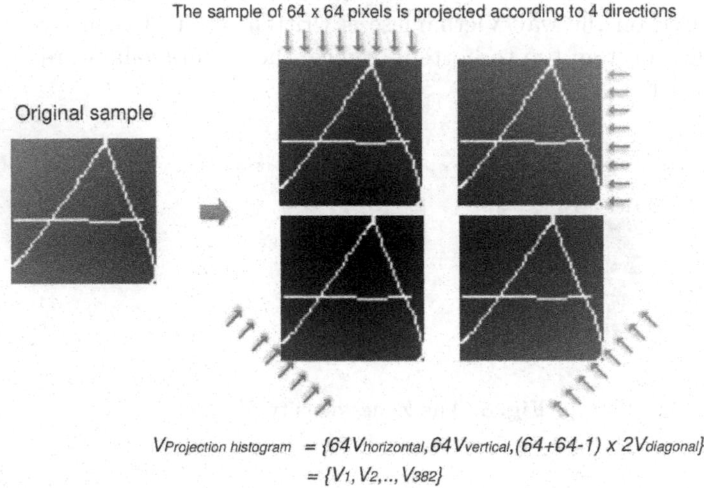

Fig. 5. The Projection histograms feature.

Haar Wavelet feature, as can be seen in Fig. 6, is conducted on the idea that each sample will be binary and standardized into $2^n \times 2^n$ pixels to give $2^n \times 2^n$ features. Therefore, 32×32 pixels after being extracted by Haar Wavelet can give 32×32 features (1024 features).

Fig. 6. The Haar Wavelet feature.

The basic steps of the Haar Wavelet used in this paper are conducted as the following Algorithm.

Algorithm 1: The Haar Wavelet feature

Input: Square matrix (A,n) level 2^n
Output: The features set $\{V_1, V_2, V_{(2^n \times 2^n)}\}$
Method
(1) Initialization
- $Queue = \emptyset$;
- $i = 1$;

(2) Calculate $F_i = Sum$ of black pixel of matrix (A,n);
- PUSH((A,n),Queue);

(3) **while** $Queue \neq \emptyset$ **do**
- POP(Queue,(A,n));
- If $(n > 1)$
  {
  $n = n \div 2$;
  Divide the image into 4 parts A1,A2,A3,A4;
  for $(j = 1; i \leq 4; j++)$
  PUSH((Aj; n), Queue);
  }
- S,S1,S2,S3 and S4 are considered as sum of the black pixels, corresponding with A,A1,A2,A3 and A4
- Calculate
  $F_{i+1} = S1 + S2$;
  $F_{i+2} = S2 + S3$;
  $F_{i+3} = S4$
- $i = i + 3$;

end

In feature extracting combination: each feature has the ability to recognize well some kinds of characters, and in each set of features, some values help to reflect the characteristic of the characters. Therefore, the combination of those features helps to take advantage of positive aspects from each one and boost the rate of the accuracy of the whole process. On that foundation, the combination procedure is done by combining the four datasets of the four methods into a dataset with 1726 features, which is performed in a kind of vectors. There are 64 features of Zones density, 256 features of Contour profiles, 382 features of Projection histogram, and 1024 features of Haar Wavelet. Figure 7 provides an overview of the whole process of combining four feature extracting methods.

The number of features is a ratio between the training time and the time recognition. With the number of features being 1726 features, the two mentioned-above processes are also too much.

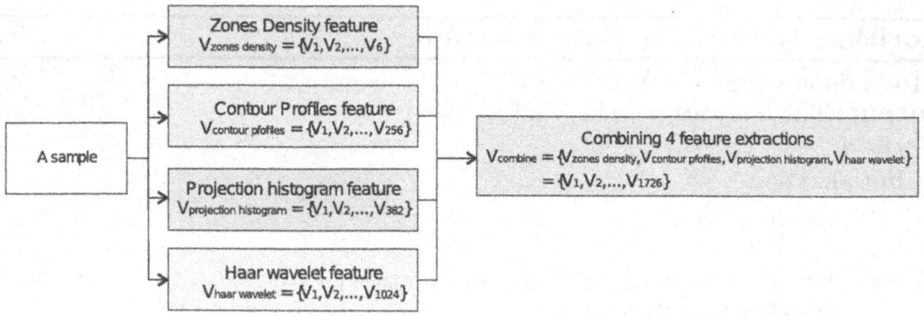

Fig. 7. Combining four feature extractions.

Those are the reasons for the two research issues. First, it is necessary to reduce the number of features, which leads to the decrease in time without making the accuracy rate down. Second, to optimize the accuracy rate, it is reasonable to build a new space where the data in this place can be performed better than those are in the original space. The Principal Component Analysis (PCA) algorithm is employed to solve those issues [3].

2.3 The Support Vector Machine (SVM)

Support Vector Machine is used in almost classification, and it is considered as a good classification technique [11]. It has more positive points than the other techniques in terms of recognition [1]. The SVM applied into the current study is the CvSVM object of the OpenCV library with the following parameters SVM type: $SVM :: C\_SVC$ kernel type: $SVM :: POLY$ (polynomial kernel function); degree: 3 (polynomial of degree 3); gamma: 0.001; coef0: 19.6; C: 0.1

3 Experiments

3.1 Purpose of Study

The current study is conducted to evaluate:

- The effectiveness of the four features extracting methods with PCA and the one without PCA
- The changes in terms of time recognition when using PCA to reduce the number of features and the influence of that reduction on the proposed model's accuracy rate. In all experimental cases in the study, dataset with 21174 samples are divided into two parts, in which 16929 samples (75%) for training and 4245 samples (25%) for recognition. This rate is also applied for each character to make sure all 99 categories are trained and tested.

3.2 Experimental Process

We do experiments with the six different cases in the same dataset to address the first research issue. Case numbers 1, 2, 3, and 4 are when we use each feature Zones density, Contour profiles, Projection Histogram, Haar Wavelet without PCA. Case number 5 is also without PCA, but this is the combination of the four features together. Case number 6 is the combined model with PCA, as described in Fig. 8.

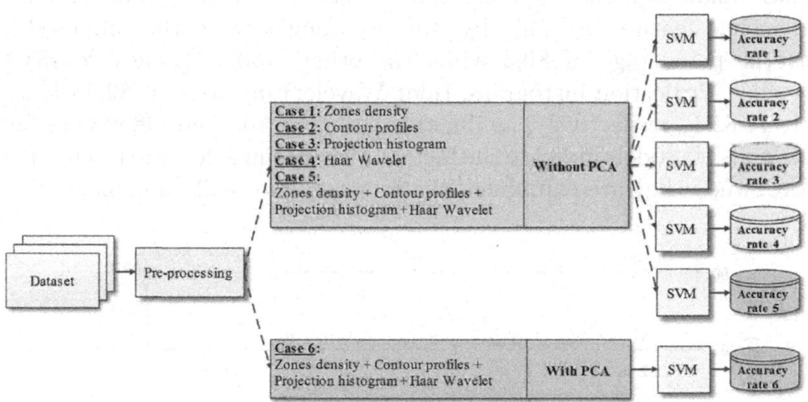

Fig. 8. Experimental process of checking the accuracy rate of every single model versus the combined model with PCA and without PCA.

Which the second research issue, to find out the changes in the time recognition when PCA is used to reduce the number of features, the recognition system experiences 4 cases with the reduced number of PCA in each case as follows: 1726 (unchanged), 512, 256, 64 (see Fig. 9).

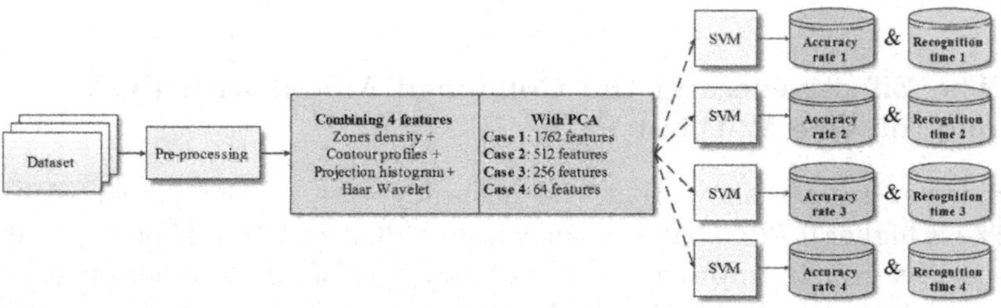

Fig. 9. Experimental process of checking the correlation between the accuracy rate and the time recognition when using PCA to change the number of features.

The recognition system is designed with Visual *C++* MFC based on Visual Studio 2012, combining with the OpenCV library (v2.4.6) of Intel - the image processing and learning machine library [2]. The experimental system is a computer having the configuration Processor Intel(R) Core(TM) i7-4720HQ CPU@2.60 GHz; RAM: 8.00 GB; OS: Windows 10 Pro 64 bit.

4 Results and Discussions

4.1 The Effectiveness of the Combined Model and Single Models

The results show that the combined model's accuracy rate is always higher than using a single feature. Specifically, the accuracy rate of the proposed model reaches the percentage of 89.3 while the other models (Zones density, Contour profiles, Projection histogram, Haar Wavelet) just stop at 82.58%, 84.44%, 78.13%, 77.82%, respectively, as illustrated in Fig. 10. The differences between the two kinds of models indicate the fact that every single feature has its strength; therefore, when they are combined, the accuracy rate will be higher.

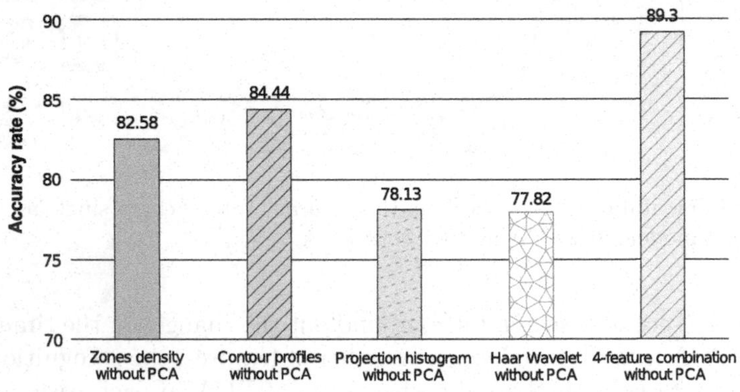

Fig. 10. The accuracy rate between every single feature versus the four-feature extracting combination.

4.2 The Effectiveness of the Combined Model with PCA and the One Without PCA

Experimental results show that the accuracy rate of the model with PCA (90.02%) is higher 0.72% than the one without PCA (89.3%). It proves that PCA has a positive role in improving the accuracy rate of the recognition system. It is appropriate to conclude that PCA can be considered as a feature extracting method, which helps to build a new feature space and data; therefore, it can be performed better (Table 2).

Table 2. The accuracy rate between the proposed model and the single feature model.

The recognition model		Accuracy (%)
Zones density	Without PCA	82.58
Contour profiles	Without PCA	84.44
Projection histogram	Without PCA	78.13
Haar Wavelet	Without PCA	77.82
Four-feature combination	Without PCA	89.3
Four-feature combination	With PCA	90.02

Table 3. The accuracy rates and time recognition from PCAs shown in the table to reduce the number of features.

The recognition model	Time recognition (s)	Accuracy (%)
With PCA-1726 features	153.13	90.02
With PCA-512 features	107.85	89.14
With PCA-256 features	94.11	89.2
With PCA-64 features	87.21	88.78

4.3 Using PCA to Reduce the Number of Features: Its Effects on the Accuracy Rate and the Time Recognition

Experimental results also show, when the number of features is reduced under PCA's impact, each case's accuracy rate is equivalent. On the other hand, comparing each case's time recognition shows that the time is a ratio with the number of features. It means that when the number of features is reduced, the recognition process is also shortened (Results are shown in Table 3). In specific, with 1726 features, the time needed is 153.13 s; when the number of features goes down to 512, the time is also down to 107.85 s (it is quicker than the first case 45.25 s, about 1/3 the initial time); similarly, the other cases with the number of

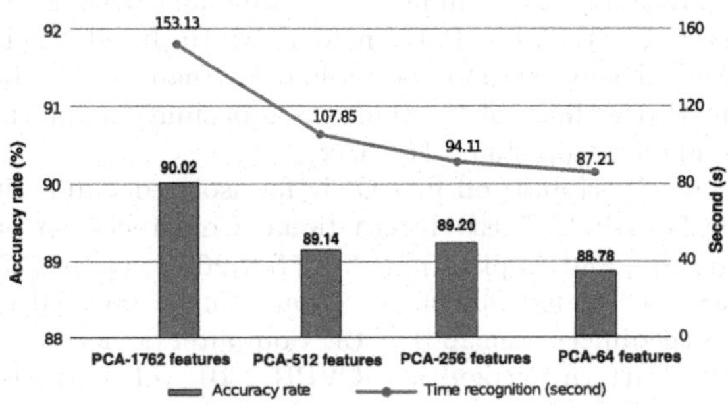

Fig. 11. The chart presents different time recognition and accuracy rates of four recognition models.

features are 256 and 64, the time is respectively standing at 94.11 and 87.21 s, as shown in Fig. 11. It is clear to conclude that the decrease in the number of features helps optimize recognition time.

5 Conclusion

The article provides an overview of the recognition issue and the recognition of Vietnamese off-line handwriting characters. The results show that the accuracy rate and the recognition time depend on selecting feature extracting methods. It is pretty positive when the combination of four features helps to improve the rate of accuracy. Simultaneously, the use of PCA reduces the recognition time remarkably while the accuracy rate remains. Those results obtained are hoped to contribute to the world of research an optimal choice for the issue of recognizing off-line handwritten characters.

References

1. Arica, N., Yarman-Vural, F.T.: One-dimensional representation of two-dimensional information for hmm based handwriting recognition. Pattern Recogn. Lett. **21**(6–7), 583–592 (2000)
2. Bradski, G., Kaehler, A.: Learning OpenCV: Computer Vision with the OpenCV Library. O'Reilly Media Inc., Newton (2008)
3. Bunke, H., Roth, M., Schukat-Talamazzini, E.G.: Off-line recognition of cursive script produced by a cooperative writer. In: Proceedings of the 12th IAPR International Conference on Pattern Recognition, vol. 3-Conference C: Signal Processing (Cat. No. 94CH3440-5), vol. 2, pp. 383–386. IEEE (1994)
4. Cakmakov, D., Gorgevik, D.: Handwritten digit recognition using classifier cooperation schemes. In: Proceedings of the 2nd Balkan Conference in Informatics, BCI, pp. 17–19 (2005)
5. Gorgevik, D., Cakmakov, D.: An efficient three-stage classifier for handwritten digit recognition. In: Proceedings of the 17th International Conference on Pattern Recognition, ICPR 2004, vol. 4, pp. 507–510. IEEE (2004)
6. Phuong, P.A., Tao, N.Q., Mai, L.C.: An efficient model for isolated Vietnamese handwritten recognition. In: 2008 International Conference on Intelligent Information Hiding and Multimedia Signal Processing, pp. 358–361. IEEE (2008)
7. Plamondon, R., Srihari, S.N.: Online and off-line handwriting recognition: a comprehensive survey. IEEE Trans. Pattern Anal. Mach. Intell. **22**(1), 63–84 (2000)
8. Tran, D.C.: An efficient method for on-line Vietnamese handwritten character recognition. In: Proceedings of the Third Symposium on Information and Communication Technology, pp. 135–141 (2012)
9. Vamvakas, G., et al.: Hybrid off-line OCR for isolated handwritten Greek characters. In: The Fourth IASTED International Conference on Signal Processing, Pattern Recognition, and Applications (SPPRA 2007), pp. 197–202 (2007)
10. Viola, P., Jones, M.: Rapid object detection using a boosted cascade of simple features. In: Proceedings of the 2001 IEEE Computer Society Conference on Computer Vision and Pattern Recognition, CVPR 2001, vol. 1. IEEE (2001)
11. Wang, G.: A survey on training algorithms for support vector machine classifiers. In: 2008 Fourth International Conference on Networked Computing and Advanced Information Management, vol. 1, pp. 123–128. IEEE (2008)

Internet of Things and Computational Technologies for Collective Intelligence

Detecting School Violence Using Artificial Intelligence to Interpret Surveillance Video Sequences

Sergazy Narynov[1], Zhandos Zhumanov[1,2], Aidana Gumar[1,3], Mariyam Khassanova[1,3], and Batyrkhan Omarov[1,2(✉)]

[1] Alem Research, Almaty, Kazakhstan
[2] Al-Farabi Kazakh National University, Almaty, Kazakhstan
[3] Department of Psychiatry and Narcology, Asfendiyarov Kazakh National Medical University, Almaty, Kazakhstan

Abstract. In this study, we present a skeleton-based approach for detecting aggressive activity. The approach does not require much powerful hardware but is very fast in realization. There are two stages in our method: feature extraction from video frames to evaluate a person's posture, and then action classification using a neural network to determine if the frames contain bullying scenes. We also selected 13 classes for identifying aggressor's and victim's behavior, created a dataset of 400 min of video data that contains actions of one person and 20 h of video data containing actions of physical bullying and aggression. The approach was tested on the assembled dataset. Results show more than 97% accuracy in determining aggressive behavior in video sequences.

Keywords: Bullying · Physical bullying · PoseNET · Neural network · Action recognition · Aggression · Video analysis

1 Introduction

One can observe different forms of bullying at school. Physical bullying is intentional pushing, hitting, kicking, beating, causing bodily harm [1]. Discussions about the extent to which a school should perform educational functions have been going on for centuries. Among the phenomena of school life that cause a vivid public reaction is bullying, or school bullying [2, 3]. Today, there is a lot of talk about the fact that it is an educational organization that should take over functions of combating that phenomenon and preventing it. Bullying is a phenomenon that covers not only the field of education; bullying is possible in any organization where there is a hierarchy and a possibility of establishing subordination relationships [4].

The world's first program to combat bullying and its consequences appeared in Norway in the 1980s and was based on the works of D. Olveus [5]. That was the reaction of the Norwegian Ministry of Education to the tragic incident — the suicide of three teenagers who were bullied at school [6]. In 1991, an evaluation of the program's

K. Wojtkiewicz et al. (Eds.): ICCCI 2021, CCIS 1463, pp. 401–412, 2021.
https://doi.org/10.1007/978-3-030-88113-9_32

effectiveness was conducted, which showed a 50% reduction in bullying [7]. At least 15 anti-bullying programs inspired by the work of D. Olveus, started in the 1990s, and today the number of programs of that type cannot be accurately calculated [8].

Traditional approaches to school bullying prevention are mainly focused on a person, that is, cases of school bullying are reported by victims or witnesses, which is usually inconvenient and untimely. Therefore, an automatic method for detecting school bullying is needed.

The development of artificial intelligence (AI) and computer vision makes it possible to detect school bullying with methods based on information from video cameras on school grounds. One such approach would be discussed in this paper. Physical abuse, emotional intimidation, damaging personal belongings, and bullying on social networks are manifestations of school bullying. Physical abuse was deemed the most dangerous to teenagers in an early study conducted by the writers' research community [9]. As a result, this paper is dedicated to the automatic detection of physical violence and aggression on school territory using artificial intelligence and computer vision techniques.

The paper is organized in the following manner: in Sect. 2 we do a review of related works that describe violence detection problem, techniques, and methods. Section 3 explains our attempt to solve the given problem and describes techniques and methods that were applied. Section 4 demonstrates experimental results for action recognition. Section 5 concludes the paper and describes directions for further research.

2 Related Works

The problem of aggressive behavior identification, which is a subclass of action recognition task, has been approached by the use of hand-crafted input feature vectors, that frequently rely on visual signals contained in frames. Vasconcelos and Lippman [10], for example, measured the difference between separate video frames in 1997. That procedure was enhanced in 2006 by identifying blood regions on the skin and measuring the motion speed of certain regions [11]. In 2002, researchers used motion direction and position of various body limbs present in a frame to identify violent actions in films [12]. In 2014, [13] proposed taking into account the acceleration of body parts. In 2016, LSTM had been used to address the issue of lacking temporal knowledge [14]. Visual features, optical flow images, and acceleration flow maps were accompanied by an LSTM and subjected to a late fusion. In 2017, the AlexNet architecture [15] was introduced. [16] followed its ideas: at each stage, the model used two subsequent frames as inputs to encode a visual representation vector before sending it to a convolutional LSTM network. After processing the frames final classification was computed using multiple fully connected layers.

State of the art research in detecting violence in the video, mostly use deep learning techniques, and their classification accuracy varies from 81% to 97% [17–20].

Eknarin et al. [17] suggested a time series image-based deep learning system. A video's degree of aggression can be identified by running a deep convolution neural network on it. Based on a movie index, they had an overall accuracy of 88.74%.

Pre-trained models along with various deep learning approaches were used by Shakil et al. [18] to detect large-scale aggression such as street protests. For abuse prevention, they merged a ResNet50 network and a long short-term memory (LSTM) network. They were able to reach an overall precision of 97.06%.

To identify aggression in the video, Chen et al. [19] used 3D CNN and SVM techniques. The proposed approach showed good results for a hockey match, crowd violence, and movie violence, and could efficiently track war, violent behavior, and violent scenes in real-time video streams. Using the UCF101 database, they were able to achieve an overall precision of 89.1%.

Accattoli et al. [20] suggested a system focused on multi-task fusion learning and various features for overall visual-audio emotion detection. In a CNN model, that approach applied multi-task learning to deep functions. The features were able to model several activities with fewer parameters all at the same time. By exchanging knowledge through activities, it could increase the sensitivity of a single recognition model to user emotion. Emotion detection quality for video and audio could surpass 81.36%.

In our research, the goal was to develop a system that detects violence in video with high accuracy and at the same time does not require a lot of hardware resources.

3 Materials and Methods

3.1 Criteria for Data Collection

Physical bullying and violence detection problem consists of several sub-tasks. Figure 1 shows a flowchart of the study. The first task is defining the characteristics of data that should be collected. For that, we created four classes of features that describe an aggressor and a victim. Characteristics of data include aggressor pattern parameters, aggressor pattern actions, victim pattern parameters, and group bullying parameters. Based on these classes we determined features of an aggressor and a victim that should be considered in the data collection process. Based on them we identified 13 classes that describe characteristics of aggressor and victim behavior.

3.2 Data Collection Process

When collecting data we searched for videos available in open access on the Internet and on social networks using keywords like "aggression", "physical aggression", "violence", "bullying", "fight", "group fight", etc. After collecting videos, we labeled temporal segments within them indicating appropriate classes, and labeling information was saved in *.json format. For that, we used software called VGG Image Annotator (https://www.robots.ox.ac.uk/~vgg/software/via/). After labeling was finished all videos were cut and arranged by classes.

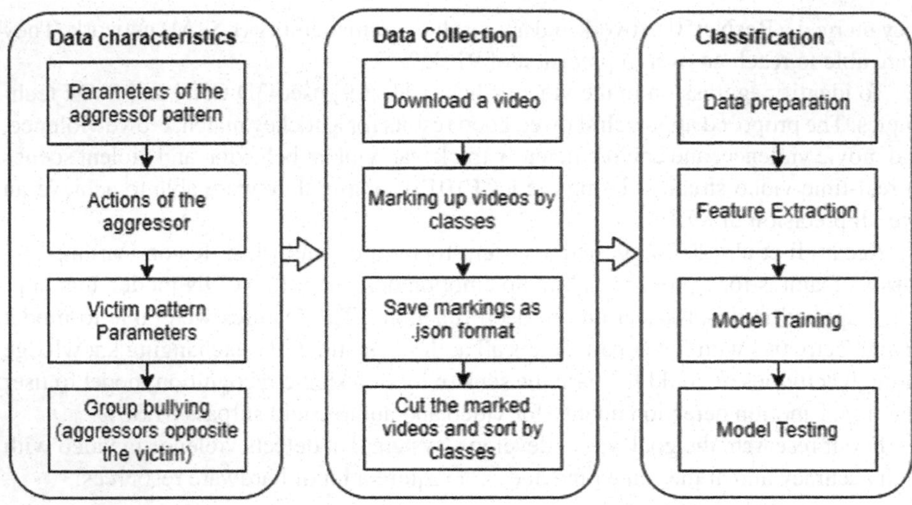

Fig. 1. Flowchart of the research

3.3 The Dataset

2,093 video files containing scenes of aggressive behavior and bullying were collected. The total duration of collected video data is 20 h 0 min 20.86 s. Distribution of collected video data by file formats:

- video in. mp4 format: 2 017 files;
- video in.mov format: 44 files;
- video in.wmv format: 32 files;

Figure 2 illustrates information about collected video data file formats.

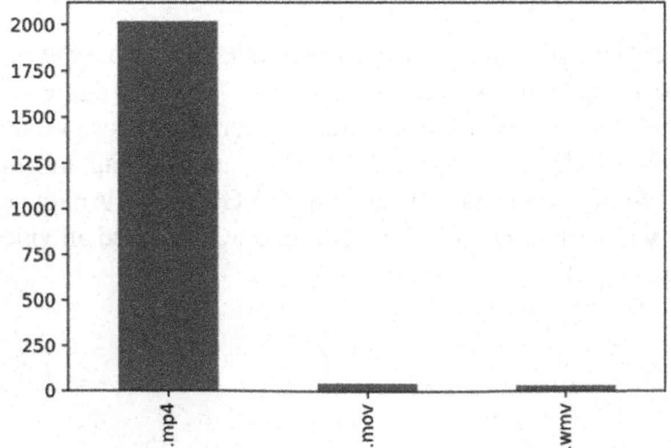

Fig. 2. Collected video data by file formats

Figure 3 demonstrates the distribution of collected video data by duration:

- shortest video clip: 1.39 s.
- longest video clip: 5,093.70 s.
- average video duration: 34.41 s.

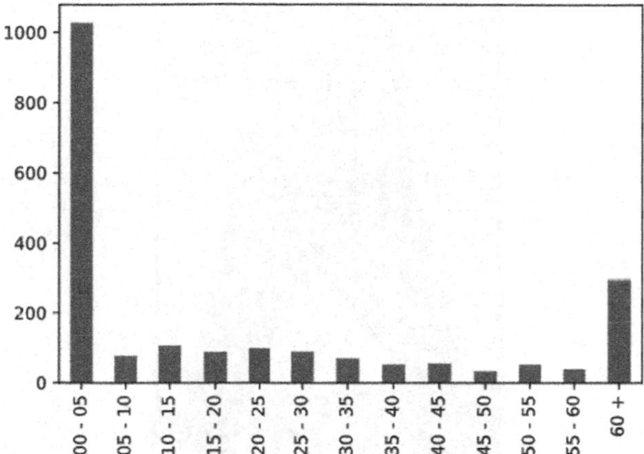

Fig. 3. Distribution of the collected video by duration

In addition to the collected data, we shot videos with imitation of aggressive actions performed by one person. Additional videos are required for the first stages of training machine learning models. The total duration of additional video data is about 400 min.

3.4 Pose Estimation

Algorithms for estimating a human body pose based on RGB images can be grouped into two categories: top-down algorithms and bottom-up algorithms. The first ones trigger human detector and evaluate body joints in detected bounding boxes. Examples of top-down methods are Possenet [21], HourglassNet [22], and Hornet [23]. Examples of bottom-up algorithms are Open space [24] and PifPaf [25].

In this paper, we used training based on a skeletal model. The proposed approach can reduce computational costs. The lightweight pre-trained PoseNET neural network is selected to provide an accurate assessment of the aggressor's or victim's figure. A pre-trained PoseNET can be used as a function extractor to transfer acquired knowledge from the source domain to the target domain. PoseNet output is a representation of the human body with positions and confidences of 17 key body points. 17 key points include nose, eyes, ears, shoulders, elbows, wrists, thighs, knees, and ankles. Figure 4 illustrates an example of 17 key points that were extracted using PoseNET. The representation of the human body can be denoted as:

$$r_b(x_i; \theta) \tag{1}$$

where θ is neural network parameters, and xi is training samples of the data set. To be able to further classify the representation of the human body $r_b(x_i; \theta)$, a fully

Fig. 4. 17 key points that extracted by PoseNET

connected neural network layer is deployed. The added neural network can be trained by minimizing categorical cross-entropy loss before being normalized by the "Softmax" layer. Figure 5 illustrates the architecture of the PoseNET artificial neural network.

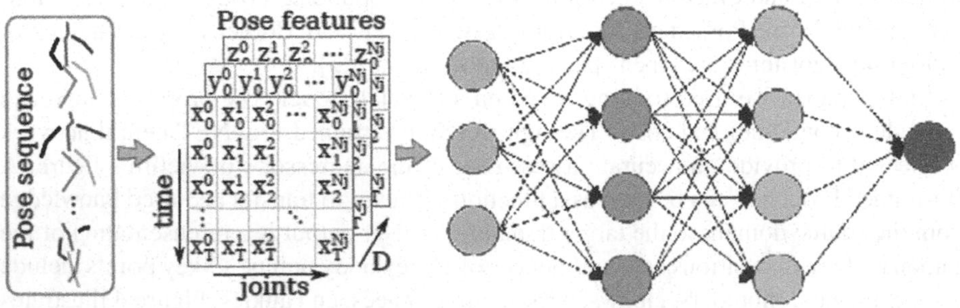

Fig. 5. PoseNET violence detection architecture

3.5 Evaluation

The findings of a prediction model can be visualized using a confusion matrix. Predicted classes are represented by rows of the matrix, whereas actual classes are represented by columns. The matrix displays values of true positives (TPc), false positives (FPc), false negatives (FNc), and true negatives (TNc) for a given class c. Several efficiency indicators, such as precision, recall, and F1-score, can be calculated using the confusion matrix [26]:

$$\text{precision} = \frac{\text{TP}}{\text{TP} + \text{FP}} \tag{2}$$

$$\text{recall} = \frac{\text{TP}}{\text{TP} + \text{FN}} \tag{3}$$

$$F1 = \frac{2 \cdot \text{precision} \cdot \text{recall}}{\text{precision} + \text{recall}} \tag{4}$$

$$\text{accuracy} = \frac{\text{TP} + \text{TN}}{\text{TP} + \text{FN} + \text{TN} + \text{FP}} \tag{5}$$

We used the weight-averaging approach to combine metrics calculated for each class into a single variable that weights values according to class proportion in results.

We used traditional train/test split to validate predictive models [27]. 80% of the data were used during training, while 20% of the data were used to test the model.

4 Experimental Results

During the experiments, we have developed and tested machine learning software models for action recognition. Machine learning software models were trained based on neural

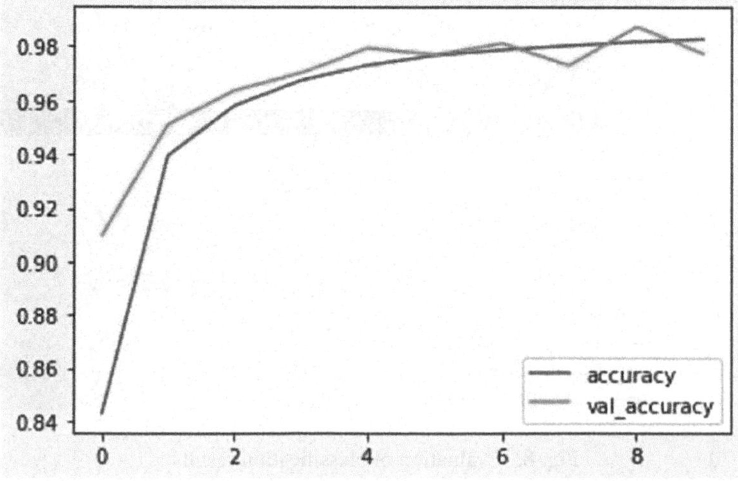

Fig. 6. Model accuracy

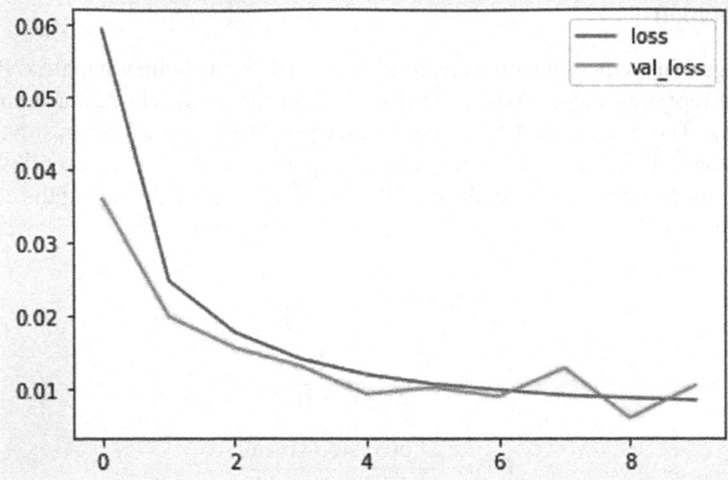

Fig. 7. Test and validation loss

networks using the PoseNet architecture. From the labeled video data, we selected 13 classes for which we had filmed additional video data. Testing the action recognition model trained on that data showed very good results in detecting aggressive behavior and physical bullying.

Figure 6 demonstrates validation and test accuracy for physical bullying detection with neural networks during 8 epochs of learning. The results show that accuracy reaches 98% after 8 epochs of training.

Figure 7 illustrates neural network loss function values during 8 epochs of training. The results show that validation loss is very low even during the first epoch of training.

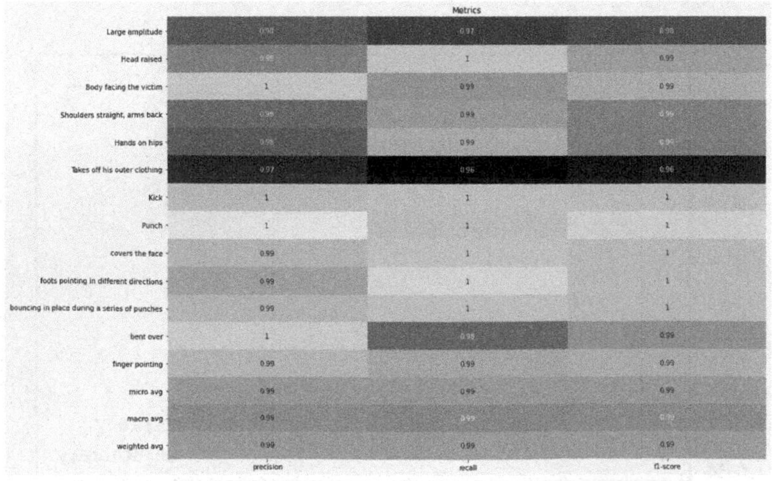

Fig. 8. Evaluation of classification results

Figure 8 demonstrates the evaluation of classification results for 13 classes. As it can be seen all the evaluation parameters show high quality. Precision varies between 0.92 to 0.98, recall varies between 0.89 to 1.0, and F1-score varies between 0.92 to 0.99.

Figure 9 shows a confusion matrix for 13 classes of videos that contain physical bullying.

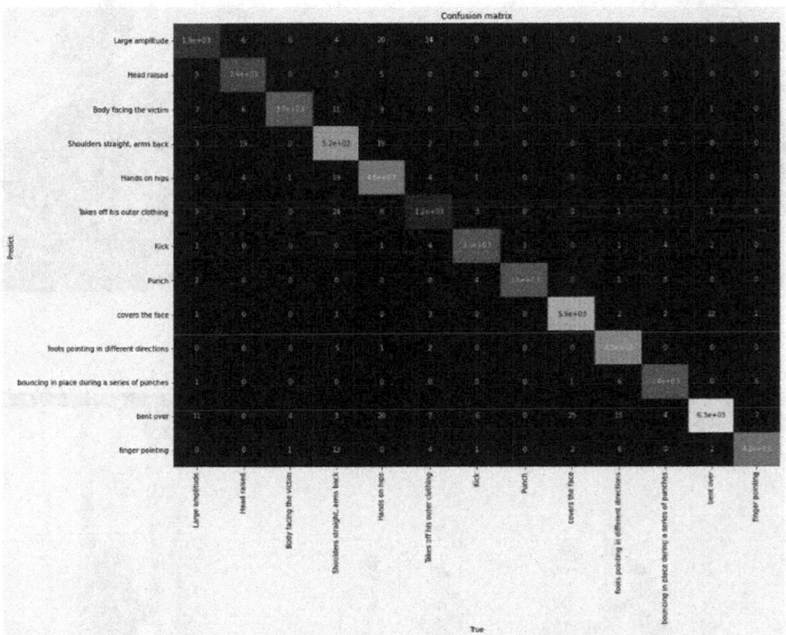

Fig. 9. Confusion matrix for multi-classification

Figures 10 and 11 demonstrate the application of the trained neural network for a group fighting scene. Figure 10 shows how the model sees the skeleton of each participant in a bullying scene. In Fig. 11 we identify the action of each person and find a class they belong to, and in real-time identify their role - aggressor or victim.

Fig. 10. Testing the proposed model

Fig. 11. Testing the proposed model

5 Conclusion and Future Work

In the paper, we propose a skeleton-based method for detecting violent behavior that does not require a lot of powerful hardware but is very easy to implement. Our process consists of two stages: attribute extraction from video frames to determine a person's pose, and then the classification of behavior using a neural network. We have collected a dataset of 400 min of video data containing activities of one individual and 20 h of video containing actions of physical bullying and violence and established 13 classes for recognizing aggressor's and victim's behavior. The method was applied and tested on the collected dataset. Findings show an accuracy of predicting aggressive behavior in video sequences of more than 97%.

Future works in this direction include collecting more video data relevant to a school environment, expanding the list of parameters the model is able to track, and experimenting with other neural network architectures.

References

1. Pande, N., Karyakarte, M.: A review for semantic analysis and text document annotation using natural language processing techniques. SSRN 3418747 (2019)
2. Alshemali, B., Kalita, J.: Improving the reliability of deep neural networks in NLP: a review. Knowl. Based Syst. 105210 (2019)
3. Yankah, S., Adams, K.S., Grimes, L., Price, A.: Age and online social media behavior in prediction of social activism orientation. J. Soc. Media Soc. **6**(2), 56–89 (2017)
4. Costello, M., Hawdon, J.: Who are the online extremists among us? Sociodemographic characteristics, social networking, and online experiences of those who produce online hate materials. Violen. Gender **5**(1), 55–60 (2018)
5. Ferrara, E.: Contagion dynamics of extremist propaganda in social networks. Inf. Sci. **418**, 1–12 (2017)
6. A Brief History of the Olweus Bullying Prevention Program. http://www.violenceprevention works.org/public/olweus_history.page
7. Olweus, D.: Bully/victim problems among schoolchildren: basic facts and effects of a school based intervention program. Developm. Treat. Childhood Aggres. **17**, 411–448 (1991)
8. Clarke, A.M., Morreale, S., Field, C., Hussein, Y., Barry, M.M.: What works in enhancing social and emotional skills development during childhood and adolescence? A review of the evidence on the effectiveness of school-based and out-of-school programmes in the UK (2015)
9. Chen, H.: Exploring extremism and terrorism on the web: the dark web project. In: Yang, C.C., et al. (eds.) Intelligence and Security Informatics, pp. 1–20. Springer, Heidelberg (2007) https://doi.org/10.1007/978-3-540-71549-8_1
10. Vasconcelos, N., Lippman, A.: Towards semantically meaningful feature spaces for the characterization of video content. Proc. Int. Conf. Image Process. **1**, 25–28 (1997). https://doi.org/10.1109/ICIP.1997.647375
11. Clarin, C.T., Dionisio, J.A.M., Echavez, M.T., Naval, P.C.: DOVE: detection of movie violence using motion intensity analysis on skin and blood. Technical report, University of the Philippines (2005)
12. Datta, A., Shah, M., Lobo, N.D.V.: Person-on-person violence detection in video data. Object Recogn. Supp. User Interact. Service Robots **1**, 433–438 (2002). https://doi.org/10.1109/ICPR.2002.1044748
13. Deniz, O., Serrano, I., Bueno, G., Kim, T.: Fast violence detection in video. In: 2014 International Conference on Computer Vision Theory and Applications (VISAPP), vol. 2, pp. 478–485 (2014)
14. Dong, Z., Qin, J., Wang, Y.: Multi-stream deep networks for person to person violence detection in videos. In: Tan, T., Li, X., Chen, X., Zhou, J., Yang, J., Cheng, H. (eds.) CCPR 2016. CCIS, vol. 662. Springer, Singapore (2016). https://doi.org/10.1007/978-981-10-3002-4

15. Krizhevsky, A., Sutskever, I., Hinton, G.E.: ImageNet classification with deep convolutional neural networks. In: Pereira, F., Burges, C.J.C., Bottou, L., Weinberger, K.Q. (eds.) Advances in Neural Information Processing Systems, vol. 25, pp. 1097–1105. Curran Associates, Inc. (2012). http://papers.nips.cc/paper/4824-imagenetclassification-with-deep-convolutional-neural-networks.pdf
16. Sudhakaran, S., Lanz, O.: Learning to detect violent videos using convolutional long short-term memory. CoRR abs/1709.06531 (2017). http://arxiv.org/abs/1709.06531
17. Eknarin, D., Luepol, P., Suwatchai, K.: Video representation learning for CCTV-based violence detection. In: Proceedings of the 2018 3rd Technology Innovation Management and Engineering Science International Conference (TIMES-iCON), Bangkok, Thailand, 12–14 December 2018
18. Sumon, S.A., Goni, R., Hashem, N.B., Shahria, T., Rahman, R.M.: Violence detection by pretrained modules with different deep learning approaches. Vietnam J. Comput. Sci. **7**, 22–23 (2020)
19. Chen, J., Xu, Y., Zhang, C., Xu, Z., Meng, X., Wang, J.: An improved two-stream 3D convolutional neural network for human action recognition. In: Proceedings of the 2019 25th International Conference on Automation and Computing (ICAC), Lancaster, UK, 5–7 September 2019
20. Accattoli, S., Sernani, P., Falcionelli, N., Mekuria, D.N., Dragoni, A.F.: Violence detection in videos by combining 3D convolutional neural networks and support vector machines. Appl. Artif. Intell. **34**, 202–203 (2020)
21. Schmidt, B., Wang, L.: Automatic work objects calibration via a global–local camera system Robot. Comput. Integr. Manuf. **30**, 678–683 (2014)
22. Paul, R.P.: Robot manipulators: mathematics, programming, and control. In: The Computer Control of Robot Manipulators Richard Paul (1981)
23. Shiu, Y.C., Ahmad, S.: Calibration of wrist-mounted robotic sensors by solving homogeneous transform equations of the form AX = XB. IEEE Trans. Robot. Autom. **5**, 16–29 (1989)
24. Zanchettin, A.M., Ceriani, N.M., Rocco, P., Ding, H., Matthias, B.: Safety in human-robot collaborative manufacturing environments: metrics and control. IEEE Trans. Automat. Sci. Eng. **13**(2), 882–893 (2016). https://doi.org/10.1109/TASE.2015.2412256
25. Hornung, A., Wurm, K.M., Bennewitz, M., Stachniss, C., Burgard, W.: OctoMap: an efficient probabilistic 3D mapping framework based on octrees. Autonom. Robots **34**(3), 189–206 (2013). https://doi.org/10.1007/s10514-012-9321-0
26. Witten, I., Frank, E., Hall, M., Pal, C.: Data Mining: Practical Machine Learning Tools and Techniques, 4th edn. Morgan Kaufmann, San Franscico (2017)
27. Ng, A.: Machine Learning Yearning. deeplearning.ai (2018)

Audio Surveillance: Detection of Audio-Based Emergency Situations

Zhandos Dosbayev[1], Rustam Abdrakhmanov[2](✉), Oxana Akhmetova[3], Marat Nurtas[4,5], Zhalgasbek Iztayev[6], Lyazzat Zhaidakbaeva[6], and Lazzat Shaimerdenova[3]

[1] Satbayev Kazakh National Technical University, Almaty, Kazakhstan
[2] Khoja Akhmet Yassawi International Kazakh-Turkish University, Turkistan, Kazakhstan
rustam.abdrakhmanov@ayu.edu.kz
[3] Al-Farabi Kazkah National University, Almaty, Kazakhstan
[4] International Information Technology University, Almaty, Kazakhstan
[5] Kazakh-British Technical University, Almaty, Kazakhstan
[6] M.Auezov South Kazakhstan University, Shymkent, Kazakhstan

Abstract. The subject of the study was the recognition of sounds of critical situations in the audio signal. The term "critical situation" is understood as an event, the characteristic sound signs of which can speak about acoustic artifacts as a shot, a scream, a glass crash, an explosion, a siren, etc.. The paper considers the scope of audio analytics, its advantages, the history of spectral analysis, as well as analyzes and selects tools for further development of system components. In the paper, we propose our dataset that consists of 14 classes that contains 1000 sounds of each, and a model to detect emergency situations using audio processing and analytics.

Keywords: Acoustic signals · Event detection · Audioanalysis · Audio surveillance

1 Introduction

In recent years, we have increasingly encountered various audio content that is distributed for both commercial and non-commercial purposes. Due to the growing availability of audio materials and the growth of computing power, automated signal-based audio processing is currently at the center of various studies [1].

Depending on the storage format, user requirements, data volume, and many other parameters, a variety of applications and trends have emerged to solve various audio analysis tasks. The following popular tasks of audio analysis can be distinguished [2]: speech recognition, speaker identification, music information search (MIR), event detection, emotion recognition, and film content analysis.

Audio information can be presented in different ways and in different formats. For example, a composer can record a work in the form of a musical score (sheet music). A note has several properties, including pitch, timbre, volume, and duration [3].

K. Wojtkiewicz et al. (Eds.): ICCCI 2021, CCIS 1463, pp. 413–424, 2021.
https://doi.org/10.1007/978-3-030-88113-9_33

MusicXML has become a universal format for storing music files for use in various music notation applications. This is a music file format, the main task of which is to correctly display the graphics, that is, to demonstrate how a piece of music will look. For electronic instruments and computers, music can be transmitted using standard protocols, such as the widely used Digital Musical Instrument Interface (MIDI) protocol, where event messages determine pitch, speed, and other parameters to generate the intended sounds [4]. Unlike symbolic representations, audio representations, such as WAV or MP3 files, do not explicitly define musical events [5]. These files encode the acoustic waves that are generated when a source (such as an instrument) makes a sound.

Another commonly used form of representation of an audio signal is the representation of a signal in the time domain. The change in the characteristics of the audio signal over time is represented as a graph. Computers can receive audio signal characteristics at specific points in time. The speed at which the computer analyzes the audio data is called the sampling rate [6].

2 Related Works

Recently, automatic systems that control a person's daily activities are becoming more common. Their main purpose is to ensure public safety, which is achieved through surveillance in public places and the recognition of potentially dangerous situations. Research in the field of automatic surveillance systems is mainly focused on the detection of events using video analytics. In turn, acoustic monitoring can be used as an additional source of information, and, being integrated with video surveillance systems, can increase the efficiency of event detection. This makes it necessary to study the problem of automated recognition of sounds of critical situations in order to further develop a system that searches for them in the audio signal in real time [7, 8].

Progress in the study of acoustic characteristics of sounds is associated with the name of the German scientist Hermann von Helmholtz. He developed the theory of resonance, on the basis of which, in the middle of the XIX century, a resonator was invented, called the Helmholtz resonator. The resonator repeatedly amplifies the amplitude of the spectral components of periodic and aperiodic signals, the frequency of which is close to its natural frequency. With a set of resonators with different natural frequencies, the researcher can perform spectral analysis of audio signals. Initially, this was done as follows: in a resonator on the opposite side of the neck, a process was created, which the researcher inserted into the ear; by listening to the sound under study using a set of such resonators, the scientist could determine which tones and with what volume are present in this sound [9–11].

The next step in the development of the technique of spectral analysis was made a few years later by Rudolf Koenig. Using a set of tunable Helmholtz resonators, he was able to provide visualization of spectral analysis using the manometric capsule he invented in 1862. The principle of operation of the capsule was as follows: in one half of the capsule, separated by an elastic membrane, the lamp gas was supplied, in the other half sound was supplied, and, thus, fluctuations in sound pressure modulated the height of the flame in the capsule: the greater the amplitude of the vibration, the higher the flame [12].

A milestone invention in the field of spectral analysis and visualization of sounds was made by American scientists. They created a new type of spectrograph called a sonograph. It made it possible to visualize a dynamic spectrogram obtained by burning an electrosensitive paper with a pen. In fact, the sonograph has completed a century of analog spectral analysis techniques [13].

The acoustic monitoring system allows you to solve the following tasks in automatic mode and in real time [14–16]:

1. selection of acoustic artifacts in the sound stream (characteristic sound signs of a particular event);
2. perform classification of acoustic artifacts (shot, scream, glass fight, explosion, siren, etc.).);
3. selection of speech and its emotional component in the audio stream (for the Russian language) with automatic recognition of keywords and phrases ("police!", "call an ambulance!", etc.);
4. determination of the approximate direction to the source of the acoustic artifact relative to the terminal device (if the terminal device is equipped with a stereo microphone);
5. determination of the coordinates of the alarm event (if the terminal device is equipped with a GPS/GLONASS signal receiver);
6. transmitting information about the recorded alarm event to the processing center with the indication of the event attributes (device ID, event time, event class, audio recording of the event, relative direction to the sound source, etc.);
7. saving information about disturbing events in the archive;
8. notification of external video surveillance systems about the registration of an alarm event.

A well-known acoustic monitoring system is the Shot Spotter system, which has been used in the United States since 2006, and although it is limited to only one class of disturbing events – shots, it is not able to recognize speech, it has proven its effectiveness. Over the years, the system has localized 39,000 firearm shots, and police have been able to respond quickly on a case-by-case basis.

3 Materials and Methods

3.1 Extracting Features from an Audio Signal

Feature extraction is an important step in both audio analysis and image recognition and machine learning in general. The goal is to extract a set of characteristics that informatively reflect the properties of the source data from the data set of interest. This allows you to reduce the dimension of the data [17].

To achieve this goal, it is important to have a good understanding of the subject area in order to decide which of the features are important and which are not. After extracting the necessary signal features for their further use, the features are normalized. In this case, well-known and theoretically studied methods of reducing the dimension of the feature vector (LDA, PCA, etc.) are used [18].

3.2 Short-Term Audio Signal Analysis

In most applications, the audio signal is analyzed using the so-called short-term (or short-term) processing technology, according to which the audio signal is divided into windows (frames) and the analysis is performed based on these frames [19] (Fig. 1).

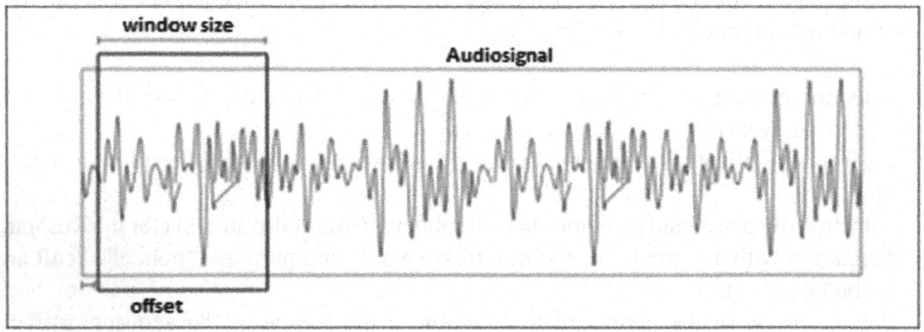

Fig. 1. Example of short-term processing using a window

During short-term processing, we focus each time on a small part (frame) of the signal, i.e., at each stage of processing, we multiply the audio signal by the shifted window function of the finite duration *w* (*n*) [20]. The resulting signal *x i* () at the *i*th stage of processing is given by the formula 1.

$$x_i(n) = x(n) * w(n - m_i),\ i = 0, \ldots, K - 1 \tag{1}$$

where *K* – number of frames, *mi* – shift delay (the number of samples by which the window is shifted to get the *i*-th frame).

Formula 1 implies that (*n*) is zero everywhere except in the region of samples with indexes *mi*,…,*mi* + *WL* − 1, where *WL* - length of the moving window. The value of *m i* depends on the step *W S* of the window. Usually *WL* varies from 10 ms to 50 ms. On the other hand, the window pitch (*S*) controls the degree of overlap between consecutive frames. If, for example, 75% overlap is required and the window length is 40 ms, then the window pitch should be 10 ms. Hence, the total number of short-term windows *K* can be obtained using the formula 2.

$$K = \begin{cases} \dfrac{N - W_L}{W_S} + 1 \\ 0,\ else \end{cases} \tag{2}$$

As for the window types, you can use a rectangular window, in which the signal is simply truncated outside the window and remains unchanged inside the window. This logic can be described by formula 3.

$$w(n) = \begin{cases} 1,\ 0 \le n \le W_L - 1 \\ 0,\ else \end{cases} \tag{3}$$

In addition to rectangular windows, you can use such windows as the Hamming window, the Bartlett window, and others.

3.3 System Architecture

The microphone's audio is constantly recorded by the device. A time limit has been set for the recording. When the user subsystem hits this time limit, it saves the freshly documented file for review, deletes the previously stored file, and starts writing the next file.

Figure 2 illustrates the proposed device architecture. Preprocessor, first stage frame classifier, and second stage frame classifier are among the components of the device.

From the initial audio signal, the preprocessor produces a series of overlapped audio frames and removes a collection of features from each frame. Each function vector is given a collection of labels by the first stage frame classifiers (frame). It's worth remembering that each frame may have several labels allocated to it. It finally group frames into intervals. Second Stage Interval Classifier conducts an interval-level classification, assigning a final prediction to each interval based on a Weighted Majority Voting (WMV) strategy within the frames that make up the interval.

The process of identifying different troubling audio incidents is broken down into two parts [21]:

- the identification (selection) of sharp pulse signals in the audio data stream from background noise;
- the assignment (recognition) of the identified signal as one of the categories of audio events.

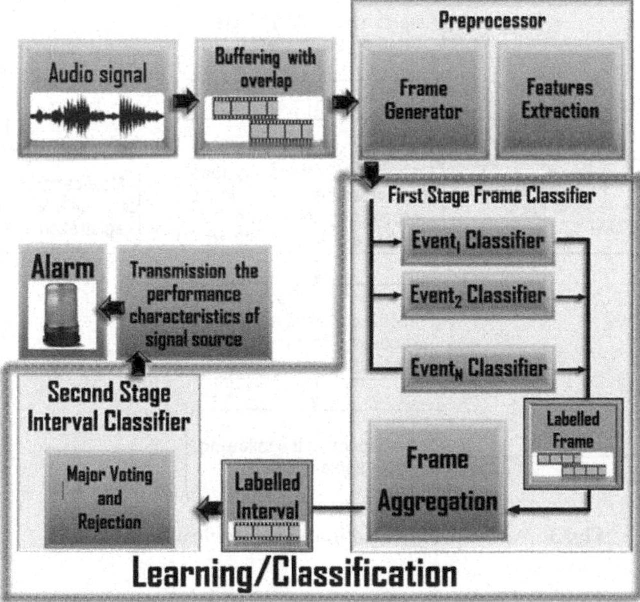

Fig. 2. System architecture

Figure 3 depicts an acoustic measurement device that detects pulsed noises and activities automatically and in real time. The machine receives a signal as well as the sound event's characteristics. Machine learning is used to classify audio patterns and identify pulsed tones. "Police," "Ambulance," and "Blast" are described as keywords in the incident. Identifying the site of possibly hazardous incidents. The next move is to submit reports regarding the warning case to the relevant authority, archive the event, and apply the evidence to the database.

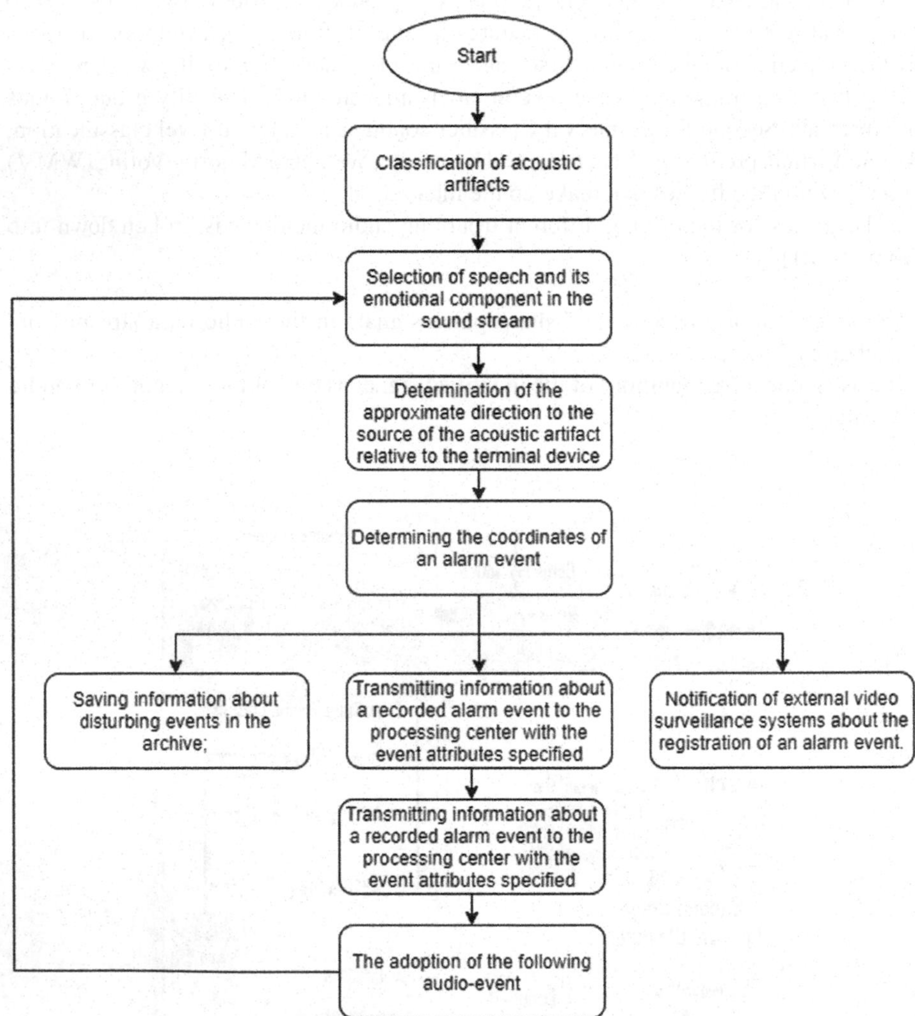

Fig. 3. Audio event detection and classification flowchart

3.4 Data Collection

The proposed system's output was assessed for an automatic monitoring program that needed to detect the following incidents (considered "abnormal" in the observed environment): shots, cries, and broken windows.

We created a data collection for this reason by combining multiple audio samples collected in different railway station scenarios.

Background noise signals such as select, shot, and broken glass make up the data collection. To accommodate for the characteristics of different device scenarios, background noise was recorded both indoors and outdoors.

The signals were divided into one-second intervals (the average time period of each occurrence of interest) for our studies, and then each interval was divided into frames of 200 MS, overlapping by 50%: each interval consists of nine frames.

Table 1 summarizes the data set's signal, frame, and interval structure in terms of signals, frames, and intervals.

4 Evaluation and Experiment Results

We selected test F as a measure of reliability for each Classifier because it is a reasonable balance between precision and recall:

$$precision = \frac{tp}{tp + fp} \tag{4}$$

True positive classified samples are referred to as tp, and false negative classified samples are referred to as fp.

$$Recall = \frac{tp}{tp + fn} \tag{5}$$

$$F_{measure} = \frac{2 * Precision * Recall}{Precision + Recall} \tag{6}$$

Table 2 illustrates experiment results of audioevent classification.

5 Discussion

One of the most critical factors for the proper running of every community is the war against violence. While video surveillance is important in this field, it only provides a visual aspect. Environmental noises that may raise situational sensitivity should be used in a more comprehensive approach.

Table 1. Samples of different impulsive sounds

Table Column Head		
Types of impulsive sounds	*Time (sec)*	*Image*
Automobile glass shattering	3.84	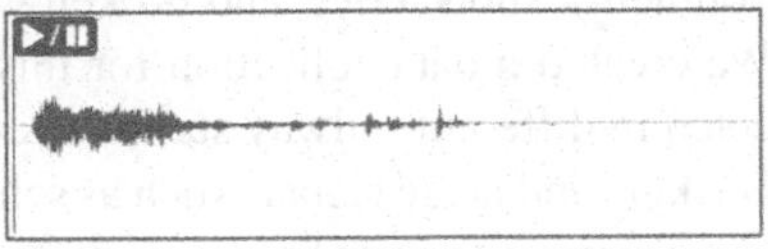
Dog barking	22.15	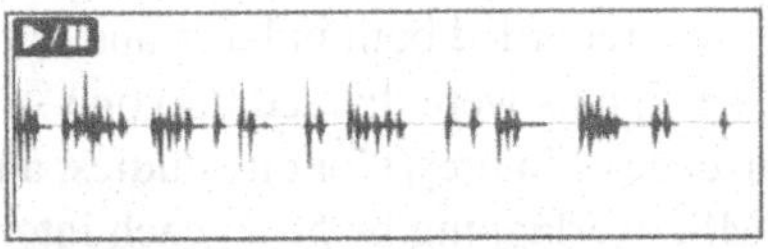
Police siren	24.19	
Ambulance siren	15.41	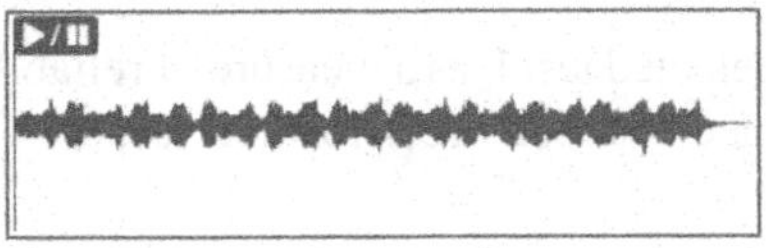
Constant Wail from Police Siren	56.87	
Single gun shot	3.84	
Explosion	7.78	
Artillery shell explosion	4	
Baby crying	6.66	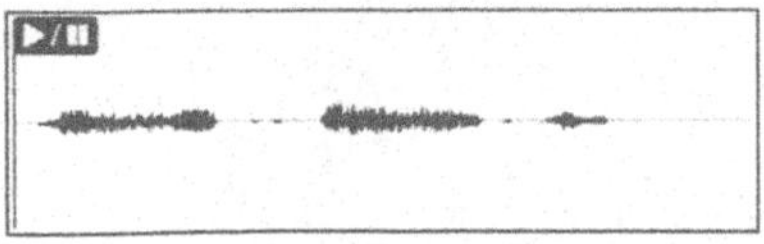

(*continued*)

Table 1. (*continued*)

Table Column Head		
Types of impulsive sounds	***Time (sec)***	***Image***
Burglar alarm	11.13	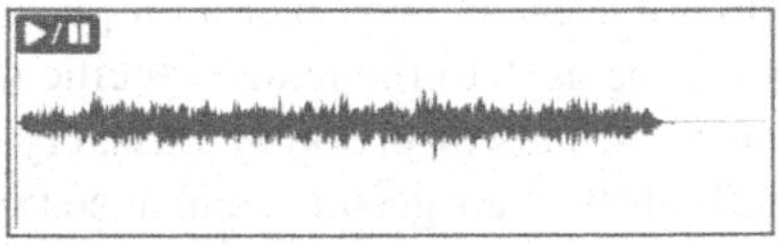
Fire alarm beeping	1.41	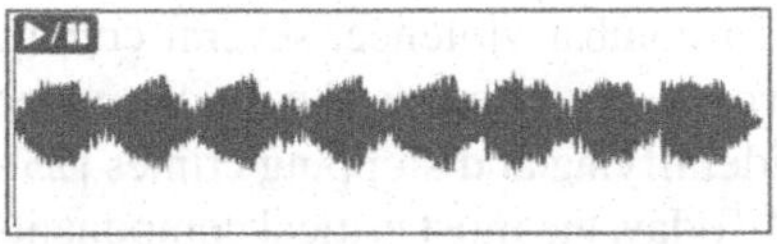
Fire alarm bell	1.59	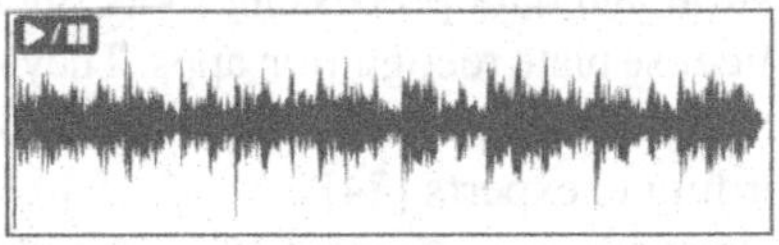
Smoke alarm	0.99	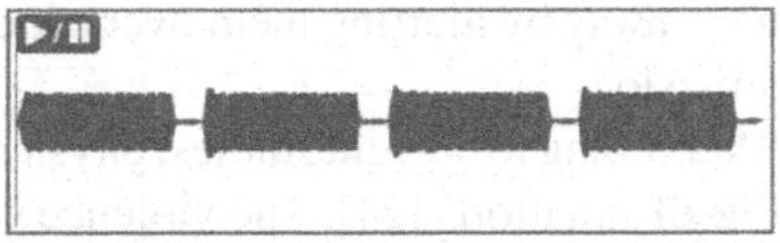
Fire alarm yelp	2.3	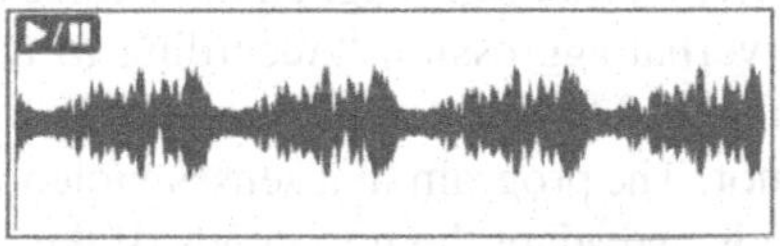

Table 2. Results of impulsive audio event type detection

Event type	Accuracy	Precision	Recall	F1 score
Gunshot	0.9178	0.9245	0.9427	0.8945
Broken glass	0.9372	0.9765	0.9215	0.9154
Fire	0.9435	0.9346	0.9215	0.9345
Siren	0.9537	0.9462	0.9876	0.9642
Explosion	0.8132	0.8254	0.8352	0.8124
Cry	0.8635	0.8524	0.8864	0.8754
Dog barking	0.8456	0.8325	0.8571	0.8254
Fire alarm bell	0.8654	0.8452	0.8576	0.8457

Both stored archives and web streams may be processed using audio analytics. Microphones are often cheaper than cameras and do not need specific requirements for positioning and repair, so they are often used as an alternative to video monitoring [21]. The system detects noises in total darkness, and microphones are much cheaper than cameras and do not need special criteria for placement and maintenance. Sound recognition systems can be used to recognize specific noises in an audio stream (screams, explosions, footsteps, sounds of breaking glass, crying), simple audio recordings of noise, identify individuals by their gestures, enhance the accuracy of the speaker's speech, and identify flaws in the function of structures [22].

To combat violence, several communities depend on video surveillance services. However, according to the article, video monitoring alone is not an adequate solution for identifying and stopping crimes [23].

"Today, the most critical components of urban defense applications are hazard identification and data processing tools, such as motion sensors, thermal imaging devices, and license plate recognition apps. They must, though, concentrate solely on visual influences. Sound sensor technology should be used in a fully robust urban defense approach, according to experts [24].

Operators may hear whether an individual is in danger, send them orders, or scare suspects away by alerting them over a loudspeaker using a surveillance solution of audio transmission.

"According to current studies, physical violence is accompanied by verbal aggression in 90% of situations [24]. The violence sound detection device is useful because it helps security staff to sense agitation in voices and other noises consistent with rage, anxiety, and verbal aggression "According to the paper. Safety and law enforcement officers would be able to use audio monitoring to decide which noises are of concern and which are not. The program that senses violence uses sophisticated algorithms to interpret the sounds and adapt them to trends. If the sound is marked as noteworthy, the app sends a warning to the monitoring team right away.

The sounds of violence (for example, physical abuse) and weapons are the two types of sounds that need to be studied the most in order to maintain city protection. Law enforcement authorities may be able to properly cope with violence by utilizing devices that identify violent noises and the use of weapons.

6 Conclusion and Future Work

The study proved the feasibility and potential of a method for automatically detecting impulsive sounds in audio files that combines the usage of amplitude-time and spectral signal parameters. Additional experiments would focus on a more detailed collection and mathematical study of low-level signal characteristics, as well as exploring the possibility of utilizing deep machine learning models to identify impulsive sounds.

References

1. Tharwat, A., Mahdi, H., Elhoseny, M., Hassanien, A.E.: Recognizing human activity in mobile crowdsensing environment using optimized k-NN algorithm. Exp. Syst. Appl. **107**, 32–44 (2018)

2. Vanus, J., et al.: Monitoring of the daily living activities in smart home care. Hum. Centr. Comput. Inf. Sci. **7**(1), 30 (2017)
3. Bux, A., Angelov, P., Habib, Z.: Vision based human activity recognition: a review. In: Angelov, P., Gegov, A., Jayne, C., Shen, Q. (eds.) Advances in Computational Intelligence Systems. AISC, vol. 513, pp. 341–371. Springer, Cham (2017). https://doi.org/10.1007/978-3-319-46562-3_23
4. Leo, M., Medioni, G., Trivedi, M., Kanade, T., Farinella, G.M.: Computer vision for assistive technologies. Comput. Vis. Image Understand. **154**, 1–15 (2017)
5. Muhammad, K., Ahmad, J., Lv, Z., Bellavista, P., Yang, P., Baik, S.W.: Efficient deep CNN-based fire detection and localization in video surveillance applications. IEEE Trans. Syst. Man Cybernet. Syst. **49**(7), 1419–1434 (2018)
6. Goldenberg, A., et al.: Use of ShotSpotter detection technology decreases prehospital time for patients sustaining gunshot wounds. J. Trauma Acute Care Surg. **87**(6), 1253–1259 (2019)
7. Weiss, A., Halevi, O., Manus, H., Springer, D.: U.S. Patent No. 10,021,457. U.S. Patent and Trademark Office, Washington, DC (2018)
8. http://www.audioanalytic.com/
9. Virtanen, T., Plumbley, M.D., Ellis, D. (eds.): Computational analysis of sound scenes and events, pp. 3–12. Springer, Berlin (2018)
10. Gabriel, D., Kojima, R., Hoshiba, K., Itoyama, K., Nishida, K., Nakadai, K.: 2D sound source position estimation using microphone arrays and its application to a VR-based bird song analysis system. Adv. Robot. **33**(7–8), 403–414 (2019)
11. Morehead, A., Ogden, L., Magee, G., Hosler, R., White, B., Mohler, G.: Low cost gunshot detection using deep learning on the raspberry pi. In: 2019 IEEE International Conference on Big Data (Big Data), pp. 3038–3044. IEEE (2019)
12. Alsina-Pagès, R.M., Navarro, J., Alías, F., Hervás, M.: homesound: Real-time audio event detection based on high performance computing for behaviour and surveillance remote monitoring. Sensors **17**(4), 854 (2017)
13. Wang, K., Yang, L., Yang, B.: Audio event detection and classification using extended R-FCN approach. In: Proceedings of the Detection and Classification of Acoustic Scenes and Events 2017 Workshop (DCASE2017), pp. 128–132 (2017)
14. Choi, I., Bae, S.H., Kim, N.S.: Deep convolutional neural network with structured prediction for weakly supervised audio event detection. Appl. Sci. **9**(11), 2302 (2019)
15. Romanov, S.A., Kharkovchuk, N.A., Sinelnikov, M.R., Abrash, M.R., Filinkov, V.: Development of an non-speech audio event detection system. In: 2020 IEEE Conference of Russian Young Researchers in Electrical and Electronic Engineering (EIConRus), pp. 1421–1423. IEEE (2020)
16. Bello, J.P., Mydlarz, C., Salamon, J.: Sound analysis in smart cities. In: Virtanen, T., Plumbley, M.D., Ellis, D. (eds.) Computational Analysis of Sound Scenes and Events, pp. 373–397. Springer International Publishing, Cham (2018). https://doi.org/10.1007/978-3-319-63450-0_13
17. Tseng, S.Y., Li, J., Wang, Y., Szurley, J., Metze, F., Das, S.: Multiple instance deep learning for weakly supervised small-footprint audio event detection (2017). https://arxiv.org/abs/1712.09673
18. Cao, Y., Iqbal, T., Kong, Q., Galindo, M., Wang, W., Plumbley, M.: Two-stage sound event localization and detection using intensity vector and generalized cross-correlation. DCASE2019 Challenge, Tech. Rep. (2019)
19. Cerutti, G., Prasad, R., Brutti, A., Farella, E.: Neural network distillation on IoT platforms for sound event detection. Proc. Interspeech **2019**, 3609–3613 (2019)
20. Zinemanas, P., Cancela, P., Rocamora, M.: MAVD: A Dataset for Sound Event Detection in Urban Environments (2019)

21. Wu, D.: An audio classification approach based on machine learning. In: 2019 International Conference on Intelligent Transportation, Big Data & Smart City (ICITBS), pp. 626–629. IEEE (2019)
22. Alías, F., Alsina-Pagès, R.M.: Review of wireless acoustic sensor networks for environmental noise monitoring in smart cities. J. Sens. **2019**, 1–13 (2019)
23. McFee, B., Salamon, J., Bello, J.P.: Adaptive pooling operators for weakly labeled sound event detection. IEEE/ACM Trans. Audio Speech Lang. Process. **26**(11), 2180–2193 (2018)
24. Sammarco, M., Detyniecki, M.: Car accident detection and reconstruction through sound analysis with Crashzam. In: Donnellan, B., Klein, C., Helfert, M., Gusikhin, O. (eds.) SMARTGREENS/VEHITS -2018. CCIS, vol. 992, pp. 159–180. Springer, Cham (2019). https://doi.org/10.1007/978-3-030-26633-2_8

Understanding Bike Sharing Stations Usage with Chi-Square Statistics

Aliya Nugumanova[1], Almasbek Maulit[1(✉)], Madina Mansurova[2], and Yerzhan Baiburin[1]

[1] S. Amanzholov East Kazakhstan University, Ust-Kamenogorsk, Kazakhstan
[2] Al-Farabi Kazakh National University, Almaty, Kazakhstan

Abstract. Bike sharing systems have both great potential and great challenge for the development of smart and green urban environment. Many problems, arising from design and operation of bike sharing systems, have no easy solutions and call for complex mathematical models. Nowadays, there are a lot of sophisticated methods for understanding and administration of bike sharing systems, based on Data mining techniques, graph computations, temporal networks models, etc. At the same time, as the digitalization is accelerating, easy and affordable old-school methods are often overlooked. This paper presents a simple but efficient Chi-square test for analyzing bike sharing stations usage in mornings and evenings. The proposed method determines stations that keep the same usage patterns over time. Experiments conducted on CitiBike trip data for New York City's bike sharing service, have shown promising performance of the proposed method.

Keywords: Bike sharing systems · Chi-square test · Citibike New York · Clustering

1 Introduction

The management of bike sharing systems is a hard and complex optimization problem. The main challenge in support and maintenance of bike sharing system is its periodic imbalance, when there are no bikes to pick-up at some stations and no free docks for returning bikes at the others [1–3]. In order to address this challenge a rebalancing procedure that consists in loading and unloading bikes to/from imbalanced stations, should be conducted daily or periodically. Such a procedure provides an operational solution to emerging problems, however, for the purposes of optimal strategic planning a long-term analysis of the situation is required.

In this paper, we propose a simple but efficient Chi-square test for analyzing morning and evening loads of stations during the one-year period. In general, the chi-square statistics is used to test a hypothesis if there is strong relation between two outcomes. We apply this statistics to determine how many bike sharing stations show stable patterns of their morning and evening usage, where these stations are located and whether their number change from month to month. The Obtained information can be useful for more accurate planning of bike sharing stations' capacities and locations.

K. Wojtkiewicz et al. (Eds.): ICCCI 2021, CCIS 1463, pp. 425–436, 2021.
https://doi.org/10.1007/978-3-030-88113-9_34

Ultimately, the goal of this paper is to separate bike sharing stations into three different classes: 1) stations that keep a high level of the morning load compared to the level of the evening load ("early birds"); 2) stations that keep a high level of the evening load compared to the level of the morning load ("night owls"); 3) stations that don't show significant difference between levels of the morning and the evening loads over time.

As the chi-square test is a universal statistical tool, the proposed approach can be expanded to determine various other patterns of stations usage. In particular, the approach is applicable to separate stations by incoming and outgoing flows: for example, to determine stations that keep a high level of incoming flows on mornings and by contrast the high level of outgoing flows on evenings.

2 Related Work

There are a huge number of publications devoted to analysis of bike sharing systems. The goal of analysis is to reveal and register temporal or spatial-temporal dependencies of pickup and return activity patterns at stations [4].

For example, in [4], five types of activity patterns are determined. The first pattern, named as "Returns Morning Pickups Evening" reflects a higher return activity in the morning compared to pick-up activity, and a slightly higher pickup activity compared to return activity in the evening. The names of the other four patterns, i.e. "Pickups Morning Returns Evening", "Active Night Pickups Morning", "AVG", "Active daytime" also speak for themselves. Station clusters, obtained according to these patterns, are visualized on the map, and a strong relation is stated between activity patterns and station locations.

In [5], bike sharing activity patterns are analyzed from both trip-based and station-based aspects. For example, trip-based aspects include information about rainy days and working or non-working days, which affect bike sharing activities. Station-based aspects include information about types of regions and environments around stations. Based on these aspects, BPNN method is applied to develop different demand prediction models according to different types of trips and stations. Weather and calendar events are used also in [6] in order to more accurate determine station usage patterns.

In [7], analyses of individual trips, trip chains, and the transition activities are combined to explore the travel pattern of bike sharing users. Three types of dominant patterns are revealed and imply that the majority of bike sharing usages might relate to commuting, and some users show an after-work shopping activity.

In [8], bike sharing stations are analyzed in order to predict their occupancy levels (i.e., critical or non-critical) in the near future. The station occupancy level is associated with various temporal factors, such as the day category (holiday or working day), the day of the week, and the daily timeslots (morning, evening, etc.). The prediction is made based on current and past station occupancy values associated with temporal factors.

In works [9–11], visual analytics frameworks to investigate bike trips and users activity patterns are introduced. In [9], bike trips and station usage footprints can be visualized for specific days, or aggregated over different time periods. The Authors of these works note that even though they don't introduce a solution to rebalancing, their analysis framework "may improve rebalancing schemes by adding instance-specific knowledge to current solutions". In [10], visual analysis is represented for more than 468 bike-sharing networks worldwide. The proposed system uses innovative interaction techniques that can help, for instance, to expose capacity bottlenecks, commuting patterns, live stations fill levels and other network characteristics. In [11], users daily activity patterns are explored based on tensor factorization. For example, the authors of this work determine one special pattern in the summer data of New York. The age distribution of this pattern is concentrated around 20 years old, and the spatial distribution is near Washington Square where New York University and Washington University are located. The pattern shows all day rental activity and the smaller flow on weekends. Hence, the authors infer that this pattern corresponds to riding to class or parks.

In [12], usage patterns of Mobike bike sharing system are extracted from spatiotemporal perspective. High traffic areas of Mibike are detected visually, informing about actual coordinates of where rebalancing is needed. In addition, three findings are inferred from the study: the major demand of Mobike is to facilitate commuting; during weekend, the highest peak is in the evening while during the weekday the highest peak is in both the morning and afternoon; during weekdays, external factors such as bad weather more strongly affect the daily flow than evening or morning flows.

3 Methodology

3.1 Structure Overview

The methodology of this work consists of 4 steps. Figure 1 shows the structure overview of the proposed methodology.

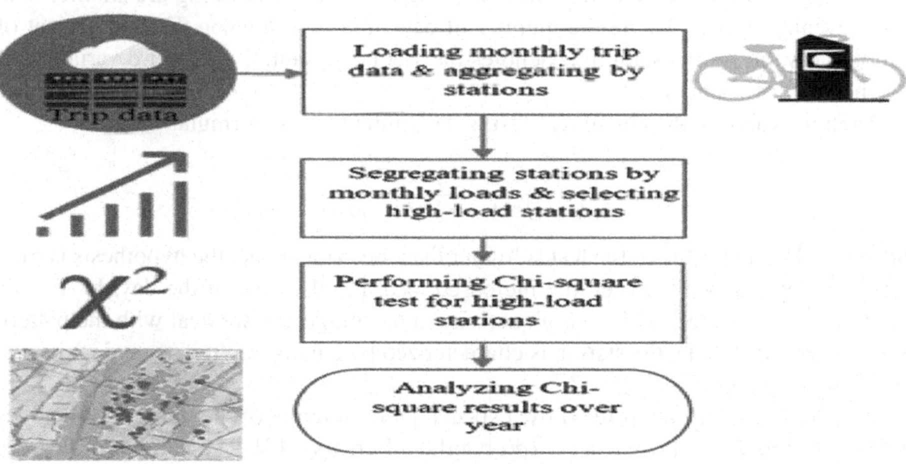

Fig. 1. The structure overview of the proposed methodology

Firstly, we load historical trip data for a month, which contains information about bike ridings, including trip duration, start time and date, stop time and date, start station id, name, longitude and latitude, stop station id, name, longitude and latitude, bike id, user's type, gender and birth year. We aggregate these data by stations and infer two types of information about stations: their total monthly loads and their loads by days and times of days. Secondly, based on four types of monthly stations loads (i.e. incoming and outgoing morning loads, incoming and outgoing evening loads), we divide stations into two clusters: high-load stations and other stations. This step may be skipped if the total number of stations is small or if it is necessary to analyze all stations. We will not describe these two steps in detail since they don't cause any difficulties.

Thirdly, for high-load stations we perform chi-square test. Meaningful values of chi-square test indicate one of the two kinds of stations usage patterns, which we call "early birds" and "night owls". Fourthly and finally, we analyze how the number and locations of the "early birds" stations and the "night owls" stations change during year. The following section describes these two steps in detail.

3.2 Chi-Square Statistics to Determine "Early Bird" and "Night Owl" Usage Patterns

In this work, we use the chi-square test to answer the question if there is a dependence between the increased activity of the station and the time of the day (morning and evening). With this aim, for each station we build a contingency table 2 * 2 in which we register the observed outcomes.

There are four variants of outcomes: 1) both the incoming and outgoing loads at the station are greater in the morning than in the evening; 2) the incoming load in the morning is greater than in the evening, but the outgoing flow is less than the outgoing flow in the evening; 3) the incoming flow in the morning is less than the incoming flow in the evening, but the outgoing flow in the morning is greater than the outgoing flow in the evening; 4) both the incoming and outgoing flows in the morning are smaller than in the evening. Let A denote the number of days in a month when the first variant of outcome is valid for the station, B denotes the second variant, C – the third variant, and D – the fourth variant.

Then the value of the chi-square test is determined by the formula:

$$\chi^2 = \frac{(A+B+C+D)(AD-BC)^2}{(A+B)(A+C)(B+D)(C+D)} \tag{1}$$

and if the obtained value of the test is higher than the critical one, the hypothesis is true, there is a dependence between the increased load and the time of the day. If $A > D$, the station is characterized by a high activity in mornings, i.e. we deal with the pattern "early birds". If $A < D$, the station is characterized by a high activity in evening, i.e. we deal with the pattern "night owl".

A critical value is determined by a special table in terms of the number of degrees of freedom and a significance level (probability of errors) [13]. The number of degrees of freedom for the table 2×2 is 1. At the significance level of 5% and one degree of freedom the critical value according to the table makes up 3.841, at the significance level of 1% – 6.635.

Table 1 shows an example of a station with an excess of morning loads over evening loads (both incoming and outgoing) during 22 days out of 31 days in the month. The value of chi-square for this station is equal to 26.30, this exceeding the critical value of 3.841.

Table 1. Contingency table for chi-square test

Number of days when...	Outgoing morning load > Outgoing evening load	Outgoing morning load ≤ Outgoing evening load	Total
Incoming morning load > Incoming evening load	A = 22	B = 1	23
Incoming morning load ≤ Incoming evening load	C = 0	D = 8	8
Total	22	9	31

Having calculated the chi-square test for every station in each month of the year, we can trace the changes in the status of the stations during a year. In particular, we can easily answer such questions: does the number of "night owl" increase in summer months, what stations show one and the same stable pattern during the whole year, what stations change the status, etc.

4 Experiments and Results

4.1 Trip Data Loading and Aggregation

In our experiments we use open data of the system CitiBike NYC [14] for 2019 as well as from January to May of 2020. The data contain information trips with an accuracy up to a second. We use two levels of data aggregation: 1) over days of the month and the time of the day (morning, afternoon, evening, night); 2) over the entire month. Table 2 contains a fragment of aggregated data for January, 2019 where the totals are presented

Table 2. Fragment of subtotal trip data aggregation for January 2019

Station ID & name	Day of month	Time of day	Number of outgoing bikes	Number of incoming bikes	Number of removed bikes	Number of added bikes
3443 - W 52 St & 6 Ave	9	Morning	62	244	1	1
3443 - W 52 St & 6 Ave	9	Evening	92	9	2	2
394 -E 9 St & Avenue C	9	Morning	69	14	30	30
394 - E 9 St & Avenue C	9	Evening	12	29	0	0

for each station over days of the month and the time of the day (morning of evening), and Table 3 contains a fragment of aggregated data for January, 2019 where totals are presented for each station over the whole month.

Table 3. Fragment of total trip data aggregation for January 2019

Station ID & name	Total of incoming morning loads	Total of outgoing morning loads	Total of incoming evening loads	Total of outgoing evening loads
3443 - W 52 St & 6 Ave	1095	451	159	604
394 - E 9 St & Avenue C	335	1283	806	364

4.2 Selecting High-Load Stations

Using the aggregated data with the totals for a month, we divide all stations into two clusters depending on their monthly load: the first cluster – high-load stations, the second cluster – low- or medium-load stations. Figure 2 shows the quantitative ratio of these clusters in January 2019 where it is seen that the number of high-load stations is smaller approximately three times.

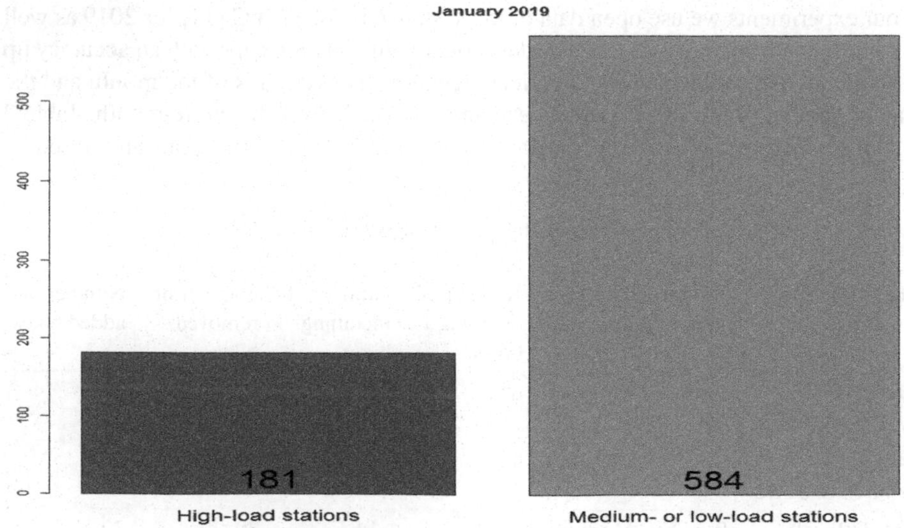

Fig. 2. The structure overview of the proposed methodology

The given ratio between the number of high-load and low-or medium-load stations is maintained in the rest months, as seen in the in the maps in Fig. 3 where high-load stations are marked with red circles, and low- or medium-load stations are marked with green circles.

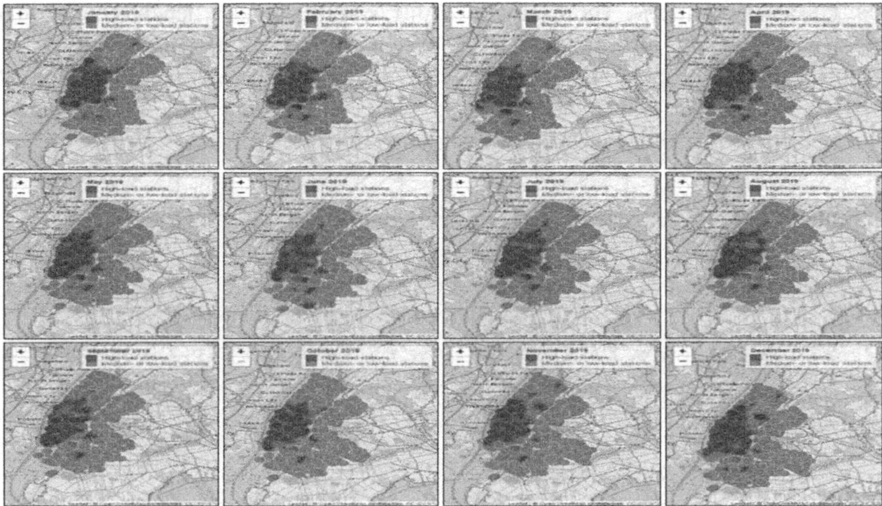

Fig. 3. The spatial distribution of high-load (red color) and low- or medium-load stations (green color) from January to December of 2019

As is seen in the Fig. 3, high-load stations are located compactly, mainly in lower Manhattan, and this trend continues throughout the year, regardless of the month. Moreover, this trend continues also in March 2020 (see Fig. 4) in spite of the fact that in this month Covid-19 outbreak began in the city.

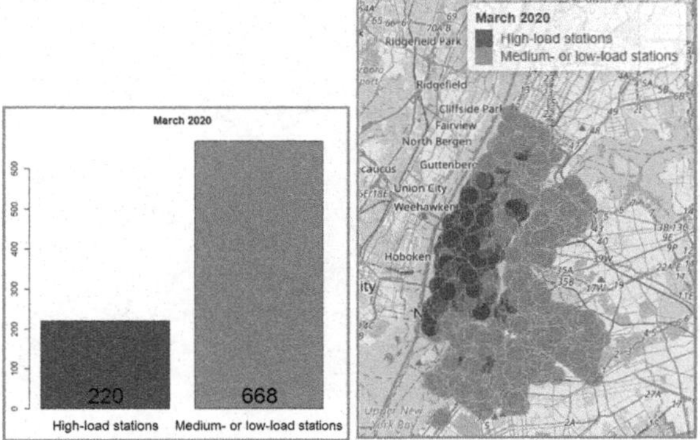

Fig. 4. The distribution of high-load (red color) and low- or medium-load stations (green color) in March 2020

4.3 Chi-Square Testing of High-Load Stations

Using the aggregated data, a fragment of which is presented in Table 2, for each station we calculate the chi-square test according to the formula (1). Then we select stations with high values of the test. These are stations the activity of which depends on the time of the day: active in mornings ("early birds") and active in evening ("night owls").

Table 4 contains Top-10 stations which keep their status of "early birds" during 12, 11 or 10 months. If you look at the map in Fig. 5, you will see that most of these stations are located along Broadway near large hotels and public houses.

Table 4. TOP-10 "early birds" stations that keeps their status for 12, 11 or 10 months

Rank	Station ID & name	Number of months when the station keeps "early birds" status	Average Chi-square
1	173 - Broadway & W 49 St	12	17.43
2	465 - Broadway & W 41 St	12	17.66
3	167 - E 39 St & 3 Ave	11	16.78
4	195 - Liberty St & Broadway	11	15.45
5	500 - Broadway & W 51 St	11	13.94
6	450 - W 49 St & 8 Ave	10	13.08
7	468 - Broadway & W 56 St	10	12.48
8	469 - Broadway & W 53 St	10	13.12
9	530 - 11 Ave & W 59 St	10	7.82
10	533 - Broadway & W 38 St	10	14.62

Fig. 5. "Early birds" stations that keep their status at least 10 months

Table 5 contains top 10 stations which keep their status of "night owls" from 7 to 10 months. In the map they are located mainly near caterings and recreation zones.

Table 5. TOP-10 Night owls stations that keeps their status for 12, 11 or 10 months

Rank	Station ID & name	Number of months when the station keeps "early birds" status	Average Chi-square
1	Carmine St & 6 Ave	10	14.45
2	2 Ave & E 31 St	10	12.94
3	Mott St & Prince St	9	7.17
4	Forsyth St & Canal St	9	13.26
5	8 Ave & W 52 St	9	10.65
6	Stanton St & Chrystie St	8	7.64
7	9 Ave & W 45 St	8	11.94
8	1 Ave & E 62 St	8	14.02
9	E 15 St & 3 Ave	7	10.08
10	Greenwich Ave & Charles St	7	6.36

4.4 Analyzing Chi-Square Results Over Year

Figure 6 presents the dynamics of the change in the number of "early birds" and "night owls" stations over months of 2019. As is seen in the Fig. 6, the number of "early birds" stations decreases in the summer period reaching minimum in June, in the rest period is at about one level with the maximum in April. The number of "night owls" stations, on the contrary, increases in summer and reaches the peak in July, decreases in winter months with the minimum in November.

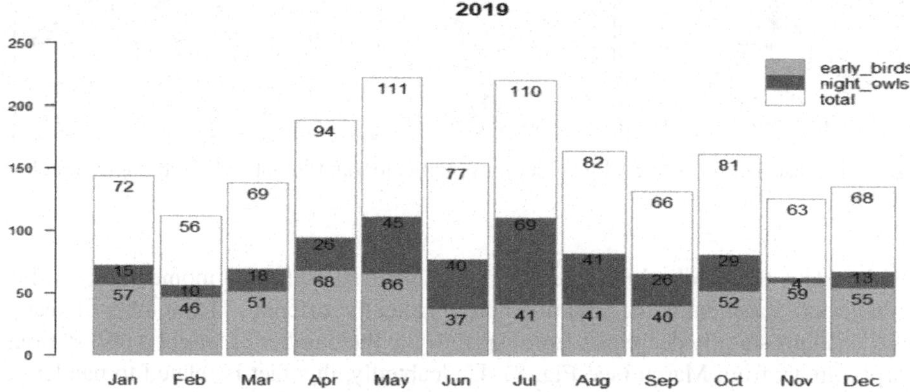

Fig. 6. The numbers of "early birds" and "night owls" stations by months of 2019

Figure 7 shows evolution in the composition of "early birds" and "night owls" stations during 2019 but in a spatial variant.

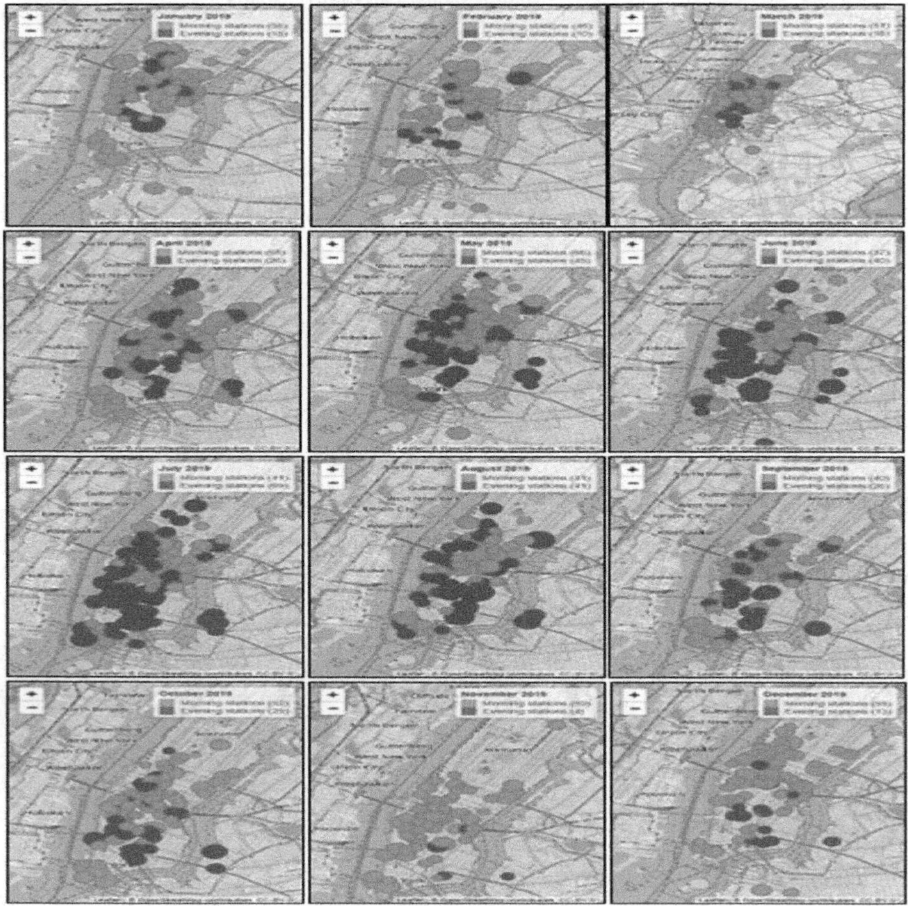

Fig. 7. The distribution of "early birds" stations (pink color) and "night owls" stations (blue color) in 2019

If we take the similar indicators for 5 months of 2020 (at the moments of writing we have only these data), the situation here if radically different. The number of "early birds" stations sharply decreases from April, while the number of "night owls" stations sharply grows from March (see Fig. 8). Undoubtedly, this fact is related to pandemic Covid-19 the peak of which in New York was observed in April.

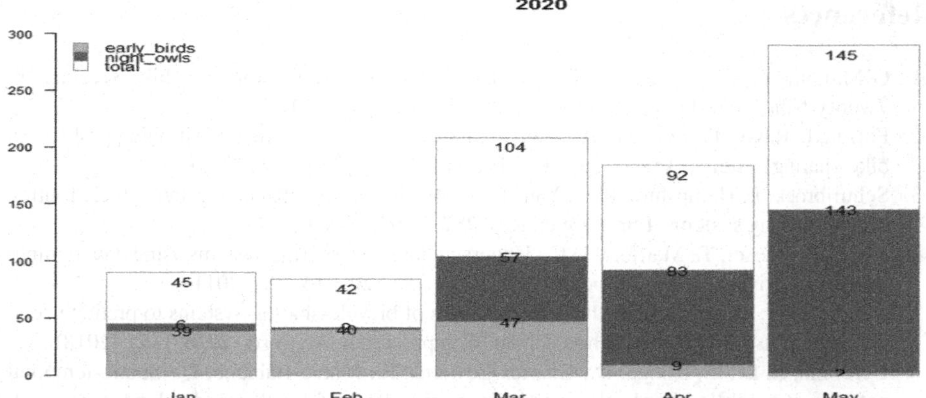

Fig. 8. The numbers of "early birds" and "night owls" stations by 5 first months of 2020

5 Conclusion

In this work we studied the applicability of the chi-square criterion for determination of activity patterns at stations of the largest bike sharing network CitiBike New York. We studied the dependence of stations activity on the time of the day and came to the following conclusions: 1) morning and evening activities of stations are seasonal, and in summer the number of stations with a high morning activity decreases but the number of stations with a high evening activity increases; 2) there is a quite clear division of high-loaded stations into 2 classes "early birds" and "night owls" and about 30 stations of the first class and 20 stations of the second class keep their class during a long period of time (from half a year and more), while only 3 stations show a mixed regime of activity throughout a year going from class "early birds" to class "night owls" and vice versa 4 and more times.

Of special attention is the period from March to May of 2020 when the outbreak of Covid-19 affected the sharp decrease in morning loads and exerted a less effect on the decrease of evening loads. Consequently, at stations where morning trips prevailed, evening trips started to dominate, therefore in April-May we observe a sharp increase in the sharp of "night owls" stations.

The obtained by us conclusions allow to confirm the fact that the chi-square test proved to be a reliable and available tool for determining temporal patterns of stations usage. In our future studies we plan to use the chi-square criterion to test other hypothesis, for example, about the presence of dependence between high incoming and outgoing loads of stations and vice versa.

Acknowledgment. This work was funded by Committee of Science of Republic of Kazakhstan AP09261344 «Development of methods for automatic extraction of geospatial objects from heterogeneous sources for information support of geographic information systems».

References

1. O'Mahony, E., Shmoys, D.B.: Data analysis and optimization for (citi) bike sharing. In: Twenty-Ninth AAAI Conference on Artificial Intelligence (2015)
2. Forma, I., Raviv, T., Tzur, M.: A 3-step math heuristic for the static repositioning problem in bike sharing systems. Transp. Res. Part B Methodol. **71**, 230–247 (2015)
3. Schuijbroek, J., Hampshire, R.C., Van Hoeve, W.: Inventory rebalancing and vehicle routing in bike sharing systems. Eur. J. Oper. Res. **257**(3), 992–1004 (2017)
4. Vogel, P., Greiser, T., Mattfeld, D.C.: Understanding bike sharing systems using data mining: exploring activity patterns. Procedia Soc. Behav. Sci. **20**, 514–523 (2011)
5. Xu, X., et al.: Understanding the usage patterns of bicycle-sharing systems to predict users' demand: a case study in Wenzhou, China. Comput. Intell. Neurosci. **2018**, 1–21 (2018)
6. Corcoran, J., Li, T., Rohde, D., Charles-Edwards, E., Mateo-Babiano, D.: Spatio-temporal patterns of a public bicycle sharing program: the effect of weather and calendar events. J. Transp. Geogr. **1**(41), 292–305 (2014)
7. Zhang, Y., Brussel, M.J., Thomas, T., van Maarseveen, M.F.: Mining bike sharing travel behavior data: an investigation into trip chains and transition activities. Comput. Environ. Urban Syst. **69**, 39–50 (2018)
8. Cagliero, L., Cerquitelli, T., Chiusano, S., Garza, P., Xiao, X.: Predicting critical conditions in bicycle sharing systems. Computing **99**(1), 39–57 (2016)
9. Oliveira, G.N., Sotomayor, J.L., Torchelsen, R.P., Silva, C.T., Comba, J.L.: Visual analysis of bike sharing systems. Comput. Graph. **60**, 119–129 (2016)
10. Oppermann, M., Möller, T., Sedlmair, M.: Bike sharing Atlas: visual analysis of bike sharing networks. Int. J. Transp. **6**(1), 1–14 (2018)
11. Yan, Y., Tao, Y., Xu, J., Ren, S., Lin, H.: Visual analytics of bike sharing data based on tensor factorization. J. Vis. **21**(3), 495–509 (2018)
12. Gorgul, E., Chen, C.: A visualization based analysis to assist rebalancing issues related to last mile problem for bike sharing programs in China: a big-data case study on mobike. In: Yuan, P.F., Xie, Y.M., Yao, J., Yan, C. (eds.) Proceedings of the 2019 DigitalFUTURES: The 1st International Conference on Computational Design and Robotic Fabrication (CDRF 2019), pp. 145–153. Springer, Singapore (2020). https://doi.org/10.1007/978-981-13-8153-9_13
13. Nugumanova, A., et al.: Automatic keywords extraction from the domain texts: implementation of the algorithm based on the MapReduce model. In: 2013 International Conference on Current Trends in Information Technology (CTIT), pp. 186–189. IEEE (2013)
14. CitBike System Data. https://www.citibikenyc.com/system-data. Accessed 17 June 2020

Intelligent System for Assessing the Socio-economic Situation in the Region

Sholpan Jomartova[1(✉)], Talgat Mazakov[2], Daryn Mukhaev[2], Aigerim Mazakova[1], and Gauhar Tolegen[1]

[1] Al-Farabi Kazakh National, Al-Farabi, 71, 050000 Almaty, Kazakhstan
[2] Institute of Information and Computing Technologies, Kurmangazy, 29, 050000 Almaty, Kazakhstan

Abstract. This article analyzes the problems of monitoring and managing the socio-economic situation. The analysis of the socio-economic situation involves the determination of the quantitative characteristics of the dynamic series, the trend of growth, decline or stabilization, the identification of causal factors, in specific territories and for different groups. The criterion of fuzzy controllability was obtained to solve the problem of forecasting and controlling the socio-economic situation. A mathematical model and algorithm for solving the task of monitoring and managing the socio-economic situation based on interval mathematics and their software implementation are described. The social effect will be expressed in improving the safety of people's lives. As a result, it will be possible to carry out preventive measures in the necessary territories.

Keywords: Social tension · Manageability · Interval mathematics · Linguistic variable · Fuzzy · Interval analysis

1 Introduction

The methodology of mathematical modeling has gained a strong position in the technological and natural science fields, and its progress is also significantly noticeable in applications to economic systems. If we talk about processes involving the «human factor» (first of all, about social processes), then the progress in this area is much more modest [1].

Therefore, the relevance of mathematical modeling of social processes and the development of intelligent information and analytical systems (IIAS) that allow monitoring indicators that characterize the socio-economic situation in the context of the country's regions is undeniable.

Mathematical modeling of socio-economic processes can be used by specialists to solve a number of applied issues, such as planning various preventive measures [2,3].

K. Wojtkiewicz et al. (Eds.): ICCCI 2021, CCIS 1463, pp. 437–447, 2021.
https://doi.org/10.1007/978-3-030-88113-9_35

2 Problem Statement

To develop a real system of automated forecasting of the socio-economic situation, a list of economic, demographic and social parameters is defined. Socio-economic indicators include, for example, gross domestic product (GDP) per capita, the index of the physical volume of GDP per capita, as a percentage of the previous year, the volume of industrial production in billion tenge, the index of the physical volume of industrial production, as a percentage of the previous year, the number of industrial enterprises and industries, etc. The following demographic indicators were taken as demographic indicators: the population, the number of people of working age, the number of births, the number of deaths, the number of emigrated citizens, the number of immigrated citizens, etc. The indicators of the crime rate in the region included, for example, the number of all registered crimes, the number of registered murders and attempted murders, the number of registered thefts, etc.

To provide automated monitoring of the socio-economic situation, the following indices were determined based on the results of the analysis and the possibility of obtaining specific data: the cost of living index; the human development index; the unemployment rate; the level of criminality; the level of medical support, etc.

As every one knows, social tension is determined not only by socio-economic factors, but also by the political activity of the population. To assess the political activity of the population, data from the media and the Internet were used. For this purpose, the following indicators of political activity have been introduced: the number of publications in regional and republican mass media with calls for acts of disobedience; the number of demonstrations, rallies and other mass protests against the leadership of the region and the country, which are of an economic nature; the number of demonstrations, rallies and other mass protests against the leadership of the region and the country that are of a political nature; the total number of participants in demonstrations, rallies and other mass demonstrations; the total number of participants in hunger strikes that are of an economic nature; the total number of participants in hunger strikes that are of a political nature; the level of activity of opposition parties. Based on the entered indicators and socio-economic indicators, the index of social tension is calculated.

Directives and measures at the national and regional levels are defined as the control parameters $u = (u_1, ..., u_l)$. In turn, the control parameters are divided into socio-economic and political ones.

3 Main Results

Using the features of the problem under study, a model is constructed in the form of a system of ordinary differential equations

$$\frac{\mathrm{d}x}{\mathrm{d}t} = f(x, u, p, t) \tag{1}$$

where u - external factors, p - parameters of binding (setting) of the mathematical model to real data.

Management restrictions are given

$$u(t) \in U = \{u(t) : -L_i \leq u_i(t) \leq L_i, i = 1, m, t \in [t_0, t_1]\} \quad (2)$$

Using the methods of the mathematical theory of identification, based on the retrospective knowledge of the values of the parameters $x = (x_1, ..., x_n)$ and $u = (u_1, ..., u_l)$, the values of the parameters p are calculated. In this case, the form of functions *f(x,u,p,t)* (up to unknown constants p) are constructed taking into account the «physics» of the studied indicators.

Thus, a mathematical model is defined that characterizes the relationship between the input and control parameters. The IAS allows you to predict the behavior (dynamics) of the input parameters under various (specially specified) specified control actions.

Knowing the values of the parameters x at the present time, which is denoted by t_0:

$$x(t_0) = x_0 \quad (3)$$

solving the obtained Cauchy problem (1)–(3) by numerical methods (in particular, the Runge-Kutta method) for given external influences u, the values of the parameters x, y at time t_1, are found, i.e., the problem of forecasting for the period $[t_0, t_1]$ is solved.

By solving the sequence of Cauchy problems (1)–(3) for various (specially defined) given external influences $u_1, ..., u_k$, it is possible to predict the corresponding behavior of the parameters x at the time t_1, i.e. to give an opportunity to get an answer to the question (lose the situation), what can happen if the strategy u_1 is chosen as opposed to the strategy u_2, etc.

In classical control theory, we usually study the controllability problem (Problem 1) [4]: is there a control that satisfies the constraint (2) and transfers the system (1) from the initial state (3) to the final given state

$$x(t_1) = x_1. \quad (4)$$

for a fixed time $t_1 - t_0$.

The initial values of the state vector x_0 in formula (3) are set from the actual measurements. At the same time, for the task of monitoring the socio-economic situation, it is not the fixed value of x_1 at the final time t_1 in formula (4) that is relevant, but the translation of the system into a certain set that allows for a convenient interpretation.

In this connection, based on the theory of fuzzy sets, we introduce the corresponding linguistic variables for the state variables x of the system (1) as follows [6].

Each state variable x_i corresponds to the linguistic variable $x_{ling}, i = \overline{1, n}$. Since in the model (1)–(4) the variables of the state of the system have a quantitative character and their greater significance increases the degree of occurrence of socio-economic danger, the following values of linguistic variables are proposed:

TermLin[1]= «optimal level»,
TermLin[2]= «moderate level»,
TermLin[3]= «acceptable level»,
TermLin[4]= «critical level» .

Each j-th value of the i-th linguistic variable $x_{lingi,j}$ corresponds to a numeric interval $(x_{min,i,j}, x_{max,i,j})$ and many $\bigcup_{j=1}^{4}(x_{min,i,j,}, x_{max,i,j})$ must cover all possible values of the variable $(x_{min,i,j}, x_{max,i,j})$. In particular, it is acceptable to $\bigcup_{j=1}^{4}(x_{min,i,j,}, x_{max,i,j}) = (-\infty, +\infty)$.

We introduce a set of indices $I_{kr} \subseteq [1, .., n]$ that defines a list of state variables that are subject to terminal constraints. For example, if for the model (1)–(4) the terminal constraints are imposed only on the variable x_2, then the set of indices $I_{kr} = [2]$ consists of a single element.

Next, we consider the following fuzzy controllability problem (Problem 2): is there a control that satisfies the constraint (2) and transfers the system (1) from the initial state (11) to the final state

$$x_{lingi}(t_1) = TermLin[i_j], i \in I_{kr} \tag{5}$$

for a fixed time $t_1 - t_0$.

In (5), the index i_j corresponds to the selected j-th linguistic fuzzy value for the i–th state variable.

Problem 1 is a special case of problem 2.

Due to the properties imposed on the right side of the system of equations of the Cauchy problem (1), (3) with a fixed control $u(t) \in U$, the conditions of the theorem of the existence and uniqueness of the solution $x(t), t \in [t_0, t_1]$ are fulfilled [5].

We rewrite the Cauchy problem (1), (3) in integral recurrent form

$$x_{k+1}(t) = x_0 + \int_{t_0}^{t} f(x_k(\tau), u(\tau), \tau)d\tau. \tag{6}$$

Due to the properties imposed on the right side of Eq. (1) and restrictions on the function *u(t)* it is proved in [7] that the method of successive approximations (5) converges to the solution to the solution absolutely and uniformly for any fixed control.

Then the controllability problem is reduced to the study of the following problem: is there at least one control $u(t) \in U$, in which the solution of the integral Eq. (6) at time t_1 satisfies the condition (5).

To solve this problem, we apply the results of the interval analysis [8,9]. Denote by $\overline{v}$ the interval from $-L$ to L, by $\overline{f}$ the interval-valued function obtained from the function $f(x_k(t), u(t), t)$.

Substituting the interval $\overline{v}$ in Eq. (6) instead of the function *u(t)*, we obtain the interval integral equation

$$\overline{x}(t) = x_0 + \int_{t_0}^{t} \overline{f}_(\overline{x}(\tau), \overline{v}, \tau)d\tau. \tag{7}$$

The solution to the integral Eq. (7) can be found by the method of successive approximations

$$\overline{x}_{k+1}(t) = x_0 + \int_{t_0}^{t} \overline{f}_(\overline{x}_k(\tau), \overline{\nu}, \tau)d\tau. \tag{8}$$

Theorem 1. *In order for the system under study was managed is necessary and sufficient that overline$x_i(t_1)$ for all $i \in I_{kr}$ had a non-empty intersection with the set $(x_{min,i,j}, x_{max,i,j})$.*

Proof. Lots of

$$X(t_1) = \left\{ x_0 + \int_{t_0}^{t} f(x_k(\tau, u(\tau), \tau)d\tau | u(t) : -L_i \leq u_i(t) \leq L_i, \right.$$
$$\left. i = 1, m, t \in [t_0, t_1] \right\}$$

coincides with the interval solution of the integral Eq. (7), where all arithmetic operations are performed using interval calculations [9]. Hence, it is obvious that the original system (1)–(4) is controllable, it is necessary and sufficient that the solution of the integral interval Eq. (7) at time t_1 for all $i \in I_{kr}$ has a non-empty intersection with the set $(x_{min,i,j}, x_{max,i,j})$, i.e.

$$\{\overline{x}_i(t_1) \cap (x_{min,i,j}, x_{max,i,j}) \neq |i \in I_{kr}\}.$$

If the system under study is controllable (i.e., there is at least one control $u \in U$ that ensures the transfer of the system (1) from state (3) to state (5), then it is advisable to choose a control that, in addition to solving the problem, would deliver a minimum to a certain criterion (this may be energy consumption, speed, etc.).

The optimal control problem under constraints (5) (6) is a problem with a movable right end.

The problem is solved by the methods of the mathematical theory of optimal control using the method of penalty functions.

In the case of several criteria for selecting optimal control actions, the multi-criteria problem with $J_i, i = \overline{1, n}$ functionals was reduced to a single-criteria optimal control problem with the functional $J = \sum_{i=1}^{n} \alpha_i J_i$. Here $\alpha_i, i = \overline{1, n}$ - global weight coefficients, are determined based on the hierarchy analysis method [10].

Next, we study the dynamical system (1) under the following assumptions: the right – hand side of the system of Eqs. (1) has the form, $f(x, u, t) = g(x, t) + Bu$. B is a constant *(n*m)*-matrix, *g(x,t)*-*n*-vector, the elements of which are continuously differentiable functions in their arguments.

Let's rewrite system (1) in the following form

$$\frac{dx}{dt} = g(x, t) + Bu. \tag{9}$$

The state of the system at the initial time t_0 is considered known (the initial state)

$$x(t_0) = x_0 \tag{10}$$

The desired state at a finite time T can be described as fixed

$$x(T) = x_T \tag{11}$$

or mobile (satisfying certain conditions)

$$\sum_{j=1}^{n} c_{ij} x_j(T) \leq d_i, i = \overline{1,k} \tag{12}$$

at the same time, the time point T can be set (fixed) or be based on certain requirements.

There are natural constraints on quantitative data

$$x_i(t) \geq 0, i = \overline{1,n}, t \in [t_0, T]. \tag{13}$$

To assess the quality of the system, the following criteria can be selected:

$$J = \int_{t_0}^{T} [u^*(t)R_0u(t) + x(t)^*R_1x(t)]\, dt \tag{14}$$

or

$$J = T - t_0 \tag{15}$$

In functional (14), R_0 is a positive – definite mxm-matrix, and R_1 is a non-negative-definite nxn matrix.

The problem of optimal control with phase constraints (13), control constraints (2) with fixed (10), (11) or movable ends (10), (12) is considered. Currently, the solution of such problems contains a number of mathematical difficulties. In this connection, we consider a number of statements of optimal control problems.

1 Optimal control problem with fixed right end and fixed time

The problem of minimizing the functional (14) under constraints is considered (9), (2), (10), (11). The time point T is considered to be set (fixed).

For the given optimal control problem, we compose the Hamilton function

$$H\left(x(t), u, \psi(t), \psi_0\right) = u^*(t)R_0u(t) + x(t)^*R_1x(t) + (g(x,t) + Bu(t))^*\psi. \tag{16}$$

Let's make a conjugate system of differential equations:

$$\frac{d\psi}{dt} = -(\frac{\partial g(t)}{\partial t})^*(t)\psi(t) - 2R_1x(t), t \in [t_0, T]. \tag{17}$$

We determine the optimal control from condition (2) and the maximum of the Hamiltonian:

$$u = \begin{cases} -L \quad if \quad R_0^{-1}B\psi < 0 \\ R_0^{-1}B\psi \; if \; 0 \leq R_0^{-1}B\psi \leq u_{max} \\ L \quad if \quad R_0^{-1}B\psi > u_{max} \end{cases} \tag{18}$$

Theorem 2. *Let the pair $(u(t), x(t)), t \in [t_0, T]$ - be the solution of the above problem. Then there must exist a vector-function $\psi(t), t \in [t_0, T]$ and a parameter ψ_0 such that*

$$\psi_0 \leq 0, |\psi_0| + |\psi(t)| \neq 0, t \in [t_0, T]$$

in this case, $x(t), \psi(t), t \in [t_0, T]$ is the solution of the boundary value problem for the system of differential Eqs. (9) and the corresponding conjugate system of differential Eqs. (17) under boundary conditions (10) and (11) and control (18).

Proof. Since all the conditions of the Pontryagin maximum principle [11] are met for the formulated optimal control problem, the validity of the theorem follows from this.

2 Optimal control problem with a movable right end

We consider the problem of minimizing the functional (14), under the constraints (9), (2), (10), (12). The time point T is considered to be set (fixed).

The optimal control is found by the formula (18).

Theorem 3. *Let the $(u(t), x(t)), t \in [t_0, T]$ - pair be the solution of the above problem. Then there must exist a vector-function $\psi(t), t \in [t_0, T]$ and a parameter ψ_0 such that*

1) $\psi_0 \leq 0, |\psi_0| + |\psi(t)| \neq 0, t \in [t_0, T]$

2) $\psi(t), t \in [t_0, T]$ is the solution of the conjugate system of differential Eqs. (17) that satisfies the condition: there are numbers $\beta_1, ..., \beta_k$ such that

$$\Psi_i(T) = \sum_{j=1}^{k} \beta_j c_{ji}, i = \overline{1, n}, \quad \beta_i \left(\sum_{j=1}^{n} c_{ij} x_j(T) - d_i \right) = 0, \ \beta_i \geq 0, \ i = \overline{1, k}$$

for each $t \in [t_0, T]$, the function $H(x(t), u, \psi(t), \psi_0)$ (16) with respect to the variable u reaches its upper edge on the set U at $u = u(t)$, i.e.

$$\sup_{u \in U} H(x(t), u, \Psi(t), \Psi_0) = H(x(t), u(t), \Psi(t), \Psi_0).$$

Proof. Since all the conditions of the Pontryagin maximum principle [11] are met for the formulated optimal control problem, the validity of the theorem follows from this.

3 Optimal performance problem with fixed right end

The problem of minimizing the functional (15) under constraints is considered (9), (2), (10), (11). The time point T is not specified and must be determined.

For the given optimal control problem, we compose the Hamilton function

$$H(x(t), u, \psi(t), \psi_0) = 1 + (g(x, t) + Bu(t))^* \psi. \tag{19}$$

Let's make a conjugate system of differential equations:

$$\frac{d\psi}{dt} = -(\frac{\partial g(t)}{\partial t})^*(t)\psi(t), t \in [t_0, T]. \tag{20}$$

Theorem 4. *Let the* $(u(t), x(t)), t \in [t_0, T]$ *- pair be the solution of the above problem. Then there must exist a vector-function* $\psi(t), t \in [t_0, T]$ *and a parameter* ψ_0 *such that*

1) $\psi_0 \leq 0, |\psi_0| + |\psi(t)| \neq 0, t \in [t_0, T]$

2) $\psi(t), t \in [t_0, T]$ *- solution of the conjugate system of differential Eqs. (20), which together with system (9) satisfies the boundary conditions (10) and (11)*

3) for each tu, the function Hx with respect to the variable u reaches its upper face on the set U at u = t, i.e.

$$\sup_{u \in U} H(x(t), u, \Psi(t), \Psi_0) = H(x(t), u(t), \Psi(t), \Psi_0).$$

Proof. Since all the conditions of the Pontryagin maximum principle [11] are met for the formulated optimal control problem, the validity of the theorem follows from this.

4 Numerical algorithm for solving the optimal control problem with fixed ends and phase constraints

The problem of optimal control with phase constraints (13), with fixed ends (10)–(11) and control constraints (2) is considered. At present, the solution of such problems contains a number of mathematical difficulties.

In this regard, for the practical solution of the optimal control problem, the method of penalty functions and the gradient method are used.

To account for the phase constraints (13) and the constraints on the end of the trajectory (11), we introduce the penalty functions $\Phi_{1k} = M_{k1} \sum_{i=1}^{n} \int_{t_0}^{T} [max\{x_i(t); 0\}]^2 dt$ and $\Phi_{2k} = M_{k2} \sum_{i=1}^{n} [x(T) - x_T)]^2$, where M_{k1}, M_{k2} are some given positive sequences tending to infinity.

Let's build a new functionality

$$J_k = \int_{t_0}^{T} \{u^*(t) R_0 u(t) + x(t)^* R_1 x(t) + M_{k1}[max\{x_i(t); 0\}]^2\} dt + M_{k2} \sum_{i=1}^{n} [x(T) - x_T)]^2$$

Replace the original problem with the following: for a given *k*, find the optimal control that minimizes the functional J_k under constraints (10), (2), and (11). The resulting problem is an optimal control problem with a free right end and a constraint on the controls. For it, we will make a Hamilton function

$$H_k = u^*(t) R_0 u(t) + x(t)^* R_1 x(t) + M_{k1}[max\{x_i(t); 0\}]^2 + (g(x, t) + Bu(t)) * \psi_k$$

The following solution algorithm is proposed.

Step 1. Let k = 0.

Step 2. Calculate the optimal control for the *k*-th iteration

$$u_k = \begin{cases} -L & if \quad R_0^{-1} B \psi_k < 0 \\ R_0^{-1} B \psi_k & if\ 0 \leq R_0^{-1} B \psi_k \leq u_{max} \\ L & if \quad R_0^{-1} B \psi_k > u_{max} \end{cases} \tag{21}$$

where ψ_k is the solution of the conjugate system of differential equations

$$\frac{d\psi_k}{dt} = -(\frac{\partial g}{\partial x})^* \psi_k - 2R_1 x_k(t) + M_{k1}[max\,\{x_{ki}(t); 0\}] \tag{22}$$

with a condition at the end

$$\Psi_k\,(T) = 2M_{k2} \sum_{i=1}^{n} [x_k(T) - x_T] \tag{23}$$

and x_k -the solution of the original system (9) under the initial conditions (10).

Step 3. When x_k and u_k are found, the value of the functional j_k is calculated.

Step 4. If $|J_k - J_{k-1}| \leq \varepsilon$ then go to step 5, otherwise k = k + 1 and go to step 2. (Here $\varepsilon > 0$ is the required calculation accuracy).

Step 5. The found pair (x_k, u_k) is the optimal solution for.

Numerical experiments on the model problem showed the convergence of the proposed algorithm already at the 6th iteration.

IIAS is developed on the MySQL DBMS [11] using the PHP WEB programming language. Currently, the IAS is in trial operation.

4 Discussion

Using the methods of correlation analysis, the IAS allows you to find the degree of dependence (correlation) between the parameters (while it is possible to take into account the lag effect). For example, you can find a correlation between: the unemployment rate and the number of crimes, the average monthly salary and the number of crimes.

To assess a number of parameters that cannot be measured in nature (for example, the social tension index), it is possible to conduct an expert study, which consists in the fact that each expert independently of the others gives an assessment of the selected parameter in a simulated or real situation, which is quantitatively characterized by the values of other parameters. For any selected parameter, a regression equation is constructed that depends on the other parameters.

The results obtained are applicable to the study of any dynamical system described by ordinary differential equations. Therefore, the application of the results of the article has great prospects for automating the solution of many problems of mathematical modeling.

5 Conclusion

The article discusses a dynamic model with a restriction on the right end based on linguistic variables, described by ordinary differential equations.

For forecasting and managing the socio-economic situation on the basis of interval mathematics, a criterion of fuzzy controllability was obtained.

Using the Pontryagin maximum principle, the optimal control and the optimal trajectory for the quadratic functional and the speed criterion are determined.

On the basis of the penalty function method and the gradient method, the optimal control problem with bounded controls and fixed ends is solved.

On the basis of the library of interval procedures [9], software has been developed for determining the controllability of a dynamic system described by ordinary differential equations.

The materials of the article are of practical value for designers of various socio-technical systems.

Acknowledgements. The work was carried out at the expense of the program-targeted funding of scientific research for 2021–2023 under the project «Development of a national system for assessing risks and threats to national security of the Republic of Kazakhstan».

For citations of references, we prefer the use of square brackets and consecutive numbers. Citations using labels or the author/year convention are also acceptable. The following bibliography provides a sample reference list with entries for journal articles [1], an LNCS chapter [2], a book [3], proceedings without editors [4], as well as a URL [5].

References

1. Malykhin, V.I.: Socio-Economic Structure of Society: Mathematical Modeling. UNITY-DANA, Moscow (2003)
2. Tsybulin, V.G., Khosaeva, Z.K.: Mathematical model of political differentiation under social tension. Comput. Res. Model. **11**(5), 999–1012 (2019)
3. Kapoguzov, E.A., Chupin, R.I., Kharlamova, M.S., Pligunova, A.V.: Social tension factors: estimation and analysis issues (case study: the city of Omsk). J. Sib. Fed. Univ. Humanit. Soc. Sci. **13**(4), 517–528 (2020)
4. Voronov, A.A.: Stability, Controllability, Observability. Nauka, Moscow (1979)
5. Schroers, B.: Ordinary Differential Equations: A Practical Guide (AIMS Library of Mathematical Sciences). Cambridge University Press, Cambridge (2011)
6. Bellman, R.E., Zadeh, L.A.: Decision-making in fuzzy environment. Manage. Sci. **17**(4), 141–164 (1970)
7. Verlan, A.F., Sizikov, V.S.: Integral Equations: Methods, Algorithms, Programs. Naukova Dumka, Kiev (1986)
8. Bairbekova, G, Mazakov, T., Jomartova, S., Nugmanova, S.: Interval arithmetic in calculations. Open Eng. Formerly Central Eur. J. Eng. Editor-in-Chief Noor Ahmed Open Eng. **6**(1), 259–263 (2016)
9. Jomartova, S., Mazakov, T., Karymsakova, N., Zhaydarova, A.: Comparison of two interval arithmetic. Appl. Math. Sci. **8**(72), 3593–3598 (2014)
10. Saaty, T.L.: Relative measurement and its generalization in decision making: why pairwise comparisons are central in mathematics for the measurement of intangible factors - the analytic hierarchy/network process. RACSAM (Rev. R. Spanish Acad. Sci. Ser. A Math.) **102**(2), 251–318 (2008)

11. Griffiths, D.F., Higham, D.J.: Numerical Methods for Ordinary Differential Equations: Initial Value Problems. Springer, London (2010). https://doi.org/10.1007/978-0-85729-148-6
12. Vaswani, V.: MySQL Database Usage & Administration. McGraw-Hill Osborne Media (2009)

Integration of PSO Algorithm and Fuzzy Logic to Reduce Energy Consumption in IoT-Based Sensor Networks

Behnam Seyedi and Octavian Postolache(✉)

Instituto Universitário de Lisboa, ISCTE-IUL, Lisbon, Portugal
Behnam_Seyedi@iscte-iul.pt, opostolache@lx.it.pt

Abstract. Wireless sensor network (WSN) is composed by a set of sensor nodes with low energy consumption and low cost which could sense quantities like humidity, temperature, pressure and send them to the central node. The routing optimization in IoT networks is required taking into account the traffic, congestion, and failure of some or all network services. In fact, low traffic and network congestion means high quality routing in that network. Increasing the network lifetime and improving the routing quality is one of the main concerns of IoT-based sensor networks. In this paper, a new clustering algorithm is proposed to increase the network efficiency in the IoT-based sensor networks using the fuzzy logic and particle swarm optimization (PSO) algorithm. In this approach, the cluster was created in WSN using energy modelling for effective routing of data packages via using fuzzy logic and (PSO). The stimulation results of the proposed method showed higher capabilities by comparison with reported algorithms (e.g. LEACH, FLCFP, HEED, FBCFP) s that were used for energy consumption optimization in WSN.

Keywords: PSO algorithm · Fuzzy logic · IoT · WSN

1 Introduction

Wireless sensor network is a set of micro devices called sensor nodes. As regards the recent progresses in sensor technology and its low-cost making, micro sensors were used in wireless sensors due to their being technical and economical [1, 2]. The sensors do action surround the environmental conditions and then they are clearly transferred to several features on the occurred phenomena [3, 4]. The network setting composing the sensor nodes transfer their data to central control station or base station so that the final user could access the data. The sensor node is a flat battery which exerts nodes to limited energy resources. Charger or sensor battery replacement may be unpleasant or say that the work setting is not possible. Therefore, when the node loses its energy, it could be efficient for measurement and supervision and it probably covers the analyses of coating and connecting of the whole network [5, 6].

Wireless sensor networks are used in IoT design to measure the environmental parameters, that means to collect data and send them to base station and computation platforms

K. Wojtkiewicz et al. (Eds.): ICCCI 2021, CCIS 1463, pp. 448–458, 2021.
https://doi.org/10.1007/978-3-030-88113-9_36

for analyses. In WSN for IoT, intelligent routing is an important phenomenon which is necessary for improving quality of services (QoS) in the network. Meanwhile, the required energy to creating connection in IoT-based sensor networks is an important challenge to prevent high packs losing and quick energy reduction and etc. which leads to reduction of node function and increasing delay related to pack delivery [7, 8].

Organizing sensor networks has been widely studies in recent years based on cluster architecture. Thus, were created a lot of group protocols with special duties. Clustering is one of the main approaches to design distributive sensor networks with high energy efficiency level. The usage of clustering generally increases the autonomy and it reduces the energy consumption and interference in sensor nodes. Therefore, this research uses combined algorithm of PSO and fuzzy for WSN nodes clustering to reduce energy consumption. Based on the proposed algorithm, we could put the nodes in clusters to create the lowest energy consumption in whole network.

The organization of the paper in Sect. 2, the previously presented methods on reducing energy consumption in sensor networks will be studies and Sect. 3 will explain the proposed method and Sect. 4 will evaluate the proposed method and study its function and finally Sect. 5 will conclude and summarize it.

2 Review of Literature

Wireless sensor networks have popularity with high penetration for different program in different regions. These small nodes have the capability for measuring, computations and possibility of limited wireless connection. The sensor nodes usually send the sensed data to base station [9, 10] but these nodes have computation resource limitations. The nodes' batteries are not easy to replace or recharge them in the context of network authonomy that made this issue one of the main concerns of wireless sensor networks. The batteries energy are used in routing and the operations of data transfer. Routing is raised as one of the challenging issues and has direct effect on energy consumption in wireless sensor networks, case networks and cellular networks. The clustering techniques are considered in wireless sensor networks for routing. These techniques have features such as efficient energy, scalability, lower delay time and etc. [11, 12].

Very diverse methods have been used to reduce the energy consumption of sensor nodes and in whole state of wireless sensor network. In some cases, these methods are classified based on where they are designed in protocol stack layer. For example, in [13], comprehensive review studies were done on the protocol of energy consumption reduction in MAC layer. Meanwhile, many methods dealt with reducing connection in network layer which are known as routing protocols.

In [14] is proposed an algorithm to assists the nodes WSN about their duties and the manner of their functions. The manner of the function of each node is improved with reinforcement learning at each stage. Sharma et al. [15] is reported the Event Driven Routing Protocol (EDRP) protocol which are designed by optimal parameters to reduce energy consumption and lengthening of the lifelong of network where head clusters and routing tree are chosen as two parameters among each sensor and its neighbors including the distance of each node and the remaining energy from nodes. Wang et al. [16] used Zigbee technology along with AODV routing to improve energy consumption in sensor network.

In [17] was presented a hierarchical routing-based method as a new method to improve the routing function in wireless sensor networks. This method has reduced the lifelong of the network upon preventing the use of extra data in routing process. Sharma et al. [18] presented a reliable combined and dynamical transfer protocol which provided the mechanism to determine the scheduling parameters to nodes as dynamically and to increase the efficiency of hybrid protocol.

In [19] Tiglao and his collages showed that using the window size related top bandwidth-delay product (BDP) can lead to desired function for saving-based protocols. Meanwhile, an exploration was presented for choosing optimal transfer window and the optimal amount is related to the average size of cache in average nodes. In [20] mentioned the optimization of cache partitioning in transfer layer. This paper connected several saving policies to distributed Transport for Sensor Networks (DTSN) transportation protocol and studied its effect on total function of the network in the cost of transferring, efficiency and fairness. The stimulation results showed that choosing cache partitioning policy has very important effect on the function and creating motivation in the need to develop more progressed policies which are compatible with dynamic network condition and complex topologies.

In [21] Anhar and his colleges presented several-phase hierarchical routing protocol to supervise on jungles firing using wireless sensor network. In [22] Vahabi, S. and his colleges proposed integration of the geographical method and hierarchical clustering with mobile sink to reduce energy consumption and increase the lifelong of the network. Having used this method, the remaining energy could be increased and it will increase the lifelong the network a lot. The results of experimental stimulation clearly showed that the proposed method increases the lifelong of the network for about 20% compared to other previously presented approaches.

In paper [23] the authors has been used evolutional techniques like genetic algorithm and PSO algorithm and presented a new method for clustering-based routing. Having used evolutionary algorithm in this paper, the optimal head clusters were recognized and based on these head clusters, the routing function was done. In another research in [24] and having used law -based clustering methods, a new routing protocol was presented in wireless sensor networks. This method has used the law-based clustering, the main clusters and also the head clusters were chosen. [25] presented a wise routing technique for routing in wireless sensor networks. In this technique, the head clusters are chosen such that the whole energy consumption in the network reduces as much as possible. Meanwhile [26] presented a dynamic and compatible routing protocol for routing in wireless sensor networks. The network nodes were divided into several clusters as dynamically and in each repetition the heads clusters are upgraded adjustably and dynamically. Meanwhile [27] has used network-based clustering technique and presented a new method for classifying the network nodes. In this method and having done primary nodes clustering, the final intermediate nodes were chosen in routing and based on these nodes, the data transfer was done in sensor network.

3 Proposed Method

This part will introduce the proposed method to reduce energy consumption and improve routing. In fact, by providing a routing method, the data transfer time between sender and receiver is reduced and as a result, network traffic is reduced. First will be presented the modelling of WSN followed by the details of the proposed method.

3.1 Modelling Wireless Sensor Network

A wireless sensor network includes several sensing nodes characterized by low computational capability that are wirelessly connected based on Radio Frequency (RF) protocols. The architecture of sensor network is such that the sensors scattered randomly (or uniformly) in a region and they identify, control and process the events and they are informed to a station called sink. Some of protocols are used in WSN to supply the requirements of the sensor networks from clustering (ex, LEACH). Thus, the sensors are divided into regions and each region has a head cluster. When an event occurred the sensors of that region send their information to the head cluster and the head cluster transmit the information dirctly to sink (Fig. 1).

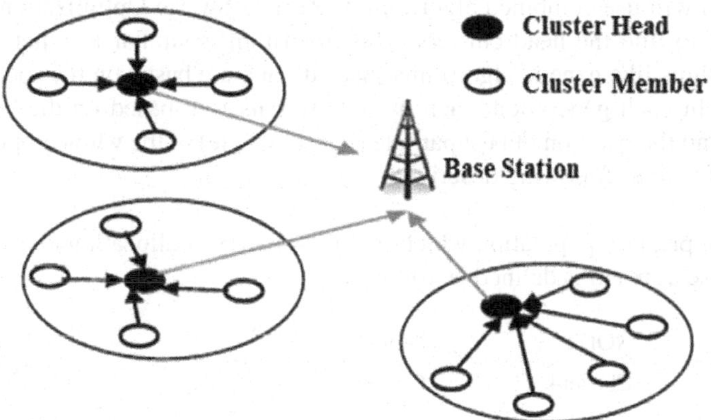

Fig. 1. Clustering in wireless sensor networks

The main and important features of the wireless sensor networks for the self-organizing in the environment and are connected to each other in small board and multi-phase routing. Meanwhile, these networks have variable topology due to breakdown, energy limitations, memory, and the capability of creating connection.

Each sensor node can transmit data with close nodes. The power, capability and capacity of sensors are usually considered similar. The pattern of energy consumption is computed according to Eqs. 1 and 2 [1].

$$E_r = E_{elec} \times l + E_{amp} \times l \times d^2 \tag{1}$$

$$E_R = E_{elec} \times l \tag{2}$$

Where Er is the consumed energy for information sending node. E_{elec} is the required energy for sending or receiving a bit of information which does not depend on distance. E_{amp} is the required energy for reinforcing the sent signal along the desired distance. l

is the length of the message that is to be sent from the sender to the receiver, d is the distance to the node that receive the information. E_R is the consumed energy by the node that received the information (Fig. 2).

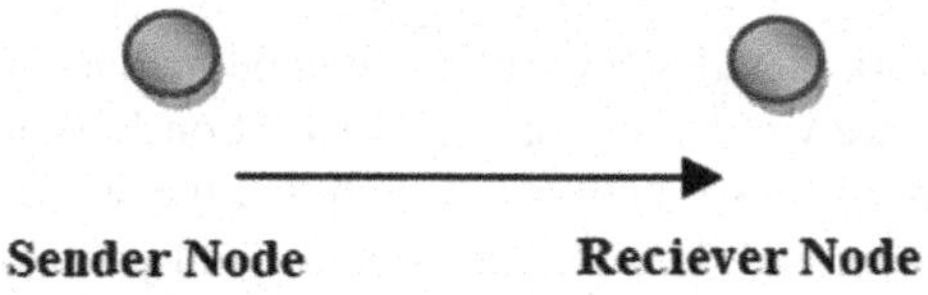

Fig. 2. Connection between two nodes

3.2 PSO and Fuzzy Logic-Based Proposed Method

This research will use combined algorithm of Particle Swarm Optimization (PSO) and Fuzzy Logic to find the head clusters. This algorithm is similar to other population-based algorithms like genetic algorithms Instead, they are based on the social behavior of particles. In each generation, each particle sets its rout based on the best location (best local) and the position of best particle (best in whole) of the whole population. The stages of PSO are as following described:

1. Choosing primary population which includes matrix of allocating clusters to nodes in this research and is defined as follow:

NOD1	NOD2	NOD3	...	NOD n
Cluster2	Cluster4	Cluster1	...	Cluster3

2. Computing of fitness function and in this research, the remaining energy is based on the following equation.

$$E_{node} = E_{currnet} - (E_r + E_R) \tag{3}$$

Where $E_{currnet}$ is the primary and remaining energy of each node and the value of the fitness function is based on the following equation for the remaining energy for each node.

$$fitness = \sum_{i=1}^{N} E_i \tag{4}$$

Where N is the number of sensors. The optimization objective is to reduce the value of fitness function.

3. Finding best GBest (The best particle found in all iterations) and PBest (The best particle found in current iteration) based on lowest value of fitness function

4. Upgrading the particle velocity (V) based on the following equation.

$$\text{Current displacement } V_{new} = C_0 \times V_{old} + C_1 \times \text{rand}() \times \left(P_{best} - P_{present}\right) + C_2 \times \text{rand}() \times (g_{best} - P_{present})$$

5. Upgrading the Particle value based on the following equation

$$\text{present}[] = \text{present}[] + \text{v}[]$$

6. Do stages 2 to 5 to the determined repeated ones.

   The output of this algorithm is the best possible clustering with lowest energy consumption. This research used Fuzzy logic to improve PSO algorithm to determine c1, c2 coefficients which will be dealt in continuing.

3.3 Fuzzy Logic to Determine Speed Coefficient

Fuzzy system is used in this research to set the velocity function coefficient in the PSO algorithm. In this regard, the difference of the particle distance from the best location the particle will be put is divided to the difference of the particle distance to the best particle among the particles and C1 and C2 parameters are allocated for the result of such division based on fuzzy law. Flowchart of this algorithm is as follow:

To compute the fuzzy system, the following equation is used.

$$D1 = \text{cost (Pbest)} - \text{cost(present)} \tag{5}$$

$$D2 = \text{cost (Gbest)} - \text{cost(present)}$$

$$D = \frac{D1}{D2}$$

Now as regards D value, proper fuzzy values could be determined for C1 and C2. According to Table 1, we could fund the fuzzy values and C1 and C2 values well based on raised fuzzy values in the Table 1, by fine-tuning these parameters (i.e. c1 and c2), the convergence speed of the optimal particle algorithm can be improved. The fuzzy system is executed and it improves the coefficients related to speed in PSO algorithm so that the particles could move toward the optimal point in higher speed [28].

Table 1. Mamdani rules

Mamadani Rules based on D value	Fuzzy	C1	C2
0 <= D <= 0.25	Very low	C1 + 0.1	C2–0.1

(continued)

Table 1. (*continued*)

Mamadani Rules based on D value	Fuzzy	C1	C2
0.25 <= D <= 0.5	Low	C1 + 0.2	C2–0.2
0.5 <= D <= 0.75	Normal	C1 + 0.3	C2–0.3
0.75 <= D <= 1	High	C1 + 0.4	C2–0.4
1 <= D	Very high	C1–0.5	C2 = 2

4 Results and Discussions

The protocol of proposed clustering was tested via simulation in MATLAB. The sensor nodes were randomly distributed in an area in $100 \times 100\ m^2$. The reason for choosing this model is that it has been studied in the basic papers of this model. The WSN parameters which are used for simulation are presented in Table 2.

Table 2. Simulation Parameters

Parameters	Values
Simulation Area	$100 \times 100\ m^2$
NO.of Sensor Nodes	100
Initial energy of nodes	0.5 J
Eelec	50 nJ/bit
ε_{fs}	10 pJ/bit/m^2
ε_{mp}	0.0013 pJ/bit/m^4
Packet size	4096

Figure 3 shows the results of the lifelong of the network. In this regard, the number of live nodes are shown based on the number of network rounds. The round number is considered between 200 to 1400 to see the value of live nodes in minimum and maximum number of rounds. In this graph, the results of four LEACH, FLCFP, HEED, FBCFP algorithms and the proposed algorithm are shown. To compare the proposed method with the studied methods, all methods were implemented, and the performance of the proposed method was evaluated.

In Fig. 3, it could be seen that the number of active nodes using the proposed algorithm is more than other available algorithms. The energy consumption of nodes in the proposed method is less than other methods . As a result, the lifespan of nodes in the proposed

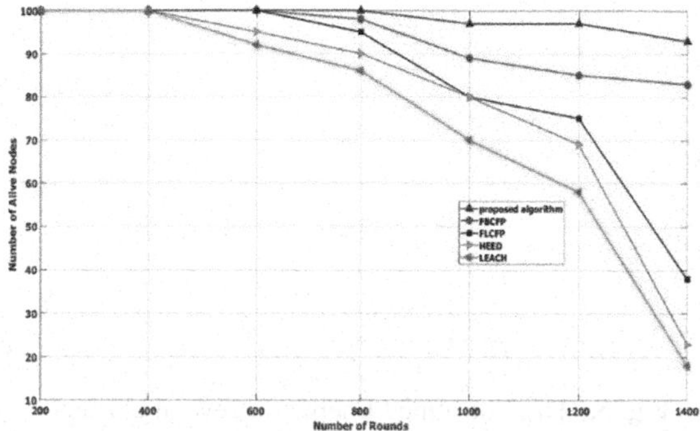

Fig. 3. Number of Live Nodes versus number of rounds

method is higher compared to other methods. Therefore, in the proposed method, the nodes save the energy upon balancing the Head Cluster (CH) load. The evolution of the number of nodes in each cluster of the network is shown in the Fig. 4. The amount of energy consumption in the proposed method is less than other methods. As result, it can be mentioned that the proposed method increases the life of the network. This is because, the energy consumption of the network nodes is reduced, which makes the nodes survive longer. In fact, in the proposed method, the nodes store their energy by balancing the load on the headers. Also, in the cluster formation stage, each node is connected to a cluster center and uses that cluster center to transmit information. As a result, energy consumption in cluster nodes will be balanced.

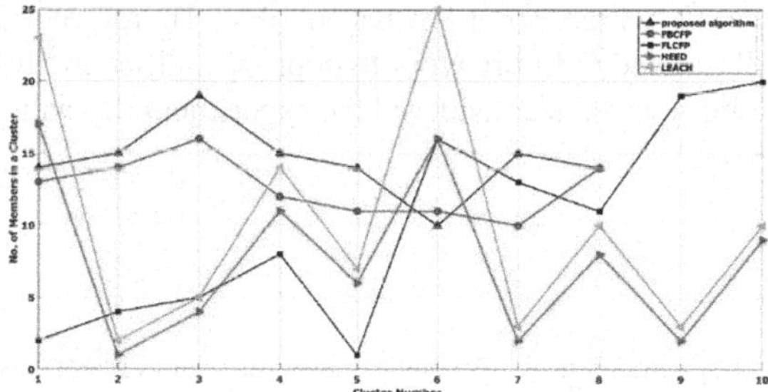

Fig. 4. Number of Nodes in Each Cluster

Moreover, average energy consumption is shown in the Fig. 5. The proposed method and FBCFB consumed lower energy for several clusters, the proposed algorithm could select the optimal cluster centers via Fuzzy and PSO algorithm and could obtain lower energy consumption compared to other algorithms.

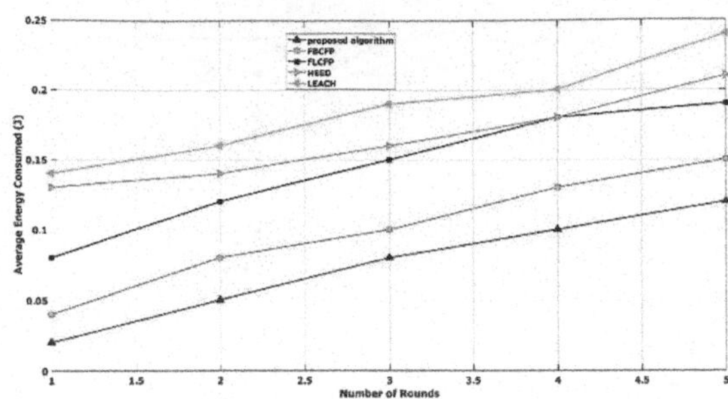

Fig. 5. The Consumed Energy for several clusters

5 Conclusion

This research proposes a new clustering algorithm for wireless sensor networks to increase the efficiency of the network. A clustering method based on fuzzy logic and PSO algorithm was considered. The clustering was done in WSN via modelling energy for effective routing of packs using fuzzy logic and PSO algorithm. Meanwhile, three components, i.e., remaining energy of head cluster, distance between head cluster and sink node and the distance between sensor node and head cluster were considered in this research. These are the important factors in optimization of energy usage for a lifelong of the network. The proposed algorithm was evaluated via simulation in MATLAB. The results of the research showed that the proposed protocol has better efficiency by comparison with FBCFP, HEED, FLCFP and LEACH in terms of energy consumption and lifelong of system. One of the limitations of this research is that all the nodes are assumed as reliable nodes which is not always possible. Therefore, it is considered that the trust criterion will be used in future work to improve and secure the routing protocol. Additionally as the future work is considered the experimentally validation of the novel proposed approach.

References

1. Tripathi, Y., Kumar, V., Prakash, A.: A robust energy-efficient cluster-based routing protocol for mobile wireless sensor network. In: Dutta, D., Kar, H., Kumar, C., Bhadauria, V. (eds.) Advances in VLSI, Communication, and Signal Processing. LNEE, vol. 587, pp. 61–69. Springer, Singapore (2020). https://doi.org/10.1007/978-981-32-9775-3_6
2. Zhou, W., Li, P., Wang, Q.J., Nabipour, N.: Research on data transmission of wireless sensor networks based on symmetric key algorithm. Measurement **153**, 107454 (2020)
3. Han, G., et al.: A dynamic ring-based routing scheme for source location privacy in wireless sensor networks. Inf. Sci. **504**, 308–323 (2019)
4. Abbas, N., Yu, F.: Design and implementation of a video surveillance system for linear wireless multimedia sensor networks. In: 2018 IEEE 3rd International Conference on Image, Vision and Computing (ICIVC) (2018)
5. Wang, M., Wang, S., Zhang, B.: APTEEN routing protocol optimization in wireless sensor networks based on combination of genetic algorithms and fruit fly optimization algorithm. Ad Hoc Netw. **102**, 102138 (2020)

6. Kalaivani, S., Tharini, C.: Analysis and implementation of novel Rice Golomb coding algorithm for wireless sensor networks. Comput. Commun. **150**, 463–471 (2020)
7. Peng, S., Wang, T., Low, C.P.: Energy neutral clustering for energy harvesting wireless sensors networks. Ad Hoc Netw. **28**, 1–16 (2015)
8. Nguyen, T.D., Khan, J.Y., Ngo, D.T.: Energy harvested roadside IEEE 802.15.4 wireless sensor networks for IoT applications. Ad Hoc Netw. **56**, 109–121 (2017)
9. Fu, X., Yao, H., Yang, Y.: Modeling and analyzing cascading dynamics of the clustered wireless sensor network. Reliab. Eng. Syst. Saf. **186**, 1–10 (2019)
10. Dong, M., et al.: Mobile agent-based energy-aware and user-centric data collection in wireless sensor networks. Comput. Netw. **74**, 58–70 (2014)
11. Sabet, M., Naji, H.: An energy efficient multi-level route-aware clustering algorithm for wireless sensor networks: a self-organized approach. Comput. Electr. Eng. **56**, 399–417 (2016)
12. Kuila, P., Jana, P.K.: Energy efficient load-balanced clustering algorithm for wireless sensor networks. Procedia Technol. **6**, 771–777 (2012)
13. Langendoen, K.: Medium access control in wireless sensor networks. In: Book Chapter in "Medium Access Control in Wireless Networks, Volume II: Practice and Standards". Nova Science Publishers, Hauppauge (2008)
14. Yau, K.-L.A., Komisarczuk, P., Teal, P.D.: Reinforcement learning for context awareness and intelligence in wireless networks: review, new features and open issues. J. Netw. Comput. Appl. **35**(1), 253–267 (2012)
15. Sharma, S., Suresh, K.: Performance improvement of OLSR protocol by modifying the routing table construction mechanism. In: International Conference on Reliability, Optimization and Information Technology - ICROIT 2014, MRIU, India, pp. 182–187 (2014)
16. Wang, D., Zhao, Y.: Network community detection from the perspective of time series. Physica A **522**, 205–214 (2019)
17. Mohanty, P., Kabat, M.R.: A hierarchical energy efficient reliable transport protocol for wireless sensor networks. Ain Shams Eng. J. **5**(4), 1141–1155 (2014)
18. Sharma, B., Aseri, T.C.: A hybrid and dynamic reliable transport protocol for wireless sensor networks. Comput. Electr. Eng. **48**, 298–311 (2015)
19. Tiglao, N.M.C., Grilo, A.M.: Transmission window optimization for caching-based transport protocols in wireless sensor networks. In: Mumtaz, S., Rodriguez, J., Katz, M., Wang, C., Nascimento, A. (eds.) WICON 2014. LNICSSITE, vol. 146, pp. 39–46. Springer, Cham (2015). https://doi.org/10.1007/978-3-319-18802-7_6
20. Tiglao, N., Grilo, A.: Optimal cache partitioning in reliable data transport for wireless sensor networks. In: NET-COOP 2010 - 4th Workshop on Network Control and Optimization, Ghent, Belgium (2010)
21. Anhar, A., Nilavalan, R.: Multi-hop hierarchical routing based on the node health status in wireless sensor network. In: Arai, K., Kapoor, S., Bhatia, R. (eds.) SAI 2018. AISC, vol. 857, pp. 849–859. Springer, Cham (2019). https://doi.org/10.1007/978-3-030-01177-2_63
22. Vahabi, S., Eslaminejad, M., Dashti, S.E.: Integration of geographic and hierarchical routing protocols for energy saving in wireless sensor networks with mobile sink. Wireless Netw. **25**(5), 2953–2961 (2019)
23. Kuila, P., Jana, P.K.: Evolutionary computing approaches for clustering and routing in wireless sensor networks: information resources management association. In: Sensor Technology: Concepts, Methodologies, Tools, and Applications, pp. 125–146. IGI Global, Hershey (2020). https://doi.org/10.4018/978-1-7998-2454-1.ch006
24. Selvi, M., Velvizhy, P., Ganapathy, S., Nehemiah, H.K., Kannan, A.: A rule based delay constrained energy efficient routing technique for wireless sensor networks. Clust. Comput. **22**(5), 10839–10848 (2017)
25. Mittal, N., Singh, U., Sohi, B.S.: An energy-aware cluster-based stable protocol for wireless sensor networks. Neural Comput. Appl. **31**(11), 7269–7286 (2018)

26. Jain, S.R., Thakur, N.V.: Cluster-based adaptive and dynamic routing protocol to enhance the performance of wireless sensor network. In: Yang, X.-S., Sherratt, S., Dey, N., Joshi, A. (eds.) Third International Congress on Information and Communication Technology. AISC, vol. 797, pp. 351–359. Springer, Singapore (2019). https://doi.org/10.1007/978-981-13-1165-9_32
27. Dhiman, S., Kakkar, D., Kaur, G.: Performance analysis of multi-hop routing protocol with optimized grid-based clustering for wireless sensor network. In: Gupta, G.P. (ed.) Nature-Inspired Computing Applications in Advanced Communication Networks, pp. 254–282. IGI Global, Hershey (2020). https://doi.org/10.4018/978-1-7998-1626-3.ch009
28. Dudeja, C.: Fuzzy-based modified particle swarm optimization algorithm for shortest path problems. Soft. Comput. **23**(17), 8321–8331 (2019)

Smart Industry and Management Systems

An Analysis of Convolutional Neural Network Models for Classifying Machine Tools

Leonid Koval[1](✉), Daniel Pfaller[1], Mühenad Bilal[1], Markus Bregulla[1], and Rafał Cupek[2]

[1] Technische Hochschule Ingolstadt, 85049 Ingolstadt, Germany
leonid koval@thi.de
[2] Silesian University of Technology, 44-100 Gliwice, Poland

Abstract. This paper analyzes the use of different Neural Network architectures on two different sets of machine tool images. The sets are either composed of images that were taken with a low-quality camera or catalog photos. The task was to classify of the different types of cutting tools, which is the first step in initiating automatic support for computer-based sharpening. The performance of different Neural Network models was evaluated using a confusion matrix and the Fl-Score. For better understanding, the ROC and PR curves were used. A final check using trained Convolutional Neural Networks was done reciprocally on each of the respective test-set. The main contribution is dedicated for the research in the Industry 4.0. Especially the application of machine learning methods. The main goal of this paper is to present an analysis of the different Deep Neural Network Models that are used to classify machine tools. Furthermore, the factor domain relevance is also briefly discussed.

Keywords: Image classification · Domain relevance · F1-score · Confusion-matrix · Machine tools

1 Introduction

Since their breakthrough in 2012 with AlexNet [1] Convolutional Neural Networks (CNN) are now the state of the art for classifying images. However, the basic idea dates back to 1943 with the McCulloch-Pitts-Neuron [11]. With different architectures and new optimization methods being developed, there has been a constant increase in the correct classification of image classes. This has enabled industry sectors that are focused on computer vision applications to develop new services or products. For example, this study [7] found that of the 17,500 companies in Germany, 49% used AI-based classification for images.

With the introduction of newer and more sophisticated network architectures, the current first place for the image classification task [14] is held by a variant of the FixEfficientNet-L2 [15] with a TOP1 Accuracy of 90.2% and a TOP5 Accuracy of 98.8%. In comparison, AlexNet achieved a TOP1 and TOP5 Accuracy of 60.3% and 81.1%, respectively. As for industry applications, there

K. Wojtkiewicz et al. (Eds.): ICCCI 2021, CCIS 1463, pp. 461–473, 2021.
https://doi.org/10.1007/978-3-030-88113-9_37

is a trend toward the Bayes optimal error for image classification. Generally, a CNN is in fact a multilayer perceptron (MLP) with many hidden layers between the input and output layers. The difference between a convolutional layer and a fully connected layer is the more efficient use of the weight connections through convolution [16]. With a fully connected layer, an MLP neuron of one layer is connected to all of the neurons of the next layer. This connectivity is a disadvantage when classifying large images compared to the CNN architectures. A CNN has smaller and shared weights, which enables an easier and less wasteful training [9]. This is because convolutional layers that connect pixels in their receptive fields are used. That architecture enables a network to concentrate on the small low-level features in the first hidden layers. The deeper layers then assemble these features into larger higher-level features in the next hidden layer. This architecture was inspired by the natural visual cortex. Other layer designs incorporate different arrangements of the width or depth of the layers of the CNN overall.

Other than the model itself, there are additional methods to boost accuracy. Examples of different methods would be data pre-processing, different loss functions or the learning rate schedule, which are discussed in [10]. Another option for obtaining better results is to improve the training and development sets. This causes missing labeled data and constraints on the availability. In most cases, a CNN needs a huge amount of available data. One solution for this is to use transfer learning. One of the most common methods is to increase the correct classification rate [17,19]. Depending on the domain, the accuracy of a CNN can be increased and the training time to be reduced.

In order to analyze the influencing factor of the domain, a new image database is built. This new database incorporates images of different machine tools, e.g., drills or mills. Therefore, this paper presents an industry-orientated application for classifying machine tools. Consequently the main contribution of this paper is regarded in the research field of "Industry 4.0". Primary a practical oriented application of CNN on a classification task in particular targeted on machine tools like drills or mills. The rest of the paper is organized as follows. Section 2 gives an overview of the current state of the art and the author gives a short review of the different CNN Architectures. In addition, the topic of transfer learning is also briefly discussed. The approach in this paper focuses on training only a few pictures. In addition, using a low-quality camera, the author also introduces a cost-efficient solution for classification tasks in an industrial context.

Section 3 explains the experimental settings. There, the author discusses the size of the database, the evaluation method and the research environment. The research experiment is introduced using the training of six different CNN Architectures on two databases. After the training, the trained models were tested on their respective databases. Additionally, their performance was evaluated by their F1-Score and confusion matrix. Subsequently, the CNN models were tested reciprocally on their respective test-sets. This experiment was done in two steps, first without transfer learning and then with transfer learning. The focus was primarily on the transferability and not on the use of any hyperparameter tuning.

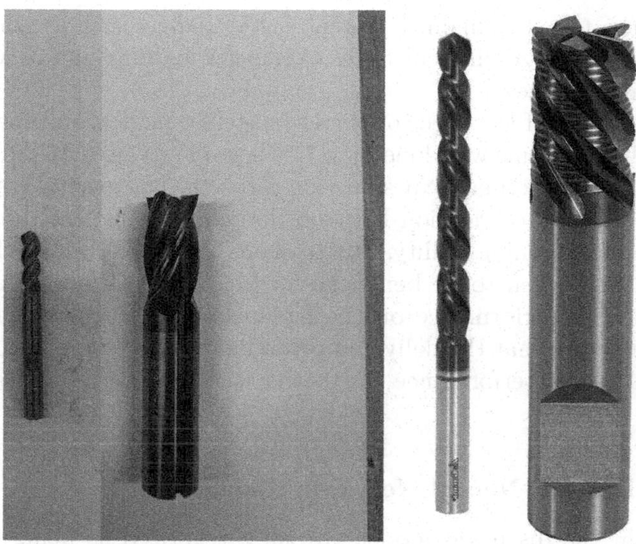

Fig. 1. From left to right, a picture of a drill that was photographed with a low-quality camera, a picture of a mill that was photographed with a low-quality camera, a picture of a drill from a catalog and a picture of a mill from a catalog.

Section 4 presents the results of the experiments and includes the diagrams of the ROC and PR curves as well as a more detailed presentation of the evaluation parameters. In addition, a brief discussion about the results is presented and the way in which the mentioned methods impact the DNN models.

In Sect. 5, the paper is summarized and an outlook for further research is presented.

2 State of the Art

The database on which the CNN was trained and tested was built with pictures that had been taken with a low-quality camera and pictures from a catalog[1]. An example of the pictures that were used in the database is presented in Fig. 1. Beginning with transfer learning, there will be a brief overview on this topic in Subsect. 2.1. Next, a short description about the neural network models that was used is given in Subsect. 2.2. Other possible approaches for the referenced small database are not the focus of this Paper. Nonetheless, an approach for small amounts of annotated pictures is discussed in ([20, 25–27]). All the above mentioned papers can be categorized as "Few-Shot-Learning".

2.1 Transfer Learning

Whenever the topic of transfer learning is mentioned, it is necessary to review the domain adaption. This means that transfer learning is beneficial if the domain is

[1] ©Hoffmann SE, 2021.

related with the target domain. Different survey papers such as [19,24,28] also suggest this and analyze different types of transfer learning and in which case it is the reasonable choice.

Another analysis of the effect of better ImageNet models and their ability to transfer to other domains was done by [17]. They investigated 16 different classification networks on 12 image classification datasets. The general statement was that there is indeed a correlation between the more sophisticated architectures and their transfer learning ability. Furthermore, they ascertained that regularizers which have proven to be beneficial for ImageNet performance are highly detrimental to the performance on the features of the penultimate layer. The third realization was that the delivered penultimate layer correlated with better models and that the performance was better when the entire network was fine tuned.

2.2 Convolutional Neural Network Models

To begin with, the discussed models are all categorized as being deep neural networks (DNN). This means that there is a certain number of different layers. These layers are often convolutional layers, max pool layers and fully connected layers. For instance, in the beginning, DNN models had a simple structure. VGG [18], for example, is simply a model in which the convolutional layers are stacked on top of one another. The most well-known variants are VGG16 and VGG19. The number indicates the depth of the network. The max pooling layers are between the convolutional layers and the fully connected layers that form the classifier are at the end. The idea is that a better accuracy is achieved with a deeper model. With each layer, a VGG-model learns the more specific features of the image content. An example is presented in Fig. 2, which shows the content of the max pooling layers of a VGG16 model.

With ongoing research, it was found that the number of convolutional layers did not improve the accuracy results. This phenomenon was called degrading and was observed for every DNN. A solution for this problem was the introduction of a shortcut between a block of convolutional layers. This was introduced by the new ResNet architecture [12]. ResNet was built on the hypotheses that it is not necessary to use the original function or vector for the successful back propagation. It was enough to use the residual, which enables the characteristic ResNet build. The results where positive and this enabled the design of various ResNet builds. The variety ranges from 32 layers up to 152 layers.

Other improvements focused on the layer design. The example that is used in this paper is the InceptionV3 architecture [6]. The base of this network is the inception layer, which was first introduced in [3] as GoogLeNet. It is a layer that is composed of multiple convolution layers in parallel. Basically, it simulates a sparsely connected architecture to reduce the computational costs. This enables the possibility to go deeper.

The concept of a newer layer and reduced computation costs enabled the XceptionNet to be designed [8]. The novelty of this network is the use of depth-separable convolution layers, which reduces the number of the necessary parameters in a

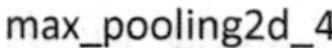

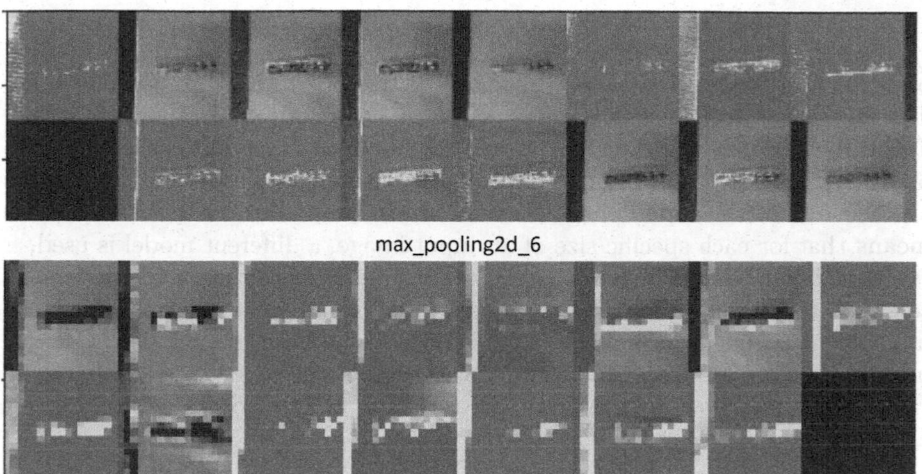

Fig. 2. An example of feature learning. At the beginning, a mill is still visible to the human eye. At the last max pooling layer, the features are transformed into high-level features that are barely recognizable to the human eye.

network. The general idea is that the analysis of the input is done in two steps. In the first step, the input is separated into its different dimensions. An example would be a color image with its red, green and blue dimensions. Each dimension is then cleared with its designated kernel, after which the intermediate result is put together and multiplied point wise. The outcome will be convoluted and will give the same result as a standard convolution, which is directly applied to an input image. The difference is that the number of multiplications is reduced, and this leads to reduced computation costs. Other ideas such as a residual build or stacking the depth-separable convolution layers are also implemented in this network which results in a reduced training time.

All the of the earlier network designs were hand engineered. The problem with this was that with each new DNN model, the time that was required to design the architecture increased. This gave rise to the idea of an automated building function for a DNN. The name of such a model is NASNet [29]. A NASNet model is built using the NAS (Neural Architecture Search) [2] algorithm. Using a recurrent network as the controller, the model was first built on the CIFAR-100 image pool. For this probabilistic approach, the best layer composition was selected for the NN architecture for a specific task. Next, its build was scaled up to be compatible for use on the ImageNet Challenge. With this new build, the complexity of the architecture increased. Although the advantage was the automated design build that could be used as a backbone for transfer learning. It was still a non-intuitive build for a human user. In addition to the large build, another small model was introduced for mobile use. In this paper, the mobile version is used. The input images are all formatted to a smaller size that corresponds with the ideal input size of the mobile NN model.

This idea of building different sized network models was adopted in [13]. They built a whole family of so-called EfficientNets from B0 to B7 with different sizes. The baseline was the use of a network search space for mobile application [21]. The difference between the other automatic build DNN models is the definition of three design parameters that have a counter dependency. These parameters are the size of the input image and the depth and width of a network. This means that for each specific size of an input image, a different model is used.

The six models that were selected were trained and tested on the two image sets. There are many more DNN models that could have been used but the main reason why these models were selected is because of their fairly simple implementation using the keras framework. All of the models are available on Keras [5], which was designed by the developer of the XceptionNet, François Chollet.

3 Research Experiments

As was mentioned earlier, the experiment was conducted using the Keras library. To summarize Keras, it is a deep-learning API that is written in Python, which can be used on top of the TensorFlow library. Additionally, Keras can be used on all Python-based platforms, which allows the application to be used in the Google Colab environment where all of the experiments are conducted. Moreover, the DNN models that were discussed in Subsect. 2.2 have already been implemented in Keras.

With the goal of investigating the usability of the DNN models to classify tools, the first step is to build a valid database. The database is composed of images from an online catalog and images from a low-quality camera. The database structure was inspired by the "dogs vs. cats" folder structure, see reference Paper [23]. In both cases, the number of images that are used is very small. For the low-quality images, the split is 856 drill- and mill-training pictures, 122 validation images and 192 test images. The catalog pictures were divided into 1,800 training pictures, 180 validation pictures and 350 test pictures. All of the sets were roughly distributed by 50% of either the drills or mills.

This small database was meant to simulate the productive industrial field in which a wide variety of tool types. The main issue is the rarity of certain tool types, which impedes a multi-classification task in an industrial use case. Therefore, there was only a general classification between the drills and mills in the first step.

The DNN models were trained on different sources and were tested on their respective test sets at the end after which the best models were tested reciprocally on each other's test sets, which meant that the NN model that was trained on the low-quality camera database was tested on the catalog database and vice versa. The performance of the DNN models was evaluated through the F1 score and a confusion matrix. The F1 score was calculated using the equation referenced in (1).

$$F1 = 2 * \frac{Precision * Recall}{Precision + Recall} = \frac{TP}{TP + \frac{FP+FN}{2}} \quad (1)$$

A perfect score values for a low-quality photo database are 104 True Negatives and 88 True Positives. A perfect score for the catalog database is 170 True Negatives and 180 True Positives. The True Positives are represented by the mill pictures. Additionally, in order to understand better, the receiver operating characteristic (ROC) curve and a precision/recall (PR) curve were used as well. The reason for selecting this combination was that in an industrial application, a false negative or a false positive usually add business costs. Therefore, an evaluation that was based solely on accuracy would not suffice in this context. This scalar metric also shows the exact results of the DNN models. For further references on the metrics see [22].

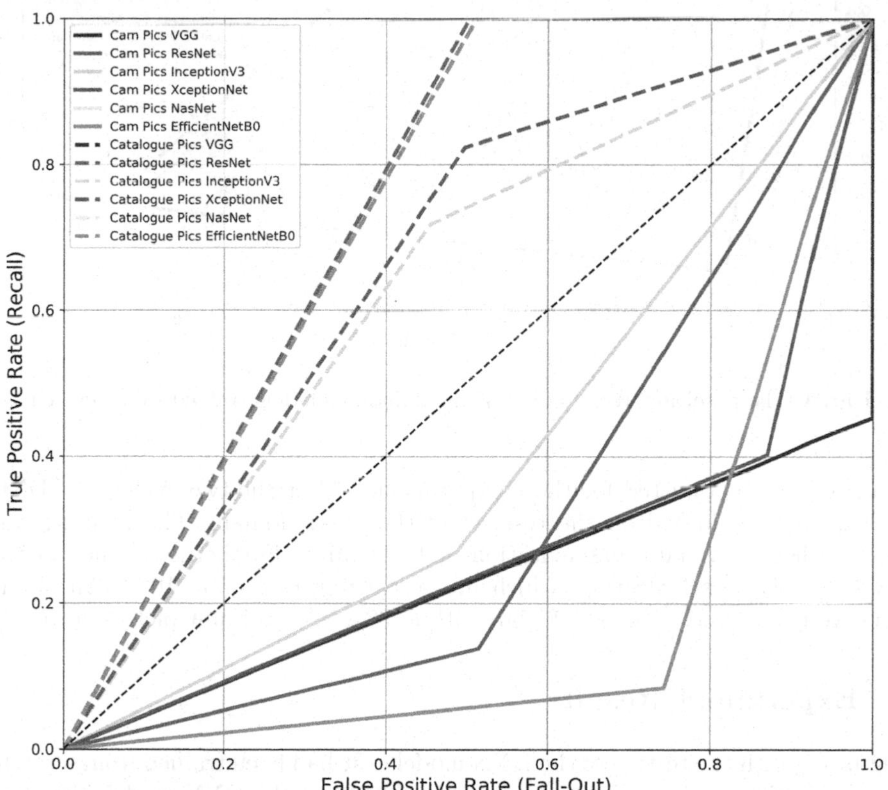

Fig. 3. The ROC-curve of the different models trained from scratch

Each of the DNN models had two cycles of training. The first cycle was done without a previous initialization with the ImageNet weights. In the second cycle, the DNN models were initialized with the ImageNet weights but are not fine-tuned. Although the recommendation for a best practice is to use a fine-tuning

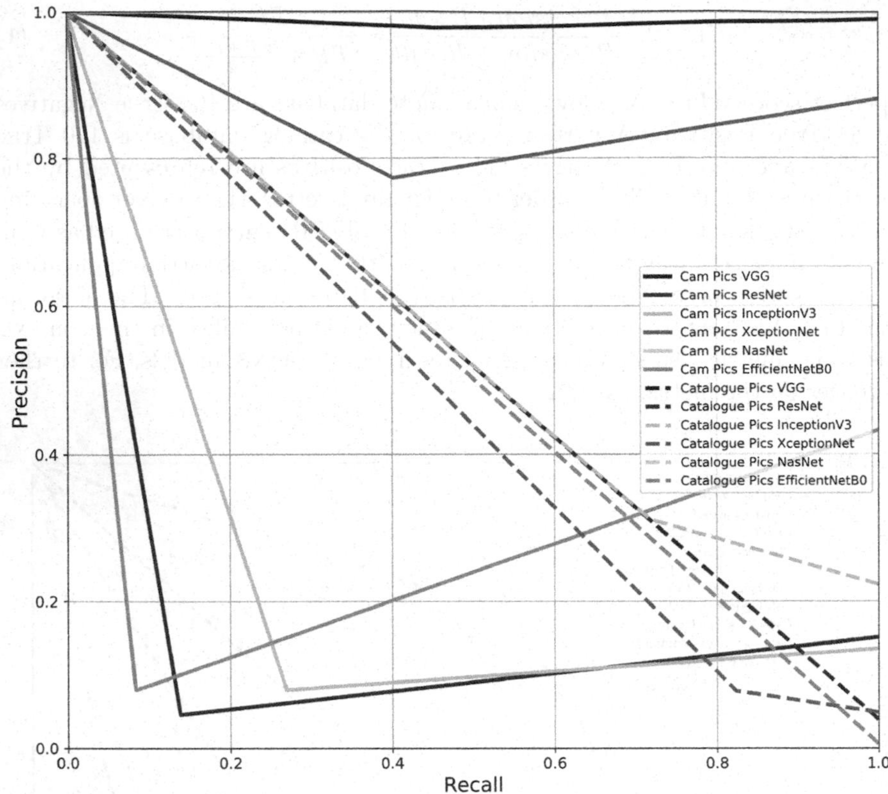

Fig. 4. The precision/recall-curve of the different models trained from scratch

phase [4], it was omitted for these experiments. After the two cycles, the DNN models were evaluated on the test set of the other domain. The training was done without any data augmentation or fine-tuning. Furthermore, each of the DNN models uses RMSprop, which has a learning rate of $1 \cdot 10^{-4}$. All of the tests were executed on google Colab with a [224, 224, 3] input picture format.

4 Experiment Results

Beginning with the testing of the DNN model that had been trained from scratch, a poor classification capability was visible. Although the DNN models that had been trained on the catalog images were above average, they could still be optimized. In addition the results presented in Figs. 3 and 4 are showing a ROC curve which is below the random classifier. If the number of images from training are taken into the account this result shows an overfitting of the classifier. In contrast, the models that are initialized with the ImageNet weights performed much better. The F1 score increased in most cases except for the VGG19 model that was tested on the low-quality picture database and the InceptionV3 model that was tested on the catalog database. The best F1 scores were obtained by the XceptionNet and NASNet. This can be seen in Figs. 5 and 6.

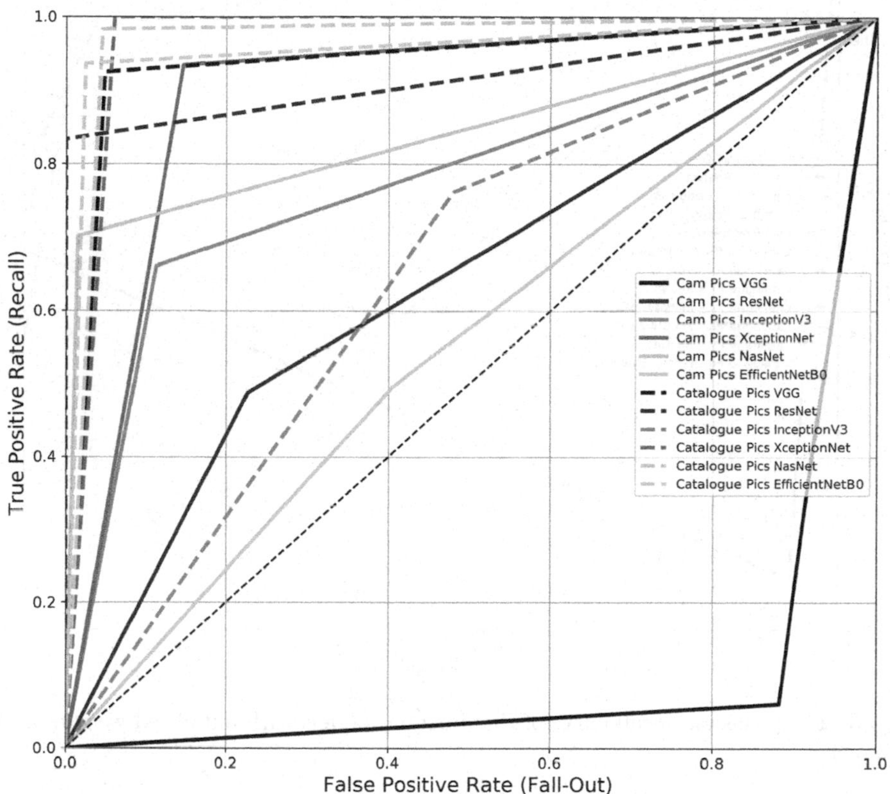

Fig. 5. The ROC-curve of the different models with initialized weights from ImageNet

The results indicate that the DNN models with a reasonable number of parameters and with the initialized weights outperformed the models that had been trained from scratch. With the exception of the InceptionV3 model that had been trained on the catalog database and the VGG19 that had been trained on the low-quality camera database, every other NN model improved significantly. The best models were the Xception and NASNet models. Furthermore, the DNN models which are trained on the catalog database gain better results compared to the DNN models trained on the smaller low quality image database. This means that even with transfer learning, a big enough database is still necessary for these industry applications.

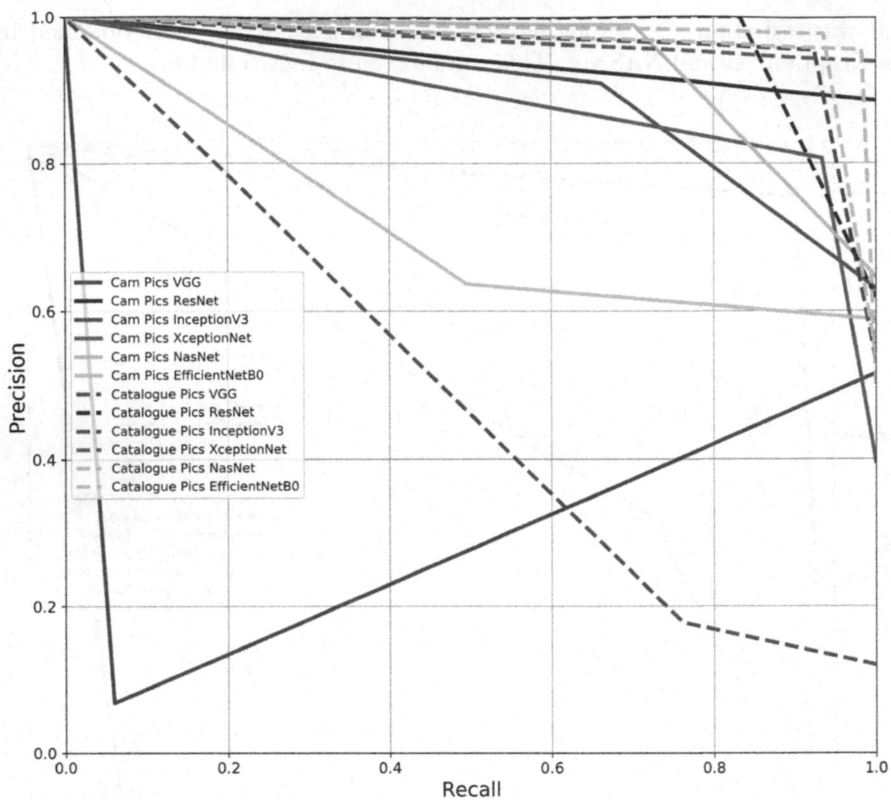

Fig. 6. The precision/recall-curve of the different models with initialized weights from ImageNet

There is also one important detail to notice. The newest model EfficientNetB0 is outperformed by the older architectures. Generally, the trend towards newer architecture equals better results can be observed from our results. This exception is interesting because based on the parameters for this model NASNet-Mobile (which is used for our training) is a smaller model than EfficientNetB0. In addition, the other good performer XceptionNet is a much larger DNN compared to EfficientNetB0. A possible explanation for these result needs to be researched and won't be further discussed in this Paper.

After the tests, the two best-performing DNN models are used reciprocally on the opposite test set. It can be observed that the results of the two Models are not very promising. The Table 1 is an excerpt of the whole test-set and shows these two DNN-Models. The other models have the same appalling results. Even though the DNN models trained on the catalog image database saw more images they cannot be used for the identification of the low-quality images.

These results are by no means surprising. The rule of thumb that a sufficient amount of domain related images is provided as training-set, can be confirmed.

Table 1. Results of the DNN-Models tested on the other test-set

DNN-Models	Metrics	Camera database	Catalogue database
		Values	
Xception	F1-Score	0.0	0.115
	C-Matrix	[[99 88]	[[170 169]
		[5 0]]	[0 11]]
NASNet	F1-Score	0.063	0.678
	C-Matrix	[[100 85]	[[11 6]
		[4 3]]	[159 174]]

This also indicates that the often-used transfer learning approach is a good method to improve the performance of the different DNN models within their own domain. Furthermore, the statements from [17] regarding transfer ability of different DNN models is being confirmed on these new databases. Provided that a sufficient number of images of the target domain is made available for the DNN-Models.

5 Conclusion

In this Paper the Authors evaluated the currently on Keras available DNN models. The evaluation is done with a F1-Score combined with the Confusion- Matrix. The results are presented in ROC and PR curves. Both metrics were selected because of their relevance for an industry application. The results showed that the use of transfer learning significantly improved the performance of the DNN models. Especially the capability of the DNN models trained from scratch with the low quality images. With the use of transfer learning the overfitting phenomena which is well visible in training from scratch presented in Fig. 3 has been reduced significantly for all models except for the VGG model as shown in Fig. 5. Particularly the best performing model for both domains was the XceptionNet model. The second best was the NASNet model. Moreover, an assertion regarding the domain relevance is also made. Even with DNN models that performed well on their own domain, without any information on the target domain, all of the DNN models failed to classify the images correctly. It is important to note that the database was very small. This was done deliberately in order to simulate a classification task in an industrial use case.

An explanation of the good performance of the two best-executed models is the overall improvement of the NN architecture that was based on the ImageNet images. However, it is questionable as to exactly why these two models outperformed the newer EfficientNet model. This suggests that there is a need for further improvement. For example, the impact factor of Data-Augmentation on a training set. Another possible research area would be to perform an in-depth analysis of the NN architectures for a given database. Further research into the use of the optimization strategies of One- and Zero-shot learning also needs to be implemented and evaluated. This could help to counter the predicament of a very small amount of labeled data.

Acknowlegments. The research leading to these results received funding from the Norway Grants 2014-2021, which is operated by the National Centre for Research and Development under the project "Automated Guided Vehicles integrated with Collaborative Robots for Smart Industry Perspective" (Project Contract no.: NOR/POLNOR/CoBotAGV/0027/2019-00).

References

1. Krizhevsky, A., Sutskever, I., Hinton, G.E.: ImageNet classification with deep convolutional neural networks. In: Pereira, F., Burges, C.J.C., Bottou, L., Weinberger, K.Q. (eds.) Advances in Neural Information Processing Systems, vol. 25, pp. 1097–1105. Curran Associates, Inc. (2012). http://papers.nips.cc/paper/4824-imagenet-classification-with-deep-convolutional-neural-networks.pdf
2. Zoph, B., Le, Q.V.: Neural architecture search with reinforcement learning. ArXiv abs/1611.01578 (2017)
3. Szegedy, C., et al.: Going deeper with convolutions. In: 2015 IEEE Conference on Computer Vision and Pattern Recognition (CVPR), pp. 1–9 (2015)
4. Chollet, F.: Deep learning with Python. Safari Tech Books Online, Manning, Shelter Island, NY (2018). http://proquest.safaribooksonline.com/9781617294433
5. Chollet, F., et al.: Keras: Simple. Flexible. Powerful (2015). https://keras.io
6. Szegedy, C., Vanhoucke, V., Ioffe, S., Shlens, J., Wojna, Z.: Rethinking the inception architecture for computer vision. In: 2016 IEEE Conference on Computer Vision and Pattern Recognition (CVPR), pp. 2818–2826 (2016)
7. Rammer, C.: Einsatz von künstlicher intelligenz in der deutschen wirtschaft: Stand der ki-nutzung im jahr 2019 (März 2020). https://www.bmwi.de/Redaktion/DE/Publikationen/Wirtschaft/einsatz-von-ki-deutsche-wirtschaft.html
8. Chollet, F.: Xception: deep learning with depthwise separable convolutions. In: 2017 IEEE Conference on Computer Vision and Pattern Recognition (CVPR), pp. 1800–1807 (2017)
9. Géron, A.: Hands-on Machine Learning with Scikit-Learn, Keras, and TensorFlow: Concepts, Tools, and Techniques to Build Intelligent Systems. 2nd edn. O'Reilly Media, Inc., Massachusetts (2019)
10. He, T., Zhang, Z., Zhang, H., Zhang, Z., Xie, J., Li, M.: Bag of tricks for image classification with convolutional neural networks. In: 2019 IEEE/CVF Conference on Computer Vision and Pattern Recognition (CVPR) (2019). https://doi.org/10.1109/cvpr.2019.00065, http://dx.doi.org/10.1109/CVPR.2019.00065
11. Schmidhuber, J.: Deep learning in neural networks: an overview. Neural Netw. Official J. Int. Neural Netw. Soc. **61**, 85–117 (2015)
12. He, K., Zhang, X., Ren, S., Sun, J.: Deep residual learning for image recognition. In: 2016 IEEE Conference on Computer Vision and Pattern Recognition (CVPR), pp. 770–778 (2016)
13. Tan, M., Le, Q.V.: Efficientnet: rethinking model scaling for convolutional neural networks. In: ICML (2019)

14. Russakovsky, O., Deng, J., Su, H., Krause, J., Satheesh, S., Ma, S., Huang, Z., Karpathy, A., Khosla, A., Bernstein, M., Berg, A.C., Fei-Fei, L.: ImageNet large scale visual recognition challenge. Int. J. Comput. Vis. **115**(3), 211–252 (2015). https://doi.org/10.1007/s11263-015-0816-y
15. Pham, H., Dai, Z., Xie, Q., Luong, M.T., Le, V.Q.: Meta pseudo labels. http://arxiv.org/pdf/2003.10580v3
16. Raschka, S., Mirjalili, V.: Machine Learning mit Python und Scikit-Learn und TensorFlow: Das umfassende Praxis-Handbuch für Data Science, Deep Learning und Predictive Analytics. mitp, Frechen, 2, aktualisierte und erweiterte auflage edn. (2018)
17. Kornblith, S., Shlens, J., Le, Q.V.: Do better ImageNet models transfer better? In: 2019 IEEE/CVF Conference on Computer Vision and Pattern Recognition (CVPR), pp. 2656–2666 (2019)
18. Simonyan, K., Zisserman, A.: Very deep convolutional networks for large-scale image recognition. http://arxiv.org/pdf/1409.1556v6
19. Pan, S.J., Yang, Q., Fan, W., Pan, S.J.: A survey on transfer learning. IEEE Trans. Knowl. Data Eng. **22**(10), 1345–1359 (2010)
20. Sung, F., Yang, Y., Zhang, L., Xiang, T., Torr, P.H.S., Hospedales, T.M.: Learning to compare: relation network for few-shot learning. In: Proceedings of the IEEE Conference on Computer Vision and Pattern Recognition, pp. 1199–1208 (2018)
21. Tan, M., et al.: MnasNet: platform-aware neural architecture search for mobile. In: 2019 IEEE/CVF Conference on Computer Vision and Pattern Recognition (CVPR) (2019). https://doi.org/10.1109/cvpr.2019.00293
22. Tharwat, A.: Classification assessment methods. Appl. Comput. Inform. **1145** (2020). ahead-of-print (ahead-of-print). https://doi.org/10.1016/j.aci.2018.08.003
23. Tushar Jajodia, P.G.: Image classification - cat and dog images. Int. Res. J. Eng. Technol. **12**, 570–572 (2019). https://www.irjet.net/archives/V6/i12/IRJET-V6I1271.pdf
24. Weiss, K., Khoshgoftaar, T.M., Wang, D.: A survey of transfer learning. J. Big Data **3**(1), 9 (2016)
25. Xian, Y., Lampert, C.H., Schiele, B., Akata, Z.: Zero-shot learning–a comprehensive evaluation of the good, the bad and the ugly. IEEE Trans. Pattern Anal. Mach. Intell. **41**(9), 2251–2265 (2018)
26. Xian, Y., Schiele, B., Akata, Z.: Zero-shot learning - the good, the bad and the ugly. In: Proceedings of the IEEE Conference on Computer Vision and Pattern Recognition (CVPR) (2017)
27. Xiao, Y., Marlet, R.: Few-shot object detection and viewpoint estimation for objects in the wild. In: Vedaldi, A., Bischof, H., Brox, T., Frahm, J.-M. (eds.) ECCV 2020. LNCS, vol. 12362, pp. 192–210. Springer, Cham (2020). https://doi.org/10.1007/978-3-030-58520-4_12
28. Zhuang, F., et al.: A comprehensive survey on transfer learning. In: Proceedings of the IEEE (2020)
29. Zoph, B., Vasudevan, V., Shlens, J., Le, Q.V.: Learning transferable architectures for scalable image recognition. In: 2018 IEEE/CVF Conference on Computer Vision and Pattern Recognition (2018). https://doi.org/10.1109/CVPR.2018.00907

Low-Level Wireless and Sensor Networks for Industry 4.0 Communication – Presentation

Anna-Lena Kampen[1(✉)], Marcin Fojcik[1], Rafal Cupek[2], and Jacek Stoj[2]

[1] Western Norway University of Applied Sciences, Bergen, Norway
{anna-lena.kampen,marcin.fojcik}@hvl.no
[2] Silesian University of Technology, Gliwice, Poland
{rafal.cupek,jacek.stoj}@polsl.pl

Abstract. Wireless communication is becoming increasingly popular in factory automation and process control systems, especially when moving components are used. One reason for this growth is the benefits that wireless communication offers, which include lower installation costs than wired networks, less mechanical wear and tear and the ability to provide critical information even about the moving components. Robust and reliable wireless communication solutions must accommodate the demanding and changing conditions of the existing industrial environment, such as the variable number of communication elements, possible interference, a large area for which to provide communication and an organic amount of available battery power. For mobile industrial environments, sensor networks appear to be candidates that can meet many or even all of these requirements. Several types of such communication solutions are available and are in use. This paper focuses on selected wireless networks that can be considered to be enabling technology for the new generation of manufacturing systems.

Keywords: Machine-to-Machine Communication (M2M) · Sensor network · Low level · Industrial wireless communication

1 Introduction

Nowadays, fundamental changes in manufacturing are being referred to as the fourth industrial revolution. The fourth industrial revolution is associated with the digitalization that transforms industry via the everyday use of individualized services tailored to particular production needs. One of the main pillars of digitalization is the broad application of cyber-physical production systems in industry, which change the architecture of production systems as well as the way in which production is performed. For the next generation of smart manufacturing systems, the information models, communication infrastructure and services have to be bound by a transparent middleware that will enable the challenge, which has been defined as "a machine connected to the market that is able to perform one-piece flow production that fits the individual requirements of a consumer," to be met.

This new paradigm for Machine-to-Machine Communication (M2M) can be defined by (i) the ***ubiquity*** of communication that is forced by agile production systems that are

K. Wojtkiewicz et al. (Eds.): ICCCI 2021, CCIS 1463, pp. 474–484, 2021.
https://doi.org/10.1007/978-3-030-88113-9_38

supported by artificial intelligence and data mining tools that require rich access to the information that is processed by individual elements of the manufacturing environment. M2M has to provide flexible communication services with a low cost of their launch and subsequent modifications. (ii) The ***automatic configuration*** of communication services, which is a requirement for effective and flexible M2M. In this area, artificial intelligence methods can effectively support the automatic configuration of the communication services that are based on wireless connections, including their automatic adaptation to the changing needs of the manufacturing system.

Unfortunately, the vast majority of contemporary IT solutions that are currently being used in manufacturing are based on a centralized architecture. Individual applications provide services and download data from other applications. The available services are rigidly determined when the system is created. Each change in the scope of the business model or the production technology forces subsequent changes in the architecture of the underlying communication system. Such a model lacks flexibility. On the one hand, the cost of making changes is high, while on the other hand, there is a high risk of the loss of the coherence of the information as well as the risk of functional errors.

This paper aims to present some low-level communication protocols that could be answers to the challenge above. The authors focus on a few communication protocols that are potential candidates for enabling communication solutions that can be used in agile manufacturing. The presentation focuses on the classical communication networks that are used in industrial control systems that can be applied for wireless communication and on sensor networks that were not created with a focus on manufacturing applications but can also be applied in M2M area. The subjective and incomplete list of communication standards presented in section two includes IEEE802.15.4, ZigBee, WirelessHART, ISA100.11a, IEEE802.11, wireless Profinet I/O and EtherCAT.

2 Presentation of the Known and Used Standards

The wireless solutions that are used in the industry consist of some known protocols. The most preferred standards in industrial networks are Wireless HART and ISA10011a, the most frequently used WSN standard is ZigBee and the standard that is probably used the most in wireless LANs is IEE802.11. 5G is a new wireless standard and because there are almost no industrial applications that use 5G as yet, the authors decided not to present this technology. The presentation includes wireless versions that are based on the communication protocols that are commonly used in industrial control systems such as Profinet or EtherCAT.

2.1 IEEE802.15.4

IEEE 802.15.4 is a popular standard for low-rate wireless personal area networks (PAN) that provides reliable and straightforward communication over short ranges. The standard offers industry the option of low-data rates, low cost and reduced energy consumption applications. It is a mature technology and the chips that support it can be bought off-the-shelf.

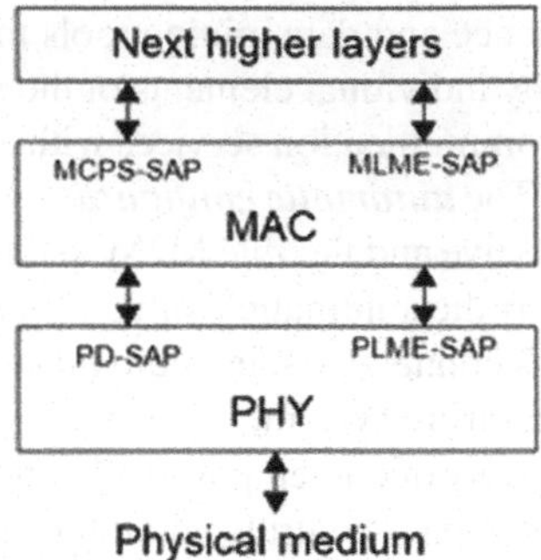

Fig. 1. Levels in IEEE802.15.4 [1]

The architecture of this standard consists of several layers. The lowest two, the physical layer (PHY) and medium access control (MAC), are defined (Fig. 1). Higher layers such as a network layer that enables network configuration, manipulation and message routing and an application layer that provides the intended function of a device. The definition of these layers is outside the scope of this standard [1].

In the IEEE802.15.4 standard, it is possible to use multiple PHYs that operate on various frequency bands. The PHY is responsible for low-level transmission operations such as activating and deactivating the radio transceiver, energy detection (ED), link quality indication (LQI), channel selection, clear channel assessment (CCA), ranging and transmitting as well as receiving packets across the physical medium [1]. The MAC layer has two services: the MAC data service and the MAC management service. The MAC services enable the transmission and reception of MAC protocol data units across the PHY data service. The features of the MAC sublayer are beacon management, channel access, guaranteed time slot (GTS) management, frame validation, acknowledged frame delivery, association and disassociation. In addition, the MAC sublayer provides hooks for implementing application-appropriate security mechanisms (Fig. 2). [1].

IEEE 802.15.4 offers star, tree, cluster-tree and mesh topologies. There are two device types, which are the standard full-function device (FFD) and the reduced-function device (RFD). An FFD device can play the role of a personal area network (PAN) coordinator. An RFD is a device that is not capable of doing this. Instead, this device type uses only simple data transfers with only a small amount of data. Because of this, an RFD uses fewer resources.

All FFDs can act as PAN coordinators. The coordinator function can be moved between FFDs – if the current coordinator is no longer available. The process of selecting a coordinator relies on beacon frames. In the beacon-enabled mode, some nodes act as personal area network coordinators (PAN) that periodically emit beacons. The time between two beacons forms a super frame, more precisely, the beacon is transmitted in the first slot of each super frame. The beacons synchronize neighboring devices and describe the super-frame structure. The time between two beacons is called the contention access period (CAP). Using slotted CSMA-CA, nodes can communicate with each other during a CAP. To run in the TDMA mode, the PAN must introduce a contention-free period (CFP) in the super-frame; the CAP is divided into a CAP and CFP period. The

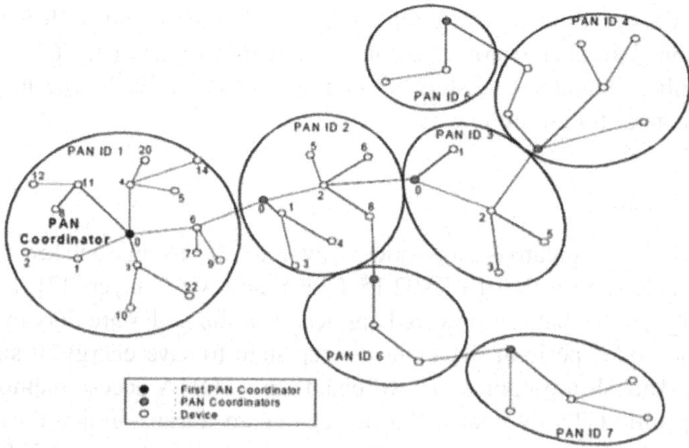

Fig. 2. Topology of IEEE 802.15.4 [1]

CFP operates in the TDMA modes because it consists of guaranteed timeslots (GTS) that are managed by a fixed PAN. The PAN shares the GTS among the nodes. The GTS is allocated to a specific node and is primarily used for communication between the dedicated node and the PAN. The CFP is used by nodes with delay-sensitive data or data that requires a specific bandwidth. A super frame can optionally have an idle period in which the coordinators can enter a sleep state.

TDMA is mainly recommended over CSMA to meet the requirements of delay-sensitive traffic in industrial networks [2]. CSMA cannot support this traffic because its medium access delay is unpredictable. Moreover, the backoff periods of CSMA make it less efficient in heavily loaded networks that have a large number of nodes [3]. However, it is a solution that distributes the medium access management to the individual nodes, reduces the complexity of a network and scaling a network up or down requires no external management. On the other hand, a well-functioning TDMA network requires tight time synchronization, which increases the network's management costs and also increases the energy consumption of the nodes. Scheduling any time-critical traffic for transmission in due time further increases the management costs. Additionally, in order to account for the large number of nodes, a TDMA should be combined with channel hopping, which adds complexity to the network management.

In order to meet the latency, reliability and robustness requirements of industry applications, the IEEE 802.15.4e working group was established in 2008 [4, 5]. The main methods that are used to fulfill the requirements are timeslot communication to reduce the number of collisions and channel hopping to reduce interference. Two main modes of operations are defined – Time-slotted Channel Hopping (TSCH) and Deterministic and Synchronous Multichannel Extension (DSME). The latter uses multi-channel communication to increase the number of GTS in the CFP periods. Our focus is on TSCH because it is mainly based on wirelessHART and ISA100.11a. TSCH defines repetitive slot frames in which each slot-frame is a collection of timeslots. The timeslots can either be dedicated or shared. The dedicated timeslots are assigned for reliable communication between two devices, one as the source the other as the receiver. The shared slot uses the

CSMA-CA access method [5] or slotted Aloha [3]. If an expected ACK is not received for transmission in the shared slot, a random backoff algorithm is activated, which counts a random number of shared timeslots before retransmission. Each timeslot is allocated a dedicated channel for communication.

2.2 ZigBee

The ZigBee wireless standard is a low-power, low-rate, short-range and low-cost wireless standard that is based on the IEEE802.15.4 PHY and MAC layers [7]. Because they are mainly targeted for battery-powered applications, the nodes are duty cycled, which means that the nodes periodically enter a sleep state to save energy. It supports star, cluster-tree and mesh topologies [7]. To enable the TDMA access method, the PAN dedicates a specific GTS to a particular device to start a transmission during the GTS without using CSMA. ZigBee uses a direct sequence spread spectrum (DSSS) and does not support channel hopping, although the PAN can change the whole network to a new channel when the current channel is severely affected by interference [4]. It operates at 868 MHz, 915 MHz and 2.4 GHz frequency bands. Zigbee Physical Devices are:

Full Function Devices FFD that can perform all of the available operations within the standard, including a routing mechanism, coordinating tasks and sensing tasks. The FFD can serve as a coordinator or router, or as an end device.

Reduced functional devices, RFD, have a low level of computing capability. The primary purpose of an RFD is to search for an available network in order to transfer the data, to determine whether there is any pending data and to send a request to the network coordinator for the data. RFDs often go into sleep mode when they are not transmitting any data, which reduces battery consumption. RFDs do not route packets and must be associated with an FFD. These are end devices such as sensors and actuators that perform limited tasks such as recording temperature data, monitoring lighting conditions or controlling external devices.

Zigbee logical devices:

Coordinators – The primary purpose of a coordinator is to setup all of the network parameters, e.g., topology, packet size, etc. It is the gateway for the outside world to interact with the network. It manages all of the nodes in the network. The inactive portion allows the coordinator to turn off its transceiver circuits to conserve battery energy (i.e., power-saving mode). The inactive portion might be void.

Zigbee Router – an intermediate device in a network that routes the data from the source to the destination. These devices route the data and also sense the data from their surrounding environments.

End Device – can be low-power/battery-powered devices that have limited computing capabilities. An end device can be an FFD or an RFD. They can collect various pieces of information from the sensors and switches. They depend on their parents to send the data (either the coordinator or a router) and cannot relay data from other devices. This reduced functionality also leads to lower costs. Each end device can have up to 240 end nodes.

2.3 WirelessHART

Wireless Highway Addressable Remote Transmission (WirelessHART) is a standard that defines the wireless interface to field devices. It is targeted toward industrial applications such as condition monitoring and flexible manufacturing. Due to its mature technology, it is based on IEEE802.15.4 at the physical layer. In order to improve the real-time and reliability characteristics, the MAC layer uses TSCH, which is the technology that was adopted into the IEEE802.15.4e standard that was described above. CSMA is typically only used in joint and shared timeslots. Otherwise, TDMA is used. A channel with high interference or noise is blacklisted and removed from the hopping sequence. Generally, the frequency or channel used is [8, 9]:

$$\text{channel} = F\left[(\text{chOffset} + \text{ASN})\ \text{modeNbChannels}\right]$$

where the higher layers allocate the channel offset (chOffset), ASN denotes the number of timeslots since the network was started and NbChannels is the number of physical channels that are used in the network.

A wirelessHART network is a hybrid wireless-wired network that consists of a wired network manager, a security manager and gateways [10]. The latter is connected to the wireless field devices and handheld devices through an access point. The wireless field devices are connected to the industrial processes and are located at the plant level. They have routing capabilities that enable a mesh or star network topology. The wired network manager is responsible for the overall network configuration, manages the routing in the network and schedules communication [11].

2.4 ISA100.11a

ISA100.11a, which was developed by the International Society of Automation (ISA), defines a wireless system for industrial automation and control applications. Like WirelessHART, it uses 802.15.4 at the physical layer, TSCH at the MAC layer and can operate with both star and mesh topologies. It supports the adaptive blacklisting of channels [10], which means that individual devices can blacklist channels autonomously unless this function is deactivated. In addition to slotted channel hopping, both slow and hybrid channel hopping are also supported. In slow hopping, a group of contiguous timeslots uses the same frequency channel. The groups can be configured with various numbers of timeslots. The group performs channel-hopping in the same way as slotted hopping, but with a slower hopping frequency since the time duration of the group is increased by including several timeslots. Slow-hopping periods are generated, and these are often used for multi-access communication using the CSMA-CA access method. These periods can be used for unscheduled traffic such as device discovery and event-based data [10]. Hybrid hopping combines periods of both slow and slotted hopping.

ISA100.11a supports five preprogrammed hopping patterns, pattern number 1 reduces interference from any co-located 802.11 networks [4] and pattern number 5 reduces interference from any co-located wirelessHART while patterns 3 and 4 are intended for slow hopping [10].

The DLL layer of ISA100.11a provides routing capabilities using routing graphs that are calculated and managed by a manager. The different graphs are individually optimized based on the requirements of different types of traffic. During transmission, the nodes choose the correct graph based on the type of traffic that is currently being transmitted. In this way, unlike WirelessHART and contrary to the OSI-model definition, the DLL layer provides a routing topology. The DLL routing is terminated at the backbone router, while the network layer's routing extends into the backbone and the plant network [10]. The network layer is based on 6LoWPAN.

The ISA100.11a network consists of wireless field devices with or without routing capabilities and handheld devices in addition to the backbone/infrastructure wired devices that include backbone routers, gateway and security and a system manager. The backbone devices are generally high-energy devices that are connected to the power outlet, while the field devices are low-energy battery-powered devices. The overall network management is centralized to the system manager, which acts as a global network clock and controls the scheduling and optimization of network operations.

Most of the security function in IAS100.11a is optional, while for WirelessHART is it mandatory [12].

2.5 IEEE802.11

In 1997, the IEEE ratified the original IEEE802.11 standards and the first IEEE802.11 standard to gain broad industry acceptance was 802.11b and the products that are certified under the IEEE802.11 standards are called Wi-Fi (Wireless Fidelity). Two basic configuration modes are supported. The first is the infrastructure mode in which communication between any station has to go through an Access Point (AP). The other is an ad-hoc mode in which the stations can communicate directly without an AP.

IEEE802.11b operate at the unlicensed 2.4 GHz instrumentation, scientific and medical (ISM) band, which supports a maximum transmission rate of 11 Mb/s using DSSS technology. The newer IEEE802.11 versions support transmission rates up to 600 Mb/s for 802.11n and 7 Gbps for 802.11ac. Some versions use the 5 GHz band and to improve the maximum throughput, more advanced technologies such as 256QAM and MIMO are used [13]. The supported network topologies are tree and star, and the mesh topology is not well supported [14]. The fundamental MAC technology that is used is the Distribution Coordination Function (DCF) and Point Coordination Function (PCF). In the DCF mode, the access method that is used is the Carrier Sense Multiple Access with Collision Avoidance (CSMA-CA) with Binary Exponential Back-off (BEB). Clear Channel Assessment (CCA) is the carrier sense method that is used to check for channel activity. Before accessing a channel, it must be idle for a random back-up period plus a DCF Interframe Space (DIFS). A parameter called the Contention Window (CW) is used to determine the length of the back-up period. The nodes choose a random number in the range [0, CW] in order to determine the number of timeslots it must let pass.

PCF provides a polling-based contention-free access method that is controlled by an AP. Periodically emitted beacons divide the time into beacon intervals, each of which is composed of Contention Free Periods (CFPs) and Contention Periods (CP). The AP polls the stations during the CFP and the stations can only transmit after being polled. The maximum frame size limits the transmission from a polled station. However, IEEE802.11 does provide multi-rate support (link adaptation) so that the transmission time is variable, which contributes to unpredictable delays and jitter.

Although the DCF and PCF approach work well for networks without real-time requirements, their latency is unpredictable, which makes them unfeasible for industrial networks. To provide real-time QoS, IEEE 802.11e introduced various new functions. A new MAC layer function called the Hybrid Coordination Function (HCF) was added [15]. The HCF uses Enhanced Distributed Channel Access (EDCA) as a contention-based medium access method that offers priority-based differentiated access. This method operates concurrently with the polling-based HCF-Controlled Channel Access (HCCA) method. Using EDCA, the traffic is divided into four different traffic categories, which are called Access Categories (AC), each with a different priority level [13]. The higher the traffic's priority, the shorter the Arbitration Inter-Frame Spacing (AIFS) and CW. AIFS is a function that is equivalent to DIFS. Shorter values mean that higher priority traffic is likely to access the medium earlier. The values of these parameters are determined by the QAP and announced periodically in the beacon frames.

HCCA represents the contention-free part of HCF and can only be used in infrastructure-mode networks [15]. The period between two beacons is divided into Control Access Periods (CAPs) and contention periods are permitted for EDCA traffic. The QoS STA (QSTA) sends a QoS request to the QoS AP (QAP) that contains the information about the QoS requirements for their upcoming traffic stream (TS) [13]. Based on the received requests, the QAP sets up a schedule for the communication in which the beacon interval is divided into suitable service intervals (SI) and the QSTA are polled during the allocated interval. In order to control the transmission time of a polled station, a Transmit Opportunity limit (TXOP) was introduced. The QoS AP (QAP) determines a time-limit TXOPLimit, which limits the time a node can use to transmit a burst of data frames. This solves the problem of an unpredictable transmission time of a polled STA in PCF.

2.6 Profinet

The development of the IEEE 802.11 specifications permitted the standard to be applicable in industrial networks. Many industrial Ethernet protocols such as Profinet can operate on wireless interfaces because specifications such as IEEE 802.11e, which was mentioned in the subsection above, enable the real-time QoS requirements to be satisfied [16].

In Profinet networks, the producer-consumer communication model is used. The producer is called the IO-Controller and a Programmable Logic Controller is most commonly used in that role. Consumers are referred to as IO-Devices. A typical architecture comprises one IO-Controller to *n* IO-Devices (where *n* depends on the number of controller resources) [17].

Most of the user data in Profinet networks is transferred cyclically with a predefined cycle time. The data transfer is initiated by the IO-Controllers. In industrial applications, it is required that the data transfer be performed in a timely manner with a determined latency and appropriate jitter. In today's Profinet networks, two real-time communication classes are distinguished RTC1 and RTC3 (the RTC2 class is now considered to be obsolete and is not used in new applications). In the RTC1 class (also referred as a RealTime RT class), the typical cycle time is less than 40ms and the jitter can be up to 15% of the cycle time.

A typical cycle time in the RTC3 communication class (called Isochronous Real-Time IRT) is 1ms with a jitter of 1 μs. [18].

Considering the temporal characteristics of the above real-time classes, it can be concluded that wireless communication is not possible for Profinet IRT communications. However, this is also the case for other reasons that are beyond the scope of this paper (synchronization of network devices, the definition of topology). However, when Profinet RT is concerned, wireless communication is quite feasible and is realized often. Any real-time requirements can be satisfied by using standards such as IEEE 802.11e for QoS.

2.7 EtherCAT

Another industrial Ethernet Protocol that is as popular and as widely used as Profinet is EtherCAT. It is often assumed that EtherCAT is not meant for wireless applications because of its high temporal characteristics with a cycle time of less than 1ms and above all because of its on-the-fly datagram processing [19, 20]. Although some research has focused on the wireless application of EtherCAT, it concerns the transfer of asynchronous traffic [21]. The concept is based on the encapsulation of user data into Type 12 PDUs or using mailbox datagrams [22].

The above remark applies to EtherCAT Device Protocol [23], which is used to exchange process data between the EtherCAT master (typically Programmable Logic Controller PLC) and EtherCAT slaves (remote Input/Output stations, drives). There is, however, the EtherCAT Application Protocol, EAP, which is used for data exchange, for example, between the PLCs. In that case, the communication is based on the Producer-Subscriber principle and wireless solutions can be used. In EAP communication, the cycle times have a value of dozens of milliseconds. Therefore, the latency that is introduced by wireless interfaces is not very critical in most common applications.

3 Conclusions

In this paper, the authors presented a few low-level communication protocols that can be used for M2M communication. On the one hand, the presentation focused on the wireless versions of the Ethernet-based communication protocols that are commonly used in industrial control systems such as Profinet or EtherCAT, while on the other hand it presented the standards that have been created for sensor networks without the primary focus being on manufacturing systems such as ZigBee and IEE802.11 (Wi-Fi). The authors presented communication solutions that can be used for M2M and that have the potential to become a critical enabling technology that will support the distributed algorithms for AI and DM. The discussion also presents some architectural issues that are related to a protocol's layers and the hardware components that are required for their implementation, some aspects related to network topologies and the ability to adapt, some issues related to the reliability and real-time support that are required for industrial control systems as well as their safety and applicability in an industrial environment. The authors believe that the presented material will support the selection of choices in wireless communication that is used in contemporary manufacturing systems and that the paper will also indicate some of the limitations in the existing solutions that require further research and development.

Acknowledgments. The research that led to these results received funding from the Norway Grants 20142021, which the National Centre operates for Research and Development under the project "Automated Guided Vehicles integrated with Collaborative Robots for Smart Industry Perspective" (Project Contract no.: NOR/POLNOR/CoBotAGV/0027/2019 00) and partially by the Polish Ministry of Science and Higher Education Funds for Statutory Research.

References

1. IEEE Standards Association: IEEE standard for low-rate wireless networks. IEEE Std. **802**, 4–2015 (2016)
2. Ovsthus, K., Kristensen, L.M.: An industrial perspective on wireless sensor networks— a survey of requirements, protocols and challenges. IEEE Commun. Surv. Tutorials **16**(3), 1391–1412 (2014)
3. Laya, A., Kalalas, C., Vazquez-Gallego, F., Alonso, L., Alonso-Zarate, J.: Goodbye, aloha! IEEE Access **4**, 2029–2044 (2016)
4. Wang, Q., Jiang, J.: Comparative examination on architecture and protocol of industrial wireless sensor network standards. IEEE Commun. Surv. Tutorials **18**(3), 2197–2219 (2016)
5. Choudhury, N., Matam, R., Mukherjee, M., Lloret, J.: A performance-to-cost analysis of IEEE 802.15. 4 MAC with 802.15. 4e MAC modes. IEEE Access. **8**, 41936–41950 (2020)
6. ZigBee Alliance. https://zigbeealliance.org/solution/zigbee. Accessed 12 Apr 2021
7. Dhillon, P., Sadawarti, H.: A review paper on Zigbee IEEE 802.15. 4 standard. Int. J. Eng. Res. Technol. **3**(4), 141–145 (2014)
8. Hermeto, R.T., Gallais, A., Theoleyre, F.: Scheduling for IEEE802. 15.4-TSCH and slow channel hopping MAC in low power industrial wireless networks: a survey. Comput. Commun. **114**, 84–105 (2017)
9. Petersen, S., Carlsen, S.: WirelessHART versus ISA100.11a: the format war hits the factory floor. IEEE Ind. Electron. Mag. **5**(4), 23–34 (2011)
10. Lennvall, T., Svensson, S., Hekland, F.: A comparison of WirelessHART and ZigBee for industrial applications. In: 2008 IEEE International Workshop on Factory Communication Systems, pp. 85–88. IEEE (2008)
11. Nixon, M., Rock, T.R.: A comparison of WirelessHART and ISA100. 11a. Whitepaper Emerson Proc. Manage. 1–36 (2012)
12. Cheng, Y., Yang, D., Zhou, H., Wang, H.: Adopting IEEE 802.11 MAC for industrial delay-sensitive wireless control and monitoring applications: a survey. Comput. Netw. **157**, 41–67 (2019)
13. Li, X., Li, D., Wan, J., Vasilakos, A.V., Lai, C.F., Wang, S.: A review of industrial wireless networks in the context of industry 4.0. Wireless Netw. **23**(1), 23–41 (2017)
14. Ni, Q.: Performance analysis and enhancements for IEEE 802.11 e wireless networks. IEEE Netw. **19**(4), 21–27 (2005)
15. Wu, X., Xie, L.: On the wireless extension of PROFINET networks. In: 2019 IEEE VTS Asia Pacific Wireless Communication Symposium APWCS, pp. 1–5 (2019)
16. Sestito, G.S., Turcato, A.C., Dias, A.L., Rocha, M.S., Brandão, D., Torres da, R.V.: Case of study of a profinet network using ring topology. In: 2016 IEEE International Symposium Consumer Electronics ISCE, pp. 91–96 (2016)

17. Müller, T., Doran, H.D.: Protecting PROFINET cyclic real-time traffic: a performance evaluation and verification platform. In: 2018 14th IEEE International Workshop Factory Communication System WFCS, pp. 1–4 (2018)
18. Wu, X., Xie, L., Lim, F.: Network delay analysis of EtherCAT and PROFINET IRT protocols. In: IECON 2014–40th Annual Conference IEEE Industrial Electronics Society, pp. 2597–2603 (2014)
19. Delgado, R., Kim, S., You, B., Choi, B.: An EtherCAT-based real-time motion control system in mobile robot application. In: 2016 13th International Conference Ubiquitous Robots Ambient Intelligent URAI, pp. 710–715 (2016)
20. Wu, X., Xie, L.: On the wireless extension of EtherCAT networks. In: 2017 IEEE 42nd Conference Local Computer Network LCN, pp. 235–238 (2017)
21. Sridevi, G., Saligram, A., Nattarasu, V.: Establishing EtherCAT communication between industrial PC and variable frequency drive. In: 2018 3rd IEEE International Conference Recent Trends Electronic Information Communication Technology RTEICT, pp. 1967–1973 (2018)
22. Patti, G., Lo, Bello, L., Alderisi, G., Mirabella, O.: An EDF-based swapping approach to enhance support for asynchronous real-time traffic over EtherCAT networks. In: IEEE International Conference Emerging Technology Factory Automation ETFA 8 (2013)
23. EtherCAT Automation Protocol, EtherCAT for Plant Automation–standard (2012)

Ontology-Based Approaches for Communication with Autonomous Guided Vehicles for Industry 4.0

Rafal Cupek[1](✉), Marcin Fojcik[2], Piotr Gaj[1], and Jacek Stój[1]

[1] Silesian University of Technology, Gliwice, Poland
{rafal.cupek,piotr.gaj,jacek.stoj}@polsl.pl
[2] Western Norway University of Applied Sciences, Bergen, Norway
marcin.fojcik@hvl.no

Abstract. Autonomous Guided Vehicles (AGV) are an enabling technology that has changed the landscape for the new generation of manufacturing systems. Because AGV must interact with a heterogenous production environment, communication between an AGV and other devices must be established dynamically. This includes the production stands, production systems, manufacturing infrastructure, and cooperation with other AGVs. The focus of this paper is the ontological approach that enables dynamic communications with an AGV that must be adapted to changing operating conditions. The aim of this work is to review the existing approaches using ontologies for industrial communication, to evoke a discussion, and to elucidate the current research opportunities by highlighting the relationship between different subareas of communication with an AGV.

Keywords: Automated Guided Vehicles · AGV · Machine-to-Machine (M2M) communication · Communication middleware

1 Introduction

The usefulness of Automated Guided Vehicles (AGV) results not only from their technical features, but also from their ability to cooperate, which determines their efficient use as a part of flexible manufacturing services. In this context, the internal logistics that are based on an AGV should be dynamically adjusted to the frequently changing production tasks [1]. An AGV has to communicate with production stands, Manufacturing Execution Systems (MES), the manufacturing infrastructure and other AGVs. For this reason, the ontological approach for communication with an AGV has to be analyzed within the context of Machine-to-Machine (M2M) communication as well as in Machine-to-System Communication. The communication services of AGV have to follow "plug and produce" paradigm [2] and therefore communication their ontology has to be built in accordance with the standards of the cooperating devices and systems. This paper presents a use case study that was focused on the ontology for an AGV that had to cover heterogenous and dynamic communications channels between the AGV and other parts of the manufacturing system.

K. Wojtkiewicz et al. (Eds.): ICCCI 2021, CCIS 1463, pp. 485–497, 2021.
https://doi.org/10.1007/978-3-030-88113-9_39

The aim of this paper is to review the existing approaches in the ontologies for industrial communication and to discuss how to apply them to the specific use case with a focus on the relationships between the different communication channels that are used by an AGV. The rest of this paper is organized as follows: the second section presents a few examples of the ontological approach in designing manufacturing systems. The ontology-based approach for communication between an AGV and Manufacturing Execution Systems (MES) is presented in section three. The fourth section presents selected tools that can be used when preparing the ontology including a discussion of their applicability in the area being considered. The conclusions are presented in section five.

2 Examples of Ontologies

An ontology is a semantic tool that is understandable by both humans and computers that consists of a formalized representation of the knowledge about a field of discourse, which is defined as "a formal, explicit specification of a shared conceptualization". Ontologies provide a shared and common understanding of a domain that can be communicated between people and heterogeneous and widely dispersed application systems. Typically, ontologies are composed of a set of terms that represent concepts (hierarchically organized) and a specification of their meaning. According to the Ontology Development Life Cycle Model presented by [3], the following steps of ontology development can be distinguished:

Specification in order to identify the purpose and scope of the ontology. In this case, the focus of the ontology was on the flexible interaction between the components of Industry4.0 systems and an AGV,

Conceptualization in order to describe the conceptual model that would meet the specification that was found in the previous step. The conceptual model consists of the concepts in the domain and the relationships among those concepts. In area that is discussed, the model had to be compliant with the other models that are used in the new generation of manufacturing systems especially with models that had been structured using the Reference Architecture Model for Industrie 4.0 (RAMI 4.0) [4],

Formalization in order to transform the conceptual description into a formal model by describing the domain that was found in the previous step that is is written in a more formal way, although not yet its final form. According to research on AGV communication, the authors analyzed several implementation tools for formalizing an ontology. Within the scope of Industry 4.0, the OPC UA standard for the address space definition is indicate as the enabling technology,

Maintenance in order to update and correct the implemented ontology,

Knowledge acquisition in order to acquire knowledge about the subject either by using elicitation techniques or consulting domain experts,

Evaluation in order to technically judge the quality of the ontology, and

Documentation in order to report it.

In the scope of this paper, the authors only focused on the first three steps of the ontology lifecycle.

There are many different ontologies, especially those for automation and robots. The IEEE 1872–2015 standard [5] defines a set of ontologies that can be combined with Robotics and Automation. Another example of an ontology is RoboEarth [6]. This is a European project about an open-source platform that enables a robot to act as part of a global system. The NIST ontology [7] from National Institute of Standards and Technology offers test methods for robotic technologies. Another example is the Intelligent Systems Ontology [8] that is used by the United States Army to describe the intelligent behavior of the cooperation of machines and humans.

Almost all of these ontologies attempt to define the entire structure of well-defined knowledge representation. There is also a definition of the relationships among the properties, rules, and constraints. These efforts have led to a definition of a complete system of operations from the most general to the most detailed aspect.

Another possibility is to define only some limited elements in a robot's behavior. The resulting ontology would not be complete, but it should cover at least some part of the problem. In this paper, the authors will attempt to show some possibilities for defining an ontology for a bottom-up definition.

3 Ontology-Based Communication Between an AGV and Manufacturing Execution Systems

Manufacturing Execution Systems (MES) are IT systems that are used in industry whose task is to ensure cooperation between industrial control systems and the systems that support the management of an enterprise. The features that distinguish MES from other industrial IT systems are (i) they operate with the production level *via* real-time, continuous communication, (ii) they perform the online conversion of information models between the different domains of their application, (iii) they are responsible for transforming the data that is presented in accordance with the business model into a form that is convenient for interpretation by industrial control systems, and (iv) they support the conversion and processing of the data that is acquired from the control systems into a form that can be used by the other IT systems of the enterprise. For this reason, MES cannot only be treated as an interface for the exchange of information. Although MES collect and store information, they are not simply a repository for the production data. MES are advanced IT solutions that provide tools for adapting the various information models that are used in industry and also provide services for transforming raw production data into information that is relevant to the operational business management and for translating business models into a number of the operations that are performed by production systems [9].

Internal logistics is a crucial part of MES that enables the successive production operations to be performed. In the context of agile manufacturing, AGV replace the classical solutions that were used in discrete manufacturing such as transport that is based on belt, slat, or bucket conveyors. AGV enable the internal logistics to be organized in a way that is fully dynamic and that can be adjusted to frequently changing production tasks. Despite the fact that AGV have many advantages as a flexible means of transport, the necessity for them to cooperate with MES creates a number of problems, which are not visible in classic (rigid) transport systems, e.g., (i) the non-deterministic time that is necessary to implement the transport tasks that is dependent on any delays that result from interactions with staff and other AGV; (ii) the increased likelihood of an error (emergency stop) because the transport routes are shared with other vehicles and human staff; (iii) the need to cooperate with many different production stands and with staff members who performing various production activities; (iv) the complexity of the transport routes that are shared and that run both inside and outside of the production buildings, which requires dynamic adjustment of the navigation and interaction with the infrastructure; and (v) the heterogeneity of communication that has to be completely wireless and that typically occurs over multiple subnets and communication standards, which causes the parameters of the communication channels to be unstable.

According to the generic ontology type classification [10], understanding the data can be done by ***representation ontology***, which defines the representation primitives of a knowledge representation system and permits an object-oriented description for all of the variables linked to an AGV and the manufacturing processes. The logical objects that combine different variables as well as conceptual elements can be defined by ***frame ontology***, which includes defining the class, for instance, of the relationship between a class and its superclass, etc.; the more general concepts, which include cooperation between the system parts such as the time point, time interval, and the relationship of any overlap between two time intervals, which can be defined by an ***upper-level*** ontology; and lastly, the concepts from the entire internal logistics that are based on an AGV including its communication with MES, which has to be described by a ***domain*** ontology. The mapping between the AGV-based internal logistics and the relevant ontology is presented in Fig. 1.

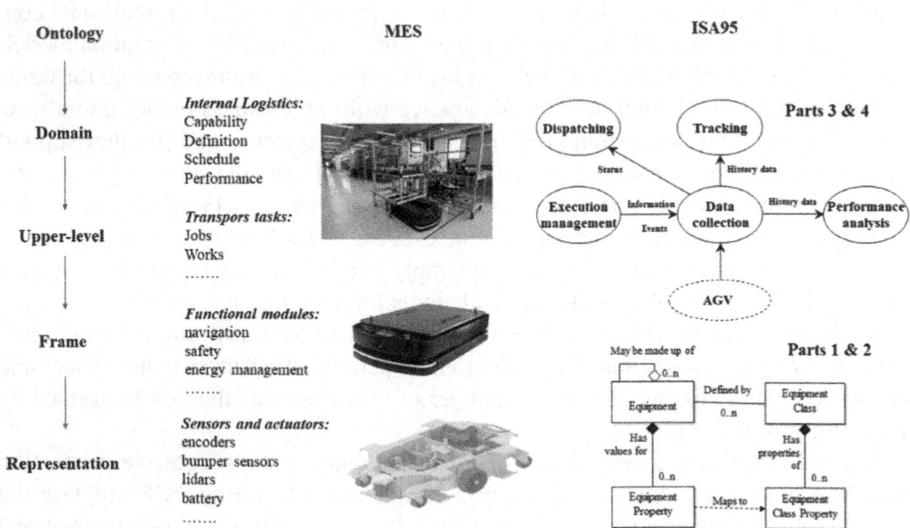

Fig. 1. Ontology for communication between an AGV and MES.

The ontology that describes the communication between an AGV and MES must, on the one hand, take into account the specificity of the internal logistics tasks that are to be performed by an AGV, while on the other hand, it must permit the easy integration between the AGV and existing MES systems. One of the enabling standards that is recommended by RAMI4.0 for MES is the ANSI/ISA-95 (IEC/ISO 62264) norm (International Society of Automation) [11], which defines the international standard for integrating enterprise and control systems [12]. The ISA95 models act as an interface between the business and manufacturing processes that define the data flow and services for MES and that can be used in all of the branches of manufacturing. These processes are separated by a clear demarcation of responsibilities and functions and combines them *via* a well-defined communication interface that is realized using B2MML [13], which is an XML implementation of the ANSI/ISA-95 family of standards. It also defines the functions and information flow within the MES. ISA95 defines the common terminology and provides a consistent set of models that are described using UML diagrams, which are understandable in both domains. ISA-95 also defines the MES data structure and MES services that are linked to the manufacturing operations: defining the product, forecasting production, managing production capability, and evaluating production performance, which are based on the PURDUE model [14].

ISA-95 defines MES ontology in terms of models and terminology. It describes the information that is exchanged between the systems for sales, finance, and logistics and the systems for production, maintenance, and quality. This information is structured in the form of UML (Unified Modelling Language) models, which were the basis for developing the standard interfaces between ERP and MES systems [15]. ISA-95 is built on an object-oriented model that defines the interface between the control systems and a business application. It also defines the services that are required for manufacturing support, which is also designed according to the object-oriented model. These services are not only based on information exchange but also on the aggregated data or the history of the realization of the process that has to be managed by the database systems. Today, ISA95 is considered to be one of the key enabling technologies for implementing manufacturing systems that are compatible with RAMI4.0 [16, 17].

The models for data and services that are defined by ISA95 enable an ontology that describes the communication and interaction between an AGV and MES at different classification levels to be built. As is shown in the bottom-up process on the right side of Fig. 1: the Equipment models that are defined by the first and second part of ISA 95 can be used for the representation and frame ontology. They enable the basic elements of AGV (e.g. sensors or actuators) as well as more complex structures responsible for navigation or energy management to be described. These models can be used to convert the technological details between control and management systems. For the upper-level and domain ontology of the internal logistics that are performed by an AGV, the relevant jobs and works models of ISA95 can be used in accordance with the services, which are defined by the third and fourth parts of the specification. This level includes both the description of the production possibilities in conjunction with the definition of the production technology that define the potential logistics tasks that are to be serviced by an AGV, the schedule for the internal logistics that directly resulted from the production plan that was provided by the ERP system, and also the logistics performance control and analysis as the on-line activity linked to the material flow analysis.

4 Ontology Editors

Usually, the correct collection of terms (vocabulary) in the form of concepts and relationships is available when common and well-known domains are described and use cases are needed including technical ones. However, sometimes, there are issues when unusual and new vocabulary must be created because of the lack of any suitable words. In many cases, not only the vocabulary, but also the relevant ontology must be created and written in a standard way. An ontology is a kind of vocabulary that is presented formally and pertains to complex things, which permits a common understanding of things.

In addition to the ontology definition itself, its description should be unambiguous and should follow a recognizable and standard ontology language. Sometimes an ontology language is needed in order to describe another language, and in this case, it is called a metalanguage. There are many formal languages and metalanguages that can be used to construct various types of ontologies. One of the most popular languages for authoring ontologies is the group that is Web Ontology Language (OWL), which is built using W3C and refers to the concepts of a semantic web and a web of linked data. OWL is based on the markup metalanguage XML. For the technical domains, and especially computer-oriented concepts, the markup languages are quite useful because of the possibility to use both data and data annotations (i.e., markups) in the same document, so that the data values and its semantic can be delivered by the same file. In many cases, this simplifies the ontology description and its processing. OWL is a standard ontology language that is able to model things and the relationships between things, and it also is general enough to be used in the areas of industrial automation, communication, processing, and manufacturing.

As an example, OWL can be the basis for developing semantic rules that extend the existing ontology that was created to describe the knowledge about manufacturing systems within the scope of ISA-95. The authors of [18] proposed a set of semantic rules that were built using the OWL concepts. Such rules can be used to automatically check an ISA-95 system during the runtime. Another interesting example is the use of OWL to build the formal semantics of PLC projects, especially the included programs. The semantic codes of even the standard languages sometimes vary in their implementations on various platforms. The authors of [19] resolved the problem of this incompatibility by defining a common semantic model that is independent of any given realizations, which could be useful for programs the automatically migrate between platforms and IDE tools. OWL is also valuable for producing M2M communication. In such a domain, a large amount of data can be transferred among various nodes, systems, and subsystems, and in different contexts. Moreover, the amount of data and the links continue to grow. As a result, the awareness of the need for ontologies has existed for many years. The initial but standardized work on this topic is presented in [20], in which there is an ontology that is based on OWL, which was designed to cope with sensors and observations. Moreover, some conceptual modules, terms, and relationships for sensor networks were also defined. For the newer concepts, in [21], the authors developed an ontology for the IoT systems and M2M communication that is based on services. OWL was also the basis for the research in [22] in which the authors built a semantic interface for M2M communication that is used when creating automation. In all of the research mentioned above, as well as in the work linked to the topic of this paper, the existence of proper semantics is necessary in order to provide automatic dialogue and data interpretation. All of these cases refer to data units that are linked together not only according to their syntax (e.g., protocols, languages, etc.) but particularly to their semantics (e.g., use cases, cooperation rules, context meaning, etc.).

4.1 A Brief Overview of the Tools

Creating an ontology requires keeping records in the selected ontology language. These can certainly be simply written on a piece of paper. However, the ontology editors that are designed for creating ontologies in a specific language are a more practical choice. More than one hundred ontology-building tools have been created in the last decade. While most of these are probably not in active use these days, dozens still have followers. There are several significant editors that are available among them, and a few support OWL. Because of the genesis of the products, they can be divided into three groups. Some of them were created because of the specific needs of research communities and are oriented to specific fields of knowledge, some were created as a result of a collaborative project and were discontinued, and some were built as a universal product that is still being developed and supported by their followers. Most of them were created by academic communities, are of open-source type, and their last released versions were published on GitHub. There are also comparative studies of these ontology building tools [23–25]. The Table 1 below lists some of these tools and their important features.

Table. 1. Comparison of the selected tools for the support of ontology design.

Editor name	Last release	OWL support	RDF/XML support	License
SWOOP	2006	+	+	open source
Neologism	2011	-	+	free
NeOn Toolkit	2011	+	+	free/open/licensed
OBO-Edit	2014	-	-	open source
Apollo	2004	-	-	open source
Hozo	2019	-	+	free
Vitro	2021	-	+	open source
OWLGrEd	2018	+	+	free
Knoodl	2012	+	+	free
Anzo Suite	2010	+	+	licensed
OntoStudio	2012	+	+	licensed
TopBraid composer	2021	+	+	licensed
VocBench + Semantic Turkey	2017	+	+	open source
Protégé	2019	+	+	open source
Fluent editor	2015	+	+	licensed

SWOOP and Neologism are lightweight and simple editors. SWOOP was developed by the Mindswap organization from the University of Maryland and was released in 2006. This web-based editor and viewer operates with OWL and the RDF and XML datasets. The architecture is open source, but without the possibility of integrating it with other tools; however, it can be extended by adding plugins. It seems that the development and support of this tool has ended.

Neologism[1] is a web-based vocabulary editor and publishing tool that is a module of the Drupal platform, which was developed by the Drupal association. It uses OWL and the resource schemas that are based on RDFS. Originally, it was developed by Digital Enterprise Research Institute (DERI) from the Science Foundation Ireland, which is now called the Data Science Institute (DSI). It no longer seems to be supported.

Another example is the NeOn Toolkit[2] that was developed and supported by the NeOn Foundation. It is also an open-source toolkit that is based on the Eclipse open development platform. It is an advanced, multi-platform and multilingual toolkit that was published in 2011. It seems that it has not been developed since then. The editor supports modelling in both F-logic and OWL, uses RDFS, and is able to operate with plugins. It potentially covers a wide range of ontology engineering activities.

Another simple editor is OBO-Edit[3], which was developed by Berkeley Bioinformatics and was funded by the Gene Ontology Consortium. This editor is optimized for ontologies in the Open Biological and Biomedical Ontologies file format.

Apollo[4] is another modelling tool that is delivered as a desktop application. It was developed by an international group united under the Knowledge Media Institute in 2004. The knowledge is built using typical abstracts as classes, relationships, etc., but the description is not in accordance with any standard OWL language. It is a standalone solution and cannot interact with other tools. The ontology can be saved in XML.

The next editor is Hozo, which is a Japanese product developed by the team of Kouji Kozaki from the Institute of Scientific and Industrial Research, Osaka University in 2011. It is still supported. Hozo is not designed to work with OWL, but it does allow the import and export of the description file formats of OWL (XML and RDF).

Vitro editor is the next web-based editor. It was developed at Cornell University, Ithaca, USA, as a core ontology platform for VIVO[5] – an open-source software for representing research and scholarship. The editor is not oriented with OWL, but it can create and load OWL ontologies. It is still supported by the VIVO community members.

OWLGrEd[6] (OWL Graphic Editor) is both a web-based and desktop tool. It can create and visualize an ontology based on OWL. It was developed at Institute of Mathematics and Computer Science, University of Latvia.

Knoodl is collaborative ontology editor oriented on communities. In Knoodle, the formal knowledge description is based on OWL while the informal knowledge collection

[1] https://www.drupal.org/project/neologism.

[2] http://neon-toolkit.org/.

[3] http://oboedit.org.

[4] http://apollo.open.ac.uk.

[5] https://duraspace.org/vivo/.

[6] http://owlgred.lumii.lv/.

is based on wiki content. It also uses RDF as a resource description and SPARQL for queries. This editor was once popular, but apparently it is not in active use.

The Anzo Suite[7] was originally developed by the Cambridge Semantics company, USA, as a set of tools for non-technical users. The suite included three products: the Anzo Data Collaboration Server, Anzo for the Web, and Anzo for Excel. The server is the core of the Anzo system, Anzo Web is a web-oriented collaborative platform, and Anzo for Excel is a plug-in for Microsoft Excel. Currently, the Anzo Platform is a scalable knowledge graph platform for data integration and analytics. The platform uses the W3C standards including RDF, OWL, SKOS and SPARQL to connect knowledge graphs of metadata and data.

OntoStudio editor is another example of professional collaborative editor for OWL that can handle RDF, RDFS, and F-Logic, and operates on the Eclipse platform. This product offered a lot of possibilities, including ontologies, rules and their processing, data sources integration, and API. However, it seems the project is no longer being supported.

An advanced and powerful ontology modeling tool is the suite of TopBraid products, which can be used as a multi-platform desktop tool called TopBraid Composer ME (Maestro Edition) and can also operate as collaborative web tool called TopBraid EDG (Enterprise Data Governance). Both can operate with the resource schemas in the RDF, RDFa, and RDFS formats, the GRDDL data transformation technique, validations in SHACL, and OWL models. The desktop version is implemented as a plug-in to the Eclipse open development platform. It can serve as a SPARQL query editor and a development environment for SPIN, SPARQLMotion, SPARQL Web Pages and more. The web-based version also has API (RESTfull and GraphQL) for integration. The editor was developed by the TopQuadrant company and it is continuously supported.

One of the brand new products is VocBench[8] [26]. Version 3 was created by the Artificial Intelligence Research Group at the University of Rome, Tor Vergata in Italy and was funded by the European Commission ISA^2 program in 2017. It is a collaborative development platform for managing the OWL ontologies and generic RDF datasets. It is a web and multilingual tool with a supporting SKOS, SKOS-XL thesaurus, and Ontolex-lemon vocabulary. It is based on Apache Karaf (implementation of OSGi – Open Services Gateway initiative[9]) and the Semantic Turkey[10] platform.

The Semantic Turkey platform is an advanced RDF service platform for Knowledge Management and Acquisition that was also developed by the ART Research Group at the University of Rome, Tor Vergata. It is the backend for the VocBench Editor.

---

7 https://www.cambridgesemantics.com/anzo-platform/.

8 http://vocbench.uniroma2.it.

9 https://www.osgi.org/.

10 http://semanticturkey.uniroma2.it/.

One of the most famous and popular products is Protégé[11] [27]. It was used by authors of [28] to record the developed ontologies. This editor is a product of a team from Stanford Center for Biomedical Informatics Research at the Stanford University School of Medicine, and it was developed as an open-source code. The editor has no special requirements or prerequisites to run. It is a tool and framework for building knowledge-based solutions in various areas, and is based on OWL. It is not explicitly devoted to communication systems but also supports knowledge engineering, and its use is not limited in practice. The editor can operate with plugins and is supported by the international community. It can be used as a dedicated desktop editor for Windows or as a web tool. It covers a variety of ontology-oriented tasks.

Another comprehensive tool for editing and manipulating complex ontologies is Fluent Editor[12], which was developed by the Cognitum company, Poland and published in 2015 as part of larger project called the Ontorion Knowledge Management framework. The editor is compatible with the W3C OWL standard, RDF and RDFS datasets, and the SWRL, SPARQL and SKOS languages data models, and can cooperate with Protégé *via* ontology import and export. It uses natural English language for knowledge modeling. The language that it uses is not fully natural but has been simplified to reduce it complexity and to remove any syntax or semantic ambiguity. It resembles a simple programming language with a restricted vocabulary and grammar. Because its descriptions are in natural language. this editor is an alternative for less natural to human XML-based OWL editors. The editor enables some non-OWL expressions to be used as a model. Therefore, it is possible to determine whether the sentences that are used are within the OWL profile.

4.2 Example Use of the Editor

In this subsection, a simple ontology is presented using different tools. The example of a simple CoBotAGV ontology was created using Fluent Editor by defining a few sentences. The corresponding graph was generated in the Fluent Editor of the T-Box and A-Box elements and the class taxonomy is presented in Fig. 2.

The presented CoBotAGV ontology in Fluent Editor and Protégé looks quite similar apart from the different distribution of the elements in the T-Box and the different graphical objects that are used for the presentation. On the other hand, in OWLGrEd the presentation corresponds to the UML diagrams. In both cases, the graphs are intuitive to read even without any in-depth knowledge in the ontology field. Importantly, the differences in the visual representation of the created ontologies does not impact the scope of usability of the presented tools in any way. All of them can claim to be universal and versatile solutions that are ready to be used in many different areas of interest, with AGV being one of them. The same ontology that was exported to Protégé is presented in Fig. 3.

[11] https://protege.stanford.edu/.

[12] Https://Www.Cognitum.Eu/Semantics/Fluenteditor/.

```
Every vehicle is a facility.
Every stand is a facility.
Every agv is a vehicle.
Every truck is a vehicle.
Cobot-Agv is an agv.
Docking is a stand.
Distribution is a stand.
Communication is-hosted-on a stand.
```

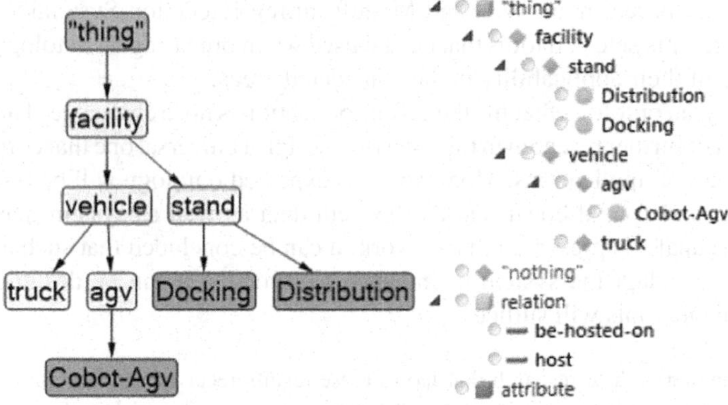

Fig. 2. An example of a simple CoBotAGV ontology that was created with Fluent Editor.

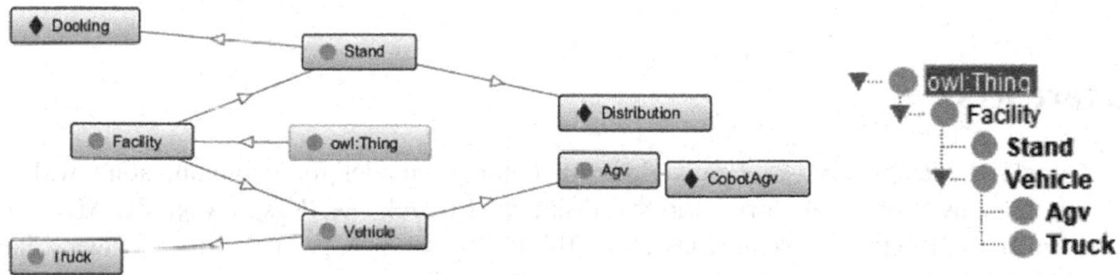

Fig. 3. An example of a simple CoBotAGV ontology that was exported to Protégé.

The same ontology as viewed by OWLGrEd as a web-tool is presented in Fig. 4.

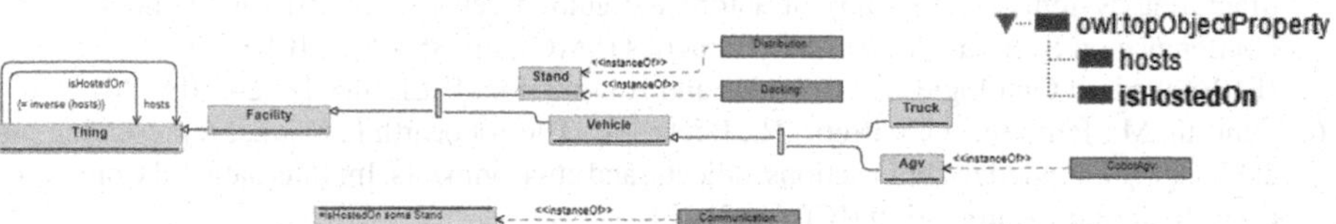

Fig. 4. An example of simple CoBotAGV ontology that was exported to Protégé.

5 Conclusions

In this paper, the authors have presented selected issues linked to the ontology-based descriptions that are used to design industrial communication systems along with a few examples for using the ontological approach in the design of manufacturing systems. The authors focused on communication with an AGV and the relationships among the different communication channels that are used by an AGV, which includes both machine-to-machine communication and the ontology-based approaches for communication design between an AGV and Manufacturing Execution Systems (MES). The paper also presents selected tools that can be used when preparing an ontology including a discussion of their applicability in the considered areas.

Generally, an ontology that fits the given application is not a challenge. Therefore, the main subject of further research in this area is to design a universal one that corresponds to the entire class of applications. Moreover, this expected ontology will be tested against the temporal and spatial consistency of system data as well as system dependencies. Based on the analysis presented in this work, it can be concluded that such an ontology is necessary to adapt the system to Industry 4.0 models, it can be designed, and the current available tools will suffice.

Acknowledgements. The research that led to these results received funding from the Norway Grants 2014–2021 operated by the National Centre for Research and Development under the project "Automated Guided Vehicles integrated with Collaborative Robots for Smart Industry Perspective" (Project Contract no.: NOR/POLNOR/CoBotAGV/0027/2019 -00).

References

1. Cupek, R., Ziebinski, A., Fojcik, M.: An ontology model for communicating with an autonomous mobile platform. In: Kozielski, S., Mrozek, D., Kasprowski, P., Małysiak-Mrozek, B., Kostrzewa, D. (eds.) BDAS 2017. CCIS, vol. 716, pp. 480–493. Springer, Cham (2017). https://doi.org/10.1007/978-3-319-58274-0_38
2. Arai, T., Aiyama, Y., Maeda, Y., Sugi, M., Ota, J.: Agile assembly system by "plug and produce." CIRP Ann. **49**(1), 1–4 (2000)
3. Pinto, H.S., Martins, J.P.: Ontologies: how can they be built? Knowl. Inf. Syst. **6**(4), 441–464 (2004)
4. Cupek, R., Drewniak, M., Ziebinski, A.: Information models for a new generation of manufacturing systems-a case study of automated guided vehicle. In: 2019 IEEE International Conference on Systems, Man and Cybernetics (SMC), pp. 858–864. IEEE (2019)
5. IEEE Standard Ontologies for Robotics and Automation. IEEE Std. 1872–2015 (2015)
6. Tenorth, M., Perzylo, A., Lafrenz, R., Beetz, M.: The roboearth language: representing and exchanging knowledge about actions, objects, and environments. In: International Conference on Robotics and Automation (ICRA) (2012)
7. Schlenoff, C., Messina, E.: A robot ontology for urban search and rescue. In: Proceedings of the CIKM 2005 Workshop on Research in Knowledge Representation for Autonomous Systems (2005)
8. Schlenoff, C., Washington, R., Barbera, T., Manteuffel, C., Dungrani, S.: A standard intelligent systems ontology. In: Proceedings of the SPIE Defense and Security Symposium, Unmanned Ground Vehicle Technology VII Conference. Orlando, FL (2005)

9. Cupek, R., Ziebinski, A., Huczala, L., Erdogan, H.: Agent-based manufacturing execution systems for short-series production scheduling. Comput. Ind. **82**, 245–258 (2016)
10. van Heist, G., Schreiber, A.T., Wielinga, B.J.: Using explicit ontologies in KBS development. Int. J. Hum. Comput. Stud. **46**(2/3), 183–292 (1997)
11. Scholten, B.: The road to integration: a guide to applying the ISA-95 standard in manufacturing. Isa (2007)
12. Harjunkoski, I., Bauer, R.: Sharing data for production scheduling using the ISA-95 standard. Front. Energy Res. **2**, 44 (2014)
13. Kannengiesser, U., Neubauer, M., Heininger, R.: Integrating business processes and manufacturing operations based on S-BPM and B2MML. In: Proceedings of the 8th International Conference on Subject-oriented Business Process Management, pp. 1–10 (2016)
14. Williams, T.J., et al.: Architectures for integrating manufacturing activities and enterprises. Comput. Ind. **24**(2–3), 111–139 (1994). https://doi.org/10.1016/0166-3615(94)90016-7
15. Prades, L., Romero, F., Estruch, A., García-Domínguez, A., Serrano, J.: Defining a methodology to design and implement business process models in BPMN according to the standard ANSI/ISA-95 in a manufacturing enterprise. Proc. Eng. **63**, 115–122 (2013)
16. Technologies, K., et al.: Smart factory of industry 4.0. Appl. Case Chall. IEEE Access **6**, 6505–6519 (2017). https://doi.org/10.1109/ACCESS.2017.2783682
17. Cupek, R., Drewniak, M., Ziebinski, A., Fojcik, M.: "Digital Twins" for highly customized electronic devices-case study on a rework operation. IEEE Access **7**, 164127–164143 (2019)
18. Seyedamir, A., Ferrer, B.R., Martinez Lastra, J.L.: An ISA-95 based Ontology for manufacturing systems knowledge description extended with semantic rules. In: 2018 IEEE 16th International Conference on Industrial Informatics (INDIN), pp. 374–380. IEEE, Porto (2018). https://doi.org/10.1109/INDIN.2018.8471929
19. An, Y., Qin, F., Chen, B., Simon, R., Wu, H.: OntoPLC: semantic model of PLC programs for code exchange and software reuse. IEEE Trans. Ind. Inf. **17**, 1702–1711 (2021). https://doi.org/10.1109/TII.2020.2997360
20. Compton, M., et al.: The SSN ontology of the W3C semantic sensor network incubator group. J. Web Semant. **17**, 25–32 (2012). https://doi.org/10.1016/j.websem.2012.05.003
21. Alaya, M.B., Medjiah, S., Monteil, T., Drira, K.: Toward semantic interoperability in oneM2M architecture. IEEE Commun. Mag. **53**, 35–41 (2015). https://doi.org/10.1109/MCOM.2015.7355582
22. Schachinger, D., Kastner, W.: Semantic interface for machine-to-machine communication in building automation. In: 2017 IEEE 13th International Workshop on Factory Communication Systems (WFCS), pp. 1–9. IEEE, Trondheim, Norway (2017). https://doi.org/10.1109/WFCS.2017.7991956
23. Kapoor, B.: A comparative study of ontology building tools in semantic web applications (2020). https://doi.org/10.5281/ZENODO.3697900
24. Clunis, J.: Comparative survey of ontology editors for the semantic web. In: iConference 2019 Proceedings iSchools (2019). https://doi.org/10.21900/iconf.2019.103300
25. Dolzhenkov, V.N.: Software tools for ontology development. IJATCSE. **9**, 935–941 (2020). https://doi.org/10.30534/ijatcse/2020/05922020
26. Alatrish, E.S.: Comparison some of ontology editors. (2014)
27. Musen, M.A.: Protégé team: the protégé project: a look back and a look forward. AI Matt. **1**, 4–12 (2015). https://doi.org/10.1145/2757001.2757003
28. Stellato, A., et al.: VocBench 3: a collaborative semantic web editor for ontologies, thesauri and lexicons. Semant. Web **11**, 855–881 (2020). https://doi.org/10.3233/SW-200370

Detecting of Minimal Changes in Physical Activity Using One Accelerometer Sensor

Pawel Mielnik[1], Marcin Fojcik[2](✉), Krzysztof Tokarz[3], Zuzanna Rodak[3], and Bjarte Pollen[2]

[1] Helse Førde, Førde, Norway
pawel.franciszek.mielnik@helse-forde.no
[2] Western Norway University of Applied Sciences, Førde, Norway
{marcin.fojcik,bjarte.pollen}@hvl.no
[3] Silesian University of Technology, Gliwice, Poland
{krzysztof.tokarz,zuzarod216}@student.polsl.pl

Abstract. This paper presents experiments using IoT systems for chronic arthritis patients monitoring using an inexpensive and convenient wristband, avoiding expensive medical equipment. The main goal is to see if it is possible to distinguish between different types of patient behavior while performing very similar exercises. The data from the wristband were collected through a communication system and statistically analyzed. The comparison of the obtained results allows for reliable, reproducible, and accurate decoding of individual cases. The publication describes the various steps in the data collection and analysis and gives the results in the form of receiver operating characteristic curves for all measured features and a comparison of performed and detected exercises.

Keywords: Accelerometer · Monitoring patients · Classification models

1 Background

Wireless tracking of human body parameters offers excellent opportunities due to the wide range of rehabilitation, medicine, and sports applications. The goal is to monitor the behavior and, more specifically, the movement of a person in a natural environment. The main problem in rehabilitation is to be able to assess the quality of treatment. Medical evaluation may be subjective and may not take progress into account. An information system consisting of sensors with accelerometers and software to evaluate the patient's exercise and behavior can make the rehabilitation process more effective. Based on the measured signals, it is possible to determine the quality and progress of rehabilitation therapy. The main problem is to accurately measure the patient's movements so that the patient's behavior can be unambiguously read.

This study is a part of the larger project using an accelerometer (ACC) to diagnose chronic arthritis exacerbation such as rheumatoid arthritis, seronegative spondylarthritis, and psoriatic arthritis. Those diseases are characterized by chronic, autoimmunologic inflammation in joints leading to mobility disturbances. It is a clear connection between

K. Wojtkiewicz et al. (Eds.): ICCCI 2021, CCIS 1463, pp. 498–508, 2021.
https://doi.org/10.1007/978-3-030-88113-9_40

such disturbances and disease activity [1]. Inflammation in joints – arthritis - reduce joint mobility and inflicts postures. Active arthritis is associated with body stiffness, most express in the morning. Those lead to characteristic clinical symptoms, which the experienced medical specialist can easily observe. We aim to find a method which can translate sign from the accelerometer in way that it makes possible to detect the disease status. As mentioned in previous work [2], we prefer an accelerometer in the form of a sport band or watch. The choice has many potential disadvantages as we obtain the signal from only one source. However, we plan to use it in everyday life, and patients can well tolerate watch-formed devices.

The main goal is to see if it is possible to unambiguously determine arthritis activity from the data recorded in the system. It had to be assessed whether it is possible to collect data with acceptable accuracy and repeatability.

2 Literature Review

It has become a platitude to say that the Internet of Things changes our life dynamically. IoT wearable devices are currently getting very popular. It sounds like a truism that one can use a device connected to the net in monitoring vital human functions. We can observe a constant increase in the number of such devices [3]. Among them, we can find smartwatches, smart wristbands, GPS trackers, used mainly to monitor sport and fitness activities, track the walking or running path of the user. Although the primary purpose of the commercially available sport wristband is to count steps and other movement activities, we can find examples of the usage of smart wearable devices to monitor health parameters in the literature. The most common research is fall detection and prediction using measurements taken with the accelerometer [4–6]. The minimization led us to use wearable devices, such as watches formed or part of clothing [2, 7]. Another popular research area is monitoring the rehabilitation process, with particular attention paid to the regularity and quality of the exercises performed by the patient [8]. Monitoring health parameters requires higher accuracy of measurements. In [9] and [10], the comparative analysis of the accuracy of a variety of motion trackers has been presented.

As mentioned above, this work is a part of the larger project developing a monitoring system for arthritis patients. For this reason, we focused in review mainly on Rheumatic and Musculoskeletal Diseases (RMD).

The wearables, specially equipped with an inertial measurement unit (IMU), can be ideal for assessing patients' physical activity (PA). Most publications use a one-point accelerometer device placed in a different place on a body. Nørgard et al. studied PA profiles of 10 to 16-year-old patients with juvenile idiopathic arthritis (JIA) using the GT1M ActiGraph device [11]. In this study, PA was estimated from overall accelerometer activity in one plane. The authors included 61 JIA patients and compared their PA with 2055 age-adjusted healthy controls. They showed that 57% of IJA participants had a below-average maximal physical capacity of healthy subjects. The accelerometer measured activity was negatively correlated with disease activity. Gilbert and colleagues used accelerometer data to validate the self-reported assessment of sedentary lifestyle in 172 rheumatoid arthritis (RA) patients [12]. Self-reported outcomes are widely used in RMD both in daily clinical practice and studies. The authors show that wearables can be a helpful validation instrument for self-report forms. In another work was an accelerometer wearable used to monitor PA activity in the systemic lupus erythematosus (SLE) patient group [13]. SLE is a disease characterized by multiorgan involvement and frequent constitutional symptoms such as fatigue [14]. Mahieu, with collaborators, used an accelerometer to assess PA[13] correlation of accelerometer registered PA with fatigue. The wearables can be used as an activity and exercise compliance monitor, as described in a study by Perraudin et al. [15]. Compliance with PA and exercise recommendation can be challenging. The authors show that participants performed only 56% of the prescribed “Five Times Sit to Stand test.” They concluded that wearables could be a useful supervising device to achieve better compliance with physician recommendations.

Another approach is to assemble a sensor-equipped device that can be worn as an item of clothing. An example is described in the work by Condell and colleagues [7]. The authors described gloves shaped system to measure finger movements in patients with arthritis. The system can be used by patients at home and is sensitive in stiffness detection. Nikitchuk et al. presented a device for automatized knee rehabilitation [16]. The device is not accelerometer-based but used electrorheological fluid.

Accelerometer-based wearables can be potentially used as a diagnostic device in RMD diseases. Andreu-Perez et al. presented a method of accelerometer signal automated tagging [17]. It was capable of differing between actigraph from RA patients and healthy controls.

Activity type recognition is usually conducted using features extracted from raw accelerometer signals. It can encompass mean value, standard deviation, energy and correlation [18]. Another feature is signal vector magnitude (SVMag), which was found effective classifier alone [19].

The literature review provides arguments that we can widely use accelerometer-based data in the diagnostic, follow-up, and treatment of RMD diseases. To our knowledge, it is, however, not known practical implementation of those methods in clinical practice. This gap is a problem that should be addressed in further work.

3 Aim

We aimed to evaluate if the accelerometer signal differs significantly enough when collected from the same subject, performing the same activities but with a small additional load. We chose this extra load in such a way that it could imitate minimal changes one can expect in patients with active inflammatory arthritis.

Because our study requires the raw data readings from the accelerometer, we decided to create our own wearable measuring device instead of adapting the commercially available wristbands. A detailed description of the developed system is provided in the method section.

4 Methods

The accelerometer signal was obtained from one subject. The subject is the study member, and no Ethical Commission approval and informed consent were necessary. The subject was asked to perform the following "exercises":

1. Repeated extensions of arms forward with and without 0.5-kilo load ("boxing")
2. Clapping in gloves, with fingers 2nd and 4th bounded together with a string and without any obstacles

The data was registered with Arduino Sense 33 developing board, equipped with 9-axis IMU LSM9DS1 from STMicroelectronics and nRF52840 microcontroller from Nordic Semiconductors. We decided to use only one sensor because, according to other studies, there is no significant quality improvement for using many similar sensors [20]. We used homebrewed software developed on the board site with Arduino IDE 1.8.13 and with Python v. 3.8 on the recorder. We recorded the signal in CSV files with a separate column for each ACC axis. The rows were marked with a timestamp. We recorded all activities in three consecutive days, in about 2.33 min for each activity, totally about 7 min. The data were analyzed with R version 4.0.3 [21]. We applied a high pass Butterworth filter to the signal to remove gravidity impact. The ACC signal was divided into smaller batches from 2.0 to 11.6 s. We analyzed the effect of the time chunk length. From the ACC signal, we extracted the following features: mean, standard deviation, median absolute deviation, variance, signal magnitude vector, signal magnitude area, skewness, kurtosis, furrier frequencies, autocorrelation coefficients, zero-crossing count, the correlation between axes, FFT energy.

5 Features Description

As mentioned above, we divided raw data into shorter chunks to make it more convenient for analysis. We calculated different statistical and mathematical parameters, called features, from data. The futures, not raw signal, was used in the making of predictive models.

5.1 Mean, Standard Deviation (SD), Median Absolute Deviation (MAD) and Variance

We calculated the arithmetic mean for each axis. Mean for n-elements data is defined as:

$$\overline{X} = \frac{1}{n}\sum\nolimits_{i=1}^{n} a_i \tag{1}$$

SD was calculated for each axis using the formula:

$$SD = \sqrt{\frac{1}{N-1}\sum\nolimits_{i=1}^{N}(x_i - \overline{x})} \tag{2}$$

Variance is defined as an SD square.
MAD was calculated using the following formula:

$$MAD = \frac{1}{n}\sum\nolimits_{i=1}^{n}|x_i - \overline{x}| \tag{3}$$

Neither mean, SD, nor variance alone plays a significant role in ACC signal analysis. They are, however, basic distribution parameters, and therefore, we used them in our work. Contrary MAD was found as an effective parameter in ACC signal analysis [17].

5.2 Kurtosis and Skewness

Kurtosis and skewness are proper parameters describing the distribution of the variable. The estimator of Pearson's measure of kurtosis was calculated using the formula:

$$Kurt[X] = E\left[\left(\frac{X-\mu}{\sigma}\right)^4\right] \tag{4}$$

The mean is expressed with μ, SD with σ. E is the expectation operator.
Skewness formula is:

$$Skew[X] = E\left[\left(\frac{X-\mu}{\sigma}\right)^3\right] \tag{5}$$

5.3 Signal Magnitude Area and Signal Vector Magnitude Variance

Signal magnitude area (SMA) was calculated as a sum of absolute values of ACC signal divide by the number of registered values. What is expressed by the formula:

$$f_{sma} = \frac{1}{T}\int_0^T |x(t) - a_x| + |y(t) - a_y| + |z(t) - a_z| \tag{6}$$

Signal vector magnitude (SVMag) is defined as a root of square axis values sum:

$$SVMag = \sqrt{x^2 + y^2 + z^2}$$

We used SVMag variance in our models.

5.4 Autoregressive Model Coefficients

Autoregressive model (AR) coefficients were calculated using the Burg method [22]. Autoregressive model is defined as:

$$X_t = c + \sum\nolimits_{i=1}^{p} \varphi_i X_{t-i} + \varepsilon_t \tag{7}$$

We use the three first AR coefficients in our analysis.

5.5 Fourier Analysis

We extracted component frequency from chunks using fast furrier transform. The transform was performed using the inbuilt R function fft(), and frequencies were extracted by the R spectrum() function—we use the three highest frequencies in further analysis.

5.6 Zero Crossing Count (ZCC) and Axis Correlation

ZCC was calculated as a simple number of switching between positive and negative values for each axis. Correlation between axes was computed using Pearson correlation for each axis par.

5.7 Data Analysis

We randomly split data in train and test set in a ratio of 80/20%. We have build logistic regression (LR) model for each feature in pair undisturbed/disturbed activity. We made a ROC curve for each LRM model. The three features with the best outcomes were used to build a predictive model to analyze the impact of signal chunk length. For this purpose, we made models with signal chunks from 2 to 11.6 s. All models were checked against the testing dataset.

To test the central scientific question, we built LR models for binary outcomes and support vector machine (SVM) models for binary and not-binary outcomes. I this part of the study, we used the caret library for R. The caret package is a "swiss knife" for predictive data analysis. The package function train() helps build quickly training models using 233 methods [23]. The function has many tuning options both for model building and underlaying methods. In our approach, we tuned data with scaling. We used K-fold cross-validation to evaluate the best training models. We next cross-validated the model with test data. For binominal output, we made ROC curves. For SVM models, we calculated accuracy with the test data.

6 Results

LR results for all "boxing" accelerometry features are shown in Fig. 1. We estimated AUC for all features separately. The three best-performing features were used in further analysis. Figure 2 shows AUC results for signal chunk length for boxing.

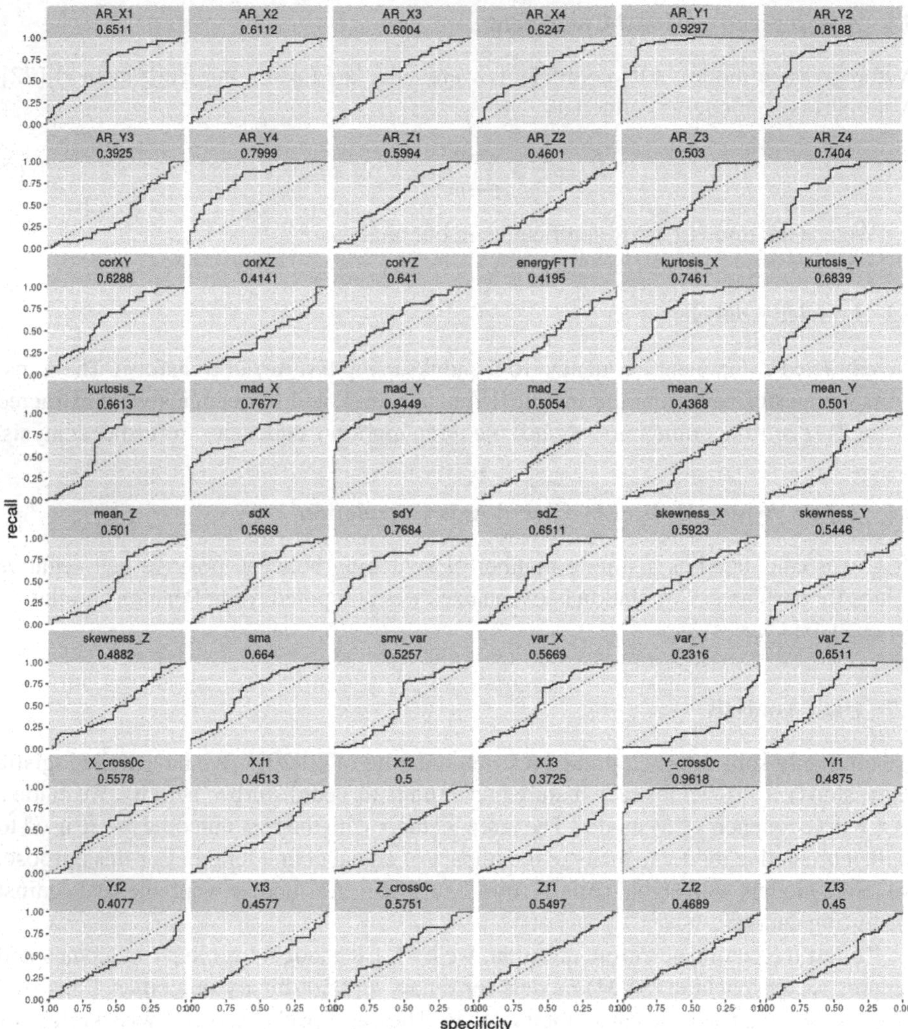

Fig. 1. ROC from cross-validation of logistic regression models separately for each feature. Models were built on "boxing" data. Numbers in the graph are AUC values. We do not present error measurement intentionally. The analysis was conducted to identify best-performing features for optimal chunk length estimation.

This analysis used LR models build on test data with the three most specific features: the first AR coefficient, MAD and ZZC for Y-axis. Models were cross-validated on test data divided into the same length. The AUC is high in the whole time compartment (> 0.95). It was, however, some instability between length 7.5–9 s. Based on this result, we chose a chunk of 6 s length for further investigation. Similar results were seen for pairs: clapping in gloves – normal and with string – normal. Those results are not depicted.

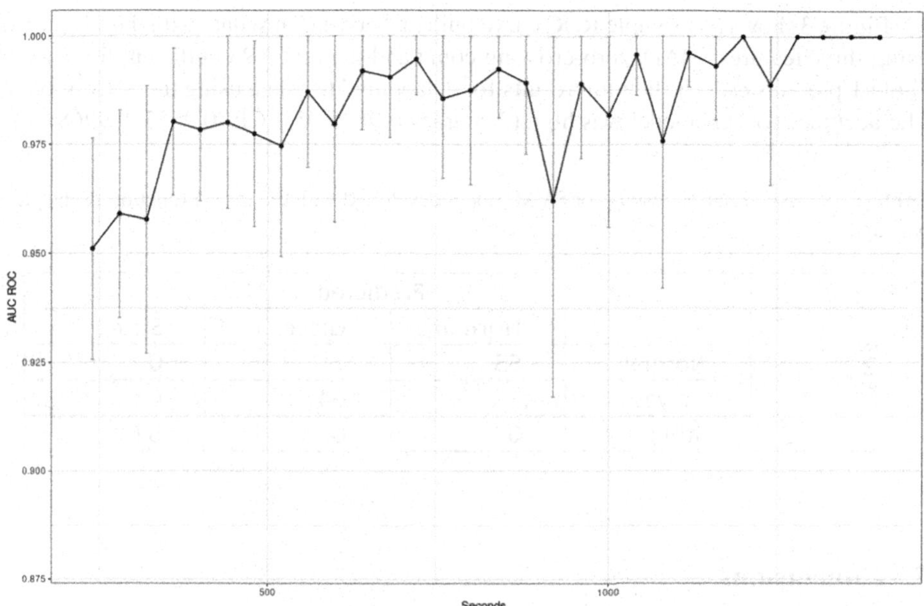

Fig. 2. AUC values for logistic models of "boxing" using three beast features for different sample time lengths. Whiskers show a 95% confidence interval. The four last results CIs are so narrow that they are not visualized.

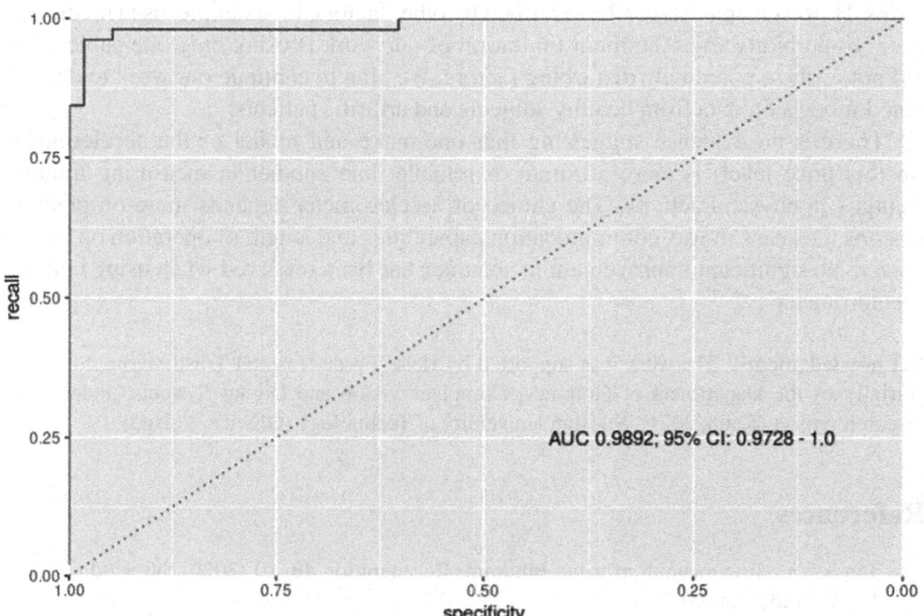

Fig. 3. ROC curve for the logistic model using MAD, zero-crossing count and the first AR coefficient for Y-axis. Cross-validation for test "boxing" data using LR model.

Figure 3 shows an example ROC curve built on "boxing" test data with the LR model using three features: MAD, zero-crossing count and the first AR coefficient for Y-axis. Table 1 presents cross-validation results for "clapping" test data using the SVM model. The accuracy for this model was high (Accuracy 0.9845 95% CI: (0.9555, 0.9968).

Table 1. Cross-validation results for SVM model developed with the train() function of the care package.

		Predicted		
Actual		Normal	Gloves	String
	Normal	63	2	0
	Gloves	1	64	0
	String	0	0	64

7 Conclusions

Our work shows that it is possible to distinguish between minimal changes in activity character. The results could be interpreted both as advantages and risks for misinterpretation. We can expect that a similar method can differentiate easily between disease states. However, analysis can be disturbed by other factors, for example, used medicines, age, co-morbidity, etc. The main limitation of our work is using only one subject. We did not analyze potentially disturbing factors. We plan to continue our work to develop tuned models on data from healthy subjects and arthritis patients.

There is no evidence suggesting that one make and model of the accelerometer (in this price level) is more accurate or reliable than another in measuring minimal changes in physical activity. The choice of accelerometer depends more on practical reasons, i.e., ease of use, communication capabilities and length of operation on battery power. No significant improvement in accuracy has been observed when using multiple accelerometers.

Acknowledgments. The work was supported by Helse Førde Hospital Trust internal funds and partially by the Department of Graphics, Computer Vision and Digital Systems, under statue research project (Rau6, 2021), Silesian University of Technology (Gliwice, Poland).

References

1. Tanaka, Y.: Rheumatoid arthritis. Inflamm. Regeneration **40**, 20 (2020). https://doi.org/10.1186/s41232-020-00133-8
2. Mielnik, P., Tokarz, K., Mrozek, D., Czekalski, P., Fojcik, M., Hjelle, A.M., Milik, M.: Monitoring of chronic arthritis patients with wearables - a report from the concept phase. In: Nguyen, N.T., Chbeir, R., Exposito, E., Aniorte, P., Trawinski, B. (eds.) ICCCI 2019. LNCS (LNAI), vol. 11684, pp. 229–238. Springer, Cham (2019). https://doi.org/10.1007/978-3-030-28374-2_20

3. Henriksen, A., Mikalsen, M.H., Woldaregay, A.Z., Muzny, M., Hartvigsen, G., Hopstock, L.A., Grimsgaard, S.: Using fitness trackers and smartwatches to measure physical activity in research: analysis of consumer wrist-worn wearables. J. Med. Internet Res. **20**(3), e110 (2018)
4. Montesinos, L., Castaldo, R., Pecchia, L.: Wearable inertial sensors for fall risk assessment and prediction in older adults: a systematic review and meta-analysis. IEEE Trans. Neural Syst. Rehabil. Eng. **26**(3), 573–582 (2018)
5. Hsieh, S.L., Yang, C.T., Li, H.J.: Combining wristband-type devices and smartphones to detect falls. In: 2017 IEEE International Conference on Systems, Man, and Cybernetics (SMC), pp. 2373–2377. IEEE (2017)
6. Park, C., Kim, J.: A location and emergency monitoring system for elder care using ZigBee. In: 2011 Seventh International Conference on Mobile Ad-hoc and Sensor Networks, pp. 367–369. IEEE (2011)
7. Condell, J., et al.: Finger movement measurements in arthritic patients using wearable sensor enabled gloves. Int. J. Human Factors Model. Simul. **2**(4), 276–292 (2011)
8. Jiang, Y.: Combination of wearable sensors and internet of things and its application in sports rehabilitation. Comput. Commun. **150**, 167–176 (2020)
9. Pardamean, B., Soeparno, H., Mahesworo, B., Budiarto, A., Baurley, J.: Comparing the accuracy of multiple commercial wearable devices: a method. Proc. Comput. Sci. **157**, 567–572 (2019)
10. Weghorn, H.: Unsubstantial health and sports monitoring reliability of commercial fitness tracker bracelets induced by their all-in-one sensing unit approach - experimental evaluation of measurement accuracy in dynamic and in steady physical effort scenarios. In: Cabri, J., Pezarat-Correia, P., Vilas-Boas, J. (eds.) icSPORTS 2016-2017. CCIS, vol. 975, pp. 55–74. Springer, Cham (2019). https://doi.org/10.1007/978-3-030-14526-2_4
11. Nørgaard, M., Twilt, M., Andersen, L.B., Herlin, T.: Accelerometry-based monitoring of daily physical activity in children with juvenile idiopathic arthritis. Scand. J. Rheumatol. **45**(3), 179–187 (2016)
12. Gilbert, A.L., et al.: Comparison of subjective and objective measures of sedentary behavior using the Yale physical activity survey and accelerometry in patients with rheumatoid arthritis. J. Phys. Act. Health **13**(4), 371–376 (2016)
13. Mahieu, M.A., et al.: Fatigue, patient reported outcomes, and objective measurement of physical activity in systemic lupus erythematosus. Lupus **25**(11), 1190–1199 (2016)
14. Więsik-Szewczyk, E., et al.: Anti-influenza vaccination in systemic lupus erythematosus patients: an analysis of specific humoral response and vaccination safety. Clin. Rheumatol. **29**(6), 605–613 (2010)
15. Perraudin, C.G., et al.: Observational study of a wearable sensor and smartphone application supporting unsupervised exercises to assess pain and stiffness. Digital Biomarkers **2**(3), 106–125 (2018)
16. Nikitczuk, J., Weinberg, B., Canavan, P.K., Mavroidis, C.: Active knee rehabilitation orthotic device with variable damping characteristics implemented via an electrorheological fluid. IEEE/ASME Trans. Mechatron. **15**(6), 952–960 (2009)
17. Andreuperez, J., et al.: Developing fine-grained actigraphies for rheumatoid arthritis patients from a single accelerometer using machine learning. Sensors **17**(9), 2113 (2017)
18. Ravi, N., Dandekar, N., Mysore, P., Littman, M.L.: Activity recognition from accelerometer data. Aaai **5**(2005), 1541–1546 (2005)
19. Mannini, A., Intille, S.S., Rosenberger, M., Sabatini, A.M., Haskell, W.: Activity recognition using a single accelerometer placed at the wrist or ankle. Med. Sci. Sports Exerc. **45**(11), 2193 (2013)

20. Rodak, Z., Tokarz, K., Mielnik, P., Fojcik, M.: Simultaneous measurements reading from more than one MiBand 3 wristbands. In: 2021 Fourth World Conference on Smart Trends in Systems, Security and Sustainability (WorldS4), London, UK
21. R Core Team, R: A Language and environment for statistical computing. Vienna, Austria: R Foundation for Statistical Computing (2017)
22. Burg, J.P.: Maximum entropy spectral analysis. Astron. Astrophys. Suppl. **15**, 383 (1974)
23. Kuhn, M., Wing, J., Weston, S., Williams, A., Keefer, C., Engelhardt, A., Benesty, M.: Package 'caret'. R J. 223 (2020)

Low Resource Languages Processing

Integrated Technology for Creating Quality Parallel Corpora

Zhandos Zhumanov(✉) and Ualsher Tukeyev

Al-Farabi Kazakh National University, Almaty, Kazakhstan

Abstract. What determines the quality of parallel corpora? Firstly, it is determined by the quality of the translation. However, in this paper, we consider not the substantial quality of the translation, but the "technical" quality of parallel texts. Parallel texts are collected from different sources and often such texts have the following disadvantages: language mixing, font mixing, text alignment problems, the need for manual correction of parallel texts. All these problems require, firstly, their recognition, and secondly, they need to be resolved, and with large volumes of parallel texts, performing these operations manually is a very time-consuming process. Therefore, the work proposes an integrated technology for creating parallel corpora, which allows to minimize the number of manual operations. The authors present the technology as an example of a new linguistic resource - an open Kazakh-English parallel corpus.

Keywords: Parallel corpora · Corpora collection · Corpora quality · Corpora comparison

1 Introduction

Corpora is a basis for a lot of linguistic research. Since Kazakh is still considered to be a low resourced language, the creation of new corpora is a very important task for the language. The main idea of this paper is to describe an integrated technology that allows collecting, cleaning, and aligning large amounts of texts from official multilingual web sites with as little manual work as possible. Our goal was to produce such technology and use it to create an open Kazakh-English parallel corpus. The developed integrated technology in the future can be used to create other parallel corpora.

In the course of our previous work we encountered a number of problems and questions: 1) which sources to use for collecting presumably parallel texts; 2) how to improve the quality of the texts; 3) how to minimize efforts for text alignment; 4) how to maximize the number of correctly aligned sentences in the result.

Our previous attempt at the creation of parallel Kazakh-English corpora using the Internet as a source of raw data revealed the following difficulties: 1) low quality of texts; 2) a mix of languages in texts; 3) alignment problems; 4) need for manual validation.

By the low quality of texts, we mean several things. First, texts in the Kazakh part of the Internet, for the most part, are initially written in Russian and then get translated into English and Kazakh. That can be seen when analyzing a number of publications on

K. Wojtkiewicz et al. (Eds.): ICCCI 2021, CCIS 1463, pp. 511–524, 2021.
https://doi.org/10.1007/978-3-030-88113-9_41

multilingual web-sites: Russian publications are the most numerous, then come English ones and a number of publications in Kazakh are a little behind a number of publications in English. That leads to the fact that content in English and Kazakh has slightly worse quality in terms of style and completeness. Second, when typing in different languages people for some reason use unusual keyboard layouts. In English texts, one might find characters from other alphabets that look similar to English letters or non-printing characters (zero-width spaces, soft hyphens, and so on). In Kazakh texts, some characters are replaced with characters from the Latin script that look similar to Kazakh ones. Symbols and misplaced characters like that are the sources of confusion during alignment.

By a mix of languages in texts we mean situations when text is written in such a way that it contains parts in different languages (addressing different parts of the audience, quotes, or incomplete translations). Such cases also make alignment more difficult.

Alignment problems were caused not only by described difficulties but also by software. We used hunalign [3] for alignment and it has its limitations. The quality of alignment depends very much on the presence of a bilingual dictionary file. When it is not present hunalign creates one using provided texts based on internal heuristics, but for languages that have different linguistic characteristics (which is the case with Kazakh and English), the created file is not even a good one. That causes misalignments and unnecessary grouping of sentences.

Described problems were the reason for manual validation of parallel data that was obtained in [2] which is a very time-consuming process.

In order to deal with described difficulties, we have adopted a number of techniques and created a set of scripts that helped to produce a notable amount of parallel Kazakh-English corpora:

- we have identified a good source of parallel texts in Kazakh and English (Sect. 3.1);
- we have created scripts that not only crawl all text from the given ULRs but also get their translations using corresponding links from the web-page and connecting each pair of translations to each other (Sect. 3.2);
- we have created scripts that clean texts which does not completely eliminate manual work, but seriously reduces it (Sect. 3.3);
- we have collected bilingual dictionary file based on word frequency list for crawled texts and grammar of Kazakh and English that improves the quality of hunalign's output (Sect. 3.4);
- we have created scripts for the post-processing of parallel sentences (Sect. 3.5).

The results are described in Sect. 4. After texts were collected and processed we have compared results with existing Kazakh-English parallel corpora (Sect. 5).

The code and the corpus are available at https://github.com/zloy-zhake/kaz-parallel-corpora.

2 Related Works

The situation with Kazakh linguistic resources gets better with every year. But it seems like it does not improve quickly enough. There are some projects aimed at the creation of linguistic resources. Among them are Almaty Corpus of Kazakh language (available at http://web-corpora.net/KazakhCorpus/), Corpus of the Kazakh Language (available at https://tbi.kz/kazcorp), Kazakh Language Corpus (available at http://kazcorpus.kz/klc web/en/) [1]. But parallel Kazakh-English corpora are not many. At the Fourth Conference on machine translation (WMT19) organizers provided two Kazakh-English parallel corpora for the Machine Translation of News Shared Task: one of about 100 000 sentences and the second one of about 500 000 sentences - both were prepared by Bagdat Myrzakhmetov of Nazarbayev University (available at https://www.statmt.org/wmt19/translation-task.html). And there is a Kazakh-English corpus of about 70 000 sentence pairs that was collected by the authors of this paper and described in [2]. After the publication, we have added sentences to our previous corpus and now it has approximately 100 000 sentence pairs.

3 Techniques and Scripts Used for Collecting Parallel Corpora

The proposed integrated technology of creation quality parallel corpora includes the next parts:

- identifying a good source of parallel texts;
- creation of scripts that not only crawl all text from the given ULRs but also get their translations using corresponding links from the web-page and connecting each pair of translations to each other;
- creation of scripts that clean texts which does not completely eliminate manual work, but seriously reduces it;
- collecting bilingual dictionary file based on word frequency list for crawled texts and grammar of Kazakh and English that improves the quality of hunalign's output;
- creation of scripts for the post-processing of parallel sentences.

These steps of proposed integrated technology are described below in detail.

3.1 Source of Quality Parallel Texts

The problem with quality parallel texts was described above in Sect. 1. In the Republic of Kazakhstan, there are some opportunities to partly solve the problem. For several years now the government has been actively promoting a policy of trilingualism [4, 5]. All government bodies are expected to publish their materials in three languages: Kazakh, Russian, and English. Judging by the quality of translations it seems like they also have been recruiting people who either studied or lived abroad. Every government website has a news section that updates regularly. And as the news from government websites are published for wide distribution crawling them for computer linguistic purposes should not cause any copyright problems.

In our work, we have used websites listed in Table 1.

Table 1. Websites used for collecting text data.

Web-site	Date crawled	Materials collected
Official site of the president of the Republic of Kazakhstan - http://www.akorda.kz/	July 25, 2019	5 428 pairs of news items
Official Information Source of the Prime Minister of the Republic of Kazakhstan - https://primeminister.kz/	December 12, 2019	257 pairs of news items
Ministry of Foreign Affairs of the Republic of Kazakhstan - http://www.mfa.gov.kz/	December 15, 2019	1 350 pairs of news items
Ministry of National Economy of the Republic of Kazakhstan - http://economy.gov.kz/	December 23, 2019	413 pairs of news items
Strategy 2050 - https://strategy2050.kz/	December 30, 2019	35 909 pairs of news items

3.2 Crawling of Parallel Texts

When crawling web pages with news we need to keep in mind that we should not download all publications in one language separately from publications in the second language. If we do that, we will end up with two large sets of texts of different sizes without obvious relations between them. We would not be able to find which sentence groups on one side correspond to which sentence groups on the other side. That might cause problems with alignment later. To avoid such problems, we downloaded texts in pairs - news item in one language and its translation into the other language. On most sites pages contain a direct link to the same content in the other language.

Crawling was performed in two steps (Fig. 1): 1) collecting URLs for news items in English; 2) gathering data from the collected URLs and from Kazakh pages that correspond to the collected English pages.

For crawling parallel web-pages we have tried using several python libraries: Scrapy (https://scrapy.org/), Beautiful Soup (https://www.crummy.com/software/BeautifulSoup/), Requests-HTML (https://requests-html.kennethreitz.org/). All of them are up to the task. By default, Scrapy works asynchronously, and that makes it difficult to fetch pairs of pages as the order of requests is not obvious at once. Beautiful Soup and Requests-HTML allow more low-level control over request order. We used Requests-HTML for crawling parallel texts. Each publication was saved into its own XML-file with the structure shown in Fig. 2. Pairs of publications that are translations of each other were named in a similar manner using integer identifiers.

From each news item, we collected news title, date published, subject section (if it was present), and news text. Titles are usually translated exactly, and that gives a certain number of already aligned sentences. The texts, unfortunately, have to be processed further.

The code that performs crawling is published on GitHub (https://github.com/zloy-zhake/kaz-parallel-corpora/tree/master/utils). It is advised not to use it regularly and during work-time hours of the agencies, whose web-sites are being crawled (or more generally during daytime in UTC + 6 time zone), as it might slow down their services.

3.3 Cleaning of Crawled Texts

We got a number of *.xml files from the previous step. Before cleaning text we had to extract it from *.xml format int *.txt format. It is done in the following steps:

1. getting file names;
2. sorting file names (as we used integer identifiers when saving the crawling result, sorting puts pairs of files on different languages together);
3. extracting title and text from each file pair:

   a. if titles in both languages exist they are written into separate files;
   b. if texts in both languages exist they are written into separate files.

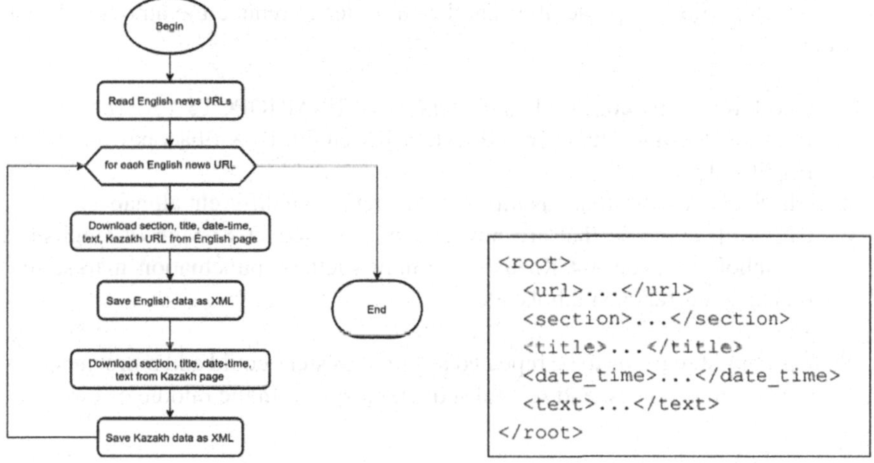

Fig. 1. Parallel data crawling

Fig. 2. Structure of XML-file with downloaded content

As a result, we got an aligned pair of files with titles and many pairs of files with texts.

To do the cleaning we combined all files with texts in each language into one file, but marking borders of each file, so they can be split back later.

Cleaning focuses on the following:

1. Spaces:

   a. Zero-width characters (here are the UNICODE codes for zero-width characters that are removed: \u2060, \u2061, \u2062, \u2063, \u180E, \u200B, \u200C, \u200D, \uFEFF, \u00AD).
   b. Unnecessary leading, trailing spaces, and several sequential spaces in the middle of lines.

2. Empty lines.
3. Quotation_marks: various quotation marks («»„“”‘’„”“❝❞‟ 〝〞 〟 ") are converted into (“), code \u0022.
4. Hyphens: various hyphens (- − – ‐ ‑ ‒ — ―) are converted into (-), code \u002D.
5. Characters that are not from the text’s primary alphabet. As there are many cases when using English characters in Kazakh texts and vice-versa is correct (organization names, person names, special terminology, etc.) this task cannot be automated and has to be performed manually using search with regular expressions. There are several strategies used one after another in order to reduce the amount of manual work:

   a. Check for easily confused characters: (АВҒЕКМНОРСТУҮХҺІЬаеорсуүхһі) from the Kazakh alphabet and (ABFEKMHOPCTYXhIbaeopcyxhi) from the English alphabet.
   b. Check every word that has mixed characters from different alphabets.
   c. Check all symbols that are not usually expected in Kazakh of English texts - symbols that are not Kazakh or English letters, punctuation marks, spaces, numbers, currency symbols, etc.

6. Spaces - this step needs to be repeated as previous steps could add more unnecessary leading, trailing spaces, and several sequential spaces in the middle of lines.

3.4 Improving Alignment Quality

After the cleaning, we split the texts into sentences. There are tools that can automate this splitting, but our tests showed that they work only in general cases and additional training is needed in order for them to work better with particular texts. As we did not have labeled training data for sentences splitting, we decided to do it semi-manually. We wrote a script that splits the text into sentences at every period that is preceded with five letters in Kazakh texts and four letters in English texts. Cases, where a period is preceded with fewer letters, had to be checked manually. Then we checked for cases where a period is preceded with or followed by a non-alphabet character with following patterns: (“.), (.“), (‘.), (.‘), (%.), ().), (<number >.), (<non-space characters >. < space > < non-space characters >), (. < space > < uppercase character >). Sentences that end with an exclamation mark and a question mark are usually very few and found and split in no time.

Unfortunately, that is the most laborious part of the work, but it is very important for getting aligned sentences. So after splitting was done we did some checks in order to make sure that there were no errors added during sentence splitting. We checked for URLs and e-mail addresses; sentences that start with lowercase letters; sentences that do not end with (.), (!) or (?); and lines that are relatively short (shorter than 30–40 characters).

After that, we received 2 files that contained a single sentence on each line.

In order to improve alignment quality, we took the following steps. Using sacremoses library (https://github.com/alvations/sacremoses) we normalized punctuation and tokenized texts. After that we transformed the text of both files into lowercase and created word frequency lists for English and Kazakh texts. Even though a word frequency list for Kazakh is usually useless without taking morphological segmentation into account, it helps to identify words and word forms most used in texts. For each website, we considered approximately 100 most used words from each side. If there were words corresponding to each other we took from frequency lists the word from the English side and all word forms of the word from the Kazakh side. Kazakh has a very rich morphology so it is a very common situation when one English word form can correspond to several dozen Kazakh word forms as translations in different circumstances. But hunalign does not take different word forms into account by default. So adding them into the dictionary file noticeably improves alignment results. Altogether we have collected 735 word form pairs. The resulting dictionary file can be found in the repository (https://github.com/zloy-zhake/kaz-parallel-corpora/blob/master/utils/en_kz.dic).

The files are then divided into original parts containing separate news items, using border marks mentioned in Sect. 3.3. After that, each file pair is aligned with hunalign, and the results of each alignment are combined into one file in *.tsv format.

3.5 Post-processing of Parallel Sentences

Post processing of parallel sentences consists of the following steps: 1) check for pairs with negative and zero hunalign scores and remove them; 2) remove duplicate sentences pairs; 3) shuffle remaining sentences pairs.

4 Results

We have applied all the techniques described in Sects. 3.2–3.5 to the websites listed in Sect. 3.1. The resulting parallel corpus contains:

- 300 702 sentence pairs;
- 5 417 135 tokens on Kazakh side;
- 6 916 062 tokens on English side.

All corpus files in *.tsv are available at https://github.com/zloy-zhake/kaz-parallel-corpora/tree/master/corpus.

Table 2. Number of unique sentence pairs

Corpus	Number of unique sentence pairs
Crawl	495 454
Kazakhtv	97 458
Old_corpus	99 109
Corpus	300 702

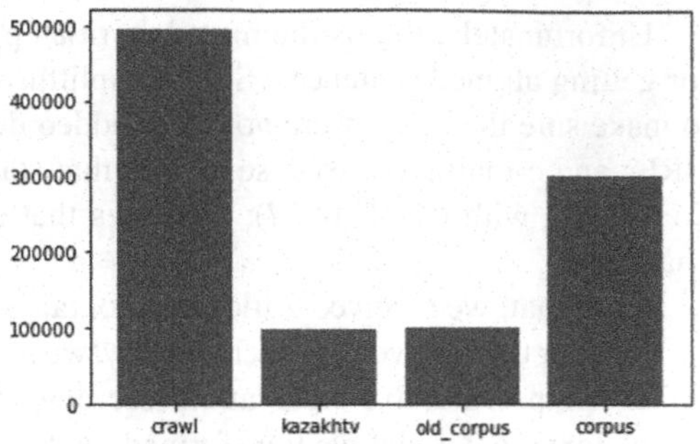

Fig. 3. Number of unique sentence pairs

5 Comparison with Existing Corpora

In order to understand how collected parallel corpus is different from existing parallel corpora we compared them according to the following criteria: number of unique sentence pairs, number of tokens in each language, most meaningful tokens according to TF-IDF statistic, hunalign scores (where available), sentence length, characters from different alphabets in the same word.

We have used 4 corpora for comparison:

- 2 corpora from WMT19 (prepared by Bagdat Myrzakhmetov from Nazarbayev University):
  - English-Kazakh crawled corpus of about 500k sentences (referred to as "crawl" based on its filename);
  - English-Kazakh crawled corpus of about 100k sentences (referred to as "kazakhtv" based on its filename);
- Kazakh-English corpus collected by the authors previously (referred to as "old_corpus");
- Kazakh-English corpus described in this paper (referred to as "corpus");

Corpora from WMT were normalized and tokenized using sacremoses library. The results of the comparison are presented in Sects. 5.1–5.6. The code that was used for comparison is available at https://github.com/zloy-zhake/kaz-parallel-corpora/tree/master/compare.

5.1 Number of Unique Sentence Pairs

A comparison of corpora sizes is shown in Table 2 and in Fig. 3. The new "corpus" is bigger than "kazakhtv" and "old corpus" combined, but 39% smaller than the "crawl" corpus.

Table 3. Number of tokens

Corpus	Number of Kazakh tokens	Number of English tokens
Crawl	9 250 219	12 038 246
Kazakhtv	1 224 434	1 516 335
Old_corpus	2 579 789	3 323 881
Corpus	5 417 135	6 916 062

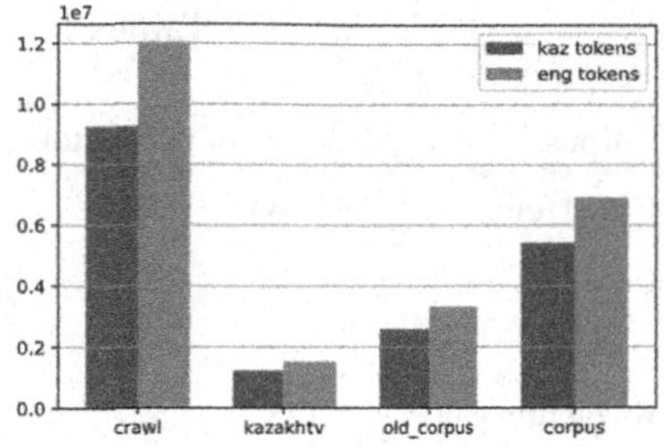

Fig. 4. Number of tokens

5.2 Number of Tokens in Each Language

The number of tokens on both sides is shown in Table 3 and in Fig. 4. All corpora have more English tokens than Kazakh tokens.

5.3 Most Meaningful Tokens According to tf-idf Statistic

In order to compare the most meaningful tokens, we trained tf-idf transformer on each side of each corpus with a number of features equal to 20. That gave us 20 presumably most meaningful tokens for each part. Then we compared the tokens from different corpora. Results for Kazakh tokens are shown in Table 4, results for English tokens are shown in Table 5. Tokens from "crawl", "kazakhtv" and "old_corpus" that are present in "corpus" are shown in bold font. In terms of selected tokens subject areas of the new "corpus" are more similar to "crawl" corpus, than to "kazakhtv" and "old_corpus". Most likely that is because "corpus" and "crawl" corpora have sources with similar text styles.

Table 4. Most meaningful Kazakh tokens

Corpus	Number of unique tokens	20 most meaningful tokens
Crawl_kaz	377 637	**'атап'**, **'ақ'**, **'басшысы'**, **'бойынша'**, **'бұл'**, **'деді'**, 'деп', **'жаңа'**, **'жылы'**, **'жұмыс'**, **'және'**, **'мемлекет'**, **'мемлекеттік'**, **'мен'**, **'туралы'**, **'қазақстан'**, **'қр'**, **'үшін'**, 'ұлттық', **'өтті'**
Kazakhtv_kaz	125 649	'end', 'tags', 'бар', 'болады', 'бір', **'бұл'**, 'да', 'де', 'деп', **'жаңа'**, **'және'**, **'мен'**, 'осы', 'отыр', 'сурет', **'халықаралық'**, 'қазақ', **'қазақстан'**, **'үшін'**, 'ұлттық'
Old_corpus_kaz	101 994	'ал', **'басшысы'**, 'бір', **'бұл'**, 'да', 'де', **'деді'**, 'деп', 'ехоба', **'және'**, **'мемлекет'**, **'мен'**, 'ол', 'олар', 'оның', 'осы', 'сол', **'туралы'**, **'қазақстан'**, **'үшін'**
Corpus_kaz	192 171	'атап', 'ақ', 'басшысы', 'бойынша', 'бұл', 'деді', 'жаңа', 'жылы', 'жұмыс', 'және', 'мемлекет', 'мемлекеттік', 'мен', 'сондай', 'туралы', 'халықаралық', 'қазақстан', 'қр', 'үшін', 'өтті'

Table 5. Most meaningful English tokens

Corpus	Number of unique tokens	20 most meaningful tokens
Crawl_eng	291 444	**'according'**, **'astana'**, **'development'**, **'head'**, 'held', **'international'**, **'kazakhstan'**, **'meeting'**, 'minister', **'national'**, **'nazarbayev'**, **'new'**, **'people'**, **'president'**, **'region'**, 'republic', **'said'**, **'state'**, 'work', **'year'**
Kazakhtv_eng	75 128	**'according'**, 'apos', **'astana'**, 'countries', **'country'**, **'development'**, 'end', **'international'**, 'kazakh', **'kazakhstan'**, **'national'**, **'new'**, **'people'**, 'photo', **'president'**, 'quot', **'region'**, 'tags', 'world', **'year'**
Old_corpus_eng	46 733	'apos', 'day', 'did', 'god', 'head', 'israel', 'jehovah', **'kazakhstan'**, 'king', 'like', 'man', **'nazarbayev'**, 'nursultan', **'people'**, **'president'**, 'quot', 'republic', **'said'**, 'son', **'state'**
Corpus_eng	100 517	'according', 'astana', 'cooperation', 'country', 'development', 'economic', 'head', 'international', 'kazakhstan', 'meeting', 'national', 'nazarbayev', 'new', 'noted', 'people', 'president', 'region', 'said', 'state', 'year'

5.4 Hunalign Scores

When aligning sentences hunalign assigns each pair a similarity score. The more similar sentences in a pair, the higher the score. So higher scores mean that the quality of alignment is better. Hunalign scores are not available for "old_corpus", so we compared only 3 corpora. The analysis is shown in Table 6. Minimum values are the same for all 3 corpora, but the "crawl" corpus has the smallest high hunalign score. The new "corpus" has higher mean and median values. The histograms show that it also has more sentence pairs with higher hunalign scores than the other two. That is the result of our work on improving alignment quality described in Sect. 3.4.

Table 6. Hunalign score analysis

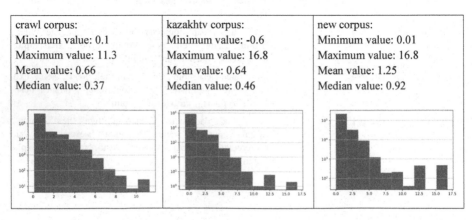

crawl corpus:	kazakhtv corpus:	new corpus:
Minimum value: 0.1 Maximum value: 11.3 Mean value: 0.66 Median value: 0.37 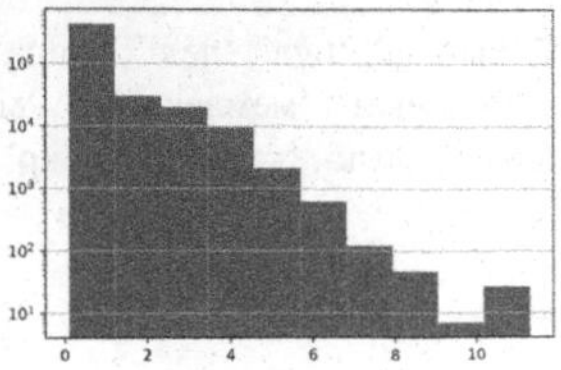	Minimum value: -0.6 Maximum value: 16.8 Mean value: 0.64 Median value: 0.46 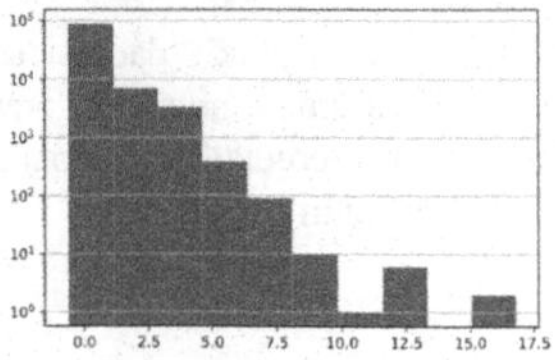	Minimum value: 0.01 Maximum value: 16.8 Mean value: 1.25 Median value: 0.92 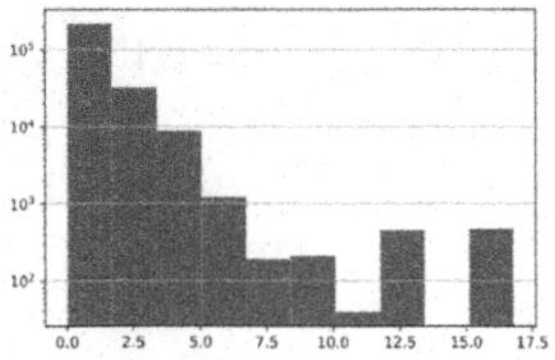

Table 7. Sentence lengths for Kazakh side

crawl corpus (Kazakh side):	kazakhtv corpus (Kazakh side):
Minimum value: 1 Maximum value: 3049 Mean value: 131.89 Median value: 115.0	Minimum value: 1 Maximum value: 611 Mean value: 86.15 Median value: 78.0
old corpus (Kazakh side): Minimum value: 1 Maximum value: 1599 Mean value: 114.54 Median value: 104.0	new corpus (Kazakh side): Minimum value: 0 Maximum value: 1773 Mean value: 130.15 Median value: 113.0

5.5 Sentence Lengths

Comparison of corpora by sentence length in characters are shown in Tables 7 and 8. "Crawl", "old_corpus" and "corpus" have similar sentence lengths. But the "kazakhtv" corpus consists of shorter sentences, the average sentence length is 25–35% smaller. The most probable reason for that is sources with different text styles.

5.6 Characters from Different Alphabets

The last comparison criterion is the characters. As we described in Sect. 3.3 Kazakh side of the new "corpus" was additionally cleaned. To analyze the results of the cleaning we looked at characters next to letters from the Kazakh alphabet. If those characters are not from the Kazakh alphabet themselves then it is likely that we have a problem with that sentence.

For example, let's take the Kazakh word "іні" (little brother). Written with Kazakh letters it will have codes (U+0456 U+043D U+0456). But it also can be written with the English letter "i" (code U+0069), and the codes for the word could be: iні (U+0069 U+043D U+0456), іні (U+0456 U+043D U+0069), iнi (U+0069 U+043D U+0069). All 4 variants look the same and are intended to have the same meaning, but they will

Table 8. Sentence lengths for English side

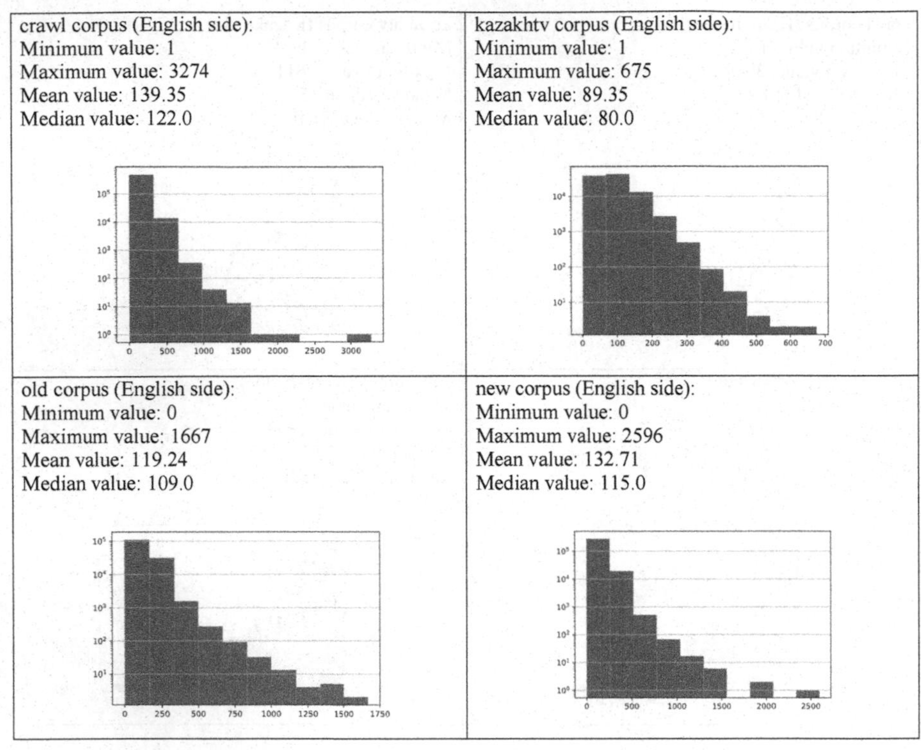

crawl corpus (English side): Minimum value: 1 Maximum value: 3274 Mean value: 139.35 Median value: 122.0	kazakhtv corpus (English side): Minimum value: 1 Maximum value: 675 Mean value: 89.35 Median value: 80.0
old corpus (English side): Minimum value: 0 Maximum value: 1667 Mean value: 119.24 Median value: 109.0	new corpus (English side): Minimum value: 0 Maximum value: 2596 Mean value: 132.71 Median value: 115.0

be different for any computer processing algorithm. Such misspellings might cause problems in the future usage of the corpus.

We analyzed and counted every character next to every Kazakh letter that is not a Kazakh letter, a digit, or any character from the following set: (.,-:\"/?!();‘$% + *№—«»[–&]’”…). That left us with characters shown in Table 9. As can be seen, the new "corpus" is much cleaner than the other 3. The particular problem with the letter "i" described in the previous paragraph is very significant in "crawl" and in "old_corpus". "Kazakhtv" corpus is relatively cleaner, compared to "crawl" and "old_corpus".

As it was shown in Sects. 5.1–5.6 the new parallel Kazakh-English corpus is the second by size out of four analyzed corpora. The ratio of English to Kazakh tokens of all corpora is comparable with each other. Comparison by the most meaningful 20 tokens shows that the new corpus is quite close semantically to the "crawl" corpus and differs from the other two. Comparison by hunalign scores showed that the new corpus has more sentences with higher scores. The sentence length of all corpora is comparable. And finally, the new corpus is the cleanest one in terms of characters from different alphabets used in the same token. Out of 6 criteria, the new corpus is comparable to others by 4 and exceeds them by 2 criteria.

Table 9. Characters from different alphabets

Corpus	Chars count	Chars
crawl_kaz	30 unique chars Total count: 31 597	(‘i’, 28803), (‘ə’, 786), (‘c’, 211), (‘x’, 208), (‘v’, 186), (‘a’, 173), (‘s’, 162), (‘r’, 136), (‘z’, 115), (‘h’, 105), (‘e’, 90), (‘g’, 75), (‘t’, 69), (‘l’, 65), (‘u’, 61), (‘n’, 60), (‘o’, 56), (‘m’, 47), (‘d’, 42), (‘p’, 37), (‘y’, 32), (‘k’, 25), (‘f’, 17), (‘ң’, 14), (‘w’, 9), (‘b’, 4), (‘\u200b’, 4), (‘^{3}’, 2), (‘ï’, 2), (‘\xad’, 1)
kazakhtv_kaz	28 unique chars Total count: 3 891	(‘z’, 1081), (‘m’, 576), (‘u’, 564), (‘i’, 344), (‘s’, 313), (‘ə’, 169), (‘a’, 139), (‘x’, 134), (‘g’, 102), (‘c’, 100), (‘t’, 77), (‘o’, 50), (‘k’, 47), (‘e’, 44), (‘v’, 30), (‘r’, 21), (‘y’, 20), (‘n’, 19), (‘p’, 14), (‘l’, 11), (‘d’, 10), (‘h’, 9), (‘f’, 8), (‘b’, 5), (‘j’, 1), (‘w’, 1), (‘q’, 1), (‘“’, 1)
old_corpus_kaz	20 unique chars Total count: 15 027	(‘i’, 13366), (‘\xad’, 1244), (‘c’, 95), (‘ə’, 74), (‘h’, 56), (‘m’, 32), (‘z’, 28), (‘v’, 20), (‘e’, 20), (‘p’, 14), (‘d’, 14), (‘k’, 10), (‘a’, 10), (‘t’, 9), (‘s’, 8), (‘r’, 8), (‘n’, 6), (‘y’, 6), (‘u’, 5), (‘l’, 2)
corpus_kaz	22 unique chars Total count: 108	(‘z’, 42), (‘i’, 10), (‘t’, 7), (‘#’, 7), (‘m’, 5), (‘u’, 4), (‘y’, 4), (‘r’, 4), (‘v’, 4), (‘c’, 3), (‘n’, 3), (‘\\’, 2), (‘g’, 2), (‘e’, 2), (‘ï’, 2), (‘l’, 1), (‘o’, 1), (‘^{2}’, 1), (‘a’, 1), (‘s’, 1), (‘d’, 1), (‘p’, 1)

6 Conclusions and Further Work

In the paper, we have described a way to collect a notable amount of parallel Kazakh-English corpus with good quality in both texts and alignment (available at https://github.com/zloy-zhake/kaz-parallel-corpora/tree/master/corpus). Although we tried to automate as many tasks as possible the quality of texts and alignment still requires some considerable amount of manual operations. But compared to our previous attempt at creating parallel Kazakh-English corpus the techniques used in this work prove to be more effective.

Nevertheless, the new corpus has its drawbacks. Among them:

- there are still sentences with low hunalign scores and they need to be dealt with before using the corpus;
- source web sites change their templates once a couple of years and usually do not keep an archive of materials so if one wants to continue the work with collecting corpora the provided code has to be updated;
- the English side of the corpus was not written by native speakers so it might contain errors;
- the cleaning process still has some parts to be improved and can be automated even more.

The texts we used for building the corpus were obtained from government sources that publish information in three languages: Kazakh, English and Russian. It gives an opportunity to build a parallel trilingual Kazakh-English-Russian corpus in the future. In the histograms of Table 6, one can see that the height of the "bars" is descending to the right naturally, but the rise that occurs at the far right is surprising. That phenomenon could be studied in the future from statistical point of view. We plan to use the collected corpus for NLP research connected with the Kazakh language. We believe that it can be useful for machine translation, segmentation, text generation, and other tasks.

References

1. Makhambetov, O., Makazhanov, A., Yessenbayev, Z., Matkarimov, B., Sabyrgaliyev, I., Sharafudinov, A.: Assembling the Kazakh language corpus. In: Proceedings of the 2013 Conference on Empirical Methods in Natural Language Processing, pp. 1022–1031 (2013)
2. Zhumanov, Z., Madiyeva, A., Rakhimova, D.: New Kazakh parallel text corpora with on-line access. In: Nguyen, N.T., Papadopoulos, G.A., Jędrzejowicz, P., Trawiński, B., Vossen, G. (eds.) Computational Collective Intelligence, pp. 501–508. Springer International Publishing, Cham (2017). https://doi.org/10.1007/978-3-319-67077-5_48
3. Varga, D., Halácsy, P., Kornai, A., Nagy, V., Németh, L., Trón, V.: Parallel corpora for medium density languages. In: Amsterdam Studies in the Theory and History of Linguistic Science Series 4, pp. 247–292 (2007)
4. The strategy for development of the Republic of Kazakhstan. https://www.akorda.kz/en/official_documents/strategies_and_programs
5. State of the Nation Address by the President of the Republic of Kazakhstan Nursultan Nazarbayev. http://www.akorda.kz/en/addresses/addresses_of_president/state-of-the-nation-address-by-the-president-of-the-republic-of-kazakhstan-nursultan-nazarbayev-january-10-2018. Accessed 10 Jan 2018

Development and Study of a Post-editing Model for Russian-Kazakh and English-Kazakh Translation Based on Machine Learning

Diana Rakhimova(✉), Kamila Sagat, Kamila Zhakypbaeva, and Aliya Zhunussova

Al-Farabi Kazakh National University, Almaty, Kazakhstan

Abstract. This work presents research in the field of machine translation for the Kazakh language. A comparative analysis of translation works of open online machine translation systems (Google translate, Yandex translate, sozdik.kz, web-tran.ru.) for English-Kazakh and Russian-Kazakh translation is presented. To improve the quality of translation for the Kazakh language a model of post-editing of the Kazakh language in machine translation has been developed, based on the neural network training approach. For machine learning parallel corpuses for the English-Kazakh and Russian-Kazakh language pairs were collected and processed. Experimental testing has been carried out. The results obtained were evaluated using the BLEU metric.

Keywords: Machine translation · Kazakh language · Post-editing machine translation (PEMT) · Neural Machine Translation (NMT) · Machine learning

1 Introduction

In recent years, the amount of data required for translation has been growing rapidly, and this factor has contributed to the growing demand for machine translation. As demand grows, so does the quality and speed of machine translation. For example, in 2010 the Executive Directorate of the European Translation Commission decided to develop a machine translation system that would be available not only to professional translators, but also to independent publishers who provide unprocessed translations. In addition, the integration of machine translation with various translation systems has allowed it to become more widespread in a professional context. Of course, it seems impossible to completely replace translators with machine translation, but working with a machine has become part of the work of professional translators today [2].

The post-edited text must be clear and concise, as well as grammatically and stylistically appropriate. With this in mind, the International Standard (ISO/CD 18587: 2017) [24] developed requirements for the process of post-editing, results and competencies of translators engaged in post-editing [3].

K. Wojtkiewicz et al. (Eds.): ICCCI 2021, CCIS 1463, pp. 525–534, 2021.
https://doi.org/10.1007/978-3-030-88113-9_42

Nowadays, it is even more important to translate data from one language to another. About three-quarters (3/4) of Internet users use free translation tools due to the availability and integration of machine translation solutions. More than 90% of English speakers use machine translation software to translate accessible English websites [4].

Despite the significant development of MT systems, the output material often requires human revision. This process is called post-processing machine translation (PEMT, post-editing) and means making corrections to the text of the machine translation in accordance with the pre-established requirements. Unlike post-editorial editing, in the first case the source text is a machine translation, and in the second case it is a human translation. The text that has passed the post-processing stage can be further submitted to the editor to correct stylistic, grammatical and lexical errors and the functional orientation of the text to the target reader. The editing specialist should be more qualified than the translator or editor. Statistics also show that interaction with MT becomes one of the most important components of the work of a professional translator [5].

2 Motivation and Related Work

Machine translation is constantly improving, faster, cheaper and more accurate. However, we still cannot compare the results of machine translation with the results of human translation. Post-editing machine translation helps to combine the best of both parties (machine translation and translator): the speed, ability and skill of trained linguists can help to process large volumes of text quickly and efficiently [7].

As a result of various experiments, scientists have come to the conclusion that post-editing takes less time than translating the whole text. However, time savings vary depending on the type of text [8]. The results of comparisons and identification of previous experiments (O 'Brien 2007; Guerberof 2009; Plitt and Masselot 2010 [22]) and recent experiments (Daems et al. 2017; Carl et al. 2011; Screen 2017 [23]) refute the notion that post-editing takes less time. However, it is important to be fair in making such statements. This is due to the fact that some experiments involved very strong translators, and some involved people with little experience in the field of translation [8]. The existence of such two-sided views is due to the linguistic differences (styles) of the texts. Often, scientific, formal, and literary texts take significantly more time than translating/post-editing a simple oral text. This is because it may take time to search for specific terms and words in specific online resources [8].

Numerous studies and experiments show that the use of the NMT method is now more successful than other methods of machine translation. Neural networks allow more accurate translation of text by context [6]. In addition, the use of special textbooks containing various scientific terms and professional words in the field related to the field in which the text to be translated in the implementation of machine learning helps to improve the quality of machine translation [6].

3 Analysis of the Translation of the Kazakh Language in Online Machine Translation Systems

The Kazakh language is an agglutinative language with a complex nominative (morphological and syntactic) participation of polysynthesis. The various machine translation systems still cannot translate completely correctly. The analysis compared various parameters - lexical, grammatical and stylistic correctness of the translation, and also revealed spelling errors, narrowing of the context and distortion of meaning. In order to assess the quality of the translation and the amount of required post-editing, an experiment was carried out to compare the translations of the most popular electronic online

Table 1. Results of the translation from Russian to Kazakh.

Source text	Names of machine translation systems and translation results			
	Google translation	Yandex translation	Sozdik.kz	Webtran.ru
Я им как младшая сестра [I'm like a little sister to them]	Мен олар үшін кішкентай әпкем сияқтымын [Men olar úshin kishkentaı ápkem sıaqtymyn]	Мен оларға kishi қарындас ретінде [Men olarǵa kishi qaryndas retinde]	мен оларға қарындасы [MEN olarǵa qaryndasy]	Мен олар үшін кішкентай әпкем сияқтымын [Men olar úshin kishkentaı ápkem sıaqtymyn]
Ударение—выделение каким-либо акустическим средством одной из сегментных единиц языка—слога, слова или синтагмы [Accent is the selection of one of the segmental units of a language-a syllable, word, or syntagma—by some acoustic means]	Стресс - бұл кез-келген акустика-лық құралдар арқылы тілдің сегменттік бірліктерінің бірін-буынды, сөзді немесесинтагманы таңдау [Stress-bul kez-kelgen akýstıka-lyq quraldar arqyly tildiń segmenttik birlikteriniń birin-býyndy, sózdi nemesesıntagmany tańdaý]	Екпін-тілдің сегменттік бірліктері-нің бірін—буынды, сөзді немесе синтагманы акустика-лық құралдармен оқшаулау [Ekpin-tildiń segmenttik birlikteri-niń birin—býyndy, sózdi nemese sıntagmany akýstıka-lyq quraldarmen oqshaýlaý]	Екпін—бөлу қандай акустическим құралы бірі сегментных бірлік тілі—буынды сөздер немесе синтагмы [Ekpin—bólý qandaı akýstıcheskım quraly biri segmentnyh birlik tili—býyndy sózder nemese sıntagmy	Стресс - бұл кез-келген акустикалық құралдар арқылы тілдің сегменттік бірліктерінің бірін - буынды, сөзді немесе синтагманы таңдау [Stress - bul kez-kelgen akýstıkalyq quraldar arqyly tildiń segmenttik birlikteriniń birin - býyndy, sózdi nemese sıntagmany tańdaý]
Лист бумаги по утрам, на квартиру носят нам [A sheet of paper in the morning, they bring us to the apartment]	Таңертең бір парақ, олар бізді пәтерге апарады [Tańerteń bir paraq, Olar bizdi páterge aparady]	Таңертең қағаз парағы, біз пәтерге киеміз [Tańerteń qaǵaz paraǵy, biz páterge kıemiz]	Бір парақ қағаз таңертең, пәтерге тағады бізге [Bir paraq qaǵaz tańerteń, páterge taǵady bizge]	Таңертең бір парақ, олар бізді пәтерге әкеледі [Tańerteń bir paraq, olar bizdi páterge ákeledi]

MT systems (translators). A comparative analysis of the translation of complex sentences was performed to identify errors that occur during machine translation. Table 1 shows the results of the translation from Russian to Kazakh. Table 2 shows the results of the translation from English to Kazakh. A total of 4 machine translation systems were selected to analyze the results [10–13].

Table 2. Results of the translation from English to Kazakh.

Source text	Names of machine translation systems and translation results		
	Google translation	Yandex translation	Sozdik.kz
Arman and Bakhyt are playing in the field	Далада Арман мен Бақыт ойнап жүр [Dalada Arman men Baqyt oınap júr]	Арман мен Бақыт аланда ойнайды. [Arman men Baqyt alańda oınaıdy]	Арман мен Бахыт ойнады далада [Arman men Bahyt oınady dalada]
When I woke up, I felt pain all over my body	Мен оянған кезде бүкіл денем ауырды [Men oıanǵan kezde búkil denem aýyrdy]	Оянғанда бүкіл денем ауырды [Men oıanǵanda búkil denem aýyrdy]	Менің оянған кезде бүкіл денем ауырды [Meniń oıanǵan kezde búkil denem aýyrdy]
The old men sat gloomy from morning to evening without saying anything to each other	Қарттар таңертеңнен кешке дейін бір-біріне ештеңе айтпастан қабағын түйіп отырды [Qarttar tańerteńnen keshke deıin bir-birine eshteńe aıtpastan qabaǵyn túıip otyrdy]	Қарттар таңертеңнен кешке дейін бір-біріне ештеңе айтпастан күңгірт отырды [Qarttar tańerteńnen keshke deıin bir-birine eshteńe aıtpastan kúńgirt otyrdy]	Қарттар таңертеңнен кешке дейін бір-біріне ештеңе айтпастан қабағын түйді [Qarttar tańerteńnen keshke deıin bir-birine eshteńe aıtpastan qabaǵyn túıdi]

Machine translation systems have advantages and disadvantages in translation. Analyzing the work of each of them, we identified possible errors in the translation from Russian to Kazakh and from English to Kazakh [14]. They are shown in Table 3:

In addition, the characteristic of the Kazakh language significantly affect the occurrence of errors in translation. Here they are:

-proximity of the lexical structure;
-the law of harmony;
-agglutination-a series of applications;
-no category;
-absence of auxiliary words (prepositions);
-special word order [19].

4 Model of Post-editing of the Kazakh Language in the MTS

Figure 1 shows the complete machine translation - based full post-editing architec-ture. Full post-editing is the process of processing the results of machine translation and

Table 3. Comparative characteristics of online machine translation systems when translating from Russian to Kazakh and from English to Kazakh.

Machine translation systems	Disadvantage	Advantage
Google translation	In some cases, there are some inconsistencies in large sentences	High quality translation of complex scientific and technical texts with minor problems of complex
Yandex translation	When translating large texts, parts of a sentence are not broken or translated	Translates very large sentences, complex texts with high quality
Sozdik.kz	Translation of large scientific texts does not give good results	Good translation results for words and short sentences
Webtran.ru	During translation, some words remain unchanged. In large sentences, the connection is incorrect	Good translation results for short sentences and phrases

producing meaningful translations. It must produce accurate translations that do not have stylistic inconsistencies and consistently use correct and approved terminology, avoiding any grammatical errors.

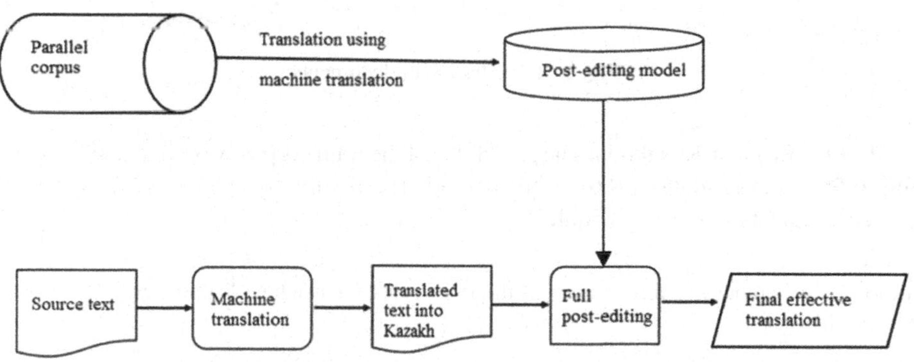

Fig. 1. Full post-editing architecture based on machine translation.

The full post-editing architecture, based on machine translation, describes in detail how a step-by-step translation from English or Russian into Kazakh using post-editing processing is done.

5 Practical Results

On the website www.akorda.kz, a parallel corpus of 80022 sentences in Russian and English was assembled using code written in the Python programming language. The assembled corpus was translated into the Kazakh language (into the Cyrillic alphabet of the Kazakh language) applying Google Translate. However, due to the fact that the Kazakh language belongs to the group of agglutinative languages, the translation quality was low. That is, the sentences are incomplete, the word order is incorrect, etc. This translation was summarized in the document «kaz». A high-quality and error-free translation of this document was created. This revised translation is summarized in the «kazedit» document. We processed the corpus, tokenized the corpus, separated the punctuation from the words. We have divided the assembled corpus into the four documents shown in Fig. 2.

1. train.kazedit, train.kaz - list of sentences for training;
2. tst2020.kazedit, tst2020.kaz - list of sentences submitted for validation;
3. tst2021.kazedit, tst2021.kaz - list of sentences submitted for testing;
4. vocab.kazedit, vocab.kaz- list of dictionaries.

Fig. 2. Distribution of documents.

For the Russian-Kazakh language, 98.9% of the total corpus was allocated for training, 0.5% - for validation, 0.6% - for testing. The number of words and sentences in these documents is shown in Table 4.

Table 4. The amount of information in the documents for machine learning for the Russian-Kazakh language.

Document name	Kaz	Kazedit
Train	77232 - sentences	77232 - sentences
tst2020	1556 - sentences	1556 - sentences
tst2021	1234 - sentences	1234 - sentences
Vocab	70508 - words	75871 - words

For the English-Kazakh language, 96.67% of the total corpus was allocated for training, 1.7% - for validation, 1.63% - for testing. The number of words and sentences in these documents is shown in Table 5.

Table 5. The amount of information in the documents for machine learning for English-Kazakh language.

Document name	Kaz	Kazedit
Train	73642 - sentences	73642 - sentences
tst2020	1302 - sentences	1302 - sentences
tst2021	1250 - sentences	1250 - sentences
Vocab	66008 - words	68803 - words

We are training this document using the seq2seq model for NMT (Neural Machine Translation).

The Seq2seq model is a model that takes sentences, words as input and returns another sequence of elements. The following example is given for the studied model (Fig. 3):

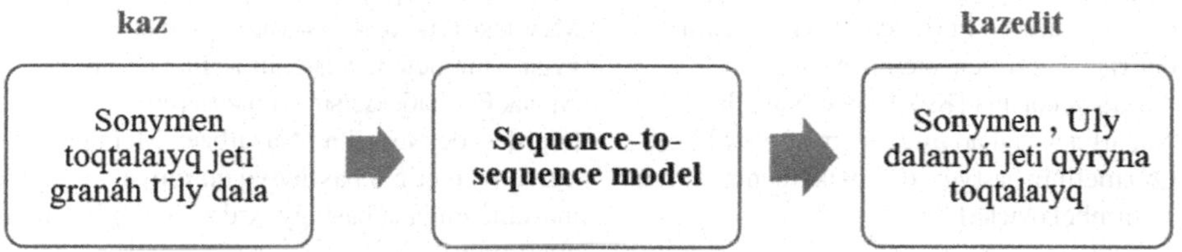

Fig. 3. Example of a sequence-to-sequence model.

The creation of the NMT model is associated with the attention mechanism, which helps to remember long sentences. The current target latent state is compared with all baseline states to obtain attention weights. Based on the attention weights, we calculate the context vector as a weighted average of the initial states and combine the context vector with the current target hidden state to get the final attention vector. This vector is supplied as input for the next time step [9].

The analysis of the results of improving machine translation was carried out using the BLEU metric. BLEU (bilingual evaluation understudy) is an algorithm for evaluating the quality of text translated from one natural language into another [15].

The main purpose of post-editing is to improve translation performance. When comparing the original translation, the results of the BLEU metric are as follows (Table 6):

The main goal of post-editing is to improve the indicator of this metric. The BLEU metric value when comparing the original enclosures is 6.6. After the training stage for post-editing into the Kazakh language, a BLEU metric value of 10.7 was obtained. Due to this, the result of translating texts has been improved.

An example of some of the sentences that appear as a result of testing is as follows (Table 7):

Analyzing the resulting sentences:

Table 6. Results of BLEU metrics.

	Google translation	Yandex translation	Post-editing
Russian-Kazakh	8.3	6.6	10.7
English-Kazakh	7.7	7.1	9.4

Table 7. Results obtained after machine learning.

kaz	kazedit
Жыл қорытындысы бойынша мемлекет басшысы бұқаралық ақпарат құралдары өкілдерімен елді [Jyl qorytyndysy boıynsha memleket basshysy buqaralyq aqparat quraldary ókilderimen eldi]	Мемлекет басшысы жыл қорытындысы бойынша еліміздің бұқаралық ақпарат құралдары өкілдерімен кездесті [Memleket basshysy jyl qorytyndysy boıynsha elimizdiń buqaralyq aqparat quraldary ókilderimen kezdesti]
Кездесуде Нұрсұлтан Назарбаев "жыл адамы" мемлекеттік күзет Қызметінің бастығы осы мекеменің Ардақ Ашимбековича [Kezdesýde Nursultan Nazarbaev "jyl adamy" memlekettik kúzet Qyzmetiniń bastyǵy osy mekemeniń Ardaq Ashımbekovıcha]	Кездесуде Нұрсұлтан Назарбаев Мемлекеттік күзет қызметінің басшылық құрамына осы мекеменің жаңа бастығы Ардақ Әшімбекұлын таныстырды [Kezdesýde Nursultan Nazarbaev Memlekettik kúzet qyzmetiniń basshylyq quramyna osy mekemeniń jańa bastyǵy Ardaq Áshimbekulyn tanystyrdy]
Сонымен тоқталайық жеті гранях Ұлы дала [Sonymen toqtalaıyq jeti granáh Uly dala]	Сонымен, Ұлы даланың жеті қырына тоқталайық [Sonymen, Uly dalanyń jeti qyryna toqtalaıyq]
Кездесу барысында тараптар ынтымақтастығының маңызды мәселелерін талқылады және одан әрі дамыту перспективалары туризм саласындағы қатынастарды [Kezdesý barysynda taraptar yntymaqtastyǵynyń mańyzdy máselelerin talqylady jáne odan ári damytý perspektıvalary týrizm salasyndaǵy qatynastardy]	Кездесу барысында тараптар ынтымақтастықтың маңызды мәселелері мен туризм саласындағы қатынастарды одан әрі дамыту перспективаларын талқылады [Kezdesý barysynda taraptar yntymaqtastyqtyń mańyzdy máseleleri men týrizm salasyndaǵy qatynastardy odan ári damytý perspektıvalaryn talqylady]

-word and word connection;
-the meaning of the sentence, and etc. can be seen to be well translated.

6 Conclusion and Future Work

Nowadays, the use of new technology and quality data is the result of machine translation. In order to improve the quality of translation, the system is constantly updated and checked, which simplifies and speeds up the work of translators. We analyzed online machine translation systems and identified common translation errors, as well as the advantages and disadvantages of machine translation systems from Russian into Kazakh and from English into Kazakh. In addition, a post-editing model was created for Russian-Kazakh and English-Kazakh translations, and a bilingual parallel corpus was assembled. The corpus, containing a total of 80022 sentences, was assembled using programming code tailored to the characteristics of each language. Various statistics are collected on the collected corpus and translation errors are grouped. After machine learning, we got the result: best bleu - 10.7.

The main contribution to this work is: automated collection of parallel corpuses for English-Kazakh and Russian-Kazakh translations. Development of a post-editing model for the Kazakh language in machine translation systems, with consider linguistic properties of the language. To improve the quality of translation and the work of the post-edit model, an approach based on a neural network was applied.

In the future, it is planned to increase the quantity of the corpus and use the Latin alphabet of the Kazakh language.

Acknowledgments. This research was performed and financed by the grant Project IRN AP08052421 Ministry of education and science of the Republic of Kazakhstan.

References

1. Chakyrova, I.I.: Post-editing in the tanslag paradigm. PNRPU Bull. Prob. Linguist. Pedag. **8**, 137–144 (2013)
2. Koponen, M.: Is machine translation post-editing worth the effort? A survey of research into post-editing and effort. J. Specialised Trans. (25), 3–5 (2016)
3. The Importance of Machine Translation Post-Editing and Its Application to Translation. WEB- Strastburg University website. [Electronic resource] (2018). https://mastertcloc.unistra.fr/2018/12/03/. Accessed 4 Apr 2021
4. ISO 18587:2017: Translation Services – Post-editing of Machine Translation Output – Requirements. International Organization for Standardization (2017)
5. Nechaeva, N.V., Svetova, S.I.ý.: Machine translation post-editing as an important area in the training of translators in universities. Questions of Teaching Methodology at the University **7**(25), 64–72 (2018)
6. Fully automated machine translation service // WEB-сайт. – [Electronic resource] (2020). https://www.semantix.com/machine-translation. Accessed 4 Apr 2021
7. Zdarek, D.: Post-editing Machine Translation Best Practices. [Electronic resource] (2020). https://www.memsource.com/blog/post-editing-machine-translation-best-practices/. Accessed 4 Apr 2021
8. How does the post-editing of neural machine translation compare with from-scratch translation? A product and process study Yanfang Jia, Hunan University Michael Carl, Kent State University Xiangling Wang, Hunan University. J. Special. Trans. **31**, 61–76 (2019)
9. Thang L., Eugene B., Rui Z.: Building Your Own Neural Machine Translation System in Tensorflow. https://github.com/tensorflow/nmt
10. https://translate.yandex.kz/
11. https://www.webtran.ru/
12. https://translate.google.kz/

13. https://sozdik.kz/
14. Rakhimova D.R. (ed.): Computational processing of the Kazakh language: collection of scientific works (materials), p. 146, Qazaq Universiteti, Almaty (2020)
15. BLUE metrics. https://en.wikipedia.org/wiki/BLEU. Accessed 4 Nov 2020
16. Rakhimova, D., Turganbayeva, A.: Auto-abstracting of texts in the Kazakh language. In: Proceedings of the 6th International Conference on Engineering & MIS, pp. 1–5 (2020). https://doi.org/10.1145/3410352.3410832
17. Diana, R., Assem, S.: Problems of semantics of words of the kazakh language in the information retrieval. In: Nguyen, N.T., Chbeir, R., Exposito, E., Aniorté, P., Trawiński, B. (eds.) ICCCI 2019. LNCS (LNAI), vol. 11684, pp. 70–81. Springer, Cham (2019). https://doi.org/10.1007/978-3-030-28374-2_7
18. Rakhimova, D., Zhumanov, Z.: Complex technology of machine translation resources extension for the Kazakh language. In: Król, D., Nguyen, N.T., Shirai, K. (eds.) Advanced Topics in Intelligent Information and Database Systems, pp. 297–307. Springer International Publishing, Cham (2017). https://doi.org/10.1007/978-3-319-56660-3_26
19. Shormakova, A., Zhumanov, Z.H., Rakhimova, D.: Post-editing of words in Kazakh sentences for information retrieval. J. Theoret. Appl. Inf. Technol. **97**(6), 1896–1908 (2019)
20. Perehodko, I.V., Máchın, D.A.: Assessment of the quality of machine translation. Bull. Orenburg State Univ. **2**(202), 92–96 (2017)
21. Goncharov, A.A., Býntman, N.V., Nýrıev, V.A.: Errors in machine translation: classification problems. Systems Means Inf. 3, 92–103 (2019)
22. https://www.researchgate.net/publication/228849469_A_Productivity_Test_of_Statistical_Machine_Translation_Post-Editing_in_a_Typical_Localisation_Context. Accessed 1 Mar 2021
23. https://www.erudit.org/en/journals/meta/2017-v62-n2-meta03191/1041023ar/. Accessed 10 Feb 2021
24. https://www.iso.org/standard/62970.html. Accessed 1 Feb 2021

Development and Study of an Approach for Determining Incorrect Words of the Kazakh Language in Semi-structured Data

Yntymak Abdrazakh[1], Aliya Turganbayeva[2], and Diana Rakhimova[1](✉)

[1] Al-Farabi Kazakh National University, Almaty, Kazakhstan
[2] Institute of Information and Computing Technologies, Almaty, Kazakhstan

Abstract. Research in the field of computer linguistics is relevant due to the rapid growth of information in natural languages on the Internet and social networks. Currently, there is an increase in the amount of information that humans and machines create in natural language. Information retrieval systems, dialog systems, machine translation, and automatic resume tools, spelling check modules analyze and process texts in natural languages. Thus, the range of automatic word processing systems is wide and covers a variety of tasks. One of the most important tasks of natural language processing (NLP) is to find errors in texts and including words, identify and correct incorrect words. The article provides an overview of semi-structured data, methods, and technologies for detecting incorrect words in natural languages. An approach for identifying incorrect words in the Kazakh language was developed and the features and capabilities of this approach were analyzed. A comparative analysis of texts on the Internet and social networks and of technologies that identify incorrect words in natural languages has been carried out.

Keywords: Kazakh language · Semi-structured data · Approach · Incorrect words · Internet · Social network · Stemming

1 Introduction

The huge flow of information on the Internet and social networks has led to the rapid development of the natural language processing industry, computer linguistics. Currently, various research mechanisms are developing their own projects, such as the exchange of information between users, machine translation of information, verification of e-mail, and the development of question-answer systems [1]. In general, the task of finding and correcting errors in texts and words in them is one of the main tasks of word processing in natural language. For more than half a century, this topic has not lost its relevance, new methods have emerged, the scope of its application is expanding. On the Internet and Instagram, Vkontakte, Twitter, and other social networks, applications are very attractive in terms of receiving and analyzing information in messages, because the information in these systems is real, it appears at this time [2]. However, the text on the Internet often differs from the generally accepted norms of the language. There

K. Wojtkiewicz et al. (Eds.): ICCCI 2021, CCIS 1463, pp. 535–545, 2021.
https://doi.org/10.1007/978-3-030-88113-9_43

are errors, deliberate distortion of words, mistakes [3]. Words with such errors, that is, incorrect words, can be processed and analyzed by identifying and correcting the necessary information. And these errors makes the text harder to read and, worse, harder to process. Natural language processing requires normalized forms of a word because incorrect spelling or digitization of text decreases informational value. A spelling error, for example, in a database of medical records, diminishes efficiency of the diagnosis process, and incorrectly written comments and publications of users on the Internet can influence research or organizational processes [4].

Due to the fact that the Kazakh language belongs to the group of low-resource languages, it is known that there are few translation systems, dictionaries, corpus (multilingual and bilingual), systems, and programs for detecting and correcting errors in words. Accordingly, today it is important to develop resources and tools, systems, as spelling errors detection programs that improve the use of languages with limited resources, such as the Kazakh language.

1.1 Semi-structured Data

Semi-structured data is data that does not conform to the rigid structure of tables and relationships in structural relational database models. Online information is not always relevant to a particular field of knowledge. In this regard, many organizations and scientists are developing specific algorithms for creating the structure of the text, which is not related to the field of education [5].

Semi-structured data becomes an important object for research, as the development of the Internet requires a data format (JSON, XML, etc.) that acts as a link between full-text documents and databases. Examples of systems with semi-structured data include comments, publications and texts written by users on the Internet, websites, and social networks [6]. Data from such systems is of great interest for research and applications, as it is possible to publish people's opinions and moods on any issue in real-time and contribute to the increase of information. It also helps to change people's attitudes towards business, politics and the social system today. Each type of data has its own characteristics, which must be taken into account when collecting, preparing, pre-processing, and describing objects.

We used information from the Internet and social media and this data is semi-structured as mentioned above. And this data has been used in research and experiments.

2 Related Works

The problems and works on spelling error detection and correction in text began in the 1960s and continues to the present day. There are good reasons to continue research in this area in order to improve quality and performance, as well as to expand the range of possible applications. For example, even though system programs (language processors, etc.) are becoming more powerful and complex, they do not help the user (with very few exceptions) to correct many obvious spelling errors in the input source data [7]. For 50 years of solving the problem of finding and correcting errors, researchers have tried a huge number of different methods. From character codes and n-gram acceptance tables and the direct application of the Damerau-Levenshtein distance to the active use of various machine learning methods, phonetic information about a word and machine translation methods. And the construction of systems for detecting and correcting errors in the text faces a number of fundamental and unresolved issues: compact storage of dictionaries, effective methods of morphological and syntactic analysis, and a system of scientific editors, i.e. a person who conducts literary and scientific processing of scientific and technical texts [8]. English text correction systems include «Grammarly», «Grammarchecker», «ReversoSpeller» and more applies. Russian text editing systems include: «Orfogramka», «Advego», «ORFO», «LINAR» and others. For agglutinative languages (such as Turkish, Kyrgyz, etc.) there are error checking systems, for example, a built-in spell checker in MS Word. But these systems are not suitable specifically for the Kazakh language. And unfortunately, there are no (in the public available) analogues of the previously listed systems for the Kazakh language.

An analysis of text verification and correction systems for English and Russian languages. During the research and analysis, texts of different styles, texts on the Internet and social networks, messages were considered. The advantages and disadvantages of the systems are shown in Table 1.

Table 1. Comparative characteristics of text verification and correction systems (system for English and Russian).

Text checking and editing systems	Disadvantages	Advantages
Microsoft.com	Recognizes some words that are not in the inserted dictionary and classifies them as incorrect words	In most cases, it identifies incorrect words in a large text
Online-spellcheck.com	In some cases, it can't correct the wrong words	Identifies different versions of incorrect words
Orfogramka - https://orfogr ammka.ru/	In some cases, it can't detect word errors	Identifies difficult errors and mistakes, different options
ORFO - https://online.orf o.ru/	Shows good results in the use of individual words, can not find some errors in large texts	Finds complex errors and mistakes, different options. Shows all possible word correction options

To date, the analysis of text correction systems has been carried out. The disadvantage of these text-correction systems is that they cannot be applied to the Kazakh language, as it is an agglutinative language with a complex morphological and lexical form [1].

To identify errors in the text and develop systems for correcting them in the Kazakh language, it is necessary to focus on the specifics of the language. Kazakh language is an agglutinative language group with the participation of morphological and syntactic rules and is a language with semantics depending on the structure of sentences.

At the same time in the process of automatic editing of Kazakh texts to ensure the correctness of the words in the text, control the correct transfer of word forms, etc. such control levels are included. As a logical result of this work, there is an electronic dictionary of the Kazakh language and systems for checking the accuracy of the Kazakh language texts, which have reached the industrial level of use. However, systems for checking the accuracy specifically for weakly structured texts in the Kazakh language are not publicly available, and even commercial software is difficult to find on the Internet [9].

2.1 Types of Spelling Errors

Spelling errors are categorized into two classes: typographic and cognitive. Cognitive errors (non-word errors) phonetic or orthographic similarity of words; a person does not know how to spell a word. Typographic errors (real word errors) are related to the keyboard and hand/finger movement where spelling errors happen because of two letters keys' closeness on the keyboard. But this is not limited to the type of error. To date, several types of errors have been identified, especially in semi-structured data [10, 11].

In the course of the study, the following cases were identified when detecting incorrect words from words of the Kazakh language obtained from semi-structured data, i.e. the following types of errors in words are indicated:

- typographic errors (кітап (kitap)– кіап (kiap));
- spelling errors (мұхит (muhit)– мухит (mýhit));
- deliberate distortion of words (алғааа (al*ǵaaa*), тағда (ta*ǵda*));
- grammatical errors;
- punctuation errors;
- spelling words with Russian alphabet;
- spelling words with Latin alphabet;
- abbreviations, etc.

3 Approach for Detecting Spelling Errors

Spelling error detection is associated with identifying a word as an incorrect word. Spelling checking methods include dictionary search methods that compare words and place them in a language dictionary. Failure to identify a word in the dictionary indicates a spelling error. Also, the most commonly used method is n-grams algorithms. Other methods used to determine to spell include morphological analysis, finite-state transducers, and machine learning algorithms. Hybrid methods are also used to check to spell [12].

There are many algorithms for checking the spelling of text documents. Figure 1 shows the use case diagram showing what types of algorithms are available to detect word errors.

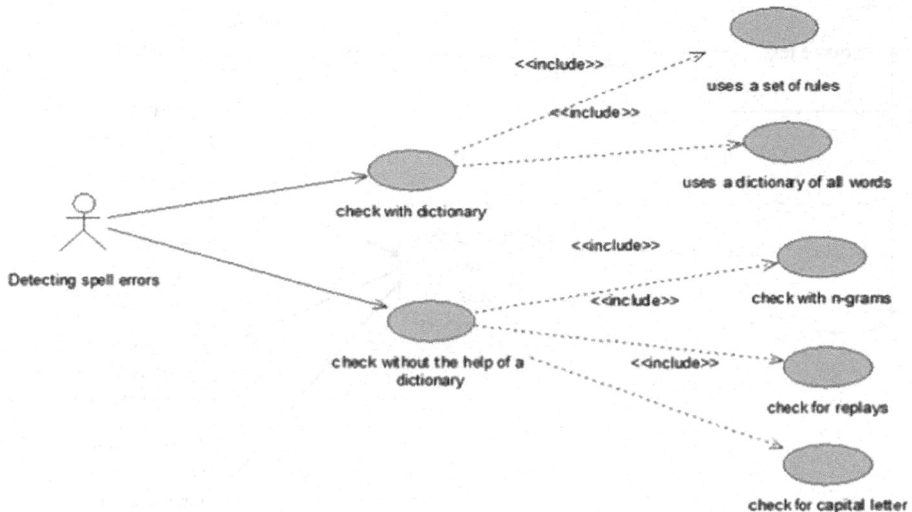

Fig. 1. Use case diagram showing the algorithm for detecting errors in word.

As shown in the diagram, the first method is to check the spelling with a dictionary. Dictionary verification is divided into verification through a dictionary of all words and verification through a dictionary using a set of rules.

Checking with the dictionary of all words. A dictionary is a file in.txt format, which contains all the words in the Kazakh language, including all forms of words. The words are arranged in alphabetical order, each word is in a new line. A dictionary check of all words is the most popular way to detect errors in the text. Checking is performed by a regular search for a word in the dictionary. If all the letters of the word match the word in the dictionary, then it is the correct word. If there is no such word, then it is wrong or incorrect [13].

Checking with a set of rules. A dictionary that uses a set of rules checks that all words are spelled correctly using language rules.

The second method is to check the spelling without the help of a dictionary, which includes checking the capital letter at the beginning of the sentence, checking the repetition of words, and checking with n-grams.

Capitalization, that is, each letter after the dot should automatically become an uppercase letter. A repeat test shows that the user wrote two identical words in a row. All letters of one word are checked for correspondence with the letters of another word, but if they match completely, it is considered an error. N-gram analysis is formulated as a method of finding misspelled words in a text array. Instead of comparing each word in the text with a dictionary, only n-grams are checked. If no or rare n-grams are detected, the word is marked as misspelled, otherwise, it is correct. This method does not depend on the language, because it does not require knowledge of the language used [14, 15].

In addition, research has been conducted on models that identify incorrect words in the language. As a result, an approach was developed to identify incorrect words in the Kazakh language. Figure 2 shows an approach of incorrect words.

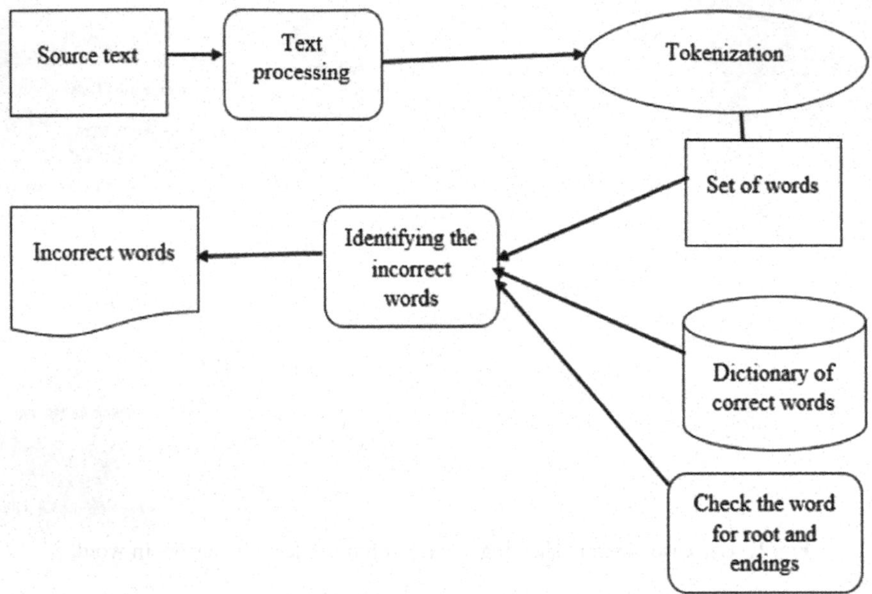

Fig. 2. Scheme of the approach for identifying incorrect words.

As shown in the approach, first the texts are collected from the semi-structured data, then the text is pre-processed, then we divide the text into sentences, sentences into words, and a set of words is formed from those words, respectively. Using the created dictionary of correct words, it is checked that the words in the set of words belong to the words in the dictionary of correct words, ie words are considered correct if they are defined in that dictionary, otherwise, they are considered incorrect. To find incorrect words for the Kazakh language, a stemming algorithm based on the CSE-model developed by Professor Ualsher Tukeyev and his team [10, 16] is used. With the help of the stemming algorithm based on the CSE-model with stems-lexicon [10] the word is separated into stem and endings, if these stem and ending of given word are found in the stem dictionaries and in the complete set of endings of the Kazakh language [17], then the word is correct, otherwise case the word is incorrect.

The proposed approach provides high performance due to the simplicity of the structure. Covers the grammar of the Kazakh language based on the CSE-model and stem dictionary, and therefore more accurately finds errors in the text. To further improve the quality, an addition to the stem dictionary is proposed.

4 Experiments and Results

During the research, a program was developed to assemble the corpus in the Kazakh language. In the Google Colab application, a corpus of 104658 sentences in the Kazakh language was compiled corpus using code written in the Python programming language. We assembled corpus from websites using Python scripts that use the BeautifulSoup and Request libraries in Python. This assembled dataset was analyzed by scripts based on the HTML structure. The corpus includes information on 1000 web pages published in the Kazakh language on the sites akorda.kz and nur.kz. Various statistical calculations were performed on the assembled corpus, the words in the corpus were analyzed and a dictionary of correct words was created, supplementing the data. Table 2 shows the information required to implement the program.

Table 2. Input data for the implementation of the program.

Text in corpus	Number of sentences
akorda.kz	81814
nur.kz	22844

The problem that arose when assembling the corpus was the need to pre-process the corpus data. This is due to the fact that information from sites comes in a variety of formats. It is necessary to consider cases of getting rid of unnecessary symbols, correcting sentences, splitting sentences into words. It will take some time.

For the experiment was used the stemming program described and available in [10, 16], also, were used the language resources of the Kazakh language, namely the dictionary of stems and stop words, complete set of endings available in [17]. The following table (Table 3) shows the files used in the experiment.

Table 3. Necessary files to run the program.

File	Description
kz_stop_words.txt	The file where the stop words are saved
stemming-for-Turkic-languages.py	Python file
affixes.xls	The file where the affixes are saved
text_for_testing.txt	The file where the source text is saved
kz_stems.txt	The file where the correct stems (stems) of words are saved
output_result.xls	The file where we will write the result (text after the steaming process)
dictionaty.txt	The file where the correct words of Kazakh language are saved

The program was tested several times. Table 4 shows the results of the experiment.

Table 4. Experimental results of the developed stemming algorithm for the Kazakh language.

Number of checked words	Number of words for which the stemming algorithm was performed correctly	Number of words for which the stemming algorithm was performed incorrectly	Accuracy, %
90	80	10	89
387	356	31	92
1339	1210	229	90
3233	3007	266	93
939	882	57	94
1239	1189	50	96
869	843	26	97
741	726	15	98

After working with the program, the results of the experiment were analyzed. Using the stemming algorithm, the roots of words (stem words) and endings were obtained. After the stemming process for words in the input text, the following errors were encountered in the analysis of the results:

- the stemming algorithm was performed on some words, assuming that there are endings on the basis of the word;
- the stemming algorithm for words was not performed correctly because some endings were not found in the affix file.

The solution of these problems was considered by adding words to the list of stem words, supplementing the set of endings. And another problem to consider is the difficulty of collecting stem words. With each experiment, we added stem words. In the next experiment, there were stems from the previous experiment. Taking them into account, it became necessary to collect universal and unique stem words with each test. It took a long time. To solve this problem, the stem words collected in each experiment were checked against the list of stem words by the program. In addition, texts in the Kazakh language of different styles were collected and experimented with to collect new stem words.

In the process of working with the program were collected stem words, stop words, as well as the ending of the Kazakh language. The following table (Table 5) lists the linguistic resources collected in the experiment.

Table 5. Linguistic resources were collected as a result of the experiment.

Linguistic resources	Number of elements of resources
Dictionary of stop words	495
Dictionary of stem words	49936
Dictionary of Kazakh language endings	3140
Dictionary of correct words	69938

Also, a dictionary of correct words was used to identify incorrect words in the Kazakh language from semi-structured data. This dictionary was created using the corpus and taking into account the morphological features of the Kazakh language. Experiments were carried out on the method of checking the dictionary and the method of checking the roots and endings of words. A comparative analysis of about 2,000 messages and texts was conducted. The following table shows (Table 6) the results of the experiment.

Table 6. Results of comparative analysis messages.

Objects that were analyzed	Percentage of errors in 400 entries, %	Common types of errors	Percentage of types of errors, %
Instagram	49,6	spelling, typography, spelling in Russian and Latin alphabets, abbreviations	spelling – 17,43, typography – 24,56, spelling in Russian and Latin alphabets – 33,88, abbreviations – 18,12, other – 6
Facebook	36,48	spelling, typography, spelling in the Russian alphabet, abbreviations	spelling – 12,13, typography – 20,87, spelling in Russian alphabet – 42,89, abbreviations – 20,11, other – 4
VKontakte	48,7	spelling in Russian and Latin alphabets, abbreviations, spelling, typography, deliberate distortion	spelling in Russian and Latin alphabets –47,93, abbreviations – 10,57, spelling – 11, typography – 16,86, deliberate distortion – 10,41, other – 3.63
https://massaget.kz/	29,92	spelling, typography, abbreviations	spelling – 24,5, typography - 51, abbreviations – 19,06, other – 5,44
https://kaz.tengri news.kz/	30,98	spelling, typography, spelling in the Russian alphabet	spelling – 19,32, typography – 28,65, spelling in the Russian alphabet – 45,91, other – 6,12

Here, at first, data from sites and social networks were collected, both automatically using the program and manually. Then the process of identifying incorrect words was carried out using the developed software product. The percentage of errors was calculated as the number of erroneous words divided by the total number of words in messages of one object. The percentage among the types of errors was calculated in this way. To classify and analyze errors, experts-linguists were involved and these experiments were carried out. As shown in the Table 6, posts on sites and social networks were considered for comparative analysis. 400 messages were received from each object, respectively, 2000 messages were received from 5 objects in total. Based on this developed approach from semi-structured data (for example, comments from social networks and news web pages) in the Kazakh language were found incorrect words and defined basic types.

5 Conclusion and Future Work

The article reviews the literature in accordance with the research and analyzes the methods and technologies for detecting incorrect words in natural languages. A comparative analysis of text correction systems was performed. The disadvantage of these systems is that they cannot be applied to the Kazakh language, as the Kazakh language is an agglutinative language with a complex morphological and lexical form. In this regard, analyzing the methods and systems for detecting errors in the text, models for detecting incorrect words in the Kazakh language were designed, a dictionary of correct words in the Kazakh language was compiled. The corpus was assembled in the Kazakh language using the program code created taking into account the peculiarities and characteristics of the Kazakh language. An approach has been developed to identify incorrect words from semi-structured data which worked based on the Stemming algorithm with stems-lexicon according to the CSE (Complete Set of Endings) morphology model and the main types of errors have been identified. The experiment was carried out on data from social networks and news web portals. Identifying incorrect words and then correcting them will increase the status of the information on your site, help your business grow, gather the target audience, as well as process the necessary information by analyzing user comments, and search engines will find keywords on your site. In general, according to the results of the experiment, the accuracy of identifying incorrect words was more than 90%.

The main contribution to this work is automated collection the corpus for Kazakh langusge. Development of an approach for identifying incorrect words of the Kazakh language, taking into account the linguistic properties of the language and creating linguistic resources and programs for collecting data in semi-structuted data.

In the future, methods will be developed and implemented to correct errors in the Kazakh language, expanding the accumulated and processed corpus and supplementing the information.

Acknowledgments. This research was performed and financed by the grant Project IRN AP09259556 Ministry of education and science of the Republic of Kazakhstan.

References

1. Rakhimova, D.R. (ed.) Computational processing of the Kazakh language: collection of scientific works (materials). Qazaq Universiteti, Almaty, p. 146 (2020)
2. Han, B., Baldwin, T.: Lexical normalisation of short text messages: Makn sens a# twitter. In: Proceedings of the 49th Annual Meeting of the Association for Computational Linguistics: Human Language Technologies, vol. 1, pp. 368–378. Association for Computational Linguistics (2011)
3. Farra, N., et al.: Generalized Character-Level Spelling Error Correction, vol. 2, pp. 161–167. ACL (2014)
4. Hladek, D., et al.: Survey of automatic spelling correction. Electronics **9**(10), 1670 (2020)
5. Peter, B.: Semistructured data. In: Proceedings of the Sixteenth ACM SIGACT-SIGMOD-SIGART Symposium on Principles of Database Systems, 11–15 May 1997, Tucson, Arizona, United States, pp. 117–121 (1997)
6. Brill, E., Moore, R.C.: An improved error model for noisy channel spelling correction. In: Proceedings of the 38th Annual Meeting on Association for Computational Linguistics, pp. 286–293. Association for Computational Linguistics (2000)
7. Ahmed, F., Luca, E.W.D., Nürnberger, A.: Revised N-Gram based automatic spelling correction tool to improve retrieval effectiveness. Polibits **40**, 39–48 (2009)
8. Kaufmann, M., Kalita, J.: Syntactic normalization of twitter messages. In: International Conference on Natural Language Processing, Kharagpur, India (2010)
9. Rakhimova, D.R.: Research of models and methods of semantics of machine translation from Russian into Kazakh language. Dissertation, Almaty (2014)
10. Tukeyev, U., Turganbayeva, A.: Universal Program of Stemming Algorithm with Stems-Lexicon According to the CSE (Complete Set of Endings) Morphology Model (2020). http://github.com/NLP-KAZNU
11. Diana, R., Assem, S.: Problems of semantics of words of the Kazakh language in the information retrieval. In: Nguyen, N.T., Chbeir, R., Exposito, E., Aniorte, P., Trawinski, B. (eds.) ICCCI 2019. LNCS (LNAI), vol. 11684, pp. 70–81. Springer, Cham (2019). https://doi.org/10.1007/978-3-030-28374-2_7
12. Shaalan, K., Aref, R., Fahmy, A.: An approach for analyzing and correcting spelling errors for non-native Arabic learners. In: 2010 The 7th International Conference on Informatics and Systems (INFOS). Published 2010, Computer Science (2010)
13. Taktashkin, D.V., Mokrousova, Y.A.: Methods and algorithms for checking the spelling of test documents (Paper in Russian). Electron. Sci. Pract. J. Mod. Sci. Res. Innov. №5 2017. https://web.snauka.ru/issues/2017/05/72892. Accessed 12 Apr 2021
14. Kumar, R., Bala, M., Sourabh, K.: A study of spell checking techniques for Indian languages. JK Res. J. Math. Comput. Sci. **1**(1), 105–113 (2018)
15. Rakhimova, D., Turganbayeva, A.: Approach to extract keywords and keyphrases of text resources and documents in the Kazakh language. In: Nguyen, N.T., Hoang, B.H., Huynh, C.P., Hwang, D., Trawinski, B., Vossen, G. (eds.) ICCCI 2020. LNCS (LNAI), vol. 12496, pp. 719–729. Springer, Cham (2020). https://doi.org/10.1007/978-3-030-63007-2_56
16. Tukeyev, U.A., Turganbaeva, A.O.: Lexicon-free stemming for the Kazakh language. In: Materials of the International Scientific Conference "Computer science and Applied Mathematics" dedicated to the 25th anniversary of the Independence of the Republic of Kazakhstan and the 25th anniversary of the Institute of Information and Computational Technologies, Part II, Almaty, September 21–24, 2016 (2016)
17. Tukeyev, U., Turganbayeva, A., Karibayeva, A., Amirova, D., Abduali, B.: Language_resources_for_Kazakh_language (2020). https://github.com/NLP-KazNU/Language_Resources_for_Kazakh_language

Conversational Machine Reading Comprehension for Vietnamese Healthcare Texts

Son T. Luu[1,2], Mao Nguyen Bui[1,2], Loi Duc Nguyen[1,2], Khiem Vinh Tran[1,2], Kiet Van Nguyen[1,2(✉)], and Ngan Luu-Thuy Nguyen[1,2]

[1] University of Information Technology, Ho Chi Minh City, Vietnam
{sonlt,kietnv,ngannlt}@uit.edu.vn

[2] Vietnam National University, Ho Chi Minh City, Vietnam
{16520724,16521722,17520634}@gm.uit.edu.vn

Abstract. Machine reading comprehension (MRC) is a sub-field in natural language processing that aims to assist computers understand unstructured texts and then answer questions related to them. In practice, the conversation is an essential way to communicate and transfer information. To help machines understand conversation texts, we present UIT-ViCoQA, a new corpus for conversational machine reading comprehension in the Vietnamese language. This corpus consists of 10,000 questions with answers over 2,000 conversations about health news articles. Then, we evaluate several baseline approaches for conversational machine comprehension on the UIT-ViCoQA corpus. The best model obtains an F1 score of 45.27%, which is 30.91 points behind human performance (76.18%), indicating that there is ample room for improvement. Our dataset is available at our website: http://nlp.uit.edu.vn/datasets/ for research purposes.

Keywords: Conversations · Question answering · Machine reading comprehension · Deep neural models · Texts

1 Introduction

Conversation is a standard method to communicate between people, and it plays an important role in human daily life. The process of asking a question and responding to an answer brings helpful information about a specific domain.

Healthcare is one of the most concerning problems for many people. Many audiences often read the healthcare news, and people tend to discuss frequently about health and medicine. Thus, based on the conversations about healthcare, we constructed a corpus named UIT-ViCoQA for conversational question answering on healthcare texts in Vietnamese. The UIT-ViCoQA contains 2,000 conversations and 10,000 questions from articles about health news in Vietnamese. This corpus is used to train the computer for understanding the conversation and giving the right answers based on the conversation context from questions of users. Besides, we implement neural-based models for conversational

K. Wojtkiewicz et al. (Eds.): ICCCI 2021, CCIS 1463, pp. 546–558, 2021.
https://doi.org/10.1007/978-3-030-88113-9_44

question answering including: DrQA [1], GraphFlow [2], FlowQA [8], and SDNet [22] on the UIT-ViCoQA corpus. Then, we evaluate the performance of those models on the UIT-ViCoQA dataset.

The main contribution in this paper includes providing a corpus for conversational machine comprehension about healthcare texts in Vietnamese and evaluating the performance of baseline MRC models on the dataset. Our paper is structured as described. Section 2 takes a literature review about the conversation machine comprehension corpora and models. Section 3 provides overview information about the UIT-ViCoQA dataset. Section 4 introduces available state-of-the-art approaches for the conversational machine comprehension task. Section 5 shows our empirical results and error analysis of question-answering models on the UIT-ViCoQA corpus. Finally, Sect. 6 concludes our works.

2 Related Works

Machine reading comprehension (MRC) is a challenging task of natural language processing (NLP) which enables machines to understand the reading text and answer the questions [16]. Many of MRC corpora are constructed on specific domains, and open domains in English such as SQuAD [16] (extractive MRC) on Wikipedia articles, RACE [11] (multiple choices MRC) on High school students English Exams domain, and NarrativeQA [9] (abstractive MRC) on books and stories domain. For the Vietnamese language, the UIT-ViQuAD [14] (Wikipedia domain), and UIT-ViNewsQA [21] (Health news domain) are two extractive MRC corpora for machine reading comprehension. Besides, the ViMMRC [13] is the multiple-choice reading comprehension corpus on the Vietnamese students' textbook for primary schools domain.

Machine reading comprehension applied in question-answering (QA) systems is another challenge that the MRC models have to understand both given texts and conversational context and then answer relevant questions. These questions are often paraphrased, contain co-reference queries, and their answers can be spans texts or free-form. This type of MRC is called Conversational Machine Comprehension (CMC) [7]. CoQA [17] and QuAC [3] are two CMC corpora in English. Based on the CoQA works, we constructed the UIT-ViCoQA for automated reading comprehension on the health news articles in the Vietnamese language.

Attention-based reasoning with sequence models and FLOW mechanism are two approaches for CMC models, according to Gupta et al. [7]. DrQA[1] and PGNet [19] are two neural attention-based models implemented in the CoQA corpus. Next, SDNet [22] is another attention-based model that combines inter-attention and self-attention to comprehend the conversation context. Finally, FlowQA [8] and GraphFlow [2] are two flow-based models that used to yield the contextual information through sequences.

3 The Corpus

Our data creation process consisting of three phases is described in Fig. 1. In the first phase, we collect news articles about health from VnExpress[1] - the most read online newspapers in Vietnam by using scrapy[2] - a web crawler tool for collecting articles from the online newspaper. In the next phase, we construct an annotation tool for creating conversational data. Our annotation tool allows two annotators to create the conversation based on the given articles. Finally, in the third phase, we hire a team of annotators who create data on our annotation tool. The detailed steps from the annotation process are described below.

3.1 Data Collection

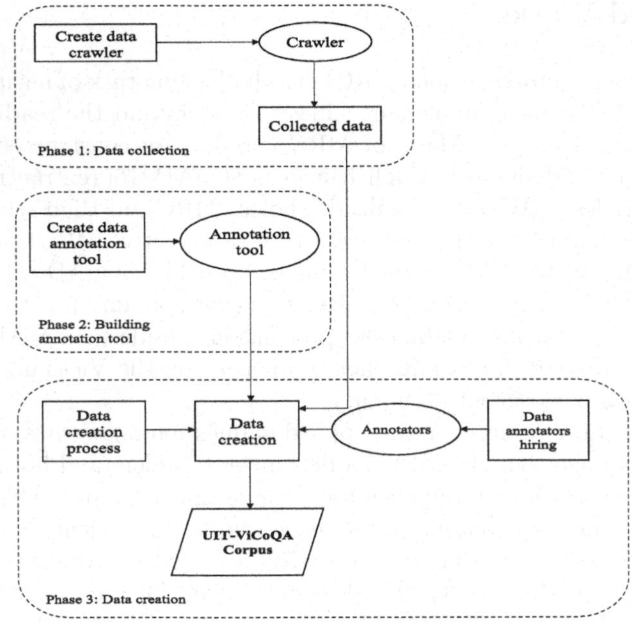

Fig. 1. The creation process of the UIT-ViCoQA corpus.

For each conversation (C), we hire two different annotators, which are questioners and answerers, respectively. The questioner goes first by asking a question (Q). The question is sent to the answerer then. After receiving the question, the answerer gives the answer by selecting a span of text from the article (S) and then submits the natural answer (A). Next, the annotation system compares the answer given by the answerer with the asked question of the questioner by character level. If the given answer matches about 70% with the asked question,

[1] https://vnexpress.net/suc-khoe.
[2] https://scrapy.org/.

it is a valid answer, and two annotators can move to the next turn. In contrast, the answerer must give another answer. There is a total of five turns for asking and answer per article.

In the data creation process, we have some requirements for questioners and answerers as: (1) The answers must be extracted from the article. Questions that cannot be answered according to the article are not allowed, (2) Questioners are encouraged to give questions with synonyms, opposite words, and coreference, and (3) The answers should be short and limited to use new words from the article content. Moreover, the selected answerers need to give full answers with complete texts, correct syntax, and punctuations.

3.2 Dataset Overview

Table 1. An example of conversation in the UIT-ViCoQA corpus

	Trạng thái "ngủ" là cách các tế bào ngay lập tức thay đổi để kháng lại phương pháp điều trị. Các phương pháp điều trị ung thư vú thường thành công, tuy nhiên một số trường hợp ung thư tái phát và tiên lượng xấu hơn. Ông Luca Magnani, Khoa Dược, Đại học Hoàng Gia London, Anh, cho biết phương pháp điều trị bằng hormone hiện được sử dụng cho phần lớn bệnh nhân ung thư vú ... (The status of "sleep" is the way when the cell changes immediately to resist treatment. The treatment methods of breast cancer are often successful. However, some cases of cancer recur, and the prognosis worsens. Mr. Luca Magnani, Faculty of Medicine, Imperial College London, says that the treatment method by using hormones is used for a huge amount of breast cancer patients ...)
Q1	Phương pháp thường được sử dụng để chữa trị ung thư vú là gì ? (What is the treatment method usually use for breast cancer treatment?)
S1	Ông Luca Magnani, Khoa Dược, Đại học Hoàng Gia London, Anh, cho biết phương pháp điều trị bằng hormone hiện được sử dụng cho phần lớn bệnh nhân ung thư vú . (Mr. Luca Magnani, Faculty of Medicine, Imperial College London, says that treatment method by using hormone is used for a huge amount of breast cancer patients.)
A1	điều trị bằng hormone (using hormone)
Q2	Các bác sĩ có lo ngại gì về phương pháp này? (What are doctors concerned about for this treatment?)
S2	Từ lâu, các nhà khoa học đã đặt câu hỏi, liệu pháp này thực chất có tiêu diệt được các tế bào ung thư vú không, hay chỉ là chuyển các tế bào sang trạng thái "ngủ yên". (Scientists have long questioned whether this therapy actually kills breast cancer cells, or just puts the cells in an "inactive" state.)
A2	nó đưa các tế bào ung thư sang trạng thái "ngủ yen" (This treatment puts the cells in an "inactive" state)
Q3	Vậy những nghiên cứu này có ý nghĩa như thế nào? (What profits from these studies?)
S3	cũng giải thích rằng những phát hiện hiện tại sẽ mở ra lộ trình mới cho việc nghiên cứu chữa trị ung thư. (explaining that current works can open new future researchs about cancer treatments)
A3	mở ra lộ trình mới cho việc nghiên cứu chữa trị ung thư (Opening new research for cancer treatments)

The UIT-ViCoQA corpus contains 2,000 conversations. Each conversation consists of a reading article and five question-answer pairs. We follow the structure of the CoQA [17] for our dataset. According to Table 1, to answer question Q2, the answerer needs to read the passage and looks back to question Q1 and answer A1 to retrieve the relevant information. Similar to question Q2, the answerer needs to read the reading passage and two previous question-answer pairs (Q1, A1) and (Q2, A2) to extract the answer A3. The chain of question-answer pairs Q1-A1, Q2-A2 is the history of the conversation.

Table 2 provides the overview of the UIT-ViCoQA corpus and compares it with the CoQA corpus. The result illustrates that although the number of questions and answers in the UIT-ViCoQA corpus is lower than the CoQA corpus, the average number of words in the UIT-ViCoQA dataset is larger than the CoQA dataset. This is because the interrogative words in English contain a single word (e.g., who?, when?, and why?) while they may have two words in Vietnamese. For example, the words "who" means "ai", "when" means "khi nào" and "why" means "tại sao". Besides, the UIT-ViCoQA is constructed on a specific domain. Hence it is not as diverse as the CoQA corpus.

Table 2. Overview information about the UIT-ViCoQA and CoQA corpus

	UIT-ViCoQA	CoQA
Domain text	Health domain	Diverse domains
Number of passages	2,000	8,399
Number of questions	10,000	127,000
Passage length	404.1	271.0
Question length	9.4	5.5
Answer length	9.7	2.7

3.3 Dataset Analysis

Table 3. The types of question in the UIT-ViCoQA corpus

Question types	**Example**	**Ratio (%)**
What	trans fat **là gì**? (what is trans fat?)	32.6
How many	Vietnam có **bao nhiêu** ca nhiễm COVID-19? (**How many** cases of COVID 19 are detected in Vietnam?)	17.2
How	DCVax hoạt động như **thế nào**? (How does DCVax work?)	7.6
Yes/No	Có **tiền sử** bị bệnh gì không ? (Have a history of any illness?)	6.6
Who	Những **người nào** dễ bị xơ gan? (Who is susceptible to cirrhosis?)	9.0
Why	**Vì sao** nhang có thể ảnh hưởng xấu tới cơ thể? (Why incense can adversely affect the body?)	7.8
Which	**Nhóm nào** chiếm tỉ lệ cao nhất? (Which group accounts for the highest percentage?)	7.0
When	**Khi nào** thì cô có thể kết thúc điều trị? (When can she finish treatment?)	2.6
Where	Zhou Xiaoying sinh sống **ở đâu?** (Where does Zhou Xiaoying live?)	4.0
Others	Còn du thuyền Diamond Princess? Kể tên một số quốc gia có số mắc cao (About the Diamond Princess yacht? Name a few countries with high risk?)	5.6

In Vietnamese, the process of interaction contains statements between two people. Each statement contains two functional elements, including the negotiatory for carrying the argument in statements that go through the conversation and the remainder to keep the rest information of statements [20]. The negotiatory is an essential part of the statement in the conversation. The negotiatory element comprises interrogatives particles, element interrogatives items, and imperative particles. The interrogatives are the characteristic of questions. In Table 3, we show all kinds of questions in Vietnamese that are usually used in daily life. The interrogative words are marked bold in the sentence. According to Table 3, the "What" type accounts for the highest ratio in the UIT-ViCoQA corpus (32.6%).

Table 4. Linguistic phenomena in UIT-ViCoQA questions

Phenomenon	Example	Ratio (%)
Relationship between a question and its passage		
Lexical match	Q: **Ai** làm giám đốc quốc gia của Hiệp hội Sảy thai? (**Who** is the director of the association of miscarriage?) A: Ruth Bender - Atik S: Ruth Bender - Atik, giám đốc quốc gia của Hiệp hội Sảy thai (Ruth Bender - Atik, national director of the association of miscarriage)	47.6
Paraphrasing	Q: **Giá** cho mỗi con robot là bao nhiêu? (**How much** is the price of each robot?) A: 500000 RMB S: Các robot có giá 500000 RMB (khoảng 72000 USD) (Robots have price 500000 RBM, about 72000 USD)	48.0
Pragmatics	Q: **Vì sao? (Why?)** A: Do sầu riêng chứa nhiều chất dinh dưỡng, nhiều năng lượng, cộng với cồn nồng độ cao làm cho nhịp tim tăng (Because durian contains lots of nutrients, energy, combining with high concentration of alcohol, make heartbeat increase.) S: Chuyên gia dinh dưỡng Nguyễn Mộc Lan cho biết sầu riêng nhiều chất dinh dưỡng, nhiều năng lượng, cộng với rượu nồng độ cao làm cho nhịp tim tăng. (Nutritionist Nguyen Moc Lan said durian has a lot of nutrients, lots of energy, plus a high concentration of alcohol makes your heart rate increase.)	4.4
Relationship between a question and its conversation history		
No coreference	Q: Phô mai có giá trị dinh dưỡng **thế nào**? (**How** does cheese have nutritional value?)	73.6
Explicit coreference	Q1: Loại bệnh **nào** Tiểu Lý mắc phải từ ban đầu? (**What** kind of illness was Tieu Ly initially?) A1: bệnh lao phổi (tuberculosis) Q2: Anh ta chữa bệnh trong thời gian **bao lâu?** (**How long** does he treat?)	20.6
Implicit coreference	Q1: Ở Hải Phòng bệnh nhân **từ đâu** trở về? (**Where** does the patient come from in Hai Phong?) A1: Quảng Đông (Guangdong) Q2: Hiện có triệu chứng **gì**? (**What** symptoms are there?)	5.8

Next, we randomly divide our corpus into training, development, and test sets with proportions 70%, 15%, and 15%, respectively. Then, we take 100 articles by random from the development set to analyze and evaluate the corpus, which is called analysis set [17]. We segment texts in the corpus by the Underthesea framework[3].

According to Gupta et al. [7], the Conversational Machine Comprehension (CMC) model answers the question by extracting information not only from the reading texts but also from conversational history. Therefore, the main linguistic

[3] https://github.com/undertheseanlp/underthesea.

phenomena in the UIT-ViCoQA are based on the relationship between questions and the reading passage and the relationship between questions and the conversation history. Table 4 displays the linguistic phenomena in the UIT-ViCoQA corpus.

For the relationship between questions and the reading texts, there are three types of phenomena: lexical match, paraphrasing, and pragmatic. The lexical match indicates that the questions contain the same words as the reading texts. In contrast, paraphrasing is the question in which their words use synonyms from the reading texts, and pragmatic means the question uses words that do not relate to the reading texts. The proportions of lexical match, paraphrasing, and pragmatic phenomenon in the UIT-ViCoQA corpus are 47.6%, 48.0%, and 4.4%, respectively, as shown in Table 4.

In addition, for the relationship between questions and the conversation history, there are three types of relational phenomena: no coreference, explicit coreference, and implicit coreference. The percentages of no coreference, explicit coreference, and implicit coreference in the UIT-ViCoQA corpus are 73.6%, 20.6%, and 5.8%, respectively, according to Table 4.

4 Methodologies

According to Gupta et al. [7], a typical conversation reading comprehension task consists of reading passage as context (C), the conversation history (H) includes multiple question-answer pairs, and the generated answers (A). Therefore, this task combines two models: the machine reading comprehension model for encoding the questions and context into neural space vectors and the question-answering model to generate and decode answers from questions to natural language.

For the machine reading comprehension model, the Document Reader (DrQA) introduced by Chen et al. [1] is a powerful model on various of machine reading comprehension corpora such as: SQuAD [16], TextWorldsQA [10], and UIT-ViQuAD [14]. The DrQA model consists of two modules: Document Retriever and Document Reader. We use the Document Reader of the DrQA to extract the answer spans for the questions.

Besides, for the conversational comprehension task, the generated answers are not only from the reading passage but also the conversation history. The model extracts the history of conversations as a special context to generate new answers. SDNeT model [22] is a contextual attention-based model based on the idea of DrQA with a special mechanism to extract the context of the conversation.

Furthermore, The FLOW mechanism enables the MRC models to encode the history of the conversation comprehensively. Hence, this mechanism integrates well the latent semantic of the conversation history. FlowQA [8] and GraphFlow [2] are two flow-based neural models that grasping the conversational history context to generate answers.

5 Experiments

5.1 Data Preparation

We pre-process the data before fitting to the model by these following steps: (1) Removing special characters and stop words, (2) Segmenting sentences into words by using the Underthesea tool, and (3) Transforming the texts into vectors by using fastText word embedding in the Vietnamese language provided by Grave et al. [6]. The dimension of fastText word embedding is 300.

5.2 Evaluation Metrics

We evaluate the performance of the models by comparing the generated answers with the accurate answers on F1-score and Exact match (EM) score. The F1-score measures the right predicted answers comparing with the correct answers. The EM score measures the exact matching of prediction answers with original answers [16].

5.3 Experiment Results

The FLOW models give optimistic results on the UIT-ViCoQA corpus. According to Table 5, FlowQA obtains the highest result by F1-score on both development and test sets. For the EM score, the SDNet model gives the highest results. However, there is a large gap between the F1 and the EM scores as well as the performance of CMC models and human performance.

Table 5. Experimental results on the UIT-ViCoQA corpus

Model	EM (%)		F1-score (%)	
	Dev	Test	Dev	Test
DrQA	13.17	13.50	43.28	37.71
SDNet	**15.40**	**15.60**	41.90	40.50
FlowQA	13.13	12.53	**44.84**	**45.27**
GraphFlow	13.77	14.73	44.69	45.16
Human performance	**35.67**	**38.66**	**73.33**	**76.18**

5.4 Error Analysis

Table 6 shows the predicted answers given by four different models, including DrQA, SDNet, FlowQA, and GraphFlow, respectively. In general, FlowQA and GraphFlow give the most relevant answer as the original answer. For example, in the question Q3 - "What the enterprise think about?", the reader needs to look

Table 6. The answers predicted by models on a sample in the UIT-ViCoQA corpus

<table>
<tr><td colspan="2">Tính đến ngày 18/2, Việt Nam có 16 ca nhiễm covid-19. Trong đó, Vĩnh Phúc có tới 5 công nhân và 6 người thân của họ bị lây nhiễm. Con số này khiến các doanh nghiệp đặt ra câu hỏi về nguy cơ lây lan virus khó lường trong môi trường doanh nghiệp. Chỉ cần một trường hợp phát hiện nhiễm Covid-19 là cả văn phòng, phân xưởng tiếp xúc với người bệnh sẽ phải cách ly cô lập, gây gián đoạn hoạt động sản xuất kinh doanh, tạo áp lực lên hệ thống y tế công. Ông Đoàn Đình Duy Khương - Tổng Giám đốc điều hành Dược Hậu Giang về vấn đề bảo vệ sức khỏe lao động cho biết, mỗi ngày họ phải dành hơn 1/3 thời gian cho nơi làm việc ... (Up to 18/2, Vietnam has 16 affected cases of covid-19. Specifically, Vinh Phuc has 5 workers and 6 relatives of whom are affected. This number makes the enterprises question about the risk of virus spreading in working environment. If only one case is detected to be affected Covid-19, the whole offices, factories which are contacted with the patients will be quarantined, disrupting production and business activities, and putting pressure on the public health system. Mr Đoàn Đình Duy Khương - General director of Hau Giang Pharmacy about protecting labor health affairs, says that, everyday they have to spend more than 1/3 of their time at work ...)</td></tr>
<tr><td>Q1</td><td>Việt Nam có bao nhiêu ca nhiễm tính đến 18/2? (How many affected cases of Vietnam have been counted up to 2/18?)</td></tr>
<tr><td>Original</td><td>Tính đến ngày 18/2, Việt Nam có 16 ca nhiễm covid-19. (Up to 18/2, Vietnam has 16 affected cases of covid-19)</td></tr>
<tr><td>DrQA</td><td>16</td></tr>
<tr><td>SDNet</td><td>16 ca nhiễm covid-19. (16 affected cases of covid-19)</td></tr>
<tr><td>FlowQA</td><td>16 ca (16 cases)</td></tr>
<tr><td>GraphQA</td><td>16 ca nhiễm covid-19 (16 affected cases of covid-19)</td></tr>
<tr><td>Q2</td><td>Cụ thể? (Detail?)</td></tr>
<tr><td>Original</td><td>Trong đó, Vĩnh Phúc có tới 5 công nhân và 6 người thân của họ bị lây nhiễm. (Specifically, Vinh Phuc has 5 workers and 6 relatives of whom are affected.)</td></tr>
<tr><td>DrQA</td><td>Vĩnh Phúc có tới 5 công nhân và 6 người thân của họ bị lây nhiễm. (Vinh Phuc has 5 workers and 6 relatives of whom are affected.)</td></tr>
<tr><td>SDNet</td><td>Trong đó, Vĩnh Phúc có tới 5 công nhân và 6 người thân của họ bị lây nhiễm. (Vinh Phuc has 5 workers and 6 relatives of whom are affected.)</td></tr>
<tr><td>FlowQA</td><td>Trong đó, Vĩnh Phúc có tới 5 công nhân và 6 người thân của họ bị lây nhiễm. (Vinh Phuc has 5 workers and 6 relatives of whom are affected.)</td></tr>
<tr><td>GraphQA</td><td>Trong đó, Vĩnh Phúc có tới 5 công nhân và 6 người thân của họ bị lây nhiễm. (Vinh Phuc has 5 workers and 6 relatives of whom are affected.)</td></tr>
<tr><td>Q3</td><td>Doanh nghiệp nghĩ gì? (What does the enterprise think about?)</td></tr>
<tr><td>Original</td><td>Con số này khiến các doanh nghiệp đặt ra câu hỏi về nguy cơ lây lan virus khó lường trong môi trường doanh nghiệp.(This number makes the enterprises question about the risk of virus spreading in working environment.)</td></tr>
<tr><td>DrQA</td><td>doanh nghiệp đặt ra câu hỏi về nguy cơ lây lan virus khó lường trong môi trường doanh nghiệp.(the enterprise questions about the risk of virus spreading in working environment.)</td></tr>
<tr><td>SDNet</td><td>ca nhiễm covid-19. (affected cases of covid-19)</td></tr>
<tr><td>FlowQA</td><td>các doanh nghiệp đặt ra câu hỏi về nguy cơ lây lan virus khó lường trong môi trường doanh nghiệp.. (the enterprises question about the risk of virus spreading in working environment.)</td></tr>
<tr><td>GraphQA</td><td>virus khó lường trong môi trường doanh nghiệp. (The virus is dangerous in working environment)</td></tr>
<tr><td>Q4</td><td>Nguy cơ là gì? (What is risk?)</td></tr>
<tr><td>Original</td><td>Chỉ cần một trường hợp phát hiện nhiễm Covid-19 là cả văn phòng, phân xưởng tiếp xúc với người bệnh sẽ phải cách ly cô lập, gây gián đoạn hoạt động sản xuất kinh doanh, tạo áp lực lên hệ thống y tế công. (If only one case is detected to be affected Covid-19, the whole offices, factories which are contacted with the patients will be quarantined, disrupting production and business activities, and putting pressure on the public health system.)</td></tr>
<tr><td>DrQA</td><td>Chỉ cần một trường hợp phát hiện nhiễm Covid-19 là cả văn phòng. (If only one case is detected to be affected Covid-19, the whole offices.)</td></tr>
<tr><td>SDNet</td><td>khó phát triển bền vững.</td></tr>
<tr><td>FlowQA</td><td>Chỉ cần một trường hợp phát hiện nhiễm Covid-19 là cả văn phòng. (If only one case is detected to be affected Covid-19, the whole offices.)</td></tr>
<tr><td>GraphQA</td><td>Chỉ cần một trường hợp phát hiện nhiễm Covid-19 là cả văn phòng. (If only one case is detected to be affected Covid-19, the whole offices.)</td></tr>
<tr><td>Q5</td><td>Đoàn Đình Duy Khương là ai? (Who is Đoàn Đình Duy Khương?)</td></tr>
<tr><td>Original</td><td>Ông Đoàn Đình Duy Khương - Tổng Giám đốc điều hành Dược Hậu Giang. (Mr. Đoàn Đình Duy Khương - General director of Hau Giang Pharmacy)</td></tr>
<tr><td>DrQA</td><td>Ông Đoàn Đình Duy Khương - Tổng Giám đốc điều hành Dược Hậu Giang về vấn đề bảo vệ sức khỏe lao động cho biết. (Mr Đoàn Đình Duy Khương - General director of Hau Giang Pharmacy about protecting labor health affairs says)</td></tr>
<tr><td>SDNet</td><td>khó phát triển bền vững. (hard to develop stably)</td></tr>
<tr><td>FlowQA</td><td>Ông Đoàn Đình Duy Khương - Tổng Giám đốc điều hành Dược Hậu Gia. (Mr Đoàn Đình Duy Khương - General director of Hau Gia)</td></tr>
<tr><td>GraphQA</td><td>Ông Đoàn Đình Duy Khương - Tổng Giám đốc điều hành Dược Hậu Giang về vấn đề bảo vệ sức khoẻ. (Mr Đoàn Đình Duy Khương - General director of Hau Giang Pharmacy about protecting health affairs)</td></tr>
</table>

back to the previous question-answer Q1-A1 and Q2-A2 to inference the context about the "affected cases of COVID-19" (Q1) and the "detailed of affected cases" (Q2). GraphFlow and FlowQA offer the most relevant answer than DrQA for the question Q3. For question Q5, GraphFlow provides the most relevant answer about the person mentioned in the reading passage, while other models give the answer with redundant information in comparison with the original answer. For the question Q4, both four models cannot give the exact answer. This is due to the ambiguity of Vietnamese interrogative words in questions where it is written in the genuine and non-genuine form. For example, the question Q2: "C th?" can be understood as "**What** is the detail?" or "**How** it happened?". Besides, the question Q4: "Nguy c l g?" can be understood as "**What** is the risk?" or "**How** bad is the risk?". This is known as the MOOD in the Vietnamese. The interrogative clause in Vietnamese consists of two main elements: the negotiatory and the remainders. The negotiatory carries the centroid of the interaction. This aspect of Vietnamese interrogative is described carefully by Thai [20].

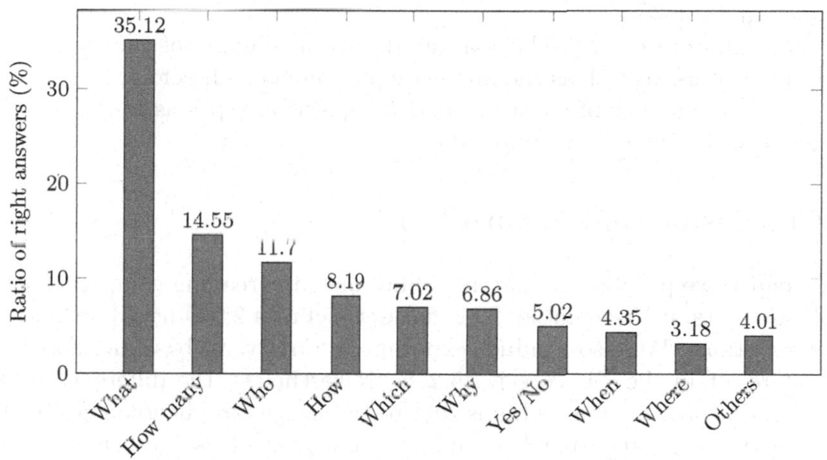

Fig. 2. The impact of question types on the performance of models.

In addition, we study the ability of the models for retrieving correct answers based on the type of questions on the development set. Figure 2 shows the ratio of correct answers by different kinds of questions in the UIT-ViCoQA corpus. A question gives the right answers if the F1-score is greater than 70%. According to Fig. 2, the question type "What" has the highest ratio, which is 35.12%. Besides, the question type "What" accounts for 32.6% as described in Table 3. Therefore, the models mostly give the correct answers to this kind of question. Furthermore, the question types "How many" and "Who" also have a high ratio.

Finally, we analyze the predicted answers on the development set. According to Table 7, there are three types of the answer given by the models, and most of the predicted answers are concentrated on the free-form type, which accounts

Table 7. Types of predicted answer given by the models

Types	Description	Example	Ratio (%)
Matching answers	The predicted answers fully match with truth answers	Q: Việc này có giúp tình trạng tốt lên không? (Does this help improve the condition?) P: Không (No) A: Không (No)	16.73
Free-form answers	The predicted answer only match the a part of truth answers	Q:Tỷ lệ ung thu Việt Nam có cao không? (Is the rate of cancer in Vietnam high?) P: cao (High) A: có (Yes)	59.93
Wrong answers	The predicted answer does not match the truth answer	Q: Béo phì có gây dậy thì sớm không? (Does obesity cause early puberty?) P: Không (No) A: Có (Yes)	23.27

for 59.93%. This is why the F1 and EM scores have a considerable difference, as described in Table 5.

In general, most error predictions are due to the number of questions and the variety of answers, as well as the linguistic phenomena. Therefore, it is necessary to increase the number of questions and the question types as well as enriching answers to make the corpus more diverse.

6 Conclusion and Future Work

In this paper, we propose the dataset about machine reading comprehension for healthcare texts in Vietnamese. This dataset includes 2,000 health articles with 10,000 questions. We also conduct experiments on several baseline models, and the best result in the F1-score is 45.27%. Nevertheless, the difference between F1 and EM scores is large. This is due to the linguistic phenomena about the Vietnamese interrogative particles and the limited answers. Therefore, it is necessary to increase the number of questions and answers as well as make questions and answers more diverse in further research. Besides, enabling the CMC models to capture and understand the contextual meaning of the conversation history is also a challenging task in the conversational machine reading comprehension model researching.

In future, we plan to increase the quantity and quality of the UIT-ViCoQA corpus as well as to conduct further experiments on deep learning and transfer learning using pre-trained language models [4,5,12,18] to enhance the performance of CMC models on the UIT-ViCoQA corpus. Inspired by the conversational question answering system [15], we suggest using this model and UIT-ViCoQA for building Vietnamese conversational question answering systems.

Acknowledgments. We would like to express our thanks to reviewers for their valuable comments to help improve our work. Besides, we would like to thank our annotators for their cooperation.

References

1. Chen, D., Fisch, A., Weston, J., Bordes, A.: Reading wikipedia to answer open-domain questions. In: Proceedings of the 55th Annual Meeting of the Association for Computational Linguistics, Vancouver, Canada, (Volume 1: Long Papers), pp. 1870–1879. Association for Computational Linguistics, July 2017
2. Chen, Y., Wu, L., Zaki, M.J.: Graphflow: exploiting conversation flow with graph neural networks for conversational machine comprehension. In: Bessiere, C. (ed.) Proceedings of the Twenty-Ninth International Joint Conference on Artificial Intelligence, IJCAI-20, pp. 1230–1236. International Joint Conferences on Artificial Intelligence Organization (2020). https://doi.org/10.24963/ijcai.2020/171
3. Choi, E., et al.: QuAC: question answering in context. In: Proceedings of the 2018 Conference on Empirical Methods in Natural Language Processing, Brussels, Belgium, pp. 2174–2184. Association for Computational Linguistics (2018)
4. Conneau, A., et al.: Unsupervised cross-lingual representation learning at scale. In: Proceedings of the 58th Annual Meeting of the Association for Computational Linguistics, pp. 8440–8451. Association for Computational Linguistics, Online, July 2020. https://doi.org/10.18653/v1/2020.acl-main.747
5. Devlin, J., Chang, M.W., Lee, K., Toutanova, K.: BERT: pre-training of deep bidirectional transformers for language understanding. In: Proceedings of the 2019 Conference of the North American Chapter of the Association for Computational Linguistics: Human Language Technologies, Minneapolis, Minnesota, Volume 1 (Long and Short Papers), pp. 4171–4186. Association for Computational Linguistics, June 2019. https://doi.org/10.18653/v1/N19-1423
6. Grave, E., Bojanowski, P., Gupta, P., Joulin, A., Mikolov, T.: Learning word vectors for 157 languages. In: Proceedings of the Eleventh International Conference on Language Resources and Evaluation (LREC 2018), Miyazaki, Japan. European Language Resources Association (ELRA) (2018)
7. Gupta, S., Rawat, B.P.S., Yu, H.: Conversational machine comprehension: a literature review. In: Proceedings of the 28th International Conference on Computational Linguistics, Barcelona, Spain, pp. 2739–2753. International Committee on Computational Linguistics (Online), December 2020
8. Huang, H.Y., Choi, E., Yih, W.t.: FlowQA: grasping flow in history for conversational machine comprehension. arXiv preprint arXiv:1810.06683 (2018)
9. Kočiský, T., et al.: The NarrativeQA reading comprehension challenge. Trans. Assoc. Comput. Linguist. **6**, 317–328 (2018)
10. Labutov, I., Yang, B., Prakash, A., Azaria, A.: Multi-relational question answering from narratives: machine reading and reasoning in simulated worlds. In: Proceedings of the 56th Annual Meeting of the Association for Computational Linguistics, Melbourne, Australia, (Volume 1: Long Papers), pp. 833–844. Association for Computational Linguistics (2018)
11. Lai, G., Xie, Q., Liu, H., Yang, Y., Hovy, E.: RACE: large-scale reading comprehension dataset from examinations. In: Proceedings of the 2017 Conference on Empirical Methods in Natural Language Processing, Copenhagen, Denmark, pp. 785–794. Association for Computational Linguistics, September 2017. https://doi.org/10.18653/v1/D17-1082
12. Nguyen, D.Q., Tuan Nguyen, A.: PhoBERT: pre-trained language models for Vietnamese. In: Findings of the Association for Computational Linguistics: EMNLP 2020, pp. 1037–1042. Association for Computational Linguistics, Online, November 2020. https://doi.org/10.18653/v1/2020.findings-emnlp.92

13. Nguyen, K.V., Tran, K.V., Luu, S.T., Nguyen, A.G.T., Nguyen, N.L.T.: Enhancing lexical-based approach with external knowledge for Vietnamese multiple-choice machine reading comprehension. IEEE Access **8**, 201404–201417 (2020)
14. Nguyen, K., Nguyen, V., Nguyen, A., Nguyen, N.: A Vietnamese dataset for evaluating machine reading comprehension. In: Proceedings of the 28th International Conference on Computational Linguistics, Barcelona, Spain, pp. 2595–2605. International Committee on Computational Linguistics (Online) (2020)
15. Qu, C., Yang, L., Chen, C., Qiu, M., Croft, W.B., Iyyer, M.: Open-retrieval conversational question answering. In: Proceedings of the 43rd International ACM SIGIR Conference on Research and Development in Information Retrieval, pp. 539–548 (2020)
16. Rajpurkar, P., Zhang, J., Lopyrev, K., Liang, P.: SQuAD: 100,000+ questions for machine comprehension of text. In: Proceedings of the 2016 Conference on Empirical Methods in Natural Language Processing, Austin, Texas, pp. 2383–2392. Association for Computational Linguistics (2016)
17. Reddy, S., Chen, D., Manning, C.D.: CoQA: a conversational question answering challenge. Trans. Assoc. Comput. Linguist. **7**, 249–266 (2019)
18. Rogers, A., Kovaleva, O., Rumshisky, A.: A primer in BERTology: what we know about how BERT works. Trans. Assoc. Comput. Linguist. **8**, 842–866 (2020)
19. See, A., Liu, P.J., Manning, C.D.: Get to the point: summarization with pointer-generator networks. In: Proceedings of the 55th Annual Meeting of the Association for Computational Linguistics, Vancouver, Canada, (Volume 1: Long Papers), pp. 1073–1083. Association for Computational Linguistics, July 2017
20. Thai, M.D.: Metafunctional profile of the grammar of Vietnamese. Lang. Typol. Funct. Perspect. **253**, 185–254 (2004)
21. Van Nguyen, K., Van Huynh, T., Nguyen, D.V., Nguyen, A.G.T., Nguyen, N.L.T.: New Vietnamese corpus for machine reading comprehension of health news articles. arXiv preprint arXiv:2006.11138 (2020)
22. Zhu, C., Zeng, M., Huang, X.: SDNet: contextualized attention-based deep network for conversational question answering. arXiv preprint arXiv:1812.03593 (2018)

Bigram Based Deep Neural Network for Extremism Detection in Online User Generated Contents in the Kazakh Language

Shynar Mussiraliyeva, Batyrkhan Omarov(✉), Milana Bolatbek, Kalamkas Bagitova, and Zhanna Alimzhanova

Al-Farabi Kazakh National University, Almaty, Kazakhstan

Abstract. Countering the spread of aggressive information and extremism in the global network is an urgent problem of society and government agencies, which is solved in particular by filtering unwanted Internet resources. A necessary condition for such filtering is the classification of the content of websites, texts and documents of the information flow. Therefore, an urgent problem of information technologies is the classification of texts in natural languages in order to detect extremist texts, such as calls for extremism and other messages that threaten the security of citizens.

Therefore, our research examines the detection of extremist messages in online content in the Kazakh language. To do this, we have collected a corpus of extremist texts from open sources, developed a deep neural network based on bigrams for detecting extremist texts in the Kazakh language. The proposed model has shown high efficiency in comparison with classical methods of machine learning and deep learning.

Keywords: Text classification · Extremism · Machine learning · Deep learning · Deep neural networks

1 Introduction

In the modern world, we accumulate a large amount of data, in particular text data. Natural language processing can be useful in many areas of activity: in industry, in banks, in medicine, etc. [1–3]. We are faced with machine processing of text data every day: search strings on the Internet, online translators, as well as chatbots that are gaining popularity [4, 5]. Traditional methods of natural language processing based on a "bag of words" cannot achieve high quality due to the lack of semantic connections in the representation of words. Recent research has focused on correlations between words, which are useful for revealing hidden semantics. For the subsequent processing of such representations, recurrent and convolutional neural networks with their various modifications are used [6].

Text processing tasks can be divided into two conditional categories. The first one includes tasks that any user faces on a daily basis: spell checking, spam filtering. From

K. Wojtkiewicz et al. (Eds.): ICCCI 2021, CCIS 1463, pp. 559–570, 2021.
https://doi.org/10.1007/978-3-030-88113-9_45

the point of view of researchers in the field of automatic text processing, all these tasks are almost solved, and today the tasks from the second category that require processing large text arrays are more relevant: analyzing opinions and reviews, finding relevant answers to questions ("question-answer" tasks), designing recommendation systems that work with large arrays of unstructured data [7]. A distinctive feature of such tasks is their complexity and lack of formalization, which leads to the fact that they do not yet have a full set of solutions, but use auxiliary methods for classifying texts and highlighting keywords and phrases [8].

At the moment, one of the most popular tasks is to understand the text. This task includes: classification, translation, answers to questions, etc. In this article, we will consider the problem of text classification by deep learning methods of neural networks for detecting extremist texts. The classification problem is one of the traditional ones in machine learning, and therefore there are training data for training neural networks. There are many solutions to this problem [9–11]. In our study, we propose possible solutions to the problem of text classification and a model based on deep learning for detecting extremist texts for the Kazakh-language segment of the Internet, with the results of testing on test samples that were collected by us from open sources.

2 Related Works

In this section, we show the works which have been done in the field of classification of texts into extremist and noon-extremist categories.

In their work, Ahmad et al. [12] proposed a system which classifies tweets into extremist and non-extremist classes using deep learning-based sentiment analysis methods. This system consists of three modules: collection of tweets, preprocessing phase and classification of tweets by LSTM + CNN model and methods of machine learning and deep learning.

Salminen et al. [13] presented a framework, which classifies comments in YouTube, Reddit, Wikipedia, and Twitter into hateful and non-hateful categories using several machine learning models such as Logistic Regression, Naïve Bayes, Support Vector Machines, XGBoost, and Neural Networks. In this research, the following features were used: Bag-of-Words, TF-IDF, Word2Vec, BERT, and their combination.

Johnston et al. [14] developed a method which classifies a text into four types of extremist speech which were used in groups: Sunni Islamic, Antifascist Groups, White Nationalists and Sovereign Citizens. Experiments conducted by LSTM models.

Duwairi et al. [15] investigated how deep learning methods such as CNN, CNN-LSTM, and BiLSTM-CNN classified and detected Arabic hate speech texts in social networks. The experiment consists of three parts: (i) the binary classification of tweets into Hate or Normal, (ii) classification of tweets into three classes (Hate, Abusive, or Normal), (iii)multi-class classification of tweets into (Misogyny, Racism, Religious Discrimination, Abusive, and Normal). In binary classification the highest accuracy obtained in the CNN model. In the classification of tweets into three classes, CNN and BiLSTM-CNN models showed the highest accuracy of 74%. In the multi-class classification task, CNN-LSTM and the BiLSTM-CNN models resulted with an accuracy of 73%.

Sharif et al. [16] presented a model which classifies Bengali text into non-suspicious and suspicious categories using machine learning methods. Authors used BoW and tf-idf feature extraction methods.

Armaan et al. [17] used an LSTM model to determine radical texts in social media. Texts were collected from news, articles and blogs, after that data were annotated by domain experts to categories Radical(R), Non-Radical (NR) and Irrelevant (I). The proposed methods showed a precision of 85.9%.

In their research, Irfan Uddin et al. [18], created models to determine the meanings of the actions of terrorists using deep neural networks. Models were conducted by single-layer neural network (NN), five-layer DNN, and three traditional machine learning algorithms, such as logistic regression, SVM, and Naıve Bayes.

Rehman et al. [19] aimed to detect radical texts in web-resources. Researchers created a new dataset in order to investigate the usage of violent and bad words in radical, neutral and random groups by using violent, terrorism and bad words dictionaries. Authors have used TF-IDF method to extract radical keywords from the radical corpus and the religious keywords from the religious corpus. In addition, unigrams and bigrams used to identify the keywords in above-mentioned categories.

Soliman et al. [20] presented a framework to predict the terrorist organizations' networks in planning terror activities in different regions. The developed approach based on several Operations Research (OR) and Decision support tools with Data Mining (DM) techniques.

Abd-Elaal et al. [21] proposed an approach, which determines ISIS online community in Twitter by using both linguistic and behavioral features of Twitter users. The proposed framework consists of two main parts: (i) crawling module, (ii) inquiring module.

3 Materials and Methods

3.1 Data Collection

The corpus is assembled on the basis of Kazakh-language posts of the Vkontakte social network platform [18]. The corpus is created to solve the problem of classifying texts into 2 classes. To train the classifier, the corpus should be divided into positive, neutral collections, each of which contains approximately the same number of texts. The corpus should be representative enough to build a dictionary of emotionally charged terms on its basis. "Sufficiently representative corpus" means that adding new posts to the collection will entail adding a very small number of new terms.

The method described in [19] showed the effectiveness of using emoticons (special symbols-icons denoting emotions in written messages) to automatically classify texts into positive and negative. With high accuracy, you can determine the emotion of a message if the author has specified a symbol indicating emotions. Therefore, first of all, dictionaries of symbols denoting the positive and negative attitude of the author were compiled.

In accordance with the written designation of emotions, a keyword search was performed and two collections were formed. These collections will be used for subsequent analysis of messages and identification of patterns of extremist texts. To form a collection of neutral messages, messages from news accounts of microblogs were taken.

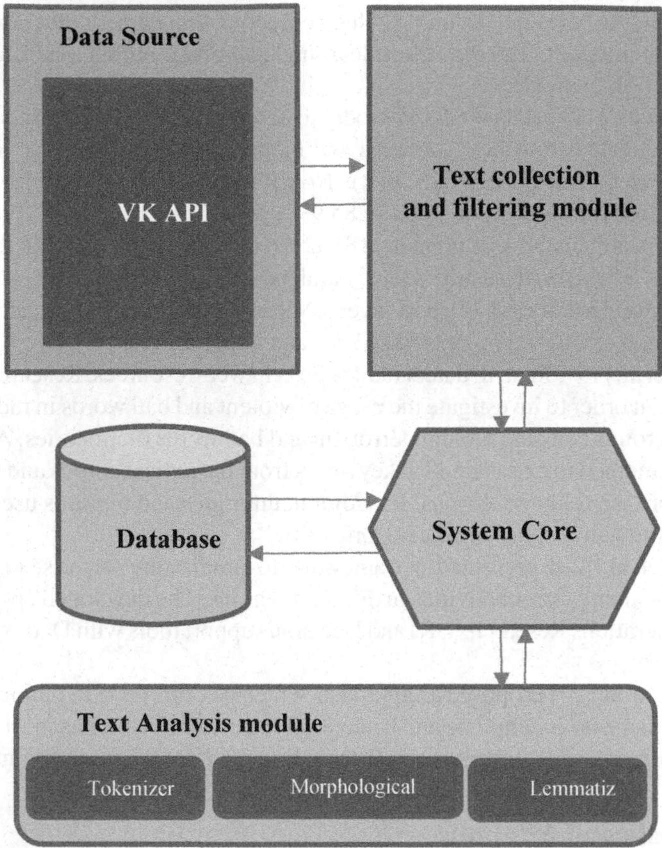

Fig. 1. Data collection and preprocessing architecture

The core of the software module is responsible for the interaction between user databases, text collection modules and their subsequent processing modules. Social system APIs return data via a web interface in JSON or XML format. To get the data from Vkontakte social network, we used VK API [20] that allows to get 1% of all data for research studies. Schematically, the architecture of the software module is shown in Fig. 1.

3.2 Dataset Exploration

To understand radicalized individuals, we analyzed the words, languages, and topics in, online user content. Figure 2 shows distribution of extremism related and neutral posts in the dataset. Figure 2a illustrates distribution of extremism related texts; Fig. 2b demonstrates neutral texts in the dataset.

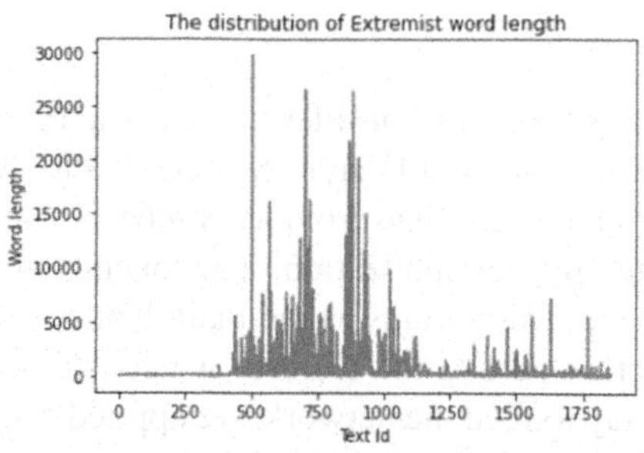

(a) Distribution of extremism related posts

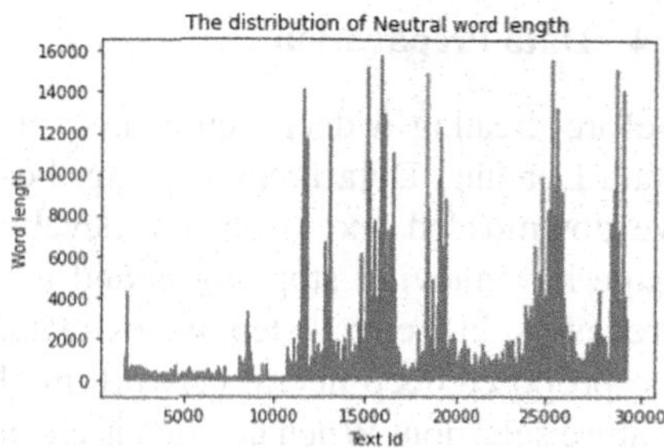

(b) Distribution of neutral posts

Fig. 2. Distribution of collected data in the dataset

Figure 3 illustrates world cloud of bigrams for the collected corpora. As it can be seen from the figure, they have quietly different result. It can lead to hypothesis that training the model based on bigrams can give good result in classification of texts.

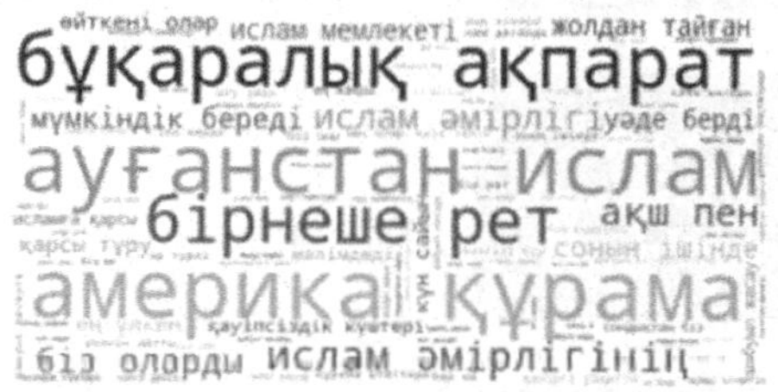

(a) Bigrams of extremism related texts

(b) Bigrams of neutral texts

Fig. 3. Worldcloud of bigrams for the collected dataset

3.3 Data Preprocessing

The primary preprocessing is to replace large letters with small ones, and to remove uninformative and rare characters. The following characters were classified as uninformative characters: tab, line feed, long sequence of identical characters (for example, a set of three or more asterisks), etc. Rare characters include characters that are used no more than a few dozen times in the entire sample.

The next stage of preprocessing is the conversion to vectors or numbers. There are various methods of preprocessing text data [21]. In this work, we used character-by-character conversion of text to vectors.

Character-by-character text conversion allows you to convert text to a vector for a neural network with the least amount of time. Each character is replaced with its corresponding vector, and no additional calculations are required. In this work, we used the Embedding layer, which converts characters to vectors automatically. Before feeding data to the layer, you need to replace the characters with their corresponding numbers.

3.4 Data Preparation

Before creating a deep neural network model we should consider several stages as Data Loading, Data Preprocessing, Feature Extraction, and Feature Selection. Firstly, we downloaded texts from the developed corpora, after that provided preprocessing stage by removing stop words and using stemming, lemmatization, and tokenization processes. In the next step, we extracted unigrams and bigrams as the main features of the proposed deep neural network model. After extracting the features we considered feature selection. When the data is clean and ready to feed the network, we applied deep neural network to classify the texts. Figure 4 describes all the mentioned data preparation process that contains Loading, Preprocessing, Feature Extraction, Feature Selection, and Classification.

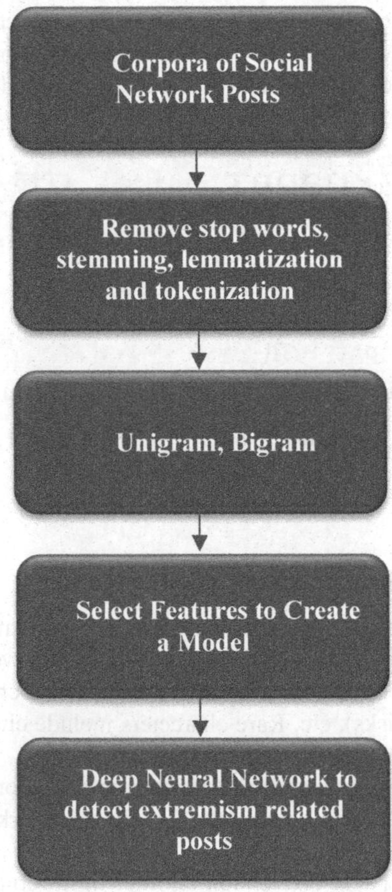

Fig. 4. Text classification flowchart.

3.5 The Proposed Model (Deep Neural Network)

This work focuses on detection of extremist messages in Kazakh language using deep learning methods in order to classify texts into extremist and non-extremist categories. During the experiments, we classified texts using classical LSTM model, but in this case, model overfitted quickly. In order to avoid this problem we combined bigrams and TF-IDF features in order to increase evaluation measures of the classification. We obtained robust results by using proposed neural network architecture with bigram and TF-IDF features on all evaluation measure than traditional LSTM model. The architecture of the proposed method shown in the Fig. 5.

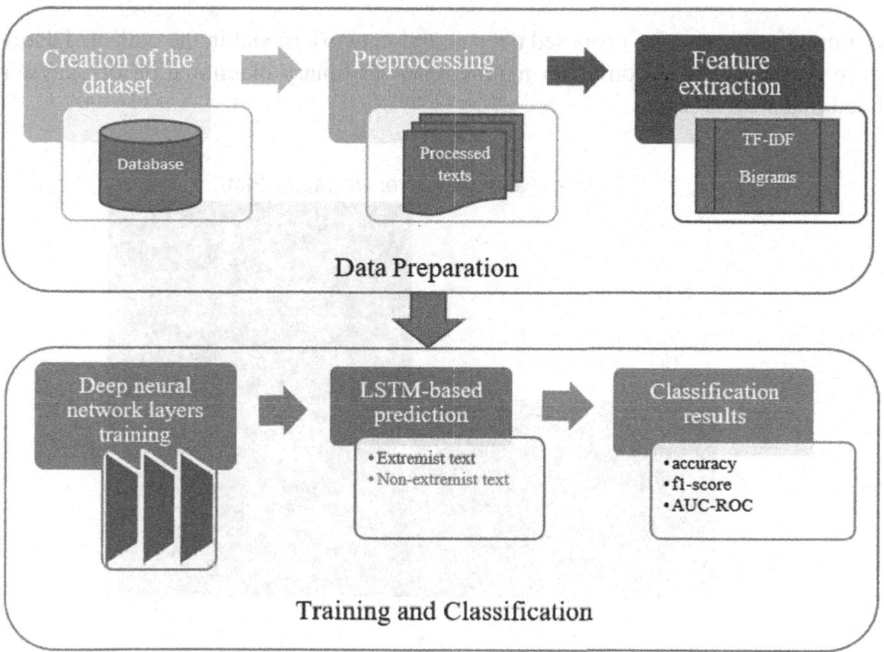

Fig. 5. Architecture of the proposed method

3.6 Evaluation

The findings of a prediction model can be visualized using a confusion matrix. The classes are represented by the rows of the matrix, whereas the actual classes are represented by the columns. The matrix displays the values of true positives (TP), false positives (FP), false negatives (FN), and true negatives (TN) for a given class. (TNc). Several efficiency indicators, such as Precision, Recall, and F1-Score, can be calculated using the confusion matrix [22]:

$$precision = \frac{TP}{TP + FP} \tag{1}$$

$$recall = \frac{TP}{TP + FN} \tag{2}$$

$$F1 = \frac{2 \cdot precision \cdot recall}{precision + recall} \tag{3}$$

$$accuracy = \frac{TP + TN}{TP + FN + TN + FP} \tag{4}$$

4 Experiment Results

We trained and tested the proposed deep neural network model in the collected dataset. Figure 6 demonstrates confusion matrix result in binary classification of extremism related and neutral posts.

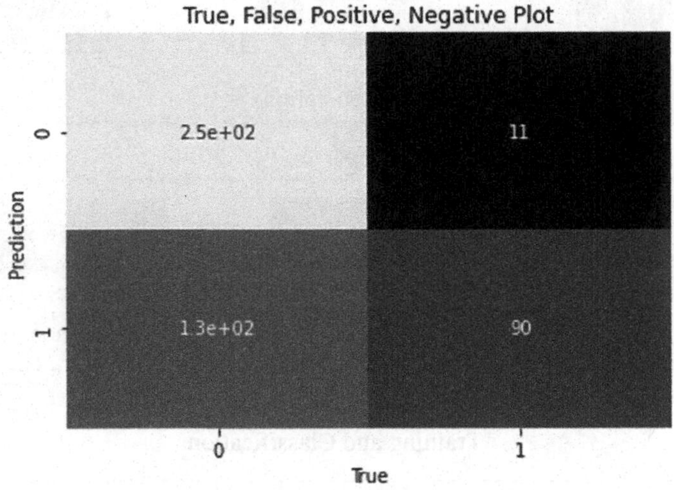

Fig. 6. Confusion matrix.

We also used Area Under the Receive Operator Curve (AUC-ROC curve) to test the result of binary classification [23]. As our model classify the texts to extremism related and neutral, AUC-ROC Curve is one of the good evaluation criteria. Figure 7 illustrates AUC-ROC curve in classification of extremism related and non-related texts. The results show that, the proposed model shows high efficiency in detecting extremism related posts.

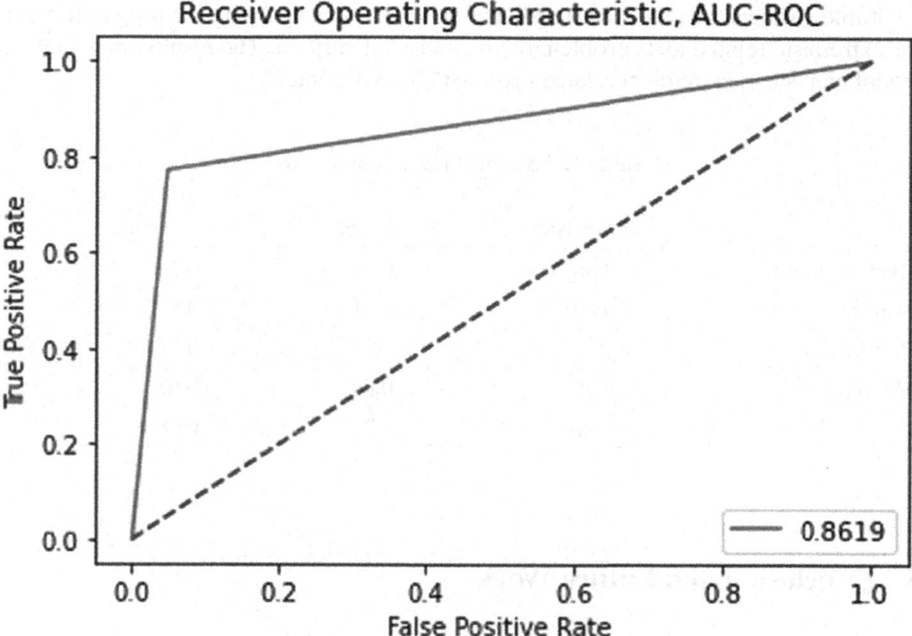

Fig. 7. AUC-ROC curve for text classification

Figure 8 compares the proposed model with classical machine learning algorithms and lstm as representative of deep learning. The proposed model shows high performance in accuracy for extremism related texts detection problem in the Kazakh language. Also, it should be noted that, applying lstm gave overfitting for the given dataset.

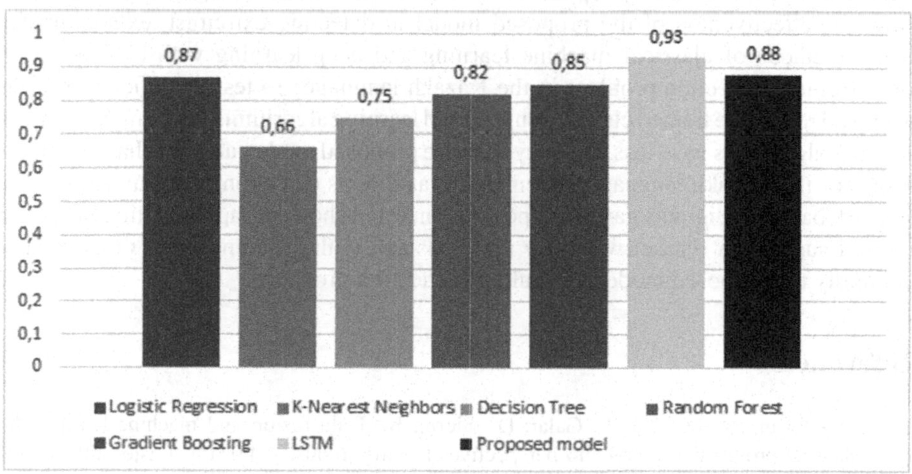

Fig. 8. Comparison of classification results of machine learning and deep learning methods

Table 1 shows the precision, recall and f1-score when applying the proposed model for extremism related texts problem on the collected corpora. The results show that our model can detect extremism related texts with 88% accuracy.

Table 1. Extremism detection in texts.

	Precision	Recall	F1-score
Extremist related	0.66	0.96	0.78
Neutral	0.89	0.41	0.57
Performance			0.71
Macro avg	0.78	0.69	0.67
Weighted avg	0.77	0.71	0.68

5 Conclusion and Future Work

As a result of the work, a software package was created for collecting and analyzing short messages in the Kazakh language to identify the content of extremist texts. With the help of the software package, a corpus of texts collected on the basis of the posts of the Vkontakte social network is built. The corpora is manually divided into two classes: extremist orientation, neutral. Each text in the corpus contains attributes that allow us to draw conclusions about the relevance of the statement and the strength of its impact on readers, the significance of the message. The second contribution of this research is the development of a deep neural network model for detecting extremist texts. We have developed a deep neural network model based on bigram and the results show the effectiveness of the proposed model in detecting extremist texts compared to the methods of classical machine learning and deep learning with 88% accuracy for extremism detection problem in the Kazakh language. To test the efficiency of the proposed results we trained classical supervised learning algorithms and lstm. Supervised learning algorithms gave less accuracy than the proposed model, and lstm has overfitted. Thus, for the Kazakh language extremism related texts detection problem deep neural network based on bigrams gave high performance and shown its applicability. In further, we will supply our dataset with new materials and with different forms of extremism and apply the proposed model for multiclassification problem.

References

1. Diez-Olivan, A., Del Ser, J., Galar, D., Sierra, B.: Data fusion and machine learning for industrial prognosis: trends and perspectives towards Industry 4.0. Inf. Fusion **50**, 92–111 (2019)
2. Da Li, X., Duan, L.: Big data for cyber physical systems in industry 4.0: a survey. Enterp. Inf. Syst. **13**(2), 148–169 (2019). https://doi.org/10.1080/17517575.2018.1442934

3. Kendzhaeva, B., Omarov, B., Abdiyeva, G., Anarbayev, A., Dauletbek, Y., Omarov, B.: Providing safety for citizens and tourists in cities: a system for detecting anomalous sounds. In: Luhach, A.K., Jat, D.S., Ghazali, K.H.B., Gao, X.-Z., Lingras, P. (eds.) Advanced Informatics for Computing Research: 4th International Conference, ICAICR 2020, Gurugram, India, December 26–27, 2020, Revised Selected Papers, Part I, pp. 264–273. Springer Singapore, Singapore (2021). https://doi.org/10.1007/978-981-16-3660-8_25
4. Sinha, S., Basak, S., Dey, Y., Mondal, A.: An educational Chatbot for answering queries. In: Mandal, J.K., Bhattacharya, D. (eds.) Emerging Technology in Modelling and Graphics. AISC, vol. 937, pp. 55–60. Springer, Singapore (2020). https://doi.org/10.1007/978-981-13-7403-6_7
5. Ait-Mlouk, A., Jiang, L.: KBot: a knowledge graph based chatBot for natural language understanding over linked data. IEEE Access **8**, 149220–149230 (2020)
6. Alshemali, B., Kalita, J.: Improving the reliability of deep neural networks in NLP: a review. Knowle. Based Syst. **191**, 105210 (2020). KBot: a Knowledge graph based chatBot for natural language understanding over linked data
7. Manogaran, G., Varatharajan, R., Priyan, M.K.: Hybrid recommendation system for heart disease diagnosis based on multiple kernel learning with adaptive neuro-fuzzy inference system. Multimedia Tools Appl. **77**(4), 4379–4399 (2017). https://doi.org/10.1007/s11042-017-5515-y
8. Mussiraliyeva, S., Bolatbek, M., Omarov, B., Bagitova, K.: Detection of extremist ideation on social media using machine learning techniques. In: Nguyen, N.T., Hoang, B.H., Huynh, C.P., Hwang, D., Trawiński, B., Vossen, G. (eds.) Computational Collective Intelligence: 12th International Conference, ICCCI 2020, Da Nang, Vietnam, November 30 – December 3, 2020, Proceedings, pp. 743–752. Springer International Publishing, Cham (2020). https://doi.org/10.1007/978-3-030-63007-2_58
9. Altınel, B., Ganiz, M.C.: Semantic text classification: a survey of past and recent advances. Inf. Process. Manage. **54**(6), 1129–1153 (2018)
10. Murzamadieva, M., Ivashov, A., Omarov, B., Omarov, B., Kendzhayeva, B., Abdrakhmanov, R.: Development of a system for ensuring humidity in sport complexes. In: 2021 11th International Conference on Cloud Computing, Data Science & Engineering (Confluence), pp. 530–535. IEEE (2021)
11. Sinoara, R.A., Camacho-Collados, J., Rossi, R.G., Navigli, R., Rezende, S.O.: Knowledge-enhanced document embeddings for text classification. Knowl. Based Syst. **163**, 955–971 (2019)
12. Ahmad, S., Asghar, M.Z., Alotaibi, F.M. et al.: Detection and classification of social media-based extremist affiliations using sentiment analysis techniques. Human-centric Comput. Inf. Sci. **9**(24) (2019). https://doi.org/10.1186/s13673-019-0185-6
13. Salminen, J., Hopf, M., Chowdhury, S.A., Jung, S.-G., Almerekhi, H., Jansen, B.J.: Developing an online hate classifier for multiple social media platforms. Human-centric Comput. Inf. Sci. **10**(1), 1–34 (2020). https://doi.org/10.1186/s13673-019-0205-6
14. Johnston, A., Marku, A.: Identifying extremism in text using deep learning. In: Pedrycz, W., Chen, S.-M. (eds.) Development and Analysis of Deep Learning Architectures. SCI, vol. 867, pp. 267–289. Springer, Cham (2020). https://doi.org/10.1007/978-3-030-31764-5_10
15. Duwairi, R., Hayajneh, A., Quwaider, M.: A deep learning framework for automatic detection of hate speech embedded in Arabic tweets. Arab. J. Sci. Eng. **46**(4), 4001–4014 (2021). https://doi.org/10.1007/s13369-021-05383-3
16. Sharif, O., Hoque, M.M., Kayes, A.S.M., Nowrozy, R., Sarker, I.H.: Detecting suspicious texts using machine learning techniques. Appl. Sci. **10**(18), 6527 (2020). https://doi.org/10.3390/app10186527
17. Armaan, K, Saini, J.K., Bansal, D.: Detecting radical text over online media using deep learning. Comput. Sci. Math. ArXiv abs/1907.12368 (2019)

18. Vk.com – Vkontakte Social Network
19. Huang, F., Zhang, S., Zhang, J., Yu, G.: Multimodal learning for topic sentiment analysis in microblogging. Neurocomputing **253**, 144–153 (2017). https://doi.org/10.1016/j.neucom.2016.10.086
20. https://vk.com/dev/methods
21. Kadhim, A.I.: Survey on supervised machine learning techniques for automatic text classification. Artif. Intell. Rev. **52**(1), 273–292 (2019). https://doi.org/10.1007/s10462-018-09677-1
22. Sun, S., Cao, Z., Zhu, H., Zhao, J.: A survey of optimization methods from a machine learning perspective. IEEE Trans. Cybern. **50**(8), 3668–3681 (2019)
23. Khan, F.A., Ibrahim, A.A., Rais, M.S., Rajpoot, P., Khan, A., Akhtar, M.N.: Performance analysis of supervised learning algorithms based on classification approach. In: 2019 IEEE 6th International Conference on Engineering Technologies and Applied Sciences (ICETAS), pp. 1–6. IEEE (2019). DOI: https://doi.org/10.1109/ICETAS48360.2019.9117394

Computational Collective Intelligence and Natural Language Processing

Cbow Training Time and Accuracy Optimization Using SkipGram

Toufik Mechouma[1(✉)], Ismail Biskri[2(✉)], Jean Guy Meunier[1(✉)], and Alaidine Ben Ayed[1(✉)]

[1] University of Quebec in Montreal, Montreal, QC, Canada
{mechouma.toufik,benayed_alaidine}@courrier.uqam.ca,
meunier.jean_guy@uqam.ca

[2] University of Quebec in Trois Rivieres, Trois Rivieres, QC, Canada
ismail.biskri@uqtr.ca

Abstract. Most word embedding techniques get their theoretical foundation from distributional semantics theory. They have been among the most popular trends of natural language processing for the last two decades. They have a large range of application. The present paper presents an overview of recent word embedding techniques. Furthermore, it proposes an optimized continuous bag of word (Cbow) model. The experiments we conducted show that the proposed approach outperforms the classic Cbow technique in terms of accuracy and training time.

Keywords: Natural language processing · Distributional semantics · Word embedding

1 Introduction

The semantic web's goal is to make machines communicate with each other across the internet [1], whereas word embedding's ultimate goal is to make machines able to capture the meaning of human language. The latter is considered to be a hard problem of AI [2]. Much concurrent research was conducted during the 1960s. Author in [3] introduced the first algebraic model of natural language understanding (NLU). A year afterward, [4] proposed an interactive natural language understanding approach. Moreover, author in [5] unveiled the conceptual dependency theory for natural language understanding. NLU has always been a multidisciplinary research area. It interfaces with other fields like psychology, cognitive sciences, philosophy of language and linguistics [6]. Word embedding techniques can be classified as a) statistical models and b) connectionist models [9]. The statistical approaches are frequency-based models [7,8], while the conntionist approaches are based on neuronal networks architectures [9]. Both

The authors would like to thank the Natural Sciences and Engineering Research Council of Canada (NSERC) as well as the Canadian Social Sciences and Humanities Research Council (SSHRC) for funding this work.

K. Wojtkiewicz et al. (Eds.): ICCCI 2021, CCIS 1463, pp. 573–585, 2021.
https://doi.org/10.1007/978-3-030-88113-9_46

models have shown impressive results. However, the perfect understanding of human language; remains far from reach.

Firstly, this paper sheds the light on current word embedding techniques by breaking down their algorithms. Secondly, it discusses the advantages and disadvantages of each approach. Finally, it proposes an optimized Cbow model.

2 Word Embedding Overview

During the last few decades, many word embedding models have appeared. Some notable ones include Word2Vec, GloVe and FastText. Also, new trends have been introduced, such as sentence embedding, context embedding and graph embedding. It seems like capturing meaning from text has become rather fashionable. There are many prolific researchers working on word embedding. We are barely able to read the related articles, as the research is moving so fast. We will first dissect Word2Vec as a connctionist model. We will explore both the SkipGram and Cbow models. Secondly we will break down the global vector GLOVE model as a statistical model. We will end with a conclusion about both statistical and connctionist models. Before we jump to the previously mentioned models, we consider prior historical overview to be necessary. We will begin with the vector space models introduced in 1970s based on the work of [8]. They are the first models that compute text documents, where each document is represented as a vector [8].

$$Vd = [W_{1d}, W_{2d}, ..., W_{Nd}] \tag{1}$$

The weight vector for document d

$$W_{td} = tf_{td} \cdot \log \frac{|D|}{|\{d' \in D \mid t \in d'\}|} \tag{2}$$

The weight computing formula

tf_{td} : is term frequency of term t in document d

$$\log \frac{|D|}{|\{d' \in D \mid t \in d'\}|} \tag{3}$$

The numerator stands for the total number of documents, while the denominator stands for the total number of documents containing the term t.

The concept of the co-occurrence matrix is used in vector space models. It assumes that columns and rows represent either documents or words. It aims to study the correlation between columns and rows [7]. Like any other model, the space vector model was impressive since it appeared. However, it suffers from many limits, particularly with large documents (known as the curse of dimensionality). In addition to lexical and semantic sensitivity, similar contexts with different terms won't be similar, etc. It would be unfair, if we focused only on the weaknesses of the vector space models. They are very simple to apprehend. They have a powerful ability to perform continuous similarity measurements on documents. Also, they allow for ranking documents based on their relevance. Years after the appearence of the space vector model, a new paradigm of word embedding was designed based on a simple artificial neural network perceptron with one hidden layer. It consists of learning word representation based on neighborhood. The Word2Vec model proved a source of inspiration and competition. A year later, author in [11] proposed GLOVE. It was like a spiritual return to vector space models because of its impressive results, however, it uses an old concept. The GLOVE team criticized the context coverage proposed by Word2Vec. They proposed incorporating the co-occurence matrix in order to ensure a global context coverage. It performed better than Word2Vec on some training datasets. In 2016, Word2Vec was extended by the work of [12]. They introduced FASTTEXT, which is another version of Word2Vec. The representation of a word is learned based on acquired n-grams through performing a windowing on the word's letters. After that, a SkipGram model is trained using the resulting samples. The challenge didn't diminish. Media Lab's team headed by Marvin Minsky since 1999; created ConceptNet. It is a sophisticated knowledge graph applied to the word embedding process [13]. The paper was published in 2017. It was ranked first in the Semantic Evaluation conference. It was the finest of knowledge graph-based word embedding models. They called it the ConceptNet NumberBatch [14]. In contrast with Word2Vec and GLOVE, the ConceptNet NumberBatch's word representation approach seems to share a perspective with ontologies. It consists of representing a portion of the world based on knowledge graphs, instead of the ordinary textual format [13]. Of course, there are several others works related to this model. However, we cannot present all of them in this paper (Fig. 1).

2.1 Word2Vec (Skip-Gram, Cbow)

For the sake of clarity, we first explain the one-hot vector representation. It is a key element of the Word2Vec approach. It consists of representing the vocabulary numerically. Given a text T of n vocabulary: $T = \{w_1, w_2, ...w_n\}$

$$\begin{bmatrix} w_1 \\ 1 \\ 0 \\ . \\ . \\ 0 \\ 0 \end{bmatrix} \begin{bmatrix} w_2 \\ 0 \\ 1 \\ . \\ . \\ 0 \\ 0 \end{bmatrix} .... \begin{bmatrix} w_n \\ 0 \\ 0 \\ . \\ . \\ 0 \\ 1 \end{bmatrix}$$

Fig. 1. One-hot vector representation

Each word w_i of the vocabulary, will have a unique corresponding vector with one as a value in a unique position compared to other words.

SkipGram: The architecture of the SkipGram model contains three layers:

1) The entry layer: it consists of a set of one- hot vectors corresponding each to a word among the training dataset vocabulary. If we assume a corpora of 10 000 vocabularies, then, the one-hot vector will have V = 10 000 as dimension, with the value of one in the position that corresponds uniquely to the related word. The one-hot vector representation is considered to be very greedy [9].
2) The hidden layer: we need to keep in mind that we are using a simple artificial neural network in Word2Vec. Hence, the hidden layer is computed from the dot product of the one-hot vector and the weights matrix W_i composed of V rows and N columns where V is the number of the vocabulary, and N is the number of the neurons in the hidden layer. The dot product result produces a vector H of N dimensions [9].

$$H = OneHotVector \cdot W_i \tag{4}$$

3) The output layer: it corresponds to the output vector. We proceed as following, we perform a dot product one more time between the vector H, which we obtained previously and the output weights matrix W_o. The result is the vector U of V dimension. After that, we apply a Softmax function on U, in order to have normal probabilistic distribution. The intuition behind this, is to maximize the likelihood function given a center word, to predict context words [9].

$$U = H \cdot W_o \tag{5}$$

$$P(w^{(c)}; w^{(t)}) = -\sum_{c=1}^{C} log \frac{exp(W_{output_{(c)}} \cdot h)}{\sum_{i=1}^{V} exp(W_{output_{(i)}} \cdot H)} \tag{6}$$

Now, we compute the error by subtracting the obtained Y vector and the prior context encoded as one-hot vectors respectively. If we assume a window of 2, then four one-hot vectors are needed for context words. After that, we sum the vectors errors to get the global error. Thus, we use it to perform back-propagation. For each iteration, we measure the loss in order to determine, whether we should stop learning or not [9].

$$W_{input}^{(new)} = W_{input}^{(old)} - \eta \cdot y \cdot (W_{output}^{T} \sum_{c=1}^{C} e_c) \tag{7}$$

$$W_{output}^{(new)} = W_{output}^{(old)} - \eta \cdot h \cdot \sum_{c=1}^{C} e_c \tag{8}$$

where η is the learning rate, h is the hidden layer vector and y is the predicted context vector. After summing the errors, we proceed to back-propagation by computing the gradient Δ, between both input and output matrices. We keep looping-back until we reach an acceptable error value.

Cbow: The architecture of the Cbow, also contains three layers, but it is slightly different:

1) The entry layer: the same as SkipGram. It consists of a set of one-hot vector correspond to a word among the vocabulary of the training dataset. The only difference, is that the input represents one-hot vectors of context words, instead of the center word. If we assume that the window's size equals 2, we will have four one-hot-vectors of context words. We multiply each one by the input weight matrix W_o, and we compute after that the average vector H.

$$H_i = OneHotVector_i \cdot W_i \tag{9}$$

$$H_i = Mean(H_1, ..., H_i) \tag{10}$$

2) The hidden layer: it contains the final result of the previous operations. In other words, we have the H vector as explained above. In the same way as SkipGram, we perform the dot product of H with the output matrix Wo, to get the U vector that we will use to produce the probability distribution, using a Softmax function.
3) The output layer: it contains the predicted vector, with a probability distribution, that we will compare to the center word's one-hot vector in order to compute the error and trigger the back-propagation loop. Both models provide, after a couple of epochs, a matrix of center words, where each row represents a unique word vector. The weakness of both models is that the created embedding vectors depend entirely on the training set. This means that if we change the training set, we may not have the same embedding vectors for the same words.

2.2 GloVe

The Global vector is a statistical model based on matrix co-occurrence and factorization. It refers to an observation. The log of the co-occurrence frequency equals the scalar value of the dot product between row and column that correspond to the pairs of words. It proposes a co-occurrence matrix for the sake of a better coverage of the global context, instead of local windowing, such in the case of Word2Vec [11]. The matrix factorization consists of a set of iterations to learn an approximated matrix to the co-occurrence matrix. At the end, GLOVE considers the two produced matrices to be center and context words matrices. They are the equivalent of W_i and W_o matrices in the Word2Vec model. Global matrix factorization is called Latent Semantic Analysis (LSA) when it is applied to term frequency matrices [7] (Fig. 2).

$$R = P \cdot Q^t \tag{11}$$

where P is the center words matrix and Q^t is the context words matrix.

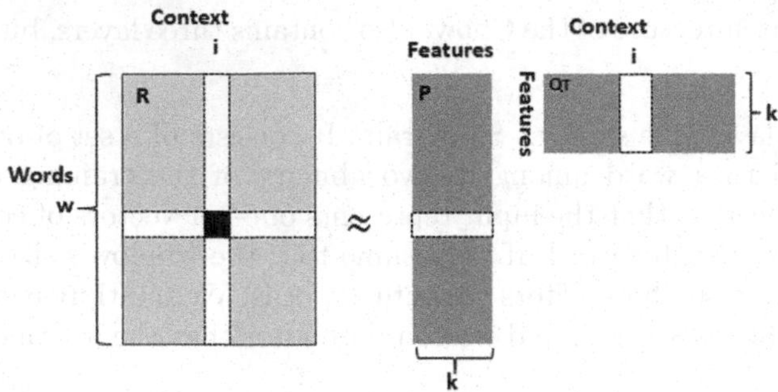

Fig. 2. Matrix factorization.

2.3 ConceptNet NumberBatch

1) ConceptNet is a word-based knowledge graph. It is composed of hyper-graphs, nodes and edges. The project of ConceptNet started in 1999, under the direction of Marvin Minsky. It is used for word embedding by Havasi and Speer in 2017 at the Semantic evaluation conference [14]. The idea of the ConceptNet NumberBatch, is to perform a word embedding on a graph, that represents a portion of the word. Here, we are talking about concepts instead of lexemes. So the word embedding of the ConceptNet NumberBatch will be different than GloVe and Word2Vec, which are data-driven approaches. The NumberBatch embedding consists of building an adjacency matrix, related to a concept represented by a lexeme. Then, a pruning is applied to the matrix to eliminate the nodes with less than 3 edges. After that, we compute the positive pointwise mutual information matrix (PPMI Matrix). The PPMI matrix is then factorized using the singular values decomposition metric [14].

$$A = U \begin{bmatrix} d & 0 & 0 \\ 0 & d_j & 0 \\ 0 & 0 & d_n \end{bmatrix} V \tag{12}$$

The singular value decomposition (SVD) is a matrix factorization process. If A is a $n \times m$ matrix, then, we may write A as a product of three factors:

$$A = U \Sigma V^* \tag{13}$$

where U is an orthogonal $n \times n$ matrix. V is an orthogonal $m \times m$ matrix. V^* is the transpose of V, and Σ is an $n \times m$ matrix, that has all zeros except for its diagonal entries, which are non-negative real numbers. If σ_{ij} is the i, j entry of Σ, then $\sigma_{ij} = 0$. Unless $i = j$ and $\sigma_{ii} = \sigma_i \geq 0$. The σ_i are the singular values and the columns of u and v. They are respectively the right and left singular vectors.

In the same way as GLOVE, the SVD factorization process of the positive pointwise mutual information matrix, will generate three matrix. We will be interested in the U and V matrix because they will respectively represent the center and context word vectors. We consider this to be a new vision of embedding. It might be classified as a hybrid approach between rule and data-driven approaches. The ConceptNet team didn't stop at this level, they tried to enhance the embedding more and more by referring to a technique called retrofitting! [14].

2) Retrofitting consists of adjusting the vectors of pretrained vectors, particularly those of Word2Vec. Retrofitting was introduced by [15]. The idea behind it is to profit from the knowledge graph's wealth of information and to combine it with the powerful learning ability of the neural networks.

The objective is to learn the matrix $Q = (q_1, q_2, ..., q_n)$ such that each q_i is both close to its counter part in Q' and Ω where Ω represents an ontology. (V,E) is an undirected graph and Q' matrix that represents the pretrained vectors for W_i. It belongs to the set of the vertices V. It's a kind of trade-off between both matrices Q and Q'.

$$\Psi(Q) = \sum_{n=1}^{n} \left[\alpha_i \left\| q_i - q_i^{\wedge} \right\|^2 + \sum_{(i,j)\in E} \beta_{ij \| q_i - q_j \|^2} \right] \tag{14}$$

where α and β values control the relative strengths of associations.

2.4 Comparison Between Word Embedding Techniques

So far, we have meticulously reviewed the Word2Vec, GLOVE and ConceptNet NumberBatch models. We may classify them as following. Both Word2Vec models are connectionist models, while GlOVE is a statistical model, and ConceptNet NumberBatch is a merge between rules and a statistical model.

Word2Vec is a powerful approach. However, it is still dependent to the training dataset, with a weak ability for generalisation. The local context windowing limits the ability to capture meaning, in addition to the failure of Cbow with rare words. On the other hand, GLOVE with its global context windowing performs better than Word2Vec in word analogy tasks. GLOVE covers the context better by considering the relationships between word pairs, rather than word to word neighborhoods. On the other hand, the model is trained on the co-occurrence matrix of words. It takes a lot of memory for storage, especially if we change the hyper-parameters related to the co-occurrence matrix, where we have to reconstruct the matrix again. This is considered to be very time-consuming. Both models are still far from achieving the ultimate objective of capturing meaning. Finally, ConceptNet NumberBatch was an innovative idea, since it allows us to perform word embedding on structured formats, which reflect concepts in the real world, rather than unstructured text. This representation is supposed to help in performing lexical disambiguation. It opens the door to multiple graph theory operations, to measure similarity between concepts represented by semantic lexicons. Meanwhile, the knowledge graphs are still related to the experts and their representation of the world, so it does not systematically represent the unique reality about the world. Furthermore, it is still so greedy in how it expresses prior knowledge about the world. It also obeys to the same limits of rule-driven approaches. We believe that in the future, developing hybrid approaches that combine the strong points of the data-driven and rule-driven approaches will help enhance word embedding.

3 The Proposed Approach

SkipGram and Cbow are considered to be a good contribution to the word representation learning community. Both are connectionist models based on neural networks. The main contrast is that SkipGram aims to learn word representation by maximization of a likelihood function and it considers a given center word and a context words to be predicted, whereas Cbow acts roughly the same way, unless, it takes context words as given words and the center word as a target. Results showed that SkipGram works well with a small set of training data, and it represents even rare words or phrases well. This is in contrast to Cbow, which is much faster to train than the skip-gram, with slightly better accuracy for frequent words [9].

Harris and Firth's hypothesis says that we shall know a word by the company it keeps [16]. Based on that, we took the risk to interpret this hypothesis in order to create a foundation for our work. Cbow stands for learning word's representation given context words. Thus, we elaborated a hypothesis that motivates our work. It might be expressed as following: Cbow stipulates that word representation learning depends on the given context words while SkipGram considers a given center word to predict context words. We wonder whether considering this as a reflexive semantic relationship could help to optimize Cbow training time and accuracy. We thoroughly believe that the initialization of the Cbow model matrices using SkipGram learned matrices might help to optimize Cbow training time and accuracy by computing a better local minimum in a shorter time, compared to the Cbow random initialization of center and context words matrices (Fig. 3).

$$Cbow : Max(\log(\frac{Center_W}{Context_W})) \tag{15}$$

$$SkipGram : Max(\log(\frac{Context_W}{Center_W})) \tag{16}$$

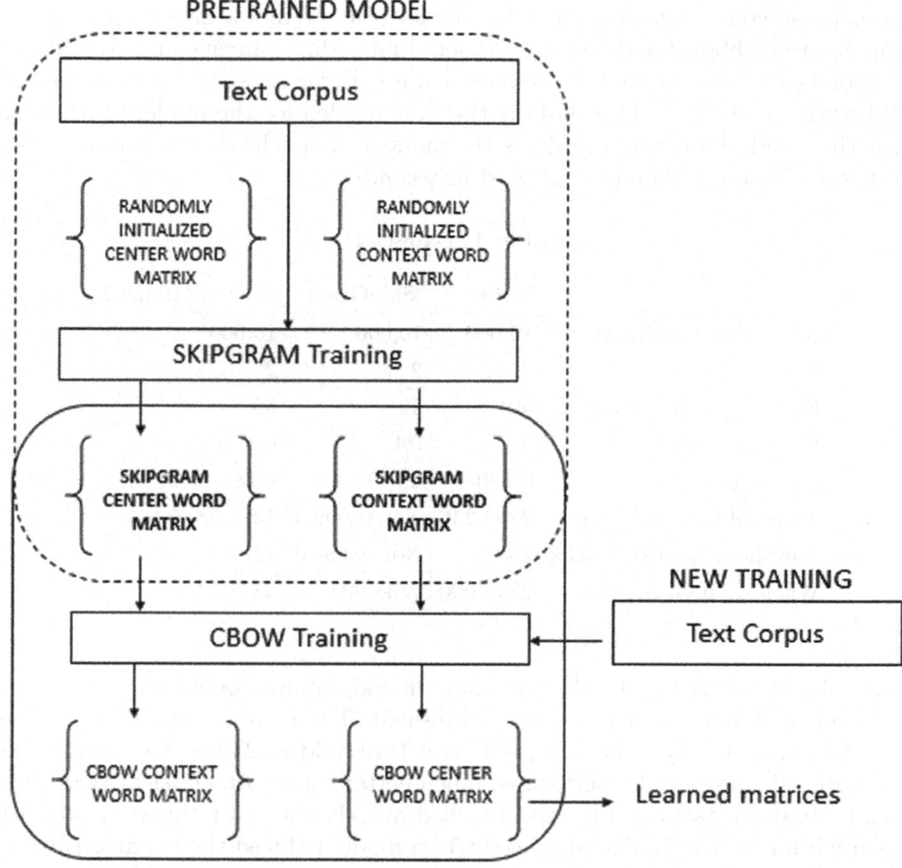

Fig. 3. Proposed model architecture.

4 Experimentations

To prove our hypothesis, we first implemented both Cbow and SkipGram models from scratch. The corpus we used is the same one used for Word2Vec300 https://code.google.com/archive/p/Word2Vec/, enwiki-latest-pages-articles.xml.bz2, it can be downloaded from https://dumps.wikimedia.org/enwiki/latest/enwiki-latest-pages-articles.xml.bz2. Due to hardware limitation, we performed an embedding of 50 dimension with less vocabulary compared to the original Word2Vec. The work is deployed on a virtual machine. It has Intel(R) Xeon(R) CPU @ 2.30 GHz as CPU of 2299.998 MHz, cache size 46080 KB, 2 CPU Cores and 25 GB of RAM.

For analysis purposes, we used three datasets with different vocabulary size, to perform a rigorous test of the proposed model. We applied the proposed technique on dataset 1, as described in Table 1. We fixed a common valid error threshold for all tests, in order, to compare the performance of the three models.

Hyper-parameters remained the same for all tests. Window size represents the number of neighbourhood words number. Embedding dimension is the length of an embedded vector that represents a word. Error threshold is the assumed valid error for all tests. Threshold is the time needed for the model to reach an error threshold. Threshold epochs is the number of epochs that occurred within the threshold time. Time is estimated in seconds.

Table 1. Dataset 1

	Cbow	SkipGram	Cbow optimized
Number of vocabular	10,000	10,000	10,000
Window size	2	2	2
Embedding dimenson	50	50	50
Learning rate	0.1	0.1	0.1
Error Threshold	0.180	0.180	0.180
Threshold needed time	2269.246	Not reached	1377.287
Threshold needed epochs	23	Not reached	14
Whole Computing time	2840.000	2836.997	2778.141

As shown in the Fig. 4. We note that the SkipGram model loss, starts from 16.46 but it didn't reach the error's threshold. The Cbow model's loss begins from 10.14 and reached the accepted error threshold in 23 epochs. Meanwhile, the proposed Cbow model performed much better than both classical Word2Vec models. Loss starts from 1.04 and reached quickly the error threshold at 14th epoch within 1377.28 s. The proposed Cbow model reduced the training time by 40%, in the meantime, the loss dropped out from 0.088 to 0.083 (Table 2).

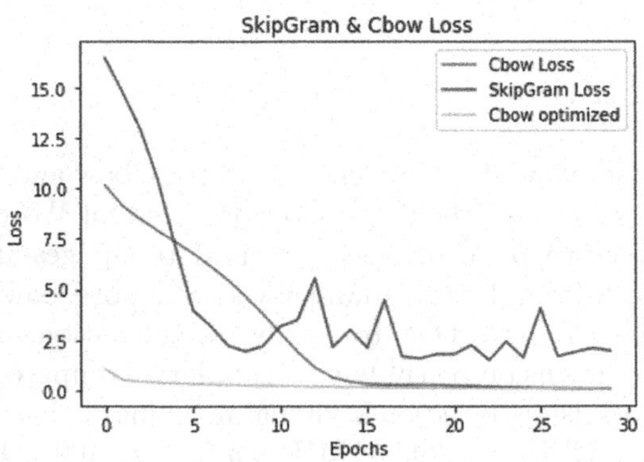

Fig. 4. Dataset 1.

For the second test, we increased the vocabulary size, in order to investigate whether the proposed model stills have the same efficiency as it did previously.

Table 2. Dataset 2

	Cbow	SkipGram	Cbow optimized
Number of vocabular	20,000	20,000	20,000
Window size	2	2	2
Embedding dimenson	50	50	50
Learning rate	0.1	0.1	0.1
Error Threshold	0.180	0.180	0.180
Threshold needed time	9267.389	Not reached	5347.418
Threshold needed epochs	23	Not reached	13
Whole Computing time	11598.00	11415.00	8450.297

During the second test, we noticed that the starting loss values increased for Cbow, SkipGram and Cbow, which at optimized 10.17, 17.42 and 1.14 respectively, compared to previous test. However, SkipGram is still didn't reach the valid error threshold. Nevertheless, the optimized Cbow model greatly reduced training time by 43% and loss remained the same for both Cbow models (Fig. 5).

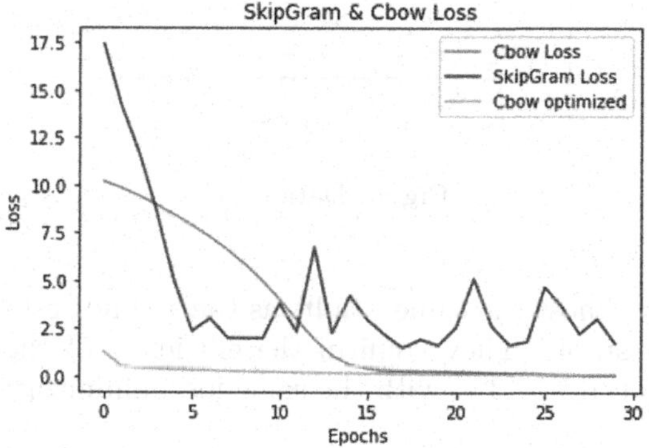

Fig. 5. Dataset 2.

In the same manner, we performed the third test by increasing the vocabulary size one more time as shown in the Table 3.

The last test consists of increasing the vocabulary size more and more, as shown in the Table 3.

Table 3. Dataset 3

	Cbow	SkipGram	Cbow optimized
Number of vocabular	30,000	30,000	30,000
Window size	2	2	2
Embedding dimenson	50	50	50
Learning rate	0.1	0.1	0.1
Error Threshold	0.180	0.180	0.180
Threshold needed time	19927.343	Not reached	18994.624
Threshold needed epochs	23	Not reached	13
Whole Computing time	24840.22	23710.02	22150.297

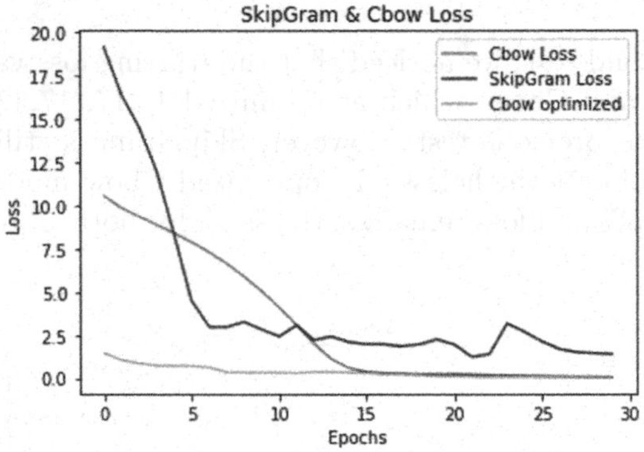

Fig. 6. Dataset 3.

Figure 6 shows almost the same results as the second test. The three models behaviour remain stable. They confirm the efficiency of the proposed model. Training time reduced by 43%, with the same loss minimization of 0.771.

5 Conclusion

Based on the three tests' results, we conclude that the usage of the SkipGram pretrained matrices to perform Cbow embedding contributes to reducing training time and error. This confirms our hypothesis about the reflexive and systematic semantic similarity, between center words and context words. The current work, shouldn't be interpreted as only a technical contribution. It has a deeper dimension. Certainly the experimentation confirms that, while the Cbow model seems to be suitable to the distributional hypothesis [16], the SkipGram model might be used as proof of the cognitive systematicity of language [17]. In other words, if something is said, it impacts all of it's neighborhood. This could explain the performance of our approach. It signifies that there is a bidirectional and reflexive semantic relationship between the word and it's neighborhood. We also note that the distributional hypothesis comes from linguistics, however it is now receiving attention in cognitive science [18].

References

1. Berners, T., Hendler, J., Lassila, O.: The semantic web. Sci. Am. **284**(5), 34–43 (2001)
2. Roman, V., Yampolskiy R.V.: Turing test as a defining feature of AI-completeness. In: Yang, X.S. (eds.) Artificial Intelligence, Evolutionary Computing and Metaheuristics. Studies in Computational Intelligence, vol. 427. Springer, Heidelberg (2013). https://doi.org/10.1007/978-3-642-29694-9_1
3. Bobrow, D.: Natural Language Input for a Computer Problem Solving System, Massachusetts Institute of Technology 201 Vassar Street, W59–200 Cambridge, MA, USA (1964)
4. Weizenbaum, J.: Computer Power and Human Reason, pp. 188–189. From Judgment to Calculation W. H. Freeman and Company, San Francisco (1976). ISBN 0-7167-0463-3
5. Schank, R.: A conceptual dependency parser for natural language. In: Proceedings of the 1969 Conference on Computational Linguistics, Sång-Säby, pp. 1–3. Sweden (1969)
6. Aaronson, D.: Computer use in cognitive psychology. Behav. Res. Meth. Instrum. Comput. **26**, 81–93 (1994)
7. Deerwester, S., Dumais, S., Furnas, G., Landauer, T., Harshman, R.: Indexing by latent semantic analysis. J. Am. Soc. Inf. Sci. (1990)
8. Salton, G., Wong, A., Yang, C.: A vector space model for automatic indexing [archive]. Commun. ACM **18**(11), 613–620 (1975)
9. Mikolov, T., Sutskever, I., Chen, K., Corrado, G., Dean, J.: Distributed representations of words and phrases and their compositionality (2013)
10. Harris, Z.: Distributional structure. Word **10**(23), 146–162 (1954)
11. Pennington, J., Socher, R., Manning, C.: Glove: global vectors for word representation. In: Empirical Methods in Natural Language Processing (EMNLP), pp. 1532–1543 (2014)
12. Bojanowski, P., Grave, P., Joulin, E., Mikolov, T.: Enriching word vectors with subword information. Trans. Assoc. Comput. Linguist. **5**, 135–146 (2017)
13. Speer, R., Chin, J., Havasi, C.: ConceptNet 5.5 an open multilingual graph of general knowledge. In: Proceedings of the AAAI Conference on Artificial Intelligence (2017)
14. Speer, R., J Duda, J.: ConceptNet extending word embeddings with multilingual relational knowledge. In: SemEval-2017 (2017)
15. Faruqui, M., Sujay, J., Jauhar, K., Hovy, C.E., Smith, N.A.: Retrofitting word vectors to semantic lexicons. In: Proceedings of NAACL (2015)
16. Harris, Z.: Distributional structure. Word **10**, 146–162 (1954). https://doi.org/10.1007/978-94-009-8467-7-1
17. Fodor, J.A., Pylyshyn, Z.W.: Connectionism and cognitive architecture: a critical analysis. Cognition **28**, 3–71 (1988)
18. McDonald, S., Ramscar, M.: Testing the distributional hypothesis: the influence of context on judgements of semantic similarity. In: Proceedings of the Annual Meeting of the Cognitive Science Society, vol. 23(23) (2001)

Erroneous Coordinated Sentences Detection in French Students' Writings

Laura Noreskal[1], Iris Eshkol-Taravella[1(✉)], and Marianne Desmets[2]

[1] MoDyCo, UMR 7114, 200 Avenue de la République, 92001 Nanterre, France
{l.noreskal,ieshkolt}@parisnanterre.fr

[2] LLF, UMR 7110, 8 Rue Albert Einstein, 75013 Paris, France
marianne.desmets@parisnanterre.fr

Abstract. This paper presents the development stages of an NLP device to be used to improve students' skills in French academic writing. Among various relevant difficulties, we focus on coordinating constructions that include or not ellipsis. We develop a tool to detect errors automatically in coordinated sentences from a corpus composed of erroneous and correct sentences. We use a deep learning approach based on the French CamemBERT model. To find the best learning environment for the classification task, we show the results obtained from training and testing datasets with different proportions of erroneous and correct sentences.

Keywords: Coordinated sentences · Error detection · Student writings · Deep learning · CamemBERT

1 The Context

1.1 The écri+ Project

In France, in order to succeed fully, mastering the written French language is crucial when entering higher education[1]. However, a significant proportion of students encounter difficulties in overcoming academic written French, which later threaten to jeopardize their professional achievements. In order to propose a conjoint response in the face of such challenge, some 15 institutions from various fields are currently developing specific training programs with new methods of remediation as a part of a national program 'The écri+ Project'. This program, the result of collective knowledge associating linguists, didacticians, experienced teachers and web developers, aims to provide a common and standardized framework for evaluation, training and certificating written and comprehension skills for academic French. It will provide innovative online progressive self-training devices for students, based on the analyses of the most prominent errors. As for teachers and researchers, the framework offers a range of shared co-constructed resources for in-class training sessions, exchange of practices, strategic and pedagogical supports.

[1] CNRS-ANR-17-NCUN-0015.

K. Wojtkiewicz et al. (Eds.): ICCCI 2021, CCIS 1463, pp. 586–596, 2021.
https://doi.org/10.1007/978-3-030-88113-9_47

1.2 Coordinated Sentences with and Without Ellipsis

Based on a preliminary linguistic analysis, it appears that complex syntactic constructions, mostly long phrasal sequences with coordination and elliptical constructions, are sensitive to errors or clumsiness in students' writings. Although ellipsis is a common linguistic phenomenon, it has been found that mastering it in writings is a struggle in some complex or long constructions. We will rely on the definition of Abeillé and Mouret [2]: "On parle d'ellipse [dans les coordinations elliptiques] lorsque l'interprétation d'une forme syntaxique requiert plus que ce qui est fourni par les éléments qui la composent et que le matériel nécessaire pour obtenir cette interprétation est récupérable dans le contexte immédiat." (We speak of ellipsis [in elliptical coordinations] when the interpretation of a syntactic form requires more than what is provided by the elements that compose it and when the material necessary to obtain this interpretation is recoverable in the immediate context.) In this sense, ellipsis is an economical linguistic system which allows to avoid any redundancy in a "target sequence" of elements present in a "source sequence".

Several works have contributed to draw a typology of ellipses in French [7] and understand their different functions [2,4,6,8,25]. They have identified different constraints imposed by the construction of ellipsis and showed that the stability and comprehension of an utterance depend on the respect of these constraints. Similarly, coordinated constructions, including or not ellipsis, have been the subject of several research that pointed out constraints related to the syntactic identities of the conjoined elements [11,15,18,23]. However, although ellipsis automatic detection and ellipsis resolution are still at the center of linguistic and NLP research works [12–14,20], to our knowledge, none has been achieved in the automatic detection of coordinated constructions including or not ellipses in French, even less in erroneous written French corpora. Many linguistic studies have investigated errors in French, proposing some analysis [10,21,22] or classificatory grids [5]. However, research on error detection in texts - which has often been limited to spelling correction [9,19] - has been abandoned by researchers in the public domain, in favor of industrialists [3,16]. Our work therefore aims at creating a tool able to automatically detect erroneous coordinating sentences including or not ellipsis in texts written by students.

2 Corpora

2.1 Data Collection

To study the coordinated constructions, including or not ellipsis in the students' writing, it was necessary to list the uses in context. Thus, we collected data that answered two main questions. First, we wanted to know the different types of coordinated constructions that include or not ellipsis in the written productions. Second, we wanted to define a typology of the frequent errors. In order to have a realistic vision of the students' difficulties in writing, we collected productions made during exams. During university studies, the writing produced varies.

Students produce personal writings (note-taking for example) but also evaluative writings. For the purposes of this research, evaluative writing was chosen because it corresponds to a very specific context of written production. In the context of higher education, evaluations are used to assess students' knowledge by giving a value to their writing. However, the grade that is given to an assignment is not totally objective because it depends on the teacher and what he or she expects from the writing. Therefore, we did not take into consideration the grades obtained by the student. We felt that the evaluative essays themselves would allow us to observe students' language skills when writing is not only a means of communication but also a means of demonstrating one's ability to express oneself and to meet the teacher's expectations. We sought to obtain a sufficiently large and diversified corpus. The data collection was therefore done on several essays from different levels of study. The writings corpus is composed on spontaneous writings (exams and exercises done in class) and prepared writings (homework assignments, internship reports and dissertations). The writings come from different fields of study such as linguistics, history, or law. The corpus is constituted from typographical sources and manuscript sources. The handwritten sources have been scanned to allow the digital exploitation of all the writings. Based on this first corpus, it was possible to create a corpus of coordinated sentences including or not ellipsis from the evaluative writings. Sentences containing coordinating conjunctions or conjunctive phrase were automatically extracted from the writings. The extracted sentences are listed in a csv document including the sentences, their source, grade level, and field of study.

2.2 Design of the Corpus

Our writings corpus contains exercises done in class (100), exams (127), homework assignments (126), internship reports (10) and dissertations (7), i.e. 370 essays from which we extracted 1455 erroneous or correct coordinated sentences. The distribution of the corpus is presented in Fig. 1.

It appears that the corpus is not homogeneous because internship reports and dissertations are very poorly represented. However, the sizes of the essays must be considered to compare the proportions of each type of writing. Indeed, dissertations and internship reports are longer than other writings. The writings' number present does not reflect the volume they represent. Despite the high probability of having errors in the internship reports or the dissertations, from the perspective of building the corpus, they represent a more expensive reading task than are exercises or exams. The ratio between processing time and the number of extracted data had to be taken into account. Therefore, an analysis was made considering the writings size in Table 1.

Thus, in exercises, an error of this type appears every 14 sentences, every 47 sentences in homework assignments, every 84 sentences in dissertations and every 424 sentences in internship reports. The data show that errors have a higher rate of occurrence in the exercises than in the other essays (7%). Homework and dissertations have a percentage of occurrence of 2% and 1% respectively. The internship reports have the lowest frequency (0.2%).

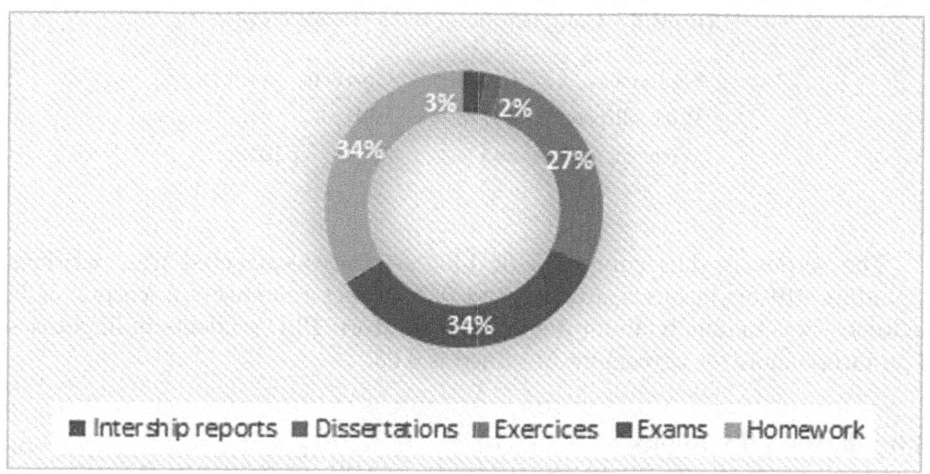

Fig. 1. Distribution of the writing's corpus

Table 1. Distribution of errors according to the size of the writing

Writings	Relative frequency errors/size	Error every x sentences
Exercises	7%	14
Homework assignments	2%	47
Dissertations	1%	84
Internship reports	0.2%	424

Among the sentences extracted from the students' writings, we distinguished coordinated sentences including ellipsis (1) and coordinated sentences not including ellipsis (2)[2].

(1) Durant ces moments, l'enseignant devra tenter au maximum de développer l'esprit critique des élèves et les pousser afin de les faire argumenter sur leur propos ou en réaction aux propos des autres, toujours avec bienveillance. (lit. During these moments, the teacher will try maximum to develop critical thinking skills and push to argue make their remarks or in response to the comments of others, always with kindness.)
(2) Chaque groupe devra théâtraliser un article et le présenter à la classe. (lit. Each group will have to dramatize an article and present it to the class.)

The composition of the corpus of coordinated sentences with or without ellipsis is presented in Table 2.

[2] We analyze example (1) as a case of erroneous coordinate sentence with ellipsis where the preposition word 'de' should be realized in front of the VP 'les pousser afin de les faire argumenter sur leur propos ou en réaction aux propos des autres'. Example (2) is a correct coordinate sentence.

Table 2. Composition of the sentence corpus

Sentences	Erroneous	Corrects	Total
With ellipse	267	149	416
Without ellipse	643	396	1039

The corpus is thus composed of 1455 sentences extracted from writings, including 910 erroneous sentences and 545 correct sentences. A corpus of 50 sentences was manually annotated by 2 annotators, PhD students in linguistics. The inter-annotator agreement obtained is 0.63.

2.3 Error's Typology

The linguistic analysis of the corpus allowed us to define a typology of recurrent syntactic errors:

- errors related to prepositions or conjunctions: sentences in which a preposition or conjunction is absent (3), is realized when not expected (4), or realized instead of another preposition or conjunction (2). The preposition errors are mainly due to the non-respect of the head verbal valence ((4) and (5)), whereas the conjunction errors are due to a problem of construction, or an erroneous coordination of subordinates.
  (3) *Dans notre cas, le discours correspond à l'événement et [abs.] la rétroaction à la réaction du récepteur. (lit. *In our case, the speech corresponds to the event and the feedback to the reaction of the receiver.)
  (4) *Pour être admis en M1, il faut obligatoirement avoir une licence de lettres, de langues ou de SDL et **d**'avoir validé le parcours en EC et didactique. (lit. *To be admitted to M1, you must obligatorily have a degree in literature, languages or SDL and of have validated the course in EC and didactics.)
  (5) *Effectivement, j'ai bien aimé la contrainte qui consistait, à la fois, **de** trouver une suite cohérente à l'incipit proposé mais aussi **de** terminer le récit par une phrase bien précise. (lit. *Indeed, I have really liked the constraint which consisted, at the same time, of finding a coherent continuation to the proposed incipit but also of ending the story with a very precise sentence.)
- errors related to sequences: sentences with a syntactic break due to the coordination of sequences that do not have the same syntactic role. In these sentences, the second sequence is not constructed like the first one and it is difficult to syntactically attach it to a part of the sentence (6). These sentences may also show an anaphora resolution problem for they contain pronouns without antecedents (7).

(6) *L'Organon est un projet politique pour que les citoyens d'etectent quand un raisonnement n'est pas valide et **ne pas se faire avoir par les sophistes**. (lit. *The Organon is a political project for that (+sub) citizens detect when a reasoning is not valid and not to be fooled by sophists.)

(7) *Les maires et les présidents des régions ne dépendent pas du ministre alors que les recteurs et **les DASEN le sont**. (lit. *The mayors and the presidents of the regions do not depend on the minister while the rectors and the DASEN are it (+pron).)

3 Automatic Detection

In testing the development of our tool for automatic detection of erroneous coordinated sentences in student writings, we tested both machine learning and deep learning methods. As the tool developed is intended to be integrated into the project device, we have favored the use of the deep learning method because it does not require external resources.

3.1 Corpora

We chose to train a classifier that could recognize two classes: Erroneous/Correct. For this task, three training corpora of 200 sentences were created: a corpus with as many correct sentences as incorrect sentences (PI), a corpus with more correct sentences than incorrect sentences (PC) and a corpus with more erroneous sentences than correct sentences (PE). In order to have a test corpus and a training corpus of 30% and 70% of the total corpus, the test corpora all contain 85 sentences. We thus have six corpora for classification, three composed of 200 sentences and three composed of 85 sentences. These corpora are used for the first tests, the goal being to increase their size by the training. Thanks to the different test corpora, we seek to observe the impact of each learning environment. We assume that the corpora with a majority class (PE and PC) will have good results on the test corpora with the same proportion correct/erroneous. For the PI training corpus, we believe that the results will depend on the test corpus. We also want to know if these different training corpora will perform well on the PI test corpus.

3.2 Deep Learning

The experiments used the Simple Transformers [1] and camemBERT [17], the French language model, as the classifier with 8 epochs. We trained our model on each training corpus (*PE train*, *PC train*, and *PI train*) and then tested it on three test corpora (*PE test*, *PC test*, and *PI test*). We considered two different inputs which were fed into the model: the tokens of each sentence and the parts of speech identified with Treetagger [24]. With these two inputs, it is possible to examine whether the classifier learns better with the tokens or the parts of speech.

3.3 Results

Experiments with the Tokens. The results of the experiments with the tokens are shown in Table 3.

Table 3. Recall, precision, and F-score of experiences with tokens

Test	PC			PE			PI		
Train	R	P	F	R	P	F	R	P	F
PC	0.32	0.50	0.39	0.28	0.89	**0.43**	0.23	0.67	0.34
PE	0.72	0.60	0.65	0.83	0.93	**0.87**	0.63	0.69	0.66
PI	0.40	0.38	0.39	0.63	1.00	**0.78**	0.42	0.82	0.55

We obtained the best results when the tokens were fed into the model as the inputs. The experiments with the PE train/PE test have given the highest F-score of 0.87. The two other training corpora (PC and PI) also achieved their best score when tested on the PE test corpus (0.43 for PC and 0.78 for PI). In general, the training with the PE corpus gave the best results in the tests of different environments. In contrast to the other training corpora, all the experiments with the PE corpus got scores higher than 0.6. Concerning the test corpus, we studied the different results on the PI corpus, which is composed of the same number of correct and erroneous sentences. Surprisingly, we obtained the best score for the PI test during the training with PE and not during the training with PI. From these results, we can conclude that having more erroneous sentences than the correct ones during training allows us to build a more robust model. Figure 2 illustrates the confusion matrix obtained during the experiments with the PE corpora and the tokens as the input.

The model successfully identified 50 erroneous sentences and 21 correct sentences, whereas it predicted the wrong class 14 times (4 times for Erroneous and 10 times for Correct).

Experiments with the Parts of Speech. The results of the experiments with the parts of speech are shown in Table 4.

The results with the parts of speech are worse than those obtained with tokens for the PC and PE training corpora. However, learning with parts of speech with the PI corpus improved the results when tested on the PI test corpus. Moreover, the PE train/PE test experiment has again given the best score (0.82) even though it is not as high as that of the experiment with tokens.

With the PC train/PI test, the classifier considered all sentences correct, which is the only experiment that found such classification errors. Other trainings with the PC corpus also gave very bad results: 0.18 for the PC test and 0.21 for the PE test. It indicates that the corpus with more correct sentences than the incorrect ones (PC) is less relevant for our classification task with either tokens or parts of speech. The PI train/PI test experiment scored better with the parts of speech. However, the difference between the two experiments (tokens

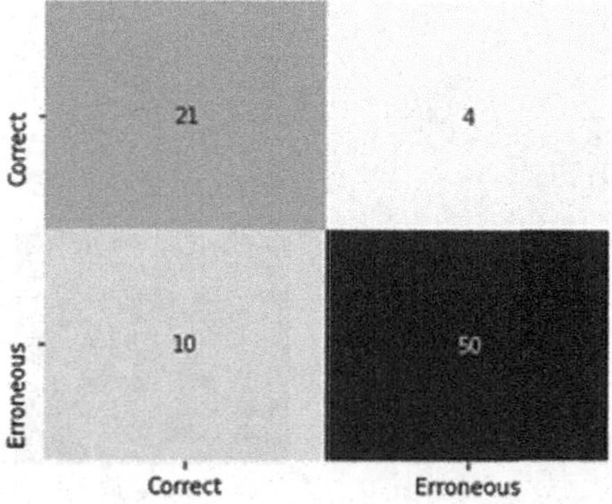

Fig. 2. Confusion matrix of PE train/PE test experiment with tokens

Table 4. Recall, precision, and F-score of experiences with Parts of speech

Test	PC			PE			PI		
Train	R	P	F	R	P	F	R	P	F
PC	0.12	0.38	0.18	0.88	0.32	**0.47**	0.44	0.32	0.37
PE	0.12	0.88	0.21	0.93	0.73	**0.82**	0.53	0.89	0.67
PI	0.00	0.00	0.00	0.95	0.51	**0.67**	0.58	0.68	0.63

and parts of speech) is relatively small. Based on the results, the PI corpus does not seem to be suitable for our task. We can hypothesize that the classification errors come from improper sequencing of the labels provided by the parser. The confusion matrices obtained during the experiments with the PE corpora with parts of speech are presented in Fig. 3.

The model identified 56 erroneous sentences and 4 correct sentences. The model predicted the wrong class 25 times (21 times for Erroneous and 4 times for Correct).

3.4 Analyses

After analyzing the misclassification errors from the best performances of our learning method, we noticed that erroneous sentences undetected as such often included errors related to prepositions and thus to verb transitivity. In view of this, our first hypothesis is that the model fails to distinguish between direct transitive verbs and indirect transitive verbs. Our second hypothesis is that the model does not have enough information about the prepositions that indirect transitive verbs expect.

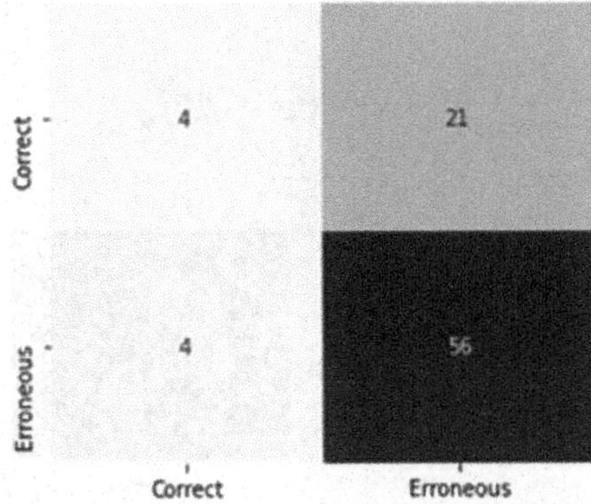

Fig. 3. Confusion matrix of PE train/PE test experiment with Parts of speech

We can observe the following two sentences that are misclassified by the model:

(3) *Nous réfléchissons sur l'expression de musulman en Chine en considérant l'essor des dispositifs socio-numériques de communication afin de répondre **les** questions suivantes.

(4) *La première partie de ce mémoire sera consacrée à une présentation synthétique de l'immigration puis **d**'une définition de la politique d'intégration linguistique des migrants adultes en France.

We face two problems: in sentence (3), the preposition "à" -which would give "aux" in this case- is absent after the verb "répondre" whereas the verb is indirect transitive and in sentence (4), the preposition ("à") expected by "être consacré" is replaced by the preposition "de". Thus, it appears that the model fails to classify errors that are related to indirect transitive verbs. These two sentences could be considered as correct if the main verbs had different transitivities but our model does not seem to be able to distinguish between the two types of verbs (indirect transitive/direct transitive). To test our hypothesis, we took from the corpus the correct sentence "L'élève doit être attentif à la portée de ses paroles et à la responsabilité de ses actes." (lit. The student must be attentive to the scope of his words and the responsibility of his actions.) which we voluntarily modified in order to observe the behavior of the model. The model predicts the class Correct when the prepositions are absent "*L'élève doit être attentif la portée de ses paroles et la responsabilité de ses actes." (lit. *The student must be attentive [abs.] the scope of his words and [abs.] the responsibility of his actions.) and when the preposition is not the correct one *L'élève doit être attentif de la portée de ses paroles et de la responsabilité de ses actes." (lit. *The student must be attentive of the scope of his words and of the responsibility of his actions.).

To overcome this problem, we would like to add this information for the next experiments in order to observe if information on verbal transitivity (direct/indirect), as well as information on the required prepositions form, improve the recognition of erroneous sentences.

Since the final task is very specific -as it is specific to the project in which this research takes place- it is difficult to compare the results with those of others researches. However, our results are very encouraging.

4 Conclusion

This paper presents a deep learning approach with CamemBERT for error detection in coordinated sentences including or not ellipsis from students' academic writings. Experiments were conducted on different learning environments to find the best environment for our classification task. During the experiments, it appeared that the corpus mainly composed of erroneous sentences was the most relevant for the training, since it obtained the best scores on all the test corpora. In the further steps in our research we are to find a way to include information on verbs subcategorization and preposition forms since it appears to play a critical part in errors, and, as suggested by a reviewer, we should investigate whether the part of speech of the element that is omitted in the ellipses impacts the result of the detection. In addition, we need to address the type of sequence errors in order to see if some structural patterns are more likely to produce errors. Finally, we plan to continue deep learning experiments by increasing the size of the training corpus.

References

1. Simple transformers homepage. https://simpletransformers.ai/. Accessed 1 Apr 2021
2. Abeillé, A., Mouret, F.: Quelques contraintes sur les coordinations elliptiques en français. Revue de sémantique et de pragmatique **24**(177–206), 89 (2010)
3. Baranes, M., Sagot, B.: Normalisation de textes par analogie: le cas des mots inconnus. In: TALN-Traitement Automatique du Langage Naturel, pp. 137–148 (2014)
4. Bîlbîie, G.: Grammaire des constructions elliptiques: une étude comparative des phrases sans verbe en roumain et en français. Language Science Press (2017)
5. Boivin, M.C., Pinsonneault, R.: La catégorisation des erreurs linguistiques: Une grille de codage fondée sur la grammaire moderne. Le Français Aujourd'hui **209**(2), 91–116 (2020)
6. Busquets, J.: Position du focus et la distinction stripping/ellipse du groupe verbal en catalan. Cahiers de grammaire **29**, 41–57 (2004)
7. Dagnac, A.: Typological case studies: French (2019)
8. Desmets, M.: Ellipses dans les constructions comparatives en comme. Linx. Revue des linguistes de l'université Paris X Nanterre **58**, 47–74 (2008)
9. Fay-Varnier, C.: Aide à la détection de fautes grammaticales par une analyse progressive des phrases. Ph.D. thesis, Institut National Polytechnique de Lorraine (1990)

10. Frei, H.: La Grammaire des Fautes. Geuthner (1931)
11. Godard, D.: Problèmes syntaxiques de la coordination et propositions récentes dans les grammaires syntagmatiques. Langages **4**, 3–24 (2005)
12. Hamza, A.: La détection et la traduction automatiques de l'ellipse : enjeux théoriques et pratiques. Theses, Université de Strasbourg, September 2019. https://tel.archives-ouvertes.fr/tel-02526670
13. Hamza, A., Bernhard, D.: Détection des ellipses dans des corpus de sous-titres en anglais (ellipsis detection in english subtitles corpora). In: Actes de la Conférence sur le Traitement Automatique des Langues Naturelles (TALN) PFIA 2019, vol. 1: Articles longs, pp. 99–112 (2019)
14. Hardt, D.: An empirical approach to VP ellipsis. Comput. Linguist. **23**(4), 525–541 (1997)
15. Hobaek Haff, M.: Coordonnants et éléments coordonnés: une étude sur la coordination en français moderne. L'information grammaticale **46**(1), 17–21 (1990)
16. Laurent, D., Nègre, S., Séguéla, P.: L'analyseur syntaxique cordial dans passage. Actes de TALN 2009 (Traitement automatique des langues naturelles) 9 (2009)
17. Martin, L., et al.: Camembert: a tasty French language model. arXiv preprint arXiv:1911.03894 (2019)
18. Mouret, F.: Grammaire des constructions coordonnées. Coordinations simples et coordinations à redoublement en français contemporain. Theses, Université Paris-Diderot - Paris VII, February 2007. https://tel.archives-ouvertes.fr/tel-00271571
19. Ndiaye, M., Faltin, A.V.: Correcteur orthographique adapté à l'apprentissage du français. Bulletin de linguistique appliquée et générale **29**, 117–134 (2004)
20. Nielsen, L.A.: A corpus-based study of verb phrase ellipsis identification and resolution. Ph.D. thesis. Citeseer (2005)
21. Perdue, C., Porquier, R.: L'analyse des erreurs: un bilan pratique. Langages **57**, 87–94 (1980)
22. Reichler-Béguelin, M.J.: L'approche des "anomalies" argumentatives. Pratiques **73**(1), 51–78 (1992)
23. Roodenburg, J.: Une coordination particulière: les syntagmes n conj n en français. Langages **4**, 93–109 (2005)
24. Schmid, H.: Probabilistic part-of-speech tagging using decision trees. In: New Methods in Language Processing, p. 154 (2013)
25. Shiraishi, A.: Discordances dans l'ellipse périphérique en français. Theses, Université Sorbonne Paris Cité, June 2018. https://tel.archives-ouvertes.fr/tel-02156083

Comprehensive Evaluation of Word Embeddings for Highly Inflectional Language

Pawel Drozda[1(✉)], Krzysztof Sopyla[2], and Juliusz Lewalski[3]

[1] Faculty of Mathematics and Computer Science, University of Warmia and Mazury in Olsztyn, Olsztyn, Poland
pdrozda@matman.uwm.edu.pl
[2] Literacka Ltd., Olsztyn, Poland
[3] Ermlab Ltd., Olsztyn, Poland

Abstract. The purpose of this paper is to present the experiments aiming at choosing the best word embeddings for highly inflectional languages. In particular, authors evaluated the word embeddings for Polish language among those available in the literature at the time of writing. The static embeddings like Word2Vec, GloVe, fasttext and their training settings were taken into account. In particular, the evaluation coverted 121 different embedding models provided by IPI PAN, OPI, Kyubyong and Facebook. The experiment phase was divided into two tasks: the first task consisted in examining word analogies and the second verified the similarities and the relatedness of pairs of words. The obtained results showed that in terms of accuracy the Facebook fasttext model learned on the Common Crawl collection should be considered the best model under assumptions of experimental session.

Keywords: Word embeddings · GloVe · Word2Vec · FastText

1 Introduction

One of the most challenging tasks in the natural language processing domain is the appropriate annotation of words, sentences or documents. There are many possibilities of using NLP in various fields, such as law, medicine or literature. The tasks that are set in the above-mentioned areas include Q&A, text classification, topic analysis, summarization. Almost all research and problems in the field of natural text processing require prior processing of the input data. In the most common cases, the preprocessing results with a representation of individual words, sentences or entire documents by means of multidimensional numerical vectors. Such action is aimed at revealing the semantic meaning of text and vectors have easy to compute form in various machine learning tasks.

There are many approaches to encode text as a vector. The newest and recognized as the best are neural networks of the BERT or ELMO type. However, utilization mentioned encoding techniques for long documents (such as books)

K. Wojtkiewicz et al. (Eds.): ICCCI 2021, CCIS 1463, pp. 597–607, 2021.
https://doi.org/10.1007/978-3-030-88113-9_48

is a very costly process, both in terms of hardware resources and time. Often the time necessary to encode a whole long document (more than 100k tokens) is not feasible. On the other hand, there are also less accurate solutions, which perform well enough in many applications and are significantly less computationally expensive. These include fasttext [11], Word2Vec [14,15] or GloVe [18], which are used for initialization of the first layers in many neural networks (e.g. LSTM) or, on the basis of their aggregation, various machine learning tasks can be performed. The most common methods that use this process are classification and regression.

In this work the main effort was directed at finding the best embeddings model for highly inflectional language. In particular, 121 models made available by different language groups (IPI PAN, OPI, Kyubyong and facebook) were examined using the state of the art datasets for the Polish language: Polish Word Analogy and MSimLex999. All considered models in the experimental session take advantage of the previously mentioned text representations: fasttext, Word2Vec and GloVe. Evaluation by analogy was used for the research, which analyzes sets of pairs of words that in a given context should be at a similar distance (for example: country name and capital of this country) and counts the differences in distance between them. As a result of the research, it turned out that the facebook-fastext-cc-300.txt model, which achieved an accuracy level of 66% in the experiment, is the best among the considered models. It should be noted, that besides accuracy, word analogies measured by correlation coefficient and relatedness were also taken into account in the experiments. In our opinion, these coefficients had a smaller impact on the quality of the model due to the fact that often the higher value of correlation and relatedness resulted from a significant reduction in the number of words from the original dictionary. This reduction is indicated by the out of vocabulary value in the experimental session. It follows, therefore, that the facebook-fastext-cc-300.txt is the best model for analyzing the sentiment among those considered in this work.

The rest of the paper is organized as follows. The Sect. 2 presents achievements obtained by other researchers in the considered domain. The Sect. 3 briefly describes datasets and methods which were used in experiments. Evaluation of the proposed solution is provided in Sect. 4. Finally, in the Sect. 5, the conclusions are made.

2 State of the Art

The main purpose of introducing word embeddings is to provide text representation which determines the semantic meaning distance between given words. The first and the simplest form is a one-hot encoding (bag-of-words) where the vector representation contains all zeros except the position where the word appears in the dictionary. The result is that the distance between words that are close in meaning is exactly the same as the distance between words that are completely different.

This indicates that the simplest representation does not reflect the semantics of the processed documents with the use of Natural Language Processing methods and its applications are very limited. In the field of Natural Language Processing, there is a lot of research around the world in the context of different languages related to finding the best possible representation of single words, sentences, or entire documents.

One of the frequently used vector representations of words are Word2Vec [14,15]. The main advantage of the Word2Vec method is the ability to process huge data sets based on dictionaries with millions of words without the need to engage significant computing resources. Moreover, this technique allows you to capture the semantic meaning in the process of word embeddings. This is done by analogy, where, for example, the distance between the vectors of the words man and king is the same as for the words woman and queen. The authors of the papers proposed two model architectures for learning word representation, which the main purpose was to minimize computational complexity. The first architecture, Continuous Bag-of-Words Model, is based on the feedforward Neural Net Language Model (NNLM), where the nonlinear hidden layer is removed and the projection layer is extended for all words. This allows achieving complexity on the level of:

$$Q = N * D + D * log_2(V),$$

where N is a number of previous words used, V is vocabulary size and D is the dimensionality of word vector representation.

The second solution, Continuous Skip-gram Model, is based on Continuous Bag of Words (CBOW), but it does not predict the current word from the context, but it tries to find the words before and after the processed word. There are many applications of these representations, which have proved their effectiveness. For example, Word2Vec has been applied in text classification [13], sentiment analysis [5] or news classification [8].

The next crucial word embedding representation in the natural language processing field was the fasttext model [11] provided by Facebook. Fasttext is one of the most popular and best-performing algorithms in text classification. In recent years, this algorithm has gained a lot of interest among researchers and is used in many scientific fields due to achieving high accuracy of calculations and the requirement of low computing resources. The main idea behind the algorithm is to use n-grams of features for the input text. It is represented by $x_1, ..., x_N$ with the bag-of-words encoding. Such data representation is applied as input to the linear classifier which uses the hierarchical softmax function for computation of probability distribution over classes and the stochastic gradient descent during training. This allows to significantly reduce the model learning time while preserving high accuracy, similar to that achieved by the best models. Fasttext has proven its use in domains such as: employment web scraping [24], social data analytics [9], typo correction [3], intent detection [2], text classification [1,6,23], sentiment analysis [20,22].

The last of the vector representations that was taken into account during this research is Global Vectors for Word Representation [18] (GloVe). Glove is a regression-based model that combines two main strands used in the vector representation of text: global matrix factorization and local context window methods. The proposed method counts global word-word co-occurrences and trains only nonzero elements. This method allows achieving high accuracy comparable to the best available solutions while ensuring a low level of computational complexity.

Recent researches have shown that one of the best representations of text for building models in natural language processing tasks is to use neural networks. As part of the use of this method, transformer neural network BERT [7] and biLSTM neural network ELMo [19] models have recently been created, which perfectly capture the context related to the semantics of the language. There are also learned models for the Polish language with the use of the aforementioned solutions [10,12]. One of the most challenging problems when teaching a model based on neural networks are the huge costs of computing power within a given language, where in many cases it is an insurmountable barrier.

Due to the importance of the field of vector representation of words in the natural language processing domain, there are also many researchers dealing with word embedding models for highly inflectional languages. For example, for the Polish language, Rogalski and Szczepaniak in [21] were the first who dealt with capturing the semantics of text using spatial relations between embeddings reflecting relations such as alternatives and analogies. Another research relating to the embedding of the Polish language [16] tests Continuous Bag of Words (CBOW) and skip-gram approaches based on Polish Wikipedia and National Corpus of Polish. In addition, in recent years, there have also appeared many models based on the above-described embeddings for the Polish language. These include Kyubyong repository, IPI PAN, OPI and Facebook.

Despite the large set of models developed for the Polish language, there is no complete comparison of their quality. This paper deals with the problem of model comparison and the selection of the best one in the context of performing sentiment analysis on long texts. The paper does not take into account models based on neural networks since in the context of processing books and long documents it is currently not possible to process the entire book (from 100,000–500,000 tokens) using BERT or ELMo models, where apart from the accuracy of the model, another critical feature is the processing time.

The first tests carried out by the authors of this paper showed that in the context of book embedding, the entire processing time needed to analyze a single book ranges from 3 to 10 days. Such a large amount of time was unacceptable for the project, so the ELMo and BERT based representations were omitted in the experimental session.

3 Datasets and Methods

This chapter describes the main contribution of the paper, which is the presentation of the methods used to evaluate the best models of Polish language embeddings: fasttext, Word2Vec, and GloVe. Two state of the art datasets were used to evaluate the embedding models for the Polish language, which are SimLex for Polish [17] and the list of analogues developed by facebook [25].

The first dataset is the polish version of the well-known SimLex-999 dataset for text embeddings translated into many languages. It contains pairs of words (like old and new), the similarities and the relatedness measured in the range from 0 to 10. All words from the original dataset were translated by three linguists and then the pairs of words were rated by independent annotators in terms of similarity and relatedness. Sample data belonging to the described dataset are presented in Table 1.

Table 1. Sample data of SimLex dataset for Polish language

No	word1	word2	Similarity	Relatedness
1	stary	nowy	0.43	7.29
2	bystry	inteligentny	8.86	9.71
3	ciezki	trudny	4.86	7.29
4	szczesliwy	radosny	8.14	8.86
5	latwy	meczacy	0.43	6.43
6	szybki	gwaltowny	3.71	7.00
7	szczesliwy	zadowolony	6.29	8.14
8	krotki	dlugi	0.43	7.43
9	glupi	tepy	7.57	9.14
10	dziwny	niesamowity	4.57	6.14
11	szeroki	waski	0.43	7.43
12	zly	okropny	6.57	8.29

As it can be seen the words "stary" and "nowy" (which means old and new) have very low similarity but are highly related. For the experimental section, the presented set required preprocessing since it was necessary to prepare an appropriate data format that could be accepted by the Python gensim library used as part of the experiments [26].

The method used on the basis of the above mentioned dataset is to evaluate the pairs of words by calculating the correlation using the model and comparing with the similarity assessments made by independent annotators. As the output metrics, two coefficients are provided: Pearson and Spearman. Moreover, the experiments also indicate the number of words that were not taken into account during the evaluation. In our opinion, it could have influenced the obtained values of the Pearson and Spearman coefficients.

The second dataset which was taken into account during the experimental session is the list of analogues. The word pair analogy was adopted as the evaluation method. As in the case of the study of similarities, the gensim library was also used for analogies [26]. Evaluation by analogy is the simplest and in fact one of the best techniques for checking the correctness of word embeddings. This method analyzes two pairs of words, e.g. "Italy" and "Rome", "France" and "Paris" or "Poland" and "Duda", "United States" and "Biden" checking the distance in the vector space between two words in each possible pair. Thereafter, it counts the difference in distance between them. The perfect model should ensure the distance is equal to 0. In the dataset provided by Facebook, there are 1000 lines of two pairs of words, arranged in categories such as, for example, "stolica_kraj". A data sample from the described set is presented in Table 2.

Table 2. Sample data of analogues dataset

No	Website	No of job offers	No of forms	No of lists
1	brat	siostra	tata	mama
2	brat	siostra	ojciec	matka
3	brat	siostra	dziadek	babcia
4	brat	siostra	wnuk	wnuczka
5	brat	siostra	pan	pani
6	brat	siostra	on	ona
7	brat	siostra	jego	jej
8	Warszawa	Polska	Teheran	Iran
9	Warszawa	Polska	Thimphu	Bhutan
10	Warszawa	Polska	Tirana	Albania
11	Warszawa	Polska	Tokio	Japonia
12	Warszawa	Polska	Tripolis	Libia
13	Warszawa	Polska	Tunis	Tunezja

As it can be seen in Table 2 the analogies between family members (brat - siostra, tata - mama) as well as capitals and countries (Warsaw - Poland, Tehran - Iran) are made. Accuracy is returned as a measure of the correctness of the above mentioned method.

4 Experimental Results

The main goal of the presented experiments and evaluation of the available word embeddings for the Polish language was to select the best ones in subsequent studies on sentiment analysis on long texts. During the research, for all evaluation processes, the 121 available embedding models for the Polish language were taken into account that have been provided in the following repositories: IPI

PAN, OPI, Kyubyong and Facebook. The annotation process in these models was performed with the use of three state of the art methodologies: fasttext, Word2Vec and GloVe.

For each model the following parameters were introduced: the size of vocabulary(vocab size), the size of the vector for embeddings set on 100, 300 or 800 (vector size) and the number of words that were excluded from vocabulary during experiments (out of vocab). Moreover, it should be noted, that the learning times of individual models are not taken into account due to the efficiency and high speed of generating results by all methods.

As was mentioned in the last section, two different tasks during the experimental session were performed. Firstly, the considered embedding models were used in order to measure the similarity and the relatedness in the SimLex for Polish dataset. The Python gensim library and the function "evaluate_word_pairs" within the library were used to perform these calculations. The obtained results were in the range from 0 to 10 and were compared with the assessments of independent annotators, who, as part of the preparation of the evaluated dataset, determined the similarity and the relatedness for the pairs of words. The next step of the experiment was to compare the retained results using embedding models with the values provided within the SimLex for Polish dataset. The comparison was made with the use of correlation coefficients: Pearson and Spearman. A higher value of the correlation coefficients indicates higher compliance of the model with the annotator's assessments, which results in an increase of the quality of the model. Moreover, for each model the number of words, which were omitted during the research, were also provided. In our opinion, a greater number of omitted words depreciates the quality of the model.

Table 3. Pearson coefficient for the best models

Name of embedding model	Vocab size	Vector size	Pearson	Out of Vocab
opi_word2vec_800_3_polish.bin	1934028	800	0.4599	11011
opi_word2vec_500_3_polish.bin	1934028	500	0.4532	11011
opi_word2vec_300_3_polish.bin	1934028	300	0.4200	11011
nkjp+wiki-lem-r-300-cbow-hs.txt	1407762	300	0.4150	16016
nkjp+wiki-lem-r-300-cbow-ns.txt	1407762	300	0.4132	16016
nkjp-lem-all-300-skipg-ns.txt	1282621	300	0.4127	16016
opi_fasttext_800_3_polish.bin	2488306	800	0.4125	11011
nkjp-lem-r-300-cbow-hs.txt	1162845	300	0.4121	16016
nkjp-lem-r-300-cbow-ns.txt	1162845	300	0.4108	16016
nkjp+wiki-lem-all-300-cbow-ns-50.txt	294182	300	0.4092	16016

Ten embedding models which achieved the greatest values of Pearson and Spearman coefficients are shown in Tables 3 and 4. Code and experiments results for all tested models are available at github: https://github.com/Ermlab/ /polish-word-embeddings-review.

Table 4. Spearman coefficient for the best models

Name of embedding model	Vocab size	Vector size	Spearman	Out of Vocab
opi_word2vec_800_3_polish.bin	1934028	800	0.5163	11011
opi_word2vec_500_3_polish.bin	1934028	500	0.5107	11011
opi_word2vec_300_3_polish.bin	1934028	300	0.5005	11011
nkjp-lemmas-all-300-skipg-ns.txt	1282621	300	0.4634	16016
opi_word2vec_100_3_polish.bin	1934030	100	0.4616	11011
nkjp+wiki-lem-r-300-cbow-hs.txt	1407762	300	0.4600	16016
nkjp+wiki-lem-all-300-cbow-ns-50.txt	294182	300	0.4600	16016
nkjp+wiki-lem-all-300-cbow-hs.txt	1549322	300	0.4597	16016
nkjp-lemmas-all-300-cbow-hs.txt	1282621	300	0.4582	16016
nkjp+wiki-lem-all-300-cbow-ns.txt	1549322	300	0.4578	16016

For each model, a name indicating the repository from which the model is derived, the method used to annotate the words in the given set, and the size of the dictionary are specified. The obtained values indicate that the best fit of the models is provided in the OPI repository, where word2vec word annotation and the feature vector size 800 were used. The results for the best three models differ slightly, and it can be noted that all three models were created in almost the same way, only with difference in vector size. This may indicate that the size of the vector is of secondary importance in such a case.

The second task performed as a part of research was to evaluate the list of analogies. The main parameter determining the quality of embedding models was the accuracy. Furthermore, as in the first phase, the "evaluate_word_analogies" function from the Python gensim library was used for the research. Ten embedding models which achieved the greatest values of accuracy are shown in Table 5.

The results show that the best model in the context of performing sentiment analysis on long texts turned out to be the one provided by Facebook using fasttext. It achieves the accuracy value of 66% in experiments with the use of the list of analogies dataset. Thus, it can be seen that depending on the choice of the processed datasets and the evaluation method, various models turn out to be the best for encoding the Polish language. In the case of determining the similarity of words, the models from the OPI set together with the word2vec method turned out to be the best, while in the case of the evaluation of the analogy of word pairs based on the Polish Word Analogy dataset provided by Facebook, the model prepared in the Facebook repository using the fasttext algorithm proved to be the most accurate.

Table 5. Accuracy for the best models

Name of embedding model	Vocab size	Vector size	Accuracy	Out of Vocab
facebook_fastext-300.txt	2000000	300	0.66	4004
nkjp+wiki-lem-r-300-skipg-ns.txt	1407762	300	0.62	16016
opi_glove_300_3_polish.txt	1926319	300	0.62	11011
nkjp+wiki-lem-all-300-skipg-ns.txt	1549322	300	0.61	16016
opi_glove_500_3_polish.txt	1926319	500	0.61	11011
nkjp+wiki-lem-r-300-cbow-ns.txt	1407762	300	0.59	16016
nkjp-lem-r-300-skipg-ns.txt	1162845	300	0.58	16016
wiki-lem-r-300-skipg-ns.txt	446608	300	0.58	21021
opi_glove_800_3_polish.txt	1926319	800	0.57	11011
nkjp-lem-all-300-skipg-ns.txt	1282621	300	0.56	16016

Thus, there are many factors to consider when choosing the best embedding model. In the authors' opinion, the best model among the evaluated models is the one provided in the Facebook repository, with the use of fasttext algorithm. The following conclusions result from the following premises: first, when calculating the similarity and the relatedness there are taken into account the opinion of annotators, which may disturb the correctness of the final results. The second important issue relates to the number of omitted words in the model's dictionary. Among all the embedding models used, the percentage of rejected words from the dictionary of Facebook model is significantly lower than others, so the correlation coefficients for this model can be significantly underestimated. Summing up, despite the multifactorial analysis of embeddings for the Polish language, in our opinion, the facebook_fastext-300.txt model should be considered the best.

5 Conclusions and Future Work

In this paper, the first attempt of finding the best word embedding for the highly inflectional language was proposed. In particular, 121 word embedding models for Polish language were evaluated. The experimental results demonstrated that facebook_fastext-300.txt model achieved the highest accuracy. Thus, under the assumptions made during the experimental phase, this model can be considered the best.

The next step of the research will address checking whether the obtained results will also be appropriate for other highly inflectional languages. Moreover, the best models obtained in the experimental session will serve as a starting point in the subsequent stages of performing sentiment analysis on long texts.

Acknowledgments. This work is part of the project No POIR.01.01.01-00-1118/17 "Automatic Reviewer - Advanced Book Recommendation System" funded by the National Centre for Research and Development.

References

1. Alessa, A., Faezipour, M., Alhassan, Z.: Text classification of flu-related tweets using FastText with sentiment and keyword features. In: IEEE International Conference on Healthcare Informatics, pp. 366–367 (2018)
2. Balodis, K., Deksne, D.: FastText-based intent detection for inflected languages. Information **10**, 161 (2019)
3. Bayrak, A., Türker, B.: Typo correction in domain-specific texts using FastText. In: 2020 Innovations in Intelligent Systems and Applications Conference, pp. 1–5 (2020)
4. Bengio, Y., Ducharme, R., Vincent, P.: A neural probabilistic language model. J. Mach. Learn. Res. **3**, 1137–1155 (2003)
5. Chen, Q., Sokolova, M.: Word2Vec and Doc2Vec in unsupervised sentiment analysis of clinical discharge summaries. arXiv, 1805.00352 (2018)
6. Dai, L., Jiang, K.: Chinese text classification based on FastText. Comput. Modern. **1693**, 012121 (2018)
7. Devlin, J., Chang, M., Lee, K., Toutanova, K.: BERT: pre-training of deep bidirectional transformers for language under-standing. arXiv, 1810.04805 (2019)
8. Dowoo, K., Moung-Wan, K.: Categorization of Korean news articles based on convolutional neural network using Doc2Vec and Word2Vec. J. KIISE **44**(7), 742–747 (2017)
9. Hammou, B., Lahcen, A., Mouline, S.: Towards a real-time processing framework based on improved distributed recurrent neural network variants with FastText for social big data analytics. Inf. Process. Manage. **57**(1), 102122 (2020)
10. Janz, A., Milkowski, P.,: ELMo Embeddings for Polish, CLARIN-PL digital repository. http://hdl.handle.net/11321/690 (2019)
11. Joulin, A., Grave, E., Bojanowski, P., Mikolov, T.: Bag of tricks for efficient text classification. arXiv, 1607.01759 (2016)
12. Kleczek, D.: Polbert: attacking Polish NLP tasks with transformers. In: Proceedings of the PolEval Workshop (2020)
13. Lilleberg, J., Zhu, Y., Zhang, Y.: Support vector machines and word2vec for text classification with semantic features. In: Proceedings of IEEE ICCI*CC, pp. 136–140 (2015)
14. Mikolov, T., Sutskever, I., Chen, K., Corrado, G., Dean, J.: Distributed representations of words and phrases and their compositionality. In: Advances in Neural Information Processing Systems, pp. 3111–3119 (2013)
15. Mikolov, T., Chen, K., Corrado, G., Dean, J.: Efficient estimation of word representations in vector space. arXiv, 1301.3781 (2013)
16. Mykowiecka, A., Marciniak, M., Rychlik, P.: Testing word embeddings for Polish. Cogn. Stud. **17**, 1468 (2017)
17. Mykowiecka, A., Marciniak, M., Rychlik, P.: SimLex-999 for Polish. In: Proceedings of LREC (2018)
18. Pennington, J., Socher, R., Manning, C.: Glove: Global vectors for word representation. In: Empirical Methods in Natural Language Processing, pp. 1532–1543 (2014)
19. Peters, M., et al.: Deep contextualized word representations. In: NAACL (2018)
20. Prabha, M., Umarani Srikanth, G.: Survey of sentiment analysis using deep learning techniques. In: International Conference on Innovations in Information and Communication Technology, pp. 1–9 (2019)

21. Rogalski, M., Szczepaniak, P.: Word embeddings for the Polish language. In: International Conference of Artificial Intelligence and Soft Computing, pp. 126–135 (2016)
22. Santos, I., Nedjah, N., de Macedo Mourelle, L.: Sentiment analysis using convolutional neural network with FastText embeddings. In: IEEE Latin American Conference on Computational Intelligence, pp. 1–5 (2017)
23. Stein, R., Jaques, P., Valiati, J.: An analysis of hierarchical text classification using word embeddings. Inf. Sci. **471**, 216–232 (2019)
24. Talun, A., Drozda, P., Bukowski, L., Scherer, R.: FastText and XGBoost content-based classification for employment web scraping. In: International Conference of Artificial Intelligence and Soft Computing, pp. 435–444 (2020)
25. Facebook analogies dataset. https://dl.fbaipublicfiles.com/fasttext/word-analogies/questions-words-pl.txt
26. Python gensim library. https://radimrehurek.com/gensim_3.8.3/

Constructing VeSNet: Mapping LOD Thesauri onto Princeton WordNet and Polish WordNet

Arkadiusz Janz, Grzegorz Kostkowski(✉), and Marek Maziarz

Wroclaw University of Science and Technology, 50-370 Wrocław, Poland
{arkadiusz.janz,grzegorz.kostkowski,marek.maziarz}@pwr.edu.pl

Abstract. Lexical resources are crucial in many modern applications of Natural Language Processing and Artificial Intelligence. We present VeSNet – a network of lexical resources resulting from the merge of Polish-English WordNet (PEWN) with several existing large electronic thesauri from the Linked Open Data cloud (DBpedia, Wikipedia, GeoWordNet, Agrovoc, Eurovoc, Gemet and MeSH). We describe the procedure of making the resource and depict its elementary properties, as well as, evaluate its quality. The created lexical network is characterised both by great coverage and high precision: nearly 1.3M new `exactMatch` links were created, including 85K to PEWN, with the estimated precision of 94%.

Keywords: Semantic network · Linked Open Data · SKOS · WordNet · Mapping · NLP

1 Introduction

In modern societies communication and information sharing and processing become every year more and more important and the necessity to obtain efficient information technologies and language processing to cope with information flood arises.

On the one hand, world becomes smaller because of the growth of the global village. The rise of the World Wide Web, globalization in various areas of human culture (like news, movie, fashion, technology), global market – all these phenomena brake borders between countries and make people to be closer, more close than in any previous time in human history, cf. [8].

On the other hand, various differences – hidden in times when the world was bigger – come to voice [1]. Diversities in cultural background make understanding sometimes impossible. Not only our perception of the same facts differs. Like after the fall of the Babel tower, we now have realised that we people spoke different languages. Delivering large and high quality linguistic resources is thus the contemporary challenge [9]. Among many efforts aiming at facilitating this information flow between people and societies, developing language technologies should be acknowledged crucial role [11]. The task is not simple, because there are 7,000 languages in the world, of which most are under-resourced [27].

K. Wojtkiewicz et al. (Eds.): ICCCI 2021, CCIS 1463, pp. 608–620, 2021.
https://doi.org/10.1007/978-3-030-88113-9_49

The Linked Open Data (LOD) initiative overcomes the abyss by providing large, of high standards and free data sets [4], among which lexical resources, like Princeton WordNet, are considered to have the pivotal role [3]. This paper presents the process of merging selected LOD resources into VeSNet – the Vocabulary Enhanced Semantic Network – a large, open, SKOS RDF-based data set, made out of the largest of existing nowadays lexico-semantic networks [19]. We describe its properties and provide information on its quality.

In brief, we took two largest and independently built wordnets (English WordNet [14] and plWordNet [20]), added labels from the Open Multilingual Wordnet [7], and heavily interlinked with a significant part of Linked Open Data network, that is with DBpedia, Wikipedia, GeoWordNet, Eurovoc, Agrovoc, Gemet and MeSH. We prepared new mappings between the resources, as well as made use of existing mappings and propagated them iteratively onto more distant concepts and resources. As a result, we obtained 1.3M new equivalence relation instances, including 85K links to Polish-English WordNet (with estimated precision of 94%).

2 Related Work

In last years several teams attempted to merge LOD resources with WordNet. De Melo and Weikum [13] combined different existing resources (several wordnets mapped onto Princeton WordNet, translational dictionaries, Wiktionary, Gemet, OWL ontologies, OmegaWiki, as well as, parallel corpora and Open Office thesauri, with frequency information from SemCor) into a large graph of lemma-synset (lemma-meaning), lemma-lemma (translational equivalents) and synset-synset (hypernymic, meronymic, antonymic etc.) links. 1.5 million lemma-synset links were created with estimated precision of 85%–91% with recall equal to 67%.

Morshed et al. [24] (cf. Caraciollo et al. [10]) described a method of linking six thesauri containing agricultural vocabulary via simple string matching (multilingual label set). According to them "simple string matching techniques are quite appropriate to provide candidate links in a Linked Data framework, as the human evaluation confirmed most of the matches found" [24]. They achieved precision above 95%.

Bond and Foster [6] linked Wiktionary and the Unicode Common Locale Data Repository with Open Multilingual WordNet. They constructed bags of words and used several Jaccard measures of similarity, manually setting parameters for heuristics. The bags were constructed from lemmas of senses/synsets and definitions. High accuracy of 85%–99% was obtained thanks "to the disambiguating power of the multiple translations" (i.e. equivalents).

McCrae and Cillessen [22] most recently have proposed a method of merging WordNet with Wikidata, based on hapax legomena identification. Hapax legomena heuristics produced 9K new equivalency links with estimated accuracy of 98.4%. The authors also tested the applicability of the Naisc system (using semantic textual similarity, see [21]) and obtained at best 85.7% accuracy, with potential coverage of most noun WordNet synsets.

Till now, Polish WordNet has not been mapped onto LOD cloud [19]. Thanks to the manual, huge coverage mapping between plWordNet and Princeton WordNet [26] we may talk now about the Polish-English WordNet (hence *PEWN*).

3 Thesauri

We decided to interlink seven Linked Open Data thesauri and PEWN. We chose only those semantic nets that were published under open licences (it enabled us to republish the whole network of inter-resource links under a Creative Commons Attribution Share-Alike licence). The final interlinked network of semantic nets included:

- Agrovoc[1] (published under the CC-BY 3.0 IGO licence),
- Eurovoc[2] (CC-BY 4.0),
- Gemet[3] (CC BY 2.5 DK),
- GeoWordNet[4] (CC-BY 3.0),
- MeSH[5] (MeSH licence, attribution requirement),
- PEWN[6] (both wordnets are published under the Princeton WordNet licence),
- Wikipedia and DBpedia[7] (both on CC-BY-SA 3.0).

In Fig. 1 we present relevant statistics. Apart from large semantic networks (such as GeoWordNet, DBpedia and Wikipedia, containing millions of nodes) we dealt also with smaller thesauri of a dozen thousand concepts each (Agrovoc, Eurovoc, Gemet and MeSH). Wordnet sizes (in terms of concepts) represented the in-between-state (ca 100K–200K concepts). We started the process of mapping from thesauri external to PEWN. In several consecutive steps involving alternating linking concepts with equivalents *via* labels and propagating newly created links through the network we obtained large numbers of the mapping links. Section 4 presents details of the whole procedure.

Two professional linguists, native speakers of Polish and proficient in English, were asked to find out the proper equivalents of thesaurus concepts in wordnets. They were presented simple random samples of thesaurus concepts, as well as, top nodes of each resource. For mapping they used the SKOS scheme and all its matching relations [23]:

1 http://www.fao.org/agrovoc/.
2 https://op.europa.eu/en/web/eu-vocabularies/dataset/-/resource?uri=http://publications.europa.eu/resource/dataset/eurovoc.
3 https://www.eionet.europa.eu/gemet/en/about/.
4 https://old.datahub.io/dataset/geowordnet.
5 https://www.ncbi.nlm.nih.gov/mesh/.
6 https://wordnet.princeton.edu/, http://plwordnet.pwr.wroc.pl/wordnet/.
7 https://www.wikipedia.org/, https://wiki.dbpedia.org/.

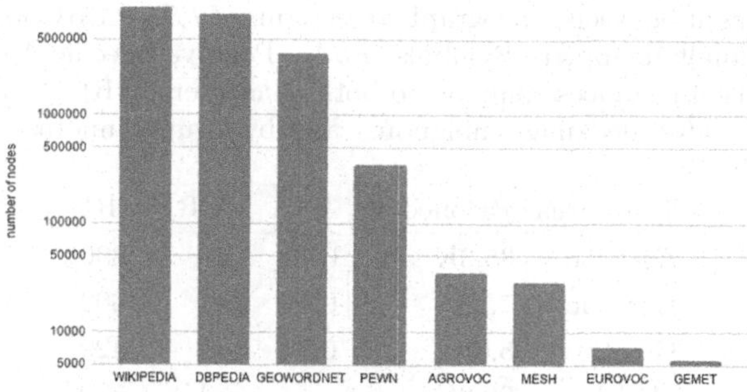

Fig. 1. Number of nodes in LOD thesauri.

1. `exactMatch` (`eM`, the exact correspondence of a concept and synset meaning);
2. `closeMatch` (`cM`, the approximate equivalence between concepts);
3. `broadMatch` (`bM`, the relation in which a thesaurus concept (the parent) has narrower term extension than the wordnet synset; `bM` has three main subtypes: hyponymy, meronymy and topic inclusion;
4. `narrowMatch` (`nM`, it is the inverse of the bM relation);
5. `relatedMatch` (`rM`, if two concepts are obviously semantically related, however the relation cannot be reduced to any of the four previously described relation types).

These `-Match` relations were organised into a ranking, exactly as in the list above. Starting from a thesaurus concepts our linguists independently looked for the best equivalents, first in WordNet and then in plWordNet. They checked applicability of `eM` and `cM` relations. If a synonymous equivalent was not found, they searched wordnets for broader and narrower terms, while *relatedMatch* relation was the last resort. From 10% to 30% of the samples overlapped. Table 1 presents the number of established relation instances in samples (#RI) and in their overlapping parts (#CRI). Each linguist linked 700 concepts a month, and the whole process of the manual annotation presented in this paper took approximately 2 person-months.

The efficiency of the mapping was evaluated on the basis of the number of thesaurus concepts shared by both annotators and – in particular – on the basis of instances of `exactMatch` and `closeMatch` established in the mapping process (with both relation types being merged[8]). The Positive Specific Agreement index [15] was calculated according to the formula:

$$PSA = \frac{2a}{2a + b + c}, \quad (1)$$

[8] Thus, we did not distinguish between them. Equaling `eM` and `cM` could be justified by the fact that "`skos:exactMatch`, defined as a transitive subproperty of `skos:closeMatch`, was intended to express a degree of similarity close enough to justify (...) propagation" [2].

Table 1. Agreement between lexicographers in terms of *PSA* (GeoWordNet and DBpedia were not manually mapped). Symbols: *PSA* – Positive Specific Agreement, #CRI – number of relation instances common to both annotators, #RI – number of relation instances in total (after deciding ambiguous cases by a superannotator).

Thesaurus	#Concepts	*PSA*	#CRI	#RI
Agrovoc	35.3K	0.78	61	890
Eurovoc	7.3K	0.90	203	602
Gemet	5.6K	0.73	146	429
MeSH	29.0K	–	0	530
Wikipedia	10.0M	0.64	49	443
in total		0.75	459	2894

where a denoted the number of shared `eM/cM` instances and b, c signified numbers of relation instances particular to one annotator. The confusion matrix for the task looked as follows:

Table 2. Confusion matrix for `eM/cM` relation instances. Symbols: #1 – first annotator, #2 – second annotator, Y – acceptance of a given `eM/cM` instance, N – rejection of the instance. Please note that d value (dual rejection) is very large (one may virtually link a thesaurus concept to any synset in a wordnet).

`eM/cM`		#1	
		Y	N
#2	Y	a	b
	N	c	d

PSA may be seen as the harmonic mean of annotator percentage agreements, calculated with regard to the decisions of the second annotator, see Sect. 6.2 for details. On the other hand, the *PSA* index could be obtained from Cohen's kappa (a measure of inter-annotator agreement corrected for chance agreement [12]) treating d cases (N-N) as infinite [16], i.e.

$$\lim_{d \to \infty} \kappa = PSA. \tag{2}$$

This assumption is justified by the fact that every thesaurus concept could be potentially linked to any synset in a wordnet. Since there are more than 100K synsets in each wordnet, the d number is indeed very large, cf. Sect. 6.1 of the *Appendix*.

Because of the dependence of the PSA index on Cohen's κ definition we adopted operational criteria proposed for the latter measure. Although there is no way to objectively assess the range of acceptable kappas, the proposal of Koch and Landis [18] to treat κ between 0.61 and 0.8 as "substantial" and $\kappa > 0.81$ as "almost perfect" is considered by many as appropriate [28]. Accordingly, the well-known rule of thumb in computational linguistics is that κ ranging between 0.67 (0.7) and 0.8 is treated as "tolerable", while $\kappa > 0.8$ is perceived as "good" [17,25].

Table 1 presents PSA values for four thesauri checked for the inter-annotator agreement (Agrovoc, Eurovoc, Gemet and Wikipedia), showing that the agreement is at least acceptable. Disagreement cases were later checked by a super-annotator (the last one author of this paper) and disambiguated.

Having taken into account all identified by annotators `eM`/`cM` cases[9] we constructed our gold standard mapping data set. The data set[10] is obtainable from the Clarin-PL site (https://clarin-pl.eu/dspace/handle/11321/790) under an open licence. We used it then to evaluate efficiency of automatic mapping procedures (Sect. 5 below).

4 Automatic Mapping Procedures

In this paper we decided to rely on simple yet effective idea of utilising multilingual resources. Our main aim was to evaluate solutions being easy to implement for any language. To effectively perform a mapping of pre-selected semantic resources onto wordnet we decided to follow the solution based on utilising available multilingual data e.g. interconnected wordnets from Open Multilingual WordNet Grid [6], multilingual encyclopedias such as Wikipedia or Wiktionary, and multilingual thesauri. The resources like Wikipedia have been frequently considered as extremely valuable resources for improving existing NLP algorithms because of their broad coverage of domain-specific and domain-independent terminology and also due to their semantic structure based on pre-defined hierarchy of topic-based categories and semantic links between concepts. The multilinguality of Wikipedia has been also very helpful in many NLP areas such as Machine Translation or Word Sense Disambiguation. Finally, the Wikipedia was used for linking with wordnet as a basis for expanding wordnets with new domain-specific terminology and introducing new semantic links between wordnet concepts. Still, the domain-specific terminology of Wikipedia can be quite limited for some domains and we believe that the Wikipedia should be not considered as the only one resource for extending wordnet with specialist terminology. However, one might use the Wikipedia as a bridge for further wordnet expansion. Let (R_1, R_2) represent a pair of input resources being aligned. The usual way of mapping semantic resources includes the following mapping steps:

[9] That is not only the shared ones.

[10] Including also other thesauri.

1. Candidate generation: a step that generates a set of possibly related concepts $C = \{(c_1, c_2) : c_1 \in R_1, c_2 \in R_2$ coming from different resources R_1 and R_2; in this step one might use available labels describing the concepts as a factor for generating candidates, thus, we can actually precise the definition of this set for our purposes and we add an additional constraint such that $\phi(c_1) \cap \phi(c_2) \neq \emptyset$ where $\phi : c \rightarrow$ labels(c),
2. Sense alignment (with sense disambiguation and rejection mechanism): a step that incorporates available sources of semantic information describing possibly related concepts (c_1, c_2); this step assumes that there exist a function $f : C \rightarrow S$ mapping generated candidates onto pre-defined SKOS classes $S = \{s_1, \ldots, s_k\}$; we also assume that the function can reject given input pair when its concepts are semantically incompatible (rejection mechanism);

We decided to extend this schema to more general case where the alignment is performed using multiple resources at the same time $R = \{R_1, R_2, \ldots, R_M\}$, where $M > 2$. In our solution we apply this schema in a recursive way since we can actually use newly discovered mappings as a source for further expansion and generating yet another alignments. However, repeating this schema can also introduce new alignment errors if we do not ensure that sense alignment step expresses a good enough performance with high precision.

Both steps can be actually seen as a supervised learning problem where the mapping function f is responsible for generating candidates and aligning possibly related concepts. Still, with this type of solutions the main issue is the lack of annotated data for training strictly supervised model and their inability to generalize well to new domains and resources. Thus, the weakly supervised solutions and representation learning techniques have gained increasing attention recently.

One of the main challenges in the area of automatic resource alignment is the problem of sense disambiguation. This problem can be partially solved by exploring new possibilities arising from multiliguality of mapped resources, especially if the resources taking part in the mapping procedure have their concepts described with multiple labels from different languages. In our procedure we explore these kind of possibilities by taking a heuristic approach to sense disambiguation of concepts being aligned and we incorporate all available pre-defined labels describing the concepts in multiple languages. We built our solution upon the idea proposed in [6], but we also expand this approach by introducing new mapping heuristics (features). Let $\phi : c \rightarrow \text{labels}(c)$

1. For each label $l \in \phi(c)$ check if it is a monosemous label with respect to its original source thesaurus R_i, $i = 1, \ldots, M$ which means that there exists only one concept $c' = c$ sharing this label (binary feature),
2. Check if a given label l is monosemous in more than one of aligned resources $\{R_1, R_2, \ldots, R_M\}$ (binary feature),
3. The feature representing the number of distinct labels linking c_1 and c_2 (or in a binary case the feature checking if the overall number of common labels taking into account different languages is greater than given threshold e.g. 2,3 etc.),

4. Semantic similarity, which represents the degree of semantic overlap of input concepts c_1 and c_2 computed as Overlap Coefficient similarity score of their word bags generated with simple graph traversal (breadth first search gathering terms appearing in given radius around c_1 and c_2 in their sources) and pre-computed definition overlap,
5. Check if a common label shared by candidate concepts is a multiword expression (MWE) or not,
6. Find if there exists a link connecting at most k-hop distant parents of input c_1 and c_2 concepts being aligned by exploring their taxonomic structure and taking into account only `broader`, `closeMatch` and `exactMatch` link types.

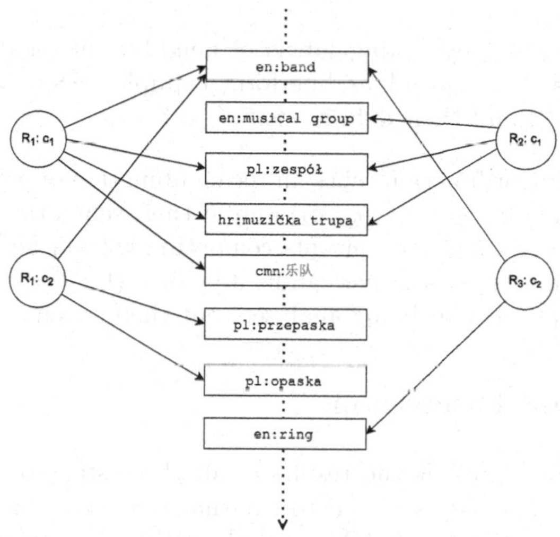

Fig. 2. Mapping concepts from different resources (R_1, R_2, and R_3) using multilingual labels. The procedure can generate possibly correct links such as $R_1 : c_1 - R_2 : c_2$, but also some negative examples like $R_1 : c_1 - R_3 : c_2$ (rejection procedure).

As the multilinguality itself might be not a sufficient factor to successfully perform the mapping we decided to support our heuristics by adding additional metrics of semantic overlap for concepts. With these metrics we are able to filter out possibly wrong mappings of concepts e.g. sharing the same labels but expressing incompatible senses. We built upon the idea proposed in [6] and we use Overlap Coefficient similarity score of label bags to measure semantic overlap of candidate concepts being linked. The label bags are built by applying the following procedure:

1. The definitions (if available) attached to input concepts; we split the definitions into single lemmatised words and add these words into our bags,

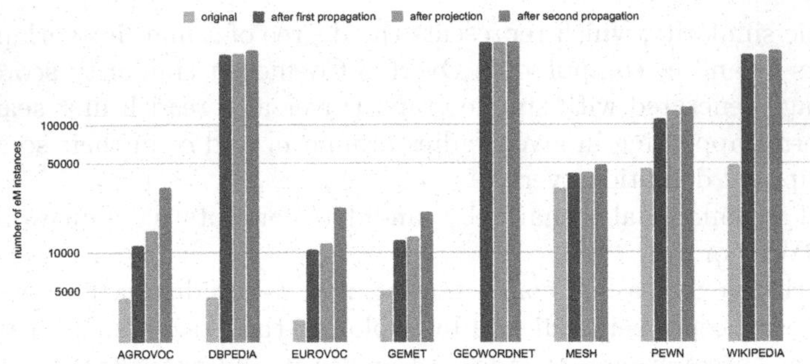

Fig. 3. Number of `skos:exactMatch` links after each phase.

2. The words gathered by taking labels of neighbouring nodes (we treat the input resources R_i as a graph and perform a simple BFS traversal with radius parameter $r = 3$) and their definitions.

Our final alignment function relies on the combination of presented heuristics and accepts candidate concepts (c_1, c_2) only if their semantic overlap is greater than semantic overlap of other concepts competing with c_1 and c_2. This usually means that there exists yet another candidate pair $(c_1\prime, c_2\prime)$ that shares the same label with input (c_1, c_2) pair being analysed, but their semantic overlap is lower.

5 Results and Discussion

Figure 3 and Table 3 present the results of all three steps of the procedure in terms of number of concepts linked to external resources through `exactMatch` instances. We obtained in total 1.3M new links within the network. Nearly 85,000 new instances of equivalency were added to PEWN. The quality of the mapping to wordnets is high, as estimated on the basis of manually mapped samples from thesauri. The 95% confidence interval for the mean precision lies in the range $[0.89, 0.99]$ with mean $P = 0.94$.[11]

Recall varies greatly from 0.22 to 0.83 (from resource to resource), which means that in some cases our label-matcher lost many proper equivalents, especially in the case of specialist thesauri with smaller number of relevant languages, like MeSH (only English labels) or Agrovoc (only few languages). Recall is positively correlated with both the percentage of `eM`/`cM` instances ("`eM` ratio",

[11] Calculated with the normality assumption and with t-Student distribution for unknown deviance, $n = 5$ observations (i.e. lexical resources).

Table 3. Evaluation of the mapping procedure. Symbols: P – precision of the class eM/cM, R – recall of the class, eM ratio – denotes the percentage of direct equivalents in each gold standard sample, *PSA* – positive specific agreement.

Thesaurus	#Concepts	# New relations	# New rels. to PEWN	P	R	eM ratio	PSA
Agrovoc	35.3K	30.8K	5.2K	0.88	0.40	0.300	0.78
Eurovoc	7.3K	16.6K	2.0K	0.95	0.83	0.930	0.90
Gemet	5.6K	13.6K	2.1K	0.93	0.60	0.228	0.73
GeoWordNet	369.8K	443.6K	2.5K	–	–	–	–
MeSH	29.0K	14.1K	2.3K	0.97	0.22	0.262	–
Wikipedia	10.0M	327.6K	11.9K	0.96	0.63	0.316	0.64
DBpedia	8.2M	370.2K	58.5K	–	–	–	–
in total:		1.3M	84.5K				

Spearman's correlation $\rho = 0.7$, p-value$= 0.066$ in a one-tailed permutation test [5, ch. 10] , as well as, with the number of labelling languages (identical parameters: $\rho = 0.7$, p-value$= 0.066$).[12]

High quality of the mapping from LOD to Polish-English WordNet, and its good coverage (1.3M equivalents in whole VeSNet, 85K for PEWN) leads to the conclusion that our resource would be a fair supplement to the Linked Open Data cloud. Yet still a lot is to be done. The work is in progress – every month our linguists annotate new lexical resources, enabling us to enhance Polish-English WordNet with vocabulary of other open-source thesauri (in plans: LCSH, DDC, UDC, Rameau, Roget's) and ontologies (UMBEL and ConceptNet). Since for many thesaurus concepts it was impossible to find exact equivalents and the annotators discovered many extension inclusion relationships, we plan to add to the automatic mapping also `broadMatch` and `narrowMatch` links, raising recall of our method. We also publish our manual as well as automatic mappings generated with the proposed solution and we share our code under an open source license[13].

Acknowledgments. This research was financed by the Polish Ministry of Education and Science, Project CLARIN-PL, and by the European Regional Development Fund as a part of the 2014–2020 Smart Growth Operational Programme, CLARIN - Common Language Resources and Technology Infrastructure, project no. POIR.04.02.00-00C002/19.

[12] The eM ratio measure is important, since it shows how 'compatible' a thesaurus is when compared to wordnets. Lower eM ratios mean more specific terms in thesauri. This might inform us on how difficult finding a proper equivalent of a thesaurus concept in a wordnet could be. On the other hand, the analysis of correlation between recall and the labelling language number leads to identical conclusions, suggesting that this could also be an important factor.

[13] The data and our code are available at https://github.com/CLARIN-PL/vesnet.

6 Appendix

6.1 PSA as the Cohen's Kappa Limit

Positive specific agreement could be derived from the definition of Cohen's kappa with the assumption that the negative class is infinitively large. We start from the definition of κ (with letters' meaning established in the confusion Table 2):

$$\kappa = \frac{A_0 - A_e}{1 - A_e},\ A_0 = \frac{a+d}{N},$$
$$A_e = p_Y + p_N = (\frac{a+b}{N} \cdot \frac{a+c}{N}) + (\frac{d+b}{N} \cdot \frac{d+c}{N}), \tag{3}$$

where $N = a + b + c + d$ is the total number of annotations, A_0 is the observed relative agreement, A_e is agreement expected by chance, and p_Y as p_N are joint probabilities of choosing "Y" and "N", respectively [15]. Hence,

$$\kappa = \frac{\frac{a+d}{N} - (\frac{a+b}{N} \cdot \frac{a+c}{N} + \frac{d+b}{N} \cdot \frac{d+c}{N})}{1 - (\frac{a+b}{N} \cdot \frac{a+c}{N} + \frac{d+b}{N} \cdot \frac{d+c}{N})} = \frac{\frac{N \cdot (a+d)}{N^2} - \frac{(a+b)\cdot(a+c)+(d+b)\cdot(d+c)}{N^2}}{\frac{N^2 - ((a+b)\cdot(a+c)+(d+b)\cdot(d+c))}{N^2}}$$
$$= \frac{N \cdot (a+d) - ((a+b) \cdot (a+c) + (d+b) \cdot (d+c))}{N^2 - ((a+b) \cdot (a+c) + (d+b) \cdot (d+c))}. \tag{4}$$

In the numerator after elementary calculations we obtain:

$$(a^2 + ab + ac + 2ad + bd + cd + d^2)$$
$$-(a^2 + ab + ac + 2bc + bd + cd + d^2) = 2(ad - bc), \tag{5}$$

while in the denominator we get:

$$a^2 + 2ab + b^2 + 2ac + 2bc + 2ad + 2bd + c^2 + 2cd + d^2$$
$$-(a^2 + ab + ac + 2bc + bd + cd + d^2) =$$
$$= ab + b^2 + ac + 2ad + bd + c^2 + cd. \tag{6}$$

Substituting the results 5 and 6 into the fraction 4 we obtain:

$$\kappa = \frac{2 \cdot (ad - bc)}{ab + b^2 + ac + 2ad + bd + c^2 + cd} = \frac{d \cdot (2a - \frac{2bc}{d})}{d \cdot (\frac{ab+b^2+ac+c^2}{d} + 2a + b + c)} \tag{7}$$

As d aproaches infinity kappa approaches PSA:

$$\lim_{d\to\infty} \kappa = \lim_{d\to\infty} \frac{2a - \frac{2bc}{d}}{\frac{ab+b^2+ac+c^2}{d} + 2a + b + c} = \frac{2a - 0}{0 + 2a + b + c} = PSA. \ \square \tag{8}$$

6.2 PSA as the Harmonic Mean of Annotator Percentage Agreements

Lets define annotator percentage agreement (APA) as the number of agreed cases divided by the total number of each annotator decisions. For the confusion Table 2 we define APA as follows:

$$APA_1 = \frac{a}{a+b},\ APA_2 = \frac{a}{a+c}, \tag{9}$$

"1" stands for the first annotator, while "2" for the second one. The PSA index could be then defined as the harmonic mean of APA_1 and APA_2:

$$PSA = \frac{2 \cdot APA_1 \cdot APA_2}{APA_1 + APA_2}. \tag{10}$$

Through elementary transformations we obtain from the definition 10:

$$PSA = \frac{2 \cdot \frac{a}{a+b} \cdot \frac{a}{a+c}}{\frac{a}{a+b} + \frac{a}{a+c}} = \frac{\frac{2a^2}{(a+b)\cdot(a+c)}}{\frac{a(a+c)+a(a+b)}{(a+b)\cdot(a+c)}} = \frac{2a^2}{a(a+c)+a(a+b)} = \frac{2a}{2a+b+c}. \quad \square \tag{11}$$

References

1. Bai, X., Ramos, M.R., Fiske, S.T.: As diversity increases, people paradoxically perceive social groups as more similar. Proc. Nat. Acad. Sci. **117**(23), 12741–12749 (2020)
2. Baker, T., Bechhofer, S., Isaac, A., Miles, A., Schreiber, G., Summers, E.: Key choices in the design of simple knowledge organization system (SKOS). Web Seman. Sci. Serv. Agents World Wide Web **20**, 35–49 (2013)
3. Ballatore, A., Bertolotto, M., Wilson, D.C.: Grounding linked open data in wordnet: the case of the OSM semantic network. In: Liang, S.H.L., Wang, X., Claramunt, C. (eds.) W2GIS 2013. LNCS, vol. 7820, pp. 1–15. Springer, Heidelberg (2013). https://doi.org/10.1007/978-3-642-37087-8_1
4. Bauer, F., Kaltenböck, M.: Linked Open Data: The essentials: A Quick Start Guide for Decision Makers. Edition mono/monochrom, Vienna, Austria (2011)
5. Berry, K.J., Johnston, J.E., Mielke, P.W.: A Primer of Permutation Statistical Methods. Springer, Cham (2019). https://doi.org/10.1007/978-3-030-20933-9
6. Bond, F., Foster, R.: Linking and extending an open multilingual wordnet. In: Proceedings of the 51st Annual Meeting of the Association for Computational Linguistics (Volume 1: Long Papers), pp. 1352–1362 (2013)
7. Bond, F., Paik, K.: A survey of wordnets and their licenses. Small, vol. 8, no. 4 (2012)
8. Buchan, N.R., Grimalda, G., Wilson, R., Brewer, M., Fatas, E., Foddy, M.: Globalization and human cooperation. Proc. Nat. Acad. Sci. **106**(11), 4138–4142 (2009)
9. Calzolari, N., Soria, C.: Preparing the field for an open and distributed resource infrastructure: The role of the FLaReNet network. LREC2010 (2010)
10. Caracciolo, C., et al.: The AGROVOC linked dataset. Seman. Web **4**(3), 341–348 (2013)

11. Cieri, C., et al.: A road map for interoperable language resource metadata (2010)
12. Cohen, J.: A coefficient of agreement for nominal scales. Educ. Psychol. Meas. **20**(1), 37–46 (1960)
13. De Melo, G., Weikum, G.: Towards a universal wordnet by learning from combined evidence. In: Proceedings of the 18th ACM Conference on Information and Knowledge Management, pp. 513–522 (2009)
14. Fellbaum, C., Miller, G. (eds.): WordNet: An Electronic Lexical Database. The MIT Press, Cambridge (1998)
15. Hripcsak, G., Heitjan, D.F.: Measuring agreement in medical informatics reliability studies. J. Biomed. Inform. **35**(2), 99–110 (2002)
16. Hripcsak, G., Rothschild, A.S.: Agreement, the f-measure, and reliability in information retrieval. J. Am. Med. Inform. Assoc. **12**(3), 296–298 (2005)
17. Krippendorff, K.: Content Analysis: An Introduction to its Methodology. Sage Publications, New York (2018)
18. Landis, J.R., Koch, G.G.: The measurement of observer agreement for categorical data. Biometrics, pp. 159–174 (1977)
19. Maziarz, M., Piasecki, M.: Towards mapping thesauri onto plWordNet. In: Proceedings of Global Wordnet Conference GWC-2018, pp. 45–53 (2018)
20. Maziarz, M., Piasecki, M., Rudnicka, E., Szpakowicz, S., Kedzia, P.: plWordNet 3.0 - a comprehensive lexical-semantic resource. In: Proceedings of COLING 2016, the 26th International Conference on Computational Linguistics: Technical Papers, pp. 2259–2268 (2016)
21. McCrae, J.P., Buitelaar, P.: Linking datasets using semantic textual similarity. Cybern. Inform. Technol. **18**(1), 109–123 (2018)
22. McCrae, J.P., Cillessen, D.: Towards a linking between WordNet and Wikidata. In: Proceedings of the 11th Global Wordnet Conference, pp. 252–257. Global Wordnet Association, University of South Africa (UNISA), January 2021
23. Miles, A., Matthews, B., Wilson, M., Brickley, D.: SKOS core: simple knowledge organisation for the Web. In: International Conference on Dublin Core and Metadata Applications, pp. 3–10 (2005)
24. Morshed, A., Caracciolo, C., Johannsen, G., Keizer, J.: Thesaurus alignment for Linked Data publishing. In: Proceedings of the International Conference on Dublin Core and Metadata Applications 2011, pp. 37–46. Dublin Core Metadata Initiative (2011)
25. Reidsma, D., Carletta, J.: Reliability measurement without limits. Comput. Linguist. **34**(3), 319–326 (2008)
26. Rudnicka, E., Witkowski, W., Piasecki, M.: A (non)-perfect match: mapping plWordNet onto princetonwordnet. In: Proceedings of the 11th Global Wordnet Conference, pp. 137–146 (2021)
27. Tracey, J., Strassel, S.: Basic language resources for 31 languages (plus English): the LORELEI representative and incident language packs. In: Proceedings of the 1st Joint Workshop on Spoken Language Technologies for Under-resourced languages (SLTU) and Collaboration and Computing for Under-Resourced Languages (CCURL), pp. 277–284 (2020)
28. Watson, P., Petrie, A.: Method agreement analysis: a review of correct methodology. Theriogenology **73**(9), 1167–1179 (2010)

Arabic Sentiment Analysis Using BERT Model

Hasna Chouikhi[1(✉)], Hamza Chniter[2(✉)], and Fethi Jarray[1,2(✉)]

[1] LIMTIC Laboratory, UTM University, Tunis, Tunisia
hasna.chouikhi@fst.utm.tn

[2] Higher Institute of Computer Science of Medenine, Medinine, Tunisia
fethi.jarray@isim.rnu.tn

Abstract. Sentiment analysis is the process of determining whether a text or a writing is positive, negative, or neutral. A lot of research has been done to improve the accuracy of sentiment analysis methods, varying from simple linear models to more complex deep neural network models. Lately, the transformer-based model showed great success in sentiment analysis and was considered as the state-of-the-art model for various languages (English, german, french, Turk, Arabic, etc.). However, the accuracy for Arabic sentiment analysis still needs improvements especially in tokenization level during data processing. In fact, the Arabic language imposes many challenges, due to its complex structure, various dialects, and resource scarcity. The improvement of the proposed approach consists of integrating an Arabic BERT tokenizer instead of a basic BERT Tokenizer. Various tests were carried out with different instances (dialect and standard). We used hyperparameters optimization by random search method to obtain the best result with different datasets. The experimental study proves the efficiency of the proposed approach in terms of classification quality and accuracy compared to Arabic BERT and AraBERT models.

Keywords: Arabic sentiment analysis · BERT model · Arabic BERT model · Arabic language · Tokenization

1 Introduction

Sentiment Analysis (SA) is a Natural Language Processing (NLP) research field that spotlights on looking over people's opinions, sentiments, and emotions. SA techniques are categorized into symbolic and sub-symbolic approaches. The former use lexica and ontologies [1] to encode the associated polarity with words and multiword expressions. The latter consist of supervised, semi-supervised and unsupervised machine learning techniques that perform sentiment classification based on word cooccurrence frequencies. Among all these techniques, the most popular are based on deep neural networks. Some hybrid frameworks leverage both symbolic and sub-symbolic approaches.

SA is based on a multi-step process including data retrieval, data extraction, data pre-processing, and feature extraction. The ultimate subtasks of sentiment

K. Wojtkiewicz et al. (Eds.): ICCCI 2021, CCIS 1463, pp. 621–632, 2021.
https://doi.org/10.1007/978-3-030-88113-9_50

classification allow three types of classification: polarity classification, intensity classification, and emotion identification. The first type classifies the text as positive, negative or neutral, while the second type identifies the polarity degree as very positive, positive, negative or very negative. The third classification identifies the emotion such as sad, anger or happy.

Pratically, arabic language has a complex nature, due to its ambiguity and rich morphological system. This nature associated to various dialects and the lack of resources represent a challenge for the progress of arabic sentiment analysis research.

In this paper, we adress the tokenization challenges of sentiment analysis for arabic language. We also tackle arabic SA by taking into account the improvement of tokenization level. The rest of this paper is organized as follows: In Sect. 2, we present specificities of arabic sentiment analysis. Section 3 overviews existing works related to ASA. Our proposed method is described in Sect. 4. Section 5 is reserved for the presentation of the results and experiments. Finaly, we end with a conclusion.

2 Specificities of Arabic Sentiment Analysis

Many researches in literature have proven that sentiment analysis is not a simple classification problem. SA is a suitcase research problem that requires tackling different NLP tasks including subjectivity detection, aspect extraction, word polarity disambiguation, and time expression recognition.

Besides the general challenges of sentiment analysis such as domain dependency, polarity fuzziness and spam [2], there are others related to arabic SA. As sentiment analysis depends significantly on the morphology of the target language, Abdul-Mageed et al. [3] listed the linguistic properties of the arabic language in terms of varieties, orthography, and morphology.

As language varieties, arabic is one of the six official languages of the united nations, and the mother tongue of about 300 million people in 22 different countries, including standard arabic and dialects. Modern standard arabic (MSA) is the formal language of communication understood by the majority of arabic speaking people, as it is commonly used in radio, newspapers, and television.

The arabic language is known by its morphological complexity and richness. The same word may carry important information using suffixes, affixes and prefixes [4]. An arabic word reveals several morphological aspects including derivation, inflection, and agglutination.

A significant factor of an accurate sentiment analysis system is the use of large annotated corpora. The accuracy increases with the quality and the size of the training corpus of the sentiment classifier. Arabic language is still poor in terms of tests corpora which represents a well known problem for sentiment analysis. In addition, the few available datasets are dialectically limited, or even free from dialectical content. To the best of our knowledge, there are no arabic corpora annotated for sentiment analysis and fully covering the different dialects.

MSA lexica are small compared to english lexica. Accordingly, many works try to translate large english lexica to arabic. However, the resulted coverage is poor regarding the morphological complexity of arabic.

While people in social media express their opinions using their local dialects, the majority of NLP tools are designed to parse MSA [5]. Dealing with dialects makes the task more complicated because there are no rules, no standard formats either.

In this paper, we will focus on overcoming the challenges relating to the nature of arabic language especially in the tokenization level.

3 Related Work for ASA

The approaches of ASA can be classified into two categories: classical machine learning approaches, and deep learning approaches.

3.1 Classical Machine Learning Approaches

Machine learning (ML) methods have broadly used for sentiment analysis. ML addresses sentiment analysis as a text classification problem. Many approaches include support vector machine (SVM), maximum entropy (ME), naïve Bayes (NB) algorithm, and artificial neural networks (ANNs). NB and SVM are the most commonly exploited machine learning algorithms for solving the sentiment classification problem [6].

Al-Rubaiee et al. [8] performed sentiment classification by two forms: polarity classification, and rating classification. They applied machine learning using SVM, MNB, and BNB. Sentiment polarity classification achieved (90% accuracy), but for rating classification, there was a lot to do for improvement in rating classification (50% accuracy).

3.2 Deep Learning Approaches

Deep learning (DL) is widely used for sentiment analysis. Socher et al. [9] proposed an RNN (Recurrent neural network) based approach, which is trained on a constructed sentiment treebank and improved the sentence-level sentiment analysis on english datasets.

Using DL is less abandon in arabic SA than in english SA, Bilal Ghanem [10] used CNN model for SA tasks and a stanford segmenter to perform tweets tokenization and normalization. They used Word2vec for word embedding with ASTD datasets.

Sarah Alhumoud [12] used a LSTM-CNN model with only two unbalanced classes (Positive and negative) among four classes (objective, subjective positive, subjective negative, and subjective mixed) form ASTD.

Ali Safaya [13] utilized a pre-trained BERT model with Convolutional Neural Networks and they present an ArabicBERT a set of pre-trained transformer language models for arabic language. They used a base version of arabic BERT model (bert-base-arabic).

ElJundi et al. [14] developed an arabic specific universal language models (ULM), hULMonA. They fine tuning multi-lingual BERT (mBERT) ULM for ASA. They collected a benchmark dataset for ULM evaluation with sentiment analysis.

Antoun et al. [15] developed an arabic language representation model to improve the state-of-the-art in several Arabic NLU tasks. They created AraBERT based on the BERT model. They used the BERT base configuration that has 12 encoder blocks, 768 hidden dimensions, 12 attention heads, 512 maximum sequence length.

Despite it is one of the main steps in any languages processing step, only few recent studies attempted to evaluate word embed ding of arabic texts. Mohamed A. Zahran [16] translated the word2vec english benchmark and used it to evaluate the different embedding techniques on a large arabic corpus. However, they reported that translating an english benchmark is not a good strategy to evaluate arabic embedding.

In this paper, we used an arabic version of the BERT model: Arabic BERT [13] that is trained from scratch and made publicly available for use. Arabic BERT was a set of BERT language models that consists of four models of different sizes trained using masked language modeling with whole word masking. Models with large, base, medium, and mini sizes [13] were trained with the same data for 4M steps (Table 1).

Table 1. Arabic BERT Models.

	Arabic BERT-Mini	Arabic BERT-Medium	Arabic BERT-Base	Arabic BERT-Large
Hidden layers	4	8	12	24
Attention heads	4	8	12	16
Hidden size	256	512	768	1024
Parameters	11M	42M	110M	340M

3.3 BERT Embedding

More recent word embedding techniques, such as FastText, Embedding from Language Models (ELMo) and BERT are yet to be fully explored for ASA despite having pre-trained arabic versions publicly available, such as FastText for 157 languages[17] and 14 Pretrained ELMo Representations for Many Languages (ELMoForManyLangs). In this work, we are interested in integrating a new word embedding techniques BERT.

A recent work Jacob Devlin and Toutanova [18] on language representation models introduced BERT (Bidirectional Encoder Representations from Transformers). BERT is pre-trained by conditioning on both left and right context in all layers, unlike previous language representation models. Applying BERT to any NLP task needs only to fine-tune one additional output layer to the downstream task. BERT needs minimal architecture changes for sequence-level and token-level natural language processing applications, such as single text classification, text tagging (e.g., part-of-speech tagging [19]), and question answering.

This makes it different from the previous word, which is applied to the task of SA as features. As this type of language representation model being new, the aim is to evaluate its performance on the task of arabic SA.

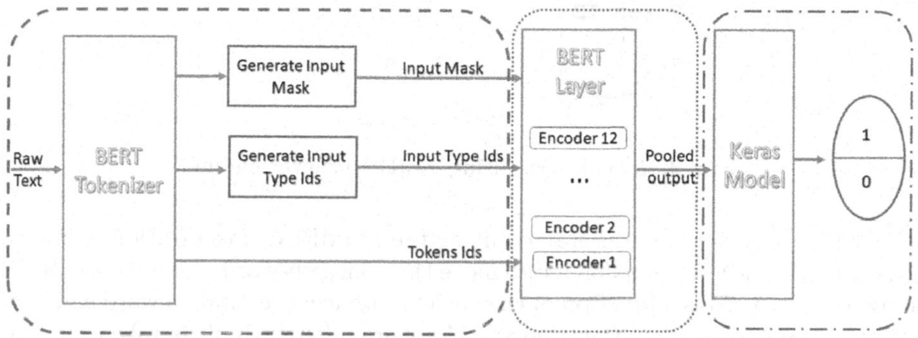

Fig. 1. BERT model architecture.

As opposed to directional models, which read the text input sequentially left-to-right or right-to-left, the transformer encoder reads the entire sequence of words at once. Therefore, it is considered bidirectional, though it would be more accurate to say that it's non-directional. This characteristic allows the model to learn the context of a word based on all of its surroundings (left and right of the word) Fig. 1.

3.4 Arabic Tokenizer

Tokenization in arabic language presents a challenge because of its rich and complex morphology. A token is usually defined as a sequence of one or more letters preceded and followed by space. This definition works well for non-agglutinative languages like english.

Arabic tokenization has been described in various researches and implemented in many solutions as it is a required preliminary stage for further processing. According to [20] there are different levels at which an arabic tokenizer can be developed, depending on the depth of the linguistic analysis involved. They presented 3 models for tokenization: (1) Tokenization combined with morphological analysis. (2) Tokenization guesser. (3) Tokenization dependent on the morphological analyser.

Abdelali et al. [21] introduced an arabic tokenizer Farasa, which uses SVM for ranking using linear kernels that uses a variety of features and lexicons to rank possible segmentation of a word. They measure the performance of the tokenizer in terms of accuracy and efficiency, in two NLP tasks, namely Machine Translation (MT) and Information Retrieval (IR).

```
Sentence : نزل جميل جدا
Tokens : ['ن', '##ز', '##ل', 'ج', '##م', '##ي', '##ل', 'ج', '##د', '##ا']
Token IDs : [590, 28483, 28495, 570, 26259, 16070, 28495, 570, 18191, 28475]
```

Fig. 2. Tokenization using BERTTokenizer method

BERT tokenizer [18] was trained using the WordPiece tokenization. It means that a word can be broken down into more than one sub-words. The vector BERT assigned to a word is a function of the entire sentence, therefore, a word can have different vectors based on the contexts.There are different built in tokenizer. The basic is character tokenizer (Fig. 2). However, the pretrained arabic BERT uses a word by word tokenizer (Fig. 3).

```
Sentence : نزل جميل جدا
Tokens : ['نزل', 'جميل', 'جدا']
Token IDs : [6120, 6889, 2791]
```

Fig. 3. Tokenization using arabic-BERT tokenizer method

The choice of this tokenizer is verified by a test on ASTD dataset where we obtained an accuracy of 81% with BERTTokenizer and 91% with pretrained arabic BERT.

4 Proposed Method

Among all cited works, the approach of Ali Safaya [13] is the most close to our approach. Figure 4 depicts the proposed architecture for arabic SA. Our architecture is composed by 3 blocks. The first block describes the text pre-processing step where we used an arabic BERT tokenizer to split the word into tokens. Second block is the training model. Arabic BERT model is used with only 8 encoder (Medium case [13]). The output of last four hidden layers is concatenated to get a size representation vector 512 × 4 × 128 with 16 batch size (32 for AJGT dataset). The pooling operation's output is concatenated and flattened to be later on crossed a dense layer and a Softmax function to get the final label. Third block is about the classifier where we used a dropout layer for some regularization and a fully-connected layer for our output. The choice of maximum token length is validated by a test with the AJGT dataset (see Fig. 5).

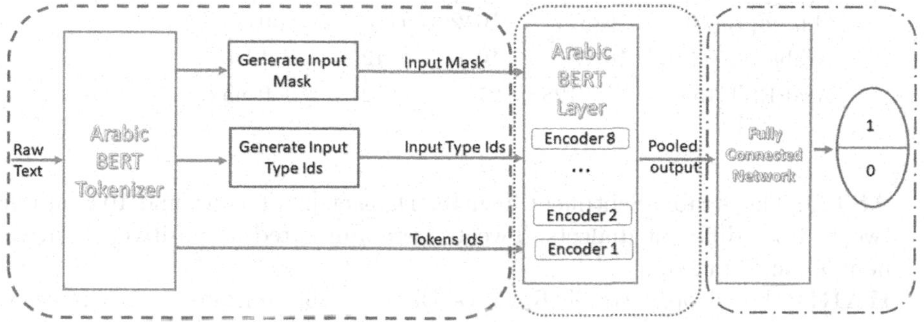

Fig. 4. Arabic BERT model architecture.

Table 2 displays the hyperparameters of the proposed model. The number of epochs varies according to the datasets and the memory reserved for the execution of the model. It can be either 10 or 20 or 50. The over all model is trained by AdamW optimizer. We note that with hyperparameters optimization by random search, we outperform the approach of [13].

Table 3 explain the differences between our model, Arabic BERT [13] and AraBERT [15] ones. It shows that with an arabic tokenizer the number of encoders in the arabic BERT model influences the accuracy value.

5 Experiments and Results

In this paper, we used five datasets in order to train the classifier, valid and test the system. All were split into three subsets: 80% for training, 10% validation, and 10% for testing.

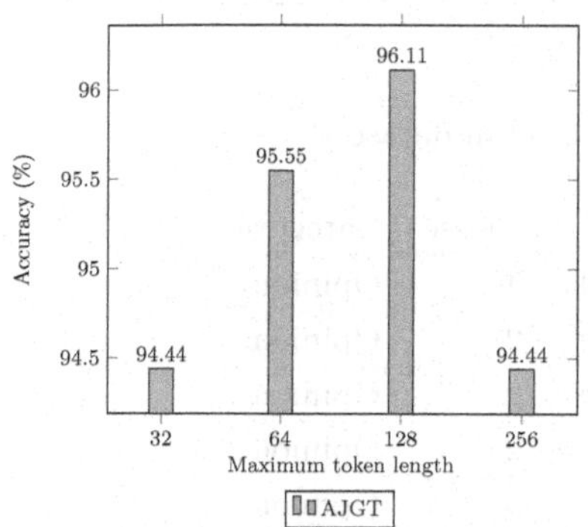

Fig. 5. Optimal value of maximum token length

Table 2. Hyper-parameters used in the approach.

Hyper-parameters	Value
Batch-size	16 (32 for AJGT)
Dropout	0.1
Max length	128
Hidden size	512
lr	2e-5
Optimizer	AdamW
Epochs	10/20/50

Table 3. Differences between the proposed approach, AraBERT [15] and Arabic BERT [13] models.

	Batch-size	Epochs	Layers	Activation function
Our approach	16/32	10/20/50	8	Softmax
Arabic BERT[13]	16/32	10	12	ReLU
AraBERT[15]	512/128	27	12	Softmax

- **ASTD**: The Arabic Sentiment Twitter Dataset [22] has around 10 K arabic tweets from different dialects. Tweets were annotated as positive, negative, neutral, and mixed.
- **HARD**: The Hotel Arabic Reviews Dataset [23] contains 93,700 reviews. Each one has two parts: positive comments and negative comments. It covers 1858 hotels contributed by 30889 users (68%positive, 13% negative, and 19% neutral).
- **LABR**: The Large-scale Arabic Book Reviews [24] contains over 63,000 book reviews in arabic.
- **AJGT**: The Arabic Jordanian General Tweets [25] contains 1,800 tweets annotated as positive and negative.
- **ArSenTD-Lev**: The Arabic Sentiment Twitter Dataset for LEVantine [26] contains 4,000 tweets written in Levantine dialect with annotations for sentiment, topic and sentiment target. We will use 3 among 5 classes.

We compare the proposed approach with two shapes of methods: classical-based and deep learning-based. The nature of the used approaches verifies this gap between the values of accuracy compared to our model.

The result of Table 5, is graphically visualized in Fig. 7 and 6, indicates the variation of the accuracy value according to the used method and datasets. It shows that we have a competition between our model and Antoun et al.[15] one. Our model gives the best result for LABR, AJGT and ArsenTD-Lev datasets; while Antoun et al. [15] works give the best result with ASTD and HARD

Table 4. Arabic language used in datasets.

Datasets	Language	Samples	Classes	Categories
ASTD	MSA	10,000	4	Opinion
LABR	DA	63,000	2	Opinion
HARD	MSA-DA	93,700	2	Opinion
AJGT	MSA-DA	1,800	2	Opinion
ArSenTD-Lev	DA	4,000	3	Opinion

Table 5. Comparison between classical and deep learning approaches.

Approaches	ASTD	LABR	AJGT	HARD	ArsenTD-Lev
CNN [10]	79%	–	–	–	–
LSTM [11]	81%	71%	–	–	–
LSTM-CNN [12]	81%	–	–	–	–
CNN-CROW [27]	72,14%	–	–	–	–
DE-CNN-G1 [28]	82,48%	–	93,06%	–	–
LR [29]	87,10%	84,97%	–	–	–
GNB [29]	86%	85%	–	–	–
SVM [24]	–	50%	–	–	–
Arabic-BERT Base [13]	71,4%	–	–	–	55,2%
hULMonA [14]	69,9%	–	–	95,7%	52,4%
AraBERT [15]	**92,6%**	86,7%	93,8%	**96,2%**	59,4%
Our approach	91%	**87%**	**96,11%**	95%	**75%**

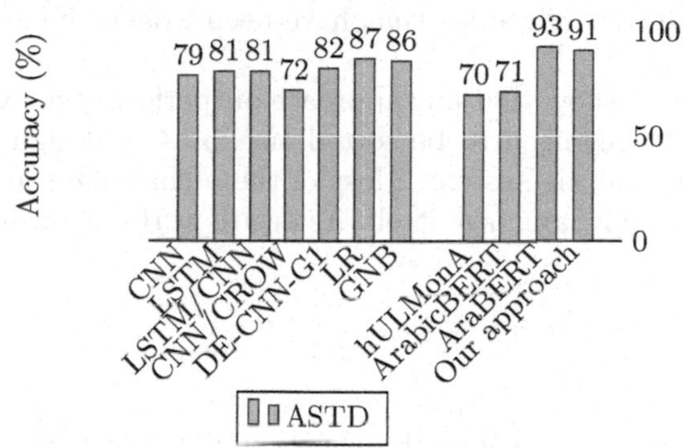

Fig. 6. Comparison between classical and deep learning approaches with ASTD datasets

datasets. We found a slight difference in the accuracy value between the two works (92,6% compared to 91% for ASTD dataset and 86,7% compared to 87% for LABR datasets). However, our model gives a very good result with ArsenTD-Lev dataset (75% compared to an accuracy value that does not exceed 60% with others models).

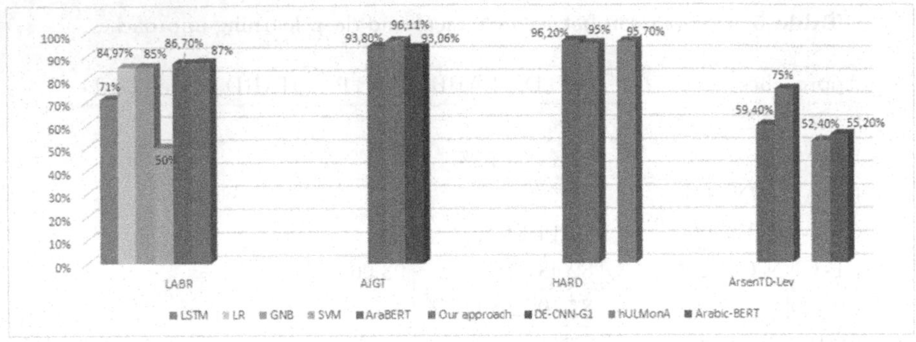

Fig. 7. Comparison between approaches with the rest of datasets.

6 Conclusion

This paper proposes a BERT based approach to sentiment analysis in arabic. This study clearly demonstrated that Arabic Sentiment Analysis (ASA) has become one of the research areas that have been drawn the attention of many researchers.

Numerical results show that our approach outperform the existing ASA approach. Many challenges need to be sorted out so as to design an effective and mature sentiment analysis system. Most of these challenges are inherited from the nature of the arabic language itself. As future works, we will try to overcome these challenges.

References

1. Dragoni, M., Poria, S., Cambria, E.: OntoSenticNet: a commonsense ontology for sentiment analysis. IEEE Intell. Syst. **33**(3), 77–85 (2018)
2. Oueslati, O., Cambria, E., Ben HajHmida, M., Ounelli, H.: A review of sentiment analysis research in Arabic language. Future Generation Comput. Syst. **112**, 408–430 (2020)
3. Abdul-Mageed, M., Diab, M., Korayem, M.: Subjectivity and sentiment analysis of modern standard Arabic. In: Proceedings of the 49th Annual Meeting of the Association for Computational Linguistics Human Language Technologies short papers-Volume 2 Association for Computational Linguistics, pp. 587–591 (2011)
4. Shoukry, A., Rafea, A.: Sentence-level Arabic sentiment analysis. In: Collaboration Technologies and Systems (CTS) 2012 International Conference on IEEE, pp. 546-550 (2012)
5. Zaghouani, W.: Critical survey of the freely available Arabic corpora (2017). https://arxiv.org/abs/1702.07835
6. Imran, A., Faiyaz, M., Akhtar, F.: An enhanced approach for quantitative prediction of personality in Facebook posts. Int. J. Educ. Manage. Eng. (IJEME) **8**(2), 8–19 (2018)
7. Alsayat, A., Elmitwally, N.: A comprehensive study for Arabic sentiment analysis (challenges and applications). Egyptian Inform. J. **21**(1), 7–12 (2020). Elsevier

8. Al-Rubaiee, H., Qiu, R., Li, D.: Identifying Mubasher software products through sentiment analysis of Arabic tweets. In: 2016 International Conference on Industrial Informatics and Computer Systems (CIICS). IEEE, pp. 1–6 (2016)
9. Socher, R., et al.: Recursive deep models for semantic compositionality over a sentiment treebank. In: Proceedings of the 2013 Conference on Empirical Methods in Natural Language Processing, pp. 1631–1642 (2013)
10. Ghanem, B., Karoui, J., Benamara, F., Moriceau, V., Rosso, P.: IDAT at FIRE2019: overview of the track on irony detection in Arabic tweets. Proceedings of the 11th Forum for Information Retrieval Evaluation, pp. 10–13 (2019)
11. Shoukry, A., Rafea, A.: Sentence-level Arabic sentiment analysis. In: Collaboration Technologies and Systems (CTS), 2012 International Conference on IEEE, pp. 546–550 (2012)
12. Alhumoud, S., Albuhairi, T., Alohaideb, W.: Hybrid sentiment analyser for Arabic tweets using R. In: 2015 7th International Joint Conference on Knowledge Discovery, Knowledge Engineering and Knowledge Management. IC3K. IEEE, pp. 417–424 (2015)
13. Safaya, A., Abdullatif, M., Yuret, D.: KUISAIL at SemEval-2020 Task 12: BERT-CNN for offensive speech identification in social media (2020). arXiv:2007.13184v1 [cs.CL]
14. ElJundi, O., Antoun, W., El Droubi, N., Hajj, H., El-Hajj, W., Shaban, K.: Hulmona: the universal language model in Arabic. In: Proceedings of the Fourth Arabic Natural Language Processing Workshop. 68–77, (2019)
15. Antoun, W., Baly, F., and Hajj, H.: AraBERT: transformer-based model for Arabic language understanding (2020). arXiv preprint arXiv:2003.00104
16. Zahran, M.A., Magooda, A., Mahgoub, A.Y., Raafat, H., Rashwan, M., Atyia, A.: Word representations in vector space and their applications for Arabic. In: Gelbukh, A. (ed.) CICLing 2015. LNCS, vol. 9041, pp. 430–443. Springer, Cham (2015). https://doi.org/10.1007/978-3-319-18111-0_32
17. Grave, E., Bojanowski, P., Gupta, P., Joulin, A., Mikolov, T.: Learning word vectors for 157 languages. In: Proceedings of the International Conference on Language Resources and Evaluation, LREC 2018 (2018)
18. Devlin, J., Chang, Ming-W., Lee, K., Toutanova, Kristina.: BERT: pre-training of deep bidirectional transformers for language understanding. In: Proceedings of the 2019 Conference of the North American Chapter of the Association for Computational Linguistics: Human Language Technologies, Minneapolis, Minnesota, June. Association for Computational Linguistics, vol. 1, pp. 4171–4186 (2019)
19. Saidi, R., Jarray, F., Mansour, M.: A BERT based approach for Arabic POS tagging. In: Rojas, I., Joya, G., Catala, A. (eds.) IWANN 2021. LNCS, vol. 12861, pp. 311–321. Springer, Cham (2021). https://doi.org/10.1007/978-3-030-85030-2_26
20. Attia, M.: Arabic tokenization system. In: Proceedings of the 2007 Workshop on Computational Approaches to Semitic Languages: Common Issues and Resources, pp. 65-72 (2007)
21. Abdelali, A., Darwish, K., Durrani, N., Mubarak, H.: Farasa: a fast and furious segmenter for Arabic. In: Proceedings of the 2016 Conference of the North American Chapter of the Association for Computational Linguistics: Demonstrations. Association for Computational Linguistics, pp. 11–16 (2016). https://www.aclweb.org/anthology/N16-3003https://doi.org/10.18653/v1/N16-3003
22. Nabil, M., Aly, M., Atiya, A.: ASTD: Arabic sentiment tweets dataset. In: Proceedings of the 2015 Conference on Empirical Methods in Natural Language Processing, pp. 2515-2519 (2015)

23. Elnagar, A., Khalifa, Y.S., Einea, A.: Hotel Arabic-reviews dataset construction for sentiment analysis applications. In: Shaalan, K., Hassanien, A.E., Tolba, F. (eds.) Intelligent Natural Language Processing: Trends and Applications. SCI, vol. 740, pp. 35–52. Springer, Cham (2018). https://doi.org/10.1007/978-3-319-67056-0_3
24. Aly, M., Atiya, A.: LABR: A Large Scale Arabic Book Reviews Dataset. Sofia, Bulgaria, Meetings of the Association for Computational Linguistics (ACL) At (2013)
25. Alomari, K.M., ElSherif, H.M., Shaalan, K.: Arabic tweets sentimental analysis using machine learning. In: Benferhat, S., Tabia, K., Ali, M. (eds.) IEA/AIE 2017. LNCS (LNAI), vol. 10350, pp. 602–610. Springer, Cham (2017). https://doi.org/10.1007/978-3-319-60042-0_66
26. Baly, R., Khaddaj, A., Hajj, H., El-Hajj, W., Shaban, B.: Arsentd-lev: a multi-topic corpus for target-based sentiment analysis in Arabic levantine tweets (2019). arXiv preprint arXiv:1906.01830
27. Eskander, R., Rambow, O.: SLSA: a sentiment lexicon for standard Arabic. EMNLP 2545–2550 (2015)
28. Abdelghani, D., Mohamed, A.E., Junwei, Z.: Arabic sentiment classification using convolutional neural network and differential evolution algorithm. Comput. Intell. Neurosci. (2019)
29. Harrat, S., Meftouh, K., Smaili, K.: Machine translation for Arabic dialects (survey). Inf. Process. Manage. **56**(2), 262–273 (2019)

Computational Intelligence for Multimedia Understanding

Infrared Thermography and Computational Intelligence in Analysis of Facial Video-Records

Aleš Procházka[1,2,4(✉)], Hana Charvátová[3], and Oldřich Vyšata[4]

[1] Department of Computing and Control Engineering, University of Chemistry and Technology in Prague, Prague, Czech Republic
A.Prochazka@ieee.org
[2] Czech Technical University in Prague, Czech Institute of Informatics, Robotics and Cybernetics, Prague, Czech Republic
[3] Faculty of Applied Informatics, Tomas Bata University in Zlín, Zlín, Czech Republic
[4] Faculty of Medicine in Hradec Králové, Department of Neurology, Charles University, Prague, Czech Republic

Abstract. Infrared thermography has a wide range of applications both in engineering and biomedicine. Resulting video-images provide immediate information about thermal conditions on the surface of the observed object but for the more sophisticated analysis the detail evaluation of separate images is necessary. The processing of thermal images is based upon data acquisition by special non-invasive sensors, efficient communication systems, and the application of selected machine learning methods in many cases. The present paper is devoted to the recognition of thermal regions in the facial area, detection of the body temperature, and evaluation of breathing frequency and its possible disorders. Data include video-sequences acquired on the home exercise bike and recorded during different load conditions. The proposed general methodology combines the use of neural networks and machine learning methods for the detection of the changing temperature ranges of the thermal camera. Selected digital signal processing methods are then used to find the mean body temperature and breathing frequency during the specified time period. Results show the temperature changes and breathing frequency between 0.48 and 0.56 Hz for selected experiments and different body loads.

Keywords: Thermography · Computational intelligence · Digital signal processing · Breathing analysis · Video-data processing

1 Introduction

Thermography [3,9,18] forms a specific research area based upon the radiation in the long infra-red region. It has a wide range of applications in the design of smart cities, construction of the low-energy buildings, and in biomedicine as well. The importance of these systems has an increasing role especially in the present situation as they allow the non-contact human temperature measurement and breathing analysis. Thermal cameras are moreover combined in some cases with

K. Wojtkiewicz et al. (Eds.): ICCCI 2021, CCIS 1463, pp. 635–643, 2021.
https://doi.org/10.1007/978-3-030-88113-9_51

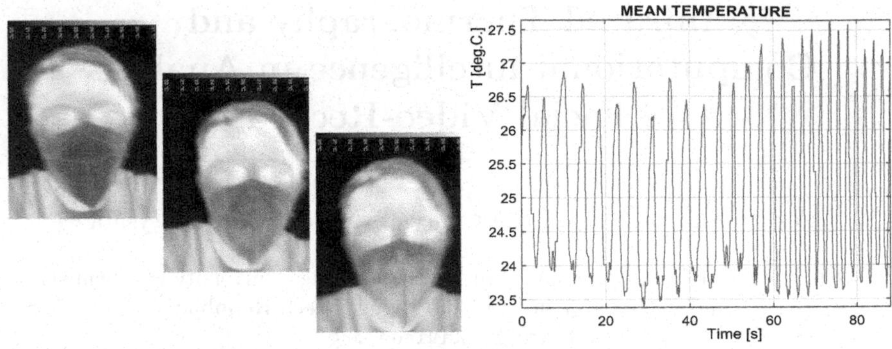

Fig. 1. Principle of the thermal video-data acquisition presenting thermal images with associated thermal bars and the time evolution of the mean value of the temperature in the veil area.

further noninvasive sensors including depth and color cameras [23,24] for motion detection related to breathing [17] and diagnosis of further specific biomedical problems. An extensive attention has been devoted to contactless monitoring of multimodal physiological signals including heart rate sensors [4] and motion recognition for analysis of the health condition and for human–computer interactions [7,15] in specific situations as well.

The present paper is devoted to the use of thermal cameras [1,16] for analysis of video-sequences recording the facial area with the mouth covered by the veil that allows the measurement of the temperature on its surface. Figure 1 presents the set of facial images recorded by a thermal camera during cycling on the home exercise bike for a selected load. The region of interest (ROI) used for evaluation of temperature changes and the detection of breathing frequency is determined by the veil covering the mouth region in this case. More sophisticated methods use adaptive specification of regions of interest [20] for the moving object. Associated image processing methods detect facial regions as areas with the most significant time changes of temperature values that specify the mouth location. More sensitive cameras moreover enable the detection of skin temperature without the need of the face mask veil.

The methodology applied for data analysis includes the use of selected preprocessing methods in the time, time-frequency and time-scale domains [10,13]. Neural networks [25] and deep learning methods [19,21] can be then used for detection of ranges of the observed temperatures from the digits projected to specific image areas at first. This approach allows the use of low-cost thermal cameras with temperatures projected to thermal images only. Standard classification methods or deep learning [8,14] with convolutional neural networks can be then used for recognition of digits in the image area. This process allows the rejection of the additional image noise in many cases. The information content of video-sequences can be then evaluated.

Thermal cameras and adaptive learning methods can be further used in many different areas [5,6,22]. Associated methods include big data processing, dimensionality reduction, parallel signal processing, and real-time respiratory rate monitoring [2] for detection of possible breathing problems both in the home environment, during physical activities, and in sleep laboratories as well.

2 Methodology

Figure 2 presents the methodology of data acquisition and its processing. The video-records acquired by the thermal camera were used for determination of the sequence of images with the selected frame rate of $f_s = 10$ fps at first.

The region of interest can be specified by the adaptive method that detects the area with the highest changes of temperature values [20]. In the more simple case and for short video-sequences the ROI was specified by the veil position.

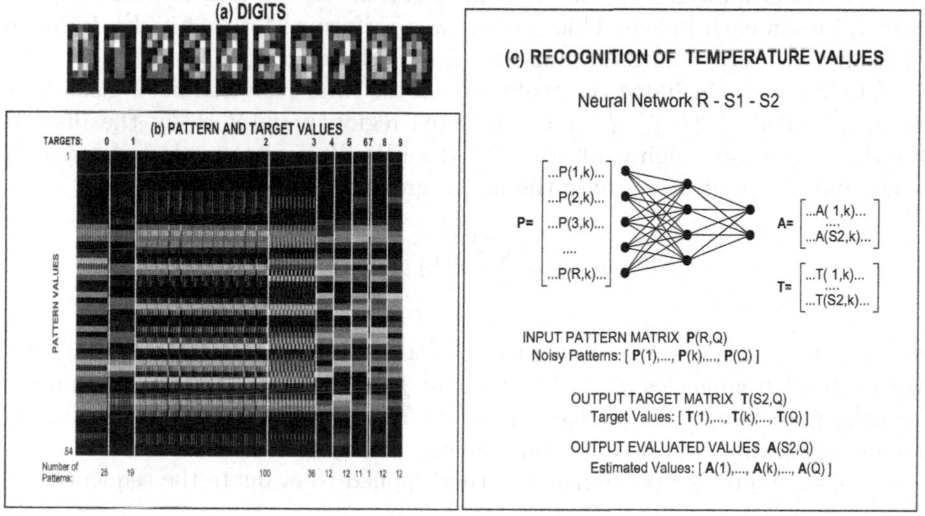

Fig. 2. Principle of the calibration of the video-sequence acquired by the thermal camera and the application of the neural network for adaptive recognition of the changing temperature ranges using (a) separate digits extracted from thermal images, (b) construction of the pattern matrix formed by column vectors of pixels defining individual digits with different noise components, and (c) the neural network structure used for recognition of digits and their association with shades of separate temperatures in the thermal image.

The initial processing stage included the association of shadow values with temperatures projected into the temperature bar inside the thermal image presented in Fig. 1. During the learning process, each digit with the additional noise (presented in Fig. 2(a)) was separated into the matrix of 9×6 pixels for a selected resolution that formed 54 values of the pattern vector (presented in Fig. 2(b)). The selected number of Q such vectors defined the pattern matrix in Fig. 2(b) that formed the input of the neural network presented in Fig. 2(c). A vector of corresponding target values $\mathbf{T}_{S2,Q}$ with $S2 = 10$ rows was defined by corresponding digit $0, 1, \cdots, 9$. The model formed by the two layer neural network was then used the evaluate values

$$\mathbf{A1}_{S1,Q} = F1(\mathbf{W1}_{\mathbf{S1,R}}\, \mathbf{P}_{\mathbf{R,Q}} + \mathbf{b1}_{\mathbf{S1,1}}\, \mathbf{ones(1,Q)}), \tag{1}$$

$$\mathbf{A2}_{S2,Q} = F2(\mathbf{W2}_{\mathbf{S2,S1}}\, \mathbf{A1}_{\mathbf{S1,Q}} + \mathbf{b2}_{\mathbf{S2,1}}\, \mathbf{ones(1,Q)}) \tag{2}$$

forming outputs of neural network layers. Network coefficients included matrix $\mathbf{W1}_{S1,R}$ of $S1$ elements of the first layer with associated vector $\mathbf{b1}_{S1,1}$ and matrix $\mathbf{W2}_{S2,S1}$ of $S2$ elements of the second layer with associated vector $\mathbf{b2}_{S2,1}$. Neural network included the sigmoidal transfer function $F1$ in the first layer and the probabilistic softmax transfer function $F2$ in the second layer. Results of the output layer provide probabilities of each class.

Owing to a well defined pattern matrix, the classification resulted in the model that was able to detect the minimal and maximal temperature values in each thermographic frame and associated gray levels for detection of temperature values in each image. This process was performed for each video-frame as temperature limits changed themselves during the recording process.

The final step included the evaluation of the time evolution of N mean temperature values $\{d(n)\}_{n=0}^{N-1}$ in the selected region of interest by the discrete Fourier transform. Digital filtering by the FIR filter of the selected order M was applied at first to evaluate the new sequence

$$y(n) = \sum_{k=0}^{M-1} b(k)\; d(n-k) \tag{3}$$

for $n = 0, 1, \cdots, N-1$ and coefficients $\{b(k)\}_{k=0}^{M-1}$ forming a band-pass filter with cut-off frequencies $f_1 = 0.2$ Hz and $f_2 = 2$ Hz to cover the estimated breathing frequency and to reject all other frequency components including the mean signal value and its additional noise.

A discrete Fourier transform was then applied to evaluate the sequence

$$Y(k) = \sum_{n=0}^{N-1} y(n)\; \exp(-j\; k\; n\; \frac{2\,\pi}{N}) \tag{4}$$

for $k = 0, 1, \cdots, N-1$ related to frequency $f_k = \frac{k}{N} f_s$. To obtain the time dependence of these values, a short time Fourier transform of the selected window length was applied. The local polynomial approximation of spectral components was then used in specified frequency ranges to detect the extremal values of the smoothing polynomial.

The associated spectrogram was then used for the time evaluation of breathing patterns for different loads during the specific physical activities on the home exercise bike.

3 Results

Extraction of the pattern and target values for the neural network to detect temperature values and associated shades was applies at first. Figure 3 presents separate digits on the thermal bar and their segmentation for definition of the pattern matrix and target values for neural network model optimization.

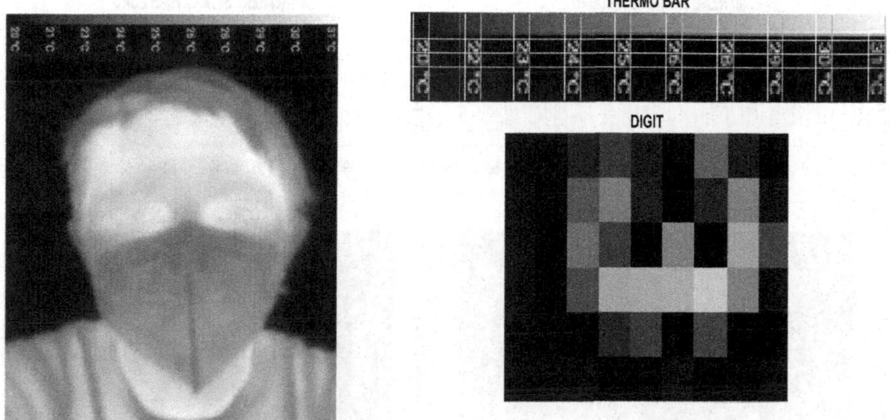

Fig. 3. Extraction of the pattern and target values for the neural network to detect separate digits on the thermal bar and associated shades of temperature values.

Figure 4 presents the performance analysis during the learning process and the confusion matrix of the final neural network model. For the selected value of $Q = 240$ pattern values, the model was able to detect the temperature values with the accuracy of 100%.

Figure 5 presents the mean temperature evolution in the mouth area in the time domain and spectral component changes for data acquired on the home exercise bike for the low and high loads. As presented in [18], the changes of the mean temperature and frequency have a delay with respect to the beginning of the activity changes. To use the observed values for classification, the upper half of the time window was used only.

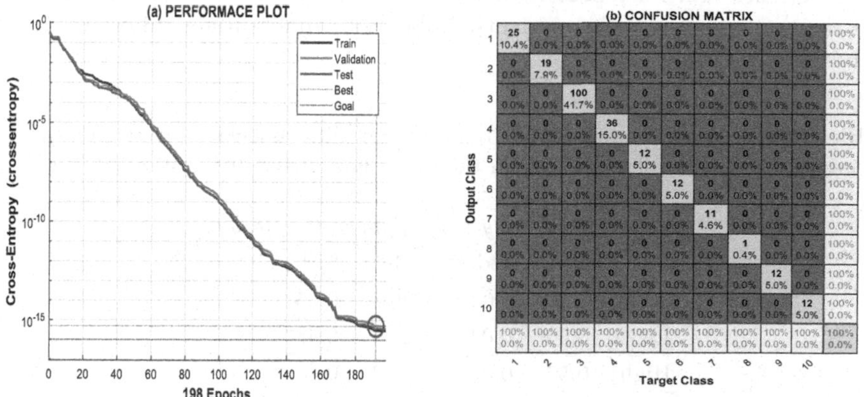

Fig. 4. Results of the neural network application for digits recognition presenting (a) the performance analysis and (b) the confusion matrix.

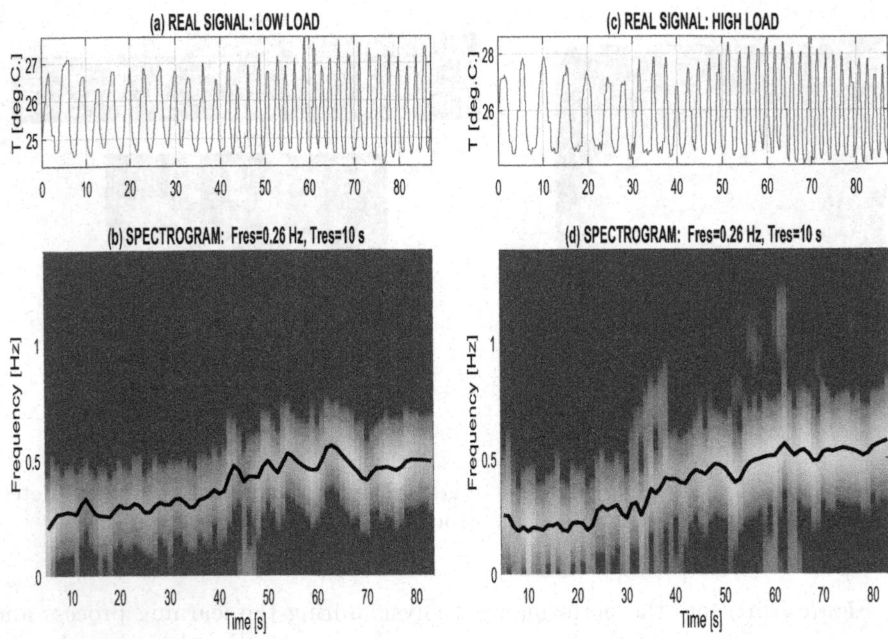

Fig. 5. Analysis of the mean temperature evolution in the mouth area presenting their time domain and spectral domain changes for data acquired on the home exercise bike for (a,b) the low load and (c,d) the high load.

Table 1 presents the mean frequency and temperature for different loads. To eliminate the time delay from the previous rest period, the upper half of the experiment was used for evaluation of breathing features only. Values in the table form features for classification of different physical loads. Further physiological characteristics can be represented by the heart rate [18], accelerometric data, and images from the color or depth cameras to differentiate different physical activities.

Table 1. The mean frequency and temperature with associated values of standard deviation (STD) for different loads in the upper half of the observation period.

Load	*Frequency [Hz]*		*Temperature [deg.C.]*	
	Mean	Std	Mean	Std
Low1	0.50	0.04	26.7	0.35
Low2	0.48	0.04	26.9	0.41
High1	0.53	0.02	27.2	0.71
High2	0.56	0.04	27.5	0.77

4 Conclusion

This paper presents the use of thermal cameras for non-contact monitoring of selected temperature changes and evaluation of breathing frequencies during different physical activities. The proposed methodology shows how video outputs of the low-cost thermal cameras with temperatures printed on images can be used in this area. The purpose of this process is to present possibilities of distant analysis of specific physiological functions and human respiratory monitoring [11,12] allowing more convenient data acquisition and their analysis.

The methods described form an alternative approach to contact biomedical data acquisition and their analysis. Increasing abilities of different bio-sensors with possibilities of wireless data transmission even increase the importance of remote data acquisition. This technology is especially important now as it allows immediate detection of specific health problems related to the increased body temperature and breathing limitations by non-contact sensors.

Further research will be devoted to the use of specific sensors and computational methods for more precise data acquisition and their processing to detect changes of selected biomedical features. It is assumed that new sensors including depth cameras and accelerometers will be used for analysis of motion, physical activities, and rehabilitation exercises.

Notes and Comments. The work has been supported by the research grant No. LTAIN19007 Development of Advanced Computational Algorithms for Evaluating Post-surgery Rehabilitation. The project was approved by the Local Ethics Committee as stipulated by the Helsinki Declaration.

References

1. Aario, S., Gorad, A., Arvonen, M., Sarkka, S.: Respiratory pattern recognition from low-resolution thermal imaging. In: The European Symposium on Artificial Neural Networks, Computational Intelligence and Machine Learning, ESANN 2020, pp. 469–474. IEEE (2020)
2. Alkali, A., Saatchi, R., Elphick, H., Burke, D.: Thermal image processing for real-time noncontact respiration rate monitoring. IET Circuits Devices Syst. **11**(2), 142–148 (2017)
3. Basu, A., Routray, A., Mukherjee, R., Shit, S.: Infrared imaging based hyperventilation monitoring through respiration rate estimation. Infrared Phys. Technol. **77**, 382–390 (2016)
4. Charvátová, H., Procházka, A., Vaseghi, S., Vyšata, O., Vališ, M.: GPS-based analysis of physical activities using positioning and heart rate cycling data. SIViP **11**(2), 251–258 (2016). https://doi.org/10.1007/s11760-016-0928-z
5. Charvátová, H., Procházka, A., Zálešák, M.: computer simulation of temperature distribution during cooling of the thermally insulated room. MDPI: Energies **11**, 3205:1–3205:16 (2018)
6. Erden, F., Velipasalar, S., Alkar, A., Cetin, A.: Sensors in assisted living. IEEE Signal Process. Mag. **33**(2), 36–44 (2016)

7. Garde, A., Karlen, W., Ansermino, J.M., Dumont, G.A.: Estimating respiratory and heart rates from the correntropy spectral density of the photoplethysmogram. PLoS ONE **9**(1), e86427:1–e86427:11 (2014)
8. Goodfellow, I., Bengio, Y., Courville, A.: Deep Learning. MIT Press, Cambridge (2016). http://www.deeplearningbook.org
9. Hanawa, D., Ohguchi, T., Oguchi, K.: Basic study on non-contact measurement of human oral breathing by using far infra-red imaging. In: N., H. (ed.) 39th International Conference on Telecommunications and Signal Processing, pp. 681–684. IEEE (2016)
10. Hošťálková, E., Vyšata, O., Procházka, A.: Multi-dimensional biomedical image denoising using Haar transform. In: Proceedings of the 15th International Conference on Digital Signal Processing, pp. 175–179. IEEE, Cardiff (2007)
11. Huang, Z., Wang, W., de Haan, G.: Nose breathing or mouth breathing? A thermography-based new measurement for sleep monitoring. In: CVPR workshop, pp. 1–7. IEEE, Eindhoven University of Technology, NL (2021)
12. Jagedev, P., Giri, L.: Human respiration monitoring using infrared thermography and artificial intelligence. Biomed. Phys. Eng. Express **6**(3), 035007 (2020)
13. Jerhotová, E., Švihlík, J., Procházka, A.: Biomedical image volumes denoising via the wavelet transform, pp. 435–458. INTECH (2011)
14. Mishra, C., Gupta, D.L.: Deep machine learning and neural networks: an overview. Int. J. Hybrid Inf. Technol. **9**(11), 401–414 (2016)
15. Monkaresi, H., Calvo, R.A., Yan, H.: A machine learning approach to improve contactless heart rate monitoring using a webcam. IEEE J. Biomed. Health Inform. **18**(4), 1153–1160 (2014)
16. Mutlu, K., Esquivelzeta Rabell, J., Martindel Olmo, P., Haesler, S.: IR thermography-based monitoring of respiration phase without image segmentation. J. Neurosci. Methods **301**, 1–18 (2018)
17. Pereira, C., Yu, X., Czaplik, M., Rossaint, R., Blazek, V.: Remote monitoring of breathing dynamics using infrared thermography. Biomed. Opt. Express **6**(11), 4378 (2015)
18. Procházka, A., Charvátová, H., Vaseghi, S., Vyšata, O.: Machine learning in rehabilitation assesment for thermal and heart rate data processing. IEEE Trans. Neural Syst. Rehabil. Eng. **26**(6), 1209–12141 (2018)
19. Procházka, A., Charvátová, H., Vyšata, O., Jarchi, D., Sanei, S.: Discrimination of cycling patterns using accelerometric data and deep learning techniques. Neural Computing and Applications (2020)
20. Procházka, A., Charvátová, H., Vyšata, O., Kopal, J., Chambers, J.: Breathing analysis using thermal and depth imaging camera video records. MDPI: Sensors) **17**, 1408:1–1408:10 (2017)
21. Procházka, A., Dostál, O., Cejnar, P., Mohamed, H., Pavelek, Z., Vališ, M., Vyšata, O.: Deep learning for accelerometric data assessment and ataxic gait monitoring. IEEE Trans. Neural Syst. Rehabilit. Eng. **29**, 33434133:1–33434133:8 (2021)
22. Procházka, A., Kuchyňka, J., Vyšata, O., Cejnar, P., Vališ, M., Mařík, V.: Multi-class sleep stage analysis and adaptive pattern recognition. MDPI: Appl. Sci. **8**(5), 697:1–697:14 (2018)
23. Procházka, A., Schätz, M., Centonze, F., Kuchyňka, J., Vyšata, O., Vališ, M.: Extraction of breathing features using MS Kinect for sleep stage detection. Signal Image Video Process. **10**(7), 1279–1286 (2016). https://doi.org/10.1007/s11760-016-0897-2

24. Procházka, A., Schatz, M., Tupa, O.: The MS kinect image and depth sensors use for gait features detection. In: The IEEE International Conference on Image Processing, ICIP 2017, pp. 2271–2274. IEEE (2014)
25. Procházka, A., Vaseghi, S., Charvátová, H., Tupa, O., Vyšata, O.: Cycling segments multimodal analysis and classification using neural networks. MDPI: Appl. Sci. **7**, 581:1–581:11 (2017)

Optimized Texture Spectral Similarity Criteria

Michal Havlíček[1] and Michal Haindl[1,2](✉)

[1] The Institute of Information Theory and Automation of the Czech Academy of Sciences, 182 08 Prague, Czechia
{havlimi2,haindl}@utia.cas.cz
[2] Faculty of Management, University of Economics, Jindřichův Hradec, Czechia
http://ro.utia.cas.cz/

Abstract. This paper introduces an accelerated algorithm for evaluating criteria for comparing the spectral similarity of color, Bidirectional Texture Functions (BTF), and hyperspectral textures. The criteria credibly compare texture pixels by simultaneously considering the pixels with similar values and their mutual ratios. Such a comparison can determine the optimal modeling or acquisition setup by comparing the original data with their synthetic simulations. Other applications of the criteria can be spectral-based texture retrieval or classification. Together with existing alternatives, the suggested methods were extensively tested and compared on a wide variety of color, BTF, and hyper-spectral textures. The methods' performance quality was examined in a long series of specially designed experiments where proposed ones outperform all tested alternatives.

Keywords: Texture spectral similarity criterion · Bidirectional texture function · Hyperspectral data · Texture modeling

1 Introduction

A fully automatic texture, or more generally image, quality assessment, i.e., mutual similarity evaluation of two or more of them, presents a fundamental but still unsolved complex problem. The validation of the state-of-the-art image and texture fidelity criteria on the web-based benchmark (http://tfa.utia.cas.cz) has demonstrated that none of the published criteria, e.g., CW-SSIM [26], STSIM-1, STSIM-2, STSIM-M [30], ζ [14] can be reliably used for this task [6]. Reliable criterion would support texture model development by comparing the original texture with a synthesized or reconstructed one to select optimal parameter settings of such a model. Such similarity metrics could also play an essential role in efficient content-based image retrieval, e.g., digital libraries or multimedia databases.

Methods based on various textural features developed and applied for texture categorization, such as Haralick's features [8], Run-Length features [2], Laws' filters [16], Gabor features [18], LBP [21], and many others cannot rank textures according to their visual similarity. These features are not descriptive, and thus they are helpful only for binary decisions: two mono-spectral textures are identical or not. Markovian textural features [7] are the rare exception. Many existing

K. Wojtkiewicz et al. (Eds.): ICCCI 2021, CCIS 1463, pp. 644–655, 2021.
https://doi.org/10.1007/978-3-030-88113-9_52

approaches are limited to mono-spectral images, which is a significant disadvantage as color is arguably the most significant visual feature.

The psychophysical evaluations [4], i.e., quality assessments performed by humans, currently represent the only reliable option. This approach requires a time-demanding experiment design setup, strictly controlled laboratory conditions, and representative sets of testers, i.e., sufficient numbers of individuals, ideally from the public, naive concerning the purpose and design of the experiment. Thus, such assessing is generally demanding, expensive, and unsuitable for daily routine practice, not feasible on demand. Moreover, human perception methods are inapplicable for hyper-spectral data due to human vision's limited tri-chromatic nature.

In this article, we assume that visual data be independent sets of pixels. The pixel values are compared as vectors while their position in the image is not considered. This restriction is called a spectral similarity comparison in the rest of the paper. It deals with the appearance and amount of pixels that occur in only one of the compared images and the ratio of pixels ratio appearing in both images to express their spectral composition difference.

The rest of the paper is organized as follows: Section 2 briefly presents published alternatives to solve image spectral similarity comparison, including some based on modifications of techniques developed for slightly different purposes. Section 3 explains in detail our approach and its optimization. Section 5 described the performed validation experiments and used test data. Section 6 shows the achieved results. Section 7 summarizes the paper with a discussion and compares our proposed criteria with the existing alternatives.

2 Related Work

Dealing with color images, i.e., containing three spectral channels, encourages using a three-dimensional (3-D) histogram or local histogram [28], which approximates the image color distribution. The most intuitive way is to compute the 3-D histogram difference (ΔH). Several other possibilities for 3-D histogram comparison have been suggested, such as the histogram intersection ($\cap H$) [24], the squared chord (d_{sc}) [13], and the Canberra metric (d_{can}) [13]. The information-theoretic measures can also be considered for evaluating the histogram difference, e.g., Jeffrey divergence (J) [22] or measure based on the χ^2 statistic (χ^2) [29].

Another possibility is represented by Earth Mover's Distance (EMD) or Wasserstein method [23] which can evaluate dissimilarity between two multi-dimensional distributions in some feature space. However, it turned out that the EMD is limited to tiny images, as demonstrated on average computing times of individual methods showed in Table 1.

The generalized colour moments (GCM) [19] and cosine distance (d_{cos}) [20, 29] suit well to the spectral similarity comparison problem. Different set-theoretic measures can serve as criteria as well, e.g., the Jaccard index (JI) [12] or the Sørensen-Dice index (SDI) [1].

Another alternative may be a modified criterion developed for texture comparison as the spectral similarity comparison might be considered an exceptional case of this task. It is possible to modify the structural similarity metric (SSIM) [25] by removing structure-related terms to obtain reduced SSIM [9].

The 3-D histogram-based criteria cannot be easily generalized to hyper-spectral data, i.e., the data having more than three spectral channels, due to the impossibility of reliably estimating such histograms from limited sample data. GCM could be used for hyperspectral image comparison, but the number of multiplication terms to be integrated significantly increases, and so does the range of possible values of the criterion. Set-theoretic, $rSSIM$ and d_{cos} based criteria can handle the hyper-spectral data with no restriction. A more detailed overview can be found in [10].

3 Computation of MEMD

A new criterion for spectral similarity comparison was proposed - the mean exhaustive minimum distance (MEMD) [10]:

$$\downarrow \zeta(A,B) = \frac{1}{M} \sum_{(r_1,r_2)\in\langle A\rangle} \min_{(s_1,s_2)\in U} \left\{ \rho\left(Y^A_{r_1,r_2,\bullet}, Y^B_{s_1,s_2,\bullet}\right)\right\} \qquad \geq 0 \ , \tag{1}$$

where $Y^A_{r_1,r_2,\bullet}$ represents the pixel at location (r_1, r_2) in the image A, $\bullet$ denotes all the corresponding spectral indices, and similarly for $Y^B_{s_1,s_2,\bullet}$. Further, ρ is an arbitrary vector metric. U is the set of unprocessed pixel indices of B (explained in detail below), $M = \min\{\sharp\{A\}, \sharp\{B\}\}$, $\sharp\{A\}$ is the number of pixels in A, and similarly for $\sharp\{B\}$ and $\min\{\emptyset\} = 0$.

The term $\zeta(A,B)$ is evaluated using raster scanning of A. The algorithm examines the pixels of A, from the upper left corner. Each pixel searches for the index in the set U for which the corresponding pixel is the closest one, in the sense of the used metric ρ. U contains all spatial indices of the image B at the beginning of the process. When such a pixel is identified at $(s_1, s_2) \in U$, the distance between this pixel and the scanned one from A, measured by ρ, is added to the sum and the index (s_1, s_2) is removed from the set U. The algorithm proceeds to the right bottom of the image A and stops when either all pixels of A are examined, or U becomes an empty set.

The criterion $\zeta(A,B)$ is not symmetrical, but can be easily symmetrized as [10]: $\zeta_S(A,B) = \frac{1}{2}(\zeta(A,B) + \zeta(B,A))$ if needed. Another analytical properties of (1) are [10]: $\zeta(A,B) = 0 \leftrightarrow A = B$ (equality), $\zeta(A,A) = 0$ (reflexivity), $\zeta(A,B) \leq \zeta(A,B')$ for $B' \subset B$ (set cardinality dependence).

Two modifications of (1), which take into account color differences just noticeable by color psychometric methods in the CIE Lab color space [27], were suggested [10]:

$$\downarrow \zeta_2(A,B) = \frac{1}{M} \sum_{(r_1,r_2)\in\langle A\rangle} \kappa(r_1,r_2) \qquad \geq 0 \ ,$$

$$\kappa(r_1,r_2) = \begin{cases} 1, & \rho^* > 2.3, \\ 0, & otherwise, \end{cases}$$

$$\rho^* = \min_{(s_1,s_2)\in N} \left\{\rho^{CIE}\left(Y^A_{r_1,r_2,\bullet}, Y^B_{s_1,s_2,\bullet}\right)\right\} , \qquad (2)$$

where the threshold 2.3 was determined in [17] and ρ^{CIE} is the Euclidean distance from pixel $Y^A_{r_1,r_2,\bullet}$ to pixel $Y^B_{s_1,s_2,\bullet}$ in the CIE Lab color space. Finally, the last suggested criterion is the weighted average of the just-noticeable differences [10]:

$$\downarrow \zeta_3(A,B) = \frac{1}{M} \sum_{(r_1,r_2)\in A} \kappa(r_1,r_2)\,\rho^* \qquad \geq 0 \ . \qquad (3)$$

The terms ζ_2 and ζ_3 are evaluated the same way as the term ζ. Notice that the proposed criterion ζ applies to any number of spectral bands, not only for the usual three spectral bands of the standard color images, while ζ_2 and ζ_3 are applicable for the images defined on CIE Lab color space.

4 Optimization

The criterion (1) and its modifications (2), (3) have been optimized to reduce time requirements without significantly increasing memory requirements while maintaining their quality. The pixels of the images to be compared are stored in the same ordered set in the optimized algorithm variant. Thus, each element of that set is assigned a variable identifying the pixel's source image. The data in the set are sorted using quicksort [11] sorting algorithm.

Table 1. The average evaluation time, on Pentium-2.8 GHz-equivalent CPU, depending on the size of compared images for individual criteria.

	8×8	16×16	32×32	64×64
ΔH, $\cap H$, d_{sc}, d_{can}, J, χ^2	0.7 s	0.7 s	0.7 s	0.7 s
EMD	1.8 ms	85.6 ms	5.7 s	7.6 min
ΔGCM^{111}_{00}	67.0 µs	0.1 ms	0.2 ms	0.5 ms
d_{cos}	32.0 µs	88.0 µs	93.0 µs	0.6 ms
JI , SDI	0.3 ms	4.0 ms	9.0 ms	48.0 ms
$rSSIM$	31.0 µs	0.1 ms	0.2 ms	1.4 ms
ζ	0.1 ms	2.0 ms	18.0 ms	0.2 s
$\zeta_{Optimized}$	39.0 µs	0.4 ms	1.2 ms	17.5 ms

Values of individual spectral channels of the given pixel form vector. The maximum metric applied on these vectors is used as an order relation. The rest of the method is formally the same, although the implementation is slightly different. The algorithm passes through the sorted set of pixels. For each pixel belonging to the first compared image, the algorithm searches a pixel belonging to the other image so that their distance is minimal in the sense of the maximum metric. During the search in the set, we use advantageously the fact that the data are sorted. Suppose a situation in the distance of the compared pixels, i.e., the pixel from the first image and the candidate for the most similar pixel from the other image, is more distant than the previous candidate. In that case, the search can be terminated, and the distance of the compared pixel from the first image and the previous candidate can be indicated as the minimum one as illustrated in Fig. 1. This step leads to a significant acceleration of the entire algorithm as shown in Table 1 comparing the computational times for both variants of the algorithm and the compared alternative criteria.

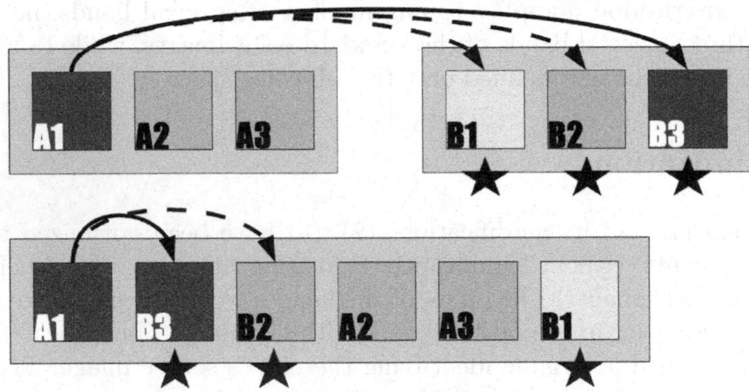

Fig. 1. The comparison of the original MEMD algorithm (upper scheme) with its optimized version (lower scheme). Comparing images A and B and their corresponding pixels A1, A1, A1 and B2, B2, B3, respectively. In the original version, there are three necessary comparisons (marked with arrows) of the pixel from the first image (A1) with the pixels from the second image B1, B2, B3 (marked with a star) to find the pixel from the second image (B3), which is the most similar to the scanned pixel (A1) from the first image (marked with solid line arrows). While there is only one necessary such comparison in the optimized version as the second pixel from the second image in the sorted set (B2) is less similar to the scanned pixel from the first image (A1) than the first pixel from the second image in the sorted set (B3), and there cannot exist a more similar one as the data are sorted.

5 Comparison

The proposed criteria (1)–(3) together with the previously published alternatives mentioned in Sect. 2 have been extensively tested on the experiments described in detail in Sect. 5.1 to investigate how the individual criteria are affected by the spectral composition changes in the compared images.

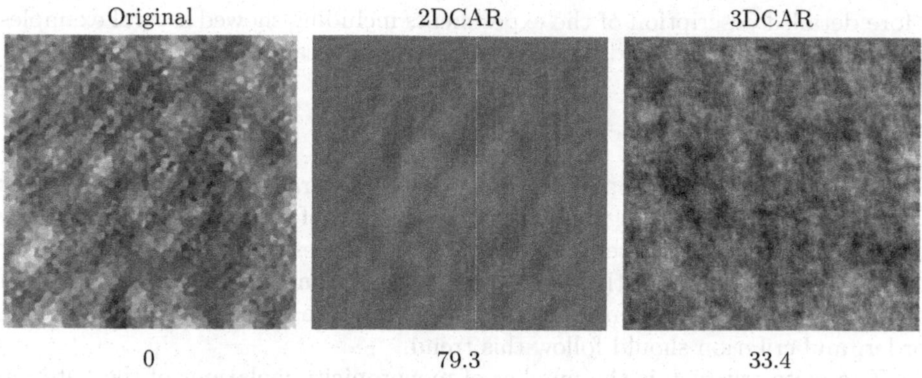

Fig. 2. Example of the use of the proposed criterion MEMD. The original image is compared with the images synthesized using 2D CAR [3] and 3D CAR [5] models, respectively. The values below individual images equal the difference between them and the original expressed by MEMD.

5.1 Controlled Degradation of the Test Data

A sequence of gradually degraded images is generated from the original test one. The original image serves as the first member of the sequence, i.e., $A_1^X = A$ and each member, except for the first one, is generated from its predecessor in the sequence as: $A_t^X = f_X\left(A_{t-1}^X\right), \quad t = 1, \ldots, l$, where l equals the length of the sequence and X is the label identifying the experiment (individual experiments described below). Further $Y_{r,t}^A$ denotes the multi-spectral pixel from the experimental image A_t^X at $r = [r_1, r_2, r_3]$ which is a multi-index with image row, column, and spectral components, respectively. X is the corresponding label of one of the following nine degradation experiments established for validation tests:

A - replacing pixel spectral intensities with the maximal value in the used colour space with the probability $p = \frac{1}{l}$
B - adding a constant $c = \frac{255}{l}$ to all pixel spectral intensities
C - adding a value $\frac{255}{l}\sin(\pi\frac{o}{l})$ depending on the order of the image in the sequence (o) to pixel spectral intensities
D - adding a constant $c = \frac{255}{l}$ to pixel spectral intensities and random mutual interchanging with probability $p = 0.5$ with 4-connected neighbourhood
E - adding a constant $c = \frac{255}{l}$ to pixel spectral intensities and randomly driven propagating with probability $p = 0.5$ with 8-connected neighbourhood
F - adding a value equals to the order of the image in the sequence (o) to pixel spectral intensities
G - adding a pseudo-random vector to each pixel
H - blurring the images using the convolution with the 3×3 Gaussian filter
I - adjusting pixel spectral intensities so as to approach average over spectral channels

More detailed description of the experiments including showed several examples of degraded images created during the experiments can be found in [10].

5.2 Evaluation Meta-criterion

The tested criteria are applied to quantifying spectral composition differences between the template image, i.e., the first member of the degradation sequence and the remaining members. As all those sequences are constructed so that monotone degradation of the original image is guaranteed, i.e., the similarity of the members of the sequence and the original image decreases with increasing order, and criterion should follow this trend.

The meta-criterion is the number of monotonicity violations of the criterion τ in the experiment X [10]:

$$\Xi^{X,\tau} = \sum_{i=1}^{l} \left[1 - \delta \left(o_i^X - o_i^{X,\tau} \right) \right] , \tag{4}$$

where τ is a tested criterion, o_i^X is the rank of a degraded image and $o_i^{X,\tau}$ its corresponding correct ordering of the τ-criterion-based ranking, and δ is the Kronecker delta function.

5.3 Test Data

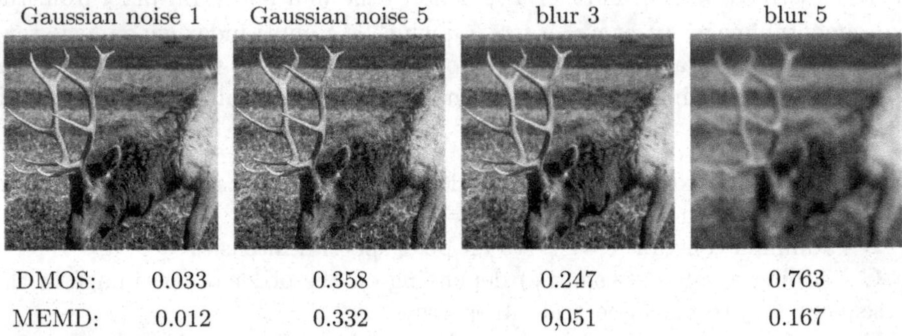

Fig. 3. Comparison between DMOS and MEMD criteria on the CSIQ image degradation examples.

Suggested criteria were validated and compared with the alternative measures on three types of visual data: color, BTF, and hyper-spectral textures, respectively. Two hundred fifty color textures, 200 BTF textures, and three hyper-spectral textures were used. Detailed information about used test data, including showed selected samples, can be found in [10]. The MEMD criterion was also compared with the differential mean opinion score (DMOS) from the CSIQ database [15] images (Fig. 3). The Spearman rank correlation between MEMD and DMOS criteria values was always 1 for all compared results (Gaussian additive noise, blurring, contrast, JPEG 2000, JPEG). Hence it suggests MEMD's high correlation with the human quality ranking.

Table 2. The average strict monotonicity violation (in percent) for 250 test color texture sequences per experiment performed in the RGB color space, the average over all experiments, and the rank for the tested criteria.

	A	B	C	D	E	F	G	H	I	⌀	Rank
$rSSIM$	43	44	46	42	42	20	47	25	47	39	9
d_{cos}	29	44	45	31	31	19	47	47	47	38	8
d_{can}	0	34	29	40	40	12	17	20	31	25	7
SDI	16	10	23	9	9	4	28	24	26	17	6
JI	10	8	26	7	7	4	28	24	26	16	5
J	7	5	9	7	7	3	14	24	14	10	4
ΔH	0	3	5	3	3	1	13	16	8	6	3
$\cap H$	0	3	5	3	3	1	13	16	8	6	3
d_{sc}	0	3	5	4	4	1	14	17	9	6	3
χ^2	0	3	5	4	4	1	14	16	9	6	3
ΔGCM_{00}^{111}	0	0	0	0	0	0	11	9	3	3	2
ζ	0	0	0	0	0	0	0	2	0	0	1

6 Results

The achieved results for the optimized MEMD criterion (1) are summarized in Tables 2, 3 and 4 showing average strict monotonicity violation, i.e., fails, for individual criteria in individual experiments, in average and their rank, using color textures in RGB color space, color textures in CIE Lab color space, and hyper-spectral textures respectively. It is apparent that the proposed criteria (1)–(3) are universally the most reliable.

It holds for the original version of the algorithm and the optimized version, i.e., Tables 2, 3 and 4 as well. Both results are the same, Tables 2, 3 and 4 as well as the corresponding tables in [10], which proves that the presented optimization does not deteriorate the original criteria outstanding performance.

Table 3. The average strict monotony violation (in percent) for 250 test color texture sequences per experiment performed in the CIE Lab color space, the average over all experiments, and rank for tested criteria.

	A	B	C	D	E	F	G	H	I	⊘	Rank
$rSSIM$	46	46	45	46	46	21	46	40	46	42	9
d_{cos}	8	46	45	46	46	21	43	46	46	39	8
d_{can}	0	14	1	45	45	5	9	4	32	17	7
SDI	3	1	2	2	2	1	37	29	18	11	6
JI	1	1	2	1	1	1	37	29	16	10	5
J	1	1	2	1	1	1	25	25	12	7	4
ΔH	0	0	0	0	0	0	10	6	2	2	3
$\cap H$	0	0	0	0	0	0	10	6	2	2	3
d_{sc}	0	0	0	0	0	0	12	5	3	2	3
χ^2	0	0	0	0	0	0	11	5	3	2	3
ΔGCM_{00}^{111}	0	0	0	0	0	0	5	5	7	2	3
ζ_2	0	0	0	0	0	0	8	2	0	1	2
ζ_3	0	0	0	0	0	0	0	0	0	0	1
ζ	0	0	0	0	0	0	0	0	0	0	1

ΔGCM_{00}^{111}, ΔH, $\cap H$, d_{sc} and χ^2 are relatively reliable and thus applicable for spectral similarity comparison. The remaining criteria are significantly worse and thus unreliable. More detailed and commented results can be found in [10]. The results achieved using BTF textures are almost the same as those achieved using color textures as presented in [10]. Figure 2 illustrates the proposed MEMD criterion values for two different color texture model synthesis of the original texture.

Table 4. The average strict monotonicity violation (in percent) for 3 test hyper-spectral data sequences per experiment, average over all experiments and the rank for the tested criteria.

	A	B	C	D	E	F	G	H	I	⊘	Rank
$rSSIM$	36	38	46	28	28	18	47	25	47	37	4
d_{cos}	30	35	41	21	22	15	47	47	47	34	3
JI	0	3	4	4	3	2	24	24	3	7	2
SDI	0	2	2	3	3	1	25	25	5	7	2
ΔGCM_{00}^{111}	0	0	0	0	0	0	0	0	0	0	1
ζ	0	0	0	0	0	0	0	0	0	0	1

7 Conclusions

Accelerated variants of the criteria for comparing the spectral similarity of the color, BTF, and hyper-spectral textures were presented. Spectral similarity comparison represents a partial solution for general visual data quality assessment as individual pixels' positions are not considered. Despite this restriction, spectral similarity comparison criteria can assist in numerous texture-analytic or synthesis applications.

The performance quality of the optimized criteria was verified and demonstrated on the extensive series of 407,700 [10] specially designed monotonically image degrading experiments, which also served to compare with the existing alternative methods. These experiments proved that optimized versions of the criteria maintain the original ones' quality although they are significantly less time demanding, decreasing the average computing time to about 20% of the average computing time of the original algorithm. On the other hand, all three proposed criteria are still slightly more time-demanding than some alternative criteria except for EMD, which is both more time- and memory-demanding in such a practically unusable way spectral similarity comparison purposes.

Unlike many existing approaches, e.g., mentioned in Sect. 2, the MEMD criterion ζ (1) and its variants ζ_2 (2), ζ_3 (3) are not based on 3-D histograms, instead representing the estimate of the image spectral distribution, and requiring a sufficiently large data set, which is seldom available. Moreover, the criterion (1) has no limit on the number of spectral bands in the compared data. The proposed criteria can be exploited in simple spectral-based texture, image retrieval, or (un)supervised classification methods as demonstrated in [10].

The presented criteria propose a reliable, fully automatic alternative to psychophysical experiments, which are highly impractical due to their cost and strict design setup, condition control, human resources, and time. Additionally, psychophysical experiments are restricted to visualize maximally three-dimensional data due to the limited tri-chromatic nature of the human vision.

Acknowledgments. The Czech Science Foundation project GAČR 19-12340S supported this research.

References

1. Dice, L.R.: Measures of the amount of ecologic association between species. Ecology **26**(3), 297–302 (1945)
2. Galloway, M.M.: Texture analysis using gray level run lengths. Comput. Graphics Image Process. **4**(2), 172–179 (1975)
3. Haindl, M., Filip, J.: A fast probabilistic bidirectional texture function model. Lect. Notes Comput. Sci. **3212**, 298–305 (2004)
4. Haindl, M., Filip, J.: Visual Texture. Advances in Computer Vision and Pattern Recognition. Springer, London (2012). https://doi.org/10.1007/978-1-4471-4902-6
5. Haindl, M., Filip, J., Arnold, M.: BTF image space utmost compression and modelling method. In: Proceedings of the 17th IAPR International Conference on Pattern Recognition, vol. 3, pp. 194–197. IEEE Press (2004)

6. Haindl, M., Kudělka, M.J.: Texture fidelity benchmark. In: 2014 International Workshop on Computational Intelligence for Multimedia Understanding (IWCIM), pp. 1–5. IEEE (2014)
7. Haindl, M., Mikeš, S.: Unsupervised texture segmentation using multispectral modelling approach. In: 18th International Conference on Pattern Recognition (ICPR'06) vol. 2, pp. 203–206. IEEE (2006)
8. Haralick, R.M., Shanmugam, K., Dinstein, I.: Textural features for image classification. IEEE Trans. Syst. Man Cybern. **6**, 610–621 (1973)
9. Havlíček, M., Haindl M.: Texture spectral similarity criteria. In: Proceedings of the 4th CIE Expert Symposium on Colour and Visual Appearance, Commission Internationale de L'Eclairage CIE Central Bureau, pp. 147–154 (2016)
10. Havlíček, M., Haindl, M.: Texture spectral similarity criteria. IET Image Proc. **13**(11), 1998–2007 (2019)
11. Hoare, C.A.R.: Algorithm 64: quicksort. Commun. ACM **4**(7), 321 (1961)
12. Jaccard, P.: Etude comparative de la distribution florale dans une portion des Alpes et du Jura. Bull. Soc. Vaudoise Sci. Nat. **37**, 547–579 (1901)
13. Kokare, M., Chatterji, B., Biswas, P.: Comparison of similarity metrics for texture image retrieval. In: TENCON 2003, Conference on Convergent Technologies for Asia-Pacific Region, vol. 2, pp. 571–575 (2003)
14. Kudělka, M., Haindl, M.: Texture fidelity criterion. In: 2016 IEEE International Conference on Image Processing (ICIP), pp. 2062–2066. IEEE (2016)
15. Larson, E.C., Chandler, D.M.: Categorical image quality (CSIQ) database (2009). http://vision.okstate.edu/csiq
16. Laws, K.I.: Rapid texture identification. In: Image Processing for Missile Guidance, vol. 238, pp. 376–381. International Society for Optics and Photonics (1980)
17. Mahy, M., Eycken, L., Oosterlinck, A.: Evaluation of uniform color spaces developed after the adoption of CIELAB and CIELUV. Color. Res. Appl. **19**(2), 105–121 (1994)
18. Manjunath, B.S., Ma, W.Y.: Texture features for browsing and retrieval of image data. IEEE Trans. Pattern Anal. Mach. Intell. **18**(8), 837–842 (1996)
19. Mindru, F., Moons, T., Gool, L.V.: Color-based moment invariants for viewpoint and illumination independent recognition of planar color patterns. In: Singh, S. (ed.) International Conference on Advances in Pattern Recognition, pp. 113–122. Springer, London (1999). https://doi.org/10.1007/978-1-4471-0833-7_12
20. Moroney, N., Gottwals, M.M., Tasti, I.: Generating Color Similarity Measures, U.S. Patent No. 10,084,941. Washington, DC: U.S. Patent and Trademark Office (2018)
21. Ojala, T., Pietikäinen, M., Mäenpää, T.: Multiresolution gray-scale and rotation invariant texture classification with local binary patterns. IEEE Trans. Pattern Anal. Mach. Intell. **24**(7), 971–987 (2002)
22. Puzicha, J., Hofmann, T., Buhmann, J.M.: Non-parametric similarity measures for unsupervised texture segmentation and image retrieval. In: Proceedings of the IEEE International Conference on Computer Vision and Pattern Recognition, pp. 267–272. IEEE (1997)
23. Rubner, Y., Tomasi, C., Guibas, L.J.: The earth mover's distance as a metric for image retrieval. Int. J. Comput. Vision **40**(2), 99–121 (2000)
24. Swain, M.J., Ballard, D.H.: Color indexing. Int. J. Comput. Vision **7**(1), 11–32 (1991)
25. Wang, Z., Bovik, A.C., Sheikh, H.R., Simoncelli, E.P.: Image quality assessment: from error visibility to structural similarity. IEEE Trans. Image Process. **13**(4), 600–612 (2004)

26. Wang, Z., Simoncelli, E.P.: Translation insensitive image similarity in complex wavelet domain. In: Proceedings, (ICASSP 2005), IEEE International Conference on Acoustics, Speech, and Signal Processing, vol. 2, pp. 573–576. IEEE (2005)
27. Wyszecki, G., Stiles, W.S.: Color Science 8. Wiley, New York (1982)
28. Yuan, J., Wang, D., Cheriyadat, A.M.: Factorization-based texture segmentation. IEEE Trans. Image Process. **24**(11), 3488–3497 (2015)
29. Zhang, D., Lu, G.: Evaluation of similarity measurement for image retrieval. In: International Conference on Neural Networks and Signal Processing, Proceedings of the 2003, pp. 928–931. IEEE (2003)
30. Zujovic, J., Pappas, T.N., Neuhoff, D.L.: Structural texture similarity metrics for image analysis and retrieval. IEEE Trans. Image Process. **22**(7), 2545–2558 (2013)

Success and Hindrance Factors of AHA-Oriented Open Service Platforms

Andrea Carboni[1], Dario Russo[1], Davide Moroni[1](✉), Paolo Barsocchi[1], Alexander Nikolov[2], Carina Dantas[3], Diana Guardado[3], Ana Filipa Leandro[3], Willeke van Staalduinen[4], Efstathios Karanastasis[5], Vassiliki Andronikou[5], Javier Ganzarain[4], Silvia Rus[6], Frederic Lievens[7], Joana Oliveira Vieira[3], Carlos Juiz[8], Belen Bermejo[8], Christina Samuelsson[9], Anna Ekström[9], Maria Fernanda Cabrera-Umpierrez[10], Silvia de los Rios Peres[10], and Ad Van Berlo[11]

[1] Institute of Information Science and Technologies, CNR, Pisa, Italy
davide.moroni@cnr.it
[2] SYNYO GmbH, Vienna, Austria
[3] Innovation Department, Cáritas Diocesana de Coimbra, Coimbra, Portugal
[4] AFEdemy, Academy on Age-friendly Environments in Europe BV, Gouda, The Netherlands
[5] Institute of Communication and Computer Systems, ICCS, Athen, Greece
[6] Fraunhofer Institute for Computer Graphics Research IGD, Darmstadt, Germany
[7] Lievens-Lanckman BVBA, Grimbergen, Belgium
[8] University of the Balearic Islands/Computer Science, Palma, Spain
[9] Linköpings Universitet, Linköping, Sweden
[10] Universidad Politécnica de Madrid, Madrid, Spain
[11] Smart Homes, Eindhoven, The Netherlands

Abstract. In the past years, there has been a flourishing of platforms dedicated to Active Assisted Living (AAL) and Active and Healthy Ageing (AHA). Most of them feature as their core elements intelligent systems for the analysis of multisource and multimodal data coming from sensors of various nature inserted in suitable IoT ecosystems. While progress in signal processing and artificial intelligence has shown how these platforms may have a great potential in improving the daylife of seniors or frail subjects, there are still several technological and non-technological barriers that should be torn down before full uptake of the existing solutions. In this paper, we address specifically this issue describing the outcome and creation process of a methodology aimed at evaluating the successful uptake of existing platforms in the field of AHA. We propose a pathway (as part of an overarching methodology) to define and select for Key Performance Indicators (KPIs), taking into account an extensive amount of parameters related to success, uptake and evolution of platforms. For this, we contribute a detailed analysis structured along with the 4 main actions of mapping, observing, understanding, and defining. Our analysis focuses on Platforms, defined as operating environments, under which various applications, agents and intelligent services

K. Wojtkiewicz et al. (Eds.): ICCCI 2021, CCIS 1463, pp. 656–668, 2021.
https://doi.org/10.1007/978-3-030-88113-9_53

are designed, implemented, tested, released and maintained. By following the proposed pathway, we were able to define a practical and effective methodology for monitoring and evaluating the uptake and other success indicators of AHA platforms. Besides, by the same token, we were able to provide guidelines and best practices for the development of the next-generation platforms in the AHA domain.

Keywords: AAL · AHA · Open service platforms · KPI Analysis · Data analysis

1 Introduction

One of the most critical socio-economic emergencies that all the countries in the world face today and will deal with soon is ageing [1]. A European Union statistic in 2019 [9] estimated that people of 55 years or more in the EU-28 would reach 40.6 % of the population by 2050, thus potentially putting the countries health systems at serious risk. To prevent this scenario, the European Union government has set aside a high level of resources for Information and Communication Technologies (ICT) projects in the AHA field. The principal idea has been to provide adaptive services to the citizens by using intelligent systems for the processing of data of various nature acquired directly from people, in their home or on the move, thanks to a wide range of sensors, including wearable as well as contact-less sensors. Following the trends in IoT, the emphasis has then shifted to the coordinated collection of information from disparate embedded devices, to the processing and correlation of multidimensional data and, finally, to the orchestration of services for the provision of superior assistance and effective guidance. In this context, computational intelligence on single-modality data has already given excellent results. To name a few, accidental falls can be automatically detected by cameras as well as mobile devices accelerometers [20], while wearable sensors might be sufficient to compute an index with very relevant prognostic value, i.e. the heart rate variability [13]. Analysis and integration of multidimensional and multimodal data may lead to advanced and smarter services in different situations ranging from the management of chronic conditions [3] to the promotion of healthier lifestyle and, in turn, to Active and Healthy Ageing (AHA) [4,15]. Considering the added value of data correlation and service orchestration, the creation of open and interoperable platforms for the integration and aggregation of data has become of growing importance. To this end, the scientific and technological community developed numerous open-source innovative platforms in AHA domain, such as universAAL [14] and FIWARE [10]. Further, during the last years, the European Union government has financed many ICT projects, such as ActivAge [12], permitting integration and interoperability across existing AHA platforms. While promising, such platforms (or meta-platforms) have not yet fully uptaken, but there still exists a mixture of technological and non-technological barriers that prevent a larger diffusion. This is a relevant issue since it jeopardizes the possibility to take advantage of the recent developments in intelligent system and artificial intelligence and use them in favour of the ageing population. The work presented here try to analyze this issue and to identify success and hindrance factors, focusing on EU funded platforms in the AHA domain. The approach consists of four main actions that define the path leading to the definition of a methodology: map, observe, understand and define. The first action was to *map* an ecosystem by collecting existing open-source platforms in the AHA domain, their end-users and related stakeholders. The next step was to *observe* common and differentiating features and characteristics of existing platforms that can act as success or hindrance factors in their uptake. Subsequently, the aim was to *understand* the links among all the information collected by running interviews and other types of consultations with platform developers to identify further hidden factors affecting their uptake and evolution. The last action was to *define* strategic KPIs to be tracked for evaluating uptake, interoperability, synergies and cost-benefit analysis of open service platforms. After all these steps, we were able to define a practical methodology for monitoring and evaluating the uptake and other success indicators of a platform in the AHA domain. In the future, the methodology will be applied to existing platforms for its validation; at the same time best practices will be identified, also using quantitative analysis, providing new input for the next-generations AHA platforms.

2 Map

The *Ecosystem Map* creation started with identifying the most representative platforms in AAL/AHA domains in the last ten years. During the selection of the platforms, we did not limit ourselves to the ones explicitly belonging to our interest domains; instead, general-purpose platforms applicable in AHA solutions were included. We found 48 platforms that meet the two main identification criteria: the extensive experience in previous projects and the in-depth research through numerous European channels, including the *eHealth Hub Platform* [6], the *DHE Catalog* [5] and specific official reports of the European Union [8]. Out of the 48 identified platforms, we selected 18 of them, discarding projects:

- with a low impact on the development of AAL/AHA technologies;
- completed ten years ago or more and no longer maintained (obsolete);
- without impact or reports on other subsequent projects;
- without the European coverage;
- aimed at specific solutions, either by type of pathology or by end-user.

However, we also included obsolete platforms that have been fundamental to developing other important selected platforms like Activage or UniversAAL. Our Ecosystem Map consists of a set of views belonging to four different domains:

- *Geographic*: the European countries (Fig. 1) involved in the selected platforms.

- *Relationship*: how different projects are related to each other. Figure 2 shows the main dependencies between the platforms. Four types of relationship are considered: *Derived from* indicates that the receiving platform was partially created using a previous platform as a basis, typically inheriting some characteristics; *Allow interoperability* indicates that the platform allows interoperability between the platforms from which the arrow starts; *Physical layer from* indicates that the receiving platform inherits the design and implementation of the layer indicated by the source platform; *Standalone platforms* are those that have no relationship with other platforms examined;
- *Application*: projects mapping according to their main domain of application. They are general-purpose, AAL and AHA.
- *Temporal*: years in which the individual projects were developed. The analysis allowed us to define three macro generations, the first from 2004 to 2010, the second from 2010 to 2015 and the third from 2015 to 2020.

3 Observe

This activity aimed to furnish a more in-depth analysis of the selected platforms to identify possible success and hindrance factors. In this task, we analyzed the eight remaining platforms of the 18 initially included in Ecosystem Map, after applying additional selection criteria regarding the development timeline and current status of the platforms and their final scope and outputs (Fig. 4).

For each project, the analysis focuses on three dimensions:

- *Technical dimension*, aiming at describing and characterizing the provided features, functionalities and services, taking into account six significant aspects of an IoT system:
  - device management capabilities, i.e. how the platform maintains the list of connected devices and track their operation status;
  - integration/interoperability, concerning the API permitting access to operations and data to expose outside of it;
  - information security, to characterize the vulnerabilities to which the data is exposed;
  - types of protocols i.e. the main used operational communication protocols;
  - data analytics, with particular concern to the way agents and intelligent services process data to produce results. It can be real-time, batch, predictive and interactive analytics;
  - visualization capabilities, the collection of human-machine interfaces supported by the platform to visualize results of the computations and analysis;
- *Contextual dimension*, aiming at the description of:
  - legal and administrative context, mainly related to administrative burdens for entry and growth, safety, health and environmental regulations, product regulation, labor market regulation, court & legal framework, procurement and reimbursement;

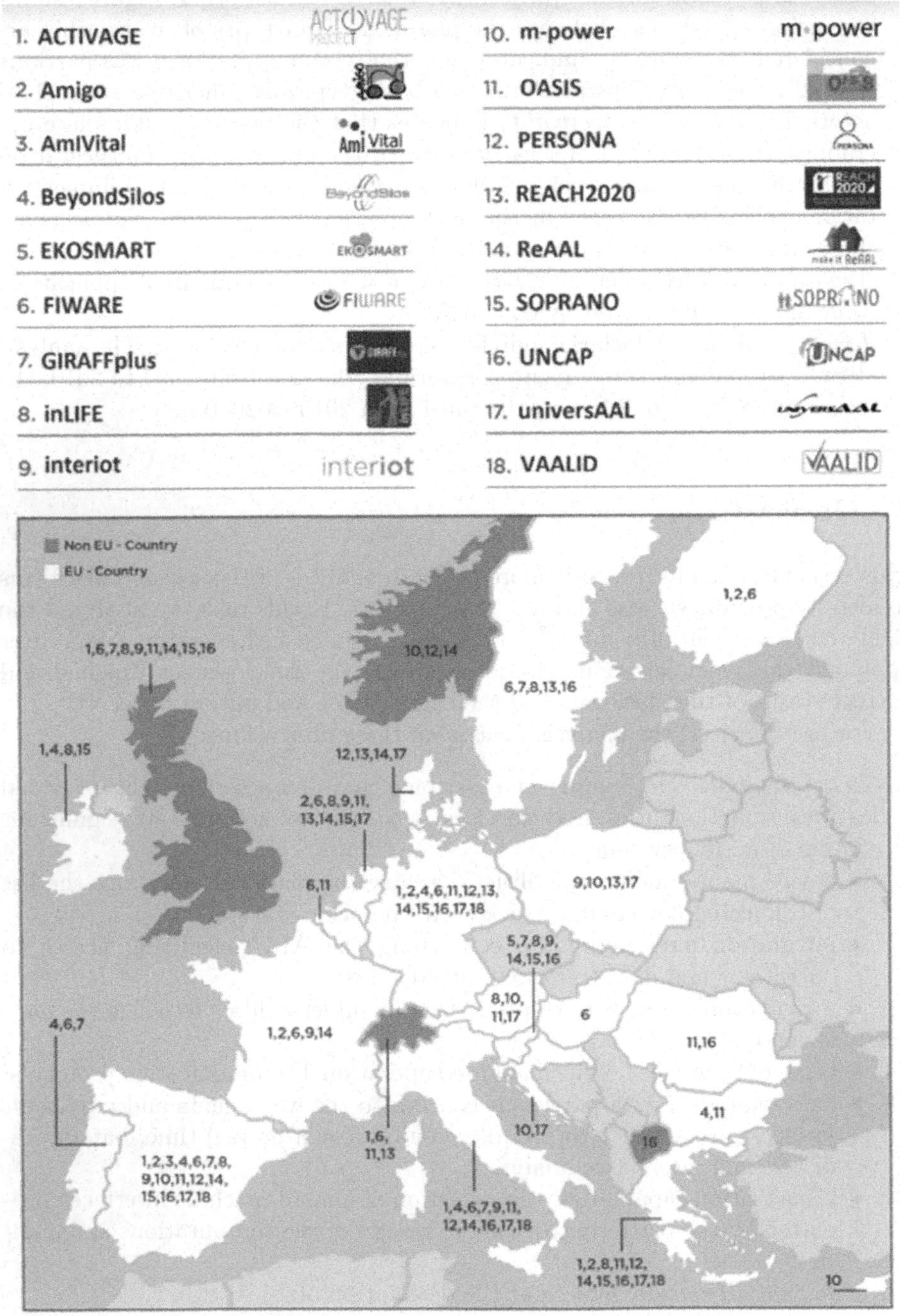

1. ACTIVAGE	10. m-power
2. Amigo	11. OASIS
3. AmIVital	12. PERSONA
4. BeyondSilos	13. REACH2020
5. EKOSMART	14. ReAAL
6. FIWARE	15. SOPRANO
7. GIRAFFplus	16. UNCAP
8. inLIFE	17. universAAL
9. interiot	18. VAALID

Fig. 1. Representation of the geographic distribution of the surveyed platforms in AAL/AHA domains i

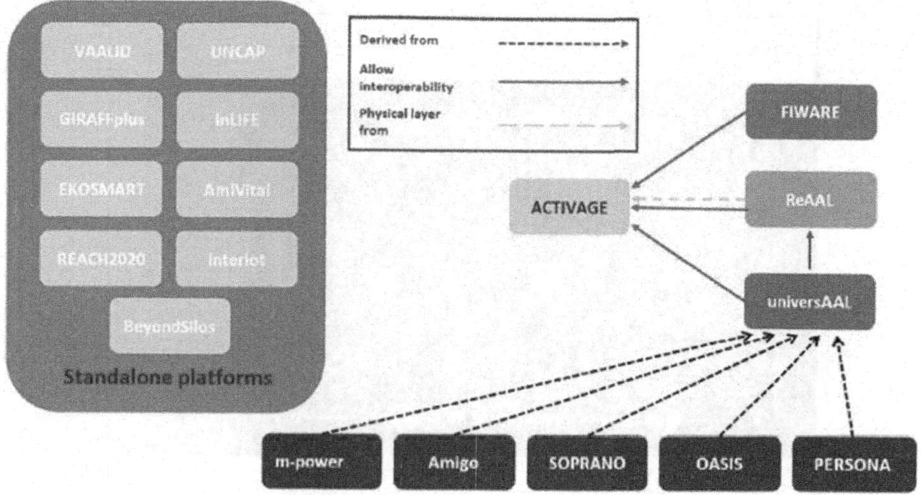

Fig. 2. View of the relationship domain. Besides standalone platform, several other have dependencies and/or interoperability features.

- ethics and privacy, about the type of data collected and information provided;
- data sharing and governance, dealing with the models (e.g. Economic, Citizenship, trusted 3rd party, collective) and data management;
- Intellectual Property Register (IPR), taking into account patents, trademarks, copyrights, and trade secrets, and open access, open-source or close access;

– *Financial & business dimension*, taking into account financial and exploitation aspects. It studies the platform's business models based on the available information acquired through existing social and professional networks as well as desk research targeting data openly accessible on the internet.

Identifying Critical Success Factors (CSFs) is a crucial step as it allows companies to focus their efforts on building their capabilities to meet those aims. By following John Rockart [22], the focus was put on industry, strategy, environmental and temporal CSFs.

Each CSF should be measurable and associated with a target goal. A critical success factor is not a KPI, but these indicators will quantify the objectives and enable the measurement of strategic performance. Evaluating the outcomes and the in-depth analysis of the examined platforms, we have identified four success criteria for an AHA platform. These are efficiency, effectiveness, fulfilment of functional requirements and stakeholder satisfaction. These criteria are formulated based on the three considered dimensions: technical, contextual and financial & business. Further, one extra dimension is considered as overarching or transversal: the resources. Stakeholders are also considered, and all areas are represented in Fig. 3.

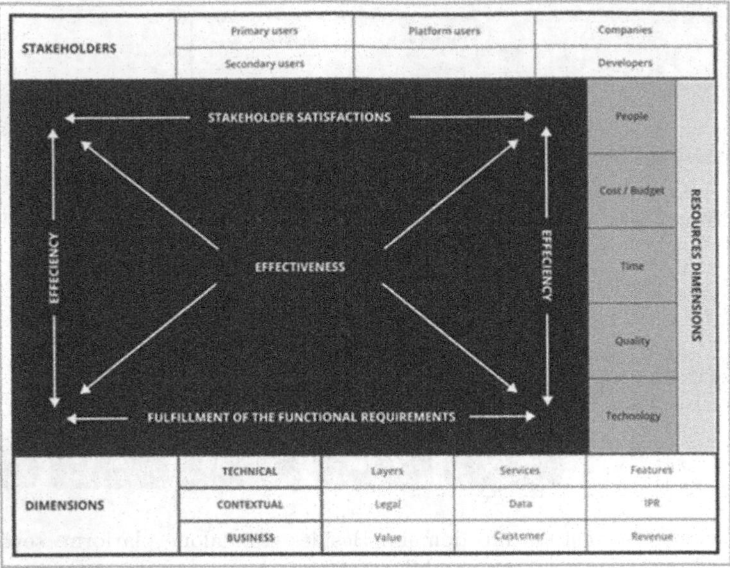

Fig. 3. Schema describing the critical success factors for open AHA platforms, their dimension and interrelation.

4 Understand

The work carried out so far has allowed us better to understand the various platforms' characteristics and differences. The purpose of this activity is to deepen the knowledge about the poll of platforms by directly questioning the professionals who took part in the creation, management, development and maintenance phases of these platforms, to try to obtain information that is hard to elicit from the official documentation. The Technical, Contextual and Business dimensions have been mapped using two questionnaires: one relating to the technical dimension to be sent to platform developers (Sect. 4.1), the other one about the contextual business dimension, dedicated to executives (Sect. 4.2).

4.1 Technical Questionnaire

The technical questionnaire is aimed primarily at platform developers and is divided into three main sets of questions. The first addresses *Development, services and devices* with the goal of collecting an overview of the platform focusing on interoperability, monitoring capabilities, real-time diagnostic, usage analytics, minimum resource requirements and communication processes between all those developing the platform. Then, *End-users and privacy* are considered since the involvement of end-users and privacy and security issues in the processing and transmitting sensitive data are of utmost importance. Finally, other miscellaneous questions are proposed regarding e.g. management or recruiting

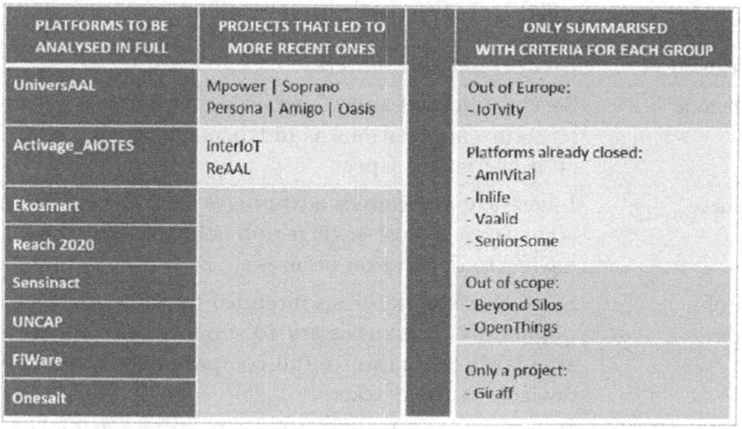

PLATFORMS TO BE ANALYSED IN FULL	PROJECTS THAT LED TO MORE RECENT ONES	ONLY SUMMARISED WITH CRITERIA FOR EACH GROUP
UniversAAL	Mpower | Soprano Persona | Amigo | Oasis	Out of Europe: - IoTvity
Activage_AIOTES	InterIoT ReAAL	Platforms already closed: - AmIVital - Inlife - Vaalid - SeniorSome
Ekosmart		
Reach 2020		
Sensinact		Out of scope: - Beyond Silos - OpenThings
UNCAP		
FiWare		Only a project: - Giraff
Onesait		

Fig. 4. List of the platforms that were selected or disregarded after thorough observation.

assignments, difficulties and problems encountered during development, and general knowledge of other AHA oriented platforms.

4.2 Contextual/Business Questionnaire

The contextual/business questionnaire is primarily aimed at platform executives and is divided into these three main sets of questions. First, a *platform overview* is sought from a high level point of view considering aspects such as competitive advantages and weaknesses of the platform, impact of the services in the AHA domain and costs related to the installation and maintenance of all the services offered. *End-users and privacy* are considered also in this questionnaire focusing on relationship with end-users and the treatment of the feedback received, security, data processing and data sharing. Finally, other miscellaneous questions are proposed concerning e.g. statistical data regarding the actual use of the platform (active or passive users, registrations, growth rates, earnings, etc.) and possible success stories.

4.3 Questionnaire Analysis and Essential Characteristics

The analysis of the information collected allowed us to establish, from an insider point of view, the characteristics of an ideal platform and to identify the main issues that might be critical and capable of compromising its functionality and purposes. In total we analyzed 14 questionnaires, completed by 12 professionals who worked on the development of the platforms examined. Table 1 reports the essential characteristics that we were able to elicit.

Table 1. Essential characteristics.

Characteristic	Description and remarks
Microservices	Service-oriented and distributed architecture permitting to structure applications as independent agents, each focused on a particular aspect
Open source	Inherently guarantees advantages such as reliability, transparency, cost savings and collaboration, without having to depend on licenses
Support of standards	Since these are systems intended for large segments of the population, it is necessary to support the existing primary standards to guarantee full compatibility with most of the devices on the market
Object-oriented	Provides natural support for software modelling of real-world objects or the abstract model to be reproduced and allows easier management and maintenance of large projects
Interoperability through semantic	Expresses the meaning of terms and concepts and finds the right relationships between them
Correct dimensions definition	It is vital that the three identified dimensions, technical, contextual and business, are thought of as separate modules but dependent on each other. The design of a platform should start from the setting of these three dimensions and their dependencies
Focused documentation	Correct documentation and its constant updating are the basis for the success of a platform over time
Tools for diagnostics and usage analytics	Fundamental both for proper maintenance and for the creation of new metadata
End-users engagement and feedback	End-users need to feel involved, they should perceive that the platform's functionalities are beneficial for improving their lives
Full GDPR compliance	Improves the protection of European data subjects' rights and clarifies what companies processing personal data must do to safeguard these rights

5 Define

In this task, a set of KPIs were defined for tracking the successful uptake and evolution of existing platforms [7,11,17–19,24,25]. These KPIs will serve as input for the revaluation and development of the final methodology. Considering the results of an analysis conducted on Google Scholar, we obtained that the current literature is mainly focused on evaluating the performance of platforms from the technical point of view. There is no related work attempting to provide KPIs or other metrics to measure the uptaking of largely diffused platforms such as

FIWARE or universAAL. As a second step, we analyzed the International Consortium for Health Outcomes Measurement (ICHOM), who has developed a group of standard sets for different health conditions and diseases to measure health-related outcomes that matter the most to patients. Based on the methodology from ICHOM [2,16,21], the process to define the KPIs has been based on a number of iterative steps: (i) the *perspectives* have been defined according to the definition of stakeholders, including Primary End Users (assisted persons, caregivers), Technology Providers (including platform developers, 3rd party developers, etc.), End-User Customers (healthcare providers, social and well-being organizations, etc.) and Government (Authorities/Policy Makers); (ii) an *initial KPI list* was collected to have an exhaustive set of potential KPIs related to the uptake and success of platforms, coming from different sources such as literature search, projects/platforms specific KPI, own authors' experience and KPI coming from benchmarking, and procedures like MAST, MAFEIP, OPEA, GLOCAL; (iii) a *revision of the initial list* of KPIs was performed, clarifying initial doubts and providing clear definitions to those KPIs that were confusing; (iv) in order to set up a priority of the initial list of KPIs, it was given a *priority* (low, medium, high) to each KPI; (v) *first analysis of KPIs*, performing an in-depth revision of the KPIs definition and measurement proposals, obtaining a clean list of KPIs; (vi) *KPI clusterization* of the clean list of KPIs, according to the perspectives defined in step (i); (vii) *Assessment of partners experts* to finalize definition and prioritization of the KPIs; (viii) *second analysis of the KPIs* by redefinition and merging of similar KPIs, new priority computation based on the average score of the initial prioritization and two partner expert assessments, approval or rejection of KPIs; (ix) *final list of KPIs* was organized per cluster according to priorities, having some KPIs shared among different clusters; (x) *partners experts' prioritization*, by rating the priority of all the KPIs per cluster with values between 1 and 10 according to the importance of this KPI per the corresponding target stakeholder of the cluster; (xi) *top-10 KPIs per cluster* were finally selected by computation of the average priority rate and the standard deviation.

The methodology described in this section can be used to identify and prioritize indicators in other domains and for different stakeholders. Moreover, the final list of KPIs can serve as a reference for current and future platforms with a focus on AHA, AAL and social health care (Fig. 5).

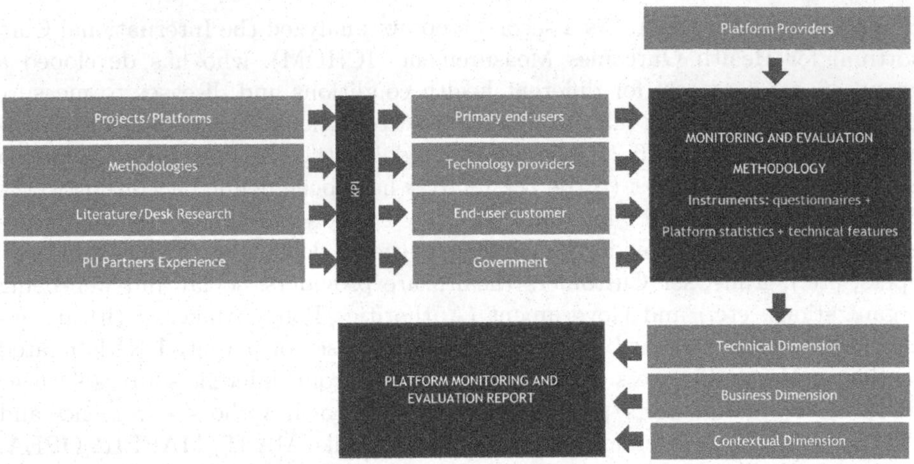

Fig. 5. Graphic representation of the proposed methodology for monitoring and evaluation of open AHA platforms.

6 Conclusions and Future Works

The pathway for the creation of the methodology considers all the performed work throughout the tasks of Map, Observe, Understand and Define. Monitoring can help the project's team to identify and solve problems and to keep track of project inputs and outputs such as activities, reporting and documentation, finances and budgets, supplies and equipment.

The monitoring methodology is based on the collection of KPI results between each dimension or platform statistics during their monitoring frequency. It keeps track of inputs and outputs of the projects according to technical, business and contextual dimensions. The evaluation seeks to understand why and how the uptake of platforms is going. Our evaluation methodology is performed by an expert jury panel, considering the monitoring results performed by the platform providers. There are 5 evaluation criteria that basically can conduct a project evaluation [23] consisting in relevance, effectiveness, efficiency, impact and sustainability.

The methodology pathway began with the identification and analysis of the existing project and open platforms in the field of AHA. More refined evaluation criteria were added in the next step, when performing the in-depth analysis, namely the combination of the technical, contextual and business analysis with the CSF model, as well as their final scope and outputs. From the firstly identified 18 platforms, 8 cooperated by responding to the questionnaires undertaken in Sect. 4 *Understand* of this document. The KPIs addressed different Open Service Platform aspects and features, mostly through validated questionnaires, according grouped in four clusters. After all the several iterations described above, including desk research, analysis of several methodologies and good practices, the pathway of our methodology was simplified and revised.

The monitoring and evaluation methodology thus combines the work performed in the previous activities, using the instruments (questionnaires, platform statistics and technical features) defined for the KPIs for Open Service Platforms Evaluation and the different layers previously defined for analysis. The results feed the technical, business and contextual dimensions of the platform monitoring and evaluation report. The monitoring and evaluation methodology presented here aims to be user-friendly, applicable and to support and collect the necessary indicators necessary to monitor and evaluate the successful uptake of an open platform in the AHA domain.

Currently, the proposed methodology is being applied to the set of available platforms (and to new ones) and is producing quantitative values with respect to different perspectives by effectively returning meaningful and consistent indicators, thus increasing our insight in success and hindrance factors.

Acknowledgments. The work developed under this article was co-funded by the project PlatformUptake.eu, under the European Union's Horizon H2020 Research and Innovation Program under the Grant Agreement n.875452.

References

1. Christensen, K., Doblhammer, G., Rau, R., Vaupel, J.W.: Ageing populations: the challenges ahead. Lancet **374**(9696), 1196–1208 (2009)
2. Ciasullo, M., Cosimato, S., Storlazzi, A., Douglas, A.: Health care ecosystem: some evidence from the international consortium for health outcomes measurement (ichom) international conference on quality and service sciences (icqss). In: 19th Toulon-Verona International Conference Excellence in Services (2016)
3. Colantonio, S., et al.: An intelligent and integrated platform for supporting the management of chronic heart failure patients. In: 2008 Computers in Cardiology, pp. 897–900. IEEE (2008)
4. Colantonio, S., et al.: Semeoticons-reading the face code of cardio-metabolic risk. In: 2015 International Workshop on Computational Intelligence for Multimedia Understanding (IWCIM), pp. 1–5. IEEE (2015)
5. Digital Health Europe: Online catalog - digital health Europe (2020). https://digitalhealtheurope.eu/catalogue/
6. EHealth Hub: Ehealth hub platform (2020). https://www.ehealth-hub.eu/
7. Eivazzadeh, S., Berglund, J.S., Larsson, T.C., Fiedler, M., Anderberg, P.: Most influential qualities in creating satisfaction among the users of health information systems: study in seven European union countries. JMIR Med. Inform. **6**(4), e11252 (2018)
8. European Union: Top 25 influential ICT for active and healthy ageing projects (2020). https://ec.europa.eu/programmes/horizon2020/en/news/top-25-influential-ict-active-and-healthy-ageing-projects
9. Eurostat: Ageing Europe: Looking at the lives of older people in the EU, 2019 edition. eurostat (2019). https://doi.org/10.2785/811048

10. Fazio, M., Celesti, A., Marquez, F.G., Glikson, A., Villari, M.: Exploiting the fiware cloud platform to develop a remote patient monitoring system. In: 2015 IEEE Symposium on Computers and Communication (ISCC), pp. 264–270. IEEE (2015)
11. Fernández, M.L.: Definición y diferencias de kpi y métricas (2020). https://www.ambit-bst.com/blog/definici%C3%B3n-y-diferencias-de-kpi-y-m%C3%A9tricas
12. Fico, G., et al.: Co-creating with consumers and stakeholders to understand the benefit of *Internet of Things* in *Smart Living Environments for Ageing Well*: the approach adopted in the Madrid *Deployment Site* of the *ACTIVAGE Large Scale Pilot*. In: EMBEC/NBC -2017. IP, vol. 65, pp. 1089–1092. Springer, Singapore (2018). https://doi.org/10.1007/978-981-10-5122-7_272
13. Georgiou, K., Larentzakis, A.V., Khamis, N.N., Alsuhaibani, G.I., Alaska, Y.A., Giallafos, E.J.: Can wearable devices accurately measure heart rate variability? A systematic review. Folia Med. **60**(1), 7–20 (2018)
14. Hanke, S., et al: universaal-an open and consolidated AAL platform. In: Ambient assisted living, pp. 127–140. Springer, Cham (2011). https://doi.org/10.1007/978-3-642-18167-2_10
15. Henriquez, P., et al.: Mirror mirror on the wall an unobtrusive intelligent multisensory mirror for well-being status self-assessment and visualization. IEEE Trans. Multimedia **19**(7), 1467–1481 (2017)
16. Kim, A.H., et al.: Developing a standard set of patient-centred outcomes for inflammatory bowel disease–an international, cross-disciplinary consensus. J. Crohn's Colitis **12**(4), 408–418 (2018)
17. Kitchenham, B., Brereton, O.P., Budgen, D., Turner, M., Bailey, J., Linkman, S.: Systematic literature reviews in software engineering-a systematic literature review. Inf. Softw. Technol. **51**(1), 7–15 (2009)
18. Marr, B.: Key Performance Indicators (KPI): The 75 measures every manager needs to know. Pearson UK (2012)
19. Marr, B.: 25 Need-to-know Key Performance Indicators. Pearson UK (2014)
20. Mubashir, M., Shao, L., Seed, L.: A survey on fall detection: principles and approaches. Neurocomputing **100**, 144–152 (2013)
21. Nijagal, M.A., et al.: Standardized outcome measures for pregnancy and childbirth, an ICHOM proposal. BMC Health Serv. Res. **18**(1), 1–12 (2018)
22. Rockart, J.F.: Chief executives define their own data needs. Harvard Busin. Rev. **57**(2), 81–93 (1979)
23. Sopact: A guide for selecting monitoring and evaluation tools (2019). https://tinyurl.com/3zp8hcpy
24. Torrenegra, A.: The best website kpi's for three different website types (2019). https://medium.com/@torrenegra/indicadores-performance-indicators-for-online-platforms-a-template-b79646a21289
25. Torrenegra, A.: Indicadores: performance indicators for online platforms (a template) (2020). https://medium.com/@torrenegra/indicadores-performance-indicators-for-online-platforms-a-template-b79646a21289

Bi-RDNet: Performance Enhancement for Remote Sensing Scene Classification with Rotational Duplicate Layers

Erdem Safa Akkul[1,3](✉), Berk Arıcan[1,3], and Behçet Uğur Töreyin[2]

[1] Faculty of Computer and Informatics Department of Computer Engineering, Istanbul Technical University, 34467 Maslak, Istanbul, Turkey
{akkul19,arican19}@itu.edu.tr

[2] Informatics Institute, Istanbul Technical University, 34467 Maslak, Istanbul, Turkey
toreyin@itu.edu.tr

[3] ASELSAN A.Ş., 06200 Yenimahalle, Ankara, Turkey

Abstract. We propose compact and effective network layer Rotational Duplicate Layer (RDLayer) that takes the place of regular convolution layer resulting up to 128× in memory saving. Along with network accuracy, memory and power constraints affect design choices of computer vision tasks performed on resource-limited devices such as FPGAs (Field Programmable Gate Array). To overcome this limited availability, RDLayers are trained in a way that whole layer parameters are obtained from duplication and rotation of smaller learned kernel. Additionally, we speed up the forward pass via partial decompression methodology for data compressed with JPEG(Joint Photograpic Expert Group)2000. Our experiments on remote sensing scene classification showed that our network achieves ∼4× reduction in model size in exchange of ∼4.5% drop in accuracy, ∼27× reduction with the cost of ∼10% drop in accuracy, along with ∼2.6× faster evaluation time on test samples.

Keywords: 1-bit DCNN · Rotational duplicate layer · Compressed domain · Remote sensing · Scene classification

1 Introduction

The popularity of artificial intelligence (AI) algorithms has begun to be felt in the avionics field. Studies in avionic AI applications have accelerated with the development of imaging technologies. Remote sensing scene classification (RSSC) is one of them in this field. RSSC is used for satellite mapping, target detection and navigation systems. Since scene images have huge amount of resolution and complex spatial information because of the remote sensing earth imaging technologies, it demands discriminative feature extractor and classifier.

Deep convolutional neural networks (DCNNs) have achieved state-of-the-art performance on RSSC tasks as well as other computer vision tasks such as image classification, object recognition, object detection, etc. Networks like ResNet50

K. Wojtkiewicz et al. (Eds.): ICCCI 2021, CCIS 1463, pp. 669–678, 2021.
https://doi.org/10.1007/978-3-030-88113-9_54

[6], DenseNet [7], VGG-16 [10], GoogLeNet [15] extract deep spatial feature representation which are then classified with fully connected layers. Such networks demand high computational power, and large memory which leads to GPU (Graphical Processing Unit) usage. Requirements for deep networks make them impractical for embedded devices such as FPGAs due to their limited resources. Researchers proposed methods to reduce computational cost by quantizing network weights [4,5,9], by designing new architectures [8,14] to overcome the limited availability of resources.

Remote sensing images are mostly extracted with JPEG2000 compression algorithm so that lossy compression with a superior performance at low bit-rates and lossless compression with progressive decoding are provided. Also this compression methodology provides different sub-bands that include different information levels. All of these sub-bands are extracted to reach original input image. [12] demonstrates that, intermediate sub-bands can be used as an image descriptor to reduce decompression time in exchange for a small accuracy drop. Lower sub-bands lead less decompression time with lower image resolution.

To meet resource requirements of embedded systems, we enhance regular convolution layer while keeping the parameter number by duplication, and keeping parameter variance by rotation. We propose RDLayer which can take place of regular convolution layer with 4× reduction in memory size using goodness of full-precision calculations, or 128× reduction in memory size using 1-bit weight representation. Furthermore we improve process time by using partial decompression method for RSSC task. The contributions of this paper can be categorized in 2 topics:

- We propose RDLayer which is obtained by learned kernel of reduced size via rotation and duplication which can replace regular convolution layer. We showed employability of RDLayers on 1-bit DCNNs for further reduction in memory. We created two networks RDNet and Bi-RDNet by adapting RDLayers to DenseNet-121 with full-precision and 1-bit weights respectively.
- We reduced the processing time of our networks by employing partial decompression method on test samples compressed with JPEG2000.

2 Related Work

2.1 Binary Networks

Many compression methods have been studied to overcome large parameters of DCNNs, and accelerate the process while keeping the loss in classification accuracy at low levels. Gong et al. [5] achieved 24 times compression of the network model proposed in [17] with only 1% loss of classification accuracy by using structured quantization methods.

XNOR-Net [13] introduced bit-wise logic operation to approximate convolution operations in 1-bit CNNs to speed up processing time.

Gao et al. [4] duplicated the input feature maps of the lower part of the network to improve the accuracy, and duplicated weights of the upper part of the network to compress model size while quantizing the input feature maps and weights to 2-bits and 1-bit respectively.

Liu et al. [9] proposed circulant filters generated by replicating learned binary weights n times channel-wisely while rotating them by $360°/(n+1)$ at each time across all convolutional layers.

2.2 Remote Sensing Scene Classification

Cheng et al. [1] proposed the large-scale benchmark dataset, NWPU-RESISC45, used for RSSC. They performed state-of-the-art scene classification methods on proposed dataset and achieved 90.36% accuracy with fine-tuned VGG-16.

Some of the works focus on the reduction of time and memory constraints in RSSC. [18] focuses network deepness. They used DenseNet as a classifier and optimized parameters with 3D pooling operation. They achieved far less parameters than other DCNNs like GoogLeNet, VGG-16 etc. with no fully connected layer. There are other RSSC approaches with feature aggregation. X. Lu et al. [11] used intermediate convolutional features that are fed into the convolutional feature encoding module to generate the convolutional representation. This representation then was merged with fully connected layer to generate the discriminative scene representation. G. Cheng et al. [2] focus to create more discriminative remote sensing scene feature representation to improve the classification accuracy. They proposed a new objective function based on the existing DCNN models without changing the DCNN architectures. They also updated cross entropy loss function for the metric learning regularization term so that discrminative DCNN model is created for RSSC task.

RSSC in the compressed domain worked by Byju et al. [12]. They generate coarsest level wavelet JPEG2000 sub-band and approximate finest level sub-bands with transposed convolutional module. In a classification step, these finest sub-bands are fed into DCNNs. They indicate that, sub-band approximation reduces the classification time dramatically while slightly decreasing the overall accuracy.

3 Approach

We adapt our RDLayer to DenseNet-121 architecture to create our network model. We create 2 new architectures: RDNet and Bi-RDNet which have full-precision and 1-bit weights respectively.

3.1 RDLayer

We propose a new convolutional layer, RDLayer, which has weights with a shape of $F \times S \times S \times (N \times D)$ without having bias vector. RDLayer is based on depth-wise duplication of learned kernel in a shape of $F \times S \times S \times D$ where F is output depth, S is height and width of convolution window, and D is output depth of learned kernel. Duplication is performed N times, depth-wise in the dimension of D. Learned kernel is rotated by $\frac{360}{N} \times k$ each time it is duplicated where $k \in \{0, 1, 2, ..(N-1)\}$. RDLayer can replace any convolutional layer, and N can be any integer value as long as equality constraint of $N \times D$ being equal to the output depth of previous layer is satisfied. We choose N as 4 in our experiments. Since input image has 3 channels and can not be divided by N, we leave first convolution layer as is which has 7×7 convolution kernel with a stride of 2.

Forward-Propagation: RDLayer behaves just like an original 2D convolution layer apart from duplication of the weights. During forward-propagation, trainable weights are duplicated N times and rotated by $\frac{360}{N} \times k$ each time it is duplicated to meet the depth size of the previous layer where $k \in \{0, 1, 2, ..(N-1)\}$. Let us assume we have an input feature map $\mathbf{X} \in \mathbb{R}^{S \times S \times (N \times D)}$, and trainable weights $\mathbf{W_t} \in \mathbb{R}^{3 \times 3 \times D}$. To compute convolution $\mathbf{X} \times \mathbf{W_t}'$, $\mathbf{W_t}'$ is obtained by duplication along with rotation of learned weights $\mathbf{W_t}$ N times which results $\mathbf{W_t}' \in \mathbb{R}^{3 \times 3 \times (N \times D)}$. Figure 1 explains the process visually.

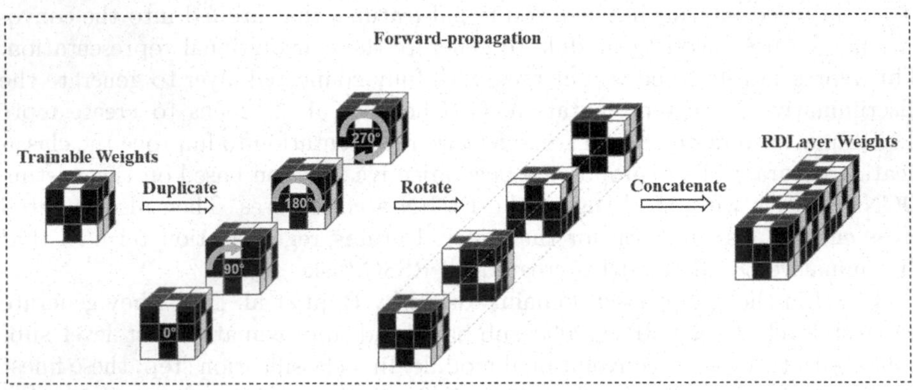

Fig. 1. Trainable kernel is duplicated 4 times while being rotated by 0° 90° 180° 270° and concatenated depth-wise to meet depth size of input features.

Back-Propagation: Gradient for each individual parameter is computed by averaging computed gradients corresponding to that individual parameter. During back-propagation, computed gradients $\frac{\partial L}{\partial \mathbf{W_t}'}$ are split into N pieces, and rotated in minus direction to correspond related trainable parameter where L is the loss of the network for given training data. Aligned gradients are averaged element-wise to obtain gradients of trainable weights $\frac{\partial L}{\partial \mathbf{W_t}} \in \mathbb{R}^{3 \times 3 \times D}$. Finally, $\mathbf{W_t}$ is updated with $\frac{\partial L}{\partial \mathbf{W_t}}$ for the next iteration. Process of back-propagation is explained visually in Fig. 2.

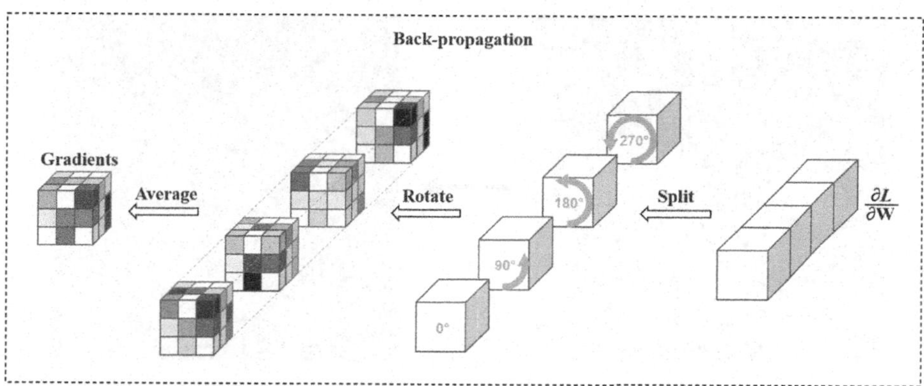

Fig. 2. Computed gradients $\frac{\partial L}{\partial W_t'}$ are split into 4 pieces, and rotated in negative direction by 0° 90° 180° 270° to align with corresponding parameter. Aligned kernels are averaged to obtain gradients of trainable weights.

1-Bit Network Training: During the training process of Bi-RDNet, full-precision weights are preserved to find optimal set of weights for RDLayers. Weights are adjusted so that every parameter in trainable weights $\mathbf{W_t}$ is an element of {-1, +1} by the training method proposed in [13] where full-precision weights $\mathbf{W_t}$ are estimated during forward propagation using the following equation:

$$\mathbf{W_t} \approx \alpha \mathbf{B} \tag{1}$$

where i^{th} element in binary weights $\mathbf{B_i} = +1$ if i^{th} element in $\mathbf{W_{t,i}} \geq 0$ and $\mathbf{B_i} = -1$ if $\mathbf{W_{t,i}} < 0$. α is a scaling factor computed analytically by $\alpha = \frac{1}{n}\|\mathbf{W_t}\|$ where n is the number of parameters in $\mathbf{W_t}$. To sum up, output of RDLayer with given input $\mathbf{X}$ is approximated by:

$$\mathbf{X} * \mathbf{W_t} \approx (\mathbf{X} \oplus \mathbf{B})\alpha \tag{2}$$

where $*$ denotes convolution, $\oplus$ denotes addition and subtraction without any multiplication since $\forall \mathbf{B_i} \in$ {-1, +1}.

3.2 JPEG2000 Sub-band Extraction

In this section, raw remote sensing (RS) images are compressed with JPEG2000 algorithm as an initial step. Instead of decompressing the whole image to feed into the model, intermediate sub-bands were used as feature descriptors to decrease decompression time. Let X be our fully decompressed image with $256 \times 256 \times 3$ dimensions. Intermediate wavelet sub-bands have 128×128 ($X^{'}$), 64×64 ($X^{''}$) and 32×32 ($X^{'''}$) resolutions. As the size of the sub-bands decreases, the spatial information it contains also decreases in exchange of an improvement in decompression time.

Fig. 3. Wavelet sub-bands are obtained during compression step. Each sub-band includes high frequency details and low resolution sub-image.

Each sub-band has high frequency information, so that intermediate sub-bands can be decompressed with these details and image itself can be obtained. An example of a sub-band extraction can be seen in as Fig. 3. $X^{'}$ is selected as a partial decompression output to find the most optimal solution. This sub-band was selected and saved for all the RS archive which is demonstrated in Fig. 4.

After partial decompression step, feature descriptors were fed into proposed RDNet and Bi-RDNet models. This allowed for a decrease in both the training time and model size. Moreover, the accuracy observed was close to the other state-of-the-art networks. Detailed observation is shared in the experiment section.

4 Dataset

We used AID [16] and NWPU-RESISC45 [1] datasets for the purpose of this work.

- **NWPU-RESISC45:** This dataset is a publicly available benchmark for the Remote Sensing Image Scene Classification (RESISC) created by Northwestern Polytechnical University (NWPU). It contains 31,500 images spanning 45 scene classes with 700 images in each class with the size of 256 $\times$ 256 $\times$ 3.
- **AID:** AID dataset is composed of 30 aerial scene types. Each class has 220–420 images with the size of 600 $\times$ 600 $\times$ 3. Total image number is 10000. Before using AID dataset, we resized each image to 256 $\times$ 256 $\times$ 3.

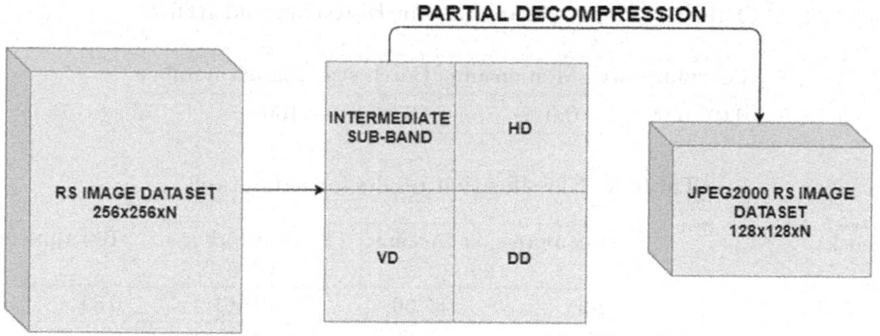

Fig. 4. Partial Decompression: 128 × 128 wavelet sub-band was extracted and saved as a new compressed image dataset. HD denotes high frequency horizontal details, VD denotes high frequency vertical details and DD denotes high frequency diagonal details.

5 Experiments

We evaluate our RDLayer on DenseNet-121 network by simply replacing all convolutional layers with our RDLayers. We also improve process time by deploying partial decompression method on training samples in exchange of small drop on accuracy. We employ AID and NWPU-RESISC45 datasets with a test ratio of 20% on RDNet, Bi-RDNet and DenseNet-121. We compare results in terms of accuracy, network size and test time. Results are presented in as Table 2 and Table 3 for AID and NWPU-RESISC45 datasets. Results pertaining to the proposed approaches are printed in boldface letters.

Before the training process, we split each dataset by moving first 20% of images in each class to test samples. Data samples for partial decompressed images are created with these train and test samples. All experiments are performed on a computer with Nvidia RTX 3070 8 GB and AMD Ryzen 5 3600XT.

We train each network for 100 epochs with batch size of 16. Learning rate is set to 0.01 initially, and dropped to one-tenth of its value after 50 epochs. SGD (Stochastic Gradient Descent) is used as optimizer with the momentum of 0.9. Table 1 summarizes the hyper-parameters for training processes.

We evaluate the test time as prediction time of the model on 800 test images along with the time spent on full and partial decompression processes.

We compare Bi-RDNet with recent models which are evaluated on AID and NWPU-RESISC45 datasets. Table 2 and Table 3 show comparison between Bi-RDNet and other full-precision models in terms of accuracy and model size. Network sizes are not mentioned in these works. Hence we estimated their network sizes in accordance with their backbone architectures. Test time and decompression information only mentioned in [12]. However their test time calculation and decompression strategy are different than ours and are not included in the table. Bi-RDNet has ∼27× to ∼502× lower network size than other approaches while having ∼9% to ∼12% lower accuracy. Our approach can be improved by pre-

Table 1. Hyper-parameters for Bi-RDNet and RDNet

Learning rate	Momentum	Batch size	Epoch number
0.01–0.001	0.9	16	100

Table 2. Classification results for aid dataset

Network	Decompression	Accuracy (%)	Network size (MByte)	Test time (sec)
DenseNet	Full	87.30	∼ 28.61	6.89
DenseNet	Partial	75.55	∼ 28.61	2.58
D-CNN with VGG-16 [2]	Full	90.82	∼ 527.57	–
ResNet50 with Approx [12]	–	92.24	∼ 98	–
DenseNet [18]	Full	95.37	∼ 28.61	–
FACNN [11]	Full	95.45	∼ 527.57	–
RDNet	**Full**	**86.05**	**∼7.08**	**6.82**
RDNet	**Partial**	**78.25**	**∼7.08**	**2.63**
Bi-RDNet	**Full**	**79.75**	**∼1.05**	**6.79**
Bi-RDNet	**Partial**	**67.95**	**∼1.05**	**2.54**

Table 3. Classification results for NWPU-RESISC45 DATASET

Network	Decompression	Accuracy (%)	Network size (MByte)	Test time (sec)
DenseNet	Full	92.38	∼28.61	6.89
DenseNet	Partial	86.62	∼28.61	2.59
D-CNN with VGG-16 [2]	Full	91.89	∼527.57	–
ResNet50 with Approx [12]	–	93.98	∼98	–
DenseNet [18]	Full	94.95	∼28.61	–
RDNet	**Full**	**87.45**	**∼7.08**	**6.81**
RDNet	**Partial**	**84.91**	**∼7.08**	**2.59**
Bi-RDNet	**Full**	**82.86**	**∼1.05**	**6.80**
Bi-RDNet	**Partial**	**76.62**	**∼1.05**	**2.57**

training on a larger dataset like ImageNet [3] and applying data augmentation techniques to training data.

6 Conclusion

In this work, we proposed a new layer RDLayer that can replace a standard convolution layer. Due to compactness of RDLayer, we achieved 4× reduction in model size on DenseNet-121 by replacing convolution layers with RDLayers. We further reduced network size by employing 1-bit weights that reduced the size of RDLayers 32× more which leads up to ∼27× reduction in total network size. Additionally, JPEG2000 partial decompression methodology is employed to reduce a considerable amount of processing time. Our experiments on RSSC datasets showed that RDNet along with the use of partial decompression method achieves ∼2.6× faster processing time, and ∼4× reduction in model size with ∼4.5% loss of classification accuracy. We also experimented ∼ 27× reduction in model size with the cost of ∼10% accuracy drop on RSSC task. Bi-RDNet has more parameters in batch normalization layers than convolution (RDLayers and the input layer) and fully connected layers combined. With the exclusion of parameters of batch normalization layers, Bi-RDNet occupies ∼65× less memory (∼0.44 MByte).

RSSC problem was handled with the fusion of RDLayer and JPEG2000 partial decompression methodology. Our RDLayer and partial decompression methodology can be applied to other tasks such as object detection, face recognition etc. We plan to combine our approach with other algorithms to explore how our methods perform on these tasks in the future work.

Acknowledgment. We would like to thank our colleagues from ASELSAN for their support.

References

1. Cheng, G., Han, J., Xiaoqiang, L.: Remote sensing image scene classification: benchmark and state of the art. Proc. IEEE **105**(10), 1865–1883 (2017)
2. Cheng, G., Yang, C., Yao, X., Guo, L., Han, J.: When deep learning meets metric learning: remote sensing image scene classification via learning discriminative CNNs. IEEE Trans. Geosci. Remote Sens. **56**(5), 2811–2821 (2018)
3. Deng, J., Dong, W., Socher, R., Li, L.-J., Li, K., Fei-Fei, L.: ImageNet: a large-scale hierarchical image database. In: 2009 IEEE Conference on Computer Vision and Pattern Recognition, pp. 248–255 (2009)
4. Gao, H., et al.: DupNet: towards very tiny quantized CNN with improved accuracy for face detection. In: Proceedings of the IEEE Conference on Computer Vision and Pattern Recognition Workshops (2019)
5. Gong, Y., Liu, L., Yang, M., Bourdev, L.: Compressing deep convolutional networks using vector quantization. arXiv preprint arXiv:1412.6115 (2014)
6. He, K., Zhang, X., Ren, S., Sun, J.: Deep residual learning for image recognition (2015)
7. Huang, G., Liu, Z., Weinberger, K.Q.: Densely connected convolutional networks. CoRR, abs/1608.06993 (2016)
8. Iandola, F.N., Han, S., Moskewicz, M.W., Ashraf, K., Dally, W.J., Keutzer, K.: SqueezeNet: AlexNet-level accuracy with 50× fewer parameters and <0.5 mb model size. arXiv preprint arXiv:1602.07360 (2016)
9. Liu, C., et al.: Circulant binary convolutional networks: enhancing the performance of 1-bit DCNNs with circulant back propagation. In: Proceedings of the IEEE Conference on Computer Vision and Pattern Recognition, pp. 2691–2699 (2019)
10. Liu, S., Deng, W.: Very deep convolutional neural network based image classification using small training sample size. In: 2015 3rd IAPR Asian Conference on Pattern Recognition (ACPR), pp. 730–734 (2015)

11. Xiaoqiang, L., Sun, H., Zheng, X.: A feature aggregation convolutional neural network for remote sensing scene classification. IEEE Trans. Geosci. Remote Sens. **57**(10), 7894–7906 (2019)
12. Byju, A.P., Sumbul, G., Demir, B., Bruzzone, L.: Remote-sensing image scene classification with deep neural networks in jpeg 2000 compressed domain. IEEE Trans. Geosci. Remote Sens. **59**(4), 3458–3472 (2021)
13. Rastegari, M., Ordonez, V., Redmon, J., Farhadi, A.: XNOR-Net: ImageNet classification using binary convolutional neural networks. In: Leibe, B., Matas, J., Sebe, N., Welling, M. (eds.) ECCV 2016. LNCS, vol. 9908, pp. 525–542. Springer, Cham (2016). https://doi.org/10.1007/978-3-319-46493-0_32
14. Redmon, J., Divvala, S., Girshick, R., Farhadi, A.: You only look once: Unified, real-time object detection. In: Proceedings of the IEEE Conference on Computer Vision and Pattern Recognition, pp. 779–788 (2016)
15. Szegedy, C., et al.: Going deeper with convolutions. In: 2015 IEEE Conference on Computer Vision and Pattern Recognition (CVPR), pp. 1–9 (2015)
16. Xia, G.-S., et al.: AID: a benchmark data set for performance evaluation of aerial scene classification. IEEE Trans. Geosci. Remote Sens. **55**(7), 3965–3981 (2017)
17. Zeiler, M.D., Fergus, R.: Visualizing and understanding convolutional networks. In: Fleet, D., Pajdla, T., Schiele, B., Tuytelaars, T. (eds.) ECCV 2014. LNCS, vol. 8689, pp. 818–833. Springer, Cham (2014). https://doi.org/10.1007/978-3-319-10590-1_53
18. Zhang, J., Chaoquan, L., Li, X., Kim, H.-J., Wang, J.: A full convolutional network based on DenseNet for remote sensing scene classification. Math. Biosci. Eng. **16**, 3345–3367 (2019)

MR Image Reconstruction Based on Densely Connected Residual Generative Adversarial Network–DCR-GAN

Amir Aghabiglou[1(✉)] and Ender M. Eksioglu[2]

[1] Graduate School, Istanbul Technical University, Istanbul, Turkey
aghabaiglou17@itu.edu.tr

[2] Electronics and Communication Engineering Department, Istanbul Technical University, Istanbul, Turkey
eksioglue@itu.edu.tr

Abstract. Magnetic Resonance Image (MRI) reconstruction from undersampled data is an important ill-posed problem for biomedical imaging. For this problem, there is a significant tradeoff between the reconstructed image quality and image acquisition time reduction due to data sampling. Recently a plethora of solutions based on deep learning have been proposed in the literature to reach improved image reconstruction quality compared to traditional analytical reconstruction methods. In this paper, a novel densely connected residual generative adversarial network (DCR-GAN) is being proposed for fast and high-quality reconstruction of MR images. DCR blocks enable the reconstruction network to go deeper by preventing feature loss in the sequential convolutional layers. DCR block concatenates feature maps from multiple steps and gives them as the input to subsequent convolutional layers in a feed-forward manner. In this new model, the DCR block's potential to train relatively deeper structures is utilized to improve quantitative and qualitative reconstruction results in comparison to the other conventional GAN-based models. We can see from the reconstruction results that the novel DCR-GAN leads to improved reconstruction results without a significant increase in the parameter complexity or run times.

Keywords: Magnetic resonance imaging · MR image reconstruction · Deep learning · Densely connected residual network

1 Introduction

Magnetic resonance (MR) imaging is one of the key non-invasive modalities among clinical imaging techniques due to its ability to acquire high-contrast images from soft tissues. Despite its popularity, MR imaging is a rather lengthy process, and it is sensitive to motion [4]. This long image acquisition time makes

This work is supported by TUBITAK (The Scientific and Technological Research Council of Turkey) under project no. 119E248.

K. Wojtkiewicz et al. (Eds.): ICCCI 2021, CCIS 1463, pp. 679–689, 2021.
https://doi.org/10.1007/978-3-030-88113-9_55

MRI susceptible to motion artifacts like ghosting and blurring because of possible motions originated from patient discomfort. Any motion during the MRI phase encoding causes ill-matching in the spatial domain [23]. Shortening the MR imaging time is one of the effective solutions for this problem. Recently, deep learning (DL) models proved their capability for solving different image processing problems [3]. In this regard, deep learning based methods [1,6,8,12,13,20] came to be an antidote for this issue. Through this path, the deep learning methods are trained using an undersampled dataset. Generative adversarial networks (GANs) as a particular DL framework have presented superb performance in imaging inverse problems in recent literature [7].

2 Related Works

GAN models predict the generative framework through an adversarial pipeline. GAN trains two networks at the same time in parallel. In MR image reconstruction, as shown in Fig. 1 the generative model G tries to reconstruct high-quality images while the discriminative network D predicts if the result is a ground truth image or it is a reconstructed one. In another point of view, G gives its best to reconstruct such a unique duplicate of a real image that fool D and push it to make mistake and accept the generator result as real one. GAN-based frameworks are proved their potential to predict undersampled k-space data and reconstruct high-resolution images [18].

In [21] a deep de-aliasing GAN has been proposed for reconstructing MR images. In DAGAN, a U-Net structure was used as the generator network [21] and the VGG (Visual Geometry Group) [19] perceptual loss was used alongside generative loss. TM Quan *et al.* [16] deployed cyclic loss in residual GAN for MR image reconstruction under name of RefineGAN. In a study, CS-based GAN (GANCS) has been provided by Mardani *et al.* [14] for MRI reconstruction. Coupling perceptual loss, pixel-wise, and the cyclic data consistency loss can improve the GAN-based model's performance for image synthesis [2]. Synthesis accuracy can be enriched using information from cross-section neighbors in each volume [2]. Recently, deep networks gained attention due to their promising performance but as they get deeper, their training becomes more challenging. They need more connections to prevent feature loss and gradient vanishment [10]. To address this drawback, layers during training can be referenced to the input layer by adding them together [9]. Huang *et al.* [11] has been demonstrated that employing dense connections among layers can prevent gradient vanishing. Dense connections concatenate receptive fields step by step from all convolutional layers and feed them into the subsequent layer as an input [11]. Then, these residual and dense connections were proved their capacity in various image processing problems. In RDN [25] residual and densely connected networks are coupled together for image restoration. In a study, dense connections are applied to a U-Net based network for image denoising problems [15]. In the MR image segmentation study, the dense connections were added into the U-Net downsampling and upsampling stages [22]. Recently, a wide multimodal dense U-Net has been put forward for reconstructing MR images related to patients who suffer from MS disease [5].

Getting inspired from the vantage points of both GAN-based and densely connected networks, we couple DCR blocks into the generative network. To the best of our knowledge, this is the the first time a DCR-GAN structure is being used for MR image reconstruction. The deep networks are applied on initial zero-filling (ZF) image estimates. The ZF images are generated directly from the undersampled k-space data via inverse DFT. For the k-space undersampling we utilize randomized Cartesian mask functions with 4-fold and 8-fold acceleration factors. In this regard, initially we developed a GAN (Fig. 1) using standard CNN with five convolutional layers as the generator (Fig. 2) and a binary classifier CNN as shown in Fig. 3 as the discriminator. We also adopted a VGG loss inside the generator loss. Secondly, we develop a densely connected residual GAN

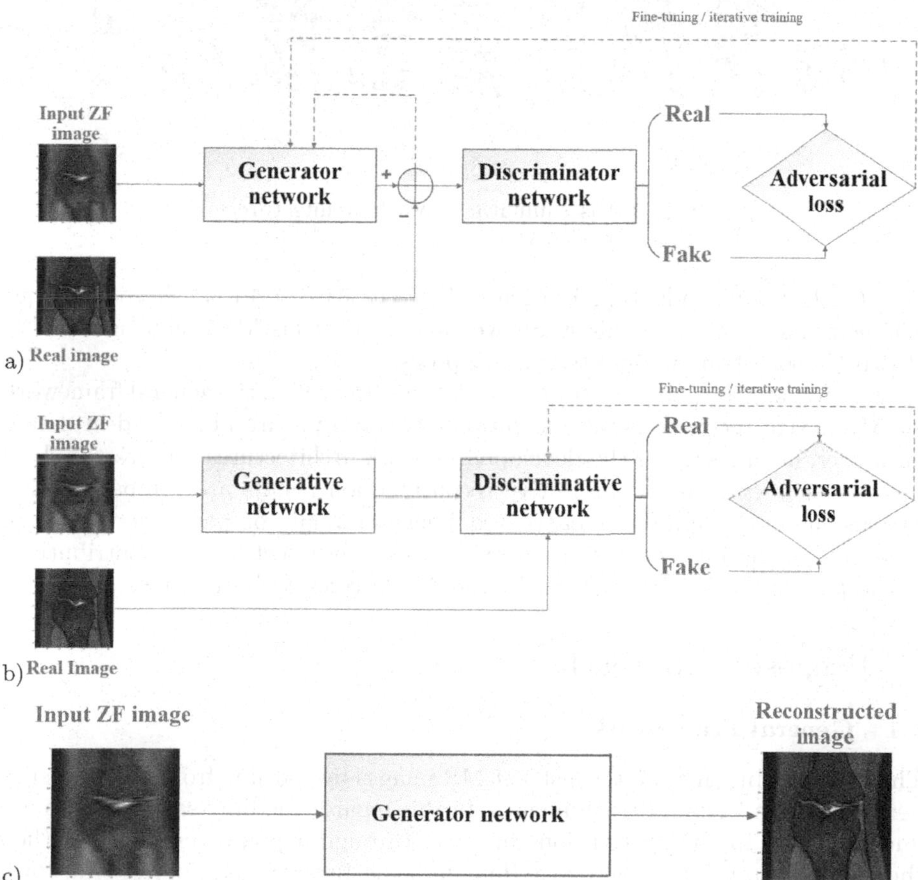

Fig. 1. GAN structure: a) Generator network during training step, b) Discriminator network during training step, c) Test step.

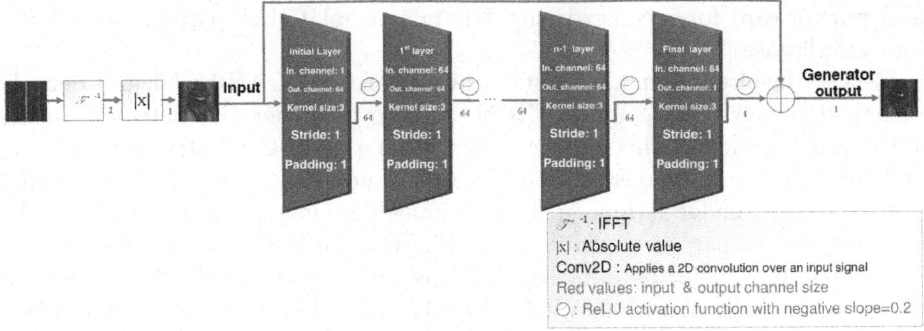

Fig. 2. Generative network architecture based on conventional CNN.

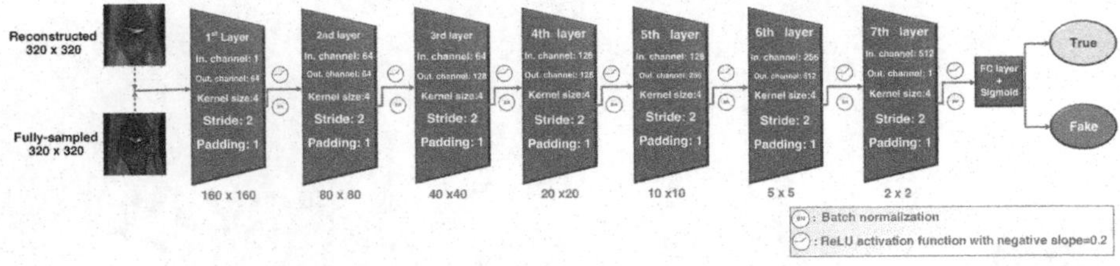

Fig. 3. Discriminator network architecture.

(DCR-GAN) and conduct qualitative and quantitative performance comparisons between these models. In this study, we have used the fastMRI challenge dataset of [24] for both training and testing purposes.

The rest of this article is arranged as follows. In Sect. 3, the general framework for MR image reconstruction and proposed structures are illustrated in detail. Moreover, in this section the developed network architectures are presented. In Sect. 4, qualitative and quantitative reconstruction results are compared using various metrics. Sample reconstructed images for all compared networks are presented in the final part of this section. In the last section, the contributions of the presented work are summarized and future research directions are given.

3 Proposed Approach

3.1 General Framework

The deep learning models reconstruct MR images by learning from the difference between ZF and ground truth images. In this regard, the fully-sampled data are undersampled in the spatial domain (x_{zf}) through a preprocessing step, then they are transported to the image domain using Inverse Fast Fourier transform (IFFT):

$$y = \mathscr{F}_{\Omega} x_{orig} \tag{1}$$

$$x_{zf} = \mathscr{F}^{-1} y \tag{2}$$

Here y is the undersampled data (observed data) in the k-space domain. $\mathscr{F}_\Omega$ indicates the undersampled Fourier transform function, $\mathscr{F}^{-1}$ is the IFFT, and x_{orig} shows the real image. MR image reconstruction model tries to complete missing points in input undersampled k-space data. This model tries to learn in the training step by minimizing the error between reconstructed image $\widetilde{x}$ and desired output. In another word, the goal is to find the best E function that minimizes the cost. So, the training process corresponds to the following optimization problem:

$$\widetilde{x} = E(x_{zf}) \tag{3}$$

$$\underset{\theta}{\operatorname{argmin}} \sum_{i=0}^{n_{data}} \|E_\theta(\widetilde{x}^{(i)} - x^{(i)})\| \tag{4}$$

Here, n_{data} refers to the number of training slices, and i is the image slice index. $E_\theta(x)$ denotes the network function, where θ represents the parameters of the underlying deep network model.

3.2 Proposed DCR-GAN

As shown in Fig. 1 the ZF images go into the proposed GAN. In general, GAN pipeline includes two competing networks, a generator (G) and a discriminator (D), with training parameters θ_G and θ_D, respectively. G should create fake images which must not be recognizable from ground truth images. To achieve this goal, network D help network G by classifying between fake and real images. Basically, this binary classifier for real samples gives value $D(x_{orig}) = 1$ and for fake data $(\widetilde{x}) = 0$. In mathematical terms, D and G play a two-player minimax game which is summarized in the following function:

$$\underset{G}{min}\,\underset{D}{max}V(D, G) = \mathbb{E}_{x \sim p_{data}}(x)[log(D(x))] + \mathbb{E}_{z \sim p_z}(Z)[1 - log(D(G(z)))] \tag{5}$$

Here, x indicates a sample slice from the fully sampled dataset distribution, and z is a sample image from ZF image distribution. Equation 5 can be optimized by training D to maximize the possibility of correct labeling, while G tries to minimize $log(1 - D(G(z)))$ and deceive D to accept the generated image as a real one. In this study, content loss was applied for generator network training. To this end, VGG loss is appended to the mean absolute error.

$$\mathcal{L}_{Total} = \alpha\mathcal{L}_{MAE} + \beta\mathcal{L}_{VGG} + \mathcal{L}_{GEN_{adv}} \tag{6}$$

$$\underset{\theta_G}{min}\mathcal{L}_{MAE}(\theta_G) = \|x_{orig} - \widetilde{x}\| \tag{7}$$

$$\underset{\theta_G}{min}\mathcal{L}_{VGG}(\theta_G) = \frac{1}{2}\|f_{vgg}(x_{orig}) - f_{vgg}(\widetilde{x})\|_2^2 \tag{8}$$

Here, f_{vgg} denotes the end-to-end function related to the pretrained VGG network. The generator adversarial loss is defined as follows.

$$\underset{\theta_G}{min} \mathcal{L}_{GEN_{adv}}(\theta_G) = -\log\left(D_{\theta_D}(G_{\theta_G}(x_{zf}))\right) \tag{9}$$

In this study, as in [21] the experimental hyperparameters α and β are set to 15 and 0.025, respectively. Here, we also applied data consistency (DC) layer [1] to improve our reconstruction results. DC layer can be defined as below:

$$x_{out} = \mathscr{F}^{-1}\{\overline{M} \circ (\mathscr{F}\widetilde{x}) + y\} \tag{10}$$

In Eq. 10, $\overline{M}$ designates the complement of the mask function used for undersampling the fully-sampled data. Here, $\circ$ is the point-wise multiplication operator, and y is defined through (1).

3.3 Architecture

The GAN model for MR reconstruction is provided in Fig. 1. As shown in Fig. 2, the generator pipeline includes five convolutional layers with the same training parameters as proposed in [17]. The discriminator network is shown in Fig. 3 and is similar to the one which is offered in [18]. This binary classifier includes 7 convolution layers that are followed by leaky-ReLU activation functions and end with a fully-connected layer. In DCR-GAN, initially the generator convolves the single channel ZF image into 64 feature-map, just like the plain CNN. Then these feature-maps are directed through three succeeding DCR blocks. The details of the DCR block can be seen in Fig. 4. In the final step, the single channel grayscale image is reconstructed through a reconstruction layer. The overall DCR-GAN generator network is seen in Fig. 5. Finally, a DC layer [1] can be applied to the resulting image to improve the reconstruction results.

4 Experimental Results

4.1 Quantitative Results

In this study, we developed a novel GAN based structure for MR image reconstruction. We have trained the proposed models using the fastMRI dataset [24]. The details for the dataset are provided in Table 1. The fully-sampled k-space is undersampled using random mask function with 4-fold and 8-fold acceleration factors. The simulation results are summarized in Table 2 for both undersampling acceleration factors. In Table 2, we have evaluated the proposed models performance using three popular performance metrics, namely Normalized Mean Squared Error (NMSE), Peak Signal to Noise Ratio(PSNR) and Structural Similarity Index Measure (SSIM) [8]. We did not utilize the VGG loss while training

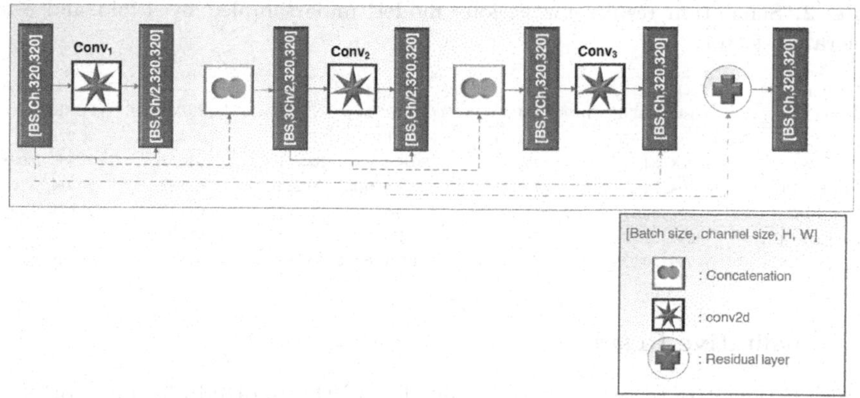

Fig. 4. DCR block structure.

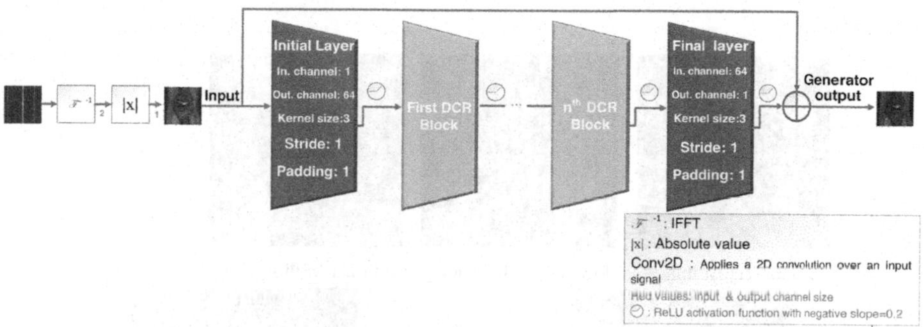

Fig. 5. Structure of the novel generator network with n DCR blocks.

the DCR-GAN. Despite this factor, the proposed structure achieved promising results in terms of all three performance indices. In Table 2, the reconstruction time is provided for 32 test image slices. The required reconstruction times indicate that these methods are suitable for real-time clinical practice.

Table 1. Number of image volumes and image slices in the fastMRI single-coil dataset [24].

Subset name	Volumes	Slices
Training	973	34742
Validation	199	7135
Test	108	3903
Challenge	92	3305

Table 2. Simulation results for various models undersampled by 4-fold and 8-fold acceleration factor.

Acceleration	4-fold				8-fold				Time (s)
Network	Loss	NMSE($\times 10^{-3}$)	SSIM($\times 10^{-3}$)	PSNR	Loss	NMSE($\times 10^{-3}$)	SSIM($\times 10^{-3}$)	PSNR	
ZF	–	41.679	711.59	29.876	–	77.751	603.37	26.921	–
GAN	0.308	34.317	755.26	30.894	0.451	69.212	637.63	27.466	0.098
GAN with VGG	0.308	34.152	755.92	30.908	0.451	69.218	639.12	27.474	0.10
GAN with VGG +DC	0.307	33.176	751.53	31.085	0.449	66.206	634.15	27.671	0.10
GAN with 3 DCR	0.297	31.273	766.34	31.413	0.432	62.106	651.63	27.972	0.29
GAN with 3 DCR +DC	0.299	30.925	759.57	31.501	0.432	59.189	643.37	28.208	0.30

4.2 Qualitative Results

In this section, the reconstructed images for all the realized methods for a particular test sample are visualized. The performance of the proposed networks is evaluated by comparing the quality of these output reconstructed images.

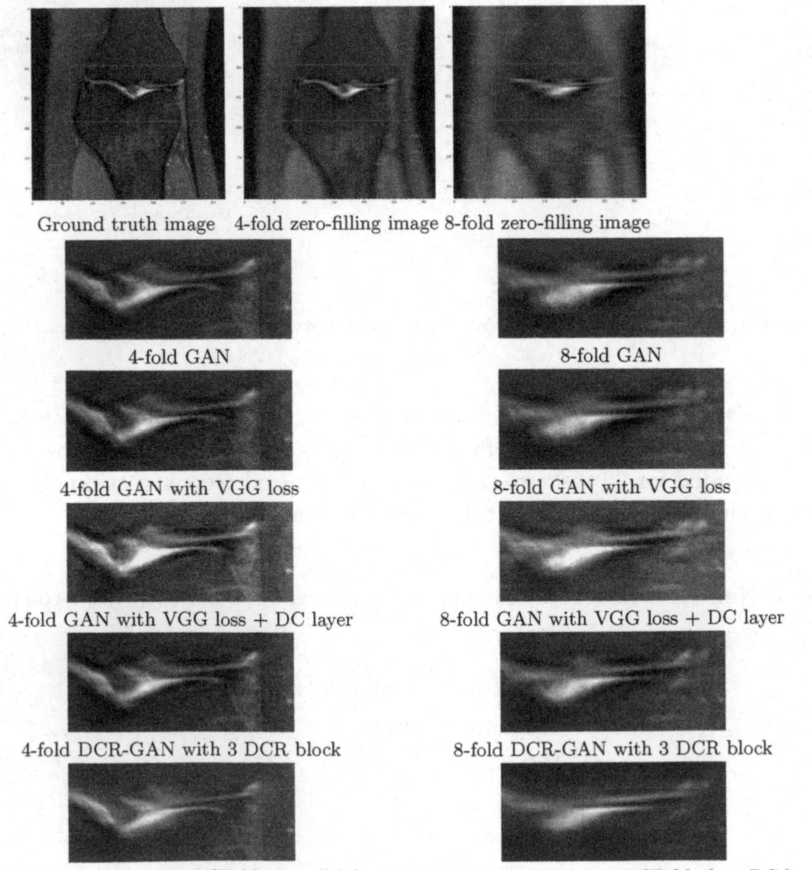

Fig. 6. Reconstructed images for 4-fold and 8-fold undersampling with random mask function.

Figure 6 depicts the original image, the ZF images (undersampled data with 4-fold and 8-fold acceleration factors), resulting images for Conventional GAN and the proposed networks. As shown in Fig. 6 the baseline GAN has not fully recovered the details while the proposed networks reconstructed images have better perceptual quality, and they have restored more detail and patterns. Moreover, the proposed structures resulting images have less severe artifacts, and most of the blurring defects have been removed. The quantitative results provided in Table 2 confirm the reconstructed images which are provided in Fig. 6.

5 Conclusion

Recently, densely connected deep residual networks have shown their capacity for improving performance results in various image processing problems. Inspired by this fact, in this work dense connections are applied inside a generative adversarial network for MR image reconstruction. Appending DCR blocks to the generative network improves the qualitative and quantitative reconstruction results of the plain CNN based generator structure. We conducted simulations comparing the quantitative and qualitative performance results for the proposed structure and other methods from literature. Results reveal that in MR image reconstruction, the proposed DCR-GAN can compete with potent models from the literature. DCR-GAN with just three DCR blocks inside the generative network can get promising results for both 4-fold acceleration factor and the more aggressive 8-fold acceleration factor. In future work, DCR-GAN can get deepened using more DCR blocks. The DCR blocks may also get utilized in conjunction with more challenging generator structures, incorporating possibly U-Net based models or cascade network structures.

Acknowledgment. This work is supported by TUBITAK (The Scientific and Technological Research Council of Turkey) under project no. 119E248.

References

1. Kocanaogullari, D., Eksioglu, E.M.: Deep learning for MRI reconstruction using a novel projection based cascaded network. In: 2019 IEEE 29th International Workshop on Machine Learning for Signal Processing (MLSP), pp. 1–6 (2019)
2. Dar, S.U., Yurt, M., Karacan, L., Erdem, A., Erdem, E., Çukur, T.: Image synthesis in multi-contrast MRI with conditional generative adversarial networks. IEEE Trans. Med. Imaging **38**(10), 2375–2388 (2019)
3. Eksioglu, E.M.: Decoupled algorithm for MRI reconstruction using nonlocal block matching model: BM3D-MRI. J. Math. Imaging Vis. **56**(3), 430–440 (2016)
4. Eksioglu, E.M., Tanc, A.K.: Denoising AMP for MRI reconstruction: BM3D-AMP-MRI. SIAM J. Imag. Sci. **11**(3), 2090–2109 (2018). https://doi.org/10.1137/18M1169655

5. Falvo, A., Comminiello, D., Scardapane, S., Scarpiniti, M., Uncini, A.: A wide multimodal dense U-Net for fast magnetic resonance imaging. In: 2020 28th European Signal Processing Conference (EUSIPCO), pp. 1274–1278. IEEE (2021)
6. Ghodrati, V., et al.: MR image reconstruction using deep learning: evaluation of network structure and loss functions. Quant. Imaging Med. Surg. **9**(9), 1516 (2019). https://doi.org/10.21037/qims.2019.08.10
7. Goodfellow, I.J., et al.: Generative Adversarial Networks. arXiv preprint arXiv:1406.2661 (2014)
8. Han, Y., Sunwoo, L., Ye, J.C.: *k*-space deep learning for accelerated MRI. IEEE Trans. Med. Imaging **39**(2), 377–386 (2019)
9. He, K., Zhang, X., Ren, S., Sun, J.: Deep residual learning for image recognition. In: Proceedings of the IEEE Conference on Computer Vision and Pattern Recognition, pp. 770–778 (2016)
10. Hochreiter, S.: The vanishing gradient problem during learning recurrent neural nets and problem solutions. Internat. J. Uncertain. Fuzziness Knowl. Based Syst. **06**(02), 107–116 (1998). https://doi.org/10.1142/S0218488598000094
11. Huang, G., Liu, Z., Van Der Maaten, L., Weinberger, K.Q.: Densely connected convolutional networks. In: Proceedings of the IEEE Conference on Computer Vision and Pattern Recognition, pp. 4700–4708 (2017)
12. Hyun, C.M., Kim, H.P., Lee, S.M., Lee, S., Seo, J.K.: Deep learning for undersampled MRI reconstruction. Phys. Med. Biol. **63**(13), 135007 (2018). https://doi.org/10.1088/1361-6560/aac71a
13. LeCun, Y., Bengio, Y., Hinton, G.: Deep learning. Nature **521**(7553), 436–444 (2015). https://doi.org/10.1038/nature14539
14. Mardani, M., et al.: Deep generative adversarial neural networks for compressive sensing MRI. IEEE Trans. Med. Imaging **38**(1), 167–179 (2019). https://doi.org/10.1109/TMI.2018.2858752
15. Park, B., Yu, S., Jeong, J.: Densely connected hierarchical network for image denoising. In: Proceedings of the IEEE/CVF Conference on Computer Vision and Pattern Recognition Workshops, pp. 2104–2113 (2019)
16. Quan, T.M., Nguyen-Duc, T., Jeong, W.K.: Compressed sensing MRI reconstruction using a generative adversarial network with a cyclic loss. IEEE Trans. Med. Imaging **37**(6), 1488–1497 (2018)
17. Schlemper, J., Caballero, J., Hajnal, J.V., Price, A.N., Rueckert, D.: A deep cascade of convolutional neural networks for dynamic MR image reconstruction. IEEE Trans. Med. Imaging **37**(2), 491–503 (2017)
18. Shaul, R., David, I., Shitrit, O., Riklin Raviv, T.: Subsampled brain MRI reconstruction by Generative Adversarial Neural networks. Med. Image Anal. **65**, 101747 (2020)
19. Simonyan, K., Zisserman, A.: Very deep convolutional networks for large-scale image recognition. arXiv preprint arXiv:1409.1556 (2014)
20. Wang, S., et al.: Accelerating magnetic resonance imaging via deep learning. In: 2016 IEEE 13th International Symposium on Biomedical Imaging (ISBI), pp. 514–517. IEEE (2016)
21. Yang, G., et al.: DAGAN: deep de-aliasing generative adversarial networks for fast compressed sensing MRI reconstruction. IEEE Trans. Med. Imaging **37**(6), 1310–1321 (2018)
22. Yuan, Y., et al.: Prostate segmentation with encoder-decoder densely connected convolutional network (Ed-Densenet). In: 2019 IEEE 16th International Symposium on Biomedical Imaging (ISBI 2019), pp. 434–437 (2019)

23. Zaitsev, M., Maclaren, J., Herbst, M.: Motion artifacts in MRI: A complex problem with many partial solutions. J. Magn. Reson. Imaging **42**(4), 887–901 (2015). https://doi.org/10.1002/jmri.24850
24. Zbontar, J., et al.: fastMRI: an open dataset and benchmarks for accelerated MRI. arXiv preprint arXiv:1811.08839 (2018)
25. Zhang, Y., Tian, Y., Kong, Y., Zhong, B., Fu, Y.: Residual dense network for image restoration. IEEE Trans. Pattern Anal. Mach. Intell. **43**(7), 2480–2495 (2021)

Underground Archeological Structures Detection

Anna Moudrá[1] and Michal Haindl[2(✉)]

[1] Faculty of Information Technology, Czech Technical University, 160 00 Prague, Czechia
moudrann@fit.cvut.cz

[2] The Institute of Information Theory and Automation of the Czech Academy of Sciences, 182 08 Prague, Czechia
haindl@utia.cas.cz
http://ro.utia.cas.cz/

Abstract. This paper introduces and compares three approaches for automatic archaeological heritage site detection hidden under soil cover from public aerial images. The methods use low quality public aerial RGB spectral data restricted by the land-use map to agricultural regions in the vegetation season to detect underground structures influencing plants growing on the surface soil layer.

Keywords: Remote sensing archeology · Underground heritage site recognition · Aerial image-based automated site detection

1 Introduction

Earth regions settled for thousands of years with numerous ancient cultures are rich in historical artifacts or their remains. Many of them are not visible, hidden under soil or vegetation cover for centuries. European countries are among the wealthiest archeological locations. The area of the former Bohemian kingdom, now the Czech Republic, is among them. Its location in the middle of Europe means close contact with many cultures and the site of many war conflicts that have destroyed many immovable monuments, the remains of which are often preserved only under a layer of protective soil. They are Celtic oppida, medieval fortresses, castles, gothic or baroque era fortifications, or commoners' houses.

Unless we have written historical records or other preserved references to such monuments, their discovery by archaeologists is a common question of chance. Modern remote sensing satellite or aerial sensors, however, offer tools that could significantly change this situation. It can be the ground penetrating radars or even simple spectral cameras because underneath materials influence plant growth on the surface due to locally change the subsoil layer's chemical composition and structure. The changes in vegetation coverage are caused by humidity and organic material content differences, and they appear as subtle spatial discontinuities or variations in the reflectance values (i.e., tones or colors) of vegetation and soil surface. Such features can be complemented with

K. Wojtkiewicz et al. (Eds.): ICCCI 2021, CCIS 1463, pp. 690–702, 2021.
https://doi.org/10.1007/978-3-030-88113-9_56

additional characteristics, such as the geometric pattern of the expected underground target. Fully automatic detection of hidden archeological heritage sites would be a solution to this problem. Furthermore, a reliable method would support a country-wide survey of unknown archeological sites, which is crucial for archeological heritage preservation and authorization of new construction and location development sites.

This article assumes only visible spectra, publicly available and low-quality aerial visual images, and land use maps, allowing us to process only meadows or cornfields and avoid irrelevant regions such as urban areas and forests. The rest of the paper is organized as follows: Sect. 2 briefly presents published alternatives to solve the automatic aerial heritage site detection. Section 3 explains in detail our approach and its optimization. Section 4 describes the performed validation experiments and used test data. Section 5 shows the achieved results. Section 6 summarizes the paper with a discussion and proposes some future research alternatives.

2 Related Work

For a brief history of 80 years of remote sensing application in archeology, see [5]. A more detailed overview of the European archeological remote sensing research literature can be found in [1]. The number of relevant publications is linearly growing during the reported 16 years.

Giardino [4] argues that multispectral and hyperspectral satellite data have provided important information for the discovery, delineation, and analysis of archaeological sites worldwide. Savage et al. [9] studied the application of hyperspectral (196 calibrated narrow bands in visible and shortwave infrared spectra) Hyperion satellite images for archeological applications. Although hyperspectral data are helpful to detect metallurgy production in the Faynan region of Jordan, their drawback is low spatial resolution. Zingman et al. [12,13] presents a method based on local Hough transform to detect approximately rectangular remains of livestock enclosures structures in panchromatic GeoEye1 satellite images while tolerating deviations from a perfect rectangular shape and incomplete or fragmented rectangles. High-resolution airborne hyperspectral images with 65–105 spectral bands between 400 nm and 1000 nm were used in [3] to detect remains of the Roman town of Carnuntum. They found beneficial hyperspectral imaging, especially at the beginning of the vegetation mark season or in a wet growing season. Lasaponara et al. [6] automatically detect buried archaeological remains of the UNESCO World Heritage Greek & Roman site at Hierapolis from the QuickBird-2 satellite panchromatic, multispectral bands. The rough regions are obtained by the K-means clustering followed by a supervised classifier, and the results were validated using the ground-penetrating radar. Lock and Pouncett [7] stresses the importance of GIS as the essential tools for data integration, manipulation and analysis, and spatial analysis for automatic site detection. Hidden linear ancient cultural relics visual detection from enhanced historical aerial photographs in the alluvial plain of Eastern Henan province is presented in [8]. Buried Roman archaeological remains detection in Llanera (Spain) using RGB and NIR cameras on the Unmanned Aerial Vehicle (UAV), multispectral (8 bands with 2 m resolution) WorldView-2 satellite data, and LiDAR data is investigated in [2]. They evaluate maps computed from various spectral indices. Stott et al. [10] proposes an automatic search for Viking age fortresses using airborne laser scanning data and Hough circle transformations and template matching.

Detection of archaeological sites previously occupied by farming communities in the Shashi-Limpopo Confluence Area of southern Africa from very high-resolution satellite WorldView-2 images is presented in [11]. They applied random forest and SVM classifiers to discriminate between bare soil, savannah woody vegetation, irrigated agricultural fields, archaeological sites with vitrified dung, and non-vitrified dung deposits.

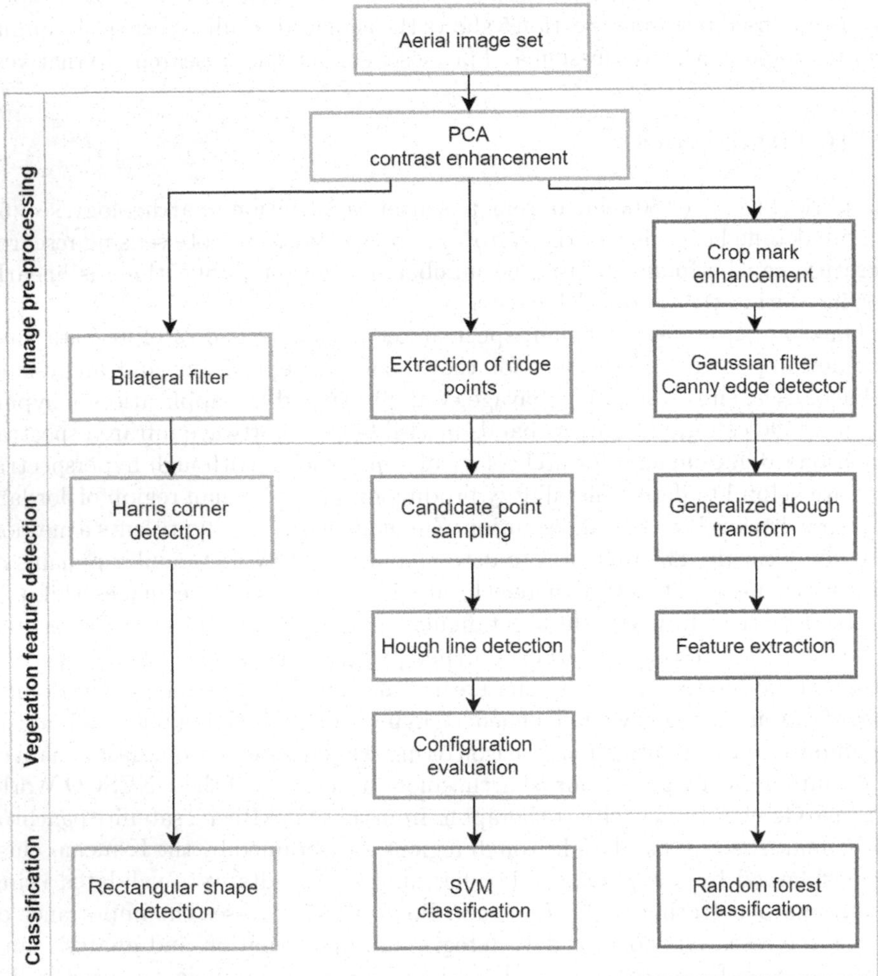

Fig. 1. The flowchart of our proposed methods. The left thread (green) represents the corner-based method (LHC/OHC), the middle thread (red) the line segment-based (RE) method, and the right thread (blue) is the template-based method. (Color figure online)

3 Proposed Approach

Three presented alternative methods together with their main functional parts are illustrated in Fig. 1. We selected the SVM and random forest classifiers to use comparable techniques standard in this application area (e.g., [11]), but the classifiers are less critical for successful archeological structures detection than the appropriate features and optimal data preprocessing.

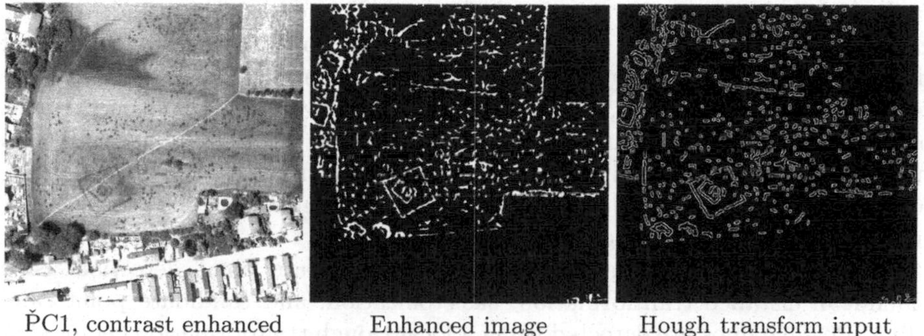

Fig. 2. Image preprocessing using the Sect. 3.3 method. Ctiněves site.

3.1 Corner Detection Based Method

Underground remains of approximately rectangular shapes can be detected using the grayscale Harris corner detector for crop mark corner extraction and subsequent geometric constraints. We propose two algorithms, each applied to a grayscale image corresponding to the first principal component of PCA applied to the original color image. Image contrast is enhanced, and a bilateral smoothing filter is applied to remove minor artifacts in our input data while preserving substantial edges. Finally, we apply the Harris corner detector to the processed, land use filtered image.

The LHC algorithm requires all four corners of a rectangular crop mark to be detected. Appropriate configurations of four corner structures, adhering to similar line length, line parallelism, and perpendicularity constraints, are considered further filtered if a line between two corners does not correspond to even a heavily fragmented edge in the original image.

In our second approach, the OHC algorithm requires finding at least three corners of an object, thus aims to overcome the issue of one undetected corner by using implicit parallelism, a similar length of these parallel lines, and the corner orientation constraint. This constraint ensures that neighboring corner orientations differ by roughly 90° moreover that the angles of corners forming a diagonal are roughly opposite.

3.2 Line Segment Based Method

The line segment-based detection referred to as the RE detection algorithm is adapted from Zingman et al., initially presented in [13] and later improved upon and reintroduced in [12]. We apply the algorithm to the grayscale, contrast-enhanced image corresponding to the first principal component (PC1) of PCA applied to the original color image. The image is prefiltered with a land-use map, a white top hat operator is applied, and the result of the operation is subtracted from the processed image to effectively suppress minor noisy artifacts such as watermarks and plough furrows. The following method, see [13], can be summarized in the following steps - black top hat operator to extract dark regions corresponding to required crop marks and other positive features in the image, thresholding, followed by morphological closing transformations, and finally, ridge extraction, is applied by selecting a point-wise maximum from morphological openings with linear structuring element of a set minimal line length at different orientations. This sequence enhances linear features in the image and suppresses background texture.

The line extraction starts with possible candidate point detection using Euclidean distance transformation, skeletonization, and candidate point sampling. Possible lines are detected using a local Hough transformation centered at each candidate point, followed by a graph construction where we consider each detected segment S, with length l, orientation θ and distance r from candidate point p_0, to be a node in a graph G. Only configurations with at least three sides, forming $\sqcup$ – like shapes and adhering to the angle and convexity constraints, see [12], are considered valid. Only the maximal cliques of each graph G we keep. The resulting rectangularity f_R (1), structure size f_S (2) measures, our proposed compactness measure f_D (3) together with the number of segments in the configuration form the feature vector used in the kernel SVM classifier.

$$f_R(G) = \Big(\sum_{S_k,S_j}^{E(G)} l_k l_j f_{90}(\beta_{k,j}) f_{cv}(\tau_{k,j}) \cdot \sum_{S_k,S_j}^{E(G)} l_k l_j f_{180}(\beta_{k,j}) f_{cv}(\tau_{k,j})\Big)^{\frac{1}{4}} , \qquad (1)$$

$$f_S(G) = \frac{\sum_j l_j r_j}{\sum_j l_j} , \qquad (2)$$

$$f_D(G) = \frac{2\sum_j l_j}{\sum_j dist(p_{0_j}, p_{1_j}) + dist(p_{0_j}, p_{2_j})} , \qquad (3)$$

where each tuple S_k, S_j is counted only once in Eq. 1, $\beta_{k,j}$ is the angle between two line segments, $\tau_{k,j}$ is a pair-wise convexity measure, p_1, p_2 are the end point coordinates of a segment, and $dist(.)$ denotes the Euclidean distance between two points. Functions $f_{cv}()$, $f_{90}()$, $f_{180}()$ are used to weight the differences in rotation and convexity from the ideal state (segments S_k, S_j are either parallel or form a perfect corner) to the allowed angle and convexity deviation thresholds, and are further described in [12].

3.3 Template Based Method

Structures with irregular but anticipated approximately circular or rectangular shapes can be detected with the generalized Hough transform. The image preprocessing, referred to as the crop mark enhancement, is applied to the PCA-based grayscale and contrast-enhanced image. Next, the white top hat is applied to extract white noise from the image as in Sect. 3.2. Median smoothing filter, adaptive thresholding, color inversion, and erosion operator are then applied, and eventually, we discard the remaining small blob-like features. The resulting image is filtered with a binary mask of land use to retrieve only relevant regions. The Gaussian filter is applied to the crop mark enhanced image to smooth the edges of the resulting contours, and the Canny edge detector is run on the smoothed image, resulting in more continuous, flat lines.

In template matching based on generalized Hough transform, we used the perfect rectangular and circular shapes of variable sizes and wall thickness. For each region localized with the generalized Hough transform, we extracted several features. The ratio of white pixels in the localized region of the crop mark enhanced image, the overlap and difference of the enhanced image and the filled out template image, the template scale, shape, and the Hough accumulator value form a feature vector used in the random forest classifier.

4 Validation

The proposed methods have been tested on the experimental sites described in Sect. 4.1 to investigate how our method's parts are affected by the quality of available images. However, this small number of known, visually detected Bohemian archeological sites can only suggest the possible large-scale performance of the automatic underneath archeological site detection method.

4.1 Test Heritage Sites

Suggested methods were validated and mutually compared on ten unique types of sites provided by courtesy of prof. Martin Gojda. Single RGB orthorectified aerial images were acquired during the vegetation season in the 2004–2016 period. Thus they have uneven illumination and had either 0.5 or 0.25 [m] resolution. The resulting crop mark dimensions are between 54 and 279 pixels, and their wall thickness ranges from 4 to 12 pixels in each image of size 1024 $\times$ 1024 pixels. The set contains 7 elliptical shapes, including 5 well defined crop marks of circular shape and two significantly fragmented crop marks of elongated ellipsoids, and 7 crop marks of approximately rectangular shape. Unfortunately, this validation set is too restrictive to propose a definitive, fully automated solution, but it can suggest further investigation (Fig. 3).

- Ledčice, district Mělník (N 50° 20′0.02, E 14° 16′42.21)
- Ctiněves, district Litoměřice (N 50° 22′33.29, E 14° 18′30.77)
- Černouček, district Litoměřice (N 50° 21′24.59, E 14° 18′2.88)

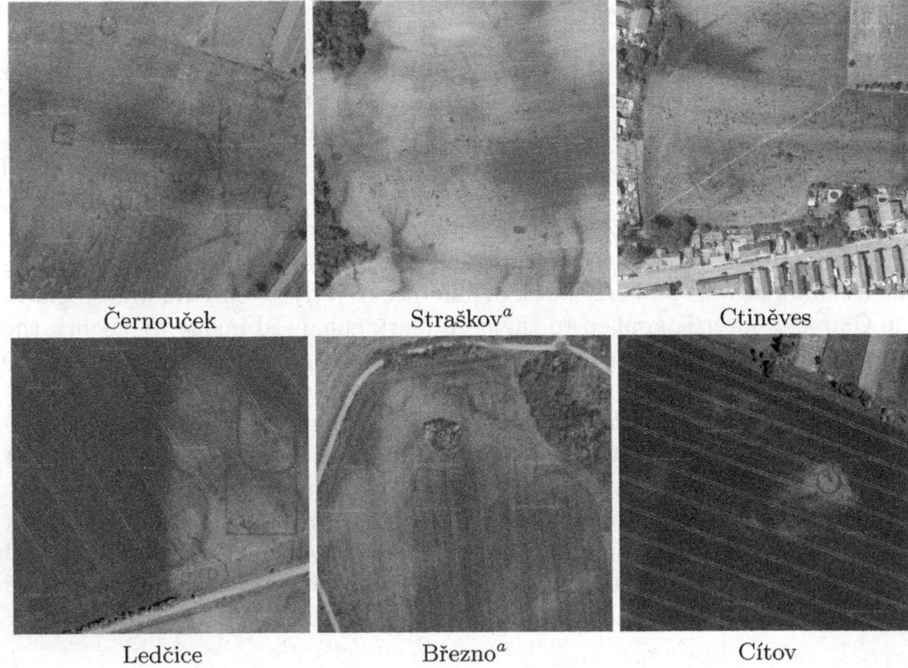

Fig. 3. Validation archeological sites.

- Straškov^a, district Litoměřice (N 50° 21′45.26, E 14° 15′18.77)
- Straškov^b, district Litoměřice (N 50° 21′55.86, E 14° 15′26.54)
- Březno^a, district Mladá Boleslav (N 50° 21′59.72, E 13° 45′1.73)
- Březno^b, district Mladá Boleslav (N 50° 22′27.57, E 13° 44′8.04)
- Cítov, district Mělník (N 50° 22′7.94, E 14° 24′7.37)
- Vražkov^a, district Litoměřice (N 50° 22′46.08, E 14° 15′7.65)
- Vražkov^b, district Litoměřice (N 50° 22′37.15, E 14° 15′51.94)

5 Results

The results achieved using the corner-based method (Sect. 3.1) tested on the single spectral first principal component images (Fig. 4). The four corners detection requirement (LHC version) was less reliable than the three corner version (OHC) because well-defined corners are sparsely present in our data. The LHC algorithm consistently detected only two crop marks[1] with one parameter setting and the OHC consistently detected three crop marks[2]. The method is susceptible to noise and extensive parameter tuning and generates many false-positive results otherwise. The minimal and maximal line length between corners was set

[1] Černouček and Ctiněves or Černouček and Březno^b sites.

[2] Černouček and Ctiněves and Březno^b sites.

Table 1. Corner-based methods: retrieval rates for most successful experimentally found parameter setting.

Algorithm	FP	TP
LHC	20	2
OHC	3	3

Table 2. Template-based method: retrieval rates with all features included.

Template type	τ	FP	TP
Rectangular	1.1	3	7
Circular	0.8	22	6

to 30 and 240 pixels for the LHC method. The maximum allowed deviation from line parallelism was set 25° and at 15° for deviation from line perpendicularity. At least 60% of an edge between two corners must be intact for a line to be considered valid. In the OHC algorithm, the minimal and maximal line length between corners was set to 30 and 270 pixels, and the maximum allowed deviation of corner orientation from the orientation of the presumed diagonal was set at 30°, as it is understood that more elongated rectangles may deviate more. The maximum allowed deviation for line perpendicularity was set at 20°. At least 85% of an edge between two corners must be intact. From our testings, the constraint placed on the completeness of the two adjacent edges was very effective in reducing false positives. The frequent limitation of the corner-based method is remaining irrelevant structures such as trees or furrows—this method requires sophisticated pre and post-processing to decrease the amount of retrieved false positives. The OHC version performs slightly better than LHC, results shown in Table 1, but the detected corner orientation precision requires further improvement. Of the three approaches, this method was the worst-performing on the tested images. From the site examples with rectangular crop marks only correct results are Černouček, Ctiněves, and Březno^b shown in Fig. 4. The remaining pictured results containing high number of false-positives are more typical for this method, as Harris corner detection results in many redundant salient points, generating rectangular configurations that remain unfiltered by the algorithms.

The line segment based method (Sect. 3.2) used in the pre-processing steps the white top hat square SE size 4×4 pixels, the black top hat was applied with square SE of size 15×15 pixels. The pixels with an intensity lower than 20 are suppressed to 0 with thresholding. The morphological closing square size SEs were set to 2×2 pixels for dilation and 3×3 pixels for erosion. The MFC operator was applied with structuring elements of size 3×3 and 10×10 pixels. The linear segments were enhanced by the composite opening with linear SE set to 30 pixels and rotated in increments of 5° the threshold set for valid ridge extraction was set to 60. The candidate points were sampled with the sampling rate five, and the window multiplier parameter was set to 1.8 see [12], all candidate points having a distance smaller than ten or greater than 170 pixels were discarded. The minimum line length for the line segment extraction was set to 20 pixels. The threshold values for angle constraint applied to $\beta_{k,j}$ is set to 15° and the convexity constraint $\tau_{k,j}$ threshold is 0.4.

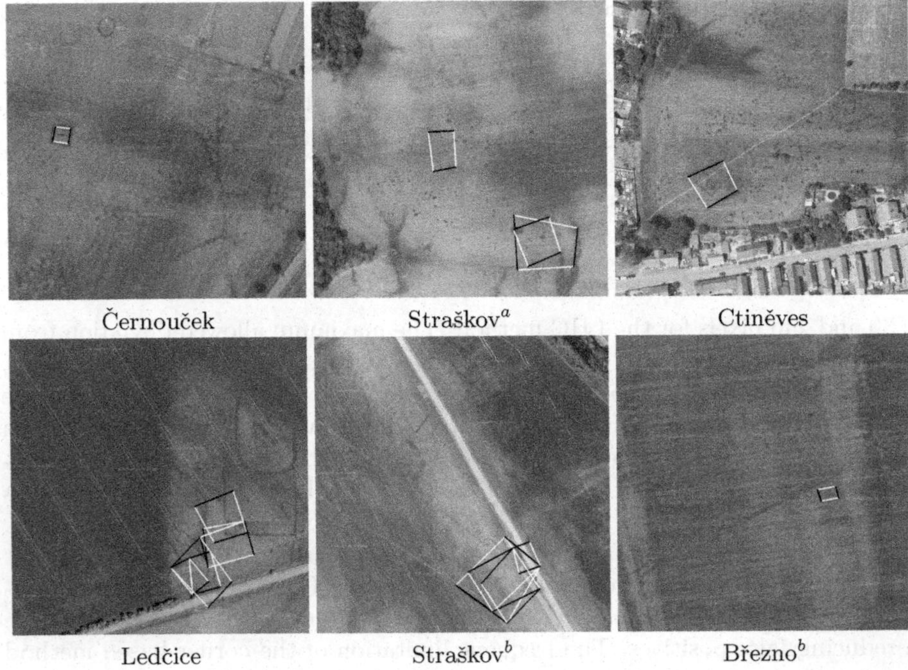

Fig. 4. Detected rectangular shapes using the Sect. 3.1 method.

Similar to [12], the method was evaluated based on the feature's ability to discriminate crop marks from irrelevant structures. We conducted this experiment by setting the parameter class weight on the SVM classifier, and results are included in Table 3. The results include some duplicity due to candidate point oversampling for significant crop marks, the unique true positives denoted as TP_u. Overall, the RE method successfully detected all seven unique rectangular crop marks across our validation data.

The methods limiting factor is its high sensitivity to noise. We encountered significantly more noise in the processed data than the original paper [12] suggested, perhaps as a result of arable land photographed at high resolution containing many more linear structures such as furrows than the original satellite data. Our modification of the original RE method, the introduced compactness measure, according to our validation, improved the ability to discriminate irrelevant structures further. However, additional improvements are needed. Another limitation of the RE method is its inability to generalize detection for other shapes than imperfect rectangles.

The template-based method (Sect. 3.3) uses in the pre-processing steps the following experimentally found parameters. First, the white top hat is square SE is set to size 4×4 pixels. Next, a median filter is applied with kernel size 5×5 pixels. Adaptive threshold of size 37×37 pixels and constant $C = 7$ is used, and the then inverted image is eroded with square SE of 2×2 pixels. Finally,

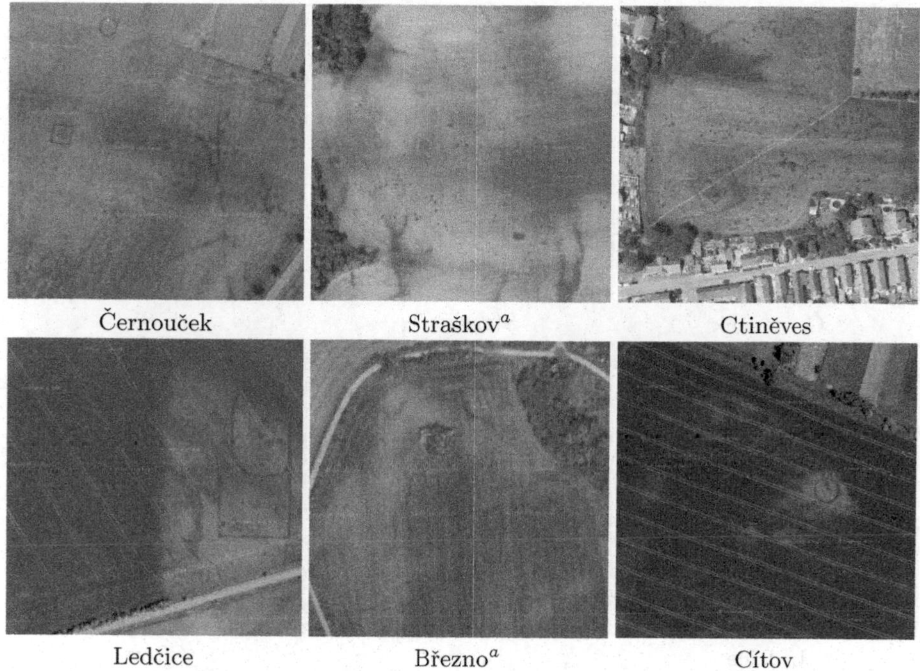

Fig. 5. Detected rectangular shapes using the Sect. 3.3 method.

blobs with an area smaller than 50 pixels are removed. Then, the crop mark enhanced image is smoothed with Gaussian filter kernel of size 9×9 pixels, and $\sigma = 1.6$ the Canny edge detector is applied with Sobel operator size set to 3×3 pixels and the lower and upper hysteresis thresholds are set to 40 and 70. The constitutive steps of pre-processing are shown in Fig. 2.

Table 3. RE: retrieval rates with all features included.

		(f_R, f_S, f_D)			(f_R, f_S)		
Dataset	Class_weight	FP	TP	TP_u	FP	TP	TP_u
PC1	0.99	16	18	7	30	18	7
PC1	0.98	1	16	7	15	15	7
PC1	0.95	0	10	6	4	13	6

We experimented with double-edged templates of rectangular and circular shapes. For the rectangular templates, the side length ratios were set to $\{0.6, 0.7, 0.8, 0.9, 1.0\}$. The rectangular shapes were rotated in three degrees steps size in the range $\langle 0°, 180° \rangle$, and the width between the template edges is set to be between 4 and 6 pixels. The total number of scales between the maximum

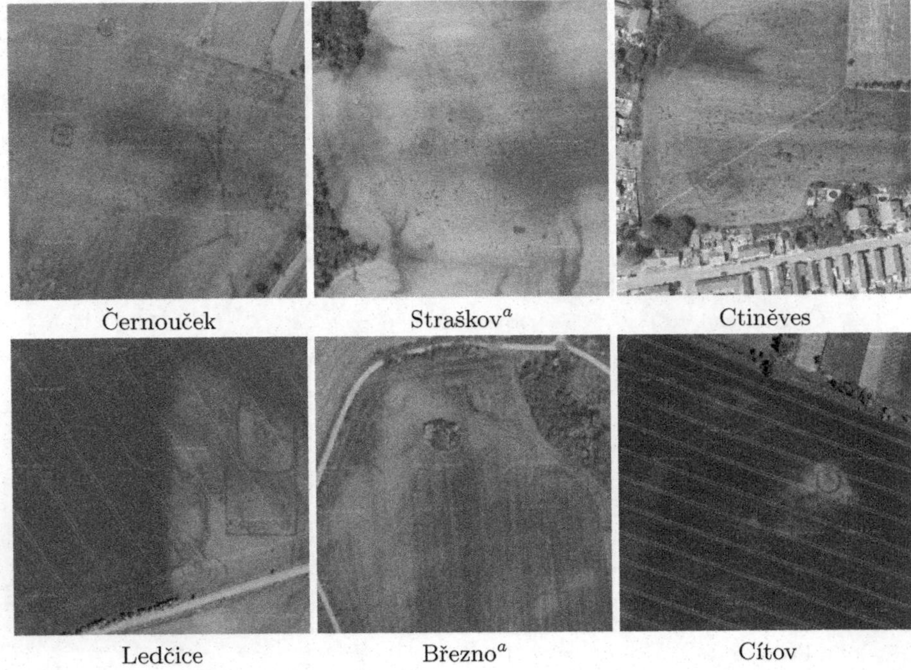

Fig. 6. Detected circular shapes using the Sect. 3.3 method.

and minimum template dimensions was set to 40 for both template types. The Hough transform threshold influences the precision-recall trade-off. Our goal was to retrieve as many crop marks as possible while allowing for a higher rate of false positives to be retrieved and later filtered out in the classification stage. Eventually, we set the value threshold value $\tau = 1.1$ for rectangular template shapes. For circular shapes, $\tau = 1.0$ proved to be a good value for crop marks that were almost entirely intact, like the two in site Černouček. The threshold needed to be lowered to 0.8 to retrieve fragmented shapes like the one in Vražkov^b. The random forest classifier was trained with 50 estimators with a maximum depth set to 3 and a class weight parameter set to 0.98. Eventually, we trained the model for each template type separately, as mixing the two led to significantly worse results.

The template-based algorithm is by a significant margin the most successful method, with seven rectangular and six circular crop marks detected and only a limited number of false positives, included in Table 2. Figure 5 illustrates the rectangular detection results with one erroneous detection on the Březno^a image while correctly missing any false negative on the Cítov image. The circular template results in Fig. 6 are worse, as the Hough transformation with a lower threshold retrieves substantially more false positives. Černouček site has two correct detections and one wrong; Straškov^a, Ctiněves, and Ledčice have false positives, and only Březno^{a} and Cítov contain correct results. However, many circular erroneous results are true archeological sites but with rectangular shapes.

The significant advantage of the template-based approach is its capability to generalize to a wider variety of shapes. Our validation experiment shows that a lack of prior knowledge of a detected crop mark's exact shape and size can be compensated for with a more extensive template set. However, this approach inevitably leads to increased computational complexity, which needs to be further mitigated with parallelization.

6 Conclusions

We present the algorithms for automatic archaeological heritage recognition hidden under the soil cover from aerial images. Three alternative methods can detect underground remains of buildings or other construction artifacts based on vegetation cover changes due to locally changed the subsoil layer's chemical composition and structure. As such, they have the potential to significantly speed up the complex and time-consuming visual detection of aerial photographs. Despite this restriction, these methods can assist in hidden archeological or construction site detections and impact the cataloging of the hitherto unknown archaeological sites.

The performance quality of the algorithms was mutually compared, verified, and demonstrated on the ten known, visually detected Bohemian archeological sites. The generalized Hough transform-based method is the most versatile and reliable approach to detect hidden archeological or construction sites belowground, provided they are not occluded by modern structures above. Multimodal and better quality data, combined with radar satellite images, interferometry, and lidar, could significantly improve detection results. Although new multispectral and high-resolution remote sensors acquire the ever-growing amount of high-quality information from a distance, the weak point is the ground truth verification of the results for calibration of the instruments or improvements of existing algorithms.

Acknowledgments. The Czech Science Foundation project GAČR 19-12340S supported this research. The archeological sites suggestion was provided by courtesy of prof. Martin Gojda from the Institute of Archaeology of the Czech Academy of Sciences, Prague.

References

1. Agapiou, A., Lysandrou, V.: Remote sensing archaeology: tracking and mapping evolution in european scientific literature from 1999 to 2015. J. Archaeol. Sci. Rep. **4**, 192–200 (2015). https://doi.org/10.1016/j.jasrep.2015.09.010
2. Calleja, J.F., et al.: Detection of buried archaeological remains with the combined use of satellite multispectral data and UAV data. Int. J. Appl. Earth Obs. Geoinf. **73**, 555–573 (2018)

3. Doneus, M., Verhoeven, G., Atzberger, C., Wess, M., Ruš, M.: New ways to extract archaeological information from hyperspectral pixels. J. Archaeol. Sci. **52**, 84–96 (2014). https://doi.org/10.1016/j.jas.2014.08.023
4. Giardino, M.J.: A history of nasa remote sensing contributions to archaeology. J. Archaeol. Sci. **38**(9), 2003–2009 (2011). https://doi.org/10.1016/j.jas.2010.09.017. Satellite remote sensing in archaeology: past, present and future perspectives
5. Kucukkaya, A.G.: Photogrammetry and remote sensing in archeology. J. Quant. Spectrosc. Radiat. Transf. **88**(1–3), 83–88 (2004)
6. Lasaponara, R., Leucci, G., Masini, N., Persico, R., Scardozzi, G.: Towards an operative use of remote sensing for exploring the past using satellite data: the case study of hierapolis (Turkey). Remote Sens. Environ. **174**, 148–164 (2016). https://doi.org/10.1016/j.rse.2015.12.016
7. Lock, G., Pouncett, J.: Spatial thinking in archaeology: Is GIS the answer? J. Archaeol. Sci. **84**, 129–135 (2017). https://doi.org/10.1016/j.jas.2017.06.002. Archaeological GIS Today: Persistent Challenges, Pushing Old Boundaries, and Exploring New Horizons
8. Lu, P., et al.: On the use of historical archive of aerial photographs for the discovery and interpretation of ancient hidden linear cultural relics in the alluvial plain of eastern henan, china. J. Cult. Heritage **23**, 20–27 (2017). https://doi.org/10.1016/j.culher.2015.09.010. Beyond the modern landscape: Earth Observation to see the unseen
9. Savage, S.H., Levy, T.E., Jones, I.W.: Prospects and problems in the use of hyperspectral imagery for archaeological remote sensing: a case study from the Faynan copper mining district, Jordan. J. Archaeol. Sci. **39**(2), 407–420 (2012). https://doi.org/10.1016/j.jas.2011.09.028
10. Stott, D., Kristiansen, S.M., Sindbæk, S.M.: Searching for Viking age fortresses with automatic landscape classification and feature detection. Remote Sens. **11**(16), 1881 (2019). https://doi.org/10.3390/rs11161881
11. Thabeng, O.L., Merlo, S., Adam, E.: High-resolution remote sensing and advanced classification techniques for the prospection of archaeological sites' markers: the case of dung deposits in the Shashi-Limpopo confluence area (Southern Africa). J. Archaeol. Sci. **102**, 48–60 (2019)
12. Zingman, I., Saupe, D., Penatti, O.A.B., Lambers, K.: Detection of fragmented rectangular enclosures in very high resolution remote sensing images. IEEE Trans. Geosci. Remote Sens. **54**(8), 4580–4593 (2016). https://doi.org/10.1109/TGRS.2016.2545919
13. Zingman, I., Saupe, D., Lambers, K.: Automated search for livestock enclosures of rectangular shape in remotely sensed imagery. In: Image and Signal Processing for Remote Sensing XIX, vol. 8892, p. 88920F. International Society for Optics and Photonics (2013)

A Deep Learning Approach for Hepatic Steatosis Estimation from Ultrasound Imaging

Sara Colantonio[1(✉)], Antonio Salvati[2], Claudia Caudai[1], Ferruccio Bonino[2,3,4,5], Laura De Rosa[2,6], Maria Antonietta Pascali[1(✉)], Danila Germanese[1], Maurizia Rossana Brunetto[2,3], and Francesco Faita[6]

[1] National Research Council, Institute of Information Science and Technologies, Pisa, Italy
sara.colantonio@isti.cnr.it
[2] Hepatology Unit, Pisa University Hospital, Pisa, Italy
[3] Department of Clinical and Experimental Medicine, University of Pisa, Pisa, Italy
[4] Fondazione Italiana Fegato, AREA Science Park, Campus Basovizza, Trieste, Italy
[5] IRCSS SDN, Naples, Italy
[6] National Research Council, Institute of Clinical Physiology, Pisa, Italy

Abstract. This paper proposes a simple convolutional neural model as a novel method to predict the level of hepatic steatosis from ultrasound data. Hepatic steatosis is the major histologic feature of non-alcoholic fatty liver disease (NAFLD), which has become a major global health challenge. Recently a new definition for FLD, that take into account the risk factors and clinical characteristics of subjects, has been suggested; the proposed criteria for Metabolic Disfunction-Associated Fatty Liver Disease (MAFLD) are based on histological (biopsy), imaging or blood biomarker evidence of fat accumulation in the liver (hepatic steatosis), in subjects with overweight/obesity or presence of type 2 diabetes mellitus. In lean or normal weight, non-diabetic individuals with steatosis, MAFLD is diagnosed when at least two metabolic abnormalities are present. Ultrasound examinations are the most used technique to non-invasively identify liver steatosis in a screening settings. However, the diagnosis is operator dependent, as accurate image processing techniques have not entered yet in the diagnostic routine. In this paper, we discuss the adoption of simple convolutional neural models to estimate the degree of steatosis from echographic images in accordance with the state-of-the-art magnetic resonance spectroscopy measurements (expressed as percentage of the estimated liver fat). More than 22,000 ultrasound images were used to train three networks, and results show promising performances in our study (150 subjects).

Keywords: Ultrasound (US) · Medical imaging · Convolutional neural network · Hepatic steatosis

K. Wojtkiewicz et al. (Eds.): ICCCI 2021, CCIS 1463, pp. 703–714, 2021.
https://doi.org/10.1007/978-3-030-88113-9_57

1 Introduction

Hepatic steatosis is the major histologic feature of MAFLD, associated with other liver diseases, as well as to type 2 diabetes, cardiovascular disease, chronic kidney disease, and some types of extrahepatic malignancies; MAFLD is diagnosed when at least two metabolic abnormalities are present [6,7,18]. Hepatic steatosis is due to the accumulation of fat within the liver and its association with inflammation, steatohepatitis causes the progression of fibrosis, to cirrhosis and hepatocellular carcinoma [8,11]. Therefore, the early detection and accurate quantification of steatosis is an essential task for prevention and monitoring of disease progression.

Liver biopsy is nowadays the standard reference diagnostic method to assess steatosis [2], though it represents an invasive procedure and it may be prone to errors, due to sampling issues in case of dishomogeneous intrahepatic distribution. To date, among the noninvasive modalities for the quantitative assessment of steatosis, the most reproducible and effective one is based on Magnetic Resonance Spectroscopy (MRS), which provides a sensitive, accurate and quantitative evaluation of liver fat content, the so-called *H-MRS index*, by using non-ionizing radiation [9]. An extensive study has demonstrated a high correlation between H-MRS index and biopsy results (Spearman's nonparametric correlation coefficient $\text{rs} = 0.9$) [5]. Hence, this modality is currently considered as the non-invasive gold-standard. Nevertheless, MRS is an expensive diagnostic procedure, and MRS devices are relatively scarcely available, thus preventing the adoption of MRS in daily clinical settings. On the other hand, UltraSound (US) imaging represents a valid approach for the assessment of liver steatosis, as demonstrated in previous studies [13]. Further to this, US is non-invasive, non-ionizing, inexpensive and widely available modality, which may fit also screening purposes.

Recently, some studies have proposed quantitative assessment of hepatic steatosis based on ultrasound imaging [12,17,19]. In these works, the US-based methodologies are generally compared to the H-MRS index. Among these, one of the most interesting result has been published in 2018 by Di Lascio et al. [10]: the authors propose and discuss the Steato-Score, a fat liver index representative of intra-hepatic fat content, which is defined by combining five different ultrasound parameters, and showed a good correlation with the H-MRS index (adjusted coefficient of determination $\text{R}^2 = 0.72$).

Artificial intelligence techniques have recently emerged as the leading tool in various research fields, and especially in general imaging analysis and computer vision, for several tasks, such as object detection, segmentation, and classification. Machine and deep learning shows huge potential for enabling the automation of the NAFLD diagnosis and staging, hence providing a viable alternative solution to traditional biomedical image processing [14]. Concerning hepatic steatosis, generally deep learning methods have been used not to estimate the liver fat fraction but to perform a classification, e.g. to discriminate normal liver vs. non-alcoholic fatty liver diseases (NAFLD, fat fraction $> 5\%$) [1,3,4,8,16]: most of them show quite desirable performances (about 95% of accuracy). Even if a coarse classification (e.g. binary classification) could support screening on large population, it is not enough accurate to have a clinical impact, e.g. for patient monitoring. Also, some of the architecture proposed are quite complex (training up to 22 layers [1], or using a transfer learning approach [3]) and are trained using small datasets (made of 63 subjects in [1], and of 55 obese patients in [3]); deeper is the learning architecture, larger should be the dataset, and using very few data could lead to unstable models (due to over-parametrization). The work of Han et al. [8], to best of our knowledge, is the most promising in this research line, developing a quantitative analysis of raw radiofrequency (RF) ultrasound signal, based on two one-dimensional CNN algorithms: a binary classifier and a fat fraction estimator. The classifier yielded a classification accuracy (96%); while the fat fraction estimator predicted fat fraction values that positively correlated with proton MRI ($r = 0.85$; $p < .001$).

The aim of the present work is to provide a CNN model able to accurately estimate from US images the liver fat fraction; the accuracy of the fat estimation is assessed with respect to the H-MRS index.

The following Section is devoted to describe the materials and methods of the present investigation, by including a description of the population study, the acquisition protocols used to collect the US data, and the preprocessing steps performed to set the input for the proposed CNN-based method. Section 2.2 provides details of the CNN architectures used in the experimentation, which is presented in Sect. 2.3. Results are reported and discussed in Sect. 3.

2 Materials and Methods

The study population included 150 consecutive patients enrolled the Hepatology Unit of the University Hospital of Pisa for evidence of hepatic steatosis at the standard ultrasound examination without with-out increased liver enzymes who gave their informed consent (their characteristics are reported in 1). Proton MRS imaging was performed with a MRI scanners (3.0 T) equipped with 32-channel receiver coils employed on patients in the supine position (Pisa: Philips Ingenia, Philips Healthcare, Best, Netherlands). The percentage of fat (H-MRS index) was assessed for each subject, normalizing the fitted signal amplitude of the fat to the sum of water and fat amplitudes [17]. The population showed different levels of steatosis: the fat percentage, assessed through the H-MRS index, ranges from 0.27% to 50.97%.

A mapping between the H-MRS and the classes routinely used in histology to estrablish the steatosis level has been established in [9] and comprises the following stratification classes:

class S0 corresponds to cases with H-MRS index <= 3.12%
class S1 to cases with H-MRS index > 3.12% and <= 8.77%
class S2 to cases with H-MRS index > 8.77% and <= 13,69%
class S3 to cases with H-MRS index > 13.69%.

In this respect, the distribution of this study population is the following:

S0: 111 subjects, corresponding to the 74% of the population study;

Table 1. Characteristics of the study population. Data were expressed as counts/percentages for categorical variable and mean ± standard deviation (sd) for continuous variables.

	n. of subjects	% of population
SEX (M:F)	73:77	48.7:51.3
	Mean ± sd	**Min-max**
AGE (years)	53.54 ± 12.66	20.0–75.3
BMI (kg/m^2)	24.86 ± 3.69	15.28–33.9
Fat (%)	4.50 ± 8.01	0.27–50.97

S1: 21 subjects, corresponding to the 14% of the population study;
S2: 6 subjects, corresponding to the 4% of the population study;
S3: 12 subjects, corresponding to the 8% of the population study.

2.1 US Data Acquisition and Preprocessing

The ultrasound data were acquired in the center of Pisa. In particular, several ultrasound images were acquired, using different projections, according to an acquisition protocol that included the acquisition of an intercostal or subcostal longitudinal scan view with subject in supine/left lateral position (named HR) and an oblique subcostal scan view (named AR). The two different scan views were chosen in such a way that in the first scan the level of ecogenicity of the ultrasound beam within both the renal and hepatic parenchyma is appreciable (i.e. the HR view in which the hepatic parenchyma and the right kidney are clearly visualized) and the second scan is the oblique subcostal scan view showing the complete liver parenchyma and diaphragm, i.e. the AR view which provides a view of the attenuation of the ultrasound beam within the liver parenchyma.

Ultrasound clips were acquired at 30 fps and their duration ranges from few frames to 224 frames, with an average of 114 frames. The clips were processed by extracting all the frames as gray images, which were centered and cropped to the size of 360 × 360 pixels. Each frame inherits a label given by the ground truth value (H-MRS index). Some remarks about the dataset:

(i) Due to the different length of the US clips, and to the uneven distribution of the H-MRS index values, the resulting datasets (HR and AR) do not have the same number of images;
(ii) Several images, namely those extracted from the same clip, are very similar because of the centrality of the sonographic cone and the acquisition with fixed probe (Fig. 1);
(iii) The ground-truth values are not uniformly distributed in the population study.

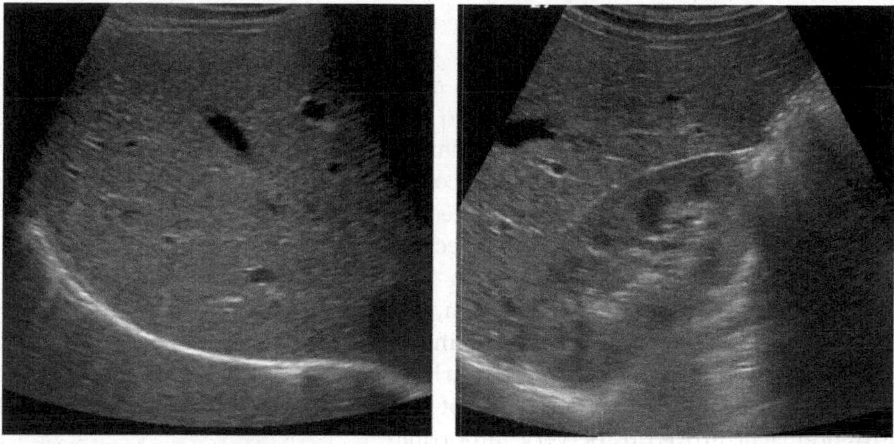

Fig. 1. Example of AR view, on the left and HR view, on the right, of the same patient.

As it usually happens, the dataset is quite unbalanced, which makes identifying the less present classes a challenging task. Nevertheless, the regression approach may help coping with this unbalance, as the CNN model learns to approximate the H-MRS index instead of the class.

2.2 The CNN Architecture

Each view was treated independently using both a single-view architecture, and coupled into a two-branch architecture, in which both AR and HR views are used to train the predictive model. This was done to understand whether the peculiarity of each single view contributes with informative content to predict the H-MRS index.

We designed two CNN architectures: a 5-layer CNN and a two-branch CNN. The first architecture is used to produce two predictive models: one trained on AR clips, and the other trained on HR clips; the latter architecture is a two-branch CNN which has been trained on both AR and HR clips:

AR CNN: 5-layer CNN trained on AR images;
HR CNN: 5-layer CNN trained on HR images;
AR & HR CNN: two-branch CNN trained on both AR and HR images.

All the CNNs have been developed in Python (version 3.7.9, Jupyter environment), using TensorFlow 2.0.0 and the learning library Scikit-learn 0.23.2.

The first architecture, in Fig. 2, is made of five convolutional layers respectively with 8, 16, 32, 64 and 128 filters. The input images, which are one-channel gray images of 360 × 360 pixels, are preliminarily regularized through a batch normalization. The padding is used to control the size of the images. The activation function is the REctified Linear Unit (ReLU) for all the convolutional layers and for the first fully connected layer, while the last fully connected layer uses a linear activation function to perform the regression. The maxpooling layers have size (2, 2) and stride 2.

The two-branch CNN, (in Fig. 3), is made of three pieces: the two branches, i.e. the AR CNN and the HR CNN, and a final tail, in which the weights associated with the best regression performances of the two branches are imported and concatenated, just before the fully connected layers: the last fully connected layer returns the regression on the subject's steatosis level.

In order to finalize the best architecture, many attempts have been made using: different hyperparameters, such as the learning rate and kernel size; the activation functions relu, elu, prelu, and swish; normalization L1, L2 and dropout; and different kinds of weight initialization. It resulted that the model was not sensitive to such changes. On the other hand, the size and number of convolutional layers and the presence of a fully connected layer before the last regression layer proved to be very important.

2.3 Model Training and Test

To each subject we associate the ultrasound clips (for each view) and the corresponding H-MRS index. This allows us to test the trained model on images extracted from different subjects, hence to assess the model performances on never-before-seen cases.

The test set is made selecting 10 patients out of 150 (resulting in 802 AR and 998 HR images). The selection was performed manually in order to have the same distribution of disease severity as the whole dataset. In more details the test set is made of: 6 cases of S0 class, 2 of S1 class, 1 of S2 and 1 of S3.

The remaining 140 subjects (13,406 AR and 16,496 HR images) were used to train independently the AR CNN and the HR CNN.

Concerning the training, the Adam optimizer, using its default parameters and the mean squared error as loss function, was used to optimize the gradient computation; all the three models have been initialized with random weights, batch size was set to 50; the number of epochs was set to 30, using the early-stopping criterion (patience = 5) to prevent overfitting.

We adopted a stratified fourfold cross-validation, recommended for regression on unbalanced datasets [15]. The values of the validation loss for the four sets of the fourfold cross-validation are reported in Table 2. Weights associated with best performances (set 1 for AR and set 4 for HR) have been imported into the two-branch architecture and used for a paired regression on the two views (Fig. 3). Finally, we evaluated the performance of the trained models using the test set of never-seen-before 10 subjects.

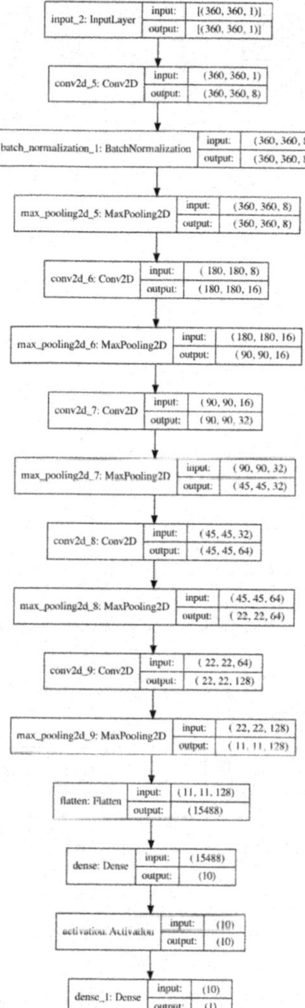

Fig. 2. Sketch of the CNN architecture used for the estimation of hepatic steatosis level from the AR views and from the HR view.

Summarizing, we trained three models to predict the hepatic steatosis level from US images: the CNN in Fig. 2 trained on AR data, the CNN in Fig. 2 trained on HR data, and the two-branch architecture (Fig. 3) trained on paired AR and HR data.

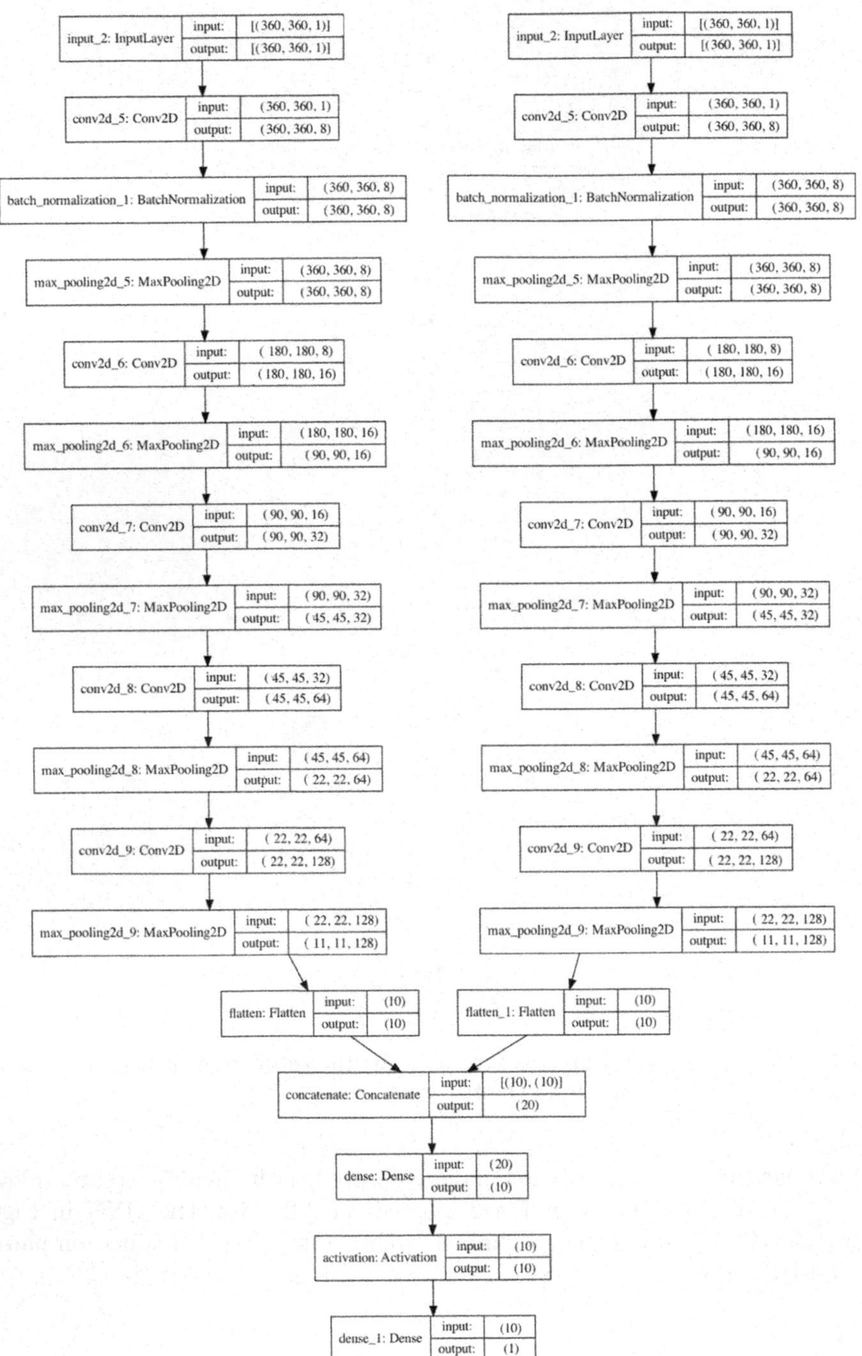

Fig. 3. Sketch of the two-branch architecture used for the estimation of hepatic steatosis level from paired AR and HR views.

3 Results and Discussion

In this work, we investigate if convolutional neural network architectures could learn to predict the H-MRS index from US sequences. For each subject, two US clips were acquired from different projections, in order to understand which one of the two is the most informative, and if the two projections may convey complementary information about the liver tissue composition.

Performances of the three approaches on the test set have been computed and reported in Table 3. The AR CNN model, trained on images representing full parenchyma, achieves the best regression performances compared to the HR CNN model, with a minimun RMSE of 1.11 and an error standard deviation of 0.77. Also the concatenated architecture, AR & HR CNN, allows to achieve very good results in regression (RMSE is 1.32 with a standard deviation of 1.11), but it does not outperform the results obtained with the AR CNN model.

This leads us to think that the HR clips do not provide additional or complementary information with respect to the information already encoded in the AR images.

A paired T-test has been used to assess the Pearson correlation between the H-MRS index and the fat fraction predicted by the AR CNN model at each frame of the test set, achieving a correlation of 0.983, with a p-value < 0.001.

Table 2. Values of the validation loss for the four sets of the 4-fold cross-validation for the CNN architectures trained on both views.

	Set 1	Set 2	Set 3	Set 4	Mean
AR CNN	**1.3274**	3.0840	2.2256	2.6277	2.3162
HR CNN	3.5108	2.9160	3.1472	**2.1721**	2.9365

In order to compare the proposed method with similar approaches, already mentioned in Sect. 1, we map the fat-liver score computed on the test set through the AR CNN, the HR CNN, and the AR & HR CNN in the classes S0-S3, introduced in [9] and described in Sect. 2.3. The accuracy of the class-mapping is 90% for all the trained CNNs. We would like to point out that choosing any of the CNN does not affect the class-mapping at all, i.e. all the CNNs predict the same class for each never-seen-before subject (see Fig. 4), misclassifying only one subject (which belongs to the less represented group, i.e. S2). Also, the classification is performed patient-level; the accuracy of 90% would increase performing a frame by frame classification, coherently with the metrics showed in Table 3 (RMSE of 1.11, and error standard deviation 0.77).

We can state that our trained CNNs achieve performances comparable to the best results in literature. In addition, we strongly believe that further improvements could be achieved by increasing the dimension of the dataset.

Table 3. The performances of the three CNN models evaluated frame by frame in the test set (RMSE is the root mean square error).

	AR CNN	HR CNN	AR & HR CNN
RMSE	**1.1127**	1.4476	1.3197
Error Std Dev	**0.7701**	1.1757	1.1068

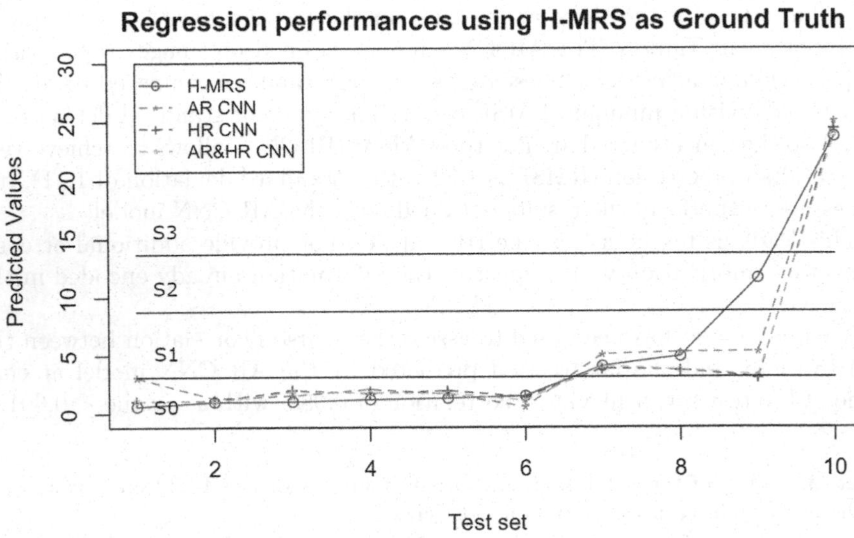

Fig. 4. Comparison of the regression performances on the test set (computed per subject).

4 Conclusions

We propose to use the deep learning to evaluate the non-alcoholic hepatic steatosis starting from US images and using H-MRS as ground truth. We started with simple CNN models to investigate the efficacy of this approach. Experimental results are encouraging and evidence that even simple models enable quite an accurate steatosis evaluation, even with US images only, without having magnetic resonance available.

In the near future, additional subjects will be included in the study population, allowing for the design of more complex and deep models, as well as for further testing and better validation of the high reliability of our approach.

References

1. Biswas, M., et al.: Symtosis: a liver ultrasound tissue characterization and risk stratification in optimized deep learning paradigm. Comput. Methods Programs Biomed. **155**, 165–177 (2018)

2. Bravo, A.A., Sheth, S., Chopra, S.: Liver biopsy. N. Engl. J. Med. **344**(7), 495–500 (2001)
3. Byra, M.: Transfer learning with deep convolutional neural network for liver steatosis assessment in ultrasound images. Int. J. Comput. Assist. Radiol. Surg. **13**(12), 1895–1903 (2018). https://doi.org/10.1007/s11548-018-1843-2
4. Cao, W., An, X., Cong, L., Lyu, C., Zhou, Q., Guo, R.: Application of deep learning in quantitative analysis of 2-dimensional ultrasound imaging of nonalcoholic fatty liver disease. J. Ultrasound Med. **39**(1), 51–59 (2019). https://doi.org/10.1002/jum.15070
5. Cowin, G., et al.: Magnetic resonance imaging and spectroscopy for monitoring liver steatosis. J. Magn. Reson. Imaging **28**(4), 937–45 (2008). https://doi.org/10.1002/jmri.21542
6. Eslam, M., et al.: A new definition for metabolic dysfunction-associated fatty liver disease: An international expert consensus statement. J. Hepatol. **73**(1), 202–209 (2020). https://doi.org/10.1016/j.jhep.2020.03.039
7. Eslam, M., et al.: MAFLD: a consensus-driven proposed nomenclature for metabolic associated fatty liver disease. Gastroenterology **158**(7), 1999.e-2014.e1 (2020). https://doi.org/10.1053/j.gastro.2019.11.312. Nonalcoholic Fatty Liver Disease in 2020
8. Han, A., et al.: Noninvasive diagnosis of nonalcoholic fatty liver disease and quantification of liver fat with radiofrequency ultrasound data using one-dimensional convolutional neural networks. Radiology **295**(2), 342–350 (2020). https://doi.org/10.1148/radiol.2020191160
9. Karlas, T., et al.: Non-invasive assessment of hepatic steatosis in patients with NAFLD using controlled attenuation parameter and 1H-MR spectroscopy. PLoS ONE **9**(3), e91987 (2014). https://doi.org/10.1371/journal.pone.0091987
10. Lascio, N.D., et al.: Steato-score: non-invasive quantitative assessment of liver fat by ultrasound imaging. Ultrasound Med. Biol. **44**(8), 1585–1596 (2018). https://doi.org/10.1016/j.ultrasmedbio.2018.03.011
11. Loomba, R., Sanyal, A.: The global NAFLD epidemic. Nat. Rev. Gastroenterol. Hepatol. **10**, 686–690 (2013). https://doi.org/10.1038/nrgastro.2013.171
12. Machado, M., Cortez-Pinto, H.: Non-invasive diagnosis of non-alcoholic fatty liver disease. A critical appraisal. J. Hepatol. **58**(5), 1007–1019 (2013). https://doi.org/10.1016/j.jhep.2012.11.021
13. Mancini, M., et al.: Sonographic hepatic-renal ratio as indicator of hepatic steatosis: comparison with (1)H magnetic resonance spectroscopy. Metab., Clin. Exp. **58**(12), 1724–1730 (2009). https://doi.org/10.1016/j.metabol.2009.05.032
14. Popa, S.L., et al.: Non-alcoholic fatty liver disease: implementing complete automated diagnosis and staging a systematic review. Diagnostics **11**(6), 1078 (2021). https://doi.org/10.3390/diagnostics11061078
15. Purushotham, S., Tripathy, B.K.: Evaluation of classifier models using stratified tenfold cross validation techniques. In: Krishna, P.V., Babu, M.R., Ariwa, E. (eds.) ObCom 2011. CCIS, vol. 270, pp. 680–690. Springer, Heidelberg (2012). https://doi.org/10.1007/978-3-642-29216-3_74
16. Reddy, D.S., Bharath, R., Rajalakshmi, P.: A novel computer-aided diagnosis framework using deep learning for classification of fatty liver disease in ultrasound imaging. In: 2018 IEEE 20th International Conference on e-Health Networking, Applications and Services (Healthcom), pp. 1–5 (2018)
17. Reeder, S., Cruite, I., Hamilton, G., Sirlin, C.: Quantitative assessment of liver fat with magnetic resonance imaging and spectroscopy. J. Magn. Reson. Imaging **34**(4), 729–749 (2011). https://doi.org/10.1002/jmri.22775

18. Targher, G., Tilg, H., Byrne, C.D.: Non-alcoholic fatty liver disease: a multisystem disease requiring a multidisciplinary and holistic approach. Lancet Gastroenterol. Hepatol. **6**(7), 578–588 (2021)
19. Xia, M.F., et al.: Standardized ultrasound hepatic/renal ratio and hepatic attenuation rate to quantify liver fat content: an improvement method. Obesity (Silver Spring, Md.) **20**, 444–452 (2012)

Sparse Progressive Neural Networks for Continual Learning

Esra Ergün(✉) and Behçet Uğur Töreyin

Informatics Institute, Istanbul Technical University, Istanbul 34467, Turkey
{ergunesr,toreyin}@itu.edu.tr

Abstract. Human brain effectively integrates prior knowledge to new skills by transferring experience across tasks without suffering from catastrophic forgetting. In this study, to continuously learn a visual classification task sequence, we employed a neural network model with lateral connections called Progressive Neural Networks (PNN). We sparsified PNNs with sparse group Least Absolute Shrinkage and Selection Operator (LASSO) and trained conventional PNNs with recursive connections. Later, the effect of the task prior on current performance is investigated with various task orders. The proposed approach is evaluated on permutedMNIST and selected subtasks from CIFAR-100 dataset. Results show that sparse Group LASSO regularization effectively sparsifies the progressive neural networks and the task sequence order affects the performance.

Keywords: Continual learning · Progressive Neural Networks · Sparse group LASSO regularization

1 Introduction

Artificial Neural Networks are addressing major problems of computer vision, natural language processing and data science in the last decade with increasing computational power and amount of data. Despite their popularity and success, when presented with a sequence of tasks with only having access to current task's data, neural networks fail to preserve their performance on previously learned tasks. This problem is called catastrophic forgetting and one of the biggest obstacle on the way of artificial general intelligence [3].

There have been numerous studies to address catastrophic forgetting in recent years [5,7,11,19]. Existing studies can be grouped into three main categories: Dynamic architectures, regularization based methods and replay based methods. Dynamic architectures aim to preserve performance by expanding the model, i.e. adding layers/neurons. For example in [18], authors proposed Dynamically Expandable Networks and prunes additional weights by group Lasso regularization. This is a complex method that requires additional hyperparameters and sub-algorithms. In Reinforced Continual Learning [17], model structure is updated

Supported by the Vodafone Future Laboratory, Istanbul Technical University (ITU), under Grant ITUVF20180901P04.

K. Wojtkiewicz et al. (Eds.): ICCCI 2021, CCIS 1463, pp. 715–725, 2021.
https://doi.org/10.1007/978-3-030-88113-9_58

with reinforcement learning and complexity-performance is balanced with the help of a reward function. A method that separates parameter estimation and finding optimal model structure proposed in [6]. This method employs various architecture search techniques to optimize the model structure. Another example of dynamic architectures is Progressive Neural Networks (PNN) [12]. PNNs initialize new set of learnable weights for each task and passes new input through all previously defined subnetworks. Purpose of PNNs is to relate new input with previously seen ones. One major disadvantage of PNNs is that the number of parameters requires grow quadratically with the number of tasks. [4] proposes a method that optimizes the neural structure and parameter learning/fine tuning component. This method searches for optimal architecture by separating architecture search and parameter estimation. Another study Bayesian Optimized Continual Learning with Attention Mechanism that dynamically expands the model capacity by Bayesian optimization and selects previous knowledge by attention mechanism [16]. Further, Strannegård et al., proposes a model with expanding, generalizing, forgetting and back propagation rules inspired by biologic neuroplasticity [15]. These studies do not require additional memory however they tend to have complex implementations.

Replay-based methods evaluates model performance and address catastrophic forgetting by keeping a subset of previous datasets. There are two types of replay-based methods: generative replay and episodic replay. Episodic replay methods rely on a sampling strategy and samples and stores a subset from each task. Gradient Episodic Memory (GEM) picks a subset from each task and uses this set to formalize a constrained optimization problem. Modifying cost function in this way prevents overfitting to pre-determined subset. Another variant of GEM is proposed in [1] modifies the cost function and achieves better performance with a new evaluation fashion. d'Autume et al. proposes an episodic memory method with local adaptation and sparse distributed experience replay to address catastrophic forgetting [2]. Reimer et al. fuses experience replay and maximization based meta learning to align gradients from different samples [10]. This approach decreases the possibility of interference of upcoming and previous gradients. Generative replay based methods captures underlying data distribution instead of sampling and generates samples. One example is Deep Generative Replay. This method captures distribution of current and previous tasks with a deep generative model and resulting model is used to preserve performance of all tasks.

Regularization based methods address catastrophic forgetting by constraining the change of model parameters. Elastic Weight Consolidation (EWC) calculates fisher information matrix after each task's training and punishes the change of important parameters proportional to Fisher Information Matrix (FIM) [5]. One disadvantage of this method is cost of calculating FIM and storing model parameters for each task on offline version. Synaptic Intelligence stores role of parameters on tasks and constrains the problem based on those stored values [19].

SI calculates this importance on each iteration while EWC makes a point estimate about it. There are also methods that employ Bayesian inference. Variational Continual Learning merges Monte Carlo approaches and variational inference [8]. Another study proposed a task based special attention mechanism to learn the current task without harming the performance of previous tasks [14].

This study investigates recursive type of PNNs and the effect of sparsity in the context of PNNs. For this purpose permutedMNIST dataset and various subsets of CIFAR-100 datasets are employed and various task orders are investigated. The organization of this paper is as follows. Section 2 briefly explains conventional Progressive Neural Networks and introduces recursive type of PNNs and explains group level sparsity. Section 3 reports the experimental results. Lastly, the conclusion is given in Sect. 4.

2 The Method

2.1 Progressive Neural Networks

The long-standing goal of continual learning is to be able to transfer knowledge obtained through previous experiences. Human brain does not suffer from catastrophic forgetting because each task builds on top of previously learned ones by effectively integrating skills, learning new ones and fine-tuning. Inspired by this, this thesis investigates various types of progressive neural networks for Continual Learning.

Initially, a PNN starts with a conventional neural network with desired number of layers and neurons that performs on a single task. Within the arrival of a new task new columns of task specific layers and weights are initialized. Previous weights of previous tasks are frozen in order to preserve knowledge. Therefore, this setting is immune to catastrophic forgetting. The purpose of lateral connections are to enable the transfer learning when possible.

In [12], the focus is reinforcement learning applications. In this study we investigated the performance of several type of PNNs on several visual classification scenarios and the effect of task order on forward transfer is investigated.

Figure 1 illustrates a conventional PNN. Dashed arrows denote inactive connections while others denote active connections. Each column belongs to a task. Here, h refers to output of a layer, hidden activations. Activation of layer i in a K task setting is calculated as follows:

$$h_k^t = f_{act}(W_k^t h_{k-1}^t + \sum_{j<t} U_k^{t:j} h_{k-1}^j) \qquad (1)$$

In this equation, f_{act} refers to element-wise non linearity, U is weight matrix transforms lateral information from previous tasks, and W is parameters of current layer. Layer h_k^t has multiple inputs. U and W matrices represent $n_i \times n_j$ dimensional spaces.

In practice, every lateral previous connection h_{k-1}^j is concatenated to a single vector as $h_{i-1}^{<k}$. Then, a multi layer perceptron, called *adapters* is employed. In this case, output of the progressive network is calculated as:

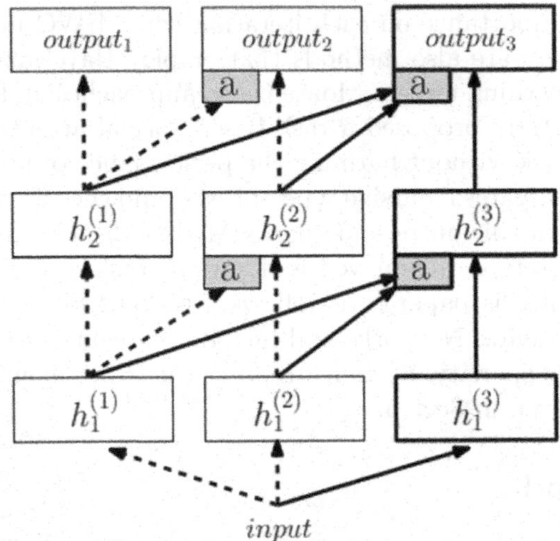

Fig. 1. Progressive Neural Network introduced in [12] with t = 3. For each task, different classification layer is used. Extracted from [12].

$$h_k^t = \sigma(W_k^t h_{k-1}^t + U_k^{t:j} \sigma(V_k^{t:j} \alpha_k h_{k-1}^{<t})) \tag{2}$$

where V is projection vector inside the MLP. Next section will explain propagation rules and structures of Progressive Neural Networks employed in this study.

2.2 Recursive Progressive Neural Networks

In this section, Recursive Progressive Neural Networks (R-PNN), a special type of PNN is introduced. An R-PNN recursively computes the outputs of prior subnetworks. The last subnetwork of the current task does not take input from any previous subtasks except the last one. Processing input recursively increases non-linearity.

Figure 2 illustrates an R-PNN trained for three sequential tasks where number of layers of each initialized subnetwork is 2. Each blue box represent a hidden layer h, where yellow box refers to task specific classification layer, o. Recursive connections are shown with orange lines. Learnable weights for lateral connections are referred with α's. In this model, input of a hidden layer h consists of two parts. First branch comes from the previous layer of the same subnetwork, the second branch comes from the last prior task. When the input is passed to h_1^1, output of this layer is given to the next subnetwork only.

In an R-PNN, output of a layer is calculated as:

$$h_k^t = f_{act}(\alpha_{d,k}^t {W_k}^t x_k^t + \alpha_{t,k}^t W_k^{t-1} x_k^{t-1}) \tag{3}$$

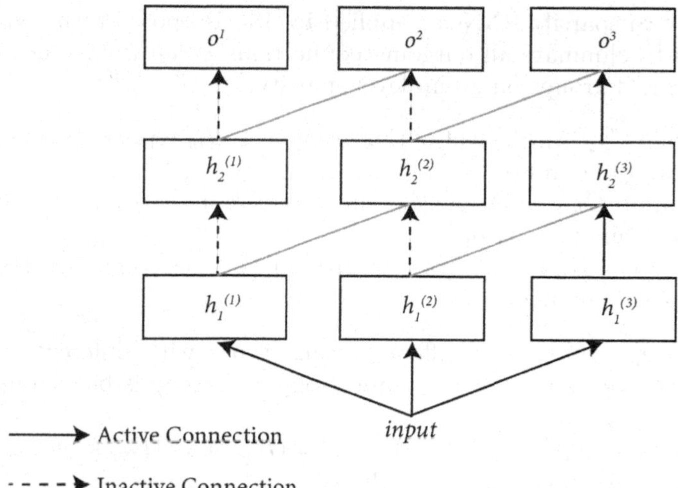

Fig. 2. Recursive Progressive Neural Networks where t = 3. Recursive connections are shown with orange lines. (Color figure online)

where t is current task and $\alpha^t_{d,k}$ and $\alpha^t_{t,k}$ are learnable parameters that weigh inputs from previous layer and previous task. f_{act} is point-wise non-linearity.

2.3 Sparse Group LASSO Regularization

There are two traditional weight regularization methods for preventing overfitting and obtaining better generalization in parametric machine learning models. One of them is using l_2 norm and its applied by adding the following term to loss function:

$$R_{l_2}(w) \triangleq \|w\|_2^2 \tag{4}$$

l_2 regularization is also called "weight decay" since parameter magnitudes are constrained and decreased through iterations. l_2 norm constitutes the ridge regression algorithm.

The second most popular approach to regularize neural network parameters is using l_1 norm. This approach stems from lasso algorithm and defined as:

$$R_{l_1}(w) \triangleq \|w|_1 \tag{5}$$

Both l_1 and l_2, *weight decay* regularizations are used to achieve generalization and can lead to sparsified neural network connections. However, employing l_1 and l_2 do not result in compact networks, since removing a neuron completely from a network requires all connections going out from that neuron to be zeroed out. A way for obtaining compact sparse networks is applying group LASSO which enables to safely remove a neuron. Therefore, *Group-level* sparsity is employed in this study to sparsify PNNs as applied in [13]. Purpose of this type of regularization is to eliminate all outgoing connections *group* from a neuron. There are three defined groups on group level sparsity:

- Input group G_{in}: An element of this group $g_i \in G_{in}$ represents set of outgoing connections of neuron i.
- Hidden group G_h: An element of this group represents all outgoing connections from a hidden neuron.
- Bias group G_b: An element of bias group is a scalar value being the bias of the corresponding neuron.

Figure 3 represents three different group types with different color coded nodes. Grey group represents the input group, red group is bias group and blue group is bias.

Defining all groups in a network as $G = G_{in} \cup G_h \cup G_b$, sparse group regularization, $L_{l_{2,1}}$, is shown in (4) as follows.

$$L_{l_{2,1}} \triangleq (\sum_{g \in G} \sqrt{|g|} \|g\|_2) \tag{6}$$

where $|g|$ is norm of a group and it ensures all groups gets weighted uniformly. Sparse group LASSO regularization, L_{SGL}, is defined as:

$$L_{SGL} \triangleq L_{l_{2,1}} + L_{p1} \tag{7}$$

Effect of this term is shown in Fig. 4. In this figure, active and inactive connections of a small weight matrix is shown for three different losses. Grey boxes refers to inactive connections. The first row demonstrates the effect of LASSO regularization. Second row shows Group Lasso, while the last row shows the Sparse Group-Lasso. While all cases obtain sparsity, Group wise removal of neurons are not achieved by Lasso and the third row reaches the highest sparsity.

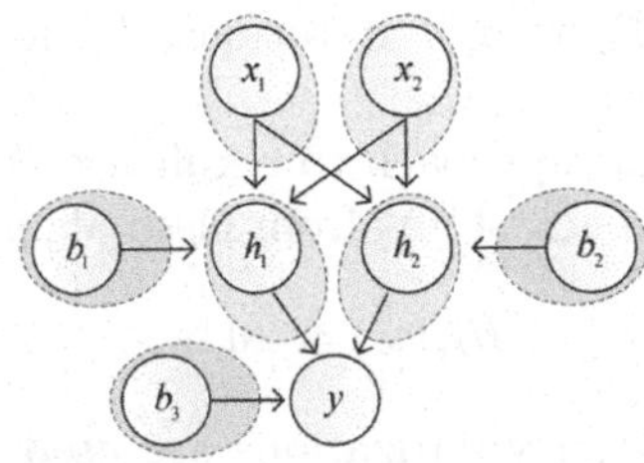

Fig. 3. Group representations in a network for group LASSO regularization. Grey, blue and red areas represent input, hidden and bias neuron groups, respectively. Here, the last node, y is output. Extracted from [13]. (Color figure online)

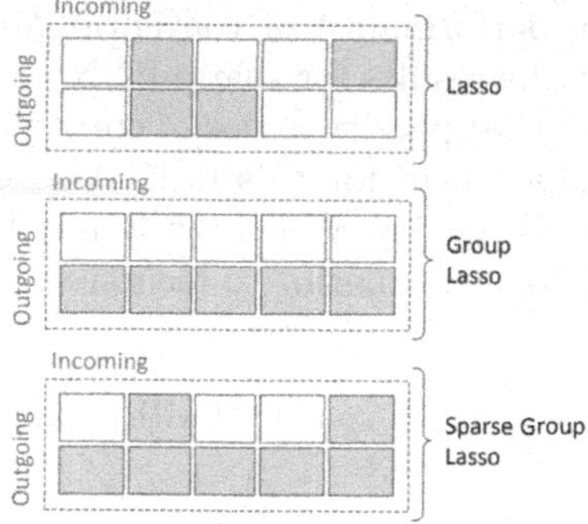

Fig. 4. Connection activities of a single weight matrix in three different regularizations. Gray represents the dead connections. White boxes refers to active connections. Extracted from [13].

Classification loss is cross entropy loss function, defined in (8):

$$E_1 = \sum_i y_i \log(p_i) \tag{8}$$

where y_i and p_i are being target and prediction vectors for an input sample x_i. In this case, we try to minimize the compound loss term, E, as follows:

$$E = E_1 + \lambda_1 L_{SGL} \tag{9}$$

3 Experimental Results

All experiments are implemented using PyTorch [9], an open source deep learning library, on Nvidia GeForce 2080Ti graphics processing unit.

On all reported results, sparsity ratios, S, on tables are calculated as in (10) where C_{act} and C_t are number of active connections and total connections, respectively.

$$S(\%) = (1 - \frac{C_{act}}{C_t}) \times 100\% \tag{10}$$

All experiments are carried out with rectified linear units. To assess effect of sparsity we did not employ dropout regularization. We employed ADAM optimizer which takes a different step for each term engaged in loss function.

3.1 Analyzing Group Sparsity for PNNs

In this section, the performance of R-PNNs and PNNs for 5 consecutive permutedMNIST tasks are reported. Each subnetwork consists of 2 convolutional layers and 2 fully connected layers. Each convolutional layer consists of 16 5×5 filters. Experiments are repeated for three seeds and average performance is reported.

Table 1 illustrates the performance of conventional PNN as well as the R-PNN. Line 3 and 5 report the results for sparse PNN and sparse R-PNN, respectively. Line 4 and 6 report the sparsity ratios of corresponding networks. RPNN do not result in performance gain for this task. As seen on line 3, sparsifying PNNs achieves up to 9.94% sparsity. When row 3 and 4 are compared, it is seen that sparsifying plain PNNs are superior to recursive PNNs.

Table 1. Performance of Sparse PNN sparsified with Group LASSO regularization for 5 consecutive permutedMNIST dataset.

	T_1	T_2	T_3	T_4	T_5
PNN	95.34	95.08	95.17	95.33	95.44
RPNN	94.71	94.80	94.34	92.28	93.77
S-PNN	94.51	94.46	94.36	93.91	94.16
S (%)	25.05	9.94	11.43	13.23	14.74
S-RPNN	94.51	94.33	93.94	93.06	90.96
S (%)	25.05	10.31	12.26	12.95	16.76

3.2 Analyzing Effect of Task Priors

The purpose in this section is to investigate the effect of prior task's similarity to current task on the performance of current classification task. For this reason we picked several superclasses from CIFAR-100 dataset and trained the model with different task orders. Table 4 shows selected superclasses and corresponding fine labels. In this section, classes are referred as scalars as shown in parenthesis in Table 4. Tables 2 and 3 show the results and sparsity ratios for 3 scenarios with various task orders for sparse PNN and recursive PNN, respectively. Table 2 shows that, the task order affects the performance and sparsity ratio for S-PNN. Learning Task 3 at last yields 26.8 % accuracy and 11.18 % sparsity while learning the same task in the third place yields 24 % accuracy and 10.81 % sparsity. Similarly, learning Task 1 at last yields 46.6 % accuracy and 13.34 % sparsity while learning the same task in the third place yields 49 % accuracy and 11.99 % sparsity. As seen from the results, increasing the number of task priors do not necessarily make positive impact over the performance or the sparsity. Changing the task order affects the average accuracy.

Table 3 reports the results for Sparse R-PNN. Similar to the previous case, task order affects the performance of the tasks. Learning Task 4 as the first task yields 57.6 % accuracy with 32.2% sparsity ratio. Learning the same task as the last task yields 46.6% accuracy and 11.72% sparsity ratio. Increasing number of prior tasks did not enhance the performance for S-RPNN. As expected, the task sequence order affects average performance. However, the contribution is not always positive.

Table 2. Performance of Sparse PNN for various CIFAR-100 task orders.

	T_1	T_2	T_3	T_4	T_5
Task	4	5	1	2	3
Acc.	57.6	41	49	46.2	26.8
S	32.32	11.64	11.99	13.55	11.18
Task	4	5	3	2	1
Acc.	57.6	41	24	45.6	46.6
S	32.32	11.64	10.81	12.89	14.0
Task	1	2	3	5	4
Acc.	61.6	44.0	27.4	45.8	42.8
S	28.78	12.07	12.47	14.92	13.34

Table 3. Performance of Sparse R-PNN for various CIFAR-100 task orders.

	T_1	T_2	T_3	T_4	T_5
Task	4	5	1	2	3
Acc.	57.6	41	52.4	45.6	22.4
S	32.32	11.64	11.20	14.19	8.05
Task	4	5	3	2	1
Acc.	57.6	41	23.8	45.6	46.6
S	32.32	11.64	11.42	10.0	11.72
Task	1	2	3	5	4
Acc.	61.6	44.0	23.0	34.6	46.6
S	32.32	11.64	11.42	10.0	11.72

Table 4. Selected subclasses and corresponding classes from CIFAR-100 dataset. Task reference is shown in paranthesis.

Superclass	Classes
medium-sized mammals (1)	fox, porcupine, possum raccoon skunk
aquatic mammals (2)	beaver, dolphin, otter, seal, whale
people (3)	baby, boy, girl, man, woman
household electronics (4)	clock, computer keyboard, lamp, telephone, television
vehicles 1 (5)	bicycle, bus, motorcycle pickup truck, train

4 Conclusion

In this study we use group sparse LASSO regularization to sparsify Progressive Neural Networks and propose a new model that recursively integrates prior task features and investigate the effect of task prior. We used permutedMNIST and medium-sized mammals, aquatic mammals, people, household electronics, vehicles 1 superclasses of CIFAR-100 dataset for investigating effect of task priors. Results show that integrating prior information recursively did not yield superior results compared to the plain PNN. Group sparse LASSO regularization effectively sparsifies both plain PNN and recursive PNN without large performance loss. Overall performance of sparsified PNN is superior to its recursive counterpart.

References

1. Chaudhry, A., Ranzato, M., Rohrbach, M., Elhoseiny, M.: Efficient lifelong learning with a-gem. arXiv preprint arXiv:1812.00420 (2018)
2. d'Autume, C.d.M., Ruder, S., Kong, L., Yogatama, D.: Episodic memory in lifelong language learning. arXiv preprint arXiv:1906.01076 (2019)
3. Goodfellow, I.J., Mirza, M., Xiao, D., Courville, A., Bengio, Y.: An empirical investigation of catastrophic forgetting in gradient-based neural networks. arXiv preprint arXiv:1312.6211 (2013)
4. Han, S., Pool, J., Tran, J., Dally, W.: Learning both weights and connections for efficient neural network. In: Advances in Neural Information Processing Systems, pp. 1135–1143 (2015)
5. Kirkpatrick, J., et al.: Overcoming catastrophic forgetting in neural networks. Proc. Nat. Acad. Sci. **114**(13), 3521–3526 (2017)
6. Li, X., Zhou, Y., Wu, T., Socher, R., Xiong, C.: Learn to grow: a continual structure learning framework for overcoming catastrophic forgetting. In: International Conference on Machine Learning, pp. 3925–3934. PMLR (2019)
7. Lopez-Paz, D., Ranzato, M.: Gradient episodic memory for continual learning. Adv. Neural Inf. Process. Syst. **30**, 6467–6476 (2017)
8. Nguyen, C.V., Li, Y., Bui, T.D., Turner, R.E.: Variational continual learning. In: International Conference on Learning Representations (2018). https://openreview.net/forum?id=BkQqq0gRb
9. Paszke, A., et al.: Automatic differentiation in Pytorch (2017)
10. Riemer, M., et al.: Learning to learn without forgetting by maximizing transfer and minimizing interference. In: International Conference on Learning Representations (2019). https://openreview.net/forum?id=B1gTShAct7
11. Ritter, H., Botev, A., Barber, D.: Online structured Laplace approximations for overcoming catastrophic forgetting. In: Advances in Neural Information Processing Systems, pp. 3738–3748 (2018)
12. Rusu, A.A., et al.: Progressive neural networks. arXiv preprint arXiv:1606.04671 (2016)
13. Scardapane, S., Comminiello, D., Hussain, A., Uncini, A.: Group sparse regularization for deep neural networks. Neurocomputing **241**, 81–89 (2017)
14. Serra, J., Suris, D., Miron, M., Karatzoglou, A.: Overcoming catastrophic forgetting with hard attention to the task. In: International Conference on Machine Learning, pp. 4548–4557. PMLR (2018)
15. Strannegård, C., Carlström, H., Engsner, N., Mäkeläinen, F., Slottner Seholm, F., Haghir Chehreghani, M.: Lifelong learning starting from zero. In: Hammer, P., Agrawal, P., Goertzel, B., Iklé, M. (eds.) AGI 2019. LNCS (LNAI), vol. 11654, pp. 188–197. Springer, Cham (2019). https://doi.org/10.1007/978-3-030-27005-6_19
16. Xu, J., Ma, J., Zhu, Z.: Bayesian optimized continual learning with attention mechanism. arXiv preprint arXiv:1905.03980 (2019)

17. Xu, J., Zhu, Z.: Reinforced continual learning. In: Advances in Neural Information Processing Systems, pp. 899–908 (2018)
18. Yoon, J., Yang, E., Lee, J., Hwang, S.J.: Lifelong learning with dynamically expandable networks. In: 6th International Conference on Learning Representations, ICLR 2018, Vancouver, BC, Canada, 30 April–3 May 2018, Conference Track Proceedings. OpenReview.net (2018). https://openreview.net/forum?id=Sk7KsfW0-
19. Zenke, F., Poole, B., Ganguli, S.: Continual learning through synaptic intelligence. In: Proceedings of the 34th International Conference on Machine Learning, vol. 70, pp. 3987–3995 (2017)

Author Index

Printed in the United States
by Baker & Taylor Publisher Services

Printed in the United States
by Baker & Taylor Publisher Services